D0875173

ENGLISH HISTORICAL DOCUMENTS

General Editor
DAVID C. DOUGLAS
M.A., F.B.A.

ENGLISH HISTORICAL DOCUMENTS

General Editor: DAVID C. DOUGLAS, M.A., F.B.A.

The following is a complete list of volumes in preparation; those marked * are already published, and those marked † are in the press.

GENERAL PREFACE

ENGLISH HISTORICAL DOCUMENTS is a work designed to meet a present need. Its purpose is to make generally accessible a wide selection of the fundamental sources of English history.

During the past half-century there has been an immense accumulation of historical material, but only a fraction of this has been made readily available to the majority of those who teach or who study history. The transcendent importance of the original authorities is recognized, but direct approach to them remains difficult, and even some of the basic texts (which are frequently quoted) are hard to consult. A gulf has thus opened between the work of the specialist scholar and those students, both at schools and universities, who best can profit by his labours. Historical studies tend too often today to consist of a commentary on documents which are not included in the available books; and, in the absence of any representative and accessible collection of the sources, the formation of opinion proceeds without that direct study of the evidence which alone can give validity to historical judgment. Correspondingly, the reading public outside schools and universities, has no adequate means of checking, by reference to the evidence itself, tendentious or partial interpretations of the past.

The editors of these volumes consider that this situation now calls for a remedy. They have striven to supply one by providing what they hope can be regarded as an authoritative work in primary reference.

An enterprise of this nature could only be effective if planned on a large scale. In scope and content, therefore, these volumes differ materially from the conventional "source-books" which usually contain only a restricted number of selected extracts. Here, within much wider limits, each editor has sought to produce a comprehensive *corpus* of evidence relating generally to the period with which he deals. His aim, in each case, has been to present the material with scholarly accuracy, and without bias. Editorial comment has thus been directed in the main towards making the evidence intelligible, and not to drawing conclusions from it. Full account has been taken of modern textual criticism to compile a reliable collection of authentic testimony, but the reader has in general been left to pass his own judgment upon this, and to appraise for himself the value of current historical verdicts. For this reason, everything in this work has been presented in such a manner as to be comprehensible by readers of English, and critical bibliographies have been added to assist further investigation.

The decision to display the texts (where necessary) in an English translation was thus dictated by the general purpose of this work. A translated text can, of course, never be a complete substitute for the original. But those who, today, can utilize a document in Anglo-Saxon, Latin or Old French are few, and are decreasing in number. This is certainly to be regretted. Nevertheless, there seems no adequate reason why the majority of those interested in English history should be arbitrarily deprived of the opportunity to consult the basic sources of their study. In this work, therefore, there is nothing that cannot be used by those who can only read English. At the same time, in every case where a translation appears, a reference is given to the place where the text in its original language may be found. In all English documents prior to 1714, and in the present volume which deals with American colonial documents of the seventeenth and eighteenth centuries, spelling and punctuation have been generally adapted to modern usage. All English documents after 1714 are given in the original form.

It will be seen that the present volume is in some sense exceptional in the series, in that it covers a period traversed by more than one of its fellows. So important, however, both in itself and for its consequences, is the theme of English colonial development in America, that it seemed desirable to provide students with the opportunity of consulting in a single volume the principal texts relating to the origin and growth of those English colonies in America, which later, having obtained independence, came to form the nucleus of the United States.

The editors of these volumes are fully aware of the magnitude of the undertaking to which they have addressed themselves. They are conscious of the hazards of selecting from the inexhaustible store of historical material. They realize also the difficulties involved in editing so large a mass of very varied texts in accordance with the exigent demands of modern scholarship. They believe, however, that the essential prerequisite for the healthy development of English historical studies is wider acquaintance with the original authorities for English history. And they are content that their work should be judged by the degree to which they have succeeded in promoting this object.

DAVID DOUGLAS

VOLUME IX

ENGLISH HISTORICAL DOCUMENTS

AMERICAN COLONIAL DOCUMENTS
TO 1776

.ENGLISH HISTORICAL DOCUMENTS

AMERICAN COLONIAL DOCUMENTS TO 1776

Edited by

MERRILL JENSEN
M.A., Ph.D.
Professor of History at the University of Wisconsin

New York
OXFORD UNIVERSITY PRESS
1955

ACKNOWLEDGEMENTS

My debt to the people who have assisted in the preparation of this volume is very great indeed. Dr. Jackson Turner Main, of San José State College, California, helped me in the preliminary bibliographical survey. During the past three years my research assistant, Dr. Arthur L. Jensen, has aided me in every way in the completion of the volume. Mrs. Elsie B. Crabb patiently typed and re-typed most of the documents. Colleagues in the field of Early American History have offered many useful suggestions. I am particularly obligated to Professor Leonard W. Labaree of Yale University, Professor Max Savelle of the University of Washington, and to Dr. Lyman Butterfield and Dr. Lester Cappon of the Institute of Early American History, Williamsburg, Virginia. Dr. Benton Wilcox, librarian, and the staff of the library of the Wisconsin State Historical Society, have eased my task immeasurably by making available at all times the materials needed.

For permission to republish materials previously published by them, I am under obligation to the following individuals and institutions: to Alfred A. Knopf, Richard J. Hooker, Perry Miller, Thomas Johnston, and Robert L. Meriwether; and to the American Antiquarian Society, the Colonial Society of Massachusetts, the Connecticut Historical Society, the Massachusetts Historical Society, the New Jersey Historical Society, the Pennsylvania Historical Society, the Virginia Historical Society, the Virginia State Library, the Institute of Early American History and Culture, the North Carolina State Department of Archives and History, the South Carolina Historical Commission, the Agricultural History Society, the Harvard University Press, the Muhlenberg Press of Philadelphia, the Princeton University Press, the Yale University Press, the Wilson-Erickson Publishing Company, and the University of North Carolina Press. I am likewise under obligation to the Public Record Office of Great Britain for permission to publish materials from their collection of manuscripts and to Her Majesty's Stationery Office for permission to reprint materials from its publications.

Randall D. Sale, cartographer at the University of Wisconsin, prepared the maps.

MERRILL JENSEN

PREFACE

THE documents contained in this volume were selected to illustrate various aspects of the internal history of the thirteen mainland colonies which declared their independence in 1776; to indicate the essential factors in the relations between them and Great Britain; and to trace the evolution of the conflict which led to the War for Independence. Certain areas relevant to the history of the American colonies have not been directly illustrated in the documents selected. These are the roles played by the colonies in European diplomacy; the relations between the colonies and their neighbours: Indian, French, and Spanish; and the relations between the mainland and the West Indian colonies. However, each of these areas has been touched upon incidentally in many of the documents. Furthermore, such matters are discussed in the various introductions, and the bibliographies contain references to relevant materials.[1]

Scholars in the field will recognize that the documents presented here are but a small sample of the number available. It would be possible to construct any number of volumes, following a similar organization, with very little duplication. It would be possible also to construct a similar volume for each of the colonies, although with variations dependent upon the individual characteristics of the colonies concerned. Moreover, a thorough documentary presentation of many of the topics illustrated here – religion, trade, agriculture, and colonial policy – would fill a volume of this size. As it is, neither all topics nor all colonies have been equally represented. The purpose has been to introduce the reader to most of the major areas of colonial history and to indicate the main threads of a complex story.

The documents have been edited to the following extent: (1) modern spelling has been used with certain exceptions which are noted in the introductions; (2) superfluous capital letters, italics, and punctuation have been removed; (3) punctuation has been supplied where it was deemed necessary to clarify meaning; (4) abbreviations have been spelled out. The verb forms are those of the sources from which the documents have been derived. Since the *Oxford Dictionary* contains virtually every word to be found in these documents, it has not been thought necessary to offer definitions of words which may seem

---

[1] *English Historical Documents*, vols. VII, VIII, and X, covering the years 1603–1783, should be consulted for documents relating to topics omitted in this volume as well as for material on many of the topics included.

strange to present-day eyes and ears. Biographical details such as dates of births and deaths are based on information in the *Dictionary of American Biography* and the *Dictionary of National Biography*. In the dating of all documents the year is taken as beginning on 1 January instead of 25 March. Otherwise, all dates are those of the sources from which the documents were derived.

Most of the documents have been given in full. One exception has been in the case of various Acts of Parliament included in this volume. Material in these Acts not relating specifically to the colonies has been deleted. Other portions have been summarized by the editor and placed in brackets. The other exception to full publication is in the case of lengthy books and pamphlets from which significant excerpts have been taken. The introductions to the individual documents indicate when this has been done.

CONTENTS

PART II. THE EVOLUTION OF COLONIAL GOVERNMENTS

A. POLITICAL THEORY IN THE COLONIES

B. THE CONSTITUTIONAL BASES OF COLONIAL GOVERNMENTS

C. BRITISH POLICY AND COLONIAL GOVERNMENTS

PART VIII. THE COMING OF THE WAR FOR AMERICAN
INDEPENDENCE, 1773-1776

A. THE BACKGROUND OF THE FIRST CONTINENTAL CONGRESS

MAPS

INTRODUCTION

INTRODUCTION

(i) THE PERIOD

THE colonial era in the history of the western hemisphere began with the first voyage of Columbus in 1492. Its end was signalled 284 years later in 1776 when thirteen of Great Britain's thirty-one American colonies declared their independence. Within a few years thereafter the New World colonies of Spain revolted and they too achieved their independence. During the first third of this colonial era England and France, who were to be the two great protagonists in the struggle for world-wide empire in the eighteenth century, played a minor role in the New World. Beset by internal weakness and difficulties, they were forced to limit themselves to sporadic raids on Spanish and Portuguese colonies, to even more sporadic voyages of discovery, and to a few futile attempts at colonization. Spain and Portugal thus dominated the New World during the sixteenth century, and the wealth in gold and silver Spain acquired from her American mines gave her the semblance if not the reality of vast power.

By the end of the sixteenth century both England and France had achieved internal unity and firmer economic foundations. Once peace was established with Spain in 1604, both countries began to establish permanent colonies in those areas of the New World not yet occupied by the Spanish and Portuguese, particularly on the smaller islands of the West Indies and along the Atlantic coastline of North America. Although the Puritan Revolution interrupted the process of English colonization, it was carried on rapidly after 1660 and was essentially complete by the end of the seventeenth century.

By the end of that century, too, the foundations were laid for the long struggle between France and England for the domination of North America. They had conflicting claims in the West Indies and on the mainland. The English colonies, ranging from Spanish Florida in the south to Maine in the north, were beginning to push into the interior. The French, from their settlements in the St. Lawrence Valley, likewise pushed into the interior until they had a vast arc of posts, forts, and settlements stretching from the mouth of the St. Lawrence to the mouth of the Mississippi, thus creating a barrier to the future expansion of the English colonies along the Atlantic seaboard. Hence it was that the initial disputes over fisheries, fur trade, and the like eventually merged into a great struggle for the control of the whole of eastern North America. The Seven Years War (1756-1763), which began in the colonies at the forks of the Ohio River in 1754, was the culmination of this long struggle.

The Treaty of Paris of 1763 ended for ever France's American empire. It gave to Britain a vast domain extending from the West Indies to Hudson's Bay and from the Atlantic Ocean to the Mississippi River. Her American empire thus reached its greatest extent 156 years after the founding of the first English colony at Jamestown in Virginia in 1607. Yet within twelve short years the war for American independence was under way. And in the Treaty of Paris in 1783, only twenty years after her great triumph over France, the heart of Britain's American empire was lost to her for ever.

Most historians of the United States consider the colonial period of its history to have ended in 1763. The years 1763–1776 are treated as a preliminary to the outbreak of the war for independence. The roots of that war are usually traced back to the Seven Years War: to the events that occurred during it, and to the colonial policies, both old and new, which Britain attempted to enforce after it.

So far as it is possible to 'periodize' history at all, there is considerable validity in such a division, for two fundamental changes took place after 1763. Britain sought to bring about in practice that subordination of the colonies which had always been complete in theory but seldom so in fact, and, in the end, to do so by armed force. The great change in the colonies was in the attitude towards the idea of independence. In 1763 few if any colonists looked upon the idea as little more than a subject for occasional speculation, as a vague possibility for some time in the distant future. Within ten years after 1763 a large and growing body of men were looking to independence in the immediate future as the only possible solution of the disputes with Great Britain.

Rooted though these two changes are in events after 1763, they can be fully understood only in terms of the whole history of the English colonies, a history quite unlike that of other European colonies, particularly in the origin and evolution of their political institutions. All European colonies were assumed to be the property of the monarch of the colonizing power. The right to establish colonies was therefore usually conveyed by a royal charter. Here the similarity between the English and other European colonies ended. Almost from the start, the colonies of France and Spain were brought under the direct control of the crown and were governed by royally appointed officials, the colonists themselves playing little or no part in the political life of the colonies. Their economic life was likewise rigidly controlled by the mother country.

The English colonies were founded by trading companies, religious groups, and private individuals who secured royal charters. But once the charters were acquired, the first group of English colonies were for the most part free of royal control, and totally lacking in government support for their enterprise. The first half-century of English colonization was therefore a period of what was, for the colonies, happy neglect by the mother country, and a period during which their political and economic institutions were firmly established.

It was only after this had come about that the mother country sought to bring the colonies under closer political and economic control. The creation of a colonial policy after 1660 was the work of both parliamentary legislation and administrative decisions, and an ever-increasing number of royal officials were appointed to carry out the policies adopted. Despite such measures, and repeated attacks on the wide powers of the colonial governments, it was clear by the eighteenth century that the effective centre of political power in the colonies lay with the colonial legislatures, and particularly in their elective branches. Because the functioning of government in the colonies, and to a large extent the implementation of many colonial policies as well, was dependent upon funds raised by these legislatures, they used that fact to maintain and increase their power. The members of these legislatures were as conscious of parliamentary traditions as any member of the House of Commons itself, and they jealously guarded their rights and privileges, most of all the right to raise money by taxation, and then to control its expenditure.

It was obvious by the middle of the eighteenth century that the several colonies were, for all practical purposes, self-governing. Not only this, but the colonies had developed a complex economic life carried on by able planters and merchants who provided most of the political leadership as well. Also participating in politics were a large number of land-owning farmers and independent artisans, craftsmen, and shopkeepers. Despite class distinctions, the Americans lived in a society where class lines were fluid, which was expanding in every direction, whose population was growing with astonishing rapidity, and whose spirit was optimistic, aggressive, and increasingly self-assertive. They were a people who resented any limitation of their activity, whether political or economic, by the mother country.

Internally, each of the colonies had always had a vigorous and sometimes violent political life. Religion, the control of land, Indian relations, paper currency, were some of the characteristic issues which occupied the time and energy of colonial legislatures. Colony fought with colony over such matters as boundary lines, and more often than not they refused to co-operate with one another in war-time. But however much they might wrangle among themselves, most Americans could unite in a moment to fight as one against interference by royal officials.

Viewed from the distance of London, and in terms of theoretical assumptions as to the proper relations that should exist between the colonies and the mother country, the American colonies, and particularly those on the mainland, seemed quite hopeless. Broad policies laid down in London were haphazardly and sometimes corruptly administered by officials in the colonies. Royal governors often found it impossible to carry out their instructions and very often did not try to, despite threats from home. Customs officers were forced to yield, or often found it profitable to do so, to the demands of colonial merchants. Support for military campaigns was as often determined by the exigencies of local politics as it was by the clear demands of imperial strategy.

Despite the independent attitude of the colonies and the confusion and inefficiency of royal administration in the colonies, America as a whole continued to contribute an ever-growing amount to the total wealth and power of Britain and consumed an ever greater proportion of the output of British industry. Furthermore, the British treasury itself gained substantial annual revenues from the flow of colonial trade through Britain. The annual net revenue derived from Virginia and Maryland tobacco alone was far greater than even the most optimistic member of any of the ministries after 1763 hoped to raise by direct parliamentary taxation of the colonies. It was only after 1763, when Britain tried to make practice conform to theory, when she tried to bring about efficiency in colonial administration, when she tried to collect pence in the form of taxes as contrasted with the pounds of private profit and government revenue arising from colonial trade, and above all when both the British and the Americans began to debate the abstract question of colonial rights as opposed to colonial privileges, that thirteen of Britain's colonies revolted and won their independence.

(ii) THE SOURCES

The sources for the colonial period of American history, both manuscript and printed, are particularly rich and varied. Manuscript sources are to be found in public and private libraries in Great Britain, on the Continent, and in the United States and other countries in North America. Printed sources in the form of sermons, pamphlets, newspapers, handbills, and the like are to be found in abundance, particularly in American libraries. Numerous guides to both the manuscript and printed materials have been prepared, and some of them are excellent indeed. Not only is there a vast body of material, but for more than a century it has received the attention of a great number of amateur and professional historians, historical societies, and government agencies.

Early in the nineteenth century, historians such as Jared Sparks and George Bancroft began to collect materials both in America and Europe and brought together great collections of original manuscripts and transcripts which are still indispensable to the scholar in early American history. Peter Force undertook the re-publication of rare pamphlets and tracts and projected a vast scheme of documentary publication called *American Archives*, of which only nine volumes covering the years 1774–1776 were ever printed. Historical societies such as that of Massachusetts began the distinguished series of documentary publications which still continue.

State governments were induced to undertake the publication of their colonial records. Not only did they publish local records such as legislative journals, but they sent agents to Europe, and particularly to England, to transcribe materials such as the correspondence of colonial governors. The result is that we have in print such major collections as the *New York Colonial Documents*, the *New Jersey Archives*, the *Pennsylvania Archives*, the *Maryland Archives*, and the *North Carolina Colonial Records*. This too is a process which continues, the most notable new project today being the publication of the journals of the South Carolina Assembly.

Such projects by American state governments were matched in importance if not in volume by the British government. The publication of such series as the *Acts of the Privy Council, Colonial Series*, the *Journal of the Board of Trade and Plantations*, and the *Calendar of State Papers, Colonial Series*, has provided indispensable tools for scholars.

During the twentieth century the interest in English and European documents relating to colonial America, which began early in the nineteenth century, was given new impetus by the projects supported by the Carnegie Institution of Washington. The most notable of these projects were the guides to materials for American history to be found in various European libraries and archives. The most important of these were the volumes containing guides to the materials in the Public Record Office, the British Museum, and other British depositories prepared by Charles M. Andrews. The Carnegie Institution likewise supported the publication of documentary series such as Elizabeth Donnan's *Documents Illustrative of the Slave Trade to America* and Leo F. Stock's *Proceedings and Debates of the British Parliament Respecting North America*.

To such activities should be added those of private collectors who have gathered together manuscripts ranging all the way from small autograph collections to the manuscript holdings of families covering centuries of time. Some of these are American collections; others are English collections bought by American collectors. The two most notable libraries of the latter kind are the Clements Library at Ann Arbor, Michigan, and the Huntington Library at San Marino, California. Thus the Clements Library contains such collections as the papers of General Thomas Gage, Lord Shelburne, and the British Headquarters Papers for the American Revolution. A notable collection at the Huntington Library is the Stowe Papers, a half-million manuscripts ranging from the twelfth to the nineteenth century, and containing, among other things, the papers of the Grenville family.

The greatest single depository of materials for American colonial history in the United States is the Library of Congress in Washington. Not only has it a great collection of original manuscripts, it has for many years been engaged in collecting transcripts, photostats, and microfilms of materials for American history in European libraries. No adequate guide to its holdings exists, but it is safe to say that the materials from European libraries alone total many millions of pages.

It is clear that the preparation of such a volume as this would have been impossible without the work of generations of scholars who have searched out and printed thousands of documents relating to the colonial period. Equally indispensable in the preparation of this volume has been the work of many scholars who have written monographs, almost without number, relating to the history of the colonies. The bibliographies in this volume represent only a selection from among the multitudes of books, articles, essays, and reviews available. Some of the greatest monuments of American historiography have been devoted to the colonial period. The eight volumes entitled *Narrative and Critical History of America*, edited by Justin Winsor, with its essays on sources and studies in cartography was the first of the great works on colonial America. It was followed by Herbert L. Osgood's seven volumes on the colonies in the seventeenth and eighteenth centuries. The most recent achievement, and within its self-established limits, the greatest, is by the man who for nearly a half-century shaped much of the thinking about American colonial history, Charles M. Andrews. His four volumes, *The Colonial Period of American History*, will not soon be, if ever, equalled. Along with such works could be named those of hundreds of scholars who have written on a vast variety of topics and on individual colonies. And the work yet goes on, for old collections in print and in manuscript have not yielded their all, while new sources of information of major importance continue to be made available to scholars almost every year.

In general the historiography of the colonies falls into two broad but not necessarily exclusive categories. Most of the work produced during the nineteenth century was characterized by a concern with the local, internal history of the colonies and tended to view Britain as little more than an external force which from time to time attempted to interfere with the course of colonial history and which eventually sought to subject the colonies to military tyranny. It was against this view that Charles M. Andrews and Herbert L. Osgood took a stand in two papers read on the same programme in 1898. In the years that followed, these two men came to be regarded as the founders of the 'imperial school' of colonial historiography, and they and their students did much to broaden the view of the colonial period and to place it in an imperial and world setting. In 1898 Andrews pointed out that historians had forgotten that the colonists were members of a great colonial empire. In an essay[1] published after his death in 1943 he declared that "our colonial history considered without a

---

[1] "On the Writing of Colonial History", *William and Mary Quarterly*, 3rd series, 1 (1944), pp. 27–48.

knowledge of the English outlook and apart from the long and continuous relationship of the colonies to the mother country loses its wider and deeper significance as a phase of English colonial expansion and becomes merely a study of conditions that preceded the history of the United States, a study that is, of the origins of democracy and the awakening of American ideals, subjects good enough in themselves but poor substitutes for the story of what happened to individuals and communities on this continent in colonial times". In the course of a lifetime devoted to his ideal, Andrews sometimes lost sight of the importance of the internal history of the colonies, of the things that were indigenous to them and which could not be explained alone in terms of the colonies as parts of the British Empire. While Osgood agreed in general with Andrews's view, his concern was with institutional history, and he paid far more attention to the internal history of the colonies.

Despite the dominance of the imperial school during the past half-century, many historians have continued to devote themselves to the exploration of the internal history of the colonies in all its aspects and with far richer results than were for the most part achieved in the nineteenth century. The continuation of this effort combined with the perspectives offered by the imperial school has not only broadened and deepened our knowledge of colonial America, but it has opened up new avenues of research for the future.

(iii) EUROPE AND THE NEW WORLD BEFORE THE SEVENTEENTH CENTURY

The discovery of the New World was in a sense an accident of the search for a sea-route to Asia, a search which Portugal led and which gave her the initial advantage. Long before the other maritime nations bordering on the Atlantic had either the political unity or the economic resources for overseas expansion, Portugal began pushing down the west coast of Africa. Under the guiding hand of Prince Henry the Navigator she established claims and added greatly to the store of geographical knowledge and practical maritime experience, and continued to do so after his death in 1460. By that time Portuguese mariners had sailed as far as Sierra Leone. The Equator was crossed in 1471, and a few years later the mouth of the Congo River had been passed. At last in 1486 Bartholomew Diaz set forth from Lisbon for the express purpose of sailing the entire distance around Africa and into the Indian Ocean. He achieved his goal but failed to reach India itself because his crew forced him to turn back. On the journey home he sighted the southernmost point of Africa, which was to be named Cape of Good Hope. When Diaz returned to Portugal, an obscure Genoese was there seeking help for his schemes. But Christopher Columbus was turned away, now that Portugal had at last mapped out a sea-route to the

2

fabulous East. In 1497–1498 Vasca da Gama carried out the task left unfinished by Diaz: he sailed around Africa and reached India.

Meanwhile Columbus at last got support from the sovereigns of Castile and Aragon, and in 1492 he sailed westward across the uncharted Atlantic. Perhaps scholars will never agree as to what Columbus was searching for: whether it was new lands rumoured to lie westward in the Atlantic, or a shorter route to India than the Portuguese had found. But whatever his goal, he established Spanish claims to what he found and in time it became clear that it was a vast new world, although centuries passed before Europeans were able to comprehend its vastness.

The news of Columbus's first voyage aroused the Portuguese, who insisted that the new discovery belonged to them. Ever since the middle of the fifteenth century the papacy had been issuing bulls confirming Portuguese possession of their discoveries. These decrees had been reinforced by a treaty between Portugal and Spain (Castile) in 1479 which confirmed the rights of Portugal to discover and possess lands and islands along the African coast, except the Canaries, which were formally ceded to Spain.

When Portugal raised its claim to the land discovered by Columbus, Ferdinand and Isabella turned to Pope Alexander VI, a Spaniard. During the year 1493 a series of papal bulls drew a boundary line between Spanish and Portuguese claims 100 leagues west of the Cape Verde Islands and granted the Spanish monarchs all the land they might find by sailing south and west until they reached India. The Portuguese protested and in 1494, in the Treaty of Tordesillas, Spain and Portugal agreed to move the boundary line 370 leagues west of the Azores, a move which made it possible for Portugal to occupy Brazil in later years.

The attempt of Spain and Portugal to divide the New World between them was ignored by other nations from the start, although Spain and Portugal were the only countries to establish permanent colonies and posts during the sixteenth century. The Spanish first established themselves on larger islands of the Caribbean Sea and then pushed to the mainland, lured on by the rumours of fabulous riches to be found there. In 1521 Cortez completed the conquest of the Aztecs of Mexico. In 1533 Pizarro broke the power of the Inca Empire in Peru. The loot from these empires was great and attracted the envy of the rest of the world, but the subsequent discovery of rich gold and silver mines was of even greater importance. Year after year the Spanish treasure fleets brought the precious metals to Spain, a fact that aroused not only the envy but the fear of other nations for it was an age that equated the possession of precious metals with national power and greatness. Actually American treasure was in the end a source of weakness and decay for Spain, but, in addition, it worked a revolution in Europe at large far more subtle than men at the time realized.

The vast increase in the supply of precious metals was followed by a steady rise in price levels, a rise that had a disrupting effect on a society where land rents and wages were relatively fixed, and that remained so during the sixteenth century. At the same time it gave an added impetus to growing commercial capitalism.

Although England, France, and other countries failed to establish permanent colonies during the sixteenth century, they did establish the claims that were to be the basis of the colonies they founded in the seventeenth century. England was the first to do so. The people of Bristol are said to have sent out expeditions even before Columbus set forth in 1492. In 1496, John Cabot, a Genoese who had become a citizen of Venice but who was then a resident of Bristol, got a grant from Henry VII. Cabot, as vassal and lieutenant of the king, was given all the lands he could find to the north, west, and east, and a monopoly of commerce. In return he was to pay one-fifth of all his gains to the Crown.

Cabot set forth from Bristol in 1497. The details of the voyage are obscure, but he seems to have touched the coast of North America – perhaps near the St. Lawrence River. On his return Henry VII granted £10 to "him that found the new Isle". In 1498 Cabot sailed again but where he went or whether or not he ever returned is unknown. England's claims to North America were thus based on Cabot's voyage of 1497, only three years after the Spanish and Portuguese had divided the unknown world between them. Further voyages were made to what soon came to be called the "new found land" or "new found island". In 1509 Sebastian, the son of John Cabot, is supposed to have set forth on a voyage for the discovery of a north-west passage to Asia. While no official evidence remains of such a voyage, the purpose of it at least indicates that the English recognized that the "new found land" was not Asia.

During the reign of Henry VIII there was little interest in the New World on the part of the English. England was preoccupied with the Reformation and with affairs on the Continent, and had little time or money to spare for exploration, nor did she have the naval strength to challenge Spain or Portugal, even if she had wished to. However, there were voyages by private vessels to Brazil, some accidental contacts with the Spanish in the West Indies, and at least three more expeditions to the "new found land".

Meanwhile the French were far more active. The struggle between Charles V and Francis I began in 1521 just as Cortez completed the conquest of Mexico. Within a few years French privateers were attacking Spanish treasure ships on the road back to Spain, and they were raiding in the Caribbean itself by the 1530's, thus long antedating the similar activities of the Elizabethan sea-dogs of the latter part of the century. In 1534 and again in 1535, Jacques Cartier was sent out by Francis I to seek for wealth in the New World. Cartier discovered the St. Lawrence River and explored it as far as present-day Montreal, but he found none of the fabled mines of gold and silver that were supposed to exist everywhere. In 1541 a third voyage left France, led by Cartier and by the Sieur de Roberval. The purpose this time was to establish a colony. Cartier established a post on the St. Lawrence above Quebec, but after a bitter winter there he started back for France. At St. Johns, Newfoundland, he met Roberval, who had sailed in the spring of 1542 with 200 colonists. Cartier refused to go back to the St. Lawrence but Roberval went on. After a winter during which the colonists suffered from disease and starvation, Roberval and the remnants also returned to France.

The French now turned their attention southward and this time the driving force behind colonizing schemes was that of the French Huguenots, and particularly Admiral de Coligny. A colony of French Protestants was sent to Brazil in 1555, but the Portuguese soon wiped it out. The French Protestants then turned to Florida. In 1562 a small colony was planted on the St. John's River but it was soon abandoned. In 1564 another group came, but, like the first group, they were more interested in gold than in colonization. Furthermore, the Spanish saw them as a threat to Spanish treasure ships and in 1565 established the fort of St. Augustine, the oldest town in what is today the United States. A French expedition sent to destroy the Spanish settlement was wrecked by a storm and the Spanish killed the survivors.

French efforts at colonization were abandoned for a time, for France was now torn by a deadly religious war. Not until the beginning of the seventeenth century were the French to turn to colonization once more, and when they did they competed with other nations for the lesser islands of the Caribbean, and, more importantly, they turned once more to the north where Cartier had explored the St. Lawrence and laid the foundation of French claims to Canada.

Meanwhile, the English began to expand in a variety of directions. In 1553 an expedition was sent to discover a north-east passage to Asia. It failed of this purpose but it did open up trade with Russia by way of the White Sea. This trade in turn led to the grant of a royal charter in 1555 to the first English joint-stock company for overseas trade, the Muscovy Company. In that same year Richard Eden published his translation of the first part of the *Decades* of Peter Martyr. Thus for the first time there was an account in English of the Spanish possessions in the New World. And it was in Spanish possessions that most Europeans were interested, for the Spanish had found gold and silver. The discovery of these metals in the hot regions of the New World merely confirmed a medieval theory that gold occurs only where the sun's rays are the hottest. Few men indeed, except unknown and unsung fishermen, were interested in the northern latitudes. Therefore a vast amount of effort was to be spent in colonizing as close to the Spanish possessions as possible, for fish and timber and even furs had not the lure of gold and silver. Decades, even centuries, elapsed before the conviction born of hope and greed was abandoned.

Meanwhile the efforts of the French Protestants to establish colonies near Spanish possessions had an impact on men who were to be leading promoters of English colonization. Among the English officers sent to France with English troops to help the Huguenots were Humphrey Gilbert, Richard Eden, and Thomas Stukeley. Such men were in touch with Admiral Coligny's plan to plant a colony in Florida. The colony sent there in 1562 attracted English interest and resulted in a scheme to take it away from the French. In 1564 John Hawkins stopped by and offered to take the starving French colonists back to Europe but they refused. Hawkins reported that treasure was not apt to be found in Florida. This report ended English interest in the colony, although they made much of Spanish brutality in murdering the remnant of the French colonists the next year, and for a century thereafter anti-Spanish feeling was an important element in English attitudes towards exploration and colonization.[1]

While English interest in overseas trade and colonization grew steadily from the 1570's onward, English activity in those fields was sporadic. The threat of Spain dominated the policies of Elizabeth, whose shifts were unpredictable and often seemed capricious. But behind those shifts lay a basic division of opinion among her advisers. One group, led by Lord Burghley, was interested in the promotion of overseas trade and the avoidance of open warfare with Spain. The other group, led by Sir Francis Walsingham, looked upon war with Spain as inevitable, favoured attacks on Spanish shipping, and looked forward to the establishment of English colonies. As a result of this division, and of changes in relations with Spain, first one policy was pushed and then another, and sometimes both at once.

In 1574 a group of west-country merchants proposed to establish a colony at their own expense in exchange for a trade monopoly, but they did not specify the location. The scheme came to a sudden end when Elizabeth, who had temporarily settled her difficulties with Philip II, demanded a heavy cash guarantee that the settlement would not be made in lands claimed by Spain. But relations with Spain soon worsened, and Humphrey Gilbert came forth with a new proposal. He published his "A Discourse of a Discovery for a new Passage to Cataia" in 1576, and in the next year proposed to the queen that an English colony be planted on the St. Lawrence River. Far more than this was involved, however. The proposed colony was a pretence to cloak a raid on French, Spanish, and Portuguese fishing fleets in Newfoundland, to be followed by a raid on the Spanish colonies in the Caribbean. In 1578 Gilbert received a patent from the queen for the purpose of exploring and colonizing "lands,

[1] No. 5.

countries, and territories not actually possessed by any Christian prince or people". Gilbert gathered together a fleet which was financed by his friends and his half-brothers, and set forth in September 1578. The leaders soon quarrelled and storms set in and by the end of November the whole project had collapsed. All that remained was the patent which was to be the legal basis for later colonizing schemes.

In November 1577, the same month in which Gilbert presented his plan to the queen, a far greater venture set forth from England. With the connivance of members of the Privy Council, and in great secrecy, Francis Drake set forth from England on the voyage that took him around the world and from which he did not return until 1580. In the course of it he captured much Spanish treasure, laid the foundations for trade with the Portuguese colonies in Asia, and whetted the appetites of Englishmen for further raids on the Spanish colonies and treasure fleets. But the queen for the moment refused to challenge Spain and leaned instead in the direction of those who favoured peaceful trade with Asia by way of the Cape of Good Hope. In fact, she invested £42,000 of her share of Drake's plunder to further this plan, which was to be carried out by the Levant Company. But as was so often the case, the commander who was sent ignored his orders. He sailed instead to the coast of Brazil, where a Spanish fleet attacked him and forced him back to England. The result was that most of the capital supplied by the queen and by London merchants was lost.

The Levant Company scheme and a proposal of the Muscovy Company that it be granted Newfoundland stirred Humphrey Gilbert to a new effort. To finance it, he granted lands under his patent of 1578 and raised capital in Southampton by promising to make it the sole port of entry for the trade of the proposed colony. His half-brother, Sir Walter Raleigh, was rapidly rising in the favour of the queen and secured permission for Gilbert to sail. He set forth in June 1583 with five ships. He landed in Newfoundland, where he read his commission to the assembled English, French, and Portuguese fishermen, and annexed the land and proclaimed the authority of the queen. He then sailed to the southward. One ship was lost and his men insisted on returning to England. On the return voyage the small ship in which Gilbert was sailing was lost in a storm off the Azores.

Gilbert's rights were inherited by his half-brother, Sir Walter Raleigh, who received a new patent from the queen in 1584. He at once sent out an exploring expedition along the North American coast and named the land Virginia in honour of the queen. The next year a second expedition was sent out. One purpose was to demonstrate the defenceless condition of the Spanish colonies, and in this it was successful. The expedition landed for a time on Puerto Rico, and then on Hispaniola. It then sailed northward and left a colony of about

100 men, under the leadership of Richard Lane, on Roanoke Island off the Carolina coast. Meanwhile, the news of the expedition's landings on the Spanish islands reached England, and the queen was at last induced to give Sir Francis Drake permission to sail on a raiding expedition. Drake sacked Cartagena and burned St. Augustine.

On his return voyage he stopped by Roanoke Island, picked up Lane and his men, and took them back to England. Short supplies and unfriendly Indians made them more than willing to go, although a few days after Drake sailed with them, new supplies and colonists arrived. Still another phase of English activity during 1585 was a raid on the foreign fishermen in Newfoundland in retaliation for the seizure of Englishmen and ships in the harbours of Spain. More than 600 Spanish and Portuguese fishermen were captured and taken to England, along with their fish, and for some years thereafter the English and French were the only competitors in the waters off Newfoundland.

The success of these raids did not lead to colonization; Raleigh, who had an exclusive patent, was losing interest and made no further efforts. However, some of the men associated with him were determined to go ahead. In 1587 John White and twelve associates bought a licence of incorporation from Raleigh as "The Governor and Assistants of the City of Raleigh", with the power to plant a colony on the shores of Virginia. During the summer of 1587 White led an expedition of 150 colonists, including women, to the New World, and once more established a settlement on Roanoke Island. White returned to England for more supplies but by now England was in the throes of open warfare with Spain. White was able to get together a relief expedition which started out in 1588, but his men mutinied and took him off on a piratical raid into the Caribbean. When at last he returned to Roanoke Island in 1591, the colony had vanished, leaving little or no trace behind it.

Colonizing projects had by now no hope of support, for the war with Spain and the superior profits from privateering occupied the time and money of all those who might have invested. Raleigh did nothing, nor would his finances have permitted him to use his patent if he had wished to.

In March 1589 he assigned virtually all of his rights under his patent to his creditors and to others, among whom were John White, Richard Hakluyt, and Sir Thomas Smythe, the great merchant capitalist. The assignment to the latter was symbolic of what was to happen in the future, for when English colonies were at last founded, they were not established by courtiers and favourites of the queen but by merchant capitalists, of whom Smythe was not only the example but the leader. He was involved in almost every overseas enterprise of the English for decades. He was a heavy investor in the Muscovy and Levant companies. He was one of the organizers of the East India Company which received its charter in 1600, and he was governor of it as well as of the

Levant Company. Finally, he was one of the men instrumental in founding the Virginia Company, and dominated its affairs for more than a decade.[1]

Although the conflict with Spain occupied most of the time of Englishmen during the latter part of the sixteenth century, and peace was not made until 1604, the foundations for rapid colonization in the seventeenth century were well laid. After the middle of the century, men such as Richard Eden, Humphrey Gilbert, and, above all, Richard Hakluyt, devoted themselves to the promotion of the idea of English colonization. By 1584, when Hakluyt wrote his "Discourse concerning Western Planting" at the behest of Raleigh in his efforts to secure the financial support of the queen, most of the basic ideas concerning the purpose and importance of English colonies had been clearly defined.[2]

Furthermore, Englishmen had acquired a certain amount of practical experience in the effort to colonize Ireland. Many of the men who urged colonization in the New World had participated in Irish ventures. Humphrey Gilbert, for instance, acquired his first colonial experience in Ireland. Even the terminology that was used in the New World plantations—words like 'planting', 'plantation', 'colony', and 'native'—were first used in Ireland, and the promotion literature of the seventeenth century had its ancestry in the advertising issued by sixteenth-century speculators in Irish lands.

Perhaps the most important foundation of all was that provided by the development of a reservoir of merchant capital in England. Despite difficulties, English merchants had freed themselves from foreign financial control by the end of the century. Beginning with the Muscovy Company in 1555, they had developed the joint-stock trading company that made possible organization to engage in successful long-range overseas trading and colonizing ventures during the seventeenth century.

Thus, when peace was made with Spain in 1604, the way was open for the sudden burst of colonizing activity which within three decades was to plant thirteen permanent English colonies in the New World. While the Spanish still claimed all of the New World, their effective control did not extend north of St. Augustine in Florida, nor did they control the lesser islands of the West Indies nor the Guiana coast of South America. It was in these three areas therefore that not only the English but the French and Dutch and others as well, established colonies during the seventeenth century.

(iv) THE FOUNDING OF THE FIRST ENGLISH COLONIES,
1607–1634

The impetus that resulted in the establishment of the first permanent English colony at Jamestown in Virginia came mainly from two groups of merchants,

[1] No. 13.   [2] No. 5.

with the assistance of certain members of the nobility such as the earl of Southampton. One group of merchants centred in London, with Thomas Smythe, of the Muscovy, Levant, and East India companies, as the most important leader. The other group centred in the west-country ports of Bristol, Exeter, and Plymouth, and had the advantage of the leadership of Chief Justice Sir John Popham, and Sir Ferdinando Gorges, governor of Plymouth. The merchants looked forward to the establishment of what were essentially a series of trading-posts which would collect fur and fish and manufacture such forest products as potash. They seemingly had little conception of the kind of colonies that would develop, in fact, would have to develop, if colonization was to be successful.[1]

After early suggestions that the government should help finance the project on the ground that colonization would render a public service by ridding England of surplus population were rejected, a royal charter was granted in 1606.[2] The charter provided for two groups commonly known as the Virginia Company of London and the Virginia Company of Plymouth. It granted them the right to settle between the thirty-fourth and forty-fifth parallels of latitude "in that part of America commonly called Virginia, and other parts and territories in America, either appertaining unto us, or which are not now actually possessed by any Christian prince or people". The Plymouth Company was to settle the northern part and the London Company the southern part.

The Plymouth Company attempted a settlement at Sagadahoc on the coast of Maine in 1607, but gave it up within a year. Thereafter the company remained inactive for years except for the dispatch of ships to fish and to explore. The London Company sent out three ships in 1607. The expedition founded Jamestown on the James River in Virginia. Despite the repeated disasters of the first years in Virginia, struggles within the company, and conflict between the company and the king, the colony managed to survive to become the first permanent English colony in the New World.[3]

The early discovery that tobacco could be grown in the colony guaranteed its permanency and radically altered its original purpose. Tobacco became the dominating concern of the economic and political life of the colony.[4] Diversified agriculture and the small farmers became a negligible element in the tidewater as a plantation economy based on large land holdings and Negro slavery developed during the seventeenth century. However, the back country, particularly during the eighteenth century, continued to be the home of an ever greater number of small farmers devoting themselves to an agriculture like that of the northern colonies.

[1] No. 6.　　[2] For a discussion of this and other charters, see Part I, A.
[3] Nos. 1, 6, 12, 13.　　[4] Nos. 44, 55 (Table VII, VIII), 66.

Politically, Virginia was of great significance in the development of the colonies for its government provided the pattern for colonial governments outside of New England. The Virginia Company created an elective legislature in the colony in 1619.[1] The Crown took over the colony in 1624, but eventually it accepted the idea of the legislative assembly as a part of the government of the colony.[2] In the years that followed, the Virginia precedent was applied to other colonies, whether royal or proprietary.

Colonies were projected in rapid succession after the founding of Virginia. In 1610 a group of London and Bristol merchants secured a charter for the colonization of Newfoundland. These men, and others to whom they sold rights, made repeated attempts to establish settlements during the next few decades, but in the long run Newfoundland remained the realm of fishermen. In 1612 the Bermuda or Somers Islands were added to Virginia in the new charter the Virginia Company received that year.[3] At once a group of the stockholders formed a voluntary association for the purpose of settling the islands and purchased the rights of the company. In 1615 they received a royal charter as the Somers Island Company, with Sir Thomas Smythe as governor. The company managed the affairs of the islands until 1684 when the company was dissolved and Bermuda became a royal colony.

English interest was not limited to the mainland–far from it. The islands of the Caribbean and the northern coast of South America continued to be as fascinating as they had been in the days of Hawkins and Drake. Repeated attempts were made to establish posts on the Guiana coast, the most notable being that of Sir Walter Raleigh. He was released from prison in 1616, and the next year he set out with a fleet. The Spanish attacked him and drove him back to England, where, upon the complaint of the Spanish ambassador, he was once more imprisoned and shortly thereafter beheaded.

English efforts to settle on the smaller islands of the Caribbean were successful. In 1625 the islands of St. Christopher and Barbados were occupied, and within the next few years Nevis, Antigua, and Montserrat as well. Conflicting grants were made to proprietors and the islands were for long torn with the struggle over rival claims to the land. Despite years of confusion, however, the islands were established on a firm economic base. By the middle of the seventeenth century they were shifting from the production of poor quality tobacco to sugar, and for a time their population far exceeded that of the mainland colonies, and their economic importance was far greater.

The conflicting claims to ownership were brought to an end after 1660. Charles II took over the proprietorship of Barbados and in 1673 it became a full-fledged royal colony. The history of Barbados is an illuminating commentary on the political attitudes and behaviour of Englishmen when transplanted

[1] Nos. 21, 39.   [2] Nos. 22, 29.   [3] No. 1.

overseas. The planters, as opposed to the proprietors, showed a sturdy independence and a desire to govern themselves, and once the island became a royal colony, the planters opposed the royal prerogative in the person of the royal governors as vigorously as did the inhabitants of the mainland colonies. Meanwhile the Leeward Islands (St. Christopher, Antigua, Nevis, and Montserrat), which had been governed from Barbados, insisted upon separation. In 1672 they were established as a royal colony. A governor-general was appointed, but each island retained its separate elective legislature and royal council, thus constituting a unique federal structure within the old empire.

The desire of merchants for profit resulted in the founding of the first mainland and West Indian colonies, but it was not the only driving force that impelled Englishmen to look to the colonies during the first half of the seventeenth century. The growing conviction on the part of various English dissenters that they must look to the New World if they were to worship as they pleased was equally important in the planting of colonies, particularly in New England. The first to move to America were an inconspicuous group of English Separatists who had gone to Holland early in the century. Their hard life, their desire to maintain their 'Englishness' and to maintain their church in a place where fellow Separatists might join them, as they would not in Holland, turned the thoughts of these people to America. In the New World they might still live within the realm of England but be far enough away to escape the eye of a king who had little use for dissenters, however inconspicuous.

These 'Pilgrims', as their descendants were to name them generations later, were so poor that they had no hope of financing a voyage. Eventually they secured the support of some hard-headed London merchants who were to exploit them unmercifully for years. They obtained a licence to settle within the bounds of Virginia, but their ship, the *Mayflower*, landed them at Cape Cod in New England at the beginning of the winter of 1620–1621. Because they landed outside the government of Virginia, they drew up a church covenant, the 'Mayflower Compact', which served as the basis of the government of the colony until it was absorbed by Massachusetts at the end of the century.[1] The colony was never significant either in numbers or economic growth, but it has occupied a major place in the history of the American past.

Of far greater importance was the founding of Massachusetts Bay in 1630 by a group of Puritan leaders who sought to establish their vision of a Bible Commonwealth far removed from the controls of the Church and State of England. The great Puritan migration from England to New England during the 1630's brought thousands of Puritans and non-Puritans to the New World and planted there certain basic political, religious, and social ideas that have been influential from that day to this.[2]

---

[1] No. 14.   [2] Nos. 2, 7, 15, 17, 20, 82, 84, 85, 89, 90.

Massachusetts Bay soon became the mother, albeit a rather grim one, of other colonies. Its leaders did not tolerate dissent; yet they were constantly tormented by men who came to the colony and dissented from the Puritan vision of the ideal commonwealth. Roger Williams came in search of religious freedom and quite logically he was banished. In 1636 he founded the town of Providence in what was to become the colony of Rhode Island.[1] Other dissenters founded other towns around Narragansett Bay. Eventually these individualistic communities were forced to unite to protect themselves from their orthodox neighbours. In 1644 Roger Williams obtained a patent from Parliament which provided for a union of the towns. After the Restoration a royal charter gave Rhode Island the status of a corporation and guaranteed to the colony its cherished ideal of religious freedom.

Still other migrations from Massachusetts resulted in the founding of the colony of Connecticut. Religious reasons were a partial element but the better lands of the Connecticut Valley were a powerful attraction as well. Several towns were soon established and, although at first they were looked upon as a part of Massachusetts Bay, the river towns established their own government when they drew up the Fundamental Orders of 1639.[2] To the south-west, along Long Island Sound, the town of New Haven was founded in 1638 by dissenters from England, who stayed in Massachusetts only long enough to discover that they did not like it. Other towns were founded near by, and these were united with New Haven in a government of their own. In 1662 a royal charter incorporated these river and coastal towns as the colony of Connecticut.

The New England colonies were unique in their origins and retained their individual quality throughout the colonial period. The New Englanders discouraged the immigration of non-English peoples, and hence most of them were of English stock, a fact of which they were intensely proud. Their political behaviour from the start was characterized by a spirit of independence, a spirit intensified by the establishment of the township form of local government. Whether or not the town governments were democratic may be a subject for debate, but there can be no question but that the New England towns provided a school of self-government unique in the colonies, and in the world, for that matter. Virtually every adult male inhabitant could participate in that school if he chose to do so.[3]

New England agriculture, at least as compared with the colonies to the southward, was subsistence agriculture. Aside from the products that were sold in the nearby towns, they produced small quantities of grain and of beef and pork for export. The character of the people, the nature of the soil and climate, all worked against the large-scale production of crops.[4] But New England had other resources which were exploited to the full by a small but aggressive group

---

[1] Nos. 18, 27.   [2] No. 26.   [3] Nos. 37, 41.   [4] No. 43.

of merchants, lumbermen, and fishermen. The forests provided timber for shipbuilding and ships were built in ever increasing numbers. The New England merchants became the carriers of an ever greater amount of the ocean-borne commerce of the whole empire. The forests, too, provided the basis for a lumber industry which produced large quantities of boards, planks, shingles, hoops, and staves which were shipped to other colonies, the West Indies, Southern Europe, and to England. The trade with the West Indies and the African slave trade were an integral part of the rum manufacture of New England. It was with some justice that John Adams remarked in his old age that molasses was an essential ingredient of the American Revolution.

The sea provided one of the major resources of New England. The cod fisheries loomed ever larger in the economy of the seaport towns and the 'Sacred Cod' of Massachusetts in time came to rival the Puritan God as a matter of concern. The products of the fisheries were a prime element in the trade with the West Indies and were of increasing importance in the trade with Southern Europe.[1]

Nothing marked off the New England colonies from the other colonies more sharply than their continued concern with religion and its ramifications. The early Puritan leaders insisted upon the idea of public responsibility for education all the way from the primary to the college level.[2] The relationship of Church to State was a basic element in the political conflict of the New England colonies. Rhode Island resolutely offered religious freedom from the start.[3] With equal resolution the colonies of Connecticut and Massachusetts denied it.[4] Connecticut for long remained the almost undisputed domain of the Congregational Church. Massachusetts was the religious storm centre of the colonies.

Much of the political history of the colony during the seventeenth century centres around religious questions, and particularly around the effort of a minority of Puritan leaders to maintain their ideal of a Puritan Commonwealth. They fought a losing battle but they fought it vigorously. As the first generation died off, the intensity of religious conviction, at least on the part of those in control of government, began to lose force. With the rise of a wealthy merchant class, more and more of the important men in the colony were found to be non-members of the Church. The abrogation of the charter of 1629 in 1684 and the grant of a new charter in 1691 opened up the way for the participation of all property owners in government. Although the Congregational Church remained powerful for generations thereafter, its ardent adherents never exercised the control over the colony that had been within the hands of its founding fathers.

The last of the English colonies to be founded before the Civil War brought

[1] Nos. 52, 53, 55.   [2] Nos. 89, 90.   [3] Nos. 83, 27.   [4] Nos. 82, 84, 85.

colonization to a halt was Maryland. Its founding was the first successful effort of still another force in English society—the landed gentry—to plant a colony on the mainland. Many of the gentry had been investors in the various schemes of colonization from the start but the joint-stock companies had been dominated by merchants whose interest was primarily in trade and only secondarily in colonization. As the gentry turned to the idea of colonization for themselves they conceived of a colony as a place to which they could transplant forms of government and land tenure which were essentially feudal in character, a place where the proprietor would be absolute lord and the colonists would be tenants for ever.

The clearest example of this ideal is to be found in the plans of Sir Ferdinando Gorges. He had been a leader in the Virginia Company of Plymouth, but after the failure at Sagadahoc in 1607–1608, the company had done nothing further to establish its claims under the charter of 1606, although members of it had sent out fishing voyages and financed explorations. It was clear by 1620 that the Plymouth group must take action if it were not to lose out completely. As an aristocrat and a member of the landed gentry, Gorges had no desire for a trading company charter that provided for government of the company by a majority vote of the stockholders. What he petitioned for and secured in 1620 was a patent incorporating a self-perpetuating group of forty as the "Council for New England".

The forty members, all of whom were of the nobility and landed gentry, were made proprietors of a vast tract extending from the fortieth to the forty-eighth parallel and running from sea to sea. They were given the land to do with as they pleased and with the power to govern any colonists who might go there. In addition, they were given a monopoly of the trading and fishing rights. The purpose of the proprietors was, as Gorges made clear in his writings, the creation of a great feudal estate, of the creation of institutions in the wilderness that were already outmoded in England. The plan was a failure. Colonists refused to go there (the landing of the Separatists at Cape Cod the month the patent was issued was an accident); the Virginia Company and the fishing towns of the west of England bitterly opposed the fishing monopoly; and the Massachusetts Bay Company Charter of 1629 carved the heart out of the grant.[1] The council achieved nothing except to divide up the lands among its members. But even these claims were whittled away. New Hampshire was made a royal colony in 1679 and Massachusetts Bay got and kept control of Maine. Thus the first effort to establish a feudal proprietorship failed utterly.

The first of the gentry to achieve success was Sir George Calvert, Lord Baltimore, who had been an investor in various overseas enterprises. He had established a settlement in Newfoundland and visited it, but gave it up because

[1] No. 2.

of the climate. He then applied for a charter to lands near Virginia but he died before it was completed, with the result that the charter for Maryland was issued to his son Cecelius.[1] The proprietary charter thus issued was to be the model for the great proprietary grants of the post-Restoration period. That neither Maryland nor the subsequent proprietary colonies developed in the direction in which their proprietors planned was due in part to changing conditions in England, and in part to the fact that the Englishmen who went to the colonies had quite another conception of the role of colonists and in a large measure were able to shape those colonies according to their conceptions.

The Maryland charter gave vast powers to the proprietor, not only of appointment but of legislation as well. The only restriction upon his legislative power was the requirement that he call the inhabitants to meet and assent to his acts. But from the start, the people of the colony demanded the right to function as a legislature. They insisted that they had the right to initiate and pass legislation and they proceeded to do so. The battle between the proprietor and the inhabitants was a long one and was punctuated by outright rebellions. Eventually the people of the colony won a legislature like that in the other colonies and during the eighteenth century the proprietors concerned themselves mainly with the very considerable economic benefits they got from the colony.

With the settlement of Maryland in 1634, the first era of English colonization came to an end. By that time thirteen colonies had been established. In addition to Maryland, there were Virginia, Bermuda, Plymouth, Barbados, St. Christopher, Antigua, Nevis, Montserrat, Massachusetts Bay, Rhode Island, Connecticut, and New Haven. Not until 1670 was another English colony to be planted. The Civil War in England and its consequences left Englishmen with little interest in or time for the colonies which, during those years, carried on their economic and political life without any serious interference from outside.

(v) RIVALS OF ENGLAND IN THE NEW WORLD

England had not been alone in colonizing in the New World during the first half of the seventeenth century. Other nations, and particularly France and Holland, had been as active as the English. The explorations of Jacques Cartier had given France a claim to the land along the St. Lawrence River. In 1605, just as the English were beginning their colonial projects, Samuel de Champlain founded Port Royal in Acadia (Nova Scotia). Three years later he founded Quebec on the site where Cartier had failed more than sixty years before. Gradually the French pushed westward, exploring and developing the fur trade. They found their way to the Great Lakes and beyond, establishing forts and

[1] Nos. 3, 8.

trading-posts. Catholic missionaries, the fur traders, and the explorers were all a part of the cutting edge of the French advance. In 1673 Joliet, a fur trader, and Father Marquette, a missionary, found their way from the Great Lakes to the Mississippi River. They were convinced that it emptied into the Gulf of Mexico, but they turned back for fear of being captured by the Spanish.

In the spring of 1682 La Salle explored the Mississippi to its mouth and took possession of the great valley and named it Louisiana in honour of the king. La Salle went to France and returned to the Gulf of Mexico with several hundred colonists in 1684. The project was a failure. La Salle was murdered by his own men and the remnants of the colonists were wiped out by the Indians. Not until the end of the century were the French able to establish themselves on the Gulf. Biloxi was founded in 1699, Mobile in 1702, and New Orleans, which became the centre of French power in the lower Mississippi Valley, in 1718. During the same years many forts and trading-posts were built along the river and its tributaries. By the end of the first quarter of the eighteenth century the French had thus constructed a vast arc of towns, forts, and trading-posts stretching from the mouth of the St. Lawrence to the mouth of the Mississippi, thus furnishing a tangible barrier to the future expansion of the English colonies along the Atlantic seaboard.

Like the English, the French were also concerned with the West Indies. They settled on St. Christopher in 1625, the same year the English established themselves on the island, and for a time they occupied it jointly. Others settled on the northern coast of Santo Domingo. During the 1630's the French occupied Guadeloupe and Martinique and expelled the English who had settled on the island of Tortuga, off the north coast of Santo Domingo. They occupied other islands as well, and by the 1660's the French held no less than fourteen of the West Indian islands. The economic history of the French islands was like that of the English. They began by raising tobacco and then they turned to sugar production. Like the English, too, the French islands were settled by companies. The French companies failed financially and eventually the islands were taken over by the French Crown. But there was one fundamental difference between French and English settlements: the French colonies, like the Spanish, were governed by royal appointees, unchecked and unhampered by representative legislatures, an institution unique to the English colonies in the New World.[1]

The Dutch interest in and development of overseas trade paralleled and often preceded the activities of the English and French, and through much of the seventeenth century, Dutch ship-owners carried a large share of the trade of western Europe and of the New World colonies as well. The Dutch voyages to Asia began before the end of the sixteenth century, and their East India

[1] Nos. 21, 22, 23, 26, 27, 28, 34, 35.

Company was chartered only two years after that of England. In 1609 the Dutch East India Company sent out Henry Hudson, an Englishman, to find a passage to Asia other than that by way of the Cape of Good Hope. Hudson sailed along the North American coast from Maine to Delaware Bay and then made his way into the river which now bears his name, and sailed up it, perhaps as far as Albany. During the next few years Dutch merchants explored and established posts to carry on the fur trade.

In 1621 the Dutch West India Company was chartered by the Estates-General. The company was given a twenty-four-year monopoly of trade with Africa, the east coasts of South and North America, and the right to colonize unsettled areas. However, colonization was always incidental to trade and to raiding Spanish and Portuguese colonies and ships. The company's interest in North America was chiefly in the fur trade. In 1624 it sent out colonists who were established in scattered trading-posts from Fort Orange (Albany) to Fort Nassau on the Delaware River. Fort Amsterdam was built on Manhattan Island.

The Dutch settlements grew slowly for the company kept a monopoly of the fur trade and agriculture was not encouraged. In 1629 it did seek to further settlement by giving vast tracts of land along the Hudson River to 'patroons' who would bring over settlers to serve as tenants on the estates. Relatively few people were attracted by the prospect of tenantry. The result was that by 1650 there were probably not more than 3,000 people in New Netherland, and they were scattered in small villages or trading-posts all the way from the Connecticut River and Albany in the north to the Delaware River in the south. It was a polyglot population that included a growing number of New Englanders who moved across Long Island Sound to the eastern end of Long Island. Most of the people, whether Dutch or English, were thoroughly discontented with the arbitrary rule of the governors sent over by the company, but their protests were ignored.

Even less successful was the effort of Sweden to establish an American colony. The Swedish government chartered the South Company in 1637, and in 1638 it established Fort Christina on the present site of Wilmington, Delaware, twenty-odd miles below the Dutch post of Fort Nassau. The colony of New Sweden never numbered more than a few hundred people, most of whom were engaged in the fur trade, and in subsistence agriculture. The Dutch objected to the colony but did nothing as long as the Dutch and Swedes were allies in the Thirty Years War. The end of the war ended consideration for the rights of former allies. In 1655 a Dutch expedition, far outnumbering the total population of New Sweden, forced its surrender and the colony became a part of New Netherland. The Dutch now held a vast domain with settlements on the two greatest rivers on the Atlantic coast, a domain that separated the two centres of English colonization. But the Dutch hold was tenuous at best and the English were soon to show that they had as little respect for Dutch claims as the Dutch had had for those of the Swedes.

(vi) THE RESTORATION COLONIES

The outbreak of the Civil War had brought an end to the first era of English colonization; the restoration of the Stuarts in 1660 inaugurated a new wave of expansion and settlement. It was preceded by the seizure of the Spanish island of Jamaica in 1655. Cromwell's "Western Design" was the result of an attitude of mind that would have been applauded by the Elizabethans (as it was not by the English merchants who opposed it). It was born of a desire for revenge on the Spaniard and of a zeal for driving the Catholics from the New World. Coupled with these was the hope, as usual a forlorn one, that enough Spanish treasure could be seized to ease the financial problems of the English nation. The capture of Jamaica did not drive the Spanish Catholics from the New World nor did it provide Spanish treasure, but it did add a new colony of vast potential wealth to England's American possessions. After 1660 New Netherland was taken from the Dutch and other colonies were founded. So rapid was the process that within twenty-five years there was a continuous line of English colonies extending along the Atlantic coast of North America from Maine on the north to the indeterminate boundaries of Spanish Florida on the south. Not only was the process rapid but it was marked by a radical shift in the character of the men who directed it. Neither the merchants nor the religious groups who had been instrumental in founding the first colonies were involved.[1] Instead, the driving force came from the nobility who had not previously, except for a few men like Lord Baltimore, been concerned directly with colonization on the mainland. Furthermore, the Restoration colonizers were for the most part friends and supporters of Charles II and his brother James, duke of York. Such men were not interested in the corporation as a colonizing device. Instead, the basis for the new colonies was the proprietary charter patterned after the grant of Maryland to Lord Baltimore in 1632.[2]

Most of the men involved had either followed Charles into exile, and thus won his favour, or had managed to shift to his side with adequate agility in 1660. The leaders of the group were Sir John Colleton, Anthony Ashley Cooper (later the earl of Shaftesbury), Arthur Hyde, earl of Clarendon and father-in-law of the duke of York, George Monck, duke of Albemarle, who had arranged

---

[1] The Quakers were an exception.

[2] The only exceptions during the Restoration were the grants of corporation charters to Connecticut (1662) and to Rhode Island (1663), but in both cases the charters were primarily a recognition of colonies already in existence. Despite repeated attacks on these two charters in the years that followed, Connecticut and Rhode Island were the only English colonies to retain their full status as corporations throughout the colonial period.

the return of Charles to the throne, and Sir George Carteret. Of lesser note were Lord John Berkeley and his brother Sir William Berkeley, governor of Virginia, and the earl of Craven. These men were involved in most of the profit-making schemes of the Restoration period. They got vast land grants in America, they were stockholders in the Royal African and Hudson's Bay companies which were chartered by Charles II, and in older organizations such as the East India Company. As advisors and intimates of the king, several of them held high offices, were members of the Privy Council, or of the various committees concerned with colonial affairs.

In 1663 these eight men were given a royal charter to Carolina, the vast tract of land lying to the south of Virginia and extending from sea to sea.[1] A second charter in 1665 widened the boundaries to latitude 36° 30' on the north and to latitude 29° on the south. The charter was a proprietary charter like that of Maryland, but it did require the grantees to include an elective legislature in whatever government they created.

The proprietors soon set forth their plans for the colony. They held out attractive terms to prospective settlers from whom they proposed to collect quitrents.[2] They envisioned an economy that would produce silk, wine, fruit, and oils. Vast estates for each of the proprietors were a part of the scheme. In essence, they proposed to create a stratified semi-feudal society in the wilderness. Their dream was embodied in the Fundamental Constitutions of 1669 which was drafted for the most part by John Locke, secretary to Lord Ashley (Shaftesbury). It proposed that the colony be divided into counties, each county to contain eight seignories which were to belong to the proprietors; eight baronies which would be given to a local nobility known as caciques and landgraves; and twenty-four colonies of 12,000 acres each, which would belong to ordinary settlers. The proprietors would hold all the chief offices. A parliament would be made up of the proprietors, the nobility, and of elected representatives of the freemen, all meeting together. Slavery of both whites and Negroes was provided for.

This scheme, drawn up before any real effort at colonization was under way, had little relation to the realities of life in the wilderness or to the nature of men who were to go there. A group of settlers from Virginia moved into the region around Albemarle Sound in the northern part of the province as early as 1663, and Sir William Berkeley appointed a governor over them. These poor but independent minded people ignored the economic plans of the proprietors. They flouted the Navigation Acts and welcomed pirates. The legislature established by the proprietors defied the officials appointed by the proprietors to sit with it. When the proprietors sent out new officials with

[1] Charles I had granted a patent to "Carolana" to Sir Robert Heath in 1629 but Heath had done nothing and his claim was presumed to have lapsed.
[2] No. 9

instructions to enforce the laws, the officials themselves were jailed. A subsequent governor was banished by the hardy people of what was to become the colony of North Carolina.

The proprietors had great hopes of the southern part of the province, but these too were thwarted. The first permanent settlers in what was to become South Carolina arrived in 1670. The bulk of those who came were not from England where the fear of depopulation was now prevalent. The West Indies contributed a good many for the rise of the sugar plantation and Negro slavery in the islands displaced men who had once been small farmers. Other settlers came from the colonies to the north. The exiled French Huguenots soon contributed an important group, as they did to other colonies.

The inhabitants of the southern part of Carolina were as indifferent to the plans of the proprietors as were those in the northern part. Instead of raising silk they raised provisions for the West Indian trade. They refused to pay quitrents. They ignored the Navigation Acts. They enslaved the Indians and carried on running warfare with those they could not capture. By 1700 the whole province had not more than 8,000 people. The great growth in wealth, particularly of South Carolina, was to come with the development of rice and indigo in the eighteenth century,[1] but by then the proprietors' cause was a lost one and North Carolina became a royal colony in 1729 and South Carolina in 1719.

English attention was not limited to the southern part of the Atlantic coastline. The vast tract of land centring on the Hudson River and thinly held by the Dutch was an object of concern. The expansion of New England, and particularly the colony of Connecticut, had shoved the Dutch back from the Connecticut River, and New Englanders had moved to the northern shore of Long Island and were constantly pushing westward towards the Dutch settlements. On the whole, the New England penetration was peaceful and the trade between Boston and New Amsterdam was mutually profitable, however offensive it might be to English officials. As early as 1653 Cromwell had sent out an agent for the purpose of conquering New Netherland, but the Massachusetts officials placed so many obstacles in the way of the plan that peace came in 1654 before any attempt could be made. After 1660, as before, New Amsterdam continued to be a centre of trade for the English colonies and as such it rendered the Navigation Act of 1660 a nullity, while Massachusetts Bay looked upon itself, implicitly if not explicitly, as an independent state quite free to do as it pleased. Clearly, from the point of view of English officials, this had to be changed.

In the spring of 1664 Charles II issued a patent making his brother, the duke of York, proprietor of the lands north of the New England colonies, the

---

[1] No. 45.

islands off the southern coast of New England, and of all the mainland between the Connecticut and Delaware rivers. The duke at once appointed Colonel Richard Nicolls deputy governor, equipped him with three warships, soldiers, and money, and sent him forth to capture New Netherland. At the same time Nicolls was given a royal commission to inquire into the affairs of New England. Nicolls appeared off New Amsterdam in August 1664. Peter Stuyvesant, the Dutch governor, got little help from the inhabitants in his efforts to defend the town, and he was forced to surrender without the firing of a shot.

Nicolls busied himself with renaming the towns, New Amsterdam becoming New York, and securing the allegiance of the inhabitants. Even Peter Stuyvesant took the oath. Nicolls established a code of laws which included trial by jury and freedom of conscience, but he had no power to establish a legislature, something the New England inhabitants were particularly anxious to have. Not until 1683 did the duke permit New York to have a legislature, and when it met, it promptly demonstrated its independence by adopting a Charter of Liberties, which the duke with equal promptness vetoed.[1] When the duke became James II in 1685, New York became a royal colony.

New York had enormous strategic importance, as the French in Canada realized. The network of waterways connecting the Hudson and St. Lawrence rivers was the main route for raiding back and forth during the wars of the eighteenth century. The competition for the fur trade between the New Yorkers and the French was a constant source of friction. New York's economic growth was slow. One dominant element in the colony was interested only in the fur trade and not in the overall economic development of the colony. In addition, the English continued the Dutch practice of making vast land grants to a few. The vast estates thus created, all too often corruptly, were held by men who looked upon themselves as feudal lords. They refused to sell land and exploited their tenants. The result was that the average immigrant who wanted to own land turned to other colonies, and particularly to Pennsylvania, rather than to New York.[2]

The rest of the domain granted to the duke of York was to become the colonies of New Jersey and Delaware. Even before New Netherland was conquered, the duke gave the land along the coast between the Hudson and the Delaware rivers to his friends Lord John Berkeley and Sir George Carteret. He named it New Jersey in honour of Carteret, who had been governor of the Isle of Jersey. The former Swedish settlements to the south became the province of Delaware, which remained a part of the duke of York's proprietary. Eventually the colony was attached to Pennsylvania, with a separate legislature but with the same governor. It was as often called the "three lower counties" as it was Delaware.

[1] No. 28.   [2] No. 50B.

The proprietors of New Jersey held out attractive terms to prospective colonists, offering among other things religious freedom and an elective legislature. A number of New Englanders settled in East Jersey and when the first legislature met in 1668, it showed itself as opposed to the claims of the proprietors as the settlers of Carolina. Berkeley, who was mainly concerned with West Jersey, soon sold his rights to the Quakers with the result that West Jersey became the first scene of Quaker colonization in the New World. In the conflict that followed, Sir Edmund Andros, governor of New York, refused to recognize the Quaker purchase and asserted his authority, but the Quakers continued to come despite his opposition. Finally, William Penn and a Quaker syndicate bought the claims of the heirs of Carteret to East Jersey. They united the two parts of the colony and the duke of York freed them from the interference of his governors in New York. In 1702, New Jersey became a royal colony. Although politically united, the colony was long divided because of overlapping claims to land and because of the conflict between the small and great landholders, a conflict that was to lead to serious riots during the eighteenth century.

The last of the mainland colonies to be founded in the seventeenth century was one of the greatest of the proprietary grants. William Penn, the son of Admiral Penn, had early become a Quaker. Yet he had retained his connexions in high places, including a sincere friendship with James, duke of York. Penn had been one of the leaders in the effort to create a refuge for Quakers in New Jersey, but he looked forward to the creation of a colony under his control and completely devoted to the idea of religious toleration. When Admiral Penn died, Charles II owed him £16,000. William Penn suggested that the debt would be cancelled if the king would grant him a tract of land lying to the west of New Jersey. The result was the issuance of a charter in 1681 making William Penn the proprietor of a colony to be called Pennsylvania.[1]

Penn set about founding a colony dedicated to his ideals and at the same time demonstrated himself to be a practical promoter of no small talent. His pamphlets setting forth the attractions of Pennsylvania were translated into many languages.[2] Farmers from all over western Europe were attracted by his promise of religious freedom and by his easy terms for land. The result was that the province grew with extraordinary rapidity. The rich farm lands produced bountiful crops which flowed to the markets of the world through Philadelphia. The capital city rapidly became the metropolis of the American colonies and by the outbreak of the Revolution was the third city in the British Empire. Politically, however, the colony had a turbulent career. Penn found it as difficult to put his political ideals[3] into practice as had Roger Williams in Rhode Island, but he showed a willingness to alter the framework

---

[1] No. 4.   [2] No. 10.   [3] No. 19.

of government to suit changing conditions.[1] As a result of the great migrations to the colony in the eighteenth century, the Quaker element soon became a minority, but its leading members became a wealthy merchant aristocracy that dominated the politics of the colony until the American Revolution.

With the founding of Pennsylvania, English colonization on the mainland was complete except for the colony of Georgia, which was chartered in 1732. Georgia was planned partly as a philanthropic enterprise and partly as a frontier outpost against the Spanish in Florida.[2] During the colonial period it remained small and weak and its philanthropic character was soon lost sight of in the rise of a plantation-slave economy in the tidewater similar to that of the other southern colonies.[3]

(vii) THE EVOLUTION OF COLONIAL POLICY

Not only were the years after 1660 a period of rapid colonization, they were years during which the foundations of English colonial policy were laid down. The overall purpose of the policy was to establish something that had not existed prior to 1660: control over the economic and political life of the colonies. The origins of economic colonial policy are to be found in the early royal proclamations requiring that colonial tobacco be brought to England, but it was the seizure of Jamaica that raised the question of overall policy for the first time. Although English merchants had opposed the venture, they now began to demand the serious attention of the government to the question of colonial trade. The conquest of Jamaica opened up the prospect of a great increase in the production of tropical produce. At the same time the early colonies were producing ever larger quantities of such tropical staples as tobacco, sugar, spice, dyewoods, and other products. It was also evident that the Dutch merchants dominated the carrying trade of most of the English colonies and that they carried colonial produce to the best markets, wherever they might be.

English merchants were no longer interested in colonization for themselves, but they did want colonial trade concentrated in English hands. Hence they demanded government action. The result was the appointment of a committee on colonial affairs in 1655. This committee, which came to be known as the "Committee for the Affairs of America", urged government regulation of colonial trade. The committee went out of existence in 1660, but it was succeeded by others and there was little break in important personnel and none at all in the policies demanded.[4] Charles II and his advisers, badly in need of revenue, were willing listeners to the merchants who talked of the national wealth and public revenue that might be derived from a restriction of colonial

[1] No. 23.   [2] No. 11.   [3] No. 79.   [4] *English Historical Documents*, vol. VIII, Nos. 202, 205.

carrying trade to the inhabitants of England and the colonies, from a requirement that certain colonial products be sent only to England or the colonies,
and from the establishment of the principle that England be the sole source of
manufactured goods used in the colonies. These were the principal ideas that
lay behind the passage of the Navigation Act of 1660 and the subsequent Acts
of Trade and Navigation,[1] and in the creation of administrative boards and the
appointment of officials to enforce them.[2]

The colonists had objected vigorously and openly to the Navigation Act
of 1651 which had been passed by the Commonwealth Parliament. They
objected as vigorously to the new legislation after 1660. The enforcement of
the policy was therefore difficult and it was made even more so by the very
manner in which the English colonies were founded and in which they had
developed. The English colonies were the result of the private enterprise of
individuals or groups of individuals who received little or no support from
either the Crown or Parliament. They acquired the right to colonize by virtue
of royal charters, but they had to provide the means themselves, or to induce
others to invest their resources.

The charters, whether corporation or proprietary, gave their holders wide
powers over and within the colonies; but at the same time they required only
the most nominal allegiance to the Crown and none at all to Parliament, since
the colonies were in law and theory the domain of the Crown. At the same
time the charters contained within them the germ of an institution–the elective
legislature–which enabled the colonists not only to defy the proprietors but to
defy both Crown and Parliament in the course of time. Within these legislatures
the colonists could and did express their own political and economic desires.
When these ran contrary to orders and laws, whether from the proprietors or
from the Crown and Parliament, as they often did, the colonial legislatures
often found ways to evade or to openly defy them.[3]

The thirteen colonies founded before 1634 had achieved a measure of independence by 1660. Their relative unimportance, their distance from England,
the Civil War, and the convictions of the colonists themselves all contributed
to this fact. The lavish proprietary grants of Charles II after 1660 in essence
contradicted the evolving colonial policies of the period. It was not until the
charter of Pennsylvania was issued that the new ideas of closer regulation and
control were to find their way into a colonial charter.[4] Meanwhile, the inhabitants of the new colonies managed to thwart the economic plans of the
proprietors, while at the same time they successfully challenged their political
authority.

When the Crown and Parliament began interfering with colonial economic
interests and with existing political institutions, the colonists were as ready to

---

[1] No. 51.   [2] No. 31.   [3] See Part II, D, The Evolution of Colonial Self-Government.   [4] No. 4.

challenge these new policies as they had been the plans of the proprietors. It became increasingly evident after 1660 that the colonial legislatures were the centre of resistance to the Navigation Acts, and nowhere was this more obvious than in New England where the corporation charters gave the governments a wide measure of authority. Massachusetts Bay was a conspicuous example. Repeated investigations, beginning with a royal commission in 1664 and continuing with the repeated reports of Edward Randolph,[1] demonstrated, to the satisfaction of English officials at least, that Massachusetts looked upon itself as virtually an independent state. Massachusetts, for instance, had legislated against the Navigation Act of 1651, and refused to admit that the Act of 1660 applied to the colony until it had been passed by its own legislature. Other colonies were less overt in their actions but showed their opposition in equally clear fashion.

Gradually the idea arose that the obvious way to combat the independence of the colonies was to cancel the charters and convert the colonies into royal provinces where the king could appoint the governors and councils, and thus, in theory at least, be able to control the elective legislatures. In 1679 the long dispute between the heirs of Gorges and Mason and Massachusetts over New Hampshire was settled by establishing it as a royal province. Massachusetts, however, was the particular problem, and in 1684 its charter was declared forfeit in a chancery suit.

The accession of James II in 1685 brought matters to a head. As duke of York he had ruled New York without having to consult a legislature, although he had finally allowed one to meet in 1683. The Dominion of New England, which eliminated all the colonial legislatures in the northern colonies and substituted for them rule by a governor appointed by the king, was the culmination of the effort to control the colonies in the seventeenth century.[2] This attack on the charter rights of the colonies was paralleled by a similar attack on corporation charters in England itself; but the plans of James II for arbitrary government were brought to a sudden end with the Revolution of 1688.

(viii) THE ENGLISH COLONIES, 1689-1763

The Revolution of 1688 altered the course of history in both England and the colonies. England's long struggle with Holland was ended, for the new English king was William of Orange, a Dutchman and son-in-law of the exiled James II, who was being aided by France in his efforts to recapture the throne. In 1689 there began a series of wars in which England and France were to be the principal protagonists for more than a century. To begin with, the wars were the outgrowth of a struggle for power in Europe, but in time the

[1] No. 30A.   [2] No. 30B.

conflict became one for world-wide empire. England's greatest triumph came in 1763 when she destroyed for ever France's American empire. England's greatest humiliation came but twenty years later when the heart of her own American empire was destroyed as she was forced to recognize the independence of the United States.

The French and English colonies were inevitably involved in the wars fought in Europe, although colonial interests were at first given little consideration in the diplomacy of war and peace. But during the eighteenth century, as the French increased their hold on the Ohio and Mississippi valleys and as the English colonists pushed westward, North America increasingly became a centre of conflict. Initially the struggle was one for control of the fur trade of the Ohio Valley, but ultimately the issue was whether or not the French were to limit the expansion of the English colonies to the narrow strip of land between the Atlantic Ocean and the western bounds of the Appalachian Mountains.

In the course of the conflict the French colonies had certain advantages over the English. Above all they functioned as a unit under the command of governors who did not need to consult legislatures since none existed. Any unified English policy, whether for offence or defence, depended not only on many governors, but on an equal number of legislatures which were responsible for raising money for military purposes. Not only were these legislatures jealous of their prerogative of raising money; most of them assumed that because they raised it they should also direct its expenditure, even to the determination of the extent and direction of military campaigns. It was inevitable, therefore, that military matters were often lost sight of in the course of disputes between legislatures and governors for the control of both money and military campaigns. Another difficulty arose from the fact that it was difficult to get legislatures to take common action, especially if a colony or a group of colonies was not subject to immediate attack.

A second advantage of the French was that they had the support of most of the Indians who had any contact with the English, and of still others who had merely heard of them. The French concentrated on the fur trade, and it was to their interest to maintain the Indian hunting grounds as they were. Although some of the English colonists were interested in the fur trade, the great majority of them were farmers who constantly pushed the Indians backward and destroyed their way of life. Such facts were obvious to most of the Indians and they objected bitterly to English encroachment.

On the other hand, the English colonies had advantages as well, and in the end they were to prove decisive. First of all, they were concentrated along the Atlantic seaboard, whereas the French were scattered in small settlements, ranging all the way from the mouth of the St. Lawrence River to the mouth of the Mississippi River. Even more important was the fact that when the struggle began the English colonists outnumbered the French by ten to one, and the disproportion was even greater by the middle of the eighteenth century.

The separatism of the English colonies and their mutual needs and antagonisms early led to the development of the idea of a union of the colonies. The New England Confederation was the first example of a union put into practice. It was a voluntary association formed in 1643 by the colonies of Massachusetts Bay, Plymouth, Connecticut, and New Haven. It was born of a need for common defence against the Indians, of a fear of conflict with the Dutch and French colonies, and of a scarcely hidden desire to eliminate the radical settlements in Rhode Island, a colony the Confederation refused to admit to membership. While the Confederation recognized the independence of each member, it assumed the sovereign powers of making war and peace and made treaties with both the Dutch and French colonists. The importance of the Confederation was ended by the 1660's, although commissioners continued to meet until the 1680's.

The second example of a colonial union was the Dominion of New England, which was imposed on the northern colonies from the outside, but its life was short and it had little result except to confirm the attachment of colonies to their political institutions and their separatism from one another.

The first plan for a union of all the colonies was set forth by William Penn in 1698. He proposed that a congress of deputies from all the colonies meet regularly and be presided over by a royal appointee who would be commander-in-chief in time of war. The congress would be given power to settle differences between colony and colony in such matters as fleeing debtors, fugitives from justice, and commercial disputes. Beyond this it would have the power to provide for the defence of the colonies, including the apportionment of quotas of men and money to be raised by each of them.

Many other plans were to follow. One of the notable suggestions was that of the Board of Trade in 1721. In an elaborate report on the state of the colonies in which the difficulties of administering any policy, whether political, economic, or military, were elaborated, the Board suggested that the colonies from Nova Scotia to South Carolina be put under one "Lord Lieutenant or Captain General from whom all other Governors of particular provinces should receive their orders, in all cases. . . ." This official would be constantly attended by two "councillors" from each province and should have a fixed salary "independent of the pleasure of the inhabitants. . . ." The benefit to be derived from such a system would be that "a general contribution of men or money may be raised upon the several Colonies, in proportion to their respective abilities".[1]

This proposal, like others for colonial union, received little or no serious

[1] This report is printed in *New York Colonial Documents*, v, pp. 591-629.

consideration. It was not until a renewal of war between France and England threatened in 1753 that the British government took action. In that year the Board of Trade instructed colonial governors to meet in a conference for the purpose of making a treaty with the Six Nations and of preparing plans for common defence against the French and their Indian allies. The four New England colonies and New York, Pennsylvania, and Maryland, sent commissioners who met at Albany, New York, in June 1754. The conference achieved little in the way of concrete plans for defence, but it adopted a plan of colonial union which proposed that Parliament pass an act whereby "one general government may be formed in America. . . ." The plan outlined a proposed constitution. It provided for a "Grand Council", to consist of delegates elected by the colonial legislatures, with the number of members in it to be in proportion to the amount contributed by each colony to the general treasury, but with no colony having more than seven nor less than two members. The constitution gave sweeping powers to the central government in matters of defence, taxation for defence, and in the granting and government of unsettled lands. The government was to be presided over by a "President General" appointed by the king, but the constitution carefully provided for the limitation of his power by the Grand Council.

The plan was ignored by the British government, which was more concerned with preparing for war than with a colonial union, and it was rejected by every colonial legislature, for the colonies had no more intention of surrendering any portion of their authority to a central government in America than they had of submitting to increased British control a few years later. The result was that the last of the wars between the French and English in the American colonies was fought as the earlier ones had been: with each colony contributing as much in the way of men and money as it thought fit.

The first of the wars in which the French and English colonists were involved was the War of the League of Augsburg (1689–1697), known in American history as King William's War. In the course of it France again sent the able Count Frontenac to Canada as governor. He at once dispatched raiding parties of French and Indians down upon the northern colonies. These attacked and burned frontier towns in New England and the town of Schenectady, New York. The English colonists retaliated. Under the leadership of Sir William Phips, Massachusetts forces captured Port Royal in Acadia (Nova Scotia). Phips then planned an attack on Quebec. The town was besieged, but the expedition ended in a miserable failure. So, too, did an expedition from the northern colonies that went up the Lake Champlain route to attack Montreal. During the next six years the French and Indians raided the frontiers of the northern colonies and forced the abandonment of many a settlement. The French also were able to cut in half the fighting strength of the Six Nations, the only powerful Indian allies of the English. When peace was made at Ryswick in 1697, colonial questions were of so little consequence that Port Royal was handed back to the French. The northern colonists were thus left with nothing for their efforts in the war except a lively fear of and deadly hatred for the French in Canada.

Within five years France and England were at war again. Louis XIV of France placed his grandson on the throne of Spain and thus united two of the world's greatest colonial empires. England and most of the rest of Europe went to war against this threat of world domination by France. The War of the Spanish Succession (1701–1713) was known to the colonists as Queen Anne's War, for William III died shortly after it began and was succeeded by his sister-in-law, Anne. As in the previous war, the French and Indians descended upon the northern colonies, burning villages and killing or capturing their inhabitants. The English colonists fought back as best they could, but they got no significant help from England until 1710, when a large fleet was sent to America. Colonial and English forces joined in capturing Port Royal once more. The next year a combined force of English and colonials besieged but was unable to take Quebec. The war was also fought on the southern frontiers. In 1702 a force of South Carolinians burned St. Augustine and shortly thereafter they successfully defended Charleston from an attack by a combined French and Spanish fleet.

The war ended with the Treaty of Utrecht in 1713. By this treaty England enlarged her American holdings at the expense of France, although the treaty did not go as far in the direction of limiting French power as some of the American colonists had hoped it would. France gave up her claims to the Hudson's Bay region and thus opened the way for the westward expansion of the Hudson's Bay Company which had been chartered in 1670. The surrender of French claims to Newfoundland and the cession of Acadia, which was renamed Nova Scotia, proved to be of great benefit to New England fishermen. A sore spot in the West Indies was eliminated by the surrender of French claims to those portions of the island of St. Christopher which Frenchmen had once occupied. From Spain, England won the *Asiento*, which had previously been given to France. This contract gave English and colonial slave traders a thirty-year monopoly of supplying the Spanish colonies with Negro slaves and opened the way for a certain amount of other trade.[1]

The long-range importance of the treaty for the colonies, however, was the fact that it established a peace that was to last for more than a quarter of a century. Warfare had been almost continuous since 1689. The French and Indian raids on the frontiers of the English colonies had forced the abandonment of many settlements, and the inhabitants who had survived were forced back

[1] No. 81.

into the already crowded older settlements. Peace after 1713 meant that they could expand in all directions and this they did with astonishing rapidity.

Nowhere was this expansion more evident than in the growth of population, a growth so rapid that the population of the colonies doubled every twenty or twenty-five years during the eighteenth century. Population had grown steadily but slowly during the seventeenth century, but it had remained concentrated in a narrow band of settlements along the coast, held there by power of the Indians and by the vastness of the task of clearing the forest as the colonists moved inland. English migration to the colonies dropped off during the last half of the century, some of the Restoration colonies being settled by migrations from other colonies. Towards the end of the century the migration of non-English peoples began to be important, but it did not reach full tide until after 1713. During the eighteenth century the great flood of people to the English colonies came from northern Ireland, the German Palatinate, Switzerland, and France. The eighteenth century witnessed also a rapid increase in the numbers of Negro slaves, an increase so great that by 1776 they constituted at least sixteen per cent of the population of the mainland colonies and an even greater proportion of that of the West Indian colonies.[1]

Peace and the rapid growth of population made for rapid geographical expansion. Frontier outposts that had been abandoned after 1689 were re-occupied and settlers pushed beyond them into new regions. Pennsylvania became the great dispersion centre for the immigrants of the eighteenth century. The Scotch-Irish and Germans settled the Pennsylvania back country and then moved south-west, providing the bulk of the inhabitants of the back country of Virginia and North Carolina, and by the middle of the century they were beginning to establish themselves in western South Carolina and Georgia as well.

Although the colonial towns grew steadily, the agrarian population grew far more rapidly, for most immigrants were farmers or men who wanted to be farmers rather than town dwellers. Thus the growth of an agricultural population was accompanied by a rapid increase in surplus crops whose chief markets were reached by water. Increasing quantities of wheat, Indian corn, barrelled beef and pork, livestock, and lumber were sent from one mainland colony to another, to the West Indies, and to the Mediterranean. The tobacco crops of Maryland and Virginia and the rice, and, later, indigo of South Carolina swelled the direct trade between the southern mainland colonies and Britain. The merchants of the northern colonies built more and more ships and took over an ever larger share of the carrying trade of the Empire. They brought manufactured goods from England and distributed them to all the colonies.[2]

[1] See Part IV: Population and Labour.
[2] See Part III, A: Colonial Agriculture and No. 55, Statistics on Colonial Trade.

The trade with the West Indies was an integral and indispensable part of the commerce of the mainland colonies, although it was not as large in either value or quantity as the direct trade with England. The West Indies played a double role in the Empire. They fitted in perfectly with the mercantilist conception of the proper role of colonies and they shaped much of English thinking about colonial policy. The tropical products, and particularly sugar, which came from them did not compete with English agriculture as did the crops of the northern mainland colonies. Nor did the West Indies ever threaten to develop manufactures. They were therefore always looked upon as more desirable than the mainland colonies, except for the southern ones with their crops of tobacco, rice, and indigo. British policy therefore always tended to favour the West Indies, even when such policy interfered harmfully with the complex web of imperial commerce.[1]

The West Indies, however, played a role quite apart from that conceived to be desirable by British theory. Since they concentrated on a few crops such as sugar, they soon became dependent upon the mainland colonies for most of their food, for the barrels and casks in which their products were shipped, for the lumber of which their houses and warehouses were built, and for the livestock used on their plantations. During the eighteenth century they were even dependent for an important part of their slave supply upon the slave traders of the mainland colonies.

The mainland colonies were in turn dependent on the West Indies as a market for their surplus wheat, corn, barrelled meats, fish, and lumber. During the eighteenth century there was a growing market in the British West Indies, but an even better market in the Dutch, Spanish, and French colonies. Not only did the foreign islands provide good markets for mainland produce, they provided bills of exchange and gold and silver as part of the profit of the trade. The profits thus acquired played an indispensable role in the direct trade between the mainland colonies and Britain. The northern colonies imported far more from Britain than they exported to her. An important part of the adverse balance of trade against them was paid from the proceeds of the trade with the West Indies, and increasingly from the trade with the foreign islands. This was a fact of which British merchants trading with the colonies were fully aware, but which few British politicians seemed to comprehend.[2]

The trade with the foreign islands, and particularly with the French, became an issue early in the eighteenth century. The French islands were reaching the peak of their production just as the English islands were entering on a long decline. The French planters were therefore able to pay higher prices for mainland produce than the British were and, in addition, they sold their products, particularly molasses, far more cheaply. The absentee British planters, who

[1] No. 51E.   [2] Nos. 52, 111.

formed a powerful *bloc* in Parliament, secured the Molasses Act of 1733 in an effort to stop the trade between the mainland colonies and the foreign islands.[1] The Act was consistent with British conceptions of the proper role of colonies, however false it was to the larger interests of imperial commerce, but the Act was never enforced effectively and so the larger issues did not have to be met.

The failure to enforce this Act was characteristic of British policy during the first half of the eighteenth century. Whatever the theory, the practice was to allow the colonies to develop pretty much as they pleased. The attempt to vacate the charters by parliamentary action was given up by 1715,[2] and although the process of royalization continued in piecemeal fashion as the various proprietors surrendered their claims, the process did not alter the course of colonial political and economic development. Laws and administrative agencies were elaborated but most of the colonies managed to achieve or maintain effective self-government during the first half of the century.[3]

During these years of peace and expansion, there were signs that the struggle between Britain and France was not over, and signs, furthermore, that the struggle for colonial empire was to loom ever larger in the making of national policies. France built the fortress of Louisbourg on Cape Breton island to guard the mouth of the St. Lawrence. New Orleans was founded in 1718 at the mouth of the Mississippi. In the Illinois country great forts were built and agricultural settlements established to provide food for French posts, including the town of New Orleans. The English colonists were pushing ever nearer to the Ohio–Mississippi Valley region, hitherto dominated by the French. The fur traders were the spearhead of the English advance, but the farmers were not far behind.

The long peace ended in 1744 with the outbreak of the War of the Austrian Succession, known to the colonists as King George's War. As before, the French and Indians raided the frontiers of the English colonies, but this time the English colonies were in a better position to carry the fight to the French. Governor William Shirley of Massachusetts was the key leader of the colonies during the war. He organized a colonial expedition against Louisbourg, a haven for French privateers. The expedition of some 4,000 colonials, led by William Pepperell, a Maine merchant, captured the fortress; and the French twice failed to retake it. Shirley then planned a major expedition against Canada in 1746, but his plans were blocked because Britain needed to use her regular troops elsewhere. When the war ended with the Treaty of Aix-la-Chapelle in 1748, Louisbourg was handed back to the French, much to the disgust of the colonists. The money grants they received from England only partially appeased them for the loss of their greatest achievement of the war.

King George's War proved to be only a preliminary so far as the colonies were concerned. No sooner was it over than the French and English colonists rushed to get control of the Ohio Valley. The French had established posts along the St. Lawrence River, the Great Lakes, and the Mississippi River before the war. They now began establishing posts nearer to the advancing English colonists. In 1749 the governor of Canada sent a French force to occupy the Ohio Valley. That same year a group of Virginia planters, including the Washingtons and the Lees, organized the Ohio Company and got a grant of land in the Ohio Valley from the British government. Meanwhile, French and English fur traders were meeting one another everywhere in the region. In 1753 Duquesne, the governor of Canada, sent a large force to build posts even closer to the English colonies. Beginning at Presque Isle (now Erie, Pennsylvania), the French thrust southward to the Allegheny River, building posts at strategic spots.

The news of the French advance stirred the Virginians to action. Governor Robert Dinwiddie sent George Washington to order the French out. Not far behind him came a company of Indian traders, who started to build a fort at the forks of the Ohio, the site of present-day Pittsburgh. Control of the forks of the Ohio meant control of the entire Ohio Valley, as both the French and English realized.

The English traders had not much more than started to build their fort when the French arrived, captured it and renamed it Fort Duquesne, and drove the traders back east of the mountains. Washington, who had returned to Virginia, now came back with troops to garrison the fort. On his way he met the retreating traders, but continued onward until he met a French force. A fight broke out and the French commander was killed. Washington then retreated to a place to which he gave the highly appropriate name of Fort Necessity. He was attacked there by a much larger French force and was forced to surrender on 4 July 1754.

Thus for the first time war had begun between France and England in their colonies, and it was no less real for being undeclared. The first round went to the French, who were left in possession of the Ohio Valley. British leaders were by now very much aware of the importance of the struggle in the colonies. They realized that the Indian support would be needed, particularly that of the Six Nations. It was the recognition of this and of the need of colonial co-operation in the coming struggle that led the Board of Trade to send out instructions in September 1753 that led to the Albany Congress in the summer of 1754.

Meanwhile, the British government worked out an elaborate plan for taking French posts in the west, although war had not yet begun officially. Simultaneous attacks on Crown Point on Lake Champlain, Fort Niagara, and Fort Duquesne were planned. General Edward Braddock, an able officer but one with no experience in the colonies, was placed in charge. He arrived in Virginia in 1755 and led a combined army of British regulars and colonial militia against

3

Fort Duquesne. By early July the army was within seven or eight miles of the fort. The officers were so sure of success with their superior force that they were wrangling as to who should have the honour of first entering the fort, and in so doing they failed to guard against a surprise attack. Suddenly the French and Indians poured fire upon them from every side and the British and colonial troops were utterly routed. Braddock was killed after bravely but helplessly trying to force his men to stand and fight. What was left of the army retreated eastward, leaving the French still in control of the Ohio Valley. And the road cut by Braddock made it even easier for the Indians to raid frontier settlements to the eastward.

The next year the Seven Years War broke out in Europe, with England and Prussia fighting against France, Austria, and Russia. The struggle was carried on in North America, the West Indies, and India, as well as in Europe. During the first two years of the war Britain suffered one disaster after another. Frederick the Great of Prussia was beaten in Europe. A British fleet in the Mediterranean was whipped. An attack on Louisbourg failed. In America much of French success was due to the Marquis de Montcalm, a man who had learned warfare in Europe but who, unlike many British generals, adapted himself easily to warfare in the American wilderness. The French captured Fort Oswego on Lake Ontario and Fort William Henry on Lake George, and shoved back every British effort to invade Canada.

The turning-point came in 1757 with the prime ministership of William Pitt. He poured men and money into the fight all over the world. He promised the American colonists that Britain would pay for the arms, ammunition, and food provided for troops raised by them. The result was far more active support by the colonists than they had ever given before.

In 1758 the war in North America took a turn for the better. A British fleet and an army took the fortress of Louisbourg. In 1760 it was destroyed, leaving Halifax, which the British had founded in 1749, as the only fort near the entry of the St. Lawrence River. While Louisbourg was under attack, another campaign was launched against Fort Duquesne. General Forbes with over a thousand Highlanders and nearly 5,000 militia from Pennsylvania, Maryland, Virginia, and North Carolina started westward. The force moved slowly, and before it reached the Ohio, France's Indian allies deserted her and the French themselves blew up the fort and left. The British took over and renamed the place Fort Pitt. Meantime Fort Frontenac on Lake Ontario had been taken by still another British force. The result of these two events was to destroy the network of posts the French had built to control the Ohio Valley. The only failure in 1758 was that of General Abercrombie, who was beaten at Fort Ticonderoga on Lake Champlain by a French garrison only a fourth the size of his army.

With the outposts of French power taken, the next blow was struck at its heart. In 1759 General Amherst was sent by the Lake Champlain route, and General Wolfe was sent by way of the St. Lawrence against Quebec. The French abandoned Ticonderoga and Crown Point as the British advanced. An expedition was sent to take Fort Niagara, which it did easily. But the French fortified themselves at the entrance to the River Richelieu, and this, with the onset of winter, stopped Amherst's advance. Wolfe was thus left to attack Quebec alone. He arrived before the town in June 1759 and bombarded it for two months, but Montcalm remained safe within its fortifications. The approach of winter forced Wolfe to more drastic action. He found a way up to the Plains of Abraham behind the town. There Montcalm met him in a battle that lasted but a few minutes and in which both generals were killed. The Quebec garrison surrendered on 17 September 1759

The British held Quebec through the winter, but more than half of their troops were ineffective by spring. In April 1760 the British lost heavily in beating off a French attack from Montreal. They managed to hold Quebec only because of the timely arrival of British ships and supplies. During the summer of 1760 three British expeditions were launched against Montreal, the last stronghold of the French in Canada. One expedition came from Quebec; another came from Oswego by way of the St. Lawrence; and a third came up the Lake Champlain route. The three forces converged early in September, and Montreal surrendered without a struggle. French power in North America was finally and for ever broken.

The year 1760 also marked the accession of George III. His attitude was soon made clear when he spoke to the Privy Council of "this bloody and expensive war". In the spring of 1761 he placed the earl of Bute in the cabinet and shortly thereafter protracted negotiations for peace got under way. When France and Spain signed the "Family Compact" in August of that year, Pitt proposed that war be declared on Spain. The cabinet and the king refused to agree. Pitt resigned in October and in January 1762 Britain declared war on Spain. During that year British expeditions took the Philippine Islands and Havana, Cuba. France and Spain were now ready for peace, although Pitt and his followers wanted to continue the war until the conquest was complete.

The Treaty of Paris in February 1763 ended the war. The treaty was clear evidence of Britain's sweeping victory and of France's crushing defeat. Canada, Cape Breton Island, and all of the region east of the Mississippi were ceded to Britain. France retained only the right to dry fish on the north and west coast of Newfoundland. France gave up the islands of Tobago, Dominica, Grenada, and St. Vincent in the West Indies, retaining Guadeloupe, Martinique, and St. Lucia. Her colonies in India, except for Pondicherry and Chandernagore, likewise went to the British. Spain too lost territory. Britain returned the

Philippines and Havana, but insisted on having Florida. The French tried to help out their ally by offering Louisiana to Britain in place of Florida, but the British refused to take it. Later, France gave Louisiana to Spain, who accepted it reluctantly. More than gratitude was involved, for France had been spending far more on the colony than it had been getting in return.

Britain's victory in the Seven Years War left her the most powerful empire in the world. France was crushed for the time being, and Spain was virtually helpless. Britain's navy dominated the seas. Her Empire in the New World reached its greatest extent. After the new possessions were organized, that empire consisted of thirty-one separate colonies: thirteen in the West Indies and eighteen in North America. All but two of these colonies, Quebec and East Florida, had elective legislatures. Twenty-six of the colonies were royal provinces with governors and councils appointed by the Crown.[1] Only two corporation colonies, Connecticut and Rhode Island, and only three proprietary colonies, Pennsylvania, Maryland, and Delaware, remained outside of direct royal control.

Yet Britain's victory carried within it the seeds of disaster. Internally, the vastly increased national debt called for rigorous new financial measures, while complex political controversies resulted in a confusion of policies. The attempt to enforce old colonial policies and the adoption of new ones met with growing opposition in the American colonies. The peace of 1763 and the acquisition of new lands opened up the way for agrarian and commercial expansion; yet Britain seemed bent on limiting both, and such limitation, to be successful, involved the limitation of the power of the virtually self-governing colonies. It happened that if one phase of British colonial policy failed to irritate a segment of colonial leaders, another inevitably achieved that result.

Coupled with this fact was the growing discontent within most of the colonies over the policies of colonial governments themselves, whether religious, economic, or political.[2] The years 1763–1776 were therefore years during which motives, policies, actions, and arguments were tangled and often seemingly contradictory. But out of the weltering confusion, two opposing views rose clear and stark. A large segment of the colonists were determined to govern themselves, yielding only nominal allegiance to the Empire. The British view, on the contrary, was that the colonies must yield to the will of king and parliament in all cases–a will which would be imposed upon the colonies by the British army and navy, if need be. Independence was ultimately the American answer.[3]

[1] Massachusetts was the only exception. Under the charter of 1691, the Massachusetts council was elected annually by the House of Representatives.

[2] See Part VI: Expansion and Social Discontent.

[3] The development of British policy and the revolutionary movement is discussed in the introductions and documents in parts seven and eight of this volume.

SELECT BIBLIOGRAPHY

of bibliographies, guides, source collections, periodicals, and modern works relating to American colonial history, 1607–1776

(a) BIBLIOGRAPHIES AND GUIDES

The most comprehensive list of the many bibliographical aids for the study of American history is to be found in HENRY P. BEERS, *Bibliographies in American History: A Guide to Materials for Research* (2nd ed., New York, 1942). The best single bibliography for the period is that contained in the first volume of *The Cambridge History of the British Empire* (Cambridge, 1929). References to important modern works published since then are contained in the bibliographies in this volume. The series of thirty-three volumes called *Writings in American History*, edited by GRACE GARDNER GRIFFIN from 1906 to 1949, and published by the American Historical Association, lists virtually all of the materials that found their way into print between 1906 and 1940. The series was preceded by two volumes for the years 1902 and 1903. As yet no volumes have been published for the years 1941–1947, but the series was resumed under the editorship of JAMES M. MASTERSON with the publication in 1952 of the volume for 1948.

Beginning with the foundation of the Massachusetts Historical Society in 1793, an ever-increasing number of local, state, and national societies have devoted themselves to the publication of historical materials. Most of their publications since 1905 have been listed in the Griffin *Writings*. For the years before 1905 the only guide is A. P. C. GRIFFIN, "Bibliography of American Historical Societies (The United States and the Dominion of Canada)", in the American Historical Association, *Annual Report* (1905), vol. II. The best modern guide to many of the printed sources for a single state is E. G. SWEM, *Virginia Historical Index* (2 vols., Roanoke, Va., 1934–1936).

There are two major bibliographies of materials printed in and about America from the time of discovery down into the nineteenth century. In 1868 JOSEPH SABIN published the first volume of *Bibliotheca Americana: A Dictionary of Books relating to America, from its Discovery to the Present Time* (New York, 1868). Sabin published the nineteenth volume of this dictionary in 1892. Publication under the editorship of WILBERFORCE EAMES was resumed in the 1920's. It was completed with the publication of vol. XXIX in 1936. Over 100,000 printed works are listed but its limitations are described in the introduction to the final volume. Far more convenient and useful for the works printed in America is CHARLES EVANS, *American Bibliography. A Chronological Dictionary of all Books, Pamphlets, and Periodical Publications Printed in the United States of America from the Genesis of Printing in 1639 down to and Including the Year 1820* (12 vols., Chicago, Ill., 1903–1934). Volumes I–IV cover the years 1639–1776. They list 15,228 printed items and indicate the libraries where known copies may be found.

The materials for English history paralleling the colonial period of American history are listed in GODFREY DAVIES, *Bibliography of British History, Stuart Period, 1603–1714* (Oxford, 1928), in STANLEY PARGELLIS and D. J. MEDLEY, *Bibliography of British History: The Eighteenth Century, 1714–1789* (Oxford, 1951) and more particularly in vols. VII–X of this series of *English Historical Documents*. For American materials in the Reports of the Royal Commission on Historical Manuscripts, see J. FRANKLIN JAMESON, "Guide to the Items Relating to American History in the Reports of the English Historical Manuscripts Commission and their Appendixes", Amer. Hist. Assoc. *Annual Report* (1898). *The Cambridge History of the British Empire*, vol. I, pp. 837–838, should also be consulted as well as the *Guide to the Reports of the Royal Commission on Historical Manuscripts, 1870–1911* (Part One, London, 1914, and Part Two, 2 vols., London, 1935–1938).

Colonial newspapers and periodicals are an invaluable source for the history of the eighteenth century. CLARENCE S. BRIGHAM, *History and Bibliography of American Newspapers, 1690–1820* (2 vols., Worcester, Mass., 1947) is indispensable. It indicates the location of all known copies at the time of the publication of the work. LYON N. RICHARDSON, *A History of Early American Magazines, 1741–1789* (New York, 1931) contains a bibliography of all the magazines of the colonial period. These have all been microfilmed and are available for purchase. The value of colonial newspapers as a source is revealed in LESTER J. CAPPON and STELLA F. DUFF, *Virginia Gazette Index, 1736–1780* (2 vols., Williamsburg, Va., 1950). The *Virginia Gazette* and an increasing number of other colonial newspapers are now available on microfilm. HENNIG COHEN, *The South Carolina Gazette, 1732–1775* (Columbia, S.C., 1953) presents some of the material from one of the better colonial newspapers.

(b) GUIDES TO MANUSCRIPT MATERIALS

The manuscripts in European and American libraries of value for the history of the American colonies, number in the millions. Fortunately for the scholar, no period of American history is as well supplied with guides to these materials, particularly those in European libraries. The Carnegie Institution of Washington for many years subsidized the necessary research and the publication of a series of guides to American materials in Europe. Of these, the most important are CHARLES M. ANDREWS, *Guide to the Materials for American History to 1783, in the Public Record Office of Great Britain* (2 vols., Washington, 1912–1914) and CHARLES M. ANDREWS and FRANCES G. DAVENPORT, *Guide to the Manuscript Materials for the History of the United States to 1783, in the British Museum, in Minor London Archives, and in the Libraries of Oxford and Cambridge* (Washington, 1908). Other guides are HERBERT C. BELL, D. W. PARKER, et al., *Guide to British West Indian Archive Materials, in London and in the Islands, for the History of the United States* (Washington, 1926); CARL RUSSELL FISH, *Guide to the Materials for American History in Roman and other Italian Archives* (Washington, 1911); WALDO G. LELAND, *Guide to Materials for American History in the Libraries and Archives of Paris, Volume I, Libraries* (Washington, 1932); WALDO G. LELAND JOHN J. MENG, and ABEL DOYSIE, *Guide to Materials for American History in the Libraries and Archives of Paris, Volume II, Archives of the Ministry of Foreign Affairs* (Washington, 1943); DAVID W. PARKER, *Guide to the Materials for United States History in Canadian Archives* (Washington, 1913); WILLIAM R. SHEPHERD, *Guide to the Materials for the History of the United States in Spanish Archives* (Washington, 1907); HERBERT E. BOLTON, *Guide to Materials for the History of the United States in the Principal Archives of Mexico* (Washington, 1913); MARION D. LEARNED, *Guide to the Manuscript Materials Relating to American History in the German State Archives* (Washington, 1912); ALBERT B. FAUST, *Guide to The Materials for American History in Swiss and Austrian Archives* (Washington, 1916). For a description of these and other guides published by the Carnegie Institution, see ROSCOE R. HILL, *American Missions in European Archives* (Mexico City, 1951).

Supplementary guides of great usefulness are CHARLES M. ANDREWS, "List of the Commissions and Instructions Issued to the Governors and Lieutenant Governors of the American and West Indian Colonies from 1609 to 1784", Amer. Hist. Assoc. *Annual Report* (1911), vol. I, and "List of Reports and Representations of the Plantation Councils, 1660–1674, the Lords of Trade, 1675–1696, and the Board of Trade, 1696–1782, in the Public Record Office", Amer. Hist. Assoc. *Annual Report* (1913), vol. I. The Library of Congress in Washington contains BENJAMIN F. STEVENS's 180 volume "Catalogue Index of MSS in the Archives of England, France, Holland,

and Spain relating to America, 1763-1783". The materials acquired in transcript, photostat, and microfilm by the Manuscript Division of the Library of Congress from British libraries is listed in GRACE GARDNER GRIFFIN, *A Guide to Manuscripts Relating to American History in British Depositories Reproduced for the Division of Manuscripts of the Library of Congress* (Washington, 1946).

Extensive though such guides are, they are by no means complete for new materials have continued to appear. A recent example in Britain is that of the Rockingham Papers which have been given to the Sheffield Public Library. Meanwhile, the Library of Congress has continued to acquire quantities of new microfilm from British and other sources which are not listed in the Griffin *Guide*.

There are useful guides to some of the many manuscript collections in libraries in the United States. Least adequate are the guides to the greatest collection of all: that of the Manuscript Division of the Library of Congress in Washington. *Handbook of Manuscripts in the Library of Congress* (Washington, 1918) with two supplements: "List of Manuscript Collections in the Library of Congress to July, 1931", in Amer. Hist. Assoc. *Annual Report* (1930), vol. 1, and "List of Manuscript Collections Received in the Library of Congress, July 1931 to July 1938", Amer. Hist. Assoc. *Annual Report* (1937), vol. 1, should be consulted. Acquisitions since then have been listed briefly in the issues of the *American Historical Review* and in the annual reports of the Librarian of Congress.

The holdings of some of the other major libraries containing valuable material for American colonial history are listed in printed guides. These include: *Handbook of the Massachusetts Historical Society, 1791-1948* (Boston, 1949); *A Guide to the Resources of the American Antiquarian Society* (Worcester, Mass., 1937); EVERTS B. GREENE and RICHARD B. MORRIS, *A Guide to the Principal Sources for Early American History, 1600-1800, in the City of New York* (2nd ed., New York, 1954); *Guide to the Manuscript Collections in the Archives of the North Carolina Historical Commission* (Raleigh, 1942); *Guide to the Manuscripts in the Southern Historical Collection of the University of North Carolina* (Chapel Hill, N.C., 1941); HELEN G. McCORMACK, "A Provisional Guide to the Manuscripts in the South Carolina Historical Society", in the *South Carolina Historical and Genealogical Magazine*, vols. XLV-XLVII (1944-1947); *Guide to the Manuscript Collections of the Historical Society of Pennsylvania* (2nd ed., Philadelphia, 1949); WILLIAM S. EWING, *Guide to the Manuscript Collections in the William L. Clements Library* (Ann Arbor, Mich., 1953); ALICE E. SMITH, *Guide to the Manuscripts of the Wisconsin Historical Society* (Madison, Wis., 1944); NORMA B. CUTHBERT, *American Manuscript Collections in the Huntington Library for the History of the Seventeenth and Eighteenth Centuries* (San Marino, Cal., 1941). Of considerable value as a check-list is the Library of Congress publication, *Manuscripts in Public and Private Collections in the United States* (Washington, 1924) which lists the papers of over 2,500 individuals in 131 different libraries. A check-list of all the available guides to manuscript collections may be found in RAY A. BILLINGTON, "Guides to American History Manuscript Collections in Libraries of the United States", *Mississippi Valley Historical Review*, vol. XXXVIII (1951).

The most comprehensive survey of manuscripts ever undertaken in America was that of the Historical Records Survey, a division of the Works Progress Administration (WPA) during the 1930's. Literally hundreds of mimeographed volumes of guides to federal, state, county, and town records; to church, school, and private manuscript collections, and the like, were prepared. As yet no bibliographical survey of this vast body of material has been prepared but it is available in the various American libraries which served as depositories for the Survey.

The public archives of the thirteen states and of the United States contain great quantities of material. Although many of the original states have published portions of their colonial records, even more remains in manuscript form. In 1899 the American Historical Association established a Public Archives Commission which undertook to survey the archives of each state, including local town, county, and court records, as well as those of the state governments. The results of its findings were printed in the annual reports of the American Historical Association between 1900 and 1917. As a result of this investigation, ADELAIDE R. HASSE published "Materials for a Bibliography of the Public Archives of the Thirteen Original States", Amer. Hist. Assoc. *Annual Report* (1906), vol. II, which is a guide to the archival materials which had been published up to that time. Recently the bulk of archival materials of the several states has been made available on microfilm in a project sponsored jointly by the Library of Congress and the University of North Carolina. Approximately 2,500,000 pages of legislative, constitutional, and administrative records, as well as legal records, are available for purchase. While the records of all forty-eight states are included, there is much for the thirteen colonies. For this, consult *A Guide to the Microfilm Collection of Early State Records* (Washington, 1950). The National Archives in Washington contains relatively little material for the years before 1774 but what it does have is valuable and can be located in *Guide to the Records in the National Archives* (Washington, 1948). In 1952 the Manuscript Division of the Library of Congress transferred to the National Archives the Papers of the Continental Congress, the basic materials relating to the history of that body from 1774 to 1789.

The Public Record Office in London contains a remarkable collection of legislative journals for the colonial period. For these, consult CHARLES M. ANDREWS, "List of the Journals and Acts of the Councils and Assemblies of the Thirteen Original Colonies, and the Floridas, in America, preserved in the Public Record Office in London", in Amer. Hist. Assoc. *Annual Report* (1908), vol. I.

(c) GENERAL WORKS

The colonial period of American history has been the subject of many histories, some of which are monuments of historiography. The writing began with the founders of the colonies themselves. CAPTAIN JOHN SMITH wrote many books. The most important, *The General Historie of Virginia, New-England, and the Summer Isles*, was first printed in London in 1624 and has been reprinted several times since then. Among the histories by the founders of New England, WILLIAM BRADFORD's *Of Plymouth Plantation* is the finest, and is perhaps the greatest of the contemporary historical works produced in and about the American colonies. It did not find its way into print until 1856. The best modern edition is that of SAMUEL ELIOT MORISON (New York, 1953). JOHN WINTHROP's *Journal, or History of New England, 1630-1649* is equally valuable if not so distinguished a piece of writing as Bradford's history. The most accessible edition is that of J. K. HOSMER (2 vols., New York, 1908, in *Original Narratives of Early American History*).

The generations that succeeded the founders wrote histories in ever greater numbers. Among the more notable are those of ROBERT BEVERLEY, *The History and Present State of Virginia* (London, 1705) which may be found in a modern edition by LOUIS B. WRIGHT (Chapel Hill, N.C., 1947) and WILLIAM SMITH, *The History of the Late Province of New York* (vol. I, London, 1757, vol. II, New York, 1826) which carries the history of New York down to the year 1762. The outstanding history written in the eighteenth century was THOMAS HUTCHINSON's *The History of the Colony and Province of Massachusetts Bay* (3 vols., Boston, 1764-1828) which is available in a modern edition by L. S. MAYO (3 vols., Cambridge, Mass., 1936). The best modern discussion of these and many other contemporary histories is to be found in JARVIS M. MORSE, *American Beginnings: Highlights and Sidelights of the Birth of the New World* (Washington, 1952).

The number of multivolume modern histories of the colonial period exceeds that for any other area of American history. The first was that of GEORGE BANCROFT, *History of the United States* (10 vols., Boston, 1834-1874), the first seven volumes of which deal with the colonial period. FRANCIS PARKMAN's several volumes subtitled *France and England in America*, which appeared between 1865 and 1884, are literary as well as historical classics. J. A. DOYLE, *English Colonies in America* (5 vols., London, 1882–1907) is the only major work by an Englishman on the American colonies. JUSTIN WINSOR, ed., *Narrative and Critical History of America* (8 vols., Boston, 1884–1889) brought together many scholars who produced many detailed studies and elaborate bibliographical and cartographical essays as well. HERBERT L. OSGOOD, *The American Colonies in the Seventeenth Century* (3 vols., New York, 1904–1907) and *The American Colonies in the Eighteenth Century* (4 vols., New York, 1924) was the first major work treating of the colonies as a whole to be printed in the present century. The second major work is that of CHARLES M. ANDREWS, *The Colonial Period of American History* (4 vols., New Haven, Conn., 1934–1938). The most important project now under way is that of LAWRENCE H. GIPSON, *The British Empire Before the American Revolution*. It begins with the middle of the eighteenth century and so far eight volumes have been printed and carry the history down to the year 1763 (vols. I–III, Caldwell, Idaho, 1936, vols. IV–VIII, New York, 1939–1954). Shorter general works are those of THOMAS J. WERTENBAKER, *The Founding of American Civilization* (*The Middle Colonies*, New York, 1938; *The Old South*, New York, 1942; *The Puritan Oligarchy*, New York, 1947). The first four volumes of *A History of American Life* cover the colonial period. They are HERBERT J. PRIESTLEY, *The Coming of the White Man, 1492–1848* (New York, 1927); THOMAS J. WERTENBAKER, *The First Americans, 1607–1690* (New York, 1927); JAMES T. ADAMS, *Provincial Society, 1690–1763* (New York, 1927); and EVERTS B. GREENE, *The Revolutionary Generations, 1763–1790* (New York, 1943). The first nine volumes of the older *The American Nation, A History* (27 vols., New York, 1904–1908) edited by ALBERT B. HART, cover the colonial period and several of these volumes are still useful. The first three volumes of EDWARD CHANNING, *A History of the United States* (New York, 1905–1912) are also valuable, and the third volume is still the best single volume on the American Revolution.

Aside from general histories, those of the particular colonies are too numerous for listing here. The best single bibliography of such histories is to be found in *The Cambridge History of the British Empire*, vol. I, which was a reasonably complete listing at the time it was published (1929). There are also many volumes on particular aspects of colonial life as a whole, and of life in individual colonies. Relevant works of this kind are listed in the various bibliographies for the subsequent parts of this volume. Of the works treating of groups of colonies, the most recent and useful are JAMES T. ADAMS, *The Founding of New England* (Boston, 1921) and *Revolutionary New England, 1691–1776* (Boston, 1923) and W. FRANK CRAVEN, *The Southern Colonies in the Seventeenth Century, 1607–1689* (*A History of the South*, vol. I, Baton Rouge, La., 1949). Many important figures in colonial history have been the subject of full length biographies, but even more have not. Indispensable for the latter, and useful as a guide to the former, are the *Dictionary of National Biography* (22 vols., and supplements, reprinted, Oxford, 1937–1949) and the *Dictionary of American Biography* (21 vols., New York, 1928–1944). A convenient reference work, although it must be used with caution, is the *Dictionary of American History* (2nd ed., 6 vols., New York, 1946. JAMES T. ADAMS and R. V. COLEMAN, ed.). Invaluable is CHARLES O. PAULLIN, *Atlas of the Historical Geography of the United States* (Washington, 1932) which includes not only many detailed maps for colonial history, but detailed discussions of such things as early maps of the new world, exploration, land grants, colonial boundary disputes, and the like.

(d) HISTORIES OF THE PARTICULAR COLONIES

The number of books, monographs, and articles on the history of individual colonies is vast and continues to grow. The best short accounts are to be found in the writings of HERBERT L. OSGOOD and CHARLES M. ANDREWS. Andrews's work has a particular value because it includes accounts of the founding of the West Indian colonies as well as those on the mainland. The following are among the more important books on individual colonies.

Connecticut: CHARLES M. ANDREWS, *The River Towns of Connecticut* (Baltimore, 1889); ISABEL M. CALDER, *The New Haven Colony* (New Haven, 1934); and NELSON P. MEAD, *Connecticut as a Corporate Colony* (Lancaster, Pa., 1906).

Delaware: Despite the fact that the early population of the region that became the colony of Dalaware numbered only in the hundreds, it has received full treatment in AMUNDUS K. JOHNSON, *The Swedish Settlements on the Delaware . . . 1638–1664* (2 vols., New York, 1911); CHRISTOPHER WARD, *The Dutch and Swedes on the Delaware, 1609–1664* (Philadelphia, 1930); and JOHN H. WUORINEN, *The Finns on the Delaware, 1638–1655* (New York, 1938).

Georgia: JAMES R. McCAIN, *Georgia as a Proprietary Province* (Boston, 1917); PERCY S. FLIPPIN, "The Royal Government in Georgia, 1752–1776", *Georgia Historical Quarterly,* vols. VIII, IX, X, XII, XIII; ALBERT B. SAYE, *New Viewpoints in Georgia History* (Athens, Ga., 1943); and VERNER W. CRANE, "The Philanthropists and the Genesis of Georgia", *Amer. Hist. Rev.,* vol. XXVII (1921–1922).

Maine: HENRY S. BURRAGE, *The Beginnings of Colonial Maine, 1602–1658* (Portland, Maine, 1914).

Maryland: BERNARD C. STEINER, *Beginnings of Maryland, 1631–1639* (Baltimore, 1903); and NEWTON D. MERENESS, *Maryland as a Proprietary Province* (New York, 1901).

Massachusetts: No colony has had its history so written and rewritten with overmuch time spent in attacking and defending the Puritan leaders. JAMES T. ADAMS, *The Founding of New England* (Boston, 1921) views the Puritans dimly, while SAMUEL E. MORISON, *Builders of the Bay Colony* (Boston, 1930) presents them in a more friendly manner. Much is still to be learned from THOMAS HUTCHINSON's eighteenth century *The History . . . of Massachusetts Bay.*

New Hampshire: JEREMY BELKNAP, *The History of New Hampshire* (3 vols., Philadelphia and Boston, 1784–1792) stands with Hutchinson's history and will remain the best history of early New Hampshire until a better one is written. See also W. H. FRY, *New Hampshire as a Royal Province* (New York, 1908).

New Jersey: E. P. TANNER, *The Province of New Jersey, 1664–1738* (New York, 1908); E. J. FISHER, *New Jersey as a Royal Province, 1738–1776* (New York, 1911); and DONALD L. KEMMERER, *Path to Freedom: The Struggle for Self-Government in New Jersey, 1703–1776* (Princeton, N.J., 1940).

New Plymouth: WILLIAM BRADFORD, *Of Plymouth Plantation,* remains the basic work. GEORGE F. WILLISON, *Saints and Strangers* (New York, 1945) is no improvement, although it has the advantage of being a history of the colony until it became a part of Massachusetts in 1691.

New York: The first two volumes of the *History of the State of New York* (10 vols., New York, 1933–1937, A. C. FLICK, ed.) are the best modern treatment.

North Carolina: JOHN S. BASSETT, *The Constitutional Beginnings of North Carolina (1663–1729)* (Baltimore, 1894); and VERNER W. CRANE, *The Southern Frontier, 1670–1732* (Philadelphia, 1929); and C. L. RAPER, North Carolina, *A Study in English Colonial Government* (New York, 1904).

Pennsylvania: W. R. SHEPHERD, *History of the Proprietary Government in Pennsylvania* (New York, 1896) and WINFRED T. ROOT, *The Relations of Pennsylvania with the British Government 1696–1765* (Philadelphia, 1912).

Rhode Island: I. B. RICHMAN, *Rhode Island, Its Making and Its Meaning* (2 vols., New York, 1902) is the most recent full-scale history, but since so much of its early history is that of Roger Williams, his biographies are indispensable. The most recent is that of SAMUEL BROCKUNIER, *The Irrepressible Democrat, Roger Williams* (New York, 1940).

South Carolina: The only modern history of early South Carolina is contained in the first two volumes of DAVID D. WALLACE, *The History of South Carolina* (4 vols., New York, 1934). See also EDWARD MCCRADY, *The History of South Carolina under the Proprietary Government, 1670–1719* (New York, 1897); *The History of South Carolina under the Royal Government, 1719–1776* (New York, 1899); and WILLIAM R. SMITH, *South Carolina as a Royal Province, 1719–1776* (New York, 1903).

Virginia: PHILIP A. BRUCE, *Institutional History of Virginia in the Seventeenth Century . . .* (2 vols., New York, 1910) presents much detail. PERCY S. FLIPPIN, *The Royal Government in Virginia 1624–1775* (New York, 1919) emphasizes political life. THOMAS J. WERTENBAKER, *Virginia Under the Stuarts, 1607–1688* (Princeton, N.J., 1914) and MARY N. STANARD, *The Story of Virginia's First Century* (Philadelphia, 1928) present contrasting interpretations.

For the West Indian colonies, see the bibliography in *The Cambridge History of the British Empire,* I, pp. 872–874. The new mainland colonies acquired as a result of the Seven Years War are treated in *The Cambridge History of the British Empire,* vol. VI, and in CECIL JOHNSON, *British West Florida, 1763–1783* (New Haven, Conn., 1943); CLINTON N. HOWARD, *The British Development of West Florida, 1763–1769* (Berkeley, Cal., 1947); and CHARLES L. MOWAT, *East Florida as a British Province, 1763–1784* (Berkeley, Cal., 1943).

(e) PRINTED PUBLIC RECORDS

The quantity of printed public records, both British and American, relating to the history of the colonies is very great indeed. The printed British records cover most of the important agencies concerned with colonial affairs. Likewise, most of the original thirteen states have undertaken, either through the state governments or historical societies, to search out and print portions of the official records of the colonies. Such printed records include legislative journals, court records, the actions of administrative bodies, the correspondence of colonial governors, and a great variety of miscellaneous material as well. In addition, many of the records include British material such as letters of the secretaries of State, reports of the Board of Trade, and the like.

A considerable amount of official material is also to be found in the proceedings and collections of historical societies and in non-official publications. Some of this material is listed elsewhere in this volume. Many local governments such as townships, counties, and cities have also published their official records but reference to the relevant ones are included in the bibliography on the evolution of colonial governments.

British Sources. The most convenient collection of legislation relating to the colonies is in DANBY PICKERING, ed., *The Statutes at Large . . .,* volumes 7–31 cover the years 1607–1776. It omits, however, the legislation during the Puritan Commonwealth. This can be found in C. H. FIRTH and R. S. RAIT, *Acts and Ordinances of the Interregnum* (3 vols., London, 1911). Debates in Parliament on the colonies, with much supplementary material, are brought together in LEO F. STOCK, ed., *Proceedings and Debates of the British Parliaments Respecting North America* (5 vols., Washington, 1924–1941) carries the debates through the year 1754. Debates subsequent to that year must still be searched for in Hansard's. The *Journals* of the House of Commons and the House of Lords are also valuable for any detailed study of British policy and action.

Administrative decisions at the highest level relating to the colonies, as well as important materials relating to colonial affairs, are to be found in W. L. GRANT and JAMES MUNRO, eds., *Acts of the Privy Council of England, Colonial Series* [1613–1783] (6 vols., London, 1908–1912). The activities of the Board of Trade are set forth in *Journal of the Commissioners for Trade and Plantations* [April, 1704–May, 1782] (14 vols., London, 1920–1938). Even more valuable are the *Calendar of State Papers, Colonial Series, 1574–1660* (London, 1860) and *Calendar of State Papers,*

Colonial Series, America and West Indies, 1661–1733 (33 vols., London, 1880–1939). Although the calendars of particular documents are often inadequate, they are an indispensable source of material as well as a guide to manuscripts.

CLARENCE S. BRIGHAM, ed., *British Royal Proclamations Relating to America, 1603–1783* (American Antiquarian Society *Transactions*, vol. XII, Worcester, Mass., 1911) contains most of the important proclamations. LEONARD W LABAREE, *Royal Instructions to British Colonial Governors, 1670–1776* (2 vols., New York, 1935) is indispensable for the study of royal governments in the colonies. FRANCES G. DAVENPORT, ed., *European Treaties Bearing on the History of the United States and its Dependencies* (4 vols., Washington, 1917–1937. C. O. PAULLIN, ed., vol. IV) contains the basic European treaties relating to American colonial history.

American Sources

Connecticut
> *The Public Records of the Colony of Connecticut* [1636–1776] (15 vols., Hartford, 1850–1890. J. H. TRUMBULL and C. J. HOADLY, eds.).
> *Records of the Colony and Plantation of New Haven from 1638 to 1649* (Hartford, 1857. C. J. HOADLY, ed.) and *Records of the Colony of Jurisdiction of New Haven, from May, 1653 to the Union* (Hartford, 1858. C. J. HOADLY, ed.).

Georgia
> *The Colonial Records of the State of Georgia* (26 vols., Atlanta, 1904–1916. ALLEN D. CANDLER, *et al.*, eds.).

Maine
> *Province and Court Records of Maine* (3 vols., Portland, 1928–1947. CHARLES T. LIBBY and ROBERT E. MOODY, eds. Published by the Maine Historical Society).

Maryland
> *Archives of Maryland* (65 vols. to date, Baltimore, 1883–1952. WILLIAM H. BROWNE, *et al.*, eds. Published by the Maryland Historical Society).

Massachusetts
> *Journals of the House of Representatives of Massachusetts* [1715–1752] (28 vols. to date, Boston, 1919–1953. Published by the Massachusetts Historical Society).
> *The Acts and Resolves, Public and Private, of the Province of the Massachusetts Bay* [1692–1780] (21 vols., Boston, 1869–1922).
> *Records of the Governor and Company of the Massachusetts Bay in New England* [1628–1686] (5 vols., Boston, 1853–1854. NATHANIEL B. SHURTLEFF, ed.).
> *Records of the Court of Assistants of the Colony of the Massachusetts Bay, 1630–1692* (3 vols., Boston, 1901–1928).

New Hampshire
> *Laws of New Hampshire . . . The Province Period* (3 vols., Manchester and Bristol, N. H., 1904–1915. A. S. BATCHELLOR and H. H. METCALFE, eds.).
> *Provincial, Town, and State Papers* (40 vols., Concord and Nashua, 1867–1943. NATHANIEL BOUTON, *et al.*, eds. The volumes are separately titled).

New Jersey
> *Archives of the State of New Jersey, First Series: Documents Relating to the Colonial History of the State of New Jersey* (33 vols., Newark, Trenton, Paterson, and Somerville, 1880–1928. WILLIAM A. WHITEHEAD, *et al.*, eds.).

New Plymouth
  Records of the Colony of New Plymouth in New England (12 vols., Boston, 1855–1861.
    NATHANIEL B. SHURTLEFF and DAVID PULSIFER, eds.).

New York
  Journal of the Votes and Proceedings of the General Assembly of the Colony of New York [1691–
    1776] (3 vols., New York and Albany, 1764–1820).
  Journal of the Legislative Council of the Colony of New York [1691–1775] (2 vols., Albany, 1861).
  The Colonial Laws of New York from the Year 1664 to the Revolution (5 vols., Albany, 1894).
  Documents Relative to the Colonial History of the State of New York (15 vols., Albany, 1856–
    1887. E. B. O'CALLAGHAN and B. FERNOW, eds.).
  The Documentary History of the State of New York (4 vols., Albany, 1850–1851. E. B.
    O'CALLAGHAN, ed.).

North Carolina
  The Colonial Records of North Carolina (10 vols., Raleigh, 1886–1890. WILLIAM L. SAUNDERS,
    ed.).

Pennsylvania
  Minutes of the Provincial Council of Pennsylvania ... (10 vols., Philadelphia and Harrisburg,
    1852).
  The Statutes at Large of Pennsylvania, 1682 to 1801 (vols. II–XVI, Harrisburg, 1896–1911.
    JAMES T. MITCHELL and HENRY FLANDERS, eds. Vol. I, 1682–1699, not printed).
  Pennsylvania Archives (119 vols. in 9 series, Philadelphia and Harrisburg, 1852–1935).

Rhode Island
  Records of the Colony of Rhode Island and Providence Plantations in New England [1636–1792]
    (10 vols., Providence, 1856–1865. JOHN R. BARTLETT, ed.).
  Rhode Island. Acts and Resolves, 1747–1776 [Binder's title] (Facsimile. 9 vols., Providence,
    n.d.).

South Carolina
  The Colonial Records of South Carolina. The Journal of the Commons House of Assembly
    [1736–1742] (3 vols. to date, Colombia, 1951–1953. J. H. EASTERBY, ed.).
  The Statutes at Large of South Carolina (10 vols., Columbia, 1836–1841. THOMAS COOPER
    and DAVID J. McCORD, eds.).

Virginia
  Journals of the House of Burgesses of Virginia [1619–1776] (13 vols., Richmond, 1905–1915.
    H. R. McILWAINE and JOHN P. KENNEDY, eds.).
  Legislative Journals of the Council of Colonial Virginia (3 vols., Richmond, 1918–1919. H. R.
    McILWAINE, ed.).
  Executive Journals of the Council of Colonial Virginia [1680–1754] (5 vols. to date, Richmond,
    1925–1945. H. R. McILWAINE and WILMER L. HALL, eds.).
  Minutes of the Council and General Court of Colonial Virginia, 1622–1632; 1670–1676 (Richmond,
    1924. H. R. McILWAINE, ed.).
  *The Statutes at Large; Being a Collection of all the Laws of Virginia, from the First Session of the
    Legislature in the Year 1619* (13 vols., Richmond, Philadelphia, and New York, 1809–1823.
    WILLIAM W. HENING, ed.).
  Calender of Virginia State Papers and Other Manuscripts, 1652–1781 (Richmond, 1875. WILLIAM
    P. PALMER, ed.).

(f) HISTORICAL SOCIETY PUBLICATIONS

Although local in origin, many historical societies have not limited their interest to a given colony or region but have ranged over the whole field of colonial history. They have published large numbers of diaries, letters, pamphlets, and in some cases, official records such as the letters of colonial governors, colonial agents, and the like. These are referred to in the separate bibliographies in this volume. Not included in the following list are the many historical societies on a county, city, or private level, although many of them have published valuable materials. A guide to those in existence in 1905 and to their publications will be found in A. P. C. GRIFFIN, "Bibliography of American Historical Societies", Amer. Hist. Assoc. *Annual Report* (1905), vol. II. Included in the following list are the names of the most important societies and their principal publications. The date of the first publications is given, and the terminal date, if publication has ceased. In the case of continuing publications, the number of volumes listed is the number completed through 1953.

Connecticut
> Connecticut Historical Society (Hartford): *Collections* (27 vols., 1860——).
> New Haven Historical Society (New Haven): *Papers* (10 vols., 1865——).

Delaware
> Historical Society of Delaware (Wilmington): *Papers* (67 vols., 1879–1922); *Delaware History* (5 vols., 1946——).

Georgia
> Georgia Historical Society (Savannah): *Collections* (10 vols., 1840——); *The Georgia Historical Quarterly* (37 vols., 1917——).

Maine
> Maine Historical Society (Portland): *Collections* (35 vols., 1831–1906).

Maryland
> Maryland Historical Society (Baltimore): *Fund Publications* (37 numbers, 1867–1901); *Maryland Historical Magazine* (48 vols., 1906——).

Massachusetts
> American Antiquarian Society (Worcester): *Proceedings*, 1812–1880 (publ. 1850–1880); *Proceedings*, New Series, 1880—— (62 vols., 1882——).
> Colonial Society of Massachusetts (Boston): *Publications* (35 vols., 1895——).
> Essex Institute (Salem): *Historical Collections* (89 vols., 1859——).
> Massachusetts Historical Society (Boston): *Proceedings*, 1791—— (68 vols., 1859——); *Collections*, 1792—— (79 vols., 1806——).

New Hampshire
> New Hampshire Historical Society (Concord): *Collections* (15 vols., 1824–1939); *Proceedings*, 1872–1912 (5 vols., 1874–1917).

New Jersey
> New Jersey Historical Society (Newark): *Collections* (10 vols., 1846–1927); *Proceedings*, 1845—— (71 vols., 1847——).

New York
> New York Historical Society (New York): *Collections*, 1809—— (84 vols., 1811——); *Quarterly Bulletin* [to 1943], *Quarterly* [since 1943] (37 vols., 1917——).
> New York State Historical Association (Cooperstown): *Proceedings*, 1900—— (50 vols., 1901——); *Quarterly Journal* [to 1932], *New York History* [since 1932] (34 vols., 1920——).

North Carolina
    State Department of Archives and History (North Carolina Historical Commission to 1943) (Raleigh): *Publications*, 1907——; *The North Carolina Historical Review* (30 vols., 1924——).

Pennsylvania
    Historical Society of Pennsylvania (Philadelphia): *Memoirs* (14 vols., 1826–1895); *The Pennsylvania Magazine of History and Biography* (77 vols., 1877——).
    Historical Society of Western Pennsylvania (Pittsburgh): *The Western Pennsylvania Historical Magazine* (36 vols., 1918——).
    Pennsylvania Historical Association: *Pennsylvania History* (20 vols., 1934——).

Rhode Island
    Rhode Island Historical Society (Providence): *Collections* (34 vols., 1827–1941); *Publications* (8 vols., 1893–1901); *Rhode Island History* (12 vols., 1942——).

South Carolina
    South Carolina Historical Society (Charleston): *Collections* (5 vols., 1857–1897); *The South Carolina Historical and Genealogical Magazine* [to 1952], *The South Carolina Historical Magazine* [since 1952] (54 vols., 1900——).
    South Carolina Historical Association (Columbia): *Proceedings*, 1931—— (unnumbered pamphlets, 1931——).

Vermont
    Vermont Historical Society (Montpelier): *Proceedings* [to 1943], *Vermont Quarterly* [since 1943] (21 vols., 1876——).

Virginia
    Virginia Historical Society (Richmond): *Collections* (11 vols., 1882–1892); *The Virginia Magazine of History and Biography* (61 vols., 1893——).
    Tyler's Quarterly Historical and Genealogical Magazine (Richmond, 33 vols., 1919–1952).
    The William and Mary College Quarterly (Williamsburg, 1st and 2nd series, 50 vols., 1892–1943). As *The William and Mary Quarterly* (Williamsburg, 3rd series, 10 vols., 1944——).

(g) PERIODICAL LITERATURE

Among the many periodicals other than those published by historical societies, the following contain important materials for colonial history. In each case the date of first publication is given after the title. *Agricultural History* (1927), *The American Historical Review* (1895), the *English Historical Review* (1886), *The Mississippi Valley Historical Review* (1914), *The New England Quarterly* (1928), *The Journal of Economic History* (1941), *The Journal of Negro History* (1916), *The Journal of Southern History* (1935), and *The South Atlantic Quarterly* (1902). In 1944 *The William and Mary Quarterly* was converted into a journal devoted exclusively to early American history to the year 1820, and its name was changed to *The William and Mary Quarterly: A Magazine of Early American History, Institutions, and Culture.*

Several periodicals containing important material for early American history which have ceased publication are: *The American Historical Record* (3 vols., Philadelphia, 1872–1874); *The Historical Magazine, and Notes and Queries Concerning the Antiquities, History and Biography of America* (23 vols., Boston and Morrisania, New York, 1857–1875); *The Magazine of History with Notes and Queries* (22 vols., New York, 1905–1922) and *Magazine of History: Extra Numbers* (50 vols., New York, 1908–1935); and *The Magazine of American History* (30 vols., New York, 1877–1893).

Part I

THE FOUNDATION OF THE ENGLISH COLONIES

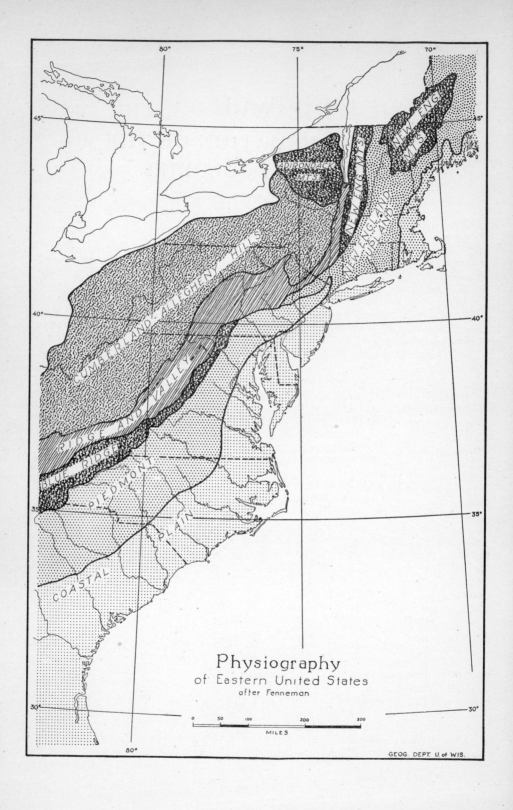

Physiography
of Eastern United States
after Fenneman

ADIRONDACK MTS.

NEW ENG. MTS.

NEW ENGLAND

NEW ENGLAND UPLAND

CUMBERLAND-ALLEGHENY HILLS

RIDGE AND VALLEY

BLUE RIDGE

PIEDMONT

COASTAL PLAIN

0   50   100   200   300

MILES

GEOG. DEPT. U. of WIS.

THE FOUNDATION OF THE
ENGLISH COLONIES

SELECT BIBLIOGRAPHY

(a) MATERIALS ON THE BACKGROUND OF ENGLISH COLONIZATION

The best single bibliography of the literature on the discovery and exploration of the New World is in *The Cambridge History of the British Empire*, I, pp. 845–857, "Exploration and Seapower". Accounts of English voyages of discovery and exploration have been published in great detail. RICHARD HAKLUYT, the great sixteenth century exponent of colonization, began the collection and printing of such documents. His *The Principal Navigations, Voyages, Traffiques and Discoveries of the English Nation* . . . has been reprinted in full (12 vols., Glasgow, 1903–1905). The Halkuyt Society has continued the work so notably begun in the sixteenth century down to the present day. SAMUEL ELIOT MORISON, *Admiral of the Ocean Sea. A Life of Christopher Columbus* (2 vols., Boston, 1942) is a notable biography. The many works of JAMES A. WILLIAMSON are of the greatest importance, as are *The Pioneer Histories*, edited by him and V. T. HARLOW. These are scholarly modern studies of important phases of discovery and exploration. Particularly useful are J. C. BEAGLEHOLE, *The Exploration of the Pacific* (London, 1934). JOHN B. BREBNER, *The Explorers of North America, 1492–1806* (London, 1933); F. A. KIRKPATRICK, *The Spanish Conquistadores* (London, 1934); ARTHUR P. NEWTON, *The European Nations in the West Indies, 1493–1688* (London, 1933); EDGAR PRESTAGE, *The Portuguese Pioneers* (London, 1933); JAMES A. WILLIAMSON, *The Age of Drake* (London, 1938).

The most convenient and scholarly studies of the immediate background of English colonization are to be found in the relevant chapters of *The Cambridge History of the British Empire*, vol. I, and in CHARLES M. ANDREWS, *The Colonial Period of American History*, vol. I. EDWARD P. CHEYNEY, *European Background of American History* (New York, 1904) is still useful for the general background, while his *The Dawn of a New Era* (New York, 1936) gives more detail. Among the most valuable of the economic histories is E. LIPSON, *The Economic History of England* (3 vols., Cambridge, 1920–1931). Among the works more specifically relating to the English colonization are ARTHUR P. NEWTON, *The Colonizing Activities of the English Puritans* (New Haven, 1914); FRANCES ROSE-TROUP, *John White: The Patriarch of Dorchester and the Founder of Massachusetts 1575–1648* (New York, 1930), and *The Massachusetts Bay Company and its Predecessors* (New York, 1930). The early explorers and ventures along the New England coast are discussed in HENRY F. HOWE, *Prologue to New England* (New York, 1943). ALEXANDER BROWN, *The Genesis of the United States* . . . (2 vols., Boston, 1890) presents a great amount of documentary material for the background of the Virginia colony, including diplomatic correspondence between England and Spain, promotion literature of the Virginia Company, and the like.

For an understanding of the trading companies which played so important a part in founding the first English colonies, W. R. SCOTT, *The Constitution and Finance of English, Scottish, and Irish Joint Stock Companies to 1720* (3 vols., Cambridge, 1910–1912) is basic. The records of the Virginia Company are to be found in SUSAN M. KINGSBURY, ed., *The Records of the Virginia Company of London* (4 vols., Library of Congress, Washington, 1906–1935). W. FRANK CRAVEN, *The Dissolution of the Virginia Company* (New York, 1932) is a detailed account of the fall of that company.

Most of the colonial charters have been reprinted in various publications by the thirteen original colonies. However, the most convenient collection is to be found in FRANCIS N. THORPE, ed., *The Federal and State Constitutions, Colonial Charters and Other Organic Laws* ... (7 vols., Washington, 1909). The collection is limited by the fact that it does not contain examples of the royal commissions and instructions which were the constitutional bases of the royal colonies. The only full-scale study of the colonial charters is the pioneer work of LOUISE P. KELLOGG, "The American Colonial Charter. A Study of English Administration in Relation thereto, chiefly after 1688", Amer. Hist. Assoc., *Annual Report* (1903), 1, pp. 185–341. The limitations of the study are explicit in its title. For the relation of such charters to the creation of governments in the colonies, see the bibliography for Part Two: The Evolution of Government in the Colonies.

Although a vast amount of literature promoting colonization is to be found in the form of pamphlets, sermons, broadsides, and 'histories', very little attention has been given to the analysis of it. The few studies that have been made are extremely useful. See VERNER W. CRANE, "Georgia Promotion Literature", in *Bibliographical Essays: A Tribute to Wilberforce Eames* (Cambridge, Mass., 1924); HOPE F. KANE, "Notes on Early Pennsylvania Promotion Literature", *Penn. Mag. of Hist. and Biog.* vol. LXIII (1939); and HOPE F. KANE, "Colonial Promotion Literature of Carolina, Pennsylvania, and New Jersey, 1660–1700" (abstract of 1930 Brown University doctoral thesis, Ann Arbor, Michigan, 1948). BROWN, *Genesis of the United States*, prints a great deal of the Virginia promotion literature. PETER FORCE, ed., *Tracts and Other Papers, Relating Principally to the Origin, Settlement, and Progress of the Colonies in North America* ... (4 vols., Washington, 1836–1846; reprinted, New York, 1947) contains much rare material including many of the early promotional tracts. Others are to be found scattered through historical society publications.

(b) PRINTED SOURCES ON THE FOUNDING OF THE COLONIES

In addition to the sources cited in the general bibliography, the following are valuable collections. The most useful is the series of volumes under the general title of *Original Narratives of Early American History*, edited by J. FRANKLIN JAMESON. Among these are *Narratives of Early Virginia 1606–1625* (New York, 1907, L. G. TYLER, ed.); *Narratives of New Netherland 1609–1664* (New York, 1909, J. F. JAMESON, ed.); *Narratives of Early Pennsylvania, West New Jersey and Delaware 1630–1707* (New York, 1912, A. C. MYERS, ed.); *Narratives of Early Maryland 1633–1684* (New York, 1910, C. C. HALL, ed.); and *Narratives of Early Carolina, 1650–1708* (New York, 1911, A. S. Salley, ed.).

Other collections are EDWARD ARBER, *The Story of the Pilgrim Fathers, 1606–1623 A.D., as told by Themselves, their Friends, and their Enemies* (London, 1897); ALEXANDER YOUNG, *Chronicles of the First Planters of the Colony of Massachusetts Bay, from 1623 to 1636* (Boston, 1846). *The Hutchinson Papers* (2 vols., Prince Society Publications, Albany, 1865) contains much valuable material for this history of Massachusetts during the seventeenth century. ALEXANDER BROWN, *The First Republic in America* ... (Boston, 1898) contains much documentary material on the first years of Virginia.

A. COLONIAL CHARTERS

EUROPEAN claims to the New World were based on the right of discovery in theory, and in practice, on the conquest of the native inhabitants. The division of the New World among various European nations was based upon the principle established by papal bulls in the fifteenth century, which held that newly discovered lands belonged to the monarch of the country making the discovery. Thus the claims of the English Crown to North America were based on the voyage of John Cabot in 1497 and were reinforced by sporadic voyages during the sixteenth century. England's claims were disputed by Spain and France and could be made good only by actual colonization. The Crown proved willing enough to grant the right to colonize, although no English monarch was ever willing to invest money to further colonization.

The right to colonize was embodied in two types of royal charters whereby the monarch granted to individuals or groups of individuals a portion of his rights and privileges in the New World lands claimed by him. The charters which were the legal basis for the first successful English colonies were those issued to trading companies. The joint-stock trading company was a device commonly used by the nations of western Europe for the promotion of overseas enterprise. Such companies had originated among the Italian city states which had used them for their colonizing ventures and this form of organization spread to the nations bordering along the Atlantic. During the sixteenth and seventeenth centuries trading companies were chartered by Holland, France, Sweden, and England in furtherance of sea-borne trade and in establishing colonies. Such enterprises involved far more expense and far greater risks than the individual investor could undertake for himself, as was demonstrated in the futile efforts of Sir Humphrey Gilbert and Sir Walter Raleigh to establish colonies based on their monopolistic charters from Queen Elizabeth. The joint-stock company was a device by which the risks and the expense, as well as the profits, could be shared among many small investors.

At least seventeen charters creating joint-stock trading companies had been granted in England before the group of men who were to establish the first permanent English colony petitioned for a charter in 1606. By that time the English joint-stock trading company for overseas enterprise had achieved a standard pattern. Such enterprises involved long voyages and the administration of affairs far from the reach of England. Hence these companies were given extensive rights of self-government and of government over lands and peoples outside of England. Such companies, as their charters declared, were bodies 'politic' as well as 'corporate'. The affairs of the company were conducted by the majority vote of its stockholders. They had the right to pass 'laws' and 'ordinances' for the government of the company, of the lands which it was granted, and of the people whom they settled on those lands. This power was subject always to the limitation that the laws and ordinances of the company be not contrary to the laws of England. The East India Company charter of 1600 provided for this kind of organization, as did most of the trading companies chartered thereafter.

But the group of men who asked for a charter to establish a colony in Virginia in

1606 were met by a new factor: the ideas of James I. James soon made it clear that he wanted a hand in the establishment of colonies within the claims of the Crown, although he had no intention of giving financial support. Thus the Virginia charter of 1606 was not a normal trading company charter: it was not even an act of incorporation. The petitioners were given the right to trade and to establish settlements. Government of both the company and the colony was placed in the hands of royal appointees, most of whom were investors in the company. The charter provided for a royal council resident in London. This council in turn was to appoint councils resident in the two colonies contemplated. The charter divided the investors into two groups, commonly known as the Plymouth and London companies. The Plymouth Company failed in its efforts to establish a colony on the coast of Maine in 1607–1608 and thereafter remained inactive for many years. The London Company established Jamestown in Virginia in 1607. By 1609 the colony was in a state of collapse and the funds of the company were exhausted. The promoters then appealed to the Crown for a new charter. The original investors in the company were dissatisfied because they had no control over the venture. New investors could not be obtained without some concessions on the part of the Crown. The result was the grant of a new charter in 1609. This charter incorporated the company and gave it direct ownership of the land. Control of the company and of the colony was handed over to the officers of the corporation, although the first officials were appointed by the Crown. Vacancies, however, were to be filled by the officials themselves from among the members of the company. The body of stockholders still did not have the privilege of governing the company as in corporations like the East India Company. Continued disaster in the colony and the need for still more funds led to an appeal for a third charter.

The Virginia charter of 1612[1] was a normal trading company charter. The governor and council were elected by a majority vote of the stockholders and were charged with carrying on the day-to-day business of the company. But for "the handling, ordering, and disposing of matters and affairs of greater weight and importance", the stockholders were to meet in four great and general courts each year. These general courts had the power to make 'laws' and 'ordinances' for the government of the company and the colony, subject only to the limitation that the laws for the colony "shall not be contrary to the laws and statutes of our realm of England". With this charter the Crown gave up its attempt at direct control of the company and of the colony in Virginia. The trading company charters granted thereafter followed the pattern of the third Virginia Company charter, the most important being that granted to the Massachusetts Bay Company in 1629.[2]

The origins of this company are complex. The land granted to it was part of the area previously granted to the Council for New England in 1620. The Council was unable to obtain colonists except for the Separatists who were landed at Plymouth, despite their intention of settling in Virginia. During the 1620's, the Council granted fishing licences to people from the west of England. Several small fishing villages were established on the New England coast, but all but one were soon abandoned. The men of Dorchester, and particularly the Reverend John White, had more than fish in mind. They declared themselves concerned with the conversion of the Indians to Christianity, and in the course of time they began looking to the formation of a colony that would be a refuge for people in England dissatisfied with the Anglican Church. In 1628 a voluntary company was organized to take over the Dorchester

[1] No. 1.   [2] No. 2.

settlement in Massachusetts Bay. It secured a somewhat dubious land grant from the Council for New England. Shortly thereafter it decided to secure a royal charter. Considerable mystery surrounds the grant of the charter to the Massachusetts Bay Company in 1629. The enemies of the colony later insisted that it was gotten surreptitiously, and there are some grounds for suspecting that bribery was involved. In any event, the company was granted lands and powers of government in complete disregard of the Council for New England, whose charter was still in effect.

The Massachusetts Bay Company charter[1] was that of a trading company much like that given to the Virginia Company in 1612. As soon as the company was organized it was clear that it contained two rival groups. A group of London merchants were interested mainly in trade. A group of country gentlemen, led by John Winthrop, were Puritans who looked forward to founding a colony which would be a refuge for Puritans. The Puritan element won out and prepared to migrate. Not only this, they decided to take the charter with them, a move of doubtful legality but entirely consistent with the Puritan desire to create a virtually independent state.

The transfer of the company to New England led to many difficulties. English enemies, including the members of the Council for New England and their heirs who had previously divided much of the land among themselves, attacked the colony continuously. Within the colony the charter was a source of embarrassment to the Puritan leaders. The structure of the trading company was essentially democratic, yet the ideals of the Puritan leaders were not.[2] Much of the political controversy that followed in Massachusetts Bay therefore centred around the effort of a Puritan minority to retain control of the government.

The second legal basis for English colonization was the proprietary charter. The landed gentry, and not merchants and religious dissenters, were the dominant social group in seventeenth-century England. Many of them had invested in the early trading company ventures, but their basic interest was not in trade. Furthermore, with few exceptions, they had little use for the democratic structure of the trading company. Their primary interest was in the acquisition of vast estates for themselves and in the making of money from the selling and renting of land. They therefore sought and got charters establishing themselves as absolute lords and proprietors, both of government and of land, in the New World. The proprietary charter was essentially a feudal grant in which the proprietors were free of all except nominal duties and rents to the Crown, but which made the colonists tenants of the proprietors and subject to their will. The extensive powers thus granted were such as the Crown did not possess, or at least dared not attempt to exercise in England.

The first proprietary charter was given to the Council for New England in 1620, a charter surrendered in 1635. In 1621 Nova Scotia was granted to Sir William Alexander, although the French had a prior claim which was recognized in 1632. In 1623 a part of Newfoundland was given to Leonard Calvert, Lord Baltimore. The failure of his attempt in Newfoundland led to the grant of Maryland in 1632. The Maryland Charter of 1632[3] is the best example of a sweeping grant of power to a proprietor.

The proprietors (except for William Penn) were given all the powers which "any bishop of Durham . . . in our kingdom of England, ever heretofore hath had, held, used, or enjoyed, or of right could, or ought to have, hold, use, or enjoy". Since the bishop of Durham had extraordinary powers of government and of granting

[1] No. 2.　　　　[2] No. 17.　　　　[3] No. 3.

lands, the American proprietors were virtually kings in their own domains. They could grant lands, confer titles of nobility, appoint all officials, create courts and hear appeals, create and command armies, establish churches, make laws and ordinances, and receive all revenues from their proprietaries. The only limitation on the power of the proprietors was that laws could be passed and taxes levied only with the consent of the freemen of their provinces.

All of the English colonies founded after 1660 were based on proprietary charters. Carolina was given to eight of the king's friends in 1663. In 1664, New Amsterdam was taken from the Dutch and the whole region between the Connecticut and Delaware rivers was given to the duke of York. The last of the great proprietary grants was that to William Penn in 1681.[1] The Georgia charter of 1732 was limited to a twenty-year period, after which the colony reverted to the Crown.

The lavish grants of the Restoration period were accompanied by the evolution of a colonial policy which in essence contradicted the nature of the charters.[2] This new policy of closer economic and political control found its first expression in a proprietary charter when Penn received his grant. The Pennsylvania charter contained many limitations that were not to be found in early charters, whether trading company or proprietary. Inhabitants of the province were expressly given the right of appeal to the Crown. All acts of the provincial legislature must be submitted to the Crown for approval within five years. The proprietor was required to keep an agent in or near London to represent his interests and those of the colony. The right of Parliament to tax the colony was clearly implied.[3]

By the end of the century it was clear that the colonial charters, of whatever kind, stood in the way of closer economic and political control stemming out of England. The Massachusetts Bay charter of 1629 was revoked by court action in 1684. When Massachusetts got a new charter in 1691, the colony's independence was limited by the addition of a royal governor and royal officials to the corporation structure of the charter of 1629, and the colony was denied the power to make church membership a prerequisite of the right to vote. During the next twenty-five years, there were repeated efforts to abolish all charters by Act of Parliament.[4] Although these efforts failed, most of the proprietary and corporation colonies were converted into royal provinces, one by one. The process was slow and halting but by the time of the American Revolution only two corporation colonies (Connecticut and Rhode Island), and only two proprietary colonies (Pennsylvania and Maryland), remained on the mainland.

The royal provinces did not have formal charters. However, they had a constitutional basis which was embodied in the commissions and instructions given to royal governors. The commissions and instructions outlined the framework of government and set forth the policies the Crown hoped to carry out in the colony.[5] They therefore served the same purpose as a charter, although they could be changed from time to time as a charter could not be, unless it were revoked. Theoretically, this method of government should have led to flexibility and closer control of the colonies from England. In practice, it led to rigidity and bad administration, for the officials in England who wrote the instructions which governors were required to obey all too seldom showed any awareness of the political and economic realities which the governors had to face. Above all, they took too little account of changing conditions in the colonies which so often rendered instructions obsolete.

---

[1] No. 4.   [2] Nos. 29, 30, 31, 32, 51.   [3] No. 4.   [4] No. 32.   [5] Nos. 22, 24, 25.

1. The third charter of the Virginia Company (12 March 1612)

Printed: William W. Hening, ed., *The Statutes at Large, Being a Collection of all the Laws of Virginia, from the First Session of the Legislature in the Year 1619* (11 vols., New York and Richmond, 1809–1823), I, pp. 98–110.

James, by the grace of God, king of England, Scotland, France, and Ireland, defender of the faith; to all to whom these presents shall come, Greeting. Whereas, at the humble suit of divers and sundry our loving subjects, as well adventurers as planters of the first colony in Virginia, and for the propagation of Christian religion, and reclaiming of people barbarous to civility and humanity, we have, by our letters patents, bearing date at Westminster the three and twentieth day of May, in the seventh year of our reign of England, France, and Ireland and the two and fortieth of Scotland, given and granted unto them, that they, and all such and so many of our loving subjects, as should from time to time for ever after be joined with them, as planters or adventurers in the said plantation, and their successors, for ever, should be one body politic, incorporated by the name of The Treasurer and Company of Adventurers and Planters of the city of London for the first Colony in Virginia.

II. And whereas also, for the great good and benefit of the said company, and for the better furtherance, strengthening, and establishing of the said plantation, we did further give, grant, and confirm, by our said letters patents, unto the said treasurer and company, and their successors, for ever, all those lands, countries, or territories, situate, lying, and being, in that part of America called Virginia, from the point of land called Cape or Point Comfort, all along the sea coasts, to the northward, two hundred miles, and from the said point of Cape Comfort all along the sea coast, to the southward, two hundred miles, and all that space and circuit of land lying from the sea coast of the precinct aforesaid, up or into the land, throughout from sea to sea, west and north-west, and also all the islands lying within one hundred miles, along the coast of both the seas of the precinct aforesaid, with divers other grants, liberties, franchises, and preheminences, privileges, profits, benefits, and commodities, granted, in and by our said letters patents, to the said treasurer and company, and their successors, for ever.

III. Now, forasmuch as we are given to understand that in those seas adjoining to the said coast of Virginia, and without the compass of those two hundred miles, by us so granted unto the said treasurer and company, as aforesaid, and yet not far distant from the said colony in Virginia, there are, or may be, divers islands, lying desolate and uninhabited, some of which are already made known and discovered, by the industry, travel, and expenses of the said company, and others also are supposed to be and remain as yet unknown and undiscovered, all and every of which it may import the said colony, both in safety and policy of trade, to populate and plant, in regard whereof, as well for the preventing of peril as for the better commodity and prosperity of the said colony, they have been humble suitors unto us that we would be pleased to grant unto them an enlargement of our said former letters patents, as well for a more ample extent of their limits and territories into the seas adjoining to and upon the coast of Virginia, as also for some other matters and articles, concerning the better government of the said company and colony, in which point our said former letters patents do not extend so far as time and experience have found to be needful and convenient.

IV. We therefore, tendering the good and happy success of the said plantation, both in regard of the general weal of human society as in respect of the good of our own estate and kingdoms, and being willing to give furtherance unto all good means that may advance the benefit of the said company, and which may secure the safety of our loving subjects, planted in our said colony under the favour and protection of God Almighty, and of our royal power and authority, have therefore, of our especial grace, certain knowledge, and mere motion, given, granted, and confirmed, and for us, our heirs, and successors, we do, by these presents, give, grant, and confirm, to the said treasurer and company of adventurers and planters of the city of London for the first colony in Virginia, and to their heirs and successors, for ever, all and singular those islands whatsoever, situate and being in any part of the ocean seas bordering upon the coast of our said first colony in Virginia, and being within three hundred leagues of any the parts heretofore granted to the said treasurer and company, in our said former letters patents, as aforesaid, and being within or between the one and fortieth and thirtieth degrees of northerly latitude, together with all and singular soils, lands, grounds, havens, ports, rivers, waters, fishings, mines, and minerals, as well royal mines of gold and silver, as other mines and minerals, pearls, precious stones, quarries, and all and singular other commodities, jurisdictions, royalties, privileges, franchises, and preheminences, both within the said tract of land upon the main, and also within the said islands and seas adjoining whatsoever, and thereunto or thereabouts, both by sea and land, being or situate; and which, by our letters patents, we may or can grant, and in as ample manner and sort as we, or any our noble progenitors, have heretofore granted to any person or persons, or to any company, body politic or corporate, or to any adventurer or adventurers, undertaker or undertakers, of any discoveries, plantations, or traffic, of, in, or into any foreign parts whatsoever, and in as large and ample manner as if the same were herein particularly named, mentioned, and expressed: Provided always, that the said islands, or any the premises herein mentioned, or by these presents intended or meant to be granted, be not actually possessed or inhabited by any other Christian prince or estate, nor be within the bounds, limits, or territories of the northern colony heretofore by us granted to be planted by divers of our loving subjects, in the north parts of Virginia. To have and to hold, possess and enjoy, all and singular the said islands, in the said ocean seas so lying and bordering upon the coast and coasts of the territories of the said first colony in Virginia, as aforesaid; with all and singular the said soils, lands, and grounds, and all and singular other the premises, heretofore by these presents granted, or mentioned to be granted, to them, the said treasurer and company of adventurers and planters of the city of London for the first colony in Virginia, and to their heirs, successors, and assigns, for ever, to the sole and proper use and behoof of them, the said treasurer and company, and their heirs, and successors, and assigns, for ever; to be holden of us, our heirs, and successors, as of our manor of East Greenwich, in free and common socage, and not *in capite*; yielding and paying therefore to us, our heirs, and successors, the fifth part of the ore of all gold and silver, which shall be there gotten, had or obtained, for all manner of services whatsoever.

V. And further, our will and pleasure is, and we do by these presents, grant and confirm, for the good and welfare of the said plantation, and that posterity may hereafter know, who have adventured and not been sparing of their purses in such a noble and generous action for the general good of their country, and at the request and with the consent of the company aforesaid, that our trusty and well beloved subjects, George, lord archbishop of Canterbury, Henry, earl of Huntington, Edward, earl of Bedford, Richard, of Clanrickard, etc., who since our said last letters patents are become adventurers, and have joined themselves with the former adventurers and planters of the said company and society, shall from henceforth be reputed, deemed, and taken to be, and shall be brethren and free members of the company, and shall and may, respectively, and according to the proportion and value of their several adventures, have, hold, and enjoy all such interest, right, title, privileges, prehemi-nences, liberties, franchises, immunities, profits, and commodities whatsoever, in as large, and ample, and beneficial manner, to all intents, constructions, and purposes as any other adventurers, nominated and expressed in any our former letters patents, or any of them, have or may have, by force and virtue of these presents or any our former letters patents whatsoever.

VI. And we are further pleased, and we do by these presents, grant and confirm, that Philip, earl of Montgomery, William, Lord Paget, Sir John Starrington, knight, etc., whom the said treasurer and company have, since the said last letters patents, nominated and set down, as worthy and discreet persons, fit to serve us as councillors, to be of our council for the said plantation, shall be reputed, deemed, and taken as persons of our said council for the said first colony, in such manner and sort, to all intents and purposes, as those who have been formerly elected and nominated, as our councillors for that colony, and whose names have been or are inserted and expressed, in our said former letters patents.

VII. And we do hereby ordain and grant, by these presents, that the said treasurer and company of adventurers and planters aforesaid, shall and may, once every week or oftener, at their pleasure, hold and keep a court and assembly for the better order and government of the said plantation, and such things as shall concern the same; and that any five persons of our council for the said first colony in Virginia, for the time being, of which company the treasurer, or his deputy, to be always one, and the number of fifteen others at the least, of the generality of the said company, assembled together in such manner as is and hath been heretofore used and accustomed, shall be said, taken, held, and reputed to be, and shall be a sufficient court of the said company, for the handling, and ordering, and dispatching of all such casual and particular occurrences, and accidental matters, of less consequence and weight as shall from time to time happen, touching and concerning the said plantation.

VIII. And that nevertheless, for the handling, ordering, and disposing of matters and affairs of greater weight and importance, and such as shall or may, in any sort, concern the weal public and general good of the said company and plantation, as namely the manner of government from time to time to be used, the ordering and disposing of the lands and possessions, and the settling and establishing of a trade there, or such like, there shall be held and kept, every year, upon the last Wednesday, save one, of Hilary term, Easter, Trinity, and Michaelmas terms, for ever, one great, general, and solemn assembly, which four assemblies shall be styled and called, The Four Great and General Courts of the Council and Company of Adventurers for Virginia; in all and every of which said great and general courts so assembled, our will and pleasure is, and we do, for us, our heirs, and successors, for ever, give and grant to the said treasurer and company and their successors, for ever, by these presents, that they, the said treasurer and company, or the greater number of them so assembled, shall and may have full power and authority, from time to time, and at all times hereafter, to elect and choose discreet persons to be of our said council, for the said first colony in Virginia, and to nominate and appoint such officers as they shall think fit and requisite for the government, managing, ordering, and dispatching of the affairs of the said company, and shall likewise have full power and authority to ordain and make such laws and ordinances for the good and welfare of the said plantation, as to them, from time to time, shall be thought requisite and meet: so always, as the same be not contrary to the laws and statutes of this our realm of England; and shall, in like manner, have power and authority to expulse, disfranchise, and put out of and from their said company and society, for ever, all and every such person and persons as having either promised, or subscribed their names, to become adventurers to the said plantation of the said first colony in Virginia, or having been nominated for adventurers, in these or any other our letters patents, or having been otherwise admitted and nominated to be of the said company, have nevertheless either not put in any adventure at all, for and towards the said plantation, or else have refused and neglected, or shall refuse and neglect, to bring in his or their adventure, by word or writing promised, within six months after the same shall be so payable and due.

IX. And whereas the failing and not payment of such moneys as have been promised in adventure for the advancement of the said plantation hath been often by experience found to be dangerous and prejudicial to the same, and much to have hindered the progress and proceeding of the said plantation, and for that it seemeth unto us a thing reasonable that such persons as by their handwriting have engaged themselves for the payment of their adventures, and afterwards neglecting their faith and promise, should be compelled to make good and keep the same; therefore our will and pleasure is that in any suit or suits, commenced or to be commenced, in any of our courts at Westminster, or elsewhere, by the said treasurer and company, or otherwise, against any such persons, that our judges for the time being, both in our court of chancery, and at the common pleas, do favour and further the said suits, so far forth as law and equity will, in any wise, further and permit.

X. And we do, for us, our heirs, and successors, further give and grant to the said treasurer and company, or their successors, for ever, that they, the said treasurer and company, or the greater part of them for the time being, so in a full and general court assembled, as aforesaid, shall and may, from time to time, and at all times for ever hereafter, elect, choose, and admit into their company and society, any person or persons, as well strangers and aliens, born in any part beyond the seas wheresoever, being in amity with us as our natural liege subjects, born in any our realms and dominions; and that all such persons so elected, chosen, and admitted to be of the said company, as aforesaid, shall thereupon be taken, reputed, and held, and shall be, free members of the said company, and shall have, hold, and enjoy, all and singular freedoms, liberties, franchises, privileges, immunities, benefits, profits, and commodities, whatsoever, to the said company in any sort belonging or appertaining, as fully, freely, and amply, as any other adventurers, now being, or which hereafter at any time shall be of the said company, hath, have, shall, may, might, or ought to have and enjoy the same, to all intents and purposes whatsoever.

XI. And we do further of our especial grace, certain knowledge, and mere motion, for us, our heirs, and successors, give and grant unto the said treasurer and company, and their successors, for ever, by these presents, that it shall be lawful and free for them and their assigns, at all and every time and times hereafter, out of any our realms and dominions whatsoever, to take, lead, carry, and transport, in and into the said voyage, and for and towards the said plantation, of our said first colony in Virginia, all such and so many of our loving subjects, or any other strangers, that will become our loving subjects and live under our allegiance, as shall willingly accompany them in the said voyages and plantation; with shipping, armour, weapons, ordnance, munition, powder, shot, victuals, and all manner of merchandises and wares, and all manner of clothing, implements, furniture, beasts, cattle, horses, mares, and all other things necessary for the said plantation, and for their use and defence, and for trade with the people there, and in passing and returning to and from, without paying or yielding any subsidy, custom, or imposition, either inward or outward, or any other duty, to us, our heirs, or successors, for the same, for the space of seven years from the date of these presents.

XII. And we do further, for us, our heirs and successors, give and grant to the said treasurer and company, and their successors, for ever, by these presents, that the said treasurer of that company, or his deputy, for the time being, or any two other of the said council for the said first colony in Virginia, for the time being, or any two other at all times hereafter and from time to time, have full power and authority to minister and give the oath and oaths of supremacy and allegiance, or either of them, to all and every person and persons, which shall at any time or times hereafter go or pass to the said colony in Virginia.

XIII. And further, that it shall be lawful likewise for the said treasurer, or his deputy, for the time being, or any two or others of our said council for the said first colony in Virginia, for the time being, from time to time, and at all times hereafter, to minister such a formal oath as by their discretion shall be reasonably devised, as well unto any person or persons employed in, for, or touching the said plantation, for their honest, faithful, and just discharge of their service, in all such matters as shall be committed unto them for the good and benefit of the said company, colony, and plantation; as also, unto such other person or persons as the said treasurer ro his deputy, with two others of the said council, shall think meet, for the examination or clearing of the truth, in any cause whatsoever concerning the said plantation, or any business, from thence proceeding, or thereunto belonging.

XIV. And furthermore, whereas we have been certified that divers lewd and ill-disposed persons, both sailors, soldiers, artificers, husbandmen, labourers, and others, having received wages, apparel, and other entertainment from the said company, or having contracted and agreed with the said company to go, or to serve, or to be employed in the said plantation of the said first colony in Virginia, have afterwards either withdrawn, hid or concealed themselves, or have refused to go thither, after they have been so entertained and agreed withal; and that divers and sundry persons also, which have been sent and employed in the said plantation of the said first colony in Virginia, at and upon the charge of the said company, and having there misbehaved themselves by mutinies, sedition, or other notorious misdemeanours, or having been employed or sent abroad by the governor of Virginia, or his deputy, with some ship or pinnace, for our provision of the said colony, or for some discovery, or other business and affairs concerning the same, have from thence most treacherously either come back again and returned unto our realm of England by stealth, or without licence of our governor of our said colony in Virginia for the time being, or have been sent hither as misdoers and offenders; and that many also of those persons, after their return from thence, having been questioned by our said council here, for such their misbehaviours and offences, by their insolent and contemptuous carriage in the presence of our said council, have showed little respect and reverence either to the place, or authority, in which we have placed and appointed them; and others, for the colouring of their lewdness and misdemeanours committed in Virginia, have endeavoured by most vile and slanderous reports, made and divulged, as well of the country of Virginia, as also of the government and estate of the said plantation and colony, as much as in them lay, to bring the said voyage and plantation into disgrace and contempt; by means whereof not only the adventurers and planters already engaged in the said plantation, have been exceedingly abused and hindered, and a great number of other our loving and well disposed subjects, otherwise well affected, and inclined to join and adventure in so noble, Christian, and worthy an action, have been discouraged from the same, but also the utter overthrow and ruin of the said enterprise hath been greatly endangered, which cannot miscarry without some dishonour to us and our kingdom.

XV. Now, forasmuch as it appeareth unto us that these insolences, misdemeanours, and abuses, not to be tolerated in any civil government, have, for the most part, grown and proceeded in regard our said council have not any direct power and authority, by any express words in our former letters patents, to correct and chastise such offenders; we therefore, for the more speedy reformation of so great and enormous abuses and misdemeanours, heretofore practised and committed, and for the preventing of the like hereafter, do, by these presents, for us, our heirs and successors, give and grant to the said treasurer and company, and their successors, for ever, that it shall and may be lawful for our said council for the said first colony in Virginia, or any two of them (whereof the said treasurer, or his deputy, for the time being, to be always one) by warrant under their hands, to send for, or to cause to be apprehended, all and every such person and persons, who shall be noted, or accused, or found, at any time or times hereafter, to offend, or misbehave themselves, in any the offences before mentioned and expressed; and upon the examination of any such offender or offenders, and just proof made by oath, taken before the said council, of any such notorious misdemeanours by them committed, as aforesaid; and also upon any insolent and contemptuous, or indecent carriage, and misbehaviour, to or against our said council, showed or used by any such person or persons, so called, convented, and appearing before them, as aforesaid; that in all such cases they, our said council, or any two of them, for the time being, shall and may have full power and authority, either here to bind them over with good sureties, for their good behaviour, and further therein to proceed, to all intents and purposes, as it is used, in other like cases, within our realm of England; or else, at their discretion, to remand and send them back, the said offenders, or any of them, unto the said colony in Virginia, there to be proceeded against and punished, as the governor, deputy, or council there, for the time being, shall think meet; or otherwise according to such laws and ordinances as are and shall be in use there, for the well ordering and good government of the said colony.

XVI. And for the more effectual advancing of the said plantation we do further, for us, our heirs, and successors, of our especial grace and favour, by virtue of our prerogative royal, and by the assent and consent of the Lords and others of our privy council, give and grant unto the said treasurer and company full power and authority, free leave, liberty, and licence, to set forth, erect, and publish, one or more lottery or lotteries, to have continuance, and to endure and be held, for the space of [one] whole year, next after the opening of the same; and after the end and expiration of the said term, the said lottery or lotteries to continue and be further kept, during our will and pleasure only, and not otherwise. And yet, nevertheless we are contented and pleased for the good and welfare of the said plantation, that the said treasurer and company shall, for the dispatch and finishing of the said lottery or lotteries, have six months' warning after the said year ended, before our will and pleasure shall, for and on that behalf, be construed, deemed, and adjudged, to be in any wise altered and determined.

XVII. And our further will and pleasure is, that the said lottery and lotteries shall and may be opened and held within our city of London, or in any other city or town, or elsewhere, within this our realm of England, with such prizes, articles, conditions, and limitations, as to them, the said treasurer and company, as their discretion shall seem convenient.

XVIII. And that it shall and may be lawful, to and for the said treasurer and company, to elect and choose receivers, auditors, surveyors, commissioners, or any other officers whatsoever, at their will and pleasure, for the better marshalling, disposing, guiding, and governing of the said lottery and lotteries; and that it shall likewise be lawful, to and for the said treasurer and any two of the said council, to minister to all and every such person so elected and chosen for officers, as aforesaid, one or more oaths, for their good behaviour, just and true dealing, in and about the said lottery or lotteries, to the intent and purpose that none of our loving subjects, putting in their names, or otherwise adventuring in the said general lottery or lotteries, may be in any wise defrauded and deceived of their said moneys, or evil and indirectly dealt withal in their said adventures.

XIX. And we further grant in manner and form aforesaid, that it shall and may be lawful, to and for the said treasurer and company, under the seal of the said council for the plantation, to publish, or to cause and procure to be published, by proclamation or otherwise (the said proclamation to be made in their name, by virtue of these presents) the said lottery or lotteries in all cities, towns, boroughs, and other places within our said realm of England; and we will and command all mayors, justices of peace, sheriffs, bailiffs, constables, and other officers and loving subjects, whatsoever, that in no wise they hinder or delay the progress and proceedings of the said lottery or lotteries, but be therein touching the premises, aiding and assisting, by all honest good and lawful means and endeavours.

XX. And further our will and pleasure is, that in all questions and doubts that shall arise upon any difficulty of construction or interpretation of anything contained in these, or any other our former letters patents, the same shall be taken and interpreted in most ample and beneficial manner for the said treasurer and company, and their successors, for ever, and every member thereof.

XXI. And lastly, we do by these presents, ratify and confirm unto the said treasurer and company, and their successors, for ever, all and all manner of privileges, franchises, liberties, immunities, preheminences, profits and commodities whatsoever, granted unto them in any our former letters patents, and not in these presents revoked, altered, changed, or abridged, although express mention of the true yearly value or certainty of the premises, or any of them, or of any other gift or grant, by us or any of our progenitors or predecessors, to the aforesaid treasurer and company heretofore made, in these presents is not made; or any statute, act, ordinance, provision, proclamation, or restraint, to the contrary thereof heretofore made, ordained, or provided, or any other matter, cause, or thing whatsoever, to the contrary in any wise notwithstanding.

In witness whereof we have caused these our letters to be made patents. Witness ourself, at Westminster, the twelfth day of March, in the ninth year of our reign of England, France, and Ireland, and of Scotland the five and fortieth.

2. The charter of the Massachusetts Bay Company (4 March 1629)

Printed: Francis N. Thorpe, ed., *The Federal and State Constitutions, Colonial Charters, and Other Organic Laws* . . . (7 vols., Washington, 1909), III, pp. 1846–1860, and in the Massachusetts Historical Society *Proceedings*, LXII, pp. 251–273.

Charles, by the Grace of God, King of England, Scotland, France, and Ireland, Defender of the Faith, etc. To all to whom these presents shall come, Greeting. Whereas, our most dear and royal father, King James of blessed memory, by his Highness's letters patents bearing date at Westminster the third day of November, in the eighteenth year of his reign, hath given and granted unto the council established at Plymouth, in the county of Devon, for the planting, ruling, ordering, and governing of New England in America, and to their successors and assigns for ever, all that part of America lying and being in breadth from forty degrees of northerly latitude from the equinoctial line, to forty-eight degrees of the said northerly latitude inclusively, and in length, of and within all the breadth aforesaid, throughout the main lands from sea to sea; together also with all the firm lands, soils, grounds, havens, ports, rivers, waters, fishing, mines, and minerals, as well royal mines of gold and silver as other mines and minerals, precious stones, quarries, and all and singular other commodities, jurisdictions, royalties, privileges, franchises, and preheminences, both within the said tract of land upon the main, and also within the islands and seas adjoining: provided always, that the said islands, or any the premises by the said letters patents intended and meant to be granted, were not then actually possessed or inhabited by any other Christian prince or state, nor within the bounds, limits, or territories of the southern colony, then before granted by our said dear father, to be planted by divers of his loving subjects in the south parts. To have and to hold, possess, and enjoy all and singular the aforesaid continent, lands, territories, islands, hereditaments, and precincts, seas, waters, fishings, with all, and all manner their commodities, royalties, liberties, preheminences, and profits that should from thenceforth arise from thence, with all and singular their appurtenances, and every part and parcel thereof, unto the said council and their successors and assigns for ever, to the sole and proper use, benefit, and behoof of them the said council, and their successors and assigns for ever: To be holden of our said most dear and royal father, his heirs and successors, as of his manor of East Greenwich in the county of Kent, in free and common socage, and not *in capite* nor by knight's service; yielding and paying therefore to the said late king, his heirs and successors, the fifth part of the ore of gold and silver which should from time to time, and at all times then after happen to be found, gotten, had, and obtained in, at, or within any of the said lands, limits, territories, and precincts, or in or within any part or parcel thereof, for or in respect of all and all manner of duties, demands, and services whatsoever, to be done, made, or paid to our said dear father the late king, his heirs and successors, as in and by the said letters patents (amongst sundry other clauses, powers, privileges, and grants therein contained), more at large appeareth.

And whereas, the said council established at Plymouth, in the county of Devon, for the planting, ruling, ordering, and governing of New England in America, have by their deed, indented under their common seal, bearing date the nineteenth day of March last past, in the third year of our reign, given, granted, bargained, sold, enfeoffed, aliened, and confirmed to Sir Henry Rosewell, Sir John Yonge, knights, Thomas Southcote, John Humfry, John Endecott, and Simon Whetcombe, their heirs and assigns, and their associates for ever, all that part of New England in America aforesaid, which lies and extends between a great river there commonly called Monomack, alias Merrimac, and a certain other river there called Charles River, being in the bottom of a certain bay there commonly called Massachusetts, alias Mattachusetts, alias Massatusetts Bay, and also all and singular those lands and hereditaments whatsoever, lying within the space of three English miles on the south part of the said Charles River, or of any or every part thereof; and also, all and singular the lands and hereditaments whatsoever lying and being within the space of three

4

English miles to the southward of the southernmost part of the said bay called Massachusetts, alias Mattachusetts, alias Massatusetts Bay; and also all those lands and hereditaments whatsoever which lie and be within the space of three English miles to the northward of the said river called Monomack, alias Merrimac, or to the northward of any and every part thereof, and all lands and hereditaments whatsoever lying within the limits aforesaid, north and south in latitude and breadth, and in length and longitude of and within all the breadth aforesaid, throughout the main lands there, from the Atlantic and Western Sea and Ocean on the east part, to the South Sea on the west part; and all lands and grounds, place and places, soils, woods and wood grounds, havens, ports, rivers, waters, fishings, and hereditaments whatsoever, lying within the said bounds and limits, and every part and parcel thereof; and also all islands lying in America aforesaid, in the said seas or either of them on the western or eastern coasts or parts of the said tracts of land, by the said indenture mentioned to be given, granted, bargained, sold, enfeoffed, aliened, and confirmed, or any of them; and also all mines and minerals, as well royal mines of gold and silver as other mines and minerals whatsoever, in the said lands and premises, or any part thereof; and all jurisdictions, rights, royalties, liberties, freedoms, immunities, privileges, franchises, preheminences, and commodities whatsoever, which they, the said council established at Plymouth in the county of Devon, for the planting, ruling, ordering, and governing of New England in America, then had, or might use, exercise, or enjoy, in or within the said lands and premises by the said indenture mentioned to be given, granted, bargained, sold, enfeoffed, and confirmed, or in or within any part or parcel thereof.

To have and to hold the said part of New England in America which lies and extends and is abutted as aforesaid, and every part and parcel thereof; and all the said islands, rivers, ports, havens, waters, fishings, mines, minerals, jurisdictions, franchises, royalties, liberties, privileges, commodities, hereditaments and premises whatsoever, with the appurtenances unto the said Sir Henry Rosewell, Sir John Yonge, Thomas Southcote, John Humfry, John Endecott, and Simon Whetcombe, their heirs and assigns, and their associates, to the only proper and absolute use and behoof of the said [men], their heirs and assigns, and their associates for evermore; to be holden of us, our heirs and successors, as of our manor of East Greenwich, in the county of Kent, in free and common socage, and not *in capite*, nor by knight's service; yielding and paying therefore unto us, our heirs and successors, the fifth part of the ore of gold and silver, which shall from time to time, and at all times hereafter, happen to be found, gotten, had, and obtained in any of the said lands, within the said limits, or in or within any part thereof, for, and in satisfaction of all manner duties, demands, and services whatsoever to be done, made, or paid to us, our heirs or successors, as in and by the said recited indenture more at large may appear.

Now know ye that we, at the humble suit and petition of the said Sir Henry Rosewell, Sir John Yonge, Thomas Southcote, John Humfry, John Endecott, and Simon Whetcombe, and of others whom they have associated unto them, have, for divers good causes and considerations, us moving, granted and confirmed and by these presents of our especial grace, certain knowledge, and mere motion, do grant and confirm unto the said Sir Henry Rosewell, Sir John Yonge, Thomas Southcote, John Humfry, John Endecott, and Simon Whetcombe, and to their associates hereafter named: (videlicet) Sir Richard Saltonstall, knight, Isaac Johnson, Samuel Aldersey, John Venn, Matthew Cradock, George Harwood, Increase Nowell, Richard Perry, Richard Bellingham, Nathaniel Wright, Samuel Vassall, Theophilus Eaton, Thomas Goffe, Thomas Adams, John Browne, Samuel Browne, Thomas Hutchins, William Vassall, William Pyncheon, and George Foxcroft, their heirs and assigns, all the said part of New England in America, lying and extending between the bounds and limits in the said recited indenture expressed, and all lands and grounds, place and places, soils, woods and wood grounds, havens, ports, rivers, waters, mines, minerals, jurisdictions, rights, royalties, liberties, freedoms, immunities, privileges, franchises, preheminences, hereditaments, and commodities whatsoever, to them the said Sir Henry Rosewell, Sir John Yonge, Thomas Southcote, John Humfry, John Endecott, and Simon Whetcombe, their heirs and assigns, and to their associates, by the said recited indenture, given granted, bargained, sold, enfeoffed, aliened, and confirmed, or mentioned, or intended thereby to be given, granted, bargained, sold, enfeoffed, aliened, and confirmed: to have, and to hold, the said part of New England in America, and other the premises hereby mentioned to be granted and confirmed, and every part and parcel thereof with the appurtenances, to the said [men], their heirs and assigns for ever, to their only proper and absolute use and behoof for evermore; to be holden of us, our heirs and successors, as of our manor of East Greenwich, aforesaid, in free and common socage, and not *in capite*, nor by knight's service; and also yielding and paying therefore to us, our heirs and successors, the fifth part only of all ore of gold and silver, which from time to time, and at all times hereafter, shall be there gotten, had, or obtained, for all services, exactions, and demands whatsoever, according to the tenure and reservation in the said recited indenture expressed.

And further, know ye, that of our more especial grace, certain knowledge, and mere motion, we have given and granted, and by these presents, do for us, our heirs and successors, give and grant unto the said [men], their heirs and assigns, all that part of New England in America, which lies and extends between a great river there commonly called Monomack River, alias Merrimac River, and a certain other river there, called Charles River, being in the bottom of a certain bay there, commonly called Massachusetts, alias Mattachusetts, alias Massatusetts Bay; and also all and singular those lands and hereditaments whatsoever, lying within the space of three English miles on the south part of the said river called Charles River, or of any or every part thereof; and also all and singular the lands and hereditaments whatsoever, lying and being within the space of three English miles to the southward of the southernmost part of the said bay, called Massachusetts, alias Mattachusetts, alias Massatusetts Bay; and also all those lands and hereditaments whatsoever which lie and be within the space of three English miles to the northward of the said river called Monomack, alias Merrimac, or to the northward of any and every part thereof, and all lands and hereditaments whatsoever lying within the limits aforesaid, north and south, in latitude and breadth, and in length and longitude, of and within all the breadth aforesaid, throughout the main lands there, from the Atlantic and Western

Sea and Ocean on the east part, to the South Sea on the west part; and all lands and grounds, place and places, soils, woods and wood grounds, havens, ports, rivers, waters, and hereditaments whatsoever, lying within the said bounds and limits, and every part and parcel thereof; and also all islands in America aforesaid, in the said seas, or either of them, on the western or eastern coasts, or parts of the said tracts of lands hereby mentioned to be given and granted, or any of them; and all mines and minerals as well royal mines of gold and silver as other mines and minerals whatsoever, in the said lands and premises, or any part thereof, and free liberty of fishing in or within any the rivers or waters within the bounds and limits aforesaid, and the seas thereunto adjoining; and all fishes, royal fishes, whales, ballan, sturgeons, and other fishes of what kind or nature soever, that shall at any time hereafter be taken in or within the said seas or waters, or any of them, by the said [men], their heirs and assigns, or by any other person or persons whatsoever there inhabiting, by them, or any of them, to be appointed to fish therein.

Provided always, that if the said lands, islands, or any other the premises hereinbefore mentioned, and by these presents, intended and meant to be granted, were at the time of the granting of the said former letters patents, dated the third day of November, in the eighteenth year of our said dear father's reign aforesaid, actually possessed or inhabited by any other Christian prince or state, or were within the bounds, limits, or territories of that southern colony, then before granted by our said late father, to be planted by divers of his loving subjects in the south parts of America, that then this present grant shall not extend to any such parts or parcels thereof so formerly inhabited, or lying within the bounds of the southern plantation as aforesaid, but as to those parts or parcels so possessed or inhabited by such Christian prince or state, or being within the boundaries aforesaid shall be utterly void, these presents or anything therein contained to the contrary notwithstanding. To have and hold, possess and enjoy the said parts of New England in America, which lie, extend, and are abutted as aforesaid, and every part and parcel thereof; and all the islands, rivers, ports, havens, waters, fishings, fishes, mines, minerals, jurisdictions, franchises, royalties, liberties, privileges, commodities, and premises whatsoever, with the appurtenances, unto the said [men], their heirs and assigns for ever, to the only proper and absolute use and behoof of the said [men], their heirs and assigns for evermore: To be holden of us, our heirs and successors, as of our manor of East Greenwich in our county of Kent, within our realm of England, in free and common socage, and not *in capite*, nor by knight's service; and also yielding and paying therefore, to us, our heirs and successors, the fifth part only of all ore of gold and silver, which from time to time, and at all times hereafter, shall be there gotten, had, or obtained, for all services, exactions, and demands whatsoever; provided always, and our express will and meaning is, that only one fifth part of the gold and silver ore above mentioned, in the whole, and no more be reserved or payable unto us, our heirs and successors, by colour or virtue of these presents, the double reservations or recitals aforesaid, or anything herein contained notwithstanding.

And forasmuch as the good and prosperous success of the plantation of the said parts of New England aforesaid intended by the said [men], to be speedily set upon, cannot but chiefly depend, next under the blessing of Almighty God, and the support of our royal authority upon the good government of the same, to the end that the affairs and businesses which from time to time shall happen and arise concerning the said lands, and the plantation of the same may be the better managed and ordered, we have further hereby of our especial grace, certain knowledge, and mere motion, given, granted, and confirmed, and for us, our heirs and successors, do give, grant, and confirm unto our said trusty and well beloved subjects [above named]; and for us, our heirs and successors, we will and ordain that the said [men], and all such others as shall hereafter be admitted and made free of the company and society hereafter mentioned, shall from time to time, and at all times for ever, hereafter be, by virtue of these presents, one body corporate and politic in fact and name, by the name of the Governor and Company of the Massachusetts Bay in New England, and them by the name of the Governor and Company of the Massachusetts Bay in New England, one body politic and corporate in deed, fact, and name; we do for us, our heirs and successors, make, ordain, constitute, and confirm by these presents, and that by that name they shall have perpetual succession, and that by the same name they and their successors shall and may be capable and enabled as well to implead, and to be impleaded, and to prosecute, demand, and answer, and be answered unto, in all and singular suits, causes, quarrels, and actions, of what kind or nature soever. And also to have, take, possess, acquire, and purchase any lands, tenements, or hereditaments, or any goods or chattels, and the same to lease, grant, demise, alien, bargain, sell, and dispose of, as other our liege people of this our realm of England, or any other corporation or body politic of the same may lawfully do.

And further, that the said governor and company, and their successors, may have for ever one common seal, to be used in all causes and occasions of the said company, and the same seal may alter, change, break, and new make, from time to time, at their pleasures. And our will and pleasure is, and we do hereby for us, our heirs and successors, ordain and grant, that from henceforth for ever, there shall be one governor, one deputy governor, and eighteen assistants of the same company, to be from time to time constituted, elected, and chosen out of the freemen of the said company, for the time being, in such manner and form as hereafter by these presents is expressed, which said officers shall apply themselves to take care for the best disposing and ordering of the general business and affairs of, for, and concerning the said lands and premises hereby mentioned, to be granted, and the plantation thereof, and the government of the people there. And for the better execution of our royal pleasure and grant in this behalf, we do by these presents, for us, our heirs and successors, nominate, ordain, make, and constitute our well beloved the said Matthew Cradock, to be the first and present governor of the said company, and the said Thomas Goffe, to be deputy governor of the said company, and the said Sir Richard Saltonstall, Isaac Johnson, Samuel Aldersey, John Venn, John Humfry, John Endecott, Simon Whetcombe, Increase Nowell, Richard Perry, Nathaniel Wright, Samuel Vassall, Theophilus Eaton, Thomas Adams Thomas Hutchins, John Browne, George Foxcroft, William Vassall, and William Pyncheon, to be the present assistants of the said company, to continue in the said several offices respectively for such time, and in such manner, as in and by these presents is hereafter declared and appointed.

And further, we will, and by these presents, for us, our heirs and successors, do ordain and grant, that the governor of the said company for the time being, or in his absence by occasion of sickness or otherwise, the deputy governor for the time being, shall have authority from time to time upon all occasions, to give order for the assembling of the said company, and calling them together to consult and advise of the businesses and affairs of the said company, and that the said governor, deputy governor, and assistants of the said company, for the time being, shall or may once every month, or oftener at their pleasures, assemble and hold and keep a court or assembly of themselves, for the better ordering and directing of their affairs, and that any seven or more persons of the assistants, together with the governor or deputy governor so assembled, shall be said, taken, held, and reputed to be, and shall be a full and sufficient court or assembly of the said company, for the handling, ordering, and dispatching of all such businesses and occurrences as shall from time to time happen, touching or concerning the said company or plantation; and that there shall or may be held and kept by the governor, or deputy governor of the said company, and seven or more of the said assistants for the time being, upon every last Wednesday in Hilary, Easter, Trinity, and Michaelmas terms respectively for ever, one great general and solemn assembly, which four general assemblies shall be styled and called the four great and general courts of the said company; in all and every or any of which said great and general courts so assembled, we do for us, our heirs and successors, give and grant to the said governor and company, and their successors, that the governor, or in his absence, the deputy governor of the said company for the time being, and such of the assistants and freemen of the said company as shall be present, or the greater number of them so assembled, whereof the governor or deputy governor and six of the assistants at the least to be seven, shall have full power and authority to choose, nominate, and appoint, such and so many others as they shall think fit, and that shall be willing to accept the same, to be free of the said company and body, and them into the same to admit; and to elect and constitute such officers as they shall think fit and requisite, for the ordering, managing, and dispatching of the affairs of the said governor and company, and their successors; and to make laws and ordinances for the good and welfare of the said company, and for the government and ordering of the said lands and plantation, and the people inhabiting and to inhabit the same, as to them from time to time shall be thought meet, so as such laws and ordinances be not contrary or repugnant to the laws and statutes of this our realm of England. And, our will and pleasure is, and we do hereby for us, our heirs and successors, establish and ordain, that yearly once in the year, for ever hereafter, namely the last Wednesday in Easter term, yearly, the governor, deputy governor, and assistants of the said company, and all other officers of the said company, shall be in the General Court or assembly to be held for that day or time, newly chosen for the year ensuing by such greater part of the said company, for the time being, then and there present, as is aforesaid. And, if it shall happen the present governor, deputy governor, and assistants, by these presents appointed or such as shall hereafter be newly chosen into their rooms, or any of them, or any other of the officers to be appointed for the said company, to die, or to be removed from his or their several offices or places before the said general day of election (whom we do hereby declare for any misdemeanour or defect to be removable by the governor, deputy governor, assistants, and company, or such greater part of them in any of the public courts to be assembled as is aforesaid) that then, and in every such case, it shall and may be lawful, to and for the governor, deputy governor, assistants, and company aforesaid, or such greater part of them so to be assembled as is aforesaid, in any of their assemblies, to proceed to a new election of one or more others of their company in the room or place, rooms or places of such officer or officers so dying or removed according to their discretion, and, immediately upon and after such election and elections made of such governor, deputy governor, assistant or assistants, or any other officer of the said company, in manner and form aforesaid, the authority, office, and power before given to the former governor, deputy governor, or other officer and officers so removed, in whose stead and place new shall be so chosen, shall as to him and them, and every of them, cease and determine.

Provided also, and our will and pleasure is, that as well such as are by these presents appointed to be the present governor, deputy governor, and assistants of the said company, as those that shall succeed them, and all other officers to be appointed and chosen as aforesaid, shall, before they undertake the execution of their said offices and places respectively, take their corporal oaths for the due and faithful performance of their duties in their several offices and places, before such person or persons as are by these presents hereunder appointed to take and receive the same; that is to say, the said Matthew Cradock, who is hereby nominated and appointed the present governor of the said company, shall take the said oaths before one or more of the masters of our court of chancery for the time being, unto which master or masters of the chancery, we do by these presents give full power and authority to take and administer the said oath to the said governor accordingly. And after the said governor shall be so sworn, then the said deputy governor and assistants, before by these presents nominated and appointed, shall take the said several oaths to their offices and places respectively belonging, before the said Matthew Cradock, the present governor, so formerly sworn as aforesaid. And every such person as shall be at the time of the annual election, or otherwise, upon death or removal, be appointed to be the new governor of the said company, shall take the oaths to that place belonging before the deputy governor, or two of the assistants of the said company at the least, for the time being, and the new elected deputy governor and assistants, and all other officers to be hereafter chosen as aforesaid from time to time, to take the oaths to their places respectively belonging, before the governor of the said company for the time being, unto which said governor, deputy governor, and assistants, we do by these presents give full power and authority to give and administer the said oaths respectively, according to our true meaning hereinbefore declared without any commission or further warrant to be had and obtained of us, our heirs or successors, in that behalf. And, we do further, of our especial grace, certain knowledge, and mere motion, for us, our heirs and successors, give and grant to the said governor and company, and their successors for ever by these presents, that it shall be lawful and free for them and their assigns, at all and every time and times hereafter, out of any our realms or dominions whatsoever, to take, lead, carry, and transport, for, in, and into their voyages, and for and towards the said plantation in New England, all such and so many of our loving subjects, or any other strangers that will become our loving subjects, and live under our allegiance, as shall willingly accompany them in the same voyages and plantation; and also shipping, armour, weapons, ordnance, munition, powder, shot, corn, victuals, and all manner of clothing, implements, furniture, beasts, cattle, horses, mares, merchandises, and all other things necessary for the said plantation, and for their use and defence, and for trade with the people there, and in passing and returning to and fro, any law or statute to the contrary hereof in any wise notwithstanding; and without paying or yielding any custom or subsidy, either inward or outward, to us, our heirs or successors, for the same, by the space of seven years from the day of the date of these presents. Provided, that none of the said persons be such as shall be hereafter by especial name restrained by us, our heirs or successors. And, for their further encouragement, of our especial grace and favour, we do by these presents, for us, our heirs and successors, yield and grant to the said governor and company and their successors, and every of them, their factors and assigns, that they and every of them shall be free and quit from all taxes, subsidies, and customs, in New England, for the like space of seven years and from all taxes and impositions for the space of twenty and one years, upon all goods and merchandises at any time or times hereafter, either upon importation thither, or exportation from thence into our realm of England, or into any other our dominions by the said governor and company, and their successors, their deputies, factors, and assigns, or any of them; except only the five pounds per centum due for custom upon all such goods and merchandises as after the said seven years shall be expired, shall be brought or imported into our realm of England, or any other of our dominions, according to the ancient trade of merchants, which five pounds per centum only being paid, it shall be thenceforth lawful and free for the said adventurers, the same goods and merchandises to export and carry out of our said dominions into foreign parts, without any custom, tax, or other duty to be paid to us, our heirs or successors, or to any other officer or ministers of us, our heirs or successors. Provided, that the said goods and merchandises be shipped out within thirteen months, after their first landing within any part of the said dominions.

And, we do for us, our heirs and successors, give and grant unto the said governor and company, and their successors, that whensoever, or so often as any custom or subsidy shall grow due or payable unto us, our heirs, or successors, according to the limitation and appointment aforesaid, by reason of any goods, wares, or merchandises to be shipped out, or any return to be made of any goods, wares, or merchandise unto or from the said parts of New England hereby mentioned to be granted as aforesaid, or any the lands or territories aforesaid, that then, and so often, and in such case, the farmers, customers, and officers of our customs of England and Ireland, and every of them for the time being, upon request made to them by the said governor and company, or their successors, factors, or assigns, and upon convenient security to be given in that behalf, shall give and allow unto the said governor and company, and their successors, and to all and every person and persons free of that company, as aforesaid, six months' time for the payment of the one half of all such custom and subsidy as shall be due and payable unto us, our heirs and successors, for the same; for which these our letters patent, or the duplicate, or the enrolment thereof, shall be unto our said officers a sufficient warrant and discharge. Nevertheless, our will and pleasure is, that if any of the said goods, wares, and merchandise, which be, or shall be at any time hereafter landed or exported out of any of our realms aforesaid, and shall be shipped with a purpose not to be carried to the parts of New England aforesaid, but to some other place, that then such payment, duty, custom, imposition, or forfeiture, shall be paid, or belong to us, our heirs and successors, for the said goods, wares, and merchandise, so fraudulently sought to be transported, as if this our grant had not been made nor granted. And we do further will, and by these presents, for us, our heirs and successors, firmly enjoin and command, as well the treasurer, chancellor and barons of the exchequer, of us, our heirs and successors, as also all and singular the customers, farmers, and collectors of the customs, subsidies, and imposts, and other the officers and ministers of us, our heirs and successors whatsoever, for the time being, that they and every of them, upon the showing forth unto them of these letters patents, or the duplicate or exemplification of the same, without any other writ or warrant whatsoever from us, our heirs or successors, to be obtained or sued forth, do and shall make full, whole, entire, and due allowance, and clear discharge unto the said governor and company, and their successors, of all customs, subsidies impositions, taxes and duties whatsoever, that shall or may be claimed by us, our heirs and successors, of or from the said governor and company, and their successors, for or by reason of the said goods, chattels, wares, merchandises, and premises to be exported out of our said dominions, or any of them, into any part of the said lands or premises hereby mentioned, to be given, granted, and confirmed, or for, or by reason of any of the said goods, chattels, wares, or merchandises to be imported from the said lands and premises hereby mentioned, to be given, granted, and confirmed into any of our said dominions, or any part thereof as aforesaid, excepting only the said five pounds per centum hereby reserved and payable after the expiration of the said term of seven years as aforesaid, and not before. And these our letters patents, or the enrolment, duplicate, or exemplification of the same shall be for ever hereafter, from time to time, as well to the treasurer, chancellor, and barons of the exchequer of us, our heirs and successors, as to all and singular the customers, farmers, and collectors of the customs, subsidies, and imposts of us, our heirs and successors, and all searchers, and other the officers and ministers whatsoever of us, our heirs and successors, for the time being, a sufficient warrant and discharge in this behalf.

And, further our will and pleasure is, and we do hereby for us, our heirs and successors, ordain, declare, and grant to the said governor and company, and their successors, that all and every the subjects of us, our heirs or successors, which shall go to and inhabit within the said lands and premises hereby mentioned to be granted, and every of their children which shall happen to be born there, or on the seas in going thither, or returning from thence, shall have and enjoy all liberties and immunities of free and natural subjects within any of the dominions of us, our heirs or successors, to all intents, constructions, and purposes whatsoever, as if they and every of them were born within the realm of England. And that the governor and deputy governor of the said company for the time being, or either of them, and any two or more of such of the said assistants as shall be thereunto appointed by the said governor and company at any of their courts or assemblies to be held as aforesaid, shall and may at all times, and from time to time hereafter, have full power and authority to minister and give the oath and oaths of supremacy and allegiance, or either of them, to all and every person and persons, which shall at any time or times hereafter go or pass to the lands and premises hereby mentioned to be granted to inhabit in the same. And, we do of our further grace, certain knowledge and mere motion, give and grant to the said governor and company, and their successors, that it shall and may be lawful, to and for the governor or deputy governor, and such of the assistants and freemen of the said company for the time being as shall be assembled in any of their general courts aforesaid, or in any other courts to be specially summoned and assembled for that purpose, or the greater part of them (whereof the governor or deputy governor, and six of the assistants to be always seven) from time to time, to make, ordain, and establish all manner of wholesome and reasonable orders, laws, statutes, and ordinances, directions, and instructions, not contrary to the laws of this our realm of England, as well for settling of the forms and ceremonies of government and magistracy, fit and necessary for the said plantation, and the inhabitants there, and for naming and styling of all sorts of officers, both superior and inferior, which they shall find needful for that government and plantation, and the distinguishing and setting forth of the several duties, powers, and limits of every such office and place, and the forms of such oaths warrantable by the laws and statutes of this our realm of England, as shall be respectively ministered unto them for the execution of the said several offices and places; as also for the disposing and ordering of the elections of such of the said officers as shall be annual, and of such others as shall be to succeed in case of death or removal, and ministering the said oaths to the new elected officers, and for impositions of lawful fines, mulcts, imprisonment, or other lawful correction, according to the course of other corporations in this our realm of England, and for the directing, ruling, and disposing of all other matters and things, whereby our said people, inhabitants there, may be so religiously, peaceably, and civilly governed, as their good life and orderly conversation, may win and incite the natives of [the] country to the knowledge and obedience of the only true God and Saviour of mankind, and the Christian faith, which in our royal intention, and the adventurers' free profession, is the principal end of this plantation. Willing, commanding, and requiring, and by these presents for us, our heirs and successors, ordaining and appointing, that all such orders, laws, statutes and ordinances, instructions and directions, as shall be so made by the governor, or deputy governor of the said company, and such of the assistants and freemen as aforesaid, and published in writing, under their common seal, shall be carefully and duly observed, kept, performed, and put in execution, according to the true intent and meaning of the same. And these our letters patents, or the duplicate or exemplification thereof, shall be to all and every such officers, superior and inferior, from time to time, for the putting of the same orders, laws, statutes, and ordinances, instructions, and directions, in due execution against us, our heirs and successors, a sufficient warrant and discharge.

And we do further, for us, our heirs and successors, give and grant to the said governor and company, and their successors by these presents, that all and every such chief commanders, captains, governors, and other officers and ministers, as by the said orders, laws, statutes, ordinances, instructions, or directions of the said governor and company for the time being, shall be from time to time hereafter employed either in the government of the said inhabitants and plantation, or in the way by sea thither, or from thence, according to the natures and limits of their offices and places respectively, shall from time to time hereafter for ever, within the precincts and parts of New England hereby mentioned to be granted and confirmed, or in the way by sea thither, or from thence, have full and absolute power and authority to correct, punish, pardon, govern, and rule all such the subjects of us, our heirs and successors, as shall from time to time adventure themselves in any voyage thither or from thence, or that shall at any time hereafter, inhabit within the precincts and parts of New England aforesaid, according to the orders, laws, ordinances, instructions, and directions aforesaid, not being repugnant to the laws and statutes of our realm of England as aforesaid. And we do further, for us, our heirs and successors, give and grant to the said governor and company, and their successors, by these presents, that it shall and may be lawful, to and for the chief commanders, governors, and officers of the said company for the time being, who shall be resident in the said part of New England in America, by these presents granted, and others there inhabiting by their appointment and direction, from time to time, and at all times hereafter for their special defence and safety, to encounter, expulse, repel, and resist by force of arms, as well by sea as by land, and by all fitting ways and means whatsoever, all such person and persons, as shall at any time hereafter attempt or enterprise the destruction, invasion, detriment, or annoyance to the said plantation or inhabitants, and to take and surprise by all ways and means whatsoever, all and every such person and persons, with their ships, armour, munition, and other goods, as shall in hostile manner invade or attempt the defeating of the said plantation, or the hurt of the said company and inhabitants. Nevertheless, our will and pleasure is, and we do hereby declare to all Christian kings, princes, and states, that if any person or persons which shall hereafter be of the said company or plantation, or any other by licence or appointment of the said governor and company for the time being, shall at any time or times hereafter, rob or spoil, by sea or by land, or do any hurt, violence, or unlawful hostility to any of the subjects of us, our heirs, or successors, or any of the subjects of any prince or state, being then in league and amity with us, our heirs and successors, and that upon such injury done and upon just complaint of such prince or state or their subjects, we, our heirs and successors shall make open proclamation within any of the parts within our realm of England, commodious for that purpose, that the person or persons having committed any such robbery or spoil, shall within the term limited by such a proclamation, make full restitution or satisfaction of all such injuries done, so as the said princes or others so complaining, may hold themselves fully satisfied and contented; and that if the said person or persons, having committed such robbery or spoil, shall not make, or cause to be made satisfaction accordingly, within such time so to be limited, that then it shall be lawful for us, our heirs and successors, to put the said person or persons out of our allegiance and protection, and that it shall be lawful and free for all princes to prosecute with hostility the said offenders, and every of them, their and every of their procurers, aiders, abettors, and comforters in that behalf. Provided also, and our express will and pleasure is, and we do by these presents for us, our heirs and successors, ordain and appoint that these presents shall not in any manner envire, or be taken to abridge, bar, or hinder any of our loving subjects whatsoever, to use and exercise the trade of fishing upon that coast of New England in America, by these presents mentioned to be granted. But that they, and every, or any of them, shall have full and free power and liberty to continue and use their said trade of fishing upon the said coast, in any the seas thereunto adjoining, or any arms of the seas or saltwater rivers where they have been wont to fish, and to build and set up upon the lands by these presents granted, such wharfs, stages, and workhouses as shall be necessary for the salting, drying, keeping, and packing up of their fish, to be taken or gotten upon that coast; and to cut down, and take such trees and other materials there growing, or being, or shall be needful for that purpose, and for all other necessary easements, helps, and advantage concerning their said trade of fishing there, in such manner and form as they have been heretofore at any time accustomed to do, without making any wilful waste or spoil, anything in these presents contained to the contrary notwithstanding. And we do further, for us, our heirs and successors, ordain and grant to the said governor and company, and their successors by these presents that these our letters patents shall be firm, good, effectual, and available in all things, and to all intents and constructions of law according to our true meaning hereinbefore declared, and shall be construed, reputed, and adjudged in all cases most favourably on the behalf, and for the benefit and behoof of the said governor and company and their successors, although express mention of the true yearly value or certainty of the premises or any of them, or of any other gifts or grants, by us, or any of our progenitors or predecessors to the aforesaid governor or company before this time made, in these presents is not made; or any statute, act, ordinance, provision, proclamation, or restraint to the contrary thereof, heretofore had, made, published, ordained, or provided, or any other matter, cause, or thing whatsoever to the contrary thereof in any wise notwithstanding.

In witness whereof, we have caused these our letters to be made patents.

Witness ourself, at Westminster, the fourth day of March, in the fourth year of our reign.

3. The charter of Maryland (20 June 1632)

Printed: Thomas Bacon, ed., *Laws of Maryland* (Annapolis, 1765), n.p. and Thorpe, *Federal and State Constitutions*, III, pp. 1669–1686.

Charles, by the Grace of God, of England, Scotland, France and Ireland, King, Defender of the Faith, etc. To all to whom these presents come, Greeting.

II. Whereas our well beloved and right trusty subject Caecilius Calvert, baron of

Baltimore, in our kingdom of Ireland, son and heir of George Calvert, knight, late baron of Baltimore, in our said kingdom of Ireland, treading in the steps of his father, being animated with a laudable and pious zeal for extending the Christian religion, and also the territories of our empire, hath humbly besought leave of us, that he may transport by his own industry and expense a numerous colony of the English nation to a certain region hereinafter described, in a country hitherto un-cultivated, in the parts of America, and partly occupied by savages, having no knowledge of the Divine Being, and that all that region, with some certain privileges, and jurisdiction, appertaining unto the wholesome government, and state of his colony and region aforesaid, may by our Royal Highness be given, granted, and confirmed unto him, and his heirs.

III. Know ye therefore, that we, encouraging with our royal favour, the pious and noble purpose of the aforesaid barons of Baltimore, of our special grace, certain know-ledge, and mere motion, have given, granted, and confirmed, and by this our present charter, for us, our heirs, and successors, do give, grant, and confirm, unto the aforesaid Caecilius, now baron of Baltimore, his heirs, and assigns, all that part of the peninsula, or chersonese, lying in the parts of America between the ocean on the east and the bay of Chesapeake on the west, divided from the residue thereof by a right line drawn from the promontory or headland called Watkin's Point, situate upon the bay aforesaid, near the river Wighco on the west, unto the main ocean on the east; and between that boundary on the south, unto that part of the bay of Delaware on the north, which lieth under the fortieth degree of north latitude from the equinoctial, where New England is terminated; and all that tract of land within the metes underwritten (that is to say) passing from the said bay, called Delaware Bay, in a right line, by the degree aforesaid, unto the true meridian of the first fountain of the river of Potomac, thence verging towards the south, unto the further bank of the said river, and following the same on the west and south, unto a certain place called Cinquack, situate near the mouth of the said river, where it disembogues into the aforesaid bay of Chesapeake, and thence by the shortest line unto the aforesaid promontory or place called Watkin's Point; so that the whole tract of land divided by the line aforesaid, between the main ocean and Watkin's Point, unto the promon-tory called Cape Charles, and every the appendages thereof, may entirely remain excepted for ever to us, our heirs, and successors.

IV. Also we do grant and likewise confirm unto the said baron of Baltimore, his heirs, and assigns, all islands and islets within the limits aforesaid, all and singular the islands, and islets, from the eastern shore of the aforesaid region, towards the east, which had been, or shall be formed in the sea, situate within ten marine leagues from the said shore; with all and singular the ports, harbours, bays, rivers, and straits belonging to the region or islands aforesaid, and all the soil, plains, woods, mountains, marshes, lakes, rivers, bays, and straits, situate, or being within the metes, bounds, and limits aforesaid, with the fishings of every kind of fish, as well of whales, sturgeons, and other royal fish, as of other fish, in the sea, bays, straits, or rivers within the premises, and the fish there taken; and moreover all veins, mines, and quarries, as well opened as hidden, already found, or that shall be found within the region, islands, or limits aforesaid, of gold, silver, gems, and precious stones, and any other whatsoever, whether they be of stones, or metals, or of any other thing, or matter whatsoever; and furthermore the patronages, and advowsons of all churches which (with the increasing worship and religion of Christ) within the said region, islands, islets, and limits aforesaid, hereafter shall happen to be built, together with licence and faculty of erecting and founding churches, chapels, and places of worship, in convenient and suitable places within the premises, and of causing the same to be dedicated and consecrated according to the ecclesiastical laws of our kingdom of England, with all and singular such, and as ample rights, jurisdictions, privileges, prerogatives, royalties, liberties, immunities, and royal rights, and temporal franchises whatsoever, as well by sea as by land, within the region, islands, islets, and limits aforesaid, to be had, exercised, used, and enjoyed, as any bishop of Durham, within the bishopric or county palatine of Durham, in our kingdom of England, ever heretofore hath had, held, used, or enjoyed, or of right could, or ought to have, hold, use, or enjoy.

V. And we do by these presents, for us, our heirs, and successors, make, create, and constitute him, the now baron of Baltimore, and his heirs, the true and absolute lords and proprietaries of the region aforesaid, and of all other premises (except the before excepted) saving always the faith and allegiance and sovereign dominion due to us, our heirs, and successors; to have, hold, possess, and enjoy the aforesaid region, islands, islets, and other the premises, unto the aforesaid now baron of Baltimore, and to his heirs and assigns, to the sole and proper behoof and use of him, the now baron of Baltimore, his heirs and assigns, for ever. To hold of us, our heirs, and successors, kings of England, as of our castle of Windsor, in our county of Berks, in free and common socage, by fealty only for all services, and not *in capite*, nor by knight's service, yielding therefore unto us, our heirs, and successors two Indian arrows of those parts, to be delivered at the said castle of Windsor every year, on Tuesday in Easter week; and also the fifth part of all gold and silver ore which shall happen from time to time, to be found within the aforesaid limits.

VI. Now, that the aforesaid region, thus by us granted and described, may be eminently distinguished above all other regions of that territory, and decorated with more ample titles, know ye, that we, of our more especial grace, certain knowledge, and mere motion, have thought fit that the said region and islands be erected into a province, as out of the plenitude of our royal power and prerogative, we do, for us, our heirs, and successors, erect and incorporate the same into a province, and nominate the same Maryland, by which name we will that it shall from henceforth be called.

VII. And forasmuch as we have above made and ordained the aforesaid now baron of Baltimore, the true lord and proprietary of the whole province aforesaid, know ye therefore further, that we, for us, our heirs, and successors, do grant unto the said now baron (in whose fidelity, prudence, justice, and provident circumspection of mind we repose the greatest confidence) and to his heirs, for the good and happy government of the said province, free, full, and absolute power, by the tenor of these presents, to ordain, make, and enact laws, of what kind soever, according to their sound discretions, whether relating to the public state of the said province or the private utility of individuals, of and with the advice, assent, and approbation of the freemen of the same province, or the greater part of them, or of their delegates or deputies, whom we will shall be called together for the framing of laws, when, and as often as need shall require, by the aforesaid now baron of Baltimore, and his heirs, and in the form which shall seem best to him or them, and the same to publish under the seal of the aforesaid now baron of Baltimore, and his heirs, and duly to execute the same upon all persons, for the time being, within the aforesaid province, and the limits thereof, or under his or their government and power, in sailing towards Maryland, or thence returning, outward-bound, either to England, or elsewhere, whether to any other part of our, or of any foreign dominions, wheresoever established, by the imposition of fines, imprisonment, and other punishment whatsoever; even if it be necessary, and the quality of the offence require it, by privation of member, or life, by him the aforesaid now baron of Baltimore, and his heirs, or by his or their deputy, lieutenant, judges, justices, magistrates, officers, and ministers, to be constituted and appointed according to the tenor and true intent of these presents, and to constitute and ordain judges, justices, magistrates, and officers, of what kind, for what cause, and with what power soever, within that land, and the sea of those parts, and in such form as to the said now baron of Baltimore, or his heirs, shall seem most fitting; and also to remit, release, pardon, and abolish all crimes and offences whatsoever against such laws, whether before or after judgment passed; and to do all and singular other things belonging to the completion of justice, and to courts, praetorian judicatories, and tribunals, judicial forms and modes of proceeding, although express mention thereof in these presents be not made; and, by judges by them delegated, to award process, hold pleas, and determine in those courts, praetorian judicatories, and tribunals, in all actions, suits, causes, and matters whatsoever, as well criminal as personal, real and mixed, and praetorian: which said laws, so to be published as abovesaid, we will, enjoin, charge, and command, to be most absolute and firm in law, and to be kept in those parts by all the subjects and liege men of us, our heirs, and successors, so far as they concern them, and to be inviolably observed under the penalties therein expressed, or to be expressed. So nevertheless, that the laws aforesaid be consonant to reason, and be not repugnant or contrary, but (so far as conveniently may be) agreeable to the laws, statutes, customs and rights of this our kingdom of England.

VIII. And forasmuch as, in the government of so great a province, sudden accidents may frequently happen, to which it will be necessary to apply a remedy, before the freeholders of the said province, their delegates, or deputies, can be called together for the framing of laws; neither will it be fit that so great a number of people should immediately, on such emergent occasion, be called together, we therefore, for the better government of so great a province, do will and ordain, and by these presents, for us, our heirs, and successors, do grant unto the said now baron of Baltimore, and to his heirs, that the aforesaid now baron of Baltimore, and his heirs, by themselves, or by their magistrates and officers, thereunto duly to be constituted as aforesaid, may, and can make and constitute fit and wholesome ordinances from time to time, to be kept and observed within the province aforesaid, as well for the conservation of the peace, as for the better government of the people inhabiting therein, and publicly to notify the same to all persons whom the same in any wise do or may affect. Which ordinances we will to be inviolably observed within the said province, under the pains to be expressed in the same. So that the said ordinances be consonant to reason and be not repugnant nor contrary, but (so far as conveniently may be done) agreeable to the laws, statutes, or rights of our kingdom of England: And so that the same ordinances do not, in any sort, extend to oblige, bind, charge, or take away the right or interest of any person or persons, of, or in member, life, freehold, goods or chattels.

IX. Furthermore, that the new colony may more happily increase by a multitude of people resorting thither, and at the same time may be more firmly secured from the incursions of savages, or of other enemies, pirates, and ravagers: we therefore, for us, our heirs, and successors, do by these presents give and grant power, licence and liberty to all the liege men and subjects, present and future, of us, our heirs, and successors, except such to whom it shall be expressly forbidden, to transport themselves and their families to the said province, with fitting vessels and suitable provisions, and therein to settle, dwell and inhabit; and to build and fortify castles, forts and other places of strength, at the appointment of the aforesaid now baron of Baltimore, and his heirs, for the public and their own defence; the statute of fugitives, or any other whatsoever to the contrary of the premises in any wise notwithstanding.

X. We will also, and of our more abundant grace, for us, our heirs, and successors do firmly charge, constitute, ordain, and command, that the said province be of our allegiance; and that all and singular the subjects and liege men of us, our heirs, and successors, transplanted, or hereafter to be transplanted into the province aforesaid, and the children of them, and of others their descendants, whether already born there, or hereafter to be born, be and shall be natives and liege men of us, our heirs, and successors, of our kingdom of England and Ireland; and in all things shall be held, treated, reputed, and esteemed as the faithful liege men of us, and our heirs, and successors, born within our kingdom of England; also lands, tenements, revenues, services, and other hereditaments whatsoever, within our kingdom of England, and other our dominions, to inherit, or otherwise purchase, receive, take, have, hold, buy, and possess, and the same to use and enjoy, and the same to give, sell, alien and bequeath; and likewise all privileges, franchises and liberties of this our kingdom of England, freely, quietly, and peaceably to have and possess, and the same may use and enjoy in the same manner as our liege men born, or to be born within our said kingdom of England, without impediment, molestation, vexation, impeachment, or grievance of us, or any of our heirs or successors; any statute, act, ordinance, or provision to the contrary thereof, notwithstanding.

XI. Furthermore, that our subjects may be incited to undertake this expedition with a ready and cheerful mind: know ye, that we, of our especial grace, certain knowledge, and mere motion, do, by the tenor of these presents, give and grant, as well as to the aforesaid baron of Baltimore, and to his heirs, as to all other persons who shall from time to time repair to the said province, either for the sake of inhabiting, or of trading with the inhabitants of the province aforesaid, full licence to ship and lade in any the ports of us, our heirs, and successors, all and singular their goods, as well movable, as immovable, wares and merchandises, likewise grain of what sort soever, and other things whatsoever necessary for food and clothing, by the laws and statutes of our kingdoms and dominions, not prohibited to be transported out of the said kingdom; and the same to transport, by themselves, or their servants or assigns, into the said province, without the impediment or molestation of us, our heirs or successors, or any officers of us, our heirs or successors (saving unto us, our heirs, and successors, the impositions, subsidies, customs, and other dues payable for the same goods and merchandises), any statute, act, ordinance, or other thing whatsoever to the contrary notwithstanding.

XII. But because, that in so remote a region, placed among so many barbarous nations, the incursions as well of the barbarians themselves, as of other enemies, pirates and ravagers, probably will be feared; therefore we have given, and for us, our heirs, and successors, do give by these presents, as full and unrestrained power as any captain-general of an army ever hath had, unto the aforesaid now baron of Baltimore, and to his heirs and assigns, by themselves, or by their captains, or other officers, to summon to their standards, and to array all men, of whatsoever condition, or wheresoever born, for the time being, in the said province of Maryland, to wage war, and to pursue, even beyond the limits of their province, the enemies and ravagers aforesaid, infesting those parts by land and by sea, and (if God shall grant it) to vanquish and captivate them, and the captives to put to death, or, according to their discretion, to save, and to do all other and singular the things which appertain, or have been accustomed to appertain unto the authority and office of a captain-general of an army.

XIII. We also will, and by this our charter, do give unto the aforesaid now baron of Baltimore, and to his heirs and assigns, power, liberty, and authority, that, in case of rebellion, sudden tumult, or sedition, if any (which God forbid) should happen to arise, whether upon land within the province aforesaid, or upon the high sea in making a voyage to the said province of Maryland, or in returning thence, they may, by themselves, or by their captains, or other officers, thereunto deputed under their seals (to whom we, for us, our heirs, and successors, by these presents, do give and grant the fullest power and authority) exercise martial law as freely, and in as ample manner and form as any captain-general of an army, by virtue of his office may, or hath accustomed to use the same, against the seditious authors of innovations in those parts, withdrawing themselves from the government of him or them, refusing to serve in war, flying over to the enemy, exceeding their leave of absence, deserters, or otherwise howsoever offending against the rule, law, or discipline of war.

XIV. Moreover, lest in so remote and far distant a region, every access to honours and dignities may seem to be precluded, and utterly barred, to men well born, who are preparing to engage in the present expedition, and desirous of deserving well, both in peace and war, of us, and our kingdom; for this cause, we, for us, our heirs, and successors, do give free and plenary power to the aforesaid now baron of Baltimore, and to his heirs and assigns, to confer favours, rewards and honours, upon such subjects, inhabiting within the province aforesaid, as shall be well deserving, and to adorn them with whatsoever titles and dignities they shall appoint (so that they be not such as are now used in England); also to erect and incorporate towns into boroughs, and boroughs into cities, with suitable privileges and immunities, according to the merits of the inhabitants, and convenience of the places; and to do all and singular other things in the premises, which to him or them shall seem fitting and convenient; even although they shall be such as, in their own nature, require a more special commandment and warrant than in these presents may be expressed.

XV. We will also, and by these presents do, for us, our heirs, and successors, give and grant licence by this our charter, unto the aforesaid now baron of Baltimore, his heirs and assigns, and to all persons whatsoever, who are, or shall be residents and inhabitants of the province aforesaid, freely to import and unlade, by themselves, their servants, factors or assigns, all wares and merchandises whatsoever, which shall be collected out of the fruits and commodities of the said province, whether the product of the land or the sea, into any the ports whatsoever of us, our heirs, and successors, of England or Ireland, or otherwise to dispose of the same there; and if need be, within one year, to be computed immediately from the time of unlading thereof, to lade the same merchandises again, in the same, or other ships, and to export the same to any other countries they shall think proper, whether belonging to us, or any foreign power which shall be in amity with us, our heirs or successors: provided always, that they be bound to pay for the same to us, our heirs, and successors, such customs and impositions, subsidies and taxes, as our other subjects of our kingdom of England, for the time being, shall be bound to pay, beyond which we will that the inhabitants of the aforesaid province of the said land, called Maryland, shall not be burdened.

XVI. And furthermore, of our more ample special grace, and of our certain knowledge, and mere motion, we do, for us, our heirs, and successors, grant unto the aforesaid now baron of Baltimore, his heirs and assigns, full and absolute power and authority to make, erect, and constitute, within the province of Maryland, and the islands and islets aforesaid, such, and so many seaports, harbours, creeks, and other places of unlading and discharge of goods and merchandises out of ships, boats, and other vessels, and of lading in the same, and in so many, and such places, and with such rights, jurisdictions, liberties, and privileges, unto such ports respecting, as to him or them shall seem most expedient; and, that all and every the ships, boats, and other vessels whatsoever, coming to, or going from the province aforesaid, for the sake of merchandising, shall be laden and unladen at such ports only as shall be so erected and constituted by the said now baron of Baltimore, his heirs and assigns, any usage, custom, or any other thing whatsoever to the contrary notwithstanding: saving always to us, our heirs, and successors, and to all the subjects of our kingdoms of England and Ireland, of us, our heirs, and successors, the liberty of fishing for sea fish, as well in the sea, bays, straits, and navigable rivers, as in the harbours, bays, and creeks of the province aforesaid; and the privilege of salting and drying fish on the shores of the same province; and for that cause, to cut down and take hedging-wood and twigs there growing, and to build huts and cabins, necessary in this behalf, in the same manner as heretofore they reasonably might, or have used to do. Which liberties and privileges the said subjects of us, our heirs, and successors, shall enjoy, without notable damage or injury in any wise to be done to the aforesaid now baron of Baltimore, his heirs or assigns, or to the residents and inhabitants of the same province in the ports, creeks, and shores aforesaid, and especially in the woods and trees there growing. And if any person shall do damage or injury of this kind, he shall incur the peril and pain of the heavy displeasure of us, our heirs, and successors, and of the due chastisement of the laws, besides making satisfaction.

XVII. Moreover, we will, appoint, and ordain, and by these presents, for us, our heirs, and successors, do grant unto the aforesaid now baron of Baltimore, his heirs and assigns, that the same baron of Baltimore, his heirs and assigns, from time to time, for ever, shall have, and enjoy the taxes and subsidies payable, or arising within the ports, harbours, and other creeks and places aforesaid, within the province aforesaid, for wares bought and sold, and things there to be laden, or unladen, to be reasonably assessed by them, and the people there as aforesaid, on emergent occasion; to whom we grant power by these presents, for us, our heirs, and successors, to assess and impose the said taxes and subsidies there, upon just cause, and in due proportion.

XVIII. And furthermore, of our special grace, and certain knowledge, and mere motion, we have given, granted, and confirmed, and by these presents, for us, our heirs, and successors, do give, grant, and confirm unto the aforesaid now baron of Baltimore, his heirs and assigns, full and absolute licence, power and authority, that he, the aforesaid now baron of Baltimore, his heirs and assigns, from time to time hereafter, for ever, may and can, at his or their will and pleasure, assign, alien, grant, demise, or enfeoff so many, such, and proportionate parts and parcels of the premises, to any person or persons willing to purchase the same, as they shall think convenient, to have and to hold to the same person or persons willing to take or purchase the same, and his and their heirs and assigns, in fee-simple or fee-tail or for term of life, lives or years; to hold of the aforesaid now baron of Baltimore, his heirs and assigns, by so many, such, and so great services, customs and rents of this kind, as to the same now baron of Baltimore, his heirs and assigns, shall seem fit and agreeable, and not immediately of us, our heirs and successors. And we do give, and by these presents, for us, our heirs, and successors, do grant to the same person and persons, and to each and every of them, licence, authority and power, that such person and persons, may take the premises, or any parcel thereof, of the aforesaid now baron of Baltimore, his heirs and assigns, and hold the same to them and their assigns, or their heirs, of the aforesaid baron of Baltimore, his heirs and assigns, of what estate of inheritance soever, in fee-simple or fee-tail, or otherwise, as to them and the now baron of Baltimore, his heirs and assigns, shall seem expedient; the statute made in the parliament of Lord Edward, son of King Henry, late king of England, our progenitor, commonly called the "Statute Quia Emptores Terrarum", heretofore published in our kingdom of England, or any other statute, act, ordinance, usage, law, or custom, or any other thing, cause, or matter, to the contrary thereof, heretofore had, done, published, ordained or provided to the contrary thereof notwithstanding.

XIX. We also, by these presents, do give and grant licence to the same baron of Baltimore, and to his heirs, to erect any parcels of land within the province aforesaid, into manors, and in every of those manors, to have and to hold a court-baron, and all things which to a court-baron do belong; and to have and to keep view of frank-pledge, for the conservation of the peace and better government of those parts, by themselves and their stewards, or by the lords, for the time being to be deputed, of other of those manors when they shall be constituted, and in the same to exercise all things to the view of frank-pledge belonging.

XX. And further we will, and do, by these presents, for us, our heirs, and successors, covenant and grant to, and with the aforesaid now baron of Baltimore, his heirs and assigns, that we, our heirs, and successors, at no time hereafter, will impose, or make or cause to be imposed, any impositions, customs, or other taxations, quotas or contributions whatsoever, in or upon the residents or inhabitants of the province aforesaid for their goods, lands, or tenements within the same province, or upon any tenements, lands, goods or chattels within the province aforesaid, or in or upon any goods or merchandises within the province aforesaid, or within the ports or harbours of the said province, to be laden or unladen; and we will and do, for us, our heirs, and successors, enjoin and command that this our declaration shall, from time to time, be received and allowed in all our courts and praetorian judicatories, and before all the judges whatsoever of us, our heirs, and successors, for a sufficient and lawful discharge, payment, and acquittance thereof, charging all and singular the officers and ministers of us, our heirs, and successors, and enjoining them, under our heavy displeasure, that they do not at any time presume to attempt any thing to the contrary of the premises, or that may in any wise contravene the same, but that they, at all times, as is fitting, do aid and assist the aforesaid now baron of Baltimore, and his heirs, and the aforesaid inhabitants and merchants of the province of Maryland aforesaid, and their servants and ministers, factors and assigns, in the fullest use and enjoyment of this our charter.

XXI. And furthermore we will, and by these presents, for us, our heirs, and successors, do grant unto the aforesaid now baron of Baltimore, his heirs and assigns, and to the freeholders and inhabitants of the said province, both present and to come, and to every of them, that the said province, and the freeholders or inhabitants of the said colony or country, shall not henceforth be held or reputed a member or part of the land of Virginia, or of any other colony already transported, or hereafter to be transported, or be dependent on the same, or subordinate in any kind of government, from which we do separate both the said province, and inhabitants thereof, and by these presents do will to be distinct, and that they may be immediately subject to our Crown of England, and dependent on the same for ever.

XXII. And if, peradventure, hereafter it may happen, that any doubts or questions should arise concerning the true sense and meaning of any word, clause, or sentence, contained in this our present charter, we will, charge and command, that interpretation to be applied, always, and in all things, and in all courts and judicatories whatsoever, to obtain which shall be judged to be the more beneficial, profitable, and favourable to the aforesaid now baron of Baltimore, his heirs and assigns: provided always, that no interpretation thereof be made, whereby God's holy and true Christian religion, or the allegiance due to us, our heirs and successors, may in any wise suffer by change, prejudice, or diminution; although express mention be not made in these presents of the true yearly value or certainty of the premises, or of any part thereof; or of other gifts and grants made by us, our heirs, and predecessors unto the said now Lord Baltimore, or any statute, act, ordinance, provision, proclamation, or restraint heretofore had, made, published, ordained, or provided, or any other thing, cause, or matter whatsoever, to the contrary thereof in any wise notwithstanding.

XXIII. In witness whereof we have caused these our letters to be made patent. Witness ourself at Westminster, the twentieth day of June, in the eighth year of our reign.

4. The charter of Pennsylvania (4 March 1681)

Printed: Thorpe, *Federal and State Constitutions*, v, pp. 3035–3044 and *Pennsylvania Archives*, 8th Series (8 vols., Harrisburg, 1931–1935), I, pp. xxvii–xl.

Charles the Second, by the Grace of God, King of England, Scotland, France, and Ireland, Defender of the Faith, &c. To all whom these presents shall come, Greeting. Whereas our trusty and well-beloved subject William Penn, Esquire, son and heir of Sir William Penn, deceased, out of a commendable desire to enlarge our English empire, and promote such useful commodities as may be of benefit to us and our dominions, as also to reduce the savage natives by gentle and just manners to the love of civil society and Christian religion, have humbly besought leave of us to transport an ample colony unto a certain country hereinafter described, in the parts of America not yet cultivated and planted; and hath likewise humbly besought our royal Majesty to give, grant, and confirm all the said country, with certain privileges and jurisdictions, requisite for the good government and safety of the said country and colony, to him and his heirs for ever: KNOW YE THEREFORE, that we, favouring the petition and good purpose of the said William Penn, and having regard to the memory and merits of his late father in divers services, and particularly to his conduct, courage, and discretion under our dearest brother James, duke of York, in that signal battle and victory fought and obtained against the Dutch fleet, command[ed] by the Heer Van Opdam, in the year one thousand six hundred and sixty-five: In consideration thereof, of our special grace, certain knowledge, and mere motion have given and granted, and by this our present charter, for us, our heirs and successors, do give and grant unto the said William Penn, his heirs and assigns, all that tract or part of land in America, with all the islands therein contained, as the same is bounded on the east by Delaware River, from twelve miles' distance northwards of New Castle Town unto the three and fortieth degree of northern latitude, if the said river doth extend so far northwards; but if the said river shall not extend so far northward, then by the said river so far as it doth extend; and from the head of the said river, the eastern bounds are to be determined by a meridian line, to be drawn from the head of the said river, unto the said three and fortieth degree. The said land to extend westwards five degrees in longitude, to be computed from the said eastern bounds; and the said lands to be bounded on the north by the beginning of the three and fortieth degree of northern latitude, and on the south by a circle drawn at twelve miles distance from New Castle northward and westward unto the beginning of the fortieth degree of northern latitude, and then by a straight line westward to the limit of longitude above-mentioned.

We do also give and grant unto the said William Penn, his heirs and assigns, the free and undisturbed use and continuance in, and passage into and out of all and singular ports, harbours, bays, waters, rivers, isles, and inlets, belonging unto, or leading to and from the country or islands aforesaid, and all the soil, lands, fields, woods, underwoods, mountains, hills, fens, isles, lakes, rivers, waters, rivulets, bays, and inlets, situate or being within, or belonging unto the limits and bounds aforesaid, together with the fishing of all sorts of fish, whales, sturgeons, and all royal and other fishes, in the sea, bays, inlets, waters, or rivers within the premises, and the fish therein taken; and also all veins, mines, and quarries, as well discovered as not discovered, of gold, silver, gems, and precious stones, and all other whatsoever, be it stones, metals, or of any other thing or matter whatsoever, found or to be found within the country, isles, or limits aforesaid. And him, the said William Penn, his heirs and assigns, we do by this our royal charter, for us, our heirs and successors, make, create, and constitute the true and absolute proprietary of the country afore-said, and of all other the premises, saving always to us, our heirs and successors, the faith and allegiance of the said William Penn, his heirs and assigns, and of all other proprietaries, tenants, and inhabitants that are or shall be within the territories and precincts aforesaid; and saving also, unto us, our heirs and successors, the sovereignty of the aforesaid country; to have, hold, possess, and enjoy the said tract of land, country, isles, inlets, and other the premises unto the said William Penn, his heirs and assigns, to the only proper use and behoof of the said William Penn, his heirs and assigns for ever, to be holden of us, our heirs and successors, kings of England, as of our castle of Windsor in our county of Berks, in free and common socage, by fealty only for all services, and not *in capite* or by knight's service, yielding and paying therefore to us, our heirs and successors, two beaver skins, to be delivered at our said castle of Windsor on the first day of January in every year; and also the fifth part of all gold and silver ore, which shall from time to time happen to be found within the limits aforesaid, clear of all charges. And of our further grace, certain knowledge, and mere motion, we have thought fit to erect, and we do hereby erect the aforesaid country and islands into a province and seigniory, and do call it Pennsylvania, and so from hence forth we will have it called.

And forasmuch as we have hereby made and ordained the aforesaid William Penn, his heirs and assigns, the true and absolute proprietaries of all the lands and dominions aforesaid, KNOW YE THEREFORE, that we reposing special trust and confidence in the fidelity, wisdom, justice, and provident circumspection of the said William Penn for us, our heirs and successors, do grant free, full, and absolute power by virtue of these presents to him and his heirs, and to his and their deputies, and lieutenants, for the good and happy government of the said country, to ordain, make, and enact, and under his and their seals to publish any laws whatsoever, for the raising of money for the public use of the said province, or for any other end, appertaining either unto the public state, peace, or safety of the said country, or unto the private utility of particular persons, according unto their best discretions, by and with the advice, assent, and approbation of the freemen of the said country, or the greater part of them, or of their delegates or deputies, whom for the enacting of the said laws, when, and as often as need shall require, we will that the said William Penn and his heirs, shall assemble in such sort and form, as to him and them shall seem best, and the same laws duly to execute, unto and upon all people within the said country and the limits thereof.

And we do likewise give and grant unto the said William Penn, and his heirs, and to his and their deputies and lieutenants, full power and authority to appoint and establish any judges and justices, magistrates and officers whatsoever, for what causes soever, for the probates of wills, and for the granting of administrations within the precincts aforesaid and with what power soever, and in such form as to the said William Penn or his heirs shall seem most convenient; also to remit, release, pardon, and abolish, whether before judgment or after, all crimes and offences whatsoever committed within the said country against the said laws, treason and wilful and malicious murder only excepted, and in those cases to grant reprieves, until our pleasure may be known therein and to do all and every other thing and things, which unto the complete establishment of justice, unto courts and tribunals, forms of judicature, and manner of proceedings do belong, although in these presents express mention be not made thereof; and by judges by them delegated, to award process, hold pleas, and determine in all the said courts and tribunals all actions, suits, and causes whatsoever, as well criminal as civil, personal, real and mixed; which laws, so as aforesaid to be published, our pleasure is, and so we enjoin, require, and command, shall be most absolute and available in law; and that all the liege people and subjects of us, our heirs and successors, do observe and keep the same inviolable in those parts, so far as they concern them, under the pain therein expressed, or to be expressed. Provided nevertheless, that the said laws be consonant to reason, and be not repugnant or contrary, but as near as conveniently may be agreeable to the laws and statutes, and rights of this our kingdom of England; and saving and reserving to us, our heirs and successors, the receiving, hearing, and determining of the appeal and appeals of all or any person or persons, of, in, or belonging to the territories aforesaid, or touching any judgment to be there made or given.

And forasmuch as in the government of so great a country, sudden accidents do often happen, whereunto it will be necessary to apply remedy before the freeholders of the said province, or their delegates or deputies, can be assembled to the making of laws; neither will it be convenient that instantly upon every such emergent occasion, so great a multitude should be called together: Therefore for the better government of the said country we will, and ordain, and by these presents, for us, our heirs and successors, do grant unto the said William Penn and his heirs, by themselves or by their magistrates and officers, in that behalf duly to be ordained as aforesaid, to make and constitute fit and wholesome ordinances, from time to time, within the said country to be kept and observed, as well for the preservation of the peace, as for the better government of the people there inhabiting; and publicly to notify the same to all persons, whom the same doth or anyway may concern. Which ordinances, our will and pleasure is, shall be observed inviolably within the said province, under pains therein to be expressed, so as the said ordinances be consonant to reason, and be not repugnant nor contrary, but so far as conveniently may be agreeable with the laws of our kingdom of England, and so as the said ordinances be not extended in any sort to bind, charge, or take away the right or interest of any person or persons, for or in their life, members, freehold, goods, or chattels. And our further will and pleasure is, that the laws for regulating and governing of property within the said province, as well for the descent and enjoyment of lands, as likewise for the enjoyment and succession of goods and chattels, and likewise as to felonies, shall be and continue the same, as they shall be for the time being by the general course of the law in our kingdom of England, until the said laws shall be altered by the said William Penn, his heirs or assigns, and by the freemen of the said province, their delegates or deputies, or the greater part of them.

And to the end the said William Penn, or his heirs, or other the planters, owners, or inhabitants of the said province, may not at any time hereafter by misconstruction of the powers aforesaid through inadvertency or design depart from that faith and due allegiance, which by the laws of this our kingdom of England, they and all our subjects, in our dominions and territories, always owe unto us, our heirs and successors, by colour of any extent or largeness of powers hereby given, or pretended to be given, or by force or colour of any laws hereafter to be made in the said province, by virtue of any such powers; our further will and pleasure is, that a transcript or duplicate of all laws, which shall be so as aforesaid made and published within the said province, shall within five years after the making thereof, be transmitted and delivered to the Privy Council, for the time being, of us, our heirs and successors: and if any of the said laws, within the space of six months after that they shall be so transmitted and delivered, be declared by us, our heirs or successors, in our or their Privy Council, inconsistent with the sovereignty or lawful prerogative of us, our heirs or successors, or contrary to the faith and allegiance due by the legal government of this realm, from the said William Penn, or his heirs, or of the planters and inhabitants of the said province, and that thereupon any of the said laws shall be adjudged and declared to be void by us, our heirs or successors, under our or their Privy Seal, that then and from thenceforth, such laws, concerning which such judgment and declaration shall be made, shall become void. Otherwise the said laws so transmitted, shall remain, and stand in full force, according to the true intent and meaning thereof.

Furthermore, that this new colony may the more happily increase, by the multitude of people resorting thither; therefore we for us, our heirs and successors, do give and grant by these presents, power, licence, and liberty unto all the liege people and subjects, both present and future, of us, our heirs and successors, excepting those who shall be specially forbidden to transport themselves and families unto the said country, with such convenient shipping as by the laws of this our kingdom of England they ought to use, with fitting provisions, paying only the customs therefore due, and there to settle themselves, dwell and inhabit, and plant, for the public and their own private advantage.

And furthermore, that our subjects may be the rather encouraged to undertake this expedition with ready and cheerful minds, KNOW YE, that we, of our especial grace, certain knowledge, and mere motion, do give and grant by virtue of these presents, as well unto the said William Penn, and his heirs, as to all others, who shall from time to time repair unto the said country, with a purpose to inhabit there, or trade with the natives of the said country, full licence to lade and freight in any ports whatsoever, of us, our heirs and successors, according to the laws made or to be made within our kingdom of England, and into the said country, by them, their servants or assigns, to transport all and singular their wares, goods, and merchandises, as likewise all sorts of grain whatsoever, and all other things whatsoever, necessary for food or clothing, not prohibited by the laws and statutes of our kingdoms and dominions to be carried out of the said kingdoms, without any let or molestation of us, our heirs and successors, or of any of the officers of us, our heirs and successors; saving always to us, our heirs and successors, the legal impositions, customs, and other duties and payments, for the said wares and merchandise, by any law or statute due or to be due to us, our heirs and successors.

And we do further, for us, our heirs and successors, give and grant unto the said William Penn, his heirs and assigns, free and absolute power to divide the said country and islands into towns, hundreds, and counties, and to erect and incorporate towns into boroughs, and boroughs into cities, and to make and constitute fairs and markets therein, with all other convenient privileges and immunities, according to the merit of the inhabitants, and the fitness of the places, and to do all and every other thing and things touching the premises, which to him or them shall seem meet and requisite, albeit they be such as of their own nature might otherwise require a more especial commandment and warrant than in these presents is expressed.

We will also, and by these presents, for us, our heirs and successors, we do give and grant licence by this our charter, unto the said William Penn, his heirs and assigns, and to all the inhabitants and dwellers in the province aforesaid, both present and to come, to import or unlade, by themselves or their servants, factors or assigns, all merchandises and goods whatsoever, that shall arise of the fruits and commodities of the said province, either by land or sea, into any of the ports of us, our heirs and successors, in our kingdom of England, and not into any other country whatsoever. And we give him full power to dispose of the said goods in the said ports; and if need be, within one year next after the unlading of the same, to lade the said merchandises and goods again into the same or other ships, and to export the same into any other countries, either of our dominions or foreign, according to law: provided always that they pay such customs and impositions, subsidies and duties for the same to us, our heirs and successors, as the rest of our subjects of our kingdom of England, for the time being, shall be bound to pay, and do observe the Acts of Navigation, and other laws in that behalf made.

And furthermore, of our most ample and especial grace, certain knowledge, and mere motion, we do, for us, our heirs and successors, grant unto the said William Penn, his heirs and assigns, full and absolute power and authority to make, erect, and constitute within the said province and the isles and islets aforesaid, such and so many seaports, harbours, creeks, havens, keys, and other places, for discharge and unlading of goods and merchandises, out of the ships, boats, and other vessels, and lading them in such and so many places, and with such rights, jurisdictions, liberties, and privileges unto the said ports belonging, as to him or them shall seem most expedient; and that all and singular the ships, boats, and other vessels, which shall come for merchandise and trade unto the said province, or out of the same shall depart, shall be laden or unladen only at such ports as shall be erected and constituted by the said William Penn, his heirs and assigns, any use, custom, or other thing to the contrary notwithstanding. Provided, that the said William Penn and his heirs, and the lieutenants and governors for the time being, shall admit and receive in and about all such ports, havens, creeks, and keys, all officers and their deputies who shall from time to time be appointed for that purpose by the farmers or commissioners of our customs for the time being.

And we do further appoint and ordain, and by these presents, for us, our heirs and successors, we do grant unto the said William Penn, his heirs and assigns, that he, the said William Penn, his heirs and assigns, may from time to time for ever, have and enjoy the customs and subsidies, in the ports, harbours, and other creeks and places aforesaid, within the province aforesaid, payable or due for merchandises and wares there to be laded and unladed, the said customs and subsidies to be reasonably assessed upon any occasion, by themselves and the people there as aforesaid to be assembled, to whom we give power by these presents, for us, our heirs and successors, upon just cause and in due proportion, to assess and impose the same; saving unto us, our heirs and successors, such impositions and customs as by Act of Parliament are and shall be appointed.

And it is our further will and pleasure that the said William Penn, his heirs and assigns, shall from time to time constitute and appoint an attorney or agent, to reside in or near our city of London, who shall make known the place where he shall dwell or may be found, unto the clerks of our Privy Council for the time being, or one of them, and shall be ready to appear in any of our courts at Westminster, to answer for any misdemeanours that shall be committed, or by any wilful default or neglect permitted by the said William Penn, his heirs or assigns, against our laws of trade or navigation; and after it shall be ascertained in any of our said courts, what damages we or our heirs or successors shall have sustained by such default or neglect, the said William Penn, his heirs and assigns shall pay the same within one year after such taxation, and demand thereof from such attorney: or in case there shall be no such attorney by the space of a year, or such attorney shall not make payment of such damages within the space of one year, and answer such other forfeitures and penalties within the said time as by the acts of Parliament in England are or shall be provided, according to the true intent and meaning of these presents; then it shall be lawful for us, our heirs and successors, to seize and resume the government of the said province or country, and the same to retain until payment shall be made thereof: but notwithstanding any such seizure or resumption of the government, nothing concerning the propriety or ownership of any lands, tenements, or other hereditaments, or goods or chattels of any the adventurers, planters, or owners, other than the respective offenders there, shall be any way affected or molested thereby.

Provided always, and our will and pleasure is, that neither the said William Penn, nor his heirs, or any other the inhabitants of the said province, shall at any time hereafter have or maintain any correspondence with any other king, prince, or state, or with any of their subjects, who shall then be in war against us, our heirs or successors; nor shall the said William Penn, or his heirs, or any other the inhabitants of the said province, make war or do any act of hostility against any other king, prince, or state, or any of their subjects who shall then be in league or amity with us, our heirs or successors.

And, because in so remote a country, and situate near many barbarous nations, the incursions as well of the savages themselves, as of other enemies, pirates and robbers, may probably be feared; therefore we have given, and for us, our heirs and successors, do give power by these presents unto the said William Penn, his heirs and assigns, by themselves or their captains or other their officers, to levy, muster and train all sorts of men, of what condition soever, or wheresoever born, in the said province of Pennsylvania, for the time being, and to make war, and to pursue the enemies and robbers aforesaid, as well by sea as by land, even without the limits of the said province, and by God's assistance to vanquish and take them, and being taken to put them to death by the law of war, or to save them, at their pleasure, and to do all and every other thing which to the charge and office of a captain-general of an army belongeth or hath accustomed to belong, as fully and freely as any captain-general of an army hath ever had the same.

And furthermore, of our especial grace and of our certain knowledge and mere motion, we have given and granted, and by these presents, for us, our heirs and successors, do give and grant unto the said William Penn, his heirs and assigns, full and absolute power, licence and authority, that he, the said William Penn, his heirs and assigns, from time to time hereafter for ever, at his or their own will and pleasure may assign, alien, grant, demise, or enfeoff of the premises so many and such parts or parcels to him or them that shall be willing to purchase the same, as they shall think fit, to have and to hold to them the said person and persons willing to take or purchase, their heirs and assigns, in fee-simple or fee-tail, or for the term of life, or lives or years, to be held of the said William Penn, his heirs and assigns, as of the said seigniory of Windsor, by such services, customs and rents as shall seem fit to the said William Penn, his heirs and assigns, and not immediately of us, our heirs and successors. And to the same person or persons, and to all and every of them, we do give and grant by these presents, for us, our heirs and successors, licence, authority and power, that such person or persons may take the premises, or any parcel thereof, of the aforesaid William Penn, his heirs or assigns, and the same hold to themselves, their heirs and assigns, in what estate of inheritance soever, in fee-simple, or in fee-tail, or otherwise, as to him, the said William Penn, his heirs and assigns, shall seem expedient: the statute made in the parliament of Edward, son of King Henry, late king of England, our predecessor, commonly called the statute QUIA EMPTORES TERRARUM, lately published in our kingdom of England in any wise notwithstanding.

And by these presents we give and grant licence unto the said William Penn, and his heirs, likewise to all and every such person and persons to whom the said William

Penn or his heirs shall at any time hereafter grant any estate or inheritance as aforesaid, to erect any parcels of land within the province aforesaid into manors, by and with the licence to be first had and obtained for that purpose, under the hand and seal of the said William Penn or his heirs; and in every of the said manors to have and to hold a court-baron, with all things whatsoever which to a court-baron do belong, and to have and to hold view of frank-pledge for the conservation of the peace and the better government of those parts, by themselves or their stewards, or by the lords for the time being of other manors to be deputed when they shall be erected, and in the same to use all things belonging to the view of frank-pledge. And we do further grant licence and authority that every such person and persons who shall erect any such manor or manors, as aforesaid, shall or may grant all or any part of his said lands to any person or persons, in fee-simple, or any other estate of inheritance to be held of the said manors respectively, so as no further tenures shall be created, but that upon all further and other alienations thereafter to be made, the said lands so aliened shall be held of the same lord and his heirs of whom the alienor did then before hold, and by the like rents and services which were before due and accustomed.

And further our pleasure is, and by these presents, for us, our heirs and successors, we do covenant and grant to and with the said William Penn, and his heirs and assigns, that we, our heirs and successors, shall at no time hereafter set or make, or cause to be set, any imposition, custom or other taxation, rate or contribution whatsoever, in and upon the dwellers and inhabitants of the aforesaid province, for their lands, tenements, goods or chattels within the said province, or in and upon any goods or merchandise within the said province, or to be laden or unladen within the ports or harbours of the said province, unless the same be with the consent of the proprietary, or chief governor, or assembly, or by act of Parliament in England.

And our pleasure is, and for us, our heirs and successors, we charge and command, that this our declaration shall from henceforward be received and allowed from time to time in all our courts, and before all the judges of us, our heirs and successors, for a sufficient and lawful discharge, payment and acquittance; commanding all and singular the officers and ministers of us, our heirs and successors, and enjoining them upon pain of our high displeasure, that they do not presume at any time to attempt anything to the contrary of the premises, or that do in any sort withstand the same, but that they be at all times aiding and assisting, as is fitting unto the said William Penn, and his heirs, and to the inhabitants and merchants of the province aforesaid, their servants, ministers, factors and assigns, in the full use and fruition of the benefit of this our charter.

And our further pleasure is, and we do hereby, for us, our heirs and successors, charge and require, that if any of the inhabitants of the said province, to the number of twenty, shall at any time hereafter be desirous, and shall by any writing, or by any person deputed for them, signify such their desire to the bishop of London for the time being that any preacher or preachers, to be approved of by the said bishop, may be sent unto them for their instruction, that then such preacher or preachers shall and may be and reside within the said province, without any denial or molestation whatsoever.

And if perchance hereafter it should happen any doubts or questions should arise concerning the true sense and meaning of any word, clause, or sentence contained in this our present charter, we will, ordain, and command that at all times and in all things such interpretation be made thereof, and allowed in any of our courts whatsoever as shall be adjudged most advantageous and favourable unto the said William Penn, his heirs and assigns: provided always that no interpretation be admitted thereof by which the allegiance due unto us, our heirs and successors, may suffer any prejudice or diminution; although express mention be not made in these presents of the true yearly value, or certainty of the premises, or of any part thereof, or of other gifts and grants made by us our progenitors or predecessors unto the said William Penn: any statute, act, ordinance, provision, proclamation, or restraint heretofore had, made, published, ordained or provided, or any other thing, cause, or matter whatsoever, to the contrary thereof in any wise notwithstanding.

B. THE PROMOTION OF COLONIZATION

THE promoters of colonies, whether trading companies or holders of proprietary charters, needed both money and men to develop successful settlements. A few men, of course, were willing to invest funds or were willing to migrate to the New World and pay their own way and that of others. But the majority of moneyed men had to be persuaded that an investment in colonies would be profitable. Equally important was the task of persuading the poor of Europe that the New World was a land of opportunity for them. No colony could be successful unless it had a growing population of farmers and labourers, and means had to be found to pay for their passage.

Thus as colony after colony was founded, the promoters wrote and printed tract after tract extolling the benefits of investment in and migration to America. Even before any English colonies were founded, Englishmen were urging the importance of colonization. One of the most effective pamphleteers was the English clergyman, Richard Hakluyt. He collected accounts of the voyages of discovery and dinned into English ears the importance of the New World to England. His *Discourse Concerning Western Planting* in 1584 contains virtually every argument in one form or another that is to be found in later discussions of the importance of colonies for the English nation. Colonies will produce raw materials not grown in England. They will free England from dependence on foreign goods. They will provide markets for English manufactures. They will provide a nursery for English seamen. They will be an outlet for idle soldiers and sailors as well as for the poor and unemployed of England.[1] Modern historians who debate whether evolving British colonial policy in the seventeenth and eighteenth centuries was concerned primarily with the colonies as sources of raw materials or as markets would do well to ponder the ideas in such early promotion literature.

As each colony was planned and established, its founders issued tracts describing it in glowing language. No matter where the colony was located or when it was founded, the ideas are essentially the same. The soil is invariably the best and ready for the plough. Crops of all kinds are bountiful and food is plentiful and cheap. The sea is filled with fish and the woods with fowl and game. The climate, whether it be New England or Carolina, is invariably healthful. There are wild beasts and snakes, it is true, but few of them are dangerous. The Indians are on the whole not unfriendly, and all of them await conversion to Christianity. Above all, the New World is a land of opportunity for both rich and poor. Landed gentry can acquire more land; the landless can become landlords in a short time. Wages are far higher than in England and every man can soon become independent.[2]

As the seventeenth century proceeded and more and more colonies were founded, the competition among colonizers became keener. The Carolina proprietors declared that the climate of Carolina was better than that of Virginia. They offered free land, freedom of religion, freedom from taxes, and the right to vote to all who would come to Carolina.[3] Perhaps the most able of all the promoters was William Penn. He wrote pamphlets himself and hired others to write for him. These pamphlets were translated

[1] No. 5.　　　　[2] Nos. 6, 7, 8, 11.　　　　[3] No. 9.

into many languages and helped to turn the great stream of eighteenth century migration to Pennsylvania.[1]

Such tracts setting forth the ease of getting land, freedom of religion, the promise of self-government, and many other things, helped fix in the minds of Europeans and Americans the idea of the New World as a place where life could be better and easier for all those who lived there. Many, of course, poked fun at promotion pamphlets throughout the colonial period. Others feared the consequences of too rapid migration from England, particularly towards the end of the seventeenth century. But such people were a minority and could not stem the flow of promotion literature or the flow of people to the American colonies.

The documents which follow are samples of the many tracts that were written. They illustrate how the image of America as the land of opportunity was firmly implanted in the literature of the times. That the ideal and the reality did not always coincide is perfectly clear, but it must be remembered that most promoters were more concerned with success than with a literal rendition of the truth about the American Colonies.

5. Richard Hakluyt: reasons for colonization, from "A Discourse Concerning Western Planting"

The following is the concluding chapter of Richard Hakluyt's book, commonly called *A Discourse Concerning Western Planting*. It was written at the request of Sir Walter Raleigh in an effort to secure the support of Queen Elizabeth for his colonizing ventures. Printed: Charles Deane, *et al.*, eds., *Documentary History of the State of Maine* (24 vols., 1869–1916, *Collections of the Maine Historical Society*, 2nd Series), II, pp. 152–161.

Chapter XX. A brief collection of certain reasons to induce her Majesty and the state to take in hand the western voyage and the planting there.

1. The soil yields and may be made to yield all the several commodities of Europe. . . .

2. The passage thither and home is neither too long nor too short, but easy, and to be made twice in the year.

3. The passage cuts not near the trade of any prince, nor near any of their countries or territories, and is a safe passage, and not easy to be annoyed by prince or potentate whatsoever.

4. The passage is to be performed at all times of the year, and in that respect passes our trades in the Levant Seas within the Straits of Gibraltar, and the trades in the seas within the King of Denmark's Strait, and the trades to the ports of Norway and of Russia, etc. . . .

5. And where England now for certain hundred years last passed, by the peculiar commodity of wool, and of later years, by clothing of the same, has raised itself from meaner state to greater wealth and much higher honour, might, and power than before, to the equalling of the princes of the same to the greatest potentates of this part of the world; it comes now so to pass that by the great endeavour of the increase of the trade of wool in Spain and in the West Indies, now daily more and more multiplying, that the wool of England, and the cloth made of the same, will become base, and every day more base than [the] other; which, prudently weighed,

[1] No. 10.

it behooves this realm, if it mean not to return to former old means and baseness, but to stand in present and late former honour, glory, and force, and not negligently and sleepingly to slide into beggary, to foresee and to plant at Norumbega[1] or some like place, were it not for anything else but for the hope of the sale of our wool. . . .

6. This enterprise may stay the Spanish king from flowing over all the face of that waste firmament of America, if we seat and plant there in time. . . . And England possessing the purposed place of planting, her Majesty may, by the benefit of the seat, having won good and royal havens, have plenty of excellent trees for masts, of goodly timber to build ships and to make great navies, of pitch, tar, hemp, and all things incident for a navy royal, and that for no price, and without money or request. How easy a matter may it be to this realm, swarming at this day with valiant youths, rusting and hurtful by lack of employment, and having good makers of cable and of all sorts of cordage, and the best and most cunning shipwrights of the world, to be lords of all those seas, and to spoil Philip's Indian navy, and to deprive him of yearly passage of his treasure to Europe, and consequently to abate the pride of Spain and of the supporter of the great Anti-christ of Rome, and to pull him down in equality to his neighbour princes, and consequently to cut off the common mischiefs that come to all Europe by the peculiar abundance of his Indian treasure, and this without difficulty.

7. This voyage, albeit it may be accomplished by bark or smallest pinnace for advice or for a necessity, yet for the distance, for burden and gain in trade, the merchant will not for profit's sake use it but by ships of great burden; so as this realm shall have by that means ships of great burden and of great strength for the defence of this realm. . . .

8. This new navy of mighty new strong ships, so in trade to that Norumbega and to the coasts there, shall never be subject to arrest of any prince or potentate as the navy of this realm from time to time has been in the ports of the empire, in the ports of the Low Countries, in Spain, France, Portugal, etc., in the times of Charles the Emperor, Francis the French king, and others. . . .

9. The great mass of wealth of the realm embarked in the merchants' ships, carried out in this new course, shall not lightly, in so far distant a course from the coast of Europe, be driven by winds and tempests into ports of any foreign princes, as the Spanish ships of late years have been into our ports of the West countries, etc. . . .

10. No foreign commodity that comes into England comes without payment of custom once, twice, or thrice, before it comes into the realm, and so all foreign commodities become dearer to the subjects of this realm; and by this course to Norumbega foreign princes' customs are avoided; and the foreign commodities cheaply purchased, they become cheap to the subjects of England, to the common benefit of the people, and to the saving of great treasure in the realm; whereas now the realm becomes poor by the purchasing of foreign commodities in so great a mass at so excessive prices.

11. At the first traffic with the people of those parts, the subjects of this realm for

---

[1] A country, city, and river, conjectured to have been occupied by Norsemen before the fourteenth century; variously located on the New England coast.

many years shall change many cheap commodities of these parts for things of high value there not esteemed; and this to the great enriching of the realm, if common use fail not.

12. By the great plenty of those regions the merchants and their factors shall lie there cheap, buy and repair their ships cheap, and shall return at pleasure without stay or restraint of foreign prince; whereas upon stays and restraints the merchant raiseth his charge in sale over of his ware. . . .

13. By making of ships and by preparing of things for the same, by making of cables and cordage, by planting of vines and olive trees, and by making of wine and oil, by husbandry, and by thousands of things there to be done, infinite numbers of the English nation may be set on work, to the unburdening of the realm with many that now live chargeable to the state at home.

14. If the sea coast serve for making of salt, and the inland for wine, oils, oranges, lemons, figs, &c., and for making of iron, all which with much more is hoped, without sword drawn, we shall cut the comb of the French, of the Spanish, of the Portuguese, and of enemies, and of doubtful friends, to the abating of their wealth and force, and to the greater saving of the wealth of the realm.

15. The substances serving, we may out of those parts receive the mass of wrought wares that now we receive out of France, Flanders, Germany, &c.; and so we may daunt the pride of some enemies of this realm, or at the least in part purchase those wares, that now we buy dearly of the French and Flemish, better cheap; and in the end, for the part that this realm was wont to receive, drive them out of trade to idleness for the setting of our people on work.

16. We shall by planting there enlarge the glory of the gospel, and from England plant sincere religion, and provide a safe and a sure place to receive people from all parts of the world that are forced to flee for the truth of God's word.

17. If frontier wars there chance to arise, and if thereupon we shall fortify, it will occasion the training up of our youth in the discipline of war, and make a number fit for the service of the wars and for the defence of our people there and at home.

18. The Spaniards govern in the Indies with all pride and tyranny; and like as when people of contrary nature at sea enter into galleys, where men are tied as slaves, all yell and cry with one voice, *Liberta, liberta,* as desirous of liberty and freedom, so no doubt whensoever the Queen of England, a prince of such clemency, shall seat upon that firmament of America, and shall be reported throughout all that tract to use the natural people there with all humanity, courtesy, and freedom, they will yield themselves to her government, and revolt clean from the Spaniard. . . .

19. The present short trades cause the mariner to be cast off, and often to be idle, and so by poverty to fall to piracy. But this course to Norumbega being longer, and a continuance of the employment of the mariner, doth keep the mariner from idleness and from necessity; and so it cuts off the principal actions of piracy, and the rather because no rich prey for them to take comes directly in their course or anything near their course.

20. Many men of excellent wits and of diverse singular gifts, overthrown by suretyship, by sea, or by some folly of youth, that are not able to live in England, may

there be raised again, and do their country good service; and many needful uses there may (to great purpose) require the saving of great numbers, that for trifles may otherwise be devoured by the gallows.

21. Many soldiers and servitors, in the end of the wars, that might be hurtful to this realm, may there be unladen, to the common profit and quiet of this realm, and to our foreign benefit there, as they may be employed.

22. The fry of the wandering beggars of England, that grow up idly, and hurtful and burdenous to this realm, may there be unladen, better bred up, and may people waste countries to the home and foreign benefit, and to their own more happy state.

23. If England cry out and affirm that there are so many in all trades that one cannot live for another, as in all places they do, this Norumbega (if it be thought so good) offers the remedy.

6. The needs of the Virginia Colony (1610)

The Virginia Company made great efforts to promote the successful establishment of the colony. It published many broadsides and pamphlets describing the advantages of the colony, explaining its needs, and defending the company against its enemies. The following broadside, " A Publication by the Counsell of Virginea, touching the Plantation there", published in 1610, is a realistic statement born of the bitter experience of the first years of failure. The source from which it is taken contains much of the promotion literature of the company as well as other documents relating to its history and that of the colony. Printed: Alexander Brown, *The Genesis of the United States* (2 vols., Cambridge, Mass., 1890), I, pp. 354-356.

Howsoever it came to pass by God's appointment, that governs all things, that the fleet of eight ships, lately sent to Virginia, by means the Admiral, wherein were shipped the chief governors, Sir Thomas Gates, Sir George Somers, and Captain [Christopher] Newport, by the tempestuous winds and forcible current, were driven so far to the westward that they could not in so convenient time recover Cape Henry, and the port in Virginia, as by the return of the same fleet to answer the expectation of the adventurers in some measure.

By occasion whereof, some few of those unruly youths sent thither (being of most lewd and bad condition) and such as no ground can hold for want of good directions there, were suffered by stealth to get aboard the ships returning thence, and are come for England again, giving out in all places where they come (to colour their own misbehaviour, and the cause of their return with some pretence) most vile and scandalous reports, both of the country itself and of the carriage of the business there.

Which hath also given occasion that sundry false rumours and despiteful speeches have been devised and given out by men that seem of better sort, being such as lie at home, and do gladly take all occasions to cheer themselves with the prevention of happy success in any action of public good, disgracing both the actions and actors of such honourable enterprises as whereof they neither know nor understand the true intents and honest ends.

Which howsoever (for a time) it may deter and keep back the hands and help of many well disposed men, yet men of wisdom and better resolution do well conceive and know that these devices infused into the tongues and heads of such devisors (by the Father of untruths) do serve for nothing else but as a cloak to cover the wretched and lewd pranks of the one sort, and the stupidity and backwardness of the other, to advance any commendable action that taxeth their purse, and tendeth not wholly to their own advantage.

And therefore those of his Majesty's Council in this honourable plantation, the lords, knights, gentlemen, and merchants interested therein (rightly considering that as in all other good services (so in this) much loss and detriment may many ways arise and grow to the due means and manner of proceeding, which yet no way toucheth nor impeacheth the action itself, nor the ends of it, which do still remain entire and safe upon the same grounds of those manifold Christian duties whereon it was first resolved) are so far from yielding or giving way to any hindrance or impeachment of their cheerful going on that many of them, both honourable and worshipful have given their hands and subscribed to contribute again and again to new supplies if need require.

And further, they do instantly prepare and make ready a certain number of good ships, with all necessaries, for the right honourable Lord de la Warr, who intendeth, God assisting, to be ready with all expedition to second the foresaid generals, which we doubt not are long since safely arrived at their wished port in Virginia.

And for that former experience hath too dearly taught how much and many ways it hurteth to suffer parents to disburden themselves of lascivious sons, masters of bad servants, and wives of ill husbands, and so to clog the business with such an idle crew as did thrust themselves in the last voyage, that will rather starve for hunger than lay their hands to labour.

It is therefore resolved that no such unnecessary person shall now be accepted, but only such sufficient, honest, and good artificers as smiths, shipwrights, sturgeon-dressers, joiners, carpenters, gardeners, turners, coopers, salt-makers, iron-men for furnace and hammer, brickmakers, bricklayers, mineral-men, bakers, gun-founders, fishermen, ploughwrights, brewers, sawyers, fowlers, vine-dressers, surgeons and physicians for the body, and learned divines to instruct the colony and to teach the infidels to worship the true God. Of which so many as will repair to the house of Sir Thomas Smythe, treasurer of the company, to proffer their service in this action before the number be full, and will put in good sureties to be ready to attend the said honourable Lord in the voyage, shall be entertained with those reasonable and good conditions as shall answer and be agreeable to each man's sufficiency in his several profession[s].

Imprinted at London by Thomas Haveland for William Welby, and are to be sold at his shop in Paul's Churchyard at the sign of the Swan. 1610.

7. Francis Higginson: New England's Plantation (1630)

The following pamphlet was written by the Reverend Francis Higginson who came to Massachusetts Bay in 1629 and who died at Salem in August 1630. The pamphlet, *New England's Plantation or a Short and True Description of the Commodities of that Country*, was published in London in 1630. It went through three editions that year. It is essentially a continuation of Higginson's journal which he sent to England in July 1629, but which was not published. Printed: Massachusetts Historical Society, *Proceedings*, LXII, pp. 307–318.

Letting pass our voyage by sea, we will now begin our discourse on the shore of New England. And because the life and welfare of every creature here below, and the commodiousness of the country whereas such creatures live, do by the most wise ordering of God's Providence, depend next unto himself, upon the temperature and disposition of the four elements, Earth, Water, Air, and Fire (for as of the mixture of all these, all sublunary things are composed; so by the more or less enjoyment of the wholesome temper and convenient use of these, consists the only well-being both of man and beast in a more or less comfortable measure in all countries under the heavens); therefore I will endeavour to show you what New England is by the consideration of each of these apart, and truly endeavour by God's help to report nothing but the naked truth, and that both to tell you of the discommodities as well as of the commodities, though as the idle proverb is, travellers may lie by authority, and so may take too much sinful liberty that way. Yet I may say of myself as once Nehemiah did in another case: Shall such a man as I lie? No verily: it becomes not a preacher of truth to be a writer of falsehood in any degree; and therefore I have been careful to report nothing of New England but what I have partly seen with my own eyes, and partly heard and inquired from the mouths of very honest and religious persons, who by living in the country a good space of time have had experience and knowledge of the state thereof, and whose testimonies I do believe as myself.

First, therefore, of the earth of New England and all the appurtenances thereof: it is a land of divers and sundry sorts all about Massachusetts Bay, and at Charles River is as fat black earth as can be seen anywhere; and in other places you have a clay soil; in other gravel; in other sandy, as it is all about our plantation at Salem, for so our town is now named, Psal. 76.2.

The form of the earth here . . . is neither too flat in the plains, nor too high in hills, but partakes of both in a mediocrity, and fit for pasture, or for plough or meadow ground, as men please to employ it: though all the country be as it were a thick wood for the general, yet in divers places there is much ground cleared by the Indians, and especially about the plantation; and I am told that about three miles from us a man may stand on a little hilly place and see divers thousands of acres of ground as good as need to be, and not a tree in the same. It is thought here is good clay to make brick and tiles and earthen pot as need to be. At this instant we are setting a brick-kiln on work to make bricks and tiles for the building of our houses. For stone, here is plenty of slates at the Isle of Slate in Massachusetts Bay, and lime-stone, freestone, and smoothstone, and ironstone, and marblestone also in such store that we have great rocks of it, and a harbour hard by. Our plantation is from thence called Marble Harbour.

Of minerals there has yet been but little trial made, yet we are not without great hope of being furnished in that soil.

The fertility of the soil is to be admired at, as appears in the abundance of grass that grows everywhere both very thick, very long, and very high in divers places; but it grows very wildly with a great stalk and a broad and ranker blade, because it never had been eaten with cattle, nor mowed with a scythe, and seldom trampled on by foot. It is scarce to be believed how our kine and goats, horses and hogs do thrive and prosper here and like well of this country.

In our plantation we have already a quart of milk for a penny; but the abundant increase of corn proved this country to be a wonderment. Thirty, forty, fifty, sixty are ordinary here: yea, Joseph's increase in Egypt is outstript here with us. Our planters hope to have more than a hundredfold this year; and all this while I am within compass. What will you say of two hundredfold and upwards? It is almost incredible what great gain some of our English planters have had by our Indian corn. Credible persons have assured me, and the party himself avouched the truth of it to me, that of the setting of 13 gallons of corn he has had increase of it 52 hogsheads, every hogshead holding 7 bushels of London measure, and every bushel was by him sold and trusted to the Indians for so much beaver as was worth 18 shillings: and so of this 13 gallons of corn which was worth 6 shillings 8 pence, he made about 327 pounds of it the year following, as by reckoning will appear: where you may see how God blessed husbandry in this land. There is not such great and plentiful ears of corn I suppose anywhere else to be found but in this country: because also of variety of colours, as red, blue and yellow, etc., and of one corn there springs four or five hundred. I have sent you many ears of divers colours that you might see the truth of it.

Little children here by setting of corn may earn much more than their own maintenance.

They have tried our English corn at New Plymouth Plantation, so that all our several grains will grow here very well, and have a fitting soil for their nature.

Our governor has store of green peas growing in his garden as good as ever I eat in England.

This country abounds naturally with store of roots of great variety and good to eat. Our turnips, parsnips and carrots are here both bigger and sweeter than is ordinarily to be found in England. Here are store of pumpkins, cucumbers, and other things of that nature which I know not. Also divers excellent pot-herbs grow abundantly among the grass, as strawberry leaves in all places of the country, and plenty of strawberries in their time, and pennyroyal, wintersavory, sorrel, brooklime, liverwort, caruell, and watercresses, also leeks and onions are ordinary, and divers physical herbs. Here are also abundance of other sweet herbs delightful to the smell, whose names we know not, etc., and plenty of single damask roses very sweet; and two kinds of herbs that bear two kinds of flowers very sweet, which they say are as good to make cordage or cloth as any hemp or flax we have.

Excellent vines are here up and down in the woods. Our governor has already planted a vineyard with great hope to increase.

Also mulberries, plums, raspberries, currants, chestnuts, filberts, walnuts, smallnuts, hurtleberries and haws of whitethorne near as good as our cherries in England, they grow in plenty here.

For wood there is no better in the world I think, here being four sorts of oak differing both in the leaf, timber and colour, all excellent good. There is also good ash, elm, willow, birch, beech, sassafras, juniper cypress, cedar, spruce, pines, and fir that will yield abundance of turpentine, pitch, tar, masts and other materials for building both of ships and houses. Also here are store of sumac trees; they are good for dyeing and tanning of leather; likewise such trees yield a precious gum called white benjamin [benzoin] that they say is excellent for perfumes. Also here be divers roots and berries wherewith the Indians dye excellent holding colours that no rain nor washing can alter. Also we have materials to make soap-ashes and saltpetre in abundance.

For beasts there are some bears, and they say some lions also for they have been seen at Cape Anne. Also here are several sorts of deer, some whereof bring three or four young ones at once, which is not ordinary in England. Also wolves, foxes, beavers, otters, martens, great wildcats, and a great beast called a molke [moose] as big as an ox. I have seen the skins of all these beasts since I came to this plantation, excepting lions. Also here are great store of squirrels, some greater, and some smaller and lesser; there are some of the lesser sort, they tell me, that by a certain skill will fly from tree to tree though they stand far distant.

Of the Waters of New England with the things belonging to the same

New England has water enough, both salt and fresh, the greatest sea in the world, the Atlantic Sea, runs all along the coast thereof. There are abundance of islands along the shore, some full of wood and mast to feed swine; and others clear of wood, and fruitful to bear corn. Also we have store of excellent harbours for ships, as at Cape Anne, and at Massachusetts Bay, and at Salem, and at many other places; and they are the better because for strangers there is a very difficult and dangerous passage into them, but to such as are well acquainted with them, they are easy and safe enough. The abundance of seafish are almost beyond believing, and sure I should scarce have believed it except I had seen it with my own eyes. I saw great store of whales and grampus, and such abundance of mackerel that it would astonish one to behold; likewise codfish [in] abundance on the coast, and in their season are plentifully taken. There is a fish called a bass, a most sweet and wholesome fish as ever I did eat; it is altogether as good as our fresh salmon, and the season of their coming was begun when we came first to New England in June, and so continued about three months' space. Of this fish our fishers may take many hundreds together which I have seen lying on the shore to my admiration; yea their nets ordinarily take more than they are able to haul to land, and for want of boats and men they are constrained to let amany go after they have taken them, and yet sometimes they fill two boats at a time with them. And besides bass we take plenty of skate and thornbacks, and abundance of lobsters, and the least boy in the plantation may both catch and eat what he will of them. For my own part I was soon cloyed with them, they were so great, and fat, and luscious. I have seen some myself that have weighed 16 pounds, but others have had divers times so great lobsters as have weighed 25 pounds, as they assure me. Also here is abundance of herring, turbot, sturgeon, cusks, haddocks, mullets, eels, crabs, mussels, and oysters. Besides there is probability that the country is of an excellent temper for the making of salt, for since our coming our fishermen have brought home very good salt which they found candied [caked] by the standing of the sea water and the heat of the sun upon a rock by the seashore, and in divers salt marshes that some have gone through they have found some salt in some places crushing under their feet and cleaving to their shoes.

And as for fresh water the country is full of dainty springs, and some great rivers, and some lesser brooks; and at Massachusetts Bay they dug wells and found water at three feet deep in most places; and near Salem they have as fine clear water as we can desire, and we may dig wells and find water where we list.

Thus we see both land and sea abound with store of blessings for the comfortable sustenance of man's life in New England.

Of the Air of New England with the temper and creatures in it

The temper of the air of New England is one special thing that commends this place. Experience doth manifest that there is hardly a more healthful place to be found in the world that agrees better with our English bodies. Many that have been weak and sickly in old England, by coming hither have been thoroughly healed and grown healthful strong. For here is an extraordinary clear and dry air that is of a most healing nature to all such as are of a cold, melancholy, phlegmatic, rheumatic temper of body. None can more truly speak hereof by their own experience than myself. My friends that knew me can well tell how very sickly I have been and continually in physic, being much troubled with a tormenting pain through an extraordinary weakness of my stomach, and abundance of melancholy humours; but since I came hither on this voyage, I thank God, I have had perfect health, and freed from pain and vomiting, having a stomach to digest the hardest and coarsest fare, who before could not eat finest meat; and whereas my stomach could only digest and did require such drink as was both strong and stale, now I can and do often times drink New England water very well; and I that have not gone without a cap for many years together, neither durst leave off the same, have now cast away my cap, and do wear none at all in the daytime; and whereas beforetime I clothed myself with double clothes and thick waistcoats to keep me warm, even in the summertime, I do now go as thin clad as any, only wearing a light stuff cassock upon my shirt, and stuff breeches of one thickness without linings. Besides I have one of my children that was formerly most lamentably handled with sore breaking out of both his hands and feet of the king's evil, but since he came hither he is very well over [sic] he was, and there is hope of perfect recovery shortly even by the very wholesomeness of the air, altering, digesting and drying up the cold and crude humours of the body; and therefore I think it is a wise course for all cold complexions to come to take physic in New England, for a sup of New England's air is better than a whole draught of old England's ale.

In the summertime in the midst of July and August, it is a good deal hotter than in old England, and in winter, January and February are much colder as they say, but the spring and autumn are of a middle temper.

Fowls of the air are plentiful here, and of all sorts as we have in England as far as I can learn, and a great many of strange fowls which we know not. While I was writing these things, one of our men brought home an eagle which he had killed in the wood; they say they are good meat. Also here are many kinds of excellent hawks, both sea hawks and land hawks, and myself walking in the woods with another in company, sprung a partridge so big that through the heaviness of his body could fly but a little way; they that have killed them say they are as big as our hens. Here are likewise abundance of turkeys often killed in the woods, far greater than our English turkeys, and exceeding fat, sweet and fleshy, for here they have abundance of feeding all the year long, as strawberries, in summer all places are full of them, and all manner of berries and fruits. In the wintertime I have seen flocks of pigeons, and have eaten of them. They do fly from tree to tree as other birds do, which our pigeons will not do in England; they are of all colours as ours are, but their wings and tails are far longer and therefore it is likely they fly swifter to escape the terrible hawks in this country. In wintertime this country doth abound with wild geese, wild ducks, and other sea-fowl, that a great part of winter the planters have eaten nothing but roast meat of divers fowls which they have killed.

Thus you have heard of the Earth, Water and Air of New England; now it may be you expect something to be said of the Fire proportionable to the rest of the elements.

Indeed, I think New England may boast of this element more than of all the rest for though it be here somewhat cold in the winter, yet here we have plenty of fire to warm us, and that a great deal cheaper than they sell billets and faggots in London; nay all Europe is not able to afford to make so great fires as New England. A poor servant here that is to possess but 50 acres of land may afford to give more wood for timber and fire as good as the world yields, than many noblemen in England can afford to do. Here is good living for those that love good fires. And although New England have no tallow to make candles of, yet by the abundance of the fish thereof, it can afford oil for lamps; yea, our pine trees that are the most plentiful of all wood, doth allow us plenty of candles which are very useful in a house and they are such candles as the Indians commonly use, having no other, and they are nothing else but the wood of the pine tree cloven into two little slices something thin, which are so full of the moisture of turpentine and pitch that they burn as clear as a torch. I have sent you some of them that you may see the experience of them.

Thus of New England commodities. Now I will tell you of some discommodities that are here to be found.

First, in the summer season for these three months, June, July, and August, we are troubled much with little flies called mosquitoes, being the same they are troubled with in Lincolnshire and the Fens, and they are nothing but gnats, which except they be smoked out of their houses are troublesome in the night season.

Secondly, in the winter season for two months' space, the earth is commonly covered with snow, which is accompanied with sharp biting frosts, something more sharp than is in old England, and therefore are forced to make great fires.

Thirdly, the country being very full of woods and wildernesses, doth also much abound with snakes and serpents of strange colours, and huge greatness; yea there are some serpents called rattlesnakes that have rattles in their tails that will not fly from a man as others will, but will fly upon him and sting him so mortally that he will die within a quarter of an hour after, except the party stung have about him some of the root of an herb called snakeweed to bite on, and then he shall receive no harm; but yet seldom falls it out that any hurt is done by these. About three years since, an Indian was stung to death by one of them, but we heard of none since that time.

Fourthly and lastly; here wants as it were good company of honest Christians to bring with them horses, kine, and sheep to make use of this fruitful land. Great pity it is to see so much good ground for corn and for grass as any is under the heavens, to lie altogether unoccupied when so many honest men and their families in old England through the populousness thereof, do make very hard shift to live one by the other.

Now, thus you know what New England is, as also with the commodities and discommodities thereof; now I will show you a little of the inhabitants thereof, and their government.

For their governors they have kings which they call sagamores, some greater and some lesser, according to the number of their subjects.

The greatest sagamores about us cannot make above three hundred men, and other less sagamores have not above fifteen subjects, and others near about us but two.

Their subjects above twelve years since were swept away by a great and grievous plague that was among them, so that there are very few left to inhabit the country.

The Indians are not able to make use of the one fourth part of the land, neither have they any settled places, as towns to dwell in, nor any ground as they challenge for their own possession, but change their habitation from place to place.

For their statures, they are a tall and strong-limbed people; their colours are tawny, they go naked, save only they are in part covered with beasts' skins on one of their shoulders, and wear something before their privates; their hair is generally black and cut before like our gentlewomen, and one lock longer than the rest, much like to our gentlemen, which fashion I think came from hence into England.

For their weapons, they have bows and arrows, some of them headed with bone, and some with brass. I have sent you some of them for an example.

The men for the most part live idly; they do nothing but hunt and fish. Their wives set their corn and do all their other work. They have little household stuff, as a kettle, and some other vessels like trays, spoons, dishes and baskets.

Their houses are very little and homely, being made with small poles pricked into the ground, and so bent and fastened at the tops and on the sides they are matted with boughs and covered on the roof with sedge and old mats, and for their beds that they take their rest on, they have a mat.

They do generally profess to like well of our coming and planting here, partly because there is abundance of ground that they cannot possess nor make use of, and partly because our being here will be a means both of relief to them when they want, and also a defence from their enemies, wherewith (I say) before this plantation began, they were often endangered.

For their religion they do worship two gods, a good god and an evil god; the good god they call Tantum, and their evil god whom they fear will do them hurt, they call Squantum.

For their dealing with us, we neither fear them nor trust them, for forty of our musketeers will drive five hundred of them out of the field. We use them kindly.

They will come into our houses sometimes by half a dozen or half a score at a time when we are at victuals, but will ask or take nothing but what we give them.

We purpose to learn their language as soon as we can, which will be a means to do them good.

Of the present condition of the Plantation, and what it is

When we came first to Nehum-kek, we found about half a score houses, and a fair house newly built for the governor, we found also abundance of corn planted by them, very good and well liking. And we brought with us about two hundred passengers and planters more, which by common consent of the old planters were all combined together into one body politic, under the same governor.

There are in all of us, both old and new planters, about three hundred, whereof two hundred of them are settled at Nehum-kek, now called Salem; and the rest have planted themselves at Massachusetts Bay, beginning to build a town there which we do call Cherton, or Charlestown.

We that are settled at Salem make what haste we can to build houses, so that within a short time we shall have a fair town.

We have great ordnance, wherewith we doubt not but we shall fortify ourselves in a short time to keep out a potent adversary. But that which is our greatest comfort, and means of defence above all others, is that we have here the true religion and holy ordinances of Almighty God taught among us. Thanks be to God, we have here plenty of preaching and diligent catechizing, with strict and careful exercise, and good and commendable orders to bring our people into a Christian conversation with whom we have to do withal. And thus we doubt not but God will be with us, and if God be with us, who can be against us?

Here ends Master Higginson's relation of New England.

8. Andrew White: A Report of the Colony of the Lord Baltimore . . . (1633)

The following document, *A Report of the Colony of the Lord Baron of Baltimore, in Maryland, near Virginia, in which the quality, nature, and condition of the region and its manifold advantages and riches are described*, was written by Father Andrew White, one of the two Jesuits who went to Maryland with the first colonists in 1634. The report was prepared for and sent to the head of the Jesuit order in Rome. Although not a promotion pamphlet, it has all the characteristics of one. Printed: Peter Force, ed., *Tracts and other Papers, Relating Principally to the Origin, Settlement, and Progress of the Colonies in North America, from the discovery of the Country to the year 1776* (4 vols., Washington, 1836–1846), IV, No. 12.

The province is near the English colony in Virginia, which, in honour of his wife Maria, his most serene Majesty of England wished to be called Maryland, or the Land of Maria. This province, his most serene Majesty, in his munificence, lately, in the month of June 1632, gave to the lord baron of Baltimore and his heirs for ever; which donation he secured, and has confirmed by the public seal of the whole realm. Therefore the most illustrious baron has resolved immediately to lead a colony into that region; first, and especially, that into the same and the neighbouring places he may carry the light of the gospel and of truth where it has been found out that hitherto no knowledge of the true God has shone; then, furthermore, with this design, that all the companions of his voyage and labours may be admitted to a participation of the profits and honour, and that the empire of the realm may be more widely extended.

For this enterprise, with all haste and diligence, he seeks companions of his voyage–as well those of fortune who may be about to experience a different condition with him, as others also. For the whole affair being carefully considered, and the counsel of men eminent for experience and prudence being called in, he has now weighed carefully and studiously all the advantages and disadvantages which hitherto advanced or impeded other colonies, and found nothing which did not greatly approve his design and promise the most happy success.

For both the writings which his most noble father left behind him, an eyewitness and most veracious–and worthy of credit, the things which those constantly report who daily come and go to us from thence or not far from thence, as well as the things which Captain [John] Smith, who first discovered that country, most veritably wrote and published, contain statements truly wonderful and almost unheard of, in relation to the fertility and excellence of its soil. There is added to this also, the common consent and testimony of innumerable men who are here from London, and who are about to return to the regions from which they had formerly come, who with one accord verify and confirm what Smith has committed to writing.

Wherefore the most noble baron, about the middle of September next succeeding, is about to make sail, God helping, into these parts; and to those whom he shall obtain as companions and followers in an undertaking so illustrious he makes the most ample and liberal promises, of which this is first and especial (to omit the titles of honour and rank which are granted to fidelity, virtue, bravery, and illustrious services), that whoever shall pay down one hundred pounds English to convey five men (which sum shall be sufficient for arms and implements, for clothes and other necessary articles), whether it shall please them to join themselves to us, or their men and money, to those to whom this gift may be transferred, or to another whom he may commission to have the care of them, and receive a division of the land–to them and to their heirs for ever, shall be assigned a possession of two thousand acres of good land; and besides, if in the first expedition they shall join themselves as companions, and exert their labours, they shall obtain their share, by no means small, in a profitable trade (of which more hereafter) with other privileges: concerning all which things, when they come to the aforesaid baron, they shall be made acquainted. But what has been before said of the one hundred pounds English, this also may be understood of a smaller or greater sum of money in proportion, whether from one person separately, or collected together and contributed by many.

The first and chief object of the most illustrious baron (which also ought to be the object of others who may be in the same ship) is, that in a land so fruitful shall be sown not so much the seeds of grain and fruit trees as of religion and piety; a design truly worthy of Christians, worthy of angels, worthy of the Angles, than which England, renowned for so many ancient victories, has undertaken nothing more noble or more glorious. Behold the regions are white unto the harvest, prepared to receive in its fruitful bosom the seed of the Gospel. From thence they are sending, on all sides, messengers to seek for suitable men who may instruct the inhabitants in the doctrine of salvation and regenerate them in the sacred font.

There are present at this very time in the city those who state that they have seen at Jamestown, in Virginia, messengers sent from their kings for this purpose, and infants carried to New England, that they might be washed in the waters of salvation. Who then can have a doubt but that by this one work so glorious many thousand souls may be led to Christ? I call the rescue and salvation of souls a glorious work, for it is a work to the glory of Christ our King. But since there are not to all the same ardour of mind and elevation of soul, so as to regard nothing but divine things, esteem nothing but heavenly things–inasmuch as most men regard rather pleasures, honours, and wealth as if in love with them–it has happened by some unseen power, or rather by the manifest remarkable wisdom of the deity, that this one undertaking should embrace all inducements that affect men–emoluments of every kind.

It is admitted that the situation of the region is the best and most advantageous; for it extends towards the north to the thirty-eighth or fortieth degree of latitude, in the same position of place with Seville, Sicily, and Jerusalem, and not unlike the best portions and climate of Arabia Felix. The air is serene and mild, neither exposed to the burning heat of Florida or ancient Virginia, nor withered by the cold of New England, but has a medium temperature between the two–enjoys the advantages of each, and is free from their inconveniences. On the east it is washed by the ocean; on the west it adjoins an almost boundless continent, which extends to the China Sea.

There are two arms of the sea on each side–bays most abundant in fish. The one whose name is Chesapeake, is twelve miles broad, and flowing between two regions, rolls from south to north one hundred and sixty miles, is able to contain great navies, and is marked by various large islands fit for grazing, where they fish actively for shad. They call the other the Delaware, where the entire year there is the fishing for codfish, but not so profitable, except only in the cold months, as those which are rather warm prevent their being cured with salt. And indeed this great plenty of fishing arises from this: the wind which sets continually from the Canaries, between the north and east, rolls the ocean and the fish with it to the Gulf of Mexico, where, since it can neither return again to the east nor the south, it is driven towards the north, and bears with it along the coasts of Florida, Virginia, Maryland, and New-foundland a great multitude of fish, which, as they avoid the cetacea, fly to shoal places, where they are more easily taken by the fishermen.

There are various and noble rivers, the chief of which they call Potomac, suitable for navigation, flowing one hundred and forty miles towards the east, where a trade with the Indians is so profitable that a certain merchant the last year shipped beaver skins at a price of forty thousand pieces of gold, and the labour of traffic is compensated by thirty-fold profit.

In the level and campaign country there is a great abundance of grass; but the region is for the most part shaded with trees; oaks and walnut trees are the most common, and the oaks are so straight and tall that beams can be made from them sixty feet long, and two feet and a half thick. Cypress trees will shoot up eighty feet before they send forth branches, and three men with extended arms scarcely encompass them. The mulberry trees that feed silkworms are very common. There is also found an Indian grain which the Portuguese call *l'ove de l'hierica*. Alders, ash trees, and chestnuts, not inferior to those which Spain, Italy, and Gaul produce–cedars equal to those which Lebanon boasts. What shall I say of the pine, laurel, fir, sassafras, and others, with various trees also which yield balsam and odoriferous gum–trees for all the most useful purposes–for architecture, for nautical uses, for plank and pitch–naptha, terebinth, and mustard, for perfumes, and for making cataplasms? But the woods are passable, not rough, with an undergrowth of thorns and shrubs, but formed by nature to afford food to beasts, and pleasure to men. There are grapes in abundance, from which wine can be pressed; you can meet with some whose juice is thick and unctuous; the inhabitants employ it as a medicine. There are cherries, with prunes, and gages very like ours. Of prunes there are three kinds. Mulberries, chestnuts, and walnuts are so abundant that they are used in various ways for food. Strawberries and esculent blackberries you will in like manner find.

Of the fishes, those that follow have already come into notice: sturgeons, herrings, phocinae, crevices, shrimp, torpedoes, trouts, mullets of three kinds, urchins, rochet-fish, white salmon, oysters, periwinkles, and others of that kind, of innumerable names and unknown species. But so great is the abundance of swine and deer that they are rather troublesome than advantageous. Cows also are innumerable, and oxen suitable for bearing burdens or for food; besides five other kinds of large beasts unknown to us, which our neighbours admit to their table. Sheep will have to be taken hence or from the Canaries; asses also, and mules and horses. The neighbouring forests are full of wild bulls and heifers, of which five hundred or six hundred thousand are annually carried to Seville from that part which lies towards New Mexico. As many deer as you wish can be obtained from the neighbouring people. Add to this muskrats, rabbits, beavers, badgers, and martens, not however destructive, as with us, to eggs and hens.

Of the birds, the eagle is the most voracious. Of hawks there are various kinds, which live in a great measure on fish. There are partridges, not larger than our quails, but almost infinite in number. Innumerable wild turkeys, which excel our tame and domestic ones, by double the size. There are also blackbirds, thrushes, and a great many little birds, of which there are various kinds, some red, some blue, &c., &c. During the winter it abounds in waterfowl: swans, geese, cranes, and herons–ostriches, owls, parrots, and many others unknown to our part of the world. It bears apples, lemons, and the best quinces. The apricots also are so abundant that an honourable man and worthy of credit positively affirmed that he had cast an hundred bushels to the hogs. What shall I say of the lupines, the most excellent beans, roots, and other things of this kind, when even in ten days peas grow to fourteen inches height? It is so fruitful in king's corn that in the most barren places it returns the seed twice an hundred fold; otherwise, and for the most part, from one grain five hundred or six hundred grains; while in the more productive years from fifteen hundred to sixteen hundred grains, and this indeed in one harvest, whereas the fertility of the soil affords three harvests. That I may draw to a close presently, it is very likely that the soil is adapted to all the fruits of Italy, figs, pomegranates, golden olives, &c., &c.

Nor are there wanting things that may be of use to conjurers and apothecaries–nor is plenty of iron, hemp, and flax wanting to their hand. There is hope also of finding gold, for the neighbouring people wear bracelets of unwrought gold, and long strings of pearls. Other advantages, both numerous and lucrative, may be expected, which sagacious industry and long acquaintance will discover.

9. A Brief Description . . . of Carolina (1666)

A Brief Description of the Province of Carolina, on the Coasts of Florida was one of several promotion tracts written for the proprietors of Carolina. It was published in London in 1666. Printed: B. R. Carroll, ed., *Historical Collections of South Carolina* (2 vols., New York, 1836), II, pp. 10–18.

Carolina is a fair and spacious province on the continent of America: so called in honour of His Sacred Majesty that now is Charles the Second, whom God preserve; and His Majesty hath been pleased to grant the same to certain honourable persons, who in order to the speedy planting of the same, have granted divers privileges and advantages to such as shall transport themselves and servants in convenient time. This province lying so near Virginia, and yet more southward, enjoys the fertility and advantages thereof, and yet is so far distant as to be freed from the inconstancy of the weather, which is a great cause of the unhealthfulness thereof; also, being in the latitude of the Bermudas, may expect the like healthfulness which it hath hitherto enjoyed, and doubtless there is no plantation that ever the English went upon in all respects so good as this, for though Bermuda be wonderful healthy and fruitful, yet is it but a prison to the inhabitants, who are much straitened for want of room, and therefore many of them are come to Carolina, and more intend to follow. There is seated in this province two colonies already, one on the River Roanoke (now called Albemarle River) and borders on Virginia; the other at Cape Fear, two degrees more southerly; of which follows a more particular description.

This province of Carolina is situate on the main continent of America, between the degrees of 30 and 36 and has on the north the south part of Virginia; on the south is bounded by the 30 degree of latitude, not yet fully discovered; on the east is *Mare Atlanticum*, part of the great ocean; and on the west the wealthy South Sea is its confines.

The particular description of Cape Fear

In the midst of this fertile province, in the latitude of 34 degrees, there is a colony of English seated, who landed there the 29 of May, *Anno* 1664, and are in all about 800 persons, who have overcome all the difficulties that attend the first attempts and have cleared the way for those that come after, who will find good houses to be in whilst their own are in building; good forts to secure them from their enemies; and many things brought from other parts there, increasing to their no small advantage. The entrance into the river, now called Cape Fear River, the situation of the Cape and trending of the land, is plainly laid down to the eye in the map annexed. The river is barred at the entrance, but there is a channel close aboard the Cape that will convey in safety a ship of 300 tons, and as soon as a ship is over the bar, the river is

5 or 6 fathom deep for 100 miles from the sea; this bar is a great security to the colony against a foreign invasion, the channel being hard to find by those that have not experience of it, and yet safe enough to those that know it.

The Earth, Water, and Air

The land is of divers sorts as in all countries of the world; that which lies near the sea is sandy and barren but beareth many tall trees, which make good timber for several uses; and this sandy ground is by experienced men thought to be one cause of the healthfulness of the place: but up the river about 20 or 30 mile where they have made a town called Charles Town, there is plenty of as rich ground as any in the world. It is a blackish mold upon a red sand, and under that a clay, but in some places is rich ground of a greyer colour. They have made brick of the clay which proves very good, and lime they have also for building. The whole country consists of stately woods, groves, marshes, and meadows; it abounds with variety of as brave oaks as eye can behold, great bodies tall and straight from 60 to 80 foot before there be any boughs, which with the little underwood makes the woods very commodious to travel in, either on horseback or afoot. In the barren sandy ground grow most stately pines, white and red cedars, ash, birch, holly, chestnut and walnut trees of great growth and very plentiful. There are many sorts of fruit trees, as vines, medlars [a wild crab-apple tree], peach, wild cherries, mulberry trees, and the silkworm breeding naturally on them, with many other trees for fruit and for building, for perfume and for medicine, for which the English have no name; also several sorts of dyeing stuff, which may prove of great advantage. The woods are stored with deer and wild turkeys of a great magnitude, weighing many times above 50 pounds apiece, and of a more pleasant taste than in England, being in their proper climate; other sorts of beasts in the woods that are good for food and also fowls whose names are not known to them. This is what they found naturally upon the place but they have brought with them most sorts of seeds and roots of the Barbados which thrive very well, and they have potatoes and the other roots and herbs of Barbados growing and thriving with them; as also from Virginia, Bermuda, and New England, what they could afford. They have indigo, tobacco, very good, and cotton wool; lime trees, orange, lemon and other fruit trees they brought, thrive exceedingly. They have two crops of Indian corn in one year and great increase every crop; apples, pears, and other English fruit grow there out of the planted kernels. The marshes and meadows are very large, from 1500 to 3000 acres and upwards, and are excellent food for cattle, and will bear any grain being prepared; some cattle both great and small, will live well all the winter and keep their fat without fodder. Hogs find so much mast and other food in the woods that they want no other care than a swineherd to keep them from running wild. The meadows are very proper for rice, rape seed, linseed, etc., and may many of them be made to overflow at pleasure with a small charge. Here are as brave rivers as any in the world, stored with great abundance of sturgeon, salmon, bass, plaice, trout and Spanish mackerel, with many other most pleasant sorts of fish, both flat and round, for which the English tongue hath no name. Also, in the little winter they have abundance of wild geese, ducks, teals, widgeons, and many other pleasant fowl, and (as it is said before) the rivers are very deep and navigable above 100 miles up; also there are wholesome springs and rivulets. Last of all, the air comes to be considered, which is not the least considerable to the well-being of a plantation, for without a wholesome air all other considerations avail nothing, and this is it which makes this place so desirable, being seated in the most temperate clime, where the neighbourhood of the glorious light of Heaven brings many advantages, and his convenient distance secures them from the inconvenience of his scorching beams. The summer is not too hot, and the winter is very short and moderate, best agreeing with English constitutions. Cape Fear lies about 34 degrees from the Equator, the nights nor days are so long, when at longest as in England, by somewhat above two hours. A remarkable instance of the healthfulness of the place is that at the first setting down of the colony, when they had no house nor harbour, but wrought hard all day in preparing wood to build, and lay in the open air all night, yet not one of them was ill but continued well all the time. They sympathize most with the Bermudas, which is the healthfullest spot in the world, and yet the last year they had a fever and ague that troubled them much, which also was at Cape Fear, but was not dangerous to any that took care of themselves, and had things convenient. This place had been aimed at many years since. Sir Walter Raleigh had a design to have planted it. Those of the Bermudas whose habitations are too strait for them, have with longing desire waited for the discovery of this place that is near their own latitude where they may expect the same healthfulness they do now enjoy, which is now perfected as to the first settlement, and wants nothing but a diligent prosecution of so noble an enterprise.

If, therefore, any industrious and ingenious persons shall be willing to partake of the felicities of this country, let them embrace the first opportunity, that they may obtain the greater advantages.

The chief of the Privileges are as follows

First, There is full and free liberty of conscience granted to all, so that no man is to be molested or called in question for matters of religious concern, but everyone to be obedient to the civil government, worshipping God after their own way.

Secondly, There is freedom from custom, for all wine, silk, raisins, currants, oil, olives, and almonds, that shall be raised in the province for 7 years, after 4 ton of any of those commodities shall be imported in one bottom.

Thirdly, Every freeman and freewoman that transport themselves and servants by the 25 of March next, being 1667, shall have for himself, wife, children, and men-servants, for each 100 acres of land for him and his heirs for ever, and for every woman-servant and slave, 50 acres, paying at most ½d. per acre, *per annum*, in lieu of all demands, to the lords proprietors; provided always, that every man be armed with a good musket full bore, 10 pounds [of] powder and 20 pounds of bullet, and six months provision for all, to serve them whilst they raise provision in that country.

Fourthly, Every man-servant at the expiration of their time is to have of the country a 100 acres of land to him and his heirs for ever, paying only ½d. per acre, *per annum*, and the women 50 acres of land on the same conditions. Their masters also are to allow them two suits of apparel and tools such as he is best able to work with, according to the custom of the country.

Fifthly, They are to have a governor and council appointed from among themselves, to see the laws of the assembly put in due execution; but the governor is to rule but three years, and then learn to obey; also he hath no power to lay any tax, or make or abrogate any law, without the consent of the colony in their assembly.

Sixthly, They are to choose annually from among themselves a certain number of men, according to their divisions, which constitute the general assembly with the governor and his council, and have the sole power of making laws and laying taxes for the common good when need shall require.

These are the chief and fundamental privileges, but the right honourable lords proprietors have promised (and it is their interest so to do) to be ready to grant what other privileges may be found advantageous for the good of the colony.

Is there, therefore, any younger brother who is born of gentle blood, and whose spirit is elevated above the common sort, and yet the hard usage of our country hath not allowed suitable fortune; he will not surely be afraid to leave his native soil to advance his fortunes equal to his blood and spirit, and so he will avoid those unlawful ways too many of our young gentlemen take to maintain themselves according to their high education, having but small estates. Here with a few servants and a small stock, a great estate may be raised; although his birth have not entitled him to any of the land of his ancestors, yet his industry may supply him so as to make him the head of as famous a family.

Such as are here tormented with much care how to get worth to gain a livelihood, or that with their labour can hardly get a comfortable subsistence, shall do well to go to this place where any man whatever that is but willing to take moderate pains, may be assured of a most comfortable subsistence, and be in a way to raise his fortunes far beyond what he could ever hope for in England. Let no man be troubled at the thoughts of being a servant for 4 or 5 years, for I can assure you that many men give money with their children to serve 7 years, to take more pains and fare nothing so well as the servants in this plantation will do. Then it is to be considered that so soon as he is out of his time, he hath land and tools and clothes given him, and is in a way of advancement. Therefore all artificers, as carpenters, wheelwrights, joiners, coopers, bricklayers, smiths, or diligent husbandmen and labourers that are willing to advance their fortunes and live in a most pleasant healthful and fruitful country, where artificers are of high esteem, and used with all civility and courtesy imaginable, may take notice that

There is an opportunity offers now by the Virginia Fleet, from whence Cape Fear is but 3 or 4 days' sail, and then a small stock carried to Virginia will purchase provisions at a far easier rate than to carry them from hence; also the freight of the said provisions will be saved and be more fresh, and there wanteth not conveyance from Virginia thither.

If any maid or single woman have a desire to go over, they will think themselves in the Golden Age when men paid a dowry for their wives, for if they be but civil and under 50 years of age, some honest man or other will purchase them for their wives.

Those that desire further advice, or servants that would be entertained, let them repair to Mr. Matthew Wilkinson, ironmonger, at the sign of the Three Feathers, in Bishopsgate Street, where they may be informed when the ships will be ready, and what they must carry with them.

Thus much was convenient to be written at present, but a more ample relation is intended to be published in due time.

10. William Penn: Some Account of the Province of Pennsilvania (1681)

Shortly after William Penn received the charter for Pennsylvania, he published the following pamphlet: *Some Account of the Province of Pennsilvania in America: lately Granted under the Great Seal of England to William Penn.* . . . It was followed by many other pamphlets written by Penn and by others to encourage the settlement of the province. Printed: Samuel Hazard, ed., *The Register of Pennsylvania* . . . (16 vols., Philadelphia, 1828–1836), I, pp. 305–308.

Since (by the good providence of God) a country in America is fallen to my lot, I thought it not less my duty than my honest interest to give some public notice of it to the world, that those of our own or other nations that are inclined to transport themselves or families beyond the seas may find another country added to their choice, that if they shall happen to like the places, conditions, and constitutions (so far as the present infancy of things will allow us any prospect) they may, if they please, fix with me in the province hereafter described. But before I come to treat of my particular concernment, I shall take leave to say something of the benefit of plantations or colonies in general, to obviate a common objection.

Colonies then are the seeds of nations begun and nourished by the care of wise and populous countries; as conceiving them best for the increase of human stock, and beneficial for commerce.

Some of the wisest men in history have justly taken their fame from this design and service: we read of the reputation given on this account to Moses, Joshua and Caleb in Scripture records; and what renown the Greek story yields to Lycurgus, Theseus, and those Greeks that planted many parts of Asia; nor is the Roman account wanting of instances to the credit of that people. They had a Romulus, a Numa Pompilius, and not only reduced, but moralized the manners of the nations they subjected, so that they may have been rather said to conquer their barbarity than them.

Nor did any of these ever dream it was the way of decreasing their people or wealth; for the cause of the decay of any of those states or empires was not their plantations, but their luxury and corruption of manners, for when they grew to neglect their ancient discipline that maintained and rewarded virtue and industry, and addicted themselves to pleasure and effeminacy, they debased their spirits and debauched their morals, from whence ruin did never fail to follow to any people. With justice therefore I deny the vulgar opinion against plantations, that they weaken England; they have manifestly enriched, and so strengthened her, which I briefly evidence thus.

1st. Those that go into a foreign plantation, their industry there is worth more than if they stayed at home, the product of their labour being in commodities of a superior nature to those of their country. For instance: what is an improved acre in Jamaica or Barbados worth to an improved acre in England? We know 'tis three times the value, and the product of it comes for England, and is usually paid for in English growth and manufacture. Nay, Virginia shows that an ordinary industry in one man produces three thousand pound weight of tobacco and twenty barrels of corn yearly. He feeds himself, and brings as much of commodity into England besides as being returned in the growth and workmanship of this country is much more than he could have spent here. Let it also be remembered that the three thousand weight of tobacco brings in three thousand twopences by way of custom to the king, which makes twenty-five pounds, an extraordinary profit.

2nd. More being produced and imported than we can spend here, we export it to other countries in Europe, which brings in money or the growth of those countries, which is the same thing, and this is the advantage of the English merchants and seamen.

3rd. Such as could not only not marry here but hardly live and allow themselves clothes, do marry there and bestow thrice more in all necessaries and conveniences (and not a little in ornamental things, too) for themselves, their wives, and children, both as to apparel and household stuff, which coming out of England, I say 'tis impossible that England should not be a considerable gainer.

4th. But let it be considered that the plantations employ many hundreds of shipping and many thousands of seamen, which must be in divers respects an advantage to England, being an island and by nature fitted for navigation above any country in Europe. This is followed by other depending trades, as shipwrights, carpenters, sawyers, hewers, trunnel-makers, joiners, slop-sellers, dry-salters, iron-workers, the Eastland-merchants, timber sellers, and victuallers, with many more trades which hang upon navigation; so that we may easily see the objection (that colonies or plantations hurt England) is at least of no strength, especially if we consider how many thousand blacks and Indians are also accommodated with clothes and many sorts of tools and utensils from England, and that their labour is mostly brought hither, which adds wealth and people to the English dominions. But 'tis further said, they injure England in that they draw away too many of the people, for we are not so populous in the countries as formerly. I say there are other reasons for that.

1. Country people are so extremely addicted to put their children into gentlemen's service, or send them to towns to learn trades, that husbandry is neglected, and after a soft and delicate usage there, they are for ever unfitted for the labour of a farming life.

2. The pride of the age in its attendance and retinue is so gross and universal that where a man of £1,000 a year formerly kept but four or five servants, he now keeps more than twice the number; he must have a gentleman to wait upon him in his chambers, a coachman, a groom or two, a butler, a man-cook, a gardener, two or three lackeys, it may be a huntsman, and a falconer; the wife a gentlewoman, and maids accordingly. This was not known by our ancestors of like quality. This hinders the plough and the dairy, from whence they are taken, and instead of keeping people to manly labour, they are effeminated by a lazy and luxurious living; but which is worse, these people rarely marry, though many of them do worse; but if they do,

'tis when they are in age, and the reason is clear, because their usual keeping at their masters is too great and costly for them with a family at their own charge, and they scarcely know how to live lower, so that too many of them choose rather to vent their lusts at an evil ordinary than honestly marry and work; the excess and sloth of the age not allowing of marriage and the charge that follows, all which hinders the increase of our people. If men, they often turn either soldiers, or gamesters, or high-way men. If women, they too frequently dress themselves for a bad market, rather than know the dairy again, or honestly return to labour, whereby it happens that both the stock of the nation decays and the issue is corrupted.

3. Of old time the nobility and gentry spent their estates in the country, and that kept the people in it, and their servants married and sat at easy rents under their master's favour, which peopled the place. Now the great men (too much loving the town and resorting to London) draw many people thither to attend them, who either don't marry, or if they do, they pine away their small gains in some petty shop, for there are so many, they prey upon one another.

4. The country being thus neglected, and no due balance kept between trade and husbandry, city and country, the poor countryman takes double toil, and cannot (for want of hands) dress and manure his land to the advantage it formerly yielded him; yet must he pay the old rents, which occasions servants, and such children as go not to trades, to continue single, at least all their youthful time, which also obstructs the increase of our people.

5. The decay of some country manufactures (where no provision is made to supply the people with a new way of living) causes the more industrious to go abroad to seek their bread in other countries, and gives the lazy an occasion to loiter and beg, or do worse, by which means the land swarms with beggars. Formerly 'twas rare to find any asking alms but the maimed, or blind, or very aged. Now thousands of both sexes run up and down, both city and country, that are sound and youthful and able to work, with false pretences and certificates; nor is there any care taken to employ or deter such vagrants, which weakens the country as to people and labour.

To which, let me add that the great debauchery in this kingdom has not only rendered many unfruitful when married, but they live not out half their time, through excess, which might be prevented by a vigorous execution of our good laws against corruption of manners. These and the like evils are the true grounds of the decay of our people in the country, to say nothing of plague and wars. Towns and cities cannot complain of the decay of people, being more replenished than ever, especially London, which with reason helps the countryman to this objection. And though some do go to the plantations, yet numbering the parishes in England, and computing how many live more than die, and are born than buried, there goes not over to all the plantations a fourth part of the yearly increase of the people, and when they are there, they are not (as I said before) lost to England, since they furnish them with much clothes, household stuff, tools, and the like necessaries, and that in greater quantities than here their condition could have needed, or they could have bought, being there well to pass that were but low here, if not poor; and now masters of families too, when here they had none and could hardly keep themselves, and very often it happens that some of them after their industry and success there have made them wealthy, they return and empty their riches into England; one in this capacity being able to buy out twenty of what he was when he went over.

Thus much to justify the credit and benefit of plantations, wherein I have not sought to speak my interest, but my judgment; and I dare venture the success of it with all sober and considering men. I shall now proceed to give some account of my own concern.

1st. I shall say what may be necessary of the place or province.

2nd. Touch upon the constitutions.

3rd. Lay down the conditions.

4th. Give my sense what persons will be fit to go.

5th. What utensils, furniture and commodities are fit to carry with them, with the charge of the voyage, and what is first to be done and expected there for some time.

And lastly, I shall give an abstract of the grant by letters patents under the great seal of England, that an account may be given of the estate and power granted to me thereby.

I. Something of the Place

The place lies 600 miles nearer the sun than England, for England begins at the 50th degree and ten minutes of north latitude, and this place begins at forty, which is about the latitude of Naples in Italy, or Montpellier in France. I shall say little in its praise, to excite desires in any, whatever I could truly write as to the soil, air and water: this shall satisfy me, that by the blessing of God, and the honesty and industry of man, it may be a good and fruitful land.

For navigation it is said to have two conveniences; the one by lying ninescore miles upon Delaware River; that is to say, about threescore and ten miles before we come to the falls, where a vessel of two hundred tons may sail (and some creeks and small harbours in that distance where ships may come nearer than the river into the country) and above the falls, for sloops and boats, as I am informed, to the extent of the patent. The other convenience is through Chesapeake Bay.

For timber and other wood there is variety for the use of man.

For fowl, fish, and wild deer, they are reported to be plentiful in those parts. Our English provision is likewise now to be had there at reasonable rates. The commodities that the country is thought to be capable of are silk, flax, hemp, wine, cider, woad, madder, licorice, tobacco, potash, and iron, and it does actually produce hides, tallow, pipe-staves, beef, pork, sheep, wool, corn, as wheat, barley, rye, and also furs, as your peltry, minks, raccoons, martens, and such like; store of furs which is to be found among the Indians that are profitable commodities in Europe.

The way of trading in those countries is thus: they send to the southern plantations corn, beef, pork, fish and pipe-staves, and take their growth and bring for England, and return with English goods to their own country. Their furs they bring for England, and either sell them here, or carry them out again to other parts of Europe where they will yield a better price; and for those that will follow merchandise and navigation there is conveniency, and timber sufficient for shipping.

II. The Constitutions

For the constitutions of the country the patent shows, first, that the people and governor have a legislative power, so that no law can be made, nor money raised but by the people's consent.

2nd. That the rights and freedoms of England (the best and largest in Europe) shall be in force there.

3rd. That making no law against allegiance (which should we, 'twere by the law of England void of itself that moment) we may enact what laws we please for the good prosperity and security of the said province.

4th. That so soon as any are engaged with me, we shall begin a scheme or draft together such as shall give ample testimony of my sincere inclinations to encourage planters, and settle a free, just, and industrious colony there.

III. The Conditions

My conditions will relate to three sorts of people: 1st; Those that will buy: 2nd; Those that take up land upon rent: 3rd; Servants. To the first, the shares I sell shall be certain as to number of acres; that is to say, every one shall contain five thousand acres free from any Indian incumbrance, the price a hundred pounds, and for the quit-rent but one English shilling or the value of it yearly for a hundred acres; and the said quit-rent not to begin to be paid till 1684. To the second sort, that take up land upon rent, they shall have liberty so to do, paying yearly one penny per acre, not exceeding two hundred acres. To the third sort, to wit, servants that are carried over, fifty acres shall be allowed to the master for every head, and fifty acres to every servant when their time is expired. And because some engage with me that may not be disposed to go, it were very advisable for every three adventurers to send an overseer with their servants, which would well pay the cost.

The dividend may be thus: if the persons concerned please, a tract of land shall be surveyed, say fifty thousand acres to a hundred adventurers, in which some of the best shall be set out for towns or cities; and there shall be so much ground allotted to each in those towns as may maintain some cattle and produce some corn. Then the remainder of the fifty thousand acres shall be shared among the said adventurers (casting up the barren for commons, and allowing for the same) whereby every adventurer will have a considerable quantity of land together; likewise everyone a proportion by a navigable river, and then backward into the country. The manner of dividend I shall not be strict in; we can but speak roughly of the matter here, but let men skilful in plantations be consulted, and I shall leave it to the majority of votes among the adventurers when it shall please God we come there, how to fix it to their own content.

IV. Those persons that Providence seems to have most fitted for plantations are:

1st. Industrious husbandmen and day labourers that are hardly able (with extreme labour) to maintain their families and portion their children.

2nd. Laborious handicrafts, especially carpenters, masons, smiths, weavers, tailors, tanners, shoemakers, shipwrights, etc., where they may be spared or low in the world, and as they shall want no encouragement, so their labour is worth more there than here, and there provision cheaper.

3rd. A plantation seems a fit place for those ingenious spirits that being low in the world, are much clogged and oppressed about a livelihood, for the means of subsisting being easy there, they may have time and opportunity to gratify their inclinations, and thereby improve science and help nurseries of people.

4th. A fourth sort of men to whom a plantation would be proper, takes in those that are younger brothers of small inheritances; yet because they would live in sight of their kindred in some proportion to their quality, and can't do it without a labour that looks like farming, their condition is too strait for them; and if married, their children are often too numerous for the estate, and are frequently bred up to no trades, but are a kind of hangers-on or retainers to the elder brother's table and charity; which is a mischief, as in itself to be lamented, so here to be remedied, for land they have for next to nothing, which with moderate labour produces plenty of all things necessary for life, and such an increase as by traffic may supply them with all conveniences.

Lastly, there are another sort of persons not only fit for, but necessary in plantations, and that is men of universal spirits, that have an eye to the good of posterity, and that both understand and delight to promote good discipline and just government among a plain and well intending people. Such persons may find room in colonies for their good counsel and contrivance, who are shut out from being of much use or service to great nations under settled customs. These men deserve much esteem and would be hearkened to. Doubtless 'twas this (as I observed before) that put some of the famous Greeks and Romans upon transplanting and regulating colonies of people in divers parts of the world; whose names, for giving so great proof of their wisdom, virtue, labour and constancy, are with justice honourably delivered down by story to the praise of our own times; though the world, after all its higher pretences of religion, barbarously errs from their excellent example.

V. The journey and its appurtenances, and what is to be done there at first coming

Next let us see what is fit for the journey and place when there, and also what may be the charge of the voyage, and what is to be expected and done there at first, that such as incline to go may not be to seek here, or brought under any disappointments there. The goods fit to take with them for use, or sell for profit, are all sorts of apparel and utensils for husbandry and building and household stuff. And because I know how much people are apt to fancy things beyond what they are, and that imaginations are great flatterers of the minds of men to the end that none may delude themselves, with an expectation of an immediate amendment of their conditions, so soon as it shall please God they arrive there; I would have them understand that they must look for a winter before a summer comes, and they must be willing to be two or three years without some of the conveniences they enjoy at home; and yet I must needs say that America is another thing than it was at the first plantation of Virginia and New England, for there is better accommodation, and English provisions are to be had at easier rates. However, I am inclined to set down particulars, as near as those inform me that know the place and have been planters, both in that and in the neighbouring colonies.

1st. The passage will come for masters and mistresses at most to 6 pounds a head, for servants 5 pounds a head, and for children under seven years of age 50 shillings, except they suck, then nothing.

Next being by the mercy of God safely arrived in September or October, two men may clear as much ground by spring (when they set the corn of that country) as will bring in that time twelve month 40 barrels, which amounts to 200 bushels, which makes 25 quarters of corn. So that the first year they must buy corn, which is usually very plentiful. They may so soon as they come, buy cows, more or less, as they want, or are able, which are to be had at easy rates. For swine, they are plentiful and cheap; these will quickly increase to a stock. So that after the first year, what with the poorer sort sometimes labouring to others, and the more able fishing, fowling, and sometimes buying, they may do very well till their own stocks are sufficient to supply them and their families, which will quickly be and to spare, if they follow the English husbandry as they do in New England and New York, and get winter fodder for their stock.

[Then follows an abstract of the patent granted by the king.][1]

To conclude, I desire all my dear countryfolks who may be inclined to go into those parts, to consider seriously the premises, as well as the present inconveniences, as future ease and plenty, that so none may move rashly or from a fickle but solid mind, having above all things an eye to the Providence of God, in the disposal of themselves. And I would further advise all such at least to have the permission, if not the good liking of their near relations, for that is both natural and a duty incumbent upon all; and by this means will natural affection be preserved and a friendly and profitable correspondence be maintained between them. In all which I beseech Almighty God to direct us, that his blessing may attend our honest endeavour, and then the consequence of all our undertaking will turn to the glory of his great name, and the true happiness of us and our posterity. Amen.

11. James Oglethorpe: Some Account of the Designs of the Trustees for Establishing . . . Georgia (1733)

The following pamphlet, *Some Account of the Designs of the Trustees for Establishing the Colony of Georgia in America*, was published in London in 1733. It was written by General James Oglethorpe who was a leader in founding the colony which, in part at least, had a quite different purpose than any previous British colony. Printed: Force, *Tracts*, vol. 1, No. 2.

In America there are fertile lands sufficient to subsist all the useless poor in England, and distressed Protestants in Europe; yet thousands starve for want of mere sustenance. The distance makes it difficult to get thither. The same want that renders men useless here prevents their paying their passage; and if others pay it for them, they become servants, or rather slaves for years to those who have defrayed the expense. Therefore, money for passage is necessary but it is not the only want, for if people were set down in America, and the land before them, they must cut down

[1] No. 4.

trees, build houses, fortify towns, dig and sow the land before they can get in a harvest, and till then they must be provided with food and kept together that they may be assistant to each other for their natural support and protection.

The Romans esteemed the sending forth of colonies among their noblest works; they observed that Rome, as she increased in power and empire, drew together such a conflux of people from all parts that she found herself overburdened with their number, and the government brought under an incapacity to provide for them or keep them in order. Necessity, the mother of invention, suggested to them an expedient which at once gave ease to the capital and increased the wealth and number of industrious citizens by lessening the useless and unruly multitude; and by planting them in colonies on the frontiers of their empire, gave a new strength to the whole; and *this* they looked upon to be so considerable a service to the commonwealth that they created peculiar officers for the establishment of such colonies, and the expense was defrayed out of the public treasury.

FROM THE CHARTER. His Majesty having taken into his consideration the miserable circumstances of many of his own poor subjects, ready to perish for want, as likewise the distresses of many poor foreigners who would take refuge here from persecution, and having a princely regard to the great danger the southern frontiers of South Carolina are exposed to by reason of the small number of white inhabitants there, has out of his fatherly compassion towards his subjects, been graciously pleased to grant a charter for incorporating a number of gentlemen by the name of *The Trustees for establishing the Colony of Georgia in America*. They are empowered to collect benefactions and lay them out in clothing, arming, sending over, and supporting colonies of the poor, whether subjects or foreigners, in Georgia. And his Majesty farther grants all his lands between the rivers Savannah and Altamaha, which he erects into a province by the name of Georgia, unto the trustees in trust for the poor and for the better support of the colony. At the desire of the gentlemen, there are clauses in the charter restraining them and their successors from receiving any salary, fee, perquisite, or profit whatsoever, by or from this undertaking; and also from receiving any grant of lands within the said district, to themselves, or in trust for them. There are farther clauses granting to the trustees proper powers for establishing and governing the colony, and liberty of conscience to all who shall settle there.

The trustees intend to relieve such unfortunate persons as cannot subsist here, and establish them in an orderly manner, so as to form a well-regulated town. As far as their fund goes, they will defray the charge of their passage to Georgia; give them necessaries, cattle, land, and subsistence till such time as they can build their houses and clear some of their land. They rely for success first on the goodness of Providence, next on the compassionate disposition of the people of England; and they doubt not that much will be spared from luxury and superfluous expenses by generous tempers, when such an opportunity is offered them by the giving of £20 to provide for a man or woman, or £10 to a child for ever.

In order to prevent the benefaction given to this purpose from ever being misapplied; and to keep up as far as human precaution can a spirit of disinterestedness, the trustees have established the following method: that each benefactor may know what he has contributed is safely lodged and justly accounted for, all money given will be deposited in the Bank of England, and entries made of every benefaction in a book to be kept for that purpose by the trustees, or if concealed, the names of those by whose hands they sent their money. There are to be annual accounts of all the money received and how the same has been disposed of laid before the Lord High Chancellor, the Lord Chief Justice of the King's Bench, the Master of the Rolls, the Lord Chief Justice of the Common Pleas, and the Lord Chief Baron of the Exchequer, or two of them, will be transmitted to every considerable benefactor.

By such a colony many families who would otherwise starve will be provided for and made masters of houses and lands; the people in Great Britain to whom these necessitous families were a burden will be relieved; numbers of manufacturers will be here employed for supplying them with clothes, working tools, and other necessaries, and by giving refuge to the distressed Salzburgers, and other persecuted Protestants, the power of Britain, as a reward for its hospitality, will be increased by the addition of so many religious and industrious subjects.

The colony of Georgia lying about the same latitude with part of China, Persia, Palestine, and the Madeiras, it is highly probable that when hereafter it shall be well peopled and rightly cultivated, England may be supplied from thence with raw silk, wine, oil, dyes, drugs, and many other materials for manufactures which she is obliged to purchase from southern countries. As towns are established and grow populous along the rivers Savannah and Altamaha, they will make such a barrier as will render the southern frontier of the British colonies on the continent of America safe from Indian and other enemies.

All human affairs are so subject to chance that there is no answering for events; yet from reason and the nature of things it may be concluded that the riches and also the number of the inhabitants in Great Britain will be increased by importing at a cheap rate from this new colony, the materials requisite for carrying on in Britain several manufactures. For our manufacturers will be encouraged to marry and multiply when they find themselves in circumstances to provide for their families which must necessarily be the happy effect of the increase and cheapness of our materials of those manufactures which at present we purchase with our money from foreign countries at dear rates; and also many people will find employment here on account [of] such farther demands by the people of this colony for those manufactures which are made for the produce of our own country, and, as has been justly observed, the people will always abound where there is full employment for them.

Christianity will be extended by the execution of this design since the good discipline established by the society will reform the manners of those miserable objects who shall be by them subsisted, and the example of a whole colony, who shall behave in a just, moral, and religious manner, will contribute greatly towards the conversion of the Indians, and taking off the prejudices received from the profligate lives of such who have scarce anything of Christianity but the name.

The trustees in their general meetings will consider of the most prudent methods for effectually establishing a regular colony, and that it may be done is demonstrable. Under what difficulties was Virginia planted? The coast and climate then unknown, the Indians numerous and at enmity with the first planters who were forced to fetch all provisions from England; yet it is grown a mighty province and the revenue receives £100,000 for duties upon the goods that they send yearly home. Within this 50 years Pennsylvania was as much a forest as Georgia is now, and in these few years by the wise economy of William Penn and those who assisted him, it now gives food to 80,000 inhabitants and can boast of as fine a city as most in Europe.

This new colony is more likely to succeed than either of the former were, since Carolina abounds with provisions, the climate is known, and there are men to instruct in the seasons and nature of cultivating the soil. There are but few Indian families within 400 miles, and those in perfect amity with the English. Port Royal (the station of his Majesty's ships) is within 30, and Charleston (a great mart) is within 120 miles. If the colony is attacked it may be relieved by sea from Port Royal or the Bahamas, and the militia of South Carolina is ready to support it by land.

For the continuing the relief which is now given, there will be lands reserved in the colony, and the benefit arising from them is to go to the carrying on of the trust. So that at the same time the money by being laid out preserves the lives of the poor and makes a comfortable provision for those whose expenses are by it defrayed; their labour in improving their own lands will make the adjoining reserved lands valuable, and the rents of those reserved lands will be a perpetual fund for the relieving more poor people. So that instead of laying out the money upon lands with the income thereof to support the poor, this is laying out money upon the poor, and by relieving those who are now unfortunate, raises a fund for the perpetual relief of those who shall be so hereafter.

There is an occasion now offered for everyone to help forward this design; the smallest benefaction will be received and applied with the utmost care; every little will do something and a great number of small benefactions will amount to a sum capable of doing a great deal of good.

If any person, moved with the calamities of the unfortunate, shall be inclined to contribute towards their relief, they are desired to pay their benefactions into the Bank of England, on account of the trustees for establishing the colony of Georgia in America, or else to any of the trustees. . . .

C. THE FOUNDING OF THE FIRST COLONIES

ENGLISHMEN of whatever class in society, when suddenly transplanted to the New World, faced problems for which little in their previous experience had prepared them. For some it meant disaster; for others it meant an opportunity to go forward. The account of the first colonies are a distinct contrast to the glowing pictures painted by the promotion pamphlets. Many of the first colonists suffered from starvation, disease, and often, from unfriendly Indians. Disaster led to bitter dissension among themselves, though it was nowhere so violent as during the first few years of the Virginia colony. Many of the early accounts found their way back to England where they were printed. While they produced scepticism, they also brought into better perspective the realities that must be met if colonization was to be successful.

The conditions described by the first colonists were repeated over and over again in successive frontier areas as settlers pushed onward from the first settlements along the coast. However, few of the accounts of later settlements are as eloquent as those of the first ones. There continued to be danger, especially from Indians who became ever more hostile, but as Englishmen learned how to live in a wilderness, the danger from starvation and disease declined. Once the first colonies were firmly established, they were able to help the later ones, as in the case of Maryland, which received aid from Virginia.[1]

12. John Smith: A True Relation of . . . Virginia (1608)

The following consists of excerpts from Captain John Smith's *A True Relation of such occurrences and accidents of noate as hath hapned in Virginia since the first planting of that Collony, which is now resident in the South part thereof, till the last returne from thence.* It was published in London in 1608. Smith (1580–1631) was one of the most vigorous and aggressive of the men who went to Virginia in 1607. The leaders fought violently with one another and many of them wrote accounts of what happened. Smith's account is prejudiced, as are the accounts of the other leaders. The bulk of his "True Relation", omitted here, describes his explorations and the difficulties of the colonists with the Indians Printed: Edward Arber, ed., *Capt. John Smith . . . Works* (The English Scholars Library, Birmingham, 1884), pp. 5–6, 7–9, 12–13, 22–23, 33–34, 39–40.

Kind Sir, commendations remembered, etc. You shall understand that after many crosses in the downs by tempests, we arrived safely upon the south-west part of the great Canaries. Within four or five days after, we set sail for Dominica the 26 of April. The first land we made, we fell with Cape Henry, the very mouth of the Bay of Chesapeake, which at that present we little expected, having by a cruel storm been put to the northward.

Anchoring in this bay, twenty or thirty went ashore with the captain, and in coming aboard [on land], they were assaulted with certain Indians, which charged them within pistol shot, in which conflict Captain Archer and Matthew Morton were shot, whereupon Captain Newport seconding them, made a shot at them, which the Indians little respected, but having spent their arrows retired without harm. And in that place was the box opened wherein the Council for Virginia was nominated, and arriving at the place [Jamestown] where we are now seated, the Council was sworn and the President elected, which for that year was Master Edmund Maria Wingfield, where was made choice for our situation, a very fit place for the erecting of a great city, about which some contention passed betwixt Captain Wingfield and Captain Gosnold. Notwithstanding, all our provision was brought ashore, and with as much speed as might be we went about our fortification.

[On 22 May, Captain Newport, Smith, and several others set forth to explore the country up the James River. They returned on 27 May.] . . . the first we heard was that 400 Indians the day before [26 May] had assaulted the fort and surprised it. Had not God (beyond all their expectations) by means of the ships (at whom they shot with their ordnances and muskets) caused them to retire, they had entered the fort with our own men, which were then busied in setting corn, their arms being then in dry fats and few ready but certain gentlemen of their own, in which conflict most of the Council was hurt, a boy slain in the pinnace, and thirteen or fourteen more hurt.

With all speed we palisadoed our fort; each other day for six or seven days we had alarms by ambuscadoes, and four or five cruelly wounded by being abroad. The Indians' loss we know not, but as they report three were slain and divers hurt.

Captain Newport, having set things in order, set sail for England the 22 of June [1607], leaving provision for 13 or 14 weeks.

The day before the ship's departure the king of Pamaunke [*i.e.* Opechancanough] sent the Indian that had met us before in our discovery, to assure us peace, our fort being then palisadoed round, and all our men in good health and comfort, albeit that through some discontented humours it did not so long continue. For the President and Captain Gosnold, with the rest of the Council, being for the most part discontented with one another, in so much that things were neither carried with that discretion nor any business effected in such good sort as wisdom would, nor our own good and safety required, whereby, and through the hard dealing of our President, the rest of the Council being diversely affected through his audacious command; and for Captain Martin, albeit very honest and wishing the best good, yet so sick and weak, and myself so disgraced through others' malice, through which disorder God (being angry with us) plagued us with such famine and sickness that the living were scarce able to bury the dead; our want of sufficient and good victuals, with continual watching four or five each night at three bulwarks, being the chief cause. Only of sturgeon we had great store, whereon our men would so greedily surfeit as it cost many their lives; the sack, *aqua vitae*, and other preservatives for our health being kept only in the President's hands, for his own diet, and his few associates.

Shortly after Captain Gosnold fell sick, and within three weeks died. Captain Ratcliffe being then also very sick and weak, and myself having also tasted of the extremity thereof, but by God's assistance being well recovered. Kendall about this time, for divers reasons, deposed from being of the Council, and shortly after it pleased God in our extremity to move the Indians to bring us corn ere it was half ripe, to refresh us, when we rather expected when they would destroy us.

About the tenth of September there was about 46 of our men dead, at which time Captain Wingfield having ordered the affairs in such sort that he was generally hated of all, in which respect with one consent he was deposed from his presidency, and Captain Ratcliffe according to his course was elected.

Our provision being now within twenty days spent, the Indians brought us great store both of corn and bread ready made, and also there came such abundance of fowls into the rivers as greatly refreshed our weak estates, whereupon many of our weak men were presently able to go abroad.

As yet we had no houses to cover us, our tents were rotten, and our cabins worse than nought. Our best commodity was iron, which we made into little chisels.

The President's and Captain Martin's sickness constrained me to be cape merchant and yet to spare no pains in making houses for the company, who notwithstanding our misery, little ceased their malice, grudging, and muttering.

As at this time were most of our chiefest men either sick or discontented, the rest being in such despair as they would rather starve and rot with idleness than be persuaded to do anything for their own relief without constraint. Our victuals being now within eighteen days spent, and the Indian trade decreasing, I was sent to the mouth of the river to Kegquouhtan, an Indian town, to trade for corn, and try the river for fish, but our fishing we could not effect by reason of the stormy weather. The Indians, thinking us near famished, with careless kindness offered us little pieces of bread and small handfuls of beans or wheat for a hatchet or a piece of copper. In like manner I entertained their kindness and in like scorn offered them like commodities, but the children, or any that showed extraordinary kindness, I liberally contented with free gift of such trifles as well contented them. [Smith continued his efforts to secure corn and achieved success.]

Having thus by God's assistance gotten good store of corn, notwithstanding some bad spirits not content with God's providence, still grew mutinous; in so much that, our President having occasion to chide the smith [James Read, the blacksmith] for his misdemeanour, he not only gave him bad language but also offered to strike him with some of his tools. For which rebellious act the smith was by a jury condemned to be hanged, but being upon the ladder, continuing very obstinate as hoping upon a rescue; when he saw no other way but death with him, he became penitent and declared a dangerous conspiracy, for which Captain Kendall as principal was by a jury condemned, and shot to death.

This conspiracy appeased, I set forward for the discovery of the river [of] Chickahominy. This third time I discovered the towns of Matapamient, Morinogh, Ascacap, Moysenock, Righkahauck, Nechanichock, Mattalunt, Attamuspincke, and divers others. Their plenty of corn I found decreased, yet lading the barge I returned to our fort.

Our store being now indifferently well provided with corn, there was much ado for to have the pinnace go for England, against which Captain Martin and myself stood chiefly against it, and in fine, after many debatings *pro et contra*, it was resolved to stay a further resolution.

This matter also quieted, I set forward to finish this discovery, which as yet I had neglected in regard of the necessity we had to take in provision whilst it was to be had. [Smith set forth with nine men in a barge. Finally he left the barge behind and pushed on with two of the men. The men were killed and Smith was captured by the Indians. Eventually he was taken before the Emperor Powhatan. Smith was well treated and returned to Jamestown.]

The next morning [8 January 1608] ere sunrise we set forward for our fort, where we arrived within an hour, where each man with the truest signs of joy they could express welcomed me, except Master Archer, and some two or three of his, who was then in my absence sworn Councillor, though not with the consent of Captain Martin.

Great blame and imputation was laid upon me by them [Archer, etc.] for the loss of our two men which the Indians slew, insomuch that they purposed to depose me. But in the midst of my miseries it pleased God to send Captain Newport, who arriving there the same night [8 January 1608], so tripled our joy as for a while these plots against me were deferred, though with much malice against me, which Captain Newport in short time did plainly see. Now was Master Scrivener, Captain Martin, and myself called Councillors [i.e. to the exclusion of Archer].

Within five or six days after the arrival of the ship [13 or 14 January 1608], by a mischance our fort was burned and the most of our apparel, lodging, and private provision. Many of our old men [became] diseased, and [many] of our new for want of lodging perished. . . .

The twenty of April [1608], being at work in hewing down trees and setting corn, an alarum caused us with all speed to take our arms, each expecting a new assault of the savages; but understanding it [to be] a boat under sail, our doubts were presently satisfied with the happy sight of Master Nelson, his many perils of extreme storms and tempests [passed], his ship well, as his company could testify, his care in sparing our provision was well; but the providence [provider] thereof, as also of our stones, hatchets, and other tools (only ours excepted) which of all the rest was most necessary, which might enforce us to think [him] either a seditious traitor to our action, or a most unconscionable deceiver of our treasures.

This happy arrival of Master Nelson in the *Phenix*, having been then about three months missing after Captain Newport's arrival, being to all our expectations lost; albeit that now at the last, having been long crossed with tempestuous weather and contrary winds, his so unexpected coming did so ravish us with exceeding joy, that now we thought ourselves as well fitted as our hearts could wish, both with a competent number of men, as also for all other needful provisions, till a further supply should come unto us. . . .

In all this time, our men being all or the most part well recovered, and we not willing to trifle away more time than necessity enforced us unto, we thought good for the better content of the adventurers, in some reasonable sort to freight home Master Nelson with cedar wood. About which, our men going with willing minds, [it] was in very good time effected and the ship sent for England [on 2 June 1608]. We now remaining being in good health, all our men well contented, free from mutinies, in love one with another, and as we hope, in a continual peace with the Indians. Where we doubt not but by God's gracious assistance, and the adventurers' willing minds and speedy furtherance to so honourable an action, in after times to see our nation to enjoy a country not only exceeding pleasant for habitation, but also very profitable for commerce in general; no doubt pleasing to Almighty God, honourable to our gracious sovereign, and commodious generally to the whole kingdom.

13. The Tragical Relation of Virginia Assembly (1624)

The Virginia Company was rent with internal dissension. Sir Thomas Smythe was replaced as treasurer by Sir Edwin Sandys in 1619. The Smythe faction, with the support of the Crown, continued to fight against the majority and helped to bring about the dissolution of the company in 1624. The "Tragical Relation" states the case of the Virginia House of Burgesses against the Smythe administration. Printed: Edward D. Neill, *History of the Virginia Company of London* . . . (Albany 1869), pp. 407–411.

The answer of the General Assembly in Virginia to a declaration of the state of the colony in the twelve years of Sir Thomas Smythe's government, exhibited by Alderman Johnson and others:

Holding it a sin against God and our own suffering, to suffer the world to be abused with untrue reports, and to give unto vice the reward of virtue, we in the name of the whole colony of Virginia, in our General Assembly, many of us having been eyewitnesses and patients of those times, have framed out of our duty to this country, and love unto truth, this dismasking of those praises which are contained in the foresaid declarations.

In those twelve years of Sir Thomas Smythe his government, we aver that the colony for the most part remained in great want and misery under most severe and cruel laws sent over in print, and contrary to the express letter of the king in his most gracious charter, and as mercilessly executed, often times without trial or judgment. The allowance in those times for a man was only eight ounces of meal and half a pint of peas for a day, the one and the other mouldy, rotten, full of cobwebs and maggots, loathsome to man and not fit for beasts, which forced many to flee for relief to the savage enemy, who being taken again were put to sundry deaths as by hanging, shooting and breaking upon the wheel, and others were forced by famine to filch for their bellies, of whom one for stealing 2 or 3 pints of oatmeal had a bodkin thrust through his tongue and was tied with a chain to a tree until he starved; if a man through his sickness had not been able to work, he had no allowance at all, and so consequently perished. Many through these extremities, being weary of life, digged holes in the earth and hid themselves till they famished.

We cannot for this our scarcity blame our commanders here, in respect that our sustenance was to come from England, for had they at that time given us no better allowance we had perished in general; so lamentable was our scarcity that we were constrained to eat dogs, cats, rats, snakes, toadstools, horse-hides and what not; one man out of the misery that he endured, killing his wife, powdered her up to eat her, for which he was burned. Many besides fed on the corpses of dead men, and one who had gotten insatiable, out of custom to that food could not be restrained, until such time as he was executed for it, and indeed, so miserable was our estate, that the happiest day that ever some of them hoped to see, was when the Indians had killed a mare, they wishing whilst she was boiling that Sir Thomas Smythe was upon her back in the kettle.

And whereas it is affirmed that there were very few of his Majesty's subjects left in those days, and those of the meanest rank, we answer that for one that now dies, there then perished five, many being of ancient houses and born to estates of 1,000 [pounds] by the year, some more, some less, who likewise perished by famine. Those who survived, who had both adventured their estates and persons, were constrained to serve the colony as if they had been slaves, 7 or 8 years for their freedoms, who underwent as hard and servile labour as the basest fellow that was brought out of Newgate.

And for discovery we say that none was discovered in those 12 years, and in these 4 or 5 last years much more than formerly.

For our houses and churches in those times they were so mean and poor by reason of those calamities that they could not stand above one or two years, the people never going to work but out of the bitterness of their spirits threatening execrable curses upon Sir Thomas Smythe, neither could a blessing from God be hoped for in those buildings which were founded upon the blood of so many Christians.

The towns were only James City, Henrico, Charles Hundred, West and Shirley Hundred, and Kiccowtan, all which in those times were ruined also, unless some 10 or 12 houses in that corporation of James City. At this present time are 4 for every one that were there, and forty times exceeding in goodness. Fortifications there were none at all against the foreign enemy, and those that were against the domestic very few and contemptible. Bridges there was only one which also decayed in that time. If through the foresaid calamities many had not perished, we doubt not but there might have been many more than 1,000 people in the land when Sir Thomas Smythe left the government.

But we conceive that when Sir George Yeardley arrived governor, he found not above 400, most of those in want of corn, nearly destitute of cattle, swine, poultry and other necessary provisions to nourish them. Ministers to instruct the people there were some whose sufficiency and ability we will not tax, yet divers of them had no orders.

We know not at any time that we exceeded in arms, powder, and munitions, but that in quality almost altogether useless. We acknowledge in those times there was a trial made of divers staple commodities, the colony as then not having means to proceed therein. We hope in time there may be some better progressions be made, and had it not been for the massacre, may by this had been brought to perfection. As for boats in the time of that government, there was only one left that was serviceable in the colony, for which one besides 4 or 5 ships and pinnaces, there are now not so few as 40. The barques and barges that then were built in number few, so unwillingly and weakly by the people effected, yet in the same time they also fished.

We never perceived that the natives of the country did voluntarily yield themselves subjects to our gracious sovereign, neither that they took any pride in that title, nor paid at any time any contribution of corn for sustentation of the colony, nor could we at any time keep them in such good respect of correspondency as we became mutually helpful each to the other but contrarily what at any [time] was done proceeded from fear and not love, and their corn procured by trade or the sword.

To what growth of perfection the colony hath attained at the end of those 22 [12] years we conceive may easily be judged by what we have formerly said. And rather to be reduced to live under the like government we desire his Majesty that commissioners may be sent over with authority to hang us.

Alderman Johnson, one of the authors of this declaration, hath reason to commend him to whose offences and infamies he is so inseparably chained.

By the general report of the country which we never heard contradicted, we affirm this to be true whereof all or the most part were eyewitnesses or resident in the country when every particular within written were effected.

14. William Bradford: From "Of Plymouth Plantation"

Plymouth Colony was founded by a group of English Separatists who had left Scrooby, England, for Holland in 1607–1608. After a short stay in Amsterdam, they moved to Leyden. In the course of time, wrote William Bradford, "they began to incline to this conclusion: of removal to some other place. Not out of any newfangledness or other such like giddy humour . . . but for sundry weighty and solid reasons. . . ." Making a living was so difficult in Holland that their friends in England refused to join them. Those in Holland were forced to work so hard that they became old before their time and their children too became decrepit because of their hard labours. Furthermore, the "great licentiousness of the youth" of Holland was a bad example for Separatist children who "were drawn away by evil examples into extravagant and dangerous courses, getting the reins off their necks and departing from their parents". "Lastly (and which was not the least)", wrote Bradford, they hoped to advance the gospel "in those remote parts of the world. . . ."

Preparations were begun in 1617. Ultimately a group of London merchants provided the necessary financial help and the Virginia Company gave them a patent to settle in Virginia. However, they landed at Cape Cod in New England in November 1620, and they decided to stay there to found their settlement.

William Bradford's "Of Plimoth Plantation" is the finest contemporary account of the founding and early history of an English colony. Bradford (1590–1657) had been a member of the original Scrooby congregation and had moved to Holland, where he worked as a weaver. He helped to make the arrangements for removal to America. In 1621 he was elected governor of the colony and was re-elected continuously except at times when he begged to be relieved of the post. His history was written in his old age. The manuscript was known to eighteenth century historians but it disappeared. It was finally located in the archives of the Bishop of London. It was printed for the first time in 1856 and in 1897 the manuscript was presented to the State of Massachusetts. The following brief excerpts describe the Mayflower Compact, the sufferings of the first winter, the early relations with the Indians, and the first planting and Thanksgiving. They are taken from the modern and definitive edition of Samuel Eliot Morison. Printed: *Of Plymouth Plantation 1620–1647*, Samuel Eliot Morison, ed. (New York 1952), pp. 75–81, 84, 85–86, 90.

The Mayflower Compact

I shall a little return back, and begin with a combination made by them before they came ashore; being the first foundation of their government in this place. Occasioned partly by the discontented and mutinous speeches that some of the strangers amongst them had let fall from them in the ship: That when they came ashore they would use their own liberty, for none had power to command them, the patent they had being for Virginia and not for New England, which belonged to another government, with which the Virginia Company had nothing to do. And partly that such an act by them done, this their condition considered, might be as firm as any patent, and in some respects more sure.

The form was as followeth:

IN THE NAME OF GOD, AMEN.

We whose names are underwritten, the loyal subjects of our dread Sovereign Lord King James, by the Grace of God of Great Britain, France, and Ireland King, Defender of the Faith, etc.

Having undertaken, for the Glory of God and advancement of the Christian Faith and Honour of our King and Country, a Voyage to plant the First Colony in the Northern Parts of Virginia, do by these presents solemnly and mutually in the presence of God and one of another, Covenant and Combine ourselves together into a Civil Body Politic, for our better ordering and preservation and furtherance of the ends aforesaid; and by virtue hereof to enact, constitute and frame such just and equal Laws, Ordinances, Acts, Constitutions and Offices, from time to time, as shall be thought most meet and convenient for the general good of the Colony, unto which we promise all due submission and obedience. In witness whereof we have hereunder subscribed our names at Cape Cod, the 11th of November, in the year of the reign of our Sovereign Lord King James, of England, France and Ireland the eighteenth, and of Scotland the fifty-fourth. Anno Domini 1620.

After this they chose, or rather confirmed, Mr. John Carver (a man godly and well approved amongst them) their governor for that year. And after they had provided a place for their goods, or common store (which were long in unlading for want of boats, foulness of the winter weather and sickness of divers) and begun some small cottages for their habitation; as time would admit, they met and consulted of laws and orders, both for their civil and military government as the necessity of their condition did require, still adding thereunto as urgent occasion in several times, and as cases did require.

In these hard and difficult beginnings they found some discontents and murmurings arise amongst some, and mutinous speeches and carriages in other; but they were soon quelled and overcome by the wisdom, patience, and just and equal carriage of things, by the governor and better part, which clave faithfully together in the main.

The starving time

But that which was most sad and lamentable was, that in two or three months' time half of their company died, especially in January and February, being the depth of winter, and wanting houses and other comforts; being infected with the scurvy and other diseases which this long voyage and their inaccommodate condition had brought upon them. So as there died some times two or three of a day in the foresaid time, that of 100 and odd persons, scarce fifty remained. And of these, in the time of most distress, there was but six or seven sound persons who to their great commendations, be it spoken, spared no pains night nor day, but with abundance of toil and hazard of their own health, fetched them wood, made them fires, dressed them meat, made their beds, washed their loathsome clothes, clothed and unclothed them. In a word, did all the homely and necessary offices for them which dainty and queasy stomachs cannot endure to hear named; and all this willingly and cheerfully, without any grudging in the least, showing herein their true love unto their friends and brethren; a rare example and worthy to be remembered. Two of these seven were Mr. William Brewster, their reverend Elder, and Myles Standish, their Captain and military commander, unto whom myself and many others were much beholden in our low and sick condition. And yet the Lord so upheld these persons as in this general calamity they were not at all infected either with sickness or lameness. And what I have said of these I may say of many others who died in this general visitation, and others yet living; that whilst they had health, yea, or any strength continuing, they were not wanting to any that had need of them. And I doubt not but their recompense is with the Lord.

But I may not here pass by another remarkable passage not to be forgotten. As this calamity fell among the passengers that were to be left here to plant, and were hasted ashore and made to drink water that the seamen might have the more beer, and one in his sickness desiring but a small can of beer, it was answered that if he were their own father he should have none. The disease began to fall amongst them also, so as almost half of their company died before they went away, and many of their officers and lustiest men, as the boatswain, gunner, three quartermasters, the cook and others. At which the Master was something strucken and sent to the sick ashore and told the Governor he should send for beer for them that had need of it, though he drunk water homeward bound.

But now amongst his company there was far another kind of carriage in this misery than amongst the passengers. For they that before had been boon companions in drinking and jollity in the time of their health and welfare, began now to desert one another in this calamity, saying they would not hazard their lives for them, they should be infected by coming to help them in their cabins; and so, after they came to lie by it, would do little or nothing for them but, "if they died, let them die". But such of the passengers as were yet aboard showed them what mercy they could, which made some of their hearts relent, as the boatswain (and some others) who was a proud young man and would often curse and scoff at the passengers. But when he grew weak, they had compassion on him and helped him; then he confessed he did not deserve it at their hands, he had abused them in word and deed. "Oh!" (saith he) "you, I now see, show your love like Christians indeed one to another, but we let one another lie and die like dogs." Another lay cursing his wife, saying if it had not been for her he had never come this unlucky voyage, and anon cursing his fellows, saying he had done this and that for some of them; he had spent so much and so much amongst them, and they were now weary of him and did not help him, having need. Another gave his companion all he had, if he died, to help him in his weakness; he went and got a little spice and made him a mess of meat once or twice. And because he died not so soon as he expected, he went amongst his fellows and swore the rogue would cozen him, he would see him choked before he made him any more meat; and yet the poor fellow died before morning.

Indian relations

All this while the Indians came skulking about them, and would sometimes show themselves aloof off, but when any approached near them, they would run away; and once they stole away their tools where they had been at work and were gone to dinner. But about the 16th of March, a certain Indian came boldly amongst them and spoke to them in broken English, which they could well understand but marvelled at it. At length they understood by discourse with him, that he was not of these parts, but belonged to the eastern parts where some English ships came to fish, with whom he was acquainted and could name sundry of them by their names, amongst whom he had got his language. He became profitable to them in acquainting them with many things concerning the state of the country in the east parts where he lived, which was afterwards profitable unto them; as also of the people here, of their names, number and strength, of their situation and distance from this place, and who was chief amongst them. His name was Samoset. He told them also of another Indian whose name was Squanto, a native of this place, who had been in England and could speak better English than himself.

Being, after some time of entertainment and gifts dismissed, a while after he came again, and five more with him, and they brought again all the tools that were stolen away before, and made way for the coming of their great Sachem, called Massasoit. Who, about four or five days after, came with the chief of his friends and other attendance, with the aforesaid Squanto. With whom, after friendly entertainment and some gifts given him, they made a peace with him (which hath now continued this 24 years) in these terms:

1. That neither he nor any of his should injure or do hurt to any of their people.
2. That if any of his did hurt to any of theirs, he should send the offender, that they might punish him.
3. That if anything were taken away from any of theirs, he should cause it to be restored; and they should do the like to his.
4. If any did unjustly war against him, they would aid him; if any did war against them, he should aid them.
5. He should send to his neighbours confederates to certify them of this, that they might not wrong them, but might be likewise comprised in the conditions of peace.
6. That when their men came to them, they should leave their bows and arrows behind them

After these things he returned to his place called Sowams, some 40 miles from this place, but Squanto continued with them and was their interpreter and was a special instrument sent of God for their good beyond their expectation. He directed them how to set their corn, where to take fish, and to procure other commodities, and was also their pilot to bring them to unknown places for their profit, and never left them till he died. He was a native of this place, and scarce any left alive besides himself. He was carried away with divers others by one Hunt, a master of a ship, who thought to sell them for slaves in Spain. But he got away for England and was entertained by a merchant in London, and employed to Newfoundland and other parts, and lastly brought hither into these parts by one Mr. Dermer, a gentleman employed by Sir Ferdinando Gorges and others for discovery and other designs in these parts.

But to return. The spring now approaching, it pleased God the mortality began to cease amongst them, and the sick and lame recovered apace, which put as [it] were new life into them, though they had borne their sad affliction with much patience and contentedness as I think any people could do. But it was the Lord which upheld them, and had beforehand prepared them; many having long borne the yoke, yea from their youth. Many other smaller matters I omit, sundry of them having been already published in a journal made by one of the company, and some other passages of journeys and relations already published, to which I refer those that are willing to know them more particularly.

Mayflower departs and corn planted

They now began to dispatch the ship away which brought them over, which lay till about this time, or the beginning of April. The reason on their part why she stayed so long, was the necessity and danger that lay upon them; for it was well towards the end of December before she could land anything here, or they able to receive anything ashore. Afterwards, the 14th of January, the house which they had made for a general rendezvous by casualty fell afire, and some were fain to retire aboard for shelter; then the sickness began to fall sore amongst them, and the weather so bad as they could not make much sooner any dispatch. Again, the governor and chief of them, seeing so many die and fall down sick daily, thought it no wisdom to send away the ship, their condition considered and the danger they stood in from the Indians, till they could procure some shelter; and therefore thought it better to draw some more charge upon themselves and friends than hazard all. The master and seamen likewise, though before they hasted the passengers ashore to be gone, now many of their men being dead, and of the ablest of them (as is before noted), and of the rest many lay sick and weak; the master durst not put to sea till he saw his men begin to recover, and the heart of winter over.

Afterwards they (as many as were able) began to plant their corn, in which service Squanto stood them in great stead, showing them both the manner how to set it, and after how to dress and tend it. Also he told them, except they got fish and set with it in these old grounds it would come to nothing. And he showed them that in the middle of April they should have store enough come up the brook by which they began to build, and taught them how to take it, and where to get other provisions necessary for them. All which they found true by trial and experience. Some English seed they sowed, as wheat and pease, but it came not to good, either by the badness of the seed or lateness of the season or both, or some other defect.

Bradford succeeds Carver

In this month of April, whilst they were busy about their seed, their governor (Mr. John Carver) came out of the field very sick, it being a hot day. He complained greatly of his head and lay down, and within a few hours his senses failed, so as he never spake more till he died, which was within a few days after. Whose death was much lamented and caused great heaviness amongst them, as there was cause. He was buried in the best manner they could, with some volleys of shot by all that bore arms. And his wife, being a weak woman, died within five or six weeks after him.

Shortly after, William Bradford was chosen Governor in his stead, and being not recovered of his illness, in which he had been near the point of death, Isaac Allerton was chosen to be an assistant unto him who, by renewed election every year, continued sundry years together. Which I here note once for all.

First Thanksgiving

They began now to gather in the small harvest they had, and to fit up their houses and dwellings against winter, being all well recovered in health and strength and had all things in good plenty. For as some were thus employed in affairs abroad, others were exercised in fishing, about cod and bass and other fish, of which they took good store, of which every family had their portion. All the summer there was no want; and now began to come in store of fowl, as winter approached, of which this place did abound when they came first (but afterward decreased by degrees). And besides waterfowl there was great store of wild turkeys, of which they took many, besides venison, etc. Besides they had about a peck a meal a week to a person, or now since harvest, Indian corn to that proportion. Which made many afterwards write so largely of their plenty here to their friends in England, which were not feigned but true reports.

[Our harvest being gotten in, our Governor sent four men on fowling, that so we might after a more special manner rejoice together, after we had gathered the fruit of our labours. They four in one day killed as much fowl as, with a little help beside, served the Company almost a week. At which time, amongst other recreations, we exercised our arms, many of the Indians coming amongst us, and amongst the rest their greatest king, Massasoit with some 90 men, whom for three days we entertained and feasted. And they went out and killed five deer which they brought to the plantation and bestowed on our Governor and upon the Captain and others.][1]

15A–B. Massachusetts in 1631

15A. Thomas Dudley to the Countess of Lincoln (12 March 1631)

Thomas Dudley had been steward to the earl of Lincoln for many years before he came to Massachusetts Bay in 1630. From 1630 until his death in 1653 he was one of the most important leaders of the colony, serving four times as governor and thirteen times as deputy governor. Omitted from the letter as given here are Dudley's comments on the Indians, the colony at Plymouth, various accidents and deaths occurring in the colony, and his account of troubles with such people as Thomas Morton. Printed: Force, *Tracts*, vol. II, No. 4, *passim*.

For the satisfaction of your honour and some friends, and for use of such as shall hereafter intend to increase our plantation in New England, I have in the throng of domestic, and not altogether free from public business, thought fit to commit to memory our present condition, and what hath befallen us since our arrival here; which I will do shortly, after my usual manner, and must do rudely, having yet no table, nor other room to write in than by the fireside upon my knee, in this sharp winter; to which my family must have leave to resort, though they break good manners and make me many times forget what I would say, and say what I would not.

Touching the plantation which we here have begun, it fell out thus about the year 1627. Some friends being together in Lincolnshire, fell into some discourse about New England and the planting of the gospel there; and after some deliberation, we imparted our reasons by letters and messages to some in London and the west country

---

[1] The paragraph in brackets is from a letter of Edward Winslow and is printed in Morison, p. 90, n. 8.

where it was likewise deliberately thought upon, and at length with often negotiation so ripened that in the year 1628 we procured a patent from his Majesty for our planting between the Massachusetts Bay and Charles River on the south; and the river of Merrimac on the north and three miles on either side of those rivers and bay, as also for the government of those who did or should inhabit within that compass and the same year we sent Mr. John Endecott and some with him to begin a plantation and to strengthen such as he should find there which we sent thither from Dorchester and some places adjoining, from whom the same year receiving hopeful news. The next year, 1629, we sent diverse ships over with about 300 people, and some cows, goats and horses, many of which arrived safely. These by their too large commendations of the country and the commodities thereof, invited us so strongly to go on that Mr. Winthrop of Suffolk (who was well known in his own country and well approved here for his piety, liberality, wisdom and gravity) coming in to us, we came to such resolution that in April, 1630, we set sail from Old England with four good ships. And in May following eight more followed, two having gone before in February and March, and two more following in June and August, besides another set out by a private merchant. These seventeen ships arrived all safe in New England, for the increase of the plantation here this year, 1630, but made a long, a troublesome, and a costly voyage, being all wind bound long in England, and hindered with contrary winds after they set sail and so scattered with mists and tempests that few of them arrived together. Our four ships which set out in April arrived here in June and July, where we found the colony in a sad and unexpected condition, above 80 of them being dead the winter before and many of those alive, weak and sick: all the corn and bread amongst them all hardly sufficient to feed them a fortnight, insomuch that the remainder of 180 servants we had the two years before sent over, coming to us for victuals to sustain them, we found ourselves wholly unable to feed them by reason that the provisions shipped for them were taken out of the ship they were put in, and they who were trusted to ship them in another failed us and left them behind; whereupon necessity enforced us to our extreme loss to give them all liberty, who had cost us about 16 or 20 [pounds] a person, furnishing and sending over. But bearing these things as we might, we began to consult of the place of our sitting down, for Salem, where we landed, pleased us not. And to that purpose some were sent to the bay to search up the rivers for a convenient place, who upon their return reported to have found a good place upon Mystic; but some other of us seconding these to approve or dislike of their judgment, we found a place liked us better three leagues up Charles River. And thereupon unshipped our goods into other vessels and with much cost and labour brought them in July to Charles Town; but there receiving advertisements by some of the late arrived ships from London and Amsterdam of some French preparations against us (many of our people brought with us being sick of fevers and the scurvy and we thereby unable to carry up our ordnance and baggage so far) we were forced to change counsel and for our present shelter to plant dispersedly, some at Charles Town, which standeth on the north side of the mouth of Charles River; some on the south side thereof, which place we named Boston (as we intended to have done the place we first resolved on); some of us upon Mystic, which we named Medford; some of us westwards on Charles River, four miles from Charles Town, which place we named Watertown; others of us two miles from Boston in a place we named Roxbury; others upon the river of Saugus between Salem and Charles Town. And the western men four miles south from Boston at a place we named Dorchester. This dispersion troubled some of us, but help it we could not, wanting ability to remove to any place fit to build a town upon, and the time too short to deliberate any longer lest the winter should surprise us before we had builded our houses. The best counsel we could find out was to build a fort to retire to, in some convenient place if any enemy pressed thereunto, after we should have fortified ourselves against the injuries of wet and cold. So ceasing to consult further for that time, they who had health to labour fell to building, wherein many were interrupted with sickness and many died weekly, yea almost daily. Amongst whom were Mrs. Pyncheon, Mrs. Coddington, Mrs. Phillips, and Mrs. Alcock, a sister of Mr. Hooker's. Insomuch that the ships being now upon their return, some for England, some for Ireland, there was, as I take it, not much less than an hundred (some think many more) partly out of dislike of our government which restrained and punished their excesses, and partly through fear of famine, not seeing other means than by their labour to feed themselves) which returned back again. And glad were we so to be rid of them. Others also afterwards hearing of men of their own disposition which were planted at Piscataway, went from us to them, whereby though our numbers were lessened, yet we accounted ourselves nothing weakened by their removal. Before the departure of the ships we contracted with Mr. Peirce, master of the *Lyon* of Bristol, to return to us with all speed with fresh supplies of victuals and gave him directions accordingly. With this ship returned Mr. Revil, one of the five undertakers here, for the joint stock of the company; and Mr. Vassall, one of the assistants, and his family; and also Mr. Bright, a minister sent hither the year before. The ships being gone, victuals wasting, and mortality increasing, we held diverse fasts in our several congregations, but the Lord would not yet be deprecated, for about the beginning of September, died Mr. Gager, a right godly man, a skilful surgeon and one of the deacons of our congregation. And Mr. Higginson, one of the ministers of Salem, a zealous and a profitable preacher; this of a consumption, that of a fever; and on the 30th of September died Mr. Johnson, another of the five undertakers (the lady Arbella his wife being dead a month before). This gentleman was a prime man amongst us, having the best estate of any, zealous for religion, and the greatest furtherer of this plantation. He made a most godly end, dying willingly, professing his life better spent in promoting this plantation than it would have been in any other way. He left to us a loss greater than the most conceived. Within a month after died Mr. Rossiter, another of our assistants, a godly man and of a good estate which still weakened us more so that there now were left of the five undertakers but the governor, Sir Richard Salstonstall, and myself and seven other of the assistants. And of the people who came over with us from the time of their setting sail from England in April, 1630, until December following, there died by estimation about 200 at the least. So low hath the Lord brought us! Well, yet they who survived were not discouraged but bearing God's corrections with humility and trusting in his mercies, and considering how after a greater ebb he had raised up our neighbours at Plymouth, we began again in December to consult about a fit place to build a town upon, leaving all thoughts of a fort, because upon any invasion we were necessarily to lose our houses when we should retire thereinto; so after diverse meetings at Boston, Roxbury, and Watertown on the 28th of December we grew to this resolution: to bind all the assistants (Mr. Endecott and Mr. Sharpe excepted, which last purposeth to return by the next ship into England) to build houses at a place a mile east from Watertown near Charles River, the next spring, and to winter there the next year, that so by our examples and by removing the ordnance and munition thither, all who were able might be drawn thither, and such as shall come to us hereafter to their advantage be compelled so to do; and so if God would, a fortified town might there grow up, the place fitting reasonably well thereto. I should before have mentioned how both the English and the Indian corn being at ten shillings a strike, and beaver being valued at 6 shilling a pound, we made laws to restrain the selling of corn to the Indians, and to leave the price of beaver at liberty which was presently sold for ten and 20 shillings a pound. I should also have remembered how the half of our cows and almost all our mares and goats sent us out of England died at sea in their passage hither, and that those intended to be sent us out of Ireland were not sent at all; all which together with the loss of our six months' building, occasioned by our intended removal to a town to be fortified, weakened our estates, especially the estates of the undertakers who were 3 or £4000 engaged in the joint stock which was now not above so many hundreds; yet many of us laboured to bear it as comfortably as we could, remembering the end of our coming hither and knowing the power of God who can support and raise us again, and useth to bring his servants low, that the meek may be made glorious by deliverance, Psalms 112.

But now having some leisure to discourse of the motives for other men's coming to this place or their abstaining from it, after my brief manner I say this: that if any come hither to plant for worldly ends that can live well at home, he commits an error of which he will soon repent him. But if for spiritual, and that no particular obstacle hinder his removal, he may find here what may well content him: vizt., materials to build, fuel to burn, ground to plant, seas and rivers to fish in, a pure air to breathe in, good water to drink till wine or beer can be made, which together with the cows, hogs, and goats brought hither already may suffice for food, for as for fowl and venison, they are dainties here as well as in England. For clothes and bedding they must bring them with them till time and industry produce them here. In a word, we yet enjoy little to be envied but endure much to be pitied in the sickness and mortality of our people. And I do the more willingly use this open and plain dealing lest other men should fall short of their expectations when they come hither as we to our great prejudice did, by means of letters sent us from hence into England, wherein honest men out of a desire to draw over others to them wrote somewhat hyperbolically of many things here. If any godly men out of religious ends will come over to help us in the good work we are about, I think they cannot dispose of themselves nor of their estates more to God's glory and the furtherance of their own reckoning, but they must not be of the poorer sort yet for diverse years. For we have found by experience that they have hindered, not furthered the work. And for profane and debauched persons their oversight in coming hither is wondered at, where they shall find nothing to content them. If there be any endued with grace and furnished with means to feed themselves and theirs for 18 months, and to build and plant, let them come into our Macedonia and help us, and not spend themselves and their estates in a less profitable employment. For others, I conceive they are not yet fitted for this business.

Upon the 5 of February arrived here Mr. Peirce with the ship *Lyon* of Bristol with supplies of victuals from England who had set forth from Bristol the first of December before. . . . By this ship we also understood the death of many of those who went from us the last year to old England, as likewise of the mortality there whereby we see there are graves in other places as well as with us.

Also to increase the heap of our sorrows we received advertisement by letters from our friends in England, and by the reports of those who came hither in this ship to abide with us (which were about 26), that those who went discontentedly from us the last year, out of their evil affections towards us have raised many false and scandalous reports against us, affirming us to be Brownists in religion and ill affected to our state at home, and that these vile reports have won credit with some who formerly wished us well. But we do desire, and cannot but hope, that wise and impartial men will at length consider that such malcontents have ever pursued this manner of casting dirt to make others to seem as foul as themselves and that our godly friends to whom we have been known will not easily believe that we are not [now] so soon turned from the profession we so long have made in our native country. And for our further clearing I truly affirm that I know no one person who came over with us the last year to be altered in his judgment and affection either in ecclesiastical or civil respects since our coming hither, but we do continue to pray daily for our sovereign lord the king, the queen, the prince, the royal blood, the council, and whole state as duty binds us to do and reason persuades others to believe, for how ungodly and unthankful should we be if we should not thus do, who come hither by virtue of his Majesty's letters patents and under his gracious protection under which shelter we hope to live safely and from whome [whose] kingdom and subjects we now have received and hereafter expect relief. Let our friends therefore give no credit to such malicious aspersions, but be more ready to answer for us than we hear they have been. We are not like those which have dispensations to lie, but as we were free enough in Old England to turn our insides outwards, sometimes to our disadvantage, very unlike is it that now (being *procul a bulmine*) we should be so unlike ourselves; let therefore this be sufficient for us to say, and others to hear in this matter.

I thought to have ended before, but the stay of the ship and my desire to inform your honour of all I can, hath caused this addition; and every one having warning to prepare for the ship's departure tomorrow, I am now this 28 of March 1631, sealing my letters.

15B. Letter to William Pond (15 March 1631)

The original spelling and punctuation in this letter from one of the less important people in the colony have been retained. Printed: Massachusetts Historical Society, *Proceedings*, XXVIII, pp. 471–473.

To my lovinge father William Ponde, at Etherston [Edwardstone] in Suffolcke give theis.

Most Loveinge & Kinde Father & Mother,—

My humble deutye remembreid unto you, trusteinge in God you are in good hellthe, & I pray remembr my love unto my brother Joseife & thanck him for his kindnes that I found at his hand at London, wich wase not the valleu of a fardin. I knowe, lovinge father, & do confese that I wase an undeuteyefull cheilld unto you when I liveied withe you & by you, for the wiche I am muche sorrowfull & greveid for it, trusteinge in God that he will geide me that I will never offend you so aney more & I truste in God that you will forgive me for it. My wreightein unto you is to lete you understand what a cuntrey theis New Eingland is whar we live. Her ar but fewoe Eingeines [Indians], a gret parte of them deyeid theis winture, it was thought it wase of the plage. Thay ar a craftey peple & thaye will cusson [cozen] & cheat, & thay ar a suttell peple, & whareas we ded expect gret stor of bever her is littell or non to be had, & thayr Sackemor John waietse it & maney of us truck with them & it leyethe us maney tymes in 8s a pound. Thay ar proper men & clenjointeide men & maney of them go nackeid with a skein abought thare loines, but now sume of them get Eingellishemenes parell; & the cuntrey is verie rockey & heilley & sume champine ground & the soile is verie flete, & her is sume good ground & marshe ground, but her is no Myckellmes. Springe cattell threive well here, but thay give small stor of mylck. The best cattell for proffeit is sweines & a good sweine is her at 5 l. preise, a goose is worthe 2 l. a good one gote. Her is teimbur good store & ackornes good stor, and her is good stor of feishe ife we had botes to goo for & leynes to serv to feishein. Her ar good stor of weield foule, but thay ar hard to come bye. It is hardur to get a shoot then it is in ould Eingland & peple her ar subjecte to deisesese, for her have deyeid of the scurveye & of the burninge fever neye too hundreid & ode; beseide as maney leyethe lame & all Sudberie men ar ded but thre & three women & sume cheildren, & proviseyones ar her at a wondurfull rat. Wheat mell is xiiij^s a bushell, & pese x^s, & mault x^s, & Einder seid wheat is xv^s & thare other wheat is x^s. Buttr xii^d a pound & chese is 8^d a pound, & all kind of speyseis verie der & allmoste non to be got. If theis ship had not cume when it ded we had bine put to a woondurfule straughte, but thanckes be to God for sendinge of it in. I reseyvied from the shipe a hogseite of mell, & the Governer tellethe me of a hundreid waight of chese the wiche I have reseyveid parte of it. I humblie thancke you for it. I ded expecte too coues, the wiche I had non, nor I do not arenestly deseyer that you shoold send me aney, becauese the cuntrey is not so as we ded expecte it. Tharefor, lovinge father, I wolld intret you that you woolld send me a ferckeine of buttr & a hogseit of mault onground, for we dreinck notheinge but walltre, & a corse clothe of fouer pound preise so it be thicke. For the fraute, if you of youer love will send them I will paye the fraute, for her is notheinge to be gote witheoughte we had cumemodeytes to go up to the Este partes amonckest the Eingeines to truck, for her whare we live her is no bever. Her is no clothe to be had to mack no parell, & shoes are at 5s a payer for me, & that clothe that is woorthe 2s 8d a yard is woorthe her 5s. So I pray, father, send me fouer or five yardes of clothe to mack us sume parell & lovinge father, thoue I be far distante from you yet I pray you remembure me as youer cheield, & we do not know how longe we may subseiste, for we can not live her witheought provyseyones from ould Eingland. Therefore, I pray do not put away youer shope stufe, for I theinck that in the eind, if I live, it must be my leveinge, for we do not know how longe theis plantatyon will stand, for sume of the magnautes that ded uphould it have turned off thare men & have givene it overe. Beseides, God hath tacken away the chefeiste stud in the land, Mr. Johnson & the ladye Arabella his wife, wiche wase the cheifeste man of estate in the land & one that woold a don moste good.

Her cam over xxv passeingares & thare cume backe agayn fouer skore & od parsones, & as maney more wolld a cume if thay had whare withe all to bringe them hom, for her ar maney that cam over the laste yere wiche wase woorthe too hundreid poundes afore thay cam ought of ould Eingland that betwine theis & Myckellmes wille be hardly worthe xxx l. So her we may live if we have suppleyes everey yere from ould Eingland, otherweyse we can not subseiste. I may, as I will, worck hard, sete an ackorne of Eindey wheat, & if we do not set it withe fishe & that will coste xx^s, if we set it witheought fishe they shall have but a por crope. So father, I pray, consedre of my cause, for her will be but a verey por beinge, no beinge witheought, lovinge father, youer helpe withe provisseyones from ould Eingland. I had thought to a cam home in theis sheipe, for my provisseyones ware allmoste all spente, but that I humbley thanck you for youer gret love & kindnes in seindinge me sume provissyones, or elles I sholld & myne a bine halef faminyshed, but now I will, if it plese God that I have my hellthe, I will plant what corne I can, & if provisseyones be not cheper betwein theis & Myckellmes & that I do not her from you what I wase beste to do, I purpose to cume hom at Myckellmes.

My wife remamburs hur humble deutey unto you & to my mother, & my love to my brother Joseife & to Sarey [?] Myler. Thus I leve you to the protectyon of Allmytey God.

From Walltmtowne [Watertown] in New Eingland the 15 of Marche, 1630 [1631].

[No signature.]

We ware wondurfule seick as we cam at sea, withe the small poxe. No man thought that I & my leittell cheilld woolld a liveid. My boye is lame & my gurell too, & thar deyeid in the sheip that I cam in xiiij persones.

16. A Relation of the Successful Beginnings of . . . Maryland (1634)

The following pamphlet, *A Relation of the successful beginnings of the Lord Baltimore's Plantation in Maryland; Being an extract of certain Letters written from thence, by some of the Adventurers to their Friends in England*, was published in London in 1634. It is notable, among other things, for its description of the Indians and for the account of the help received from the colony of Virginia. Printed : *Shea's Early Southern Tracts* (Baltimore, 1865), No. 1.

On Friday, the 22 of November 1633 a small gale of wind coming gently from the northwest, weighed from the Cowes, in the Isle of Wight, about ten in the morning; and (having stayed by the way twenty days at the Barbados, and fourteen days at St. Christophers, upon some necessary occasions) we arrived at Point Comfort in Virginia on the 24 of February following, the Lord be praised for it. At this time one Captain [William] Claiborne was come from parts where we intended to plant, to Virginia, and from him we understood that all the natives of these parts were in preparation of defence, by reason of a rumour somebody had raised amongst them of six ships that were come with a power of Spaniards, whose meaning was to drive all the inhabitants out of the country.

We had good letters from his Majesty to the governor and Council of Virginia, which made him favour us and show us as noble usage as the place afforded, with promise that for their cattle and hogs, corn and poultry, our plantation should not want the open way to furnish ourselves from thence. He told us likewise that when his lordship should be resolved on a convenient place to make himself a seat, he should be able to provide him with as much brick and tile as he should have occasion to employ, until his lordship had made of his own. Also that he had to furnish his lordship with two or three hundred stocks ready grafted with pears, apples, plums, apricots, figs, and peaches, and some cherries; that he had also some orange and lemon trees in the grounds which yet thrived; also filberts, hazelnuts, and almonds; and in one place of the colony, quince trees, wherewith he could furnish his lordship; and, in fine, that his lordship should not want anything that colony had.

On the 3 of March we came into Chesapeake Bay and made sail to the north of Potomac River, the Bay running between two sweet lands in the channel of 7, 8 and 9 fathom deep, 10 leagues broad, and full of fish at the time of the year. It is one of the delightfulest waters I ever saw, except Potomac, which we named St. Gregory's. And now being in our own country, we began to give names to places, and called the southern point Cape Saint Gregory; and the northerly point, Saint Michaels.

This river, of all I know, is the greatest and sweetest, much broader than the Thames; so pleasant as I, for my part, was never satisfied in beholding it. Few marshes or swamps, but the greatest part solid good earth, with great curiosity of woods which are not choked up with undershrubs, but set commonly one from the other in such distance as a coach and four horses may easily travel through them.

At the first looming of the ship upon the river, we found (as was foretold us) all the country in arms. The king of the Paschattoways had drawn together 1500 bowmen, which we ourselves saw; the woods were fired in manner of beacons the night after; and for that our vessel was the greatest that ever those Indians saw, the scouts reported we came in a canoe as big as an island, and had as many men as there be trees in the woods.

We sailed up the river till we came to Heron Islands so called from the infinite swarms of that fowl there. The first of those islands we called Saint Clement's, the second Saint Katherine's, and the third, Saint Cicilie's. We took land first in Saint Clement's which is compassed about with a shallow water and admits no access without wading; here by the overturning of the shallop, the maids which had been washing at the land were almost drowned, beside the loss of much linen, and amongst the rest, I lost the best of mine which is a very main loss in these parts. The ground is covered thick with pokickeries (which is a wild walnut very hard and thick of shell; but the meat (though little) is passing sweet), with black walnuts, and acorns bigger than ours. It abounds with vines and sallets, herbs and flowers, full of cedar and sassafras. It is but 400 acres big, and therefore too little for us to settle upon.

Here we went to a place where a large tree was made into a cross and taking it on our shoulders, we carried it to the place appointed for it. The governor and commissioners putting their hands first on it, then the rest of the chiefest adventurers. At the place prepared we all kneeled down and said certain prayers; taking possession of the country for our Saviour, and for our sovereign lord the king of England.

Here our governor had good advice given him not to land for good and all before he had been with the emperor of Paschattoway and had declared unto him the cause of our coming: which was first to learn them a divine doctrine which would lead their souls to a place of happiness after this life were ended; and also to enrich them with such ornaments of a civil life wherewith our country doth abound: and this emperor being satisfied, none of the inferior kings would stir. In conformity to this advice he took two pinnaces, his own and another hired in Virginia; and leaving the ship before St. Clement's at anchor, went up the river and landing on the south side, and finding the Indians fled for fear, came to Potomac Town, when the king being a child, Archihau, his uncle, governed both him and his country for him. He gave all the company good welcome and one of the company having entered into a little discourse with him touching the errors of their religion, he seemed well pleased therewith and at his going away desired him to return unto him again, telling him he should live at his table, his men should hunt for him, and he would divide all with him.

From hence they went to Paschattoway. All were here armed: 500 bowmen came to the waterside. The emperor himself, more fearless than the rest, came privately aboard where he was courteously entertained, and understanding we came in a peaceable manner, bade us welcome, and gave us leave to sit down in what place of his kingdom we pleased. While this king was aboard, all the Indians came to the waterside, fearing treason, whereupon two of the king's men that attended him in our ship were appointed to row on shore to quit them of this fear; but they refusing to go for fear of the popular fury, the interpreters standing on the deck showed the king to them that he was in safety, wherewith they were satisfied. In this journey the governor entertained Captain Henry Fleete and his three barks; who accepted a proportion in beaver trade to serve us, being skilful in the tongue, and well beloved of the natives.

Whilst the governor was abroad the Indians began to lay aside fear and to come to our court of guard, which we kept night and day upon St. Clement's Isle; partly to defend our barge, which was brought in pieces out of England, and there made up, and partly to defend the captain's men, which were employed in felling of trees and cleaning pales for the palisado; and at last they ventured to come aboard our ship. It was worth the hearing for those who understood them to hear what admiration at our ship; calling it a canoe and wondering where so great a tree grew that made it, conceiving it to be made of one piece, as their canoes are. Our great ordnance was a great and fearful thunder, they had never heard any before; all the country trembles at them.

The governor being returned, we came some nine leagues lower to a river on the north side of that land, as big as the Thames, which we called Saint Gregory's River. It runs up to the north about 20 miles before it comes to the fresh. This river makes two excellent bays for 300 sail of ships of 1,000 ton, to harbour in with great safety. The one bay we named Saint George's; the other (and more inward) Saint Mary's. The king of Yaocomico dwells on the left hand or side thereof, and we took up our seat on the right, one mile within the land. It is as brave a piece of ground to set down on as most is in the country, and I suppose as good (if not much better), than the primest parcel of English ground.

Our town we call Saint Mary's and to avoid all just occasion of offence and colour of wrong, we bought of the king for hatchets, axes, hoes, and clothes, a quantity of some 30 miles of land which we call Augusta Carolina; and that which made them the more willing to sell it was the wars they had with the Susquehannas, a mighty bordering nation, who came often into their country to waste and destroy, and forced many of them to leave their country and pass over Potomac to free themselves from peril before we came. God no doubt disposing all this for them, who were to bring his law and light among the infidels. Yet, seeing we came so well prepared with arms, their fear was much less, and they could be content to dwell by us; yet do they daily relinquish their houses, lands and cornfields and leave them to us. Is not this a piece of wonder that a nation which a few days before was in arms with the rest against us should yield themselves now unto us like lambs, and give us their houses, lands and livings for a trifle? *Digitus Dei est hic*: and surely some great good is intended by God to his nation. Some few families of Indians are permitted to stay by us till next year, and then the land is free.

We had not been long time seated there ere Sir John Harvey, governor of Virginia, did our Governor the honour (in most friendly manner) to visit him, and during the time of his being there, the king of Patuxent also came to visit us, and being come aboard the *Ark* and brought into the great cabin, and seated between the two governors (Captain Fleete and Master Golding the interpreters being present) he began his speech as followeth:

"When I heard that a great werowance of the English was come to Yaocomico, I had a great desire to see him. But when I heard the werowance of Pasbie-haye was come thither also to visit him, I presently start up, and without further counsel came to see them both."

In the time of his stay at St. Mary's we kept the solemnity of carrying our colours on shore and the king of Patuxent accompanying us, was much taken with the ceremony. But the same night (he and Captain Fleete being at the Indian House) the *Ark*'s great guns, to honour the day, spoke aloud, which the king of Patuxent with great admiration hearing, counselled his friends the Yaocomico Indians to be careful that they break not their peace with us and said: "When we shoot, our bowstrings give a twang that's heard but a little way off; but do you not hear what cracks their bowstrings give?" Many such pretty sayings he used in the time of his being with us, and at his departure he thus expressed his extraordinary affection unto us:

"I do love the English so well that if they should kill me, so that they left me with so much breath as to speak unto my people, I would commend them not to revenge my death."

As for the natives, they are proper tall men of person; swarthy by nature but much more by art; painting themselves with colours in oil, like a dark red, which they do to keep the gnats off, wherein, I confess, there is more ease than comeliness.

As for their faces, they have other colours at times, as blue from the nose upward, and red downward, and sometimes contrariwise in great variety and in very ghastly manner; sometimes they have no beards till they come to be very old, and therefore draw from each side of their mouths lines to their very ears, to represent a beard; and this sometimes of one colour and sometimes of another.

They wear their hair generally very long, and it is as black as jet; which they bring up in a knot to the left ear and tie it about with a large string of wampampegge [wampum], or roanoke, or some other of the best jewels among them. Upon their forehead some use to wear a fish of copper and some wear other figures.

About their necks they use to wear many bugle chains, though these begin now not to be esteemed among them for truck. Their apparel generally is deerskin and some fur, which they wear like loose mantles; yet under this about their middle all women and men, at man's estate, wear perizomata (or round aprons) of skins, which keep them decently covered, that without any offence to chaste eyes we may converse with them.

All the rest of their bodies are naked, and at times, some of the youngest sort both of men and women have just nothing to cover them. Their feet are as hard as any horn; when they run over prickles and thorns they feel it not. Their arms is a bow with a bunch of arrows of a yard long, furnished with three feathers at the top and pointed either with the point of a deer's horn, or a sharp three-cornered white flint; the rest is a small cane, or straight stick. They are so expert at these that I have once seen one a good distance off, strike a very small bird through the middle; and they used to cast a thing up from hand and before it came to the ground, to meet it with a shaft. Their bows are but weak and carry not level very far; yet these are their livelihood, and every day they are abroad after squirrels, partridges, turkeys, deer and the like game, whereof there is a wonderful plenty; though we dare not yet be so bold ourselves as to fetch fresh meat by this means, far off.

The Indian houses are all build here in a long half oval; nine or ten foot high to the middle top where, as in ancient temples, the light is admitted by a window half a yard square; which window is also the chimney which giveth passage to the smoke, the fire being made in the midst of the floor (as in our old halls of England) and about it they use to lie. Save only that their kings and great men have their cabins and a bed of skins well dressed (wherein they are excellent) set on boards and four stakes driven into the ground. And now at this present, many of us live in these witchotts (as they term them) conveniently enough till better be set up: but they are dressed up something better than when the Indians had them.

The natural wit of this nation is good and quick, and will conceive a thing very readily; they excel in smell and taste, and have far sharper sight than we. Their ordinary diet is pone and hominy, both made of corn, to which they add at times fish, fowl, and venison.

They are of great temperance, especially from hot waters or wine which they are hardly brought to taste, save only whom the English have corrupted with their own vices.

For modesty, I must confess, I never saw from man or woman any action tending to levity, and yet daily the poor souls are here in our houses and take content to be with us, bringing sometimes turkeys, sometimes squirrels as big as English rabbits, but much more dainty; at other times fine white cakes, partridges, oysters, ready boiled and stewed; and do run unto us with smiling countenance when they see us, and will fish and hunt for us, if we will; and all this with intercourse of very few words, but we have hitherto gathered their meaning by signs.

It is lawful among them to have more wives than one, but all keep the rigour of conjugal faith unto their husbands. The women's very aspect is modest and grave.

Generally the nation is so noble that you cannot do them any favour or good turn but they return it. There is small passion among them, but they weigh all with a calm and quiet reason. And to do this the better, in great affairs they are studying in a long silence what is best to be said or done, and then they answer yea or no, in two words, and stand constantly to their resolution.

If these people were once Christians (as by some signs we have reason to think nothing hinders it but want of language) it would be a right virtuous and renowned nation.

As for their religion, we have not language ourselves to find it out; Master Thoroughgood, who drives his lordship's trade upon the river Patuxent, hath related somewhat.

First they acknowledge one God of Heaven which they call (our) God; and cry a thousand shames upon those Christians that so lightly offend so good a God. But they give no external honour unto him but use all their might to please an Okee (or frantic spirit) for fear of harm from him. They adore also wheat and fire as two gods very beneficial unto man's nature.

In the Machicomoco, or temple of Patuxent, there was seen by our traders this ceremony. Upon a day appointed all the towns met and a great fire being made, about it stood the younger sort, and behind them again the elder. Then taking a little deer suet, they cast it into the fire, crying "Taho, Taho", and lifting their hands to heaven. After this was brought before them a great bag filled with a large tobacco pipe and poke, which is the word they use for our tobacco. This was carried about the fire, the youth following, and singing "Taho, Taho" in very good tune of voice and comely gesture of body.

The round ended, one comes reverently to the bag and opening it, takes out the pipe and divides the poke from one to one. As every one took his draught, he breathed his smoke upon the limbs of his own body, as it were to sanctify them by this ceremony, to the honour and service of their God, whomsoever they meant.

This is all I can say touching their religion; save only that they seem to have some knowledge by tradition of a flood wherein the world was drowned for sin.

And now to return to the place itself, chosen for our plantation. We have been upon it but one month, and therefore can make no large relation of it. Yet thus much I can say of it already: For our own safety we have built a good strong fort or palisado, and have mounted upon it one good piece of ordnance, and four murderers, and have seven pieces of ordnance more ready to mount forthwith. For our provision, here is some store of pease and beans and wheat left on the ground by the Indians, who had satisfaction for it.

We have planted since we came as much maize (or Indian wheat) as will suffice (if God prosper it) much more company than we have. It is up about knee high above ground already, and we expect return of 1,000 for one, as we have reason for our hope from the experience of the yield in other parts of this country, as is very credibly related to us.

We have also English pease, and French beans, cotton, oranges, lemons, melocotones, apples, pears, potatoes, and sugar-canes of our own planting, beside hortage coming up very finely.

But such is the quantity of vines and grapes now already upon them (though young) as I dare say if we had vessels and skill we might make many a tun of wine, even from about our plantation, and such wine, as those of Virginia say (for yet we can say nothing) as is as good as the wine of Spain. I fear they exceed, but surely very good. For the clime of this country is near the same with Seville and Cordova, lying between 38 and 40 degrees of northerly latitude.

Of hogs we have already got from Accomack (a plantation in Virginia) to the number of 100, and more, and some 30 cows, and more we expect daily, with goats and hens; our horses and sheep we must have out of England or some other place by the way, for we can have none in Virginia.

For the commodities I will speak more when I see further; only we have sent over a good quantity of ironstone for a trial, which, if it prove well, the place is likely to yield infinite store of it. And for that flax and hemp which we have sowed, it comes up, and we hope will thrive exceedingly well. I end with the soil, which is excellent, covered with store of large strawberries, raspises, vines, sassafras, walnuts, acorns, and the like, and this in the wildest woods, too.

The mould is black, a foot deep, and then comes after a red earth. All is high wood but in the Indian fields, which are some parcels of ground cleared for corn. It abounds with good springs, which is our drink. Of beasts I have seen deer, raccoons, and squirrels, beside which there are many others which I have not yet seen. Of birds diversely feathered there are infinite: eagles, bitterns, herons, swans, geese, partridge, ducks; red, blue, parti-coloured birds, and the like. By all which it appeareth the country aboundeth not only with profit but with pleasure. And to say truth, there wanteth nothing for the perfecting of this hopeful plantation but greater numbers of our countrymen to enjoy it.

From Saint Mary's in Maryland,
27 May 1634.

Part II

THE EVOLUTION OF COLONIAL GOVERNMENTS

THE EVOLUTION OF COLONIAL GOVERNMENTS

SELECT BIBLIOGRAPHY

Detailed accounts of the evolution of colonial governments will be found in the general histories and the histories of particular colonies listed in the general bibliography. The basic source materials are in the printed records of the individual colonies, also listed in the general bibliography.

(a) POLITICAL THEORY AND CONSTITUTIONAL HISTORY

The English background of the political ideas of the English colonists is discussed at length in J. W. ALLEN, *Political Thought in the Sixteenth Century* (3rd ed., New York, 1951), and in his *English Political Thought, 1603–1660* (London, 1938). G. P. GOOCH, *English Democratic Ideas in the Seventeenth Century* (2nd ed., Cambridge, 1927) is suggestive but often inaccurate in details, as is CHARLES BORGEAUD, *The Rise of Modern Democracy in Old and New England* (London, 1894). Although old, E. P. CHEYNEY, *European Backgrounds of American History*, has very useful chapters on the heritage of political and constitutional thought carried by the English colonists to America.

The most recent and best work on political thought in the colonies is CLINTON ROSSITER, *Seedtime of the Republic. The Origin of the American Tradition of Political Liberty* (New York, 1953) which contains important chapters on Roger Williams, Thomas Hooker, John Wise, Jonathan Mayhew, and Richard Bland. The notes to this volume are a comprehensive survey of the source and secondary materials on the subject. Of special studies, that of HERBERT L. OSGOOD, "The Political Ideas of the Puritans", *Political Science Quarterly*, vol. VI (1891), has influenced much writing but is no longer acceptable. A comprehensive discussion of Puritan political theory in the colonies with supporting documents may be found in PERRY MILLER and THOMAS H. JOHNSON, *The Puritans* (New York, 1938). On the political thought of particular individuals in addition to the discussions in ROSSITER, see STANLEY GRAY, "The Political Thought of John Winthrop", *New England Quarterly*, vol. III (1930); JAMES ERNST, *The Political Thought of Roger Williams* (Seattle, 1929); PERRY MILLER, *Roger Williams* (New York, 1953), which contains long excerpts from WILLIAMS's writings; and GEORGE A. COOK, *John Wise: Early American Democrat* (New York, 1952).

On the creation of elective legislatures in the colonies, and on American attachment to the idea of a written constitution, W. C. MOREY, "The Genesis of a Written Constitution", *Annals of the American Academy of Political and Social Science*, vol. I (1891) is a significant pioneer essay, although it needs to be corrected as to details. Also to be consulted are ANDREW C. McLAUGHLIN, *The Foundations of American Constitutionalism* (New York, 1932); CHARLES BORGEAUD, "The Origin and Development of Written Constitutions", *Pol. Sci. Quarterly*, vol. VII (1892); BENJAMIN F. WRIGHT, "The Early History of Written Constitutions in America", in *Essays in History and Political Theory in Honour of Charles Howard McIlwain* (Cambridge, Mass., 1936); and CHARLES H. McILWAIN, "The Transfer of the Charter to New England, and its Significance in American Constitutional History", *Mass. Hist. Soc. Proceedings*, vol. LXIII (1931).

Of the general works covering the constitutional history of the colonies as a whole, THOMAS POWNALL, *The Administration of the Colonies* (London, 1764, and subsequent editions) is significant. POWNALL, governor of Massachusetts, 1757–1760, understood the problems of government in the colonies as did few contemporaries. A. B. KEITH, *Constitutional History of the First British Empire* (Oxford, 1930), and LEONARD W. LABAREE, *Royal Government in America. A Study of the British Colonial System before 1783* (New Haven, Conn., 1930) are two basic modern works.

(b) BRITISH COLONIAL THEORY AND POLICY

The most recent and comprehensive study of British colonial theories is KLAUS E. KNORR, *British Colonial Theories 1570–1850* (Toronto, 1944). The notes contain valuable references to contemporary writings from the sixteenth to the nineteenth centuries. CHARLES M. ANDREWS, *The Colonial Period of American History*, vol. IV, subtitled "England's Commercial and Colonial Policy", is the most detailed and scholarly account available at the present time. ANDREWS's two chapters in *The Cambridge History of the British Empire*, vol. I, on "The Acts of Trade" and "The Government of the Empire, 1660–1763" are concise accounts. Among the older works, those of GEORGE LOUIS BEER are still important. These include *The Origins of the British Colonial System 1578–1660* (New York, 1908) and *The Old Colonial System 1660–1754* (2 vols., New York, 1912). The latter work was never completed. Volume II carries only through the revolution of 1688–1689.

In addition to LOUISE P. KELLOGG's study of the American colonial charter already cited, special aspects of colonial policy are discussed in VIOLA F. BARNES, *The Dominion of New England, a Study in British Colonial Policy* (New Haven, Conn., 1923); G. H. GUTTRIDGE, *The Colonial Policy of William III in America and the West Indies* (Cambridge, 1922); and in KATE HOTBLACK, *Chatham's Colonial Policy* (London, 1917).

(c) BRITISH ADMINISTRATION OF THE COLONIES

The works of the Lords Commissioners of Trade and Plantations–the Board of Trade–and its predecessors have been treated in detail in the following: CHARLES M. ANDREWS, *British Committees, Commissions, and Councils of Trade and Plantations, 1622–1675* (Baltimore, 1908); W. T. ROOT, "The Lords of Trade and Plantations, 1675–1696", *Amer. Hist. Rev.*, vol. XXIII (1917–1918); RALPH BIEBER, *The Lords of Trade and Plantations, 1675–1696* (Allentown, Pa., 1919); O. M. DICKERSON, *American Colonial Government, 1696–1765. A Study of the British Board of Trade in its relation to the American Colonies* . . . (Cleveland, 1912); A. H. BASYE, *The Lords Commissioners of Trade and Plantations* . . . *1748–1782* (New Haven, Conn., 1925); MARY P. CLARKE, "The Board of Trade at Work", *Eng. Hist. Rev.*, vol. XXVI (1911); and MARGARET MARION SPECTOR, *The American Department of the British Government, 1768–1782* (New York, 1940).

The colonial governors represented British administration within the colonies and were instructed to carry out British policies. LEONARD W. LABAREE's *Royal Instructions to British Colonial Governors* is an invaluable collection of the various kinds of instructions sent to the governors. The official correspondence of several of the governors is to be found in the published colonial records of many of the colonies. In addition to such material, there are several valuable collections of governors' letters, and of other officials connected with colonial affairs which have been printed. Among these are: SIR EDMUND ANDROS, *The Andros Tracts* (Prince Society Publications, 3 vols., Boston, 1868–1874); JONATHAN BELCHER, *The Belcher Papers* (Mass. Hist. Soc., *Collections*, 6th Series, vols. VI and VII, Boston, 1893–1894); SIR FRANCIS BERNARD, *The Barrington-Bernard Correspondence and Illustrative Matter, 1760–1770* (Cambridge, Mass., 1912. E. CHANNING and A. C. COOLIDGE, eds.); CADWALLADER COLDEN, *Letterbooks* (2 vols., New York Hist. Soc. *Collections*, 1876, 1877) and *Papers, 1711–1775* (9 vols., New York Hist. Soc. *Collections*, 1917–1923, 1934, 1935); ROBERT DINWIDDIE, *The Official Records of Robert Dinwiddie* . . . (Va. Hist. Soc. *Collections*, new Series, vols. III and IV, Richmond, 1883–1884); THOMAS FITCH, *The Fitch Papers* (Conn. Hist. Soc., *Collections*, vols. XVII and XVIII, Hartford, 1918, 1920); THOMAS HUTCHINSON, *The Diary and Letters of his Excellency Thomas Hutchinson* . . . (2 vols., London, 1883, P. O. HUTCHINSON, ed.); Jonathan Law, *The Law Papers* (Conn. Hist. Soc. *Collections*, vols. XI, XIII, XV, Hartford, 1907, 1911, 1914); LEWIS MORRIS, *The Papers of Lewis Morris, Governor of the Province of New Jersey from 1738 to 1746* (New Jersey Hist. Soc. *Collections*, vol. IV, New York, 1852); WILLIAM PENN, *Correspondence Between William Penn and James Logan* . . . *and others. 1700–1750* (Memoirs of the Historical Society of Pennsylvania, vols. IX and X, Philadelphia, 1870, 1872); WILLIAM PITKIN, *The Pitkin Papers* (Conn. Hist. Soc. *Collections*, vol. XIX, Hartford, 1921); GERTRUDE S. KIMBALL, ed., *Correspondence of William Pitt, when*

Secretary of State, with Colonial Governors and Military and Naval Commissioners in America (2 vols., New York, 1906); ROBERT N. TOPPAN and A. T. S. GOODRICK, eds., *Edward Randolph: Including his Letters and Official Papers from the New England, Middle and Southern Colonies in America* . . . (Prince Society Publications, 7 vols., Boston, 1898, 1909); GERTRUDE S. KIMBALL, ed., *The Correspondence of the Colonial Governors of Rhode Island, 1723-1775* (2 vols., Boston, 1902); WILLIAM SHIRLEY, *Correspondence of William Shirley, Governor of Massachusetts and Military Commander in America, 1730-1760* (2 vols., New York, 1912, C. H. LINCOLN, ed.); ALEXANDER SPOTSWOOD, *The Official Letters of Alexander Spotswood* . . . (Virginia Hist. Soc. *Collections*, new Series, vols. I and II, Richmond, 1882, 1885); JOSEPH TALCOTT, *The Talcott Papers* (Conn. Hist. Soc. *Collections*, vols. IV and V, Hartford, 1892, 1896); JOHN WINTHROP, *The Winthrop Papers* (5 vols. to date, Mass. Hist. Soc., Boston, 1929-1947); and ROGER WOLCOTT, *The Wolcott Papers* (Conn. Hist. Soc. *Collections*, vol. XVI, Hartford, 1916).

The biographies of most of the colonial governors are to be found in brief form in the *Dictionary of American Biography*. These sketches are accompanied by bibliographical notes and references to more extended biographies where such exist. The *Dictionary of National Biography* likewise contains material on many of the colonial governors and officials. EVARTS B. GREENE, *The Provincial Governor in the English Colonies of North America* (New York, 1898) discusses the colonial governors in relation to the workings of colonial government. LEONARD W. LABAREE, "The Early Careers of the Royal Governors" in *Essays in Colonial History Presented to Charles McLean Andrews* . . . and LOUISE B. DUNBAR, "The Royal Governors in the Middle and Southern Colonies on the Eve of the Revolution . . ." in RICHARD B. MORRIS, ed., *The Era of the American Revolution* (New York, 1939) are valuable shorter essays. JOHN F. BURNS, *Controversies Between Royal Governors and their Assemblies in the Northern American Colonies* (Boston, 1923) is an account of an almost continuous struggle.

The colonial agent, who was the legal representative of a colony in London, was particularly important during the eighteenth century. A good deal of the correspondence of such agents has been published in historical society collections. References to such sources and to unprinted materials may be found in the following monographs: LILIAN M. PENSON, *The Colonial Agents of the British West Indies* . . . (London, 1924); J. J. BURNS, *The Colonial Agents of New England* (Washington, 1935); and ELLA LONN, *The Colonial Agents of the Southern Colonies* (Chapel Hill, N.C., 1945). M. WOLFF, *The Colonial Agency of Pennsylvania, 1712-1757* (Philadelphia, 1933) deals with a single colony. BEVERLY W. BOND, "The Colonial Agent as a Popular Representative", *Pol. Sci. Quarterly*, vol. XXXV (1920) emphasizes the role of the agent as a representative of the elected branches of colonial legislatures.

The appeal of judicial cases from colonial courts to the Privy Council and the veto of colonial legislation by the Privy Council were two important devices of political control. Both have been the subject of important monographs. H. D. HAZELTINE, "Appeals from Colonial Courts to the King in Council, with especial reference to Rhode Island", Amer. Hist. Assoc., *Annual Report* (1894), G. A. WASHBURNE, *Imperial Control of the Administration of Justice in the Thirteen American Colonies, 1684-1776* (New York, 1923), and ARTHUR M. SCHLESINGER, "Colonial Appeals to the Privy Council", *Pol. Sci. Quarterly*, vol XXVIII (1913) are earlier studies. The most detailed study is J. H. SMITH, *Appeals to the Privy Council from the American Plantations* (New York, 1950). There is need of a thorough study of the review of colonial legislation by the Privy Council. E. B. RUSSELL, *The Review of American Colonial Legislation by the King in Council* (New York, 1915) covers the subject in a general way. See also ARTHUR G. DORLAND, *The Royal Disallowance in Massachusetts* (Queen's University, Kingston, Ontario, 1917, History and Political and Economic Science, *Bulletin* No. 22); and CHARLES M. ANDREWS, "The Royal Disallowance", American Antiquarian Society *Proceedings*, new Series, vol. XXIV (1914).

(d) GOVERNMENT WITHIN THE COLONIES
(i) The Evolution of Colonial Legislatures
From the beginning, members of colonial legislatures assumed they had the privileges of members of Parliament and that the legislatures as collective bodies had the rights of Parliament.

This is treated fully in MARY P. CLARKE, *Parliamentary Privilege in the American Colonies* (New Haven, 1943). The development of the two-house legislature is discussed in THOMAS F. MORAN, *The Rise and Development of the Bicameral System in America* (Baltimore, 1895); FRANKLIN L. RILEY, *The Colonial Origins of New England Senates* (Baltimore, 1896); and in detail for one colony in ELLEN E. BRENNAN, "The Massachusetts Council of Magistrates", *New England Quarterly*, vol. IV (1931). Other aspects of the development of legislatures are discussed in C. F. BISHOP, *History of Elections in the American Colonies* (New York, 1893); HUBERT PHILLIPS, *The Development of a Residential Qualification for Representatives in Colonial Legislature* (Cincinnati, 1921), and FRANK H. MILLER, "Legal Qualifications for Office in America, 1619–1899", Amer. His. Assoc. *Annual Report* (1899), vol. I. The procedures of colonial legislatures are discussed by RALPH V. HARLOW, *The History of Legislative Methods in the Period before 1825* (New Haven, 1917). STANLEY M. PARGELLIS, "The Procedure of the Virginia House of Burgesses", *William and Mary Quarterly*, 2nd Series, vol. VII (1927) is an invaluable detailed study for one colony. FLORENCE COOK, "Procedure in the North Carolina Colonial Assembly, 1731–1770", *N.C. Hist. Rev.*, vol. VIII (1931) is also useful.

The development of what amounted to an office-holding aristocracy is discussed in LEONARD W. LABAREE, *Conservatism in Early American History* (New York, 1948); ELLEN E. BRENNAN, *Plural Office Holding in Massachusetts, 1760–1780* (Chapel Hill, N.C., 1945); and in Donald M. Owings, *His Lordships Patronage: Offices of Profit in Colonial Maryland* (Baltimore, 1953). CHARLES S. SYDNOR, *Gentlemen Freeholders: Political Practices in Washington's Virginia* (Chapel Hill, N.C., 1952) is an illuminating study of political leadership in Virginia. See also ROBERT MUNFORD, *The Candidates*, a revealing eighteenth-century comedy satirizing a Virginia election which has been reprinted in the *William and Mary Quarterly*, 3rd Series, vol. V (1948) with an introduction by J. B. HUBBELL and DOUGLASS ADAIR.

The right to vote in elections and extension of representation in colonial legislatures to newly settled areas were two important political issues and have been the subject of several important studies. ALBERT E. MCKINLEY, *The Suffrage Franchise in the Thirteen English Colonies in America* (Philadelphia, 1905) is based primarily on legislation and his estimates as to the size of voting population have been questioned. Several of the colonies have been the subject of separate studies. Among these are J. A. C. CHANDLER, *The History of Suffrage in Virginia* (Baltimore, 1901); DONALD L. KEMMERER, "The Suffrage Franchise in Colonial New Jersey", N. J. Hist. Soc. *Proceedings*, vol. LII (1934). G. H. HAYNES, *Representation and Suffrage in Massachusetts 1620–1691* (Baltimore, 1894) discusses both topics for that colony. ROBERT E. BROWN, "Democracy in Colonial Massachusetts", *New England Quarterly*, vol. XXV (1952) argues that the right to vote in Massachusetts was very democratic. W. NEIL FRANKLIN, "Some Aspects of Representation in the American Colonies", *N.C. Hist. Rev.*, vol. VI (1929) is a general discussion. The most detailed and useful discussion of representation is W. A. SCHAPER, "Sectionalism and Representation in South Carolina", Amer. Hist. Assoc. *Annual Report* (1900), vol. I. Other studies of individual colonies are J. A. C. CHANDLER, *Representation in Virginia* (Baltimore, 1896), and LAWRENCE F. LONDON, "The Representation Controversy in Colonial North Carolina", *N.C. Hist. Rev.*, vol. XI (1934).

(ii) Local Governments in the Colonies

Local governments were studied intensively at the Johns Hopkins University in the late nineteenth century under the guidance of HERBERT BAXTER ADAMS, but have not received the detailed treatment since then that their importance warrants. Among the pioneer studies at John Hopkins were GEORGE E. HOWARD, *An Introduction to the Local Constitutional History of the United States* (Baltimore, 1889), and several other works cited elsewhere in this bibliography. Aside from the emphasis on the idea of Germanic origins of New England towns, which is no longer accepted, these pioneer studies are still useful.

TOWN GOVERNMENT

Town or township government was the primary form of local government in New England. Many of the New England towns have published their records as well as town histories. A notable example of the former are the Boston Town Records. These are embodied in *Reports of the Records Commissioners of the City of Boston* (39 vols., Boston, 1876-1909) and include records of the town meetings, 1634-1822, the selectmen's minutes, marriage and birth lists, tax and census lists, and miscellaneous papers. The most comprehensive bibliography of materials on local government in New England is the *Bibliography on State and Local Governments in New England* (Boston University Bureau of Public Administration, *Bulletin* No. 1, Boston, 1952). This covers colonial times as well as recent ones, but does not list the published town records nor many of the town histories.

Theories as to the origin of New England town government are subjected to critical analysis in JOHN F. SLY, *Town Government in Massachusetts, 1620-1930* (Cambridge, Mass., 1930). KENNETH COLEGROVE, "New England Town Mandates: Instructions to the Deputies in Colonial Legislatures", Col. Soc. Mass. *Publications*, vol. XXI (1920) discusses one of the most important political devices in colonial America.

COUNTY GOVERNMENT

Counties were the basic unit of government and of representation in the colonies south of New England, except for South Carolina, where the parish served the same purpose. Counties were governed by a county court made up of justices of the peace appointed by the governor for the various districts within a county. These county courts served as both governing and judicial bodies. Portions of colonial county records have been published, but all too often they are mere lists of names. The bulk of county records that remain are in manuscript. An excellent example of published records is LEWIS P. SUMMERS, ed., *Annals of Southwest Virginia, 1769-1800* (Abingdon, Va., 1929). MORGAN P. ROBINSON, *Virginia Counties . . .* (Virginia State Library *Bulletin*, vol. IX, Richmond, 1916) gives the history of the creation of Virginia counties, and ALBERT O. PORTER, *County Government in Virginia, a Legislative History, 1607-1904* (New York, 1947) discusses the evolution of county governments. "County Government in Massachusetts" in *Bulletins for the Constitutional Convention 1917-1918* (2 vols., Boston, 1918-1919), vol. I, No. 8, discusses the county in Massachusetts.

The chief administrative officer of the county was the sheriff. The office is discussed in CYRUS H. KARRAKER, *The Seventeenth Century Sheriff: A Comparative Study of the Sheriff in England and the Chesapeake Colonies, 1607-1689* (Chapel Hill, N.C., 1930) and in JULIAN P. BOYD, "The Sheriff in Colonial North Carolina", *N.C. Hist. Rev.*, vol. V (1928).

The vestry of the Anglican Church, in those colonies where it was established, was also an important unit of local government. Vestrymen supervised morals and were responsible for the care of the poor and of orphans. Several Virginia vestry records have been published. A good example is W. L. HALL, ed., *The Vestry Book of the Upper Parish, Nansemond County, Virginia, 1743-1793* (Richmond, 1949). Hall's introduction is an excellent account of the role of the parish in local government.

CITY GOVERNMENT

ERNEST S. GRIFFITH, *History of American City Government, The Colonial Period* (New York, 1938) is a detailed discussion, primarily of the cities with charters, which thus excludes consideration of such cities as Boston which had a town meeting form of government. The bibliography is a valuable guide to published city records and to secondary materials. Two important collections of city records are *Minutes of the Common Council of the City of Philadelphia, 1704-1776* (Philadelphia, 1847), and *Minutes of the Common Council of the City of New York, 1675-1776* (8 vols., New York, 1907). CARL BRIDENBAUGH, *Cities in the Wilderness, The First Century of Urban Life in America, 1625-1742* (New York, 1938) is a valuable scholarly study concentrating on the histories of Boston, New York, Newport, Philadelphia, and Charleston. Three nineteenth-century histories are of great value: JUSTIN WINSOR, ed., *The Memorial History of Boston . . .* (4 vols., Boston, 1880-1881); JAMES G. WILSON, *The Memorial History of the City of New York* (4 vols., New York, 1892-1893); and J. T. SCHARF and THOMPSON WESTCOTT, *History of Philadelphia* (3 vols., Philadelphia, 1884). Modern works on colonial cities are A. E. PETERSON, *New*

York as an Eighteenth Century Municipality Prior to 1731 (New York, 1917); G. W. EDWARDS, *New York as an Eighteenth Century Municipality, 1731–1776* (New York, 1917); JAMES D. PHILLIPS, *Salem in the Seventeenth Century* (Boston, 1933), and *Salem in the Eighteenth Century* (Boston, 1937); CARL BRIDENBAUGH and JESSICA BRIDENBAUGH, *Rebels and Gentlemen. Philadelphia in the Age of Franklin* (New York, 1942); and GERTRUDE S. KIMBALL, *Providence in Colonial Times* (Boston, 1912).

LEGAL HISTORY

A representative sample of the work of colonial courts has been published. Josiah Quincy, Jr., *Reports of Cases Argued and Adjudged by the Superior Court of Judicature of the Province of Massachusetts Bay, between 1761 and 1772* (Boston, 1865) and R. T. BARTON, ed., *Virginia Colonial Decisions: the Reports by Sir John Randolph and by Edward Barradall of Decisions of the General Court of Virginia, 1728–1741* (2 vols., Boston, 1909) are important older works. The American Historical Association has recently undertaken the publication of a series of volumes of *American Legal Records*. CARROLL T. BOND, ed., *Proceedings of the Maryland Court of Appeals, 1695–1729* (Washington, 1933); RICHARD B. MORRIS, ed., *Select Cases of the Mayor's Court of New York City, 1674–1784* (Washington, 1935); JOHN T. FARRELL, ed., *The Superior Court Diary of William Samuel Johnson, 1772–1773* . . . (Washington, 1942); REED H. CLAY and GEORGE J. MILLER, eds., *The Burlington Court Book: A Record of Quaker Jurisprudence in West New Jersey, 1680–1709* (Washington, 1944); and ANNE KING GREGORIE, *Records of the Court of Chancery of South Carolina, 1671–1779* (Washington, 1950) are among those that have been published to date. *Rhode Island Court Records . . . 1647–1670* (2 vols., Providence, 1920–1922) cover the early court records of that colony. A good example of the records of a county court is the *Records and Files of the Quarterly Courts of Essex County Massachusetts* (8 vols., Salem, Mass., 1911–1921). In addition, a variety of colonial court records are to be found in various historical society publications and in periodicals. For example, see "Abstracts from the Records of the Court of Ordinary of the Province of South Carolina" covering the years 1692–1771 in the *South Carolina Historical and Genealogical Magazine*, vols. VIII–XLV (1908–1944). In New York and Maryland, manorial courts existed for a time. A. J. F. VAN LAER, trans. and ed., *Minutes of the Court of Rennselaerswyck, 1648–1652* (Albany, N.Y., 1922) is an example.

Vice-admiralty courts were important institutions for local matters relating to commerce as well as for the enforcement of the Navigation Acts. Records of such courts are to be found in CHARLES M. HOUGH, ed., *Reports of Cases in the Vice-Admiralty of the Province of New York and in the Court of Admiralty of the State of New York, 1715–1788* (New Haven, 1925) and in DOROTHY S. TOWLE, ed., *The Records of the Vice-Admiralty Court of Rhode Island, 1716–1752* (Washington, 1936. *American Legal Records*, vol. III). This volume also contains an introduction by CHARLES M. ANDREWS. H. J. CRUMP, *Colonial Admiralty Jurisdiction in the Seventeenth Century* (New York, 1931) and JOHN NOBLE, "A Few Notes on Admiralty Jurisdiction in the Colony and in the Province of the Massachusetts Bay", Col. Soc. Mass. *Publications*, vol. VIII (1906) discuss aspects of these courts.

Legal history of the colonies needs much more attention than it has received. Among the important studies are PAUL S. REINSCH, *English Common Law in the Early American Colonies* (Madison, Wis., 1899); RICHARD B. MORRIS, *Studies in the History of American Law* . . . (New York, 1930); and *Select Essays in Anglo-American Legal History* (3 vols., Boston, 1907), which contains important sections relating to colonial law. Special aspects are treated in A. H. CARPENTER, "Habeas Corpus in the Colonies", *Amer. Hist. Rev.*, vol. VIII (1902–1903); and ARTHUR L. CROSS, "Benefit of Clergy in the American Criminal Law", Mass. Hist. Soc. *Proceedings*, vol. LXI (1928). E. A. JONES, *American Members of the Inns of Court* (London, 1924) gives an account of the Americans who received their legal training in England.

Important studies for individual colonies are CHARLES J. HILKEY, *Legal Development in Colonial Massachusetts, 1630–1686* (New York, 1910); F. W. GRINNELL, "The Bench and Bar in Colony and Province", in A. B. HART, ed., *Commonwealth History of Massachusetts* (5 vols., New York, 1927–1930), vol. II; JULIUS GOEBEL and T. R. NAUGHTON, *Law Enforcement in Colonial New York*

... (New York, 1944); RICHARD S. FIELD, *The Provincial Courts of New Jersey* ... (N.J. Hist. Soc. *Collections*, vol. III, New York, 1849); ST. GEORGE L. SIOUSSAT, *The English Statutes in Maryland* (Baltimore, 1903); OLIVER P. CHITWOOD, *Justice in Colonial Virginia* (Baltimore, 1905); and GEORGE L. CHUMBLEY, *Colonial Justice in Virginia* ... (Richmond, 1938).

A. POLITICAL THEORY IN THE COLONIES

POLITICAL thinking in the English colonies stemmed from two main sources: the concepts derived from the political and constitutional history of England, and the concepts, both religious and political, of English religious dissenters. Englishmen, of whatever class in society or variety of religious belief, were imbued with certain ideas of the 'rights' of Englishmen as individuals, and of the 'rights' of Englishmen when meeting in legislative assemblies. The seventeenth-century colonists were keenly aware of the issues at stake between the rival claims of Crown and Parliament, and, with few exceptions, supported Parliament in the struggle. This was made abundantly plain as colonial legislatures were established. They insisted on freedom of elections, on freedom from arrest during sessions, freedom of speech in debate, and the right of petition to the sovereign: either to the king himself, or to the governor as representative of the king. While colonial legislatures were not always able to maintain such ideas in practice, they never surrendered the principles and grew ever clearer in the statement of them.

As individuals, the colonists insisted on the "rights of Englishmen" which the first charters guaranteed to them. They claimed the right of petition against grievances, freedom from arrest and imprisonment except on specific charges and by due process of law, trial by jury, and, above all, of freedom from taxation except by elected representatives meeting in legal assemblies. Such ideas, in one form or another, are to be found in the proceedings of colonial legislatures beginning with that of Virginia in 1619.[1] While legislative proceedings are not ordinarily looked upon as statements of political theory, they do in fact contain a great deal of evidence for the basic political assumptions of the English colonists.[2]

While, in general, the colonists were imbued with the parliamentary tradition, many of them went far beyond this in their political thinking. Much of this stems from the religious turmoil of sixteenth- and seventeenth-century England. Various religious groups were concerned with the problem of religious toleration, with the relationship of Church and State, and ultimately with the nature of man and of government suitable for him. The Separatists, the Puritans, and the Quakers each had firm convictions, and since they founded colonies in America, they were able to put their theories into practice.

The English Puritans who settled in Massachusetts Bay were clear and firm in their convictions. They sought to establish what they called a theocracy in which the Church and State were intertwined. They did not believe in toleration of dissenters and they abhorred the idea of democracy.[3] The Reverend John Cotton stated their convictions succinctly when he declared that "Democracy I do not conceive that ever God did ordain as a fit government either for church or commonwealth. If the people be governors, who shall be governed? As for monarchy, and aristocracy, they are both of them clearly approved, and directed in scripture, yet so as referreth the sovereignty to himself, and setteth up theocracy in both, as the best form of government in the commonwealth, as well as in the church."

The ablest spokesman among the Puritan leaders in Massachusetts Bay was John

[1] No. 39.   [2] Nos. 26, 27, 28, 35.   [3] Nos. 17, 82, 84.

Winthrop. His statements of the Puritan philosophy of government and society are among the most lucid written during the seventeenth century. As clearly as John Cotton he makes it plain that the Puritans did not believe in democracy.[1]

Despite the statements of Puritan leaders and their political actions, the idea has persisted that American democracy stems from Puritanism. It is an idea which can be maintained only by making the Puritan label broad enough to include men of quite different political and religious convictions. The transplanting of the democratic idea to America was the work of English dissenters far more radical in their convictions than the leaders of Massachusetts Bay. Such people believed that the only true church was voluntary association of like-minded believers and that association was expressed in a written compact signed by all the members. This idea was revolutionary enough in an age in which Protestants and Catholics alike were convinced that a state could not exist without a state church to which all must be compelled to belong. But the idea was even more revolutionary when it was applied to civil affairs. Thus the settlers at Plymouth drew up the Mayflower Compact which they deemed a good and sufficient basis for government.[2] Such people did not believe that the permission of higher authority was necessary to create government, and thus in state as in religion they flew in the face of the dominant opinion of the seventeenth century. Believers in compacts did not always believe in democracy nor can the Plymouth people be said to have done so. The step, however, was but a short one, and it was taken by the settlers of the towns in Rhode Island, and, above all, by Roger Williams. He carried the idea of compact to its logical conclusion when he declared that "the foundation of civil power lies in the people" and that "a people may erect and establish what form of government seems to them most meet for their civil condition. . . ."[3] That this meant democracy was stated specifically when a General Court at Newport, Rhode Island, declared in 1641 that "the government which this body politic doth attend unto in this island . . . is a democracy or popular government. . . ." When the towns of Rhode Island formed a Confederation in 1647, they declared the government to be "democratical; that is to say, a government held by the free and voluntary consent of all, or the greater part of the free inhabitants".[4]

In the seventeenth century the implementation of such ideas was possible only in remote places far from the controls of an older society. The American frontier was such an area. There religious and political dissenters from Europe could practice their belief in the separation of Church and State and in political democracy. Towards the end of the century the Quakers were to put their weight behind the idea of religious toleration and self-government. William Penn, in founding government in Pennsylvania, was as eloquent as Roger Williams had been earlier in the century,[5] although in practice he did not go so far as the people of Rhode Island.

The concept that people may meet together and create government without permission from higher authority, although frowned upon by England and by many colonials, remained a strong current in the political and constitutional thinking of the American colonists. It was no better expressed than in Thomas Jefferson's phrases in the Declaration of Independence in 1776[6] which repeat, almost word for word, Roger Williams's declaration in 1644.[7]

Much of the political thinking of the seventeenth century had been concerned with the relationship of Church to State, and with the question of religious toleration. Early in the century men reasoned from the rightness of self-government in church

[1] No. 17.   [2] No. 14.   [3] No. 18.   [4] No. 27.   [5] Nos. 18, 19.   [6] No. 179.   [7] No. 18.

affairs to self-government in civil affairs. John Wise is a significant figure because in his defence of the self-government of the Congregational churches of New England he reasons from the assumption that democracy in politics is good, and goes on to argue that therefore democracy in church government must also be good.[1]

Political thinking in the eighteenth century produced no basic alterations in the pattern laid down during the preceding century. It represents, rather, a change in emphasis away from religious concerns to political matters, and increasingly an emphasis on the problems of the relationship between the colonies and the mother country. The revolutionary crisis after 1763 was accompanied by a flood of tracts and pamphlets reiterating many of the basic ideas set forth earlier. These ideas were embodied in the many actions and resolutions of colonial legislatures and revolutionary bodies and are included in Part VII.

17A–B. Puritan political theory

John Winthrop (1587–1649) was an English country gentleman, trained in the law, who became a part of the Puritan movement in England. When it was decided to move the Massachusetts Bay Company to New England in 1629, he was elected governor and came to Massachusetts in 1630. From then until his death he played a leading role, acting as governor, deputy-governor, and as magistrate. The Puritan leaders dominated the council of the company and were called magistrates or assistants. From the start there were disputes between the representatives of the towns and the magistrates, who sat together in meetings of the General Court. The magistrates claimed the right to veto the actions of the representatives. The dispute came to a head in 1642 when a case concerning a strayed sow was appealed to the General Court. Mistress Sherman claimed that Robert Keayne, a wealthy merchant, had killed a sow belonging to her. The merchant denied this. The majority of the deputies from the towns sided with Mistress Sherman; the majority of the magistrates sided with the merchant. In the course of the dispute Winthrop wrote his treatise on the negative vote, of which the part containing his statement on democracy is included here (17A).

The dispute between the magistrates and the deputies was settled in 1644 when it was agreed that thereafter they would sit as two bodies, each with a right to veto the legislation of the other. Thus began a two-house legislature in Massachusetts. Meanwhile, the inhabitants of the colony continued to be alarmed at the power of the magistrates. In 1645 the citizens of Hingham got into a wrangle over the election of a militia captain. The magistrates backed the losing candidate and jailed his opponents. Thereupon the citizens of the town appealed to the General Court and accused Winthrop, then deputy-governor, of exceeding his authority as magistrate. Winthrop agreed to stand trial. It lasted from May until August 1645, and was extremely bitter. In the end the Hingham offenders were fined and Winthrop was acquitted. It was upon the occasion of his acquittal that he made the speech given here, one of the classic statements of Puritan political thought (17B).

17A. John Winthrop: from "Defence of the Negative Vote" (1642)

Printed: Robert C. Winthrop, *Life and Letters of John Winthrop* (2 vols., Boston, 1869), II, pp. 429–430.

That which makes a specific difference between one form of government and another is essential and fundamental. But the negative vote in the magistrates doth so in our government; therefore it is essential and fundamental.

The assumption is proved by this, that if the negative vote were taken away, our government would be a mere democracy, whereas now it is mixed. This I prove thus:

Where the chief ordinary power and administration thereof is in the people, there is a democracy. This I prove thus: if it be in the deputies, it is in the people, but it will be in the deputies, governor, etc., for they are but the representative body of the people, and the matter lies not in the number of the people assembled, but in their power. Again the people are not bound to send their deputies, but they may come themselves, if they will. And though the magistrates be joined with them in the court,

[2] No. 20.

as they were in Athens and other popular states in Greece, etc., yet they serve but as councillors, seeing they shall have but their single votes, as every one of the people hath. Lastly the answer: himself confesseth that the deputies are the democratic part of our government.

Now if we should change from a mixed aristocracy to a mere democracy: first, we should have no warrant in Scripture for it; there was no such government in Israel.

We should hereby voluntarily abase ourselves, and deprive ourselves of that dignity which the providence of God hath put upon us, which is a manifest breach of the fifth commandment; for a democracy is among most civil nations accounted the meanest and worst of all forms of government; and therefore in writers it is branded with reproachful epithets as *Bellua mutoru capitu*, a monster, etc., and histories do record that it hath been always of least continuance and fullest of troubles.

17B. John Winthrop: speech on authority and liberty (1645)

Printed: John Winthrop, *The History of New England from 1630 to 1649* (James Savage, ed., 2 vols., Boston, 1853), II, pp. 279–282.

I suppose something may be expected from me upon this charge that is befallen me, which moves me to speak now to you; yet I intend not to intermeddle in the proceedings of the court, or with any of the persons concerned therein. Only I bless God that I see an issue of this troublesome business. I also acknowledge the justice of the court and for mine own part I am well satisfied; I was publicly charged, and I am publicly and legally acquitted, which is all I did expect or desire. And though this be sufficient for my justification before men, yet not so before the God who hath seen so much amiss in my dispensations (and even in this affair) as calls me to be humble. For to be publicly and criminally charged in this court is matter of humiliation (and I desire to make a right use of it) notwithstanding I be thus acquitted. If her father had spit in her face (saith the Lord concerning Miriam) should she not have been ashamed seven days? Shame had lien upon her, whatever the occasion had been. I am unwilling to stay you from your urgent affairs, yet give me leave (upon this special occasion) to speak a little more to this assembly. It may be of some good use to inform and rectify the judgments of some of the people, and may prevent such distempers as have arisen amongst us. The great questions that have troubled the country are about the authority of the magistrates and the liberty of the people. It is yourselves who have called us to this office, and being called by you, we have our authority from God, in way of an ordinance, such as hath the image of God eminently stamped upon it, the contempt and violation whereof hath been vindicated with examples of divine vengeance. I entreat you to consider that when you choose magistrates you take them from among yourselves, men subject to like passions as you are. Therefore when you see infirmities in us, you should reflect upon your own, and that would make you bear the more with us, and not be severe censurers of the failings of your magistrates when you have continual experience of the like infirmities in yourselves and others. We account him a good servant who breaks not his covenant. The covenant between you and us is the oath you have taken of us, which is to this purpose: that we shall govern you and judge your causes by the rules of God's laws and our own, according to our best skill. When you agree with a workman to build you a ship or house, etc., he undertakes as well for his skill as for his faithfulness, for it is his profession, and you pay him for both. But when you call one to be a magistrate, he doth not profess nor undertake to have sufficient skill for that office, nor can you furnish him with gifts, etc., therefore you must run the hazard of his skill and ability. But if he fail in faithfulness, which by his oath he is bound unto, that he must answer for. If it fall out that the case be clear to common apprehension and the rule clear also; if he transgress here, the error is not in the skill, but in the evil of the will: it must be required of him. But if the case be doubtful, or the rule doubtful, to men of such understanding and parts as your magistrates are, if your magistrates should err here, yourselves must bear it.

For the other point concerning liberty, I observe a great mistake in the country about that. There is a twofold liberty, natural (I mean as our nature is now corrupt) and civil or federal. The first is common to man with beasts and other creatures. By this, man as he stands in relation to man, simply, has liberty to do what he lists; it is a liberty to evil as well as to good. This libery is incompatible and inconsistent with authority, and cannot endure the least restraint of the most just authority. The exercise and maintaining of this liberty makes men grow more evil, and in time to be, worse than brute beasts: *omnes sumus licentia deteriores*. This is that great enemy of truth and peace, that wild beast which all the ordinances of God are bent against, to restrain and subdue it. The other kind of liberty I call civil or federal; it may also be termed moral, in reference to the covenant between God and man in the moral law, and the politic covenants and constitutions amongst men themselves. This liberty is the proper end and object of authority and cannot subsist without it, and it is a liberty to that only which is good, just, and honest. This liberty you are to stand for, with the hazard not only of your goods but of your lives, if need be. Whatsoever crosseth this is not authority but a distemper thereof. This liberty is maintained and exercised in a way of subjection to authority; it is of the same kind of liberty wherewith Christ hath made us free. The woman's own choice makes such a man her husband; yet being so chosen, he is her lord and she is to be subject to him, yet in a way of liberty, not of bondage, and a true wife accounts her subjection her honour and freedom, and would not think her condition safe and free but in her subjection to her husband's authority. Such is the liberty of the church under the authority of Christ, her king and husband; his yoke is so easy and sweet to her as a bride's ornaments; and if through forwardness or wantonness, etc., she shake it off at any time, she is at no rest in her spirit until she take it up again; and whether her lord smiles upon her and embraceth her in his arms, or whether he frowns, or rebukes, or smites her, she apprehends the sweetness of his love in all and is refreshed, supported, and instructed by every such dispensation of his authority over her. On the other side, you know who they are that complain of this yoke and say, let us break their bands, etc., we will not have this man to rule over us. Even so, brethren, it will be between you and your magistrates. If you stand for your natural corrupt liberties and will do what is good in your own eyes, you will not endure the least weight of authority, but will murmur, and oppose, and be always striving to shake off that yoke; but if you will be satisfied to enjoy such civil and lawful liberties such as Christ allows you, then will you quietly and cheerfully submit to that authority which is set over you, in all the administrations of it, for your good. Wherein, if we fail at any time we hope we shall be willing by God's assistance to hearken to good advice from any of you, or in any other way of God; so shall your liberties be preserved in upholding the honour and power of authority amongst you.

The deputy governor having ended his speech, the court arose, and the magistrates and deputies retired to attend their other affairs. Many things were observable in the agitation and proceedings about this case. It may be of use to leave a memorial of some of the most material, that our posterity and others may behold the workings of Satan to ruin the colonies and churches of Christ in New England, and into what distempers a wise and godly people may fall in times of temptation; and when such have entertained some false and plausible principles, what deformed superstructures they will raise thereupon, and with what unreasonable obstinacy they will maintain them.

18. Roger Williams: from "The Bloudy Tenent, of Persecution, for Cause of Conscience" (1644)

Roger Williams (1603 ?–1687) contributed much to the political theory of both the American colonies and the Puritan Revolution. He was born in London, the son of a merchant tailor. He came to the attention of Sir Edward Coke who helped him get an education. He went to Cambridge University in 1624 and eventually took Holy Orders. In 1629 he went as chaplain to the country estate of Sir Edward Masham in Essex. There he became the friend of men like Oliver Cromwell, John Hampden, Edward Whalley, and Sir Thomas Barrington. Later on these men were to protect him and the colony of Rhode Island. Late in 1630, already imbued with the ideas that were to make him a storm centre, he left for Massachusetts Bay.

At once he was in difficulties. He was, said John Cotton, "the first rebel against the divine church order in the wilderness". He denied that civil magistrates could punish people for not keeping the Sabbath. He insisted that the New England churches must proclaim their complete separation from the Church of England. Soon he insisted that the king of England had no right to grant away the land of the Indians and that the colonists must purchase it to have legal title. He led a successful movement to defeat the imposition of a resident's oath law. He preached the separation of Church and State.

Such ideas were anathema to the Puritan leaders, yet Williams was a man of great personal charm and had influence with important Puritans in England. Therefore the Massachusetts leaders were for a time at a loss as to what to do, but eventually he was tried and banished, the General Court declaring that his "dangerous opinions subverted the fundamental state and government of the country . . . and tended to unsettle the kingdoms and Commonwealths of Europe".

As one of the founders of Rhode Island he was able to put many of his ideas into practice, and through the rest of his long life his was the guiding hand that kept that tempestuous colony on the path that he set for it. In his many writings he upheld the ideas of freedom of conscience, the separation of Church and State, and the sovereignty of the people; and his writings had influence in both England and America.

One of his most eloquent pleas for freedom of conscience was *The Bloudy Tenent, of Persecution, for cause of Conscience, discussed in A conference betweene Truth and Peace. Who In all tender Affection, present to the High Court of Parliament, (as the Result of their Discourse) these, (amongst other Passages) of highest consideration.* It was written and published while he was in England in 1644 in his successful attempt to get a charter for Rhode Island. It appeared the same year as John Milton's *Areopagitica*, but Williams goes further than Milton in his plea for toleration for Milton would have exempted Catholics from consideration. Chapter XCII, which follows, contains Williams's basic convictions concerning the origin and nature of government, convictions which are fundamental to the idea of democracy. Printed: *Publications of the Narragansett Club* (1st Series, Providence, 1867), III, pp. 247–250.

Peace. The fourth head is the proper means of both these powers to attain their ends. First, the proper means whereby the civil power may and should attain its end are only political, and principally these five.

First, the erecting and establishing what form of civil government may seem in wisdom most meet, according to general rules of the Word and state of the people.

Secondly, the making, publishing, and establishing of wholesome civil laws, not only such as concern civil justice, but also the free passage of true religion: for outward civil peace ariseth and is maintained from them both, from the latter as well as from the former.

Civil peace cannot stand entire where religion is corrupted, 2 Chronicles, 15: 3, 5, 6; Judges, 8. And yet such laws, though conversant about religion, may still be counted civil laws, as on the contrary, an oath doth still remain religious, though conversant about civil matters.

Thirdly, election and appointment of civil officers, to see execution of those laws.

Fourthly, civil punishments and rewards of transgressors and observers of these laws.

Fifthly, taking up arms against the enemies of civil peace.

Secondly, the means whereby the church may and should attain her ends are only ecclesiastical, which are chiefly five.

First, setting up that form of church government only of which Christ hath given them a pattern in his Word.

Secondly, acknowledging and admitting of no lawgiver in the church but Christ, and the publishing of his laws.

Thirdly, electing and ordaining of such officers only as Christ hath appointed in his Word.

Fourthly, to receive into their fellowship them that are approved, and inflicting spiritual censures against them that offend.

Fifthly, prayer and patience in suffering any evil from them that be without who disturb their peace.

So that magistrates, as magistrates, have no power of setting up the form of church government, electing church officers, punishing with church censures, but to see that the church doth her duty herein. And on the other side, the churches as churches, have no power (though as members of the commonweal they may have power) of erecting or altering forms of civil government, electing of civil officers, inflicting civil punishments (no not on persons excommunicate) as by deposing magistrates from their civil authority, or withdrawing the hearts of the people against them to their laws, no more than to discharge wives, or children, or servants, from due obedience to their husbands, parents, or masters: or by taking up arms against their magistrates, though he persecute them for conscience. For though members of churches who are public officers also of the civil state may suppress by force the violence of usurpers as Iehoiada did Athaliah, yet this they do not as members of the church, but as officers of the civil state.

Truth. Here are divers considerable passages which I shall briefly examine, so far as concerns our controversy.

First, whereas they say that the civil power may erect and establish what form of civil government may seem in wisdom most meet, I acknowledge the proposition to be most true, both in itself, and also considered with the end of it, that a civil government is an ordinance of God, to conserve the civil peace of people, so far as concerns their bodies and goods, as formerly hath been said.

But from this grant I infer (as before hath been touched) that the sovereign, original, and foundation of civil power lies in the people (whom they must needs mean by the civil power distinct from the government set up). And if so, that a people may erect and establish what form of government seems to them most meet for their civil condition. It is evident that such governments as are by them erected and established have no more power, nor for no longer time, than the civil power or people consenting and agreeing shall betrust them with. This is clear not only in reason, but in the experience of all commonweals where the people are not deprived of their natural freedom by the power of tyrants.[1]

And if so, that the magistrates receive their power of governing the church from the people; undeniably it follows that a people as a people naturally considered (of what nature or nation soever in Europe, Asia, Africa, or America) have fundamentally and originally, as men, a power to govern the church, to see her do her duty, to correct her, to redress, reform, establish, etc. And if this be not to pull God and Christ and Spirit out of Heaven, and subject them to natural, sinful, inconstant men, and so consequently to Satan himself, by whom all peoples naturally are guided, let Heaven and earth judge.[2]

Peace. It cannot by their own grant be denied but that the wildest Indians in America ought (and in their kind and several degrees do) to agree upon some forms of government, some more civil, compact in towns, etc., some less. As also that their civil and earthly governments be as lawful and true as any governments in the world, and therefore consequently their governors are keepers of the church or both tables (if any church of Christ should arise or be amongst them), and therefore lastly (if Christ have betrusted and charged the civil power with his church), they must judge according to their Indian or American consciences, for other consciences it cannot be supposed they should have.[3]

19. William Penn: preface to the first Frame of Government (1682)

The political philosophy of William Penn (1644–1718), like that of Roger Williams, stemmed from his religious convictions. His father, Admiral William Penn, was a man of wealth and social standing, and a friend of James, duke of York, and of Charles II, to whom he lent large sums of money. His son soon showed signs of religious radicalism, which horrified the admiral and led to endless quarrels and reconciliations. Young Penn was thrown out of Oxford for associating with religious nonconformists. He was sent to Ireland, where he was converted to Quakerism. Once back in England he became a close associate of George Fox and an open apostle of Quakerism. This led to repeated arrests and imprisonments. He was involved in Fox's plans for Quaker colonization, and was one of the proprietors of West Jersey.

---

[1] Civil power originally and fundamentally in the people. [Williams's marginal note.]

[2] Mr. Cotton and the New-English ministers give the government of Christ's church or spouse into the hands of the people or commonweal. [Williams's marginal note.]

[3] The very Indian Americans made governors of the church by the authors of these positions. [Williams's marginal note.]

When his father died, he inherited the estate, which included the large debt owed to it by Charles II. The king granted Pennsylvania to William Penn in payment of the debt, and named the province Pennsylvania in honour of the admiral. William Penn looked upon the founding of the colony as an opportunity to carry out what he called a "Holy Experiment": a colony devoted to the ideal of religious freedom. The development of the government of the colony was an experimental process in which Penn showed his complete lack of doctrinaire conviction as to forms of government. The 'Preface' to the 'first frame' of government in 1682 which follows, is a clear statement of Penn's basic political convictions. Printed: *Minutes of the Provincial Council of Pennsylvania* (10 vols., Philadelphia and Harrisburg, 1852–1853), I, pp. 29–32.

When the great and wise God had made the world, of all his creatures it pleased him to choose man his deputy to rule it, and to fit him for so great a charge and trust he did not only qualify him with skill and power, but with integrity to use them justly. This native goodness was equally his honour and his happiness, and whilst he stood here, all went well; there was no need of coercive or compulsive means; the precept of divine love and truth in his bosom was the guide and keeper of his innocency. But lust prevailing against duty, made a lamentable breach upon it, and the law that before had no power over him, took place upon him and his disobedient posterity, that such as would not live conformable to the holy law within, should fall under the reproof and correction of the just law without, in a judicial administration.

This the apostle teaches us in divers of his epistles. The law (says he) was added because of transgression; in another place, knowing that the law was not made for the righteous man but for the disobedient and ungodly, for sinners, for unholy and profane, for murderers, for whoremongers, for them that defile themselves with mankind, and for menstealers, for liars, for perjured persons, etc. But this is not all. He opens and carries the matter of government a little further: let every soul be subject to the higher powers for there is no power but of God. The powers that be are ordained of God: whosoever therefore resisteth the power, resisteth the ordinance of God. For rulers are not a terror to good works, but to evil; wilt thou then not be afraid of the power? Do that which is good, and thou shalt have praise of the same. He is the minister of God to thee for good. Wherefore ye must needs be subject, not only for wrath, but for conscience' sake.

This settles the divine right of government beyond exception, and that for two ends: first, to terrify evil-doers; secondly, to cherish those that do well, which gives government a life beyond corruption and makes it as durable in the world as good men shall be. So that government seems to me a part of religion itself, a thing sacred in its institution and end. For if it does not directly remove the cause, it crushes the effects of evil, and is as such (though a lower yet) an emanation of the same Divine Power that is both author and object of pure religion; the difference lying here, that the one is more free and mental, the other more corporal and compulsive in its operations, but that is only to evil-doers; government itself being otherwise as capable of kindness, goodness and charity as a more private society. They weakly err that think there is no other use of government than correction, which is the coarsest part of it; daily experience tells us that the care and regulation of many other affairs more soft and daily necessary make up much the greatest part of government and which must have followed the peopling of the world had Adam never fell, and will continue among men on earth under the highest attainments they may arrive at, by the coming of the blessed second Adam, the Lord from heaven. Thus much of government in general, as to its rise and end.

For particular frames and models it will become me to say little, and comparatively I will say nothing. My reasons are: first, that the age is too nice and difficult for it, there being nothing the wits of men are more busy and divided upon. 'Tis true, they seem to agree in the end, to wit, happiness, but in the means they differ as to divine, so to this human felicity, and the cause is much the same, not always want of light and knowledge, but want of using them rightly. Men side with their passions against their reason, and their sinister interests have so strong a bias upon their minds that they lean to them against the good of the things they know.

Secondly, I do not find a model in the world that time, place, and some singular emergences have not necessarily altered; nor is it easy to frame a civil government that shall serve all places alike.

Thirdly, I know what is said by the several admirers of monarchy, aristocracy and democracy, which are the rule of one, a few, and many, and are the three common ideas of government, when men discourse on that subject. But I choose to solve the controversy with this small distinction, and it belongs to all three: any government is free to the people under it (whatever be the frame) where the laws rule, and the people are a party to those laws, and more than this is tyranny, oligarchy, and confusion.

But lastly, when all is said, there is hardly one frame of government in the world so ill designed by its first founders that in good hands would not do well enough, and story tells us the best in ill ones can do nothing that is great or good; witness the Jewish and Roman states. Governments, like clocks, go from the motion men give them, and as governments are made and moved by men, so by them they are ruined too. Wherefore governments rather depend upon men than men upon governments. Let men be good, and the government cannot be bad; if it be ill, they will cure it. But if men be bad, let the government be never so good, they will endeavour to warp and spoil to their turn.

I know some say, let us have good laws and no matter for the men that execute them. But let them consider that though good laws do well, good men do better; for good laws may want good men, and be abolished or invaded by ill men; but good men will never want good laws, nor suffer ill ones. 'Tis true, good laws have some awe upon ill ministers, but that is where they have not power to escape or abolish them, and the people are generally wise and good; but a loose and depraved people (which is to the question) love laws and an administration like themselves. That, therefore, which makes a good constitution, must keep it; viz., men of wisdom and virtue, qualities that because they descend not with worldly inheritances, must be carefully propagated by a virtuous education of youth, for which after ages will owe more to the care and prudence of founders, and the successive magistracy, than to their parents for their private patrimonies.

These considerations of the weight of government, and the nice and various opinions about it, made it uneasy to me to think of publishing the ensuing frame and conditional laws, foreseeing both the censures they will meet with from men of differing humours and engagements, and the occasion they may give of discourse beyond my design.

But next to the power of necessity (which is a solicitor that will take no denial) this induced me to a compliance that we have (with reverence to God and good conscience to men) to the best of our skill, contrived and composed the FRAME and LAWS of this government to the great end of all government, viz., to support power in reverence with the people and to secure the people from the abuse of power, that they may be free by their just obedience, and the magistrates honourable for their just administration; for liberty without obedience is confusion, and obedience without liberty is slavery. To carry this evenness is partly owing to the constitution, and partly to the magistracy; where either of these fail, government will be subject to convulsions; but where both are wanting, it must be totally subverted: then where both meet, the government is like to endure. Which I humbly pray and hope God will please to make the lot of this of Pennsylvania.

20. John Wise: from "A Vindication of the Government of New England Churches" (1717)

John Wise (1652?–1725), was graduated from Harvard in 1673, and from 1680 until his death was pastor of the second church at Ipswich, Massachusetts. He distinguished himself during the Dominion of New England by telling his people to refuse to pay the taxes levied by the Andros régime, and was imprisoned. Early in the eighteenth century there was a movement on foot, led by a group of Congregational clergymen, to overthrow the congregational system of church government and to replace it with a presbyterian organization. Wise opposed the movement and wrote two books defending the congregational form of church government. In 1712 he published *The Churches Quarrel Espoused* and in 1717 *A Vindication of the Government of New England Churches.* Historically, he justifies the congregational form because it had been established by the founding fathers of New England. But he goes beyond this and declares that democracy in church and state are according to the dictates of 'right reason'. Whatever his personal political convictions, his writing is in the tradition of Roger Williams and William Penn and is a link between them and the theorists of the Revolutionary era. Printed: John Wise, *A Vindication of the Government of New England Churches* (4th ed., Boston, 1860), pp. 37–45.

2. To consider man in a civil state of being wherein we shall observe the great difference between a natural and political state; for in the latter state many great disproportions appear, or at least many obvious distinctions are soon made amongst men, which doctrine is to be laid open under a few heads.

(1) Every man, considered in a natural state, must be allowed to be free and at his own disposal; yet to suit man's inclinations to society, and in a peculiar manner to gratify the necessity he is in of public rule and order he is impelled to enter into a civil community, and divests himself of his natural freedom, and puts himself under government, which, amongst other things, comprehends the power of life and death over him, together with authority to enjoin him some things to which he has an utter aversion, and to prohibit him other things for which he may have as strong an inclination–so that he may be often, under this authority, obliged to sacrifice his private for the public good; so that though man is inclined to society, yet he is driven to a combination by great necessity. For that the true and leading cause of forming governments and yielding up natural liberty, and throwing man's equality into a common pile to be new cast by the rules of fellowship, was really and truly to guard

themselves against the injuries men were liable to interchangeably; for none so good to man as man, and yet none a greater enemy. So that,

(2) The first human subject and original of civil power is the people; for as they have a power every man over himself in a natural state, so upon a combination they can and do bequeath this power unto others, and settle it according as their united discretion shall determine. For that this is very plain, that when the subject of sovereign power is quite extinct, that power returns to the people again. And when they are free, they may set up what species of government they please; or if they rather incline to it, they may subside into a state of natural being, if it be plainly for the best. In the eastern country of the Mogul, we have some resemblance of the case, for upon the death of an absolute monarch they live so many days without a civil head; but in that interregnum those who survive the vacancy are glad to get into a civil state again, and usually they are in a very bloody condition when they return under the covert of a new monarch; this project is to endear the people to a tyranny from the experience they have so lately had of an anarchy.

(3) The formal reason of government is the will of a community yielded up and surrendered to some other subject, either of one particular person or more, conveyed in the following manner.

Let us conceive in our mind a multitude of men, all naturally free and equal, going about voluntarily to erect themselves into a new commonwealth. Now their condition being such, to bring themselves into a politic body they must needs enter into divers covenants.

1. They must interchangeably each man covenant to join in one lasting society, that they may be capable to concert the measures of their safety by a public vote.

2. A vote or decree must then nextly pass to set up some particular species of government over them. And if they are joined in their first compact upon absolute terms to stand to the decision of the first vote concerning the species of government, then all are bound by the majority to acquiesce in that particular form thereby settled, though their own private opinions incline them to some other model.

3. After a decree has specified the particular form of government, then there will be need of a new covenant whereby those on whom sovereignty is conferred engage to take care of the common peace and welfare; and the subjects, on the other hand, to yield them faithful obedience; in which covenant is included that submission and union of wills by which a state may be conceived to be but one person. So that the most proper definition of a civil state is this, namely: A civil state is a compound moral person whose will (united by those covenants before passed) is the will of all, to the end it may use and apply the strength and riches of private persons towards maintaining the common peace, security, and well-being of all, which may be conceived as though the whole state was now become but one man; in which the aforesaid covenants may be supposed, under God's providence, to be the divine fiat pronounced by God, "Let us make man." And by way of resemblance the aforesaid being may be thus anatomized.

(1) The sovereign power is the soul infused, giving life and motion to the whole body.

(2) Subordinate officers are the joints by which the body moves.

(3) Wealth and riches are the strength.

(4) Equity and laws are the reason.

(5) Counsellors the memory.

(6) *Salus Populi*, or the happiness of the people is the end of its being, or main business to be attended and done.

(7) Concord amongst the members and all estates, is the health.

(8) Sedition is sickness, and civil war death.

4. The parts of sovereignty may be considered thus:

(1) As it prescribes the rule of action, it is rightly termed legislative power.

(2) As it determines the controversies of subjects by the standard of those rules, so is it justly termed judiciary power.

(3) As it arms the subjects against foreigners, or forbids hostility, so it is called the power of peace and war.

(4) As it takes in ministers for the discharge of business, so it is called the right of appointing magistrates. So that all great officers and public servants must needs owe their original to the creating power of sovereignty; so that those whose right it is to create may dissolve the being of those who are created, unless they cast them into an immortal frame, and yet must needs be dissoluble if they justly forfeith their being to their creators.

(5) The chief end of civil communities is that men thus conjoined may be secured against the injuries they are liable to from their own kind; for if every man could secure himself singly, it would be great folly for him to renounce his natural liberty, in which every man is his own king and protector.

(6) The sovereign authority, besides that it inheres in every state as in a common and general subject, so further according as it resides in some one person, or in a council (consisting of some select persons, or of all the members of a community) as in a proper and particular subject, so it produceth different forms of commonwealths, namely, such as are either simple and regular, or mixed.

The forms of a regular state are three only, which forms arise from the proper and particular subject in which the supreme power resides. As,

1. A democracy, which is when the sovereign power is lodged in a council consisting of all the members, and where every member has the privilege of a vote. This form of government appears in the greatest part of the world to have been the most ancient. For that reason seems to show it to be most probable that when men (being originally in a condition of natural freedom and equality) had thoughts of joining in a civil body, would without question be inclined to administer their common affairs by their common judgment, and so must necessarily, to gratify that inclination, establish a democracy; neither can it be rationally imagined that fathers of families being yet free and independent, should in a moment, or little time, take off their long delight in governing their own affairs and devolve all upon some single sovereign commander; for that it seems to have been thought more equitable that what belonged to all should be managed by all, when all had entered by compact into one community. The original of our government, says Plato (speaking of the

Athenian commonwealth) was taken from the equality of our race. Other states there are composed of different blood, and of unequal lines, the consequences of which are disproportionable sovereignty, tyrannical or oligarchical sway, under which men live in such a manner as to esteem themselves partly lords and partly slaves to each other. But we and our countrymen, being all born brethren of the same mother, do not look upon ourselves to stand under so hard a relation as that of lords and slaves; but the parity of our descent inclines us to keep up the like parity by our laws, and to yield the precedency to nothing but to superior virtue and wisdom. And moreover, it seems very manifest that most civil communities arose at first from the union of families that were nearly allied in race and blood. And though ancient story makes frequent mention of kings, yet it appears that most of them were such that had an influence rather in persuading, than in any power of commanding. So Justin describes that kind of government as the most primitive which Aristotle styles an heroical kingdom, namely, such as is no ways inconsistent with a democratical state. De Princip. Reru. I.L. I.C.

A democracy is then erected when a number of free persons do assemble together in order to enter into a covenant for uniting themselves in a body. And such a preparative assembly hath some appearance already of a democracy; it is a democracy in embryo properly in this respect: that every man hath the privilege freely to deliver his opinion concerning the common affairs. Yet he who dissents from the vote of the majority is not in the least obliged by what they determine till by a second covenant a popular form be actually established, for not before then can we call it a democratical government, namely, till the right of determining all matters relating to the public safety is actually placed in a general assembly of the whole people; or by their own compact and mutual agreement, determine themselves the proper subject for the exercise of sovereign power. And to complete this state and render it capable to exert its power to answer the end of a civil state, these conditions are necessary.

(1) That a certain time and place be assigned for assembling.

(2) That when the assembly be orderly met as to time and place, that then the vote of the majority must pass for the vote of the whole body.

(3) That magistrates be appointed to exercise the authority of the whole for the better dispatch of business of every day's occurrence; who also may with more mature diligence search into more important affairs, and if in case anything happens of greater consequence, may report it to the assembly; and be peculiarly serviceable in putting all public decrees into execution. Because a large body of people is almost useless in respect of the last service and of many others, as to the more particular application and exercise of power. Therefore it is most agreeable with the law of nature that they institute their officers to act in their name and stead.

2. The second species of regular government is an aristocracy; and this is said then to be constituted when the people, or assembly united by a first covenant, and having thereby cast themselves into the first rudiments of a state, do then, by common decree, devolve the sovereign power on a council consisting of some select members; and

these having accepted of the designation, are then properly invested with sovereign command, and then an aristocracy is formed.

3. The third species of a regular government is a monarchy, which is settled when the sovereign power is conferred on some one worthy person. It differs from the former because a monarch who is but one person in natural as well as in moral account, and so is furnished with an immediate power of exercising sovereign command in all instances of government; but the forenamed must needs have particular time and place assigned, but the power and authority is equal in each.

B. THE CONSTITUTIONAL BASES OF COLONIAL GOVERNMENTS

FROM the British point of view government in the colonies could exist only as a result of grants from the Crown. At first the power to create government in the colonies was given to the holders of corporation and proprietary charters who could govern as they pleased, subject to certain general restrictions set forth in their charters.[1] The result was a considerable amount of experimentation before a relatively stable pattern of government evolved. Eventually, governments were to be created directly through the issuance of royal commissions and instructions to the governors appointed for the colonies taken over by the Crown.[2]

Under the charter of 1606 Virginia was governed by a resident council appointed by the Crown. From 1609 to 1619 the colony was under the absolute control of a series of governors appointed by the Virginia Company in London. The colonists were increasingly discontented, particularly with the corrupt and tyrannical rule of Samuel Argall, who was governor from 1617 to 1619. A change in control of the company brought about a change in policy towards the colony. Sir Edward Sandys is usually given credit for this change, which involved the creation of the first legislative assembly in the New World.

In 1618 the company drew up a 'charter' for the colony and sent it out with Sir George Yeardley, who went to replace Argall as governor. This charter has been lost, but it is presumed that the ordinance of 1621 is more or less similar in character.[3] Yeardley arrived in the spring of 1619. He issued a proclamation freeing the colonists from public service, abrogating the "cruel laws" by which they had been governed, and declaring that the colonists were "now governed by those free laws which his Majesty's subjects live under in England". The proclamation went on to state that "in order that they might have a hand in the governing of themselves . . . a general assembly should be held yearly once, whereat were to be present the governor and council with two burgesses freely to be elected by the inhabitants thereof: this assembly to have power to make and ordain whatsoever laws and orders should by them be thought good and profitable for our subsistence". The assembly met at Jamestown, 30 July 1619.[4]

In effect the company set up a duplicate of its own organization except that the governor and council in the colony were appointed by the company. In 1624 the charter of the company was annulled. The next year Charles I issued a proclamation in which he declared that the aim of King James had been to "reduce that government into such a right course, as might best agree with that form which has held in the rest of his royal monarchy. . . ." Furthermore, he proclaimed that the government of Virginia "shall immediately depend on ourself" and not be committed to any company or corporation "to whom it may be proper to trust matters of trade and commerce, but cannot be fit or safe to communicate the ordering of state affairs, be they of never so mean consequence. . . ."[5]

However, no settled form of government was agreed upon at first. The king continued to appoint governors as the company had done. Various commissions

[1] See Part I, A: Colonial Charters.　　[2] Nos. 22, 24, 25.　　[3] No. 21.　　[4] No. 39.　　[5] No. 29.

investigated the problem, but the idea of an elected assembly was not at first accepted. However, the colonists in petition after petition asked for the continuation of the assembly. Furthermore, the governors called the colonists in for consultation from time to time. Finally, in 1638, when Sir Francis Wyatt was sent out as governor, he was authorized to call an assembly. In 1642 Sir William Berkeley was sent out as governor and he was instructed to call an assembly "as formerly, once a year or oftener".[1] Thus the pattern of government established by the Virginia Company in 1619 was at last accepted by the Crown. In the future, as other colonies were brought under royal control, the framework established in Virginia provided the precedent for their governments.

The same development took place in the proprietary colonies. Lord Baltimore was required to call his colonists together to 'assent' to his legislation, but he had no intention of allowing a semi-independent legislative assembly. Yet one developed in Maryland. The colonists pointed to English precedents, they had the example of Virginia across the river from them, and in time they won out over the proprietor. The proprietors of Carolina promised a representative assembly as one of the inducements to prospective colonists. William Penn, as we have seen, had profound convictions as to the nature of government.[2] Furthermore, his charter gave him the power to make laws "by and with the advice, assent, and approbation of the freemen of the said country, or the greater part of them, or of their delegates or deputies. . . ."[3] After considerable experimentation with constitutions, his Charter of Privileges in 1701[4] provided a framework of government which was to serve as the constitution of the colony until 1776.

With the exception of Virginia, which was given a royal charter in 1676, the colonies which came under royal control did not receive charters. Instead, the framework of government was embodied in the commissions issued to royal governors when they were appointed to a colony. The form of these commissions was virtually the same for all colonies by the eighteenth century.[5] They were supplemented by elaborate instructions which were issued when commissions were granted.[6] These commissions and instructions functioned as constitutions for the royal colonies. This was formally recognized by a court decision in 1764, which held that such documents had the same force as a charter, and that the rights granted to the colonists, such as that to a local legislature, could not be revoked arbitrarily by the Privy Council.[7]

There was never any agreement, however, between England and the colonists as to the precise nature of 'right' in the case of the colonial legislatures. The colonists held that it was a right which they had as Englishmen, and that the commissions and instructions were merely recognition of that right and that the colonial legislature was an equal and independent part of government. English officials held, on the other hand, that the colonial legislatures were the creation of the Crown and could have no powers other than those granted in the commissions and instructions.[8] In practice, whatever the theory, the colonial legislatures did play an independent role, and increasingly so in the eighteenth century.

In the case of corporation colonies the situation was entirely different. The Massachusetts Bay Company charter was moved to the colony. The trading company charter gave all governmental power to the members of the corporation. The only

---

[1] No. 22. [2] No. 19. [3] No. 4. [4] No. 23. [5] No. 24. [6] No. 25.
[7] Louise P. Kellogg, "The American Colonial Charter", in American Historical Association, *Annual Report* (1903), I, p. 209.
[8] Leonard W. Labaree, *Royal Government in America* (New Haven, 1930), pp. 174–175.

problem therefore was the extent to which membership was extended to the colonists. The Puritan leaders of Massachusetts Bay possessed a constitution which was essentially democratic in structure but they had no intention of allowing anything that smacked of democratic rule.[1] They therefore adopted the device of church membership as a prerequisite to citizenship in an effort to keep the control of the colony in the hands of the Puritan leaders. Connecticut and Rhode Island, in their charters of 1661 and 1663, were established as corporations, and the governmental powers in those colonies remained in the hands of the voters throughout the colonial period.

While, in the strictest sense, no government could exist in the colonies without a grant from the Crown, there did exist in the colonies from the start a concept and a practice which assumed that there was a more basic foundation of society and government than that offered by grants from higher authority. This was the essentially democratic idea that people could associate voluntarily together in the formation of government by means of a compact. This idea was one of the great contributions of English religious dissenters to America. It was an idea which men such as Robert Browne had maintained was the only true basis of church government, and the transfer from the religious sphere was easy. This was the case of the Separatists on the *Mayflower*, who arrived at Massachusetts Bay in the autumn of 1620. The "Pilgrim Fathers" drew up a compact which all men on board were required to sign. Bradford in his history explained that the compact was occasioned partly by the "discontented and mutinous speeches" of some of the "strangers" on board, who insisted they would be free to do as they pleased once on shore since they were outside of Virginia, from which the Separatists had a patent; and "partly that such an act by them done (this their condition considered) might be as firm as any patent, and in some respects more sure".[2] The Separatists thus made an easy transition from a church compact to a simple document, which was the only basis of government in Plymouth until it was absorbed by Massachusetts Bay by the charter of 1691.

The settlers of the towns in Connecticut acted upon the same assumption when in 1639 they met and agreed to "associate and conjoin ourselves to be as one public state or commonwealth. . . ."[3] The founders of the several towns in Rhode Island likewise acted on the assumption that compacts among themselves were the only necessary basis for valid government.[4] When they did agree to seek a charter from the government of England in 1644, it was not because they had changed their convictions, but because they were convinced they needed protection from their neighbours in Massachusetts, Plymouth, and Connecticut.

As the colonies grew, there was ever more evidence of growing self-consciousness and of an insistence that the colonies had 'rights' of which they could not be deprived legally. The colonists of New York had had no experience whatsoever with self-government, yet when at last a legislative assembly was called by the duke of York in 1683, the members of the legislature at once drafted a "Charter of Liberties and Privileges". Implicit in these is the assumption that the 'rights' of Englishmen are inherent rights, not a gift from higher authority.[5] This 'Charter' is not a constitution in any strict sense of the word, yet it does set forth a 'constitutional' platform to which the inhabitants of New York, like those of the other colonies, were to adhere throughout the colonial period.

The concern with a specific written document as the basis of government, whether it was a charter from the Crown, a compact, or the commission of a royal governor,

[1] No. 17.   [2] No. 14.   [3] No. 26.   [4] See Introduction, Part II, A.   [5] No. 28.

firmly implanted in American colonial thought the idea of a single written constitution as the basis of government. When the Revolution came, Americans regarded the drafting of constitutions as one of the most important things they had to do, and to many of them the nature of the constitutions to be written seemed as important as fighting the War for Independence.

21. Ordinance for Virginia (24 July 1621)

The "Great Charter" of 1618, authorizing the calling of an assembly in 1619, has been lost. It is presumed that the Ordinance of 1621 is essentially the same. Printed: Hening, *Statutes . . . of Virginia*, I, pp. 110–113.

I. To all people to whom these presents shall come, be seen, or heard, the Treasurer, Council, and Company of Adventurers and Planters for the City of London for the first Colony of Virginia, send greeting. Know ye that we, the said treasurer, council, and company, taking into our careful consideration the present state of the said Colony of Virginia, and intending, by the divine assistance, to settle such a form of government there as may be to the greatest benefit and comfort of the people, and whereby all injustice, grievances, and oppression may be prevented and kept off as much as possible from the said colony, have thought fit to make our entrance, by ordering and establishing such supreme councils as may not only be assisting to the governor for the time being in the administration of justice, and the executing of other duties to this office belonging but also by their vigilant care and prudence may provide as well for a remedy of all inconveniences growing from time to time, as also for advancing of increase, strength, stability, and prosperity of the said colony.

II. We therefore, the said treasurer, council, and company, by authority directed to us from his Majesty under the great seal, upon mature deliberation, do hereby order and declare, that from hence forward there shall be two supreme councils in Virginia, for the better government of the said colony aforesaid.

III. The one of which councils to be called the Council of State (and whose office shall chiefly be assisting with their care, advice, and circumspection, to the said governor) shall be chosen, nominated, placed, and displaced, from time to time, by us, the said treasurer, council, and company, and our successors: which Council of State shall consist, for the present, only of these persons, as are here inserted, viz. Sir Francis Wyatt, governor of Virginia; Captain Francis West; Sir George Yeardley, knight; Sir William Neuce, knight, marshal of Virginia; Mr. George Sandys, treasurer; Mr. George Thorpe, deputy of the college; Captain Thomas Neuce, deputy for the company; Mr. Powlet, Mr. Leech, Captain Nathaniel Powel, Mr. Christopher Davidson, secretary; Doctor Potts, physician to the company; Mr. Roger Smith; Mr. John Berkeley; Mr. John Rolfe; Mr. Ralph Hamer; Mr. John Pountis; Mr. Michael Lapworth; Mr. Harwood; Mr. Samuel Macock. Which said councillors and Council we earnestly pray and desire, and in his Majesty's name strictly charge and command, that (all factions, partialities, and sinister respect laid aside) they bend their care and endeavours to assist the said governor; first and principally in the advancement of the honour and service of God, and the enlargement of his kingdom against the heathen people; and next, in erecting of the said colony in due obedience to his Majesty, and all lawful authority from his Majesty's directions; and lastly, in maintaining the said people in justice and Christian conversation amongst themselves, and in strength and ability to withstand their enemies. And this council to be always, or for the most part, residing about or near the governor.

IV. The other council, more generally to be called by the governor once yearly, and no oftener, but for very extraordinary and important occasions, shall consist for the present, of the said Council of State, and of two burgesses out of every town, hundred, or other particular plantation, to be respectively chosen by the inhabitants: which council shall be called the General Assembly, wherein (as also in the said Council of State) all matters shall be decided, determined, and ordered, by the greater part of the voices then present; reserving to the governor always a negative voice. And this General Assembly shall have free power to treat, consult, and conclude, as well of all emergent occasions concerning the public weal of the said colony and every part thereof, as also to make, ordain, and enact such general laws and orders for the behoof of the said colony, and the good government thereof, as shall, from time to time, appear necessary or requisite.

V. Whereas, in all other things we require the said General Assembly, as also the said Council of State, to imitate and follow the policy of the form of government, laws, customs, and manner of trial, and other administration of justice used in the realm of England, as near as may be, even as ourselves, by his Majesty's letters patent, are required.

VI. Provided, that no law or ordinance, made in the said General Assembly, shall be or continue in force or validity, unless the same shall be solemnly ratified and confirmed in a general quarter court of the said company here in England and so ratified, be returned to them under our seal; it being our intent to afford the like measure also unto the said colony, that after the government of the said colony shall once have been well framed and settled accordingly, which is to be done by us, as by authority derived from his Majesty, and the same shall have been so by us declared, no orders of court afterwards, shall bind the said colony unless they be ratified in like manner in the general assemblies. In witness whereof we have hereunto set our common seal the 24th of July, 1621.

22. Instructions to Sir William Berkeley as governor of Virginia (1642)

The instructions to Sir Francis Wyatt, 1639, authorized him to call an assembly as the company had done. The instructions to Berkeley confirm those to Wyatt. Thereafter, although instructions were to become increasingly elaborate, there is no change in the essential character of the structure of government in royal colonies except for the interlude of the Dominion of New England (No. 30). Printed: *The Virginia Magazine of History and Biography*, II (1894–1895), pp. 281–288.

That in the first place you be careful Almighty God may be duly and daily served according to the form of religion established in the Church of England both by yourself and all the people under your charge, which may draw down a blessing on all your endeavours. And let every congregation that hath an able minister build for him a convenient parsonage house, to which for his better maintenance over and above the usual pension you lay 200 acres of glebeable lands; for the clearing of that ground every of his parishioners for three years shall give some days labours of themselves and their servants, and see that you have a special care that the glebe land be set as near the parsonage house as may be and that it be of the best conditioned land. Suffer no invasion in matters of religion and be careful to appoint sufficient and conformable ministers to each congregation, that you catechise and instruct them in the grounds and principles of religion.

2. That you administer the Oaths of Allegiance and Supremacy to all such as come thither with intention to plant themselves in the country, which if he shall refuse he is to be returned and shipped from thence home and certificate made to the Lords of the Council; the same oath is to be administered to all other persons when you shall see it fit, as mariners, merchants, etc., to prevent any danger of spies.

3. That justice be equally administered to all his Majesty's subjects there residing and as near as may be after the form of this realm of England, and vigilant care to be had to prevent corruption in officers tending to the delay or perverting of justice.

4. That you and the councillors, as formerly once a year or oftener, if urgent occasion shall require, do summon the burgesses of all and singular plantations there, which together with the Governor and Council makes the Grand Assembly, and shall have power to make acts and laws for the government of that plantation correspondent, as near as may be, to the laws of England, in which assembly the governor is to have a negative voice, as formerly.

That you and the Council assembled are to set down the fittest months of the quarterly meeting of the Council of State, whereas they are to give their attendance for one and consult upon matter of council and state and to decide and determine such causes as shall come before them, and that free access be admitted to all suitors to make known their particular grievances, being against what persons soever, wherein the governor for the time being, as formerly, is to have but a casting voice if the number of the councillors should be equally divided in opinion; besides the quarterly meeting of the Council it shall be lawful for you to summon from time to time extraordinary meetings of the Council according to emergent occasions.

6. In case there shall be necessary cause to proceed against any of the Council for their own persons, they are in such cases to be summoned by you the governor to appear at the next sessions of the Council holden there to abide their censure; or otherwise, if you shall think it may concern either the safety or quiet of that state to proceed more speedily with such an offender, it shall be lawful to summon a council extraordinary whereat six of the Council at least are to be present with you, and by the major part of their voices commit my councillors to safe custody or upon bail to abide the order of the next quarter Council.

7. For the ease of the country and quicker despatch of business, you, the governor and Council, may appoint in places convenient, inferior courts of justice and commissioners for the same, to determine of suits not exceeding the value of ten pounds, and for the punishments of such offences as you and the Council shall think fit to give them the power to hear and determine.

8. The governor shall appoint officers of sealing of writs and subpoenas and such officers as shall be thought necessary for the execution [of] orders.

And also the acts and laws of the General Assembly and for punishing any neglect or contempt of the said orders, acts, or laws respectively. And shall nominate and appoint all other public officers under the degree of the Council, the captain of the fort, master and surveyor-general excepted.

9. That since the Council attend his Majesty's service and the public business to the great hindrance of the private, that they and ten servants for every councillor be exempted from all public charges and contributions assessed and levied by the General Assembly (a war defensive, assistance towards the building of a town or churches, or the ministers' dues excepted).

10. To avoid all questions concerning the estates of persons dying in Virginia, it shall be lawful as it hath been used heretofore, to make probates of wills and, [in] default of a will, to grant letters of administration in the colony : provided always that such to whom administration is granted do put in sufficient security to be accountable to such persons in England or elsewhere unto whom of right those estates shall belong. And that such probate of wills and letters of administration shall be and abide in full force and virtue to all intents and purposes.

11. To the end the country may be the better served against all hostile invasions it is requisite that all persons from the age of 16 to 60 be armed with arms, both offensive and defensive. And if any person be defective in this kind, we strictly charge you to command them to provide themselves of sufficient arms within one year or sooner, if possible it may be done, and if any shall fail to be armed at the end of the term limited, we will that you punish them severely.

12. And for that arms without the knowledge of the use of them are of no effect, we ordain that there be one muster master general, appointed by us for the colony, who shall 4 times in the year and oftener (if cause be) not only view the arms, ammunition, and furniture of every person in the colony, but also train and exercise the people, touching the use and order of arms, and shall also certify the defects, if any be, either of appearance or otherwise, to you the governor and Council. And being informed that the place is vacant by the death of George Dunn, we do nominate and appoint our trusty and beloved John West, Esq., being recommended to us for his sufficiency and long experience in the country, to be muster master of the said colony. And for his competent maintenance we will that you, the governor and Council, so order the business at a General Assembly that every plantation be rated equally according to the number of persons, wherein you are to follow the course practised in the realm of England.

13. That you cause likewise 10 guarders to be maintained for the port at Point Comfort. And that you take course that the captain of the said port have a competent allowance for his services there. Also that the said fort be well kept in reparation and provided with ammunition.

14. That newcomers be exempted the first year from going in person or contributing to the wars save only in defence of the place where they shall inhabit and that only when the enemies shall assail them, but all others in the colony shall go or be rated to the maintenance of the war proportionately to their abilities; neither shall any man be privileged for going to the war that is above 16 years old and under 60,

respect being had to the quality of the person, that officers be not forced to go as private soldiers or in places inferior to their degrees, unless in case of supreme necessity.

15. That you may better avoid and prevent the treachery of the savages, we strictly forbid all persons whatsoever to receive into their houses the person of any Indian or to converse or trade with them without the especial licence and warrant given to that purpose according to the commissioner, inflicting severe punishment upon the offenders.

16. For preventing of all surprises, as well as of the treacherous savages as of any foreign enemy, we require you to erect beacons in several parts of the countries by firing whereof the country may take notice of their attempts of their beacons or their watching them to bear the charge of the country as shall be determined by a General Assembly, or otherwise, by the shooting off 3 pieces, whereby they may take the alarm as shall be found most convenient.

17. That for raising of towns everyone ye [who] have and shall have a grant of 500 acres of land, shall within a convenient time, build a convenient house of brick of 24 feet long and 16 feet broad, with a cellar to it, and so proportionately for grants of larger or lesser quantity. And the grounds and platforms for the towns to be laid out in such form and order as the governor and Council shall appoint. And that you cause at the public charge of the country a convenient house to be built where you and the Council may meet and sit for the dispatching of public affairs and hearing of causes. And because the buildings at James Town are for the most part decayed and the place found to be unhealthy and inconvenient in many respects, it shall be in the power of you and the Council, with the advice of the General Assembly, to choose such other seat for your chief town and residence of the governor as by them shall be judged most convenient, retaining the ancient name of James Town.

18. That you shall have power to grant patents and to assign such proportion of land to all adventurers and planters as have been useful heretofore in the like cases, either for adventurers of money, transportation of people thither, according to the orders of the late company and since allowed by his Majesty.

And that there likewise be the same proportion of fifty acres of land granted and assigned for every person transported thither since midsummer, 1625. And that you continue the same course to all persons transported thither until it shall be otherwise determined by his Majesty.

19. Whereas the greatest part of the land on James River hath been formerly granted unto particular persons or public society, but being by them either not planted at all or for many years deserted, divers planters have by orders and leave of the governor and Council of Virginia set down upon these lands or some part of them which was absolutely necessary for the defence and security of the colony against the Indians, that the governor confirm those lands to the present planters and possessors thereof. And that the like course be taken for planting new patents in any other places so unplanted and deserted as aforesaid where it shall be found necessary. And in case former proprietors make their claims thereunto that there be assigned to them the like quantities in any other part of the colony not actually possessed where they shall make choice.

20. That you call for the charter parties that masters of ships bring along with and strictly examine whether they have truly performed the conditions of their contracts. And further, diligently to inquire and examine whether they have given sufficient and wholesome food and drink with convenient room to the passengers during the voyage. And that no servants be discharged the ships and turned ashore as formerly until their masters have notice and sufficient time to send for them. And that upon complaint in any of these particulars you give such redress as justice shall require.

21. That in regard you may daily expect the coming of a foreign enemy, we require you soon after the first landing, that you publish by proclamation throughout the colony that no person whatsoever upon the arrival of any ships shall dare to go on board without the express warrant from you, the governor and Council, lest by the means they be surprised to the great prejudice, if not the overthrow, of the plantation.

22. And to avoid that intolerable abuse of engrossing commodities, of forestalling the market, that you require all masters of ships not to break bulk until they arrive off Saint James city, or otherwise without special orders from you, the governor and Council, and that care be taken that there be sufficient storehouses and warehouses for the same and convenient laying of their goods as they shall arrive.

23. That you endeavour by severe punishment to suppress drunkenness; and that you be careful the great quantity of wine and strong waters be not sold into the hands of those that be likeliest to abuse it, but that so near as you can it may be equally disposed of for the relief of the whole plantation. And if any merchant or other for private lucre shall bring in any corrupt or unwholesome wines, waters, or any other liquors, such as may endanger the health of the people, and shall so be found upon the oaths of sufficient persons appointed for the trial, that the vessel be staved.

24. That especial care be taken for the preservation of neat cattle and that the females be not killed up as formerly, whereby the colony will in short time have such plenty of victuals, that much people may come thither for the setting up of iron works and other staple commodities. That you cause the people to plant great store of corn, as there may be one whole year's provision beforehand in the colony, lest in relying upon one single harvest, drought, blasting, or otherwise, they fall into such wants or famine as formerly they have endured. And that the plough may go and English be sowed in all places convenient. And that no corn nor cattle be sold out of the plantation without leave from the governor and Council.

25. That they apply themselves to the impaling of orchards and gardens for roots and fruits which that country is so proper for, and that every planter be compelled for every 500 acres granted unto him to enclose and sufficiently fence either with pales or quickset and dikes, and so from time to time to preserve, enclosed and fenced, a quarter of an acre of ground in the most convenient place near his dwelling-house for orchards and gardens.

26. That whereas your tobacco falleth every day more and more to a baser price, that it be stinted into a far less proportion than hath been made in the last year 1637, not only to be accounted by the plants but by the quantity when 'tis cured. And because of great debts of the planter in tobacco, occasioned by the excessive rates of

commodities have been the stinting thereof, so hard to be put into execution that the course commanded by his Majesty in his letter of the 22nd of April, in the 13th year of his reign for regulating the debts of the colony be duly observed. And also not to suffer men to build slight cottages as heretofore have been there used. And to remove from place to place, only to plant tobacco. That tradesmen and handicrafts be compelled to follow their several trades and occupations, and that you draw you into towns.

27. We require you to use your best endeavour to cause the people there to apply themselves to the raising of more staple commodities as hemp and flax, rope, seed and madder, pitch and tar, for tanning of hides and leather. Likewise every plantation to plant a proportion of vines, answerable to their numbers, and to plant white mulberry trees, and attend silkworms.

28. That the merchant be not constrained to take tobacco at any price in exchange for his wares. But that it be lawful for him to make his own bargain for his goods he so changeth, notwithstanding any proclamation here published to the contrary.

29. That no merchant shall be suffered to bring in ten pounds' worth of wine or strong waters that brings not one hundred pounds' worth of necessary commodities and so rateably. And that every merchant that deserves a warrant for the recovery of his debt shall bring in a bill of parcels with the rates of the several commodities, whereby the certainty of the debt and the commodities thereof may the better appear.

30. That whereas many ships laden with tobacco and other merchandise from thence carry the same immediately into foreign countries, whereby his Majesty loseth the custom and duties thereupon due, nothing being answered in Virginia, you be very careful that no ship or other vessel whatsoever depart from thence, freighted with tobacco or other commodities which that country shall afford, before bond with sufficient sureties be taken to [his] Majesty's use to bring the same directly unto his Majesty's dominions, and not elsewhere, and to bring a bill of lading from home that the staple of those commodities may be made here, whereby his Majesty, after so great expense upon that plantation, and so many of his subjects transported thither, may not be defrauded of what shall be justly due unto him for custom and other duties upon those goods. These bonds to be transmitted to the Council here, and from thence to the Exchequer, that the delinquent may be proceeded with according to due course of law.

31. Next that you strictly and resolutely forbid all trade or trucking for any merchandise whatsoever with any ship other than his Majesty's subjects that shall either purposely or casually come to any of your plantations. And that if upon some unexpected occasions and necessity the governor and Council shall think fit to admit such intercourse, which we admit not but upon some extremity, that good caution and bond be taken, both of the master and also the owner of the said tobacco or other commodities so laden that they shall (damages of the sea excepted) be brought to our port of London, there to pay unto us such duties as are due upon the same.

And to conclude, that in all things accordingly to your best understanding you endeavour the extirpation of vice and encouragement of religion, virtue, and goodness.

23. The Pennsylvania Charter of Privileges (28 October 1701)

Previous to this charter, William Penn had issued three "frames of government", as he called them. Each had proven unsatisfactory. This fourth "frame" provided the constitution for the colony until 1776. Printed: *Minutes of the Provincial Council of Pennsylvania*, II, pp. 56–60.

Whereas, King Charles the Second, by his letters patents under the great seal of England, bearing date the fourth day of March, in the year one thousand six hundred and eighty, was graciously pleased to give and grant unto me, my heirs, and assigns, for ever, this province of Pennsylvania, with divers great powers and jurisdictions for the well government thereof; and whereas the king's dearest brother James, duke of York and Albany, etc., by his deed of feoffment under his hand and seal, duly perfecting, bearing date the twenty-fourth day of August, one thousand six hundred eighty and two, did grant unto me, my heirs, and assigns, all that tract of land now called the territories of Pennsylvania, together with powers and jurisdictions for the good government thereof; and whereas, for the encouragement of all the freemen and planters that might be concerned in the said province and territories, and for the good government thereof, I, the said William Penn, in the year one thousand six hundred eighty and three, for me, my heirs and assigns, did grant and confirm unto all the freemen, planters and adventurers therein divers liberties, franchises and properties, as by the said grant entitled the Frame of the Government of the Province of Pennsylvania and Territories Thereunto Belonging, in America, may appear; which charter or frame, being found in some parts of it not so suitable to the present circumstances of the inhabitants, was in the third month in the year one thousand seven hundred delivered up to me by six parts of seven of freemen of this province and territories, in General Assembly met, provision being made in the said charter for that end and purpose; and whereas, I was then pleased to promise that I would restore the said charter to them again with necessary alterations, or in lieu thereof give them another better adapted to answer the present circumstances and condition of the said inhabitants, which they have now by their representatives in General Assembly met at Philadelphia requested me to grant; know ye therefore, that I, for the further well-being and good government of the said province and territories, and in pursuance of the rights and powers before mentioned, I, the said William Penn, do declare, grant and confirm unto all the freemen, planters, and adventurers, and other inhabitants in this province and territories, these following liberties, franchises and privileges, so far as in me lieth, to be held, enjoyed, and kept by the freemen, planters, and adventurers, and other inhabitants of and in the said province and territories thereunto annexed, for ever;

First. Because no people can be truly happy, though under the greatest enjoyment of civil liberties, if abridged of the freedom of their consciences as to their religious profession and worship; and Almighty God being the only Lord of conscience, father of lights and spirits, and the author as well as object of all divine knowledge, faith and worship, who only doth enlighten the mind and persuade and convince the understandings of people, I do hereby grant and declare that no person or persons inhabiting in this province or territories, who shall confess and acknowledge one Almighty God, the creator, upholder, and ruler of the world, and profess him or themselves obliged to live quietly under the civil government, shall be in any case molested or prejudiced in his or their person or estate because of his or their conscientious persuasion or practice, nor be compelled to frequent or maintain any religious worship, place, or ministry contrary to his or their mind, or to do or suffer any other act or thing contrary to their religious persuasion. And that all persons who also profess to believe in Jesus Christ the Saviour of the world shall be capable (notwithstanding their other persuasions and practices in point of conscience and religion) to serve this government in any capacity, both legislatively and executively, he or they solemnly promising, when lawfully required, allegiance to the king as sovereign, and fidelity to the proprietor and governor, and taking the attests as now established, by the law made at New Castle in the year one thousand seven hundred, entitled an act directing the attests of several offices and ministers, as now amended and confirmed by this present assembly.

Secondly. For the well governing of this province and territories, there shall be an assembly yearly chosen by the freemen thereof, to consist of four persons out of each county of most note for virtue, wisdom, and ability (or of a greater number at any time as the governor and Assembly shall agree) upon the first day of October, for ever; and shall sit on the fourteenth day of the said month, at Philadelphia, unless the governor and Council for the time being shall see cause to appoint another place within the said province or territories, which Assembly shall have power to choose a speaker and other their officers, and shall be judges of the qualifications and elections of their own members, sit upon their own adjournments, appoint committees, prepare bills in or to pass into laws, impeach criminals, and redress grievances; and shall have all other powers and privileges of an assembly, according to the rights of the freeborn subjects of England, and as is usual in any of the king's plantations in America. And if any county or counties shall refuse or neglect to choose their respective representatives, as aforesaid, or if chosen do not meet to serve in assembly, those who are so chosen and met shall have the full power of an assembly in as ample manner as if all the representatives had been chosen and met; provided they are not less than two thirds of the whole number that ought to meet; and that the qualifications of electors and elected, and all other matters and things relating to elections of representatives to serve in assemblies, though not herein particularly expressed, shall be and remain as by a law of this government made at New Castle in the year one thousand seven hundred, entitled an act to ascertain the number of members of assembly, and to regulate the elections.

Thirdly. That the freemen in each respective county, at the time and place of meeting for electing their representatives to serve in assembly, may as often as there shall be occasion, choose a double number of persons to present to the governor for sheriffs and coroners, to serve for three years, if they so long behave themselves well, out of which respective elections and presentments the governor shall nominate and commissionate one for each of the said officers the third day after such presentment, or else the first named in such presentment for each office, as aforesaid, shall stand and serve in that office for the time before respectively limited; and in case of death or default, such vacancies shall be supplied by the governor to serve to the end of the said term: provided always, that if the said freemen shall at any time neglect or decline to choose a person or persons for either or both the aforesaid offices, then and in such case the persons that are or shall be in the respective offices of sheriff or coroner at the time of election, shall remain therein until they shall be removed by another election, as aforesaid. And that the justices of the respective counties shall or may nominate and present to the governor three persons to serve for clerk of the peace for the said county when there is a vacancy, one of which the governor shall commissionate within ten days after such presentment, or else the first nominated shall serve in the said office during good behaviour.

Fourthly. That the laws of this government shall be in this style, viz: [By the governor with the consent and approbation of the freemen in General Assembly met] and shall be, after confirmation by the governor, forthwith recorded in the rolls office and kept at Philadelphia, unless the governor and Assembly shall agree to appoint another place.

Fifthly. That all criminals shall have the same privileges of witnesses and counsel as their prosecutors.

Sixthly. That no person or persons shall or may, at any time hereafter, be obliged to answer any complaint, matter or thing whatsoever relating to property before the governor and Council, or in any other place but in the ordinary courts of justice, unless appeals thereunto shall be hereafter by law appointed.

Seventhly. That no person within this government shall be licensed by the governor to keep ordinary, tavern, or house of public entertainment but such who are first recommended to him under the hand of the justices of the respective counties, signed in open court, which justices are and shall be hereby empowered to suppress and forbid any person keeping such public house, as aforesaid, upon their misbehaviour, on such penalties as the law doth or shall direct, and to recommend others from time to time as they shall see occasion.

Eighthly. If any person, through temptation or melancholy, shall destroy himself, his estate, real and personal, shall notwithstanding, descend to his wife, and children or relations as if he had died a natural death; and if any person shall be destroyed or killed by casualty or accident, there shall be no forfeiture to the governor by reason thereof; and no act, law or ordinance, whatsoever, shall at any time hereafter be made or done to alter, change, or diminish the form or effect of this charter, or of any part or clause therein, contrary to the true intent and meaning thereof, without the consent of the governor for the time being, and six parts of seven of the Assembly met. But because the happiness of mankind depends so much upon the enjoying of liberty of their consciences, as aforesaid, I do hereby solemnly declare, promise, and grant for me, my heirs and assigns, that the first article of this charter relating to liberty of conscience, and every part and clause therein, according to the true intent and meaning thereof, shall be kept and remain without any alteration, inviolably for ever.

And lastly, I, the said William Penn, proprietor and governor of the province of Pennsylvania and territories thereunto belonging, for myself, my heirs and assigns, have solemnly declared, granted, and confirmed, and do hereby solemnly declare, grant, and confirm, that neither I, my heirs or assigns, shall procure or do anything or things whereby the liberties in this charter contained and expressed, nor any part thereof, shall be infringed or broken; and if anything shall be procured or done by any person or persons, contrary to these presents, it shall be held of no force or effect.

In witness whereof, I, the said William Penn, at Philadelphia in Pennsylvania, have unto this present Charter of Liberties set my hand and broad seal this twenty-eighth day of October, in the year of our Lord one thousand seven hundred and one, being the thirteenth year of the reign of King William the third, over England, Scotland, France, and Ireland, etc., and in the twenty-first year of my government. And notwithstanding the closure and test of this present charter, as aforesaid, I think fit to add this following proviso thereunto as part of the same, that is to say: that notwithstanding any clause or clauses in the above-mentioned charter, obliged the province and territories to join together in legislation, I am content and do hereby declare that if the representatives of the province and territories shall not hereafter agree to join together in legislation, and if the same shall be signified to me or my deputy, in open assembly or otherwise, from under the hands and seals of the representatives (for the time being) of the province or territories, or the major part of either of them, any time within three years from the date hereof; that in such case the inhabitants of each of the three counties of this province shall not have less than eight persons to represent them in assembly for the province, and the inhabitants of the town of Philadelphia (when the said town is incorporated) two persons to represent them in assembly; and the inhabitants of each county in the territories shall have as many persons to represent them in a distinct assembly for the territories as shall be by them requested, as aforesaid, notwithstanding which separation of the province and territories in respect of legislation, I do hereby promise, grant, and declare that the inhabitants of both province and territories shall separately enjoy all other liberties, privileges, and benefits granted jointly to them in this charter; any law, usage, or custom of this government heretofore made and practised, or any law made and passed by this General Assembly to the contrary hereof, notwithstanding.

24. Commission to George Clinton as governor of New York (3 July 1741)

By the eighteenth century, the commissions of royal governors had arrived at a standard pattern. The following commission issued in 1741 to George Clinton as governor of New York is character-istic. Printed: E. B. O'Callaghan, ed., *Documents Relative to the Colonial History of the State of New York* (15 vols., Albany, 1856–1887), VI, pp. 190–195.

. . . And our will and pleasure is that you, the said George Clinton, after the publica-tion of these, our letters patents, do in the first place take the oaths mentioned to be taken by an act passed in the 1st year of our late royal father's reign entitled "An Act for the further security of his Majesty's Person and Government and the Succession of the Crown in the Heirs of the late Princess Sophia, being Protestants, and for extinguishing the Hopes of the pretended Prince of Wales and his open and Secret Abettors." As also that you make and subscribe the declaration mentioned in an act of Parliament made in the 25th year of the reign of King Charles the second entitled "An Act for preventing Dangers which may happen from Popish Recusants" and likewise that you take the usual oath for the due execution of the office and trust of our captain-general and governor-in-chief in and over our said province of New York and territories depending thereon for the due and impartial administration of justice, and further that you take the oath required to be taken by governors of plantations to do their utmost that the several laws relating to trade and the plantations be observed, which said oaths and declaration our Council in our said province or any three of the members thereof have hereby full power and authority, and are requested to tender and administer unto you, and in your absence, to our lieutenant-governor, if there be any upon the place [all which being duly performed, you shall administer to each of the members of our said Council, as also to our lieutenant-governor, if there be any upon the place], the oaths mentioned in the said act . . . as also to cause them to make and subscribe the forementioned declaration, and to adminster to them the oath for the due execution of their places and trusts.

And we do hereby give and grant unto you full power and authority to suspend any of the members of our said Council from sitting, voting, and assisting therein, if you shall find joint cause for so doing, and if there shall be any lieutenant-governor, him likewise to suspend from the execution of his command, and to appoint another in his stead until our pleasure be known.

And if it shall at any time happen that by the death, departure out of our said province, or suspension of any of our said councillors, or otherwise, there shall be a vacancy in our said Council (any three whereof we do hereby appoint to be a quorum), our will and pleasure is that you signify the same unto us by the first opportunity that we may, under our signet and sign manual, constitute and appoint others in their stead. But that our affairs may not suffer at that distance for want of a due number of councillors, if ever it shall happen that there be less than seven of them residing in our said province: we do hereby give and grant unto you, the said George Clinton, full power and authority to choose as many persons out of the principal freeholders, inhabitants thereof, as will make up the full number of our said Council to be seven and no more; which persons so chosen and appointed by you shall be to all intents and purposes councillors in our said province, until either they shall be confirmed by us, or that by the nomination of others by us, under our sign manual and signet, our said Council shall have seven or more persons in it.

And we do hereby give and grant unto you full power and authority, with the advice and consent of our said Council, from time to time as need shall require, to summon and call general assemblies of the said freeholders and planters within your government, according to the usage of our province of New York.

And our will and pleasure is that the persons thereupon duly elected by the major part of the freeholders of the respective counties and places, and so returned, shall before their sitting take the oaths mentioned in the said act . . . as also to make and subscribe the forementioned declaration, which oaths and declaration you shall commissionate fit persons under our seal of New York to tender and administer unto them, and until the same shall be so taken and subscribed, no person shall be capable of sitting though elected; and we do hereby declare that the persons so elected and qualified shall be called and deemed the General Assembly of that our province and the territories depending thereon.

And you, the said George Clinton, with the consent of our said Council and Assembly, or the major part of them respectively, shall have full power and authority to make, constitute and ordain laws, statutes, and ordinances for the public peace, welfare, and good government of our said province and of the people and inhabitants thereof, and such others as shall resort thereto, and for the benefit of us, our heirs and successors; which said laws, statutes, and ordinances are not to be repugnant but as near as may be agreeable unto the laws and statutes of this our kingdom of Great Britain; provided that all such laws, statutes, and ordinances of what nature or duration soever be within three months or sooner after the making thereof, transmitted unto us under our seal of New York for our approbation or disallowance of the same. As also duplicates thereof by the next conveyance.

And in case any or all of the said laws, statutes, and ordinances (being not before confirmed by us), shall at any time be disallowed and not approved and so signified by us, our heirs and successors, under our or their sign manual or signet, or by order of our or their Privy Council unto you, the said George Clinton, or to the commander-in-chief of our said province, for the time being, then such and so many of the said laws, statutes, and ordinances as shall be so disallowed and not approved shall from thenceforth cease, determine, and become utterly void and of none effect, anything to the contrary thereof notwithstanding.

And to the end that nothing may be passed or done by our said Council or Assembly to the prejudice of us, our heirs, and successors, we will and ordain that you, the said George Clinton, shall have and enjoy a negative voice in the making and passing of all laws, statutes, and ordinances as aforesaid.

And you shall and may likewise from time to time as you shall judge it necessary, adjourn, prorogue, and dissolve all general assemblies as aforesaid.

And our further will and pleasure is that you shall and may use and keep the Public Seal of our province of New York for sealing all things whatsoever that pass the Great Seal of our said province under your government.

And we do further give and grant unto you, the said George Clinton, full power and authority from time to time and at any time hereafter by yourself, or by any other to be authorized by you in that behalf, to administer and give the aforementioned oaths to all and every such person and persons as you shall think fit, who shall at any time or times pass into our said province or shall be resident or abiding there.

And we do further by these presents give and grant unto you full power and authority, with the advice and consent of our said Council, to erect, constitute, and establish such and so many courts of judicature and public justice within our said province under your government as you and they shall think fit and necessary for the hearing and determining of all causes, as well criminal as civil, according to law and equity, and for awarding of execution thereupon, with all reasonable and necessary powers and authorities, fees, and privileges belonging thereto, as also to appoint and commissionate fit persons in the several parts of your government to administer the oaths mentioned in the aforesaid act. . . . As also to tender and administer the aforesaid declarations unto such persons belonging to the said courts as shall be obliged to take the same.

And we do hereby authorize and empower you to constitute and appoint judges, and (in cases requisite) commissioners of oyer and terminer, justices of the peace, and other necessary officers and ministers in our said province for the better administration of justice and putting the laws in execution; and to administer or cause to be administered unto them such oath or oaths as are usually given for the due execution and performance of offices and places, and for the clearing of truth in judicial cases.

And we do hereby give and grant unto you full power and authority where you shall see cause or shall judge any offender or offenders in criminal matters, or for any fines or forfeitures due unto us, fit objects of our mercy, to pardon all such offenders, and to remit all such offences, fines, and forfeitures, treason and wilful murder only excepted, in which cases you shall likewise have power upon extraordinary occasions to grant reprieves to the offenders until and to the intent our royal pleasure may be known therein.

And we do by these presents authorize and empower you to collate any person or persons to any churches, chapels, or other ecclesiastical benefices within our said province and territories aforesaid as often as any of them shall happen to be void.

And we do hereby give and grant unto you, the said George Clinton, by yourself or by your captains or commanders by you to be authorized, full power and authority to levy, arm, muster, command, and employ all persons whatsoever residing within our said province of New York and other the territories under your government, and as occasion shall serve, to march from one place to another, or to embark them for the resisting and withstanding of all enemies, pirates, and rebels, both at sea and land, and to transport such forces to any of our plantations in America (if necessity shall require) for the defence of the same against the invasion or attempts of any of our enemies and such enemies, pirates, and rebels, if there shall be occasion to pursue or prosecute in or out of the limits of our said province and plantations, or any of them, and, if it shall so please God, them to vanquish, apprehend, and take, and being taken either according to law, to put to death or keep and preserve alive at your discretion, and to execute martial law in time of invasion, or other times, when by law it may be executed, and to do and execute all and every other thing and things which to our captain-general and governor-in-chief doth or ought of right to belong.

And we do hereby give and grant unto you full power and authority, by and with the advice and consent of our said Council, to erect, raise, and build in our said province of New York and territories depending thereon, such and so many forts and platforms, castles, cities, boroughs, towns, and fortifications as you by the advice aforesaid shall judge necessary, and the same, or any of them, to fortify and furnish with ordnance, ammunition, and all sorts of arms fit and necessary for the security and defence of our said province, and by the advice aforesaid the same again, or any of them, to demolish or dismantle as may be most convenient.

And forasmuch as divers mutinies and disorders may happen by persons shipped and employed at sea during the time of war and to the end that such as shall be shipped and employed at sea during the time of war may be better governed and ordered: we do hereby give and grant unto you, the said George Clinton, full power and authority to constitute and appoint captains, lieutenants, master of ships and other commanders and officers, and to grant unto such captains, lieutenants, masters of ships, and other commanders and officers commissions to execute the law martial according to the directions of an act passed in the 13th year of the reign of King Charles the second entitled "An Act for the Establishing Articles and Orders for the Regulation and better Government of His Majesty's Navies, Ships of War, and Forces by Sea", during the time of war, and to use such proceedings, authorities, punishments, corrections, and executions upon any offender or offenders who shall be mutinous, seditious, disorderly, or any way unruly, either at sea or during the time of their abode or residence in any of the ports, harbours, or bays of our said province and territories, as the cause shall be found to require, according to the martial law and the said directions during the time of war as aforesaid.

Provided that nothing herein contained shall be construed to the enabling you or any by your authority, to hold plea or have any jurisdiction of any offence, cause, matter, or thing, committed or done upon the high sea, or within any of the havens, rivers, or creeks of our said province or territories, under your government, by any captain, commander, lieutenant, master, officer, seaman, soldier, or other person whatsoever, who shall be in actual service and pay in or on board any of our ships of war or other vessels acting by immediate commission or warrant from our commissioners for executing the office of our High Admiral, or from our High Admiral of Great Britain for the time being under the seal of our Admiralty; but that such captain, commander, lieutenant, master, officer, seaman, soldier, or other person so offending shall be left to be proceeded against and tried as their offences shall require, either by commission under our great seal of Great Britain, as the statute of the 28th of Henry the 8th directs, or by commission from our said commissioners for executing the office of our High Admiral, or from our High Admiral of Great Britain for the time being according to the aforementioned act for the establishing articles and orders for the regulating and better government of his Majesty's navies, ships of war, and forces by sea, and not otherwise.

Provided nevertheless that all disorders and misdemeanours committed on shore by any captain, commander, lieutenant, master, officer, seaman, soldier, or other person whatsoever belonging to any of our ships of war or other vessels, acting by immediate commission or warrant from our said commissioners for executing the office of our High Admiral or from our High Admiral of Great Britain, for the time being, under the seal of our Admiralty, may be tried and punished according to the laws of the place where any such disorders, offences, and misdemeanours shall be committed on shore, notwithstanding such offender be in our actual service and born in our pay on board any such our ships of war or other vessels acting by immediate commission or warrant from our said commissioners for executing the office of our High Admiral or from our High Admiral of Great Britain for the time being as aforesaid, so as he shall not receive any protection for the avoiding of justice for such offences committed on shore from any pretence of his being employed in our service at sea.

And our further will and pleasure is that all public money raised or which shall be raised by any act to be hereafter made within our said province and other the territories depending thereon, be issued out by warrant from you, by and with the advice and consent of our Council, and disposed of by you for the support of the government, and not otherwise.

And we do hereby likewise give and grant unto you full power and authority, by and with the advice and consent of our said Council, to settle and agree with the inhabitants of our province and territories aforesaid, for such lands, tenements, and hereditaments as now are or hereafter shall be in our power to dispose of, and them to grant to any person or persons upon such terms and under such moderate quit rents, services, and acknowledgements to be thereupon reserved unto us, as you, by and with the advice aforesaid, shall think fit; which said grants are to pass and be sealed by our seal of New York, and being entered upon record by such officer or officers as you shall appoint, shall be good and effectual in law against us, our heirs, and successors.

And we do hereby give you, the said George Clinton, full power and authority to order and appoint fairs, marts, and markets, as also such and so many ports, harbours, bays, havens, and other places for the convenience and security of shipping and for the better loading and unloading of goods and merchandises as by you, with the advice and consent of our said Council, shall be thought fit and necessary.

And we do hereby require and command all officers and ministers, civil and military, and all other inhabitants of our said province and territories depending thereon, to be obedient, aiding and assisting unto you, the said George Clinton, in the execution of this our commission, and of the powers and authorities herein contained, and in case of your death or absence out of our said province and territories depending thereon, to be obedient, aiding and assisting unto such person as shall be appointed by us to be our lieutenant-governor or commander-in-chief of our said province, to whom we do therefore by these presents, give and grant all and singular the powers and authorities herein granted to be by him executed and enjoyed during our pleasure or until your arrival within our said province and territories.

And if upon your death or absence out of our said province and territories depending thereon, there be no person upon the place commissionated or appointed by us to be our lieutenant-governor or commander-in-chief of our said province, our will and pleasure is that the eldest councillor whose name is first placed in our said instructions to you, and who shall be at the time of your death or absence, residing within our said province of New York, shall take upon him the administration of the government and execute our said commission and instructions and the several powers and authorities therein contained in the same manner, and to all intents and purposes as other our governor or commander-in-chief of our said province should or ought to do in case of your absence until your return, or in all cases until our further pleasure be known therein.

And we do hereby declare, ordain, and appoint that you, the said George Clinton, shall and may hold, execute, and enjoy the office and place of our captain-general and governor-in-chief in and over our province of New York and the territories depending thereon, together with all and singular the powers and authorities hereby granted unto you for and during our will and pleasure.

And whereas there are divers colonies adjoining to our province of New York, for the defence and security whereof it is requisite that due care be taken in time of war, we have therefore thought it necessary for our service and for the better protection and security of our subjects inhabiting those parts, to constitute and appoint, and we do by these presents constitute and appoint you, the said George Clinton, to be our captain-general and commander-in-chief of the militia and of all the forces by sea and land within our colony of Connecticut and of all our forts and places of strength within the same.

And for the better ordering, governing, and ruling our said militia and all our forces, forts, and places of strength within our said colony of Connecticut, we do hereby give and grant unto you, the said George Clinton, and in your absence, to our commander-in-chief of our province of New York, all and every the like powers as in these presents are before granted and recited for the ruling, governing, and ordering our militia and all our forces, forts, and places of strength within our province of New York, to be exercised by you, the said George Clinton, and in your absence from our territory and dominion of New York, by our commander-in-chief of our province of New York within our said colony of Connecticut, for and during our pleasure.

25. Instructions to Lord Dunmore as governor of Virginia (7 February 1771)

Every governor, in addition to his commission, was given instructions setting forth in detail the manner in which he was to administer the colony to which he had been appointed. Such instructions were remarkably uniform for all the colonies in the eighteenth century, with only occasional variations in detail. Governors were expected to obey their instructions implicitly and were given relatively little discretion. If a governor obeyed his instructions he was in trouble with the local legislature; if he did not, he was in trouble with the Board of Trade. That "the inflexibility and uniformity of the instructions contributed directly to the failure of the royal system of government in America" is the measured conclusion of L. W. Labaree in his study of royal government in America. Printed: Massachusetts Historical Society *Collections*, 4th Series, x, pp. 630–666.

First. With these our instructions you will receive our commission under our great seal of Great Britain, constituting you our lieutenant and governor-general of our colony and dominion of Virginia in America. You are therefore to fit yourself with all convenient speed, and to repair to our said colony of Virginia; and being there arrived, you are to take upon you the execution of the place and trust we have reposed in you, and forthwith to call together the following persons by name, whom we do hereby appoint to be the members of our said Council in our said colony, viz.: William Nelson, Thomas Nelson, Richard Corbin, William Byrd, Philip Ludwell Lee, Robert Carter, Robert Burwell, George William Fairfax, and John Page, esquires, the Reverend James Horrocks, clerk, and Ralph Wormley, esquire.

2. You are with all due and usual solemnity to cause our said commission constituting you our lieutenant and governor-general, as aforesaid, to be read and published at the said meeting of our Council, which being done, you shall then take, and also administer unto each of the members of our said Council, the oaths mentioned in an act passed in the first year of the reign of his late Majesty King George the first, entitled "An Act for the further security of His Majesty's Person and Government, and the Succession of the Crown in the Heirs of the late Princess Sophia, being

Protestants, and for extinguishing the hopes of the pretended Prince of Wales, and his open and secret Abettors", and in an act passed in the sixth year of our reign, entitled "An Act for altering the oath of abjuration, and the Assurance, and for amending so much of an Act of the seventh year of Her late Majesty Queen Anne, intituled, 'An Act for the improvement of the Union of the two Kingdoms', as, after the time therein limited, requires the delivery of certain Lists and Copies therein mentioned, to Persons indicted of High Treason, or misprision of Treason"; as also make and subscribe and cause the members of our said Council to make and subscribe the declaration mentioned in an act of Parliament made in the twenty-fifth year of the reign of King Charles the second, entitled "An Act for preventing dangers which may happen from Popish Recusants". And you and every of them are likewise to take an oath for the due execution of your and their places and trusts, as well as with regard to your and their equal and impartial administration of justice; and you are also to take the oath required by an act passed in the seventh and eighth years of the reign of King William the third, to be taken by governors of plantations, to do their utmost that the acts relating to the plantations be observed.

3. You shall administer, or cause to be administered, the oaths appointed in the aforesaid acts, entitled "An Act for the further security of His Majesty's Person, and Government; and the succession of the Crown in the Heirs of the late Princess Sophia, being Protestants: and for extinguishing the hopes of the pretended Prince of Wales, and his open and secret Abettors", and, "An Act for altering the Oath of Abjuration, and the Assurance: and for amending so much of an Act of the seventh year of Her late Majesty Queen Anne, intituled 'An Act for the improvement of the Union of the two Kingdoms', as, after the time therein limited, requires the delivery of certain Lists and Copies therein mentioned to Persons indicted of High Treason, or misprision of Treason"; to the members and officers of the Assembly, and to all judges, justices, and other persons that hold any office or place of trust or profit in our said colony, whether by virtue of any patent under our great seal of Great Britain, or the public seal of Virginia, or otherwise. And you shall also cause them to make and subscribe the aforesaid declaration, without the doing all which you are not to admit any person whatsoever into any public office, nor suffer those that have been admitted formerly, to continue therein.

4. You are forthwith to communicate unto our said Council such and so many of these our instructions wherein their advice and consent are required; as likewise all such others from time to time as you shall find convenient for our service to be imparted to them.

5. You are to permit the members of our said Council, to have and enjoy freedom of debate and vote in all affairs of public concern that may be debated in Council.

6. And, although by our commission aforesaid we have thought fit to direct that any three of our councillors shall make a quorum, it is nevertheless our will and pleasure that you do not act with a quorum of less than five members, unless upon extraordinary emergencies, when a greater number cannot be conveniently had.

7. And, that we may always be informed of the names and characters of persons fit to supply the vacancies that may happen in our said Council, you are from time to time, when any vacancies shall happen therein, forthwith to transmit unto us, by one of our principal secretaries of state, the names of three persons, inhabitants of our said colony, whom you shall esteem the best qualified for that trust.

8. And whereas by our commission you are empowered, in case of the death or absence of any of our Council of the said colony, to fill up the vacancies in the said Council to the number of nine, and no more; you are from time to time to send to us, by one of our principal secretaries of state, the names and qualities of any member or members by you put into our said Council, by the first conveyance after your so doing.

9. And in the choice and nomination of the members of our said Council, as also of the chief officers, judges, assistant justices, and sheriffs, you are always to take care that they be men of good life, well-affected to our government, of good estates, and of abilities suitable to their employments.

10. You are neither to augment nor diminish the number of our said Council as it is hereby established, nor to suspend any of the members thereof without good and sufficient cause, nor without the consent of the majority of the said Council, signified in Council after due examination of the charge against such councillor, and his answer thereunto; and in case of suspension of any of them you are to cause your reasons for so doing, together with the charges and proofs against the said persons and their answers thereunto, to be duly entered upon the council books, and forthwith to transmit copies thereof to us by one of our principal secretaries of state.

Nevertheless if it should happen that you should have reasons for suspending of any councillor, not fit to be communicated to the Council, you may in that case suspend such person without their consent; but you are thereupon immediately to send to us by one of our principal secretaries of state an account of your proceedings therein, with your reasons at large for such suspension, as also for not communicating the same to our Council, and duplicates thereof, by the next opportunity.

11. And whereas we are sensible that effectual care ought to be taken to oblige the members of our Council to a due attendance therein, in order to prevent the many inconveniences that may happen for want of a quorum of the Council to transact business, as occasion may require, it is our will and pleasure that if any of the members of our said Council residing in our said colony, shall hereafter willfully absent themselves from our said colony and continue absent above the space of twelve months without leave from you or from the commander-in-chief of the said colony for the time being, first obtained under your or his hand and seal, or shall remain absent for the space of two years successively without our leave, given them under our royal signature, their place or places in our said Council shall immediately become void; and that if any of the members of our said Council residing within our said colony shall hereafter wilfully absent themselves from the council board, when duly summoned, without a just and lawful cause, and shall persist therein after admonition, you suspend the said councillors so absenting themselves until our further pleasure shall be known, giving timely notice thereof to us by one of our principal secretaries

of state. And we do hereby will and require that this, our royal pleasure, be signified to the several members of our said Council, and that it be entered on the Council books of the said colony as a standing rule.

12. And whereas complaint hath formerly been made that the members of our said Council, in all matters of civil right where any of them are defendants, claim a privilege of exemption from the ordinary forms of process by writ so that they cannot be arrested, and to be summoned to appear by letters from the secretary of our said colony, which they comply with, or neglect at their pleasure, by which means the cause of justice is obstructed and the plaintiffs are frequently left destitute of relief: you are therefore to take especial care that a letter of summons to any of the said councillors, signed either by yourself or by the secretary of our said colony, or by the clerk of any court of record within our said colony, be deemed as binding and as strict in law for their appearance as a writ, and that, upon their neglect to comply with any such summons, except only in times of general assembly, they be liable to the ordinary forms of common process.

13. Whereas a practice hath of late years prevailed in several of our colonies and plantations in America of passing laws for raising money by instituting public lotteries; and whereas it hath been represented to us that such practice doth tend to disengage those who become adventurers therein from that spirit of industry and attention to their proper callings and occupations on which the public welfare so greatly depends; and whereas it further appears that this practice of authorizing lotteries by acts of legislature hath been also extended to the enabling private persons to set up such lotteries by means whereof great frauds and abuses have been committed: it is therefore our will and pleasure that you do not give your assent to any act or acts for raising money by the institution of any public or private lotteries whatsoever until you shall have first transmitted unto us, by one of our principal secretaries of state, a draft or drafts of such act or acts, and shall have received our directions therein.

14. Whereas laws have at several times been passed in many of our colonies and plantations in America, by which certain parishes and districts have been empowered and authorized to send representatives to the general assemblies of the respective colonies in which the said parishes and districts lie, and sundry other regulations have been introduced by those laws relative to the said assemblies, it is our will and pleasure, and we do hereby require and command that you do not, upon any pretence whatsoever, give your assent to any law or laws to be passed in our colony under your government by which the number of the assembly shall be enlarged or diminished, the duration of it ascertained, the qualification of the electors or the elected, fixed or altered, or by which any regulations shall be established with respect thereto, inconsistent with our instructions to you, our governor, as prejudicial to that right or authority which you derive from us in virtue of our royal commission and instructions.

15. And whereas the members of several assemblies in our plantations have frequently assumed to themselves privileges no ways belonging to them, especially of being protected from suits at law, during the term they remain of the assembly, to the great prejudice of their creditors and the obstruction of justice, and some

assemblies have presumed to adjourn themselves at pleasure without leave from our governor first obtained for that purpose; which is highly detrimental to our royal prerogative and may be very prejudicial to the public service: you are to signify to the general assemblies of our said colony of Virginia, if occasion should require, that it is our express will and pleasure that you do not allow any protection to any members of assembly further than in their persons, and that only during the session of the assembly, and that you are not to allow them to adjourn themselves otherwise than *de die in diem*, except Sundays and holidays, without leave from you, our governor or the governor or commander-in-chief of our said colony for the time being first asked and obtained.

16. You are to observe in the passing of all laws that the style of enacting the same be by the Governor, Council and Assembly. You are also as much as possible to observe in the passing of all laws that whatever may be requisite upon each different matter be provided for by a different law without intermixing in one and the same act such things as have no proper relation to each other. And you are more especially to take care that no clause or clauses be inserted in or annexed to any act which shall be foreign to what the title of such act imports. And that no perpetual clause be made part of any temporary law. And that no act whatever be suspended, altered, continued, revived, or repealed by general words but that the title and date of such act so suspended, altered, continued, revived, or repealed be particularly mentioned and expressed in the enacting part.

17. And whereas several laws have formerly been enacted in several of our plantations in America for so short a time that the royal assent or refusal could not be had thereupon before the time for which such laws were enacted did expire; you shall not therefore give your assent to any law that shall be enacted for a less time than two years except in the cases hereinafter mentioned; and it is our further will and pleasure that you do not re-enact any law to which the assent of us or our royal predecessors has once been refused without express leave for that purpose first obtained from us, upon a full representation by you to be made to us, by one of our principal secretaries of state, of the reason and necessity of passing such a law, nor give your assent to any law for repealing any other law passed within your government, whether the same has or has not received the royal approbation, unless you take care that a clause be inserted therein suspending and deferring the execution thereof until our pleasure shall be known concerning the same.

18. And whereas great mischiefs do arise by passing bills of an unusual and extraordinary nature and importance in the plantations, which bills remain in force there from the time of enacting until our pleasure be signified to the contrary; we do hereby will and require you not to pass or give your assent to any bill or bills in the assembly of our said colony of unusual and extraordinary nature and importance, wherein our prerogative, the property of our subjects, or the trade and shipping of this kingdom may be any ways prejudiced, until you shall have first transmitted unto us by one of our principal secretaries of state the draft or drafts of such a bill or bills, and shall have received our royal pleasure thereupon; unless you take care in the passing of any bill of such nature, as before mentioned, that there be a clause inserted

therein suspending and deferring the execution thereof until our pleasure shall be known concerning the same.

19. You are also to take care that no private act whereby the property of any private person may be affected be passed in which there is not a saving of the right of us, our heirs and successors, all bodies politic and corporate, and of all other persons except such as are mentioned in the said act, and those claiming by, from, and under them. And further, you are to take care that no such private act be passed without a clause suspending and deferring the execution thereof until the same shall have received our royal approbation. It is likewise our will and pleasure that you do not give your assent to any private act until proof be made before you in Council, and entered on the council books, that public notification was made of the party's intention to apply for such act in the several parish churches where the premises in question lie, for three Sundays at least, successively, before such act was brought into the Assembly; and that a certificate under your hand be transmitted with, and annexed to every such private act, signifying that the same has passed through all the forms above-mentioned.

20. You are to take care that in all acts or orders to be passed within our said colony in any case for levying money, or imposing fines or penalties, express mention be made that the same is granted or reserved to us, our heirs and successors, for the public uses of that, our colony, and the support of the government thereof, as by the said act or order shall be directed. And you are particularly directed not to pass any law or do any act by grant, settlement, or otherwise, whereby our revenue may be lessened or impaired, without our especial licence or command therein.

21. You are not to suffer any public money whatsoever to be issued or disposed of otherwise than by warrant under your hand, by and with the advice and consent of our Council. But the Assembly may nevertheless be permitted from time to time to view and examine the accounts of money or value of money disposed of by virtue of laws made by them, which you are to signify unto them as there shall be occasion.

22. You are not to permit any clause whatsoever to be inserted in any law for levying money, or the value of money, whereby the same shall not be liable to be accounted for unto us and to our commissioners of our treasury, or to our high treasurer for the time being, and audited by our auditor-general of our plantations, or his deputy for the time being. And we do particularly require and enjoin you, upon pain of our highest displeasure, to take care that fair books of accounts of all receipts and payments of all public moneys be duly kept, and the truth thereof attested upon oath. And that all such accounts be audited and attested by our auditor-general of our plantations or his deputy, who is to transmit copies thereof to us by one of our principal secretaries of state, and to our commissioners of our treasury, or our high treasurer for the time being: in which books shall be specified every particular sum raised or disposed of, together with the names of the persons to whom any payment shall be made, to the end we may be satisfied of the right and due application of the revenue of our said colony, with the probability of the increase or diminution of it, under every head or article thereof.

23. Whereas several inconveniences have arisen to our governments in the

plantations by gifts and presents made to our governors by the general assemblies; it is our express will and pleasure that neither you, our governor, nor any governor, lieutenant-governor, or commander-in-chief, or president of our Council of our said colony for the time being, do give your or their consent to the passing any law or act for any gift or present to be made to you or them by the Assembly; and that neither you nor they do receive any gift or present from the Assembly or others, on any account or in any manner whatsoever, upon pain of our highest displeasure, and of being recalled from that our government.

24. And it is our express will and pleasure that no law for raising any imposition upon wines or other strong liquors be made to continue for less than one whole year. And also that all other laws made for the supply and support of the government shall be without limitation of time, except the same be for a temporary service, and which shall expire and have their full effect within the time therein prefixed.

25. Whereas it hath been represented to us by our commissioners for executing the office of Lord High Admiral of this kingdom that by an act passed in our colony of Virginia on the first of May, 1765, entitled, "An Act to prevent frauds in the Drawback of the Duties on Liquors imported into that Colony", it is enacted that no person whatever shall be entitled to the drawback of the duties of any liquors purchased for the use of any ship or vessel whatsoever; by which prohibition of the drawback, as aforesaid, the merchants, contractors for victualling our ships in our said colony, would, in consequence of former laws therein passed, be obliged to pay a duty or tax of four pence per gallon upon all rum furnished by them to our said ships, contrary to what hath been the practice from the time of first laying a duty on that commodity, whereby an extraordinary expense would be incurred in victualling our navy, equal at least to the amount of the said duty; and whereas we have thought fit, upon a consideration of the said memorial, as well as upon a representation of our commissioners for trade and plantations thereupon, to repeal the said law; in order therefore to prevent any extraordinary expense being brought upon the service by any future act of the legislature of our said colony of Virginia, it is our will and pleasure, and you are hereby strictly enjoined and required, on no pretence whatsoever, to give your assent to any law or laws for imposing taxes or duties upon liquors, or any species of provisions or victual, unless it be therein expressly provided, that the said taxes or duties shall not extend to any such provisions or victual as shall be bought up in, or exported from our said colony for the use and supply of our ships of war.

26. Whereas acts have been passed in several of our plantations in America for striking bills of credit and issuing out the same in lieu of money in order to discharge their debts, and for other purposes from whence several inconveniences have arisen; it is therefore our will and pleasure that you do not give your assent to, or pass any act in our colony and dominion of Virginia under your government, whereby bills of credit may be struck or issued in lieu of money, or for payment of money either to you, our governor, or to any lieutenant-governor or commander-in-chief, or to any of the members of our Council, or of the Assembly, or to any other person whatsoever, except to us, our heirs and successors, without a clause be inserted in such

act declaring that the same shall not take effect until the said act shall have been approved and confirmed by us, our heirs or successors.

27. And whereas complaints have heretofore been made by the merchants of the city of London in behalf of themselves and of several others our good subjects of Great Britain trading to our plantations in America, that greater duties and impositions are laid on their ships and goods than on the ships and goods of persons who are natives and inhabitants of the said plantations: it is therefore our will and pleasure that you do not, upon any pretence whatsoever, upon pain of our highest displeasure, give your assent to any law whereby the natives or inhabitants of our colony of Virginia under your government may be put on a more advantageous footing than those of this kingdom, or whereby any duties shall be laid upon British shipping, or upon the product or manufacture of Great Britain, upon any pretence whatsoever.

28. Whereas acts have been passed in some of our plantations in America for laying duties on the importation and exportation of Negroes, to the great discouragement of the merchants trading thither from the coast of Africa; and whereas acts have likewise been passed for laying duties on felons imported, in direct opposition to an act of Parliament passed in the fourth year of the reign of King George the first "for the further preventing Robbery, Burglary, and other Felonies, and for the more effectual transportation of Felons, &c"; it is our will and pleasure that you do not give your assent to, or pass any law imposing duties upon Negroes imported into our colony of Virginia, payable by the importer, or upon any slaves exported, that have not been sold in our said colony, and continued there for the space of twelve months. It is our further will and pleasure that you do not give your assent to, or pass any act whatsoever for imposing duties on the importation of any felons from this kingdom into Virginia.

29. You are to transmit authentic copies of all laws, statutes, and ordinances which at any time hereafter shall be made or enacted within our said colony, each of them separately under the public seal, unto us, by one of our principal secretaries of state, within three months, or sooner after their being enacted; together with duplicates thereof by the next conveyance, upon pain of our highest displeasure, and of the forfeiture of that year's salary, wherein you at any time, or upon any pretence whatsoever omit to send over the said laws, statutes, and ordinances as aforesaid, within the time above limited, as also of such other penalty as we shall please to inflict. But if it shall happen that no shipping shall come from our said colony within three months after the making such laws, statutes, and ordinances, whereby the same may be transmitted as aforesaid, then the said laws, statutes, and ordinances are to be transmitted by the next conveyance after the making thereof, whenever it may happen, for our royal approbation or disallowance of the same.

30. And you are to take especial care that the copies and duplicates of the said acts so to be transmitted as aforesaid, be fairly abstracted in the margins, and that in every act the dates or respective times, when the same passed the Assembly and the Council, and received your assent, be particularly expressed. And you are to be as explicit as may be in your observations upon every act, that is to say, whether the same be introductive of a new law, declaratory of a former law, or does repeal a law

then before in being. And you are likewise to send to us, by one of our principal secretaries of state, the reasons for passing of such law, unless the same do fully appear in the preamble thereof.

31. You are to require the secretary of our said colony, or his deputy for the time being, to furnish you with transcripts of all such acts and public orders as shall be made from time to time, together with a copy of the journals of our Council, and that all such transcripts and copies be fairly abstracted in the margins, to the end the same may be transmitted unto us by one of our principal secretaries of state, which he is duly to perform, upon pain of incurring the forfeiture of his office.

32. You are also to require from the clerk of the Assembly, or other proper officer, transcripts of all journals and other proceedings of the Assembly, fairly abstracted in the margins, to the end the same may be in like manner transmitted as aforesaid.

33. Whereas an act of Parliament was passed in the sixth year of the reign of Queen Anne, entitled, "An Act for ascertaining the rates of foreign Coins in Her Majesty's Plantations in America", which act the respective governors of all our plantations in America have from time to time been instructed to observe and carry into due execution; and whereas, notwithstanding the same, complaints have been made that the said act has not been observed as it ought to have been in many of our colonies and plantations in America, by means of which neglect many indirect practices have grown up and various and illegal currencies have been introduced in several of our said colonies and plantations contrary to the true intent and meaning of the said act, and to the prejudice of the trade of our subjects: it is therefore our will and pleasure and you are hereby strictly required and commanded, under pain of our highest displeasure, and of being removed from your government, to take the most effectual care for the future that the said act be punctually and *bona fide* observed and put in execution, according to the true intent and meaning thereof.

34. You are to examine what rates and duties are charged and payable upon any goods exported and imported within our said colony, whether of the growth or manufacture of the said colony, or otherwise. And you are to suppress the engrossing of commodities as tending to the prejudice of that freedom which trade and commerce ought to have, and to use your best endeavours in the improving the trade of those parts by settling such orders and regulations therein, with the advice of our said Council, as may be most acceptable to the generality of the inhabitants. And it is our express will and pleasure that you do not, upon any pretence whatever, upon pain of our highest displeasure, give your assent to any law or laws for setting up any manufactures, and carrying on any trades which are hurtful and prejudicial to this kingdom, and that you do use your utmost endeavours to discourage, discountenance and restrain any attempts which may be made to set up such manufactures, or establish any such trades.

35. And whereas by an act passed in our said colony of Virginia in the 32d year of the reign of King Charles the 2d, entitled "An Act for raising a public Revenue for the better Support of the Government of this His Majesty's Colony of Virginia",

a duty of two shillings current money of this kingdom is imposed on every hogshead of tobacco exported out of our said colony, the same to be to his said majesty, his heirs and successors for ever, to and for the better support of the government of the said colony; and whereas it hath been heretofore represented that great frauds and abuses have formerly been committed in our said revenue, as well in the payment of the said duty by the masters of ships and other persons on whom the same is chargeable as in the collection thereof by our officers appointed to receive and collect the said duty: you are therefore to take especial care that the several provisions in the said act, made and established for the better discovering and preventing of frauds, be strictly observed and duly carried into execution: and that all persons, employed in the receipt and collection of our said revenue, do take a solemn oath faithfully to execute their respective offices in their own persons, and not by deputies, unless in cases of absolute necessity, and in such cases that the deputies be likewise sworn to the faithful and diligent execution of the trusts reposed in them respectively. And it is our further will and pleasure that, if you shall find any person employed in the receipt of our said revenue to be guilty of any fraud or neglect in the execution of his office, you do immediately remove such person from his place and appoint a fit person in his stead, giving unto us by one of our principal secretaries of state, and to our commissioners of our Treasury, or to our high treasurer for the time being, speedy notice of your proceedings therein.

36. And you are to transmit unto us by one of our principal secretaries of state, and to our commissioners of our Treasury, or our high treasurer for the time being, every half year, an account of the amount of our said revenue, specifying how the same has been disposed of.

37. Whereas it is necessary that our rights and dues be preserved and recovered, and that speedy and effectual justice be administered in all cases relative to our revenue; you are to take care that a court of exchequer be called and do meet at all such times as shall be needful. And you are to inform us by one of our principal secretaries of state whether our service may require that a constant court of exchequer be settled and established there.

38. You shall not erect any court or office of judicature not before erected or established, nor dissolve any court or office already erected or established, without our especial order.

39. And whereas frequent complaints have been made of great delays and undue proceedings in the courts of justice in several of our plantations whereby many of our subjects have very much suffered; and it being of the greatest importance to our service, and to the welfare of our plantations, that justice be every where duly and speedily administered, and that all disorders, delays, and other undue practices in the administration thereof be effectually prevented: we do particularly require you to take especial care that in all courts where you are authorized to preside, justice be impartially administered, and that in all other courts established within our said colony all judges and other persons therein concerned do likewise perform their several duties without delay or partiality.

40. You are to take care that no court of judicature be adjourned but upon good

grounds, as also that no orders of any court of judicature be entered or allowed which shall not be first read and approved by the magistrates in open court; which rule you are in like manner to see observed with relation to the proceedings of our Council of Virginia, and that all orders there made be first read and approved in Council before they are entered upon the council books.

41. Our will and pleasure is that you or the commander-in-chief of our said colony for the time being do, in all civil causes, on proper application being made to you or the commander-in-chief for the time being for that purpose, permit and allow appeals to be made from any of the inferior courts of common law in our said colony, unto you or the commander-in-chief, and the members of our Council of our said colony in supreme court assembled, according to the regulations and directions of such acts as having been passed in our colony and ratified and confirmed by us, are now in force within the same. And if either party in such appeal or in any cause which shall have been originally brought into the said supreme court of our said colony shall not rest satisfied with the judgment of you or the commander-in-chief for the time being, and of our Council, as aforesaid, our will and pleasure is that such party may then appeal unto us in our Privy Council, provided the sum or value so appealed for unto us do exceed five hundred pounds sterling; and that such appeal be made within fourteen days after sentence given by you or the commander-in-chief, and by our Council, as aforesaid, and that good and sufficient security be given by the appellant that he will effectually prosecute the same and answer the condemnation, as also pay such costs and damages as shall be awarded by us, in case the sentence of you or the commander-in-chief for the time being, and of our Council be affirmed; provided nevertheless, that in all cases where the matter in question relates to the taking or demanding any duty payable to us or to any fee of office, or annual rent, or other such like matter or thing where our rights *in futuro* may be bound, you are to admit appeals to us in our Privy Council, although the immediate sum or value appealed for be of a less value. And it is our further will and pleasure that in all cases where, by these our instructions, you are to admit appeals unto us in our Privy Council, execution be suspended until the final determination of such appeals, unless good and sufficient security be given by the appellee to make ample restitution of all that the appellant shall have lost by means of such judgment or decree, in case, upon the determination of such appeal, such decree or judgment should be reversed, and restitution awarded to the appellant.

42. You are also to permit appeals unto us in our Privy Council, in all cases of fines imposed for misdemeanours, provided the fines so imposed amount to, or exceed the sum of one hundred pounds sterling, the appellant first giving good security that he will effectually prosecute the same and answer the condemnation if the sentence by which such fines were imposed shall be confirmed.

43. You shall not remit any fines or forfeitures whatever above the sum of ten pounds, nor dispose of any forfeiture whatever, until you signify unto us, by one of our principal secretaries of state, and to the commissioners of our Treasury, or our high treasurer for the time being, the nature of the offence, and the occasion of such fines and forfeitures, with the particular sums of value thereof (which you are to do

with all speed) you shall have received our directions therein; but you may in the meantime suspend the payment of the said fines and forfeitures.

44. It is our will and pleasure that you do not dispose of any forfeitures or escheats to any person until the sheriff or other proper officer shall have made enquiry by a jury upon their oaths into the true value thereof; nor until you shall have transmitted unto us by one of our principal secretaries of state, and to our commissioners of our Treasury, or our high treasurer for the time being, a particular account of such forfeitures, or escheats, and the value thereof, and shall have received our directions thereupon. And you are to take care that the produce of the said forfeitures or escheats, in case we shall think proper to give directions to dispose of the same, be duly paid to our receiver-general of our said colony, and a full account transmitted unto us by one of our principal secretaries of state, and to our commissioners of our Treasury, or our high treasurer for the time being, with the names of the persons to whom disposed. And provided that in the grants of all forfeited and escheated lands there be a clause obliging the grantee to such terms and conditions of cultivation and improvement as are required by the several laws now in force within our said colony relative to the seating and cultivating of lands; and likewise that there be proper savings and reservations of quit-rents to us, our heirs and successors.

45. You shall not appoint any person to be a judge or justice of the peace without the advice and consent of at least three members of our Council, signified in Council; nor shall you execute yourself or by your deputy any of the said offices; and it is our further will and pleasure that all commissions to be granted by you to any person or persons to be judges, justices of the peace, or other necessary officers, be granted during pleasure only.

46. You shall not displace any of the judges, justices, sheriffs, or other our officers or ministers within our said colony without good and sufficient cause, to be signified in the fullest and most distinct manner to us by one of our principal secretaries of state, by the first opportunity after such removal.

47. You shall not suffer any person to execute more offices than one by deputy.

48. And you are, with the advice and consent of our Council, to take especial care to regulate all salaries and fees belonging to places, or paid upon emergencies, that they be within the bounds of moderation; and that no exaction be made upon any occasion whatsoever; as also that tables of all fees be publicly hung up in all places where such fees are to be paid; and you are to transmit copies of all such tables of fees to us by one of our principal secretaries of state.

49. Whereas there are several offices in our plantations granted under the great seal of Great Britain, and the public seals of the said colonies, and our service may be very much prejudiced by reason of the absence of the patentees and by their appointing deputies not fit to officiate in their stead; you are therefore to inspect such of the said offices as are in our said colony under your government, and enquire into the capacity and behaviour of the persons exercising them, and to report thereupon to us by one of our principal secretaries of state what you think fit to be done or altered in relation thereto. And you are, upon the misbehaviour of any of the patentees or their deputies, to suspend them from the execution of their places until you shall have represented

the whole matter unto us and received our directions therein. And in case of the death of any such deputy, it is our express will and pleasure that you take care that the person appointed to execute the place until the patentee can be informed thereof, and appoint another deputy, to give sufficient security to the patentee, or in case of suspension, to the person suspended, to be answerable for the profits accruing during such interval by death, or during such suspension, in case we shall think fit to restore the person suspended to his place. It is nevertheless our will and pleasure that the person executing the place during such interval by death or suspension, shall for his encouragement receive the same profits as the person dead or suspended did receive. And it is our further will and pleasure that in case of the suspension of a patentee, the person appointed by you to execute the office during such suspension shall for his encouragement receive a moiety of the profits which would otherwise have accrued and become due to such patentee, giving security to such patentee to be answerable to him for the other moiety, in case we shall think fit to restore him to his place again.

50. And whereas complaints have formerly been made of several undue practices in the office of secretary or register of that our colony by the clerks or other persons employed therein; you are therefore from time to time to make inspection into the state and management of the said office and report to us by one of our principal secretaries of state how you find the same; together with your opinion by what methods any mismanagements may for the future be best prevented; and in the meantime to take all possible care that the records of the said office be well and faithfully kept; and in order thereunto that not only the secretary or register himself, but his clerks also be under oath for the due execution of the trust reposed in them and that they accordingly give sufficient security for their faithful performance.

51. You shall not, by colour of any power or authority hereby or otherwise granted or mentioned to be granted unto you, take upon you to give, grant, or dispose of any place or office within our said colony which now is or shall be granted under the great seal of this kingdom, or to which any person is or shall be appointed by warrant under our signet or sign manual, any further than that you may, upon the vacancy of any such office or place, or upon the suspension of any such officer by you, as aforesaid, put in any fit person to officiate in the interval, 'till you shall have represented the matter unto us by one of our principal secretaries of state; which you are to do by the first opportunity, and till the said office or place be disposed of by us, our heirs or successors under the great seal of this kingdom, or until some person shall be appointed thereto under our signet and sign manual or that our further directions be given therein. And it is our express will and pleasure that you do countenance and give all due encouragement to all our patent officers in the enjoyment of the legal and accustomed fees, rights, privileges, and emoluments, according to the true intent and meaning of their patents.

52. And whereas several complaints have been made by the officers of our customs in our plantations in America that they are frequently obliged to serve on juries, and personally to appear in arms, whenever the militia is drawn out, and thereby are much hindered in the execution of their employments; our will and pleasure is that you take effectual care, and give the necessary directions, that the several officers of

our customs be excused and exempted from serving on any juries, or personally appearing in arms in the militia, unless in cases of absolute necessity, or serving any parochial offices which may hinder them in the execution of their duties.

53. You are to transmit to us, by one of our principal secretaries of state, with all convenient speed, a particular account of all establishments of jurisdictions, courts, offices, powers and authorities, fees and privileges granted and settled within our said colony; together with an account of all the expenses attending the establishment of the said courts, and of such funds as are settled and appropriated for discharging such expenses.

54. Whereas it has at all times been a great hindrance to the peopling and settling of our said colony that large tracts of land have been engrossed by particular persons, a great part whereof remaining uncultivated, the colony is thereby deprived of many inhabitants that would otherwise have settled there; in order to remedy this inconvenience for the future it is our will and pleasure that in all grants of land to be made by you, you do not grant more than one thousand acres to any one person, either in his own name or in the name of any other person in trust for him. And that you do take especial care for the reservation of our quit-rents, and for settling and cultivating the lands according to the several regulations prescribed by such laws as now are in force in our said colony relative to the clearing, settling and cultivating of lands.

55. And whereas it has been represented to us that a very irregular practice hath prevailed in our said colony of taking out surveys for lands and neglecting to pass patents for the same, whereby we have been defrauded of our quit-rents, and the lands so surveyed have remained uncultivated: it is therefore our will and pleasure that you do take especial care, and give positive directions to the proper officers, that, immediately upon the return of each survey, a patent be made out and passed, and a docket or copy entered in the offices of the auditor general of our plantations, and of the receiver-general of our quit-rents, to the end that such lands may be immediately carried to and borne upon the rent-roll. And you are earnestly to recommend it to the Council and Assembly of our said colony to make proper provision of law, in case it hath not been already done, for compelling and obliging the surveyors of land in the several districts of our said colony to make a return of their surveys into the secretary's office of our said colony within a reasonable time to be limited in such law.

56. You shall, with the advice of our Council, take care to appoint men fitly qualified to be surveyors throughout all the several districts of our said colony, and that they be sworn to make true and exact surveys of all lands required to be set out, according to the best of their skill. And you shall likewise take care that a general survey be made of all our said colony, and of each county, with the several plantations and fortifications in it; and that an exact map or maps thereof be transmitted to us by one of our principal secretaries of state.

57. And you are to take the most effectual care for the discovery of our quit-rents, and for making in each county a perfect rent-roll of the same, by empowering the several receivers to administer an oath to all such as they account with, to declare what other lands they may have, either in their own right, or in the right of others

unaccounted for, or by such other means as you, with the advice of our said Council, shall think most conducive to this service. And you are further to take care that an exact account be forthwith made out of all arrears of quit-rents due unto us, expressing from what persons, for what quantity of land, and for what time those arrears are due; and likewise an account specifying what particular persons in our said colony are possessed of more than twenty thousand acres each, by what title they respectively hold such land, and how much each of them is possessed of above that quantity; both which accounts you are with all convenient speed to transmit to us by one of our principal secretaries of state and to our commissioners of our Treasury or to our high treasurer for the time being.

58. And it is our express will and pleasure, and you are strictly charged and required not to dispose of any part of our said revenue of quit-rents, nor to suffer the same to be issued out upon any occasion until, upon your certifying unto us the value of what shall remain thereof from time to time in our Treasury, or be due unto us, we shall order the same to be disposed of as we shall find occasion for our service.

59. And whereas there are several nations, cantons, or tribes of Indians inhabiting the western parts of our said colony under your government, you are upon all occasions to give them all proper encouragement, so as to induce them to trade with our subjects in preference to any others of Europe, and to become not only peaceable neighbours but useful and faithful allies. And you are, with the advice of our Council of our said colony, to establish such regulations with respect to the trade carried on with the said Indians, as may best conduce to the restriction or prevention of fraud and imposition in those persons by whom such trade is carried on.

60. And whereas private persons in several of our colonies in America have frequently purchased lands from the Indians without any licence from us, or from any person acting under our authority; which practice is inconsistent with our rights and may endanger the peace and security of our said colonies, it is therefore our will and pleasure that you do not, upon any pretence whatsoever, make a grant or grants to any person or persons of any lands within our colony of Virginia which may or shall have been purchased of the Indians, without a licence first had and obtained from you or the commander-in-chief for the time being. And when any application shall be made to you for a licence to purchase lands of the Indians, you shall, before the issuing of such licence, cause the land proposed to be purchased to be carefully and publicly surveyed by a sworn surveyor in the presence of the Indians who claim a right to such lands, and in the presence of an interpreter properly authorized, which said surveyor shall within a reasonable time, not exceeding three months, make a return to you of such survey, signed or otherwise attested and certified by such Indians, with a plot or description of the land and the exact buttings and boundings thereof, the particulars whereof shall be fully inserted in the licence by you to be granted for that purpose. And you are to take especial care that in all licences to be granted by you for the purchase of lands from the Indians, the quantity of land to be purchased by any one person either in his or her own name or in the names of any person or persons in trust for him or her, do not exceed one thousand acres. And you are further to take care that in passing patents for land purchased of the Indians under

a licence from you, as aforesaid, you do strictly observe the regulations prescribed in the aforegoing articles of these our instructions to you relative to the form, method, terms and conditions of all grants of land.

61. Whereas you will receive from our commissioners for executing the office of High Admiral of Great Britain, and of our plantations, a commission constituting you vice-admiral of our said colony of Virginia, you are hereby required and directed carefully to put in execution the several powers thereby granted you.

62. And whereas we have been informed that the fees for the condemnation of a prize ship in our courts of admiralty in our plantations are considerably greater than those demanded on the like occasion in our High Court of Admiralty here; and whereas we are willing that our subjects in the plantations should have the same ease in obtaining the condemnation of prizes there as in this kingdom, you are to signify our will and pleasure to the officers of our Admiralty Court in Virginia that they do not presume to demand or exact other fees than such as are taken in this kingdom, which amount to about ten pounds for the condemnation of each prize, according to the list of such fees.

63. And there having been great irregularities in the manner of granting commissions in the plantations to private ships of war, you are to govern yourself whenever there shall be occasion according to the commissions and instructions granted in this kingdom. But you are not to grant commissions of marque or reprisal against any prince, or state, or their subjects in amity with us, to any person whatever without our especial command. And you are to oblige the commanders of all ships having private commissions to wear no other colours than such as described in an Order in Council of the 7th of January, 1730, in relation to colours to be worn by all ships of war.

64. Whereas commissions have been granted unto several persons in our respective plantations in America for the trying of pirates in those parts, pursuant to the several acts for the more effectual suppression of piracy; and by a commission already sent to our colony of Virginia, you (as our lieutenant and governor-general of our said colony) are empowered, together with others therein mentioned, to proceed accordingly in reference to the said colony of Virginia; our will and pleasure is that in all matters relating to pirates you govern yourself according to the intent of the said acts and commission aforementioned.

65. And whereas we have thought it necessary for our royal service to constitute and appoint a receiver-general of our rights and perquisites of the admiralty: it is therefore our will and pleasure that you be aiding and assisting to our said receiver-general, his deputy or deputies, in the execution of the said office of receiver-general. And we do hereby require and enjoin you to make up your accounts with him, his deputy or deputies, of all rights of admiralty (effects of pirates included) as you or your officers have received, or shall or may receive; and to pay over to the said receiver-general, his deputy or deputies, for our use all such sum or sums of money as shall appear upon the foot of such accounts to be and remain in your hands or in the hands of any of your officers. And whereas our said receiver-general is directed, in case the parties chargeable with any part of such our revenue, refuse, neglect, or

delay payment thereof, by himself or sufficient deputy to apply in our name to our governors, judges, attorneys-general, or any other our officers or magistrates to be aiding and assisting to him in recovering the same; it is therefore our will and pleasure that you our governor, our judges, our attorneys-general, and all other our officers whom the same may concern, do use all lawful authority for the recovering and levying thereof.

66. You are to permit a liberty of conscience to all persons (except papists) so they be contented with a quiet and peaceable enjoyment of the same, not giving offence or scandal to the government.

67. You shall take especial care that God Almighty be devoutly and duly served throughout your government, the Book of Common Prayer, as by law established, read on each Sunday and holiday; and the blessed sacrament administered according to the rites of the Church of England.

68. You shall be careful that the churches already built there be well and orderly kept, and that more be built, as the province shall, by God's blessing, be improved; and that, besides a competent maintenance to be assigned to the minister of each orthodox church, a convenient house be built at the common charge for each minister, and a competent proportion of land assigned him for a glebe, and exercise of his industry.

69. You are not to prefer any minister to any ecclesiastical benefice in that our colony without a certificate from the right reverend father in God, the lord bishop of London, of his being conformable to the doctrine and discipline of the Church of England, and of a good life and conversation; and if any person, preferred already to a benefice, shall appear to you to give scandal, either by his doctrine or manners, you are to use the proper and usual means for the removal of him.

70. You are to give orders forthwith (if the same be not already done) that every orthodox minister within your government be one of the vestry in his respective parish; and that no vestry be held without him except in case of sickness, or that after notice of a vestry summoned, he omit to come.

71. You are to enquire whether there be any minister within your government who preaches and administers the sacrament in any orthodox church or chapel, without being in due orders, and to give an account thereof to the said lord bishop of London.

72. And to the end the ecclesiastical jurisdiction of the said lord bishop of London may take place in that colony, so far as conveniently may be; we do think fit that you do give all countenance and encouragement to the exercise of the same, excepting only the collating to benefices, granting licences for marriages, and probate of wills, which we have reserved to you, our governor, and to the commander-in-chief of our said colony for the time being.

73. We do further direct that no schoolmaster be henceforth permitted to come from England and to keep school in the said colony without the licence of the said bishop of London; and that no other person now there, or that shall come from other parts, shall be admitted to keep school in that our said colony of Virginia without your licence first obtained.

74. And you are to take especial care that a table of marriages, established by the canons of the Church of England, be hung up in every orthodox church and duly observed; and you are to endeavour to get a law passed in the Assembly of that colony (if not already done) for the strict observation of the said table.

75. The right reverend father in God, Edmund, late lord bishop of London, having presented a petition to his late majesty, King George the first, humbly beseeching him to send instructions to the governors of all the several plantations in America, that they cause all laws already made against blasphemy, profaneness, adultery, fornication, polygamy, incest, profanation of the Lord's day, swearing, and drunkenness in their respective governments, to be vigorously executed; and we thinking it highly just that all persons who shall offend in any of the particulars aforesaid should be prosecuted and punished for their said offences; it is therefore our will and pleasure that you take due care for the punishment of the aforementioned vices and that you earnestly recommend it to the Assembly of Virginia to provide effectual laws for the restraint and punishment of all such of the aforementioned vices against which no laws are as yet provided; and also you are to use your endeavours to render the laws in being more effectual by providing for the punishment of the aforementioned vices by presentment on oath to be made to the temporal courts by the churchwardens of the several parishes at proper times of the year, to be appointed for that purpose. And for the further discouragement of vice and encouragement of virtue and good living, that by such example the infidels may be invited and desire to embrace the Christian religion, you are not to admit any person to public trusts or employments in the colony under your government whose ill fame and conversation may occasion scandal. And it is our further will and pleasure that you recommend to the Assemby to enter upon proper methods for the erecting and maintaining of schools in order to the training up of youth to reading, and to a necessary knowledge of the principles of religion.

76. You shall send to us, by one of our principal secretaries of state, an account of the present number of inhabitants: men, women, and children, as well masters as servants, free and unfree, and of the slaves in our said colony, as also a yearly account of the increase or decrease of them, and how many of them are fit to bear arms in the militia of our said colony.

77. You shall also give unto us, by one of our principal secretaries of state, an account every half year of what number of Negroes our said colony is supplied with and at what rates sold.

78. You shall not upon any occasion whatever establish or put in execution any articles of war, or other law martial upon any of our subjects, inhabitants of our said colony of Virginia, without the advice and consent of our Council there.

79. Whereas it is absolutely necessary that we be informed of the state of defence of all our plantations in America, as well in relation to the stores of war that are in each plantation, as to the forts and fortifications there; and what more may be necessary to be built for the defence and security of the same; you are as soon as

possible to prepare an account thereof with relation to our said colony of Virginia in the most particular manner. And you are therein to express the present state of the arms, ammunition, and other stores of war belonging to the said colony, either in any public magazines, or in the hands of private persons, together with the state of all places either already fortified or that you judge necessary to be fortified for the security of our said colony. And you are to transmit the said accounts to us by one of our principal secretaries of state, as also a duplicate thereof to our master-general, or principal officers of our ordnance; which accounts are to express the particulars of ordnance, carriages, ball, powder, and all other sort of arms and ammunition in our public stores at your arrival, and so from time to time of what shall be sent to you, or bought with the public money, and to specify the time of the disposal, and the occasion thereof; and other like accounts half yearly in the same manner.

80. You are to take especial care that fit storehouses be settled throughout our said colony for receiving and keeping of arms, ammunition, and other public stores.

81. Whereas by a clause in the act above recited, passed in our colony of Virginia in the year 1680, "for raising a public Revenue for the better support of the Government of His Majesty's Colony of Virginia", a duty of powder and shot, or an equivalent in money in lieu thereof is laid on the tonnage of any ship or vessel coming to our said colony, which act is perpetual; and whereas it hath been found by experience that the raising the said duty in kind only, where gunpowder can possibly be had, has been of great service in furnishing the magazines with powder for the defence of our colonies in times of danger; it is our royal will and pleasure, and you are hereby required and directed to recommend it to the Assembly of our said colony to pass a new law for imposing and collecting a duty of powder and shot; and that such law be made perpetual; that a certain time not exceeding twelve months be allowed by the said act for giving notice thereof to the several masters of vessels trading to our said colony; and that for the more ample notification thereof a proclamation be also published there, declaring that from and after the time limited in the said act, no commutation shall be allowed but upon evident necessity, which may sometimes happen, whereof you or the commander-in-chief of our said colony, for the time being, are to be the judge, in which case the master shall pay the full price gunpowder sells for there, and the money so collected shall be laid out as soon as may be in the purchase of gunpowder. And you are also to transmit every six months to us, by one of our principal secretaries of state, an account of the particular quantities of powder collected under the said act, and also a duplicate thereof to the master-general or principal officers of our ordnance.

82. You shall cause a survey to be made of all the considerable landing places and harbours in our said colony, and with the advice of our Council there, erect in any of them such fortifications as shall be necessary for the security and advantage of the said colony, which shall be done at the public charge. And you are accordingly to move the General Assembly to the passing of such acts as may be requisite for the carrying on that work, in which we doubt not their cheerful concurrence from the common security and benefit they will receive thereby.

83. And in case of the distress of any other of our plantations, you shall, upon

application of the respective governors thereof to you, assist them with what aid the condition and safety of our colony under your government can spare.

84. Whereas we have been informed that in times of war our enemies have frequently got intelligence of the state of our plantations by letters from private persons to their correspondents in Great Britain, taken on board ships coming from the plantations, which has been of dangerous consequence, our will and pleasure is that you signify to all merchants, planters, and others, that they be very cautious in time of war, whenever that shall happen, in giving any account by letters of the public state and condition of our colony of Virginia. And you are further to give directions to all masters of ships, or other persons to whom you may intrust your letters that they put such letters into a bag with a sufficient weight to sink the same immediately in case of imminent danger from the enemy. And you are also to let the merchants and planters know how greatly it is for their interest that their letters should not fall into the hands of the enemy, and that they should give the like orders to masters of ships in relation to their letters. And you are further to advise all masters of ships that they do sink all letters in case of danger in the manner before-mentioned.

85. And whereas the merchants and planters in America have, in time of war, corresponded and traded with our enemies and carried intelligence to them, to the great prejudice and hazard of the British plantations, you are therefore by all possible methods to hinder such trade and correspondence in time of war.

86. You are likewise from time to time to give unto us, by one of our principal secretaries of state, an account of the wants and defects of our said colony, what are the chief products thereof, what new improvements are made therein by the industry of the inhabitants or planters, and what further improvements you conceive may be made, or advantages gained by trade, and which way we may contribute thereunto.

87. If anything shall happen which may be for the advantage and security of our said colony which is not herein or by our commission provided for, we do hereby allow unto you, with the advice and consent of our said Council, to take order for the present therein, giving unto us, by one of our principal secretaries of state, speedy notice thereof, that so you may receive our ratification if we shall approve the same; provided always that you do not, by colour of any power or authority hereby given you, commence or declare war without our knowledge and particular commands therein, except it be against Indians upon emergencies, wherein the consent of our Council shall be had, and speedy notice given thereof to us by one of our principal secretaries of state.

88. And for the maintenance and support of you, our lieutenant and governor-general of our colony and dominion of Virginia, and of the dignity of that our government, our will and pleasure is that you do take to yourself, out of our revenue arising from the duty of two shillings per hogshead on tobacco, the sum of two thousand pounds sterling per annum by quarterly payments. And you shall also cause to be paid out of our said revenue to the members of our Council, the judges and other officers, as well civil as military, and to the marshal, clerk of assembly, gunners and matrosses, the usual salaries and allowances, as already established, or such other

as you, with the advice of our Council, shall think requisite and reasonable, a true account whereof you shall transmit every six months unto us by one of our principal secretaries of state, and to our commissioners of our Treasury, or to our high treasurer for the time being.

89. And whereas great prejudice may happen to our service and to the security of our said colony by the absence of you, our lieutenant and governor-general, or the commander-in-chief of our said colony for the time being from those parts; our will and pleasure is that neither you, our lieutenant and governor-general, nor our commander-in-chief for the time being, shall, upon any pretence whatsoever, come to Europe without having first obtained leave for so doing from us under our sign manual and signet, or by our order in our Privy Council. Yet, nevertheless, in case of sickness, you or he may go to New York, or any other of our neighbouring plantations, and there stay for such a space as the recovery of your or their health may absolutely require.

90. And whereas we have thought fit by our commission to direct that in case of your death or absence from our said colony, and in case there be at that time no person upon the place commissionated or appointed by us to be our lieutenant-governor or commander-in-chief, the eldest councillor, who shall be at the time of your death or absence residing within our said colony or dominion of Virginia, shall take upon him the administration of the government, and execute our said commission and instructions, and the several powers and authorities therein contained in the manner thereby directed. It is nevertheless our express will and pleasure that in such case the said president shall forbear to pass any acts but what are immediately necessary for the peace and welfare of our said colony, without our particular order for that purpose, and that he shall not take upon him to dissolve the Assembly then in being, nor to remove nor suspend any of the members of our said Council, nor any judges, justices of the peace, or other officers, civil or military, without the advice and consent of at least seven of the Council. And the said president is to transmit to us by one of our principal secretaries of state by the first opportunity the reasons of such alterations, signed by himself and by our Council.

91. And whereas we are willing in the best manner to provide for the support of the government of our said colony, by setting apart a sufficient allowance to such as shall be our lieutenant-governor or president of our Council, commanding in chief, residing for the time being within the same, our will and pleasure therefore is that when it shall happen that you shall be absent from our said colony, one full moiety of the salary, and of all perquisites and emoluments whatsoever which would otherwise become due unto you, shall, during the time of your absence from our said colony, be paid and satisfied unto such lieutenant-governor, or president of our Council commanding in chief, who shall be resident upon the place for the time being, which we do hereby order and allot unto him towards his maintenance and for the better support of the dignity of that our government.

92. And you are upon all occasions to send to us by one of our principal secretaries of state a particular account of all your proceedings, and of the condition of affairs within your government.

26. The Fundamental Orders of Connecticut (14 January 1639)

Connecticut was founded by settlers from Massachusetts. The government was in operation three years before the Fundamental Orders were drawn up. The preamble is essentially a compact such as that adopted by Rhode Island settlers, and the remainder is a body of law rather than a constitution. Connecticut, unlike Rhode Island, showed few democratic tendencies during its colonial history. The basis of government was popular but the colony was in fact ruled by a tight-knit aristocracy for nearly two centuries. Printed: John H. Trumbull, Charles J. Hoadly, *et al.*, eds., *Public Records of the Colony of Connecticut, 1636–1776* (15 vols., Hartford, 1850–1890), I, pp. 20–25.

Forasmuch as it hath pleased the almighty God by the wise disposition of his divine providence so to order and dispose of things that we the inhabitants and residents of Windsor, Hartford, and Wethersfield are now cohabiting and dwelling in and upon the River of Connecticut and the lands thereunto adjoining; and well knowing where a people are gathered together the word of God requires that to maintain the peace and union of such a people there should be an orderly and decent government established according to God, to order and dispose of the affairs of the people at all seasons as occasion shall require: do therefore associate and conjoin ourselves to be as one public state or commonwealth; and do, for ourselves and our successors, and such as shall be adjoined to us at any time hereafter, enter into combination and confederation together, to maintain and preserve the liberty and purity of the gospel of our Lord Jesus which we now profess, as also the discipline of the churches, which according to the truth of the said gospel is now practised amongst us; as also in our civil affairs to be guided and governed according to such laws, rules, orders, and decrees as shall be made, ordered and decreed, as followeth:

1. It is ordered, sentenced, and decreed that there shall be yearly two general assemblies or courts, the one the second Thursday in April, the other the second Thursday in September, following; the first shall be called the court of election, wherein shall be yearly chosen from time to time so many magistrates and other public officers as shall be found requisite: whereof one to be chosen governor for the year ensuing and until another be chosen, and no other magistrate to be chosen for more than one year; provided always there be six chosen besides the governor, which being chosen and sworn according to an oath recorded for that purpose, shall have power to administer justice according to the laws here established, and for want thereof, according to the rule of the word of God; which choice shall be made by all that are admitted freemen and have taken the oath of fidelity and do cohabit within this jurisdiction (having been admitted inhabitants by the major part of the town wherein they live), or the major part of such as shall be then present.

2. It is ordered, sentenced, and decreed that the election of the aforesaid magistrates shall be on this manner: every person present and qualified for choice shall bring in (to the persons deputed to receive them) one single paper with the name of him written in it whom he desires to have governor, and he that hath the greatest number of papers shall be governor for that year. And the rest of the magistrates or public officers to be chosen in this manner: the secretary for the time being shall first read the names of all that are to be put to choice and then shall severally nominate them distinctly, and every one that would have the person nominated to be chosen shall bring in one single paper written upon, and he that would not have him chosen

shall bring in a blank; and every one that has more written papers than blanks shall be a magistrate for that year; which papers shall be received and told by one or more that shall be then chosen by the court and sworn to be faithful therein; but in case there should not be six chosen as aforesaid, besides the governor, out of those which are nominated, then he or they which have the most written papers shall be a magistrate or magistrates for the ensuing year, to make up the foresaid number.

3. It is ordered, sentenced, and decreed that the secretary shall not nominate any person, nor shall any person be chosen newly into the magistracy which was not propounded in some general court before, to be nominated the next election; and to that end it shall be lawful for each of the towns aforesaid by their deputies to nominate any two whom they conceive fit to be put to election; and the court may add so many more as they judge requisite.

4. It is ordered, sentenced, and decreed that no person be chosen governor above once in two years, and that the governor be always a member of some approved congregation, and formerly of the magistracy within this jurisdiction; and all the magistrates, freemen of this commonwealth; and that no magistrate or other public officer shall execute any part of his or their office before they are severally sworn, which shall be done in the face of the court if they be present, and in case of absence, by some deputed for that purpose.

5. It is ordered, sentenced, and decreed that to the aforesaid court of election the several towns shall send their deputies, and when the elections are ended they may proceed in any public service as at other courts. Also the other general court in September shall be for making of laws, and any other public occasion which concerns the good of the commonwealth.

6. It is ordered, sentenced, and decreed that the governor shall, either by himself or by the secretary, send out summons to the constables of every town for the calling of these two standing courts one month at least before their several times; and also if the governor and the greatest part of the magistrates see cause upon any special occasion to call a general court, they may give order to the secretary so to do within fourteen days' warning; and if urgent necessity so require, upon a shorter notice, giving sufficient grounds for it to the deputies when they meet, or else be questioned for the same; and if the governor and major part of magistrates shall either neglect or refuse to call the two general standing courts or either of them, as also at other times when the occasions of the commonwealth require, the freemen thereof, or the major part of them, shall petition to them so to do: if then it be either denied or neglected the said freemen or the major part of them shall have power to give order to the constables of the several towns to do the same, and so may meet together, and choose to themselves a moderator, and may proceed to do any act of power which any other general court may.

7. It is ordered, sentenced, and decreed that after there are warrants given out for any of the said general courts, the constable or constables of each town shall forthwith give notice distinctly to the inhabitants of the same, in some public assembly or by going or sending from house to house, that at a place and time by him or them limited and set, they meet and assemble themselves together to elect and choose

certain deputies to be at the general court then following to agitate the affairs of the commonwealth; which said deputies shall be chosen by all that are admitted inhabitants in the several towns and have taken the oath of fidelity; provided that none be chosen a deputy for any general court which is not a freeman of this commonwealth.

The foresaid deputies shall be chosen in manner following: every person that is present and qualified as before expressed, shall bring the names of such, written in several papers, as they desire to have chosen for that employment, and these 3 or 4, more or less, being the number agreed on to be chosen for that time, that have greatest number of papers written for them shall be deputies for that court; whose names shall be endorsed on the back side of the warrant and returned into the court, with the constable or constables hand unto the same.

8. It is ordered, sentenced, and decreed that Windsor, Hartford, and Wethersfield shall have power, each town, to send four of their freemen as their deputies to every general court; and whatsoever other towns shall be hereafter added to this jurisdiction, they shall send so many deputies as the court shall judge meet, a reasonable proportion to the number of freemen that are in the said towns being to be attended therein; which deputies shall have the power of the whole town to give their votes and allowance to all such laws and orders as may be for the public good, and unto which the said towns are to be bound.

9. It is ordered and decreed that the deputies thus chosen shall have power and liberty to appoint a time and a place of meeting together before any general court to advise and consult of all such things as may concern the good of the public, as also to examine their own elections, whether according to the order, and if they or the greatest part of them find any election to be illegal, they may seclude such present from their meeting, and return the same and their reasons to the court; and if it prove true, the court may fine the party or parties so intruding and the town, if they see cause, and give out a warrant to go to a new election in a legal way, either in part or in whole. Also the said deputies shall have power to fine any that shall be disorderly at their meetings, or for not coming in due time or place according to appointment; and they may return the said fines into the court if it be refused to be paid, and the treasurer to take notice of it, and to estreat or levy the same as he doth other fines.

10. It is ordered, sentenced, and decreed that every general court, except such as through neglect of the governor and the greatest part of magistrates, the freemen themselves do call, shall consist of the governor, or some one chosen to moderate the court, and 4 other magistrates at least, with the major part of the deputies of the several towns legally chosen; and in case the freemen or major part of them through neglect or refusal of the governor and major part of the magistrates shall call a court, it shall consist of the major part of freemen that are present or their deputies, with a moderator chosen by them: in which said general courts shall consist the supreme power of the commonwealth, and they only shall have power to make laws or repeal them, to grant levies, to admit of freemen, dispose of lands undisposed of, to several towns or persons, and also shall have power to call either court or magistrate or any other person whatsoever into question for any misdemeanour, and may for just causes displace or deal otherwise according to the nature of the offence; and also may

deal in any other matter that concerns the good of this commonwealth, except election of magistrates, which shall be done by the whole body of freemen. In which court the governor or moderator shall have power to order the court to give liberty of speech, and silence unseasonable and disorderly speakings, to put all things to vote, and in case the vote be equal, to have the casting voice. But none of these courts shall be adjourned or dissolved without the consent of the major part of the court.

11. It is ordered, sentenced, and decreed that when any general court, upon the occasions of the commonwealth, have agreed upon any sum or sums of money to be levied upon the several towns within this jurisdiction, that a committee be chosen to set out and appoint what shall be the proportion of every town to pay of the said levy, provided the committees be made up of an equal number out of each town.

27. The federation of Rhode Island Towns (May 1647)

The town of Providence was founded by Roger Williams and his followers in 1636. Other towns were founded during the next few years by other refugees and exiles, mostly from Massachusetts. The leaders in each of the towns were men and women of strong convictions and disputatious character. The result was that towns were rent with internal dissension, while disputes over land and other matters meant quarrels between town and town. Most of the people believed in democratic government and in freedom of religion. Rhode Island was thus looked upon as a sinkhole of iniquity by the other New England settlements and they made it plain that they would take over the little settlements whenever opportunity offered.

The only chance of survival for Rhode Island was to get a charter from England. Roger Williams was firmly convinced that the compacts among the settlers themselves were the only necessary basis of government, yet he was a practical man as well. Therefore he went to England and secured a charter of incorporation in 1644 from the Commissioners of Plantations, headed by the earl of Warwick. The charter named the colony the "Incorporation of Providence Plantations" and gave the inhabitants the right to rule themselves by "such civil laws and constitutions" as they might think fit, subject only to the restriction that such laws "be conformable to the laws of England, so far as the nature and constitution of the place will admit". Armed with this charter, Williams returned to Rhode Island with a safe conduct through Massachusetts. In 1647 a federation of Rhode Island towns was brought about. The general assembly which met at Portsmouth in May 1647, was made up of freemen from the four towns in the colony. The assembly created a federation and drafted a code of laws embodying the precedents set by the laws and statutes of England, including a bill of rights.

The section of the proceedings of the assembly which follow sets forth the philosophy of government and the rights of individuals. Printed: John R. Bartlett, ed., *Records of the Colony of Rhode Island and Providence Plantations in New England* (10 vols., Providence, 1856–1865), I, pp. 156–160.

FOR THE PROVINCE OF PROVIDENCE

Forasmuch as we have received from our noble lords and honoured governors, and that by virtue of an ordinance of the Parliament of England, a free and absolute charter of civil incorporation, etc., we do jointly agree to incorporate ourselves, and so to remain a body politic by the authority thereof, and therefore do declare to own ourselves and one another to be members of the same body, and to have right to the freedom and privileges thereof by subscribing our names to these words, following:

We, whose names are hereunder written, do engage ourselves to the utmost of our estates and strength, to maintain the authority and to enjoy the liberty granted to us by our charter, in the extent of it according to the letter, and to maintain each other by the same authority, in his lawful right and liberty.

And now since our charter gives us power to govern ourselves and such other as come among us, and by such a form of civil government as by the voluntary consent, etc., shall be found most suitable to our estate and condition.

It is agreed, by this present assembly thus incorporate, and by this present act declared, that the form of government established in Providence Plantations is democratical; that is to say, a government held by the free and voluntary consent of all, or the greater part of the free inhabitants.

And now to the end that we may give, each to other (notwithstanding our different consciences, touching the truth as it is in Jesus, whereof, upon the point we all make mention), as good and hopeful assurance as we are able, touching each man's peaceable and quiet enjoyment of his lawful right and liberty, we do agree unto, and by the authority above said, enact, establish, and confirm these orders following.

Touching Laws

1. That no person in this colony shall be taken or imprisoned, or be disseized of his lands or liberties, or be exiled, or any other otherwise molested or destroyed, but by the lawful judgment of his peers, or by some known law, and according to the letter of it, ratified and confirmed by the major part of the General Assembly lawfully met and orderly managed.

2. That no person shall (but at his great peril) presume to bear or execute any office that is not lawfully called to it and confirmed in it; nor though he be lawfully called and confirmed, presume to do more or less than those that had power to call him, or did authorize him to do.

3. That no Assembly shall have power to constitute any laws for the binding of others, or to ordain officers for the execution thereof but such as are founded upon the charter and rightly derived from the General Assembly, lawfully met and orderly managed.

4. That no person be employed in any service for the public administration of justice and judgment upon offenders, or between man and man, without good encouragement, and due satisfaction from the public, either out of the common stock, or out of the stocks of those that have occasioned his service; that so those that are able to serve, may not be unwilling, and those that are able and willing, may not be disabled by being overburdened. And then, in case a man be called unto office by a lawful Assembly, and refuse to bear office, or be called by an officer to assist in the execution of his office, and refuse to assist him, he shall forfeit as much again as his wages would have amounted unto, or be otherwise fined by the judgment of his peers, and to pay his fine or forfeiture unless the colony or that lawful Assembly release him. But in case of eminent danger, no man shall refuse.

And now, forasmuch as our charter gives us power to make such laws, constitutions, penalties, and officers of justice for the execution thereof as we, or the greater part of us shall, by free consent, agree unto, and yet does premise that those laws, constitutions, and penalties so made shall be conformable to the laws of England, so far as the nature and constitution of our place will admit, to the end that we may show ourselves not only unwilling that our popularity should prove (as some conjecture it will) an anarchy, and so a common tyranny, but willing and exceedingly desirous to preserve every man safe in his person, name, and estate; and to show ourselves, in so doing, to be also under authority, by keeping within the verge and limits prescribed us in our charter, by which we have authority in this respect to act; we do agree and by this present act determine, to make such laws and constitutions so conformable, etc., or rather to make those laws ours, and better known among us; that is to say, such of them and so far as the nature and constitution of our place will admit.

Touching the Common Law

It being the common right among common men, and is profitable either to direct or correct all, without exception; and it being true which that great doctor of the Gentiles once said, that the law is made or brought to light, not for a righteous man, who is a law unto himself, but for the lawless and disobedient in the general, but more particularly for murderers of fathers and mothers, for manslayers, for whoremongers, and those that defile themselves with mankind; for menstealers, for liars and perjured persons, unto which, upon the point, may be reduced the common law of the realm of England, the end of which is, as is propounded, to preserve every man safe in his own person, name, and estate; we do agree to make, or rather to bring such laws to light for the direction or correction of such lawless persons, and for their memories sake to reduce them to these five general laws or heads, viz.:

1. Under that head of murdering fathers and mothers, being the highest and most unnatural, are comprehended those laws that concern high treason, petty treason, rebellion, misbehaviour, and their accessories.

2. Under the law for manslayers are comprehended those laws that concern self-murder, murder, homicide, misadventure, casual death, cutting out the tongue or eyes, witchcraft, burglary, robbery, burning of houses, forcible entries, rescues and escape, riots, routs and unlawful assemblies, batteries, assaults and threats and their accessories.

3. Under the law for whoremongers, and those that defile themselves with mankind, being the chief of that nature, are comprehended those laws that concern sodomy, buggery, rape, adultery, fornication, and their accessories.

4. Under the law for menstealers, being the chief of that nature, are comprehended those laws that concern theft of men, larceny, trespasses by men or beasts, fraudulent dealing by deceitful bargain, covenants, conveyances by barratry, conspiracy, champerty and maintenance, by forging or raising records, writs, deeds, leases, bills, etc., and by using false weights and measures and their accessories.

5. Under the law for liars and perjured persons, being the chief of that nature, are comprehended such as concern perjury itself, breach of covenant, slander, false witness-bearing, and their accessories.

And as necessary concomitants hereof, to prevent murder, theft, and perjury, we do jointly agree in this present Assembly, to make or produce such laws as concern provision for the poor, so that the impotent shall be maintained and the able employed. And to prevent poverties it is agreed that such laws be made and produced as concerns the ordering of alehouses and taverns, drunkenness and unlawful gaming therein; and instead of such, to propagate archery, which is both man-like and profitable; and to prevent whoredom and those evils before mentioned, it is agreed by this present Assembly to constitute and establish some ordinance touching marriage, probate of wills, and intestates.

28. The New York Charter of Liberties and Privileges (30 October 1683)

When New York was taken from the Dutch in 1664, it was given to the duke of York as a proprietary province. He appointed a series of governors who ruled without a local legislature. The inhabitants protested more and more vigorously because they did not have the privileges of other English colonists, and particularly because they did not have a legislature. By 1681 men were refusing to pay customs duties and taxes. The duke of York finally conceded that the colony should have a legislature. He sent out Colonel Thomas Dongan as governor with instructions to call an assembly.

As soon as the assembly met it drafted a charter of liberties and privileges. The governor approved and sent it to the duke of York. Apparently he at first approved, but before final action was taken, he became King James II. The Privy Council then vetoed the charter and declared that New York was to have the same form of government as the Dominion of New England (No. 30). Thus the legislature was abolished. When it was re-established in 1691 it soon agreed upon another charter of liberties almost identical with that of 1683. This new charter was also vetoed, the Privy Council declaring that it gave unreasonable privileges to members of the assembly during its sessions, that all except innholders were exempted from the quartering of troops, and because it contained "several large and doubtful expressions".

While these "charters of liberties" are not strictly compacts such as those of New England, they are nevertheless clear statements of what were conceived to be the rights of Englishmen and colonists, and they can be matched by similar statements from virtually every other English colony. Printed: *The Colonial Laws of New York from the Year 1664 to the Revolution* (5 vols., Albany, 1894), I, pp. 111–116.

For the better establishing the government of this province of New York, and that justice and right may be equally done to all persons within the same:

Be it enacted by the Governor, Council, and Representatives now in General Assembly met and assembled, and by the authority of the same: that the supreme legislative authority under his Majesty and Royal Highness, James, duke of York, Albany, etc., lord proprietor of the said province, shall for ever be and reside in a Governor, Council, and the people met in General Assembly.

That the exercise of the chief magistracy and administration of the government over the said province shall be in the said Governor, assisted by a Council with whose advice and consent, or with at least four of them, he is to rule and govern the same according to the laws thereof.

That in case the governor shall die or be absent out of the province and that there be no person within the said province commissionated by his Royal Highness, his heirs or successors to be governor or commander-in-chief there, that then the Council for the time being, or so many of them as are in the said province, do take upon them the administration of the governor and the execution of the laws thereof, and powers and authorities belonging to the governor and Council, the first in nomination in which Council is to preside until the said governor shall return and arrive in the said province again, or the pleasure of his Royal Highness, his heirs or successors shall be further known.

That according to the usage, custom, and practice of the realm of England, a sessions of a General Assembly be held in this province once in three years at least.

That every freeholder within this province, and freeman in any corporation, shall have his free choice and vote in the electing of the representatives without any manner of constraint or imposition. And that in all elections the majority of voices shall carry it, and by freeholders is understood everyone who is so understood according to the laws of England.

That the persons to be elected to sit as representatives in the General Assembly from time to time for the several cities, towns, counties, shires, or divisions of this province, and all places within the same, shall be according to the proportion and number hereafter expressed: that is to say for the city and county of New York four; for the county of Suffolk two; for Queens county two; for Kings county two; for the county of Richmond two; for the county of West Chester two; for the county of Ulster two; for the county of Albany two, and for Schenectady within the said county one; for Dukes county two; for the county of Cornwall two, and as many more as his Royal Highness shall think fit to establish.

That all persons chosen and assembled in manner aforesaid, or the major part of them, shall be deemed and accounted the representatives of this province, which said representatives together with the governor and his Council, shall for ever be the supreme and only legislative power under his Royal Highness of the said province.

That the said representatives may appoint their own times of meeting during their sessions and may adjourn their house from time to time to such time as to them shall seem meet and convenient.

That the said representatives are the sole judges of the qualifications of their own members, and likewise of all undue elections, and may from time to time purge their house as they shall see occasion during the said sessions.

That no member of the General Assembly or their servants during the time of their sessions and while they shall be going to and returning from the said Assembly, shall be arrested, sued, imprisoned, or any ways molested or troubled, nor be compelled to make answer to any suit, bill, plaint, declaration, or otherwise (cases of high treason and felony only excepted), provided the number of the said servants shall not exceed three. That all bills agreed upon by the said representatives, or the major part of them, shall be presented to the governor and his Council for their approbation and consent; all and every which said bills so approved of, consented to by the governor and his Council, shall be esteemed and accounted the laws of the province, which said laws shall continue and remain of force until they shall be repealed by the authority aforesaid: that is to say, the Governor, Council, and Representatives in General Assembly, by and with the approbation of his Royal Highness, or expire by their own limitations.

That in all cases of death or removal of any of the said representatives, the governor shall issue out summons by writ to the respective towns, cities, shires, counties, or divisions for which he or they so removed or deceased were chosen, willing and requiring the freeholders of the same to elect others in their place and stead.

That no freeman shall be taken and imprisoned or be disseized of his freehold or liberty or free customs, or be outlawed or exiled, or any other ways destroyed, nor shall be passed upon, adjudged, or condemned but by the lawful judgment of his peers and by the law of this province. Justice nor right shall be neither sold, denied, or deferred to any man within this province.

That no aid, tax, tallage, assessment, custom, loan, benevolence, or imposition whatsoever shall be laid, assessed, imposed, or levied on any of his Majesty's subjects within this province or their estates, upon any manner of colour or pretence, but by the act and consent of the Governor, Council, and representatives of the people in General Assembly met and assembled.

That no man of what estate or condition soever shall be put out of his lands or tenements, nor taken, nor imprisoned, nor disherited, nor banished, nor any ways destroyed without being brought to answer by due course of law.

That a freeman shall not be amerced for a small fault, but after the manner of his fault, and for a great fault, after the greatness thereof, saving to him his freehold; and a husbandman saving to him his wainage, and a merchant likewise saving to him his merchandise. And none of the said amercements shall be assessed but by the oath of twelve honest and lawful men of the vicinage, provided the faults and misdemeanours be not in contempt of courts of judicature.

All trials shall be by the verdict of twelve men, and as near as may be, peers or equals; and of the neighbourhood and in the county, shire, or division where the fact shall arise or grow; whether the same be by indictment, information, declaration, or otherwise against the person, offender, or defendant.

That in all cases capital or criminal there shall be a grand inquest, who shall first present the offence, and then twelve men of the neighbourhood to try the offender, who after his plea to the indictment shall be allowed his reasonable challenges. That in all cases whatsoever bail by sufficient sureties shall be allowed and taken, unless for treason or felony plainly and specially expressed and mentioned in the warrant of commitment; provided always that nothing herein contained shall extend to discharge out of prison upon bail any person taken in execution for debts, or otherwise legally sentenced by the judgment of any of the courts of record within the province.

That no freeman shall be compelled to receive any mariners or soldiers into his house and there suffer them to sojourn against their wills, provided always it be not in time of actual war within this province.

That no commissions for proceeding by martial law against any of his Majesty's subjects within this province shall issue forth to any person or persons whatsoever, lest by colour of them any of his Majesty's subjects be destroyed or put to death, except all such officers, persons, and soldiers in pay throughout the government.

That from henceforward no lands within this province shall be esteemed or accounted a chattel or personal estate, but an estate of inheritance, according to the custom and practice of his Majesty's realm of England.

That no court or courts within this province have or at any time hereafter shall have any jurisdiction, power, or authority to grant out any execution or other writ whereby any man's land may be sold or any other way disposed of without the owner's consent, provided always that the issues or mean profits of any man's lands shall or may be extended by execution or otherwise to satisfy just debts, anything to the contrary hereof in any wise notwithstanding.

That no estate of a feme covert shall be sold or conveyed but by deed, acknowledged by her in some court of record, the woman being secretly examined if she doth it freely without threats or compulsion of her husband.

That all wills in writing attested by two credible witnesses shall be of the same force to convey lands as other conveyances, being registered in the secretary's office within forty days after the testator's death.

That a widow after the death of her husband shall have her dower and shall and may tarry in the chief house of her husband forty days after the death of her husband, within which forty days her dower shall be assigned her, and for her dower shall be assigned unto her the third part of all the lands of her husband during coverture, except she were endowed of less before marriage.

That all lands and heritages within this province and dependencies shall be free from all fines and licences upon alienations, and from all heriots, wardships, liveries, primer seisins, year day and waste escheats and forfeitures upon the death of parents and ancestors, natural, unnatural, casual, or judicial, and that for ever; cases of high treason only excepted.

That no person or persons which profess faith in God by Jesus Christ shall at any time be any ways molested, punished, disquieted, or called in question for any difference in opinion or matter of religious concernment, who do not actually disturb the civil peace of the province; but that all and every such person or persons may from time to time and at all times freely have and fully enjoy his or their judgments or consciences in matters of religion throughout all the province, they behaving themselves peaceably and quietly, and not using this liberty to licentiousness nor to the civil injury or outward disturbance of others, provided always that this liberty or anything contained therein to the contrary shall never be construed or improved to make void the settlement of any public minister on Long Island, whether such settlement be by two thirds of the voices in any town thereon, which shall always include the minor part, or by subscriptions of particular inhabitants in said towns, provided they are the two thirds thereon; but that all such agreements, covenants, and subscriptions that are there already made and had, or that hereafter shall be in this manner consented to, agreed, and subscribed shall at all time and times hereafter be firm and stable. And in confirmation hereof it is enacted by the Governor, Council, and Representatives, that all such sums of money so agreed on, consented to, or subscribed as aforesaid, for maintenance of said public ministers by the two thirds of any town on Long Island shall always include the minor part who shall be regulated thereby, and also such subscriptions and agreements as are before mentioned, are and shall be always ratified, performed, and paid. And if any town on said island in their public capacity of agreement with any such minister or any particular persons by their private subscriptions as aforesaid shall make, default, deny, or withdraw from such payment so covenanted to, agreed upon, and subscribed: that in such case, upon complaint of any collector appointed and chosen by two thirds of such town upon Long Island, unto any justice of that county, upon his hearing the same he is hereby authorized, empowered, and required to issue out his warrant unto the constable or his deputy, or any other person appointed for the collection of said rates or agreement, to levy upon the goods and chattels of the said delinquent or defaulter all such sums of money so covenanted and agreed to be paid, by distress with costs and charges without any further suit in law, any law, custom, or usage to the contrary in any wise notwithstanding. Provided always the said sum or sums be under forty shillings, otherwise to be recovered as the law directs.

And whereas all the respective Christian churches now in practice within the city of New York, and the other places of this province, do appear to be privileged churches and have been so established and confirmed by the former authority of this government: be it hereby enacted by this General Assembly and by the authority thereof, that all the said respective Christian churches be hereby confirmed therein, and that they and every of them shall from henceforth for ever be held and reputed as privileged churches, and enjoy all their former freedoms of their religion in divine worship and church discipline; and that all former contracts made and agreed upon for the maintenances of the several ministers of the said churches, shall stand and continue in full force and virtue; and that all contracts for the future to be made shall be of the same power. And all persons that are unwilling to perform their part of the said contract shall be constrained thereunto by a warrant from any justice of the peace, provided it be under forty shillings, or otherwise, as this law directs; provided also that all Christian churches that shall hereafter come and settle within this province shall have the same privileges.

C. BRITISH POLICY AND COLONIAL GOVERNMENTS

WITH the exception of a brief effort to control the founding of Virginia, the Crown did not interfere with colonization until the Virginia Company charter was revoked in 1624. In 1625 Charles I issued a proclamation declaring that the government of Virginia should depend upon the Crown, but specific details were not worked out.[1] That Charles I had no intention of allowing colonial self-government was made plain in 1634 when he created a special commission on plantations. This commission was given power to make laws, ordinances, and constitutions "concerning either the state public of the said colonies, or utility of private persons and their lands, goods, debts, and successions". It also had the power to remove governors, establish courts, examine and pass upon letters patent, and support the clergy. However, the commission achieved little. It attempted to vacate the Massachusetts charter of 1629, it forbade emigration without licence, and it restored John Harvey to the governorship of Virginia after the inhabitants had thrown him out.

By the time the commission was appointed, thirteen English colonies had been planted in the New World and no new ones were to be founded until after 1660. Because of the Puritan Revolution the first thirteen colonies were allowed to go their own way and to govern themselves as they pleased. Virginia was granted a legislative assembly in 1639.[2] Rhode Island was given a charter allowing it to govern itself in 1644.[3] Such indifference ended with the Restoration. Then came a new surge of colonizing activity carried on by the close supporters of Charles II, who gave them huge proprietary grants. But at the same time the legal and administrative framework for imperial administration was developed. Between 1660 and 1696 Parliament passed the basic Acts of Trade and Navigation.[4] During the same period administrative agencies under control of the Crown were set up to supervise colonial affairs.

The king in Council, that is the Privy Council, exercised ultimate authority over the colonies, but other agencies also played a part. A committee of the Privy Council, known as the Lords of Trade and Plantations, was established in 1675.[5] It was vigorous at first, but soon lost its effectiveness. English merchants grew increasingly indignant. They demanded a board filled with "knowing men of business" and appealed to Parliament. The House of Commons investigated and was on the point of creating a council for colonial trade by Act of Parliament when William III created the Board of Trade and Plantations in 1696.[6] This board was charged with the general supervision of colonial political and economic affairs, but it had no executive authority. It functioned as an investigating and advisory body. However, its recommendations could be carried out only through action by the Privy Council. The Board of Trade was a hard-working and effective body for a time, but it became a spot for placemen and declined in importance. Shortly before the Seven Years War it once more took an active interest in colonial affairs only to have its efforts nullified by the outbreak of war in 1756.

There were in addition many other agencies and offices in England concerned

[1] No. 29.   [2] No. 22.   [3] No. 27.   [4] No. 51.
[5] *English Historical Documents*, vol. VIII, No. 205.   [6] No. 31.

with colonial affairs. The Secretary of State for the southern department, as direct representative of the Crown, issued warrants for the appointment of colonial governors and carried on the bulk of correspondence with colonial governors, except in matters relating to trade. The Treasury Board had general oversight of moneys expended for colonial affairs. The Customs Board collected duties in the colonies through its own agents and prepared trade instructions for colonial governors. The Admiralty Board was concerned with naval stores in the colonies, piracy, illegal trade, and had jurisdiction over colonial admiralty courts. British officials in the colonies were thus responsible to many different offices and agencies in Great Britain and the result was often vast confusion and inefficiency which made it difficult to carry out clear-cut colonial policies.

Two important institutional devices were of great importance in British control of colonial life: the disallowance of colonial legislation by the Privy Council, and the appeal of cases from colonial courts to the Privy Council. The disallowance was an exercise of the royal veto upon colonial legislation. It was used to defend the prerogatives of royal officials, to check colonial manufacturing, to prohibit discrimination against British trade and subjects, to limit colonial money issues, and to regulate laws affecting the inheritance of property. Appeals to the Privy Council from courts of final appeal in the colonies were limited to causes worth more than £500. In practice this meant that the bulk of final decisions were made by colonial courts. It is impossible to say how effective these institutions were in controlling colonial legislation, but it is clear that the colonies often had their own way despite the limitations imposed upon them.

Within the colonies themselves there was an ever-increasing number of officials appointed by the Crown or by agents of the Crown in the colonies. In the royal colonies, the governor and council, the secretary of the province, the attorney-general, the surveyor-general, the receiver-general, and the chief justice were usually Crown appointees. Beyond these, the customs service accounted for an ever-increasing number of men concerned with the collection of revenue in the colonies and the enforcement of the Acts of Trade and Navigation.

Despite legislation and the multiplication of administrative agencies and offices, the colonies were never brought under effective control for any length of time. After 1660, Massachusetts provided a centre of resistance. That colony sheltered some of the regicides. It opposed the appeal of cases from its courts to the Privy Council. It objected to the Navigation Acts. Other colonies likewise opposed efforts at control, but in this period none were so strenuous as Massachusetts. The Stuarts made increasingly serious efforts to bring all colonies under royal control. Many investigations were made of trade and economic conditions in the colonies. A key figure in this work was Edward Randolph, who wrote innumerable reports on affairs in the colonies. He was convinced that the existence of the corporation and proprietary colonies was the chief obstacle to better control of the colonies and he urged their abolition.[1]

The Stuart effort at centralization culminated in the Dominion of New England. The Massachusetts Charter was vacated in 1684. The Dominion of New England wiped out the legislatures of the New England colonies and substituted for them a royal governor and council who were given the power to rule without consulting the inhabitants. New York and New Jersey were added to the Dominion under the

[1] Nos. 30A and 32A.

governorship of Sir Edmund Andros.[1] Resistance to this arbitrary government grew steadily, and when the news of the Revolution of 1688 reached the colonies, a series of revolutions took place there. Sir Edmund Andros and his supporters in Massachusetts were jailed. Connecticut and Rhode Island resumed their former governments. Jacob Leisler in New York organized a rebellion, expelled Deputy-Governor Francis Nicholson, and took over the government for a time, but was later hanged for treason. Other colonies as well seized upon the opportunity offered. The Protestants in Maryland overthrew the proprietary government and excluded Catholics from the political life of the colony. Virginians protested against the power given to the royal governor.

The Revolution of 1688 ended the effort to abolish colonial legislatures, but it did not end the effort to increase royal control over the colonies. After 1696 the Board of Trade campaigned steadily to bring about the abolition of corporation and proprietary colonies by act of Parliament, and thus to convert them into royal colonies.[2] The effort to secure parliamentary legislation did not succeed but the policy of royalization was continued. By the middle of the eighteenth century only two proprietary colonies and two corporation colonies remained outside direct royal control. Despite the increase in officials, the policy of royalization, and an increasing amount of parliamentary legislation, colonial governments were able to maintain and to increase their control over the internal affairs of the colonies. This fact was clearly recognized in both Great Britain and the colonies by the middle of the eighteenth century.[3]

29. Royal proclamation for Virginia (13 May 1625)

The Proclamation of 1625 sets forth the idea that all colonies should be under royal control and supervision. Virginia is to be governed by a colonial council, subject to a special council in England, which in turn is to be under the control of the Privy Council. However, this plan was given up in 1639 when Virginia was given a government essentially like that provided for it by the Virginia Company in 1619 (Nos. 21, 22). Printed: Clarence S. Brigham, ed., *British Royal Proclamations Relating to America, 1603–1783* (Worcester, Mass., 1911), pp. 52–55.

Whereas the colony of Virginia, planted by the hands of our most dear father of blessed memory, for the propagation of Christian religion, the increase of trade, and the enlarging of his royal empire, hath not hitherto prospered so happily as was hoped and desired; a great occasion whereof his late Majesty conceived to be, for that the government of that colony was committed to the company of Virginia, incorporated of a multitude of persons of several dispositions, amongst whom the affairs of greatest moment were, and must be ruled by the greater number of votes and voices; and therefore his late Majesty, out of his great wisdom and depth of judgment, did desire to resume that popular government, and accordingly the letters patents of that incorporation were by his highness' direction in a legal course questioned, and thereupon judicially repealed and adjudged to be void; wherein his Majesty's aim was only to reduce that government into such a right course as might best agree with that form which was held in the rest of his royal monarchy, and was not intended by him to take away, or impeach the particular interest of any private planter, or adventurer, nor to alter the same, otherwise than should be of necessity for the good of the public; and whereas we continue the like care of those colonies

---

[1] No. 30B.   [2] No. 32.   [3] See D. The Evolution of Colonial Self-Government.

and plantations as our late dear father did, and upon deliberate advice and considera-tion, are of the same judgment that our said father was of, for the government of that colony of Virginia. Now lest the apprehension of former personal differences which have heretofore happened (the reviving and continuing whereof we utterly disallow, and strictly forbid) might distract the minds of the planters and adventurers, or the opinion that we would neglect those plantations might discourage men to go or send thither, and so hinder the perfecting of that work wherein we hold the honour of our dear father deceased and our own honour to be deeply engaged; we have thought fit to declare, and by our royal proclamation to publish our own judgment and resolution in these things, which by God's assistance we purpose constantly to pursue. And therefore we do by these presents publish and declare to all our loving subjects, and to the whole world, that we hold those territories of Virginia and the Summer Islands, as also that of New England where our colonies are already planted, and within the limits and bounds whereof our late dear father, by his letters patents, under his great seal of England, remaining of record, hath given leave and liberty to his subjects to plant and inhabit, to be a part of our royal empire, descended upon us and undoubtedly belonging and appertaining unto us; and that we hold ourself as well bound by our regal office, to protect, maintain, and support the same, and are so resolved to do, as any other part of our dominions.

And that our full resolution is, to the end that there may be one uniform course of government in and through our whole monarchy, that the government of the colony of Virginia shall immediately depend upon ourself, and not be committed to any company or corporation to whom it may be proper to trust matters of trade and commerce, but cannot be fit or safe to communicate the ordering of state affairs, be they of never so mean consequence. And that therefore we have determined that our commissioners for those affairs shall proceed according to the tenor of our commission directed unto them until we shall declare our further pleasure therein. Nevertheless we do hereby declare that we are resolved, with as much convenient expedition as our affairs of greater importance will give leave, to establish a Council consisting of a few persons of understanding and quality, to whom we will give trust for the immediate care of the affairs of that colony, and who shall be answerable to us for their proceedings, and in matters of greater moment, shall be subordinate and atten-dant unto our Privy Council here; and that we will also establish another Council to be resident in Virginia, who shall be subordinate to our Council here for that colony; and that at our own charge we will maintain those public officers and ministers, and that strength of men, munition, and fortification, as shall be fit and necessary for the defence of that plantation, and will by any course that shall be desired of us, settle and assure the particular rights and interests of every planter and adventurer, in any of those territories which shall desire the same, to give them full satisfaction for their quiet and assured enjoying thereof.

And lastly, whereas it is agreed on all sides that the tobacco of those plantations of Virginia and the Summer Islands (which is the only present means for their subsisting) cannot be managed for the good of the plantations unless it be brought into one hand, whereby the foreign tobacco may be carefully kept out, and the tobacco of those plantations may yield a certain and ready price to the owners thereof; we do hereby declare, that to avoid all differences and contrariety of opinions, which will hardly be reconciled amongst the planters and adventurers themselves, we are resolved to take the same into our own hands, and by our servants or agents for us, to give such prices to the planters and adventurers for the same as may give them reasonable satisfaction and encouragement; but of the manner thereof, we will determine hereafter at better leisure. And when we shall have concluded the same, we shall expect that all our loving subjects will readily conform themselves thereunto.

And in the meantime, because the importation and use of foreign tobacco, which is not of the growth of those plantations, or one of them, will visibly and assuredly undermine and destroy those plantations by taking away the means of their subsistence, we do hereby strictly charge and command that our late proclamation, bearing date the ninth day of April last, entitled (A Proclamation Touching Tobacco) shall in all points and parts thereof be duly and strictly observed upon pain of our high displeasure, and such further penalties and punishments as by the said proclamation are to be inflicted upon the offenders. And we do hereby advise all our loving subjects, and all others whom it may concern, not to adventure the breach of our royal commandment in any of the premises, we being fully resolved, upon no importunity or intercession whatsoever, to release or remit the deserved punishment of such as shall dare to offend against the same, seeing we hold not ourself only, but our people interested therein.

30A–B. The Dominion of New England

The Dominion of New England was the climax of the policy of increasing control over the colonies after 1660. Massachusetts, the most important northern colony, was virtually independent, and showed every intention of remaining so if possible. Commissioners sent over in 1664 to investigate were treated badly, and three of the four of them recommended that the charter of the colony be annulled. In 1674 Edward Randolph was sent over to investigate, and he too was treated badly. His reports on conditions in New England, of which No. 30A, dated 6 May 1677, is an example, provided evidence for those who wished to annul the Massachusetts charter, and this was done in 1684. The local legislatures were abolished and government by a royal governor and council was provided for. Joseph Dudley of Massachusetts was appointed governor temporarily and was replaced by Sir Edmund Andros in 1686. The Andros Commission of 1688 (No. 30B) represents the culmination of the dominion idea. Andros was made governor over all the region from the Delaware River to the French possessions in Canada.

30A. Edward Randolph: report on the state of affairs in New England (6 May 1677)

Printed: Robert N. Toppan, *Edward Randolph, including his Letters and Official Papers* (5 vols., Boston, 1898–1899, published by the Prince Society), II, pp. 265–268.

The present state of the affairs of New England depending before the lords of the Committee for Plantations are reduced to two heads, viz., matter of law and fact.

Matter of law ariseth from the title of lands and government claimed by Mr. Mason and Mr. Gorges in their several provinces of New Hampshire and Maine, and also what right and title the Massachusetts have to either land or government in any part of New England; these are referred to the Lords Chief Justices of the King's Bench and Common Pleas for their opinion.

Matters of fact concern as well his Majesty as Mr. Mason and Mr. Gorges, and against the government of the Massachusetts these following articles will be proved.

1. That they have no right either to land or government in any part of New England and have always been usurpers.

2. That they have formed themselves into a commonwealth, denying any appeals to England, and contrary to other plantations do not take the oath of allegiance.

3. They have protected the late king's murderers, directly contrary to his Majesty's royal proclamation of the 6th of June 1660 and of his letters of 28th June 1662.

4. They coin money with their own impress.

5. They have put his Majesty's subjects to death for opinion in matters of religion.

6. In the year 1665 they did violently oppose his Majesty's commissioners in the settlement of New Hampshire and in 1668 by armed forces turned out his Majesty's justices of the peace in the province of Maine in contempt of his Majesty's authority and declaration of the 10th of April 1666.

7. They impose an oath of fidelity upon all that inhabit within their territories to be true and faithful to their government.

8. They violate all the Acts of Trade and Navigation by which they have engrossed the greatest part of the West India trade whereby his Majesty is damaged in his customs above £100,000 yearly and this kingdom much more.

Reasons inducing a speedy hearing and determination

1. His Majesty hath an opportunity to settle that country under his royal authority with little charge, Sir John Berry being now at Virginia not far distant from New England, and it lies in his way home where are many good harbours free from the worms, convenient towns for quartering of soldiers, and plentiful accommodation for men and shipping.

2. The earnest desire of most and best of the inhabitants (wearied out with the arbitrary proceedings of those in the present government) to be under his Majesty's government and laws.

3. The Indians upon the settlement of that country, it is presumed, would unanimously submit and become very serviceable and useful for improving that country, there being upward of three hundred thousand English [Indians?] inhabiting therein.

Proposals for the settling of that country

1. His Majesty's gracious and general pardon upon their conviction of having acted without and in contempt of his Majesty's authority will make the most refractory to comply to save their estates.

2. His Majesty's declaration of confirming unto the inhabitants the lands and houses they now possess upon payment of an easy quit-rent and granting liberty of conscience in matters of religion.

3. His Majesty's commission directed to the most eminent persons for estates and loyalty in every colony to meet, consult and act for the present peace and safety of that country during his Majesty's pleasure, and that such of the present magistrates be of the council as shall readily comply with his Majesty's commands in the settling

of the country, and a pension to be allowed them out of the public revenue of the country with some title of honour to be conferred upon the most deserving of them, will cause a general submission.

30B. Commission to Sir Edmund Andros as governor of the Dominion of New England (7 April 1688)

Printed: *New York Colonial Documents*, III, pp. 537–542.

James the second, by the Grace of God, king of England, Scotland, France, and Ireland, Defender of the Faith, etc. To our trusty and well-beloved Sir Edmund Andros, knight, Greeting: whereas by our commission under our Great Seal of England, bearing date the third day of June in the second year of our reign, we have constituted and appointed you to be our captain-general and governor-in-chief in and over all that part of our territory and dominion of New England in America known by the names of our colony of the Massachusetts Bay, our colony of New Plymouth, our provinces of New Hampshire and Maine, and the Narragansett country or King's Province; and whereas since that time we have thought it necessary for our service and for the better protection and security of our subjects in those parts to join and annex to our said government the neighbouring colonies of Rhode Island and Connecticut, our province of New York and East and West Jersey, with the territories thereunto belonging, as we do hereby join, annex, and unite the same to our said government and dominion of New England. We therefore reposing especial trust and confidence in the prudence, courage, and loyalty of you, the said Sir Edmund Andros, out of our especial grace, certain knowledge, and mere motion, have thought fit to constitute and appoint, as we do by these presents constitute and appoint you, the said Sir Edmund Andros, to be our captain-general and governor-in-chief in and over our colonies of the Massachusetts Bay and New Plymouth, our provinces of New Hampshire and Maine, the Narragansett country or King's Province, our colonies of Rhode Island and Connecticut, our province of New York and East and West Jersey, and of all that tract of land, circuit, continent, precincts, and limits in America lying and being in breadth from forty degrees of northern latitude from the equinoctial line to the river of St. Croix eastward, and from thence directly northward to the river of Canada, and in length and longitude by all the breadth aforesaid throughout the mainland from the Atlantic or Western sea or ocean on the east part, to the South Sea on the west part, with all the islands, seas, rivers, waters, rights, members and appurtenances thereunto belonging (our province of Pennsylvania and country of Delaware only excepted), to be called and known as formerly by the name and title of our territory and dominion of New England in America.

And for your better guidance and direction we do hereby require and command you to do and execute all things in due manner, that shall belong unto the said office and the trust we have reposed in you, according to the several powers, instructions and authorities mentioned in these presents, or such further powers, instructions, and authorities as you shall herewith receive or which shall at any time hereafter be granted or appointed you under our signet and sign manual, or by our order in our Privy

Council, and according to such reasonable laws and statutes as are now in force or such others as shall hereafter be made and established within our territory and dominion aforesaid.

And our will and pleasure is that you, the said Sir Edmund Andros, having, after publication of these our letters patents, first taken the oath of duly executing the office of our captain-general and governor-in-chief of our said territory and dominion, which our Council there or any three of them are hereby required, authorized, and impowered to give and administer unto you, you shall administer unto each of the members of our Council the oath for the due execution of their places and trusts.

And we do hereby give and grant unto you full power and authority to suspend any member of our Council from sitting, voting and assisting therein, as you shall find just cause for so doing.

And if it shall hereafter at any time happen that by the death, departure out of our said territory, or suspension of any of our councillors, or otherwise, there shall be a vacancy in our said Council (any five whereof we do hereby appoint to be a quorum), our will and pleasure is that you signify the same unto us by the first opportunity, that we may under our signet and sign manual constitute and appoint others in their room.

And we do hereby give and grant unto you full power and authority, by and with the advice and consent of our said Council or the major part of them, to make, constitute and ordain laws, statutes and ordinances for the public peace, welfare, and good government of our said territory and dominion and of the people and inhabitants thereof, and such others as shall resort thereto, and for the benefit of us, our heirs and successors. Which said laws, statutes, and ordinances are to be, as near as conveniently may be, agreeable to the laws and statutes of this our kingdom of England: provided that all such laws, statutes, and ordinances of what nature or duration soever, be within three months, or sooner, after the making of the same, transmitted unto us, under our Seal of New England, for our allowance or disapprobation of them, as also duplicates thereof by the next conveyance.

And we do by these presents give and grant unto you full power and authority by and with the advice and consent of our said Council, or the major part of them, to impose, assess and raise and levy such rates and taxes as you shall find necessary for the support of the government within our territory and dominion of New England, to be collected and levied and to be employed to the uses aforesaid in such manner as to you and our said Council, or the major part of them, shall seem most equal and reasonable.

And for the better supporting the charge of the government of our said territory and dominion, our will and pleasure is, and we do by these presents authorize and impower you, the said Sir Edmund Andros, and our Council, to continue such taxes and impositions as are now laid and imposed upon the inhabitants thereof; and to levy and distribute or cause the same to be levied and distributed to those ends in the best and most equal manner, until you shall by and with the advice and consent of our Council agree on and settle such other taxes as shall be sufficient for the support of our government there, which are to be applied to that use and no other.

And our further will and pleasure is that all public money raised or to be raised or appointed for the support of the government within our said territory and dominion, be issued out by warrant or order from you, by and with the advice and consent of our Council as aforesaid.

And our will and pleasure is that you shall and may keep and use our Seal appointed by us for our said territory and dominion.

And we do by these presents ordain, constitute, and appoint you or the commander-in-chief for the time being, and the Council of our said territory and dominion for the time being, to be a constant and settled court of record for the administration of justice to all our subjects inhabiting within our said territory and dominion, in all causes, as well civil as criminal, with full power and authority to hold pleas in all cases, from time to time, as well in pleas of the Crown and in all matters relating to the conservation of the peace and punishment of offenders, as in civil causes and actions between party and party, or between us and any of our subjects there, whether the same do concern the realty and relate to any right of freehold and inheritance, or whether the same do concern the personalty and relate to matter of debt, contract, damage, or other personal injury; and also in all mixed actions which may concern both realty and personalty; and therein, after due and orderly proceeding and deliberate hearing of both sides, to give judgement and to award execution, as well in criminal as in civil cases as aforesaid, so as always that the forms of proceedings in such cases and the judgment thereupon to be given, be as consonant and agreeable to the laws and statutes of this our realm of England as the present state and condition of our subjects inhabiting within our said territory and dominion and the circumstances of the place will admit.

And we do further hereby give and grant unto you full power and authority, with the advice and consent of our said Council, to erect, constitute, and establish such and so many courts of judicature and public justice within our said territory and dominion as you and they shall think fit and necessary for the determining of all causes, as well criminal as civil, according to law and equity, and for awarding of execution thereupon, with all reasonable and necessary powers, authorities, fees, and privileges belonging unto them.

And we do hereby give and grant unto you full power and authority to constitute and appoint judges and, in cases requisite, commissioners of oyer and terminer, justices of the peace, sheriffs, and all other necessary officers and ministers within our said territory for the better administration of justice and putting the laws in execution, and to administer such oath and oaths as are usually given for the due execution and performance of offices and places and for the clearing of truth in judicial causes.

And our further will and pleasure is and we do hereby declare that all actings and proceedings at law or equity heretofore had or done, or now depending within any of the courts of our said territory, and all executions thereupon, be hereby confirmed and continued so far forth as not to be avoided for want of any legal power in the said courts; but that all and every such judicial actings, proceeding, and execution shall be of the same force, effect, and virtue as if such courts had acted by a just and legal authority.

And we do further by these presents will and require you to permit appeals to be made in cases of error from our courts in our said territory and dominion of New England unto you, or the commander-in-chief for the time being and the Council, in civil causes: provided the value appealed for do exceed the sum of one hundred pounds sterling, and that security be first duly given by the appellant to answer such charges as shall be awarded in case the first sentence shall be affirmed.

And whereas we judge it necessary that all our subjects may have liberty to appeal to our royal person in cases that may require the same: our will and pleasure is that if either party shall not rest satisfied with the judgment or sentence of you (or the commander-in-chief for the time being) and the Council, they may appeal unto us in our Privy Council: provided the matter in difference exceed the value and sum of three hundred pounds sterling and that such appeal be made within one fortnight after sentence, and that security be likewise duly given by the appellant to answer such charges as shall be awarded in case the sentence of you (or the commander-in-chief for the time being) and the Council be confirmed; and provided also that execution be not suspended by reason of any such appeal unto us.

And we do hereby give and grant unto you full power where you shall see cause and shall judge any offender or offenders in capital and criminal matters, or for any fines or forfeitures due unto us, fit objects of our mercy, to pardon such offenders and to remit such fines and forfeitures, treason and wilful murder only excepted, in which case you shall likewise have power upon extraordinary occasions to grant reprieves to the offenders therein until and to the intent our pleasure may be further known.

And we do hereby give and grant unto you the said Sir Edmund Andros, by yourself, your captains and commanders, by you to be authorized, full power and authority to levy, arm, muster, command, or employ, all persons whatsoever residing within our said territory and dominion of New England, and as occasion shall serve, them to transfer from one place to another for the resisting and withstanding all enemies, pirates, and rebels, both at land and sea, and to transfer such forces to any of our plantations in America or the territories thereunto belonging, as occasion shall require, for the defence of the same against the invasion or attempt of any of our enemies, and then, if occasion shall require, to pursue and prosecute in or out of the limits of our said territories and plantations or any of them; and if it shall so please God, them to vanquish; and, being taken, according to the law of arms, to put to death or keep and preserve alive, at your discretion. And also to execute martial law in time of invasion, insurrection, or war, and during the continuance of the same, and upon soldiers in pay, and to do and execute all and every other thing which to a captain-general doth or ought of right to belong, as fully and amply as any our captain-general doth or hath usually done.

And we do hereby give and grant unto you full power and authority to erect, raise and build within our territory and dominion aforesaid, such and so many forts, platforms, castles, cities, boroughs, towns, and fortifications as you shall judge necessary; and the same or any of them to fortify and furnish with ordnance, ammunition, and all sorts of arms, fit and necessary for the security and defence of our said territory;

and the same again or any of them to demolish or dismantle as may be most convenient.

And we do hereby give and grant unto you, the said Sir Edmund Andros, full power and authority to erect one or more court or courts admiral within our said territory and dominion, for the hearing and determining of all marine and other causes and matters proper therein to be heard and determined, with all reasonable and necessary powers, authorities, fees, and privileges.

And you are to execute all powers belonging to the place and office of Vice-Admiral of and in all the seas and coasts about your government; according to such commission, authority, and instructions as you shall receive from ourself under the seal of our Admiralty or from our High Admiral of our foreign plantations for the time being.

And forasmuch as divers mutinies and disorders do happen by persons shipped and employed at sea, and to the end that such as shall be shipped or employed at sea may be the better governed and ordered: we do hereby give and grant unto you, the said Sir Edmund Andros, our captain-general and governor-in-chief, full power and authority to constitute and appoint captains, masters of ships, and other commanders, and to grant unto such captains, masters of ships, and other commanders commissions to execute the law martial, and to use such proceedings, authorities, punishment, correction, and execution upon any offender or offenders who shall be mutinous, seditious, disorderly, or any way unruly, either at sea or during the time of their abode or residence in any of the ports, harbours, or bays of our said territory and dominion, as the cause shall be found to require, according to martial law. Provided that nothing herein contained shall be construed to the enabling you or any by your authority to hold plea or have jurisdiction of any offence, cause, matter, or thing committed or done upon the sea or within any of the havens, rivers, or creeks of our said territory and dominion under your government, by any captain, commander, lieutenant, master, or other officer, seaman, soldier, or person whatsoever, who shall be in actual service and pay in and on board any of our ships of war or other vessels acting by immediate commission or warrant from ourself under the seal of our Admiralty, or from our High Admiral of England for the time being; but that such captain, commander, lieutenant, master, officer, seaman, soldier and other person so offending shall be left to be proceeded against and tried, as the merit of their offences shall require, either by commission under our Great Seal of England as the statute of 28 Henry VIII directs, or by commission from our said High Admiral, according to the act of Parliament passed in the 13th year of the reign of the late king, our most dear and most entirely beloved brother of ever blessed memory (entitled an act for the establishing articles and orders for the regulating and better government of his Majesty's navies, ships of war, and forces by sea) and not otherwise. Saving only, that it shall and may be lawful for you, upon such captains or commanders refusing or neglecting to execute, or upon his negligent or undue execution of any the written orders he shall receive from you for our service and the service of our said territory and dominion, to suspend him, the said captain or commander, from the exercise of the said office of commander and commit him into safe custody, either on board his own ship or elsewhere, at the discretion of you, in order to his being brought to answer for the same by commission either under our Great Seal of England or from our said High Admiral, as is before expressed. In which case our will and pleasure is that the captain or commander so by you suspended, shall during such his suspension and commitment be succeeded in his said office, by such commission or warrant officer of our said ship appointed by ourself or our High Admiral for the time being, as by the known practice and discipline of our navy doth and ought next to succeed him, as in case of death, sickness, or other ordinary disability happening to the commander of any of our ships, and not otherwise; you standing also accountable to us for the truth and importance of the crimes and misdemeanours for which you shall so proceed to the suspending of such our said captain or commander. Provided also that all disorders and misdemeanours committed on shore by any captain, commander, lieutenant, master, or other officer, seaman, soldier or person whatsoever belonging to any of our ships of war or other vessel acting by immediate commission or warrant from ourself under the Great Seal of our Admiralty or from our High Admiral of England for the time being, may be tried and punished according to the laws of the place where any such disorders, offences, and misdemeanours shall be so committed on shore, notwithstanding such offender be in our actual service and borne in our pay on board any such our ships of war or other vessels acting by immediate commission or warrant from ourself or our High Admiral as aforesaid; so as he shall not receive any protection (for the avoiding of justice for such offences committed on shore) from any pretence of his being employed in our service at sea.

And we do likewise give and grant unto you full power and authority by and with the advice and consent of our said Council to agree with the planters and inhabitants of our said territory and dominion concerning such lands, tenements, and hereditaments as now are or hereafter shall be in our power to dispose of, and them to grant unto any person or persons for such terms and under such moderate quitrents, services, and acknowledgments to be thereupon reserved unto us as shall be appointed by us. Which said grants are to pass and be sealed by our Seal of New England and, being entered upon record by such officer or officers as you shall appoint thereunto, shall be good and effectual in law against us, our heirs and successors.

And we do give you full power and authority to appoint so many fairs, marts, and markets as you with the advice of the said Council shall think fit.

As likewise to order and appoint within our said territory such and so many ports, harbours, bays, havens and other places for the convenience and security of shipping, and for the better loading and unloading of goods and merchandise as by you with the advice and consent of our Council shall be thought fit and necessary; and in them or any of them to erect, nominate, and appoint custom houses, warehouses, and officers relating thereto; and them to alter, change, place or displace from time to time, as with the advice aforesaid shall be thought fit.

And forasmuch as pursuant to the laws and customs of our colony of the Massachusetts Bay and of our other colonies and provinces aforementioned, divers marriages have been made and performed by the magistrates of our said territory; our royal will and pleasure is hereby to confirm all the said marriages and to direct that they be held good and valid in the same manner, to all intents and purposes whatsoever, as if they had been made and contracted according to the laws established within our kingdom of England.

And we do hereby require and command all officers and ministers, civil and military, and all other inhabitants of our said territory and dominion to be obedient, aiding, and assisting unto you, the said Sir Edmund Andros, in the execution of this our commission and of the powers and authorities therein contained, and upon your death or absence out of our said territory, unto our lieutenant-governor, to whom we do, therefore, by these presents give and grant all and singular the powers and authorities aforesaid to be exercised and enjoyed by him in case of your death, or absence during our pleasure, or until your arrival within our said territory and dominion; as we do further hereby give and grant full power and authority to our lieutenant-governor to do and execute whatsoever he shall be by you authorized and appointed to do and execute, in pursuance of and according to the powers and authorities granted to you by this commission.

And if in case of your death or absence there be no person upon the place, appointed by us to be commander-in-chief; our will and pleasure is that the then present Council of our territory aforesaid, do take upon them the administration of the government and execute this commission and the several powers and authorities herein contained; and that the first councillor who shall be at the time of your death or absence residing within the same, do preside in our said Council, with such powers and preheminences as any former president hath used and enjoyed within our said territory, or any other our plantations in America, until our pleasure be further known, or your arrival as aforesaid.

And lastly, our will and pleasure is that you, the said Sir Edmund Andros, shall and may hold, exercise, and enjoy the office and place of captain-general and governor-in-chief in and over our territory and dominion aforesaid, with all its rights, members, and appurtenances whatsoever, together with all and singular the powers and authorities hereby granted unto you, for and during our will and pleasure.

31. The commission of the Board of Trade (15 May 1696)

This commission created the agency which was to concern itself with almost every phase of colonial life from 1696 until the American Revolution. It investigated economic, political, social, and religious questions, it wrote reports to the Privy Council and to Parliament, and it corresponded with colonial governors on economic matters. Its effectiveness varied with its personnel and the support it received from other agencies, but on the whole it worked steadily for closer supervision of the colonies. Printed: *New York Colonial Documents*, IV, pp. 145-148.

His Majesty's Commission for promoting the trade of this kingdom and for inspecting and improving his plantations in America and elsewhere.

William the third, by the grace of God, king of England, Scotland, France, and Ireland, Defender of the Faith, etc. To our Keeper of our Great Seal of England or Chancellor of England for the time being; our President of our Privy Council for the time being; our first commissioner of our Treasury and our Treasurer of England for the time being; our first commissioner of our Admiralty and our Admiral of

England for the time being; and our Principal Secretaries of State for the time being, and our Chancellor of our Exchequer for the time being; to our right trusty and right well beloved cousin and councillor, John, earl of Bridgewater, and Ford, earl of Tankerville; to our trusty and well beloved Sir Philip Meadows, knight, William Blathwayt, John Pollexfen, John Locke, Abraham Hill, and John Methuen, esquires, Greeting:

Whereas we are extremely desirous that the trade of our kingdom of England, upon which the strength and riches thereof do in a great measure depend, should by all proper means be promoted and advanced; and whereas we are persuaded that nothing will more effectually contribute thereto than the appointing of knowing and fit persons to inspect and examine into the general trade of our said kingdom and the several parts thereof, and to inquire into the several matters and things hereinafter mentioned relating thereunto, with such powers and directions as are hereinafter specified and contained.

Know ye therefore that we, reposing especial trust and confidence in your discretions, abilities, and integrities, have nominated, authorized, and constituted, and do by these presents nominate, authorize, and appoint [you] . . . or any other three or more of you, to be our commissioners during our royal pleasure, for promoting the trade of our kingdom and for inspecting and improving our plantations in America and elsewhere.

And to the end that our royal purpose and intention herein may the better take effect, our will and pleasure is, and we do hereby order, direct, and appoint that you do diligently and constantly as the nature of the service may require, meet together at some convenient place in our palace of Whitehall, which we shall assign for that purpose, or at any other place which we shall appoint for the execution of this our commission.

And we do by these presents authorize and empower you our said commissioners, or any three or more of you, to inquire, examine into and take an account of the state and condition of the general trade of England, and also of the several particular trades in all foreign parts, and how the same respectively are advanced or decayed, and the causes or occasions thereof; and to inquire into and examine what trades are or may prove hurtful, or are or may be made beneficial to our kingdom of England, and by what ways and means the profitable and advantageous trades may be more improved and extended, and such as are hurtful and prejudicial rectified or discouraged; and to inquire into the several obstructions of trade, and the means of removing the same. And also in what manner and by what proper methods the trade of our said kingdom may be most effectually protected and secured in all the parts thereof; and to consider by what means the several useful and profitable manufactures already settled in our said kingdom may be further improved, and how and in what manner new and profitable manufactures may be introduced.

And we do further by these presents authorize and require you, our said commissioners, or any three or more of you, to consider of some proper methods for setting on work and employing the poor of our said kingdom and making them useful to the public, and thereby easing our subjects of that burden; and by what ways and means such design may be made most effectual; and in general, by all such methods and ways as you in your discretions shall think best, to inform yourselves of all things relating to trade and the promoting and encouraging thereof; as also to consider of the best and most effectual means to regain, encourage, and establish the fishery of this kingdom.

And our further will and pleasure is that you, our said commissioners, or any five or more of you, do from time to time make representations touching the premises to us, or to our Privy Council, as the nature of the business shall require, which said representations are to be in writing, and to be signed by five or more of you.

And we do hereby further empower and require you, our said commissioners, to take into your care all records, grants, and papers remaining in the plantation office or thereunto belonging.

And likewise to inform yourselves of the present condition of our respective plantations, as well with regard to the administration of the government and justice in those places as in relation to the commerce thereof; and also to inquire into the limits of soil and product of our several plantations and how the same may be improved, and of the best means for easing and securing our colonies there, and how the same may be rendered most useful and beneficial to our said kingdom of England.

And we do hereby further empower and require you, our said commissioners, more particularly and in a principal manner to inform yourselves what naval stores may be furnished from our plantations and in what quantities and by what methods our royal purpose of having our kingdom supplied with naval stores from thence may be made practicable and promoted; and also to inquire into and inform yourselves of the best and most proper methods of settling and improving in our plantations such other staples and other manufactures as our subjects of England are now obliged to fetch and supply themselves withal from other princes and states; and also what staples and manufactures may be best encouraged there, and what trades are taken up and exercised there which are or may prove prejudicial to England, by furnishing themselves or other our colonies with what has been usually supplied from England; and to find out proper means of diverting them from such trades, and whatsoever else may turn to the hurt of our kingdom of England.

And to examine and look into the usual instructions given to the governors of our plantations, and to see if anything may be added, omitted, or changed therein to advantage; to take an account yearly by way of journal of the administration of our governors there, and to draw out what is proper to be observed and represented unto us; and as often as occasion shall require to consider of proper persons to be governors or deputy governors, or to be of our council or of our council at law, or secretaries, in our respective plantations in order to present their names to us in council.

And we do hereby further authorize and empower you, our said commissioners, to examine into and weigh such acts of the assemblies of the plantations respectively as shall from time to time be sent or transmitted hither for our approbation; and to set down and represent as aforesaid the usefulness or mischief thereof to our Crown and to our said kingdom of England, or to the plantations themselves, in case the same should be established for laws there; and also to consider what matters may be recommended as fit to be passed in the assemblies there; to hear complaints of oppressions and maladministrations in our plantations in order to represent as aforesaid what you in your discretions shall think proper; and also to require an account of all moneys given for public uses by the assemblies in our plantations, and how the same are and have been expended or laid out.

And we do by these presents authorize and empower you, our said commissioners, or any three of you, to send for persons and papers for your better information in the premises; and as occasion shall require to examine witnesses upon oath, which oath you are hereby empowered to administer in order to the matters aforesaid.

And we do declare our further will and pleasure to be, that you our said commissioners do from time to time report all your doings in relation to the premises in writing under the hands of any five of you as aforesaid, to us or to our Privy Council, as the nature of the thing shall require.

And we do hereby further authorize and empower you our said commissioners to execute and perform all other things necessary or proper for answering our royal intentions in the premises.

And we do further give power to you our said commissioners, or any three or more of you as aforesaid, from time to time, and as occasion shall require, to send for and desire the advice and assistance of our Attorney or Solicitor-General, or other our counsel at law.

And we do hereby further declare our royal will and pleasure to be that we do not hereby intend that our Chancellor of England or Keeper of our Great Seal for the time being, the President of our Privy Council for the time being, the Keeper of our Privy Seal for the time being, the Treasurer or first commissioner of our Treasury for the time being, our Admiral or first commissioner for executing the office of Admiral for the time being, our Principal Secretaries of State for the time being, or our Chancellor of the Exchequer for the time being, should be obliged to give constant attendance at the meeting of our said commissioners, but only so often and when the presence of them or any of them shall be necessary and requisite, and as their other public service will permit.

IN WITNESS whereof we have caused these our letters to be made patents, witness Thomas, archbishop of Canterbury, and the rest of the guardians and justices of the realm. At Westminster the fifteenth day of May in the eighth year of our reign.

32A–B. The attack upon the colonial Charters (1701–1715)

Despite the collapse of the dominion of New England the demand for increased control over the colonies continued to grow. After 1696 the Board of Trade was convinced that the charter governments should be abolished. Since the use of the courts was a slow process, it was decided that the only solution was an act of Parliament. Again, Edward Randolph provided the materials for attacks upon the colonial charters. His report in March 1701 (No. 32A) is an example of the charges made. Such evidence and other similar materials were the basis of the report by the Board of Trade to the Privy Council in 1701 (No. 32B). This report was the foundation for a bill introduced in Parliament voiding those clauses in proprietary and corporation charters by which the Crown had granted any governmental authority to individuals or groups of individuals in the colonies. The death of the King in March 1702 ended the first attempt. A second attempt to limit sharply the powers given in most of the charters was made in 1706, but this too failed. The last attempt was made in 1715, but the colonial agents and the representatives of the proprietors produced a host of petitions and opposition in Parliament. Thus ended the effort to vacate the powers given to the chartered colonies by Parliamentary action, although the Board of Trade urged such legislation from time to time. However, it continued the policy of converting individual colonies into royal colonies whenever the opportunity offered.

32A. Edward Randolph: crimes and misdemeanours of the proprietary governors (24 March 1701)

Printed: Toppan, *Edward Randolph*, v, pp. 263–268.

Articles of high crimes: misdemeanours charged upon the governors in the several proprieties, on the continent of America and islands adjacent.

Bahama Islands. Pirates entertained there and illegal trade maintained and carried on by the inhabitants.

Every, the pirate, and his men were entertained when Colonel Trott was governor of Providence, and had liberty to depart or stay there upon their giving bond of £1,000 to appear when called. Some of those were bound, one for another. They carry from those islands the braziletto and other dyeing woods to Curaçao.

Colonel Nicholas Webb, his successor, was a cruel oppressor and imprisoned his Majesty's subjects at pleasure, by which means he got a great deal of money and they and their families were ruined. Read Elding, the present governor, stands charged with piracy lately committed upon a New England vessel richly loaded, bound from Jamaica to Boston.

He tyrannically beat and wounded Mr. Thomas Gower, the present secretary, and soon after kept him in prison 17 days.

He seized and condemned small vessels belonging to the inhabitants, having made Parker, one of Every's men (and his brother-in-law), marshal.

Dolton, a Red Sea man, is judge, and Warren, another Red Sea man, his attorney-general. They have sold the vessels and put the money in their pockets.

South Carolina. 70 pirates were entertained there about 8 years ago.

Mr. Archdale, the late governor, harboured pirates. He countenanced Day, the master of a Bristol ship, to defraud his owners of vessel and loading, and afterwards Day, being bound to the Red Sea, Mr. Archdale provided for him a Moschetto engine, against his master's will, to catch fish for his voyage.

He gave his permit to Simon Tristrant, a Frenchman born, who imported a rich loading of wine, sugars and cocoa, to sell his vessel and cargo, for which he was well paid.

Mr. Joseph Blake, late governor deceased, was a great Indian trader and took 6 barrels of powder in the late French wars and sent them by his agents to purchase skins of the Indians, having but 4 barrels in the store, all which was purchased for defence of the country.

He caused some vessels and their loading to be seized and condemned upon pretence of their acts of trade, and getting them to be appraised at half the value, he and his accomplices got them into their hands, denying to the owners appeal to his Majesty in council.

He caused other vessels to be seized upon the same pretence and upon private contract with the masters to pay him half the value of their vessels (which they did) he discharged their vessels, defrauding his Majesty thereby of his third part, with many other like misdemeanours committed by him.

North Carolina. They have no settled government amongst them. About 4 years ago the *Swift* frigate being drove out of Virginia by storm and coming ashore upon the sands in that province, the inhabitants robbed her and fired great guns into her and disabled her from getting off. The chief offender was banished only. 'Tis a place which receives pirates, runaways, and illegal traders.

Maryland. His Majesty took the government of that province out of the hands of the Lord Baltimore, the proprietor, because Colonel Talbott, his governor, murdered the collector of his Majesty's customs in cool blood.

The three lower counties on Delaware Bay. Mr. Penn usurps government and lays taxes upon his Majesty's loyal subjects inhabiting there.

There were not long since, two persons tried and condemned, the judges and juries not being sworn, and afterwards executed in those counties.

Pennsylvania. Another person was tried, condemned, and executed in Mr. Penn's own province, the judge and jury not being sworn.

It has been and still is the only receptacle for pirates and illegal traders.

Mr. Penn, in defiance of the authority of the Court of Admiralty there erected, has appointed a person to execute the office of marshal by warrant under his hand and seal.

I was made a prisoner by Mr. Markham (Mr. Penn's governor) because I would not deliver to him two bonds, one of £1,000, the other of £500 forfeited to his Majesty, which I had given orders to be put in suit.

Mr. Penn, about October last, intercepted and detained letters and packets from the commissioners of the customs, to Mr. Birch, their officer at Newcastle.

He likewise charged Mr. Swift, bound from Pennsylvania to England, who Mr. Penn knew had letters from the judge of the Admiralty in Pennsylvania for the said commissioners, not to deliver them till one month after his arrival.

Provinces of East and West Jersey. They are all in confusion for want of government and humbly pray to be taken under his Majesty's immediate government and protection. They likewise receive and harbour pirates.

Colony of Connecticut. Receive and countenance illegal traders and lately intended to oppose with force persons legally empowered to seize and carry away prohibited goods in order to be tried in his Majesty's Court of Admiralty at New York.

Rhode Island. They have all along harboured pirates. Walter Clark, the late governor, refused to take the oath enjoined by the Acts of Trade to be taken by all governors, etc.

Samuel Cranston, the present governor, openly opposed the authority of the Court of Admiralty, ordered by act of Parliament to be there erected.

Province of the Massachusetts Bay. They having obtained a new grant, made void and destroyed all those laws made not long before for the maintenance and support of his Majesty's governors of that province, on purpose to discourage gentlemen of honour and abilities to serve his Majesty in that country, having thereby made that government precarious only.

They enrich themselves by their continued breach of the Acts of Trade, some of the members of the council being illegal traders, sit judges in the courts upon trial of seizures for his Majesty, and do likewise deny appeals to his Majesty in council to those who are empowered and directed to prosecute them.

They have likewise turned out Mr. Byfield, a man zealous for having the Acts of Trade duly executed, who by commission under the great seal of the Admiralty was judge of the Court of Admiralty in that province. And made Mr. Wait Winthrop (a small practitioner in physic) to be judge of that court though in no sort qualified for the office, instead of Mr. Byfield, against whom they had nothing to object. Some of the first pirates I ever heard of in the northern plantations were set out from Boston, who brought in a great deal of riches from the Spanish plantations.

Province of New Hampshire. Mr. William Partridge, the present lieutenant-governor, and several of the inhabitants of that province are notorious illegal traders.

32B. Report of the Board of Trade on proprietary governments (26 March 1701)

Printed: William L. Saunders, ed., *The Colonial Records of North Carolina* (10 vols., Raleigh, 1886–1890), I, pp. 535–537.

Having formerly on several occasions humbly represented to your Majesty the state of the government under proprietors and charters in America; and perceiving the irregularities of these governments daily to increase, to the prejudice of trade and of your Majesty's other plantations in America, as well as of your Majesty's revenue arising from the customs here, we find ourselves obliged at present humbly to represent to your Majesty:

That those colonies in general have no ways answered the chief design for which such large tracts of land and such privileges and immunities were granted by the Crown.

That they have not conformed themselves to the several acts of Parliament for regulating trade and navigation, to which they ought to pay the same obedience and submit to the same restrictions as the other plantations which are subject to your Majesty's immediate government; on the contrary, in most of these proprieties and charter governments the governors have not applied themselves to your Majesty for your approbation, nor have taken the oaths required by the acts of trade, both which qualifications are made necessary by the late act for preventing frauds and regulating abuses in the plantation trade.

That they have assumed to themselves a power to make laws contrary and repugnant to the laws of England, and directly prejudicial to trade, some of them having refused to send hither such laws as they had enacted, and others having sent them but very imperfectly.

That divers of them have denied appeals to your Majesty in Council, by which not only the inhabitants of those colonies but others your Majesty's subjects are deprived of that benefit enjoyed in the plantations under your Majesty's immediate government, and the parties aggrieved are left without remedy from the arbitrary and illegal proceedings of their courts.

That these colonies continue to be the refuge and retreat of pirates and illegal traders, and the receptacle of goods imported thither from foreign parts, contrary to law; in return of which commodities those of the growth of these colonies are likewise, contrary to law, exported to foreign parts; all which is likewise much encouraged by their not admitting appeals as aforesaid.

That by raising and lowering their coin from time to time to their particular advantage, and to the prejudice of other colonies; by exempting their inhabitants from duties and customs to which the other colonies are subject, and by harbouring of servants and fugitives, these governments tend greatly to the undermining the trade and welfare of the other plantations, and seduce and draw away the people thereof; by which diminution of hands the rest of the colonies more beneficial to England do very much suffer.

That these independent colonies do turn the course of trade to the promoting and propagating woollen and other manufactures proper to England, instead of applying their thoughts and endeavours to the production of such commodities as are fit to be encouraged in these parts according to the true design and intention of such settlements.

That they do not in general take any due care for their own defence and security against an enemy, either in building forts or providing their inhabitants with sufficient arms and ammunition, in case they should be attacked, which is every day more and more to be apprehended, considering how the French power increases in those parts.

That this chiefly arises from the ill use they make of the powers entrusted to them by their charters and the independency which they pretend to, and that each government is obliged only to defend itself without any consideration had of their neighbours, or of the general preservation of the whole.

That many of them have not a regular militia, and some (particularly the colonies of East and West New Jersey) are no otherwise at present than in a state of anarchy and confusion.

And because the care of these and other great mischiefs in your Majesty's plantations and colonies aforesaid, and the introducing such an administration of government and fit regulation of trade as may put them into a better state of security and make them duly subservient and useful to England, does every day become more and more necessary, and that your Majesty's frequent commands to them have not met with due compliance: we humbly conceive it may be expedient that the charters of the several proprietors and others entitling them to absolute government be reassumed to the Crown and these colonies put into the same state and dependency as those of your Majesty's other plantations, without prejudice to any man's particular property and freehold. Which being no otherwise so well to be effected as by the legislative power of this kingdom.

D. THE EVOLUTION OF COLONIAL SELF-GOVERNMENT

COLONIAL self-government had several bases: the creation of local legislatures based on trading company charters, as in Virginia and Massachusetts, and the acceptance of this idea by the Crown; the religious ideas of English dissenters; and the convictions which the colonists derived from the political and constitutional experience of the mother country. From the start colonists claimed and their charters guaranteed the "rights of Englishmen". As time went on, the maintenance of those rights became a vital portion of the activity of every elected legislature in the colonies. In the royal colonies these 'lower' houses represented local and popular interests as opposed to appointed governors and councils, and the administrative orders and parliamentary legislation flowing out of England. In the proprietary colonies the elected assemblies played the same role in opposition to the wishes of the proprietors. In the corporation colonies, where outside control was relatively unimportant, the same conflicts appear between the assemblies and the governors and councils elected by them.

The basic issue in the royal colonies was the very foundation of the assembly: the colonists insisted that an elected assembly was a 'right'; the British insisted that an assembly could exist only as an act of the royal prerogative expressed through the commissions and instructions of a royal governor. The difference of opinion was fundamental and was not to be finally settled until the war for independence. The outstanding issue around which most of the conflicts centred was the control of taxation and the expenditure of money in the colonies. The maintenance of royal officials and policies in most of the colonies depended upon grants from the local legislatures. The elected assemblies in every colony insisted that they alone had the right to raise money by taxation and to direct how that money should be spent, no matter what a governor's instructions might say. Not only did the assemblies insist upon such control, they were able to maintain it and thereby to defeat both governors and councils, and often to usurp both their executive and legislative powers.

By the middle of the eighteenth century royal officials in most of the colonies were virtually at the mercy of the local assemblies. The statement of the Privy Council in 1754 on the situation in New York sums up what had happened in nearly every colony. It said: "the assembly have taken to themselves not only the management and disposal of such public money, but have also wrested from your majesty's governor the nomination of all officers of government, the custody and direction of all military stores, the mustering and regulating of troops raised for your Majesty's service, and in short almost every other executive part of government. . . ."

33. The maladministration of Governor Nicholson of Virginia

One important factor in the development of colonial self-government was the plight of any royal governor who crossed the wills of the dominant political leaders in a colony. An independent governor who followed his instructions was doomed to trouble, and often to the loss of his post. There was virtually no limit to the virulence of colonists bent on ridding themselves of a man who refused to co-operate with them. Francis Nicholson (1655–1728) was as near to being a professional colonial governor as any man in the eighteenth century. In the course of his career he was successively lieutenant-governor of the Dominion of New England (1688–1689), lieutenant-governor of

Virginia (1692), governor of Maryland (1694–1698), governor of Virginia (1698–1705), and governor of South Carolina (1720–1725). Nicholson was a man of great ability, but was possessed of a violent temper. He was popular with the elected legislatures of both Virginia and South Carolina, but alienated the aristocracy. The following document, written some time after 1702, was signed by six members of the Virginia Council: J. Lightfoot, Matthew Page, Benjamin Harrison, Robert Carter, James Blair, and Philip Ludwell. These men were leaders of one of the most powerful aristocracies in the American colonies and no governor could thwart their wills for long. As a result of their opposition, Nicholson was recalled in 1705. Printed: *The Virginia Magazine of History and Biography*, III (1895–1896), pp. 373–382.

A Memorial Concerning the Maladministrations of His Excellency Francis Nicholson, Esq., Her Majesty's Lieutenant and Governor-General of Virginia

Not to speak of the vast number of instances of his injustice, oppression, and insolence to particular persons which would require a large volume, we shall limit our observations to his behaviour toward ourselves in the several capacities wherein we act, whether as members of her Majesty's Council, or as the Upper House of Assembly, or as judges of the General Court, with some few more of the most public and notorious abuses of his government and bad examples of his life and conversation because he would offer nothing on so tender a subject that may be improper to be taken notice of by persons in that station wherein her Majesty has thought fit to place us in this country.

HIS BEHAVIOUR IN THE COUNCIL

Whereas heretofore it was the constant practice, agreeable to her Majesty's royal instructions, that the government of this country (though in chief committed to the governor for the time being) was administered by the advice and consent of the Council, he, the said governor, has altered this good and wholesome method by engrossing all power to himself and by acting alone in most of the chief affairs of the government. For instance, justices of the peace all over the country who used always to be nominated in Council and by the Council's advice and consent are now privately appointed by himself, and sometimes blank commissions are signed and sealed for that purpose, to be filled up by particular favourites. The same method is used for striking anyone out of the peace without any fault known or communicated to the Council, and of late a whole court was in this manner turned out at once (two only excepted) and very insufficient and undeserving men substituted into their places, to the general dissatisfaction of the people and endangering of the peace in that part of the country.

All the sheriffs are of late nominated by his excellency in private, without asking the advice of the Council contrary to all former practices.

All colonels, lieutenant-colonels, majors, captains, and other officers of the militia are put in and turned out in like manner.

Naval officers are put in and turned out at pleasure without any advice of the Council.

Orders and proclamations of all sorts are issued out in her Majesty's name and published at court and churches all over this government without any advice in Council.

Precepts and warrants are drawn upon the receiver-general, not only without the previous advice but without the subsequent privity and knowledge of the Council.

The whole accounts of her Majesty's revenue (if passed at all) are passed by his excellency without the knowledge or consent of the Council.

Particular agents are sent home for England by his excellency and paid out of her Majesty's revenues, without the knowledge of or consent of the Council.

A standing agent is named by his excellency in England, and allowed one hundred pounds per annum out of her Majesty's revenues of two shillings per hogshead without the consent of the Council, or any other body of men in this country, though he goes under the character of the agent of Virginia.

Rules of limitation in taking up of land have been prescribed to surveyors, against both law and custom, and without any advice in Council.

Surveyors of land have been directed, limited, and totally restrained in the execution of their office, against law and without any advice in Council, to the great prejudice of her Majesty's subjects.

Many things have been put on record both in the Secretary's and Council's offices, and others forbid to be put upon record, without any advice in Council, what shall or shall not be so recorded.

His excellency alone recommends home such persons as he thinks fit to be put upon the Council, without the knowledge or advice of the Council.

By his excellency's interposition with the secretary the clerks of the county courts are put in and removed at pleasure, without any advice in Council, and much to the dissatisfaction of the courts they are to serve.

And in short all methods are taken to engross all power into his own hands and to render the Council insignificant cypher, which is a great alteration of government, much to the dissatisfaction of this country, and as we conceive, very dangerous and unsafe to her Majesty's service.

II. Many matters of great moment are transacted by his excellency expressly contrary to advice in Council particularly. The calling so many General Assemblies, and at such unseasonable times of the year, to the great trouble and charge of the inhabitants.

The exasperating of Assembly with harsh speeches and irritating propositions to the great obstruction of her Majesty's business.

The keeping the land on Blackwater and Pamunkey Neck shut up without any instruction, contrary to the advice of both Council and burgesses.

When afterwards by an order of himself and Council (notified by proclamation all over the country) the Blackwater land was opened, and a great many people had been at the charge of purchasing rights of her Majesty and of making entries and surveys, he by his private orders, contradicted and retracted all, forbidding the surveyors to proceed, without taking any notice to the Council of this prohibition, either before or after issuing thereof, to the great loss of her Majesty in her quit-rents.

III. He signs many orders, warrants, patents, commissions, and other things in Council (on purpose to have the colour of the Council's name) which are never so much as read in Council, and the Council knows nothing of them.

IV. There is now no check nor control upon the accounts of her Majesty's revenue in this country, whereas formerly they used to be examined and passed in Council at a solemn audit appointed for that purpose.

V. He is impatient of all just freedom of dispute or debate in Council, that if anyone of the Council presumes to differ in opinion from him, though he expresses himself in never so modest and submissive terms, he is commonly treated with reproof and threats in the most rude, insolent, and abusive manner, as if it were a great crime to pretend to that freedom of debate and vote which is allowed us by her Majesty's instructions and is so necessary for her service.

VI. To the end he may act without control he carefully conceals from the Council the knowledge of his instructions by which (as we humbly conceive) we ought to be directed in giving and he in taking our advice.

VII. He has endeavoured upon all occasions to debase and vilify the Council before the people by giving them gross and abusive language (such as rogues, villains, rascals, cowards, dogs, etc.) to their faces and behind their backs; reflecting upon them as if they had got their estates by cheating the people, swearing that he valued the Council no more than the dirt under his feet and that he would reduce them to their primitive nothing, and likewise advancing men of inferior stations to the chief commands of the militia; by which trusts and honours the Council alone used formerly to be dignified and distinguished, to her Majesty's great security in times of danger. By these means endeavouring not only to regain the good opinion of the common people, but also to beget in them such jealousies and distrusts of the Council as might render them incapable to withstand his arbitrary designs.

HIS BEHAVIOUR IN THE UPPER HOUSE OF ASSEMBLY

I. Whereas that House humbly conceives that they ought to be left to the freedom of their own debates without being swayed and overawed by the governor's interposition: he is not only continually present but takes upon himself to preside and debate and state the questions and overrule, as if he were still in Council, which the said House takes to be a great encroachment upon their liberties and privileges.

II. His usual high, haughty, passionate, and abusive way of browbeating, discouraging, and threatening all that speak anything contrary to his opinion or designs is another great encroachment on the liberties of that House.

III. His endeavouring to beget or feed a bad understanding between the two Houses; his downright interposing and siding, sometimes with one House and sometimes with the other, and making entries to that purpose in the Assembly books, we take to be a great encroachment on the liberties of both Houses.

IV. His closeting of the members and using all the arts of cajoling and threatening for his own ends, not sticking sometimes to threaten the cutting of their throats and their utter ruin, we take to be another intolerable encroachment on the liberties of that House.

V. He makes several extemporary rash speeches to both Houses of Assembly, cajoling or irritating, promising or threatening, which though they have great influence in making or marring the business of Assemblies, yet are never put into writing, nor appear anywhere in the minutes of either House of Assembly.

HIS BEHAVIOUR IN THE GENERAL COURTS

I. He uses gross and visible partiality in most cases of his friends or enemies, abusing the counsel at the bar, and often hectoring his fellow judges if they happen to differ in opinion from him.

II. He keeps courts at most unseasonable hours in the night, to the great dissatisfaction and endangering the health of judges, lawyers, and people.

III. He sends for his creatures from the country and gives directions to the sheriff to put them upon the grand jury and tampers with these juries to procure flattering encomiums of himself, that by the sending of these for England his true character may be concealed.

IV. He often makes particular entries contrary to the opinion of the rest of the court, and in very abusive and reflecting terms.

OTHER PUBLIC ABUSES IN HIS GOVERNMENT

I. He makes her Majesty's name cheap and contemptible by using it to every frivolous, unnecessary, or arbitrary command; *e.g.*, if he wants to speak with any man, the message is brought him in these words: his excellency commands you in the queen's name to come to him immediately. If he wants a horse, or boat and hands, etc., he sends presently to press a horse, or boat and hands in her Majesty's name, or whatsoever other command he gives, though no manner of way relating to the government, they are all given in the queen's name, and the more illegal, arbitrary, or unjust they are, so much the surer are they to be backed with the authority of her Majesty's name.

II. He encourages all sorts of sycophants, tattlers, and talebearers, takes their stories in writing, and if he can persuade or threaten them to swear to them, without giving the accused person any opportunity of knowing his accusation or accuser.

III. He has privately issued several commissions to examine witnesses against particular men *ex parte*; he has forced men upon oath to turn informers, and if witnesses do not swear up to what is expected, they are tampered with and additional depositions are taken, but all this while the person accused is not admitted to be confronted with, or defend himself against his defamers.

IV. As he encourages these sycophants and tell-tales, and has some such in most parts of the country, so he is a man so subject to suspicion and jealousy that he readily believes and mightily improves all such stories, and studies and pursues revenge to the utmost against all whom he suspects and all their kindred, friends and acquaintance.

V. He makes it a great part of his business, by most malicious stories of his own coining, to blast the reputation of all such persons of either sex against whom he has any manner of prejudice, and by that means prostitutes his own honour and honesty.

VI. He endeavours mightily to make parties, and foment divisions in the country, to the utter destruction of good neighbourhood and the manifest endangering of the peace.

VII. He is exceedingly self-willed and utterly uncounselable by any person or persons whatsoever.

VIII. He values not how arbitrary and illegal his commands are. If the ordinary attorney for her Majesty will not undertake his designs as being against law, he employs others that will. Upon an attorney-general declining one of his commands as being against law, he took him by the collar and swore by God that he knew of no law we had and that his commands should be obeyed without hesitation or reserve.

IX. His haughty, furious, and insolent behaviour to the best gentlemen in the country is more like downright madness than anger or passion. He has told us sometimes that he knew how to govern the Moors and that he would beat us into good manners. And sometimes upon very trivial occasions he has threatened very considerable gentlemen to try them for their lives, swearing that he must hang one half of these rogues before the other would learn to obey his commands. He has not only in rash words threatened to cut gentlemen's throats, but sent them formal messages and made solemn vows that he would be their death or their ruin, and to assure them that he should be borne out in all these things. And he has been heard to make his brags that, right or wrong, he could by his authority ruin any private man.

X. He is so abusive in his words and actions as not only to treat our best gentlemen with the scurrilous names of dogs, rogues, villains, dastards, cheats, and cowards, and our best women with the names of whores, bitches, jades, etc., but actually to beat and buffet some gentlemen in a most public, insolent, and tyrannical manner.

XI. In his rage he most arbitrarily committed men into custody without any cause of commitment assigned, and without prosecution thereon.

XII. His profane custom of bloody cursing and swearing, and that often immediately before or after prayers, and perhaps the same or next day after receiving the blessed sacrament, convinces all people that he has no sense of religion, and that he is a great scandal to the Church of England for which he pretends to set up.

XIII. This is further confirmed by many gross immoralities and pranks of lewdness and rudeness to women that he is notoriously known to be guilty of in several parts of the country.

XIV. His rash and profane swearing ensnares him sometimes in the higher sin of forswearing, particularly upon the pretence that a great deal of injustice has been done by executors and administrators in the execution of their trusts. He swore several times that he would never sign any more probates or commissions of administrations, saying it was against his conscience, and in this humour he continued for several months, often repeating solemn oaths that he would never do it; yet afterwards when he found the complaints in the country grew very loud, and feared the bad influence of them on a General Assembly then called, he got over all his oaths and signed them again as himself and other governors before had used to do, and by such rash oaths and solemn promises upon public occasions which he hath afterwards thought fit to break, he hath so ruined his credit that neither his promise nor oath are now any more regarded.

XV. He has extremely ensnared the consciences of the clergy by urging, persuading, bribing, and terrifying them into such eulogies and encomiums of himself in highflown flattering addresses as must make them forfeit their honour and honesty if they comply with them, or expose them to his fury and revenge, and consequently their own ruin, if they refuse them.

XVI. To oblige his flatterers he breaks through the clearest instructions, and the greatest ground of merit with him is to be forward in promoting of any flattering address to recommend him to the Court of England. For this reason the foreman of a grand jury that had drawn one of the most fulsome of these addresses was lately immediately rewarded with a naval officer's place worth about one hundred pounds per annum, taken on purpose from an honest gentleman that had blamelessly managed it, and one of the greatest traders of this country (because he is a tool of his) was by him preferred and has been all along kept in the possession of such another naval officer's place, expressly contrary to the royal instruction on that subject, which positively forbids the bestowing of these places on any men much in trade, by that means to cut off from them the many opportunities they have of playing tricks in their office.

XVII. His ordinary housekeeping is most scandalously penurious, no way suiting the dignity of her Majesty's governor, having but one dish of meat at his table, though at public times when he has any flattering address to procure, or any other design in hand, he prepares such feasts as he thinks may best contribute to the carrying on of his sinister purposes.

XVIII. Though this is his true character, he takes all imaginable care to conceal the same in England.

1. By giving out terrible threatenings against all that shall offer to accuse him there.

2. By endeavouring to stop all from going out of the country that he suspects will give an unfavourable character of him.

3. By giving the falsest and blackest characters of all such as he fears will dare to write the truth, as if they were men of scandalous lives, or disaffected to her Majesty's government, though they are men of never so known loyalty and good credit and reputation.

4. By procuring flattering addresses from packed grand juries, for which he rewards them with places of honour and profit in the government.

5. By calling clandestine meetings of such of the clergy as will join in the like flattering addresses, and managing them with treats and presents and protection of such as are obnoxious and promotion of such as are desirous of better preferment.

6. By intercepting letters in hopes of discovering the intelligence for or from England concerning his conduct in this country, to the unspeakable hindrance of friendship, trade, and business.

7. By procuring the commendatory letters of the few Church of England ministers that are in New England, New York, and Pennsylvania, to whom and their churches he sends now and then a present when he wants any of their flattering recommendations.

8. Especially by employing Sir Thomas Lawrence in Maryland, and Colonel

Robert Quary in Pennsylvania (men linked in interest with him) to varnish over his unjustifiable life and government for which he repays them both with his own favours and by employing his interest in England to promote theirs; the intercourse between him and them being kept up at her Majesty's charge, as may appear by the extraordinary disbursements for messages to the northward in the accounts of her Majesty's revenue.

If the truth of any of the particulars of this memorial requires any further proof besides our own representation (being the major part of the Council) we pray that some course may be contrived that witnesses may be examined here and may be enabled to deliver their testimony free from the terror and resentments of his arbitrary government, and that we may have free access to the Council and Assembly books, and all other public records, and we doubt not we shall make out a great deal more than we do now attest under our hands.

And moreover we humbly pray that her Majesty will be graciously pleased by her royal instructions to her future governors to provide that the several particular grievances before mentioned may not hereafter be drawn in consequence to prejudice the just rights and liberties of ourselves and other her Majesty's dutiful and loyal subjects in this her Colony and Dominion.

34A–B. Self-government in Massachusetts

The rise of colonial self-government in the eighteenth century is told best by the colonial governors in endless letters and memorials to the authorities in England. There is little variation from colony to colony. Massachusetts continued to be, as it had been, one of the most independent minded of the colonies. Samuel Shute (1662–1742), after a military career in Marlborough's armies, was made governor of Massachusetts and New Hampshire in 1716. In 1723 he returned to England to present a memorial to the king (No. 34A). This memorial was turned over to the Board of Trade which reported the facts to be correct and declared that the people of Massachusetts "are daily endeavouring to wrest the small remains of power out of the hands of the Crown, and to become independent of their Mother Kingdom". Once more it recommended the intervention of Parliament.

Jonathan Belcher (1682–1757) was born in Massachusetts and was a graduate of Harvard. He accumulated a fortune as a merchant and was elected to the Massachusetts Council for the first time in 1718. He was one of the leaders against Governor William Burnet in the perennial dispute over the governor's salary, and in 1729 he was sent to England to present the colony's side of the argument. Shortly thereafter, Governor Burnet died and Belcher secured the appointment as governor of Massachusetts and New Hampshire. His administration was a prolonged series of disputes, the nature of which is illustrated by his letters (No. 34B). He was removed in 1741. In 1746 he became governor of New Jersey where his administration was relatively peaceful.

34A. Memorial of Governor Shute to the King (1723)

Printed: Cecil Headlam, et al., eds., Calendar of State Papers, Colonial Series, America and West Indies, 1722–1723 (London, 1934), pp. 324–330.

[Upon arrival in the Massachusetts Bay in October 1716] I soon called the General Assembly together. I found the House of Representatives, who are chosen annually, possessed of all the same powers of the House of Commons, and of much greater, they having the power of nominating once a year the persons that constitute your Majesty's Council, etc., and giving the salary of the governor and lieutenant-governor but from six months to six months; and likewise giving such only as is no way suitable to the rank of your Majesty's governor and lieutenant-governor, or to the known abilities of the province, and this notwithstanding your Majesty's instructions, directing them to settle a salary suitable to their stations and for such time as they shall continue in [them?]. The said House likewise appoint the salary of the treasurer every year whereby they have in effect the sole authority over that important office, which they often use in order to intimidate the treasurer from obeying the proper orders for issuing money, if such orders are not agreeable to their views and inclinations. By all which means the House of Representatives are in a manner the whole legislative, and in a good measure the executive power of the province. This House consists of about one hundred, who by an act of Assembly must be persons residing in the respective towns which they represent, whereby it happens that the greatest part of them are of small fortunes and mean education; men of the best sense and circumstances generally residing in or near Boston; so that by the artifice of a few designing members, together with the insinuations of some people in the town of Boston, the country representatives are easily made to believe that the House is barely supporting the privileges of the people, whilst they are invading the undoubted prerogatives of the Crown. Were it not for this act, the Assembly would certainly consist of men of much better sense, temper, and fortune than they do at present. The Assembly usually sit at Boston, the capital of this province, a large and populous town supposed to contain about 18,000 inhabitants, under no magistracy, by the want of which many of the inhabitants become too much disposed to a levelling spirit, too apt to be mutinous and disorderly, and to support the House of Representatives in any steps they take towards encroaching on the prerogative of the Crown. That this is too much the prevailing temper in the majority of the inhabitants of this town is plain from hence, that if I have at any time, according to the known power vested in your Majesty's governor of that province, with the strongest reasons, given my negative to any person nominated to be of your Majesty's Council there, the said town have hardly ever failed to choose him their representative. Three negatived councillors are the present representatives of the town of Boston. This practice is so notoriously known and justified that it is a common maxim that a negatived councillor makes a good representative. The House of Representatives thus constituted and abetted, notwithstanding the many uncommon privileges they enjoy by virtue of their charter, far from being contented therewith, have for some years last past been making attempts upon the few prerogatives that have been reserved to the Crown; which for that reason, as well as from the obligation of my oath and the trust reposed in me by your Majesty, I have endeavoured to my utmost to maintain against all invasions whatsoever.

I would humbly beg leave to lay before your Majesty some instances in which they have endeavoured to wrest those prerogatives out of your royal hands. (1) The House of Representatives have denied your Majesty's right to the woods in the province of Maine, contrary to the reservations in their charter, to an act of Parliament of Great Britain, and the instructions I received from your Majesty, etc. The said House having received an account of a great quantity of trees that were felled and cut into logs in the county of York, many of them fit for masting the royal navy, voted that a committee of that House should be joined with a committee of the

Council to make inquiry into that affair, and to dispose of those logs for the use of the province. To which the Council, at my instance, made the following amendment, viz., "saving to his Majesty his right". But the House of Representatives refused to agree to that amendment. After which, without either my consent or the Council's, they sent a committee of their own with orders to dispose of the said logs for the use of the province. (2) The House of Representatives would have refused me the power of a negative on the choice of their Speaker, which I thought it necessary to make use of against Mr. Cooke when he was chosen to that office, he having publicly opposed your Majesty's known rights to those woods. And the said House, insisting on their choice notwithstanding the negative I had given it, I dissolved that Assembly and then made a representation of the whole matter to the right honourable, the Lords of Trade, who sent me the opinion of your Majesty's Attorney-General, that the power was vested in your Majesty's governor for the time being. And when they acquainted me at the next meeting of the House of Representatives by a message, that they had chosen Mr. Clarke for their Speaker, and I had returned them for answer that I approved their said choice, the House of Representatives sent me this message, viz., "that they did not send up the foregoing message for my approbation, but for my information only", and since that time, whenever the Speaker has been absent by sickness, or otherwise, they have never failed to choose the said Mr. Cooke Speaker *pro tempore*. (3) The House of Representatives voted a public fast throughout your Majesty's said province, a thing never attempted by any of their predecessors; it being very well known that that power was always vested in and exercised by your Majesty's governor in that and all other colonies in America. (4) Though the royal charter has vested in the governor only the power of proroguing the General Assembly, yet the House of Representatives sent up a vote to the Council adjourning the General Assembly to the town of Cambridge; to which I refused to give my assent, and yet after this they adjourned themselves for several days without my consent or privity, and did not meet me on the day to which I had adjourned the General Assembly. (5) I had hoped that the House of Representatives, upon making due reflection on the several attempts they had unwarrantably made against these, your Majesty's undoubted prerogatives, and the constant opposition they had met with from me therein, would have desisted from any further attempts of this kind. But to my great surprise they have endeavoured to wrest the sword out of your royal hands, as will appear by the following instances. Though the charter, as well as your Majesty's commission, gives the command of all the forts in the said province to your Majesty's governor, and the sole power of building and demolishing such forts; yet the House of Representatives voted [in margin, 13, 29, and 14 June 1722] that a committee of their House should go down to your Majesty's Castle William to take an account of all the stores there, and to take receipts from the officers for the same, without any application made to me for my leave, and in the same manner without asking my consent, ordered the treasurer that he should pay no more subsistence money to the officers and soldiers of Fort Mary at Winter Harbour; and directed him to take speedy care that the provisions of ordnance, arms, and ammunition, and all other stores of war at that fort, should be transported to Boston, and lodged with him.

Upon which, I must beg leave to observe to your Majesty that the last of these is the only fort and harbour that can secure the fishing vessels of your Majesty's subjects in the eastern parts. The inhabitants have been so sensible of the danger of dismantling this fort that one hundred and thirty-two persons at Marblehead have petitioned the House of Representatives since my departure that the said fort may not be dismantled; whereupon the House has desisted from any further attempts that way, and ordered it to be supported. [In margin, 20 December, 10 January 1722.] This instance may serve at the same time to show the disposition of the House to wrest the sword out of your royal hands, and that by their assuming this undue power to themselves, the people are taught to address them in cases where they should only apply to him that has the honour of commanding in chief over your forces there. (6) The House of Representatives voted [in margin, 17 August 1722] that Mr. Moody, a major in your [Majesty's for]ces there should be suspended, and that even unheard; which vote they sent up to the [Council for their?] concurrence. But the Council nonconcurring, the said House of Representatives ordered [the salary of Maj?] or Moody should be no longer paid. And upon my expostulating with the House on their proceeding against a major in your Majesty's service, so manifestly contrary to all rules of justice, they sent me a message justifying their proceedings against him, in terms that have not been usually given to one that has the honour of being your Majesty's governor in that province. And to [   ] your Majesty's governor there of less weight, they have of late addressed the chair in terms much less respectful than any of their predecessors. (7) The House of Representatives ordered a committee [in margin, 17 and 20 November 1720] to command the officers at the eastern and western parts of the province to draw out their forces and muster them only under colour of an order signed by their Speaker. And the said House has been so far from returning to a just sense of their duty, and from acknowledging this unprecedented violation of the most important and undoubted right of your Crown, that they have since my departure from the said province, by your Majesty's leave, repeated this unprecedented attempt by pretending to the power of drawing off the forces from the place where they were [in margin, 8 January 1722]. Which bold pretence of theirs has not gone without a proper animadversion and reprimand from your Majesty's lieutenant-governor. These charges may be made good by their own votes. I would with humble submission, further lay before your Majesty, that upon my arrival I had good reason given to me to expect that they would allow me for my salary, £1,500 per annum of the money current there. But they gave me no more the first year than £1,200 of that money. At which time £160 there was equal in value to £100 sterling, and they did likewise continue the same allowance for two years after; and though provisions have been much dearer since, they have given me no more than £1,000 per annum of that money, which is now so much reduced in its value that £260 is but equal to £100 sterling, and therefore is now above a third less in value than when I first arrived there, so that £385 sterling per annum is all which they in reality now allow me. They vote me that sum by moieties at each session of their Assembly, which is once in six months, but even that they don't give me till I have passed the bills in the respective sessions, thereby to constrain me as far as they can to consent to any bills they lay before me. In the last sessions of the Assembly they have voted me no salary at all, so that I have been, and must be, without any support from them for some time. And because I did all in my power to prevent their encroachments on your Majesty's just prerogative, they have endeavoured to make me uneasy by other ways, as well as by reducing the salary or allowance which they formerly gave me, as appears by comparing the salary of the three first years with the salary or allowance of the three last, and as might be made appear to your Majesty by other instances, if that was necessary. They voted the lieutenant-governor for his service of three years no more than £35 of that country money, which he thought below the honour of his commission to accept, for which unjust treatment I know no other reason than that he is firmly attached to the just prerogatives of the Crown.

It is but justice to the province, after making these observations on the House of Representatives, and on too great a part of the town of Boston, humbly to acquaint your Majesty that the whole clergy of the province, as well as the generality of the people, are zealously affected to your Majesty's person and government, and the succession of the Crown in your royal family. And that the unjustifiable proceedings of the House of Representatives are disapproved by those in the province who are most distinguished for their wealth, understanding, and probity; though by reason of the constitution of that government which in effect excludes many of the richest [   ] of representatives, they are not able to prevent or redress [   ]. I am also humbly of opinion that this province may deserve your Majesty's attention, the rather because it is of great extent, well peopled, capable of being made a strong frontier to several of your Majesty's other colonies; furnishes pitch, tar, masts, and planks for your royal navy, and other valuable commodities which they exchange for British manufactures.

34B. Letters of Governor Belcher to the Board of Trade (1732–1733)

Printed: Massachusetts Historical Society *Collections*, 6th Series, VI, pp. 226–228, 240–242, 307–309.

My Lords: I had the honour of writing to your lordships the 21 of the last month, of which a duplicate is also gone. The General Assembly of this province being still sitting, I cannot by this conveyance write your lordships so fully on the state of the public affairs as I hope to do when the General Court rises, and which will be in a few days. The speech I made at the opening of this session will show your lordships what a miserable condition the province is in for want of the Assembly's making the proper and seasonable supplies of money to the public treasury, where there has not been a shilling for nineteen months past, although there is now upwards of £40,000 due to the officers and soldiers of the king's forts and garrisons, the judges, the secretary of the province, and other people; nor am I yet able to judge whether the Assembly will raise any money before they rise; but as they have, my lords, taken a very extraordinary step upon his Majesty's royal instructions to me (the 16 and 30) by addressing his Majesty a third time to withdraw them, and in case his Majesty will not hear them, then their agent is instructed to apply to the House of Commons.

This, my lords, is what I take to be very extraordinary, to complain to his Majesty's dutiful and faithful Commons of the severity of his Majesty's proceedings with his people here. I believe, I say, this is without precedent. Nor have I ever heard that any of the king's plantations have presumed upon anything of this nature. Nor is there that I can see any occasion for treating his Majesty so indecently and disrespectfully. The justice and strength of his royal orders will undoubtedly appear plain to all men of sense and understanding by comparing them with the charter of this province, and if the construction of any paragraph thereof falls into dispute, or seems dubious, why cannot the judges of England determine such points? I know no reason unless that the Assembly here love to be clamorous and troublesome. His Majesty's 16 and 30 instructions to me in my humble opinion are excellently calculated for supporting the honour of his government, and for the peace, welfare, and happiness of his people. I therefore hope in justice, mercy, and favour to his good subjects he will not recede from any part of them.

As to the 16 instruction, which limits or restrains the striking of credit bills, I believe every man of thought and substance is highly thankful that the Assembly are kept from ruining all the estates of the province by issuing out floods of those pernicious bills. At an emission of 50 or £60,000, every man that has outstanding debts sinks at least a fifth part of his capital, the bills growing in 3 or 4 months' time of so much less value than before such an emission. And whereas £125 of the lawful money of the province would purchase £100 sterling, yet £350 of the vile bills that have been issued by the government will not at this day purchase that sum; so that to allow any further liberty of making these bills than for the annual expense of the province, or to extend the calling them in beyond the year in which they are issued, would have a direct tendency to ruin the king's government and people, and would prove a fraud and cheat upon all the merchants of England, who have always large effects in this country.

As to the 30 instruction, my lords, I think nothing can be plainer than that it exactly quadrates with the charter; and for his Majesty to give it up or condescend to the House of Representatives examining the public accounts of charge of the government, I should think it would be as well to suffer them to appoint their own governor. For really, my lords, all the struggle in that matter is for power. If every account of the province must be subjected to a House of Representatives, the king's governor will be of very little signification. They that have the control of the money will certainly have the power; and I take the single question on this head to be, whether the king shall appoint his own governor, or whether the House of Representatives shall be governor of the province? I have, my lords, with the best assistance and information I could get, drawn up the state of the case respecting the 30 instruction in the enclosed sheets, which is humbly submitted to your correction, and to be used as your lordships shall judge proper. When the sitting of the Assembly is over, I shall do myself the honour of writing your lordships the further needful for his Majesty's service in the government under my care. And in the meantime I remain with all possible respect and esteem, my lords, your lordships' most obedient and most humble servant.

10

Boston, December 23, 1732

Your lordships have enclosed the journals of the House of Representatives from the time that I last sent them.

*   *   *

My Lords: The captain to whom I delivered mine to your lordships of 23 last month, being to this day embargoed by the ice, gives me the opportunity of acquainting your lordships that after the Assembly's sitting here upwards nine weeks, I dismissed them yesterday by their own request, and now cover to your lordships the remaining journals of their House; upon which I think your lordships will easily observe that the House of Representatives of this province are continually running wild, nor are their attempts for assuming (in a manner) the whole legislative, as well as the executive part, of the government into their own hands to be endured with honour to his Majesty. Your lordships will find upon the king's Council's not agreeing to their vote of taking the public affairs of the government into their hands in the recess of the Court, they made a vote yesterday fully empowering a committee of their own House to write the agent from time to time on the address and memorial of both Houses. This, most certainly, is assuming a power they have no right to, unless the address and memorial had been only from themselves. Had they sat a few days longer I should have expected they would have voted his Majesty's Council an useless part of the legislature.

I have, my lords, according to my duty to the king, been representing to your lordships for 18 months past the great difficulty under which this province labours through the perverseness and obstinacy of the House of Representatives (or rather of a few designing men of influence among them), and really, my lords, matters seem now to be hastening to a crisis, that I cannot apprehend the king's government can subsist any longer without his Majesty's immediate care. The officers and soldiers will certainly desert all the forts and garrisons, being naked and unable to do their duty for want of their just pay; and this your lordships will see by the several enclosed petitions from the officers and soldiers which I have laid before the Assembly to no purpose.

About two years ago I sent the lieutenant-governor of the province with a number of other gentlemen to survey all the forts of the province and to make a report to me, which they did; and according to his Majesty's royal instructions I sent the report they made to your lordships. And about six months ago I made a tour into the eastern frontiers and surveyed all the forts there, and since that, Castle William in this harbour (the principal fortification and key of this country). The forts on the frontier are all dropping down, and Castle William wants a large repair. To all these things I have had no answer from your lordships; but since the province is come into the condition in which I now represent it, I must beg your lordships to be no longer silent. For really, my lords, if things thus continue (or still grow worse) this government and province is in a fair way to fall into all confusion and be lost. I humbly beg your lordships seriously to consider all I have and do write, and that you would lay the state of this government before his Majesty, according to your wonted justice and wisdom.

As to their long address and memorial, they are mainly filled up with the old history of this country, which seems to me very impertinent and calculated more to move the passions than anything else. The dispute as to the supply of the Treasury I think must entirely turn upon the words and sense of the charter, and I hope his Majesty will steadily abide by his royal orders for the safety and honour of his government, and for the best good of his subjects here.

Your lordships may entirely depend, as I have through the whole course of my administration, done everything to support his Majesty's just right and authority, as well as to protect the liberties of his people, so I shall still proceed. Praying this dispute may have a speedy issue, and that I may receive the result from your lordships, I have the honour to be with great respect, my lords,

Your lordships' most obedient and most humble servant.

Boston, January 5, 1732/3.

*   *   *

My Lords:

Since I last wrote your lordships I have met the new Assembly of this province, and I humbly refer your lordships to their journal herewith for their proceedings, by which your lordships will see they seem resolved to supply no money in support of the king's government or for paying their just debts till there comes a conclusive answer to their Address to the King and of their Memorial to the House of Commons. I must therefore again beseech your lordships that these affairs may have dispatch, and thereby the king's government and his people be delivered from the dangers and difficulties they now lie exposed to. I have faithfully done all in my power in obedience to the king's royal orders, and what remains must be from his Majesty. I now beg leave to repeat to your lordships the great distress and extremity the people of this province are brought to for want of a good medium to carry on end their trade and commerce, and think it would be a good service to his Majesty's subjects that your lordships would send me the king's leave to sign a bill of the nature of that I sent your lordships in January last, which would make an emission of the best sort of credit bills that were ever yet put forth in this province; and I could wish the leave might also extend to New Hampshire, which would be a great ease and relief to his Majesty's good subjects there. For really, my lords, it is impossible for the traffic to be carried on end without something of this kind, nor does the restriction the king has laid me under fully answer the end of preventing a multiplication of paper currency of the low, mean value it constantly is, since Connecticut and Rhode Island issue out what of it they please, without control. Let me therefore again entreat your lordships that the king's good people under my care may be supported in their trade and business by the benefit of such a bill as I have mentioned; and I should rejoice that your lordships would put the line betwixt this province and New Hampshire into a method of settling, according to my letter of 13 January last, which would be doing a very kind part to the people of New Hampshire. And I would pray your lordships that the mandamuses for Messrs. Sherburne and Husk may be made out and delivered to Mr. Partridge.

Your lordships will observe by the votes of the Massachusetts Assembly that there arose a difficulty the 6 current about their voting my support, and some men of great influence were entirely against my having any, unless I would break the king's instructions and sign the bill for supply of the Treasury in the way they are contending for, and contrary to the charter. And the question put for my support was first of all without those words, *at this time*, but when the violent opposers to any peace in the government looked on the question so standing, it's supposed they thought it was too bold and barefaced upon the king to whom they have made so many public and solemn promises of amply and honourably supporting his governor, and to do it the first thing at their May session; therefore after the vote was passed of 6 current, they proposed an amendment to it of these words, *at this time*, and yet when the motion came forward again on the 15 the same set of men opposed any bill for the governor's support, unless it were tacked to a bill for supply of the Treasury in the manner before mentioned. Thus your lordships see the difficulty I labour with for paying a strict duty and obedience to his Majesty, and it shall be my care, my lords, that this people shall never have any other complaint against me; and notwithstanding the opposition made to it, yet I now enclose your lordships a bill passed by the House of Representatives and by his Majesty's Council the 20 current for £3,000 for my support, and I again pray your lordships' favour that I may have the royal leave for giving my assent to this bill, and would hope your lordships will think it most consistent with the king's honour that the leave be general for the future, and which will save your lordships a great deal of trouble and me a great expense of soliciting leave to take my bread; and I must freely repeat to your lordships that there is not the least prospect of a governor's ever being supported by an Assembly here in any other manner, and I believe your lordships will allow that it is a great hardship on a governor to spend his salary a year before he gets it, as has been my case hitherto; and as I have often said to your lordships, should my mortality happen while soliciting for leave, the Assembly seems to me to have so little justice or honour as that I don't expect the grant would ever be revived, and the hard fate of Governor Burnet's family must convince the world of what I say in this matter. I therefore entreat your lordships that the royal leave may have as much dispatch as possible, for by the delay of it the last year it arrived but 5 days before the then Assembly must have expired, according to the royal charter, when that grant would have been lost.

I remain with great deference and respect, my lords, your lordships' most obedient and most humble servant.

Boston, June 28, 1733.

35. Sir John Randolph: the constitution of Virginia (6 August 1736)

The election of a speaker of the House of Burgesses was an occasion for much ceremony. In 1736 when Sir John Randolph was re-elected, he was presented to Lieutenant-Governor William Gooch for approval. Randolph's speech upon this occasion is a lucid statement of the constitutional thinking of the political leaders of the colony. Randolph (1693 ?-1737) was one of the most distinguished lawyers of the time. He was knighted in 1732, the only Virginian so honoured during the colonial period. Printed: H. R. McIlwaine, ed., *Journals of the House of Burgesses of Virginia, 1727-1734, 1736-1740* (Richmond, 1910), pp. 241-242.

Mr. Speaker elect, with the House, went to attend the governor in the Council Chamber and spake as followeth:

The House of Burgesses have, in obedience to your commands, proceeded to the choice of a speaker; and having elected me, do now present me for your approbation. And as I have never yet tried my strength in perverting the use of speech, which was given us for the true discovering, and not to disguise our minds, I dare not make my first essay in this place, and before this assembly; but without arraigning the small abilities I have, I humbly submit myself to your judgment.

Then the governor spake thus:

Gentlemen, the choice you have made of a speaker is greatly to my satisfaction.

After the governor's speech, Mr. Speaker replied:

I humbly thank you for this your favourable opinion, which I don't pretend to deserve, but will use it as a proper admonition, whereby I ought to regulate my conduct in the exercise of the office you are now pleased to confirm me in, which I do not intend to magnify to the degree some have done, feeling we are no more than the representative body of a colony, naturally and justly dependent upon the mother kingdom, whose power is circumscribed by very narrow bounds, and whose influence is of small extent. All we pretend to is to be of some importance to those who send us hither, and to have some share in their protection and the security of their lives, liberties, and properties.

The planters who sustained the heat and burden of the first settlement of this plantation were miserably harassed by the government in the form it was then established, which had an unnatural power of ruling by martial law, and constitutions passed by a Council in England, without the consent of the people, which were no better. This made the name of Virginia so infamous that we see the impressions of those times hardly yet worn out in other countries, especially among the vulgar. And such have been in all ages and for ever must continue to be the effects of an arbitrary despotic power, of which the Company in London, in whom all dominion and property was then lodged, were so sensible that they resolved to establish another form of government more agreeable and suitable to the temper and genius of the English nation. And accordingly, in July, 1621, passed a charter under their Common Seal, which was founded upon powers before granted by charters under the Great Seal of England, whereby they ordered and declared that for preventing injustice and oppression for the future and for advancing the strength and prosperity of the colony there should be two supreme councils; one to be called the Council of State, consisting of the governor and certain councillors, particularly named, to serve as a council of advice to the governor; the other to be called by the governor yearly, consisting of the Council of State and two burgesses, to be chosen by the inhabitants of every town, hundred, or other plantation, to be called the General Assembly. And to have free power to treat, consult, and conclude of all things concerning the public weal; and to enact such laws for the behoof of the colony and the good government thereof as from time to time should appear necessary or requisite, commanding them to imitate and follow the policy, form of government, laws, customs, manner of trial, and other administration of justice used in England; and providing that no orders of their

General Court should bind the colony unless ratified in the General Assemblies.[1] This is the original of our constitution, confirmed by King James the first, by King Charles the first, upon his accession to the throne, and by all the crowned heads of England and Great Britain, successively, upon the appointment of every new governor, with very little alteration. Under it we are grown to whatever we now have to boast of. And from hence, the House of Burgesses do derive diverse privileges which they have long enjoyed, and claim as their undoubted right. Freedom of speech is the very essence of their being because without it nothing could be thoroughly debated, nor could they be looked upon as a council; an exemption from arrests, confirmed by a positive law; otherwise their counsels and debates might be frequently interrupted and their body diminished by the loss of its members; a protection for their estates to prevent all occasions to withdraw them from the necessary duty of their attendance; a power over their own members, that they may be answerable to no other jurisdiction for anything done in the House; and a sole right of determining all questions concerning their own elections lest contrary judgments in the courts of law might thwart or destroy theirs.

All these I say, besides others which spring out of them, are incident to the nature and constitution of our body; and I am commanded by the House to offer a petition in their behalf that you will be pleased to discountenance all attempts that may be offered against them and assist us with your authority in supporting and maintaining them against all insults whatsoever. And lastly, I must beg your favour to myself, that you will not construe my actions with too much severity, nor impute my particular errors and failings to the House.

To which the governor answered:

The House of Burgesses may always depend upon my care to support them in their ancient rights and privileges.

And then Mr. Speaker went on:

We have long experienced your love and good will to the people of this country, and observe with what readiness you exert it upon all occasions.

The art of governing well is thought to be the most abstruse, as well as the usefullest science in the world, and when it is learnt to some degree of perfection it is very difficult to put it in practice, being often opposed by the pride and interest of the person that governs. But you have showed how easy it is to give universal satisfaction to the people under your government. You have met them and heard their grievances in frequent assemblies and have had the pleasure of seeing none of them proceed from your administration. You have not been intoxicated with the power committed to you by his Majesty but have used it like a faithful trustee for the public good and with proper cautions; raised no debates about what it might be able to do of itself, but on all important occasions have suffered it to unite with that of the other parts of the legislature. You never propose matters without supposing your opinion subject to the examination of others, nor strove to make other men's reason blindly and implicitly obedient to yours, but have always calmly acquiesced in the contrary opinion. And lastly, you have extirpated all factions from among us by discountenancing

[1] See No. 21.

public animosities, and plainly proved that none can arise, or be lasting, but from the countenance and encouragement of a governor. *Hinc illae Artes.*

I do not mention these things for the sake of enlarging my periods nor for flattery, nor for conciliating favour, for if I know myself at all I have none of the arts of the first nor the address that is necessary for the other. And I hope I shall never be one of those who bestow their commendations upon all men alike; upon those who deserve it as well as those who do not.

Permit me then, sir, to beseech you to go on in the same steady course. Finish the character you have been almost nine years establishing. Let it remain unblemished and a pattern to those who shall come after you. Make us the envy of the king's other plantations and put those governors out of countenance who make tyranny their glory, and though they know their master's will, fancy it a dishonour to perform it.

36. Thomas Pownall: from "The Administration of the Colonies" (1764)

The outstanding eighteenth-century account of the problems of colonial government was written by Thomas Pownall (1722–1805). After leaving Cambridge University he worked for a time at the Board of Trade where his brother John was secretary. In 1753 he went to the colonies as secretary to Sir Danvers Osborne, who had been appointed governor of New York. Within two days after taking over the government Osborne committed suicide. Pownall then travelled about the colonies and became acquainted with many colonial leaders. In 1755 he was appointed lieutenant-governor of New Jersey to assist the ailing governor, Jonathan Belcher. In 1756 he returned to England where he impressed William Pitt with his ideas of military strategy. In 1757 he was appointed governor of Massachusetts. There he won the favour of the popular leaders and got their support in fighting the war. He left Massachusetts for England in 1760, never to return to the colonies, although he was offered the governorships of South Carolina and of Jamaica. The book from which the following selection is taken appeared anonymously in 1764 and was published under his own name in five successive editions between 1765 and 1777. Printed: *The Administration of the Colonies* (4th ed., London, 1768), pp. 67–80.

The above is the actual and rightful relation between the king and the American colonies; and by the rule of this relation, we ought to review and decide those several points wherein the Crown, or its governors acting under its commission and instruction, differ with the people.

Upon such review it will appear, under this first general head, in various instances, that the two great points which the colonists labour to establish, is the exercise of their several rights and privileges, as founded in the rights of an Englishman; and secondly, as what they suppose to be a necessary measure in a subordinate government, the keeping in their own hands the command of the revenue, and the pay of the officers of government, as a security for the conduct of those officers towards them.

Under the first head come all the disputes about the king's instructions, and the governor's power, as founded on them.

The king's commission to his governor, which grants the power of government, and directs the calling of a legislature, and the establishing courts, at the same time that it fixes the governor's power, according to the several powers and directions granted and appointed by the commission and instructions, adds "and by such further powers, instructions, and authorities, as shall, at any time hereafter, be granted or appointed you, under our signet or sign manual, or by our order in our Privy Council". It should here seem that the same power which framed the commission, with this clause in it, could also issue its future orders and instructions in consequence thereof: but the people of the colonies say that the inhabitants of the colonies are entitled to all the privileges of Englishmen; that they have a right to participate in the legislative power; and that no commands of the Crown, by orders in Council, instructions, or letters from secretaries of state, are binding upon them, further than they please to acquiesce under such, and conform their own actions thereto; that they hold this right of legislature, not derived from the grace and will of the Crown, and depending on the commission which continues at the will of the Crown; that this right is inherent and essential to the community, as a community of Englishmen: and that therefore they must have all the rights, privileges, and full and free exercise of their own will and liberty in making laws which are necessary to that act of legislation, uncontrolled by any power of the Crown, or of the governor, preventing or suspending that act; and, that the clause in the commission, directing the governor to call together a legislature by his writs, is declarative and not creative; and therefore he is directed to act conformably to a right actually already existing in the people, etc., and therefore that such clause ought not to be in the commission, or to be understood as being of no effect, so far as concerns the colonists.

When I speak of full uncontrolled independent powers of debate and result, so far as relates to the framing bills and passing them into laws, uncontrolled by any power of the Crown or of the governor, as an essential property of a free legislature, I find some persons in the colonies imagine that I represent the colonies as claiming a power of legislature independent of the king's or governor's negative. These gentlemen knowing that it is not my intention to do injustice to the colonies, wish me so to explain this matter that it may not bear even the interpretation of such a charge. I do therefore here desire that the reader will give his attention to distinguish a full, free, uncontrolled, independent power, in the act of legislation, from a full, free, uncontrolled, independent power of carrying the results of that legislation into effect, independent either of the governor's or king's negative. The first right is that which I represent the colonists claiming as a right essential to the very existence of the legislature. The second is what is also essential to the nature of a subordinate legislature, and what the colonists never call in question. That therefore the point here meant to be stated as in debate is, whether a subordinate legislature can be instructed, restricted, and controlled, in the very act of legislation? Whether the king's instructions or letters from secretaries of state, and such like significations of his Majesty's will and pleasure, is a due and constitutional application of the governor's or of the royal negative? The colonists constantly deny it, and ministry, otherwise such instructions would not be given, constantly maintain it. After experience of the confusion and obstruction which this dubitable point hath occasioned to business, it is time surely that it were some way or other determined. Or whether in fact or deed, the people of the colonies, having every right to the full powers of government, and to a whole legislative power, are not under this claim entitled in the powers of legislature and the administration of government, to use and exercise in conformity to the laws of Great Britain, the same full, free, independent, unrestrained power and legislative will in their several corporations, and under the king's commission and their respective charters, as the government and legislature of Great Britain holds by its constitution, and under the Great Charter.

Every subject, born within the realm, under the freedom of the government of Great Britain, or by adoption admitted to the same, has an essential indefeasible right to be governed, under such a mode of government as has the unrestrained exercise of all those powers which form the freedom and rights of the constitution; and therefore "the Crown cannot establish any colony upon–or contract it within a narrower scale than the subject is entitled to, by the Great Charter of England". The government of each colony must have the same powers and the same extent of powers that the government of Great Britain has, and must have, while it does not act contrary to the laws of Great Britain, the same freedom and independence of legislature, as the Parliament of Great Britain has. This right (say they) is founded not only in the general principles of the rights of a British subject, but is actually declared, confirmed, or granted to them in the commissions and charters which gave the particular frame of their respective constitutions. If therefore, in the first original establishment, like the original contract, they could not be established upon any scale short of the full and complete scale of the powers of the British government, nor the legislature be established on anything less than the whole legislative power; much less can this power of government and legislature, thus established, be governed, directed, restrained, or restricted by any posterior instructions or commands by the letters of secretaries of state. But upon the supposition that a kind of general indetermined power in the Crown, to superadd instructions to the commissions and charter be admitted, where the colonists do not make a question of the case wherein it is exerted, yet there are particular cases wherein both directive and restrictive instructions are given, and avowedly not admitted by the colonists. It is a standing instruction, as a security of the dependence of the government of the colonies, on the mother country, that no acts wherein the king's rights, or the rights of the mother country or of private persons can be affected, shall be enacted into a law without a clause suspending the effect thereof till his Majesty's pleasure shall be known. This suspending clause is universally rejected on the principles above because such suspension disfranchises the inherent full power of legislature, which they claim by their rights to the British liberties, and by the special declarations of such in their charters. It does not remove this difficulty by saying that the Crown has already in its hands the power of fixing this point, by the effect of its negative given to its governor. It is said that if the Crown should withdraw that instruction which allows certain bills to be passed into laws with a suspending clause, which instruction is not meant as a restriction upon, but an indulgence to the legislature; that if the Crown should withdraw this instruction and peremptorily restrain its governor from enacting laws, under such circumstances as the wisdom of government cannot admit of, that then these points are actually fixed by the true constitutional power; but wherever it is so said, I must repeat my idea that this does not remove the difficulty. For waiving the doubt which the colonists might raise, especially in the charter colonies, how far the governor ought, or ought not, to be restricted from giving his assent in cases contrary only to instructions, and not to the laws of Great Britain; waiving this point, let administration consider the effects of this measure. In cases where the bills, offered by the two branches, are for providing laws absolutely necessary to the continuance, support, and exercise of government, and where yet the orders of the Crown and the sense of the people are so widely different as to the mode, that no agreement can ever be come to in these points—is the government and administration of the government of the colonies to be suspended? The interest, perhaps the being of the plantations, to be hazarded by this obstinate variance, and can the exercise of the Crown's negative, in such emergencies, and with such effect, ever be taken up as a measure of administration? And when everything is thrown into confusion, and abandoned even to ruin by such measure, will administration justify itself by saying that it is the fault of the colonists? On the contrary, this very state of the case shows the necessity of some other remedy.

In the course of examining these matters, will arise to consideration the following very material point. As a principal tie of the subordination of the legislatures of the colonies on the government of the mother country, they are bound by their constitutions and charters to send all their acts of legislature to England to be confirmed or abrogated by the Crown; but if any of the legislatures should be found to do almost every act of legislature, by votes or orders, even to the repealing the effects of acts, suspending establishments of pay, paying services, doing chancery and other judicatory business; if matters of this sort, done by these votes and orders, never reduced into the form of an act, have their effect without ever being sent home as acts of legislature, or submitted to the allowance or disallowance of the Crown; if it should be found that many, or any of the legislatures of the colonies carry the powers of legislature into execution, independent of the Crown by this device, it will be a point to be determined how far, in such cases, the subordination of the legislatures of the colonies to the government of the mother country is maintained or suspended; or if, from emergencies arising in these governments, this device is to be admitted, the point, how far such is to be admitted, ought to be determined; and the validity of these votes and orders, these Senatus Consulta so far declared. For a point of such great importance in the subordination of the colony legislatures, and of so questionable a cast in the valid exercise of this legislative power, ought no longer to remain in question.

The next general point yet undetermined, the determination of which very essentially imports the subordination and dependence of the colony governments on the government of the mother country, is the manner of providing for the support of government, and for all the executive officers of the Crown. The freedom and right efficiency of the constitution require that the executive and judicial officers of government should be independent of the legislative; and more especially in popular governments where the legislature itself is so much influenced by the humours and passions of the people; for if they do not, there will be neither justice nor equity in any of the courts of law, nor any efficient execution of the laws and orders of government in the magistracy; according, therefore, to the constitution of Great Britain, the Crown has the appointment and payment of the several executive and judicial officers, and the legislature settles a permanent and fixed appointment for the support of government and the civil list in general. The Crown therefore has, *à fortiori*, a right to require of the colonies, to whom, by its commission or charter, it gives the power of government such permanent support, appropriated to the offices, not the officers of government, that they may not depend upon the temporary and arbitrary will of the legislature.

The Crown does, by its instructions to its governors, order them to require of the legislature a permanent support. This order of the Crown is generally, if not universally rejected, by the legislatures of the colonies. The assemblies quote the precedents of the British constitution, and found all the rights and privileges which they claim on the principles thereof. They allow the truth and fitness of this principle in the British constitution where the executive power of the Crown is immediately administered by the king's Majesty; yet say, under the circumstances in which they find themselves, that there is no other measure left to them to prevent the misapplications of public money than by an annual voting and appropriation of the salaries of the governor and other civil officers, issuing from moneys lodged in the hands of a provincial treasurer appointed by the Assemblies. For in these subordinate governments, remote from his Majesty's immediate influence, administered oftentimes by necessitous and rapacious governors who have no natural, although they have a political connection with the country, experience has shown that such governors have misapplied the moneys raised for the support of government, so that the civil officers have been left unpaid, even after having been provided for by the Assembly. The point then of this very important question comes to this issue: whether the inconveniencies arising, and experienced by some instances of misapplications of appropriations (for which however there are in the king's courts of law due and sufficient remedies against the offender), are a sufficient reason and ground for establishing a measure so directly contrary to the British constitution; and whether the inconveniencies to be traced in the history of the colonies through the votes and journals of their legislatures, in which the support of governors, judges, and officers of the Crown will be found to have been withheld or reduced on occasions, where the Assemblies have supposed that they have had reason to disapprove the nomination, or the person, or his conduct; whether, I say, these inconveniencies have not been more detrimental and injurious to government; and whether, instead of these colonies being dependent on, and governed under, the officers of the Crown, the sceptre is not reversed, and the officers of the Crown dependent on and governed by the Assemblies, as the colonists themselves allow, that this measure "renders the governor, and all the other servants of the Crown, dependent on the Assembly". But the operation of this measure does not end here; it extends to the assuming by the Assemblies the actual executive part of the government in the case of the revenue, than which nothing is more clearly and unquestionably settled in the Crown. In the colonies the treasurer is solely and entirely a servant of the Assembly or General Court; and although the moneys granted and appropriated be, or ought to be, granted to the Crown on such appropriations, the treasurer is neither named by the Crown, nor its governor, nor gives security to the Crown or to the Lord High Treasurer (which seems the most proper), nor in many of the colonies, is to obey the governor's warrant in the issue, nor accounts in the auditor's office, nor in any one colony is it admitted that he is liable to such account. In consequence of this supposed necessity, for the Assembly's taking upon them the administration of the treasury and revenue, the governor and servants of the Crown, in the ordinary revenue of government, are not only held dependent on the Assembly, but all services where special appropriations are made for the extraordinaries which such services require, are actually executed and done by commissioners appointed by the Assembly, to whose disposition such appropriations are made liable. It would be perhaps invidious, and might tend to prejudging on points which ought very seriously and dispassionately to be examined, if I were here to point out in the several instances of the actual execution of this assumed power, how almost every executive power of the Crown lodged in its governor, is, where money is necessary, thus exercised by the Assembly and its commissioners. I therefore rest the matter here.

E. GOVERNMENT WITHIN THE COLONIES

IN addition to the colonial governments with their governors, councils, judiciaries, and assemblies, there were local governments of considerable variety and importance. The two basic agencies of local government were the towns of New England and the counties of the southern colonies. Every New England town was a little state within itself, whose powers were established by the colonial assemblies.[1] The towns chose their own officers, levied taxes, controlled church and school, distributed lands, and elected representatives to the colonial assemblies in their town meetings.[2] The town meeting was a primary assembly of the qualified inhabitants of the town. Administrative business of the towns was carried on by select men who were elected annually and could exercise only the power delegated to them by the town meeting. As a training school in self-government, the town meeting was a unique institution in the American colonies. When New Englanders moved to other colonies they carried their township form of government with them and established it as they did in New Jersey and parts of New York. After the Revolution, the system was carried westward, and township government is still a living institution in many parts of the United States outside of New England.

The county of the southern colonies was the basis of local government, but it did not provide for elective self-government as the township did. The county court was the governing body of the county.[3] This body, which usually met once a month, was both a judicial and an administrative body whose members were also justices of the peace. As individuals they could try minor cases; meeting as a body they had both criminal and civil jurisdiction in more important cases. The county court also administered the civil affairs of a county. It laid out roads apportioned taxes, made lists of taxpayers and voters, licensed taverns, and, in general, oversaw the running of affairs.[4] The members of the county court were usually appointed by the colonial governors, and their tenure tended to be for life. Almost invariably the court was made up of the political leaders of the county, and usually the county representatives in the colonial legislatures were chosen from this small group of men. The executive officer of the county was the sheriff. Like the members of the county court, he too was appointed by the governor. The sheriff collected taxes, arrested and jailed criminals, supervised elections, and carried out the orders of the county court.

Counties were organized in all the colonies. In the middle colonies the county was the unit of representation as it was in the south, but it was never so well organized as a governmental agency. Counties were created in New England too, but they were primarily judicial districts.

In the south the parish was an agency which had a political as well as religious function. It was most fully developed in Virginia. The vestry, usually of twelve men, became in time self-perpetuating. Not only did it concern itself with the church, it was responsible for the care of the poor, it apportioned and collected a parish levy, and in general had oversight of the manners and morals of the parish. The parish was an inheritance from England. So too were the hundreds of Maryland and the manors of Maryland and New York. The hundred in Maryland was a subdivision of the

[1] No. 37.   [2] No. 41.   [3] No. 38.   [4] No. 42.

parish which collected taxes and regulated the local militia. The first manors or patroonships, as they were called in New York, were created by the Dutch West India Company, and other manorial grants were made by the duke of York after 1664. The manors thus created extended down to the nineteenth century. The lords of the manors had wide powers of government over their tenants, including the right to hold courts. In Maryland, the proprietors set up manors for themselves in every county, and in addition granted manorial estates to others. The inhabitants of the estates were tenants and the manor lords had the right to hold court leet and court baron. However, such institutions were of no great significance in the overall pattern of local government.

The governments of the growing colonial towns were diverse in character. In New England the town meeting form of government was retained, even for the large cities, down to the nineteenth century. Some colonial cities, notably Philadelphia, were governed by closed corporations consisting of a mayor, aldermen, and councilmen. Charleston, South Carolina, was governed by the legislature of the colony until after the Revolution.

The right to vote and to hold office was subject to a variety of restrictions that tended to increase during the colonial period. In early Virginia and Maryland all free men seem to have had the right to vote. In Massachusetts church membership was the prerequisite for voting imposed on the colony by the Puritan leaders and maintained until the revocation of the charter in 1684. After the Restoration, both the English government and the rising colonial aristocracy agreed that the ownership of property should be made the prerequisite of the franchise. In 1670 Virginia passed a law limiting voting to landowners and Maryland passed a similar law a little later. The requirement spread to other colonies. By the beginning of the eighteenth century the property qualification for both the suffrage and office-holding was universal. It varied from 50 to 100 acres of land or was described as a freehold worth £40 or yielding forty shillings a year. On the whole, the property qualification for office-holding was the same as for voting. South Carolina was an extreme example where eventually a member of the legislature had to own 500 acres in a "settled plantation", or ten slaves, or other property worth £1,000. Aside from property qualifications, the most common ones were religious, Catholics being excluded everywhere from voting.

Considerable uncertainty exists as to how many people were disfranchised by the property qualification. The older view was that large numbers were thus prevented from voting. The newer view is that the franchise was relatively democratic because property ownership was so widespread. The evidence to support either view is fragmentary at best. It would seem that the property qualification was particularly effective in the colonial towns, but that it did not seriously affect the rural areas. During the eighteenth century the refusal to grant adequate representation to newly settled areas by the creation of counties and townships was clearly more effective in preventing the mass of the people from participating in colonial governments than was the property qualification. The lack of representation in colonial legislatures was one of the basic grievances of western settlers in most of the colonies during the eighteenth century.[1] Both the British government and the colonial aristocracies along the coast quite consciously sought to maintain the control of an ever smaller minority of the population over the governments of the colonies. The issue was an explosive

[1] See for example, Nos. 95A and 96B.

one during the American Revolution and for long afterwards it remained an important issue in American political life.

The documents that follow are examples of the creation of local governments by colonial legislatures, and of the proceedings of some types of local government and of the legislatures themselves.

37. The creation of township government in Massachusetts

The system of township government was established in Massachusetts between 1635 and 1670 in a number of legislative enactments and in the Body of Liberties of 1641. In 1692 an elaborate law outlined the system in detail, but the foundations for it are in the documents which follow. Printed: Nathaniel B. Shurtleff, ed., *Records of the Governor and Company of the Massachusetts Bay in New England* (5 vols., Boston, 1853–1854), I, p. 172; II, pp. 197, 208; IV, pt. I, p. 336; IV, pt. II, p. 464. The excerpts from the Body of Liberties are printed in Massachusetts Historical Society *Collections*, 3rd Series, VIII, pp. 218, 225, 227, 228. For the steps in the creation of one township, see No. 47.

General Court, 3 March 1635/36

Whereas particular towns have many things which concern only themselves, and the ordering of their own affairs, and disposing of businesses in their own town, it is therefore ordered that the freemen of every town, or the major part of them, shall only have power to dispose of their own lands and woods with all the privileges and appurtenances of the said towns to grant lots and make such orders as may concern the well ordering of their own towns not repugnant to the laws and orders here established by the General Court; as also to lay mulcts and penalties for the breach of these orders, and to levy and distrain the same, not exceeding the sum of twenty shillings; also to choose their own particular officers as constables, surveyors for the highways, and the like; and because much business is like to ensue to the constables of several towns by reason they are to make distresses and gather fines, therefore that every town shall have two constables where there is need, that so their office may not be a burden unto them, and they may attend more carefully upon the discharge of their office, for which they shall be liable to give their accounts to this court when they shall be called thereunto.

Body of Liberties, Sec. 12

Every man, whether inhabitant or foreigner, free or not free, shall have liberty to come to any public court, council, or town meeting, and either by speech or writing to move any lawful, seasonable, and material question, or to present any necessary motion, complaint, petition, bill, or information whereof that meeting hath proper cognizance, so it be done in convenient time, due order, and respective manner.

Body of Liberties, Sec. 56

If any man shall behave himself offensively at any town meeting, the rest of the freemen then present shall have power to sentence him for his offence. So be it the mulct or penalty exceed not twenty shillings.

Body of Liberties, Sec. 66

The freemen of every township shall have power to make such by-laws and constitutions as may concern the welfare of their town, provided they be not of a criminal, but only of a prudential nature, and that their penalties exceed not 20 shillings for one offence. And that they be not repugnant to the public laws and orders of the country. And if any inhabitant shall neglect or refuse to observe them, they shall have power to levy the appointed penalties by distress.

Body of Liberties, Sec. 74

The freemen of every town or township shall have full power to choose yearly or for less time out of themselves a convenient number of fit men to order the planting or prudential occasions of that town, according to instructions given them in writing, provided nothing be done by them contrary to the public laws and orders of the country, provided also the number of such select persons be not above nine.

General Court, 26 May 1647

This court, taking into consideration the useful parts and abilities of divers inhabitants amongst us which are not freemen, which, if improved to public use, the affairs of this commonwealth may be the easier carried an end, in the several towns of this jurisdiction, doth hereby declare that henceforth it shall and may be lawful for the freemen within any of the said towns to make choice of such inhabitants, though non-freemen, who have taken or shall take the oath of fidelity to this government to be jury men, and to have their vote in the choice of the selectmen for town affairs, assessment of rates, and other prudentials proper to the selectmen of the several towns, provided still that the major part of all companies (of selectmen be freemen) from time to time that shall make any valid act, as also where no selectmen are to have their vote in ordering of schools, herding of cattle, laying out of highways, and distributing of lands, any law, usage, or custom to the contrary notwithstanding; provided also that no non-freeman shall have his vote until he have attained the age of 24 years; provided also that none that are or shall be detected and convicted in any court of any evil carriage against the government, or commonwealth, or churches (it being intended to be immediately done) shall be capable to vote until the court where he was convicted or sentenced hath restored him to his former liberty.

General Court, 11 November 1647

There being within this jurisdiction many members of churches, who, to exempt themselves from all public service in the commonwealth, will not come in to be made freemen, it is therefore ordered by this court, and the authority thereof, that all such members of churches in the several towns within this jurisdiction shall not be exempted from such public service as they are chosen to by the freemen of the several towns, as constables, jurors, selectmen, and surveyors of highways; and if any person shall refuse to serve such office he shall pay for every such refusal, being legally chosen thereunto, such fine as the town shall impose, not exceeding 20 shillings, as freemen are liable unto in such cases.

General Court, 26 May 1658

For explanation and emendation of two laws in the printed book, title Townships, relating to the liberty of such as have taken the oath of fidelity to vote in town affairs, which seems not well to consist together, the latter also repealing the former, and finding inconvenience in the execution of that, have therefore ordered, and be it hereby ordered and enacted that for time to come all Englishmen that are settled inhabitants and householders in any town of the age of 24 years, and of honest and good conversation, being rated at £20 estate in a single country rate, that hath taken the oath of fidelity to this government, and no other, except freemen, may be chosen jury men or constables, and have their vote in the choice of the selectmen for the town affairs, assessments of rates, and other prudentials proper to the selectmen of the several towns, provided still that the major part of all companies of selectmen be freemen from time to time that shall make a valid act, as also where no selectmen are to have their vote in ordering of schools, herding of cattle, laying out of highways, and distributing of lands, any law, use, or custom to the contrary notwithstanding, and the former laws, so far as they relate to the liberty of such as are non-freemen, are hereby repealed.

General Court, 12 October 1670

It is ordered that instead of the sum of twenty pounds in the fourth section, title Townships, it shall be inserted instead thereof, eighty pounds, provided this change of that sum be not interpreted to exclude any person from the privilege granted him formerly in that law.

38A–B. The creation of counties in Virginia

In 1634 Virginia was divided into eight shires, to be governed like the shires in England. The law provided for the appointment of lieutenants and sheriffs and other officials with the same powers as those of England. Courts were provided to try minor causes. It was not long before the name county was adopted, and as each one was created the legislature provided the regulations for its organization and government.

38A. Northumberland County (1648)

Printed: Hening, *Statutes of Virginia*, i, pp. 352–353.

It is enacted by the Governor, Council, and Burgesses of this Grand Assembly that the 9th act of Assembly [1644/45] for the reducing of the inhabitants of Chickeun and other parts of the neck of land between Rappahanock River and Potomac River be repealed, and that the said tract of land be hereafter called and known by the name of the county of Northumberland; and that from henceforth they have power of electing burgesses for the said county to serve at assemblies upon lawful summons from the governor, which they are authorized to do by virtue of this act to the next sessions of this Assembly; and it is further thought fit that patents be granted unto them for their lands with such reservations and provisos and upon such certificates of right as is usual granted to the planters by virtue of his Majesty's instructions or otherwise; and it is further enacted that the said inhabitants *de futuro* be rated proportionably in all levies to the rest of the inhabitants of the colony, and that they make payment of all assessments made by this Assembly and all arrears due from them, for which their so doing Captain Francis Poythers hath undertaken to the Assembly, who is therefore authorized to collect the same, with power to distrain in case of refusal either of the said arrears or of the levy ordered at this session of Assembly.

38B. Spotsylvania and Brunswick counties (1720)

Printed: Hening, *Statutes of Virginia*, IV, pp. 77–79.

Preamble, that the frontiers towards the high mountains are exposed to danger from the Indians, and the late settlements of the French to the westward of the said mountains.

Enacted, Spotsylvania County bounds upon Snow Creek up to the mill, thence by a south-west line to the River North Anna, thence up the said river as far as convenient, and thence by a line to be run over the high mountains to the river on the north-west side thereof, so as to include the northern passage through the said mountains, thence down the said river until it comes against the head of Rappahannock, thence by a line to the head of Rappahannock River, and down that river to the mouth of Snow Creek; which tract of land from the first of May 1721 shall become a county by the name of Spotsylvania County.

Brunswick County begins on the south side the River Roanoke at the place where the line lately run for ascertaining the uncontroverted bounds of this colony towards North Carolina, intersects the said River Roanoke, and to be bounded by the direction of the governor with consent of Council, so as to include the southern pass; which land from and after the time that it shall be laid off and bounded, shall become a county by the name of Brunswick County.

That fifteen hundred pounds, current money of Virginia, be paid by the treasurer to the governor to these uses, viz.

Five hundred pounds for a church, court house, prison, pillory, and stocks where the governor shall appoint them in the county of Spotsylvania, and the governor to employ workmen, provide materials, etc.

One thousand pounds to be distributed in arms and ammunition amongst such persons as shall hereafter go to seat the said counties, that is, to each Christian tithable, one firelock musket, one socket, bayonet fitted thereto, one cartouche box, eight pounds [bullets], two pounds powder, until the whole one thousand pounds be laid out. The account whereof is to be desired to be laid before the General Assembly.

Those arms are appropriated to the defence of the said counties, and the land as well as personal estate of the parties that take them is made liable to see them forthcoming in good order.

The arms to be stamped with the name of the county, and liable to the seizure of any militia officer if found within the bounds.

That five hundred pounds more be paid by the treasurer to Nathanial Harrison, Esq., Jonathan Allen, Henry Harrison, and William Edwards, gentlemen, or the survivors of them, or in case of their refusal, to such others as the governor shall name, to make up the like number, to be by them laid out for a church, court house, prison, pillory, and stocks where they shall think fit in the county of Brunswick and are required to account to the General Assembly.

Inhabitants of the said counties are made free of public levies for ten years from the first of May 1721.

The whole county of Spotsylvania made one parish, by the name of St. George; and that of Brunswick one, by the name of St. Andrew.

Because foreign Protestants may not understand English readily, if any such shall entertain a minister of their own, they and their tithables shall be free for ten years from the said first of May 1721.

Until the governor shall settle a court in Spotsylvania, the justices of the several counties of Essex, King and Queen, and King William take power over them by their warrants, and the clerks of the said courts by their process returnable to their said courts in the same manner as before the said county was constituted, directing the process always to the sheriff. And the court of Prince George County has the same power in Brunswick: but the sheriff of Prince George to have double fees.

Court day of Spotsylvania is the first Tuesday of the month and Brunswick the first Thursday.

39. Proceedings of the Virginia General Assembly (30 July–4 August 1619)

The first legislative assembly in the New World met in Virginia at the call of Governor Sir George Yeardley, acting under orders from the Virginia Company in London. The members were inhabitants of settlements variously known as 'hundreds', 'towns', and 'plantations', to which the company applied the collective name of 'boroughs'. These boroughs went out of existence but the term 'burgess' came to mean a member of the elective branch of the legislature, which was known as the House of Burgesses throughout the colonial period.

At this first meeting the governor and Council appointed by the company and the elected members sat as one body and decided matters by majority vote, although the governor had the power to veto its actions.

The account which follows is not the journal kept by the clerk. If there was one, it was lost. It consists of an account sent to England by John Pory, who was both Speaker of the House and Secretary of the colony. Printed: *Journals of the House of Burgesses, 1619–1658/59* (Richmond, 1915), pp. 3–16, and in L. L. Tyler, ed., *Narratives of Early Virginia*, pp. 245–278.

A report of the manner of proceeding in the General Assembly convened at James City in Virginia, July 30, 1619, consisting of the Governor, the Council of Estate, and two Burgesses, elected out of each incorporation and plantation, and being dissolved the 4th of August next ensuing.

First. Sir George Yeardley, Knight, Governor and Captain-General of Virginia, having sent his summons all over the country, as well to invite those of the Council of Estate that were absent as also for the election of burgesses, there were chosen and appeared.

For James City	Captain William Powell
	Ensign William Spense
For Charles City	Samuel Sharpe
	Samuel Jordan
For the city of Henrico	Thomas Dowse
	John Polentine
For Kiccowtan	Captain William Tucker
	William Capp
For Martin Brandon, Capt. John Martin's Plantation	Mr. Thomas Davis
	Mr. Robert Stacy

For Smythe's Hundred	Captain Thomas Graves
	Mr. Walter Shelley
For Martin's Hundred	Mr. John Boys
	John Jackson
For Argall's Gift	Mr. Pawlett
	Mr. Gourgaing
For Flowerdieu Hundred	Ensign Rossingham
	Mr. Jefferson
For Captain Lawne's Plantation	Captain Christopher Lawne
	Ensign Washer
For Captain Warde's Plantation	Captain Warde
	Lieutenant Gibbes

The most convenient place we could find to sit in was the choir of the church where Sir George Yeardley, the governor, being set down in his accustomed place, those of the Council of Estate sat next him on both hands except only the secretary, then appointed speaker, who sat right before him, John Twine, clerk of the General Assembly, being placed next the speaker, and Thomas Pierse, the sergeant, standing at the bar, to be ready for any service the Assembly should command him. But forasmuch as men's affairs do little prosper where God's service is neglected, all the burgesses took their places in the choir till a prayer was said by Mr. Buck, the minister, that it would please God to guide us and sanctify all our proceedings to his own glory and the good of this plantation. Prayer being ended, to the intent that as we had begun at God Almighty, so we might proceed with awful and due respect towards his lieutenant, our most gracious and dread sovereign, all the burgesses were entreated to retire themselves into the body of the church, which being done, before they were fully admitted, they were called in order and by name, and so every man (none staggering at it) took the oath of supremacy, and then entered the Assembly. At Captain Warde the speaker took exception, as at one that without any commission or authority had seated himself, either upon the company's, and then his plantation could not be lawful, or on Captain Martin's land, and so he was but a limb or member of him, and so there could be but two burgesses for all. So Captain Warde was commanded to absent himself till such time as the Assembly had agreed what was fit for him to do. After much debate, they resolved on this order following:

An order concluded by the General Assembly concerning Captain Warde, July 30th, 1619, at the opening of the said Assembly.

At the reading of the names of the burgesses, exception was taken against Captain Warde as having planted here in Virginia without any authority or commission from the treasurer, council, and company in England. But considering he had been at so great charge and pains to augment this colony, and had adventured his own person in the action, and since that time had brought home a good quantity of fish, to relieve the colony by way of trade, and above all, because the commission for authorizing the General Assembly admitteth of two burgesses out of every plantation without restraint or exception. Upon all these considerations, the Assembly was contented to admit of him and his lieutenant (as members of their body and burgesses) into their society. Provided, that the said Captain Warde with all expedition, that is to say between this and the next General Assembly (all lawful impediments excepted), should procure from the treasurer, council, and company in England a commission lawfully to establish and plant himself and his company as the chiefs of other plantations have done. And in case he do neglect this he is to stand to the censure of the next General Assembly. To this Captain Warde, in the presence of us all, having given his consent and undertaken to perform the same, was, together with his lieutenant, by the voices of the whole Assembly, first admitted to take the oath of supremacy, and then to make up their number and to sit amongst them.

This being done, the governor himself alleged that before we proceeded any further it behooved us to examine whether it were fit that Captain Martin's burgesses should have any place in the Assembly, forasmuch as he hath a clause in his patent which doth not only exempt him from that equality and uniformity of laws and orders which the great charter says are to extend over the whole colony, but also from divers such laws as we must be enforced to make in the General Assembly. That clause is as followeth: Item. that it shall and may be lawful to and for the said Captain John Martin, his heirs, executors, and assignees to govern and command all such person or persons as at this time he shall carry over with him, or that shall be sent him hereafter, free from any command of the colony, except it be in aiding and assisting the same against any foreign or domestic enemy.

Upon the motion of the governor, discussed the same time in the Assembly, ensued this order following:

An order of the General Assembly touching a clause in Captain Martin's patent at James City, July 30, 1619.

After all the burgesses had taken the oath of supremacy and were admitted into the house and all set down in their places, a copy of Captain Martin's patent was produced by the governor out of a clause whereof it appeared that when the General Assembly had made some kind of laws requisite for the whole colony, he and his burgesses and people might deride the whole company and choose whether they would obey the same or no. It was therefore ordered in court that the aforesaid two burgesses should withdraw themselves out of the Assembly till such time as Captain Martin had made his personal appearance before them. At what time, if upon their motion, if he would be content to quit and give over that part of his patent, and contrary thereunto would submit himself to the general form of government as all others did, that then his burgesses should be readmitted, otherwise they were utterly to be excluded as being spies rather than loyal burgesses, because they had offered themselves to be assistant at the making of laws which both themselves and those whom they represented might choose whether they would obey or not.

Then came in a complaint against Captain Martin, that having sent his shallop to trade for corn into the bay, under the command of Ensign Harrison, the said ensign should affirm to one Thomas Davis, of Paspaheighs, Gent. (as the said Thomas Davis deposed upon oath) that they had made a hard voyage, had they not met with a canoe coming out of a creek where their shallop could not go. For the Indians refusing to sell their corn, those of the shallop entered the canoe with their arms and took it by force, measuring out the corn with a basket they had into the shallop and, as the said Ensign Harrison saith, giving them satisfaction in copper beads and other trucking stuff.

Hitherto Mr. Davis upon his oath.

Furthermore it was signified from Opechancanough to the governor that those people had complained to him to procure them justice. For which considerations and because such outrages as this might breed danger and loss of life to others of the colony which should have leave to trade in the bay hereafter, and for prevention of the like violences against the Indians in time to come, this order following was agreed on by the General Assembly:

A second order made against Captain Martin, at James City, July 30, 1619.

It was also ordered by the Assembly the same day that in case Captain Martin and the ging of his shallop could not thoroughly answer an accusation of an outrage committed against a certain canoe of Indians in the bay, that then it was thought reason (his patent notwithstanding, the authority whereof he had in that case abused), he should from henceforth take leave of the Governor as other men, and should put in security that his people shall commit no such outrage any more.

Upon this a letter or warrant was drawn in the name of the whole Assembly to summon Captain Martin to appear before them in the form following:

By the Governor and General Assembly of Virginia.

Captain Martin, we are to request you upon sight hereof, with all convenient speed to repair hither to James City to treat and confer with us about some matters of especial importance which concern both us and the whole colony and yourself. And of this we pray you not to fail. . . .

These obstacles removed, the speaker, who a long time had been extremely . . . sickly, and therefore not able to pass through long harangues, delivered in brief to the whole Assembly the occasions of their meeting. Which done he read unto them the commission for establishing the Council of Estate and the General Assembly, wherein their duties were described to the life.

Having thus prepared them he read over unto them the great charter, or commission of privileges, orders, and laws sent by Sir George Yeardley out of England. Which for the more ease of the committees, having divided into four books, he read the former two the same forenoon, for expedition's sake a second time over, and so they were referred to the perusal of two committees, which did reciprocally consider of either, and accordingly brought in their opinions. But some man may here object to what end we should presume to refer that to the examination of committees which the council and company in England had already resolved to be perfect, and did expect nothing but our assent thereunto. To this we answer that we did it not to the end to correct or control anything therein contained, but only in case we should find aught not perfectly squaring with the state of this colony or any law which did press or bind too hard, that we might by way of humble petition seek to have it redressed, especially because this great charter is to bind us and our heirs for ever.

The names of the committees for perusing the first book of the four:

1. Captain William Powell
2. Ensign Rossingham
3. Captain Warde
4. Captain Tucker
5. Mr. Shelley
6. Thomas Dowse
7. Samuel Jordan
8. Mr. Boys

The names of the committees for perusing the second book:

1. Captain Lawne
2. Captain Graves
3. Ensign Spense
4. Samuel Sharpe
5. William Capp
6. Mr. Pawlett
7. Mr. Jefferson
8. Mr. Jackson

These committees thus appointed, we brake up the first forenoon's assembly.

After dinner the governor and those that were not of the committees sat a second time, while the said committees were employed in the perusal of those two books. And whereas the speaker had propounded four several objects for the Assembly to consider on: namely, first, the great charter of orders, laws, and privileges; secondly, which of the instructions given by the council in England to my Lord de la Warr, Captain Argall, or Sir George Yeardley, might conveniently put on the habit of laws; thirdly, what laws might issue out of the private conceit of any of the burgesses, or any other of the colony; and lastly, what petitions were fit to be sent home for England. It pleased the governor for expedition sake to have the second object of the four to be examined and prepared by himself and the non-committee. Wherein, after having spent some three hours conference, the two committees brought in their opinions concerning the two former books (the second of which beginneth at these words of the charter: And forasmuch as our intent is to establish one equal and uniform kind of government over all Virginia etc.) which the whole Assembly because it was late, deferred to treat of till the next morning.

Saturday July 31

The next day, therefore, out of the opinions of the said committees, it was agreed, those petitions ensuing should be framed, to be presented to the treasurer, council, and company in England. Upon the committees' perusal of the first book, the General Assembly do become most humble suitors to their lordships and to the rest of that honourable council and renowned company, that albeit they have been pleased to allot unto the governor to themselves, together with the Council of Estate here, and to the officers of incorporations, certain large portions of land to be laid out within the limits of the same, yet that they would vouchsafe also, that such grounds as heretofore hath been granted by patent to the ancient planters by former governors that had from the company received commission so to do, might not now after so much labour and cost, and so many years habitation be taken from them. And to the end that no man might do or suffer any wrong in this kind, that they would favour us so much (if they mean to grant this our petition) as to send us notice, what commission or authority for granting of lands they have given to each particular governor in times past.

The second petition of the General Assembly framed by the committees out of the second book is that the treasurer and company in England would be pleased with as much convenient speed as may be to send men hither to occupy their lands belonging to the four incorporations, as well for their own behoof and profit as for the maintenance of the Council of Estate, who are now to their extreme hindrance often drawn far from their private business and likewise that they will have a care to send tenants to the ministers of the four incorporations to manure their glebe, to the intent that the allowance they have allotted them of £200 a year may the more easily be raised.

The third petition humbly presented by this General Assembly to the treasurer, council, and company is that it may plainly be expressed in the great commission (as indeed it is not) that the ancient planters of both sorts, viz., such as before Sir Thomas Dale's departure were come hither upon their own charges, and such also as were brought hither upon the company's cost, may have their second, third, and more divisions successively in as large and free manner as any other planters. Also that they will be pleased to allow to the male children, of them and of all others begotten in Virginia, being the only hope of a posterity, a single share apiece, and shares for their wives as for themselves, because that in a new plantation it is not known whether man or woman be the most necessary.

Their fourth petition is to beseech the treasurer, council, and company that they would be pleased to appoint a sub-treasurer here to collect their rents, to the end that the inhabitants of this colony be not tied to an impossibility of paying the same yearly to the treasurer in England, and that they would enjoin the said sub-treasurer not precisely according to the letter of the charter to exact money of us (whereof we have none at all, as we have no mint), but the true value of the rent in commodity.

The fifth petition is to beseech the treasurer, council, and company that, towards the erecting of the university and college, they will send, when they shall think most convenient, workmen of all sorts, fit for that purpose.

The sixth and last is, they will be pleased to change the savage name of Kiccowtan, and to give that incorporation a new name.

These are the several petitions drawn by the committees out of the two former books which the whole General Assembly, in manner and form above set down, do most humbly offer up and present to the favourable construction of the treasurer, council, and company in England.

These petitions thus concluded on, those two committees brought in a report what they had observed in the two latter books, which was nothing else but that the perfection of them was such as they could find nothing therein subject to exception, only the governor's particular opinion to myself in private hath been as touching a clause in the third book, that in these doubtful times between us and the Indians, it would behoove us not to make so large disances between plantation and plantation as ten miles, but for our more strength and security to draw nearer together. At the same time, there remaining no farther scruple in the minds of the Assembly touching the said great charter of laws, orders, and privileges, the speaker put the same to the question, and so it had both the general assent and the applause of the whole Assembly, who, as they professed themselves in the first place most submissively thankful to Almighty God, therefore so they commanded the speaker to return (as now he doth) their due and humble thanks to the treasurer, council, and company for so many privileges and favours as well in their own names as in the names of the whole colony whom they represented.

This being dispatched we fell once more to debating of such instructions given by the council in England to several governors as might be converted into laws, the last whereof was the establishment of the price of tobacco, namely, of the best at 3s. and the second at 18d. the pound. At the reading of this the Assembly thought good to send for Mr. Abraham Persey, the cape merchant, to publish this instruction to him, and to demand of him if he knew any impediment why it might not be admitted of. His answer was that he had not as yet received any such order from the adventurers of the magazine in England. And notwithstanding he saw the authority was good, yet was he unwilling to yield till such time as the governor and Assembly had laid their commandment upon him, out of the authority of the aforesaid instructions as follows:

By the General Assembly

We will and require you, Mr. Abraham Persey, cape merchant, from this day forward to take notice, that, according to an article in the instructions confirmed by the treasurer, council, and company in England at a general quarter court, both by voices and under their hands and the common seal, and given to Sir George Yeardley, Knight, this present governor, December 1, 1618, that you are bound to accept of the tobacco of the colony, either for commodities or upon bills, at three shillings the best and the second sort at 18d. the pound, and this shall be your sufficient discharge.

At the same time the instructions convertible into laws were referred to the consideration of the above named committees, viz., the general instructions to the first committee and the particular instructions to the second, to be returned by them into the Assembly on Monday morning.

Sunday, August 1

Mr. Shelley, one of the Burgesses, deceased.

Monday, August 2

Captain John Martin (according to the summons sent him on Friday, July 30) made his personal appearance at the bar, when, the speaker having first read to him the orders of the Assembly that concerned him, he pleaded largely for himself to them both and endeavoured to answer some other things that were objected against his patent. In fine, being demanded out of the former order whether he would quit that clause of his patent which (quite otherwise than Sir William Throckmorton's, Captain Christopher Lawne's, and other men's patents) exempteth himself and his people from all services of the colony except only in case of war against a foreign or domestic enemy. His answer was negative, that he would not infringe any part of his patent. Whereupon it was resolved by the Assembly that his burgesses should have no admittance.

To the second order his answer was affirmative, namely, that (his patent notwithstanding) whensoever he should send into the bay to trade, he would be content to put in security to the governor for the good behaviour of his people towards the Indians.

It was at the same time further ordered by the Assembly that the speaker, in their names, should (as he now do) humbly demand of the treasurer, council, and company an exposition of this one clause in Captain Martin's patent, namely, where it is said that he is to enjoy his lands in as large and ample a manner, to all intents and purposes, as any lord of any manors in England doth hold his ground, out of which some have collected that he might by the same grant protect men from paying their debts and from divers other dangers of law. The least the Assembly can allege against this clause is, that it is obscure, and that it is a thing impossible for us here to know the prerogatives of all the manors in England. The Assembly therefore humbly beseecheth their lordships and the rest of the honourable board that in case they shall find anything in this or in any other part of his grant whereby that clause towards the conclusion of the great charter (viz., that all grants as well of the one sort as of the other respectively, be made with equal favour, and grants of like liberties and immunities as near as may be, to the end that all complaint of partiality and unindifferency may be avoided), might in any sort be contradicted or the uniformity and equality of laws and orders extending over the whole colony might be impeached, that they would be pleased to remove any such hindrance as may divert out of the true course the free and public current of justice.

Upon the same ground and reason their lordships, together with the rest of the council and company, are humbly besought by this General Assembly that if in that other clause which exempteth Captain Martin and his people from all services of the colony, etc., they shall find any resistance against that equality and uniformity of laws and orders intended now by them to be established over the whole colony, that they would be pleased to reform it.

In fine, whereas Captain Martin, for those ten shares allowed him for his personal adventure and for his adventure of £70 besides, doth claim 500 acres a share, that the treasurer, council, and company would vouchsafe to give notice to the governor here what kind of shares they meant he should have when they gave him his patent.

The premises about Captain Martin thus resolved, the committee appointed to consider what instructions are fit to be converted into laws, brought in their opinions, and first of some of the general instructions.

> Here begin the laws drawn out of the instructions given by his Majesty's
> Council of Virginia in England to my Lord de la Warr, Captain Argall,
> and Sir George Yeardley, Knight.

By this present General Assembly be it enacted that no injury or oppression be wrought by the English against the Indians whereby the present peace might be disturbed and ancient quarrels might be revived. And further be it ordained that the Chickahominy are not to be excepted out of this law, until either that such order come out of England, or that they do provoke us by some new injury.

Against idleness, gaming, drunkenness, and excess in apparel the Assembly hath enacted as followeth:

First, in detestation of idlers be it enacted, that if any man be found to live as an idler or runagate, though a freedman, it shall be lawful for that incorporation or plantation to which he belongeth to appoint him a master to serve for wages till he show apparent signs of amendment.

Against gaming at dice and cards be it ordained by this present Assembly that the winner or winners shall lose all his or their winnings, and both winners and losers shall forfeit ten shillings a man, one ten shillings whereof to go to the discoverer, and the rest to charitable and pious uses in the incorporation where the faults are committed.

Against drunkenness be it also decreed that if any private person be found culpable thereof, for the first time he is to be reproved privately by the minister, the second time publicly, the third time to lie in bolts 12 hours in the house of the provost-marshal and to pay his fees, and if he still continue in that vice, to undergo such severe punishment as the governor and Council of Estate shall think fit to be inflicted on him. But if any officer offend in this crime, the first time he shall receive an reproof from the governor, the second time he shall openly be reproved in the church by the minister, and the third time he shall first be committed and then degraded. Provided it be understood that the governor hath always power to restore him when he shall in his discretion think fit.

Against excess of apparel that every man be cessed in the church for all public contributions, if he be unmarried according to his own apparel; if he be married, according to his own and his wife's, or either of their apparel.

As touching the instruction of drawing some of the better disposed of the Indians to converse with our people and to live and labour amongst them, the Assembly who know well their dispositions think it fit to enjoin, at least to counsel those of the colony, neither utterly to reject them nor yet to draw them to come in. But in case they will of themselves come voluntarily to places well peopled, there to do service in killing of deer, fishing, beating corn, and other works, that then five or six may be admitted into every such place, and no more, and that with the consent of the governor. Provided that good guard in the night be kept upon them, for generally (though some amongst many may prove good) they are a most treacherous people and quickly gone when they have done a villainy. And it were fit a house were built for them to lodge in apart by themselves, and lone inhabitants by no means to entertain them.

Be it enacted by this present Assembly that for laying a surer foundation of the conversion of the Indians to Christian religion, each town, city, borough, and particular plantation do obtain unto themselves by just means a certain number of the natives' children to be educated by them in true religion and civil course of life, of which children the most towardly boys in wit and graces of nature to be brought up by them in the first elements of literature, so as to be fitted for the college intended for them that from thence they may be sent to that work of conversion.

As touching the business of planting corn this present Assembly doth ordain that year by year all and every householder and householders have in store for every servant he or they shall keep, and also for his or their own persons, whether they have any servants or no, one spare barrel of corn to be delivered out yearly, either upon sale or exchange as need shall require. For the neglect of which duty he shall be subject to the censure of the governor and Council of Estate. Provided always that the first year of every new man this law shall not be of force.

About the plantation of mulberry trees, be it enacted that every man as he is seated upon his division, do for seven years together, every year plant and maintain in growth six mulberry trees at the least, and as many more as he shall think convenient, and as his virtue and industry shall move him to plant, and that all such persons as shall neglect the yearly planting and maintaining of that small proportion shall be subject to the censure of the governor and the Council of Estate.

Be it farther enacted as concerning silk-flax, that those men that are upon their division or settled habitation, do this next year plant and dress 100 plants, which being found a commodity, may farther be increased. And whosoever do fail in the performance of this shall be subject to the punishment of the governor and Council of Estate.

For hemp also, both English and Indian, and for English flax and anise seeds, we do require and enjoin all householders of this colony that have any of those seeds to make trial thereof the next season.

Moreover be it enacted by this present Assembly, that every householder do yearly plant and maintain ten vines until they have attained to the art and experience of dressing a vineyard, either by their own industry or by the instruction of some vigneron. And that upon what penalty soever the governor and Council of Estate shall think fit to impose upon the neglectors of this act.

Be it also enacted that all necessary tradesmen, or so many as need shall require, such as are come over since the departure of Sir Thomas Dale, or that shall hereafter come, shall work at their trades for any other man, each one being paid according to the quality of his trade and work, to be estimated, if he shall not be contented, by the governor and officers of the place where he worketh.

Be it further ordained by this General Assembly, and we do by these presents enact, that all contracts made in England between the owners of the land and their tenants and servants which they shall send hither, may be caused to be duly performed, and that the offenders be punished as the governor and Council of Estate shall think just and convenient.

Be it established also by this present Assembly that no crafty or advantageous means be suffered to be put in practice for the enticing away the tenants and servants of any particular plantation from the place where they are seated. And that it shall be the duty of the governor and Council of Estate most severely to punish both the seducers and the seduced, and to return these latter into their former places.

Be it further enacted that the orders for the magazine lately made be exactly kept, and that the magazine be preserved from wrong and sinister practices, and that according to the orders of court in England, all tobacco and sassafras be brought by the planters to the cape merchant till such time as all the goods now or heretofore sent for the magazine be taken off their hands at the prices agreed on. That by this means the same going for England into one hand, the price thereof may be upheld the better. And to that end that all the whole colony may take notice of the last order of court made in England, and all those whom it concerneth may know how to observe it, we hold it fit to publish it here for a law among the rest of our laws. The which order is as followeth:

Upon the 26 of October, 1618, it was ordered that the magazine should continue during the term formerly prefixed, and that certain abuses now complained of should be reformed, and that for preventing of all impositions save the allowance of 25 in the hundred profit, the governor shall have an invoice as well as the cape merchant, that if any abuse in the sale of the goods be offered, he, upon intelligence and due examination thereof, shall see it corrected. And for encouragement of particular hundreds, as Smythe's hundred, Martin's hundred, Lawnes' hundred, and the like, it is agreed that what commodities are reaped upon any of these several colonies, it shall be lawful for them to return the same to their own adventurers. Provided that the same commodity be of their own growing, without trading with any other, in one entire lump and not dispersed and that at the determination of the joint stock, the goods then remaining in the magazine shall be bought by the said particular colonies before any other goods which shall be sent by private men. And it is moreover ordered that if the Lady de la Warr, the Lady Dale, Captain Bargrave and the rest, would unite themselves into a settled colony, they might be capable of the same privileges that are granted to any of the foresaid hundreds. Hitherto the order.

All the General Assembly by voices concluded not only the acceptance and observation of this order, but of the instruction also to Sir George Yeardley next preceding the same. Provided first, that the cape merchant do accept of the tobacco of all and every the planters here in Virginia, either for goods or upon bills of exchange at three shillings the pound the best, and 18d. the second sort. Provided also that the bills be duly paid in England. Provided, in the third place, that if any other besides the magazine have at any time any necessary commodity which the magazine doth want, it shall and may be lawful for any of the colony to buy the said necessary commodity of the said party, but upon the terms of the magazine, viz.: allowing no more gain than 25 in the hundred, and that with the leave of the governor. Provided lastly, that it may be lawful for the governor to give leave to any mariner, or any other person that shall have any such necessary commodity wanting to the magazine to carry home for England so much tobacco or other natural commodities of the country as his customers shall pay him for the said necessary commodity or commodities. And to the end we may not only persuade and incite men, but enforce them also thoroughly and loyally to cure their tobacco before they bring it to the magazine, be it enacted, and by these presents we do enact, that if upon the judgment of four sufficient men of any incorporation where the magazine shall reside (having first taken their oaths to give true sentence, two whereof to be chosen by the cape merchant and two by the incorporation), any tobacco whatsoever shall not prove vendible at the second price, that it shall there immediately be burned before the owner's face. Hitherto such laws as were drawn out of the instructions.

Tuesday, August 3, 1619

This morning a third sort of laws (such as might proceed out of every man's private conceit) were read and referred by halves to the same committees which were from the beginning.

This done, Captain William Powell presented to the Assembly a petition to have justice against a lewd and treacherous servant of his, who, by false accusation given up in writing to the governor, sought not only to get him deposed from his government of James City and utterly (according to the proclamation) to be degraded from the place and title of a captain, but to take his life from him also. And so out of the said petition sprang this order following:

Captain William Powell presented a petition to the General Assembly against one Thomas Garnett, a servant of his, not only for extreme neglect of his business to the great loss and prejudice of the said captain, and for openly and impudently abusing his house, in sight of both master and mistress, through wantonness with a woman servant of theirs, a widow, but also for falsely accusing him to the governor both of drunkenness and theft, and besides for bringing his fellow servants to testify on his side, wherein they justly failed him. It was thought fit by the General Assembly (the governor himself giving sentence) that he should stand four days with his ears nailed to the pillory, viz.: Wednesday, August 4, and so likewise Thursday, Friday, and Saturday next following, and every of those four days should be publicly whipped. Now, as touching the neglect of his work, what satisfaction ought to be made to his master for that is referred to the governor and Council of Estate.

The same morning the laws above written, drawn out of the instructions, were read, and one by one thoroughly examined, and then passed once again the general consent of the whole Assembly.

This afternoon the committees brought in a report what they had done as concerning the third sort of laws, the discussing whereof spent the residue of that day. Except only the consideration of a petition of Mr. John Rolfe against Captain John Martin for writing a letter to him wherein (as Mr. Rolfe alleges) he taxeth him both unseemly and amiss of certain things wherein he was never faulty, and besides, casteth some aspersion upon the present government, which is the most temperate and just that ever was in this country, too mild indeed, for many of this colony whom unwonted liberty has made insolent and not to know themselves. This petition of Mr. Rolfe's was thought fit to be referred to the Council of State.

Wednesday, August 4th

This day (by reason of extreme heat, both past and likely to ensue, and by that means of the alteration of the healths of divers of the General Assembly) the governor, who himself also was not well, resolved should be the last of this first session; so in the morning the speaker (as he was required by the Assembly) read over all the laws and orders that had formerly passed the house, to give the same yet one review more, and to see whether there were anything to be amended or that might be excepted against. This being done, the third sort of laws which I am now coming to set down, were read over and thoroughly discussed, which, together with the former, did now pass the last and final consent of the General Assembly.

A third sort of laws, such as may issue out of every man's private conceits.

It shall be free for every man to trade with the Indians, servants only excepted, upon pain of whipping, unless the master redeem it off with the payment of an angel, one fourth part whereof to go to the provost-marshal, one fourth part to the discoverer, and the other moiety to the public uses of the incorporation.

That no man do sell or give any Indians any piece, shot, or powder, or any other arms, offensive or defensive, upon pain of being held a traitor to the colony, and of being hanged as soon as the fact is proved, without all redemption.

That no man do sell or give any of the greater howes [sic] to the Indians, or any English dog of quality, as a mastiff, greyhound, bloodhound, land or water spaniel, or any other dog or bitch whatsoever, of the English race, upon pain of forfeiting £5 sterling to the public uses of the incorporation where he dwelleth.

That no man may go above twenty miles from his dwelling-place, nor upon any voyage whatsoever shall be absent from thence for the space of seven days together without first having made the governor or commander of the same place acquainted therewith, upon pain of paying twenty shillings to the public uses of the same incorporation where the party delinquent dwelleth.

That no man shall purposely go to any Indian towns, habitations, or places of resort without leave from the governor or commander of that place where he liveth, upon pain of paying 40s. to public uses as aforesaid.

That no man living in this colony but shall between this and the first of January next ensuing come or send to the secretary of state to enter his own and all his servants' names, and for what term or upon what conditions they are to serve, upon penalty of paying 40s. to the said secretary of state. Also, whatsoever masters or people come over to this plantation that within one month of their arrival (notice being first given them of this very law) they shall likewise resort to the secretary of state and shall certify him upon what terms or conditions they be come hither, to the end that he may record their grants and commissions, and for how long time and upon what conditions their servants (in case they have any) are to serve them, and that upon pain of the penalty next above mentioned.

All ministers in the colony shall once a year, namely in the month of March, bring to the secretary of estate a true account of all christenings, burials, and marriages, upon pain, if they fail, to be censured for their negligence by the governor and Council of Estate; likewise, where there be no ministers, that the commanders of the place do supply the same duty.

No man, without leave of the governor, shall kill any neat cattle whatsoever, young or old, especially kine, heifers or cow-calves, and shall be careful to preserve their steers and oxen, and to bring them to the plough and such profitable uses, and without having obtained leave as aforesaid, shall not kill them, upon penalty of forfeiting the value of the beast so killed.

Whoever shall take any of his neighbours' boats, oars, or canoes without leave from the owner shall be held and esteemed as a felon and so proceeded against; also he that shall take away by violence or stealth any canoes or other things from the Indians shall make valuable restitution to the said Indians, and shall forfeit, if he be a freeholder, five pound; if a servant, 40s. or endure a whipping; and anything under the value of 13d. shall be accounted petty larceny.

All ministers shall duly read divine service, and exercise their ministerial function according to the ecclesiastical laws and orders of the Church of England, and every Sunday in the afternoon shall catechize such as are not yet ripe to come to the communion. And whosoever of them shall be found negligent or faulty in this kind shall be subject to the censure of the governor and Council of Estate.

The ministers and churchwardens shall seek to prevent all ungodly disorders, the committers whereof if, upon good admonitions and mild reproof, they will not forbear the said scandalous offences, as suspicions of whoredoms, dishonest company keeping with women and such like, they are to be presented and punished accordingly.

If any person after two warnings do not amend his or her life in point of evident suspicion of incontinency or of the commission of any other enormous sins, that then he or she be presented by the churchwardens and suspended for a time from the church by the minister. In which interim, if the same person do not amend and humbly submit him or herself to the church, he is then fully to be excommunicate and soon after a writ or warrant to be sent from the governor for the apprehending of his person and seizing all his goods. Provided always, that all the ministers do meet once a quarter, namely, at the feast of St. Michael the Archangel, of the nativity of our Saviour, of the Annunciation of the blessed Virgin, and about midsummer, at James City or any other place where the governor shall reside, to determine whom it is fit to excommunicate, and that they first present their opinion to the governor ere they proceed to the act of excommunication.

For reformation of swearing, every freeman and master of a family, after thrice admonition, shall give 5s. or the value upon present demand, to the use of the church where he dwelleth; and every servant after the like admonition, except his master discharge the fine, shall be subject to whipping. Provided, that the payment of the fine notwithstanding, the said servant shall acknowledge his fault publicly in the church.

No man whatsoever, coming by water from above, as from Henrico, Charles City, or any place from the westward of James City, and being bound for Kiccowtan, or any other part on this side, the same shall presume to pass by, either by day or by night, without touching first here at James City to know whether the governor will command him any service. And the like shall they perform that come from Kiccowtanward, or from any place between this and that, to go upward, upon pain of forfeiting ten pound sterling a time to the governor. Provided, that if a servant having had instructions from his master to observe this law, do notwithstanding, transgress the same, that then the said servant shall be punished at the governor's discretion; otherwise, that the master himself shall undergo the aforesaid penalty.

No man shall trade into the bay, either in shallop, pinnace, or ship, without the governor's licence, and without putting in security that neither himself nor his company shall force or wrong the Indians, upon pain that, doing otherwise, they shall be censured at their return by the governor and Council of Estate.

All persons whatsoever upon the Sabbath day shall frequent divine service and sermons both forenoon and afternoon, and all such as bear arms shall bring their pieces, swords, powder and shot. And everyone that shall transgress this law shall forfeit three shillings a time to the use of the church, all lawful and necessary impediments excepted. But if a servant in this case shall wilfully neglect his master's command he shall suffer bodily punishment.

No maid or woman servant, either now resident in the colony or hereafter to come, shall contract herself in marriage without either the consent of her parents, or her master or mistress, or of the magistrate and minister of the place both together. And whatsoever minister shall marry or contract any such persons without some of the foresaid consents shall be subject to the severe censure of the governor and Council of Estate.

Be it enacted by this present Assembly that whatsoever servant hath heretofore or shall hereafter contract himself in England, either by way of indenture or otherwise, to serve any master here in Virginia, and shall afterward, against his said former contract, depart from his master without leave, or being once embarked, shall abandon the ship he is appointed to come in, and so, being left behind, shall put himself into the service of any other man that will bring him hither, that then at the same servant's arrival here, he shall first serve out his time with that master that brought him hither and afterward also shall serve out his time with his former master according to his covenant.

Here end the laws.

All these laws being thus concluded and consented to as aforesaid, Captain Henry Spelman was called to the bar to answer to certain misdemeanours laid to his charge by Robert Poole, interpreter, upon his oath (whose examination the governor sent into England in the *Prosperus*) of which accusations of Poole, some he acknowledged for true, but the greatest part he denied. Whereupon the General Assembly having thoroughly heard and considered his speeches, did constitute this order following against him:

This day Captain Henry Spelman was convented before the General Assembly and was examined by a relation upon oath of one Robert Poole, interpreter, what conference had passed between the said Spelman and Opechancanough at Poole's meeting with him in Opechancanough's court. Poole chargeth him he spoke very unreverently and maliciously against this present governor, whereby the honour and dignity of his place and person, and so of the whole colony, might be brought into contempt, by which means what mischiefs might ensue from the Indians by disturbance of the peace or otherwise, may easily be conjectured. Some things of this relation Spelman confessed, but the most part he denied, except only one matter of importance, and that was that he had informed Opechancanough that within a year there would come a governor greater than this that now is in place. By which and by other reports it seems he has alienated the mind of Opechancanough from this present governor, and brought him in much disesteem, both with Opechancanough and the Indians, and the whole colony in danger of their slippery designs.

The General Assembly upon Poole's testimony only, not willing to put Spelman to the rigour and extremity of the law which might, perhaps both speedily and deservedly, have taken his life from him (upon the witness of one whom he much excepted against), were pleased, for the present, to censure him rather out of that his confession above written than out of any other proof. Several and sharp punishments were pronounced against him by divers of the Assembly, but in fine the whole court by voices united did incline to the most favourable, which was that for this misdemeanour he should first be degraded of his title of captain, at the head of the troop, and should be condemned to perform seven years' service to the colony in the nature of interpreter to the governor.

This sentence being read to Spelman, he, as one that had in him more of the savage than of the Christian, muttered certain words to himself, neither showing any remorse for his offences, nor yet any thankfulness to the Assembly for their so favourable censure, which he at one time or another (God's grace not wholly abandoning him), might with some one service have been able to have redeemed.

This day also did the inhabitants of Paspaheigh, alias Argall's town, present a petition to the General Assembly to give them an absolute discharge from certain bonds wherein they stand bound to Captain Samuel Argall for the payment of £600 and to Captain William Powell, at Captain Argall's appointment, for the payment of £50 more to Captain Argall for 15 score acres of woody ground, called by the name of Argall's town or Paspaheigh; to Captain Powell in respect of his pains in clearing the ground and building the houses, for which Captain Argall ought to have given him satisfaction. Now, the General Assembly being doubtful whether they have any power and authority to discharge the said bonds, do by these presents (at the instance of the said inhabitants of Paspaheigh, alias Martin's hundred people) become most humble suitors to the treasurer, council, and company in England that they will be pleased to get the said bonds for £600 to be cancelled; forasmuch as in their great commission they have expressly and by name appointed that place of Paspaheigh for part of the governor's land. And whereas Captain William Powell is paid his £50 which Captain Argall enjoined the said inhabitants to present him with, as part of the bargain, the General Assembly, at their entreaty, do become suitors on their behalf, that Captain Argall, by the council and company in England, may be compelled either to restore the said £50 from thence, or else that restitution thereof be made here out of the goods of the said Captain Argall.

The last act of the General Assembly was a contribution to gratify their officers, as follows:

It is fully agreed at this General Assembly that in regard of the great pains and labour of the speaker of this Assembly (who not only first formed the same Assembly and to their great ease and expedition reduced all matters to be treated of into a ready method, but also, his indisposition notwithstanding, wrote or dictated all orders and other expedients and is yet to write several books for all the several incorporations and plantations both of the great charter, and of all the laws), and likewise in respect of the diligence of the clerk and sergeant, officers thereto belonging: that every man and manservant of above 16 years of age shall pay into the hands and custody of the burgesses of every incorporation and plantation, one pound of the best tobacco, to be distributed to the speaker and likewise to the clerk and sergeant of the Assembly, according to their degrees and ranks, the whole bulk whereof to be delivered into the speaker's hands, to be divided accordingly. And in regard to the provost-marshal of James City hath also given some attendance upon the said General Assembly, he is also to have a share out of the same. And this is to begin to be gathered the 24th of February next.

In conclusion, the whole Assembly commanded the speaker (as now he doth) to present their humble excuse to the treasurer, council, and company in England for being constrained by the intemperature of the weather and the falling sick of divers of the burgesses, to break up so abruptly—before they had so much as put their laws to the engrossing. This they wholly committed to the fidelity of their speaker, who therein (his conscience tells him) hath done the part of an honest man; otherwise he would be easily found out by the burgesses themselves, who with all expedition are to have so many books of the same laws as there are both incorporations and plantations in the colony.

In the second place, the Assembly doth most humbly crave pardon that in so short a space they could bring their matter to no more perfection, being for the present enforced to send home titles rather than laws, propositions rather than resolutions, attempts than achievements, hoping their courtesy will accept our poor endeavour, and their wisdom will be ready to support the weakness of this little flock.

Thirdly, the General Assembly doth humbly beseech the said treasurer, council and company, that albeit it belongs to them only to allow or to abrogate any laws which we shall here make, and that it is their right so to do, yet that it would please them not to take it in ill part if these laws which we have now brought to light, do pass current and be of force till such time as we may know their further pleasure out of England; for otherwise this people (who now at length have gotten the reins of former servitude into their own swing) would in short time grow so insolent as they would shake off all government, and there would be no living among them.

Their last humble suit is that the said council and company would be pleased, so soon as they shall find it convenient, to make good their promise set down at the conclusion of their commission for establishing the Council of Estate and the General Assembly, namely, that they will give us power to allow or disallow of their orders of court, as his Majesty has given them power to allow or to reject our laws.

In sum, Sir George Yeardley, the governor prorogued the said General Assembly till the first of March, which is to fall out this present year of 1619, and in the mean season dissolved the same.

40. Proceedings of the Massachusetts House of Representatives (21 June 1735)

The following selection illustrates the great variety of business taken care of by a colonial legislature in the course of a single day. Printed: *Journals of the House of Representatives of Massachusetts, 1735-1736* (Boston, 1932), pp. 57-60.

A bill entitled an Act for dividing the Town of Concord, and erecting a new town there by the name of Acton. Read a second time and a third time, and passed a concurrence.

A bill entitled An Act for erecting the Plantation called the Elbows into a township by the name of..................... Read a first time and a second time.

A petition of James Pierson of Newbury, praying he may have the sole privilege of making linseed oil in the county of Essex, for a term of years, for the reasons mentioned. Read, and the question was put, whether the prayer of the petition shall be granted? It passed in the negative.

A bill entitled An Act for the more effectual amending and keeping in Repair the Sea Wall or Wharves from the Sconce or South Battery in the town of Boston, to Captain Samuel Scarlett's Wharf, heretofore commonly so-called in Boston aforesaid. Read a third time and passed to be engrossed.

Sent up for concurrence.

William Dudley, Esq., brought down a bill entitled An Act to prevent unnecessary Charge in the Trial of Small Causes, passed in Council, viz. In Council June 20th. 1735. Read a first time and a second time, and passed to be engrossed. Sent down for concurrence. Read a first time.

Jeremiah Moulton, Esq., brought down a petition of John Penhallow, of Portsmouth, Esq., guardian to Lydia Watts, a minor, and daughter of John Watts, Esq., deceased, and Elizabeth, his wife, late wife of the said John Watts, and sole executrix of his last will; Caleb Richardson and Elizabeth, his wife, and John Watts of Portsmouth, mariner, which said Elizabeth and John are also the children of the said John Watts, deceased, showing that the said John Watts died seized of three-eighths and one thirty-second part of Charlestown Grist Mills, so-called, and a lot of land belonging to said mills situate in Charlestown aforesaid, which mills are very much out of repair and would require a great sum of money to put them in repair, more than they are able to pay, as they set forth, that their interest therein is of no profit to them, but the proceeds thereof if sold would be very advantageous, praying leave to make sale of their interest in the premises, for the reasons mentioned. Passed in Council, viz. In Council June 16th. 1735. Read and ordered, that the prayer of the petition be granted, and the petitioners are accordingly enabled to execute a good deed of the estate within mentioned, which shall to all intents and purposes convey the property to the purchaser and his heirs and assigns; provided John Penhallow, in behalf of Lydia Watts, and Caleb Richardson in behalf of Elizabeth, his wife, give security in double the value to the Judge of Probate for the county of Middlesex that the said Elizabeth and Lydia shall receive the full value of their part of the premises at their arrival at the age of twenty-one years, or in case of the decease of both or either of them before that age, that then their legal representatives shall receive the same and that the interest or use of Lydia's proportion in the meantime shall be improved for her benefit. Sent down for concurrence.

Read and concurred.

A petition of Mary Legg, spinster, Edward Bulkley, mariner, and Martha, his wife, and Joseph Brandon, guardian to Elizabeth Legg, a minor, which said Mary, Martha, and Elizabeth, are children of John Legg, late of Boston, and Martha, his wife, both deceased, and grandchildren of Simeon Stoddard, late of Boston aforesaid, Esq., deceased, showing that the said Simeon, by his last will duly proved, approved and allowed, bequeathed one-fourth part of his estate to his said grandchildren, the children of his said daughter Martha, by force whereof the petitioners are entitled to a certain piece or parcel of land behind the testator's buildings in Cornhill, and to one other piece of land in Sudbury Street, both which pieces they hold in common and undivided, that they cannot enjoy and improve the same to advantage equal to what the produce thereof would amount to if sold, praying leave to make sale of the same, for the reasons mentioned. Read and ordered, that the prayer of the petition be granted, and the petitioners are accordingly enabled to execute a good deed or deeds of the estate within mentioned, which shall to all intents and purposes convey the property to the purchaser or purchasers, his and their heirs and assigns respectively; provided Joseph Brandon in behalf of Elizabeth Legg, give security in double the value to the Judge of Probate for the county of Suffolk, that the said Elizabeth shall receive the full value of her part of the proceeds of the sale of the premises at her arrival at the age of twenty-one years, or marriage, or in case of the decease of the said Elizabeth before that, then her legal representative shall receive the same, and the interest or use of the said Elizabeth's proportion in the meantime shall be employed for her benefit.

Sent up for concurrence.

A bill entitled An Act for the more effectual preventing of Theft. Read a second time, and voted an amendment on the bill.

Col. Prescot from the committee on the affair of the School Farms reported.

Voted, that Mr. William Fairfield be of the committee on the two petitions from several of the inhabitants of Boxford, as entered the 3d current, in the room of Samuel Danforth, Esq; who desires to be excused from that service.

Sent up for concurrence.

A petition of George Ledain of Boston, mariner, praying he may be allowed to review an action of debt pursued against him by one Samuel Norton of Boston, shipwright, for the recovery of forty pounds for house rent, which was prosecuted while the petitioner was at sea, and judgment was given against him by default, and execution awarded thereon, the petitioner, as he suggests, having bona fide paid the rent sued for. Read and ordered, that the petitioner serve Samuel Norton, the adverse party, with a copy of the petition, that he show cause on Thursday next, the 26th current, at three o'clock afternoon, why the prayer thereof should not be granted, and that the execution within mentioned be stayed in the meantime.

Sent up for concurrence.

A petition of Isaac Royal, William Crane, and Elkanah Billings, a committee in behalf of the town of Stoughton, praying that a certain number of families, formerly of the western end of Dorchester, but now intermixed with the westerly end of Stoughton, which were by order of this court Anno 1724, joined with their estates to the town of Wrentham, may be continued to Wrentham with the whole tract of land by the line set forth and described in the petition, excepting the School Farm therein contained, or that the said families so set off may be returned to Stoughton to do duties with them, excepting ministerial charges, for the reasons mentioned. Read and ordered, that the petitioners serve the town of Wrentham with a copy of the petition, that they show cause, if any they have, on the first Friday of the next sitting of the court, why the prayer thereof should not be granted, and the petition is referred in the meantime for consideration.

Sent up for concurrence.

A petition of Robert Eliot, John Dinsdale, and several others, prisoners for debt in his Majesty's gaol in Boston, setting forth many extreme hardships and unreasonable abuses they suffer from the cruel treatment of the keeper of the gaol, as particularly therein set forth, praying the compassionate consideration of the Court, for the reasons mentioned. Read and ordered, that Col. Wainwright, Major Brattle, Col. Chandler, and Mr. Cushing, with such as the honourable board shall appoint, be a committee to inquire into the matters of grief within complained of and suggested against the prison-keeper, and report what may be proper for the Court to do thereon.

Sent up for concurrence.

Ezekiel Lewis, and Anthony Stoddard, Esq., brought down the bill entitled An Act for Apportioning and Assessing a tax of three thousand ninety-nine pounds, fourteen shillings and three pence, with an additional tax of twenty-six pounds, five shillings, ordered by the General Court in April last, to be put on the town of Falmouth in the county of York, and also for apportioning and assessing a further tax of two thousand eight hundred and six pounds, nine shillings, paid the representatives for their service and attendance in the General Court in the years 1734 and 1735. Passed in Council, viz.: In Council June 20th, 1735. Read. 21st. Read a second time and nonconcurred; with a message to acquaint the House, the reason the board had nonconcurred the bill was because they had observed that some of the maritime towns of the province were taxed in a higher proportion than heretofore they had been in the land tax.

The vote of Council was read, and the House insist on the bill as first sent up. Sent up for concurrence by Col. Wainwright, Col. Chandler, Col. Brown, Col. Saltonstall, and Capt. Choate, with a message to the honourable board to inform them the House had considered their reasons for nonconcurring the House's vote on the bill; and to acquaint the honourable board that as the right of taxing the people according to their known ability in order for making good the grants to his Majesty, and discharging the public funds, is undoubtedly with the House, who are the representative body of the people, so they have proceeded in that manner in proportioning the present tax, and the House desire the board would therefore pass on the bill; for if those funds are not complied with, and the public funds made good, the failure will not be in the House: who returned they had carried up the bill and delivered the message.

A bill entitled An Act in further Addition to and Explanation of the Act made and passed in the fourth year of the reign of King William and Queen Mary, entitled, An Act for regulating Townships Choice of Town Officers, &c.

Read a first time.

Then the House adjourned till Monday next three o'clock afternoon.

41. Braintree, Massachusetts town meeting (3, 17 March 1766)

The documents which follow are perhaps a unique combination, for not only is there the official record of the regular spring meeting of the town of Braintree, 3 and 17 March 1766; there is also an account of the political manœuvring incident to it from the diary of John Adams. Printed: Samuel A. Bates, ed., *Records of the Town of Braintree, 1640 to 1793* (Randolph, Mass., 1886), pp. 407–411; and Charles F. Adams, ed., *The Works of John Adams* (10 vols., Boston, 1850–1856), II, pp. 185–187, 188–189.

The Anniversary Town Meeting for the choice of town officers, March 3d 1766. Warrants. The freeholders and other inhabitants of the town of Braintree qualified to vote in town affairs being assembled at the meeting-house in the middle precinct of said town for the choice of town officers and the transacting other affairs of said town, the particulars whereof, as inserted in the warrants, are as follows, viz.:

After a moderator chosen, etc., etc.

First, to choose all such town officers for the ensuing year as the law directs, also a county treasurer and a register of deeds, for said county.

Secondly, to make provision for leasing out the town's lands, as the present leases are nigh expired; also to see if the town will remit to the purchasers of the North Commons the interest on their bonds for one year.

Thirdly, to see if the town will repair the highways within said town in the same manner it was done the two last years.

Fourthly, to see if the town will allow the surveyors that served for the year 1764 a reward for their extraordinary service.

Fifthly, to consider of and resolve upon some effectual means for a passage for the fish called ale-wives up Monotaquot River (so called).

Sixthly, to see if the town will discontinue the way from the town's way leading to the town landing, so called, along by Mr. Benoni Spears to the brook.

Seventhly, to hear the report of any committee or choose any committees that may be necessary.

Assembled as aforesaid, chose Samuel Niles Esq., Moderator.

Elisha Niles chosen clerk & also treasurer for the town.

Constables. Chosen Mr. Joseph Cleverly, Ensign Thomas Thayer and Benjamin Spear Jr.

Wardens. Mr. Robert Williams, Jonathan Bass 2d, Balch Cowen, John Vinton, Capt. Peter Thayer, Ensign Jonathan Wild.

Ensign Thomas Thayer presenting to the town Stephen Penniman to serve in the office of a constable in his, the said Thayer's, stead.

Voted the said Stephen Penniman be accepted to serve the town in the office of a constable the ensuing year, provided said Thomas Thayer lodge a bond with the town's treasurer for the town's security as has been usual.

Selectmen chosen: Mr. Norton Quincy, John Adams, Esq., Deacon James Penniman, Ebenezer Thayer, Esq., Mr. Benjamin Porter.

Then the following officers were chosen by nomination, viz.:

Tithingmen: Peter Adams, William Bowditch, Lt. Seth Turner.

Fence Viewers: Ebenezer Miller, Esq., Oliver Gay, Caleb Hobart, Jr., Abijah Allen, Joseph Wales, Jr., Elijah French.

Fire Wardens: Ephraim Blancher, Moses French, Jr., William Harmon.

Surveyors of Lumber: William Field, Jr., Benjamin Thayer, John Clark, Lt. Seth Turner.

Sealers of Leather: Abijah Allen, Benjamin Cleverly, Jr.

Cullers of Staves: Benjamin Thayer, Lt. Joseph White, Lt. Seth Turner.

Sealer of Shingles: Benjamin Thayer.

Hog-reeves: Joseph Nightingale, Jr., Benjamin Baxter, Christopher Thayer, Jr., Thomas Vinton, Jr., Edward Cheesman, Naphtali Thayer, Hezekiah Thayer, Jr., Isaac Smith.

Surveyors of Highways: Ebenezer Miller, Esq., Benjamin Bass, Daniel Arnold, Josiah Vesey, William White, Silas Wild, Elisha Niles, Thomas Newcomb, James Thayer, Jonathan Thayer, John Stetson, Ephraim Thayer 2d, Elihu Adams, Hezekiah Thayer, Jr., Moses Spear.

Voted. The highways within said town be repaired the ensuing year by a tax laid on the inhabitants and freeholders in the same proportion as the last years.

Separately, voted, Ebenezer Miller, Esq., Samuel Niles, Esq., and Capt. Thomas Wales, a committee to lease out the town's land and to give and take security in the name and behalf of the town, said committee to determine respecting planting said land the next term.

The affair respecting the fish referred to the adjournment of this meeting.

The motion of discontinuing the way in the sixth article negatived, as was also the motion of the North Common purchasers for a remittance under the second article.

Votes, for a county register were collected and delivered to Daniel Arnold, constable.

Then the meeting was adjourned to Monday the seventeenth inst., three o'clock P.M. at this place.

1766 March 17.

The freeholders and other inhabitants of the town of Braintree qualified by law to vote in town affairs being assembled by adjournment from 3d of March instant.

Voted, Mr. Joseph Cleverly be excused serving constable, he paying into the town treasury three pounds lawful money.

Then James Brackett, Jr., was chosen constable.

Voted, said James Brackett be allowed out of the town treasury four pounds, lawful money, provided he serve the town in the office of a constable. Benjamin

Spear, Jr., presenting Eliphalet Sawin to the town to serve in the office of constable in the said Benjamin's stead.

Voted, the said Eliphalet Sawin be accepted to serve as constable provided the said Spear give bond for the town's security; also voted, the said Benjamin Spear be allowed forty shillings lawful money.

Oliver Gay excused serving as fence viewer; Elijah Belcher, Tompson Baxter, chosen.

Voted, that no owner of any mill or dam across or upon Monotaquot or Moor's Farm Rivers (so-called) nor any other person upon any pretence whatsoever shall draw up or shut down any gate or make any weir or any obstruction whatsoever that may obstruct the passage of the fish called ale-wives up said rivers or any branch of said rivers for the space of thirty days to begin from and after the last day of April the ensuing year without leave of the committee of the town appointed for that purpose, upon the penalty of twenty shillings for each and every such offence, to be sued for and recovered in any court proper to try the same, or before any justice of the peace in the county of Suffolk; one moiety of said penalty to be to the use of the town, one fourth part thereof to the use of the town's committee, who are hereby authorized to sue for and recover the same, and the other fourth part to the informer.

Also, voted, that no person be permitted to fish for ale-wives in any part of said rivers within the said term of thirty days, excepting on Tuesdays and Fridays, and every person or persons presuming to fish on any other days for every such offence shall forfeit and pay twenty shillings to be sued for as aforesaid and appropriated as aforesaid.

Also, voted, the above votes respecting the fish be presented to the Court of General Sessions of the Peace for their approbation and confirmation for the year ensuing as a by-law, according to the law of this province in such cases made and provided.

Then Capt. John Hayward, Mr. Jonathan Thayer, and Mr. John French were separately nominated and chosen a committee to prevent obstructions to the fish in the rivers as aforesaid, as also to pursue and prosecute the town's resolves respecting said affair.

The town treasurer offered a report to the town respecting a province note which has been lodged in the treasury, as follows:

March 17th. 1766

Agreeable to the town's order in August last, I then returned a province note that I was charged with as town treasurer, into the province treasury, and received the principal sum twenty-seven pounds, which I have placed out at interest for the town's use and have a bond for the same from Lieut. Joseph Hayward, Ensign Jonathan Wild and Mr. Isaac Niles; the interest of said note one pound, eighteen shillings and five pence, I received and improved for the discharge of the town's debt and have credited the town for the same.

Elisha Niles, Town Treasurer

The above report was voted accepted.

Then the town appointed Deacon James Penniman, Ebenezer Miller, Esq., and Mr. Azariah Faxon, a committee to settle accounts with the town treasurer.

The selectmen offered a report to the town respecting ways laid out as follows, viz. :

Braintree Febry. 28th. 1766

We, the subscribers, selectmen of the town of Braintree, being requested by sundry of the inhabitants of said town, on the day above said, went and viewed a way lately obtained by a number of the inhabitants of this town, of Samuel Belcher on the southerly side of the westerly part of his home place next Mr. Sawen's land, of which way they have a deed of said Mr. Belcher, of one rod and half wide. They desire it may be a town way to help them mend said way, there being no other charge arising therefrom; which motion we look upon reasonable and recommend to the town for their acceptance.

We also proceeded and laid out a way two rods wide through Jonathan Thayer's land from Captain Moses Curtis' land that was formerly Daniel Thayer's, to the Patten line, so called, to Bridgewater line, running as the way is now improved, from Captain Curtis' land southerly until we come near a brook where is a large white oak stump with stones upon it; we laid from thence to a white oak tree, from thence to a black oak tree, from thence to a white oak tree, from thence to a second white oak tree, from thence to a third white oak tree, from thence to a fourth white oak tree, and from thence to a black oak tree in said Patten Line, all which trees are marked. The way to be on the west side of said bounds, the said Jonathan Thayer consenting and assisting in laying out said way, there being but little alteration, only to make it straight from what hath been long improved.

James Penniman
Ebenezer Miller
Ebenezer Thayer, Jr.
Norton Quincy

The above report was voted accepted.

1766 May 19th.

Representative. The freeholders and other inhabitants of the town of Braintree qualified to vote in the choice of a representative, being assembled (pursuant to a precept directed to the selectmen), made choice of Ebenezer Thayer Esq. to serve for and represent them in the Great and General Court or assembly the year ensuing.

(Excerpts from Diary of John Adams)

March 1. Saturday. Spent a part of last evening with Mr. Joseph Cleverly. He is a tiptoe for town-meeting; he has many schemes and improvements in his head; namely, for separating the offices of constable and collector; collecting taxes has laid the foundation for the ruin of many families. He is for five selectmen, and will vote for the old ones, Mr. Quincy and Major Miller. He hears they are for turning out all the old selectmen and choosing a new set; they for having but three, etc. The only way is to oppose schemes to schemes, and so break in upon them. Cleverly will become a great town-meeting man, and a great speaker in town-meeting. Q. What effect will this have on the town affairs?

Brother tells me that William Veasey, Jr., tells him he has but one objection against Jonathan Bass and that is, Bass is too forward. When a man is forward, we may conclude he has some selfish view, some self ends. Brother asked him if he and his party would carry that argument through. It holds stronger against Captain Thayer and Major Miller than it ever did against anybody in this town, excepting Colonel Gooch and Captain Mills. But I desire the proof of Bass's forwardness. Has he been more so than Major Miller? Come, come, Mr. Veasey, says Master Joseph Cleverly, don't you say too much; I an't of that mind. *Ego*. Bass is an active, capable man, but no seeker by mean begging or buying of votes.

3. Monday. My brother Peter, Mr. Etter, and Mr. Field, having a number of votes prepared for Mr. Quincy and me, set themselves to scatter them in town-meeting. The town had been very silent and still, my name had never been mentioned, nor had our friends ever talked of any new selectmen at all, excepting in the south precinct; but as soon as they found there was an attempt to be made, they fell in and assisted; and, although there were six different hats with votes for as many different persons, besides a considerable number of scattering votes, I had the major vote of the assembly the first time. Mr. Quincy had more than one hundred and sixty votes. I had but one vote more than half. Some of the church people—Mr. Joseph Cleverly, his brother Ben and son, etc., and Mr. Ben Veasey, of the middle precinct, Mr. James Faxon, etc.—I found were grieved and chagrined for the loss of their dear Major Miller. Etter and my brother took a skilful method; they let a number of young fellows into the design, John Ruggles, Peter Newcomb, etc., who were very well pleased with the employment, and put about a great many votes. Many persons, I hear, acted slyly and deceitfully; this is always the case.

I own it gave me much pleasure to find I had so many friends, and that my conduct in town has been not disapproved. The choice was quite unexpected to me. I thought the project was so new and sudden that the people had not digested it, and would generally suppose the town would not like it, and so would not vote for it. But my brother's answer was, that it had been talked of last year and some years before, and that the thought was familiar to the people in general, and was more agreeable than anything of the kind that could be proposed to many, and for these reasons his hopes were strong.

But the triumph of the party was very considerable, though not complete; for Thayer, and Miller, and the late lessees of the North Commons, and many of the church people, and many others had determined to get out Deacon Penniman; but instead of that, their favourite was dropped, and I, more obnoxious to that party than even Deacon Penniman or any other man, was chosen in his room, and Deacon Penniman was saved with more than one hundred and thirty votes, a more reputable election than even Thayer himself had.

Mr. Jonathan Bass was extremely sorry for the loss of Major Miller; he would never come to another meeting. Mr. Joseph Cleverly could not account for many things done at town-meetings. His motion for choosing collectors was slighted; his motion for lessening his fine was thrown out; and he made no sort of figure as a speaker; so that I believe Mr. Cleverly will make no hand.

Elisha Niles says, set a knave to catch a knave. A few days before a former March meeting he told Thayer that he had a mind to get in Deacon Penniman. Thayer asked him who he would have with him? he answered, Captain Allen. Thayer made him no answer, but when the meeting came, was chosen himself. Mr. Thomas Faxon, of this end of the town, told my wife he never saw anybody chosen so neatly in his life–not a word, not a whisper beforehand. Peter Newcomb gave him a vote; he had one before for Miller, and had heard nothing of me; but he thought I should have one. So he dropped that for Miller. Jo Nightingale asked my wife, "Mr. Adams will have too much business, will he not; the courts to attend, selectman, and representative at May, etc.?" Mr. John Baxter, the old gentleman, told me he was very well pleased with the choice at the north end, etc. Old Mr. John Ruggles voted for me; but says that Thayer will [be chosen] at May. If I would set up, he would vote for me, and I should go, but Mr. Quincy will not. Lieutenant Holbrook, I hear, was much in my favour, etc. Thus the town is pretty generally disputing about me, I find.

But this choice will not disconcert Thayer, at May, though it will weaken him. But, as I said before, the triumph was not complete; Cornet Bass had the most votes the first time, and would have come in the second, but the north end people, his friends, after putting in their votes the first time, withdrew for refreshment, by which accident he lost it, to their great regret.

Mark the fruits of this election to me. Will the church people be angry, and grow hot and furious, or will they be cooler and calmer for it? Will Thayer's other precinct friends resent it and become more violent, or will they be less so? In short, I cannot answer these questions; many of them will be disheartened, I know; some will be glad. . . .

. . . I find the late choice has brought upon me a multiplicity of new cares. The schools are one great object of my attention. It is a thing of some difficulty to find out the best, most beneficial method of expending the school money. Captain Adams says that each parish's proportion of the school money has not been settled since my father's day. Thomas Faxon says it would be more profitable to the children to have a number of women's schools about than to have a fixed grammar school. Q. Whether he has not a desire that his wife should keep one? Jonathan Bass says the same. Q. His wife is a schoolmistress. So that two points of examination occur; the portion between the parishes, that is, the sum which this parish ought to have; and whether a standing grammar school is preferable to a number of schoolmistresses part of the year, and a grammar school part.

Another great object is the poor; persons are soliciting for the privilege of supplying the poor with wood, corn, meat, &c. The care of supplying at cash price, and in weight and measure, is something; the care of considering and deciding the pretensions of the claimants is something.

A third, and the greatest, is the assessment; here I am not so thorough; I must inquire a great while before I shall know the polls and estates, real and personal, of all the inhabitants of the town or parish. The highways, the districts to surveyors, and laying out new ways or altering old ones, are a fourth thing. Perambulations of lines are another thing. Dorchester, Milton, Stoughton, Bridgewater, Abington, Weymouth–orders for services of many sorts to, &c.

It will increase my connections with the people.

42. Proceedings of Botetourt county court, Virginia (10 March 1770)

The county court was both the governing and judicial body of a county in the southern colonies. The following proceedings of a Virginia county court illustrate the variety of business handled by such courts. Printed: Lewis P. Summers, ed., *Annals of Southwest Virginia, 1769–1800* (Abingdon, Virginia, 1929), pp. 70–74.

Present:
Andrew Lewis, William Preston, Israel Christian, Philip Love, John Montgomery, and Anthony Bledsoe, gentlemen.

John Trimble produced a commission from the president and masters of William and Mary College appointing him deputy surveyor of this county; and thereupon he, having taken the usual oaths to his Majesty's person and government and repeated and subscribed to the test, entered into and acknowledged bond with James Trimble and James Gilmore, his securities in the sum of five hundred pounds to his Majesty, conditioned as the law directs, and also took the oath of deputy surveyor.

James Trimble proved a certificate according to law for one thousand pounds of winter rotted hemp made on his plantation in this county, which is certified to his excellency the governor.[1]

William McClure proved a certificate according to law for five hundred thirty pounds of winter rotted hemp made on his plantation in this county.

John McClure proved certificates according to law for two thousand eight hundred and seven pounds of hemp, part winter rotted and part water rotted, made on his plantation in this county.

Andrew Lewis proved certificates according to law for three thousand and ninety-seven pounds of neu [net] and eight hundred eighty-six pounds of gross hemp made on his plantation in this county.

Patrick Denny proved a certificate according to law for one thousand and seventy-eight pounds of hemp made on his plantation in this county.

Thomas McAlister proved a certificate according to law for one thousand seven hundred ninety pounds of hemp made on James McAlister's plantation in this county.

Charles Kirkpatrick proved a certificate according to law for one thousand nine hundred and ten pounds of winter rotted hemp made in this county.

Robert Erwin proved a certificate according to law for two thousand three hundred nineteen pounds made in this county.

John Mills proved a certificate according to law for four hundred twenty-eight pounds of gross hemp made on the plantation of John Mills in this county.

John Armstrong proved a certificate according to law for four hundred nineteen pounds of winter rotted hemp made on his plantation in this county.

Upon the petition of Thomas Barns a licence is granted him to keep an ordinary at his house in this county, whereupon the said Thomas, together with William Christian, his security, entered into and acknowledged bond according to law.

---

[1] The Virginia legislature offered a bounty for hemp grown in the colony. To secure it, the grower had to obtain a certificate from his county court.

Upon the petition of William Christian a licence is granted him to keep an ordinary at his house in this county for the term of one year and from thence till the next court held for this county, whereupon he, together with Stephen Trigg, his security, entered into and acknowledged bond according to law.

This court doth appoint Robert Breckenridge to be constable for that precinct on Reed Creek in the room of Abraham Bledsoe, who is discharged from that office.

Margaret Kirkham, orphan of Henry Kirkham, deceased, has leave of the court to choose Michael Kirkham her guardian, upon his giving security according to law.

Elizabeth and Benjamin Kirkham, orphans of Henry Kirkham, deceased, have leave of the court to choose Daniel Evans their guardian upon his giving security according to law.

Upon the petition of Arthur Campbell he hath leave to build a mill on the Royal Oak plantation on Holston's River.

Ordered that Alexander Collier do lay off a road from James Gilmore Jr.'s place into the main road passing Robert Young's, and that he, together with the tithables on both sides thereof, within two miles, do open and keep the same in repair.

Ordered that John Robinson, Abraham Crismon, and Samuel Willson do view the road from William Robinson's to the head waters of Catawba and make report of the nearest and best way to the next court.

Philip Love, Hugh Crocket, and Jacob Kent to do the same from William Robinson's to the road leading from Han's Meadows to Vance's.

Francis Smith, John Armstrong, Joseph Cloyd, and Bryan McDonald to view and lay off the nearest and best way from the first ford on Catawba to the head waters thereof and make report thereof to the court.

This court doth appoint James Caghee to be surveyor of the road leading to Captain Doggal's, and it is ordered that the tithables belonging to that precinct do attend him accordingly.

Samuel McClanachan proved a certificate according to law for David McClanachan for four hundred and seven pounds of winter rotted hemp made on the said David's plantation in this county.

Andrew Woods the same for eleven hundred and sixty-four pounds winter rotted hemp made on his plantation in this county.

Francis Smith the same for three thousand six hundred forty-two pounds of hemp as above.

Ordered that William Thompson, Joseph How, John Draper, Joseph Montgomery, and Samuel Scott, or any three of them, to view the ground from Michael Price's by Taylors and the Buffalo Pound ford by the head waters of Peek Creek to Buchanan's plough on Reed Creek, and make report of the conveniences and inconveniences attending the same, especially of the fords to the next court. And the former order relating to the same set aside.

Henry Paulin, one of the persons appointed to view the way from Thomas McFarran's by Patterson's Creek to Henry Paulin's on Craig's Creek, having made report that a wagon road might easily be made there, it is ordered that upon one other of the viewers signing the said report before any one of the justices of the peace of this county, Samuel McFarran with the tithables belonging to that precinct, do open and keep the same in repair from Craig's Creek wagon road to Patterson's Creek, and that Henry Paulin with the tithables belonging to his precinct, do open and keep the same in repair from Patterson's Creek to his own house, and that John McFarran and John Potts do appoint the tithables to each precinct.

Ordered that Samuel Crocket, Samuel Woods, and Charles Stapleton, or any two of them being sworn, do view the road from Vausses to Stapleton's and report the conveniences and inconveniences to the next court, and that the former order relating hereto be set aside.

Ordered that Thomas Acres, John McAdo, and Daniel McNeill, or any two of them, being first sworn, do view the way from the long lick to the Bedford line to join the road leading to Pates settlement, and make report of the conveniences and inconveniences attending the same to the next court.

Ordered that William Bryants shall make what alterations he shall think fit in the road between James Nielly and James Bryans so as not to prejudice any person.

This court doth appoint Francis Kincannon to be surveyor of the road from Stalnakers to the Eleven Mile Creek, Thomas Ramsay from the said creek to Beaver Creek, and David Looney from Beaver Creek to Fall Creek, and it [is] ordered that Anthony Bledsoe do appoint the tithables to each precinct.

This court doth appoint James Brigham to be constable for that precinct below Beaver Creek, Stephen Jordon from Beaver Creek to Eleven Mile Creek, James Thompson on the waters of Buffalo Creek in the room of Joseph Davis, and James Johnston on Macks Run in the room of James Kerr, who are discharged therefrom.

Ordered that Andrew Lewis, Robert Brackenridge, Israel Christian, John Howard, Francis Smith, and Stephen Trigg, or any five or more of them, do agree, with workmen, to build a prison and court-house according to such plan as they shall think fit and on such plan at Millers Mill as they shall appoint.

Ordered that the Sheriff summon twenty-four freeholders of this county qualified by law to serve on a grand jury at May Court next for this county.

John Bowyer, David Robinson, James Cloyd, Francis Smith, Robert Doak, Philip Love, Matthew Aruikle, Anthony Bledsoe, Walter Crocket, and Arthur Campbell produced commissions from his excellency the governor appointing them captains in the militia, whereupon they took the oaths, etc., and subscribed the test respectively.

Henry Paulin and James McAfee produced commissions from his excellency the governor appointing them lieutenants in the militia, and John May produced a commission from his excellency the governor appointing him quartermaster in the militia, and thereupon they severally took the usual oaths to his Majesty's person and government, and repeated and subscribed the test.

William Fleming, James Rowland, William Ingles, Bryan McDonald, John Bowyer, John Armstrong, John May, Thomas Barnes, Luke Bowyer, Anthony Bledsoe, Thomas Roland, and Philip Love, vestrymen for the parish of Botetourt, took the usual oaths to his Majesty's person and government, and repeated and subscribed the test.

Ordered that the court be adjourned till the court in course.

Part III

THE ECONOMIC DEVELOPMENT OF THE COLONIES

THE ECONOMIC DEVELOPMENT OF
THE COLONIES

SELECT BIBLIOGRAPHY

(a) ECONOMIC POLICY: ENGLISH AND AMERICAN

In addition to the works listed in the bibliography on "British Colonial Theory and Policy" preceding Part Two, the following are important. The most detailed study of mercantilism is E. F. HECKSCHER, *Mercantilism* (2 vols., London, 1935). KLAUS KNORR, *British Colonial Theories, 1570–1850* contains detailed references to contemporary mercantilist writings as well as critical analyses of scholarly work on the subject. PHILIP W. BUCK, *The Politics of Mercantilism* (New York, 1942) is a short account with many useful references. The best over-all view of the administration of British policy is CHARLES M. ANDREWS, *The Colonial Period of American History*, vol. IV. The most detailed discussion of the Navigation Acts is LAWRENCE A. HARPER, *The English Navigation Laws: A Seventeenth Century Experiment in Social Engineering* (New York, 1939).

Broadly speaking, writers on the economic aspects of English policy fall into two groups: those who believe it harmed the colonies, and those who believe it was beneficial, or at least did not hamper them greatly. OLIVER M. DICKERSON, *The Navigation Acts and the American Revolution* (Philadelphia, 1951) argues vigorously that the Navigation Acts were not harmful to the colonies. LAWRENCE A. HARPER, "The Effect of the Navigation Acts on the Thirteen Colonies" in R. B. MORRIS, ed., *The Era of the American Revolution*, presents evidence to the contrary; and LOUIS M. HACKER, *The Triumph of American Capitalism* . . . (New York, 1946) argues that it was capitalistic exploitation of the colonies that led to the war for independence.

There are many older works which are still useful but they must be considered in the light of new points of view and new evidence offered in the foregoing. Among the older works are the several volumes of GEORGE LOUIS BEER, G. B. HERTZ, *The Old Colonial System* (Manchester, 1905) and *British Imperialism in the Eighteenth Century* (London, 1908); W. J. ASHLEY, *Surveys Historic and Economic* (London, 1900); and the various chapters in *The Cambridge History of the British Empire*, vol. I.

There are several noteworthy studies of particular phases of English policy. ELEANOR H. LORD, *Industrial Experiments in the British Colonies of North America* (Baltimore, 1898) discusses the attempt to develop a naval stores industry in the colonies, as does JUSTIN WILLIAMS, "English Mercantilism and Carolina Naval Stores, 1705–1776", *Journal of Southern History*, vol. I (1935). Even more specific phases of the naval stores policy are discussed in R. G. ALBION, *Forests and Sea Power: The Timber Problem of the Royal Navy* (Cambridge, Mass., 1926), and LAWRENCE S. MAYO, "The King's Woods", Mass. Hist. Soc. *Proceedings*, vol. LIV (1922).

ARTHUR C. BINING, *British Regulation of the Colonial Iron Industry* (Philadelphia, 1933) is a model study of a particular policy. ALBERT B. SOUTHWICK, "The Molasses Act–a Source of Precedents", *William and Mary Quarterly*, 3rd Series, vol. VIII (1951) is a clear analysis of the issues involved in the passage of the act of 1733. Many of the works cited in the following topical bibliographies also discuss various aspects of economic policy, both British and colonial.

American economic thought during the colonial period is discussed in EDGAR A. J. JOHNSON, *American Economic Thought in the Seventeenth Century* (London, 1932), in volume one of JOSEPH DORFMAN, *The Economic Mind in American Civilization* (3 vols., New York, 1946–1949), and in CLIVE DAY, "Capitalistic and Socialistic Tendencies in the Puritan Colonies", Amer. Hist. Assoc. *Annual Report* (1920).

General economic histories specifically relating to the colonial period are WILLIAM B. WEEDEN, *Economic and Social History of New England 1620–1789* (2 vols., Boston, 1890), and

PHILLIP A. BRUCE, *Economic History of Virginia in the Seventeenth Century* (2 vols., New York, 1895). Studies of prices have resulted in the publication of valuable materials in G. R. TAYLOR, "Wholesale Commodity Prices at Charleston, South Carolina, 1732–1791", *Journal of Economic and Business History*, vol. IV (1931–1932); ANNE BEZANSON, R. D. GRAY, and M. HUSSEY, *Prices in Colonial Pennsylvania* (Philadelphia, 1935); and ARTHUR H. COLE, *Wholesale Commodity Prices in the United States, 1700–1861* (Cambridge, Mass., 1938).

B. H. MEYER, *et al.*, *History of Transportation in the United States Before 1860* (Washington, 1917) has important material on the development of internal economic life in the colonies.

(b) COLONIAL AGRICULTURE

Two bibliographies on colonial agriculture are indispensable. These are EVERETT E. EDWARDS, "References on American Colonial Agriculture" (U.S. Dept. of Agric., *Bibliographical Contributions*, No. 33, Washington, 1938), and his "Agriculture of the American Indians: A Classified List of Annotated Historical References" (U.S. Dept. of Agric., *Bibliographical Contributions*, No. 23, Washington, 1933).

Two major sources are the anonymous *American Husbandry* (1775) (H. J. CARMAN, ed., New York, 1939); and JARED ELIOT, *Essays upon the Field Husbandry in New England . . .* (1748) (H. J. CARMAN and R. TUGWELL, eds., New York, 1934). PETER KALM, the Swedish botanist-economist who came to the colonies in the middle of the eighteenth century, has left a remarkable record. His writings are edited by ADOLPH BENSON as *Peter Kalm's Travels in North America* (2 vols., New York, 1937). The first two volumes of *A Documentary History of American Industrial Society* (11 vols., Cleveland, 1910–1911, JOHN R. COMMONS, *et al.*, eds.) edited by U. B. PHILLIPS, contain valuable material for plantation and frontier life in colonial America. EDWIN M. BETTS, ed., *Thomas Jefferson's Farm Book* (Princeton, 1953) is a first-rate account of and by one of eighteenth-century America's leading farmers.

Two major works cover the history of colonial agriculture. P. W. BIDWELL and J. I. FALCONER, *History of Agriculture in the Northern United States, 1620–1860* (Washington, 1925) needs amplification. LEWIS H. GRAY, *History of Agriculture in the Southern United States to 1860* (2 vols., Washington, 1933) is far superior on all phases. Lyman Carrier, *The Beginnings of Agriculture in America* (New York, 1923); and EVERETT E. EDWARDS, "American Indian Contributions to Civilization", *Minnesota History*, vol. XV (1934) are both important for the beginnings.

Special studies for particular areas are R. R. WALCOTT, "Husbandry in Colonial New England", *New England Quarterly*, vol. IX (1936); A. L. OLSON, *Agricultural Economy and the Population in Eighteenth-Century Connecticut* (Connecticut Tercentenary Commission, Pamphlet No. 40, New Haven, 1935); U. P. HEDRICK, *A History of Agriculture in the State of New York* (Albany, 1933); WILLIAM D. MILLER, "The Narragansett Planters", Amer. Antiq. Soc. *Proceedings*, new Series, vol. XLIII (1933); C. R. WOODWARD, *The Development of Agriculture in New Jersey 1640–1880* (New Brunswick, N. J., 1927), and his *Ploughs and Politicks: Charles Read of New Jersey and his Notes on Agriculture, 1715–1774* (New Brunswick, N. J., 1941); S. W. FLETCHER, *Pennsylvania Agriculture and Country Life, 1640–1840* (Harrisburg, Pa., 1950); AVERY O. CRAVEN, *Soil Exhaustion as a Factor in the Agricultural History of Virginia and Maryland 1606–1860* (Urbana, Ill., 1925); J. S. BASSETT, "The Relation Between the Virginia Planter and the London Merchant", Amer. Hist. Assoc. *Annual Report* (1901), vol. I; THOMAS J. WERTENBAKER, *The Planters of Colonial Virginia* (Princeton, 1922); W. NEIL FRANKLIN, "Agriculture in Colonial North Carolina", *N.C. Hist. Rev.*, vol. III (1926); and A. S. SALLEY, *The Introduction of Rice Culture into South Carolina* (Columbia, S.C., 1919).

Special aspects are treated in RICHARD H. SHRYOCK, "British Versus German Traditions in Colonial Agriculture", *Miss. Valley Hist. Rev.*, vol. XXVI (1939–1940); A. H. HIRSCH, "French Influence on American Agriculture in the Colonial Period . . .", *Agricultural History*, vol. IV (1930); ALFRED TRUE, *A History of Agricultural Experimentation and Research in the United States, 1607–1925 . . .* (U.S. Dept. of Agric. Miscellaneous Pamphlet, No. 251, Washington, 1937); U. P. HEDRICK, *History of Horticulture in America to 1860* (New York, 1950); GEORGE K. HOLMES

"Some Features of Tobacco History", and G. N. COLLINS, "Notes on the Agricultural History of Maize", Amer. Hist. Assoc. *Annual Report* (1919) vol. 1; EARL D. ROSS, "Benjamin Franklin as an Eighteenth-Century Agricultural Leader", *Journal of Political Economy*, vol. XXXVII (1929); and D. D. BRAND, "The Origin and Early Distribution of New World Cultivated Plants", *Agricultural History*, vol. XIII (1939).

(c) LAND SYSTEMS AND LAND POLICY

Land systems and policies are discussed in many of the works already cited on agriculture, particularly in that of L. H. GRAY. The following are special studies relating to various regions and to various phases. Legal aspects are discussed in VIOLA F. BARNES, "Land Tenure in the English Colonial Charters of the Seventeenth Century", in *Essays in Colonial History Presented to Charles McLean Andrews . . .*; RICHARD B. MORRIS, "Primogeniture and Entailed Estates in America", *Columbia Law Review*, vol. XXVII (1927) and in his *Studies in the History of American Law*, and in G. L. HASKINS, "The Beginnings of Partible Inheritance in the American Colonies", *Yale Law Review*, vol. LI (1942). The most recent study is MARSHALL HARRIS, *Origin of the Land Tenure System in the United States* (Ames, Iowa, 1953). It is deficient in knowledge of the historical setting but has many useful references.

Land systems of particular regions and colonies are treated in MELVILLE EGLESTON, *The Land System of the New England Colonies* (Baltimore, 1886), which is old but useful. ROY H. AKAGI, *The Town Proprietors of the New England Colonies . . .* (Philadelphia, 1924) and FLORENCE M. WOODWARD, *The Town Proprietors of Vermont: The New England Town Proprietorship in Decline* (New York, 1936) discuss the evolution of township grants from those to actual settlers to the development of speculative grants. CHARLES W. SPENCER, "The Land System of Colonial New York", N.Y. State Hist. Assoc. *Proceedings*, vol. XVI (1917); S. G. NISSENSON, *The Patroon's Domain* (New York, 1937); and IRVING MARK, *Agrarian Conflicts in Colonial New York, 1711–1775* (New York, 1940) discuss various aspects of the colony where the great manorial estate with tenant farmers was the dominant form of landholding. Mark's work is particularly valuable. DONALD L. KEMMERER, *Path to Freedom* discusses the conflict over land in New Jersey.

Pennsylvania's land system is discussed in WILLIAM R. SHEPHERD, *History of Proprietary Government in Pennsylvania*, and in ALAN C. GREGG, "The Land Policy and System of the Penn Family in Early Pennsylvania", *Western Penn. Hist. Mag.*, vol. VI (1923), and JAMES N. FULLERTON, "Squatters and Titles to Land in Early Western Pennsylvania", *ibid.*, vol. VI. CLARENCE P. GOULD *The Land System in Maryland, 1720–1765* (Baltimore, 1913); PAUL H. GIDDENS, "Land Policies and Administration in Colonial Maryland, 1753–1769", *Md. Hist. Mag.*, vol. XXVIII (1933); and V. J. WYCKOFF, "The Sizes of Plantations in Seventeenth-Century Maryland", *ibid.*, vol. XXXII (1937) give the essential material for Pennsylvania and Maryland.

L. H. GRAY, *History of Agriculture in the Southern United States* has the best over-all account of the distribution of land in the southern colonies. Studies of importance in addition are FAIRFAX HARRISON, *Virginia Land Grants: A Study of Conveyancing in Relation to Colonial Politics* (Richmond, 1925); MANNING C. VOORHIS, "Crown versus Council in the Virginia Land Policy", *William and Mary Quarterly*, 3rd Series, vol. III (1946); JOHN S. BASSETT, "Landholding in Colonial North Carolina", *Law Quarterly Review*, vol. XI (1895); and the relevant sections of DAVID D. WALLACE, *History of South Carolina*, vols. I and II. VOORHIS's short article on Virginia is a particularly valuable study.

The subject of quit rents in the colonies is discussed at length in BEVERLY W. BOND, *The Quit-Rent System in the American Colonies* (New Haven, 1919), and in virtually all writings on colonial land systems.

(d) COLONIAL COMMERCE

The basic sources for policies and decisions affecting colonial commerce are the legislative and administrative records of both England and the colonies. The letter and account books of the merchants of the Atlantic world are the basic sources for the realities of colonial trade.

Large bodies of such mercantile papers exist today, most of them in manuscript form. Here and there in periodicals and historical society proceedings, scattered letters have been printed. There are a few notable publications in book form. *The Commerce of Rhode Island, 1726–1800* (2 vols., Boston, 1914–1915, Mass. Hist. Soc. *Collections*, 7th Series, vol. IX–X); FRANCIS N. MASON, ed., *John Norton & Sons, Merchants of London and Virginia . . . 1750 to 1795* (Richmond, 1937); ANNE R. CUNNINGHAM, ed., *Letters and Diary of John Rowe, Boston Merchant, 1758–1762, 1764–1779* (Boston, 1903), and DOROTHY C. BARCK, ed., *Letter Book of John Watts . . . of New York . . . 1762–1765* (N.Y. Hist. Soc. *Collections*, 1928) are important, not only for the colonies concerned, but for colonial trade as a whole. The most comprehensive and valuable of all collections is ELIZABETH DONNAN, *Documents Illustrative of the Slave Trade to America* (4 vols., Washington, 1930–1935), which offers the foundation for a much needed modern study of the topic. DAVID MACPHERSON, *Annals of Commerce, Manufactures, Fisheries, and Navigation . . .* (4 vols. London, 1805) is the source to which most historians have gone for printed statistical material on colonial trade and it is still useful for it was based on records which have since been destroyed. Users of colonial trade statistics should consult G. N. CLARK, *Guide to English Commercial Statistics, 1696–1782* (London, 1938).

The first portion of EMORY R. JOHNSON, et al., *History of Domestic and Foreign Commerce of the United States* (2 vols., Washington, 1915) covers the colonial period. CHARLES M. ANDREWS, "Colonial Commerce", and his "Anglo-French Commercial Rivalry, 1700–1750: the Western Phase", all in *Amer. Hist. Rev.*, vol. XX (1914–1915) should not be missed. Several chapters in CURTIS P. NETTELS, *The Money Supply of the American Colonies before 1720* (Madison, Wis., 1934) are indispensable for the study of commerce.

Specialized studies relating to particular areas and topics are RALPH G. LOUNSBURY, "Yankee Trade at Newfoundland", *New England Quarterly*, vol. III (1930); W. F. CRAWFORD, "The Commerce of Rhode Island with the Southern Continental Colonies in the Eighteenth Century", R. I. Hist. Soc. *Collections*, vol. XIV (1921); Roland M. Hooker, *The Colonial Trade of Connecticut* (Conn. Tercentenary Commission, Pamphlet No. 50, New Haven, 1936); Margaret E. Martin, *Merchants and Trade of the Connecticut River Valley, 1750–1820* (Smith College *Studies in History*, vol. XXIV, Northampton, Mass., 1938–1939); Virginia D. Harrington, *The New York Merchant on the Eve of the Revolution* (New York, 1935); MARY A. HANNA, *Trade of the Delaware District before the Revolution* (Smith College *Studies in History*, vol. II, Northampton, 1917); HARRY D. BERG, "The Organization of Business in Colonial Philadelphia", *Pennsylvania History*, vol. X (1943); M. S. MORRISS, *Colonial Trade of Maryland, 1689–1715* (Baltimore, 1914); PAUL H. GIDDENS, "Trade and Industry in Colonial Maryland, 1753–1769", *Journal of Economic and Business History*, vol. IV (1931–1932); PAUL R. KELBAUGH, "Tobacco Trade in Maryland, 1700–1725", *Md. Hist. Mag.*, vol. XXVI (1931); V. J. WYCKOFF, "Ships and Shipping of Seventeenth Century Maryland", *Md. Hist. Mag.*, vol. XXXIII–XXXIV (1938–1939); ARTHUR P. MIDDLETON, *Tobacco Coast: A Maritime History of Chesapeake Bay in the Colonial Era* (Newport News, Va., 1953) covers the commerce of the Virginia-Maryland area in great detail with bibliographical citations to monographic articles. C. M. MACINNES, *The Early English Tobacco Trade* (London, 1926) gives the English setting. CHARLES C. CRITTENDEN, *The Commerce of North Carolina 1763–1789* (New Haven, 1936); LEILA SELLERS, *Charleston Business on the Eve of the Revolution* (Chapel Hill, N. C. 1934); and CHARLES J. GAYLE, "The Nature and Volume of Exports from Charleston 1724–1774", S.C. Hist. Assoc. *Proceedings* (1937) are important for the colonies concerned.

Among the studies of individual merchants are W. T. BAXTER, *The House of Hancock: Business in Boston, 1724–1775* (Cambridge, Mass., 1945) which contains indispensable chapters on eighteenth-century business methods; EDWARD EDELMAN, "Thomas Hancock, Colonial Merchant", *Journal of Economic and Business History*, vol. I (1928–1929) which should be read despite BAXTER's work; JAMES D. PHILLIPS, *The Life and Times of Richard Derby, Merchant of Salem, 1712–1783* (Cambridge, Mass., 1929); JAMES B. HEDGES, *The Browns of Providence Plantations, Colonial Years* (Cambridge, Mass., 1952), the best of all the studies of individual merchants that we now have; B. M. BIGELOW, "Aaron Lopez: Colonial Merchant of Newport", *New England Quarterly*, vol. IV (1931); MARGARET L. BROWN, "William Bingham, Eighteenth

Century Magnate", *Penn. Mag. of Hist. and Biog.*, vol. LXI (1937); JOHN H. MORGAN, "John Watson Painter, Merchant, and Capitalist of New Jersey 1685–1768", Amer. Antiq. Soc. *Proceedings*, vol. L (1940). FREDERICK B. TOLLES, *Meeting House and Counting House: The Quaker Merchants of Colonial Philadelphia 1682–1763* (Chapel Hill, N.C., 1948) places more emphasis on the meeting house than on the strictly economic aspects of Philadelphia, but is invaluable, nonetheless. ARTHUR L. JENSEN, "The Maritime Commerce of Colonial Philadelphia", a doctoral thesis in the library of the University of Wisconsin (1954) is the most thorough study that has yet been made.

The slave trade was a major economic activity of the eighteenth century in which American colonists played an important part. Elizabeth Donnan's introductions to the four volumes of her *Documents Illustrative of the History of the Slave Trade to America* are the best accounts of the trade. To this should be added her "The Slave Trade into South Carolina before the Revolution", *Amer. Hist. Rev.*, vol. XXXIII (1927–1928). L. H. GRAY, *History of Agriculture* . . . discusses the colonial attitude towards the slave trade and slavery. These materials render obsolete most of the older studies although material of value may be found in such works as U. B. PHILLIPS, *American Negro Slavery* (New York, 1918). The best modern account of Negro history is that of JOHN HOPE FRANKLIN, *From Slavery to Freedom: A History of the American Negroes* (New York, 1947), which contains a critical bibliography on the slave trade as well as on other matters relating to Negro history.

The fur trade was important in the early years of colonization and continued to be in newly opened areas, both economically and in terms of international rivalries.

There is no thorough study of the colonial fur trade such as that of HARROLD A. INNIS, *The Fur Trade in Canada* (New York, 1930). INNIS's "Interrelations between the Fur Trade of Canada and the United States", *Miss. Valley Hist. Rev.*, vol. XX (1933–1934) points the way to a much needed study. Specialized regional studies are the introduction by C. H. MCILWAIN in his edition of PETER WRAXALL's *An Abridgement of the Indian Affairs . . . of New York . . .* (Cambridge, Mass., 1915); HELEN BROSHAR, "The First Push Westward of the Albany Traders", *Miss. Valley Hist. Rev.*, vol. VII (1920–1921); C. A. HANNA, *The Wilderness Trail . . .* (2 vols., New York, 1911); A. T. VOLWILER, *George Croghan and the Westward Movement, 1741–1782* (Cleveland, 1926); J. A. ADAMS, "The Indian Trader of the Upper Ohio Valley", *Western Penn. Hist. Mag.*, vol. XVII (1934); WAYNE E. STEVENS, *The Northwest Fur Trade 1763–1800* (Urbana, Ill., 1928); V. W. CRANE, *The Southern Frontier, 1670–1732*.

Colonial fisheries have been given the thorough treatment their importance warrants. HAROLD INNIS, *The Cod Fisheries . . .* (New Haven, 1940) is a major economic study. CHARLES B. JUDAH, *The North American Fisheries and British Policy to 1713* (Ubana, Ill., 1933) is an excellent survey. The earlier portions of RAYMOND MCPARTLAND, *A History of the New England Fisheries* (New York, 1911); W. S. TOWER, *A History of the American Whale Fishery* (Philadelphia, 1907) and E. P. Hohman, *The American Whaleman . . .* (New York, 1928) cover the colonial period.

During the eighteenth century, trade with the West Indies played an ever more important role in the economic life of the mainland colonies. That trade is discussed in many of the works previously cited. Two major monographs on the West Indies are F. W. PITMAN, *The Development of the British West Indies, 1700–1763* (New Haven, 1917) and L. J. RAGATZ, *The Fall of the Planter Class in the British Caribbean, 1763–1833* (New York [1928]). Richard Pares, *War and Trade in the West Indies, 1739–1763* (Oxford, 1936) emphasizes the international aspects of the period covered. HERBERT C. BELL, "The West India Trade before the American Revolution", *Amer. Hist. Rev.*, vol. XXII (1916–1917) is a convenient summary. AGNES M. WHITSON, "The Outlook of the Continental American Colonies on the British West Indies, 1760–1775", *Pol. Sci. Quarterly*, vol. XLV (1930) offers a different perspective. Not to be ignored is BRYAN EDWARDS, *The History, Civil and Commercial, of the British Colonies in the West Indies* (2 vols., London, 1793), the work of a West Indian planter fully aware of the close relationships between the islands and the mainland colonies.

On the customs service, ELIZABETH E. HOON, *The Organization of the English Customs System, 1696–1786* (New York, 1938) is a thorough account of its subject. The fourth volume of

ANDREWS, *The Colonial Period*, discusses customs administration within the colonies. WILLIAM S. McCLELLAN, *Smuggling in the American Colonies at the Outbreak of the American Revolution, with special reference to the West Indies Trade* (New York, 1912); and J. F. JAMESON, ed., *Privateering and Piracy in the Colonial Period: Illustrative Documents* (New York, 1923) illustrate various aspects of illegal trade.

(e) COLONIAL MANUFACTURES

The best modern work which deals in detail with colonial manufactures is the early portion of VICTOR S. CLARK, *History of Manufactures in the United States* (rev. ed., 3 vols., New York, 1929). The old work of J. L. BISHOP, *A History of American Manufactures* . . . (rev. ed., 3 vols., Philadelphia, 1868) has much useful detail. ROLLA M. TYRON, *Household Manufactures in the United States 1640–1860* . . . (Chicago, 1917) emphasizes the great importance of domestic production. CARL BRIDENBAUGH, *The Colonial Craftsman* (New York, 1950) is a first-rate account of growth and importance of the artisan class and their productions. ARTHUR C. BINING, *Pennsylvania Iron Manufacture in the Eighteenth Century* (Harrisburg, 1938) and the early portion of KATHLEEN BRUCE, *Virginia Iron Manufacture in the Slave Era* (New York, 1930) are thorough studies. CURTIS NETTELS, "The Menace of Colonial Manufacturing", *New England Quarterly*, vol. IV (1931), is a brief statement of the British attitude towards colonial manufactures.

(f) COLONIAL MONEY PROBLEMS

Most older studies of colonial currency were written in the midst of the gold standard controversy in the nineteenth century and sought to demonstrate the horrors of 'fiat' money. Newer studies have shown how distorted these older works were by the preconceptions of the times. They emphasized the bad experience of the New England colonies and ignored the successful practices of the middle colonies. These latter are pointed out in RICHARD A. LESTER, *Monetary Experiments, Early American and Recent Scandinavian* (Princeton, 1939), which discusses the use of money issues to overcome depressions in the eighteenth century. E. JAMES FERGUSON, "Currency Finance: an Interpretation of Colonial Monetary Practices", *William and Mary Quarterly*, 3rd Series, vol. X (1953) is a thorough discussion of the older and new points of view and the notes constitute an excellent bibliography of writings on the subject.

The most thorough study of colonial currency is the as yet unpublished doctoral thesis of LESLIE VAN HORN BROCK, "The Currency of the American Colonies, 1700 to 1764" (University of Michigan, 1941). CURTIS NETTELS, *The Money Supply of the American Colonies before 1720* (Madison, Wis., 1934) is an invaluable study of trade and its relation to monetary problems. ANDREW M. DAVIS, *Currency and Banking in the Province of the Massachusetts Bay* (Amer. Econ. Assoc. Publications, 3rd Series, vol. I, New York, 1900) takes the older view but does not exclude evidence. C. W. McFARLANE, "Pennsylvania Paper Currency", *Annals of the American Academy of Political and Social Science*, vol. VIII (1896) is the only study for Pennsylvania. CLARENCE P. GOULD, *Money and Transportation in Maryland, 1720–1765* (Baltimore, 1915); and KATHRYN L. BEHRENS, *Paper Money in Maryland, 1727–1789* (Baltimore, 1923) give thorough coverage for that colony. W. Z. RIPLEY, *The Financial History of Virginia, 1609–1776* (New York, 1893) and P. S. FLIPPIN, *The Financial Administration of the Colony of Virginia* (Baltimore, 1915) are general and do not treat Virginia's experience adequately. Special studies of consequence do not exist for other colonies but the various histories treat of monetary matters. For these, see the article of Ferguson cited above.

Special monographs of interest are W. G. SUMNER, "The Spanish Dollar and the Colonial Shilling", *Amer. Hist. Rev.*, vol. III (1897–1898); C. M. ANDREWS, "Current Lawful Money of New England", *ibid.*, vol. XXIV (1918–1919); and W. R. RIDDELL, "Benjamin Franklin and Colonial Money", *Penn. Mag. of Hist. and Biog.*, vol. LIV (1930).

The role of taxation in colonial economic life has received only slight attention in most of the general histories and but few special studies have been made. These are L. H. GIPSON, *Connecticut Taxation, 1750–1775* (Conn. Tercentenary Commission, Pamphlet No. 10, New

Haven, 1933); F. R. JONES, *History of Taxation in Connecticut, 1636–1776* (Baltimore, 1896); E. R. A. SELIGMAN, "The Income Tax in the American Colonies and States", *Pol. Sci. Quarterly*, vol. x (1895).

(g) COLONIAL REGULATION OF ECONOMIC LIFE

Various economic histories already listed discuss economic regulation in some detail, particularly L. H. GRAY in his study of southern agriculture, and V. S. CLARK in his history of manufactures. A. A. GIESECKE, *American Commercial Legislation before 1789* (Philadelphia, 1910) is a brief study. V. J. WYCKOFF, *Tobacco Regulation in Colonial Maryland* (Baltimore, 1936) and A. L. JENSEN, "The Inspection of Exports in Colonial Pennsylvania", *Penn. Mag. of Hist. and Biog.*, vol. LXXVIII (1954) are thorough accounts of economic regulation in the colonies concerned. RICHARD B. MORRIS, *Government and Labor in Early America* (New York, 1946) is a vastly detailed study of great importance.

A. COLONIAL AGRICULTURE

MOST of the Englishmen who looked to the founding of English colonies did not conceive of them as agricultural communities. Their vision was distracted by the precious metals and tropical produce which the Spanish and Portuguese had found in their part of the New World; they hoped to find gold and silver, to exploit the fur trade and fisheries, to develop forest products such as naval stores, and to produce silk and wines. But the first colonists, whether they came to fish or engage in the fur trade or to find gold, were soon forced to the realization that the only basis of permanent colonization was agriculture. The tragic experience of the first Englishmen in Virginia, who starved because they depended for their food upon supplies from England and from the Indians, drove this fact home.[1] Within a few years the discovery that tobacco could be grown profitably in Virginia turned that colony from a dismal failure into a success and focused the attention of prospective colonizers and colonists on the agricultural possibilities of America.[2] In the colonies that were founded afterwards it was taken for granted that they would have an agricultural base.

The fur trade, fishing, and lumbering were integral parts of colonial economy. The fur trade was a source of quick returns, especially in the newly founded colonies, but it declined in relative importance as they grew. The fisheries and lumber and forest products grew steadily in importance throughout the colonial period. But, taken altogether, they never came near to equalling the importance of agriculture. The most important products for export during the eighteenth century were tobacco, rice, wheat, bread and flour, Indian corn, lumber, fish, and indigo. These were sent to Britain, southern Europe, and the West Indies in ever-increasing quantities.[3]

Therefore, although rising merchant and artisan classes played an increasingly important role, colonial society was essentially agrarian. At the end of the colonial period at least ninety per cent of the population still lived on farms and plantations.[4] The existence and growth of colonial commerce was directly dependent upon export of agricultural surpluses to the markets of the world and upon the importation of British and foreign manufactures which were sold to a growing farm population.

In the development of agriculture, the English colonists brought with them a knowledge of English crops and methods, but these did not always fit American conditions. Colonial agriculture was therefore to a high degree experimental. Different soil and climatic conditions led the colonists to try out a great variety of plants, often in unlikely places. The hope of producing tropical crops that had antedated colonization led to efforts to raise indigo, cotton, and rice in New England. Repeated but futile efforts were made to produce commercially profitable amounts of wine and silk, particularly in the southern colonies.

Wheat, barley, oats, and rye were brought from Europe and were grown everywhere in the colonies. So too were cattle, horses, sheep, and swine, although for long it was held that European livestock degenerated in the New World. But the plants indigenous to America were of at least equal, if not far greater, importance than imported plants in the agriculture of the colonies. Many of the American Indians were skilful farmers, and the Atlantic coastline of North America was dotted with

[1] Nos. 6, 13.   [2] No. 44.   [3] No. 55, Table III.   [4] No. 73.

323

agricultural clearings made by the Indians. They knew how to preserve foods and how to make clothes from animal skins. They practised seed selection and, in arid areas, engaged in irrigation. In other words, the Indians had developed an agriculture suited to American conditions and plants, and much of their knowledge they taught to the white men who came to America.

The Indians of North and South America had cultivated maize or Indian corn, sweet potatoes, and tobacco for centuries, and many other crops as well, including white potatoes, onions, squash, gourds, watermelons, red peppers, tomatoes, peanuts (ground nuts), pineapples, and beans. Europeans thus came to a new world rich in crops and with a native population skilled in the fine art of raising them. Indian corn was a vital part of the food supply of America before white men came. The Indians taught the secrets of its culture to the colonists as they did at Plymouth, and Indian corn continued to be for white men, as it had been for Indians, a basic food crop.[1] Indigenous to America too was tobacco, the value of which exceeded that of any other single crop produced in the mainland colonies throughout the colonial period.[2]

Because the land was cheap and plentiful and labour was always expensive, the colonists followed the Indian practice of rotating fields rather than crops. Usually the same crop was planted in a field until the soil was worn out. Then a new field was cleared and the process repeated. It was a wasteful process much criticized by the eighteenth-century European proponents of the new ideas of scientific agriculture. However, such ideas did make their way to the colonies during the latter part of the colonial period and were put into practice here and there in many of the colonies.[3]

By the end of the seventeenth century, colonial agriculture had taken on sectional characteristics. Most of the farms of New England were small from the beginning, partly because most New Englanders came from small villages and farms in England, and in a measure patterned their lives after that of the mother country, and partly because the soil and climate made small farms a necessity. A wide diversity of crops was raised, but very little was produced for export except livestock and barrelled beef and pork, which was sent to other mainland colonies, and to the West Indies. The New Englanders turned to the sea and the forests early in the seventeenth century with the result that more than half of New England's exports consisted of fish and lumber products.[4] Many of the New England farms were subsistence farms or at best farms that supplied local villages with food. The town of Boston, for instance, found it necessary to import grain from colonies to the south throughout the eighteenth century.

The Middle Colonies (New York, New Jersey, Pennsylvania, and Delaware) were known as the 'bread colonies' during the eighteenth century for they produced great quantities of Indian corn, wheat, and bread products for export to the West Indies, southern Europe, and to the other mainland colonies.[5] This was in part due to the far better soil and climatic conditions of the Middle Colonies, and in part to the migration of non-English farmers, particularly to Pennsylvania. Contemporary observers were in agreement that the Palatine Germans who came to Pennsylvania in the eighteenth century brought with them agricultural methods far superior to those commonly used in the colonies and that such improved farming methods contributed substantially to the rapid rise of Pennsylvania.

The Southern Colonies (Maryland, Virginia, North Carolina, and South Carolina) were known as the 'staple colonies'. Maryland and Virginia were the great

[1] No. 46.   [2] No. 44 and No. 55, Tables VII and VIII.
[3] No. 43.   [4] No. 55, Table III.   [5] No. 55, Table III.

producers of tobacco for the world market. South Carolina early began to produce rice for export, and during the 1740's added indigo as a 'second staple' to its exports.[1] Tobacco was the most important single crop grown in the mainland colonies. By law all tobacco had to be shipped to Great Britain although by the end of the colonial period perhaps ninety per cent of it was re-exported each year. This meant profits for the British merchants who handled the trade. It also meant large revenues for the British government, for the various duties on tobacco were heavy. Between 1765 and 1775 the net revenues accruing to the British treasury averaged about £200,000 a year.[2]

Although the raising of tobacco made possible the growth of the powerful planter aristocracy of Virginia and Maryland, the planters were beset with problems which seemed insoluble. Tobacco wore out the soil rapidly, and this meant a never-ending search for new land and the accumulation of vast landholdings, all too often by corrupt means. Even more important was the fact that within a few years, as production increased, the price of tobacco began to fall. The tobacco planters tried all sorts of devices to raise the price-level. Throughout the seventeenth century they tried to limit production, but the effort failed. During the eighteenth century they were more successful in their attempts to improve the quality of the tobacco exported.[3] Meanwhile, the small farmers in the tidewater were unable to compete with the planters who acquired slaves and were thus able greatly to increase production. By the end of the first quarter of the eighteenth century the small farmer had virtually disappeared from the tidewater. He either moved on to the frontiers or became a farm labourer.

However, the great planters of the tidewater remained in difficulties. By the middle of the eighteenth century many of them were saddled with what amounted to hereditary debts to British and Scottish merchants. A part of the debt was due to extravagance, according to contemporary observers, but a part of it was due to the heavy toll taken by freights, commissions, handling charges, and British duties which absorbed between fifty and ninety per cent of the price paid by the ultimate consumer. In the effort to extricate themselves the tobacco planters turned to diversified farming and to domestic manufactures.

Meanwhile, the southern back country was settled rapidly by people who developed a diversified agriculture as contrasted with the single crop economy which had characterized the tidewater. With the development of roads to the points on the rivers which could be reached by boats and ships, an increasing amount of grain and meat for export helped to alter the pattern of southern agriculture. By the 1760's wheat was looked upon as a second 'staple' of Virginia and Maryland. In addition a growing export trade in forest products, and particularly naval stores, added to the variety of southern economy, notably in the case of North and South Carolina.[4]

Colonial agriculture was a complex way of life whose patterns were constantly changing. The domestic market was small, for the urban market was negligible and the ordinary farm was self-sufficient so far as colonial crops were concerned. The prosperity of colonial agriculture was therefore dependent upon the sale of surplus crops all over the Atlantic world and hence upon sea-borne commerce. At the same time the methods of agriculture and the phenomenal growth of population in the eighteenth century meant a constant drive onward to new land on the seemingly endless frontiers. The only natural limitations were the understandable opposition of the Indian inhabitants and the necessity of clearing the tangled forest land which extended from the sea-coast to the mountains and far beyond.

[1] No. 45.   [2] No. 55, Table VII.   [3] No. 66.   [4] No. 55, Table III.

43. The agriculture of New England, from "American Husbandry" (1775)

The following account of New England agriculture is taken from *American Husbandry*, printed in London in 1775. The author is unknown although the title page says that the book is "By an American". Efforts to identify the author have failed. Lyman Carrier believed the book was written by Dr. John Mitchell who came to America early in the eighteenth century and returned to England in 1746. Mitchell, a botanist, the maker of the map of North America published in 1755, and the author of several works on the colonies, died in 1768. Harry J. Carman inclines to the view that the author was Arthur Young. Whoever the author, the probability is that he was an Englishman. He had a good deal of information about the colonies although some of it was not accurate. He looks on the plantation colonies with favour and on the northern colonies with disfavour because their crops and their fishermen compete with those of Great Britain. Nevertheless, the book remains the single most valuable source for the history of colonial agriculture. A modern edition, edited by Professor Harry J. Carman, was published in 1939. It includes a highly uncritical review published in *The Monthly Magazine* for January 1776, Lyman Carrier's review published in 1918 in which he argues that Dr. John Mitchell was the author, and Professor Carman's own discussion of the authorship. The following excerpt is from the first edition of *American Husbandry* (2 vols., London, 1775), I, pp. 50–58.

The particulars of the husbandry of this province are extremely worthy of attention, because it is as it were between the most northerly colonies and the central ones, which are of an acknowledged merit in climate, etc. The crops commonly cultivated are first, maize, which is the grand product of the country, and upon which the inhabitants principally feed. It is not however to the exclusion of common wheat, which in a few districts is cultivated with success. It would be useless to give a particular description of this plant, which is so generally known. Its [*i.e.* maize] culture has something particular in it, and therefore should be mentioned more particularly. It is a very large branching plant, which requires a great share of nourishment, so as to be planted singly at the distance of four or five feet square; it requires good land, and much dung, if plentiful crops would be gained; and the soil must be kept clean from weeds by frequent hoeings, besides ploughing cross and cross between the plants. This is practised only by good farmers, but it is pity it is not universal among all the cultivators of this plant, for none in the world pays better for good treatment, proportioned to the value of its produce. Had Mr. Tull, the inventor of the horse-hoeing husbandry, known it, or rather had he lived in a country where it was commonly cultivated, he would have exhibited it particularly as the plant of all others which was most formed for his method of culture. Even common farmers in some parts of New England have been struck with the excellency of the practice of ploughing between the rows of this grain that they have been presently brought to practise it in common, so that it is now no longer an unusual method. One peck of the seed is the common quantity for an acre of land; and the produce varies from twenty to forty bushels, but from twenty-five to thirty are very generally gained. The expenses of this culture per acre have been thus stated:

	£	s.	d.
Seed	0	0	6
Culture	0	11	8
Harvesting, etc.	0	3	6
Conveyance to market	0	4	6
Sundries	0	2	6
	1	2	8

And the value, straw included, amounts to from 50s. to £4 sterling per English acre, which is certainly very considerable; but then their management in other respects renders the culture not so cheap as it may appear at first sight for the New England farmers practise pretty much the same system as their brethren in Canada; they have not a just idea of the importance of throwing their crops into a proper arrangement so as one may be a preparation for another, and thereby save the barren expense of a mere fallow. Maize is a very exhausting crop; scarce anything exhausts the land more, and this to so great a degree that their being obliged to depend on this for their food renders them more than any other circumstance unable to raise hemp and flax in sufficient quantities for exportation, or even for rigging their own ships, and clothing themselves with linen. Nor have they sufficient quantities of rich land upon which they can practise a management that would include both.

Besides maize, they raise small quantities of common wheat; but it does not produce so much as one would apprehend from the great richness of the soil. This is owing to the peculiarity of the climate, for we have lands in Europe that, to appearance, could bid fairer to produce large crops. But as I before observed, the new settlers in the north-east part of the province have found that wheat is to be raised with no contemptible success.

Barley and oats are very poor crops, yet do they cultivate both in all parts of New England. The crops are such as an English farmer, used to the husbandry of the eastern parts of the kingdom, would think not worth standing. This I attribute entirely to climate, for they have land equal to the greatest productions of those plants. Their common management of these three sorts of grain, wheat, barley, and oats, is to sow them chiefly on land that has laid fallow for two or three years, that is, left undisturbed for weeds and all sorts of trumpery to grow; though at other times they sow oats or barley after maize, which they are enabled to do by the culture they give the latter plant while it is growing. All their corn here is in general sown in spring, from the common idea that the climate will not admit of an autumnal sowing, but this is with exceptions; for of late years some of the more intelligent *gentlemen farmers* have, in various instances, broken through the old methods and substituted new ones in their room. These have, in various parts of the province, substituted the autumnal instead of the spring sowing, and with great advantage. In some parts of Connecticut and Rhode Island, they have introduced the English system of making clovers a preparation for corn. They leave the grass upon the land as many years as it will yield tolerable crops, and then plough it up and sow wheat, which is found a much better management than the common one. The clover affords good crops of hay once a year, besides an advantageous eatage for their cattle, which is much better than leaving the land to cover itself with weeds.

Summer fallowing is in some parts of the province not an uncommon practice, but it is not executed so well as in England. They give this preparation to land that is pretty much exhausted, and which they design for maize or for hemp, which latter also requires the addition of much manuring. What they produce is good, though not equal to the Russian, or even to that of old England; but its requiring the very best rich lands in the province, and also dunging, prevents them raising even enough for their own use, as their numerous shipping demands large supplies of it. They have been urged by several counties [bounties], even to a large amount, to go largely into the culture of hemp, which would certainly be a very national object, since there is no staple that any colony could raise would be more advantageous to Great Britain, or save her the expenditure of larger sums of money.

Flax they raise with much better success, as it does not demand near so rich a soil as hemp; but the more southern colonies much exceed New England, even in this article, for what is there raised is not sufficient for the home consumption of this very populous colony, whereas more to the south they export considerable quantities of flax-seed.

In the best cultivated parts of New England, turnips are introducing in the field culture, but not in the manner they ought to do. This is an article that demands their attention greatly, but as I shall be more particular on them when I speak of the defects of their husbandry, I shall not enlarge on it here.

Pease, beans, and tares are sown variously through the province, but scarcely anywhere managed as they are in the well cultivated parts of the mother country. But every planter or farmer grows enough of the food for fattening hogs, for supplying his own family, and driving some fat ones to market. Hogs are throughout the province in great plenty, and very large; a considerable export from the province constantly goes on in barrelled pork, besides the vast demand there is for the fishery, and the shipping in general.

Apples may be mentioned as an article of culture throughout New England, for there is no farmer, or even cottager, without a large orchard. Some of them of such extent that they make three or four hundred hogsheads of cider a man, besides exporting immense quantities of apples from all parts of the province. The orchards in New England are reckoned as profitable as any other part of the plantation. Among the other productions of this province, I should not forget the woods, which in the parts not brought into culture, are very noble. They consist of oak, ash, elm, chestnut, cypress, cedar, beech, fir, ash, sassafras, and sumac. The oak is very good, and employed chiefly in shipbuilding; and the fir yields very greatly for masts, yards, and plank; even the royal navy is supplied from hence with masts of an extraordinary size; and the export of lumber to the West Indies is one of [the] greatest articles in the province.

A large portion of every farm in New England consists of meadow and pasture land, wherein it much resembles the better parts of the mother country. In the low lands, the meadows are rich, yielding large quantities of hay, which though apparently coarse, is yet much liked by all cattle. The common herbage of many of these is a grass which has made much noise in England under the name Timothy grass. Two or three tons of hay an acre are not an uncommon produce in these meadows. The farmers find great advantage in keeping a large part of their farms for pasturage, as they are thereby enabled to support large herds of cattle and flocks of sheep, which much improve their farms.

The cattle commonly kept here are the same as in Great Britain: cows, oxen, horses, sheep, and hogs. They have large dairies, which succeed quite as well as in

Old England; oxen they fat to nearly as great a size; their mutton is good, and the wool which their sheep yield is long but coarse, but they manufacture it into coarse cloths that are the common and only wear of the province, except the gentry who purchase the fine cloths of Britain. No inconsiderable quantities of these coarse New England cloths are also exported to other colonies, to the lower people of whom, especially to the northward, they answer better than any we can send them. The horses are excellent, being the most hardy in the world. Very great numbers are exported to the West Indies and elsewhere.

44. The growing of tobacco, from "American Husbandry" (1775)

The following account is one of the best of the contemporary descriptions of tobacco culture and the problems of the planter. Printed: *American Husbandry*, I, pp. 222–231.

This plant is cultivated in all parts of North America, from Quebec to Carolina, and even the West Indies; but, except in Maryland, Virginia, and North Carolina, they plant no more than for private use, making it an object of exportation only in these provinces, where it is of such immense consequence.

It was planted in large quantities by the Indians when we first came to America, and its use from them brought into Europe; but what their method of culture was is now no longer known, as they plant none but buy what they want of the English.

Tobacco is raised from the seed, which is sown in spring upon a bed of rich mould; when about the height of four or five inches, the planter takes the opportunity of rainy weather to transplant them. The ground which is prepared to receive it is, if it can be got, a rich black mould; fresh woodlands are best: sometimes it is so badly cleared from the stumps of trees that they cannot give it any ploughings; but in old cultivated lands they plough it several times and spread on it what manure they can raise. The Negroes then hill it; that is, with hoes and shovels they form hillocks, which lie in the manner of Indian corn, only they are larger and more carefully raked up. The hills are made in squares, from six to nine feet distance, according to the land; the richer it is the further they are put asunder, as the plants grow higher and spread proportionably. The plants in about a month are a foot high, when they prune and top them; operations in which they seem to be very wild and to execute them upon no rational principles; experiments are much wanting on these points for the planters never go out of the beaten road but do just as their fathers did, resembling therein the British farmers, their brethren. They prune off all the bottom leaves, leaving only seven or eight on a stalk, thinking that such as they leave will be the larger, which is contrary to nature in every instance throughout all vegetation. In six weeks more the tobacco is at its full growth, being then from four and a half to seven feet high. During all this time the Negroes are employed twice a week in pruning off the suckers, clearing the hillocks from weeds, and attending to the worms, which are a great enemy to the plant. When the tobacco changes its colour, turning brown, it is ripe and they then cut it down and lay it close in heaps in the field to sweat one night. The next day they are carried in bunches by the Negroes to a building called the tobacco house, where every plant is hung up separate to dry, which takes a month or five weeks. This house excludes the rain but is designed for the admission of as much air as possible. They are then laid close in heaps in the tobacco houses for a week or a fortnight to sweat again, after which it is sorted and packed up in hogsheads. All the operations after the plants are dried must be done in moist or wet weather, which prevents its crumbling to dust.

There are among many inferior distinctions of sorts two generally attended to, Oronoko and sweet scented; the latter is of the finest flavour and most valued, growing chiefly in the lower parts of Virginia, viz. on James River and York River, and likewise on the Rappahannock, and the south side of the Potomac. The Oronoko is principally in use on Chesapeake Bay, and the back settlements on all the rivers. It is strong and hot; the principal markets for it are Germany and the North.

One of the greatest advantages attending the culture of tobacco is the quick, easy, and certain method of sale. This was effected by the inspection law, which took place in Virginia in the year 1730, but not in Maryland till 1748.[1] The planter, by virtue of this, may go to any place and sell his tobacco without carrying a sample of it along with him, and the merchant may buy it, though lying a hundred miles, or at any distance from his store, and yet be morally sure both with respect to quantity and quality. For this purpose, upon all the rivers and bays of both provinces, at the distance of about twelve or fourteen miles from each other, are erected warehouses to which all the tobacco in the country must be brought, and there lodged, before the planters can offer it to sale, and inspectors are appointed to examine all the tobacco brought in, receive such as is good and merchantable, condemn and burn what appears damnified or insufficient. The greatest part of the tobacco is prized, or put up into hogsheads by the planters themselves, before it is carried to the warehouses. Each hogshead, by an act of assembly, must be 950 lb. neat, or upwards; some of them weigh 14 cwt. and even 18 cwt., and the heavier they are the merchants like them the better because four hogsheads, whatsoever their weight be, are esteemed a tun, and pay the same freight. The inspectors give notes of receipt for the tobacco and the merchants take them in payment for their goods, passing current indeed over the whole colonies; a most admirable invention which operates so greatly that in Virginia they have no paper currency.

The merchants generally purchase the tobacco in the country by sending persons to open stores for them; that is, warehouses in which they lay in a great assortment of British commodities and manufactures. To these, as to shops, the planters resort and supply themselves with what they want, paying in inspection receipts or taking on credit according to what will be given them, and as they are in general a very luxurious set of people, they buy too much upon credit; the consequence of which is, their getting in debt to the London merchants, who take mortgages on their plantations, ruinous enough, with the usury of eight per cent. But this is apparently the effect of their imprudence in living upon trust.

Respecting the product of tobacco, they know very little of it themselves by the acre, as they never calculate in that manner and not many tobacco grounds were ever measured. All their ideas run in the proportion per working hand. Some are hired labourers, but in general they are Negro slaves, and the product, from the best

[1] See No. 66.

information I have gained, varies from a hogshead and a half to three and a half per head. The hogshead used to be of the value of £5 but of late years it is £8. The variation is therefore from £12 to £28 per head, according to the goodness of the lands, and other circumstances. But the planters, none of them depend on tobacco alone, and this is more and more the case since corn has yielded a high price and since their grounds have begun to be worn out. They all raise corn and provisions enough to support the family and plantation, besides exporting considerable quantities; no wheat in the world exceeds in quality that of Virginia and Maryland. Lumber they also send largely to the West Indies. The whole culture of tobacco is over in the summer months. In the winter the Negroes are employed in sawing and cutting timber, threshing corn, clearing new land, and preparing for tobacco, so that it is plain they make a product per head, besides that of tobacco.

Suppose each Negro makes two hogsheads of tobacco, or £16, and £4 in corn, provisions, and lumber, besides supporting the plantation. This is a moderate supposition and if true, the planter's profit may be easily calculated. The Negro costs him £50; his clothing, tools, and sundries £3. In this case the expense of the slave is only the interest of his cost, £2 10s., and the total only makes £5 10s. a year. To this we must add the interest of the planter's capital, province taxes, etc., which will make some addition, perhaps thirty or forty shillings per head more There will then remain £12 10s. a head profit to the planter, which is more than cent per cent profit, but this being a point of considerable importance, shall be further examined.

There is no plant in the world that requires richer land or more manure than tobacco. It will grow on poorer soils but not to yield crops that are sufficiently profitable to pay the expenses of Negroes, etc. The land they found to answer best is fresh woodlands, where many ages have formed a stratum of rich black mould. Such land will, after clearing, bear tobacco many years without any change, prove more profitable to the planter than the power of dung can do on worse lands. This makes the tobacco planters more solicitous for new land than any other people in America, they wanting it much more. Many of them have very handsome houses, gardens, and improvements about them, which fixes them to one spot; but others, when they have exhausted their grounds, will sell them to new settlers for cornfields and move backwards with their Negroes, cattle, and tools, to take up fresh land for tobacco. This is common and will continue so as long as good land is to be had upon navigable rivers. This is the system of business which made some, so long ago as 1750, move over the Allegheny Mountains and settle not far from the Ohio, where their tobacco was to be carried by land some distance, which is a heavy burden on so bulky a commodity, but answered by the superior crops they gained. The French encroachments drove these people all back again, but upon the peace, many more went, and the number increasing, became the occasion of the new colony which has been settled in that country.

A very considerable tract of land is necessary for a tobacco plantation; first, that the planter may have a sure prospect of increasing his culture on fresh land; secondly, that the lumber may be a winter employment for his slaves and afford casks for his crops. Thirdly, that he may be able to keep vast stocks of cattle for raising provisions in plenty, by ranging in the woods, and where the lands are not fresh, the necessity is yet greater, as they must yield much manure for replenishing the worn-out fields. This want of land is such that they reckon a planter should have 50 acres of land for every working hand; with less than this they will find themselves distressed for want of room.

45. The growing of rice and indigo, from "A Description of South Carolina" (1761)

Rice and indigo were the two chief agricultural products of South Carolina, and one of the main exports from the mainland colonies. The following account was written by James Glen (1701–1777), governor of South Carolina from 1738 to 1756. The account originated as a result of a series of questions sent by the Board of Trade in 1749. Glen wrote his replies and submitted them to the legislature for amendments and corrections before sending them to the Board of Trade. In 1761 the clerk in the office of the secretary of the colony took a copy of the report to England. The copy was edited and additions were made to it from other sources. It was printed in 1761 as *A Description of South Carolina* . . . without the knowledge or consent of Glen, who returned to England in that year. The following account is from Section II of the pamphlet. Printed: Chapman J. Milling, ed., *Colonial South Carolina. Two Contemporary Descriptions by Governor James Glen and Doctor George Milligen-Johnston* (South Carolina Sesquicentennial Series, No. 1, Robert L. Meriwether, general editor, Columbia, S.C., 1951), pp. 5–10.

The land of South Carolina for a hundred or a hundred and fifty miles back is flat and woody; intersected with many large rivers, some of which rise out of the Cherokee Mountains, and after a winding course of some hundreds of miles, discharge themselves into the sea.

It is remarkable for the diversity of its soil; that near the coast is generally sandy, but not therefore unfruitful; in other parts there is clay, loam, and marl; I have seen of the soil of some high bluffs, near the sides of rivers, that exactly resembles castile soap, and is not less variegated with red and blue veins, nor less clammy.

There are dispersed up and down the country several large Indian old fields, which are lands that have been cleared by the Indians, and now remain just as they left them.

There arise in many places fine savannahs, or wide extended plains, which do not produce any trees; these are a kind of natural lawns, and some of them as beautiful as those made by art.

The country abounds everywhere with large swamps, which, when cleared, opened, and sweetened by culture, yield plentiful crops of rice. Along the banks of our rivers and creeks there are also swamps and marshes, fit either for rice, or, by the hardness of their bottoms, for pasturage.

It would open too large a field to enter very minutely into the nature of the soil; and I think that this will sufficiently appear by the following account of what the labour of one Negro employed on our best lands will annually produce in rice, corn, and indigo.

The best land for rice is a wet, deep, miry soil such as is generally to be found in cypress swamps; or a black, greasy mould with a clay foundation; but the very best lands may be meliorated by laying them under water at proper seasons.

Good crops are produced even the first year when the surface of the earth appears in some degree covered with the trunks and branches of trees. The proper months for sowing rice are March, April, and May. The method is to plant it in trenches or rows made with a hoe, about three inches deep. The land must be kept pretty clear from weeds and at the latter end of August or the beginning of September it will be fit to be reaped.

Rice is not the worse for being a little green when cut. They let it remain on the stubble till dry, which will be in about two or three days, if the weather be favourable, and then they house or put it in large stacks.

Afterwards it is threshed with a flail, and then winnowed, which was formerly a very tedious operation, but it is now performed with great ease by a very simple machine, a wind-fan, but lately used here and a prodigious improvement.

The next part of the process is grinding, which is done in small mills made of wood of about two feet in diameter. It is then winnowed again, and afterwards put into a mortar made of wood, sufficient to contain from half a bushel to a bushel, where it is beat with a pestle of a size suitable to the mortar and to the strength of the person who is to pound it. This is done to free the rice from a thick skin, and is the most laborious part of the work.

It is then sifted from the flour and dust, made by the pounding, and afterwards by a wire sieve called a market sieve it is separated from the broken and small rice, which fits it for the barrels in which it is carried to market.

They reckon thirty slaves a proper number for a rice plantation, and to be tended with one overseer. These in favourable seasons and on good land will produce a surprising quantity of rice; but that I may not be blamed by those who being induced to come here upon such favourable accounts and may not reap so great a harvest; and that I may not mislead any person whatever, I choose rather to mention the common computation throughout the province, *communibus Annis*; which is, that each good working hand employed in a rice plantation makes four barrels and a half of rice, each barrel weighing five hundred pounds weight, neat; besides a sufficient quantity of provisions of all kinds, for the slaves, horses, cattle, and poultry of the plantation, for the ensuing year.

Rice last year bore a good price, being at a medium about forty-five shillings of our currency per hundred weight; and all this year it hath been fifty-five shillings and three pounds; though not many years ago it was sold at such low prices as ten or twelve shillings per hundred.

Indian corn delights in high loose land. It does not agree with clay, and is killed by much wet. It is generally planted in ridges made by the plough or hoe, and in holes about six or eight feet from each other. It requires to be kept free from weeds, and will produce, according to the goodness of the land, from fifteen to fifty bushels an acre; some extraordinary rich land in good seasons will yield eighty bushels, but the common computation is that a Negro will tend six acres and that each acre will produce from ten to thirty-five bushels. It sells generally for about ten shillings currency a bushel, but is at present fifteen.

Indigo is of several sorts. What we have gone mostly upon is the sort generally cultivated in the Sugar Islands, which requires a high loose soil, tolerably rich, and is an annual plant; but the wild sort, which is common in this country, is much more hardy and luxuriant, and is perennial. Its stalk dies every year, but it shoots up again next spring. The indigo made from it is of as good a quality as the other, and it will grow on very indifferent land, provided it be dry and loose.

An acre of good land may produce about eighty pounds weight of good indigo, and one slave may manage two acres and upwards, and raise provisions besides, and have all the winter months to saw lumber and be otherwise employed in. But as much of the land hitherto used for indigo is improper, I am persuaded that not above thirty pounds weight of good indigo per acre can be expected from the land at present cultivated. Perhaps we are not conversant enough in this commodity, either in the culture of the plant or in the method of managing or manufacturing it, to write with certainty.

I am afraid that the limewater which some use to make the particles subside, contrary as I have been informed to the practice of the French, is prejudicial to it by precipitating different kinds of particles, and consequently incorporating them with the indigo.

But I cannot leave this subject without observing how conveniently and profitably, as to the charge of labour, both indigo and rice may be managed by the same persons; for the labour attending indigo being over in the summer months, those who were employed in it may afterwards manufacture rice in the ensuing part of the year, when it becomes most laborious; and after doing all this they will have some time to spare for sawing lumber, and making hogshead and other staves to supply the Sugar Colonies.

46. Peter Kalm: maize in colonial agriculture (1751-1752)

Maize, or Indian corn, or corn, as it is known today, was a crop indigenous to the New World. It was of ever-increasing importance in colonial economy as food for both men and animals, and as a product for export. It attracted the attention of Europeans because of its great productivity as compared with other crops, and because of the great variety of uses to which it could be put. The Swedish economist and botanist, Kalm, was one of the most thorough investigators of plant life in the English colonies. The results of his studies during a trip to America, 1748-1751, were presented in his *Travels in North America*, first published in Sweden in 1753-1761. The account of maize which follows was first published in Sweden in 1751-1752. The translation is by Esther Louise Larsen. Printed: *Agricultural History*, IX (1935), pp. 109-110, 111-116, passim.

Now I will come to the uses of maize, which are so numerous. I doubt if any other species of grain exists which alone may be used for so many purposes both for man and animals.

To begin with, it is one of the most productive plants in the whole world, wherefore it is called by some "the lazy man's crop". I have counted on a single ear 650 clean and healthy kernels, and on each stalk commonly two to three ears. An ear is rarely found which has less than 300 kernels. In addition, this crop has this advantage –the kernels do not spill away as in the case of rye and other grains. On the contrary, great difficulty is apt to be encountered in loosening the kernels. In America this crop is considered a failure if it does not yield two hundred times the corn planted. It is to be noted that a large household seldom plants over 2 bushels, in fact, rarely this much in order to raise food for an entire year, and in addition, some for other purposes.

Let us recall what has previously been discussed: maize can freeze several times during the spring and still come up from the same root; it stands more heat and drought than any other crop plant; it grows in much poorer soil; it grows rapidly in dry and sandy places; it is not subject to injury by excess moisture as other crops, etc.

If the leaves of maize are removed from the stalk while they are still green, *i.e.* before they have dried by themselves in the sun, and put together in a covered stack, they will provide food for horses and cows which is preferable to clover or other good hay. On the other hand, if the leaves dry by themselves out on the stalks, the horses and cattle will not eat them, unless they lack all other food. Warm water poured on maize leaves which are dried green makes a fodder which provides the cows with both food and drink, and increases the amount of milk considerably. During the winter these leaves are cut in pieces, just as we cut straw for provender for horses. Horses prefer this fodder to clover hay.

When the maize ears are large, but the kernels on them still soft, it is customary to remove the ears from the stalks on which they are growing in the field. The husks covering the kernels are torn off. The ears are then placed in front of a fire to roast until they become light brown. These ears are considered a delicacy by both Europeans and savages. The savages plague strangers and guests who visit them at that time by offering them roasted ears. If maize had been known to the Israelites, I would say that these ears were the same as the dried ears mentioned in the Bible. But here there is no room for conjecture. Later in the season the savages do not roast the green ears, but cook and eat them, and they actually taste quite good. It is even customary with many to take these green ears where they stand in the field and eat them immediately, raw as they are. I have often done so myself, and to my taste, the kernels are as good as sweet-sugared milk.

While the maize stalks are green, and before the ears are ripe, there is a clear water between the nodes of the stalk, which is as sweet as sugar. Various people have made both syrups and sugar from maize, but this conversion has not been considered profitable. I have seen the Europeans, as well as the American savages cut off the maize stalks in the field, chew them to pieces between their teeth, and suck out the sweet juice. [John] Lawson, in his *Description* [*i.e. History*] *of Carolina,* p. 75 [(London, 1714)], says that some people crush the stalks and make from them a very palatable drink.

In most of the English colonies the farmers make their bread from maize. In Maryland even the aristocracy and the wealthy eat hardly any other bread. If a stranger comes to them, they place before him both wheat and maize bread, allowing him the freedom to choose whichever he prefers; they themselves prefer the maize bread. But if the bread is made entirely of maize, one does not find it so good. The best is made of rye and maize flour mixed. From wheat and maize flour one also gets fine bread. In America this bread is commonly baked in the form of large loaves. It is a very wholesome bread and always keeps the bowels well regulated. I know that various people, describers of plants as well as travellers, who have written about maize, have said that too much maize for food causes constipation, and even skin eruptions, scurvy, and itch. This I had read and heard discussed, here at home in

Sweden, before I left for America. I had also read those who claim that maize had been unjustly criticized. When I reached America and observed people who ate almost nothing but maize and looked as well and happy as those who eat the best and cleanest rye or wheat bread, I often told them what I had read and heard about maize. At the same time I asked them if it did not cause constipation and skin eruptions. They answered all of one accord that no more wholesome food exists and that they had never had these symptoms which are attributed to maize. I then determined to experiment on myself. Maize was a food which I had scarcely seen, much less tasted. I had just come to a strange climate; it should certainly show its effect on me. I ate, then, during the whole first winter I was in America, hardly any other bread, only maize alone or maize and rye flour mixed. However, I had no digestive disturbances, at least not more than usual. I found no such effects as those attributed to maize–quite the opposite. I can never wish to be in better health than I was at that time. The boy, Jungstrom, who accompanied me, reacted similarly. Others who have written of North America attribute to maize the same laxative quality which I found and for that reason they recommend that it be mixed with wheat, to counteract the binding constipating effect of the latter. The results attributed to the use of maize are due either to climate or to some other factor, which man has not carefully investigated.

Occasionally people make bread of different kinds of pumpkin and maize mixed. This bread is very fine and sweet. Usually the maize flour is scalded first and the pumpkins cooked, and then both are kneaded together. When bread is made of rye flour, a mush is first cooked of the maize flour, which must stand until cool, then the rye is kneaded in.

Most mush which is used in America is cooked from maize flour, and although nothing is added except water, it is very white and similar to our mush cooked with milk. To my taste its flavour is more delicious than the mush cooked from any other flour. During the time I spent with the Dutch who live north of Albany, I never had any other food in the evening but maize mush and milk, and scarcely any other breakfast but the same maize mush, either browned in butter or warmed in sweet milk. The Dutch ate nothing else for long periods. During the previous summer, when I was with them, they cooked part mush, part gruel, from maize flour and buttermilk mixed together, which tasted well enough to the hungry stomach. From grits of maize a mush or gruel is made which is cooked with water, buttermilk or sweet milk, and all of these types of gruels or mush almost vie with that cooked of rice. Occasionally syrup or sugar is mixed with the buttermilk to make it more tasty. Maize mush is quite nourishing.

From the American savage the Europeans have learned to make a grit soup of maize, which is generally esteemed as a delicacy. The French call it *Sagamité*; the English and several savage tribes, *Hommony* [hominy]; the Swedes and some wild tribes, *Sapaan*.

Some people in America make near beer from maize. They commonly consider blue maize to be better and more productive for this purpose than any other kind of maize. Maize malt is prepared in the same manner as any other malt, but malting takes longer. If much near beer is to be produced the maize should be allowed to sprout until the shoots are quite green. Malting maize should be washed thoroughly once a day in order to prevent moulding. The malt of maize tastes exactly like that of barley. A quantity of blue maize is planted by some people solely for the purpose of making this drink. The ale brewed from maize is not inferior in strength and flavour to that which is brewed from barley. This near beer has a quality which vies with other near beer. A near beer is also made of broken-up maize bread. In addition to the fact that blue maize is considered to be more suitable for making near beer, it has the advantage of ripening in a week or fourteen days. Fine spirits are distilled from maize, although this is a property of less importance.

Horses like maize quite well. One must be on guard, however. When the maize kernels are still green and in the milk, they are not especially healthful for horses. They claim in America that when the maize is ripe a horse gets as much nourishment from a bushel of maize as from 2 bushels of oats. Yet maize is considered better for a horse which is to be fattened, and oats better for one which is to be ridden on a journey. The kernels of maize are pounded from the ears in a mortar, as previously described. One or two of these mortars are to be found on each farm. The kernels are pounded loose from maize ears, especially for journeys, so the horses may eat them more quickly. A few whole ears are mixed in for the horses. Although it goes slowly the horse must take the trouble to chew the kernels loose. If a horse gets into a field of maize, when the ears have formed, he leaves the most desirable grass and clover pasture and turns entirely to picking maize ears. This I myself have seen.

Nothing is better for fattening cows and oxen than maize bran and maize flour, which are frequently mixed. Sheep are unbelievably greedy for maize, as I have observed in amazement many times. For swine, maize is considered to be the best fodder, in that it is very fattening and the flavour of the meat is far superior to that produced by any other fodder.

Chickens, doves, ducks, and geese prefer this feed to all others. Chickens also lay better when they are fed maize. In a word, without exception, I know of no cultivated plant which is so universally and greedily sought by all domestic animals.

How delicious this food is to all sorts of animals is to be inferred from this: I hardly know of any cultivated plant which has so many enemies as maize from the time it begins to ripen, and even after it is stored. For example, rats and mice leave wheat rye and all other foods untouched as long as they have access to maize in the field or storehouse. Crows also prefer maize to all other types of food. Maize thieves are of three types—the grey and black American squirrels, ground squirrels, or those which live for the most part in the soil and do not climb trees. Woodpeckers of various sorts, and other birds, are so greedy for maize that it is almost impossible to scare them away from the field by any method of frightening or trapping. The birds are present during the day and the squirrels during the night. In a few nights, if undisturbed, squirrels can cart away from the granary half a tub or more to their nests. When the maize is ripe, but still in the fields, I have myself seen a farmer with his gun go to the end of the field and shoot at the maize thieves, who do not allow themselves to be frightened from the delicious maize. Finally, the whole swarm of them move forward from one end of the field to the other. When the farmer returns, they fly back to the part of the field where they were before, and so they switch from one end of the field to the other, entirely according to how the farmer pursues them. They almost wear the farmer out before he is able to scare them away, although now and then he shoots one of them. In order to rid the maize of all these destructive pests, the governing bodies in all parts of that country have been called upon to set a definite bounty to be paid on squirrels, crows, maize thieves, woodpeckers, and other pests. An almost inconceivable sum was paid in Pennsylvania alone for squirrel heads for a single year, namely, from January 1, 1749, to that same date, 1750. When the representatives from all regions in Pennsylvania met at the beginning of 1750 to make necessary laws, they received complaints from all regions that the treasuries were empty solely because of squirrels. Previously a law had been enacted that 3d. (which is about 12 to 14 öre kopp:mt) should be paid from the general coffers for each squirrel head. So high had the spirit of vengeance gone against these animals, that during the one year £8,000 in Pennsylvania currency had been paid. This is 40,000 plåtar in our money. When I heard this discussed above all else in the city, it was inconceivable to me until Mr. Franklin, who has gone so far in experiments with electricity, and who is one of their outstanding legislators, convinced me of the truth directly from the documents. The high expenditure was attributed to the fact that when one received 3d. for each squirrel, it paid to go into the woods to hunt these creatures. Many young people in particular gave up all other work and went to the woods to shoot squirrels. The legislature was therefore forced to repeal the law and change it from 3d. bounty to half that sum for a head.

A very similar law was passed against maize thieves in New England. As a result, the maize thieves were almost wholly and entirely exterminated. During the summer of 1749, a multitude of grass worms spread over the entire country, destroying all the hay crop for that year. The inhabitants were forced to write to England for a ship loaded with hay. They began to regret that they had been so hard on the maize thieves because they believed, as they had previously observed, that the maize thieves for a good deal of the summer before the maize ripened, lived on these insects and thus hindered their increase. The people of New England were conscience-stricken because they believed this to be a punishment for meddling in the providence of the Almighty Creator.

For swellings the following is used: A mush of maize meal and milk is cooked. While the mush is on the fire suet or other fats are added. The mush is spread on a cloth and is placed on the swollen part as hot as one can stand it. It should remain until cold. This is held to be an unequalled aid in the treatment of swellings, for it relieves the ache, brings down the swelling, or ripens the swelling, if it is a boil, so the pus drains out. I have tried both. With my own eyes I have seen others obtain relief by using this treatment for swellings caused by toothache or colds.

B. THE ACQUISITION OF LAND

THE promise of land on easy terms, or free of purchase price, more than any other single thing, was the lure which brought ever greater numbers of Europeans to the English mainland colonies. The colonial promoters of the seventeenth century held out glowing hopes to would-be immigrants, hopes that had no chance of realization in the Europe of that and later times.[1] The promoters, with a few exceptions, were not idealists; to profit from their domains they had to have settlers upon them and hence the easy terms they offered.

The Virginia Company established the pattern of land policy that was to be characteristic in the southern colonies. The company promised that a man might acquire land in the colony by becoming an 'adventurer': that is, by buying shares of stock in the company, or by going to the colony as a 'planter'. Eventually fifty acres was the amount agreed upon for each share of stock in the company and for each settler going to the colony. To further encourage settlement, the company promised too that anyone who paid for the transportation of poor people to the colonies should have fifty acres for each person so transported. This came to be known as a 'headright'[2] and was the chief means of acquiring land during the seventeenth century. The indentured servants thus brought in never seem to have acquired head-rights for themselves, although the English government usually instructed the governors to grant such rights. In fact, the headright system became a source of corruption and led to the acquisition of great tracts of land by a rising aristocracy. Not only did the importers of servants acquire headrights, but even the ship captains who brought them in and the planters who purchased them got headrights, and some did not balk at the forgery of such certificates.[3] In 1699 the Virginia legislature gave up the pretence of granting land to encourage settlement and established the 'treasury right'. This provided that anyone who paid five shillings was entitled to fifty acres.

The proprietors of Carolina offered fifty acres of land to each person moving to their province, and the colony retained that method until the Revolution.[4] In Pennsylvania lands were sold on easy terms, and large grants were made to those who helped others to emigrate.

In New England the prevailing practice in the seventeenth century was for the legislatures to grant townships to groups of individuals who settled in small, well-defined communities and who divided the lands among themselves.[5] In New York the common practice, which began with the Dutch, was the creation of vast manors on which the farmers were tenants.[6] While there were manorial estates in Maryland the proprietors also used the headright system to attract settlers.[7] Entirely apart from the legal means of getting land, large numbers of people settled on land as 'squatters' without observing legal formalities. This was particularly true in back-country Pennsylvania and in the south. In many cases such people were able to maintain their 'squatter's rights' despite the opposition of proprietors and other claimants.

As compared with Europe, land was unbelievably easy to acquire in the English

[1] Nos. 9 and 10.   [2] No. 48.   [3] No. 50A.   [4] Nos. 9 and 49.
[5] No. 47.   [6] No. 50B.   [7] No. 74A.

colonies. The very ease of acquisition, of course, led to abuses and the concentration of great landholdings in a few hands as in portions of Virginia, South Carolina, and New York. The rise of the mania for land speculation in the eighteenth century altered even the New England system. The free grant to actual communities was characteristic of the seventeenth century; but by the middle of the eighteenth century legislatures were, in effect, selling townships to speculators rather than granting them free of charge to actual settlers.[1]

The concentration of great landholdings and the rise of great speculative holdings in the eighteenth century was a source of increasing discontent everywhere among small farmers. The shift in the New England land system resulted in the rise of a class of absentee proprietors who not only owned the land but exercised the powers of government as well, thus leaving the actual settlers at their mercy. The great landlords of New York refused to sell land. Instead they insisted that the farmers on their lands must remain as tenants. The opposition to tenantry and to the unfair exactions of the landlords became so great that the tenants on many of the manors rebelled during the 1760's. So widespread did the revolt become that it could be suppressed only by using British troops. A similar rebellion had occurred in New Jersey in the 1740's. The land policy of the Penns was liberal, but even in Pennsylvania there was discontent on the part of back-country settlers, many of whom settled on the reserved lands of the Penns and refused to buy it or to pay rents. The southern back country was covered by a great patchwork of vast holdings, but here too the actual settlers located without consideration for the tidewater owners.

During the first half of the eighteenth century the British government sought to prevent great speculative holdings and to encourage small farmers, especially after the revelation of the corruption of the land system in Virginia.[2] The primary concern of British officials was the collection of quit-rents in the royal colonies. In law, ultimate ownership of the land in the royal colonies lay with the Crown, and the right to hold land was dependent upon the payment of a quit-rent. It was obvious that the holders of great tracts had no intention of paying such rents, and used every means possible to evade doing so. The British policy of encouraging small holdings was based on the reasonable assumption that it would be far easier to collect quit-rents from small farmers than from great landholders.

Theoretically the king granted all land in the royal colonies, but in fact it was done by the royal governors and colonial councils, and the councils were dominated by men interested in acquiring large tracts of land. Therefore the attempt to encourage small holdings was a failure. Laws requiring that three acres out of every fifty granted be cultivated, or calling for the erection of a building on each plot of a certain size, were ignored or cleverly evaded. Not until after 1763 did British control of colonial land granting threaten to become effective. The promised opening up of new land in the Ohio Valley beyond the Appalachian Mountains led to the organization of great speculative land companies, and to plans for new colonies.

In all these schemes British political leaders, as well as Americans, were avid participants, and their membership in such projects helps to account for the erratic western policy followed by Britain after 1763.[3] Nevertheless, British efforts at controlling or limiting colonial expansion into this great new region, and British favouritism of one project as opposed to another, were contributing factors in the development of colonial antagonism to the mother country. The problem of the disposal of this

[1] No. 50C.   [2] No. 50A.   [3] Cf. Nos. 98 and 118.

great domain was, in the end, left to be solved by the United States in the first years of independence.

47A–C. Grant of a Massachusetts township (1660–1667)

During the seventeenth century land in New England was given and not sold, and given to groups, rather than individuals. This was done by the colonial legislatures as new communities were planned, or to recognize groups who had settled in communities without a prior grant of land. In Massachusetts such communities were usually called either districts or towns. Both were given the right to govern themselves in local affairs and to divide the lands given them as they saw fit. The town or township was a full fledged corporate community, for unlike the district, it had the right to elect two representatives to the colonial legislature. This community system of settlement was to be altered during the eighteenth century when the legislatures began selling towns to speculative groups who did not plan to settle the land themselves but to sell it to others (No. 50C).

The following documents relate to the founding of the town of Mendon, Massachusetts. In 1659 several inhabitants of the town of Braintree petitioned the General Court for the establishment of a 'new plantation'. The Court gave them permission to seek out ungranted lands. On 15 October 1660, the General Court gave them permission to settle on the land they had located, and appointed commissioners to oversee the plantation (No. 47A). On 22 December 1662 a meeting was held at which rules and regulations for the settlement of the plantation were adopted (No. 47B). By 1667 several new members had been admitted and the plantation had been surveyed. The map with a description of the boundaries was presented to the General Court, and on 15 May 1667 the General Court incorporated the plantation as the Town of Mendon (No. 47C).

47A. Authorization of the plantation at Mendon (16 October 1660)

Printed: *Records of Massachusetts Bay*, IV, pt. i, p. 445.

In answer to the petition of the inhabitants of Braintree, *i.e.* Gregory Belchar, James Penneman, Thomas Mekins, Moses Paine, Edmond Quinsey, Robert Twelves, and Peter Brackett, the Court judgeth it meet to encourage the petitioners to proceed in their settling themselves, and an able minister with them, in the place desired for a new plantation, within their time limited; and that those that begin the said plantation may not want due encouragement in their accommodation, and yet the place preserved from unnecessary waste, it is ordered that Captain Daniel Gookin, Mr. Wm. Parkes, Lt. Roger Clap, Ephraim Child, and Wm. Stiltson, or any three of them, shall be and hereby are appointed a committee, and hereby empowered to appoint unto each inhabitant there, any time within this three years, as they shall see meet, and that when a full number of persons appear, this Court will, on the committee's information, order them due bounds. In further answer to said Braintree petition, the Court declares that they judge meet to grant a plantation of eight miles square, and that the persons named have liberty to enter thereupon, and make a beginning thereof, and to take such persons into their society as they shall judge meet, and that Major Humphrey Atherton, Lt. Roger Clap, Captain Eliazer Lusher, and Deacon Parkes, or any three of them, shall and hereby are appointed commissioners, and empowered to make a valid act there.

47B. Rules for the settlement of the plantation (22 May 1662)

Printed: John G. Metcalf, comp., *Annals of the Town of Mendon, from 1659 to 1880* (Providence, 1880), pp. 3–4.

Dorchester, 22 : 5 : 1662

We whose names are hereunto subscribed, being the committee empowered by the General Court to assist the ordering and settling the plantation granted at Netmocke, do agree and declare as followeth, viz.:

  1. That the divisions of land there shall be by these ensuing rules, that one hundred

pounds estate be granted one hundred and fifty acres of land, viz.: thirty acres to the house lot, and ten acres of meadow and five acres of swampy or low land, being capable of being made meadow, and more, one hundred and five acres for the great lot; and according to this proportion for all estates be they more or less, and this to be the rule for the division of all the lands of the plantation that shall be divided before the place or the people there shall be allowed to be a township and enjoy the privileges thereof.

2. That the public charges already disbursed, or that shall be disbursed before the time of town privileges aforesaid shall be borne and defrayed according to the proportion of allotments provided as before said.

3. The persons whose names are presented being (as we understand) of honest and good report are accepted and allowed to take up allotments in said plantation.

4. That it shall not be in the power of an inhabitant now accepted or hereafter to be accepted before the time of privileges aforesaid, to sell, lease, or alienate his said allotment, or any part or parcel thereof to any person whatsoever without the consent or approbation of the major part of the inhabitants, or of those then chosen to regulate the affairs of the plantation upon penalty of forfeiting to the said plantation all and every part and parcel so sold or alienated.

5. There shall be an able and approved minister settled with them there according to the order of Court in that case made and provided.

6. That whereas experience shows it not to be the best expedient for transaction of public work to be left to the whole number of inhabitants, we therefore advise that the said inhabitants now accepted should in their first opportunity make choice of 5 or 7 meet persons for the management of their said occasions for the space of one year, and that Mr. Peter Brackett and Ensign Moses Paine be 2 of them, and the men so chosen should have the whole power of accepting inhabitants and disposing lands according to the rules above written.

7. And whereas it appears that the said Mr. Brackett and Mr. Paine hath already taken much pains and been at charges to promote this plantation, and we suppose must yet continue their assistance therein, we judge but just and equal that each of them be gratified with convenient farms of uplands and meadow proportionable to the quantities of each in the plantation to be laid out to them at convenient distance from the seat of the town, that is, not less than two miles, and in such places as they shall accept and that the quantity of these be not above 300 acres to each of them.

8. It is also further agreed and ordered that each of the persons now accepted to allotments there, and all others that shall be so accepted before the time of obtaining town privileges, shall be settled at the said plantation before the end of the seventh month 1663 with these persons and estates.

47C. Incorporation of the town of Mendon (15 May 1667)

Printed: *Records of Massachusetts Bay*, IV, pt. II, pp. 341–342.

The return of Joshua Fisher, that laid out the Court's grant to Qunshapage, is an explanation of this plot, being the township of Qunshapage as it was laid out according to the grant of the General Court. From A to B it is bounded by Charles

River; a white oak, being marked, on the south side of Charles River at A, and a black oak, on the north side of Charles River at B; Charles River east, and a line of four miles, want forty rod, from B to C, with marked trees and heaps of stones; the country's land north from C to D, a line of marked trees and heaps of stones, running eight miles and a half; the country's land west, and so from D to E, eight miles; the country's land south, and so from E to F; the country's land east; a parcel of meadow, of thirty acres by estimation, on the north line from Charles River, laid out and deciphered in the plat. That the name thereof be Mendon; and it is ordered that Mendon be settled as part of the county of Middlesex, and that they and their successors be invested with town privileges, as other towns of this jurisdiction do enjoy; and in respect of the distance from the bay, and low estate of the inhabitants there, shall be freed from country charges the space of three years from the time of this grant.

48. The Virginia headright patent (1710)

The headright was based on the theory that each settler, or each man who brought in a settler, was entitled to a tract of land, usually fifty acres. It was the common method of procuring land in seventeenth-century Virginia and was also used in the Carolinas. The method led to corruption and engrossment (No. 50A) and in 1699 the Virginia legislature gave up the pretence of granting land to encourage settlement. It established the 'treasury right' whereby anyone who paid five shillings was entitled to fifty acres. The following form of headright patent was worked out early in the eighteenth century, and although little used thereafter, represents a summation of seventeenth-century practice. Printed: [Fairfax Harrison] *Virginia Land Grants* (Richmond, 1925), pp. 39-40.

Anne, by the Grace of God, of Great Britain, France, and Ireland, Queen, Defender of the Faith, etc.

To all to whom these presents shall come, Greeting.

Know ye that for divers good causes and considerations, but more especially for and in consideration of the importation of one person to dwell within this our colony of Virginia, whose name is William Shoreman,

We have given, granted, and confirmed, and by these presents for us, our heirs and successors, do give, grant, and confirm unto John Wade of the county of James City one certain tract or parcel of land in same, containing 47 acres, and bounded as follows, to wit: [Description of boundaries]

With all woods, underwoods, swamps, marshes, low grounds, meadows, feedings, and his due share of all veins, mines, and quarries, as well discovered as not discovered, within the bounds aforesaid, same being part of the said quantity of 47 acres of land and also the rivers, waters, and watercourses therein contained, together with the privileges of hunting, hawking, fishing, fowling, and all other profits, commodities, and hereditaments whatsoever to the same or any part thereof belonging or in any wise appertaining.

To have, hold, possess, and enjoy the said tract or parcel of land, and all other the before-mentioned and granted premises and every part thereof, with their and every of their appurtenances unto the said John Wade and to his heirs and assigns for ever, to the only use and behoof of him, the said John Wade, his heirs and assigns for ever.

To be held of us, our heirs and successors, as of our manor of East Greenwich in the county of Kent, in free and common socage and not *in capite* or by knight's service.

Yielding and paying unto us, our heirs and successors, for every fifty acres of land (and so proportionably for a lesser or greater quantity than fifty acres) the fee rent of one shilling yearly, to be paid upon the Feast of Saint Michael the Archangel.

And also cultivating and improving three acres part of every fifty of the tract above-mentioned within three years after the date of these presents.

Provided always that if three years of the said fee rent shall at any time be in arrear and unpaid, or if the said John Wade, his heirs or assigns do not within the space of three years next coming after the date of these presents, cultivate and improve three acres part of every fifty of the tract above-mentioned, then the estate hereby granted shall cease and be utterly determined; and thereafter it shall and may be lawful to and for us, our heirs and successors, to grant the same lands and premises with the appurtenances unto such other person or persons as we, our heirs and successors, shall think fit.

In witness whereof we have caused these our letters patent to be made.

Witness our trusty and well-beloved Alexander Spotswood, esquire, our lieutenant-governor and commander-in-chief of our said colony and dominion at Williamsburg, under the seal of our said colony the 12th day of December, one thousand seven hundred and ten, in the ninth year of our reign.

49. North Carolina land patent (1767)

From the beginning the proprietors of Carolina held out the promise that each person coming to the colony was entitled to fifty acres of land (No. 9). In essence they adopted the Virginia headright system. At the same time they gave large grants to individuals who brought over settlers or who had influence with the proprietors, and, after the establishment of royal governments, with the governors and councils. The following standard form of land patent was sent to England by Governor William Tryon in 1767 in answer to queries as to the forms and methods of land granting in the colony. The form was printed. The italicized portions were left blank and filled in when the grant was made. The patent was accompanied by maps of surveys showing the location of the land granted. From: British Public Record Office, C.O. 5/112.

North-Carolina, ff.   No.

George the Third, by the Grace of God, of Great-Britain, France and Ireland, King, Defender of the Faith, etc. To all to whom these Presents shall come, Greeting: KNOW YE, That We, for and in Consideration of the Rents and Duties herein reserved, Have Given and Granted, and by these Presents for Us, Our Heirs and Successors, DO Give and Grant, unto *James Fulsher* a Tract of Land, containing *Two Hundred* Acres, lying and being in the County of *Craven* in our Province of NORTH-CAROLINA.

[Space here for description of location.]

As by the Plat hereunto annexed doth appear; together with all Woods, Waters, Mines, Minerals, Hereditaments and Appurtenances to the said Land belonging or appertaining (one Half of all Gold and Silver Mines, excepted;) To hold to *him* the said *James Fulsher his* Heirs and Assigns, for ever, as of our Manor of EAST-GREENWICH, in our County of KENT, in free and common Soccage, by Fealty only; YIELDING AND PAYING, unto Us, our Heirs and Successors, for ever, the Yearly Rent of Four Shillings, Proclamation Money, for every Hundred Acres hereby granted; to be paid unto Us, our Heirs and Successors, on the second Day of FEBRUARY in each Year, at such Places in our said Province, as our Governor for the Time being, with the Advice and

Consent of our Council, shall think fit to direct and appoint. PROVIDED ALWAYS, That in Case the said *James Fulsher his* Heirs and Assigns, shall not within Three Years from the Date hereof, clear and cultivate according to the Proportion of three Acres for every Hundred; and also, That if a Minute or Docket of these our Letters Patent, shall not be entered in the Office of our Auditor-General, for the Time being, in our said Province, within Six Months from the Date hereof; that then, and in either of the said Cases, these our Letters Patent, shall be void and of none Effect. IN TESTIMONY whereof, We have caused the Seal of our said Province to be hereunto affixed. WITNESS our trusty and well-beloved WILLIAM TRYON, Esquire, Captain-General, Governor and Commander in Chief, in and over our said Province, this......Day of April, in the Seventh Year of our Reign. Annoque Domini, one Thousand, seven Hundred and Sixty-seven.

50A–C. The engrossment of land

Since land granting was a function of colonial governments, people with influence used it to acquire land without regard for the welfare of the actual settlers or the revenues of the governments. During the eighteenth century ever larger amounts of the available land fell into the hands of speculators and the small farmers were increasingly forced to buy from them rather than to acquire lands directly from governments. Since land speculation was a process characterized by fraud and favouritism, it was doubly a cause of discontent on the part of small landholders and would be landholders.

The accounts that follow illustrate what happened in Virginia, New York, and New England.

The Present State of Virginia, and the College was written by Henry Hartwell, James Blair, and Edward Chilton at the request of the Board of Trade. These men were Virginia officials who were at the time in England. The report was not published until 1727, but it had influence on the Board of Trade and the policies it attempted to carry out. The section relating to land granting, which is given below (No. 50A), resulted in a serious effort to limit the acquisition of vast landholdings in Virginia. It led the Board of Trade to promote what amounted to a homestead policy, for it was obvious that quit-rents could be collected more easily from small farmers than from a great landed aristocracy. The attempt failed, for the Virginia leaders were able to dominate royal governors who were instructed to bring about reform measures.

Cadwallader Colden (1688–1776) was one of the most extraordinary men of the eighteenth century. For a half-century he was an office-holder in New York. He controlled the land office; he acted as governor several times and was the power behind other governors; and he was a leader in intellectual movements of his time. He consistently supported the power of the Crown in the colonies. He looked upon the great landholdings as the source of the power of the social group whose existence threatened the very foundation of royal government in the colony (No. 50B).

Thomas Hutchinson (1711–1780) was an outstanding political figure in Massachusetts in the middle of the eighteenth century. He was made royal governor of the colony in 1770, but he had won for himself the enmity of popular leaders. He left the colony at the outbreak of the Revolution and never returned. He was a student of the history of the colony in which his family had played so important a part; and his *History . . . of Massachusetts Bay*, published first in 1764, is still one of the better histories of the colony. His account of the change in the purpose of land granting in Massachusetts is applicable in general to the other New England colonies as well (No. 50C).

50A. Henry Hartwell, James Blair, and Edward Chilton: from "The Present State of Virginia" (1697)

Printed: *The Present State of Virginia, and the College* (ed., Hunter Dickinson Farish, Williamsburg, Va., 1940), pp. 16–20.

The method settled by the king from the first seating of that country was to allot 50 acres of land to everyone that should adventure into that country; which, if it had been punctually observed, would have been a lasting encouragement to adventurers, till the country had come to be well peopled; but as the matter has been managed, the land is now gone from the king, and yet the country but very ill peopled. The first great abuse of this design was by the ignorance and knavery of surveyors, who often gave out draughts of surveys without ever actually surveying it, or ever coming on the land; only they gave the description, by some natural bounds, and were sure to allow large measure, that so the persons for whom they surveyed might enjoy larger tracts of land than they were to pay quit-rent for. Then all courts were very lavish in allowing certificates for rights; for if a master of a ship came into any court and made oath that he had imported himself and so many seamen and passengers at divers times into the country, and that he never elsewhere made use of those rights; he had presently an order granted him for so many rights (*i.e.* so many times 50 acres of land), and these rights he would sell and dispose of for a small matter. Perhaps the same seamen made oath that they had adventured themselves so many times into the country, and had not elsewhere proved their rights, and upon this they had an order for so many rights *toties quoties*. The masters likewise that bought the servants so imported would at another court make oath that they had bought so many persons that had ventured themselves into the country, and upon this so many rights were ordered them: so that still the land went away, and the adventurers themselves, who remained in the country, for whom it was originally designed, had the least share. Then great liberty was used in issuing out certificates for rights, by the country clerks, and especially by the clerks of the secretary's office, which was and is still a constant mint of these rights, where they may be purchased at very easy rates, of the clerks, from five shillings to one shilling per right.

These things were not unknown to the government, who connived at them, thinking it a very pardonable crime that the king's land was given away to people that really and truly had no right to it, since by this means the land was taken up, and so the king had so much more quit-rents paid him, whereas that which was not taken up, paid nothing. But they little considered that the small profit which comes by quit-rents doth not balance the great damage of leaving the country without inhabitants, which is the effect of the methods they have followed, for the king and kingdom of England gain near 200 times as much by an ordinary planter as the king would have got by the quit-rents of the 50 acres he should have had, which may be made out thus: an usual crop of tobacco for one head is 2,000 pounds weight, which at sixpence per pound, the present duty in England, amounts to 50 pounds. Then supposing this 2,000 pounds of tobacco to be put into 3 hogsheads, here is six shillings of Virginia duty to the king, by the 2 shillings per hogshead; then the freight of this at 8 pounds per tun comes to six pound, which is commonly paid into England; in all 56 pounds, 6 shillings; besides the increase of ships and seamen, and the multitudes maintained by the manufacture of tobacco here in England, and the manufacture of English goods sold to the planters. To find out, on the other hand, how many acres of land it will require to make up the bare 56 pounds, 6 shillings out of the quit-rents of it in quit-rent tobacco, sold *communibus annis* at 5 shillings per hundred, and 24 pounds of tobacco for every hundred acres; at that rate, 56 pounds 6 shillings, will purchase 22,520 pounds of tobacco, which is the quit-rent for 93,833 acres of land; so that one man's labour is equivalent to the quit-rents of near a hundred thousand acres of land, which was the quantity allotted for 2,000 men. Besides the quit-rents would not have been lost, but would have been paid at last when the country came to be peopled. This fundamental error of letting the king's land lie waste, together with another of not seating in townships, as they did in some other colonies, is the cause that Virginia at this day is so badly peopled.

Everyone that takes out a patent for any dividend or tract of king's land, is, in the patent, obliged to two things. One is to seat or plant upon it within three years after the date of the patent, otherwise it lapses again to the king. The other is, to pay the quit-rents, at the rate of a shilling for every 50 acres *per annum*. Seating, by their law, is reckoned the building of a house, and keeping a stock one whole year. They matter not how small an house it is; if it be but a hoghouse, it serves the turn; and planting, their law reckons the planting and tending one acre of ground, it is no matter how badly, and either of these; viz. either seating or planting, within the three years, saves the whole tract, if it be never so large, which is the cause that though all the good land of the country is taken up, yet there is very little improvement on it.

The land which is neither seated nor planted within the three years, lapses to the king, and it is called lapsed land, but it never comes into the king's hands, being due, by their law, to any one that first petitions the general court for it.

When a man dies seized of land in fee, without will or heirs, such land escheats to the king. The way of disposing of it is thus: the person in possession hath by the king's charter, the right of the grant. But of late, it depends on the governor's favour, who, among the several petitions that are presented to him, for the benefit of the escheat, accepts of anyone he pleases, and underwrites it thus. This petition is granted, paying composition to the auditor, according to law. Then a warrant issues from the governor to the escheator of the precinct, who makes inquisition and finds the office by a jury of 12 men. Which inquisition being returned by the escheator to the secretary's office, lies there nine months, that any person concerned may come and traverse the office, and if nobody appears in that time, a patent passeth according to the petitioner's request. The escheator's fee is five pounds sterling, and the composition by the charter is two pounds of tobacco per acre.

50B. Cadwallader Colden: from " State of the Lands in the Province of New York " (1732)

The following account of land granting practices in New York was written while Colden was surveyor-general of the New York land office. The portion of the document given here is preceded by an historical account of land granting by royal governors since 1664 and is followed by Colden's suggestions for solving the problems he describes. Printed: E. B. O'Callaghan, ed., *The Documentary History of the State of New York* (4 vols., Albany, 1850–1851), I, pp. 251–253.

I shall now proceed to some more particular account of the great grants of lands, I mean of such as contain fifty thousand acres and upwards to a million of acres, for if I be not very much misinformed, there is more than one that contain that quantity.

No quantity of land or number of acres, for the most part, are mentioned in any of these grants, nor is it possible to discover the quantity by inspection of the patents, as it may be done in those grants which are founded on a previous survey, and where any quantity is expressed it seems to be done more with design to hide the real quantity (if their present claims be truly conformable to their original bounds) than to set forth the truth, for I have heard of one instance at least where the patent grants 300 acres, and the patentee now claims upwards of sixty thousand acres within the bounds of his grant. Others suspecting that such disproportion between the real quantity and the quantity expressed in the grant might invalidate the grant, got the quantity of land to be expressed in the following manner, containing for example, one thousand acres of profitable land, besides woodland, and waste, and yet when these lands were granted, perhaps there was not ten acres that was not woodland, or one acre that at the time of the grant yielded any profit or one acre that by improvement might not be made profitable. Others guard against this exception to their grant by adding to the quantity of land expressed in the grant these words, *Be it more or less*, or some such words, and by virtue of these they not only claim a small quantity more than is expressed in the patent but claim twice as much, and often ten times as much, and sometimes above one hundred times the quantity of land that is expressed in the grant, but as I said before, generally no quantity of land is expressed in the large grants.

There being no previous survey to the grants, their boundaries are generally expressed with much uncertainty by the Indian names of brooks, rivulets, hills, ponds, falls of water, etc., which were and still are known to very few Christians, and which adds to this uncertainty is, that such names as are in these grants taken to be the proper name of a brook, hill, or fall of water, etc., in the Indian language signifies only a large brook or broad brook, or small brook or high hill, or only a hill or fall of water in general, so that the Indians show many places by the same name. Brooks and rivers have different names with the Indians at different places, and often change their names, they taking their names often from the abode of some Indian near the place where it is so called. This has given room to some to explain and enlarge their grants according to their own inclinations by putting the names mentioned in their grants to what place or part of the country they please, of which I can give some particular instances where the claims of some have increased many miles, in a few years, and this they commonly do by taking some Indians in a public manner to show such places as they name to them, and it is too well known that an Indian will show any place by any name you please for the small reward of a blanket or bottle of rum, and the names as I observed, being common names in the Indian language, and not proper ones as they are understood to be in English, gives more room to these frauds.

Several of the great tracts lying on Hudson's River are bounded by that river on the east or west sides, and on the north and south sides by brooks or streams of water which, when the country was not well known, were supposed to run nearly perpendicular to the river, as they do for some distance from their mouths, whereas many of these brooks run nearly parallel to the river and sometimes in a course almost directly opposite to the river. This has created great confusion with the adjoining patents, and frequently contradictions in the boundaries, as they are expressed in the same patent.

Sometimes the grant is of the land that belonged to such an Indian by name or is bounded by such an Indian land, but to prove that any particular spot belonged to any particular Indian, or to show the bounds of any particular Indian, I believe is beyond human skill, so as to make it evident to any indifferent man.

I shall next recite what have been the consequences of these large grants. It is evident that thereby the king has been deprived of almost all his quit-rents, which it appears by the powers given to the governors to grant lands, the king designed to reserve. But the consequence I think has been much worse as to the improvement of the country for though this country was settled many years before Pennsylvania and some of the neighbouring colonies, and has many advantages over them as to the situation and conveniencies of trade, it is not near so well cultivated, nor are there near such a number of inhabitants as in the others in proportion to the quantity of land; and it is chiefly if not only where these large grants are made where the country remains uncultivated–though they contain some of the best of the lands, and the most conveniently situated. And every year the young people go from this province and purchase land in the neighbouring colonies, while much better and every way more convenient lands lie useless to the king and country. The reason of this is that the grantees themselves are not nor ever were in a capacity to improve such large tracts, and other people will not become their vassals or tenants for one great reason as peoples (the better sort especially) leaving their native country was to avoid the dependence on landlords, and to enjoy lands in fee to descend to their posterity that their children may reap the benefit of their labour and industry. There is the more reason for this because the first purchase of unimproved land is but a trifle to the charge of improving them.

It may perhaps deserve the consideration of those who are more capable of political foresight than I am whether if these large grants take place as they are designed, and become great lordships with large dependencies and revenues, whether this will secure or endanger the dependency of the colonies on their mother country. I think few instances can be given where great changes were brought to effect in any state but when they were headed by rich and powerful men; any other commotions generally produced only some short-lived disorders and confusions.

50C. Thomas Hutchinson: from "The History . . . of Massachusetts Bay"

Printed: *The History of the Colony and Province of Massachusetts Bay* (3 vols., London, 1765–1828), II, pp. 331–332.

The government, under the old charter and the new, had been very prudent in the distribution of the territory. Lands were granted for the sake of settling them. Grants for any other purpose had been very rare and, ordinarily, a new settlement was contiguous to an old one. The settlers themselves, as well as the government, were inclined to this for the sake of a social neighbourhood, as well as mutual defence against an enemy. The first settlers on Connecticut River, indeed, left a great tract of wilderness between them and the rest of the colony, but they went off in a body, and a new colony, Connecticut, was settling near them at the same time. Rivers were also an inducement to settle, but very few had ventured above Dunstable, upon the fine river Merrimac, and the rivers in the province of Maine had no towns at any distance from the sea into which they empty. But all on a sudden, plans are laid for grants of vast tracts of unimproved land and, the last session of Mr. Dummer's administration, a vote passed the two houses appointing a committee to lay out three lines of towns, each town of the contents of six miles square, one line to extend from Connecticut River above Northfield to Merrimac River above Dunstable, another line on each side Merrimac as far as Penicook, and another from Nichewanock River to Falmouth in Casco Bay.

Pretences were encouraged, and even sought after, to entitle persons to be grantees. The posterity of all the officers and soldiers who served in the famous Narragansett expedition in 1675 were the first pitched upon, those who were in the unfortunate attempt upon Canada in 1690 were to come next. The government of New Hampshire supposed these grants were made in order to secure the possession of a tract of country challenged by them as within their bounds. This might have weight with some leading men who were acquainted with the controversy, but there was a fondness for granting land in any part of the province. A condition of settling a certain number of families in a few years, ordinarily, was annexed to the grants, but the court, by multiplying their grants, rendered the performance of the condition impracticable, there not being people enough within the province willing to leave the old settled towns, and the grantees not being able to procure settlers from abroad.

The settlement of the province was retarded by it, a trade of land jobbing made many idle persons, imaginary wealth was created, which was attended with some of the mischievous effects of the paper currency, viz., idleness and bad economy, a real expense was occasioned to many persons, besides the purchase of the grantees' title, for every township by law was made a propriety, and their frequent meetings, schemes for settlement, and other preparatory business, occasioned many charges. In some few towns, houses were built and some part of the lands cleared. In a short time, a new line being determined for the northern boundary of the Massachusetts colony, many of these townships were found to be without it. The government of New Hampshire, for the Crown, laid claim to some of them, and certain persons, calling themselves proprietors under Mason, to others, and the Massachusetts people, after a further expense in contesting their title, either wholly lost the lands or made such composition as the new claimers thought fit to agree to.

C. COLONIAL COMMERCE

WHILE the economic life of the colonies rested upon the broad base of agriculture, its prosperity and growth were dependent upon ocean-borne commerce. Once the problem of raising enough food to eat had been solved in the first colonies, they began to produce a surplus for which the only outlet was outside of the colonies. The plantation colonies had a ready market from the start for such products as tobacco and sugar, and, later on, for rice and indigo. The Acts of Trade and Navigation[1] declared such products to be "enumerated articles", which could be shipped only to England or to other colonies. Thus the increase in production in the plantation colonies meant an increase in the direct trade with England and (after 1707) with Scotland. In return, these colonies received large quantities of manufactured goods.[2] The plantation colonies with their 'staple' crops therefore fitted in with the prevalent conception of the nature of desirable colonies.

Such was not the case with the northern colonies. Because of the soil, the climate, and the inclination of their inhabitants, they produced crops which competed directly with those of England and were therefore denied entry into the British Isles except in times of shortages. It was necessary for their well-being that they find markets elsewhere, and this their merchants did with remarkable success, both inside and outside the British Empire. Trade outside the empire, and particularly with the foreign colonies in the Caribbean area, led to repeated charges that the northern merchants were violators of the Navigation Acts. Only two things are clear. One is that the northern merchants had little use for laws which hampered their trade. The other is that British officials had a fixed opinion that all northern merchants were either actual or incipient smugglers.[3] The fact seems to be that the bulk of colonial trade flowed in legal channels, but the existence of the two opposing views was equally real and influential in the determination of policies.

Within the empire itself the northern merchants had certain competitive advantages. The New England fishermen and merchants came to play a dominating role in the cod fisheries and fish were marketed all the way from the West Indies to the Mediterranean countries. The plentiful timber supply in the colonies led to the growth of a colonial shipbuilding industry which competed favourably with English shipbuilders and enabled the colonial merchants to take an ever larger share of the carrying trade of the empire.

Although at least half of the total trade of the colonies was still with the British Isles at the end of the colonial period, there were other areas of trade equally important, not only to the colonies, but to Britain as well. The trade among the mainland colonies themselves grew steadily. Merchants carried food, lumber, and manufactured products ranging all the way from imports from Britain to the things produced in colonial homes and in the shops of a growing artisan class. Colonial manufactures ranged all the way from hand-hammered nails to furniture and fine silver.

During the eighteenth century there was a steady rise in the trade with southern Europe. The colonies exported fish and grain and imported salt, wines, and cash in return. By the end of the colonial period the trade with the Mediterranean, for some

[1] No. 51.　　　　[2] No. 55, Tables I and II.　　　　[3] No. 53.

colonies at least, equalled in importance the trade with the West Indies.[1] Equally specialized but even more lucrative was the slave trade to the west coast of Africa, in which the colonies shared, and upon which was founded more than one colonial fortune.[2] However, it was the West India trade which was for so long indispensable to the mainland colonies. It was the trade too which caused more trouble between the colonies and Britain than any other branch of colonial commerce, and for years after the independence of the United States quarrels over it embittered Anglo-American relations.

As the West Indies concentrated on the production of sugar and other tropical crops, they largely gave up the production of food. In time they became almost completely dependent on the mainland colonies, not only for food but for livestock and for the lumber they used for buildings and for the casks and barrels in which they shipped their crops. The merchants of the mainland colonies carried such things to the islands and in return took cargoes of molasses, rum, sugar, and dyewoods. In addition, they usually received bills of exchange on London and specie, much of which came from the trade with the Spanish and French colonies in the Caribbean area.[3]

The profits of the West India trade had an intimate relation to the direct trade between the northern colonies and Britain. From year to year those colonies imported far more from Britain than they exported to her, and thus they always had an adverse balance of trade against them. They made it up in many ways. They sold their imports everywhere in the colonies. They built and sold ships. They earned freights. But the most important factor, or at least the one with which they showed the most concern, was the profits of the West India trade, and particularly the bills of exchange and specie they acquired in the course of it.

The trade of the colonial merchants was therefore an intricate process[4] whose nature and difficulties were not revealed by simple figures of imports and exports into and out of Britain.[5] Yet British policy makers all too often looked only at such figures and came to the too simple conclusion that the northern colonies did not fit into the empire as did the plantation colonies. Never did such figures reveal the complex web by which the commerce of the empire was carried on. Any interference with that web was bound to cause alarm and to interfere with the whole structure of trade, yet all too few people realized it. Such was the case with the Molasses Act of 1733 by which Parliament sought to hamper the trade between the mainland colonies and the foreign West Indies for the benefit of the British West India planters.[6] It was passed at a time when the British islands had begun their decline and could not begin to consume the products of the mainland colonies. Furthermore, they could not supply the demand for sugar and other produce, at least in competition with the cheaper sugar of the French islands. If the Act had ever been enforced it might have proved disastrous, not only for the mainland colonies, but for their direct trade with Britain as well. As it was, when an attempt was made to enforce it in the Revenue Act of 1764, it was given up within two years. British merchants realized, as the politicians did not, how important the foreign islands were to their own trade with the mainland colonies.[7]

Despite such underlying realities, the commerce of the northern colonies, like their agriculture, was always looked upon askance by British officials. Either they did not

---

[1] No. 55, Table III.   [2] No. 81.   [3] No. 55, Tables III, IV, V.   [4] No. 54.
[5] No. 55, Tables I and II.   [6] No. 51E.   [7] Nos. 99, 111, and 114.

fit in with their ideas of the proper role of colonies or they competed with economic interests in England. However shortsighted they might be in terms of the larger interests of the empire, such views did exist, and were influential in the determination of colonial policies. The plantation colonies were consistently favoured at the expense of the northern ones, while the colonies as a whole were expected to subordinate their interests to those of English farmers, merchants, and manufacturers.

The colonists were seldom willing to accept such subordination, and when it was to their advantage they ignored or evaded British restrictions as best they could. The contemporary arguments resulting from the conflict of interests have found their way into most of the subsequent histories of the period.

Some writers argue that membership in the empire was a benefit to the colonies. Others argue that the colonies were simply the victims of selfish exploitation by Britain and that they would have advanced far more rapidly if they had been free to trade as they pleased. There is doubtless some truth in both positions, much depending on the particular branch of commerce under discussion. But to achieve a balanced view, one must turn from the theory and purpose embodied in legislation to the underlying economic facts which shaped colonial commerce in particular, and colonial development in general. Too often the historians, like contemporary pamphleteers, have not done so.

On the whole, it would seem a valid generalization to say that the course of colonial commerce was as much determined by such factors as natural resources, the relative costs of labour and land in the colonies, and the cheapness of English manufactured goods, as it was by parliamentary legislation.

51A–E. The Acts of Trade and Navigation

An elaborate discussion of the principles of mercantilism is unnecessary, for whatever they were, *mercantilism* their concrete application in the form of specific legislation and regulations was what concerned the colonies. The aim of mercantilism was a self-sufficient state. It involved restraints on the natural course of economic development. Those restraints meant that (1) goods and produce going to and coming from the colonies must be shipped only in the ships of the mother country or the colonies; (2) certain specific colonial goods must be shipped only to the mother country; (3) the mother country should have a monopoly of shipping manufactured goods to the colonies; (4) preferential treatment should be granted to certain colonial products in the markets of the mother country; (5) the colonies should be forbidden to engage in manufactures competing with those of the mother country, and should be encouraged to develop manufactures supplementary to them.

The English Acts of Trade and Navigation and Acts relating to colonial manufactures are embraced within such general principles. As early as the fourteenth century, legislation provided that goods coming into England must be brought in English ships. In 1621 Virginia tobacco was ordered brought only to England, and soon tobacco growing in England was forbidden. The first legislation specifically relating to the colonies came during the Commonwealth. In 1650 foreign ships were forbidden to trade with the colonies and in 1651 it was provided that ships bringing goods to England or her colonies must be English owned, with the captain and the "major part" of the crew being English. This legislation was aimed primarily at the Dutch, who had a large share of the carrying-trade of the western world, including the English colonies.

The Navigation Act of 1660 (12 Charles II, c. 18) (No. 51A) embodied the principles of the Acts of 1650–1651 and made them more specific. The captains must be English and the crews of the ships must be three fourths English. The colonists were regarded as Englishmen under such legislation. The new idea in the Act was the inclusion of 'enumerated articles': colonial produce which could be shipped only to England or to other English colonies. The Act of 1663 (15 Charles II, c. 7) (No. 51B) was known as the 'staple Act' for it provided that European goods shipped to the colonies must be laden in England. A few exceptions such as salt for colonial fisheries and wines from the Madeiras and Azores were allowed. The Act of 1673 (25 Charles II, c. 7) (No. 51C) was passed for the purpose of plugging a loop-hole in the Act of 1660. According to that Act, enumerated articles shipped from one colony to another were free of duty. Having thus technically obeyed the law, merchants and shipowners continued to ship enumerated articles directly from colonial ports to Europe. The Act of 1673 therefore levied duties, afterwards known as 'plantation duties', if shippers did not post bonds to carry enumerated articles directly to England from the colony of origin. The Act of 1696 (7 & 8 William III, c. 22) (No. 51D) was primarily an administrative measure to tighten up enforcement of previous legislation. This was the final Act of Trade and Navigation although it was to be followed by multitudes of orders, regulations, and instructions to clarify the uncertainties of it and of previous acts.

The Molasses Act of 1733 (6 George II, c. 13) (No. 51E) did not fall within the general principles outlined above. The Act was the direct result of the activity of a specific pressure group: the West India planters. They were alarmed at the competition of the foreign sugar islands and the rapid growth of their trade with the mainland colonies, and they tried to stop it. It is a clear example of the use of Parliamentary action to exploit one part of an empire for the benefit of another. It was an attempt that failed for the Act was never effectively enforced. Discriminatory duties against foreign molasses were made 'perpetual' in the Revenue Act of 1764 (No. 91) and more effective enforcement provided for, but discrimination was given up in the 'Sugar Act' of 1766 (No. 114) when both British and foreign molasses were required to pay the same duty on entering colonial ports.

The following documents consist for the most part of only those portions of the Navigation Acts relating specifically to the American colonies. The sections relating to other than colonial policies are omitted. The Act of 1660 (No. 51A) is printed more fully in *English Colonial Documents*, vol. VIII, No. 203, wherein both the colonial and the more specifically English policies are set forth.

In the following selections the editor has occasionally summarized portions of the Acts. Such editorial summaries are included within square brackets.

51A. The Navigation Act of 1660 (13 September 1660) (12 Chas. II, c. 18)

Printed: Danby Pickering, ed., *The Statutes at Large*, VII, pp. 452–454, 459–460.

For the increase of shipping and encouragement of the navigation of this nation wherein, under the good providence and protection of God, the wealth, safety, and strength of this kingdom is so much concerned; (2) be it enacted by the king's most excellent Majesty, and by the Lords and Commons in this present Parliament assembled, and by the authority thereof, that from and after the first day of December, one thousand six hundred and sixty, and from thence forward, no goods or commodities whatsoever shall be imported into or exported out of any lands, islands, plantations, or territories to his Majesty belonging or in his possession, or which may hereafter belong unto or be in the possession of his Majesty, his heirs, and successors, in Asia, Africa, or America, in any other ship or ships, vessel or vessels whatsoever, but in such ships or vessels as do truly and without fraud belong only to the people of England or Ireland, dominion of Wales or town of Berwick upon Tweed, or are of the built of and belonging to any the said lands, islands, plantations, or territories, as the proprietors and right owners thereof, and whereof the master and three fourths of the mariners at least are English; (3) under the penalty of the forfeiture and loss of all the goods and commodities which shall be imported into or exported out of any the aforesaid places in any other ship or vessel, as also of the ship or vessel, with all its guns, furniture, tackle, ammunition, and apparel; one third part thereof to his Majesty, his heirs and successors; one third part to the governor of such land, plantation, island, or territory where such default shall be committed, in case the said ship or goods be there seized, or otherwise that third part also to his Majesty, his heirs and successors; and the other third part to him or them who shall seize, inform, or sue for the same in any court of record, by bill, information, plaint, or other action, wherein no essoin, protection, or wager of law shall be allowed; (4) and all admirals and other commanders at sea of any the ships of war or other ship having commission from his Majesty or from his heirs or successors, are hereby authorized and strictly required to seize and bring in as prize all such ships or vessels as shall have offended contrary hereunto, and deliver them to the court of admiralty, there to be proceeded against; and in case of condemnation, one moiety of such forfeitures shall be to the use of such admirals or commanders and their companies, to be divided and proportioned amongst them according to the rules and orders of the sea in case of ships taken prize; and the other moiety to the use of his Majesty, his heirs and successors.

II. And be it enacted, that no alien or person not born within the allegiance of our sovereign lord the king, his heirs and successors, or naturalized, or made a free denizen, shall from and after the first day of February, which will be in the year of our Lord one thousand six hundred sixty-one, exercise the trade or occupation of a merchant or factor in any the said places; (2) upon pain of the forfeiture and loss of all his goods and chattels, or which are in his possession; one third to his Majesty, his heirs and successors; one third to the governor of the plantation where such person shall so offend; and the other third to him or them that shall inform or sue for the same in any of his Majesty's courts in the plantation where such offence shall be committed; (3) and all governors of the said lands, islands, plantations, or territories, and every of them, are hereby strictly required and commanded, and all who hereafter shall be made governors of any such islands, plantations, or territories, by his Majesty, his heirs or successors, shall before their entrance into their government take a solemn oath to do their utmost, that every the afore-mentioned clauses, and all the matters and things therein contained, shall be punctually and *bona fide* observed according to the true intent and meaning thereof; (4) and upon complaint and proof made before his Majesty, his heirs or successors, or such as shall be by him or them thereunto authorized and appointed, that any the said governors have been willingly and wittingly negligent in doing their duty accordingly, that the said governor so offending shall be removed from his government.

III. And it is further enacted by the authority aforesaid, that no goods or commodities whatsoever, of the growth, production or manufacture of Africa, Asia, or America, or of any part thereof, or which are described or laid down in the usual maps or cards of those places, be imported into England, Ireland, or Wales, islands of Guernsey and Jersey, or town of Berwick upon Tweed, in any other ship or ships, vessel or vessels whatsoever, but in such as do truly and without fraud belong only to the people of England or Ireland, dominion of Wales, or town of Berwick upon Tweed, or of the lands, islands, plantations or territories in Asia, Africa, or America, to his Majesty belonging, as the proprietors and right owners thereof, and whereof the master, and three fourths at least of the mariners are English; (2) under the penalty of the forfeiture of all such goods and commodities, and of the ship or vessel in which they were imported, with all her guns, tackle, furniture, ammunition, and apparel; one moiety to his Majesty, his heirs and successors; and the other moiety to him or them who shall seize, inform or sue for the same in any court of record, by bill, information, plaint or other action, wherein no essoin, protection or wager of law shall be allowed.

XVIII. And it is further enacted by the authority aforesaid, that from and after the first day of April, which shall be in the year of our Lord one thousand six hundred sixty-one, no sugars, tobacco, cotton-wool, indigoes, ginger, fustic, or other dyeing wood, of the growth, production, or manufacture of any English plantations in America, Asia, or Africa, shall be shipped, carried, conveyed, or transported from any of the said English plantations to any land, island, territory, dominion, port, or place whatsoever, other than to such other English plantations as do belong to his Majesty, his heirs and successors, or to the kingdom of England or Ireland, or principality of Wales, or town of Berwick upon Tweed, there to be laid on shore; (2) under the penalty of the forfeiture of the said goods, or the full value thereof, as also of the ship, with all her guns, tackle, apparel, ammunition, and furniture; the one moiety to the king's Majesty, his heirs and successors, and the other to moiety to him or them that shall seize, inform, or sue for the same in any court of record, by bill, plaint, or information, wherein no essoin, protection, or wager of law shall be allowed.

XIX. And be it further enacted by the authority aforesaid, that for every ship or vessel, which from and after the five and twentieth day of December in the year of our Lord one thousand six hundred and sixty shall set sail out of or from England, Ireland, Wales, or town of Berwick upon Tweed, for any English plantation in America, Asia, or Africa, sufficient bond shall be given with one surety to the chief officers of the custom-house of such port or place from whence the said ship shall set sail, to the value of one thousand pounds, if the ship be of less burden than one hundred tons; and of the sum of two thousand pounds, if the ship shall be of greater burden; that in case the said ship or vessel shall load any of the said commodities at any of the said English plantations, that the same commodities shall be by the said ship brought to some port of England, Ireland, Wales, or to the port or town of Berwick upon Tweed, and shall there unload and put on shore the same, the danger of the seas only excepted; (2) and for all ships coming from any other port or place to any of the aforesaid plantations, who by this act are permitted to trade there, that the governor of such English plantations shall before the said ship or vessel be permitted to load on board any of the said commodities, take bond in manner and to the value aforesaid, for each respective ship or vessel, that such ship or vessel shall carry all the aforesaid goods that shall be laden on board in the said ship to some other of his Majesty's English plantations, or to England, Ireland, Wales, or town of Berwick upon Tweed; (3) and that every ship or vessel which shall load or take on board any of the aforesaid goods, until such bond given to the said governor, or certificate produced from the officers of any custom-house of England, Ireland, Wales, or of the town of Berwick, that such bonds have been there duly given, shall be forfeited with all her guns, tackle, apparel, and furniture, to be employed and recovered in manner as aforesaid; and the said governors and every of them shall twice in every year after the first day of January one thousand six hundred and sixty, return true copies of all such bonds by him so taken, to the chief officers of the custom in London.

51B. The Navigation Act of 1663 (27 July 1663) (15 Chas. II, c. 7)

Printed: Pickering, *Statutes at Large*, VIII, pp. 161–163.

V. And in regard his Majesty's plantations beyond the seas are inhabited and peopled by his subjects of this his kingdom of England; for the maintaining a greater correspondence and kindness between them, and keeping them in a firmer dependence upon it, and rendering them yet more beneficial and advantageous unto it in the further employment and increase of English shipping and seamen, vent of English woollen and other manufactures and commodities, rendering the navigation to and from the same more safe and cheap, and making this kingdom a staple, not only of the commodities of those plantations, but also of the commodities of other countries and places, for the supplying of them; and it being the usage of other nations to keep their plantations trade to themselves.

VI. Be it enacted, and it is hereby enacted, that from and after the five and twentieth day of March one thousand six hundred sixty-four, no commodity of the growth, production, or manufacture of Europe shall be imported into any land, island, plantation, colony, territory, or place to his Majesty belonging, or which shall hereafter belong unto or be in the possession of his Majesty, his heirs and successors, in Asia, Africa, or America (Tangier only excepted) but what shall be *bona fide*, and without fraud, laden and shipped in England, Wales, or the town of Berwick upon Tweed, and in English built shipping . . .; and whereof the master and three fourths of the mariners at least are English, and which shall be carried directly thence to the said lands, islands, plantations, colonies, territories, or places, and from no other place or places whatsoever; any law, statute, or usage to the contrary notwithstanding; (2) under the penalty of the loss of all such commodities of the growth, production, or manufacture of Europe, as shall be imported into any of them from any other place whatsoever, by land or water; and if by water, of the ship or vessel also in which they were imported, with all her guns, tackle, furniture, ammunition, and apparel; one third part to his Majesty, his heirs and successors; one third part to the governor of such land, island, plantation, colony, territory, or place, into which such goods were imported, if the said ship, vessel, or goods be there seized or informed against and sued for; or otherwise that third part also to his Majesty, his heirs and successors; and the other third part to him or them who shall seize, inform, or sue for the same in any of his Majesty's courts in such of the said lands, islands, colonies, plantations, territories, or places where the offence was committed, or in any court of record in England, by bill, information, plaint, or other action, wherein no essoin, protection, or wager of law shall be allowed.

VII. Provided always, and be it hereby enacted by the authority aforesaid, that it shall and may be lawful to ship and lade in such ships, and so navigated, as in the foregoing clause is set down and expressed, in any part of Europe, salt for the fisheries of New England and Newfoundland, and to ship and lade in the Madeira's wines of the growth thereof, and to ship and lade in the Western islands of Azores wines of the growth of the said islands, and to ship and take in servants or horses in Scotland or Ireland, and to ship or lade in Scotland all sorts of victual of the growth or production of Scotland, and to ship or lade in Ireland all sorts of victual of the growth or production of Ireland, and the same to transport into any of the said lands, islands, plantations, colonies, territories, or places; anything in the foregoing clause to the contrary in any wise notwithstanding.

VIII. And for the better prevention of frauds, be it enacted and it is hereby enacted, that from and after the five and twentieth day of March one thousand six hundred sixty and four, every person or persons importing by land any goods or commodities whatsoever into any the said lands, islands, plantations, colonies, territories, or places, shall deliver to the governor of such land, island, plantation, colony, territory, or place, or to such person or officer as shall be by him thereunto authorized and appointed, within four and twenty hours after such importation, his and their names and surnames, and a true inventory and particular of all such goods or commodities; (2) and no ship or vessel coming to any such land, island, plantation, colony, territory, or place, shall lade or unlade any goods or commodities whatsoever, until the master or commander of such ship or vessel shall first have made known to the governor of such land, island, plantation, colony, territory, or place, or such other person or officer as shall be by him thereunto authorized and appointed, the arrival of the said ship or vessel, with her name, and the name and surname of her master or commander, and have shown to him that she is an English built ship, or made good by producing such certificate, as abovesaid, that she is a ship or vessel *bona fide* belonging to England, Wales, or the town of Berwick, and navigated with an English master, and three fourth parts of the mariners at least Englishmen, and have delivered to such governor or other person or officer a true and perfect inventory or invoice of her lading, together with the place or places in which the said goods were laden or taken into the said ship or vessel. . . .

51C. The Navigation Act of 1673 (29 March 1673) (25 Chas. II, c. 7)

Printed: Pickering, *Statutes at Large*, VIII, pp. 398–400.

II . . .

(2) And whereas by one act passed in this present parliament in the twelfth year of your Majesty's reign, entitled, An act for encouragement of shipping and navigation, and by several other laws passed since that time, it is permitted to ship, carry, convey, and transport sugar, tobacco, cotton-wool, indigo, ginger, fustic, and all other dyeing-wood of the growth, production, and manufacture of any of your Majesty's plantations in America, Asia, or Africa, from the places of their growth, production, and manufacture, to any of your Majesty's plantations in those parts (Tangier only excepted), and that without paying of custom for the same, either at the lading or unlading of the said commodities, by means whereof the trade and navigation in those commodities, from one plantation to another, is greatly increased; (3) and the inhabitants of divers of those colonies, not contenting themselves with being supplied with those commodities for their own use, free from all customs (while the subjects of this your kingdom of England have paid great customs and imposition for what of them hath been spent here) but contrary to the express letter of the aforesaid laws, have brought into divers parts of Europe great quantities thereof, and do also daily vend great quantities thereof, to the shipping of other nations who bring them into divers parts of Europe, to the great hurt and diminution of your Majesty's customs, and of the trade and navigation of this your kingdom; (4) for the prevention thereof, . . . that from and after the first day of September which shall be in the year of our Lord one thousand six hundred seventy and three,

if any ship or vessel which by law may trade in any of your Majesty's plantations, shall come to any of them to ship and take on board any of the aforesaid commodities, and that bond shall not be first given with one sufficient surety to bring the same to England or Wales, or the town of Berwick upon Tweed, and to no other place, and there to unload and put the same on shore (the danger of the seas only excepted) that there shall be answered and paid to your Majesty, your heirs and successors, for so much of the said commodities as shall be laded and put on board such ship or vessel, these following rates or duties: that is to say, for sugar white the hundredweight, containing one hundred and twelve pounds, five shillings; and brown sugar and muscovadoes, the hundredweight, containing one hundred and twelve pounds, one shilling and six pence; (5) for tobacco, the pound, one penny; for cotton-wool, the pound, one halfpenny; for indigo, the pound, two pence; for ginger, the hundredweight, containing one hundred and twelve pounds, one shilling; (6) for logwood, the hundredweight, containing one hundred and twelve pounds, five pounds; for fustic and all other dyeing-wood, the hundredweight, containing one hundred and twelve pounds, six pence; and also for every pound of cocoanuts, one penny; (7) to be levied, collected, and paid at such places and to such collectors and other officers as shall be appointed in their respective plantations to collect, levy, and receive the same, before the lading thereof, and under such penalties both to the officers and upon the goods, as for nonpayment of or defrauding his Majesty of his customs in England.

IV. And in case any person or persons liable by this law to pay any of the duties aforementioned, shall not have moneys wherewith to answer and pay the same, be it further enacted by the authority aforesaid, that the officers appointed to collect the same shall accept instead of such moneys such a proportion of the commodities to be shipped as shall amount to the value thereof, according to the current rate of the said commodities in such plantation respectively.

51D. The Navigation Act of 1696 (10 April 1696) (7 & 8 Wm. III, c. 22)

Printed: Pickering, *Statutes at Large*, IX, pp. 428–437.

Whereas notwithstanding divers acts made for the encouragement of the navigation of this kingdom, . . . great abuses are daily committed to the prejudice of the English navigation, and the loss of a great part of the plantation trade to this kingdom, by the artifice and cunning of ill-disposed persons: for remedy whereof for the future. . . .

II. Be it enacted, . . . that after the five and twentieth day of March, one thousand six hundred and ninety-eight, no goods or merchandises whatsoever shall be imported into, or exported out of, any colony or plantation . . . or shall be laden in, or carried from any one port or place in the said colonies or plantations to any other port or place in the same, the kingdom of England, dominion of Wales, or town of Berwick upon Tweed, in any ship or bottom but what is or shall be of the built of England, or of the built of Ireland, or the said colonies or plantations, and wholly owned by the people thereof, or any of them, and navigated with the masters and three fourths of the mariners of the said places only (except such ships only as are or shall be taken as prize, and condemnation thereof made in one of the courts of admiralty in England, Ireland, or the said colonies or plantations, to be navigated by the master and three fourths of the mariners English, or of the said plantations as aforesaid, and whereof the property doth belong to Englishmen; and also except for the space of three years, such foreign built ships as shall be employed by the commissioners of his Majesty's navy for the time being, or upon contract with them, in bringing only masts, timber, and other naval stores for the king's service from his Majesty's colonies or plantations to this kingdom, to be navigated as aforesaid, and whereof the property doth belong to Englishmen), under pain of forfeiture of ship and goods; one third part whereof to be to the use of his Majesty, his heirs and successors, one third part to the governor of the said colonies or plantations, and the other third part to the person who shall inform and sue for the same, by bill, plaint or information, in any of his Majesty's courts of record at Westminster, or in any court in his Majesty's plantations, where such offence shall be committed.

IV. [Colonial governors were required to take an oath by the [Navigation Act of 1660] to enforce the clauses of the Act preceding the oath, but were not "strictly obliged by that oath to put in execution the subsequent clauses of the said act, although some of the clauses following are of great importance, and tend greatly to the security of the plantation trade" and since other laws have been passed since then for regulating and securing the plantation trade, all present and future governors and commanders-in-chief in the colonies must take an oath to do their utmost to enforce all the acts of Parliament relating to the colonies and plantations. If any governor or commander-in-chief neglects to take the oath or is "wittingly or willingly negligent" he shall be removed from office and forfeit one thousand pounds sterling.]

V. [Whereas by the [Navigation Act of 1663] colonial governors were empowered to appoint an officer to carry out provisions of the Act, which officer "is there commonly known by the name of the naval officer" and whereas through connivance or negligence, frauds and abuses have been committed, all such officers must give security to the Commissioner of Customs in England for the faithful performance of their duty. Colonial governors are to be answerable for "offenses, neglects or misdemeanours" of persons appointed by them.]

VI. And for the more effectual preventing of frauds, and regulating abuses in the plantation trade in America, be it further enacted by the authority aforesaid, that all ships coming into, or going out of, any of the said plantations, and lading or unlading any goods or commodities, whether the same be his Majesty's ships of war, or merchant ships, and the masters and commanders thereof, and their ladings, shall be subject and liable to the same rules, visitations, searches, penalties, and forfeitures, as to the entering, lading or discharging their respective ships and ladings, as ships and their ladings, and the commanders and masters of ships, are subject and liable unto in this kingdom, by virtue of an act of Parliament made in the fourteenth year of the reign of King Charles the second, entitled, An Act for preventing frauds, and regulating abuses in his Majesty's customs; and that the officers for collecting and managing his Majesty's revenue, and inspecting the plantation trade, in any of the said plantations, shall have the same powers and authorities, for visiting and searching of ships, and taking their entries, and for seizing and securing or bringing on shore any of the goods prohibited to be imported or exported into or out of any the said plantations, or for which any duties are payable, or ought to have been paid, by any of the before mentioned acts, as are provided for the officers of the customs in England by the said last mentioned act made in the fourteenth year of the reign of King Charles the second, and also to enter houses or warehouses, to search for and seize any such goods; and that all the wharfingers, and owners of quays and wharfs, or any lighter-men, bargemen, watermen, porters, or other persons assisting in the conveyance, concealment or rescue of any of the said goods, or in the hindering or resistance of any of the said officers in the performance of their duty, and the boats, barges, lighters, or other vessels, employed in the conveyance of such goods, shall be subject to the like pains and penalties as are provided by the same act made in the fourteenth year of the reign of King Charles the second, in relation to prohibited or uncustomed goods in this kingdom; and that the like assistance shall be given to the said officers in the execution of their office, as by the said last mentioned act is provided for the officers in England; and also that the said officers shall be subject to the same penalties and forfeitures, for any corruptions, frauds, connivances, or concealments, in violation of any the before mentioned laws, as any officers of the customs in England are liable to, by virtue of the said last mentioned act; and also that in case any officer or officers in the plantations shall be sued or molested for any thing done in the execution of their office, the said officer shall and may plead the general issue, and shall give this or other custom acts in evidence, and the judge to allow thereof, have and enjoy the like privileges and advantages, as are allowed by law to the officers of his Majesty's customs in England.

VII. And it is hereby further enacted, that all the penalties and forfeitures before mentioned, not in this act particularly disposed of, shall be one third part to the use of his Majesty, his heirs and successors, and one third part to the governor of the colony or plantation where the offence shall be committed, and the other third part to such person or persons as shall sue for the same, to be recovered in any of his Majesty's courts at Westminster, or in the kingdom of Ireland, or in the court of admiralty held in his Majesty's plantations respectively, where such offence shall be committed, at the pleasure of the officer or informer, or in any other plantation belonging to any subject of England, wherein no essoin, protection, or wager of law, shall be allowed; and that where any question shall arise concerning the importation or exportation of any goods into or out of the said plantations, in such case the proof shall lie upon the owner or claimer, and the claimer shall be reputed the importer or owner thereof.

VIII. And whereas in some of his Majesty's American plantations, a doubt or misconstruction has arisen upon the before mentioned act, made in the five and twentieth year of the reign of King Charles the second, whereby certain duties are laid upon the commodities therein enumerated (which by law may be transported from one plantation to another for the supply of each others wants), as if the same were by the payment of those duties in one plantation, discharged from giving the securities intended by the aforesaid acts, made in the twelfth, two and twentieth, and

13

three and twentieth years of the reign of King Charles the second, and consequently be at liberty to go to any foreign market in Europe, without coming to England, Wales, or Berwick: it is hereby further enacted and declared, that notwithstanding the payment of the aforesaid duties in any of the said plantations, none of the said goods shall be shipped or laden on board, until such security shall be given as is required by the said acts, made in the twelfth, two and twentieth and three and twentieth years of the reign of King Charles the second, to carry the same to England, Wales, or Berwick, or to some other of his Majesty's plantations, and so *toties quoties*, as any of the said goods shall be brought to be reshipped or laden in any of the said plantations, under the penalty and forfeiture of ship and goods, to be divided and disposed of as aforesaid.

IX. And it is further enacted and declared by the authority aforesaid, that all laws, by-laws, usages or customs, at this time, or which hereafter shall be in practice, or endeavoured or pretended to be in force or practice, in any of the said plantations, which are in any wise repugnant to the before mentioned laws, or any of them, so far as they do relate to the said plantations, or any of them, or which are any ways repugnant to this present act, or to any other law hereafter to be made in this kingdom, so far as such law shall relate to and mention the said plantations, are illegal, null and void, to all intents and purposes whatsoever.

X. [Great frauds have been committed by Scotchmen and others by counterfeiting certificates of security to bring plantation goods to England or Wales; and certificates of having discharged plantation goods in England or Wales or of having loaded European goods in England or Wales, thereby evading transshipment through England. Therefore it is further enacted that when governors or customs officers in the colonies have reasonable suspicion that certificates of having given security in England are false, they shall require sufficient security for discharge in England or Wales. Where there is cause to suspect that the certificate of having loaded plantation goods in Britain is false, such officers shall not vacate the security given in the plantation until they are informed by the customs commissioners in England that the certificate is true. Persons counterfeiting or altering any such certificate or permit or knowingly use such shall forfeit five hundred pounds and the certificate or permit shall be invalid.]

XI. And for the better executing the several acts of Parliament relating to the plantation trade, be it enacted by the authority aforesaid, that the Lord Treasurer, Commissioners of the Treasury, and the Commissioners of the Customs in England for the time being, shall and may constitute and appoint such and so many officers of the customs in any city, town, river, port, harbour or creek, of or belonging to any of the islands, tracts of land and proprieties, when and as often as to them shall seem needful; be it further also enacted, that upon any actions, suits, and informations that shall be brought, commenced, or entered in the said plantations, upon any law or statute concerning his Majesty's duties, or ships or goods to be forfeited by reason of any unlawful importations or exportations, there shall not be any jury, but of such only as are natives of England or Ireland, or are born in his Majesty's said plantations; and also that upon all such actions, suits, and informations, the offences may be laid or alleged in any colony, province, county, precinct, or division of any of the said plantations where such offences are alleged to be committed, at the pleasure of the officer or informer.

XII. Provided always, that all places of trust in the courts of law, or what relates to the treasury of the said islands, shall, from the making of this act, be in the hands of the native-born subjects of England or Ireland, or of the said islands.

XIII. [By the act of 1670–71, Ireland is left out of the condition of the bonds therein required; the same Act required that prior to loading enumerated goods in the plantation, ships should give bond that all such goods would be carried to another English plantation or to Great Britain. No time limit had been set for returning certificates of proof that goods were discharged as required by the bond, and the sureties for said bonds had often been persons of uncertain and unknown residence, rendering the bonds ineffectual to the intended purposes: it is therefore enacted that in all such bonds hereafter given in the plantations, the sureties are to be persons of known residence and of known ability for the value of the bond. And the condition of the bonds shall be that within 18 months of their date (the danger of the seas excepted) certificate be produced that the goods mentioned have been discharged in a proper port.]

XIV. [Ships carrying American produce have been unloaded in Scotland and Ireland, contrary to existing law, under the pretence they were driven there by weather, lack of provisions, or other cause. After December 1, 1696, it shall be unlawful under any pretext to unload in Scotland or Ireland any goods or merchandise the growth or product of the American plantations unless they have first been landed in England or Wales and the proper duties paid. Penalty to be forfeiture of the ship and goods, with three-fourths to the crown and the other fourth to him or them bringing the action.]

XVI. [Persons claiming any right or propriety in any islands or tracts of land upon the continent of America, by charter or letters patent, shall not sell them to any other than natural-born subjects of England, Ireland, Wales, or Berwick without prior consent of the Crown by order in council. Governors nominated or appointed by such proprietors to be approved of by the king and take the oaths required of governors in the king's other colonies, before entering upon the government.]

XVII. And for a more effectual prevention of frauds which may be used to elude the intention of this act, by colouring foreign ships under English names; be it further enacted by the authority aforesaid, that from and after the five and twentieth day of March, which shall be in the year of our Lord one thousand six hundred ninety-eight, no ship or vessel whatsoever shall be deemed or pass as a ship of the built of England, Ireland, Wales, Berwick, Guernsey, Jersey, or any of his Majesty's plantations in America, so as to be qualified to trade to, from, or in any of the plantations, until the person or persons claiming property in such ship or vessel shall register the same . . . [with proper proof and oath of ownership as herein prescribed].

XVIII. [This oath, attested by the governor or custom officer administering it, shall be registered and delivered to the master of the ship, with a duplicate of the register transmitted for entry in the general register of the customs commissioners in

London. After March 25, 1798, any ship engaging in trade with the American colonies without such proof shall be liable to such prosecution and forfeiture as any foreign ship (except prizes condemned in the High Court of Admiralty) would be liable to for trading to these plantations.]

XIX. [Ships taken at sea and condemned as prizes in the High Court of Admiralty to be specially registered, with proper oaths and proof of entire English ownership, before being allowed the privileges of an English built ship.]

XX. Provided also, that nothing in this act shall be construed to require the registering any fisher-boats, hoys [coasting vessels], lighters, barges, or any open boats or other vessels (though of English or plantation built) whose navigation is confined to the rivers or coasts of the same plantation or place where they trade respectively, but only of such of them as cross the seas to or from any of the lands, islands, places, or territories, in this act before recited, or from one plantation to another.

XXI. [No ship's name registered shall be changed without new registration. Such new registration also is required if ownership is transferred to another port. If there is any change of ownership in the same port, by the sale of one or more shares in any registered ship, this is to be acknowledged by endorsement on the registration certificate before two witnesses, to prove that the entire ownership remains English.]

51E. The Molasses Act (17 May 1733) (6 Geo. II, c. 13)

Printed: Pickering, *Statutes at Large*, XVI, p. 374.

Whereas the welfare and prosperity of your Majesty's sugar colonies in America are of the greatest consequence and importance to the trade, navigation, and strength of this kingdom; and whereas the planters of the said sugar colonies have of late years fallen under such great discouragements that they are unable to improve or carry on the sugar trade upon an equal footing with the foreign sugar colonies without some advantage and relief be given to them from Great Britain; for remedy whereof, . . . be it enacted, . . . that from and after the twenty-fifth day of December, one thousand seven hundred and thirty-three, there shall be raised, levied, collected and paid, unto and for the use of his Majesty, his heirs and successors, upon all rum or spirits of the produce or manufacture of any of the colonies or plantations in America, not in the possession or under the dominion of his Majesty, his heirs and successors, which at any time or times within or during the continuance of this act, shall be imported or brought into any of the colonies or plantations in America, which now are or hereafter may be in the possession or under the dominion of his Majesty, his heirs or successors, the sum of nine pence, money of Great Britain, to be paid according to the proportion and value of five shillings and six pence the ounce in silver, for every gallon thereof, and after that rate for any greater or lesser quantity; and upon all molasses or syrups of such foreign produce or manufacture as aforesaid, which shall be imported or brought into any of the said colonies or plantations of or belonging to his Majesty, the sum of six pence of like money for every gallon thereof, and after that rate for any greater or lesser quantity; and upon all sugars and paneles of such foreign growth, produce or manufacture as aforesaid, which shall be imported into any of the said colonies or plantations of or belonging to his Majesty, a duty after the rate of five shillings of like money, for every hundredweight avoirdupois, of the said sugar and paneles, and after that rate for a greater or lesser quantity.

52. Robert Dinwiddie: report on the trade of the colonies (April 1740)

The Board of Trade constantly gathered materials on the state of colonial trade. Customs officials and colonial governors were required to report on every aspect of economic life in the colonies and they did so with varying degrees of thoroughness. Much of this reporting is highly interpretative, for the men of the eighteenth century did not have adequate statistical evidence. Nevertheless, they understood the patterns of trade and its significance.

One of the ablest officials in the customs service was Robert Dinwiddie (1693–1770). He was born in Scotland and worked in his father's counting-house. In 1727 he was appointed a collector of customs for Bermuda. He proved so competent that in 1738 he was made surveyor-general of customs for the southern district, which meant that the area from Maryland and Virginia to the West Indies was under his supervision. His report to the Board of Trade in 1740 was thus based on wide experience with colonial trade. While the accuracy of some of his statistics may be questioned, the general picture of trade which he presents seems to be valid. Later on, Dinwiddie was made lieutenant-governor of Virginia, a post he filled with distinction, although not without difficulty, from 1751 to 1758. Printed: William A. Whitehead, ed., *Documents Relating to the Colonial History of the State of New Jersey*, VI (Newark, 1882), pp. 83–91.

I have been at a great deal of trouble and expense to inform myself of the trade of his Majesty's American Empire, and the annual amount of the national produce of each colony or plantation. I give you the following thoughts, observations, and calculations, which is partly from my own knowledge and from the best informations I possibly could get. If it's thought worthy your notice, it will fully answer my hopes. I shall therefore, to make it somewhat regular. . . .

First: Give you an account of the number of vessels belonging to his Majesty's subjects in America, distinguished by each respective colony, beginning with New-foundland and ending with Barbados.

Secondly. An account of the number of vessels belonging to Great Britain and Ireland trading to the American colonies and plantations.

Thirdly. An estimate of the value of the vessels belonging to America, and those trading from Great Britain and Ireland thereto.

Fourthly. An account of the amount of the natural produce of each plantation by the improvement and manufacturing of the British subjects in those parts.

Fifthly. An estimate of the amount of goods from Great Britain and Ireland annually carried to the plantations in America, and to the coast of Guinea.

Sixthly. The amount of cash, dye woods, drugs, cocoa, etc., brought into our plantations, being the consequence of a trade with Spanish and French colonies.

Seventhly. The whole brought into an account by which you will be able to observe the considerable value of our American trade.

I then shall endeavour to give an account of the number of subjects in each colony fit to carry arms, this entirely from information, and then the account of slaves used in the sugar plantations, their value and value of the works, etc., necessary for sugar plantations.

First. Is account of the vessels belonging to his Majesty's subjects in America distinguished by each colony, beginning at Newfoundland and ending at Barbados:

	Vessels
Belonging to Newfoundland	25
The government of New England vessels of different denominations used in foreign trade ..	750
In the same government entirely employed in fishing and coasting being sloops and schooners ..	350
In Connecticut and Rhode Island in foreign trade	260
In Ditto, used in fishing and coasting sloops and schooners ..	150
In New York and Jerseys, in foreign trade and in coasting, etc.	60
In Pennsylvania and the lower counties	70
In Maryland	60
In Virginia	80
In North Carolina	25
In South Carolina	25
In Bermuda	75
In Providence and Bahama Islands	20
In Jamaica	30
In Leeward and Virgin Islands	35
In Barbados	20
	2,035

You'll please to observe there is two thousand and thirty-five sail of vessels of all dimensions and denominations belonging to his Majesty's subjects in America, which, I believe, is rather under than above the exact number, but must notice that upwards of five hundred of them are small and used in the fishery and coasting trade, which will be noticed when we come to the valuation of them.

Secondly. Here follows the account from information of the ships, etc., trading to and from America belonging to Great Britain and Ireland distinguished by the trade they are concerned in:

	Vessels
To Newfoundland with the fishermen and those employed in carrying fish to the different markets ..	80
To New England and Nova Scotia	20
To Connecticut and Rhode Island	6
To New York and the Jerseys	8
To Pennsylvania	10
To Maryland	95
To Virginia	120
To North Carolina	30
To South Carolina	200
To Jamaica	100
To Leeward Islands	151
To Barbados	80
	900

Add to the above one hundred and fifty sail⎫ *Vessels*
from Great Britain and Ireland to the Coast ⎬ 150
of Guinea, and so to the plantations ⎭

                   1,050

Thirdly. An estimate of the value of the vessels belonging to the subjects of America and those belonging to Great Britain and Ireland trading to the different colonies, etc.:

1065 —	Ships, snows, and brigantines belonging to the American subjects trading to foreign parts, valued at a medium £1,000 sterling each is	£1,065,000
970 —	Sloops and schooners of smaller size and burden, valued one with the other at £400 sterling each is	388,000
900 —	Ships, snows, etc., from Great Britain and Ireland to and from the plantations, valued at £1,200 each	1,080,000
150 —	Ditto from Great Britain and Ireland to the coast of Guinea and the plantations with extraordinary outfits £1,500 each	225,000
3,085	Sail	£2,758,000

Fourthly. An estimate of the natural and improved annual produce of his Majesty's American colonies and plantations, distinguished into each colony or plantation:

Newfoundland by fish and oil	..	..	..	.. £100,000
New England and Nova Scotia by fish, oil, whalebone, cattle, lumber, pitch, tar, turpentine, building of vessels, etc.)		..	..	800,000
Connecticut and Rhode Island, with the same commodities and sheep, corn, bread, flour, cheese, and butter		..	..	150,000
New York and the Jerseys with the same, and tar, copper-ore, iron, and wheat		..	..	250,000
Pennsylvania and the lower counties the same, and tobacco		..	..	280,000
Maryland, in the same	..	..	..	200,000
Virginia in the same, with pitch, tar, and turpentine		..	..	250,000
North Carolina in the same	..	..	..	60,000
South Carolina in ditto with rice	..	..	..	200,000
Bermuda, in plett, live stock, fish, oil, cabbage, onions, and stones for building		..	..	10,000

Bahama Islands in salt, timber, plank, bark, turtle-shell, Brazil wood, and fruit	.. ..	£15,000
Jamaica in sugar, molasses, rum, cotton, lime-juice, ginger, indigo, coffee, aloes, pimento, turtle-shell, mahogany timber, and plank	.. ..	500,000
Antigua in the same commodities	.. .. ..	250,000
St. Christopher's in ditto	.. ..	220,000
Nevis in ditto	.. ..	50,000
Montserrat in ditto	.. ..	50,000
Anguilla in ditto	.. ..	15,000
Tortola in ditto	.. ..	30,000
Spanish Town in ditto	.. ..	15,000
Barbados in ditto	.. ..	300,000
		£3,745,000

Fifthly.   The amount of the value of goods shipped from Great Britain and Ireland to our British plantations and the coast of Guinea is annually by computation £2,550,000

Sixthly.   A calculation of the amount of cash, dye woods, drugs, cocoa, etc., imported to the British plantations, being the consequence of a trade carried on to Spanish and French dominions in America. That trade in New England, Connecticut, and Rhode Island in dye woods from Honduras, some cash and cocoa amounting to yearly..   100,000

To New York (*circa*)	.. ..	25,000
To Bermuda ..	.. ..	10,000
To Jamaica ..	.. ..	250,000
To Leeward Islands (*circa*) ..	.. .. ..	20,000
To Barbados (*circa*) ..	.. ..	20,000
		£425,000

It's to be observed that as this is the produce of foreign colonies, it's mentioned by itself to show the amount of that private branch of trade, and though it's carried on with goods from Britain and Negroes, which is before considered in the calculate, yet it's conceived that the addition of this will not overrate our American trade.

Seventhly. The whole brought into an account by which you may see the amount of the above American trade:

The amount of the computed value of the vessels trading in America, including those belonging to the merchants of Great Britain and Ireland being 3,085, which amounts to..   ..   ..£2,758,000

The amount of the natural and improved produce of
the British colonies which employ the above vessels .. £3,745,000
The amount of goods from Great Britain and Ireland
to the plantations and coast of Guinea annually 2,550,000
The amount of a casual trade carried on to the Spanish
and French settlements in America annually (*circa*) .. 425,000

£9,478,000

You will please to observe that the whole trade to and in America, belonging to his Majesty's British and American subjects (Hudson's Bay only excepted) amounts yearly to nine million four hundred and seventy-eight thousand pounds. This includes the value of the whole navigation, the annual supplies from Great Britain and Ireland, the natural and improved produce remitted to Europe from the plantations and colonies, as well as the supplies given each other by their traffic and commerce from one colony or plantation to the other.

I now come to give an account of the number of fighting men in the British Empire in America, distinguished by each different colony and plantation, including his Majesty's regular forces as well as Palatines, Germans, etc. The calculate is taken from the years of sixteen to sixty, by information given me from each colony and plantation:

In Newfoundland ..	..	..	..	..	..	400
New England and Nova Scotia	..	..	..			38,000
Connecticut and Rhode Island	..	..	..			8,000
New York and the Jerseys	..	..	..	..		10,000
Pennsylvania and the lower counties		..	..			50,000
Maryland	..	..	..	..	..	10,000
Virginia ..	..	..	..	..	..	12,000
North Carolina	..	..	..	..	..	2,000
South Carolina ..	..	..	..	..	..	4,000
Georgia ..	..	..	..	..	..	1,000
Bermuda	..	..	..	..	..	800
New Providence	..	..	..	..	..	450
Jamaica ..	..	..	..	..	..	5,000
Antigua ..	..	..	..	..	..	2,200
Montserrat	..	..	..	..	..	600
Nevis ..	..	..	..	..	..	600
St. Christopher's	..	..	..	..	..	1,200
Anguilla ..	..	..	..	..	..	150
Spanish Town ..	..	..	..	..	..	150
Tortola ..	..	..	..	..	..	200
Barbados	..	..	..	..	..	4,500

151,250

I believe there is not less than one hundred thousand Negroes in the colonies on the main of America.

I presume it will not be disagreeable to give you a small detail of the charges attending the sugar islands in planting and manufacturing their sugars; as their charge in Negro slaves is the greatest of their expense, I shall hereafter give you the numbers from the exactest accounts, and that distinguished by each different plantation or island.

Jamaica has Negroes	90,000
Antigua	28,000
St. Christopher's	20,000
Nevis	9,000
Montserrat	9,000

Virgin Islands

(viz.) Anguilla	800	
Spanish Town	700	3,000
Tortola	1,500	
Barbados		72,000

231,000

You'll please to observe there are two hundred and thirty-one thousand Negro slaves belonging and employed in the British sugar colonies, which being valued at £20 sterling per head amounts to £4,620,000. The value of their sugar works, mills, stills, worms, horses, cattle, and all other necessaries belonging to a sugar plantation, may justly be valued at one third the amount of the Negro slaves, which at that calculation amounts to £1,540,000, which added together makes £6,160,000, which is the value of the sugar plantations, abstract of the soil.

Upon the foregoing observations and calculations, I believe, you will think that the British Empire of America is of inestimable value to the nation of Great Britain. Please to observe the trade and fishery of America, abstract of Hudson's Bay, employs 3,085 sail of vessels of different denominations and burden; allowing eight men to navigate each vessel, there is employed in that trade only, 24,680 mariners, which I think is a fine nursery for our sailors.

As for the revenue arising from the American trade, I must refer to those that are acquainted with the receipts thereof.

If the foregoing be acceptable and agreeable to you, it fully answers my intent; if any errors in the calculations, it is wholly owing to my informations, though I have reason to think it's pretty just; but that and the whole is entirely submitted to your superior judgment. . . .

53. William Shirley and William Bollan: report on illegal trade in the colonies (26 February 1743)

From the passage of the first Navigation Act in 1660 down to the Revolution, British officials were much concerned with colonial infractions of commercial laws and regulations. It was a concern disproportionate to the actual amount of illegal trade for, with the exception of the Molasses Act of 1733, it is probable that the vast bulk of colonial commerce was carried on within legal channels. Nevertheless, whenever a colonial merchant was accused of breaking a law, whether rightly or wrongly, a great deal of heat was generated and hence the question of illegal trade is of importance in understanding opinion in both Britain and the colonies

The merchants of the northern colonies were more often involved in such disputes than any others because their trade was of great complexity. They functioned as importers, exporters, distributors, and carriers, and traded outside of the empire as well as within it. Entirely apart from the smuggling which some of them engaged in, the rules were so complex that honest disputes over the interpretation of them were constantly arising. The two letters which follow are from the governor and the advocate-general of Massachusetts, a colony in which disputes over trade matters were probably more serious than in any other colony. The letters were written in answer to one of the periodic questionnaires sent by the Board of Trade to the colonial governors.

William Shirley (1674–1771) was born in England and lived there until financial difficulties caused him to move to Massachusetts in 1731. He had been a lawyer in England and was soon appointed judge of the colonial court of vice-admiralty. He joined the enemies of Governor Jonathan Belcher (see No. 34B) in a successful effort to unseat him. In 1741 Shirley replaced Belcher as governor, a post he held until 1757. Shirley was one of the abler colonial governors and did much to organize colonial support during both the War of the Austrian Succession and the Seven Years War. William Bollan (c. 1710–c. 1776) was born in England and studied law there. He came to Massachusetts, married Shirley's daughter, and was appointed advocate-general. Later on he was the Massachusetts Agent in England. Printed: Colonial Society of Massachusetts *Publications*, VI, pp. 297–304.

[Governor William Shirley to the Board of Trade.]

Boston, New England
February 26, 1742/3

My Lords:

The seventh of the queries lately sent by your lordships to be answered, is this, viz.:

What methods are used in the province under your government to prevent illegal trade; and are the same effectual?

I have singled out this query to answer in the first place because the illicit trade which appears to have been carried on in this province and some of the neighbouring colonies (within this last year more especially) is such as without the speedy inter- position of the Parliament to stop it, must be highly destructive of the interests of Great Britain, by lessening the vent of her woollen and other manufactures and commodities in her own plantations, making her cease to be a staple of the European commodities for supplying them, letting foreigners into the profits of the plantation trade, and finally weakening the dependence which the British northern colonies ought to have upon their mother country.

That the main benefits and advantages arising to Great Britain from her planta- tions, which I have above enumerated, and which have constantly employed the attention of the British Parliament to secure to her by keeping particularly the Euro- pean trade to and from her plantations to herself (as has been the usage of other nations with regard to their plantations), are in very imminent danger of being lost to her by the frauds and abuses lately practised here in that trade, I think will appear to your lordships upon your perusal of the enclosed account of them given by the advocate- general pursuant to my orders, and which he has chose to cast into the form of a letter to your lordships.

I am sensible that the advocate's letter is very long, but I hope its length may be excused by your lordships on account of the importance of its subject and the necessity there is of laying before your lordships a full and particular account of the mischiefs represented in it, with their causes and proper remedies, as they appear to persons upon the spot who have had the conduct of prosecutions for breaches of the Acts of

Trade in this and the neighbouring colonies for several years, and form their judgment upon a long experience of the effect of those Acts as they have been construed by the provincial courts of law and evaded by illicit traders.

I shall only add to the enclosed letter that until all breaches of the Acts of Trade which extend to the plantations, or at least those of the 15th Charles II, chap. 7th, are made tryable in the courts of vice-admiralty here (without which it is in vain to hope that the illicit trade complained of can be suppressed), it may be expected that it will be carried on in New England, and perhaps grow, if not timely prevented, to so strong an head as that it will be no easy matter wholly to subdue it.

The prosecution of the importers of the goods brought in the brigantine *Hannah* (mentioned in the advocate's letter) from Rotterdam into this port, for the value of the goods imported in her, would doubtless discourage the illicit traders to a very great degree, and must deter 'em exceedingly by showing 'em their insecurity even after they have safely landed their goods; and I am of opinion it can't fail of having a great tendency to break up the trade. But as I think it more proper that the Commissioners of the Customs should be troubled with the care of procuring this evidence from Rotterdam for the prosecution of this affair, than your lordships, I have directed him to recommend it to them to take that trouble upon themselves; and if your lordships should be of opinion that this prosecution would be for the service of the Crown, your signifying that to the Commissioners of the Customs must effectually procure the desired evidence, and the action upon the receipt of it, shall be forthwith brought here and prosecuted to effect.

[William Bollan to the Board of Trade.]
Boston, New England, Feb. 26, 1742/43

My Lords:

Mr. Shirley, the governor and vice-admiral of this province, soon after his being made such, was pleased to appoint me the King's Advocate and according to the practice here it is the duty of the person filling that place to prosecute all offenders against the Acts of Trade, the discharge of which trust has been lately attended with such discoveries, and is at present accompanied with so many difficulties, that after communicating them to his excellency, he gave me orders to make them particularly known to your lordships, and indeed I conceive 'em to be of such nature and consequence that had I not received his commands to that end, I should have thought myself obliged in faithfulness to the Crown to lay them before your lordships. After mentioning which I shall make no further apology for giving your lordships this trouble but proceed to inform you that there has lately been carried on here a large illicit trade (destructive to the interest of Great Britain in her trade to her own plantations and contrary to the main intent of all her laws made to regulate that trade) by importing into this province large quantities of European goods of almost all sorts from diverse parts of Europe, some of which are by the laws wholly prohibited to be imported into the plantations, and the rest are prohibited to be imported there unless brought directly from Great Britain. To show forth to your lordships the rise, progress, and extent of this pernicious practice would, I fear, far exceed the proper compass of a letter from me to your lordships, and therefore I shall content myself with saying, first, that a considerable number of ships have, contrary to the 15th Charles II, chap. 7th, lately come into this country directly from Holland, laden some wholly, some in part, with reels of yarn or spun hemp, paper, gunpowder, iron, and goods of various sorts used for men and women's clothing; secondly, that some vessels have also come directly from other foreign parts of Europe with like cargoes; thirdly, that some of those vessels were laden chiefly and others in part with the goods of the produce and manufacture of old Spain prohibited under large penalties to be imported into Great Britain during the present war; fourthly, that to carry on this sort of trade, diverse vessels have been fitted out here laden with provisions, and though they appear wholly English in the plantations; yet by means of their being commanded and navigated by French refugees naturalized, or such persons as may easily pass for Frenchmen and by the help of French papers and passes procured by French merchants concerned in the matter, they have carried the English provisions to their open enemies and landed them out of those vessels in the ports of Spain; fifthly, that a considerable part of the illicit trade from Holland is carried on by factors here for the sake of their commissions, Dutch merchants having the property in the goods imported; sixthly, that one of these illicit traders, lately departed hence for Holland, proposed to one of the greatest sellers of broadcloths here (and to how many others I can't say) to supply him with black cloths from thence, saying that this country might be better and cheaper supplied with broadcloths of that colour from Holland than from England; but to prevent, or rather increase your lordships' surprise on this head I need only to acquaint you that I write this clad in a superfine French cloth which I bought on purpose that I might wear about the evidence of these illegal traders having already begun to destroy the vital parts of the British commerce, and to use as a memento to myself and the custom-house officers to do everything in our power towards cutting off this trade so very pernicious to the British nation; seventhly, that the persons concerned in this trade are many, some of them of the greatest fortunes in this country, and who have made great gains by it, and having all felt the sweets of it, they begin to espouse and justify it, some openly, some covertly; and having persuaded themselves that their trade ought not to be bound by the laws of Great Britain, they labour, and not without success, to poison the minds of all the inhabitants of the province, and matters are brought to such a pass that it is sufficient to recommend any trade to their general approbation and favour that it is unlawful; and as examples of this kind soon spread their influence on the other plantations around, 'tis too plain almost to need mentioning that if care be not soon taken to cure this growing mischief, the British trade to these plantations and their proper dependence on their mother country will in a great measure, ere long, be lost. I shall now recount to your lordships the difficulties which attend the suppression of this mischief. The first and one of the principal whereof is that the breaches of the statute of the 15th Charles II, chap. 7th, entitled an Act for the Encouragement of Trade, and made purposely to keep the plantations in a firm dependence upon England, and to render them advantageous to it in the vent of English woollen and other commodities, and which provides that all European goods and manufactures imported into the plantations shall be shipped in England, are not cognizable in the Court of Admiralty, and a prosecution in the common law courts here will be unavoidably attended with great delay and too many difficulties and discouragements to be generally overcome. For in the first place, by the course of judicial proceedings established in this province, there will be a necessity for the prosecutor to pass through various trials (and frequently in distant counties) in courts disinclined to the prosecution, and with scarce any hopes of success; for, in the next place, the prosecutor cannot there have process to compel an appearance of unwilling witnesses (and all witnesses for the Crown in cases of this nature are generally such), and finally, a trial by jury here is only trying one illicit trader by his fellows, or at least his well-wishers. How it happened that the offences against this statute which is the main ligament whereby the plantation trade is fastened and secured to Great Britain, should not be cognizable in the Court of Admiralty, when the cognizance of other Acts of Trade of much less consequence to the nation are given to that court from the common consideration of the interest, or desire that the juries have here to defeat all seizures and prosecutions for the Crown, I cannot say; but the inconveniences that at present proceed from the Court of Admiralty's want of jurisdiction over offences against that statute, are certainly very great. Another difficulty that attends the suppressing this illegal trade arises from the nature and situation of the country which abounds with outports, where vessels employed in this trade unlade their cargoes into small vessels, wherein they afterwards carry their prohibited goods with ease into some proper places of safety; and a further difficulty grows out of the corruption of those who are employed to carry on this trade, which is become so great that we have had some late instances of oaths taken at the custom-house by masters of vessels in direct contradiction to their certain knowledge of the truth, and to this crime these illicit traders have lately added this contrivance, viz., to conceal or spirit away the seamen who might otherwise be witnesses and by their testimony possibly cause a condemnation of some of the vessels employed this way; and thus when vast quantities of goods are illegally imported here, after they are unladen and secured, the master appears boldly and is ready to swear anything for the good of the voyage, and the sailors are dispersed and gone, and there is nothing to be found but an empty vessel, against which no proof can be obtained. Having thus laid before your lordships the principal difficulties that attend the carrying the Acts of Trade into execution here, it may perhaps be expected that I should propose some remedies which appear to us who are upon the spot, and there observe the working of these things, to be most likely to effect the cure of these mischiefs; wherefore I shall now proceed to mention 'em for the consideration of your lordships.

The first thing that seems necessary to be done, and that by Parliament, is to grant to the Court of Admiralty cognizance of all past and future offences against the above-mentioned statute 15th Charles II, or (which would be much better) to provide by act of Parliament that all offences whatever, past and future, against the Acts of Trade committed in the plantations, and the penalties and forfeitures arising therefrom, may be prosecuted for and recovered in any court of admiralty in the plantations. There is really a greater want of a certain and general jurisdiction in the courts of admiralty in the plantations over breaches of the Acts of Trade there than at first may be imagined. For among other things the statute made in the seventh and eighth of William the third for preventing frauds and regulating abuses in the plantation trade is so obscurely penned in the point of the admiralty's jurisdiction that it has received different constructions, and that court has been frequently prohibited in this province to take cognizance of some of the main offences against that statute, and of late I hear that like prohibitions have been granted in the province of New York, though the intent of the Parliament that made that statute (as I think) doubtless was to give that admiralty jurisdiction of all offences against it. The granting to the Admiralty a general jurisdiction over all breaches of the Laws of Trade will, without question, be of advantage to the Crown and kingdom and save much trouble to the officers prosecuting illicit traders, and indeed no reason can be assigned for giving the Admiralty cognizance of offences against some of the Acts of Trade, but what holds equally good for giving the like jurisdiction over the rest. But let what will be done with respect to granting the admiralty courts in the plantations such general jurisdiction, I think it is very plain that to suffer the offences against 15th Charles II, to remain only punishable in the courts of common law, is to leave it in the power of illicit traders (notwithstanding that statute) to import into these plantations any European goods directly from any foreign countries to their great profit and with little peril. Another thing I would propose to your lordships as a cure of this mischievous trade is that actions of detinue be brought against some of the principal offenders importing here goods from foreign parts in order to recover the goods imported, or their value, against the importer of them. Such actions will be warranted by the judgment given in Westminster Hall by the Court of King's Bench, 8th William third, in the case of Roberts against Wetheral, as reported by Mr. Salkeld, and others. The effect of a few such actions properly pursued and recoveries thereupon had, will, I think, unquestionably have the greatest possible tendency to break up this trade; for the security of the persons concerned in it according to their understanding of the matter rests in this: that if they can but prevent the officers scizing the goods illegally imported (and therein they generally meet with no great difficulty, as has been already observed), then they are, according to their present judgments, safe in all respects. But when once the importers come to find that they are chargeable with actions for the goods illegally imported, or their value, after they have imported them safely and disposed of them, I think they cannot but be deterred from making such unlawful importations; for then they will see a new danger, great and of long duration, such as upon the whole they will have but little (if any) hopes to secure themselves from. The most favourable case wherein the first action of this kind can be commenced and prosecuted, in my opinion, will be that of the brigantine *Hannah* which arrived here in December 1741 and came directly from Rotterdam, which place she left in October, proceeding laden with hemp spun into yarn, paper, Ozenbrigs, gunpowder, and other goods. After her arrival here she was seized, but she had first unladen and secured her cargo, and with great difficulty we got some of the crew, and by their oaths proved such facts against her that she was condemned, and as we have already secured considerable evidence of what goods were imported in her,

I think nothing will be wanting to support an action to be brought against the owners of her for the goods by them imported in her, or their value, but the proof of the particular goods taken in by her at Rotterdam; and if your lordships will be pleased to give orders for obtaining that, I think the Crown will be greatly served by it. In such case it will be necessary to have such evidence of this point as the lords of the Committee of Council will finally receive and adjudge sufficient, for with regard to the success of such actions here, I think there is but little reason to expect any recovery on a trial by our juries, though the proof of such action and the law for the support of it, be ever so plain; but on an appeal to his Majesty in Council, law and justice will without question be rightly administered. The condemnation of this vessel was owing in a great measure to accident, the advocate employed by the claimers not knowing that upon application to the Superior Court here, he might have had a prohibition to the Court of Admiralty. Had that method of defence been used, the vessel would have been certainly acquitted in the common law courts. For the only thing which worked her condemnation was our catching some of the crew flying, and holding them by such compulsory process as we could not have had anywhere but in the Admiralty Court. This is the only vessel which has been condemned for being employed in this illicit trade, and it is very remarkable that though she sold for about four hundred pounds sterling, and so the owners of her lost that sum, yet they have continued that trade ever since to a very great degree, though somewhat more warily, and other persons have been no wise deterred by this loss and the peril which the owners were in of having their goods taken, but on the contrary, more illicit trading ships have come in here from Holland only this last summer and fall than from London. So near is Great Britain to being quite worked out of this part of her trade. And though I have said so much to your lordships touching this matter, yet I cannot avoid adding that this illicit trade is carried on to so great a degree and in so many various shapes that I make no doubt but if proper preventive measures be not soon taken, a great part of the bounty money given by Great Britain to the importers of naval stores from the plantations will in a short time be laid out in Holland or other parts of Europe in the purchase of goods there, to be illegally imported here, if that has not been already practised.

I cannot conclude without observing to your lordships that unless effectual measures are speedily taken to stop this growing evil, the illicit traders will by their numbers, wealth, and wiles have got such power in these parts that laws and orders may come too late from Great Britain to have their proper effect against it.

Your lordships' commands to me (if you have any touching these matters) signified to his excellency the governor, or in whatever manner you please, shall be obeyed with the utmost care and dispatch. . . .

54. The conduct of trade (1774–1776)

The following documents are selections from the correspondence relating to the voyages of the *Union*, owned by Joseph Lee and Company of Beverly and Salem, Massachusetts, and captained by Zachariah Burchmore. Although the letters were written just at the beginning of the Revolution, when conditions were not normal, they do illustrate many of the methods and problems of colonial merchants and ship captains in carrying on the intercolonial and transatlantic trade. Printed: Massachusetts Historical Society *Proceedings*, LIX, pp. 211–232, *passim*.

[Orders to Captain Burchmore.]

Beverly, Nov. 26, 1774.

Captain Zachariah Burchmore: As you command our brigantine, we direct you to proceed immediately for Charleston, and there make sale of our rum if the market should be such as to pay the first cost and charges, but if otherwise, and you judge it prudent to proceed to Winyah for the benefit of getting rice cheaper, reserve 25 hogsheads rum to carry with you, as it helps ballast the vessel and with your cask may be put off at a tolerable price. The advantages, however, that arise from dispatch we esteem so great as to advise not to leave Charleston unless rice is higher than 57/6 per cwt. as the detention will be much longer in any other place, and perhaps be more than a balance for the saving of 10/ on each cask, which is the principal advantage gained at Winyah. These things would have you weigh well in your own mind and determine according to your judgment. When you have fixed on the place for loading, lay the whole of our interest out in rice and proceed with all possible dispatch for Cadiz. If the market should be as high as 62 reals Vellon [a quarter of a peseta, about five cents] per cwt. clear on board, it would not be prudent to go further unless our friends Messrs. Bewick, Timmerman, and Romero strongly advise to it. Bear it in mind that whoever receives your cargo must either advance the money or give bills on Malaga so as to enable you to load there with fruit and wine; and after the discharge of your rice, proceed directly for Malaga and apply to our friends Messrs. Kirkpatrick & Escott for 150 quarter casks wine, 20 fanegas [a bushel to a bushel and a half] of almonds, and if oil is cheap take 10 quarter casks, the balance in raisins unless they are much higher than usual, in which case you will take more wine and less fruit. But should they be at 75 or 80 reals Vellon, take only two or three hundred barrels with the other things above-mentioned and desire them to give you a letter of credit to their friends at Lisbon for the balance in lemons. Call in there in your way to Falmouth and take the balance in fruit. When in England desire Mr. Banfield to get a licence for another voyage to load with rice and endeavour to sell so much of your cargo there as to pay the charges. It will not be worth while to wait any time for the licence, but as soon as you are reloaded, return immediately for Beverly where shall hope in due time to see you safely arrive.

[Captain Burchmore to Joseph Lee & Co.]

Charleston, So. Carolina, Jan'y 10, 1775

Gentlemen: This day I received yours per Capt. Thrash, and now having an opportunity by the way of Newport, I would inform you that I arrived here after 25 days' passage where I find markets for rum very dull at present and no possibility of selling it at present, and I thought it most for your interest to value myself on some merchant and accordingly I have on Crouch & Gray with giving them one half commissions. We have not sold any rum yet on account of Christmas holidays, there being no vendue. The last rum sold here at 13/. But since that there is large quantities arrived from Philadelphia so that I'm afraid we shan't obtain more than 11/6. I have stored all the rum, and as Crouch & Gray has agreed to load me with rice at 50/,

I shall make all the dispatch I can consistent with your interest, and shall sail in about ten days for Cadiz where I should be glad of your further advice. I learn by Capt. George [Cabot's] letter that the house you advised to in Cadiz is broke and by his advice I shall go to Duff & Welsh. I have now 200 casks of rice on board and all the rest engaged. I am your humble servant.⌡

P.S. Your certificate came here in March last and your bonds is cancelled. I believe I shall make the rice licence answer.

[Received 7 February 1775.]

[Crouch & Gray to Joseph Lee & Co.]

Charlestown, So. Carolina
January 18, 1775.

Gentlemen: Your Brigt. *Union*, Captain Zachariah Burchmore, arrived here the 21 ulto. with a cargo of rum and some money in order to purchase a load of rice. The captain finding it impossible to dispose of his rum so as to get away in a reasonable time, applied to our house to do his business, upon sharing the commissions, that is to say 2½ per cent. for selling and 1¼ for purchasing, which however is not the custom of the place, the established charge being 5 per cent. for selling and 5 per cent. for purchasing, besides 2½ per cent. for storage of inward cargo, which we must have charged had the vessel been consigned to us, and we have only derogated from custom in this instance merely to oblige the captain and to serve you, as it would have been out of the captain's power to have loaded till he had disposed of his rum, which there was not the least probability of his doing for a month or two to come. We have put on board 412 barrels of excellent rice purchased for ready money at 50/ our currency per 100 lb., and he is now waiting for a wind. We could have dispatched him at least ten days sooner had not the holidays intervened and prevented the rice coming to town from the country.

As soon as we have disposed of the rum (which is now a glut) we shall immediately close the sales and transmit them to you. We are fearful that the rum will be sold to a loss, notwithstanding we have done all in our power to prevent it by keeping it up for a better price, for there has been such an amazing quantity in within this six weeks that people supplied themselves before Christmas with a sufficient stock to last them for a considerable time. Had your vessel arrived here a month sooner she would have come to a good market, having ourselves sold a cargo of near 7,000 gallons for Mr. Derby in November for more than two shillings sterling a gallon round, and could at that time have sold as much more at the same price. Let this be your government in future, that about a month or six weeks before Christmas is the time for New England vessels to arrive here. We have not yet received a single shilling upon the rum; however, we shall not be discouraged, but will keep it a little longer in hopes of a better price. At present we suppose that we could not obtain 11/ for the whole of it, which is above 3/ less than we sold for six weeks ago. Your Capt. George Cabot arrived here about a fortnight since from Cadiz, and intends purchasing [*torn*] part and letting out the remainder. We will be happy to see him and should be glad to render him or any of your connections every service in our power, being at all times with very great respect and esteem, gentlemen, your most obedt. servants.

P.S. We have sent you certificate to cancel your bond.

[Received 14 February 1775.]

[Captain Burchmore to Joseph Lee & Co.]
Charleston, So. Carolina,
Jany. 19, 1775.

Gentlemen: This my second via New York. In which I would inform you that I am loaded and ready for sea the first wind. I have on board 412 casks of rice on cargo containing 220,007 lbs. wt. We have sold but very little rum yet and that at 12/ as the place is full of it. I have settled with Messrs. Crouch & Gray as near as possible, but have not closed the accounts. I have advised with Capt. Cabot and he thinks as there is so many vessels gone to Lisbon, Cadiz, and the straits that there is the best prospect at Croina [Corunna] or Bilbao where, with his advice, I shall proceed thinking it most for your interest, and as I'm obliged to go to England, I may possibly get a freight that way which may help the voyage. You mentioned my taking a load of salt and coming home or going to the West Indies. The latter he advises me to pursue if when I am [in] Spain I judge it for your interest. I'm your humb. servant.

[Received 14 February 1775.]

[Crouch & Gray to Joseph Lee & Co.]
Charleston, So. Carolina,
14th Febry, 1775.

Gentlemen: We wrote you the 18th of last month to which we refer, since when we have finished the sales of your rum, and enclosed we furnish you with the accounts, balance due us two hundred and three pounds seventeen shillings and three pence our currency, or twenty-nine pounds two shillings and six pence sterling for which we shall draw upon you very soon. You will please observe that we have saved for you the duty upon near two thousand gallons of the rum, which is at least five and twenty guineas in your pocket, and which is not effected but by considerable pains, and being upon the best terms with the officers here.

We are sorry it was not in our power to render you more acceptable sales, but the great quantities of rum that has arrived here within two months past has knocked down the price of that article from 15/ to 10/ this money, several whole cargoes having been sold for the latter price, though we are thankful we have not been necessitated to sell *any* so low.

Your Capt. George Cabot sailed over our bar last Friday, after having been detained a fortnight by contrary winds. We sincerely wish you better sale in your next adventure and beg leave to repeat our assurances of rendering you every service here we are capable of, being very respectfully, gentlemen, Your most obedt. servants.

[Received 12 March 1775.]

[Captain Burchmore to Joseph Lee & Co.]

Lisbon, March 14, 1775.

Gentlemen: This by the way of Philadelphia in which I would inform you that I arrived at Corunna after 27 days where the rice would have sold very well had not a ship arrived 3 weeks before me with 600 casks from Philadelphia. I lay in Corunna 8 days in which time we had news from Bilbao, Ferrol, Vigo, but found it would not answer, and with the advice of Messrs. O'Reilly & Smith, I proceeded to Cascais where I got news from Lisbon in a letter from Mr. Houston in which he told me he knew of no better prospect than this, as his friendly correspondents to the southward had not for some time quoted the value of rice. He in short advised me to come in and declare I was put in by distress of weather till he could hear from Barcelona, which was the next day, in which his friends told him they had a plentiful supply, and Mr. Houston told me he could get 3100 for my rice but must give 4 month credit. I told him the necessity of having more money for my cargo and that I could not deliver it without. The next day arrived 2 ships from Cadiz loaded with rice, so I thought it would not be prudent to leave this, and an opportunity offered, my cargo is sold at 3,000, the cash to be paid in 10 days; and as I cannot learn that matters is likely to be settled between Europe and America, I shall take in 100 moys of salt and proceed to Falmouth to pay the Dalys [duties?] on the rice and proceed home, without counter orders from you should advise otherwise. We cannot learn here that matters will be settled but that this is 11 sail of ships fitting out for America, and it is the opinion of the merchants here that the acts will all be enforced. But as I shall be better able to hear when I get in England. Till then I shall make all the dispatch I can consistent with your interest, and am your humble servant.

[Received 16 May 1775.]

[Captain Burchmore to Joseph Lee & Co.]

Lisbon, March 28. 1775.

Gentlemen: I should be glad to give you such information as would be more agreeable than to tell you that Mr. Houston has not acted like the gentleman I took him for from his invitation. I came here as he wrote me a letter to Cascais in which he said he knew not any market so good as this as he was selling at 3100. When I came in with the vessel and talked with him, he told me that if I would leave the cargo with him he could get 3100 m for it. I told him I could not deliver it without having the money for it. The next day he told me he could obtain 3,000 m for the cargo, and notwithstanding the duties and charges, it would pay a very handsome freight. When I come to deliver it, we found 5 or 6 casks something damaged, which he has since made a great difficulty about and tells me he cannot close my accounts on that account, but that he will remit home to you the account [of] sales and the balance in Capt. Collyer of Marblehead. He has advanced me about 460 half Joes and given me a bill for £80 sterling to pay the duties in Falmouth, and I have 100 moys salt on board and this day shall sail for Falmouth and am your humble servt.

[Received 26 May 1775.]

[Captain Burchmore to Joseph Lee & Co.]

Falmouth, May 4, 1775.

Gentlemen: Since I arrived here I find by the late Acts that it is inconsistent with your interest to proceed home at present, and impossible to bring home the salt I had on board. Therefore have sold it for something better than the first cost and taking in ballast, and this day I shall with the advice of Capt. John Cabot who arrived here 4 days ago, proceed for the West Indies where I shall take in such goods as I judge most for your interest and proceed home or return back to Europe again as I can best judge when I'm there; and for as the present state of affairs stands between Great Britain and the Colonies, we cannot think of any better way to proceed, for it is the opinion of most here that a civil war will commence in America as there is great preparations making here for it. I expected to have had advice from you when I arrived at Falmouth but have found none nor have I received a letter since I left Carolina, so that in these critical times I have been greatly at a loss what to do. I have at present the satisfaction of advising with Capt. John Cabot on the matter and pray God the resolutions we have taken may turn to your interest and satisfaction. That is all I wish and am your most Humble Servant.

[Received 12 July 1775.]

[Joseph Banfield to Joseph Lee & Co.]

Falmouth, May 6th, 1775.

Dear Sir: The present serves to acquaint you that on the 16th ulto. your Brig. *Union*, Capt. Zach. Burchmore, arrived here from Lisbon with a ballast of salt, and in order to deliver up his rice licence and cancel the bond. Upon his arrival here he applied to me to sell his salt, which having advertised I sold at public sale at 15d¼. per bushel which was 1d¼. per bushel higher than a parcel had just before been sold at. I furnished him with account sales of the same and paid him the neat proceeds in specie. This parcel of salt fell considerably short of the weight, having turned out only 1264 bushels, when, had it made out as usual, the quantity would have been 1500 bushels, it commonly turning out 15 bushels to the moy, whereas yours per *Union* did not make out 13. Salt is very cheap here on account of the failure in the fishery, and no encouragement for stocking salt, the old stocks lying on hand. I have 2/3 of the salt by me in the cellar which I bought of you in the year 1772.

Capt. Burchmore was at a loss, on account of the critical situation of public affairs, which track to pursue. I furnished him with an abstract of the late restraining Act on your province and neighbouring ones, upon which he resolved to proceed for the West Indies and carry the amount of his cargo of rice sold at Lisbon which he brought in specie with him. He sailed yesterday with a fair wind. I sincerely wish him a successful and safe voyage.

Mr. John Cabot is now here clearing out a cargo of tobacco in the *Tryall*, Capt. Higginson, from Virginia for Spain, and will be ready to sail from hence in about a week from this. We now wait with eager expection the result of the late Acts to know in what manner they will be received in America. It is now the crisis, and we anxiously look towards America. Indeed the eyes of all Europe are upon America to see how she will behave in this last grand trial. I beg my best compliments to your brother and all friends and I pray God to keep you under his protection, being very sincerely, Dear Sir, your most Obedient Servt.

[Received 12 July 1775.]

[Captain Burchmore to Joseph Lee & Co.]

St. Eustatia, June 19, 1775.

Gentlemen: I am at present in the utmost confusion to determine what to do as I find it will be imprudent to come home without too great a risk of having your interest confiscated. I have about nine hundred pounds sterling which I shall lay out in sugar and cocoa and proceed to Bilbao where I think your interest will be safest. The gentlemen here that I take to be my friends think it the prudentest course I can take. I should been very glad to have had your advice when I arrived here, but as I suppose the letters from Falmouth is not come to hand, I can't expect it. I am this day bound for St. Martin's for sugar and I hope to get out of the West Indies in ten days. Should my wife be in want of money, as it is possible she will before I can come home, I should be glad if you would supply her and will do the utmost that lays in my power with your interest and am your Humble Servt.

[Received 24 July 1775.]

[Captain Burchmore to Joseph Lee & Co.]

Philadelphia, July 17, 1775.

Sir: I arrived here the 11th of this month from the West Indies with sugar and cocoa which I purchased there in order to go to Europe as per advice. I wrote you by Capt. Allcock that I should go to Bilbao, but after I had been out a few day I spoke [a] brigantine from Gilbraltar who said that he expected there was a Spanish war by this time, and as the goods I had on board would not answer anywhere else but in Spain, I thought it would not be prudent for me to proceed, and when I came here I found Mr. Andrew Cabot and am very happy to find one who can act with more propriety than myself in those difficult times, and I shall deliver up all the accounts to Mr. Cabot for a settlement and for the rest, refer you to his letter. As I don't expect to come I should be glad if you would supply my wife with twelve guineas which I will reduct from my wages and I wish you would write me if you can tell me where she is. I am your most Hum. Servant.

[Received 28 July 1775.]

[Captain Burchmore to Joseph Lee & Co.]

Philadelphia, July 20, 1775.

Sir: I wrote you by the last post in which I gave the reasons for my coming here, but since I have been here I find I could have come home, which in all probability would have been more for your interest as the goods I brought here are very dull at present, and when I came in the river I came immediately up to town where

Mr. Cabot told me I could not go home and said I had took the most prudent step
I possibly could in coming here. I have discharged all hands but the mate and now
wait for your answer what to do. I have cleared out for Gibraltar and shall grave the
vessel, which must be done if you send her out again or not. If you send her out again,
I shall settle all accounts with Mr. Cabot and the whole of my wages I shall leave,
which, if you think proper, pay to my wife which will be adding to your stock here
and save me the trouble and risk of sending it home. Whatever you order to be done
with your vessel I wish may turn more for your interest than it has hitherto. Your
Most Hum. Servant.

[Received 5 August 1775.]

[Orders to Captain Burchmore.]
Philadelphia, 21st August, 1775.

Capt. Burchmore: You having the command of our Brigt. *Union*, our orders are
that you immediately proceed to Cadiz and deliver your letters to Messrs. Duff and
Welsh and advise with them respecting the delivery of your cargo there, or proceeding to any other port. I have in my letter to Messrs. Duff and Welsh desired them to
advance you the amount of your cargo nearly or quite, as the present disputes between
Great Britain and her Colonies may prevent your returning home; therefore it's
absolutely necessary you should have it in your power to go upon some voyage on
our account which you cannot possibly effect unless the merchants that receive your
cargo advance you the value thereof. If after your cargo is delivered, and you can with
safety (by the disputes being at an end), and it is not forbid by the Congress, go to
Malaga and Falmouth, we would have you do it. Your cargo from Malaga should
advise to consist of 150 quarter casks of wine, 60 ditto figs, one ton of almonds,
20 casks of olive oil, if the price does not exceed 2/6 sterling per gallon, and the
remainder, after having reserved money enough to pay your duties in Falmouth, in
raisins. After having been to Falmouth, make the utmost dispatch for Beverly. But
if the disputes should remain as they now are, or if the Congress should not give
liberty for such a voyage, then endeavour to procure some advantageous freight or
freights and order your money deposited in the hands of Messrs. Kirkpatrick and
Escott of Malaga. But if neither of the before mentioned plans answer, and upon
inquiry you can see any probability of making a freight from the West Indies back
to Europe, we would have you proceed to the West Indies, and if upon your arrival
in the West Indies you find you can with safety return to Beverly, we would have you
with a load molasses, sugar, etc., as the prices may be. But if you cannot return home,
then purchase coffee, cocoa, and sugar or such other articles as you may learn in
Europe are best calculated for their markets. Remember that cocoa, if it is of the
yellow shell, it will not answer. It must be the dark black shell and should it be as
low as 10 or 11 pieces of eight, would have you take largely of it unless our friends
in Europe advise to the contrary. Desire them to give you a memorandum of such
articles as will answer the quantity and particular kind. As it's very probable you will
meet Mr. John or Capt. George Cabot, advise with them and obey their directions
and advice respecting every matter. By no means whatever break one single act or

resolution of the Continental [Congress] or any other Congress Committee etc. Nor any Acts of Trade. I wish you a good voyage, etc.   AND: CABOT.

Our friends at Cadiz, Messrs. Duff & Welsh & Co.

Malaga,	Kirkpatrick & Escott.
Gibraltar,	Robert Anderson.
Barcelona,	Wambwells & Arabet.
Lisbon,	James Houston (unless further orders).
Bilbao,	Joseph Gardoqui & Sons.

Remember upon your arrival to desire your merchants to draw upon Mr. Houston for the balance of your last voyage.

[Captain Burchmore to Joseph Lee & Co.]

Cadiz, Octo. 22d, 1775.

Gentlemen: I wrote you per Capt. Jones of Marblehead that I could not tell where I should go from here, but since that I have the good fortune to get a freight of wheat for Ferrol, which is more than I expected, where I may make about 600 dollars. I am now almost unloaded and my cargo comes out in good order. The prices of flour I mentioned in my first, that is ten dollars per barrel for common, eleven and half for superfine, staves at 50 dollars per M. With respect to politics, we find by the last London papers that the Parliament is determined to pursue matters in America as the greatest part of the people in England have publicly declared they will stand by the king with their lives and fortunes, so there is no prospect of an accommodation so I shall order the money for the cargo deposited as you ordered me, and proceed with my freight. I shall in all things advise with your friends in respect to your interest. And am your most obedt. humble servant.

[Received 27 December 1775.]

[James Houston, Jr., to Joseph Lee & Co.]

Lisbon, Oct. 27, 1775.

Gentlemen: By last post I received a letter from Capt. Zachariah Burchmore, dated Cadiz the 6 inst. He therein gives me orders to remit the balance of your adventure per the *Union* to Messrs. Duff and Welsh of that place, which you may depend I shall comply with the first proper opportunity, and I embrace with pleasure the present one of forwarding you account sales of that one cargo, the net proceed whereof being 3859 $258[1] is carried to the credit of your account current annexed in which you'll see charged 90 $803 for the abatements I have been obliged to make on account of the damaged rice. However considerable you may deem this drawback, I assure you it is much less than I apprehended would have been the case from the miserable situation of the cargo, nor is it easy to conceive the trouble and vexation I have experienced with the Health Office on that account. In short, this speculation has proved a disagreeable one to you, gentlemen, as well as to me, for it always gives me pain to be prevented from serving my friends as I could wish; and I can assure

---

[1] In this and subsequent references to Portuguese money the numbers before the dollar sign indicate milreis and those after the sign indicate reis; one milreis equals 1,000 reis.

you from my certain knowledge that the purchaser with whom the Health Office has not been quite so indulgent, and what with abatements he also has been obliged to make for damage in barrels, which appeared to be sound and good, does not see the interest of his money in the profits he makes.

I must observe that Capt. Burchmore hints as if he had before given me directions how to remit your balance, which, if he did, never came to my hands, and though they had, it would not have been practicable sooner. He carried, it seems, a cargo of flour which, by what he mentions, is not like to meet a favourable issue; here the value is at present at 3100 per bl. and a large quantity on hand. Rice had advanced to 3800 per bl. at which I doubt not but it will make a stand for some time.

Our market is not destitute of fish, but the intelligence received of the damage sustained at the land by the equinoctial hurricane, has induced holders to keep back their best quality and to demand even 5600 per bl. for the second sort; these are certainly most extravagant terms but if too much don't drop in, the value of this article must, I think, be very high during the season.

We are impatiently waiting the sitting of the Parliament in hopes that some healing measures may be thought of to cure the breach made by the present unhappy disturbances, which God in his infinite goodness inspire. I am truly, gentlemen, your most obedient servant.

Wine at present 12500 per cask, but will be, I think, extremely cheap very soon as the vintage has been abundant. Oil the same—it may be now quoted at about 18 $000 per cask. Lemons abundant and will be shipped, I dare say, cheaper than has been known for many years. Salt about 1400 per moy.

[Received 26 December 1775.]

[Duff & Welsh to Joseph Lee & Co.]
Cadiz the 30 October 1775.

Sir: We had the pleasure of writing you under date of the 6 inst. advising the safe arrival here of your Brig. *Union*, Captn. Zachariah Burchmore, and that we would do everything in our power relative to the sale of the cargo and promoting such other voyage for the Brig. as might judge most suitable to your advantage. We have now the pleasure to inform you that we have had the good fortune to sell the whole cargo of flour to Messrs. Moeraert Van de Vennet & Cordon, an house of undoubted solidity here, at 12/m credit with 3 per cent interest for the last 6 months; the common flour at $10, and the superfine do., and Treil [?] at $11½, and the whole is now delivered; and we have further obtained a freight for the *Union* of wheat and provisions for the king's account for Ferrol, with which she is now loaded and will be ready to proceed, we expect, tomorrow. Shall recommend Captn. Burchmore to our friend at Ferrol to assist him in endeavouring to procure him a freight from thence to the Mediterranean, in defect thereof he must return here to see what further will be best to be done, according to the turn public affairs may take. In consequence of the faculty which you give us, and with a view to secure your property at all events, we have judged it convenient to pass a sale of the Brig. before our Consul (*pro forma*) in favour of William Dalrymple, Esqr. of this city, a British subject, and have made out new articles for Captn. Burchmore and the crew and given him instructions signed by said Mr. Dalrymple, Esqr. for his further regulation. Shall be happy that it may so turn out as to render said precautions unnecessary, but it's good to guard against the worst, when it can be done at a small expense. Have not heard from your brothers since our last, but believe they were at Barcelona and expect hearing from them by the next post. Flour continues quite heavy here, and little appearance of being otherways, and wheat is a drug at all markets, and affords us a particular satisfaction to have had it in our power to serve you so effectually at such a juncture as the present when flour is next to invendible, and so many vessels lying by the weeks. We are with esteem, Sir, your obedt. humble servts.

By a vessel will be sailing in 8 or 10 days hence will send you account sales of the *Union*'s cargo and advise you the freight she may make which will go to from 5 to 600 hard dollars.

To the use of Messrs. Dan'l & Mich'l Rundle.

Account Sales Charges and net proceeds of Cargo of Flour and Staves per the Brigt. *Union*, Zack'h Burchmore, for Account of Messrs. Joseph Lee Co.

1775	389 barrels Superfine flour to Moeraert		*Reals Vellon*
Oct. 31	VandeVennet in 12/m at 11 1/2		35788
	628 Ditto Common to Ditto at 10		50240
			86028
	Interest for the last 6/m at 3%		2580
			88608
Nov. 30	2 M 250 Staves at 52 ps.		1227·8
barr	3 [barrels]		160
	2 „		240
			90235·8
Charges	Paid his Account port Charges	280	
	National Dutys on 100 tons 2 ps.	200	
	Primage to the Capt. 5 Guineas at		
	39	258·17	
	Brokerage on 87655 at [1] per cent	876·17	
	Commissions 3 per cent	2629·21	4244·21

To the Owner account for Net proceeds   85990·21
Errors Excepted.
Cadiz the 15 Decem. 1775   DUFF & WELSH
[Received 30 November 1776]

[Captain Burchmore to Joseph Lee & Co.]
Cadiz, February 7th, 1775 [1776]
Gentlemen: I take this opportunity fearing it will be the last I shall have until those unhappy differences subside, as the late diabolical act of Parliament is to take all

American ships. And would inform you that I arrived at Cadiz the 8 of January from Ferrol where I went with a freight of wheat and flour on the King Spain acct., the particulars of which I wrote you in my last from Cadiz of the 22d. Octr. And I have this day engaged a freight from this to Alicant of sugar and cocoa where I shall make but a poor freight as the times are very dull and all freights very low. There is many ships here without employ and have been this some time. But as I am to a very good house, and I think with prejudice the best in Cadiz, I shall not be without a freight if there is any stirring. My sails begins to be very old and bad so that I shall be under necessity of getting some new ones very soon. But I shall make them do as long as I can and not go to any expense for fear of the worst, though I have with the advice of Messrs. Duff & Welsh taken all the precautions that I can to secure your interest. I have not heard from Capt. George Cabot since the 5 of Novr. Then he was at Barcelona without a freight and had been for some time. Please to let my friends know that I'm well if they may be found, and if my wife should want money you'll please to supply her with it.

And I am, gentlemen, with the Cordial Respect Your most obedt. and Humb. Servant.

[Received 27 March 1776.]

[James Houston to Joseph Lee & Co.]
Lisbon, March 12, 1776.

Gentlemen: I wrote you under the 27 October, which as I understand the vessel arrived in safety, I hope you have received in course. Agreeable thereto I remitted under the 7th of the following month the balance of your account to Messrs. Duff & Welsh in a good bill for Dubs (?) 39.28.32 making at 2390 per Dn. 95 $373 which you'll please to pass in conformity. Although Cap. Burchmore did not complain to me of the measure of his salt, yet my correspondent at Falmouth hinted it to me, on settling therefore my accounts with the shipper, I insisted on his making me an allowance in part of the deficiency, and with some difficulty I obtained an abatement of 28 $800, which sum I carry to your credit and hope some future opportunity may arise to enable my remitting it to you; but *at present* there's no very great appearance of the present troubles being accommodated as I could wish. The value of rice is up at 4 $000 to 4200 per bl. very little of the Carolina growth in town. Flour continues moderate on account of the very inferior quality of what remains on hand, and this affects the price of grain exceedingly. Being what at present offers, I have only to assure you of my wishes for your happiness, that I am truly, Gentlemen, your most obedt. Servant.

[Received 16 May 1776.]

[Captain Burchmore to Joseph Lee & Co.]
Bilbao, Sepr. 10, '76.

Gentlemen: I arrived at Bilbao the 5th of July from Dunkirk, where I found letter from you under the 6th of April ordering me on the receipt of it to proceed to some convenient port to load salt. But as I had no register on board, nor by no means sufficiently covered (had I met a king's ship), I thought it would not be prudent to run the risk merely for the profits on a load salt as there was not anyone at Bilbao that would freight my vessel. However, I determined to lay till I could have Messrs. John and George Cabot's approbation (who I learnt were at Cadiz) and had the satisfaction to receive it, adding they were much pleased with my tarrying there till a proper time to proceed homewards. I have got a new main topsail to the Brign. and shall before I sail furnish her with new sails and everything that may be necessary, and have wrote to France for 6 swivel guns as they are not to be had here. Messrs. John, George, and Francis Cabot arrived here the 1st ins. from Cadiz and are all on board of *Union* and probably will take passage with me. The 400 muskets you ordered in memorandum will be hard to get here, if not impossible. All the other goods are plenty excepting duck. That is scarce and dear at present. But there is vessels daily expect with that article and handkerchiefs are 118 R. Vellon. The stock in Cadiz will be considerable more than by your letter you expected, as I have remitted to Cadiz at several different times the amount of £260 sterling, besides a small balance from James Houston of Lisbon of my rice voyage, so that the whole stock is about two thousand pounds sterling, but as I have a large portlage bill to pay, and shall be at considerable expense to put the vessel in good order, there will be about eighteen hundred pounds sterling to lay out in such goods as you ordered and which I shall advise with Messrs. Cabots about in every respect. And as I shall sail the middle of November as you ordered I must beg you to get one hundred pounds sterling insured for me, or to put my wife in a way how she may do it as it is a piece of business she is not acquainted with.

Salt is scarce here at present but as there is vessels expected from Cadiz it will be plenty soon. The last sold here was at 10 RV per fanaque [fanega]. I shall write you soon after this per Capt. Flitcher of Newbury and be more particular. I remain, Gentlemen, your most Obedient and very Humble Servant.

[Received 30 October 1776.]

[Captain Burchmore to Joseph Lee & Co.]
Bilbao, Octr. 17th 1776.

Gentlemen: I wrote you this day per Capt. Barker of the schooner *Two Brothers* of Marblehead, the true state of my affairs, and would only add that I shall take all possible care in executing your orders and be punctual to the time limited, please God.

I have enclosed you a copy of account from Duff & Welsh in Cadiz to Messrs. Cabots for your government, and shall in my next by Capt. Flitcher of Cape Ann, send a copy of my freights since I have been in Spain. And remain your humble servant.

[Received 30 November 1776.]

[Captain Burchmore to Joseph Lee & Co.]
Bilbao, Oct. 18 1776.

Gentlemen: I this day wrote you by Capt. George Cabot with which I enclosed to you a copy of my flour voyage, and here you have a copy of my freights, made since with the charges in Cadiz. My expenses here will be considerable as I wrote you in my former letters. The stock will be about £1800 sterling, a little more or less, to lay out in goods which I shall take care to have on board by the 10 of November so as not to lose the first opportunity of sailing, as I am very desirous of getting home as soon as possible. Everything you wrote for will be got excepting the arms which cannot be got here. The swivel I wrote to France about I have had no answer to yet. But if they do not come I shall be able to get some old ones here which will be better than none. The only thing I want now is men, but as I have wrote to a friend in Cadiz for some, I expect to hear every day which will be my complement. I remain, Gentlemen, your most Obli'd and very Humble Servant.

[Received 10 December 1776.]

55. Statistics of Colonial Trade

The following tables have several purposes: (a) to offer a basis for comparison of the extent of trade between Britain and the colonies early in the eighteenth century and the years 1763–1775; (b) to show the importance of the trade between the mainland colonies and the British and foreign West Indies; (c) to illustrate the important role of tobacco in the trade of Britain and in its public finances; (d) to present a panoramic picture of the nature and extent of colonial commerce in 1772–1773, including the quantities of the most important products exported, the places to which they were shipped, and the differences among the various colonies.

The tables that follow are based on documents to be found in the Public Record Office of Great Britain. The originals consist for the most part of official reports made by customs house officers at the request of one or another of the governmental agencies concerned with colonial affairs. With a few exceptions, the tables given here are not literal reproductions of the originals. The long titles have been omitted, and in the case of tables of great length, many of the details of lesser importance have been excluded because of lack of space. Table III, for instance, includes only those exports from the colonies in 1772 which in terms of either value or of quantity were of major significance in colonial commerce. The original report, "Exports and Imports, America, 1768–1773" (PRO, Customs 16/1) is a vastly detailed document, presumably the work of the American Board of Customs which was established in Boston in 1767 (No. 116). It lists hundreds of small items whose quantity and value were small. Anyone who wishes a detailed picture of colonial commerce must consult the original report, or the photostatic copy in the Library of Congress in Washington.

A major omission in the tables is an account of the quantities of goods imported into the colonies from Great Britain during the year 1772. The reason for the omission is that the list of items is too lengthy to be compressed in a comprehensible table of reasonable size. However, the following statement of the value of British exports to the mainland colonies is a rough index to the character of British trade to them. It is derived from Customs 17/1 in the Public Record Office.

Value of all Exports to Mainland Colonies, 1772:

Value of Cloth exported:	
Woollens	£1,117,354
Linens	755,433
Silk	159,754
Cotton	90,585
Wearing Apparel (coats, hats, haberdashery, etc.)	231,647
Total	£2,354,773
Value of Ironware	540,450
Miscellaneous	1,428,928
Total value of British exports	£4,324,151
Value of foreign goods exported from Britain to mainland colonies	771,637
Total value of all British exports to mainland colonies	£5,155,178

Of this total, the exports from Scotland amounted to £268,225.

A word of caution concerning eighteenth-century value figures is necessary. These figures are based on rates established by law or by customs procedures, and since these rates were seldom changed, they do not reflect the rise and fall of prices or the ultimate selling price of goods. Any adequate analysis of value would have to include such items as the original purchase price, commissions, handling charges, warehouse charges, freights, insurance, and the profit margins of the merchants who handled the goods. Nevertheless, official values such as given in the following tables are important. They offer a basis for estimating the growth and decline of trade and they make it possible to determine the relative importance of various branches of commerce for Britain and for the colonies.

TABLE I

Exports of English and Foreign Goods to the American Colonies, 1715-1726

From: British Public Record Office, T/64, Bundle 273.

Year	New England, New York and Pennsylvania			Maryland, Virginia, North and South Carolina			The British West Indies		
	English	Foreign	Total	English	Foreign	Total	English	Foreign	Total
1715	£166,196	£69,263	£235,459	£150,119	£65,787	£215,906	£259,692	£147,541	£407,233
1716	130,615	64,554	195,169	144,793	62,079	206,872	288,905	216,762	505,667
1717	125,666	72,979	198,645	167,264	73,756	241,020	267,605	155,407	423,012
1718	149,050	68,516	217,566	151,609	56,157	207,766	442,428	129,902	572,330
1719	151,617	57,122	208,739	132,329	51,932	184,261	217,382	121,558	338,940
1720	122,484	68,210	190,694	95,892	33,115	129,007	187,814	112,942	300,756
1721	130,166	56,657	186,823	100,826	44,254	145,080	192,073	148,728	340,801
1722	135,000	82,595	217,595	137,884	69,244	207,128	216,363	191,609	407,972
1723	147,536	97,954	245,490	112,820	53,279	166,099	282,632	164,805	447,437
1724	181,264	80,586	261,850	127,947	71,786	199,733	313,414	222,560	535,974
1725	208,249	106,376	314,625	154,387	80,679	235,066	360,297	235,851	596,148
1726	208,763	116,616	325,379	144,199	85,717	229,916	234,785	153,041	387,826

TABLE II

Value of Colonial Exports To and Imports From England, 1762–1775

From: British Public Record Office, T64, Bundle 273; and David MacPherson, *Annals of Commerce.* . . . (4 vols., London, 1805), III, *passim.*

Year	New England		New York		Pennsylvania	
	Exports	Imports	Exports	Imports	Exports	Imports
1762	£41,733	£247,385	£58,882	£288,046	£38,091	£206,199
1763	74,815	258,854	53,988	238,560	38,228	284,152
1764	88,157	459,765	53,697	515,416	36,258	435,191
1765	145,819	451,299	54,959	382,349	25,148	363,368
1766	141,733	409,642	67,020	330,829	26,851	327,314
1767*	128,207	406,081	61,422	417,957	37,641	371,830
1768	148,375	419,797	87,115	482,930	59,406	432,107
1769	129,353	207,993	73,466	74,918	26,111	199,909
1770*	148,011	394,451	69,882	475,991	28,109	134,881
1771*	150,381	1,420,119	95,875	653,621	31,615	728,744
1772*	126,265	824,830	82,707	343,970	29,133	507,909
1773	124,624	527,055	76,246	289,214	36,652	426,448
1774*	112,248	562,476	80,008	437,937	69,611	625,652
1775	116,588	71,625	187,018	1,228	175,962	1,366

* Figures from MacPherson, *Annals of Commerce*, III.

TABLE IIa

Year	Virginia and Maryland		North and South Carolina and Georgia		British West Indies	
	Exports	Imports	Exports	Imports	Exports	Imports
1762	£415,709	£417,599	£188,217	£217,931	£2,590,020	£1,404,659
1763	642,294	555,391	296,835	295,040	3,268,485	1,149,596
1764	559,408	515,192	373,052	324,146	2,467,492	918,480
1765	505,671	383,224	420,101	363,874	2,286,173	1,029,173
1766	461,693	372,548	346,661	364,000	2,821,604	1,037,644
1767*	437,926	437,628	430,883	267,427	2,705,623	1,049,853
1768	406,048	475,954	550,510	346,430	2,956,848	1,183,932
1769	361,892	488,362	469,384	364,940	2,710,684	1,263,604
1770*	435,094	717,782	334,439	202,466	3,131,880	1,268,468
1771*	577,848	920,326	484,121	479,662	2,716,569	1,151,357
1772*	528,404	793,910	492,006	542,016	3,304,452	1,378,021
1773	589,803	328,904	541,904	407,791	2,764,642	1,265,789
1774*	612,030	528,738	499,949	435,634	3,454,614	1,350,906
1775	758,356	1,921	682,996	120,022	3,411,200	1,634,002

* Figures from MacPherson, *Annals of Commerce*, III.

TABLE III

Major Exports of the Mainland Colonies, 1772

From: British Public Record Office, Customs 16/1

WHEAT (BUSHELS)

From	To British and Foreign West Indies	To Southern Europe, Wine Is., and Africa	To England and Ireland	Coastwise	Total
New England	16			5,447	5,463
New York	96	45,054		390	45,540
Pennsylvania, New Jersey, Delaware	48	82,888	1,644	124	84,704
Maryland and Virginia		165,635	26,465	108,981	301,081
Carolinas and Georgia				13,358	13,358
Total	160	293,577	28,109	128,300	450,146

INDIAN CORN (BUSHELS)

From	To British and Foreign West Indies	To Southern Europe, Wine Is., and Africa	To England and Ireland	Coastwise	Total
New England	5,995	3,018		29,803	38,816
New York	20,495	46,907	45	8,719	76,166
Pennsylvania, New Jersey, Delaware	42,887	80,471		28,809	152,167
Maryland and Virginia	396,650	123,239		226,074	745,963
Carolinas and Georgia	73,907	7,942	4,355	134,639	220,843
Total	539,934	261,577	4,400	428,044	1,233,955

Table IIIa

BREAD AND FLOUR (TONS)

From	To British and Foreign West Indies	To Southern Europe, Wine Is., and Africa	To England and Ireland	Coastwise	Total
New England	970	104		772	1,846
New York	6,890	3,623	3	4,220	14,736
Pennsylvania, New Jersey, Delaware	12,819	11,148	125	7,229	31,321
Maryland and Virginia	2,707	3,183	332	2,559	8,781
Carolinas and Georgia	118	5	5	90	218
Total	23,504	18,063	465	14,870	56,902

BEEF AND PORK (BARRELS)

From	To British and Foreign West Indies	To Southern Europe, Wine Is., and Africa	To England and Ireland	Coastwise	Total
New England	6,555	248	40	8,068	14,911
New York	2,340	39		4,322	6,701
Pennsylvania, New Jersey, Delaware	2,737		2	1,094	3,833
Maryland and Virginia	5,305			1,493	6,798
Carolinas and Georgia	3,834			5,048	8,882
Total	20,771	287	42	20,025	41,125

TABLE IIIb

FISH, DRIED (QUINTALS)

From	To British and Foreign West Indies	To Southern Europe, Wine Is., and Africa	To England and Ireland	Coastwise	Total
New England	251,720	94,330	7	23,831	369,888
New York	4,537	12		171	4,720
Pennsylvania, New Jersey, Delaware	1,837			192	2,029
Maryland and Virginia	108	30		24	162
Carolinas and Georgia	62	46		72	180
Total	258,264	94,418	7	24,290	376,979

FISH, PICKLED (BARRELS)

From	To British and Foreign West Indies	To Southern Europe, Wine Is., and Africa	To England and Ireland	Coastwise	Total
New England	22,644	90		6,651	29,385
New York	2,747	87		223	3,057
Pennsylvania, New Jersey, Delaware	5,083	50	12	27	5,172
Maryland and Virginia	5,050	163	10	1,722	6,945
Carolinas and Georgia	4,460	620		412	5,492
Total	39,984	1,010	22	9,035	50,051

TABLE IIIc

RUM (GALLONS)

From	To British and Foreign West Indies	To Southern Europe, Wine Is., and Africa	To England and Ireland	Coastwise	Total
New England	1,090	397,846		1,577,126	1,976,062
New York	960	25,306	3,039	194,773	224,078
Pennsylvania, New Jersey, Delaware	360	4,435	18,495	219,824	243,114
Maryland and Virginia		1,400	540	56,563	58,503
Carolinas and Georgia	1,500	16,193		70,372	88,065
Total	3,910	445,180	22,074	2,118,658	2,589,822

BOARDS AND PLANK (FEET)

From	To British and Foreign West Indies	To Southern Europe, Wine Is., and Africa	To England and Ireland	Coastwise	Total
New England	28,297,527	283,250	2,082,405	4,161,370	34,824,552
New York	1,543,068	111,500	247,176	230,496	2,132,240
Pennsylvania, New Jersey, Delaware	4,853,164	8,200	401,214	88,700	5,351,278
Maryland and Virginia	2,254,945	50,495	217,595	105,136	2,628,171
Carolinas and Georgia	4,517,322	14,000	104,873	308,842	4,945,037
Total	41,466,026	467,445	3,053,263	4,894,544	49,881,278

TABLE IIId

SHINGLES (PIECES)

From	To British and Foreign West Indies	To Southern Europe, Wine Is., and Africa	To England and Ireland	Coastwise	Total
New England	19,035,742			2,016,700	21,052,442
New York	1,608,000			139,300	1,747,300
Pennsylvania, New Jersey, Delaware	4,865,033	7,000		1,171,000	6,043,033
Maryland and Virginia	9,020,445	81,300		102,200	9,203,945
Carolinas and Georgia	8,850,305	5,000		1,887,770	10,743,075
Total	43,379,525	93,300		5,316,970	48,789,795

HOOPS AND STAVES (PIECES)

From	To British and Foreign West Indies	To Southern Europe, Wine Is., and Africa	To England and Ireland	Coastwise	Total
New England	8,292,938	196,300	1,269,751	845,050	10,604,039
New York	2,396,500	264,000	806,000	726,580	4,193,080
Pennsylvania, New Jersey, Delaware	4,317,071	373,661	1,217,000	109,165	6,016,897
Maryland and Virginia	3,728,477	267,423	4,356,981	264,400	8,617,281
Carolinas and Georgia	2,037,735	362,800	467,894	1,224,986	4,093,415
Total	20,772,721	1,464,184	8,117,626	3,170,181	33,524,712

TABLE IIIe

PITCH, TAR, AND TURPENTINE (BARRELS)

From	To British and Foreign West Indies	To Southern Europe, Wine Is., and Africa	To England and Ireland	Coastwise	Total
New England	347	128	11,544	1,877	13,896
New York	375	52	3,161	1,911	5,499
Pennsylvania, New Jersey, Delaware	832	169	5,532	437	6,970
Maryland and Virginia	3,883		22,461	1,781	28,125
Carolinas and Georgia	4,149	930	72,583	53,019	130,681
Total	9,586	1,279	115,281	59,025	185,171

PIG IRON (TONS)

From	To British and Foreign West Indies	To Southern Europe, Wine Is., and Africa	To England and Ireland	Coastwise	Total
New England			119	273	392
New York			779	558	1,337
Pennsylvania, New Jersey, Delaware	20		450		470
Maryland and Virginia	4		2,402	302	2,708
Carolinas and Georgia					
Total	24		3,750	1,133	4,907

TABLE IIIf

BAR IRON (TONS)

From	To British and Foreign West Indies	To Southern Europe, Wine Is., and Africa	To England and Ireland	Coastwise	Total
New England	4			99	103
New York	119	8	497	240	864
Pennsylvania, New Jersey, Delaware	82	13	45	967	1,107
Maryland and Virginia	28		462	480	970
Carolinas and Georgia				3	3
Total	233	21	1,004	1,789	3,047

TOBACCO (POUNDS)

From	To British and Foreign West Indies	To Southern Europe, Wine Is., and Africa	To England and Ireland	Coastwise	Total
New England	2,537	8,101		28,703	39,341
New York	6,707	15,331		36,634	58,672
Pennsylvania, New Jersey, Delaware		4,050		22,259	26,309
Maryland and Virginia	149,514		104,351,417	40,542	104,541,473
Carolinas and Georgia	19,165	5,518	2,222,625	64,321	2,311,629
Total	177,923	33,000	106,574,042	192,459	106,977,424

TABLE IIIg

RICE (BARRELS)

From	To British and Foreign West Indies	To Southern Europe, Wine Is., and Africa	To England and Ireland	Coastwise	Total
New England	12	46	6	186	250
New York	277	278		163	718
Pennsylvania, New Jersey, Delaware	27,932		1,281	102	29,315
Maryland and Virginia					
Carolinas and Georgia	21,607	9,768	96,084	9,755	137,214
Total	49,828	10,092	97,371	10,206	167,497

INDIGO (POUNDS)

From	To British and Foreign West Indies	To Southern Europe, Wine Is., and Africa	To England and Ireland	Coastwise	Total
New England				20	20
New York				3,731	3,731
Pennsylvania, New Jersey, Delaware					
Maryland and Virginia			2,423		2,423
Carolinas and Georgia	4,000		758,677	15,694	778,371
Total	4,000		761,100	19,445	784,545

TABLE IV

Imports of the British West Indies from the Mainland Colonies, 1772

From : British Public Record Office, B.T. 6/86, No. 11 : Dated 15 March 1775

Colony	Lumber Feet	Shingles Number	Staves Number	Hoops Number	Corn Bus.
Newfoundland					
Canada	22,680	16,000	450	4,750	8
Nova Scotia	61,000	31,000			
New England	17,691,416	10,374,569	6,214,096	1,926,860	5,993
New York	538,140	500,813	1,395,591	83,825	17,500
Pennsylvania	1,655,008	1,359,332	3,620,192	84,546	28,010
Maryland	693,900	299,900	375,434	19,750	21,874
Virginia	1,976,709	5,667,918	2,630,170	39,155	239,743
North Carolina	2,891,529	1,586,700	3,730,107	3,000	43,269
South Carolina	688,740	591,866	1,559,290	7,200	7,254
Georgia	919,385	508,090	1,635,131		1,649
Total	27,138,507	20,936,188	21,160,461	2,169,086	365,300

TABLE IVa

Colony	Oats	Peas and Beans	Bread and Flour		Rice	
	Bus.	Bus.	Bbls.	Kegs	Bbls.	Tierces
Newfoundland						
Canada	68	288	172			
Nova Scotia						
New England	1,780	713	5,542	520	82	66
New York	1,443	1,686	12,969	406	86	106
Pennsylvania	306	351	90,453	3,874	222	138
Maryland		50	7,458	157		
Virginia	2,571	11,272	8,852			
North Carolina		3,784	189	3	53	133
South Carolina		1,976	639		6,526	4,033
Georgia			25		687	901
Total	6,168	20,120	126,299	4,960	7,656	5,377

TABLE IVb

Colony	Fish				Beef and Pork	Poultry	Horses	Oxen
	Hhds.	Bbls.	Quints.	Kegs	Bbls.	Doz.	No.	No.
Newfoundland	1,406	42	4,391					
Canada	111	67	394	195	3			
Nova Scotia	52	94	108			10	28	
New England	14,210	8,820	5,760	836	2,013	779	1,896	1,204
New York	534	1,296	182	233	911	12	65	20
Pennsylvania	549	3,071	91	84	2,717	12	14	
Maryland	160	1,572			177	17		
Virginia	1,918	726	2		4,178		6	
North Carolina	2,244	1,811			1,217	105	38	
South Carolina		248	26	10	860		94	12
Georgia		3			499	4	79	60
Total	21,184	17,750	10,954	1,358	12,575	939	2,220	1,296

TABLE IVc

Colony	Sheep and Hogs	Oil	Pitch, Tar & Turp.	Masts	Spars	Shook Hhds. & Water Casks	Soap & Candles	Ox-bows and Yokes	House Frames	Iron
	No.	Bbl.	Bbls.	No.	No.	No.	Boxes	No.	No.	Tons and Bars
Newfoundland		46								
Canada		37								
Nova Scotia		7								
New England	3,364	646	313	30	976	17,140	3,000	240	200	13 tons
New York		25	162		2		753			47½ tons 314 bars
Pennsylvania		190	549			6	3,000			72¾ tons 288 bars
Maryland	20					14	11	133		14 tons
Virginia			1,269	5			2		1	9½ tons
North Carolina	154		3,754				24			2 tons
South Carolina	39		1,427			51				
Georgia	116		247				56			2½ tons
Total	3,693	951	7,721	35	978	17,211	6,846	373	201	161¼ tons 602 bars

TABLE V

Imports of the Mainland Colonies from the British and Foreign West Indies, 1772

From : British Public Record Office, Customs 16/1

Colony	Cocoa (pounds)		Coffee (pounds)*		Cotton (pounds)	
	British	Foreign	British	Foreign	British	Foreign
New Hampshire	4,650	63,300	19,734		16,330	33,260
Massachusetts	82,594	166,393	13,740	166	19,900	127,171
Rhode Island		37,652		593	2,767	15,892
Connecticut		192,952	23,086		1,050	26,944
New York		25,600	20,245	1,528	1,900	27,480
New Jersey	800					
Pennsylvania	28,300	30,510	291,016		15,874	11,900
Maryland			5,751		400	
Virginia	7,400		59,269		8,950	
North Carolina		430	6,214	980	1,000	
South Carolina	3,050		36,120			
Georgia			8,298			

* Converted to pounds from the original figures given in hundredweight, quarters, and pounds.

TABLE Va

| Colony | Mahogany | | Molasses (gals.) | | Rum (gals.) |
	Cubic Measure (tons. ft.)	Short Measure (feet)	British	Foreign	British
New Hampshire		200	9,783	521,538	165,875
Massachusetts		28,580	32,660	2,047,529	178,756
Rhode Island	5·30	9,600	30,539	586,329	155,750
Connecticut		27,800	1,700	269,805	313,690
New York		902,531	8,426	417,198	374,167
New Jersey		1,700	750	1,200	19,870
Pennsylvania	125·16	498,390	18,194	551,639	899,520
Maryland			2,730	24,018	256,060
Virginia			6,640	145,498	549,360
North Carolina		10,600	2,546	33,550	72,636
South Carolina		106,159	2,164	91,493	350,650
Georgia		36,800		6,694	45,044

TABLE Vb

Colony	Salt (Bushels)		Brown Sugar (Pounds)*	
	From West Indies	From So. Europe	British	Foreign
New Hampshire	64,648	5,600	168,372	106,085
Massachusetts	204,267	175,440	709,004	2,356,590
Rhode Island	65,110	10,300	149,544	148,922
Connecticut	126,625		108,614	103,558
New York	59,490	42,200	537,544	1,201,344
New Jersey	1,407		16,872	1,792
Pennsylvania	19,028	105,398	1,990,252	1,254,572
Maryland	22,900		209,400	66,359
Virginia	42,729		668,609	56,500
North Carolina	40,761	3,000	87,597	47,256
South Carolina	13,626		290,012	280,997
Georgia	2,700		64,165	31,604

* Converted to pounds from the original figures given in hundredweight, quarters, and pounds.

TABLE VI

Exports of the British West Indies to the Mainland Colonies and to Great Britain, 1773

From: British Public Record Office, B.T. 6/83

	Sugar		Rum		Molasses	
	Pounds	Equal to hhds. of 1,600 lb.	Gals.	Equal to puncheons of 110 gals.	Hhds. of unknown contents	Gals.
To England and Scotland	190,265,088	118,915	2,792,785	25,389	44	140
To North America	6,042,710	3,776	3,549,152	32,265	1,277	2,450
Total	196,307,798	122,691	6,341,937	57,654	1,321	2,590

	Pimento	Coffee		Cotton		Ginger
	Casks and bags of unknown weight	Casks and bags of unknown weight	Pounds	Bags of unknown weight	Pounds	Pounds
To England and Scotland	18,263	235	3,444,371	1,184	846,810	462,171
To North America	1,521	53	364,236	184	50,080	90
Total	19,784	288	3,808,967	1,368	896,890	462,261

TABLE VII

English Imports and Exports of Colonial Tobacco, 1761–1776

From: British Public Record Office, T/64, Bundle 276 B: Dated Custom House, London,
26 January 1778

Year	Pounds Imported	Pounds Exported	Gross Duties Collected	Net Duties
1761	47,065,787	36,788,944	£1,225,671	£267,626
1762	44,102,491	36,445,951	1,148,502	199,389
1763	65,173,752	40,940,312	1,697,233	631,079
1764	54,433,318	54,058,336	1,417,534	9,765
1765	48,306,593	39,121,423	1,257,984	239,197
1766	43,307,453	32,986,790	1,127,798	268,767
1767	39,140,639	36,400,398	1,019,287	71,360
1768	35,545,708	30,864,536	925,669	121,905
1769	33,784,208	23,793,272	879,797	260,180
1770	39,188,037	33,238,437	1,020,495	154,911
1771	58,079,183	41,439,386	1,512,478	433,328
1772	51,493,522	49,784,009	1,340,977	44,518
1773	55,928,957	50,349,967	1,456,983	145,786
1774	56,048,393	44,829,835	1,459,593	292,149
1775	55,965,463	43.880,865	1,457,433	} 73,886
1776	7,275,037	16,522,412	189,454	

TABLE VIII

Tobacco Imported Into England and Scotland, 1772–1775

From: British Public Record Office, Customs 17/1, 2, 3, 4

Year	England		Scotland		Total	
	Quantity (pounds)	Value*	Quantity (pounds)	Value*	Quantity (pounds)	Value*
1772	51,493,522	£482,751	45,259,675	£471,454	96,753,197	£954,206
1773	55,928,957	£542,540	44,543,050	£463,990	100,472,007	£1,006,530
1774	56,048,393	£525,453	41,348,295	£430,711	97,396,688	£956,164
1775	55,965,463	£525,187	45,863,154	£477,741	101,828,617	£1,002,929

* Based on valuation as follows:

1772 — 2d.   per lb.
1773 — 2¼d. per lb.
1774 — 2¼d. per lb.
1775 — 2¼d. per lb.

D. MANUFACTURING IN THE COLONIES

ONE of the earliest arguments for the founding of English colonies was that they would become markets for the manufactures of England. It was hoped too that colonies would produce raw materials such as iron, potash, and dyewoods that could be used in English industry.[1] British policy after 1660 consistently opposed the manufacture of finished products in the colonies and sought to make Britain the only source of the colonial supply of manufactured goods, whether they were produced in England or in Europe. This policy was expressed in legislation and in the veto of colonial laws which sought to encourage manufactures, either directly or indirectly. Thus in 1766 the Privy Council disallowed a Virginia law which encouraged the export of dressed hides and skins. The Privy Council declared that such efforts "to check or interfere with the manufactures of this country ought in policy and reason to be discouraged and suppressed".

There were certain controlling facts, aside from British opposition, which stood in the way of the development of large-scale manufacturing in the colonies. Either the capital was lacking or there were far more profitable outlets for it in trade and land speculation. The price of labour was high as compared with the price of English labour. There was a vast extent of cheap and relatively available land, and the desire of most people who came to the colonies was to become landowners and farmers. The Board of Trade repeatedly queried the colonial governors about manufactures in their provinces, and the testimony of the governors was virtually unanimous in reporting that these were the factors that prevented the development of large-scale manufactures.[2]

Nevertheless, manufactures did develop in the colonies despite the obstacles provided by colonial conditions and British policy. Such manufactures were the result of both economic advantages and economic obstacles which were to be found in the colonies. A sizeable hat industry developed because of the availability and cheapness of beaver. In the age of the beaver hat the colonial hatmakers were able to compete so favourably with English hatmakers that the hatmakers of London petitioned Parliament to save them from poverty. Parliament responded with the Hat Act of 1732, which was apparently the only piece of legislation against colonial manufacturing that was effective.[3]

The shipbuilding industry was a natural outgrowth of the existence of a great supply of fine ship timber at a time when English timber was becoming scarce and expensive. By the end of the colonial period, even the southern colonies were building an increasing number of ships. The overall result was that perhaps a third of the tonnage in the carrying trade of the empire, just before the American Revolution, had been built in the colonies. English shipbuilders repeatedly demanded protection from Parliament, but Parliament refused for colonial shipbuilding was all too obviously an indispensable element in the commercial and naval strength of the empire.

The colonial iron industry grew steadily from the early part of the seventeenth century. Great deposits of bog iron existed in most of the colonies, along with a

---

[1] No. 5.   [2] No. 57.   [3] No. 56B.

seemingly endless supply of wood for smelting. Various groups in the iron industry of England wrangled for decades over the question of parliamentary regulation. English raw iron producers wanted to eliminate colonial competition. English producers of finished iron products wanted the raw iron industry in the colonies encouraged and its product brought into England as cheaply as possible. Owners of woodlands lined up with the iron producers, and so on. The only point upon which English interests could agree at all was that the colonists must not be allowed to produce finished iron products for themselves. In the Iron Act of 1750 the English producers of finished iron won out. The importation of raw iron into England was encouraged and the colonists were forbidden to erect any more slitting mills.[1] The Act did not serve either purpose. There was a steady increase in iron production, but most of it was used in the colony where it was produced or was shipped to other colonies, where it was made into finished products by local artisans. The prohibition of slitting mills was ignored, and colonial governors either could not find them or conveniently closed their eyes to the fact.

There was one area, however, in which Parliament sought to encourage colonial industry, and this was in the production of naval stores. One purpose of the Naval Stores Act of 1704 was to divert the colonies from developing other manufactures and to provide them with additional means of paying for imports. A second purpose was to free Britain from dependence on the Baltic countries for supplies of naval stores such as pitch, tar, and turpentine.[2] The Act seems to have been successful in the case of these three products for ever greater quantities were exported to Britain, and of course were used in the colonial shipbuilding industry.

The major industry of England was the cloth industry, and at least fifty per cent of the value of British exports to the colonies throughout the colonial period consisted of cloth. The concern of Parliament was accordingly great. The Woollen Act of 1699[3] was aimed at the exportation of cloth from Ireland and the colonies. Whatever its effects on Ireland, it had little apparent effect on the colonies. In general, the English cloth industry did not need to fear American competition because its product was cheaper than anything that could be produced in America. However, there were certain economic facts that resulted in a large production of cloth in the colonies. During times of depression throughout the colonial period there were movements for the production and wearing of domestic clothing in order to reduce imports from England. It is doubtful that these were of any significance until after 1763 when political motives were joined to economic. The bulk of the cloth production was carried on in the homes of American farmers and was the result of economic necessity. Farmers' wives, like the farmers, were forced to produce as much as possible on the farm. Hence, not only the clothing but the shoes, tools, furniture, and buildings of the average small farm family were made from the materials at hand. If there was any surplus production, it went to nearby trading areas and seldom found its way into intercolonial, much less transatlantic, commerce. It was therefore difficult to either regulate or limit by any means available to the British government.

In addition to domestic manufactures, there was a steady growth of an artisan class in the colonial towns. There is no dependable information as to the quantity of manufactured goods produced by the artisans but the contemporary evidence agrees that the artisans were of vital importance in every community. The products of their skill were of great variety. The increasing exports of shingles, staves, barrels, and

[1] No. 56c.   [2] No. 56D.   [3] No. 56A.

boards and the growth of the shipbuilding industry are an index to one area of production. Shoemakers in increasing numbers were to be found in shops as well as in homes. Furniture makers, blacksmiths, silversmiths, printers, paper makers, and bookbinders all grew in number and skill and produced much that was not only useful but beautiful for colonial homes.

The outbreak of the Revolution brought a clear demonstration of the importance of the artisan class in the colonies, and of the average farmer as well, for he too, of necessity, was a 'mechanick' as well as farmer. The war shut off the normal supply of manufactured goods from Britain, but the Americans turned to and produced materials needed to fight the war. They were never able to produce all that was needed, but without the contribution of a myriad of small 'manufacturers' the war could not have been fought to a successful conclusion.

56A–D. British legislation on colonial manufactures

The following documents are excerpts from British legislation relating to manufactures in the colonies. The portions in brackets are editorial summaries. The omitted portions of the Woollen Act relate to Ireland.

56A. The Woollen Act (4 May 1699) (10 and 11 William III, c. 10)

Printed: Pickering, *Statutes at Large*, x, pp. 249, 256.

Forasmuch as wool and the woollen manufactures of cloth, serge, bays, kerseys, and other stuffs made or mixed with wool, are the greatest and most profitable commodities of this kingdom, on which the value of lands, and the trade of the nation do chiefly depend; and whereas great quantities of the like manufactures have of late been made, and are daily increasing in the kingdom of Ireland, and in the English plantations in America, and are exported from thence to foreign markets, heretofore supplied from England, which will inevitably sink the value of lands, and tend to the ruin of the trade, and the woollen manufactures of this realm; for the prevention whereof, and for the encouragement of the woollen manufactures within this kingdom. . . .

XIX. And for the more effectual encouragement of the woollen manufacture of this kingdom; be it further enacted by the authority aforesaid, that from and after the first day of December, in the year of our Lord, one thousand six hundred ninety-nine, no wool, wool-fells, shortlings, mortlings, woolflocks, worsted, bay, or woollen yarn, cloth, serge, bays, kerseys, says, friezes, druggets, cloth-serges, shalloons, or any other drapery stuffs, or woollen manufactures whatsoever, made or mixed with wool or woolflocks, being of the product or manufacture of any of the English plantations in America, shall be loaden or laid on board in any ship or vessel, in any place or parts within any of the said English plantations, upon any pretence whatsoever; as likewise that no such wool, wool-fells, shortlings, mortlings, woolflocks, worsted, bay, or woollen yarn, cloth, serge, bays, kerseys, says, friezes, druggets, cloth-serges, shalloons, or any other drapery stuffs, or woollen manufactures whatsoever, made up or mixt with wool or woolflocks, being of the product or manufacture of any of the English plantations in America as aforesaid, shall be loaden upon any horse, cart, or other carriage, to the intent and purpose to be exported, transported, carried, or conveyed out of the said English plantations to any other of the said plantations, or to any other place whatsoever. . . .

56B. The Hat Act (1 June 1732) (5 Geo. II, c. 22)

Printed: Pickering, *Statutes at Large*, XVI, pp. 304-305, 307-308.

Whereas the art and mystery of making hats in Great Britain hath arrived to great perfection, and considerable quantities of hats manufactured in this kingdom have heretofore been exported to his Majesty's plantations or colonies in America, who have been wholly supplied with hats from Great Britain; and whereas great quantities of hats have of late years been made, and the said manufacture is daily increasing in the British plantations in America, and is from thence exported to foreign markets, which were heretofore supplied from Great Britain, and the hatmakers in the said plantations take many apprentices for very small terms, to the discouragement of the said trade, and debasing the said manufacture; wherefore for preventing the said ill practices for the future, and for promoting and encouraging the trade of making hats in Great Britain, be it enacted by the king's most excellent Majesty, by and with the advice and consent of the Lords Spiritual and Temporal, and Commons in this present Parliament assembled, and by the authority of the same, that from and after the twenty-ninth day of September in the year of our Lord one thousand seven hundred and thirty-two, no hats or felts whatsoever, dyed or undyed, finished or unfinished, shall be shipt, loaden, or put on board any ship or vessel in any place or parts within any of the British plantations, upon any pretence whatsoever, by any person or persons whatsoever, and also that no hats or felts, either dyed or undyed, finished or unfinished, shall be loaden upon any horse, cart, or other carriage, to the intent or purpose to be exported, transported, shipped off, carried, or conveyed out of any of the said British plantations to any other of the British plantations, or to any other place whatsoever, by any persons or persons whatsoever.

VII. And it is hereby further enacted by the authority aforesaid, that no person residing in any of his Majesty's plantations in America shall, from and after the said twenty-ninth day of September, one thousand seven hundred and thirty-two, make or cause to be made, any felt or hat of or with any wool or stuff whatsoever, unless he shall have first served as an apprentice in the trade or art of feltmaking during the space of seven years at the least; neither shall any feltmaker or hatmaker in any of the said plantations employ, retain, or set to work, in the said art or trade, any person as a journeyman or hired servant, other than such as shall have lawfully served an apprenticeship in the said trade for the space of seven years; nor shall any feltmaker or hatmaker in any of the said plantations have, take, or keep above the number of two apprentices at one time, or take any apprentice for any less term than seven years, upon pain to forfeit and pay the sum of five pounds for every month that he shall continue offending in the premises contrary to the true meaning of this act, of which one moiety shall go and be applied to the use of his Majesty, his heirs, and successors, and the other moiety thereof to such person or persons as will sue for the same by action of debt, bill, plaint, or information, to be commenced, brought, or prosecuted in any court in the said plantations, wherein no essoin, protection, or wager of law, or more than one imparlance shall be admitted or allowed for the defendant.

VIII. And be it further enacted by the authority aforesaid, that no person or persons inhabiting in the said plantations, from and after the said twenty-ninth day of September, one thousand seven hundred and thirty-two, shall retain or set on work, in the said art of hat or feltmaking, any black or Negro, upon pain to forfeit and pay the sum of five pounds for every month wherein such person or persons shall so offend, contrary to the meaning of this act; and to be recovered and applied in manner, and to the uses aforesaid.

IX. Provided always, that nothing in this act contained shall extend to charge any person or persons lawfully exercising the said art, with any penalty or forfeiture for setting or using his or their own son or sons to the making or working hats or felts in his or their own house or houses, so as every such son or sons be bound by indenture of apprenticeship, for the term of seven years at the least, which term shall not be to expire before he shall be of the full age of twenty-one years; anything herein contained to the contrary notwithstanding.

X. Provided also, and be it enacted by the authority aforesaid, that every felt-maker residing in the said plantations, who at the beginning of this present session of Parliament was a maker or worker of hats or felts, and being an householder, and likewise all such as were at the beginning of this present session apprentices, covenant servants, or journeymen in the same art or mystery of feltmaking so as such apprentices serve or make up their respective apprenticeships, shall and may continue and exercise the trade or art of making hats and felts in the said plantations, although the same persons were not bound apprentices to the same art for the term of seven years; anything in this act to the contrary notwithstanding.

XI. And be it further enacted by the authority aforesaid, that this present act shall be deemed, and is hereby declared to be a public act, of which all judges and justices are to take notice without special pleading the same.

56C. The Iron Act (12 April 1750) (23 Geo. II, c. 29)

Printed: Pickering, *Statutes at Large*, xx, pp. 97, 99–100.

Whereas the importation of bar iron from his Majesty's colonies in America, into the port of London, and the importation of pig-iron from the said colonies into any port of Great Britain, and the manufacture of such bar and pig-iron in Great Britain, will be a great advantage not only to the said colonies, but also to this kingdom, by furnishing the manufacturers of iron with a supply of that useful and necessary commodity, and by means thereof large sums of money, now annually paid for iron to foreigners, will be saved to this kingdom, and a greater quantity of the woollen, and other manufactures of Great Britain, will be exported to America in exchange for such iron so imported; be it therefore enacted by the king's most excellent Majesty, by and with the advice and consent of the Lords Spiritual and Temporal, and Commons, in this present Parliament assembled, and by the authority of the same, that from and after the twenty-fourth day of June, one thousand seven hundred and fifty, the several and respective subsidies, customs, impositions, rates, and duties, now payable on pig-iron, made in and imported from his Majesty's colonies in America, into any port of Great Britain, shall cease, determine, and be no longer paid; and that from and after the said twenty-fourth day of June, no subsidy, custom, imposition, rate, or duty whatsoever shall be payable upon bar-iron made in and imported from the said colonies into the port of London; any law statute, or usage to the contrary thereof in any wise notwithstanding.

IX. And, that pig and bar-iron made in his Majesty's colonies in America may be further manufactured in this kingdom, be it further enacted by the authority aforesaid, that from and after the twenty-fourth day of June, one thousand seven hundred and fifty, no mill or other engine for slitting or rolling of iron, or any plating-forge to work with a tilt hammer, or any furnace for making steel, shall be erected, or after such erection, continued, in any of his Majesty's colonies in America; and if any person or persons shall erect, or cause to be erected, or after such erection, continue, or cause to be continued, in any of the said colonies, any such mill, engine, forge, or furnace, every person or persons so offending, shall for every such mill, engine, forge, or furnace, forfeit the sum of two hundred pounds of lawful money of Great Britain.

56D. The Naval Stores Act (14 March 1705) (3 and 4 Anne, c. 10)

Printed: Pickering, *Statutes at Large*, XI, pp. 109–111.

Whereas the royal navy and the navigation of England, wherein, under God, the wealth, safety, and strength of this kingdom is so much concerned, depends on the due supply of stores necessary for the same, which being now brought in mostly from foreign parts, in foreign shipping, at exorbitant and arbitrary rates, to the great prejudice and discouragement of the trade and navigation of this kingdom, may be provided in a more certain and beneficial manner from her Majesty's own dominions; and whereas her Majesty's colonies and plantations in America were at first settled, and are still maintained and protected at a great expense of the treasure of this kingdom, with a design to render them as useful as may be to England, and the labour and industry of the people there, profitable to themselves; and in regard the said colonies and plantations, by the vast tracts of land therein, lying near the sea, and upon navigable rivers, may commodiously afford great quantities of all sorts of naval stores, if due encouragement be given for carrying on so great and advantageous an undertaking, which will likewise tend not only to the further employment and increase of English shipping and seamen, but also to the enlarging, in a great measure, the trade and vent of the woollen and other manufactures and commodities of this kingdom, and of other her Majesty's dominions, in exchange for such naval stores, which are now purchased from foreign countries with money or bullion; and for enabling her Majesty's subjects, in the said colonies and plantations, to continue to make due and sufficient returns in the course of their trade; be it therefore enacted . . . that every person or persons that shall, within the time appointed by this act, import or cause to be imported into this kingdom, directly from any of her Majesty's

English colonies or plantations in America, in any ship or ships that may lawfully trade to her Majesty's plantations, manned as by law is required, any of the naval stores hereafter mentioned, shall have and enjoy, as a reward or premium for such importation, after and according to the several rates for such naval stores. . . .

II. [Lists premiums for tar, pitch, rosin or turpentine, hemp, masts, yards, and bowsprits.]

III. Which several rewards or premiums, for each species aforementioned, shall be paid and answered by the commissioners or principal officers of her Majesty's navy, who are hereby empowered and required to make out bill or bills, to be paid in course for the same, upon certificate of the respective chief officer or officers of the customs, in any port of this kingdom where such naval stores shall be imported, as aforesaid; such bill or bills to be made out and given to the person or persons importing the same. . . .

VI. And for the better preservation of all timber fit for the uses aforesaid, be it further enacted and ordained by the authority aforesaid; that no person or persons within her Majesty's colonies of New Hampshire, the Massachusetts Bay, Rhode Island and Providence Plantation, the Narragansett Country or King's Province, and Connecticut in New England, and New York, and New Jersey, do or shall presume to cut, fell, or destroy any pitch, pine trees, or tar trees, not being within any fence or actual enclosure, under the growth of twelve inches diameter, at three foot from the earth, on the penalty or forfeiture of five pounds for each offence, on proof thereof to be made by one or more credible witnesses on oath, before one or more justice or justices of the peace within or nearest to such place where such offence shall be committed; one moiety of such penalty or forfeiture to be to her Majesty, her heirs or successors, the other moiety to the informer or informers.

57A–C. Reports of governors on colonial manufactures (1766–1768)

At the time of the Stamp Act the colonists passed resolutions declaring their intention to promote colonial manufactures. The usual alarm was created in Great Britain. As a result of resolutions passed by the House of Commons, the Board of Trade ordered all colonial governors to report on manufactures developed in the colonies since 1734 and on legislative encouragement. The letters to the Board of Trade which follow are typical of the reports sent back by the governors. It has been charged that colonial governors underestimated colonial manufactures in order to defend their administrations. Whatever the merit of the charge, the governors' reports indicate the essential facts standing in the way of large-scale industrial development in the colonies.

57A. Governor Francis Bernard: manufactures in Massachusetts (15 November 1766, 21 March 1768)

To the Board of Trade, 15 November 1766. From: British Public Record Office, C.O. 5/892.

I have received your lordships' letter dated August 1 commanding me to transmit to your lordships a particular account of the several manufactures which have been set up and carried on in this province since the year 1734, and of the public encouragements which have been given thereto. As this inquiry lay for the most part out of the reach of my knowledge, I ordered the secretary to search the books for public encouragements and make inquiry of manufactures set up without them. For my own part I could have immediately answered that since I have been governor I have known of no new manufactures set up here except potash, which I presume is not an object of the present inquiry.

The secretary has now made his report to me, which consists of a very few articles and really shows the impracticability of carrying on manufactures here to any purpose, and is as follows:

The greatest manufactory which has been attempted here was set up at Boston in the year [   ] by a subscription of the principal gentlemen there, for spinning and weaving linen. They built a large brick building for that purpose and in the year 1750 the General Court granted the sum of £1500 to pay for the building, to be raised by a tax upon coaches, chaises, etc., for five years. The tax did not raise half the money; the manufactory entirely failed; and the General Court has since paid the rest of the £1500 with interest, to indemnify the creditors of the building, and have taken it to themselves. They have lately put it up for sale, but cannot find a purchaser.

In the year [   ] a manufactory for making glass bottles was set up at Germantown, a place so called by Germans settled there under English taskmasters. In the year 1754, upon a petition that some of their buildings had been destroyed by fire or otherwise, the General Court granted them £1215 to be raised by lottery. The bottle manufactory is now quite at an end, and a stocking manufactory which was set up at the same place has had little better success.

In the year 1754, upon the petition of Franklin and others, that they had introduced foreign Protestants and settled them within the province for carrying on several manufactures, and particularly potash, the General Court granted them 1500 acres of land upon condition that they carried on the same manufactures which they were engaged in in Germantown. This came to nothing but the acquiring 1500 acres of land, which probably would have sold for no more than so many shillings.

In the year 1763, upon the petition of the owners of a paper mill at Milton, the General Court lent them £400, to be paid again at stated times without interest. All this grant, which cost the province nothing, by interest at 6 per cent amounts only to 60 guineas.

These are all the encouragements that I can learn have been granted to manufactories since 1734; and these discouragements, and perhaps some others which had no bounty and have not come to my knowledge, seem to have put a stop to attempts of this kind, and to have disposed people to pursue those businesses which are sure to make them better returns than manufactories are like to do. And it is remarkable that the opposers of the Stamp Act in this province, among their several practices to obtain a repeal, did not threaten Great Britain with setting up manufactories against her in the manner some other provinces did; for they knew that the futility of such a threat was too open. They threatened to be more sparing in the use of British manufactures; but did not pretend to rival them.

To the earl of Shelburne, 21 March 1768. From: British Public Record Office, C.O. 5/757.

. . . There is such confidence in the success of this combination that the business of manufactures seems to be dropped; at least it is not now talked of. I cannot be answerable for all America; it is possible that in Pennsylvania, which advances much faster in arts than other colonies, there may be some rivalry with Great Britain. But for New England to threaten the mother country with manufactures is the idlest bully that ever was attempted to be imposed upon sensible people. Notwithstanding all the puffs flung in the newspapers, there is not as yet the least apparent advance of any one work. They have neither materials nor hands nor inclination for such works. All the wool in the province would not make two pair of stockings a year for each person. It always has been worked up, chiefly in the families where it grows, and there used, not being fit for any market; all the advantage being its being done in the dead time of the year when there is no work to be done out of doors. There is no probability of any increase or improvement in this than what has been time out of mind. There has been an attempt to make nails; it is found they cannot be brought within a saleable price; paper, there is but one mill, and that can scarce keep itself going. There is now an attempt to set up a manufactory of duck or sailcloth at Boston in order to employ the poor, who are so ill managed as to be a great burden. If that should succeed it can only be by the town making good the loss in the price of labour, and thereby gaining something in aid of the poor rate. And this, as it is a foreign manufacture, cannot hurt Great Britain. Whatever therefore may be the motives to induce Great Britain to submit to the present advanced claims of the Americans, let not the fear of American manufactories be one of them.

57B. Governor Henry Moore: manufactures in New York (12 January 1767)
Printed: *New York Colonial Documents*, VII, pp. 888–889.

Having received your lordships' command in a letter dated the first of August last, in which I was directed to prepare and transmit as soon as possible an account of the several manufactures set up and carried on within this colony since the year 1734, I took the liberty of giving Mr. Peter Hasenclever a letter of introduction to your lordships, as he was then ready to sail for England, imagining that from his character and knowledge of the country, a more perfect account might be obtained from him of what was required in the before mentioned letter than I could possibly give by that opportunity. I have since made all the inquiries I could, and the whole of the information given to me may be reduced to the following heads.

There is a small manufactory of linen in this city under the conduct of one Wells, and supported chiefly by the subscriptions of a set of men who call themselves the Society of Arts and Agriculture. No more than fourteen looms are employed in it, and it was established in order to give bread to several poor families which were a considerable charge to the city, and are now comfortably supported by their own daily labour, in spinning of flax. It does not appear that there is any established fabric of broadcloth here; and some poor weavers from Yorkshire who came over lately in expectation of being engaged to make broadcloths, could find no employment. But there is a general manufactory of woollen carried on here, and consists of two sorts, the first a coarse cloth entirely woollen, three fourths of a yard wide; and the other a stuff which they call linsey woolsey. The warp of this is linen, and the woof woollen; and a very small quantity of it is ever sent to market. Last year when the riots and

disorders here were at their height on the occasion of the Stamp Act, these manufactures were greatly boasted of, and the quantity then made greatly magnified by
those who were desirous of distinguishing themselves as American patriots, and would
wear nothing else. They were sometimes sold for three times their value; but the
manufacturers themselves showed that they had more good sense than the persons
who employed them, for they never clothed themselves with the work of their own
hands but readily brought it to market, and selling it at an extravagant price there,
bought English cloth for themselves and their families. The custom of making these
coarse cloths in private families prevails throughout the whole province, and almost
in every house a sufficient quantity is manufactured for the use of the family without
the least design of sending any of it to market. This I had an opportunity of seeing
during the late tour I made, and had the same accounts given me by all those persons
of whom I made any inquiry, for every house swarms with children who are set to
work as soon as they are able to spin and card; and as every family is furnished with
a loom, the itinerant weavers who travel about the country put the finishing hand
to the work.

There is a manufactory of hats in this city which is very considerable; for the hats
are not so good as those made in England, and are infinitely dearer. Under such
disadvantages as these it is easy to imagine with what difficulty it is supported, and
how short the duration of it is like to be; the price of labour is so great in this part
of the world that it will always prove the greatest obstacle to any manufactures
attempted to be set up here, and the genius of the people in a country where everyone
can have land to work upon leads them so naturally into agriculture that it prevails
over every other occupation. There can be no stronger instances of this than in the
servants imported from Europe of different trades; as soon as the time stipulated in
their indentures is expired, they immediately quit their masters and get a small tract
of land, in settling which for the first three or four years they lead miserable lives, and
in the most abject poverty, but all this is patiently borne and submitted to with the
greatest cheerfulness, the satisfaction of being landholders smooths every difficulty
and makes them prefer this manner of living to that comfortable subsistence which
they could procure for themselves and their families by working at the trades in which
they were brought up.

The master of a glass house which was set up here a few years ago, now a bankrupt, assured me that his ruin was owing to no other cause than being deserted in this
manner by his servants, which he had imported at a great expense; and that many
others had suffered and been reduced as he was, by the same kind of misfortune.

The little foundry lately set up near this town for making small iron pots is under
the direction of a few private persons, and as yet very inconsiderable.

, As to the foundries which Mr. Hasenclever has set up in the different parts of this
country, I do not mention them as he will be able to give your lordships a full account
of them and of the progress he has already made; I can only say that I think this
province is under very great obligations to him for the large sums of money he has
laid out here in promoting the cultivation of hemp, and introducing the valuable
manufactures of iron and potash.

57C. Lieutenant-Governor Wiillam Bull: manufactures in South Carolina
(6 September 1768)

From: British Public Record Office, C.O. 5/379.

In obedience to his Majesty's commands signified by the right honourable the earl
of Hillsborough, his Majesty's Principal Secretary of State for America, in his
lordship's letter No. 4 to Lord Charles Montagu, governor in chief of this province,
requiring a particular and exact account of the several manufactures which have been
set up and carried on in this province from the year 1734, and of the public encouragements that have been given thereto, which in the absence of Lord Charles Montagu
for recovery of his health, came into my hands the 8th of August last, I have now the
honour to transmit to your lordships the fullest information I have been able to
procure.

Upon the most particular inquiry I cannot learn that any manufactures have been
set up in this province except three rope-walks and two houses for baking or refining
sugar; and after the most diligent search into our records I cannot find that any
public encouragement has ever been given to any manufactures, although in some of
our laws the term manufacture has been applied, perhaps improperly, to the raising
silk, hemp, and indigo.

One of the rope-walks was set up near Charleston twenty years ago in order to
have assortments of cordage for shipping, and on receiving some unfavourable
accounts of sales of hemp sent to London, two other rope-walks have lately been set
up. One sugar house was set up about eighteen years ago, and the other about ten.
These are all carried on at the private expense of the proprietors, without any public
encouragement given them.

Looms, it is true, are to be seen in almost every house in our western settlements,
where most of the inhabitants, being emigrants from the northern colonies, have been
accustomed to employ some part of their time in weaving coarse cloths of flax,
cotton, and wool for their own families.

The frequent captures of our shipping in the Spanish and French War in 1744,
raising the insurance to and from this place to 33 per cent, whereby the price of our
rice which *communibus annis* was 6s. 6d. sterling the hundred, sunk so low that one
hundredweight of rice was often bartered for a yard or less of coarse Welch plains
that cost in England 12d. or 14d. the yard. The people of Carolina were driven by
this distress to the necessity of weaving coarse cloths of cotton and wool for their
Negroes. But in this calamitous situation the Assembly did not encourage manufactures but bent their thoughts to the improvement of agriculture; and gave a
bounty of 9d. sterling for every pound of indigo raised in this province; and bounties
for the raising silk, wine, oil, barley, wheat, hemp, flax, cotton, indigo, and ginger.
Soon after this, peace restored our trade and brought it into its usual course and the
generous bounty given by Parliament to the making indigo gave fresh vigour to our
industry. All home made cloths were then laid aside; and at this day above five
hundred thousand yards of Welch plains are consumed yearly in this province, chiefly
in clothing our Negroes.

We have no glass house, paper, or fulling-mill in the province; the only mills erected here are sawmills, grist, and bolting mills for flour, and mills for pounding rice. Public rewards have at various times been given for improvements made in the latter from principles both of humanity and interest in preventing the loss of Negroes by such heavy labour.

To support my allegation that the attention of this province has been confined to staple commodities for exportation to Great Britain, and not to manufactures for home consumption, I have taken the liberty to add as an appendix a copy of the titles of all the acts, and the votes of Assembly with the dates when passed, which have given any public encouragement since the year 1734, except the bounty given to poor Protestants from Europe to become settlers in Carolina.

E. THE PROBLEM OF COLONIAL MONEY SUPPLY

MUCH of the business of the colonies was carried on by means of credit. Colonial merchants bought from British merchants on credit and paid balances by shipping cargoes of colonial produce. Colonial merchants in turn sold to their customers on credit and accepted in return a vast variety of products. Much of the economic life of the colonies could be summed up by saying that it represented a complex series of book-keeping transactions, with a periodic balancing of accounts between debtors and creditors. Yet from the start there was also the need for some form of circulating medium. The colonists turned naturally to commodity money. Beginning with the wampum of the Indians, they used beaver skins, tobacco, rum, wheat, and other products for money. The amounts of taxes, wages, and debts were expressed in such things as a certain number of pounds of tobacco, and were often paid in such media. Although various forms of commodity money were used throughout the colonial period, they were obviously inadequate in an increasingly complex economy, and other means were devised and used.

The growing trade with the West Indies brought increasing amounts of bills of exchange and specie into the mainland colonies. However, neither bills of exchange nor specie served the purpose of a general circulating medium for they were used primarily to settle accounts among merchants within the colonies and to pay balances owing to British merchants. There was a great deal of competition among the merchants of the various colonies to secure foreign specie and this led them to overvalue it in terms of sterling. British merchants were concerned with such practices and demanded regulation and a uniformity of valuation. Thus, in 1704, a royal proclamation established uniform rates of exchange for all the colonies.[1] The proclamation was futile, and it was followed by an Act of Parliament to achieve the same purpose (6 Anne, c. 30). This was equally futile, for though colonial governors were instructed to enforce obedience, the colonists managed to evade the law in the ordinary course of private business transactions.

Far more important were the efforts of colonial governments to provide a circulating medium by the issuance of various forms of paper money. The practice began in 1690 when Massachusetts issued paper money to pay soldiers who had gone on an expedition to Canada. From that time on throughout the eighteenth century, the issuance of paper money for war-time expenses was common in the colonies. The second phase in the development of paper currency was for colonial governments to issue 'bills of credit' to pay the ordinary expenses of government, with taxes collected at some specified date in the future set aside to pay these bills as they came due. This practice was likewise inaugurated by Massachusetts in the 1690's. During the next quarter-century all of the colonies, except Maryland, Pennsylvania, and Virginia, issued paper money in some form to finance the expense of fighting the wars with the French and the Indians and for ordinary expenses of government.

Still another problem of money supply in the colonies was that of credit for private individuals, and particularly for farmers. Wealthy people, both merchants and planters, lent money as individuals, but this did not meet the demand for loans.

[1] No. 58.

Colonists therefore turned to their governments. The answer to the demand was the creation of 'land banks' for the purpose of lending money on farm mortgages. There were a good many schemes for private land banks in the colonies. The major example of a private bank was the one established in Massachusetts. It was violently opposed by the creditor interests in the colony, and in 1741 they secured an Act of Parliament which extended the Bubble Act of 1720 to the colonies. The bank was thus destroyed by a piece of *ex post facto* legislation, and it lent bitterness to the internal politics of the colony for years thereafter, for the father of Samuel Adams was one of the chief backers of the Land Bank, and Thomas Hutchinson was its chief enemy.

But in other colonies, and notably in Pennsylvania, government loan offices and land banks were established and worked well. Money issues created by legislatures were lent out on farm mortgages at low rates of interest. Small annual payments were required until the principal was repaid. Such loans added to the circulating medium, for the borrowers could use the money to pay taxes and to buy land. The government loan office of Pennsylvania was so profitable that from the 1720's to the 1750's it paid most of the expenses of the provincial government, thus rendering negligible taxation for that purpose.

Convenient though it was, and even necessary during war-time, one problem involved in the use of paper currency was abundantly clear by 1715: when issued in large quantities, it depreciated in terms of gold and silver money. This was particularly the case in the New England colonies and in South Carolina. This aroused creditor interests in the colonies and in England, and there were reiterated demands for restriction of colonial currency issues. The political struggles over paper money in the colonies were the basis of some of the most conspicuous battles between governors and councils on one hand, and elected assemblies on the other, during the first half of the eighteenth century. The former usually took the side of restriction of issues while the latter usually supported an 'easy money' policy. This was particularly true in New England.

Most of the subsequent histories of colonial money problems have been written in terms of what happened in New England and were written by nineteenth-century historians who supported the gold standard side of the money argument of the times in which they lived. They therefore ignored the fact that paper currency worked well in the middle colonies where it was well regulated and did not depreciate significantly. Furthermore, the middle colonies, in quite modern fashion, issued paper money in times of depression and did so with apparently successful results.

The money supply problem of the colonies inevitably involved the British government, for British merchants concerned with colonial trade were always afraid that their interests would be adversely affected. From time to time they appealed for restrictions and regulations to protect them. The first interference came in the seventeenth century when a mint established by Massachusetts was abolished. The next attempt was the royal proclamation of 1704 regulating the value of foreign coins brought into the colonies, and this was followed by an Act of Parliament for the same purpose.[1] The enforcement of this policy was left to the colonial governors, who were instructed to carry out the policy. However, the governors more often than not were forced to surrender to their legislatures despite such instructions. In 1740 forceful instructions were sent to the governors. They were told to obey previous instructions

[1] No. 58.

with regard to the valuation of foreign coins and to refuse their assent to bills issuing paper money unless such bills contained a suspending clause providing for royal approval before going into effect. The governors were told that if they did not obey these instructions they would be summarily removed.[1] These instructions were little more effective than previous ones.[2]

A half-century of experience with this method did little more than prove its inadequacy when pitted against the wishes of determined colonial assemblies. In 1751, therefore, Parliament in effect enacted the policy embodied in governors' instructions into law. In that year it passed an Act restricting the power of the New England governments to issue paper money. The Act required that all outstanding issues of paper money be redeemed strictly according to the laws emitting them. The second and more fundamental restriction in the law was the provision that no bills whatever could be issued and used as legal tender in the payment of private debts. But the law did not abolish paper money in New England. The colonies were allowed to issue money for the "current service of the year", providing the bills were paid within two years. Furthermore, they were allowed to issue paper money in time of war or invasion (24 Geo. II, c. 53).

Within the colonies the chief opposition to paper money came from the creditor interests of New England where depreciation had been relatively unchecked. Governor Jonathan Belcher in 1732 stated in summary form the arguments of colonial opponents of paper currency.[3] Outside of New England, where paper money was better regulated, its defence was undertaken not only by important merchants and landowners, but by British officials as well. In 1742 Governor William Burnet of New York stated the case for his approval of a paper money bill in that colony, and in doing so summed up the needs and the arguments for paper money in able fashion.[4] One of the ablest defences came from Virginia, which was the last of the colonies to issue paper money, although it had had a long experience with tobacco notes previously. The Virginia planters were well aware of the demands of the British merchants which led to the Currency Act of 1764,[5] and they presented vigorous statements of the colonial position.[6]

With the outbreak of the Seven Years War, British efforts to control colonial currency emissions were suspended in order to encourage colonial support of the war. The colonies issued paper money as never before, and once the war was over, the policy of imperial restriction was renewed, a renewal which contributed to the intensification of the controversy between Britain and the colonies.[7]

58. Royal proclamation regulating the value of foreign coins (18 June 1704)

Printed: Brigham, *British Royal Proclamations Relating to America*, pp. 161–163.

We having had under our consideration the different rates at which the same species of foreign coins do pass in our several colonies and plantations in America, and the inconveniences thereof, by the indirect practice of drawing the money from one plantation to another to the great prejudice of the trade of our subjects; and being sensible that the same cannot be otherwise remedied than by reducing of all foreign coins to the same current rate within all our dominions in

[1] No. 59.   [2] See No. 34B.   [3] No. 60.   [4] No. 61.
[5] No. 100.   [6] No. 62.   [7] See Introduction to No. 100.

America; and the principal officers of our mint having laid before us a table of the value of the several foreign coins which usually pass in payments in our said plantations, according to their weight and the assays made of them in our mint, thereby showing the just proportion which each coin ought to have to the other, which is as followeth, viz.: Seville pieces of eight, old plate, seventeen pennyweight twelve grains, four shillings and six pence; Seville pieces of eight, new plate, fourteen pennyweight, three shillings seven pence one farthing; Mexico pieces of eight, seventeen pennyweight twelve grains, four shillings and six pence; Pillar pieces of eight, seventeen pennyweight twelve grains, four shillings and six pence three farthings; Peru pieces of eight, old plate, seventeen pennyweight twelve grains, four shillings and five pence, or thereabouts; cross dollars, eighteen pennyweight, four shillings and four pence three farthings; ducatoons of Flanders, twenty pennyweight and twenty-one grains, five shillings and six pence; ecus of France, or silver louis, seventeen pennyweight twelve grains, four shillings and six pence; crusadoes of Portugal, eleven pennyweight four grains, two shillings and ten pence one farthing; three guilder pieces of Holland, twenty pennyweight and seven grains, five shillings and two pence one farthing; old rix-dollars of the Empire, eighteen pennyweight and ten grains, four shillings and six pence; the half, quarters and other parts in proportion to their denominations, and light pieces in proportion to their weight. We have therefore thought fit for remedying the said inconveniences, by the advice of our Council, to publish and declare, that from and after the first day of January next ensuing the date hereof, no Seville, Pillar, or Mexico pieces of eight, though of the full weight of seventeen pennyweight and a half, shall be accounted, received, taken or paid within any of our said colonies or plantations, as well those under proprietors and charters, as under our immediate commission and government, at above the rate of six shillings per piece current money, for the discharge of any contracts or bargains to be made after the said first day of January next, the halfs, quarters, and other lesser pieces of the same coins to be accounted, received, taken, or paid in the same proportion. And the currency of all pieces of eight of Peru, dollars, and other foreign species of silver coins, whether of the same or baser alloy, shall, after the said first day of January next, stand regulated, according to their weight and fineness, according and in proportion to the rate before limited and set for the pieces of eight of Seville, Pillar, and Mexico; so that no foreign silver coin of any sort be permitted to exceed the same proportion upon any account whatsoever. And we do hereby require and command all our governors, lieutenant-governors, magistrates, officers, and all other our good subjects, within our said colonies and plantations, to observe and obey our directions herein, as they tender our displeasure.

Given at our castle at Windsor, the eighteenth day of June 1704 in the third year of our reign.

59. Instruction to governors on colonial currency (5 August 1740)

The additional instruction which follows was sent to all colonial governors in 1740 after investigation showed that they were not obeying their instructions with regard to colonial financial matters. Printed: *Documents Relating to the Colonial History of the State of New Jersey*, VI, pp. 94–98.

Whereas an Act of Parliament was passed in the sixth year of her late Majesty Queen Anne entitled *An Act for Ascertaining the Rates of Foreign Coins in her Majesty's Plantations in America*, which act the respective governors of all the plantations in America have from time to time been instructed to observe and carry into due execution; and whereas notwithstanding the same, complaints have been made that the said Act has not been observed as it ought to have been in many of his Majesty's colonies and plantations in America, by means whereof many indirect practices have grown up and various and illegal currencies have been introduced in several of the said colonies and plantations, contrary to the true intent and meaning of the said Act and to the prejudice of the trade of his Majesty's subjects. In consequence of which complaints, an humble address was presented the last sessions by the House of Commons to his Majesty that he would be graciously pleased to require and command the respective governors of his colonies and plantations in America effectually to observe his Majesty's Royal Instruction, directing them that the Act of the sixth year of the reign of her Majesty Queen Anne entitled *An Act for Ascertaining the Rate of Foreign Coins in her Majesty's Plantations in America* be punctually and *bona fide* observed and put in execution according to the true intent and meaning of the said Act. It is therefore his Majesty's royal will and pleasure, and you are hereby strictly required and commanded, under pain of his Majesty's highest displeasure and of being removed from your government, to take the most effectual care for the future that the said Act be punctually and *bona fide* observed and put in execution according to the true intent and meaning thereof.

And to the end that his Majesty's commands herein may be fully made known to all his subjects within your government, and that none of them may pretend ignorance thereof, you are hereby further required and commanded to publish this instruction in such manner as may best answer his Majesty's gracious intentions herein signified.

And whereas, for preventing the many and great inconveniences that had arisen in some of his Majesty's colonies and plantations in America by passing laws for striking bills of credit and issuing out the same in lieu of money, the respective governors and commanders-in-chief of his Majesty's colonies and plantations for the time being have been particularly instructed not to give their assent to or pass any such laws for the future without a clause be inserted in such act declaring that the same shall not take effect until the said act shall have been approved and confirmed by his Majesty, his heirs, or successors. And whereas notwithstanding such his Majesty's commands to the said governors in that behalf, paper bills of credit have been created and issued in his Majesty's said colonies and plantations by virtue of acts of assembly there, making it obligatory on all persons to take such bills of credit in payment for debts, dues, and demands, whereby the good intention of the aforementioned Act of the 6th of her late Majesty Queen Anne for ascertaining the rates of foreign coins in her Majesty's plantations in America has been frustrated, and a great discouragement has been brought on the commerce of this kingdom by occasioning a confusion in dealings and a lessening of credit in those parts. And whereas an humble address was presented the last session by the House of Commons to his Majesty that he would be graciously pleased to require and command the respective governors of his colonies and plantations in America, punctually and effectually to observe his Majesty's royal instructions not to give assent to or to pass any act whereby bills of credit may be issued in lieu of money without a clause be inserted in such act declaring that the same shall be approved by his Majesty:

It is therefore his Majesty's will and pleasure, and you are hereby also further required and commanded under pain of his Majesty's highest displeasure and of being removed from your government, punctually and effectually to observe his Majesty's royal instruction not to give assent to or pass any act whereby bills of credit may be issued in lieu of money without a clause be inserted in such act declaring that the same shall not take effect until the said act shall be approved by his Majesty, his heirs, or successors.

60. Governor Jonathan Belcher: objections to paper currency (23 December 1732)

The opposition of New England merchants to unlimited issues of paper currency grew ever stronger as the value of the currency depreciated. Many tracts and pamphlets were written to support that opposition. Governor Jonathan Belcher, a native of the colony, summed up those arguments in an unusually brief fashion in a letter to the Board of Trade. Printed: "The Belcher Papers", Massachusetts Historical Society *Collections*, 6th Series, VI, p. 227.

As to the 16 instruction, which limits or restrains the striking of credit bills, I believe every man of thought and substance is highly thankful that the Assembly are kept from ruining all the estates of the province by issuing out floods of those pernicious bills. At an emission of 50 or £60,000, every man that has outstanding debts sinks at least a fifth part of his capital – the bills growing in three or four months' time of so much less value than before such an emission. And whereas £125 of the lawful money of the province would purchase £100 sterling, yet £350 of the vile bills that have been issued by the government will not at this day purchase that sum; so that to allow any further liberty of making these bills than for the annual expense of the province, or to extend the calling them in beyond the year in which they are issued, would have a direct tendency to ruin the king's government and people, and would prove a fraud and cheat upon all the merchants of England, who have always large effects in this country.

61. Governor William Burnet: defence of colonial paper currency (21 November 1724)

Burnet (1683–1729) was governor of New York, 1720–1728. His letter to the Board of Trade which follows is a clear and objective statement by a man thoroughly familiar with colonial conditions. Printed: *New York Colonial Documents*, V, pp. 735–738.

With my last of the 11th November I sent your lordships duplicates of the authentic acts of Assembly passed 1723. Now I enclose herewith to Mr. Popple the authentic [acts] of Assembly passed in July last.

1. The first of these is an act for raising and levying the sum of six thousand six hundred and thirty pounds for the supplying the deficiencies of his Majesty's revenue, and for the several uses and purposes therein mentioned, and for making of bills of credit for that value.

This act sets forth in the preamble the several uses, and in the body of the bill, the sums provided for those uses, which are:

1st. To supply the deficiency in his Majesty's revenue, £2521.15.3/4.

2nd. To repair the buildings of the fort, £2000.0.0.

3rd. To pay the arrears of salary due to the agents in England, £600.0.0.

4th. Towards encouraging the far Indians to trade with us and keep the 5 Nations true to his Majesty's interest, £200.0.0.

5th. To supply the deficiency in the fund for cancelling bills of credit struck in 1715, the sum of £1200.0.0.

6th. For the charges of printing and signing these bills of credit, £108.4.1/4.

Which makes up the sum total of £6630.

After the uses of the money are explained, the reasons for striking bills are next expressed—that the officers of the government must otherwise be kept out of their money for a very long time and have difficulty to subsist, that the buildings of the fort are so ruinous as to want immediate repairs, and that there is danger in all delays to engage the Indians in our interest.

The means of assessing these levies on the real and personal estates of the inhabitants has nothing in it different from former acts, and the nature of the circulation of these bills, and the provision for sinking them do not at all deviate from the acts formerly passed for the same purpose, so that there is no further need of explanation of these particulars.

But this being an act for making paper money, though within my additional instruction, which allows of such acts when they are for raising or levying a public revenue, I think myself obliged to offer to your lordships reasons that are, in my poor opinion, sufficient to justify it and other acts of this nature with the same precaution.

I am very sensible of the disadvantage I lie under in writing upon this argument, and the misfortune it is to any cause to have already appeared in an odious light, as I am but too well convinced is the case of paper money acts in the plantations, by your lordships' last words in your letter of the 17 of June—that bills for increasing of paper money will meet with no encouragement. I hope your lordships will not think it presumption in me, even after this declaration, to endeavour to give you a more favourable opinion of such acts, and if I go too far in this it is owing to the encouragement your lordships have given me by receiving what I have offered on all occasions in so kind a manner, and admitting the best constructions that my weak reasoning will bear.

I have already in my letter of the 12th of May last used several arguments to justify the paper act in New Jersey, and therein I observed how well the bills of New York keep up their credit and the reasons why they have not fallen in value as those of Carolina and New England, and that under a good regulation, these acts are both of service to the trade of the plantations and of Great Britain, for which, that I may not repeat, I beg leave to refer to my said letter of the 12th of May last, and desire your lordships would again take into your consideration when you are to determine your opinion on this present act.

But there are many things there only hinted at which I shall now lay before your lordships, and in which I shall chiefly argue from what is to be gathered from experience in Great Britain itself from observing the nature of credit and the events it has undergone, and in this I hope I may be the more patiently heard because what experience I have was purchased at no very cheap rate.

Credit ought to be supported, if it is possible, both by *reason* and *common opinion*. Reason, though ever so strong, will not always do alone in the beginning if common opinion is against it, but it will carry all before it at the long run. Common opinion or humour will generally do for a time without reason, nay, against it. But then it is often attended with vast mischief and danger. Of this we have a fatal instance in the famous South Sea scheme, which being left to common opinion without any restraint, has produced the most terrible effects possible. If there had been a positive law making all bargains for South Sea stock above some fixed price as 150 void, and making it a legal tender at 100, all these mischiefs would have been avoided, but this would have been called *compulsive paper credit*; yet because in reason it is worth so much as long as the nation stands, and because the Parliament has always kept their engagements, all clamours against this would soon have blown over, and no enemies would have been found to it but brokers.

To make this appear, it is enough to prove that at the bottom all the present voluntary credit stand upon this very foundation at last, and no other.

It is very certain that there is no proportion between the specie and the great quantity of bank bills and bankers' notes commonly current, who lend their notes on the several branches of government securities, and seldom at a rate under par–very often above par. When the government is safe, this would do; when there is any danger, common opinion pulls down her own work, and bankers break in abundance, and the Bank itself is put to extremities. An instance of this I remember at the time of the Preston affair. The Bank would have broke in a few days if the victory there had not happened as soon as it did.

And the reason was plainly this, because when they had paid away all their specie, they had nothing left but exchequer notes and such other securities to exchange for their remaining bank notes, and these would have been at such a discount that they must have broke, and compounded for such payment at the best.

Thus it is plain that the foundation in reason of the credit of the Bank itself, not to speak of private goldsmiths, is the government security remaining at par, and yet the Parliament is so good as to provide an interest on these exchequer bills, and to pay the Bank so much more per cent for circulation; whereas in fact when foul weather comes, the Bank is a staff of reed, and must lean on the government to prop itself up and so increase the load instead of easing it.

And this humour keeps up the imaginary value when there is no real occasion for it; all government securities being at the same time commonly above par. But upon any ill news the like humour beats down all voluntary credit in the same manner as it does exchequer bills, etc., and really carries the general discredit as much further than it ought as it had advanced credit beyond its reasonable bounds before, and if once the Bank had broke, then all this would have appeared to a demonstration. But the Bank is yet a virgin, and the exchequer was once shut up in King Charles's reign, though I think she has since fully made up for the sins of her youth by punctual payment for thirty or forty years last past.

If, then, instead of these secondary instruments of circulation, the Parliament should think fit to make all parliamentary paper credit a tender at par, and that it be received in all taxes as well as paid, which is doing with private persons as the public is done by, I cannot see that it would be any injustice nor more liable to danger than the present methods of circulation are. It may be objected that this is a French way of proceeding to declare the value of money by edict, but it is easy to answer that the laws of a free government are not at all like the edicts of an arbitrary one, and that it is as unsafe in France to trust the bankers as the government, for when the government refuses to pay them, then they must break, and so it would be in England. The first breach of engagements in the legislature to the creditors of the public would break all the bankers at once, and therefore what the government does by their hands, and in which it is in effect their support, it is capable of doing for itself, and if founded on reason, though against the present humour, it will prevail in the end.

I have already endeavoured to show the danger of common opinion in money matters, when no ways restrained by law, by the instance of the South Sea.

I may add that it is the same thing with liberty in general. If mobs are entirely left to their common opinion or humour, it is well known how fatal they may be to the public safety, and if the liberty of the poor which is now grown to such a pitch of licentiousness as to be the greatest tax and grievance to the nation, were regulated by as severe and as practicable laws as in Holland, it would be of great use to the public.

From all which I beg leave to conclude that [it] is not the names things get for the present, but the real nature of them that will be found to hold against all events, and that in the instance of paper money where it is regulated by just laws, and where the public have not acted contrary to them, their credit is in reason better established than the credit of any private persons or society, and that the method used to catch the common opinion of mankind by offering them their money when they please, is nothing but a fashionable bubble which people are every day sufferers by when a banker breaks, and that even the best founded societies cannot maintain their credit when there is the greatest need of them, but that all credit finally centres in the security of the government.

I take the liberty further to observe to your lordships on how many occasions the government of Great Britain has found it impracticable to raise all the money wanted within the year, from whence all the present debts of the nation have arisen. The same necessity lies often upon the plantations where frequently a sum of ready money is wanted which it would be an intolerable tax to raise at once, and therefore they are forced to imitate the Parliament at home in anticipating upon remote funds. And as there is no Bank nor East India Company nor even private subscribers capable of lending the province the money they want, at least without demanding the extravagant interest of 8 per cent, which is the common interest here, but would ruin the public to pay. Since this is a case, there is no possible way left to make distant funds provide ready money when it is necessarily wanted but making paper bills to be sunk by such funds. Without this, Carolina would have been ruined by their Indian war, Boston could not now support theirs, nor could any of the provinces have furnished such considerable sums to the expeditions against Canada. Nor could at present any of the necessary repairs of this fort be provided for, nor the arrears of the revenue be discharged, which is done by this act in a tax to be levied in 4 years; nor indeed, any public service readily and sufficiently effected.

And I may add one thing more: that this manner of compulsive credit does in fact keep up its value here, and that it occasions much more trade and business than would be without it, and that more specie is exported to England by reason of these paper bills than could be if there was no circulation but of specie, for which reason all the merchants here seem now well satisfied with it.

I hope your lordships will excuse my being so long and earnest upon this head because it is a subject of the greatest importance to all the plantations, and what I humbly conceive has been often misrepresented by the merchants in London.

62. Defence of paper money by the Virginia Committee of Correspondence (1759, 1763)

Virginia issued paper money for the first time during the Seven Years War. British merchants trading to Virginia soon objected. The two documents which follow consist of a set of instructions and a letter sent to the Virginia agent in London by the Committee of Correspondence of the Virginia House of Burgesses. Printed: *The Virginia Magazine of History and Biography*, XI (1903), pp. 1–5, 345–349.

[Instructions to the Virginia Agent (12 December 1759)]

We are informed that the merchants of Great Britain are much alarmed at our Assembly's passing some acts for emitting large quantities of paper money, which is made a legal tender for all debts (the king's quit-rents excepted), and they are very apprehensive that they may be great sufferers thereby in collecting their debts due here.

These apprehensions of the merchants proceed from a mistaken notion of our having a law in force for paying off sterling debts in current money at 25 per cent exchange.

No loss can arise to the merchants from making this paper money a legal tender for sterling debts as the law now stands, and they are in a much better condition and less liable to losses in collecting their debts than if nothing but sterling or lawful money of Great Britain were held a tender for such debts, as by the Act of the 6th of Queen Anne, which they so much rely on to be a good precedent in such case.

If this can be shown, it is to be hoped the gentlemen in the trade will be satisfied that there is no necessity to solicit their memorial so far as to procure an instruction about this matter.

True it is that before this war, and when exchange was rarely above 25 per cent, we had a law to settle the payment of judgments for sterling debts at that rate, and it was passed to prevent disputes about the exchange, and as a direction to the sheriffs in levying executions on these judgments. There was likewise a further view: to prevent creditors from taking an unreasonable advantage of the necessity of the debtor for his forbearing to execute the judgment perhaps 10 or 15 per cent above the then current exchange which, as it was a kind of traffic about bills of exchange, did not come under the penalties of our laws against usury, or at least was hard to be come at and punished by them. But when at the breaking out of the present war exchange began to rise, or rather it was foreseen that it would do so, and it was found that injustice would be done to many, especially the merchants in Great Britain, if that law remained in force, it was repealed by an Act of the 28th George II, entitled "An Act to amend an Act entitled An Act declaring the law concerning executions, and for the relief of insolvent debtors and for other purposes therein mentioned." The preamble of which shows its intention to take care of the merchants' interest, and the principal enacting clause is "That in any action which hath been or shall be commenced, and is or shall be depending for the recovery of any sterling money, in any court of record within this dominion wherein the plaintiff or plaintiffs shall recover, such court shall have power, and are hereby directed by rule to be entered at the foot of their judgment in such action, to order such judgment to be discharged or levied in current money, at such a difference of exchange as they shall think just, any law, usage, or custom to the contrary thereof in any wise notwithstanding." And what rate of exchange can a court under the direction of this act think just but that which is current at the time of entering the judgment, or such a one that the merchant may have his whole debt remitted to him without those losses they so much apprehend?

If our notable agent at the other end of the town had known and stated these things to the merchants, they would hardly have thought it necessary to present any memorial about it. And this it was his duty to have known and done, as he has an allowance of £200 per annum to negotiate the affairs of the country; and these acts above mentioned are regularly transmitted, as he knows, to the Board of Trade, and were remaining in that office at the very time the memorial was presented.

But it may be thought that the greatest difficulty is yet to come, viz., to obviate the heavy complaint, and that which seems to carry weight at first view, that the Assembly have passed a law, *ex post facto*, to declare paper bills of credit a good tender even for sterling debts contracted before the passing such law, whereas the merchants think that nothing less than sterling or lawful money of Great Britain should be allowed to be a good tender, agreeable to the Act of the 6th of Queen Anne, especially for such precontracted debts. This is to be done, and at the same time it is to be shown that the merchants are in a better condition and less liable to losses in receiving their sterling debts under our laws than they would be if nothing but sterling or lawful money of Great Britain were held a tender.

For this purpose let us suppose that a merchant in London obtains a judgment here for £100 sterling; the debtor is obliged by the 6th of Queen Anne and therefore procures £100 sterling or lawful money of Great Britain, and pays this debt. Now this sum being only of equal value to £125 current money and exchange being now at 35 per cent (and in war-time it is rarely lower) the agent here must in that case give £10 current money more to purchase a bill of exchange to remit this debt to his principal, which £10 is so much real loss to the merchant; whereas by the provision of our law, no such loss is incurred, but the creditor hath his whole £135 decreed to him, with which a bill is bought and the full debt remitted.

Thus it is hoped the proposition is proved, and that our legislature have conceived just apprehensions of the interest of the merchants, and all other creditors for sterling debts, and have made a proper provision for their security.

But to set this matter still in a stronger light: the merchants in their memorial quote the provisions in the Act of the 6th of Queen Anne, that even foreign gold and silver coin, made current by that Act, was not to be held a legal tender for sterling debts, much less ought paper bills of credit, which are, they say, of a local, uncertain, and fluctuating value. But give us leave to tell them that if they had no better dependence than that Act affords for collecting their sterling debts, they might be great sufferers indeed; for though that Act when it was made, and for many years after, was a good provision for them in that respect (nothing but sterling or lawful British money being a legal tender for sterling debts) inasmuch as the exchange then current here was under the rate settled by that Act, viz., 25 per cent, or one shilling passed for 1s. 3d., but since exchange hath been higher than that, which is always the case in time of war, a tender exactly agreeable to that Act would occasion a loss to the merchants of so much as 25 per cent falls short of the highest exchange, viz., 10, 15 or perhaps 20 per cent.

Let it be observed that however contemptibly the merchants look upon this paper money as of a local, uncertain, and fluctuating value, yet it is emitted on such funds that every one is glad to receive it in any kind of payment, and exchange is now ten per cent lower than it was last war, when we had nothing current but gold and silver coin, a circumstance very favourable to the credit of our paper. And although the king's quit-rents, as the merchants rightly observe, are not payable in paper by that act, that was done because his Majesty had by instruction to the governor and officers of his revenue, directed them to be received only in sterling, or gold and silver coin at a certain rate, which instruction the governor durst not contravene by including them in the act; yet the Receiver-General never refuses paper money for the quit-rents because he can readily procure bills of exchange for it.

[Letter to the Virginia Agent (16 June, 1763)]

In our last we advised you of the receipt of yours enclosing the merchants' memorial, together with the resolutions of the Board of Trade thereupon. They also were by the same conveyance transmitted to the governor, who immediately convened the Assembly, and in his speech at the opening of the session recommended it to them in the strongest terms to secure the interest of the British merchants in such a manner as to remove all future cause of complaint. The House of Burgesses pressed thereto by the warm remonstrances of the governor, who in every instance of his administration has given proofs of his zeal for his Majesty's service and his attention to the interest of the colony and at the same time being desirous of supporting the character of honest men, proceeded to consider the matter complained of, but after some days' deliberation, and duly examining the state of the taxes, which they found fully sufficient to sink the notes at the respective periods expressed in the several acts of Assembly; they were of opinion that the merchants were well secured in their property here and consequently had not the least foundation for a complaint, and indeed they were persuaded that their unjust and unreasonable clamours on this account took its rise from a protest of some of the council casting the most severe reflections on the conduct of the legislature under a pretence that the taxes imposed for sinking the money emitted were inadequate to the purposes intended. What might induce these gentlemen to blow up the coals at that time, we shall not pretend to determine, but we may be allowed to hope they had no interested views.

Nothing occurring to the Assembly whereby they could better secure the interest of the British merchants than they had already done, they came to several resolutions and agreed upon a representation to his honour the governor, explaining the reasons of their conduct, all which will be transmitted to you. If they should be of what end to divert their lordships from taking the measures with which they in their resolutions are pleased to threaten us, we shall consider it as an happy event, but on the contrary, if they should persist in their interests and succeed therein, we may venture to assert that the memorialists will in some degree feel the calamities and distresses we shall be involved in.

We have upon another occasion been very full and explicit to you upon the subject of paper money, and we will besides have the perusal of our representations to the governor so that we scarce think there is a necessity of adding thereto, but that an affair of such importance may not be neglected, we shall also transmit to you a state of the taxes, an exact account of the said judgments, and of the exchange offered by the General Court from April, '57 to April, '63, faithfully taken from the records of that court. You will from thence see the amount of the said judgments, which to us appears too trifling to justify an application to abolish paper money, more especially when we consider that many of them arise from bills of exchange negotiated with the same money. We can with truth say the greatest losses have been sustained through the ignorance or inadvertency of some factors who, while bringing suits, have too hastily received said debts before the exchange was either settled by the purchasers of bills or the court. Against the misconduct of these gentlemen it is impossible for the legislature to provide. A prudent manager would always insist on such an exchange as would purchase a good bill, leaving that point to be settled when it could be done with certainty.

Let us suppose that paper money was no legal tender in the payment of debts, which seems to be the only thing aimed at by the merchants, and many your designing men who have large outstanding debts due to them in the colony, and having sold their goods at a most extraordinary advance during the war, are now desirous of reaping the benefit of a low exchange. What would be the consequence to a country quite exhausted of its specie and when bills of exchange are very justly not allowed to be a legal tender? Would it not be in the power of avaricious men, determined at all events to enrich themselves by the misfortunes of their fellow subjects, to take the most injurious and oppressive advantage of their debtors who had not the power of procuring specie to discharge their debts? Would they not say when paper money was offered them in discharge of a debt, that is no legal tender and if I take it I must have 5 for 1, or perhaps carry it [to] greater lengths: And if the debtor should stand out the whole process and suffer him to levy his execution when the estate is seized, who are to be the purchasers? Only such as can provide specie. How few there would be in number we can easily suggest, and they would undoubtedly have it in their power to combine together and purchase on their own terms, which must inevitably terminate in the ruin of the debtor, so that possibly a man of £90,000 fortune in land and slaves owing only £1,000, might by these means be reduced to beggary.

His Majesty's revenue of quit-rents has undoubtedly sustained great loss by the rise of exchange, and if that should be attributed to the large emission of paper money, the Assembly may with justice be exculpated as they have by all their acts provided that paper money should be no legal tender in payment of quit-rents. We therefore presume the officers of the revenue have taken paper in payment from a thorough conviction that nothing else could be procured.

The merchants in their memorial represent that the settling the exchange by the determination of the judges is a new mode of justice. In answer thereto we beg leave to observe that if differences of that kind were submitted to juries who consist of different men, it would introduce confusion as there would be probably a great variety of opinions. It was therefore thought more eligible to give the courts that power, who at the conclusion thereof have always fixed the exchange at the highest rate given that court.

Thus, sir, we have given you an impartial account of our situation which will convince you the Assembly acted prudently in adhering to their former resolutions; and however the Lords of Trade may have considered the matter at the first view, we are not without hopes that when they again take it into consideration they will think it more just that the difference of exchange should be settled by the determination of disinterested judges than to leave it to the arbitrary will of the creditor. And we are the more sanguine in our expectations of the alteration in their opinion as we by no means appear in the light of the northern colonies who emitted their money for the payment of their debts without establishing proper funds for sinking their notes. His Majesty's requisition first introduced paper money into the colonies, and had the objections been made to it then that now are, we should not only have escaped censure, but saved a great part of the exchange we were loaded with during the war. And as we have readily and cheerfully complied with everything required of us, and our method of doing it was never objected to so long as our assistance was necessary, it must be very afflicting to us to find our faithful services like to be represented to his Majesty in such a light as to draw on us his displeasure, which cannot fail of being attended with disagreeable consequences.

F. COLONIAL GOVERNMENTS AND COLONIAL ECONOMY

OVERMUCH attention to the Acts of Trade and Navigation has too often led us to forget that colonial governments played a role in the development of colonial economy far more comprehensive and effective than that of the British government. From the beginning, English colonists assumed that their local governments should be concerned with wages and prices and the regulation of public utilities. This was in large part due to the fact that they were accustomed to such regulation in England, but, in addition, it was reinforced by ethical concepts, particularly during the seventeenth century. Such concepts were believed in and expressed in all the colonies, but nowhere so forcefully as in New England.[1]

Colonial legislatures everywhere enacted laws creating public roads and ferries and establishing the fees that might be charged. They sought, particularly in the seventeenth century, to regulate wages and prices,[2] and there were continuous efforts to establish the fees to be charged by government officials. 'Assizes' of beer, ale, and bread, an effective form of local economic regulation, were found in all the colonies.[3]

The attempt to shape the direction of colonial economy lay behind much colonial legislation, beginning with the first legislative assembly in Virginia in 1619 which required every landholder to plant six mulberry trees a year for the purpose of laying a foundation for a silk industry.[4] From time to time land grants, cash loans, and exemptions from taxes were offered to help in the development of manufactures. Cash bounties were offered for the development of certain new crops such as hemp.

However, the most significant and effective area of regulation was that relating to the standards of colonial exports. The purpose of such legislation was to maintain a high level of quality and thus to secure and retain good foreign markets and better prices for colonial produce. The colonies exporting barrelled beef and pork required that it be inspected by public officials. Even crops such as rice and indigo, which had a ready market, were subject to inspection. In colonies such as Pennsylvania, where wheat, flour, and bread products were an important part of the export trade, the inspection system was increasingly rigorous. The Pennsylvania inspection law of 1725 is characteristic of this type of legislation and served as a model for similar legislation in other colonies.[5] That law and its subsequent amendments were given much of the credit in the eighteenth century for Philadelphia's pre-eminent position in the export of wheat products. Philadelphia "superfine" flour had an international reputation which was envied by colonial rivals. The exporters of New York, for instance, were particularly concerned. They bought samples of Philadelphia flour and even tried to acquire the same type of millstones in the hope of discovering Philadelphia's secret. New York, too, tried inspection laws in an effort to match its ever more successful rival.

The regulation and inspection of export staples was as characteristic in the south as in the north. The crop of greatest concern was tobacco, the most important export from the mainland colonies and the very centre of the economic life of Virginia and

[1] No. 63.   [2] No. 64.   [3] No. 67.   [4] No. 39.   [5] No. 65.

Maryland. It was a crop constantly beset with difficulties ranging from insects and the weather to the ever present spectre of low prices. Within ten years after tobacco was first grown commercially in Virginia the economic problems created brought about the intervention of the colonial government. As early as 1621 Governor Wyatt ordered production limited to 1,000 plants with no more than nine leaves to the plant for each head of family and labourer. From this time until the eighteenth century periodic but futile efforts were made to limit production in order to keep up the price-level.[1]

Far more successful were the efforts to improve the quality of tobacco exported. 'Tasters' and 'viewers' were appointed as early as 1619, but government control did not become effective until the eighteenth century. In 1712 an Act of the legislature established public warehouses and regulated the rates charged by them. An Act of 1713 establishing public inspectors at the warehouses was vetoed by the Privy Council. Nevertheless, the demand for inspection continued and in May 1730 the House of Burgesses passed a stringent inspection law.[2] During the 1740's Maryland adopted similar legislation.

With this law the colonial government took complete charge of the export of tobacco. After its passage no planter could ship his tobacco independently. He had to take it to a public warehouse where it must pass inspection by government employees. Bad tobacco was destroyed. The size of casks was standardized. The crews of ships were forbidden to load the tobacco: it must be done by the owner. Crews could load ships only if the captain or his agents bought tobacco directly as a cargo for the vessel concerned.

It is clear from the examples given that the American colonists took it for granted that government should play an important part in the development of the economic life of the colonies. Both the assumption and the practice remained a part of American thought and action long after the end of the colonial era.

63. John Winthrop: account of Puritan attitudes toward mercantile practice (1639)

Robert Keayne was a well to do Boston merchant who was brought before both the legislature and his church in 1639 for charging exorbitant prices. John Winthrop's account of the affair illustrates the Puritan attitude towards excessive profit-taking and towards mercantile practices in general. Printed: Winthrop, *History of New England* (Savage, ed.), I, pp. 377–382.

Mo. 9 (November). At a general court holden at Boston, great complaint was made of the oppression used in the country in sale of foreign commodities; and Mr. Robert Keayne, who kept a shop in Boston, was notoriously above others observed and complained of; and, being convented, he was charged with many particulars; in some, for taking above six pence in the shilling profit; in some above eight pence; and in some small things, above two for one; and being hereof convict (as appears by the records) he was fined £200, which came thus to pass. The deputies considered, apart, of his fine, and set it at £200; the magistrates agreed but to £100. So the court being divided, at length it was agreed that his fine should be £200, but he should pay but £100, and the other should be respited to the further consideration

---

[1] During the course of the seventeenth century it became settled English policy to forbid the growing of tobacco in England to give the American colonies a monopoly of the English market. See *English Historical Documents*, vol. VIII, No. 204.

[2] No. 66.

of the next general court. By this means the magistrates and deputies were brought to an accord, which otherwise had not been likely, and so much trouble might have grown and the offender escaped censure. For the cry of the country was so great against oppression, and some of the elders and magistrates had declared such detestation of the corrupt practice of this man (which was the more observable because he was wealthy and sold dearer than most other tradesmen, and for that he was of ill report for the like covetous practice in England that incensed the deputies very much against him). And sure the course was very evil, especial circumstances considered: 1. he being an ancient professor of the gospel; 2. a man of eminent parts; 3. wealthy, and having but one child; 4. having come over for conscience' sake, and for the advancement of the gospel here; 5. having been formerly dealt with and admonished, both by private friends and also by some of the magistrates and elders, and having promised reformation; being a member of a church and commonwealth now in their infancy, and under the curious observation of all churches and civil states in the world. These added much aggravation to his sin in the judgment of all men of understanding. Yet most of the magistrates (though they discerned of the offence clothed with all these circumstances) would have been more moderate in their censure: 1. because there was no law in force to limit or direct men in point of profit in their trade; 2. because it is the common practice in all countries for men to make use of advantages for raising the prices of their commodities; 3. because (though he were chiefly aimed at, yet) he was not alone in this fault; 4. because all men through the country, in sale of cattle, corn, labour, etc., were guilty of the like excess in prices; 5. because a certain rule could not be found out for an equal rate between buyer and seller, though much labour had been bestowed in it, and divers laws had been made, which upon experience, were repealed, as being neither safe nor equal. Lastly, and especially, because the law of God appoints no other punishment but double restitution; and in some cases, as where the offender freely confesseth and brings his offering, only half added to the principal. After the court had censured him, the church of Boston called him also in question, where (as before he had done in the court) he did, with tears, acknowledge and bewail his covetous and corrupt heart, yet making some excuse for many of the particulars which were charged upon him, as partly by pretence of ignorance of the true price of some wares, and chiefly by being misled by some false principles, as 1. That if a man lost in one commodity, he might help himself in the price of another; 2. that if through want of skill or other occasion his commodity cost him more than the price of the market in England, he might then sell it for more than the price of the market in New England, etc. These things gave occasion to Mr. Cotton in his public exercise the next lecture day, to lay open the error of such false principles, and to give some rules of direction in the case.

Some false principles were these:

1. That a man might sell as dear as he can, and buy as cheap as he can.

2. If a man lose by casualty of sea, etc., in some of his commodities, he may raise the price of the rest.

3. That he may sell as he bought, though he paid too dear, etc., and though the commodity be fallen, etc,

4. That, as a man may take the advantage of his own skill or ability, so he may of another's ignorance or necessity.

5. Where one gives time for payment, he is to take like recompense of one as of another.

The rules for trading were these:

1. A man may not sell above the current price, *i.e.* such a price as is usual in the time and place, and as another (who knows the worth of the commodity) would give for it if he had occasion to use it; as that is called current money, which every man will take, etc.

2. When a man loseth in his commodity for want of skill, etc., he must look at it as his own fault or cross, and therefore must not lay it upon another.

3. Where a man loseth by casualty of sea, or etc., it is a loss cast upon himself by providence, and he may not ease himself of it by casting it upon another; for so a man should seem to provide against all providences, etc., that he should never lose; but where there is a scarcity of the commodity, there men may raise their price; for now it is a hand of God upon the commodity, and not the person.

4. A man may not ask any more for his commodity than his selling price, as Ephron to Abraham, the land is worth thus much.

The cause being debated by the church, some were earnest to have him excommunicated, but the most thought an admonition would be sufficient. Mr. Cotton opened the causes which required excommunication out of that in 1 Cor. 5: 11. The point now in question was, whether these actions did declare him to be such a covetous person, etc. Upon which he showed that it is neither the habit of covetousness (which is in every man in some degree) nor simply the act, that declares a man to be such, but when it appears that a man sins against his conscience, or the very light of nature, and when it appears in a man's whole conversation. But Mr. Keayne did not appear to be such, but rather upon an error in his judgment, being led by false principles, and besides, he is otherwise liberal, as in his hospitality, and in church communion, etc. So, in the end, the church consented to an admonition.

64A–B. Regulation of prices and wages in New England

The two laws which follow are indicative of the methods used in New England in the attempt to limit profits and wages and to provide consumers with a legal method of redress if they believe they have been victimized by merchants and labourers.

64A. Massachusetts Law (3 November 1675)

Printed: *Massachusetts Bay Records*, v, pp. 62–63.

Whereas there is oppression in the midst of us, not only by such shopkeepers and merchants who set excessive prices on their goods, also by mechanics, but *also by mechanics* and day labourers who are daily guilty of that evil, for redress whereof and as an addition to the law, title Oppression, it is ordered by this court that any person that judgeth himself oppressed by shopkeepers or merchants in setting excessive prices on their goods, have hereby liberty to make their complaint to the grand jurors, or otherwise by petition to the county court immediately, who shall send to the person accused, and if the court, upon examination, judge the person complaining injured, they shall cause the offender to return double the overplus, or more than the equal price, to the injured person, and also impose a fine on the offenders at the discretion of the court; and if any person judge himself oppressed by mechanics or day labourers, they may make complaint thereof to the selectmen of the town, who if upon the examination do find such complaint just, having respect to the quality of the pay, and the length or shortness of the day labour, they shall cause the offender to make double restitution to the party injured, and pay a fine of double the value exceeding the due price.

64B. Connecticut Law (May 1676)

Printed: *Public Records of the Colony of Connecticut*, v, pp. iv–v.

Whereas a great cry of oppression is heard amongst us, and that principally pointed at workmen and traders, which is hard to regulate without a standard prepared both for advance and for pay duly set as money, it is therefore ordered that the price of provision be duly set at each of our General Courts annually, according to true intelligence from Boston, for money sold, and then for such pay within six months paid, no merchant or trader shall advance above two pence upon the shilling for profit, charge and venture from Boston, or other market of like distance, for goods well bought with ready money; trustings and trifles under a shilling being left to each man's agreement, discretion, and moderation, according to a good conscience, to deal. All goods as are subject to waste, the waste to be allowed as part of the first price or cost of the goods. And all breaches of this order to be punished proportionable to the value of the oppression, treble to the oppression; one third to be restored to the party oppressed, and the residue half of it to the complainer that shall prove the fact, and half to the county treasury where the offence is committed. And as for those tradesmen whose commodities are partly their own labour, and partly materials they work upon, as tanners, shoemakers, smiths, and such like, as also such whose day's labour cannot ordinarily be known how much they daily effect, as weavers, tailors, and such like, and day labourers, there being great difficulty to regulate the prices of their ware and work, this court, purposing in season to state orders respecting those things which at present is not attainable, do in the interim recommend it to all such tradesmen and labourers to consider the religious end of their callings, which is that receiving such moderate profit as may enable them to serve God and their neighbours with their arts and trades comfortably, they do not enrich themselves suddenly and inordinately (by oppressing prices and wages, to the impoverishing their neighbours and rendering them in great measure uncapable of convenient subsistence) live in the practice of that crying sin of oppression, but avoid it.

65. Pennsylvania Flour Inspection Law (20 March 1725)

The following document was the first Pennsylvania law by which the inspection of flour intended for export was made mandatory. Subsequent laws amplified and corrected this law but did not substantially change it. The inspection system seems to have worked well, for "Philadelphia superfine" flour was the standard of quality at which other colonies aimed in their own similar legislation. Printed: James T. Mitchell and Henry Flanders, eds., *The Statutes at Large of Pennsylvania* (12 [11] vols., Harrisburg, 1896–1908), IV, pp. 3–8.

Whereas by the laws of this province lately made and provided for preventing the exportation of flour not merchantable, the credit of the trade of this province in one of its most considerable branches hath in some good measure been retrieved, but forasmuch as those laws continue in force no longer than three years from the publication thereof;

Therefore, to the end that the said credit of our trade and the benefits thence arising may be continued and improved:

[Section I.] Be it enacted . . . that every bolter of flour and baker of bread residing, or at any time hereafter during the continuance of this present act, to reside within this province, shall each one for himself provide and have a distinguishable brand-mark; and shall therewith brand each and every cask of flour or biscuit of his own bolting or baking before the same shall be removed from the place where the same was so as aforesaid bolted or baked. But before any such bolter or baker shall bolt any flour or bake any bread for exportation out of this province, every such bolter and baker shall cause such his brand-mark, together with his name and place of abode, to be entered with the clerk of the court of quarter-sessions for the county where he doth reside (if not already entered), and so from time to time as often as any such bolter or baker shall move the place of his residence from one county of this province into another he shall there cause his mark, name, and place of residence to be entered with the clerk of the respective county, for recording whereof the said clerk shall have and receive one shilling each and no more; and every bolter and baker offending in all or any of the premises on due proof thereof made shall forfeit and pay the sum of five shillings for every such offence.

[Section II.] And be it enacted . . . that all wheat flour bolted and packed for exportation from and after the thirteenth day of May next ensuing the publication of this act, shall by the bolter thereof be and be made merchantable and of due fineness, without any mixture of coarser or other flour, and honestly and well packed in well-seasoned cask with the tare thereof thereupon marked, the cask being first weighed by weights tried by or made according to the standard of weights in this province, wherewith the flour and bread packed shall be also weighed. And if any bolter shall offend therein he shall forfeit and pay for every such offence the sum of one shilling per cask.

[Section III.] And be it enacted . . . that if any person or persons shall be convicted of any other wilful fraud or cheat in packing of flour or bread, or of wilfully making a fraudulent invoice of the net proceeds or weight of any flour or bread, the person offending therein shall forfeit and pay the sum of five pounds for every such offence.

[Section IV.] And be it enacted . . . that no merchant or person whatsoever shall lade or ship any flour for exportation out of this province before he shall first submit the same to the view and examination of the officer appointed by or by the direction of this act, who shall search and try the same in order to judge of its goodness; and if the said officer shall judge the same to be merchantable, according to the direction of this present act, he shall brand every such cask of flour on the quarter with the provincial brand-mark, which the said officer shall provide and have for that end and purpose, sufficient and capable to impress in a fair and distinguishable manner the arms of the province of Pennsylvania with the letter P on each side, for which trouble of the said officer he shall have and receive of the shipper one penny per cask, and no more.

Provided always nevertheless, that if any dispute shall happen to arise between the said officer and possessor of such flour concerning the fineness or goodness thereof, application being made to one of the magistrates of the city or county where the said dispute arises, who shall issue his warrant to two indifferent, judicious persons of skill and integrity to view and search the said flour and make report forthwith according as they find the same, and the said magistrate is hereby empowered and required to give judgment accordingly. And in case the said flour is judged not fit to be exported, the said magistrate shall order it not to be exported under the penalty of forfeiture of all such flour, and shall also award and order the owner or possessor of the said flour to pay the said officer one shilling per cask for all such flour as shall be adjudged not fit for exportation as aforesaid, with reasonable charges, who shall recover the said costs and charges from the bolter and maker thereof. But in case the said flour upon trial shall be found to be good and merchantable according to the directions of this act, the charges of prosecution shall be paid by the said officer. And in case any flour shall upon trial be found not merchantable or fit to be exported, the officer shall take the bolter's brand and the marks and numbers of such casks of flour; and if the same flour be afterwards shipped in order for exportation, the proof that it is not the said flour shall lie wholly on the owner or shipper thereof and shall not be incumbent on the said officer.

[Section V.] And be it enacted . . . that the said officer [or his deputies] shall have full power and authority by virtue of this act and without any further or other warrant, to enter on board any ship, sloop, or vessel whatsoever lying or being in any port or place of this province, and into any house, store, or place whatsoever within the province aforesaid, to search for and make discovery of any flour shipped or intended to be shipped for exportation; and if the owner or possessor thereof or their servants or others shall deny him or them entrance, or if the said officer or his deputies shall be anyways molested in making such discovery as aforesaid, or if such merchant or owner shall refuse to permit the said officer or his deputies to view and examine any flour or not permit him or them to brand the same if merchantable, according to the directions of this act, every such person so offending shall forfeit and pay the sum of ten pounds; or shall ship off any cask or casks of flour not branded with the provincial brand-mark aforesaid, every such person so offending shall forfeit and pay the sum of five shillings for every cask of flour so shipped.

[Section VI.] [Inspecting officer's salary provided.]

[Section VII.] [Inspecting officer appointed.]

[Section VIII.] [Officer may appoint deputies.]

[Section IX.] And be it enacted by the authority aforesaid, that no owner, possessor, or occupier of any grist-mill in this province shall by himself, servant, or others presume to grind or suffer to be ground into meal for bolting for exportation out of this province any unsound, ill-dressed, or unmerchantable wheat; and whatsoever owner, possessor, or occupier of any such mill as aforesaid shall so grind or suffer to be ground any such unsound, ill-dressed, or unmerchantable wheat, to be bolted for exportation out of this province contrary to the true intent and meaning of this act, he, she, or they so offending in the premises shall forfeit and pay for every such offence the sum of thirty-five shillings on due proof thereof by one or more credible witnesses before any one justice of the peace in this province.

[Section X.] [Penalty for counterfeiting brand-mark.]

[Section XI.] And be it enacted . . . that all and singular the fines, forfeitures, and charges mentioned in this act, where the same respectively exceed not forty shillings, the same shall be recovered in the same manner as other debts under forty shillings by the Laws of this province; and where the same shall exceed forty shillings, they may be sued for and shall be recovered in any court of record in this province by bill, plaint, or information, wherein no essoin, protection, or wager of law nor any more than one imparlance shall be allowed. All which said forfeitures not herein-before directed how to be applied shall be paid to the prosecutor, one half thereof for the use of the poor, which he is hereby strictly required immediately on receipt thereof to pay to the overseers of the poor of the place where the forfeiture shall happen, and the other half for the said prosecutor, which he may detain to his own use as prosecutor, any law, usage, or custom to the contrary in any wise notwith-standing.

66. Virginia Tobacco Inspection Law (May 1730)

The Virginia law of 1730 was the culmination of a century of effort to regulate the production of tobacco and to improve the quality of the export crop. With this law the colonial government took complete charge of the export of tobacco. The law was amended from time to time but its basic ideas were not altered and it served as a model for similar legislation in Maryland. The sections of the law omitted here relate to penalties for violations, the maintenance of the integrity of inspectors, the location of the public warehouses, and the rates at which tobacco notes issued by inspectors for tobacco brought to the warehouses in payment of public and private debts should circulate in the colony. Printed: Hening, *Statutes of Virginia*, IV, pp. 247–271, *passim*.

Whereas the laws heretofore made have been found ineffectual to prevent the exportation of bad and trash tobacco, and the many frauds in deceiving his Majesty of his customs, which of late years have greatly increased, to the great decay of the trade of this colony:

II. Be it enacted by the Lieutenant-Governor, Council, and Burgesses of this present General Assembly, and it is hereby enacted by the authority of the same, that for the more effectual preventing the exportation of all trash, bad, unsound, and unmerchantable tobacco, all tobacco which from and after the first day of August, which shall be in the year of our Lord one thousand seven hundred and thirty-one, shall be exported out of this colony and dominion, shall be first brought to some public warehouse hereinafter mentioned, and there shall be viewed and inspected by persons thereunto appointed, in such manner as herein is expressed.

III. And be it further enacted by the authority aforesaid, that no person shall put on board, or receive into any ship, sloop, boat, or other vessel, in order to be exported therein, any tobacco not packed in hogsheads, casks, or cases, upon any pretence whatsoever; nor in any hogshead, cask, or case, to be in that or any other ship, sloop, or vessel, exported out of this colony, before the same shall have been viewed and inspected, according to the directions of this act; but that all tobacco whatsoever, to be received or taken on board any ship, sloop, or other vessel, and to be therein exported, or to be carried or put on board any other ship, sloop, or vessel, for exportation as aforesaid, shall be received or taken on board at the several warehouses for that purpose hereinafter mentioned, or some, or one of them, and at no other place or places whatsoever. And every master, mate, and boatswain, which shall arrive in this colony, in order to lade tobacco, during the continuance of this act, shall, before the said ship or vessel be permitted to take on board any tobacco whatsoever, make oath before the naval officer of the district wherein such ship or vessel shall arrive (which oath the said naval officer is hereby impowered and required to administer) that they will not permit any tobacco whatsoever to be taken on board their respective ships or vessels, except the same be packed in hogsheads, casks, or cases, stamped by some inspector legally thereunto appointed.

X. And be it further enacted by the authority aforesaid, that all tobacco which shall be brought to any warehouse hereinafter mentioned, shall be viewed by three fit and able persons who are reputed to be skilful in tobacco, to be appointed for that purpose by the governor or commander-in-chief for the time being, with the advice and consent of the council; who shall be called inspectors, and shall break every hogshead, cask, or case of tobacco, and diligently view and examine the same; and if they, or any two of them shall agree that the same is good, sound, well-conditioned, and merchantable, and free from trash, sand, and dirt; and if in leaf, tied up with a leaf of equal goodness, then such tobacco shall be weighed in scales with weights of the lawful standard. And the said inspectors, or one of them, shall stamp every such hogshead, cask, or case wherein is contained any tobacco, by them so as aforesaid weighed, and allowed to be good, or shall cause the same to be done in their presence, or the presence of one of them, with the name of the warehouse at which such hogshead, cask, or case of tobacco shall be so stamped as aforesaid; and shall also stamp in like manner thereon the tare of the hogshead, cask, or case, and quantity of net tobacco therein contained.

XI. And be it further enacted by the authority aforesaid, that if any tobacco shall be brought to any of the said warehouses for the discharge of any public or private debt or contract, the said inspectors, or one of them, after they have viewed, examined, and weighed the said tobacco, according to the directions of this act, shall be obliged to deliver to the person bringing the same, as many promissory notes, under the hands and seals of the said inspectors, or the stamp of the warehouse to which the same shall be brought, as shall be required for the full quantity of tobacco received by them; in which shall be expressed whether the tobacco so received be sweet scented, or Oronoko, stemmed or leaf. Which notes shall be, and are hereby declared to be current and payable in all tobacco payments whatsoever, according to the species expressed in the note, within the county where such inspectors shall officiate, or in any other county next adjacent thereto, and not separated therefrom by any of the great rivers or bay hereinafter mentioned; that is to say, James River below the mouth of Appomattox; York River below West Point; Rappahannock River below

Taliaferro's Mount, or by the great bay of Chesapeake; and shall be transferable from one to another in all such payments; and shall be paid and satisfied by the inspector or inspectors who signed the same, upon demand. And for every hogshead of tobacco brought to any public warehouse for the discharge of any public or private debt, in good cask, of such dimensions as are hereinafter expressed, there shall be allowed by the inspectors thereof to the person bringing the same, thirty pounds of tobacco for the cask. And for every hogshead of tobacco by them paid away, well lined, and nailed, fit for shipping, there shall be paid by the person receiving such hogshead, five shillings, so as such hogshead so paid away and received do not contain less than eight hundred pounds of net tobacco, whether the same be sweet scented or Oronoko; who shall also allow thirty pounds of tobacco to the person demanding the same for every hogshead of tobacco so received, for the cask. And moreover there shall be allowed to the said inspectors by the person taking the same away, two pounds of tobacco for every hundred pounds of tobacco so paid away as aforesaid, and proportionably for a less quantity, for shrinking and wasting, if the said tobacco be paid at any time within two months after the date of the note given for the same; and one pound of tobacco per hundred for every month the same shall be unpaid, after the said two months, so as such allowance for shrinking and wasting do not exceed in the whole six pounds of tobacco per centum.

XIII. And forasmuch as it is evident that the owners of ships trading to this country will reap great benefit by having tobacco put on board their ships by the inhabitants of this colony, whereby the great trouble and delay in fetching the same on board will be prevented, and the charge of craft, wages, and provisions saved to them, in the expense of each voyage.

XIV. Be it further enacted by the authority aforesaid, that no master of a ship or other vessel shall carry to any warehouse, or fetch from thence, or any place whatsoever, in any boat or vessel to him belonging, or in any vessel manned by the sailors of the ship or vessel whereof he is master, any tobacco to be shipped upon freight, upon pain of forfeiting ten pounds of lawful money for every hogshead so carried, fetched, or put on board; to be recovered by action of debt, in any court of record; one moiety whereof shall be to our sovereign lord the king, his heirs and successors, to be applied towards defraying the expense of the execution of this act, and the other moiety to the person who will sue for the same. But all tobacco shipped on board any ship or vessel whatsoever, shall be put on board by, or at the charge of, the owners of the tobacco respectively; for which a reward of four shillings for every hogshead so put on board shall be paid by the master of such ship or vessel on which the same shall be laden and put on board.

XXVII. And be it further enacted by the authority aforesaid, that all tobacco brought to any of the said warehouses in hogsheads, casks, or cases, to be exported, on the account and for the use of the owners thereof, after the same shall have been examined, viewed, and weighed, and found to be good, shall be stamped as is hereinbefore directed. And the said inspectors, or one of them, shall deliver to the person bringing the same, as many receipts, signed, sealed, or stamped as aforesaid, as shall be required, for the number of hogsheads so brought and stamped. And for every hogshead, cask, or case of tobacco brought to any of the said warehouses, to be exported, on the account and for the use of the owners thereof, there shall be paid to the inspectors there attending three shillings lawful money for viewing, examining, stamping, and nailing.

XXVIII. And, for restraining the undue practice of mixing trash with stemmed tobacco, and preventing the packing tobacco in unsizeable cask, be it enacted, and declared, that all stemmed tobacco, not laid straight, whether the same be packed loose, or in bundles; and all tobacco packed in hogsheads, which exceed eight and forty inches in the length of the stave, or thirty inches at the head, within the croes, making reasonable allowance for prising, which allowance shall not exceed two inches above the gauge, in the prising head, shall be accounted unlawful tobacco, and shall not be passed or received, but the owner of such tobacco, packed in cask of greater dimensions than is hereinbefore expressed, shall be obliged to repack the same in sizeable casks, at his own cost and charge, before the same shall be stamped by the said inspectors.

XXIX. And be it further enacted by the authority aforesaid, that when any tobacco shall be brought to any of the said public warehouses, and refused by the said inspectors there officiating, the owner of such tobacco shall not be permitted to take or carry away the same from the warehouse to which the same shall be brought; but the said inspectors shall permit and suffer the owner of such tobacco, or other person bringing the same, to sort and separate the tobacco so refused, in the same warehouse, without demanding any fee or reward; and so much of the said tobacco as shall be separated and taken apart from the rest, as bad, unsound, or unmerchantable tobacco shall, in the presence of the said inspectors there officiating, or of one of them, be immediately burnt. And if any owner of, or other person, bringing such tobacco so refused, will not sort and separate the same, then every such hogshead, or parcel of tobacco, shall be immediately burnt, as is hereinbefore directed.

XXX. And if any tobacco packed in cask by an overseer, or the hands under his care, shall be burnt by the said inspectors, by the reason of its being bad, unsound, or not in good condition, the overseer who had the care of making and packing the same, shall bear the loss of the tobacco so burnt, and make satisfaction for the same out of his share of the crop, or otherwise.

67. South Carolina assize of bread (16 March 1749)

Assizes of bread and of such things as beer and ale were common in the colonies. The South Carolina Act which follows is characteristic. Omitted from the following copy is an elaborate table which sets forth the weights of each of the various priced loaves of bread, and providing a scale indicating how much the weight of loaves in each price class may be varied in relationship to the rise and fall of the price of fine flour on the Charleston market. Printed: Thomas Cooper, ed., *The Statutes at Large of South Carolina*, III (Columbia, S.C., 1838), pp. 715–718.

Whereas, no Act of Assembly of this Province hath hitherto been made and provided for regulating the price and assize of bread, whereby little or no observance hath been made either of the due assize or reasonable price of bread made for sale within the same, and covetous and evil-disposed persons, taking advantage thereof, have for their own gain and lucre, deceived and oppressed his Majesty's subjects, and more especially the poorer sort of people; for remedy whereof for the future, and that a plain and constant rule and method may henceforward be duly observed and kept, in the making and assizing the several sorts of bread made for sale within this province, and hereinafter mentioned;

I. Therefore be it enacted, that from and after the expiration of thirty days next ensuing the day of the passing of this act, no person or persons whatsoever shall make for sale, or sell or expose to sale within this province, any sort or sorts of soft bread made of wheat, other than the several sorts hereinafter mentioned, that is to say, white, wheaten, and household bread; all which several sorts of soft bread shall be made in their several and respective degrees, according to the goodness and fineness of the several sorts of flour whereof the same ought to be made; and when fine wheat flour is ordinarily sold for money at Charlestown at any of the rates hereafter mentioned, the assize and weight of the said white, wheaten, and household bread respectively, are and shall be set and ascertained according to the following table in avoirdupois weight, and so proportionably when fine flour shall be ordinarily sold at Charlestown for more or less money than is specified in the said table, wherein the white loaves shall always be one half and the wheaten three quarters of the weight of household loaves.

II. Obsolete.

III. And to the intent that the good design of this act may be effectually complied with, be it further enacted, that every common baker and other person who shall make or bake for sale, or any ways expose to sale, any of the sorts of bread hereinbefore mentioned, shall, from and after the expiration of the said thirty days nextensuing the passing of this act, fairly imprint or mark, or cause to be fairly imprinted or marked, on every loaf, so by him or her made or exposed to sale, the price of such loaf, together with the initial letters of the name of the baker thereof, whereby the said baker and price of such bread may be distinctly known; and if any baker or bakers, or other person or persons, baking or making such bread for sale and exposing the same to sale, shall not observe the assize ascertained by virtue of this act, or shall bake or make for sale, or sell or expose to sale, any soft white, wheaten or household bread, wanting the due weight, or that shall not be marked according to the direction of this act, or shall in any sort or way break or infringe any of the matters or things appointed by the same, he, she, or they so doing, being thereof convicted by the confession of the party, or by the oath of one or more credible witness or witnesses, before one or more justice or justices of the peace for the county wherein the offence shall be committed, shall for every such offence forfeit the sum of twenty shillings proclamation money, to be levied by way of distress, upon the goods and chattels of every such offender, by warrant from the said justice or justices before whom such conviction shall be made, which forfeiture shall be for the use of and given to the informer and informers.

IV. And if any baker or seller of bread, in this act mentioned, shall put into any such bread by him or her sold or exposed to sale, any mixture of any other grain than what shall be absolutely necessary for the well making or baking thereof, to be judged of by the justice or justices trying and examining the same, every such person so offending shall for every such offence forfeit all such bread so fraudulently mixed, for the use of the poor of the parish where the offence shall be committed, and also the sum of 20s. proclamation money, for the use of the informer or informers; to be had and recovered in the manner and form hereinbefore mentioned. Provided always, that no person shall be convicted in manner aforesaid, for any of the before mentioned offences, unless the prosecution in order to such conviction be commenced in three days next after the offence committed.

V. And that the good design of this act may be the more effectually accomplished, be it further enacted, that it shall and may be lawful to and for any one or more justice or justices of the peace, within their respective counties, at all times hereafter, in the daytime, to enter into any house, shop, stall, bakehouse, warehouse, or out-house, of or belonging to any baker or seller of bread, there to search for, view, weigh, and try all or any of the bread mentioned in this act, of such person, or which shall there be found; and if any such bread shall be found wanting either in the goodness of the materials whereof the same should be made, or be deficient in the due baking or working thereof, or shall be wanting in the due weight, or shall not be truly marked according to the directions of this act, or shall be mixed with any other grain, or of any other sort than is allowed by virtue of this act, then and in every such case, it shall and may be lawful to and for such justice or justices of the peace, to seize and take the said bread so found, and cause the same to be forthwith given and distributed to the poor of the parish where such seizure shall be made. And if any baker or seller of bread, or other person or persons, shall not permit or suffer such search or seizure to be made, or shall oppose, hinder, or resist the same, he, she, or they so doing, shall for every such offence forfeit the sum of £4 proclamation money aforesaid, to the use of the poor of the parish where the offence shall be committed, to be had and recovered in the summary manner and form hereinbefore first mentioned.

VI. Provided, that if any person convicted of any offence against this act, shall think him or herself aggrieved, he or she shall or may immediately, or within three days after such conviction, make his or her appeal in writing to any three justices of the peace for the parish or county where such conviction shall be made, by whom the same shall be heard and finally determined, within ten days after such appeal made; and if the said person so appealing shall not make good his or her appeal, or prosecute it with effect, the said justices shall award such costs as they shall think reasonable to the prosecutor or informer, and commit the offender to the common gaol until he or she shall make payment of the said costs, and also of the penalty adjudged on the conviction to the informer; but in case the said appellant shall make good his or her appeal, and be discharged of his or her said conviction, the like reasonable costs shall be awarded to the appellant against such informer, who should in case of conviction have been entitled to the said penalty, to be recovered as aforesaid.

VII. If any action or suit shall be commenced or brought against any person or persons whatsoever for doing or causing to be done anything in pursuance or execution of this act, or relating thereto, the defendant in every such action or suit may plead the general issue, and give the special matter and this act in evidence; and if the plaintiff be nonsuited or discontinue his action, or a verdict be given against him, or judgment be otherwise given for the defendant, every such defendant shall have and be allowed his double costs. Provided, that no person punished by virtue of this act shall be for the same offence prosecuted by any other law, statute, usage, or custom whatsoever.

Part IV
POPULATION AND LABOUR

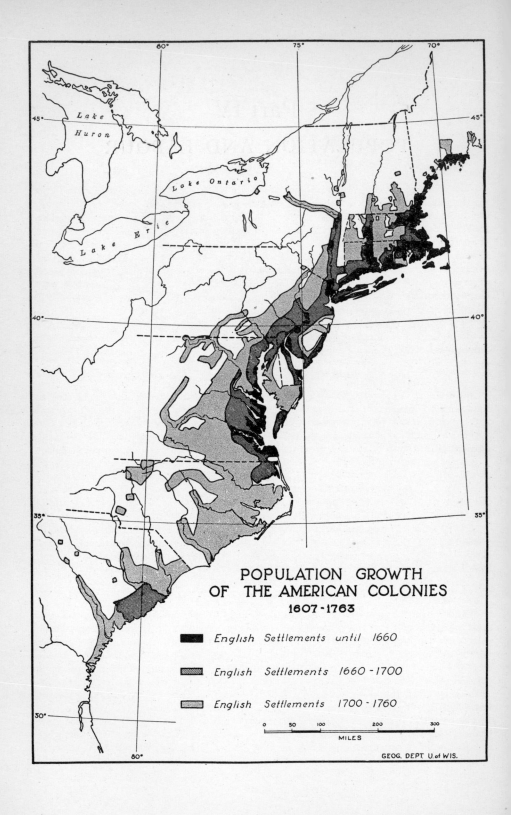

POPULATION GROWTH
OF THE AMERICAN COLONIES
1607-1763

■ English Settlements until 1660

▨ English Settlements 1660-1700

▨ English Settlements 1700-1760

0   50   100   200   300
MILES

GEOG. DEPT U. of WIS.

POPULATION AND LABOUR

SELECT BIBLIOGRAPHY

(a) THE SOURCES

The various printed records already cited contain much material on this topic. In addition, the descendants of various national and religious groups which came to the colonies have at one time or another founded historical societies which have recorded, and often exaggerated, the roles played by particular groups in early American history. Among the societies founded at one time or another, and some of which still continue to publish materials, are the Pennsylvania German Society (Lancaster, Pa.); the German-American Historical Society (Philadelphia); Society for the History of Germans in Maryland (Baltimore); The Huguenot Society of America (New York); the American-Irish Historical Society (Boston); the American Jewish Historical Society (Washington); and the Association for the Study of Negro Life and History (Washington), which publishes the excellent *Journal of Negro History*.

Such organizations have published valuable materials for the history of early colonization. In addition, much source material has been published in magazines and historical society publications listed in the General Bibliography.

(b) GENERAL WORKS ON POPULATION AND IMMIGRATION

Estimates of population growth in the colonies are brought together in E. B. Greene and Virginia D. Harrington, *American Population Before the Federal Census of 1790* (New York, 1932) and in Stella H. Sutherland, *Population Distribution in Colonial America* (New York, 1936). The latter book is particularly valuable because it includes maps showing population distribution and short histories of population growth and movements in individual colonies.

Of the one-volume histories of immigration, the most useful are Marcus L. Hansen, *The Atlantic Migration, 1607–1860* (Cambridge, Mass., 1940); Carl Wittke, *We Who Built America* . . . (New York, 1939); and Edith Abbott, ed., *Historical Aspects of the Immigration Problem* . . . (Chicago, 1926). Immigration to New England is discussed in C. K. Shipton, "Immigration to New England, 1680–1740", *Journal of Political Economy*, vol. xliv (1936).

Special aspects of immigration are discussed in E. E. Proper, *Colonial Immigration Laws* . . . (New York, 1900); A. H. Carpenter, "Naturalization in England and the American Colonies", *Amer. Hist. Rev.*, vol. ix (1903–1904); and W. F. Dunaway, "Pennsylvania as an Early Distributing Center of Population", *Penn. Mag. of Hist. and Biog.*, vol. lv (1931).

(c) WORKS ON NATIONAL, RELIGIOUS, AND RACIAL GROUPS

Various national groups whose ancestors migrated to colonial America have produced a great variety of histories and a literal flood of articles in periodicals. Oddly enough, English emigration has received little attention except for the studies of the transportation of convicts. For this see Abbott E. Smith, *Colonists in Bondage: White Servitude and Convict Labor in America, 1607–1776* (Chapel Hill, N.C., 1947). A brief discussion of emigration from England in the colonial period is in S. C. Johnson, *A History of Emigration from the United Kingdom to North America, 1763–1912* (London, 1913) and in W. F. Dunaway, "The English Settlers in Colonial Pennsylvania", *Penn. Mag. of Hist. and Biog.*, vol. lii (1928).

On the other hand such groups as the Scotch-Irish and the Germans have produced a plethora of materials. The following are some of the books on the Scotch-Irish which have appeared in the twentieth century. C. A. Hanna, *The Scotch-Irish, or, The Scot in North Britain*,

North Ireland and North America (2 vols., New York, 1902); C. K. BOLTON, *Scotch Irish Pioneers in Ulster and America* (Boston, 1910); H. J. FORD, *The Scotch-Irish in America* (Princeton, 1915); MAUDE GLASGOW, *The Scotch-Irish in Northern Ireland and in the American Colonies* (New York, 1936); W. F. DUNAWAY, *The Scotch Irish of Colonial Pennsylvania* (Philadelphia, 1944).

Scotch-Irish historians have struggled valiantly to distinguish their colonial ancestors from the 'Irish' Irish while historians of the latter group have denied the claims of the former, going so far as to declare that 38 per cent of the soldiers in the American Revolutionary armies were Irish Irish. See MICHAEL J. O'BRIEN, *A Hidden Phase of American History, Ireland's Part in America's Struggle for Liberty* (New York, 1919) and THOMAS H. MAGINNISS, *The Irish Contributions to America's Independence* (New York, 1913).

The role of Scots in America is treated inadequately in JOHN P. MCLEAN, *An Historical Account of the Settlements of Scotch Highlanders in America* . . . (Cleveland, 1900); G. S. PRYDE, "The Scots in East New Jersey", *N. J. Hist. Soc. Proceedings*, new Series, vol. XV (1930), and MARGARET I. ADAM, "The Highland Emigration of 1770", *Scottish Historical Review*, vol. XVI (1918–1919).

Productive though the Scotch-Irish historians have been, their output pales to nothing beside that of the German-Americans. They, and particularly the Pennsylvania Germans, or 'Dutch', have produced histories, books on folk lore, folk art, cookery, poetry, pottery, architecture, church music, and the like. The Pennsylvania German Society and the Lancaster County Historical Society have between them published at least 100 volumes of records and articles. *The Pennsylvania Magazine of History and Biography* has dozens of articles on the subject. Furthermore, many works have been written and published in Germany. A major bibliography is that of EMIL MEYNEN, *Bibliographie des Deutschtums der kolonialzeitlichen Einwanderung in Nordamerika* . . . (Leipzig, Germany, 1937). For references to the variety of material on the Germans in colonial times see WITTKE, *We Who Built America*, chap. 6, "The Colonial Germans".

The following are some of the works written during the twentieth century. F. R. DIFFENDERFER, *The German Immigration into Pennsylvania through the Port of Philadelphia from 1700 to 1775* (Lancaster, Pa., 1900); LUCY F. BITTINGER, *The German and Swiss Settlements in Pennsylvania. A Study of the So-Called Pennsylvania Dutch* (New York, 1901); A. B. FAUST, *The German Element in the United States* . . . (2 vols., New York, 1909); J. O. KNAUSS, *Social Conditions Among the Pennsylvania Germans in the Eighteenth Century as revealed in the German Newspapers Published in America* (Lancaster, Pa., 1922); J. L. ROSENBERGER, *The Pennsylvania Germans* . . . (Chicago, 1923); W. A. KNITTLE, *The Early Eighteenth Century Palatine Emigration* . . . (Philadelphia, 1936); RALPH WOOD, ed., *The Pennsylvania Germans* (Princeton, 1942); DIETER CUNZ, *The Maryland Germans: A History* (Princeton, 1948), part one of which deals with the colonial period; and FREDERICK KLEES, *The Pennsylvania Dutch* (New York, 1950).

The bulk of the Germans were Lutherans, but they included also a great variety of sects and considerable writing has been done from the approach of sectarian history. Examples are J. F. SACHSE, *The German Sectarians of Pennsylvania, 1708–1800* . . . (2 vols., Philadelphia, 1899–1900); J. M. LEVERING, *A History of Bethlehem, Pennsylvania, 1741–1792* . . . (Bethlehem, 1903); C. H. SMITH, *The Mennonite Immigration to Pennsylvania in the Eighteenth Century* (Norristown, Pa., 1929). The Moravians, who played an important role in the southern back country, have had their records published in part in ADELAIDE L. FRIES, ed., *Records of the Moravians in North Carolina* (7 vols., Raleigh, N.C., 1922–1947), the first two volumes of which cover the colonial period.

Among groups of less numerical importance who came to the American colonies were the French Huguenots, the Swiss, the Jews, and people from Scandinavia. French immigration is treated in CHARLES W. BAIRD, *History of the Huguenot Emigration to America* (2 vols., New York, 1885); LUCIEN J. FOSDICK, *The French Blood in America* (New York, 1919); A. H. HIRSCH, *The Huguenots of Colonial South Carolina* (Durham, N.C., 1928). The Virginia Historical Society *Collections*, new Series, vol. V (1886) contains documents on Huguenot emigration, as do the publications of the Huguenot Society of South Carolina, and other organizations devoted to their history.

The considerable Swiss emigration of the eighteenth century has not been given thorough study. A. B. FAUST, "Swiss Emigration to the American Colonies in the Eighteenth Century" and "Documents in Swiss Archives relating to Emigration to American Colonies in the Eighteenth Century", *Amer. Hist. Rev.*, vol. XXII (1916–1917) point the way to further study. OSCAR KUHNS, *The German and Swiss Settlements in Colonial Pennsylvania* ... (New York, 1901) has material on the Swiss in that colony.

Jewish immigration was small but it has been thoroughly studied. Like other groups, Jewish historians have tended to over-emphasize the role played by their colonial ancestors. See LEE M. FRIEDMAN, *Early American Jews* (Cambridge, Mass., 1934), ANITA L. LEBESON, *Jewish Pioneers in America, 1492–1848* (New York, 1931), and the *Publications* of the American Jewish Historical Society. The most recent and thorough studies are those of JACOB R. MARCUS, *Early American Jewry: The Jews of New York, New England, and Canada, 1649–1794* and *Early American Jewry: The Jews of Pennsylvania and the South, 1655–1790* (Philadelphia, The Jewish Publication Society of America, 1951, 1953).

Welsh immigration is treated in CHARLES H. BROWNING, *Welsh Settlement of Pennsylvania* (Philadelphia, 1912). Colonial settlers from Sweden and Finland are given elaborate treatment in the works of AMANDUS K. JOHNSON, CHRISTOPHER WARD, and JOHN WUORNINEN, cited in the Select Bibliography at the end of the general introduction.

(d) WORKS ON LABOUR IN THE COLONIES

The most thorough modern study of labour is RICHARD B. MORRIS, *Government and Labor in Early America*. Volume one of JOHN R. COMMONS, *et al.*, eds., *History of Labor in the United States* (New York, 1918); M. W. JERNEGAN, *The Laboring and Dependent Classes in Colonial America, 1607–1783* (Chicago, 1931); and *History of Wages in the United States from Colonial Times to 1928* (U.S. Bureau of Labor Statistics, *Bulletin*, Washington, 1929) should also be consulted.

The system of white servitude whereby so many people came to the colonies has received much attention. The most recent and best study is ABBOT E. SMITH, *Colonists in Bondage: White Servitude and Convict Labor in America, 1607–1776*. The bibliography of manuscript and printed sources and secondary works is the most thorough available. Other works dealing with particular colonies are SAMUEL MCKEE, *Labor in Colonial New York, 1664–1776* (New York, 1935); E. I. MCCORMAC, *White Servitude in Maryland, 1634–1820* (Baltimore, 1904); K. F. GEISER, *Redemptioners and Indentured Servants of the Colony and Commonwealth of Pennsylvania* (New Haven, 1901); C. A. HERRICK, *White Servitude of Pennsylvania* ... (Philadelphia, 1926); J. C. BALLAGH, *White Servitude in the Colony of Virginia* (Baltimore, 1895).

(e) WORKS ON SLAVERY IN THE COLONIES

The most recent book dealing with slavery in America is JOHN HOPE FRANKLIN, *From Slavery to Freedom: A History of American Negroes* (New York, 1947), the early portion of which deals with the colonies. It is particularly important for its bibliography. U. B. PHILLIPS, *American Negro Slavery* (New York, 1918) and his *Life and Labor in the Old South* (New York, 1929) are also valuable. Specialized works dealing with particular colonies are L. J. GREENE, *The Negro in Colonia New England, 1620–1776* (New York, 1942); E. R. TURNER, *The Negro in Pennsylvania* ... (Washington, 1911); J. R. BRACKETT, *The Negro in Maryland* (Baltimore, 1889); JAMES M. WRIGHT, *The Free Negro in Maryland, 1634–1860* (New York, 1921); J. C. BALLAGH, *A History of Slavery in Virginia* (Baltimore, 1902); JOHN S. BASSETT, *Slavery and Servitude in the Colony of North Carolina* (Baltimore, 1896); R. H. TAYLOR, *Slaveholding in North Carolina: An Economic View* (*James Sprunt Historical Publications*, vol. XVIII, Chapel Hill, N. C., 1926); EDWARD MCCRADY "Slavery in the Province of South Carolina, 1670–1770", *Amer. Hist. Assoc. Annual*

Report (1895). In addition, most colonial histories have something to say of slavery. Among the works already cited which should be mentioned again are ELIZABETH DONNAN, ed., *Documents Illustrative of the Slave Trade to America*, and L. H. GRAY, *History of Agriculture in the Southern United States*. In addition, there are many monographic articles in periodicals and historical society publications, and particularly in the *Journal of Negro History*.

The attempts of the colonists to enslave the Indians are discussed in A. W. LAUBER, *Indian Slavery in Colonial Times within the Present Limits of the United States* (New York, 1913).

A. IMMIGRATION TO THE COLONIES

WITHIN two years of the founding of Virginia John Smith begged the Virginia Company to "send but thirty carpenters, husbandmen, gardners, fishermen, black-smiths, masons, and diggers up of trees' roots well provided, than a thousand such as we have. . . ." Gentlemen and adventurers were not the stuff of which successful colonies were made, and while men of fortune did migrate throughout the colonial period they never did so in large numbers. The vast majority of the people who came to the colonies were farmers, artisans, and labourers. The founders and promoters of colonies held out many inducements, the chief of which was cheap or free land.[1] In the southern colonies land was promised to all who came as a 'headright'.[2] Land was also given to men of wealth who assisted poor people to emigrate. In fact, many land grants were made contingent upon the importation and settlement of a specified number of people. The founders of Massachusetts Bay financed the immigration of large numbers during the 1630's.

During the seventeenth century the bulk of the people who came to the colonies was English, although many nationalities were represented from the start. Thus when the English took over New Amsterdam in 1664, they found fourteen different languages spoken there. Aside from the economic benefits to be derived from coloni-zation, English propagandists for colonies looked upon the colonies as a place to send undesirables. Unemployment was a growing problem during the sixteenth century, and colonies would provide an outlet for potentially dangerous people.[3] This attitude began to change towards the end of the seventeenth century. The Puritan Revolution and the plague had partially solved the problem while the development of industry and commerce provided a growing market for labour. Alarm began to be expressed at the drain of population although few measures were taken to stop migration. Meanwhile, the British government continued to look upon the colonies as dumping ground for convicts of various sorts. The transportation of convicts was regularized by an Act of Parliament in 1718.[4] The colonies always objected to the importation of convicts, but their legislation against the traffic was invariably vetoed.[5]

The great tide of migration to the colonies during the eighteenth century was non-English. The two main streams came from Northern Ireland and from the Rhine Valley of Germany. Minor streams were made up of Swiss, French Huguenots, and Jews. All these groups added much to the variety and richness of colonial life. The Scots-Irish in particular were the cutting edge of frontier expansion. The Germans did much for the development of colonial agriculture. The Huguenots and Jews became prominent in commerce. The other great migration of the eighteenth century was the forced transportation of Negro slaves from Africa. Slaves were to be found almost from the start, although they were not brought in in great numbers until towards the end of the seventeenth century. Slavery existed in all the colonies, but it was the predominant labour supply in the tidewater sections of the plantation colonies during the eighteenth century. By 1775, slaves made up nearly twenty per cent of the population of the colonies as a whole, and a far greater percentage of the population of the southern colonies.[6]

[1] See Part I, B.   [2] Nos. 48, 49.   [3] No. 5.   [4] No. 68.   [5] No. 69.   [6] No. 73.

After a relatively slow growth during the seventeenth century, the population of the colonies grew with extraordinary rapidity during the eighteenth century. The bulk of the immigrants came to Pennsylvania, settled in western Pennsylvania, and then flowed south-westward into the southern back country. The increase of population north of Pennsylvania was much less rapid. New England never received large numbers after the 1630's. On the whole, those colonies were content with the natural increase of their original population, and, in fact, made every effort to keep out religiously and economically undesirable immigrants. New York, because of the monopolization of land by a few owners, was unpopular with immigrants.

Nevertheless, all the colonies had a remarkable admixture of national and economic groups. Many came for religious and political reasons; perhaps most came because to them America represented economic opportunity such as they could never hope for in their Old World homes.[1] While the realities did not always live up to their hopes,[2] there was still more opportunity for the ordinary individual in the English colonies than anywhere else in the world at the time. The optimism generated by opportunity and the peaceable mixture of so many different kinds of people, produced something that was new: the American. What it meant is stated best, if perhaps too optimistically, by a Frenchman, Hector St. Jean Crèvecoeur, in one of his *Letters from an American Farmer*.[3]

68. British law authorizing the transportation of convicts to the colonies (21 March 1718) (7 Geo. I, c. 11)

The transportation of convicts to Virginia was authorized as early as 1618. During the Commonwealth political prisoners as well as vagrants, rogues, and paupers were sent to the colonies. The practice was continued and legalized after 1660. The first legislation was an Act (13 and 14 Charles II, c. 12) that provided for the transportation of such "rogues, vagabonds, and sturdy beggars, as shall be duly convicted and adjudged incorrigible, to any of the English plantations beyond the seas". The transportation of convicts was finally elaborated and regularized by an Act of Parliament in 1718 entitled "An act for the further preventing robbery, burglary, and other felonies, and for the more effectual transportations of felons, and unlawful exporters of wools; and for declaring the law upon some points relating to pirates." The extracts which follow relate to the transportation of convicts to the colonies. Printed: Pickering, *Statutes at Large*, XIII, pp. 471-474.

Whereas it is found by experience that the punishments inflicted by the laws now in force against the offences of robbery, larceny, and other felonious taking and stealing of money and goods, have not proved effectual to deter wicked and evil-disposed persons from being guilty of the said crimes; and whereas many offenders to whom royal mercy hath been extended, upon condition of transporting themselves to the West Indies, have often neglected to perform the said condition, but returned to their former wickedness and been at last for new crimes brought to a shameful and ignominious death; and whereas in many of his Majesty's colonies and plantations in America there is great want of servants, who by their labour and industry might be the means of improving and making the said colonies and plantations more useful to this nation: be it enacted . . . that where any person or persons have been convicted of any offence within the benefit of clergy before the twentieth day of January one thousand seven hundred and seventeen, and are liable to be whipt or burnt in the hand, or have been ordered to any workhouse, and who shall be therein on the said twentieth day of January; as also where any person or persons shall be hereafter

[1] No. 71.   [2] No. 70.   [3] No. 72.

convicted of grand or petit larceny, or any felonious stealing or taking of money or goods and chattels, either from the person or the house of any other, or in any other manner, and who by the law shall be entitled to the benefit of clergy and liable only to the penalties of burning in the hand or whipping (except persons convicted for receiving or buying stolen goods, knowing them to be stolen), it shall and may be lawful for the court before whom they were convicted, or any court held at the same place with the like authority, if they think fit, instead of ordering any such offenders to be burnt in the hand or whipt, to order and direct, that such offenders, as also such offenders in any workhouse, as aforesaid, shall be sent as soon as conveniently may be to some of his Majesty's colonies and plantations in America for the space of seven years. . . .

II. And be it further enacted by the authority aforesaid that if any offender or offenders so ordered by any such court to be transported for any term of seven years or fourteen years, or other time or times as aforesaid, shall return into any part of Great Britain or Ireland before the end of his or their said term, he or she so returning as aforesaid, shall be liable to be punished as any person attainted of felony without the benefit of clergy; and execution may and shall be awarded against such offender or offenders accordingly. Provided nevertheless, that his Majesty, his heirs and successors, may pardon and dispense with any such transportation, and allow of the return of any such offender or offenders from America, he or they paying their owner or proprietor at the time of such pardon, dispensation, or allowance, such sum of money as shall be adjudged reasonable by any two justices of the peace residing within the province where such owner dwells; and where any such offenders shall be transported and shall have served their respective terms, according to the order of any such court as aforesaid, such services shall have the effect of a pardon to all intents and purposes, as for that crime or crimes for which they were so transported, and shall have so served, as aforesaid.

V. And whereas there are many idle persons who are under the age of one and twenty years lurking about in divers parts of London and elsewhere who want employment and may be tempted to become thieves, if not provided for; and whereas they may be inclined to be transported, and to enter into services in some of his Majesty's colonies and plantations in America; but as they have no power to contract for themselves and therefore that it is not safe for merchants to transport or take them into such services; be it enacted by the authority aforesaid, that where any person of the age of fifteen years or more, and under the age of twenty-one, shall be willing to be transported, and to enter into any service in any of his Majesty's colonies or plantations in America, it shall and may be lawful for any merchant, or other, to contract with any such person for any such service, not exceeding the term of eight years. . . .

69. Maryland law regulating convict servants (October 1723)

Although the colonies needed labour and accepted convicts to begin with, opposition to their importation grew steadily. In 1670 Virginia passed a law forbidding their importation on the ground that it was to prevent the "danger which apparently threatens us, from the barbarous designs and the felonious practices of such wicked villains . . ." (Hening, II, p. 509). Other colonies passed similar laws but the British government vetoed them regularly. The colonists called the convicts "jail birds" or "New-gate birds", the latter being a reference to the fact that large numbers were sent from Newgate prison in London. It is estimated that Old Bailey prison alone supplied about 10,000 convicts for the colonies between 1717 and 1775. All told, perhaps a total of 50,000 convicts were sent to the colonies.

The Maryland law of 1723 requiring bonds from the owners of convict servants and regulating their importation was typical. Its veto by the proprietor was likewise indicative of British policy. Printed: Bernard C. Steiner, ed., *Archives of Maryland*, xxxviii (Baltimore, 1918), pp. 320–322; xxxv (Baltimore, 1915), p. 212.

An Act to prevent the great evils arising by the importation of convicts into this province and for the better discovery of such when imported:

Whereas the great number of convicts of late years imported into this province have not only committed several murders, burglaries, and other felonies, but debauched the minds and principles of several of the ignorant and formerly innocent inhabitants thereof, so far as to induce them to commit several of the like crimes, the perpetration whereof are now become so common and frequent that honest people are very insecure in their lives or properties; and whereas the greatest part of the magistrates' time is taken up in the trial and prosecution of the said convicts and their proselytes, to the great delay of all civil business and the insupportable expense of the country, which evils are in a great measure occasioned by the masters or owners of such convicts not taking care to keep them within due bounds and restraining them from injuring their neighbours, for remedy whereof:

Be it enacted by the right honourable the lord proprietor by and with the advice and consent of his lordship's governor and the upper and lower houses of Assembly, and the authority of the same: that every inhabitant of this province that hereafter shall buy any convict servant, shall be and is by this act obliged, within twenty days after the publication hereof, or purchase of such convict servant, to give and enter into recognizance, in the sum of thirty pounds current money of Maryland, before some justice of the provincial or county court, for the good behaviour of such convict servant for the space of one whole year from the date of such recognizance, which recognizances are to be renewed yearly, and every year during the time of the servitude of such convict servant. And to be returned by the several magistrates taking the same to the county clerks respectively where the persons recognizing reside, to be by him entered upon record.

And be it enacted by the authority, advice, and consent aforesaid that any person that shall hereafter buy any convict servant that shall neglect or refuse to give a recognizance according to the directions of this act by the space of twenty days after the publication thereof, or purchase of such convict servant, and renew the same recognizance yearly as aforesaid, shall forfeit the quantity of four thousand pounds of tobacco; one half to the lord proprietor for and towards defraying the public charge of this province; the other half to the informer or him that will sue for the same, to be recovered by action of debt, bill, plaint, or information wherein no essoin, protection, or wager of law shall be allowed, and to the end that it may be known when and to whom any convict servants are sold.

Be it enacted that every person having the sale of any such convict servant within this province shall be and is hereby obliged to make oath, or affirmation, if a Quaker, before one justice of the provincial or county court within six days after such sale of the time of the sale of such convict servant, and to whom sold; which deposition or affirmation shall be by such magistrate transmitted to the clerk of the county who is hereby obliged to enter the same on record without fee or reward, and that an exemplification of such deposition or affirmation shall be received as evidence to prove the fact therein contained. And that the person selling such convicts and neglecting to do what is by this act required, shall forfeit twenty thousand pounds of tobacco to the use aforesaid, to be recovered as aforesaid. And for the better discovery of convict servants: be it enacted that every master of a ship or other vessel that shall hereafter import any servants into this province shall be obliged at the time of the entry of his ship or other vessel, as aforesaid, to declare upon oath or affirmation (if a Quaker) which the naval officer of the port is by this act empowered to administer, whether he knows of any convicts among the servants by him imported, and to give a list of their names to the naval officer, to be by him transmitted to the clerk of the county court within twenty days after the entry of such ship or other vessel, to be entered upon record; and that every master of a ship that shall refuse to make oath or affirmation according to the directions of this act, shall forfeit one hundred and fifty pounds sterling for the use aforesaid, to be recovered as aforesaid. And be it further enacted by the authority aforesaid, by and with the advice and consent aforesaid, that every magistrate taking any recognizance or depositions in pursuance to the directions of this act shall for every recognizance or deposition by him so taken, have and receive from the person entering into such recognizance, or causing such deposition to be taken as aforesaid, the sum of five shillings current money of Maryland as a fee or reward for the same, to be paid by the purchaser or owner of such convict servant.

PROPRIETOR'S VETO

Charles, absolute lord and proprietary of the provinces of Maryland and Avalon, lord baron of Baltimore, etc., to our right trusty and well-beloved Charles Calvert, Esq., our lieutenant-governor of our said province of Maryland, and to our right trusty and well-beloved the upper and lower houses of our General Assembly there and to all others of our said province of Maryland for the time being, greeting.

Whereas at a sessions of Assembly begun and held in our province of Maryland the 23 day of September and ending the 26th day of October in the eighth year of our dominion over the said province, Annoq Domini 1723, an act passed entitled an act to prevent the great evils arising by the importation of convicts into this province and for the better discovery of such when imported:

And whereas it hath been represented to us that the said act may and will in a great measure disable the contractor with the government of England for transporting of felons to his Majesty's plantations from performing his said contract, and that the said act does in great measure destroy the intent of the acts of Parliament made for that purpose in England; and their excellencies the Lords Justices in Council having last August disallowed an act the like nature in his Majesty's colony of Virginia, we on due consideration of the aforesaid act made in Maryland have thought fit to dissent to the same and do hereby declare the said act to be null, void, and of no effect.

Given under our hand and seal at arms at London the 8th day of June in the ninth year of our dominion over the said province of Maryland, Annoq Dni 1724.

70. Gottlieb Mittelberger: on immigration to America (c. 1750)

Gottlieb Mittelberger, a German pastor, came to Pennsylvania to investigate the lot of his fellow Germans who were migrating to the colonies in such large numbers. His description of the passage across the Atlantic in an eighteenth-century immigrant ship is one of the most grim and vivid which has come down to us. Printed: Mittelberger, *Journey to Pennsylvania in the Year 1750 and Return to Germany in the Year 1754* (translated by Carl T. Eben, Philadelphia, 1898), pp. 16–29.

But the most important occasion for publishing this little book was the wretched and grievous condition of those who travel from Germany to this new land, and the outrageous and merciless proceeding of the Dutch man-dealers and their man-stealing emissaries; I mean the so-called newlanders, for they steal, as it were, German people under all manner of false pretences, and deliver them into the hands of the great Dutch traffickers in human souls. These derive a large, and the newlanders a smaller profit from this traffic. This, I say, is the main cause why I publish this book. I had to bind myself even by a vow to do so. For before I left Pennsylvania, when it became known that I was about to return to Wurtemberg, many Wurtembergers, Durlachers, and Palatines, of whom there are a great number there who repent and regret it while they live that they left their native country, implored me with tears and uplifted hands, and even in the name of God, to make this misery and sorrow known in Germany, so that not only the common people, but even princes and lords, might learn how they had fared, to prevent other innocent souls from leaving their fatherland, persuaded thereto by the newlanders, and from being sold into a like slavery. And so I vowed to the great God, and promised those people, to reveal to the people of Germany the pure truth about it, to the best of my knowledge and ability. I hope, therefore, that my beloved countrymen and all Germany will care no less to obtain accurate information as to how far it is to Pennsylvania, how long it takes to get there; what the journey costs, and besides, what hardships and dangers one has to pass through; what takes place when the people arrive well or ill in the country; how they are sold and dispersed; and finally, the nature and condition of the whole land. I relate both what is good and what is evil, and I hope, therefore, to be considered impartial and truthful by an honour-loving world.

When all this will have been read I do not doubt that those who may still desire to go there, will remain in their fatherland, and carefully avoid this long and tedious journey and the fatalities connected with it; as such a journey involves with most a loss of their property, liberty, and peace; with not a few even a loss of life, and I may well say, of the salvation of their souls. . . .

. . . This journey lasts from the beginning of May to the end of October, fully half a year, amid such hardships as no one is able to describe adequately with their misery.

The cause is because the Rhine-boats from Heilbronn to Holland have to pass by

36 custom-houses, at all of which the ships are examined, which is done when it suits the convenience of the custom-house officials. In the meantime the ships with the people are detained long, so that the passengers have to spend much money. The trip down the Rhine alone lasts therefore 4, 5 and even 6 weeks.

When the ships with the people come to Holland, they are detained there likewise 5 or 6 weeks. Because things are very dear there, the poor people have to spend nearly all they have during that time. Not to mention many sad accidents which occur here; having seen with my own eyes how a man, as he was about to board the ship near Rotterdam, lost two children at once by drowning.

Both in Rotterdam and in Amsterdam the people are packed densely, like herrings so to say, in the large sea-vessels. One person receives a place of scarcely 2 feet width and 6 feet length in the bedstead, while many a ship carries four to six hundred souls; not to mention the innumerable implements, tools, provisions, water-barrels and other things which likewise occupy much space.

On account of contrary winds it takes the ships sometimes 2, 3 and 4 weeks to make the trip from Holland to Kaupp [Cowes] in England. But when the wind is good, they get there in 8 days or even sooner. Everything is examined there and the custom-duties paid, whence it comes that the ships ride there 8, 10 to 14 days and even longer at anchor, till they have taken in their full cargoes. During that time every one is compelled to spend his last remaining money and to consume his little stock of provisions which had been reserved for the sea; so that most passengers, finding themselves on the ocean where they would be in greater need of them, must greatly suffer from hunger and want. Many suffer want already on the water between Holland and Old England.

When the ships have for the last time weighed their anchors near the city of Kaupp [Cowes] in Old England, the real misery begins with the long voyage. For from there the ships, unless they have good wind, must often sail 8, 9, 10 to 12 weeks before they reach Philadelphia. But even with the best wind the voyage lasts 7 weeks.

But during the voyage there is on board these ships terrible misery, stench, fumes, horror, vomiting, many kinds of sea-sickness, fever, dysentery, headache, heat, consti-pation, boils, scurvy, cancer, mouth-rot, and the like, all of which come from old and sharply salted food and meat, also from very bad and foul water, so that many die miserably.

Add to this want of provisions, hunger, thirst, frost, heat, dampness, anxiety, want, afflictions and lamentations, together with other trouble, as c.v. the lice abound so frightfully, especially on sick people, that they can be scraped off the body. The misery reaches the climax when a gale rages for 2 or 3 nights and days, so that every one believes that the ship will go to the bottom with all human beings on board. In such a visitation the people cry and pray most piteously.

When in such a gale the sea rages and surges, so that the waves rise often like high mountains one above the other, and often tumble over the ship so that one fears to go down with the ship; when the ship is constantly tossed from side to side by the storm and waves, so that no one can either walk, or sit, or lie, and the closely packed people in the berths are thereby tumbled over each other, both the sick and the well–it will be readily understood that many of these people, none of whom had been prepared for hardships, suffer so terribly from them that they do not survive it.

I myself had to pass through a severe illness at sea, and I best know how I felt at the time. These poor people often long for consolation, and I often entertained and comforted them with singing, praying and exhorting; and whenever it was possible and the winds and waves permitted it, I kept daily prayer-meetings with them on deck. Besides, I baptized five children in distress, because we had no ordained minister on board. I also held divine service every Sunday by reading sermons to the people; and when the dead were sunk in the water, I commended them and our souls to the mercy of God.

Among the healthy, impatience sometimes grows so great and cruel that one curses the other, or himself and the day of his birth, and sometimes come near killing each other. Misery and malice join each other, so that they cheat and rob one another. One always reproaches the other with having persuaded him to undertake the journey. Frequently children cry out against their parents, husbands against their wives and wives against their husbands, brothers and sisters, friends and acquaintances against each other. But most against the soul-traffickers.

Many sigh and cry: "Oh, that I were at home again, and if I had to lie in my pig-sty!" Or they say: "O God, if I only had a piece of good bread, or a good fresh drop of water." Many people whimper, sigh and cry piteously for their homes; most of them get home-sick. Many hundred people necessarily die and perish in such misery, and must be cast into the sea, which drives their relatives, or those who persuaded them to undertake the journey, to such despair that it is almost impossible to pacify and console them. In a word, the sighing and crying and lamenting on board the ship continues night and day, so as to cause the hearts even of the most hardened to bleed when they hear it.

No one can have an idea of the sufferings which women in confinement have to bear with their innocent children on board these ships. Few of this class escape with their lives; many a mother is cast into the water with her child as soon as she is dead. One day, just as we had a heavy gale, a woman in our ship, who was to give birth and could not give birth under the circumstances, was pushed through a loop-hole [port-hole] in the ship and dropped into the sea, because she was far in the rear of the ship and could not be brought forward.

Children from 1 to 7 years rarely survive the voyage; and many a time parents are compelled to see their children miserably suffer and die from hunger, thirst, and sickness, and then to see them cast into the water. I witnessed such misery in no less than 32 children in our ship, all of whom were thrown into the sea. The parents grieve all the more since their children find no resting-place in the earth, but are devoured by the monsters of the sea. It is a notable fact that children, who have not yet had the measles or small-pox, generally get them on board the ship, and mostly die of them.

Often a father is separated by death from his wife and children, or mothers from their little children, or even both parents from their children; and sometimes whole families die in quick succession; so that often many dead persons lie in the berths beside the living ones, especially when contagious diseases have broken out on board the ship.

Many other accidents happen on board these ships, especially by falling, whereby people are often made cripples and can never be set right again. Some have also fallen into the ocean.

That most of the people get sick is not surprising, because, in addition to all other trials and hardships, warm food is served only three times a week, the rations being very poor and very little. Such meals can hardly be eaten, on account of being so unclean. The water which is served out on the ships is often very black, thick and full of worms, so that one cannot drink it without loathing, even with the greatest thirst. O surely, one would often give much money at sea for a piece of good bread, or a drink of good water, not to say a drink of good wine, if it were only to be had. I myself experienced that sufficiently, I am sorry to say. Towards the end we were compelled to eat the ship's biscuit which had been spoiled long ago; though in a whole biscuit there was scarcely a piece the size of a dollar that had not been full of red worms and spiders' nests. Great hunger and thirst force us to eat and drink everything; but many a one does so at the risk of his life. The sea-water cannot be drunk, because it is salt and bitter as gall. If this were not so, such a voyage could be made with less expense and without so many hardships.

At length, when, after a long and tedious voyage, the ships come in sight of land, so that the promontories can be seen, which the people were so eager and anxious to see, all creep from below on deck to see the land from afar, and they weep for joy, and pray and sing, thanking and praising God. The sight of the land makes the people on board the ship, especially the sick and the half dead, alive again, so that their hearts leap within them; they shout and rejoice, and are content to bear their misery in patience, in the hope that they may soon reach the land in safety. But alas!

When the ships have landed at Philadelphia after their long voyage, no one is permitted to leave them except those who pay for their passage or can give good security; the others, who cannot pay, must remain on board the ships till they are purchased, and are released from the ships by their purchasers. The sick always fare the worst, for the healthy are naturally preferred and purchased first; and so the sick and wretched must often remain on board in front of the city for 2 or 3 weeks, and frequently die, whereas many a one, if he could pay his debt and were permitted to leave the ship immediately, might recover and remain alive.

Before I describe how this traffic in human flesh is conducted, I must mention how much the journey to Philadelphia or Pennsylvania costs.

A person over 10 years pays for the passage from Rotterdam to Philadelphia 10 pounds, or 60 florins. Children from 5 to 10 years pay half price, 5 pounds or 30 florins. All children under 5 years are free. For these prices the passengers are conveyed to Philadelphia, and, as long as they are at sea, provided with food, though with very poor, as has been shown above.

But this is only the sea-passage; the other costs on land, from home to Rotterdam, including the passage on the Rhine, are at least 40 florins, no matter how economically one may live. No account is here taken of extraordinary contingencies. I may safely assert that, with the greatest economy, many passengers have spent 200 florins from home to Philadelphia.

The sale of human beings in the market on board the ship is carried on thus: every day Englishmen, Dutchmen and High-German people come from the city of Philadelphia and other places, in part from a great distance, say 20, 30, or 40 hours away, and go on board the newly arrived ship that has brought and offers for sale passengers from Europe, and select among the healthy persons such as they deem suitable for their business, and bargain with them how long they will serve for their passage-money, which most of them are still in debt for. When they have come to an agreement, it happens that adult persons bind themselves in writing to serve 3, 4, 5 or 6 years for the amount due by them, according to their age and strength. But very young people, from 10 to 15 years, must serve till they are 21 years old.

Many parents must sell and trade away their children like so many head of cattle; for if their children take the debt upon themselves, the parents can leave the ship free and unrestrained; but as the parents often do not know where and to what people their children are going, it often happens that such parents and children, after leaving the ship, do not see each other again for many years, perhaps no more in all their lives.

When people arrive who cannot make themselves free, but have children under 5 years, the parents cannot free themselves by them; for such children must be given to somebody without compensation to be brought up, and they must serve for their bringing up till they are 21 years old. Children from 5 to 10 years, who pay half price for their passage, viz. 30 florins, must likewise serve for it till they are 21 years of age; they cannot, therefore, redeem their parents by taking the debt of the latter upon themselves. But children above 10 years can take part of their parents' debt upon themselves.

A woman must stand for her husband if he arrives sick, and in like manner a man for his sick wife, and take the debt upon herself or himself, and thus serve 5 to 6 years, not alone for his or her own debt, but also for that of the sick husband or wife. But if both are sick, such persons are sent from the ship to the sick-house [hospital], but not until it appears probable that they will find no purchasers. As soon as they are well again they must serve for their passage, or pay if they have means.

It often happens that whole families, husband, wife, and children, are separated by being sold to different purchasers, especially when they have not paid any part of their passage-money.

When a husband or wife has died at sea, when the ship has made more than half of her trip, the survivor must pay or serve not only for himself or herself, but also for the deceased.

When both parents have died over half-way at sea, their children, especially when they are young and have nothing to pawn or to pay, must stand for their own and their parents' passage, and serve till they are 21 years old. When one has served his or her term, he or she is entitled to a new suit of clothes at parting; and if it has been so stipulated, a man gets in addition a horse; a woman, a cow.

When a serf has an opportunity to marry in this country, he or she must pay for each year which he or she would have yet to serve, 5 to 6 pounds. But many a one who has thus purchased and paid for his bride, has subsequently repented his bargain, so that he would gladly have returned his exorbitantly dear ware, and lost the money besides.

If some one in this country runs away from his master, who has treated him harshly, he cannot get far. Good provision has been made for such cases, so that a runaway is soon recovered. He who detains or returns a deserter receives a good reward.

If such a runaway has been away from his master one day, he must serve for it as a punishment a week, for a week a month, and for a month half a year. But if the master will not keep the runaway after he has got him back, he may sell him for so many years as he would have to serve him yet.

Work and labour in this new and wild land are very hard and manifold, and many a one who came there in his old age must work very hard to his end for his bread.

71. Motives for Scotch emigration to America (1774)

In December 1773 John Robinson, secretary of the treasury, directed customs officials in England and Scotland to supply him with information concerning people leaving for the colonies. The reports of the customs officials indicate that the economic factor was the principal cause of migration. It shows that people were attracted to the colonies by the promise of high wages, cheap land, and plentiful food. The following report consists of the examinations of emigrants from the counties of Caithness and Sutherland in Scotland. They were on board the ship *Bachelor* which put in at Port Lerwick in the Shetland Islands *en route* to Wilmington, North Carolina. Printed: *The North Carolina Historical Review*, XI (1934), pp. 130–138.

William Gordon saith that he is aged sixty and upwards, by trade a farmer, married, hath six children who emigrate with him, with the wives and children of his two sons John and Alexander Gordon. Resided last at Wymore in the parish of Clyne in the county of Sutherland, upon lands belonging to William Baillie of Rosehall. That having two sons already settled in Carolina, who wrote him encouraging him to come there, and finding the rents of lands raised in so much that a possession for which his grandfather paid only eight merks Scots, he himself at last paid sixty, he was induced to emigrate for the greater benefit of his children, being himself an old man and lame so that it was indifferent to him in what country he died. That his circumstances were greatly reduced not only by the rise of rents but by the loss of cattle, particularly in the severe winter [of] 1771. That the lands on which he lived have often changed masters, and that the rents have been raised on every change, and when Mr. Baillie bought them they were farmed with the rest of his purchase to one tacksman at a very high rent, who must also have his profits out of them. All these things concurring induced him to leave his own country in hopes that his children would earn their bread more comfortably elsewhere. That one of his sons is a weaver and another a shoemaker, and he hopes they may get bread for themselves and be a help to support him.

William McKay, aged thirty, by trade a farmer, married, hath three children from eight to two years old, besides one dead since he left his own country, resided last at —— in the parish of Farr in the county of Strathnaver upon the estate of the countess of Sutherland. Intends to go to Wilmington in North Carolina because his stock being small, crops failing, and bread excessively dear, and the price of cattle low, he found he could not have bread for his family at home and was encouraged to emigrate by the accounts received from his countrymen who had gone to America before him, assuring him that he might procure a comfortable subsistence in that country. That the land he possessed was a wadset of the family of Sutherland to Mr. Charles Gordon of Skelpick, lying in the height of the country of Strathnaver, the rents were not raised.

William Sutherland, aged forty, a farmer, married, hath five children from 19 to 9 years old, lived last at Strathalidale in the parish of Rea, in the county of Caithness, upon the estate of the late Colonel McKay of Bighouse; intends to go to North Carolina; left his own country because the rents were raised, as soldiers returning upon the peace with a little money had offered higher rents; and longer fines or grassums [a premium paid to a feudal superior on entering the holding]; besides the services were oppressive in the highest degree. That from his farm which paid 60 merks Scots, he was obliged to find two horses and two servants from the middle of July to the end of harvest solely at his own expense, besides ploughing, cutting turf, making middings, mixing dung and leading it out in seed time, and besides cutting, winning, leading and stacking 10 fathoms of peats yearly, all done without so much as a bit of bread or a drink to his servants.

John Catanoch, aged fifty years, by trade a farmer, married, hath 4 children from 19 to 7 years old; resided last at Chabster in the parish of Rae in the county of Caithness, upon the estate of Mr. Alexander Nicolson, minister at Thurso, intends to go to Wilmington, North Carolina; left his own country because crops failed, bread became dear, the rents of his possession were raised from two to five pounds sterling; besides his pasture or common grounds were taken up by placing new tenants thereon, especially the grounds adjacent to his farm, which were the only grounds on which his cattle pastured. That this method of parking and placing tenants on the pasture grounds rendered his farm useless; his cattle died for want of grass, and his corn farm was unfit to support his family after paying the extravagant tack duty. That beside the rise of rents and scarcity of bread, the landlord exacted arbitrary and oppressive services, such as obliging the declarant to labour up his ground, cart, win, lead and stack his peats; mow, win and lead his hay, and cut his corn and lead it in the yard, which took up about 30 or 40 days of his servants and horses each year, without the least acknowledgment for it, and without victuals, save the men that mowed the hay who got their dinner only. That he was induced to emigrate by advices received from his friends in America; that provisions are extremely plenty and cheap, and the price of labour very high, so that people who are temperate and laborious have every chance of bettering their circumstances. Adds that the price of bread in the country he hath left is greatly enhanced by distilling, that being for so long a time so scarce and dear, and the price of cattle at the same time reduced full one half while the rents of lands have been raised nearly in the same proportion, all the smaller farms must inevitably be ruined.

Elizabeth McDonald, aged 29, unmarried, servant to James Duncan in Mointle in the parish of Farr in the county of Sutherland; intends to go to Wilmington in North Carolina, left her own country because several of her friends having gone to

Carolina before her, had assured her that she would get much better service and greater encouragement in Carolina than in her own country.

Donald McDonald, aged 29 years, by trade a farmer and tailor, married, hath one child six years old. Resided last at Chapter in the parish of Rae in the county of Caithness upon the estate of Mr. Alexander Nicolson, minister at Thurso; intends to go to Carolina; left his own country for the reasons assigned by John Catanoch, as he resided in the same town and was subjected to the same hardships with the other. Complains as he doth of the advanced price of corn, owing in a great measure to the consumption of it in distilling.

John McBeath, aged 37, by trade a farmer and shoemaker, married; hath 5 children from 13 years to 9 months old. Resided last in Mault in the parish of Kildonnan in the county of Sutherland, upon the estate of Sutherland. Intends to go to Wilmington in North Carolina; left his own country because crops failed, he lost his cattle, the rent of his possession was raised, and bread had been long dear; he could get no employment at home whereby he could support himself and family, being unable to buy bread at the prices the factors on the estate of Sutherland and neighbouring estates exacted from him. That he was encouraged to emigrate by the accounts received from his own and his wife's friends already in America, assuring him that he would procure comfortable subsistence in that country for his wife and children, and that the price of labour was very high. He also assigns for the cause of bread being dear in his country that it is owing to the great quantities of corn consumed in brewing risquebah [whiskey].

James Duncan, aged 27 years, by trade a farmer, married, hath two children, one 5 years, the other 9 months old. Resided last at Mondle in the parish of Farr in the shire of Sutherland, upon the estate of Sutherland; intends to go to Wilmington in North Carolina; left his own country because crops failed him for several years and among the last years of his labouring he scarce reaped any crop; bread became dear and the price of cattle so much reduced that one cow's price could only buy a boll [a measure of 6 bushels] of meal. That the people on the estate of Sutherland were often supplied with meal from Caithness but the farmers there had of late stopped the sale of their meal because it rendered them a much greater profit by distilling. That he could find no employment at home whereby he could support his family. That he has very promising prospects by the advices from his friends in Carolina, as they have bettered their circumstances greatly since they went there by their labours, lands being cheap and good provisions plenty, and the price of labour very encouraging.

Hector McDonald, aged 75, married, a farmer, hath three sons who emigrate with him, John, Alexander, and George from 27 to 22 years old; also two grandchildren, Hector Campbell, aged 16, and Alexander Campbell, aged 12, who go to their mother already in Carolina. Resided last at Langwall in the parish of Rogart in the county of Sutherland, upon the estate of Sutherland. Intends to go to North Carolina. Left his own country because the rents of his possession had been raised from one pound seven shillings to four pounds, while the price of the cattle raised upon it fell more than one half, and not being in a corn country, the price of bread was so far advanced that a cow formerly worth from 50 shillings to 3 pounds could only purchase a boll of meal. He suffered much by the death of cattle, and still more by oppressive services exacted by the factor, being obliged to work with his people and cattle for 40 days and more each year without a bit of bread. That falling into reduced circumstances, he was assured by some of his children already in America that his family might subsist more comfortably there, and in all events they can scarce be worse. Ascribes the excessive price of corn to the consumption of it in distilling.

William McDonald, aged 71, by trade a farmer, married, hath 3 children from 7 to 5 years old, who emigrate with him. Resided last at Little Savall in the parish of Lairg in the county of Sutherland, upon the estate of Hugh Monro of Achanny. Intends to go to Wilmington in North Carolina; left his own country because crops failed, bread became dear, the rents of his possession were raised, but not so high as the lands belonging to the neighbouring heritors, by which and the excessive price of meal, the lowness of the price of cattle, and still further by a Cautionary [personal security] by which he lost 30 pounds sterling; his circumstances were much straightened, so that he could no longer support his family at home, though Mr. Monro used him with great humanity. That his friends already in Carolina have given him assurance of bettering his condition, as the price of labour is high and provisions very cheap. Ascribes the high price of corn to the consumption of it in distilling.

Hugh Matheson, aged 32, married, hath 3 children from 8 to 2 years old, also a sister Katherine Matheson aged 16, who emigrate with him; was a farmer last at Rimsdale in the parish of Kildonan in the county of Sutherland; leaves his country and goes to Carolina because upon the rise of the price of cattle some years ago, the rent of his possession was raised from 2 pounds 16 shillings to 5 pounds 10 shillings. But the price of cattle has been of late so low and that of bread so high that the factor who was also a drover would give no more than a boll of meal for a cow, which was formerly worth from 50 shillings to 3 pounds, and obliged the tenants to give him their cattle at his own price. That in these grassing counties little corn can be raised, and for some years past the little they had was in a great measure blighted and rendered useless by the frost which is common in the beginning of autumn in the inland parts of the country. That in such circumstances it seems impossible for farmers to avoid ruin, and their distresses heightened by the consumption of corn in distilling in a grassing country where little can be raised. That encouraged by his friends already in America, he hath good hopes of bettering his condition in that country.

William McKay, aged 26, married, a farmer last at Craigie in the parish of Rae and county of Caithness, upon the estate of George McRay, Handa Island; goes to Carolina because the rent of his possession was raised to double at the same time that the price of cattle was reduced one half, and even lower, as he was obliged to sell them to the factor at what price he pleased; at the same time his crop was destroyed by bad harvests and bread became excessive dear, owing in a great measure to the consumption by distilling. That the services were oppressive, being unlimited and arbitrary, at the pleasure of the factor, and when by reason of sickness the declarant could not perform them, he was charged at the rate of one shilling per day. He had assurances from his friends in America that the high price of labour and cheapness of provisions would enable him to support himself in that country.

Alexander Sinclair, aged 36, married, hath 3 children from 18 to 2 years old, a farmer last at Dollochcagy in the parish of Rae and county of Caithness, upon the estate of Sir John Sinclair of Murkle. Left his own country and goes to Carolina, because the tacksman of Sir John Sinclair's estate, demanded an advanced rent and arbitrary services, which in the present distresses of the country could not be complied with without ruin. That he is encouraged by his friends in America to hope to better his circumstances there.

George Grant, aged 20, married, a farmer last at Aschog in the parish of Kildonan in the county of Sutherland on the estate of ——. Intends to go to North Carolina because crops failed so that he was obliged to buy four months' provisions in a year, and at the same time the price of cattle was reduced more than one half. That his brothers-in-law, already in America, have assured him that from the cheapness of provisions and the high price of labour, he may better his circumstances in that country.

William Bain, aged 37, a widower, by trade a shopkeeper, resided last in Wick in the county of Caithness. Intends to go to Carolina. Left his own country because he could not get bread in his employment, the poverty of the common people with whom he dealt disabling them to pay their debts. Hopes to better his condition in America, but in what business he cannot determine till he comes there.

George Morgan, aged 37, married, hath two children, one 7, the other 1 year old; a farmer last at Chabster in the parish of Rae and county of Caithness, upon lands belonging to Mr. Alexander Nicolson, minister at Thurso. Goes to Carolina, leaving his country for the same reasons and upon the same motives assigned by John Catanoch, who was his neighbour. See pages 3rd and 4th of this report.

William Monro, aged 34, married, emigrates with his wife, a servant maid, and a servant boy; by trade a shoemaker; resided last at Borgymore in the parish of Tongue and county of Sutherland. Left his own country as his employment was little and he had no hopes of bettering his circumstances in it, which he expects to do in America.

Patrick Ross, aged 35, unmarried, lately schoolmaster in the parish of Farr, in the county of Sutherland. Goes to America on the assurance of some of his friends already in that country of procuring a more profitable school for him.

Alexander Morison, aged 60, married; hath one son and a servant maid who emigrate with him; resided last at Kinside in the parish of Tongue and county of Sutherland, on the estate of Sutherland, by occupation a farmer. Left his country as the rents of his possession were near doubled, the price of cattle low, and little being raised in that country, what they bought was excessive dear; besides the tenants were in various ways oppressed by Lord Rae's factors; and by the reports from America he is in hopes of bettering his circumstances in that country.

George McKay, aged 40, married, hath one child a year old; by trade a tailor and farmer; last at Strathoolie in the parish of Kildonan and county of Sutherland, upon that part of the estate of Sutherland set in tack to George Gordon by whom his rent was augmented and great services demanded, viz., 12 days work yearly over and above what he paid to the family of Sutherland. That the price of cattle on which he chiefly depended was greatly reduced and the little corn raised in the country almost totally blighted by frost for two years past, by which the farmers in general were brought into great distress. In these circumstances he had no resource but to follow his countrymen to America as the condition can scarce be worse.

Donald Gun, aged 33, married, hath 3 children from 8 years to 5 weeks old; by trade a tailor; resided last at Achinnaris in the parish of Halerick in the county of Caithness. Finding he cannot make bread in his own country, intends to go to America in hopes of doing it better there.

John Ross, aged 47, a widower hath 6 children from 20 to 5 years old who emigrate with him; by trade a farmer; last at Kavel in the parish of Farr and county of Sutherland, upon the estate of Sutherland. Goes to Carolina because the rent of his possession was greatly advanced; the price of cattle which must pay that rent reduced more than one half, and bread which they must always buy excessively dear. The evil is the greater that the estate being parcelled out to different factors and tacksmen, these must oppress the sub-tenants in order to raise a profit to themselves, particularly on the article of cattle, which they never fail to take at their own prices, lately at 20/ or 20 merks, and seldom or never higher than 30/ though the same cattle have been sold in the country from 50 to 55 shillings. By these means reduced in his circumstances and encouraged by his friends already in America, he hopes to live more comfortably in that country.

James Sinclair, aged 21 years, a farmer, married, hath no children, resided last at Forsenain in the parish of Rea and county of Caithness upon the estate of Bighouse, now possessed by George McRay of Island Handa, upon a farm, paying 8 pounds sterling rent; that he left his own country because crops of corn had [failed] and bread was very dear; he had lost a great part of his cattle two years ago; the rearing cattle being his principal business, the prices of cattle were reduced one half while the rents were nevertheless kept up and in many places, advanced. In such circumstances it was not possible for people of small stock to avoid ruin. His father, mother and sisters and some other friends go along with him to Carolina, where he is informed land and provisions are cheap, labour dear, and crops seldom fail. What employment he shall follow there he hath not yet determined, but thinks it will be husbandry.

Aeneas McLeod, aged 60, a farmer, married, hath one daughter 15 years old. Resided last in the parish of Tongue in the county of Sutherland upon the estate of Lord Rae. Goes to Wilmington in North Carolina where he proposes to live by day labour, being informed that one day's wages will support him a week. Left his own country because upon the rise of the price of cattle some years ago, the rent of his possession was raised from 28/ to 38/ a year, but thereafter when the price of cattle was reduced one half, the rent was nevertheless still kept up. Moreover being near the house of Tongue, he was harassed and oppressed with arbitrary services daily called for without wages or maintenance.

Aeneas Mackay, aged 20, single, resided last with his father in the parish of Tongue and county of Sutherland; hath been taught to read, write and cipher, and goes to

Carolina in hopes of being employed either as a teacher or as a clerk. He has several relations and acquaintances there already who inform him he may get from 60 to 70 pounds a year in this way, which is much better than he had any reason to expect at home.

Donald Campbell, aged 50, a farmer, married, has one son 12 years old; resided last in the parish of Adrachoolish, in the county of Sutherland on the estate of Rea. Intends to go to Carolina because the small farm he possessed could not keep a plough and he could not raise so much corn by delving as [would] maintain his family and pay his rent, which was advanced from 21/ to 30/. Has hopes of meeting an uncle in America who will be able to put him in a way of gaining his bread.

William McRay, aged 37, a farmer, married, has 4 children from 8 years to 18 months old and one man servant, who emigrate with him; resided last at Shathale-dale in the parish of Rea, and county of Caithness upon the estate of George McRay of Bighouse. Left his country because the rent of his possession was raised from 30 to 80 pounds Scots, while at the same time the price of cattle upon which his subsistence and the payment of his rent chiefly depended had fallen in the last seven years at least one half. In the year 1772 he lost of the little crop his farm produced and in cattle to the value of 40 pounds sterling. Under these losses and discouragements he had assurances from a brother and sister already in Carolina that a sober, industrious man could not fail of living comfortably, lands could be rented cheap, and grounds not cleared purchased for 6 pence an acre; that the soil was fertile and if a man could bring a small sum of money with him he might make rich very fast. He proposes to follow agriculture, but has not yet determined whether he will purchase or rent a possession.

William McLeod, aged 26, a farmer, married, has one son 2 years old; resided last in the parish of Adrachoolish in the county of Sutherland, upon the estate of Bighouse; intends to go to Wilmington in North Carolina where he has a brother settled who wrote him to come out, assuring him that he would find a better farm for him than he possessed at home (the rent of which was considerably raised upon him) for one fourth of the money, and that he will live more comfortably in every respect.

Hugh Monro, aged 26, a shoemaker, married, hath no children. Resided last in the parish of Tongue and county of Sutherland. Goes to Carolina upon assurance that tradesmen of all kinds will find large encouragement.

William Sutherland, aged 24, married, left an only child at home. Resided last in the parish of Latheron and county of Caithness, upon the estate of John Sutherland of Forse. Goes to Carolina because he lost his cattle in 1772, and for a farm of 40/ rent, was obliged to perform with his family and his horses so many and so arbitrary services to his landlord at all times of the year, but especially in seedtime and harvest, that he could not in two years he possessed it, raise as much corn as serve his family for six months. That his little stock daily decreasing, he was encouraged to go to Carolina by the assurances of the fertility of the land which yields three crops a year; by which means provisions are extremely cheap, wheat being sold at 3 shillings a boll; potatoes at 1 shilling so that one man's labour will maintain a family of twenty persons. He has no money; therefore proposes to employ himself as a day labourer; his wife can spin and sew, and he has heard of many going out in the same way who are now substantial farmers. At any rate, he comforts himself in the hopes that he cannot be worse than he has been at home.

James McKay, aged 60, a shoemaker, married, has one child. Resided last on Lord Rae's estate in Strathnaver. Left his own country, being exceeding poor, and assured by his friends who contributed among them the money required to pay for his passage, that he would find better employment in Carolina.

This and the 20 preceding pages contain the examination of the emigrants on board the Ship *Bachelor* of Leith, Alexander Ramage, Master; taken by the officers at the Port of Lerwick.

15 April 1774.

72. Crèvecoeur: from "What is an American" (1782)

Michel-Guillaume Jean de Crèvecoeur (1735–1813) sensed as did few others the fact that a new people had evolved in the American colonies. This young Frenchman came to America during the Seven Years War and fought in the French army. He stayed on, travelled widely, and in 1765 became a citizen of New York. He married an American and became a prosperous farmer. During the Revolution his sympathies were loyalist and in 1780 he went to France. In 1783 he came back to New York as French consul. In 1790 he returned to France where he remained until his death. His *Letters from an American Farmer* were published in London in 1782. The first American edition appeared in 1793. The following are excerpts from the third letter: "What is an American". Printed: *Letters from an American Farmer* (Philadelphia, 1793), pp. 42–47.

I wish I could be acquainted with the feelings and thoughts which must agitate the heart and present themselves to the mind of an enlightened Englishman, when he first lands on this continent. He must greatly rejoice that he lived at a time to see this fair country discovered and settled; he must necessarily feel a share of national pride, when he views the chain of settlements which embellishes these extended shores. When he says to himself, this is the work of my countrymen, who, when convulsed by factions, afflicted by a variety of miseries and wants, restless and impatient, took refuge here. They brought along with them their national genius, to which they principally owe what liberty they enjoy, and what substance they possess. Here he sees the industry of his native country displayed in a new manner, and traces in their works the embryos of all the arts, sciences, and ingenuity which flourish in Europe. Here he beholds fair cities, substantial villages, extensive fields, an immense country filled with decent houses, good roads, orchards, meadows, and bridges, where an hundred years ago all was wild, woody, and uncultivated! What a train of pleasing ideas this fair spectacle must suggest; it is a prospect which must inspire a good citizen with the most heartfelt pleasure. The difficulty consists in the manner of viewing so extensive a scene. He is arrived on a new continent; a modern society offers itself to his contemplation, different from what he had hitherto seen. It is not composed, as in Europe, of great lords who possess everything, and of a herd of people who have nothing. Here are no aristocratical families, no courts, no kings, no bishops, no ecclesiastical dominion, no invisible power giving to a few a very visible one, no great manufacturers employing thousands, no great refinements of luxury. The rich and the poor are not so far removed from each other as they are in Europe. Some few towns excepted, we are all tillers of the earth, from Nova Scotia to West Florida. We are a people of cultivators, scattered over an immense territory, communicating with each other by means of good roads and navigable rivers, united by the silken bands of mild government, all respecting the laws, without dreading their power, because they are equitable. We are all animated with the spirit of an industry which is unfettered and unrestrained, because each person works for himself. If he travels through our rural districts he views not the hostile castle, and the haughty mansion, contrasted with the clay-built hut and miserable cabin, where cattle and men help to keep each other warm, and dwell in meanness, smoke, and indigence. A pleasing uniformity of decent competence appears throughout our habitations. The meanest of our log-houses is a dry and comfortable habitation. Lawyer or merchant are the fairest titles our towns afford; that of a farmer is the only appellation of the rural inhabitants of our country. It must take some time ere he can reconcile himself to our dictionary, which is but short in words of dignity, and names of honour. There, on a Sunday, he sees a congregation of respectable farmers and their wives, all clad in neat homespun, well mounted, or riding in their own humble waggons. There is not among them an esquire, saving the unlettered magistrate. There he sees a parson as simple as his flock, a farmer who does not riot on the labour of others. We have no princes, for whom we toil, starve, and bleed: we are the most perfect society now existing in the world. Here man is free as he ought to be; nor is this pleasing equality so transitory as many others are. Many ages will not see the shores of our great lakes replenished with inland nations, nor the unknown bounds of North America entirely peopled. Who can tell how far it extends? Who can tell the millions of men whom it will feed and contain? For no European foot has as yet travelled half the extent of this mighty continent!

The next wish of this traveller will be to know whence came all these people? They are a mixture of English, Scotch, Irish, French, Dutch, Germans, and Swedes. From this promiscuous breed, that race now called Americans have arisen. The eastern provinces must indeed be excepted, as being the unmixed descendants of Englishmen. I have heard many wish that they had been more intermixed also: for my part, I am no wisher, and think it much better as it has happened. They exhibit a most conspicuous figure in this great and variegated picture; they too enter for a great share in the pleasing perspective displayed in these thirteen provinces. I know it is fashionable to reflect on them, but I respect them for what they have done, for the accuracy and wisdom with which they have settled their territory; for the decency of their manners; for their early love of letters; their ancient college, the first in this hemisphere; for their industry; which to me who am but a farmer, is the criterion of everything. There never was a people, situated as they are, who with so ungrateful a soil have done more in so short a time. Do you think that the monarchical ingredients which are more prevalent in other governments, have purged them from all foul stains? Their histories assert the contrary.

In this great American asylum, the poor of Europe have by some means met together, and in consequence of various causes; to what purpose should they ask one another what countrymen they are? Alas, two thirds of them had no country. Can a wretch who wanders about, who works and starves, whose life is a continual scene of sore affliction or pinching penury; can that man call England or any other kingdom his country? A country that had no bread for him, whose fields procured him no harvest, who met with nothing but the frowns of the rich, the severity of the laws, with jails and punishments; who owned not a single foot of the extensive surface of this planet? No! urged by a variety of motives, here they came. Every thing has tended to regenerate them; new laws, a new mode of living, a new social system; here they are become men: in Europe they were as so many useless plants, wanting vegetative mould, and refreshing showers; they withered, and were mowed down by want, hunger, and war; but now by the power of transplantation, like all other plants they have taken root and flourished! Formerly they were not numbered in any civil lists of their country, except in those of the poor; here they rank as citizens. By what invisible power has this surprising metamorphosis been performed? By that of the laws and that of their industry. The laws, the indulgent laws, protect them as they arrive, stamping on them the symbol of adoption; they receive ample rewards for their labours; these accumulated rewards procure them lands; those lands confer on them the title of freemen, and to that title every benefit is affixed which men can possibly require. This is the great operation daily performed by our laws. From whence proceed these laws? From our government. Whence the government? It is derived from the original genius and strong desire of the people ratified and confirmed by the Crown. This is the great chain which links us all, this is the picture which every province exhibits, Nova Scotia excepted. . . .

What attachment can a poor European emigrant have for a country where he had nothing? The knowledge of the language, the love a few kindred as poor as himself, were the only cords that tied him: his country is now that which gives him land, bread, protection, and consequence: *Ubi panis ibi patria*, is the motto of all emigrants. What then is the American, this new man? He is either an European, or the descendant of an European, hence that strange mixture of blood, which you will find in no other country. I could point out to you a family whose grandfather was an Englishman, whose wife was Dutch, whose son married a French woman, and whose present four sons have now four wives of different nations. *He* is an American, who, leaving behind him all his ancient prejudices and manners, receives new ones from the new mode of life he has embraced, the new government he obeys, and the new rank he holds. He becomes an American by being received in the broad lap of our great *Alma Mater*. Here individuals of all nations are melted into a new race of men, whose labours and posterity will one day cause great changes in the world. Americans are the western pilgrims, who are carrying along with them that great mass of arts, sciences, vigour, and industry which began long since in the east; they will finish the great circle. The Americans were once scattered all over Europe; here they are incorporated into one of the finest systems of population which has ever appeared, and which will hereafter become distinct by the power of the different climates they inhabit. The American ought therefore to love this country much better than that wherein either he or his forefathers were born. Here the rewards of his industry follow with equal steps the progress of his labour; his labour is founded on the basis of nature, *self-interest*; can it want a stronger allurement? Wives and children, who before in vain demanded of him a morsel of bread, now, fat and frolicsome, gladly help their father to clear those fields whence exuberant crops are to arise to feed and to clothe them all; without any part being claimed, either by a despotic prince, a rich abbot, or a mighty lord. Here religion demands but little of him; a small voluntary salary to the minister and gratitude to God; can he refuse these? The American is a new man, who acts upon new principles; he must therefore entertain new ideas, and form new opinions. From involuntary idleness, servile dependence, penury, and useless labour, he has passed to toils of a very different nature, rewarded by ample subsistence. – This is an American. . . .

73. Statistics of colonial population

Not until the United States census of 1790 are there any reliable figures for the population of what had been the thirteen mainland colonies. In that year the United States had 3,929,214 people, of whom 757,208 were Negroes. Of this number, 697,681 were slaves. The Indians were not enumerated. Before 1790 the estimates of population varied widely. Very few of the colonies had anything resembling a modern census. Colonial governors from time to time estimated the population of the colonies. Various bases were used: number of houses, the colonial militia, tax lists, and the like. The figures given below are in round numbers and represent approximations of various estimates except where it is indicated that they are based on a census. They are compiled from the two basic studies of population in the colonies: Evarts B. Greene and Virginia D. Harrington, *American Population Before the Federal Census of 1790* (New York, 1932), *passim*; and Stella H. Sutherland, *Population Distribution in Colonial America* (New York, 1936), *passim*.

a. The Population of the Colonies in 1715

Colony	White	Negro	Total
New Hampshire	9,500	150	9,650
Massachusetts	94,000	2,000	96,000
Rhode Island	8,500	500	9,000
Connecticut	46,000	1,500	47,500
New York	27,000	4,000	31,000
New Jersey	21,000	1,500	22,500
Pennsylvania and Delaware	43,300	2,500	45,800
Maryland	40,700	9,500	50,200
Virginia	72,000	23,000	95,000
North Carolina	7,500	3,700	11,200
South Carolina	6,250	10,500	16,750
Total	375,750	58,850	434,600

b. The Population of the Colonies in 1774–1775

Colony	White	Negro	Total
New Hampshire	80,000	500	80,500*
Massachusetts	355,000	5,000	360,000*
Rhode Island	54,500	5,000	59,500*
Connecticut	191,500	8,000	199,500*
New York	161,000	21,000	182,000
New Jersey	117,000	3,000	120,000
Pennsylvania and Delaware	298,000	2,000	300,000
Maryland	190,000	60,000	250,000
Virginia	300,000	200,000	500,000
North Carolina	260,000	10,000	270,000
South Carolina	120,000	80,000	200,000
Georgia	18,000	15,000	33,000
Total	2,145,000	409,500	2,554,500

c. Colonial Cities

Boston	(1700)	6,700	(1765)	15,500*
Newport	(1708)	2,203*	(1774)	9,100*
New Haven	(1706)	1,100*	(1774)	8,300*
New York (city and county)	(1700)	5,480*	(1771)	19,800*
Philadelphia	(1722)	10,000	(1769)	28,000
Baltimore	(1752)	100	(1775)	5,900*
Charleston	(1705)	3,000	(1775)	14,000

* Based on census reports.

B. INDENTURED SERVITUDE IN THE COLONIES

A BASIC fact in the peopling of the colonies was that the majority of the people who came to the colonies did not pay their way. The ordinary Englishman or European could not save enough in a lifetime to purchase his own passage across the Atlantic, much less that of a family. Therefore they came at the expense of others. This was made possible by the system of indentured servitude which lasted down into the nineteenth century. In its simplest form the immigrant signed a contract to work, usually from four to seven years, in payment for his passage. The system was begun by the Virginia Company and was well established by 1624. Its importance is indicated by a Virginia census of 1624–1625 which showed that 487 out of a total population of 1,227 were indentured servants. In 1671, Governor William Berkeley reported that Virginia had a total population of 40,000, of whom 6,000 were indentured servants and 2,000 were Negro slaves.

The system was extended to other colonies and was of the greatest importance in the settling of Pennsylvania. Although there are few reliable statistics, it has been estimated that two-thirds of the people who came to Pennsylvania came as indentured servants. During the eighteenth century a new type of indentured servant appeared: the redemptioner. The redemptioners were usually people who could pay part of their own way and who were allowed a period of time after arrival to dispose of their services to pay for the balance of their passage. If they could not do so, the ship captain could sell them as indentured servants to satisfy the remaining debt. This method was first used by German immigrants but spread to the Scotch-Irish and others who came to Pennsylvania during the eighteenth century. It differed also from indentured servitude in that it was a method most often used by families, whereas indentured servitude usually applied to individuals. The most recent scholarly estimate declares that between one-half and two-thirds of all the white immigrants to the colonies were indentured servants, redemptioners, or convicts.

The indenture or contract was a standard printed form. It usually provided for the conditions of service and for the compensation to be awarded to the servant at the end of his term of service.[1] The compensation varied. In most of the southern colonies tools and fifty acres of land were commonly promised, but the available evidence indicates that very few ex-servants settled on the land promised to them.

The traffic in servants became a highly organized business, engaged in by both European and colonial shipowners and merchants. In general, the conditions on the immigrant ships were horrible,[2] and various colonies passed a considerable amount of legislation for improvement of the traffic.[3]

There is a considerable diversity of opinion as to the lot of indentured servants.[4] Many were badly treated, and there was colonial legislation to improve conditions. On the other hand, legislation provided for strict punishment of recalcitrant and runaway servants. Eighteenth-century newspapers are replete with unflattering descriptions of runaway servants. The ire of colonists was particularly aroused by the

---

[1] No. 74A.　　[2] No. 70.　　[3] No. 76.　　[4] Nos. 70, 75, 77.

many convicts sent over to the colonies as servants. And large numbers were sent. London and the home circuit shipped over 17,000 convicts to the colonies between 1718 and 1772. Maryland alone received over 9,000 convict servants from Britain between 1748 and 1775. Yet all colonial efforts to end this traffic were consistently vetoed.[1]

Very little evidence exists as to the fate of servants, once they had worked out their contracts. Perhaps a greater proportion had a chance for advancement in the early days of the colonies than was true in the eighteenth century. Seven burgesses in the Virginia Assembly of 1629 were former servants. But even in the eighteenth century there are examples of servants or their descendants who were people of importance. The maternal grandmother of Benjamin Franklin was an indentured servant. Tradition has it that at least one signer of the Declaration of Independence, Matthew Thornton of New Hampshire, was an indentured servant, as well as Charles Thomson, the secretary of the Continental Congress from 1774 to 1789, but the evidence is not clear. What is clear is that by the end of the colonial period, families or individuals who had started as indentured servants, sought to hide the fact if they had achieved any prominence. As for servants as a group, a modern scholar has estimated that perhaps a tenth became land-owning farmers and that another tenth became artisans. The proportion of redemptioners achieving ultimate independence was probably greater since most of them had property when they came to the colonies. As to convicts, American records are understandably non-existent, and even the most indefatigable genealogists have shown no interest in the English records of convicts shipped to America.

74A–D. Indentures and apprenticeship contracts

The traffic in indentured servants to the colonies was so well established by the 1630's that in England one could get printed forms with blank spaces to be filled in with the names of the servant and the master and the terms of service (No. 74B). In the colonies contracts were bought and sold but had to be registered with the proper officials. Thus Richard Smyth registered two contracts with the Provincial Court of Maryland before sending two servants from England on to Virginia (No. 74A).

Apprenticeship was a common means of training artisans in the colonies. The contracts vary little from those of indentured servants except that specialized training is called for (Nos. 74C and D).

74A. Maryland indentures (1659–1660)

Printed: *Archives of Maryland*, XLI, pp. 385–386.

Richard Smyth came this day, being the 19th of December, 1660, and demands the ensuing indentures to be recorded among the records of the Provincial Court, in regard he is to send them to Virginia, viz.: This indenture made the eighth day of August in the year of our Lord one thousand six hundred fifty and nine, between Richard Smyth of Potomac in the island of Virginia in the parts beyond the seas, planter, on the one part; and Thomas Allison, son of Thomas Allison of Gaston in the county of Lancaster, husbandman, on the other part. Witnesseth that the said Thomas Allison doth covenant, promise, and grant to and with the said Richard Smyth, his executors and assigns, by these presents from the day of the date hereof

[1] No. 69.

until his first and next arrival in the island of Virginia aforesaid, and after, for, and during the term of seven years to serve, in such service and employment as he, the said Richard Smyth or his assigns shall there employ him, according to the custom of the country in the like kind; in consideration whereof the said Richard Smyth doth hereby covenant and grant to and with the said Thomas Allison to pay for . . . and lodging, with other necessaries during the said term, and at the end of the said term to pay the said Thomas Allison two suits of apparel, three barrels of good merchantable corn, and fifty acres of land. In witness whereof the said parties to these present indentures have interchangeably set their hands and seals the day and year abovesaid. Signed Richard Smyth.

Sealed and delivered in presence of us Andrew A. Dickinson, his mark.

George Flouke, his mark X.

Locus Sigilli X.

This indenture made the 24th day of August in the year of our Lord 1659, between Richard Smyth of Virginia, planter, of the one part, and Margaret Williams of Bristol, spinster, of the other part: Witnesseth that the said Margaret doth hereby covenant, promise, and grant to and with the said Richard, his executors and assigns, from the day of the date hereof, until her first and next arrival at Virginia, and after, for and during the term of four years, to serve in such service and employment as the said Richard or his assigns shall there employ her, according to the custom of the country in the like kind. In consideration whereof the said master doth hereby covenant and grant to and with the said servant to pay for her passing, and to find and allow her meat, drink, apparel, and lodging, with other necessaries during the said term; and at the end of the said term to pay unto her one axe, one hoe, double apparel, fifty acres of land, one year's provision, according to the custom of the country. In witness whereof the parties above-named to these indentures have interchangeably set their hands and seals the day and year above written. ·

Sealed & d[elivere]d in presence of George Hawkins. Md worth.

The mark of Margaret Williams.

74B. New York indenture (21 February 1683)

The following indenture is a typical printed form. The portions in italics were filled in by the signers of the contract. Printed: Abbot E. Smith, *Colonists in Bondage: White Servitude and Convict Labour in America, 1607–1776* (Chapel Hill, North Carolina, 1947), p. 18.

This Indenture made the *21st February 1682/3* between *Rich. Browne aged 33 years* of the one party, and *Francis Richardson* of the other party, witnesseth, that the said *Rich. Browne* doth thereby covenant, promise, and grant to and with the said *Francis Richardson*, his executors and assigns, from the day of the date hereof until *his* first and next arrival *at New York or New Jersey* and after, for and during the term of *four* years, to serve in such service and employment, as he, the said *Francis Richardson* or his assigns shall there employ *him* according to the custom of the country in the like kind: in consideration whereof the said *Francis Richardson* doth hereby covenant and grant to and with the said *Richard Browne* to pay for *his* passing, and to find and allow *him* meat, drink, apparel, and lodging, with other necessaries, during the said term, and at the end of the said term to pay unto *him according to the custom of the country*.

In Witness thereof the parties above mentioned to these indentures have interchangeably set their hands and seals the day and year above written.

74C. New Jersey apprentice contract (1 May 1680)

Printed: New Jersey Historical Society *Proceedings*, new Series, xv (1930), pp. 269–270.

This indenture made the first day of May in the year of our Lord 1680. Between Nathaniel Bunn of the town of Woodbridge, in the province of New Jersey, by and with the consent of his mother Hester Bunn, widow, the one party, and Bernerd Filder of the abovesaid town and province, potter, the other party, witnesseth that the above-named Nathaniel Bunn, by and with the consent of his mother abovesaid, doth by these presents covenant, agree and bind himself an apprentice unto the above-named Bernerd Filder until the abovesaid Nathaniel be of the age of one and twenty years, which will be the five and twentieth day of March, one thousand six hundred eighty and six, during which time of five years, ten months and upwards, the above-said Nathaniel doth by these presents engage to be true and faithful in his said master's service, and mistress's during her widowhood and not longer; his master and mistress's secrets to keep and not purloin or embezzle any of his master's estate, nor consent to the purloining or embezzlement of any part thereof by any person or persons whatsoever, his said master's lawful commands obey and not absent himself from his master's service, neither by day nor night, without his said master's leave, but in all things behave himself as a faithful apprentice ought to do during the full time and term abovesaid.

In consideration whereof the above-named Bernerd Filder doth by these presents covenant, promise, and engage to find and allow the above-named Nathaniel Bunn, during the time and term abovesaid, sufficient meat, drink, washing, and lodging, and at the expiration of the term abovesaid to allow him two suits of apparel, one of good cloth or stuff fit for holy days, and to pay or cause to be paid unto him, the abovesaid Nathaniel, the full and just sum of five pounds sterling, in good pay of this country, and the abovesaid Bernerd doth by these presents engage not to sell the said Nathaniel to any man whatsoever, nor to carry him out of this government of New Jersey, except into the government of New York, or some part of New England, and the abovesaid Bernerd doth by these presents engage to learn, teach, and instruct the abovesaid Nathaniel the art, trade, and mystery of a potter and of tile making, if he goes upon that, and also to teach him to write and cipher, and if the said Bernerd should marry and decease within the time abovesaid, then the abovesaid Nathaniel to serve his mistress during the time of her widowhood and no longer. In witness whereof the parties to these presents have interchangeably set, too, their hands and seal the day and year above-written and the said Bernerd is to let the abovesaid Nathaniel, at his going away from him, have his military arms that the said Nathaniel trains with whilst an apprentice and furnish him with a new Bible.

74D. Massachusetts apprentice contract (1 September 1713)
Printed: *Historical Collections of the Essex Institute*, 1 (Salem, Mass., 1859), pp. 14-15.

This indenture, made the first day of September, RRae, Anno Nunc Magna Brittania Duodecimo annoq Dom., 1713, witnesseth that Nicholas Bourguess, a youth of Guernsey, of his own free and voluntary will, and by and with the consent of his present master, Captain John Hardy of Guernsey, aforesaid, mariner, has put himself a servant unto Mr. William English, of Salem, in the county of Essex, within the province of the Massachusetts Bay in New England, mariner, for the space of four years from the day of the date hereof until the aforesaid term of four years be fully complete and ended; during all which time the said servant, his said master, his heirs, executors, administrators, or assignees dwelling within the province aforesaid, shall well and faithfully serve, their lawful commands obey. He shall not absent himself from his or their service without leave or licence first had from him or them; his master's money, goods, or other estate he shall not purloin, embezzle, or waste; at unlawful games he shall not play; taverns or alehouses he shall not frequent; fornication he shall not commit, nor matrimony contract; but in all things shall demean himself as a faithful servant during the term aforesaid, and the aforesaid master on his part, doth for himself, his heirs, and assignees, covenant, promise, and agree to and with the said servant: that he or they shall and will provide and find him with sufficient meat, drink, clothing, washing, and lodging, and in case of sickness, with physic and attendance during the term aforesaid, and to learn him to read a chapter well in the Bible, if he may be capable of learning it, and to dismiss him with two suits of apparel for all parts of his body–the one for Lord's Days, the other for working days. In testimony and for confirmation whereof the parties aforenamed have interchangeably set their hands and seals the day and year first above written.

Nicholas Bourguess, John Hardy.

Signed, sealed and delivered in presence of us
 Margaret Sewall, Jr.
 Susannah Sewall.
 Stephen Sewall, Notary Public and Justice Peace.

75. Peter Kalm: on servants in the colonies (c. 1750)
Printed: Adolph Benson, ed., *Peter Kalm's Travels in North America* (2 vols., New York, 1937), I, pp. 204-206.

Servants. The servants which are employed in the English-American colonies are either free persons or slaves, and the former, again, are of two different classes.

1. Those who are entirely free serve by the year. They are not only allowed to leave their service at the expiration of their year, but may leave it at any time when they do not agree with their masters. However, in that case they are in danger of losing their wages, which are very considerable. A man servant who has some ability gets between sixteen and twenty pounds in Pennsylvania currency, but those in the country do not get so much. A maidservant gets eight or ten pounds a year. These servants have their food besides their wages, but they must buy their own clothes, and whatever they get of these as gifts they must thank their master's generosity for.

Indenture. 2. The second kind of free servants consists of such persons as annually come from Germany, England and other countries, in order to settle here. These newcomers are very numerous every year: there are old and young of both sexes. Some of them have fled from oppression, under which they have laboured. Others have been driven from their country by religious persecution, but most of them are poor and have not money enough to pay their passage, which is between six and eight pounds sterling for each person. Therefore, they agree with the captain that they will suffer themselves to be sold for a few years on their arrival. In that case the person who buys them pays the freight for them; but frequently very old people come over who cannot pay their passage, they therefore sell their children for several years, so that they serve both for themselves and for their parents. There are likewise some who pay part of their passage, and they are sold only for a short time. From these circumstances it appears that the price on the poor foreigners who come over to North America varies considerably, and that some of them have to serve longer than others. When their time has expired, they get a new suit of clothes from their master and some other things. He is likewise obliged to feed and clothe them during the years of their servitude. Many of the Germans who come hither bring money enough with them to pay their passage, but prefer to be sold, hoping that during their servitude they may get a knowledge of the language and character of the country and the life, that they may the better be able to consider what they shall do when they have gotten their liberty. Such servants are preferable to all others, because they are not so expensive. To buy a Negro or black slave requires too much money at one time; and men or maids who get yearly wages are likewise too costly. But this kind of servant may be gotten for half the money, and even for less; for they commonly pay fourteen pounds, Pennsylvania currency, for a person who is to serve four years, and so on in proportion. Their wages therefore are not above three pounds Pennsylvania currency per annum. These servants are, after the English, called *servingar* by the Swedes. When a person has bought such a servant for a certain number of years, and has an intention to sell him again, he is at liberty to do so, but is obliged, at the expiration of the term of servitude, to provide the usual suit of clothes for the servant, unless he has made that part of the bargain with the purchaser. The English and Irish commonly sell themselves for four years, but the Germans frequently agree with the captain before they set out, to pay him a certain sum of money, for a certain number of persons. As soon as they arrive in America they go about and try to get a man who will pay the passage for them. In return they give according to their circumstances, one or several of their children to serve a certain number of years. At last they make their bargain with the highest bidder.

76. Pennsylvania law regulating conditions on immigrant ships (27 January 1750)

The bad conditions on immigrant ships, so well described by Mittelberger (No. 70) led various colonies to pass laws regulating conditions on immigrant ships entering the colonies. The first Pennsylvania law of 1750 is a typical example of such legislation. It is entitled: "An act for prohibiting the importation of Germans or other passengers in too great numbers in any one vessel." Printed: Mitchell and Flanders, *The Statutes at Large of Pennsylvania*, v, pp. 94–97.

Whereas it hath been too frequently practised by masters and owners of vessels trading within this province to import so great a number of Germans or other passengers in one vessel that through want of necessary room and accommodations they have often contracted mortal and contagious distempers, and thereby have occasioned not only the death of great numbers of such passengers in their passage, but also by these means have so infected those who survived as on their arrival into this province they have spread the contagion and been the cause of the death of many of the inhabitants:

To the end, therefore, that the like evil practices may be prevented and inconveniencies thence arising avoided as much as may be for the future:

[Section I.] Be it enacted . . . that from and after the publication of this act no master or commander of any ship or other vessel whatsoever, bound to the port of Philadelphia, or elsewhere within this province, shall import into the river Delaware or into any port within the province of Pennsylvania any greater number of passengers in any one ship or other vessel than such only as shall be well provided with good and wholesome meat, drink, and other necessaries for passengers and others during the whole voyage; and shall have room therein to contain for single freight or passengers of the age of fourteen years or upwards, at least six feet in length and one foot six inches in breadth, and if under the age aforesaid, to contain the same length and breadth for every two such passengers. And if any master or commander of any ship or vessel against the tenor of this act shall import into this province any one or a greater number of passengers not accommodated or provided during his voyage with good and wholesome meat, drink, room, and other necessaries as aforesaid, such master or commander shall forfeit and pay for every such passenger imported into this province the sum of ten pounds, to be recovered by action of debt with full costs of suit in any court of record within this province, the one half of the said forfeiture to any one who will sue for the same to effect, and the other half to the trustees of Province Island, to be applied towards the payment of the expenses which shall arise by the placing of sick passengers or others there; provided such action shall be commenced within the space of one month next after any such offence shall be committed, or the delinquent may be indicted for the same in the next quarter-sessions of the peace of the county where the offence shall be committed, and on due conviction be fined at the discretion of the court, in any sum not exceeding ten pounds for each passenger exceeding the number by this act allowed to be imported as aforesaid.

And to the end this act and the provisions herein made may be the more punctually observed:

[Section II.] Be it further enacted by the authority aforesaid, that the officer appointed for collecting of the duties to arise by the act, entitled "An act for imposing duties on persons convicted of heinous crimes", etc., or his deputy, in going on board any ship or other vessel importing of passengers, either by his or their view or otherwise, shall and is hereby required to inform himself of the condition and circumstances of the passengers on board, and whether they have been provided for and accommodated with the provisions, room, and other necessaries herein directed; and where at any time a deficiency shall appear to him or any of them, he or they shall forthwith give notice of the same to the mayor or recorder, or any one of the aldermen of the city of Philadelphia, or to some one or more of the justices of the peace of the county where the offence is committed, to the end the person or persons delinquent may be sent for and bound over to the next general quarter-sessions of the peace, then and there to answer the premises as is herein directed and enacted.

[Section III.] And be it further enacted by the authority aforesaid, that every master or commander of any ship or other vessel importing any passenger or passengers to be landed within this province, who in their passage hither or soon after may happen to die, leaving goods, chattels, money, or other effects on board or in the hands or custody of any such master or commander, every such master or commander, within the space of twenty days next after his arrival, or after the decease of every such passenger, shall exhibit to the register-general, or to some one of his deputies of the county where such effects shall lay, a true and perfect inventory of all such goods, chattels, money and other effects, to the end that after payment of all just demands which shall be due to the said master, commander, or to his or their owner or owners, the remainder of the said goods or effects may be committed to the custody of some proper person or persons for the benefit of the wife or children, next of kin, or creditors of the deceased, as the case may require and the law in such case shall direct.

[Section IV.] And be it further enacted by the authority aforesaid, that if any such master or commander of any such ship or other vessel shall neglect or refuse to exhibit a true and perfect inventory of the goods and effects of any such passenger or passengers so dying as aforesaid, every such master or commander shall forfeit and pay the sum of one hundred pounds, to be recovered and applied as aforesaid.

77. Letters of indentured servants

While contemporary sources have much to say about indentured servants, the servants themselves have left virtually no records. One of the few is John Harrower, "Diary, 1773-1776", published in the *Amer. Hist. Rev.*, VI (1900-1901), pp. 65-107. The two letters which follow are from the papers of the High Court of Admiralty, 30/258, in the Public Record Office, of which there are photostats in the Library of Congress. They are also printed in Isabel M. Calder, ed., *Colonial Captivities Marches and Journeys* (New York, 1935), pp. 151-152, 155-157. The original spelling and punctuation have been retained.

To Mr. John Sprigs White Smith in White Cross Street
near Cripple Gate, London

Maryland Sept'r 22'd 1756

Honred Father
    My being for ever banished from your sight, will I hope pardon the Boldness I now take of troubling you with these, my long silence has been purely owing to my undutifullness to you, and well knowing I had offended in the highest Degree, put a tie to my tongue and pen, for fear I should be extinct from your good Graces and add a further Trouble to you, but too well knowing your care and tenderness for me so long as I retaind my Duty to you, induced me once again to endeavour if possible, to kindle up that flame again. O Dear Father, belive what I am going to

relate the words of truth and sincerity, and Ballance my former bad Conduct my sufferings here, and then I am sure you'll pitty your Destress Daughter, What we unfortunat English People suffer here is beyond the probability of you in England to Conceive, let it suffice that I one of the unhappy Number, am toiling almost Day and Night, and very often in the Horses druggery, with only this comfort that you Bitch you do not halfe enough, and then tied up and whipp'd to that Degree that you'd not serve an Annimal, scarce any thing but Indian Corn and Salt to eat and that even begrudged nay many Neagroes are better used, almost naked no shoes nor stockings to wear, and the comfort after slaving dureing Masters pleasure, what rest we can get is to rap ourselves up in a Blanket and ly upon the Ground, this is the deplorable Condition your poor Betty endures, and now I beg if you have any Bowels of Compassion left show it by sending me some Relief, Cothing is the principal thing wanting, which if you should condiscend to, may easely send them to me by any of the ships bound to Baltimore Town Patapsco River Maryland, and give me leave to conclude in Duty to you and Uncles and Aunts, and Respect to all Friends.

Honred Father
Your undutifull and Disobedient
Child
Elizabeth Sprigs

Please to direct for me
at Mr. Rich'd Crosses to
be left at Mr. Luxes Merc't
in Baltimore Town Patapsco River
Maryland

To Mr. Edmond Hector, Surgeon in Birmingham,
Warwickshire, England

Augusta Court House
Octob'r 10 1756
(Frontiers of Virginia)

Hon'ble Sir
    This Day I Rec'd a Letter from my Wife bearing date April 21st 1755. and w'd have s'd Answ'r Immediately but fear'd Mr. Freeman w'd be gone therefore I humbly hope you'l Excuse me for this Freedom knowing y'r Character and that I might have greater dependance of its coming to You than to her. Hon'd Sir You must know that I am an Indented Serv't have 2 yrs 1/2 of my Time to come from 3d of Nov'r next to give a Description of my Servitude is Impossible so as to Expect you w'd Credit it. But will give You an Acc't of one Years Employ. I was Surgeon to 300 Men who went out against the Shauneeb Indians Town but we had 500 Miles to go and having a bad Pilate out of 200 Horses we broug't in but 4 or 5 the chief of the Rest we were forc'd to Eat being all like to Perish Several Times since I have been upon Scouts I have fasted 3 or 4 Days together as for Beding and Cloathing I am so [u]sd to it now if I get a Blanket I am satisfy'd, the French Ind's have killd our Men and Inhab's

all round the Camp and they are [so] much of the Nature of a Wolf that if we dont come on them while at there Prey its needless They'l lye in Ambush and Fire on us before we are Sensible. My first Mast. Colo. Patton was killd and 12 Men close by our Camp we foll'd them 200 Miles but to know purpose Our County is reduc'd to one half of the Inhabitants there is 150 Miles Leng: 300 or 400 in Curcumference laid Waste most of them Killd and the rest fled w'th Difficulty Its in this Wastepts we Range but as Yet w'th little Success having not Killd above 10 of our Enemy and they have killd some Hundreds of our People. The Hand of God seems to Cooperate with the Heath'n perhaps as a Scourge for our Sins. Pensylvania is likewise sorely Handled.

My Wife writes to me to s'd some Money but I cannot having not had 5s. this Year and half I humbly beg you'l do y'r Endeav'rs to get my Friends to contribute to the Value of £20 Sterl'g for me and Commission Mr. Wm. Freeman to pay it to me who will have freqt. Opportunity of sending it to me from Philadelphia.

You need not be Scrupulous on my former Follies for I am sensibly Fam'd. The Gentle'n above can give you an Acc't of my Pst Character I expect he'll be in Birmingham before this. Your Civility to my Wife is a Mark of y'r good Character (w'ch never can be Extinguishd) I Hope You'l do y'r utmost for me per Mr. Freeman and Assure Y'rself I shall always be ready to Acknowledge it. From Sir

Y'r most Ob't and Hble Serv't

Thomas Lloyd

P.S. Please to Remember my Duty to my Mother Love to Bro'rs and Sisters and Hble Service to Mrs. Hector and 2 Mas'r Careless.

N.B Sir I wish youd send me a Case of Launces and a common Case of Pocket Instrum'ts: if my Mother will pay for them, by Mr. Freeman.

Whether you send the Money or know or the Launces and Instrument Case (I Beleive you may get them for 18s. plain and a Bistoury. I Beg you'l doit if you can If not be pleasd to Honour me w'th a Letter from You. and it will be great Consolation to my Distressd Heart

Thomas Lloyd

If they dont send money to purchase my Time if I get the above it will be great Satisfaction and Advantage to me the[y] are so Dear here. I cou'd raise as much Money as w'd pay that but have no Opportunity of send'g it y'r Honour

C. NEGRO SLAVERY IN THE COLONIES

ALTHOUGH a few Negro slaves were brought to Virginia as early as 1619, indentured servants rather than slaves were a major source of labour in all the colonies until well towards the end of the seventeenth century, and remained so during the eighteenth century in the northern colonies. While slavery existed in all the colonies, the great concentration of slave holdings was to be found in the plantation colonies during the eighteenth century.[1] Slaves were regarded as an indispensable labour supply on the tobacco, indigo, and rice plantations of Maryland, Virginia, and South Carolina. The demand for slaves throughout the New World was so great that the slave trade played a major role in world commerce during the eighteenth century. In the year 1768, for instance, more than 100,000 slaves were exported from Africa. Of this number, English and colonial slave-traders carried approximately 53,000 to the West Indies, and 6,000 to the mainland colonies. It was a branch of trade in which many colonial merchants participated, and it was a lucrative one.[2]

Legally, slavery was never established as an institution. In law, the Negroes were servants for life. Yet the existence of slavery was recognized in a great variety of legislation. Virginia and Maryland adopted the principle that conversion to Christianity did not affect the status of the slave. Legislation provided that the child of a slave mother was also a slave. Marriage between whites and blacks was forbidden. With the great increase in the number of slaves during the eighteenth century, the colonies passed increasingly rigorous laws for their control. South Carolina, where the fear of slave insurrections was constant, enacted the strictest codes.

The colonies also adopted various laws affecting the slave trade. Maryland and Virginia both passed laws to encourage it during the seventeenth century. During the next century the southern colonies passed many acts levying duties on slaves imported, but most such legislation was primarily for the purpose of raising revenue, not an effort to block the trade. Furthermore, the policy of the British government was consistently opposed to any effort of the colonies to place any limitation on the trade.

Few colonists could be found who were willing to justify slavery. Even many of the slaveholders deplored it, but at the same time they defended it as an economic necessity.[3] The Georgia settlers, despite the prohibition of slavery there, demanded it on such grounds.[4] The most serious attacks on slavery came from the early Quakers[5] although even Quakers became slaveholders before the Revolution. The first serious attacks on slavery came during the American Revolution, and its abolition in the northern states was well under way before the end of the war.

78. Protest of German Quakers against slavery (18 April 1688)

While few colonials were willing to defend slavery, neither was there any widespread and effective opposition to the institution. Rhode Island sought to abolish it in 1652 but the move failed and Rhode Island became a centre of the slave trade. Samuel Sewall of Massachusetts published his "The Selling of Joseph" in 1701 but it had no apparent effect. Baptists and Methodists disapproved of slavery but consistent opponents of the institution were to be found only among the Quakers.

---

[1] No. 73.   [2] No. 81.   [3] No. 80.   [4] No. 79.   [5] No. 78.

However, many Quakers were slaveowners and it was not until 1776 that the Quakers as a group were committed to the principle of abolition.

The document which follows is the first protest of a Quaker group against slavery. It was prepared in 1688 at Germantown, Pennsylvania by a group of German Quakers. Printed: *Pennsylvania Magazine of History and Biography*, IV (1880), pp. 28–30.

This is to the monthly meeting held at Richard Worrell's:

These are the reasons why we are against the traffic of mens-body, as follows: Is there any that would be done or handled at this manner? viz., to be sold or made a slave for all the time of his life? How fearful and faint-hearted are many on sea, when they see a strange vessel, being afraid it should be a Turk and they should be taken and sold for slaves in Turkey. Now what is *this* better done than Turks do? Yea, rather it is worse for them which say they are Christians; for we hear that the most part of such Negroes are brought hither against their will and consent, and that many of them are stolen. Now, though they are black, we cannot conceive there is more liberty to have them slaves as it is to have other white ones. There is a saying that we shall do to all men like as we will be done ourselves; making no difference of what generation, descent or colour they are. And those who steal or rob men, and those who buy or purchase them, are they not all alike? Here is liberty of conscience, which is right and reasonable; here ought to be likewise liberty of the body, except of evil-doers, which is another case. But to bring men hither, or to rob and sell them against their will, we stand against. In Europe there are many oppressed for conscience sake; and here there are those oppressed which are of a black colour. And we who know that men must not commit adultery–some do commit adultery *in* others, separating wives from their husbands, and giving them to others: and some sell the children of those poor creatures to other men. Oh! do consider well this thing, you who do it, if you would be done at this manner–and if it is done according to Christianity! You surpass Holland and Germany in this thing. This makes an ill report in all those countries of Europe, where they hear of [it], that the Quakers do here handle men like they handle there the cattle. And for that reason some have no mind or inclination to come hither. And who shall maintain this your cause, or plead for it? Truly, we cannot do so except you shall inform us better hereof, viz.: that Christians have liberty to practise these things. Pray, what thing in the world can be done worse towards us than if men should rob or steal us away and sell us for slaves to strange countries; separating husbands from their wives and children. Being now this is not done at that manner we will be done at; therefore, we contradict, and are against this traffic of mens-body. And we who profess that it is not lawful to steal, must, likewise, avoid to purchase such things as are stolen, but rather help to stop this robbing and stealing, if possible. And such men ought to be delivered out of the hands of the robbers and set free as well as in Europe. Then is Pennsylvania to have a good report; instead, it has now a bad one for this sake in other countries; especially whereas the Europeans are desirous to know in what manner *the Quakers* do rule in *their* province; and most of them do look upon us with an envious eye. But if this is done well, what shall we say is done evil?

If once these slaves (which they say are so wicked and stubborn men), should join themselves–fight for their freedom, and handle their masters and mistresses as they did handle them before; will these masters and mistresses take the sword at hand and war against these poor slaves, like we are able to believe, some will not refuse to do? Or, have these Negroes not as much right to fight for their freedom as you have to keep them slaves?

Now, consider well this thing, if it is good or bad. And in case you find it to be good to handle these blacks in that manner, we desire and require you hereby lovingly that you may inform us herein, which at this time never was done, viz., that Christians have liberty to do so. To the end we shall be satisfied on this point, and satisfy likewise our good friends and acquaintances in our native country, to whom it is a terror or fearful thing, that men should be handled so in Pennsylvania.

This is from our meeting at Germantown, held the 18 of the 2 month, 1688, to be delivered to the monthly meeting at Richard Worrell's.

Gerret Hendericks Francis Daniel Pastorius

Derick op de Graeff Abraham op den Graeff

79. The demand for slavery in Georgia (1743)

The founders of Georgia were determined to develop a colony of small farmers. They limited the size of land holdings and forbade the importation of rum and slaves. The colonists of Georgia soon demanded slavery. The Georgia trustees fought a losing battle and eventually gave up the restriction. The following excerpt is a characteristic argument for the establishment of slavery in Georgia. It is from *A Brief Account of the Causes have that Retarded the Progress of the Colony of Georgia in America* . . . (London, 1743). Printed: *Collections of the Georgia Historical Society*, II (Savannah, 1842), pp. 93–94.

. . . But as if the difficulties arising from indifferent lands, and discouraging tenures, were not sufficient to humble and prepare them for the other severities they have met with, they were totally prohibited the importation, use, or even sight of Negroes. In spite of all endeavours to disguise this point, it is as clear as light itself, that Negroes are as essentially necessary to the cultivation of Georgia, as axes, hoes, or any other utensil of agriculture. So that if a colony was designed able but to subsist itself, their prohibition was inconsistent; if a garrison only was intended, the very inhabitants were needless. But all circumstances considered, it looked as if the assistance of human creatures, who have been called slaves, as well as subject to the treatment of such, were incongruous with a system that proceeded to confer the thing, but to spare the odium of the appellation. Experience would too soon have taught them the parity of their conditions, in spite of a mere nominal difference. The only English clergymen, who were ever countenanced there, declared they never desired to see Georgia a rich, but a godly colony; and the blind subjection the poor Salzburgers are under to the Rev. Mr. Boltzius, who has furnished such extraordinary extracts in some accounts of Georgia, published here, will be too evident from some of the annexed depositions to call for any descant.

The pretended content and satisfaction of the people of Ebenezer, without Negroes, will plainly appear to be the dictates of spiritual tyranny, and only the wretched acquiescence of people, who were in truth unacquainted with the privilege of choosing for themselves.

It is acknowledged indeed that the present war, and late invasion, may furnish the enemies of the colony with the most plausible objections that could occur, against the allowance of black slaves; but these reasons have not always existed, nor have the trustees ever declared any resolution to admit them, at any other juncture. But if it plainly appears that Georgia, as a colony, cannot barely exist without them, surely an admission of them under limitations, suitable to the present situation of affairs, is absolutely necessary to its support; since want and famine must be more dreadful and insuperable invaders, than any living enemy. Besides, the honourable trustees were informed by a letter from Mr. Stirling and others, of the falsehood of the contented and comfortable situation the people of Darien were affirmed to be in; and that they were bought with a number of cattle, and extensive promises of future rewards when they signed their petition against Negroes.

80. Peter Fontaine: defence of slavery in Virginia (30 March 1757)

The following is an excerpt from a letter of the Reverend Peter Fontaine of Westover, Virginia, 30 March 1757, to his brother Moses. Printed: Ann Maury, ed., *Memoirs of a Huguenot Family* (New York, 1853), pp. 351-352.

As to your second query, if enslaving our fellow creatures be a practice agreeable to Christianity, it is answered in a great measure in many treatises at home, to which I refer you. I shall only mention something of our present state here.

Like Adam we are all apt to shift off the blame from ourselves and lay it upon others, how justly in our case you may judge. The Negroes are enslaved by the Negroes themselves before they are purchased by the masters of the ships who bring them here. It is to be sure at our choice whether we buy them or not, so this then is our crime, folly, or whatever you will please to call it. But, our Assembly, foreseeing the ill consequences of importing such numbers amongst us, hath often attempted to lay a duty upon them which would amount to a prohibition, such as ten or twenty pounds a head, but no governor dare pass such a law, having instructions to the contrary from the Board of Trade at home. By this means they are forced upon us, whether we will or will not. This plainly shows the African Company hath the advantage of the colonies, and may do as it pleases with the ministry.

Indeed, since we have been exhausted of our little stock of cash by the war, the importation has stopped; our poverty then is our best security. There is no more picking for their ravenous jaws upon bare bones, but should we begin to thrive, they will be at the same again. All our taxes are now laid upon slaves and on shippers of tobacco, which they wink at while we are in danger of being torn from them, but we durst not do it in time of peace, it being looked upon as the highest presumption to lay any burden upon trade. This is our part of the grievance, but to live in Virginia without slaves is morally impossible. Before our troubles, you could not hire a servant or slave for love or money, so that unless robust enough to cut wood, to go to mill, to work at the hoe, etc., you must starve, or board in some family where they both fleece and half starve you. There is no set price upon corn, wheat and provisions, so they take advantage of the necessities of strangers, who are thus obliged to purchase some slaves and land. This of course draws us all into the original sin and curse of the country of purchasing slaves, and this is the reason we have no merchants, traders, or artificers of any sort but what become planters in a short time.

A common labourer, white or black, if you can be so much favoured as to hire one, is a shilling sterling or fifteen pence currency per day; a bungling carpenter two shillings or two shillings and sixpence per day; besides diet and lodging. That is, for a lazy fellow to get wood and water, £19. 16. 3, current per annum; add to this seven or eight pounds more and you have a slave for life.

81. The conduct of the slave trade (1752–1756)

The following documents including letters, instructions, accounts of sales of slaves and of cargoes, illustrate the method of carrying on the slave trade in the middle of the eighteenth century and also something of the profits obtained. The sections of the text within square brackets are the editorial comments of the compiler of the material. Printed: George C. Mason, "The African Slave Trade in Colonial Times", *American Historical Record*, 1 (1872), pp. 311–319, 338–345. (Selections.)

[Certificate of Ownership]

Newport
Rhode Island
[SEAL]

In pursuance of an Act of Parliament made and passed in the 7th and 8th years of the reign of King William the Third, entitled, An Act for preventing fraud and regulating abuses in the plantation trade.

Jurat: William Johnston, of Newport, in the colony of Rhode Island, etc., merchant.

That the brigantine called the *Sanderson*, whereof David Lindsay is at present master, being a square sterned vessel of the burden of about forty tons, was built at Portsmouth, in the colony aforesaid, in the year seventeen hundred and forty-five, as appears by a former register, now cancelled, and that this deponent at present is sole owner thereof, and that no foreigner, directly or indirectly, hath any share or part or interest therein.

William Johnston

[SEAL] Which oath abovesaid, was made before us, William Greene, Esq., Governor of the Colony aforesaid, and Joseph Wanton, Esq., collector and principal officer of his Majesty's customs in said Colony.

Given under our hands and seals at Newport, abovesaid, this twelfth day of March, Anno Dom. 1752, in the twenty-fifth year of his Majesty's reign.

W. Greene

Custom House, Newport, R.I.
Rec'd, Ex'd, and Del.

J. Wanton

[Instructions to Captain David Lindsay]

Newport, March 13, 1752.

Capt. David Lindsay,

You being master of my brigantine *Sanderson* and ready to sail, my orders are that you embrace the first opportunity of wind and weather and proceed for the island of St. Vincent, where, please God, you arrive; there dispose of your cargo on the best terms you can. What you can't get money for, take good cocoa. When you have disposed of your cargo and receive your pay, proceed to St. Eustatia, there lay out your money in good molasses, and proceed home with all possible dispatch. Should you not have money enough to load you with molasses, you may sell what cocoa you have in order to purchase molasses, if it be plenty. If not, desire you'll only employ your money in molasses and bring the cocoa home with you.

Notwithstanding my order to sell at St. Vincent, if you find your cargo is not in demand, desire you will proceed to Dominica (taking care not to go within three leagues of Martinique) and endeavour to sell what part of your cargo you may have left there for money, if you think it will answer better than at St. Eustatia. You must take care not to take any of the produce of the French islands on board, or any goods from old France, before you arrive at St. Eustatia (St. Vincent and Dominica are not understood to be French islands).

You must observe to set your cooper to work as soon as you arrive at St. Vincent, and let him have all the assistance you can in order to get a sufficient number of casks made. Should you meet with any Frenchman who has got a good permission to carry a vessel amongst them, you may go if you can agree to our advantage, but not otherwise. Be careful not to go without having a firm agreement, and should you sell them your cargo, you must have your load of molasses, and the remainder in anything that will answer best, taking care to agree for so much molasses, etc., clear of all charges, to be delivered on board, or at least at the bay where you may lay. You may, perhaps, meet with some Frenchman who has French papers, who may propose to make a French bottom of your vessel; but desire that you will not take up with any such proposal, as I would not have you go on any illicit trade. On the whole, if you find that your cargo will not answer tolerably well at some of the aforementioned ports, desire you will proceed to Jamaica, there do the best you can, and proceed home with all possible dispatch. After getting what molasses you can, your boards and horses you must sell at the first port, if possible, as the horses will not do to carry to Jamaica, as it will be too long to keep them on board. I shall not add but desire you to let me have from you by all opportunities. I wish you a good voyage and am your loving owner and humble servant.

William Johnston

Above is a copy of orders, which I promise to follow.

David Lindsay

[Captain Lindsay to the Owners]
Anamaboe, 28 February, 1753

This third of mine to you and now I am to let you know my proceedings since my last dated, 3 January, and I have got 13 or 14 hogsheads of rum yet left aboard and God knows when I shall get clear of it. The trade is so dull it is actually enough to make a man crazy. My chief mate after making four or five trips in the boat was taken sick and remains very bad yet; then I sent Mr. Taylor and he got not well and three more of my men has sick. James Dixon is not well now and worse than that, have wore out my small cable, also oakum, and have been obliged to buy one here, for I thought the consequence of your interest on board this vessel was too great to risk without a cable to trust to; therefore I beg you not blame me in so doing. I should be glad I could come right home with my slaves, for my vessel will not last to proceed far. We can see daylight all round her bow under deck. However, I hope she will carry me safe home once more. I need not enlarge. Here lies Captain Hamlet, James Jepson, Carpenter, Butler, and Lindsay. Gardner is done. Firginson is gone to Leeward. All these is rum ships. Butler is in a brig with 150 hogsheads from Barbados, belongs to Cape Coast Castle. I've sent a small boy to my wife. I conclude with my best endeavours for interest. Gentlemen, your faithful servant at command.

N.B. On the whole I never had so much trouble in all my voyages. I shall write to Barbados in a few days.

[Susanna and Elias Merivielle to the Owners]

Barbados, March 16, 1753

Slaves are now in lots from £33 to £56 per head and £37. We shall be glad to have your further orders about Captain Lindsay, as they may be here before he arrives. Lumber, horses, and all sorts of provisions plenty and cheap. Our new crops rum is now 2s, molasses 20d., very little here. Sugar in barrels 27/6 to 28/9 per cwt. Price of hogsheads not broke yet, nor the price of cotton and ginger. Bills 40 per cent.

Barbados, April 27, 1753

We have not heard from the Gold Coast since our last per Captain Nichols. Our produce now very plenty and if the vessels does not come in too fast, hope it will fall. Good slaves are now wanted. We daily expect three vessels to our address, from the Coast. We had a snow belonging to us and some of our friends here last week, from Gambia. We sold the greater part of her cargo at about £33 per head. She brought 135 slaves. Sold about 100 at the above price. The rest were old and sickly, which were sold cheaper, at about £23, per head round. We shall be glad to embrace all opportunities to serve you and your friends here.

[Captain Lindsay to the Owners]

Barbados, June 17 N.S. 1753

These are to acquaint you of my arrival here the day before yesterday in 10 weeks from Anamaboe. I met on my passage 22 days of very squally winds and continued rains, so that it beat my sails all to pieces, so that I was oblige[d] several days to have sails unbent to mend them. The vessel likewise is all open round her bows under deck. For these reasons am oblige[d] to enter my vessel here and have valued myself on Mr. Elias Merivielle who is to despatch me in three or four week's time. My slaves is not landed as yet. They are 56 in number for owners, all in health and fat. I lost one small girl. I've got 40 oz. gold dust and eight or nine hundred weight malabar pepper for owners.

Not to enlarge, shall write in a day or two. We are all well aboard. Mr. Sanford died the 3 day of March, and one John Wood who went in the boat with him, died the 3d of April at sea. I left Captain Hamlet at Cape Coast, sick. His slaves had rose and they lost the best of what they had. Here is no slaves at market now. I conclude with my best endeavours for your interest and am your faithful servant at command.

[Account of sales of cargo of *Sanderson*]

Sales of forty-seven Negroes, and a parcel of lumber and water casks, imported in the brigantine Sanderson, *and put into my hands by Captain David Lindsay, on the proper account and risk of Messrs. William Johnston and Peter Brown of Rhode Island, owners of said brigantine.*

Date	Men	Women	Men Boys	Small Boys	Girls	Small Girls	Ft. of Boards	Staves	Shingles	Water Casks	Prices	£ s. d.
June 18 1753	10	4	11								£35	875
		1										30
						1						25
				2							29	58
				1								28
	1											30
						1						22 10
				1								22 10
				1								22 10
		1										29
				1								24 2 6
						1						21
					1							30
	2	1			1						Ord'y £25	100
	1	2		1							,, ,,	100
				1								15
[Total]	14	9	11	8	2	3						1,432 12 6
							4,256	1,353			@ £4 per m.	22 13 6
									8,500	20	@ 15s. and 5s.	11 7 6
											[Total]	£1,466 13 6

Charges deduced viz.

		£		
To cash paid for permit to land the slaves		00	5	
„	Duty on 47 slaves at 5s.	11	15	0
„	for drummer attending sales		5	
„	paid for carrying notes into the country, for liquor at the sales & for wherry hire	1	19	5
To the captain's coast commission on £1432 12 6		55	2	2
To commissions on £1466 13 5 at 6 per cent		73	6	8
		142	15	3

Net proceeds carried to the credit of
Mssrs. William Johnston and Peter Brown,
Rhode Island; their account current.   £1,324   0   3
Barbados July 10 1753
      Errors excepted
            Elias Merivielle

[Captain Lindsay took on board 55 hogsheads of rum, 3 hogsheads and 27 barrels of sugar, amounting in all to £911, 17s, 2½d, and received bills on Liverpool for the balance due the owners and returned to Rhode Island in safety, notwithstanding the defects in his vessel. His good management produced so favourable an impression that a new vessel was tendered him, and he was placed in command of the schooner *Sierra Leone*, about forty tons burden, owned jointly by Newport and Boston merchants, and June 19, 1754, he signed the following bill of lading, comprising his outward cargo.]

[Bill of Lading]

"Shipped by the grace of God, in good order and well-conditioned, by William Johnston & Co., owners of the schooner *Sierra Leone*, in and upon the said schooner, called the *Sierra Leone*, whereof is master under God for this present voyage, David Lindsay, and now riding at anchor in harbour of Newport, and by God's grace bound for the coast of Africa: To say, thirty-four hogsheads, ten tierces, eight barrels and six half-barrels rum, one barrel sugar, sixty muskets, six half-barrels powder, one box beads, three boxes snuff, two barrels tallow, twenty-one barrels beef, pork and mutton, 14 cwt. 1 qr. 22 lbs. bread, one barrel mackerel, six shirts, five jackets, one piece blue calico, one piece checks, one mill, shackles, handcuffs, etc.

Being marked and numbered as in the margin, and are to be delivered in like good order and well condition, at the aforesaid port of the coast of Africa (the dangers of the seas only excepted) unto the said David Lindsay, or to his assigns, he or they paying freight for the said goods, notting [sic], with primage and average accustomed.

In witness whereof, the master or purser of the said schooner hath affirmed unto three bills of lading, all of this tenor and date, one of which three bills of lading being accomplished the other two stand void. And so God send the good schooner to her desired port in safety. Amen.

Dated in Newport in Rhode Island, June 19 1754.

David Lindsay

·

[Instructions to Captain Lindsay]

Newport, June 10, 1754

Captain David Lindsay:

Sir, You being master of our schooner *Sierra Leone*, and ready to sail, our orders are that you embrace the first opportunity of wind and weather and proceed for the coast of Africa, where, please God you arrive there, dispose of your cargo on the best terms you can for gold, good slaves, etc. When you have finished your trade on the coast (which we desire may be with all convenient dispatch) proceed for the island of Barbados, where you will find letters lodged for you in the hands of Mr. Elias Merivielle, with whom consult in regard to the sale of your slaves, and if they will fetch 26 pounds sterling per head, round, you may dispose of them there, and invest the produce as per your orders you will find lodged there. But if you cannot sell at the above price, proceed without loss of time to St. Vincent, there dispose of your slaves if they will fetch nine hundred livres round in money, and in case you sell there, you may purchase as much cocoa as you can carry under your half deck and proceed to St. Eustatia, there load with molasses, and if an opportunity of freight, ship the remainder of the net proceeds in molasses to this port or to Boston. Should you find it will detain you long at St. Eustatia to accomplish this, send the schooner home as soon as possible after she is loaded and come passenger after you have finished your business. But if they will not fetch the above price, proceed directly for the island of Jamaica; there you will find orders lodged for you, and dispose of your slaves on the best terms you can and invest as much of the proceeds in good Muscovado sugar as will load you, in such casks as you can stow with most convenience, and proceed home with all possible dispatch. You are to have four out of 104 for your coast commission and five per cent for sale of your cargo in the West Indies and five per cent for the goods you purchase for return cargo. You are to have five slaves privilege, your chief mate two, if he can purchase them, and your second mate two.

We desire you will omit no opportunity of letting us hear from you. We wish you a good voyage and are your loving owners.

William Johnston & Co.

Above is a copy of orders received, which I promise to follow.

David Lindsay

[Boston owners to their associates in Newport]

Boston, April 28, 1755.

Lindsay's arrival is very agreeable to us, and we wish we may never make a worse voyage. Our account of the sugar you may ship round when it suits best, believe the sooner the better, as the price here will soon fall, except a war should open. The bills for us you may also enclose us, and may depend upon our observing the directions of keeping them till the time limited.

How many hogsheads of rum can the schooner *Sierra Leone* carry? Are you determined to get a larger vessel for Lindsay? The reason of these questions is that we may possibly find a purchaser, if she is big enough.

[Captain Lindsay to Owners]

[Cape Coast Road, 1756]

Gentlemen:

These are to acquaint you I sail this night, please God, with all my slaves well, as likewise white people. Have got 57 slaves on board and expect one or two more. Here is no news. Here is not one hogshead rum on the Gold Coast to sell. Buffum and Wanton both ready to sail. I need not add, having just wrote to you via *Siranand*, from, gentlemen, your faithful servant at command.

[Owners in Boston to their associates in Newport]

May 26, 1756.

We have yours of the 21st inst. which gives us the agreeable advice of Lindsay's completing his voyage. Please not to omit sending his certificate of his not proceeding to Jamaica and South Carolina. . . .

. . . Mr. Brown, of Plymouth, has a vessel on the stocks of about 90 tons, designed for a schooner, has a long quarterdeck, comes home to the main mast, and lays high enough to stow fish hogsheads. She has a row of ports on each side, and may be launched in a few days. He says she is an exceedingly well-built vessel and designed for his own use, but the approach of war inclines him to sell. We know not his price. We are sensible of the cost and trouble of sending rigging and stores there to equip her, and the expense of the hands, etc., to get her to your port, therefore mention it only on account of the dispatch.

The snow of Mr. Quincey's, which we wrote you about last year, is expected from London. She is about 112 tons, a fine vessel for the Guinea trade and possibly may go cheap, but if you think that as many rum vessels are going to the Coast this spring, it will be best to stay till the fall before we fit out. The brigantine you mention may probably be the best and cheapest.

As for the schooner [the *Sierra Leone*] we should like to dispatch her the same way again, if she is sufficient, if not, we can't at present think what to do with her, as she is too small for most branches of trade.

[Account of sales of cargo of *Sierra Leone*]

[June 24, 1756]

Sales of forty-four slaves imported in the schooner Sierra Leone, *David Lindsay master, from Anamaboe, and sold by John Willett for account of owners in Rhode Island.*

1756 April	To whom sold	Men	Women	Men Boys	Boys	Girls	Price £	£ Sterling
5	Benj. Wilson Esq.	6					at 34	204
			1	5			30	180
				2			28	56
	John Baker	6					32.5	193.10
		2					31	62
				5			28	140
					3	1	20	80
	David Dalrymble				1			23
	John Hamm				1			24
	Sam'l Deleon					1		25.10
	Wm. Woodley				10			200
		14	6	7	15	2		£1188

Charges on the above sales.

To cash paid Capt. Lindsay, his coast commission of £4
    in £104   £   15   13   10
To my commission on sales at 5 per cent   39   8   0
Bill in favour of owners for net proceeds   1082   18   2
                             £1188

St. Christopher's, April 6 1756
    Errors excepted

                     John Willett

Sales of three refuse slaves imported in the schooner Sierra Leone, *David Lindsay, master, from Anamaboe, and sold by John Willett for account of the owners in Rhode Island.*

1756

April 19	Abr. Douglass, 1 man boy and 2 boys	£66	0	0
	Charges on the above sale			
	To cash paid Capt. Lindsay his coast			
	commission	2	6	5
	My commission of 5 per cent	3	0	0
	Bill in favour of owner for net proceeds	54	13	7
		£60		

St. Christopher's, April 19th 1756.
   Errors excepted.
                    John Willett

[Invoice of Goods shipped to Owners]

Invoice of sundry merchandise shipped by John Willett on board the schooner *Sierra Leone*, David Lindsay, Master, for account and risk of the owners in Rhode Island.

	at	£		
5495 sugar net	35	96	3	3
5625 „ „	35/6	99	16	10
5745 „ „	36	103	8	2
5686 „ „	34	96	13	2
1392 gals. rum	2	139	4	0
12 rum hogsheads	30	18	0	0
duty and cocket		5		
16 sugar hogsheads	20	16	0	0
duty at 4 1/2 per cent and				
enumerated duty 30s. per hogshead		31	4	0
Commission 5 per cent		30	5	5
—		£635	14	10

St. Christopher's, April 17 1756.
   Errors excepted.
                    John Willett

[Owners to Agent in St. Christopher's]
[Boston, Oct. 4, 1756]

We have your favour per post, and glad to hear the *Sierra Leone* gone. Think you have given her dispatch, and wish the voyage may prove fortunate. Slaves ought to rise 50 per cent to pay the extra charges on the African trade, and all West Indies goods must rise near as much, otherwise it won't be of any avail to fit out.

[Captain Lindsay to Owners]

[Barbados]

Gentlemen:

Thank God I have the pleasure once more to give you a line or two in regard to the proceedings of my present voyage.

I hope these will find you and both yours in good health, as they leave me. I sailed from Anamaboe the 28 May and arrived here in 51 days. I purchased 151 slaves and have shipped from here a bill exchange for £103 sterling I sold my gold for, and I've got some gold dust, the just sum I can't tell, for I carried neither scales nor weights. I lost 18 slaves and sold 133 slaves. I applied myself to Messrs. Merivielle, Wood, and Simmons. The condition of our bargain is that I'm to be paid a bill exchange one thousand pounds sterling and the rest in produce. I sail the   of September. Pray my love to my family and all friends, while I am, gentlemen, your humble servant at command.

Part V
RELIGION AND EDUCATION IN THE COLONIES

RELIGION AND EDUCATION IN THE COLONIES

SELECT BIBLIOGRAPHY

(a) INTELLECTUAL BACKGROUND

While much of the intellectual life of the early colonies was centred about matters of religion, it was increasingly affected by new ideas from Europe and by changing conditions in the colonies themselves. The broad setting is presented in THOMAS J. WERTENBAKER, *The First Americans, 1607–1690,* and J. T. ADAMS, *Provincial America, 1690–1760,* both of which contain bibliographies on religion, education, and related matters. It is presented also in greater detail in the three volumes of THOMAS J. WERTENBAKER's *The Founding of American Civilization.* Works concentrating primarily on the eighteenth century are MICHAEL KRAUS, *The Atlantic Civilization: Eighteenth Century Origins* (Ithaca, N.Y., 1949) which emphasizes the interrelations between the colonies and Europe in such matters as religion, education, scientific thought; MAX SAVELLE, *Seeds of Liberty: The Genesis of the American Mind* (New York, 1948), a broad survey concentrating on the mid-eighteenth century; and MICHAEL KRAUS, *Intercolonial Aspects of American Culture on the Eve of the Revolution* . . . (New York, 1928). Works specifically emphasizing urban culture are CARL BRIDENBAUGH, *Cities in the Wilderness;* THOMAS J. WERTENBAKER, *The Golden Age of Colonial Culture* (2nd ed., New York, 1949); F. P. BOWES, *The Culture of Early Charleston* (Chapel Hill, N.C., 1942); CARL BRIDENBAUGH, *Rebels and Gentlemen: Philadelphia in the Age of Franklin.* LOUIS B. WRIGHT, *The First Gentlemen of Virginia: Intellectual Qualities of the Early Colonial Ruling Class* (San Marino, Cal., Huntington Library, 1940) and "The Classical Tradition in Colonial Virginia", Bibliographical Society of America *Papers,* vol. XXXIII (1939), and CARL BRIDENBAUGH's "The Chesapeake Society" and "The Carolina Society" in *Myths and Realities: Societies of the Colonial South* (Baton Rouge, La., 1952) are important discussions of the nature of intellectual life in the Southern colonies. PERRY MILLER, *The New England Mind: From Colony to Province* (Cambridge, Mass., 1953) is a thorough study of changes in New England from about 1650 to 1720.

New religious currents are discussed in F. A. CHRISTIE, "The Beginnings of Arminianism in New England", American Society of Church History *Papers,* 2nd Series, vol. III (1912); HERBERT M. MORAIS, *Deism in Eighteenth Century America* (New York, 1934), as well as elsewhere.

The impact of scientific ideas is treated in MICHAEL KRAUS, *The Atlantic Civilization;* THEODORE HORNBERGER, *Scientific Thought in the American Colleges, 1638–1800* (Austin, Texas, 1945); L. W. McKEEHAN, *Yale Science, the First Hundred Years, 1701–1800* (New York, 1947); I. BERNARD COHEN, *Some Early Tools of American Science* . . . [on Harvard] (Cambridge, Mass., 1950); F. E. BRASCH, "The Royal Society of London and its Influence upon Scientific Thought in the American Colonies", *Scientific Monthly,* vol. XXXIII (1931), and "The Newtonian Epoch in the American Colonies (1680–1783)", Amer. Antiq. Soc. *Proceedings,* new Series, vol. XLIX (1939), C. E. JORGENSON, "The New Science in the Almanacs of Ames and Franklin", *New England Quarterly,* vol. VIII (1935). R. P. STEARNS, "Colonial Fellows of the Royal Society of London, 1661–1788", *William and Mary Quarterly,* 3rd Series, vol. III (1946), lists the colonial members. I. BERNARD COHEN, ed., *Benjamin Franklin's Experiments* . . . (Cambridge, Mass., 1940) reprints Franklin's experiments with electricity and has an informative introduction.

Colonial literature has been the subject of many studies. The most recent work, which is particularly valuable for its bibliographies, is ROBERT E. SPILLER, et al., eds., *Literary History of the United States* (3 vols., New York, 1948). The old work of MOSES COIT TYLER, *A History of*

American Literature, 1607–1765 (2 vols., New York, 1879), which integrates literature with the life of the times, has still to be supplanted. THOMAS G. WRIGHT, *Literary Culture in Early New England, 1620–1730* (New Haven, Conn., 1920), and KENNETH MURDOCK, *Literature and Theology in Colonial New England* (Cambridge, Mass., 1949) are recent studies concentrating on the seventeenth century and emphasizing the cultural and theological backgrounds. LOUIS B. WRIGHT, *The First Gentlemen of Virginia*, discusses literary interests and achievements in that colony. VERNON L. PARRINGTON, *Main Currents in American Thought*, vol. I, *The Colonial Mind* (New York, 1927) is much criticized for antagonism towards the Puritans and for errors in detail, but it remains a monument of interpretation and literary style.

Books, reading, and libraries are discussed in a variety of useful studies. T. G. WRIGHT, *Literary Culture in Early New England, 1620–1730*, is replete with comments on books and libraries. Additional references may be found in MILLER and JOHNSON, *The Puritans*. Books and libraries in other colonies are discussed in A. B. KEEP, *The Library in Colonial New York* (New York, 1909); E. V. LAMBERTON, "Colonial Libraries of Pennsylvania", *Penn. Mag. of Hist. and Biog.*, vol. XLII (1918); AUSTIN K. GRAY, *Benjamin Franklin's Library . . .* (New York, 1937); G. K. SMART, "Private Libraries in Colonial Virginia", *American Literature*, vol. X (1938–1939); BERNARD C. STEINER, "Rev. Thomas Bray and his American Libraries", *Amer. Hist. Rev.*, vol. II (1896–1897). LAWRENCE C. WROTH, *An American Bookshelf, 1755* (New York, 1934) is a learned essay on the works published in America around the year 1755. STEPHEN B. WEEKS, "Libraries and Literature in North Carolina in the Eighteenth Century", Amer. His. Assoc. *Annual Report* (1895), gives much detail for a colony little celebrated in such matters.

The growth of printing, newspapers, and magazines was ever more rapid during the eighteenth century. ISAIAH THOMAS, *The History of Printing in America . . .* (2 vols., Worcester, Mass., 1810; reprinted, 2 vols., Albany, 1874) is a valuable work by one of the eighteenth century's great printers and editors. JOHN T. WINTERICH, *Early American Books and Printing* (New York, 1935); LAWRENCE C. WROTH, *The Colonial Printer* (2nd ed., Portland, Me., 1938); and SIDNEY KOBRE, *The Development of the Colonial Newspaper* (Pittsburgh, 1944) are modern accounts. DANIEL MILLER, "Early German American Newspapers", Pennsylvania German American Society *Proceedings*, vol. XIX (1910), discusses that important development. Closely related to the development of printing was the paper industry which is given definitive treatment in DARD HUNTER, *Papermaking in Pioneer America* (Philadelphia, 1952). C. S. BRIGHAM, *History and Bibliography of American Newspapers, 1690–1820* is the indispensable guide to early newspapers, an increasing number of which are available on microfilm.

The struggle for liberty of the Press is discussed in L. R. SCHUYLER, *The Liberty of the Press in the American Colonies Before the Revolutionary War* (New York, 1905) and C. A. DUNIWAY, *The Development of Freedom of the Press in Massachusetts* (New York, 1906). The trial of PETER ZENGER in New York in 1735, in which freedom of the Press was vindicated, is conveniently summarized in RICHARD B. MORRIS, *Fair Trial* (New York, 1952), chap. iii, "The Case of the Palatine Printer".

LYON RICHARDSON, *A History of Early American Magazines, 1741–1789* is thorough. All of the available copies of early American magazines have been reproduced on microfilm.

(b) RELIGION

For the vast literature on the Puritans, both printed sources and scholarly writing, see the bibliographies in MILLER and JOHNSON, *The Puritans*, which includes, as well, representative examples of Puritan writing on a great many topics. Materials on the Anglican Church are to be found in W. S. PERRY, ed., *Historical Collections Relating to the American Colonial Church* (5 vols., Hartford, Conn., 1870–1878) and in F. R. HAWKS and W. S. PERRY, eds., *Documentary History of the Protestant Episcopal Church in the United States of America* [Connecticut] (2 vols., New York, 1863–1864). WILLISTON WALKER, *The Creeds and Platforms of Congregationalism* (New York, 1893) has essential documents and commentary. *Ecclesiastical Records, State of New York* (7 vols., Albany, 1901–1916) has a great mass of material on the religious history of that colony.

ADELAIDE M. FRIES, *Records of the Moravians of North Carolina* contains material on religious history as well as other matters. G. L. BURR, ed., *Narratives of the Witchcraft Cases, 1648–1706 (Original Narratives of American History*, New York, 1914) is a convenient collection, with ample references to other sources. In addition, the published colonial records, historical society publications, and periodicals have quantities of source material for religious history of the colonies.

Of individual religious leaders, the most voluminous writers were the father and son, Increase and Cotton Mather, who between them dominated the printing in Boston for more than half a century, if for no other reason than sheer quantity of output. Their writings have been the subject of two great bibliographies by THOMAS J. HOLMES: *Increase Mather: A Bibliography of his Works* (2 vols., Cleveland, 1931) and *Cotton Mather: A Bibliography of his Works* (3 vols., Cambridge, Mass., 1940). COTTON MATHER'S Diary is published in Mass. Hist. Soc. *Collections*, 7th Series, vol. VII–VIII (1911–1912). Excerpts from his writings are published in KENNETH MURDOCK, ed., *Selections from Cotton Mather* (New York, 1926). COTTON MATHER, *Magnalia Christi Americana; or the Ecclesiastical History of New England* . . . (London, 1702, and subsequent editions) is the subject of widely varying opinions among critics but it is safe to say that it reveals much of both New England and its author.

The writings of ROGER WILLIAMS, including a volume of his letters, are to be found in *Publications of the Narragansett Club*, 1st Series (6 vols., Providence, R. L., 1866–1874). Brief excerpts from the writings with a commentary are to be found in PERRY MILLER, *Roger Williams* (New York, 1953).

There is no modern edition of JONATHAN EDWARD'S writings although four multivolumed editions were published in the first part of the nineteenth century. Brief selections may be found in C. H. FAUST and R. H. JOHNSON, eds., *Jonathan Edwards; Representative Selections* (New York, 1935). For a thorough bibliography on EDWARDS, see OLA E. WINSLOW, *Jonathan Edwards, 1705–1758* (New York, 1941).

AMELIA M. GUMMERE, ed., *The Journal and Essays of John Woolman* (New York, 1922) is a modern collection of the writings of a remarkable eighteenth-century Quaker.

Of the general works on the religious history of the colonies, THOMAS C. HALL, *The Religious Background of American Culture* (Boston, 1930) stresses the importance of the English dissenting tradition running back to JOHN WYCLIF; W. W. SWEET, *Religion in Colonial America* (New York, 1942) and *Religion in the Development of American Culture, 1765–1840* (New York, 1952) offer a general survey, and the first volume of A. P. STOKES, *Church and State in the United States* (3 vols., New York, 1950) is an intensive study of Church-State relationship and other related questions.

Of the various denominations and religious groups, the Puritans have received the most attention and are the subject of a greater variety of contradictory interpretations. The bibliographies in MILLER and JOHNSON, *The Puritans*, reveal this. Two outstanding modern studies of the English background are M. M. KNAPPEN, *Tudor Puritanism* . . . (Chicago, 1939) and WILLIAM HALLER, *The Rise of Puritanism* . . . *1570–1643* (New York, 1938). RAYMOND P. STEARNS, "The New England Way in Holland", *New England Quarterly*, vol. VI (1933) emphasizes the importance of the experience of Puritan leaders in Holland. PERRY MILLER, *Orthodoxy in Massachusetts, 1630–1650* . . . (Cambridge, Mass., 1933) and *The New England Mind: The Seventeenth Century* (New York, 1939) set forth with finality the conception of church organization and the nature of the theology of the founders of Massachusetts Bay. H. W. SCHNEIDER, *The Puritan Mind* (New York, 1930) is a clear survey which should be read in the light of Miller's work. A classic statement of the anti-Puritan view is to be found in BROOKS ADAMS, *The Emancipation of Massachusetts* (Boston, 1887). Williston Walker, *A History of the Congregational Churches in the United States* (New York, 1898) is old but reliable.

There are a great number of denominational histories relating wholly or in part to the colonial period. Most of them are nineteenth-century works by authors who show the same kind of 'patriotism' shown by writers on colonial immigration. W. W. SWEET, *Religion in Colonial America* is a good guide to such books, only a few of which are cited hereafter. There are also several religious historical societies which publish materials. Among them are the

Presbyterian Historical Society, the Moravian Historical Society, the Protestant Episcopal Historical Society, the American Catholic Historical Society, and the American Society of Church History. Much material on religious life in the colonies is also to be found in the works on immigration listed.

While the Anglican Church was legally established in several of the colonies, it was important only in Virginia. GEORGE M. BRYDON, *Virginia's Mother Church and the Political Conditions Under Which it Grew* (vol. I, Richmond, Va., 1947, vol. II, Philadelphia, 1952) is a scholarly modern study and contains many documents. ARTHUR L. CROSS, *The Anglican Episcopate and the American Colonies* (Cambridge, Mass., 1902) discusses the role of the Bishop of London who had charge of Anglican churches in the colonies, and the various proposals to establish an American bishopric. ELIZABETH H. DAVIDSON, *The Establishment of the English Church in the Continental American Colonies* (Durham, N.C., 1936) is a useful survey. The Society for the Propagation of the Gospel which did missionary and educational work in the colonies is discussed in C. S. PASCOE, *Two Hundred Years of the S.P.G.: An Historical Account of the Society for the Propagation of the Gospel . . . 1701–1900* (2 vols., London, 1901) and H. P. THOMPSON, *Into All Lands: The History of the Society for the Propagation of the Gospel in Foreign Parts, 1701–1950* (London, 1951) which are essentially 'official' histories. Pascoe's work is detailed and valuable. The latter work ignores the considerable American scholarship on the work of the Society. For this, see FRANK J. KLINGBERG, *Anglican Humanitarianism in Colonial New York* (Philadelphia, 1940. The Church Historical Society *Publications*, No. 11), and the various studies cited in the bibliography. The beginnings of the Methodist Church are discussed in W. W. SWEET, *Men of Zeal: The Romance of American Methodist Beginnings* (New York, 1935).

The best overall study of the Quakers is RUFUS M. JONES, *The Quakers in the American Colonies* (New York, 1911). The first half of THOMAS E. DRAKE, *Quakers and Slavery in America* New Haven, Conn., 1950), is an excellent account of Quaker opposition to slavery in the colonial period. FREDERICK B. TOLLES, "Quaker History Enters its Fourth Century", *William and Mary Quarterly*, 3rd Series, vol. X (1953) is a critical review article on the achievements and the needs of Quaker historiography.

Baptists appeared in the colonies even before the Quakers. A modern study is needed. Material on them may be found in ISAAC BACKUS, *History of New England with particular reference to the . . . Baptists* (3 vols., Boston, 1777–1796, and Newton, Mass., 1871), and R. B. SEMPLE, *A History of The Rise and Progress of the Baptists in Virginia* (Richmond, 1810). Since the Baptists were among the most vigorous fighters for religious freedom, much material on them may be found in the studies on the relations between Church and State listed hereafter.

The most recent study of the Presbyterians is LEONARD J. TRINTERUD, *The Forming of an American Tradition, A Re-examination of Colonial Presbyterianism* (Philadelphia, 1949), which replaces most earlier studies. See also, GUY S. KLETT, *Presbyterians in Colonial Pennsylvania* (Philadelphia, 1937) and "The Presbyterian Church and the Scotch-Irish on the Pennsylvania Colonial Frontier", *Pennsylvania History*, vol. VIII (1941), and HENRY D. FUNK, "The Influence of the Presbyterian Church in Early American History", Presbyterian Historical Society *Journal*, vol. XII (1924–1927).

Among the books on the small number of Catholics in the Colonies are JOHN D. G. SHEA, *The Catholic Church in Colonial Days* (New York, 1886), and SISTER MARY AUGUSTINA RAY, *American Opinion of Roman Catholicism in the Eighteenth Century* (New York, 1936).

A great variety of Protestant sects from the Continent, and particularly from Germany, came to Pennsylvania and spread from there into the southern back country. LUCY F. BITTINGER, *German Religious Life in Colonial Times* (Philadelphia, 1906), is a general survey. Particular sects are discussed in C. H. SMITH, *The Mennonite Immigration to Pennsylvania in the Eighteenth Century* (Norristown, Pa., 1929); J. T. HAMILTON, *A History of the Church Known as the Moravian Church . . .* (Bethlehem, Pa., 1900); JOHN J. SESSLER, *Communal Pietism Among Early American Moravians* (New York, 1933); DANIEL MILLER, *Early History of the Reformed Church in Pennsylvania* (Reading, Pa., 1906); T. E. SCHMAUK, "The Lutheran Church in Pennsylvania, 1638–1800",

Penn. German Soc. *Proceedings*, vol. XI–XII (1902–1903); M. G. BRUMBAUGH, *A History of the German Baptist Brethren in Europe and America* [Dunkers] (Mt. Morris, Ill., 1899); H. W. KRIEBEL, "The Schwenkfelders in Pennsylvania, A Historical Sketch", Penn. German Soc. *Proceedings*, vol. XIII (1904); GEORGE B. WATTS, *The Waldenses in the New World* (Durham, N.C., 1941).

Studies of the relationship between Church and State, of the struggle for religious freedom and toleration, are numerous. The English background is given in W. K. JORDAN, *The Development of Religious Toleration in England* . . . (4 vols., Cambridge, Mass., 1932–1940). EVARTS B. GREENE, *Religion and The State: The Making and Testing of an American Tradition* (New York, 1941) and S. H. COBB, *The Rise of Religious Liberty in America; A History* (New York, 1902), discuss the colonies as a whole.

Special studies for particular colonies are SUSAN M. REED, *Church and State in Massachusetts, 1691–1740* (Urbana, Ill., 1914); J. C. MEYER, *Church and State in Massachusetts from 1740 to 1833* . . . (Cleveland, 1930); A. B. SEIDMAN, "Church and State in the Early Years of the Massachusetts Bay Colony", *New England Quarterly*, vol. XVIII (1945); M. LOUISE GREENE, *The Development of Religious Liberty in Connecticut* (Boston, 1905); THOMAS F. O'CONNOR, "Religious Toleration in New York, 1664–1700", N.Y. State Hist. Assoc. *Proceedings*, vol. XXXIV (1936); C. J. STILLÉ, "Religious Tests in Provincial Pennsylvania", *Penn. Mag. of Hist. and Biog.*, vol. IX (1885); ALBERT W. WERLINE, *Problems of Church and State in Maryland During the Seventeenth and Eighteenth Centuries* (South Lancaster, Mass., 1948); H. R. McILWAINE, *The struggle of Protestant Dissenters for religious Toleration in Virginia* (Baltimore, 1894); W. T. THOM, *The Struggle for Religious Freedom in Virginia: The Baptists* (Baltimore, 1900); C. F. JAMES, *Documentary History of the Struggle for Religious Liberty in Virginia* (Lynchburg, Va., 1900); H. J. ECKENRODE, *Separation of Church and State in Virginia* . . . (Richmond, Va., 1910); S. B. WEEKS, *The Religious Development in the Province of North Carolina* (Baltimore, 1892); REBA C. STRICKLAND, *Religion and the State in Georgia in the Eighteenth Century* (New York, 1939).

Witchcraft in the colonies has been the subject of much writing, particularly the outbreak in Massachusetts in 1692. GEORGE L. KITTREDGE, *Witchcraft in Old and New England* (Cambridge, Mass., 1929) defends New England by tracing the history of witchcraft from ancient times and detailing witchcraft trials in Old England. MARION L. STARKEY, *The Devil in Massachusetts* (New York, 1949) is a sprightly modern account with ample references to sources on the subject.

The most significant event in the religious history of the colonies was the Great Awakening in the 1730's and 1740's. Joseph Tracy, *The Great Awakening* . . . (Boston, 1841) is the only account of the whole movement and is valuable in addition for documentary material. PERRY MILLER, "Jonathan Edwards and the Great Awakening" in DANIEL AARON, ed., *America in Crisis* (New York, 1952) interprets the movement in broad terms and links it up with the revivalistic movement in Europe. CHARLES H. MAXSON, *The Great Awakening in the Middle Colonies* (Chicago, 1920) and WESLEY M. GEWEHR, *The Great Awakening in Virginia, 1740–1790* (Durham, N.C., 1930) are solid studies for those areas. LEONARD W. LABAREE, "The Conservative Attitude toward the Great Awakening", *William and Mary Quarterly*, 3rd Series, vol. I (1944) and FREDERICK B. TOLLES, "Quietism versus Enthusiasm: the Philadelphia Quakers and the Great Awakening", *Penn. Mag. of Hist. and Biog.*, vol. LXIX (1945) are special studies of particular merit.

Biographies of many of the important religious figures in the colonies are nonexistent. However, most of them have been discussed in the *Dictionary of American Biography*. Among the worthwhile biographies are JAMES E. ERNST, *Roger Williams, New England Firebrand* (New York, 1932); S. H. Brockunier, *The Irrepressible Democrat, Roger Williams* (New York, 1940); KENNETH B. MURDOCK, *Increase Mather, The Foremost American Puritan* (2 vols., Cambridge, Mass., 1925); RALPH and LOUISE BOAS, *Cotton Mather, Keeper of the Puritan Conscience* (New York 1928); GEORGE A. COOK, *John Wise, Early American Democrat* (New York, 1952); OLA E. WINSLOW, *Jonathan Edwards* . . . (New York, 1940); PERRY MILLER, *Jonathan Edwards* (New York 1949), a study of Edwards's thought. LUKE TYERMAN, *The Life of the Rev. George Whitefield* (2 vols., London, 1876–1877) is the only worthwhile biography of an extraordinary man.

The Reverend ALBERT D. BELDEN, *George Whitefield: The Awakener*, was printed in England and published in New York in 1953 without indicating previous publication in London in 1930. The preface to the current edition says that its chief justification is "the intense desire to quicken the forces of religious revival in modern society". Mention should be made of the excellent essays, with full references, on Thomas Hooker, Roger Williams, John Wise, and Jonathan Mayhew, in CLINTON ROSSITER, *Seedtime of the Republic: The Origin of the American Tradition of Political Liberty*.

(c) EDUCATION

Printed source material for the history of education in the colonies is scanty. Printed legislative journals and statutes contain the official actions. The only available collection for the southern colonies is EDGAR W. KNIGHT, ed., *A Documentary History of Education in the South Before 1860* (5 vols., Chapel Hill, N.C., 1949–1953), which is very useful. R. F. SEYBOLT, *Source Studies in American Colonial Education: The Private School* (Urbana, Ill., 1925) is thin but useful for the brief selections not otherwise easily available. Harvard College records may be found in the Colonial Society of Massachusetts *Publications*, vol. XV, XVI, XXXI (Boston, 1925–1935). Sources for the early history of Yale are in FRANKLIN B. DEXTER, *Documentary History of Yale University . . . 1701–1745* (New Haven, Conn., 1916). The writings of the first president of what became Columbia University are in HERBERT W. and CAROL C. S. SCHNEIDER, eds., *Samuel Johnson, President of King's College . . .* (4 vols., New York, 1929). A selection from Puritan writings on education is given in MILLER and JOHNSON, *The Puritans*, which also contains a bibliography of primary and secondary writings.

Much of the considerable writing on colonial education is of questionable value because of inadequate research or lack of understanding. Among the worthwhile general works are PAUL MONROE, *Founding of the American Public School System. A History of Education in the United States from the Early Settlements to the Close of the Civil War Period* (New York, 1940); ELSIE W. CLEWS PARSONS, *Educational Legislation and Administration of the Colonial Governments* (New York, 1899); ALLEN O. HANSEN, *Liberalism and American Education in the Eighteenth Century* (New York, 1926); M. W. JERNEGAN, "Factors Influencing the Development of American Education before the Revolution", Miss. Valley Hist. Assoc. *Proceedings*, vol. V (1912). The education of the poor and of apprentices is well treated in several chapters of M. W. JERNEGAN, *Laboring and Dependent Classes in Colonial America* and in R. F. SEYBOLT, *Apprenticeship and Apprenticeship Education in Colonial New England and New York* (New York, 1917). SAMUEL ELIOT MORISON, *The Puritan Pronaos: Studies in the Intellectual Life of New England in the Seventeenth Century* (New York, 1936) offers many rebuttals of old ideas about colonial education.

Most studies of New England education are centred on Massachusetts. The old work of GEORGE H. MARTIN, *The Evolution of the Massachusetts Public School System* (New York, 1894) is one of the best. VERA M. BUTLER, *Education as revealed by New England Newspapers Prior to 1850* (Philadelphia, 1935) has many useful quotations from newspapers. CLIFFORD K. SHIPTON, "Secondary Education in the Puritan Colonies", *New England Quarterly*, vol. VII (1934) offers much sharp criticism of previous writing on the subject. R. F. SEYBOLT, *The Public Schools of Colonial Boston, 1635–1775* (Cambridge, Mass., 1935) and *The Private Schools of Colonial Boston* (Cambridge, 1935) are full studies. WILLIAM H. KIRKPATRICK, *The Dutch Schools of New Netherlands and Colonial New York* (Washington, 1912) and W. W. KEMP, *The Support of Schools in Colonial New York by the Society for the Propagation of the Gospel in Foreign Parts* (New York, 1913) are thorough studies. Among the studies of education in Pennsylvania, the most important are THOMAS WOODY, *Early Quaker Education in Pennsylvania* (New York, 1920); S. E. WEBER, *The Charity School Movement in Colonial Pennsylvania* (Philadelphia 1905); F. G. LIVINGOOD, "Eighteenth Century Reformed Church Schools", Penn. German Soc. *Proceedings*, vol. XXXVIII (1930); CHARLES L. MAURER, "Early Lutheran Education in Pennsylvania", Penn. German Soc. *Proceedings*, vol. XL (1932); R. F. SEYBOLT, "Schoolmasters of Colonial Philadelphia", *Penn. Mag. of Hist. and Biog.*, vol. LII (1928).

Education in the southern colonies has received relatively little study. EDGAR W. KNIGHT, *Education in the South* (Chapel Hill, N.C., 1924) discusses the colonial period in a general way, but much more of value is to be found in his *Documentary History of Education in the South,* previously cited. PHILIP A. BRUCE *Institutional History of Virginia in the Seventeenth Century* has several chapters relevant to education in that colony. G. F. WELLS, *Parish Education in Colonial Virginia* (New York, 1923) discusses the role of the Anglican vestries. C. L. RAPER, *The Church and Private Schools of North Carolina: A Historical Study* (Greensboro, N.C., 1898) has a section on the colonial period. FREDERICK BOWES, *The Culture of Early Charleston,* has some material on education in that city.

Most of the colonial colleges need thorough modern histories. SAMUEL E. MORISON, *The Founding of Harvard College* (Cambridge, Mass., 1935) and *Harvard College in the Seventeenth Century* (2 vols., Cambridge, 1936) are models, and among other things, demonstrate that Harvard was not merely a nursery of Puritan clergymen. EDWIN OVIATT, *The Beginnings of Yale (1701–1726)* (New Haven, Conn., 1916) needs to be continued. EDWARD P. CHEYNEY, *History of the University of Pennsylvania, 1740–1940* (Philadelphia, 1940), and THOMAS J. WERTENBAKER, *Princeton, 1746–1896* (Princeton, 1946) complete the list of modern studies of colonial colleges. A history of Columbia University is now being written. William and Mary, Brown, Rutgers and Dartmouth need similar histories.

A unique series of biographies, useful for much more than the history of education, are the volumes known as *Sibley's Harvard Graduates.* JOHN L. SIBLEY prepared the first three volumes (Cambridge, Mass., 1873–1885). CLIFFORD K. SHIPTON is continuing the project and has completed volumes four through eight (Cambridge and Boston, 1933–1951). Volume VIII contains the biographies of the classes graduating between 1726 and 1730.

A. RELIGION IN THE COLONIES

THE part played by religion in the founding and development of the American colonies is difficult to over-estimate although it is too little appreciated by people of the twentieth century, whose concern is more often with economic orthodoxies than it is with those values and beliefs which were at the core of the thought and feeling of the seventeenth and eighteenth centuries. A variety of religious convictions was the driving force behind the establishment of the New England colonies and helped to shape their social and political institutions in fundamental ways. The religious impulse was operative in other colonies as well, although it was not so pervasive. The founding of Virginia, for instance, was supported by many clergymen who looked forward to the Christianization and education of the Indians. Most promoters of colonies did in fact at least bow in the direction of carrying the gospel to the heathen, although for the most part the practice of the actual colonists was to exterminate rather than to convert the Indians.

Once the colonies were established, religion continued to play an all-important role. Much of the political thought of the seventeenth century was the outgrowth of or closely related to the religious convictions of various colonists.[1] Education was a major interest of religious groups and, with one exception, all the colonial colleges were founded or controlled by colonial churches.[2] They also supported the founding and maintenance of most of the elementary schools in the colonies.[3] The effort to control wages and prices during the seventeenth century was at least partially based on religious convictions.[4]

However, the most significant fact in the religious history of the English colonies is that they became the home of a great number of the religious sects which were one of the consequences of the Protestant Reformation.[5] These sects held a great variety of views, but most of them were opposed to state churches and therefore they ran afoul of national governments supporting national churches, for the dominant conviction of the ruling classes was that the state could not exist without a state church to which all conformed. The dissenting sects were persecuted in one way or another and an extraordinary number of them turned to the English colonies as a refuge from persecution and as a place where they could practise their beliefs as they pleased. Dissenters came to America in such numbers that their very presence as well as their religious ideas were to exert a profound effect on the course of colonial development.

The English dissenters of the seventeenth century led the way to the colonies. Since they held to differing ideas about the nature of man, the relationship that should exist between church and state, and the question of religious toleration, they soon came into conflict with one another in the New World. Although the English Puritans disagreed with Anglicans and Catholics on matters of church government, ritual, and theology, they were in fundamental agreement on one point: the church must be established and maintained by the state, and to it all must conform. Thus the Puritan leaders of the Massachusetts Bay colony looked upon the idea of the

[1] Nos. 17, 18, 19, 20.　　　　[2] See Part V, B.
[3] Part V, B.　　　[4] Nos. 63, 64.　　　[5] No. 87.

separation of church and state with horror and the toleration of religious dissenters was declared a "prodigious impiety".[1]

But Puritanism was not the only force let loose by the Reformation in England. The most radical of the English dissenters were the people variously known as Separatists, Independents, or Brownists. One of their basic convictions was that no state could establish a true church. In their eyes a true church could be established only by the creation of a covenant signed willingly by like-minded believers. The number of such people who came to the colonies was small as compared with the Puritans; yet their example was a beacon to those who believed in religious freedom. The Separatists who landed at Plymouth in 1620 looked upon themselves as a church. Their government was an outgrowth of their church covenant, but they never faced or were forced to face the implications of it.[2] It was Roger Williams who carried out to a logical conclusion the ideas implicit in Separatist thought. He argued powerfully for the separation of church and state, for the toleration of all religions, and for basing all government on the consent of the governed.[3] In Rhode Island he established a colony openly dedicated to such ideas. Although he obtained a charter from Parliament in 1644 and a royal charter in 1663, they represented no surrender of his basic convictions but rather a practical recognition of the need for protecting the colony from external and internal enemies who did not have his vision of society.

Within a short time two more religious groups which believed in religious toleration and in the separation of church and state found their way to the colonies: the Baptists and the Quakers. The Baptists were the leading opponents of established churches in every colony in which they settled. William Penn dedicated Pennsylvania to the idea of toleration for all religions and the colony soon contained an extraordinary variety of religious sects.[4] Other promoters of colonies, and notably those of Carolina, held out the promise of religious toleration, not from personal conviction but in order to attract settlers.[5] Lord Baltimore, in establishing Maryland, hoped that it would be a refuge for Catholics, but he provided for the toleration for all sects.

The ideal of toleration was persistent in the colonies but there was also bitter opposition to it, and most of the colonies had established churches. The Congregational Church was established by law in Massachusetts and Connecticut, and all were taxed to support it, whether they were members or not. The Anglican Church was relatively unimportant in the seventeenth century except in Virginia, where it remained the established church until after the American Revolution. The colonies as a whole were a part of the diocese of the bishop of London, and his commissaries in the colonies promoted the interest of the church with varying degrees of success. The Society for the Propagation of the Gospel in Foreign Parts, which was founded in 1701, sent missionaries to the colonies who worked vigorously to increase the influence of the Anglican Church, particularly in the southern colonies. The reports of these missionaries represent one of the most illuminating pictures of the religious diversity of the colonies, and at the same time reveal that the lot of the Anglican missionary was one of almost unrelieved gloom and despair, even in colonies where the church was established by law.[6] By 1776 the Anglican Church was the established church of Virginia, Maryland, North Carolina, South Carolina, Georgia, and in part of New York, although in none of these colonies did it represent a majority of the inhabitants. The effort to establish the Anglican Church in New Jersey failed.

[1] No. 82.   [2] No. 14.   [3] Nos. 18, 83.   [4] Nos. 19, 87A.   [5] No. 9.   [6] No. 87B.

Rhode Island, Pennsylvania, and Delaware remained devoted to the ideal of religious freedom.

In every English colony with an established church, whether Congregational or Anglican, the effort was made to suppress dissenters or to force them to conform, at least to the extent of paying taxes to support the state church. Entirely apart from dissenting sects, there was the problem of dissenters within the ranks of the established churches themselves. This was nowhere more evident than in Massachusetts, which attracted many independent-minded people who were soon at odds with the Puritan leaders of the colony. Some of these, like Roger Williams and Anne Hutchinson, were banished. Still others were subjected to such pressure that they left voluntarily. The difficulty of maintaining orthodoxy in a colony where each of the churches was relatively independent, led to a variety of laws including laws defining the nature of heresy.[1]

Even greater were the difficulties created by members of other religions who came into colonies with established churches. The early Quakers were aggressive expounders of their religious and political views and were persecuted everywhere, although nowhere more violently than in Massachusetts.[2] The Baptists, who denied the validity of infant baptism, aroused the orthodox to splenetic fury, and their attacks on state churches guaranteed their persecution wherever they appeared. The Catholics, although small in numbers, were subjected to legal disabilities in every colony. Even Maryland, which was open to them at the beginning and which had adopted an act of toleration, soon came to be dominated by Protestants. By the eighteenth century, Maryland had stricter laws against Catholics than any other colony. Priests, and particularly Jesuits, were forbidden in most of the colonies. Only Pennsylvania allowed Mass to be said publicly. Catholic laymen were denied the franchise, forbidden to hold office, or serve in the militia in every colony. The severity of the laws and the effectiveness of their enforcement varied from colony to colony, but on the whole the Catholics were the one religious group which did not share in the broadening toleration that was characteristic of the eighteenth century.

A number of factors were involved in the spread of religious freedom, in practice if not in law, during the eighteenth century. Rhode Island and Pennsylvania continued to be examples of flourishing colonies where toleration was the rule. The English Toleration Act of 1689[3] did not apply to the colonies, but it was used by Protestant dissenters in every colony to justify their demand for religious freedom. Far more important in breaking down religious restrictions was the great migration of an increasing number of Protestant sects to the colonies during the eighteenth century. The bulk of them settled in the back country from Pennsylvania to Georgia in such numbers that the established Anglican Church found it simply impossible to achieve conformity. The Scotch-Irish Presbyterians in particular could not be subjected and their numbers were so great, as in Virginia, that they not only achieved toleration but even became members of the Anglican vestries in the back country.

The other great factor in growing toleration had its roots in changing theological convictions, and nowhere were the results more striking than in Massachusetts. The Quakers and Baptists kept the colony under constant fire, and Charles II, who had other reasons for disliking the colony, supported them. In 1691, when Massachusetts received its new charter, it provided for the liberty of all Christians "except Papists". Meanwhile the leading clergymen of the generation of the end of the seventeenth

[1] No. 84.   [2] No. 85.   [3] *English Historical Documents*, vol. VIII, No. 151.

century were exhibiting views quite unlike those of the founding fathers of the colony. This is strikingly illustrated in the case of Increase Mather and his son Cotton Mather, who were for decades the two most important clergymen in Massachusetts. During the 1680's Increase Mather was still justifying the persecution of the Baptists, but in 1718 he and his son were invited to assist in the ordination and installation of the minister of a Baptist church in Boston, and Cotton Mather preached the ordination sermon.

This represented a remarkable shift in temper on the part of many New England leaders. During the eighteenth century the New England colonies exempted Baptists, Quakers, and Anglicans from the payment of taxes for the support of the Congregational Church, although the exemptions were so difficult to obtain that the laws were not particularly effective.

The most disruptive experience in the religious history of the colonies was the Great Awakening.[1] Theologically, it was a movement inaugurated by clergymen who sought to defend the orthodoxy of Calvinist thought against the doctrines of Arminianism which had spread from Europe to America, where they were receiving wide acceptance among the clergy and laymen of various colonial churches. In the course of their defence of orthodoxy, the 'New Light' clergymen became evangelists who stirred up audiences by emotional appeals that would have been inconceivable in the seventeenth century. During the height of the movement, churches from one end of the colonies to the other were split into 'Old Light' and 'New Light' groups.

The religious diversity of the colonies thus became even more diverse and the power of the established churches was weakened accordingly. With the rise of the revolutionary movement, the proponents of religious freedom drew the obvious parallels between the political ideas of the Revolution and their own demand for the separation of church and state.[2] The demand was so powerful and was supported by so many political leaders of widely varying political and religious convictions that within a few years after independence was achieved, state churches were abolished in the United States and the religious freedom of all the inhabitants was guaranteed by the state and national constitutions.

82. Nathaniel Ward: The argument against toleration, from "The Simple Cobler of Aggawam" (1647)

The Puritans' argument against religious toleration was stated over and over. One of the best presentations of their views was that of Nathaniel Ward (1578–1652). Born in England and educated at Cambridge, he practised law before becoming a minister in 1618. He was one of the organizers of the Massachusetts Bay Company, came to the colony in 1634, and served as minister of the church at Ipswich for two years. In 1646 he returned to England. His tract was written in 1645 and published in London in 1647. Aggawam was the Indian name for Ipswich. Printed: The Simple Cobler of Aggawam in America, facsimile edition, with introduction by Lawrence C. Wroth, New York, 1937), pp. 1–10.

Either I am in an apoplexy, or that man is in a lethargy, who doth not now sensibly feel God shaking the heavens over his head, and the earth under his feet: the heavens so, as the sun begins to turn into darkness, the moon into blood, the stars to fall down to the ground; so that little light of comfort or counsel is left to the sons of men: the earth so, as the foundations are failing, the righteous scarce know where

---

[1] No. 86.   [2] No. 88.

to find rest, the inhabitants stagger like drunken men. It is in a manner dissolved both in religions and relations, and no marvel; for they have defiled it by transgressing the laws, changing the ordinances, and breaking the everlasting covenant. The truths of God are the pillars of the world, whereon states and churches may stand quiet if they will; if they will not, he can easily shake them off into delusions and distractions enough.

Satan is now in his passions, he feels his passion approaching; he loves to fish in roiled waters. Though that Dragon cannot sting the vitals of the elect mortally, yet that Beelzebub can fly-blow their intellectuals miserably. The finer religion grows, the finer he spins his cobwebs, he will hold pace with Christ so long as his wits will serve him. He sees himself beaten out of gross idolatries, heresies, ceremonies, where the Light breaks forth with power; he will therefore bestir him to prevaricate evangelical truths and ordinances, that if they will needs be walking, yet they shall *laborare varicibus,* and not keep their path: he will put them out of time and place; assassinating for his engineers, men of Paracelsian parts, well complexioned for honesty; for such are fittest to mountebank his chemistry into sick churches and weak judgments.

Nor shall he need to stretch his strength overmuch in this work. Too many men having not laid their foundation sure, nor ballasted their spirits deep with humility and fear, are pressed enough of themselves to evaporate their own apprehensions. Those that are acquainted with story know it hath ever been so in new editions of churches: such as are least able are most busy to pudder in the rubbish, and to raise dust in the eyes of more steady repairers. Civil commotions make room for uncivil practices; religious mutations, for irreligious opinions; change of air discovers corrupt bodies; reformation of religion, unsound minds. He that hath any well-faced fancy in his crown, and doth not vent it now, fears the pride of his own heart will dub him dunce for ever. Such a one will trouble the whole Israel of God with his most untimely births, though he makes the bones of his vanity stick up to the view and grief of all that are godly wise. The devil desires no better sport than to see light heads handle their heels, and fetch their careers in a time when the roof of liberty stands open.

The next perplexed question, with pious and ponderous men, will be: what should be done for the healing of these comfortless exulcerations. I am the unablest adviser of a thousand, the unworthiest of ten thousand; yet I hope I may presume to assert what follows without just offence.

First, such as have given or taken any unfriendly reports of us New English, should do well to recollect themselves. We have been reputed a colluvies of wild opinionists, swarmed into a remote wilderness to find elbow-room for our fanatic doctrines and practices; I trust our diligence past, and constant sedulity against such persons and courses, will plead better things for us. I dare take upon me to be the herald of New England so far as to proclaim to the world, in the name of our colony, that all Familists, Antinomians, Anabaptists, and other enthusiasts, shall have free liberty to keep away from us, and such as will come, to be gone as fast as they can, the sooner the better.

Secondly, I dare aver, that God doth nowhere in his word tolerate Christian states to give tolerations to such adversaries of his truth, if they have power in their hands to suppress them.

Here is lately brought us an extract of a Magna Charta, so called, compiled between the subplanters of a West Indiana island, whereof the first article of constipulation, firmly provides free stable-room and litter for all kinds of consciences, be they never so dirty or jadish; making it actionable, yea, treasonable, to disturb any man in his religion, or to discommend it, whatever it be. We are very sorrow to see such professed profaneness in English professors, as industriously to lay their religious foundation on the ruin of true religion, which strictly binds every conscience to contend earnestly for the truth: to preserve unity of spirit, faith, and ordinances, to be all like minded, of one accord; every man to take his brother into his Christian care; to stand fast with one spirit, with one mind, striving together for the faith of the Gospel, and by no means to permit heresies or erroneous opinions. But God abhorring such loathsome beverages, hath in his righteous judgment blasted that enterprise, which might otherwise have prospered well, for aught I know. I presume their case is generally known ere this.

If the devil might have his free option I believe he would ask nothing else but liberty to enfranchise all other religions, and to embondage the true, nor should he need. It is much to be feared, that lax tolerations upon state pretences and planting necessities, will be the next subtle stratagem he will spread, to disstate the truth of God and supplant the peace of the churches. Tolerations in things tolerable, exquisitely drawn out by the lines of the Scripture, and pencil of the Spirit, are the sacred favours of truth, the due latitudes of love, the fair compartments of Christian fraternity; but irregular dispensations, dealt forth by the facilities of men, are the frontiers of error, the redoubts of schism, the perilous irritaments of carnal enmity.

My heart hath naturally detested four things: The standing of the Apocrypha in the Bible; foreigners dwelling in my country, to crowd out native subjects into the corners of the earth; alchemized coins; tolerations of divers religions, or of one religion in segregant shapes. He that willingly assents to the last, if he examines his heart by daylight, his conscience will tell him, he is either an atheist, or an heretic or an hypocrite, or at best a captive to some lust; polypiety is the greatest impiety in the world. True religion is *Ignis probationis*, which doth *congregare homogenea & segregare heterogenia.*

Not to tolerate things merely indifferent to weak consciences, argues a conscience too strong: pressed uniformity in these, causes much disunity. To tolerate more than indifferents, is not to deal indifferently with God. He that doth it, takes his sceptre out of his hand, and bids him stand by. The power of all religion and ordinances, lies in their purity; their purity in their simplicity; then are mixtures pernicious. I lived in a city where a Papist preached in one church, a Lutheran in another, a Calvinist in a third; a Lutheran one part of the day, a Calvinist the other, in the same pulpit. The religion of that place was but motley and meagre, their affections leopard like.

If the whole creature should conspire to do the Creator a mischief, or offer him an insolency, it would be in nothing more than in erecting untruths against his truth, or by sophisticating his truths with human medleys; the removing of some one iota in Scripture may draw out all the life and traverse all the truth of the whole Bible; but to authorize an untruth by a toleration of state, is to build a sconce against the walls of Heaven, to batter God out of his chair. To tell a practical lie is a great sin, but yet transient; but to set up a theorical untruth, is to warrant every lie that lies from its root to the top of every branch it hath.

I would willingly hope that no member of the Parliament hath skilfully ingratiated himself into the hearts of the House, that he might watch a time to midwife out some ungracious toleration for his own turn, and for the sake of that, some others. I would also hope that a word of general caution should not be particularly misapplied. Yet, good gentlemen, look well about you and remember how Tiberius played the fox with the Senate of Rome, and how Fabius Maximus cropped his ears for his cunning.

That state is wise that will improve all pains and patience rather to compose, than tolerate differences in religion. There is no divine truth but hath much celestial fire in it from the spirit of truth; nor no irreligious untruth, without its proportion of antifire from the spirit of error to contradict it. The zeal of the one, the virulency of the other, must necessarily kindle combustions. Fiery diseases seated in the spirit embroil the whole frame of the body; others more external and cool are less dangerous. They which divide in religion, divide in God; they who divide in him divide beyond *Genus Generalissimum*, where there is no reconciliation without atonement; that is, without uniting in him who is one, and in his truth, which is also one.

Wise are those men who will be persuaded rather to live within the pale of truth where they may be quiet, than in the purlieus, where they are sure to be hunted ever and anon, do authority what it can. Every singular opinion hath a singular opinion of itself, and he that holds it, a singular opinion of himself, and a simple opinion of all contra-sentients; he that confutes them must confute all three at once, or else he does nothing, which will not be done without more stir than the peace of the state or church can endure.

And prudent are those Christians that will rather give what may be given than hazard all by yielding nothing. To sell all peace of country, to buy some peace of conscience unseasonably, is more avarice than thrift, imprudence than patience; they deal not equally that set any truth of God at such a rate, but they deal wisely that will stay till the market is fallen.

My prognostics deceive me not a little if once within three seven years' peace prove not such a pennyworth at most marts in Christendom that he that would not lay down his money, his lust, his opinion, his will, I had almost said the best flower of his crown, for it, while he might have had it, will tell his own heart he played the very ill husband.

Concerning Tolerations I may further assert

That persecution of true religion, and toleration of false, are the *Jannes* and *Jambres* to the Kingdom of Christ, whereof the last is far the worst. Augustine's tongue had not owed his mouth one penny rent though it had never spake word more in it but this, *Nullum malum pejus libertate errandi.*

He that is willing to tolerate any religion, or discrepant way of religion, besides his own, unless it be in matters merely indifferent, either doubts of his own or is not sincere in it.

He that is willing to tolerate any unsound opinion, that his own may also be tolerated, though never so sound, will for a need hang God's Bible at the devil's girdle.

Every toleration of false religions, or opinions, hath as many errors and sins in it as all the false religions and opinions it tolerates, and one sound one more.

That state that will give liberty of conscience in matters of religion, must give liberty of conscience and conversation in their moral laws, or else the fiddle will be out of tune and some of the strings crack.

He that will rather make an irreligious quarrel with other religions than try the truth of his own by valuable arguments, and peaceable sufferings, either his religion, or himself, is irreligious.

Experience will teach churches and Christians that it is far better to live in a state united, though somewhat corrupt, than in a state whereof some part is incorrupt and all the rest divided.

I am not altogether ignorant of the eight rules given by orthodox divines about giving tolerations, yet with their favour I dare affirm:

That there is no rule given by God for any state to give an affirmative toleration to any false religion or opinion whatsoever; they must connive in some cases, but may not concede in any.

That the state of England (so far as my intelligence serves) might in time have prevented with ease, and may yet without any great difficulty deny both toleration and connivances *salva Republica*.

That if the state of England shall either willingly tolerate, or weakly connive at such courses, the church of that kingdom will sooner become the devil's dancing-school than God's Temple; the civil state a bear-garden than an exchange: the whole realm a *Pays bas*, than an England. And what pity it is that that country which hath been the staple of truth to all Christendom should now become the aviary of errors to the whole world, let every fearing heart judge.

I take liberty of conscience to be nothing but a freedom from sin and error. *Conscientia in tantum libera, in quantum ab errore liberata*. And liberty of error nothing but a prison for conscience. Then small will be the kindness of a state to build such prisons for their subjects.

The Scripture saith there is nothing makes free but truth, and truth saith there is no truth but one. If the states of the world would make it their sumoperous care to preserve this one truth in its purity and authority it would ease them of all other political cares. I am sure Satan makes it his grand, if not only task, to adulterate truth; falsehood is his sole sceptre, whereby he first ruffled, and ever since ruined the world.

If truth be but one, me thinks all the opinionists in England should not be all in that one truth, some of them I doubt are out. He that can extract an unity out of such a disparity, or contract such a disparity into an unity had need be a better artist than ever was *Drebell*.

If two centres (as we may suppose) be in one circle, and lines drawn from both to all the points of the compass, they will certainly cross one another and probably cut through the centres themselves.

There is talk of an universal toleration. I would talk what I could against it did I know what more apt and reasonable sacrifice England could offer to God for his late performing all his heavenly truths than an universal toleration of all hellish errors, or how they shall make an universal reformation but by making Christ's academy the devil's university, where any man may commence heretique *per saltum*; where he that is *filius Diabolicus*, or *simpliciter pessimus*, may have his grace to go to hell *cum Publico Privilegio*; and carry as many after him as he can.

83. Roger Williams: defence of religious freedom, from "The Bloody Tenent Yet More Bloody" (1652)

While Roger Williams was in England in 1644 securing a charter for the Rhode Island settlements, he wrote two essays in defence of religious toleration. The first, *Queries of Highest Consideration*, was in the form of questions addressed to Parliament and was an eloquent attack on the doctrine of a national church. The second, *The Bloudy Tenent of Persecution for Cause of Conscience*, was an answer to the Reverend John Cotton's defence of Williams's banishment from Massachusetts. When it was published, Parliament ordered it burned by the common hangman. A copy of the book got to Massachusetts where Cotton wrote a reply called *The Bloudy Tenent, washed, And made white in the bloud of the Lambe* which was published in England in 1647. To this Williams wrote a reply which was also published there in 1652. The document which follows is from the concluding chapter of that work. The work as a whole is one of the most eloquent pleas for religious toleration written in the seventeenth century. Printed: *The Bloody Tenent Yet More Bloody by Mr. Cottons endevour to wash it white in the BLOOD of the LAMBE* . . . (ed. by Samuel L. Caldwell, *Publications of the Narragansett Club*, IV, Providence, 1870), pp. 493–501.

Truth. Dear Peace, our golden sand is out, we now must part with a holy kiss of heavenly peace and love. Mr. Cotton speaks and writes his conscience, yet the Father of lights may please to show him that what he highly esteems as a tenet washed white in the Lamb's blood, is yet more black and abominable, in the most pure and jealous eye of God.

Peace. The blackamoor's darkness differs not in the dark from the fairest white.

Truth. Christ Jesus, the Son of Righteousness, has broke forth, and daily will to a brighter and brighter discovery of this deformed Ethiopian. And for myself I must proclaim before the most holy God, angels and men, that (whatever other white and heavenly tenets Mr. Cotton holds) yet this is a foul, a black, and a bloody tenet.[1]

A tenet of high blasphemy against the God of Peace, the God of Order, who hath of one blood made all mankind to dwell upon the face of the earth, now all confounded and destroyed in their civil beings and subsistences by mutual flames of war from their several respective religions and consciences.

A tenet warring against the Prince of Peace, Christ Jesus, denying his appearance and coming in the flesh to put an end to and abolish the shadows of that ceremonial and typical Land of Canaan.

A tenet fighting against the sweet end of his coming, which was not to destroy

[1] The Portraiture of the Bloody Tenent.

men's lives for their religions, but to save them, by the meek and peaceable invitations and persuasions of his peaceable wisdom's maidens.

A tenet foully charging his wisdom, faithfulness and love in so poorly providing such magistrates and civil powers all the world over, as might effect so great a charge preterded to be committed to them.

A tenet lamentably guilty of his most precious blood, shed in the blood of so many hundred thousand of his poor servants by the civil powers of the world, pretending to suppress blasphemies, heresies, idolatries, superstition, etc.

A tenet fighting with the spirit of love, holiness, and meekness, by kindling fiery spirits of false zeal and fury, when yet such spirits know not of what spirit they are.

A tenet fighting with those mighty angels who stand up for the peace of the saints, against Persia, Greece, etc., and so consequently all other nations, who fighting for their several religions, and against the truth, leave no room for such as fear and love the Lord on the earth.

A tenet against which the blessed souls under the altar cry loud for vengeance, this tenet having cut their throats, torn out their hearts, and poured forth their blood in all ages, as the only heretics and blasphemers in the world.

A tenet which no uncleanness, no adultery, incest, sodomy, or bestiality can equal, this ravishing and forcing (explicitly or implicitly) the very souls and consciences of all the nations and inhabitants of the world.

A tenet that puts out the very eye of all true faith, which cannot but be as free and voluntary as any virgin in the world in refusing or embracing any spiritual offer or object.

A tenet loathsome and ugly (in the eyes of the God of Heaven and serious sons of men) I say, loathsome with the palpable filths of gross dissimulation and hypocrisy: thousands of peoples and whole nations, compelled by this tenet to put on the foul vizard of religious hypocrisy, for fear of laws, losses and punishments, and for the keeping and hoping for of favour, liberty, worldly commodity, etc.

A tenet woefully guilty of hardening all false and deluded consciences (of what-soever sect, faction, heresy, or idolatry, though never so horrid and blasphemous) by cruelties and violences practised against them: all false teachers and their followers (ordinarily) contracting a brawny and steely hardness from their sufferings for their consciences.

A tenet that shuts and bars out the gracious prophecies and promises and dis-coveries of the most glorious Son of Righteousness, Christ Jesus, that burns up the holy Scriptures, and forbids them (upon the point) to be read in English, or that any trial or search, or (truly) free disquisition be made by them: when the most able, diligent, and conscionable readers must pluck forth their own eyes and be forced to read by the (whichsoever predominate) clergies' spectacles.

A tenet that seals up the spiritual graves of all men, Jews and Gentiles (and conse-quently stands guilty of the damnation of all men), since no preachers, nor trumpets of Christ himself may call them out, but such as the several and respective nations of the world themselves allow of.

A tenet that fights against the common principles of all civility, and the very civil being and combinations of men in nations, cities, etc., by commixing (explicitly or implicitly) a spiritual and civil state together, and so confounding and overthrowing the purity and strength of both.

A tenet that kindles the devouring flames of combustions and wars in most nations of the world, and (if God were not infinitely gracious) had almost ruined the English, French, the Scotch and Irish, and many other nations: Germans, Poles, Hungarians, Bohemians, etc.

A tenet that bows down the backs and necks of all civil states and magistrates, kings and emperors, under the proud feet of that man and monster of sin and pride, the Pope, and all popish and proud clergymen rendering such laics and seculars (as they call them) but slavish executioners (upon the point) of their most imperious synodical decrees and sentences.

A tenet that renders the highest civil magistrates and ministers of justice (the fathers and Gods of their countries) either odious or lamentably grievous unto the very best subjects, by either clapping or keeping on the iron yokes of cruellest oppression. No yoke or bondage comparably so grievous as that upon the soul's neck of men's religion and consciences.

A tenet, all besprinkled with the bloody murders, stabs, poisonings, pistolings, powder-plots, etc., against many famous kings, princes, and states, either actually performed or attempted, in France, England, Scotland, Low Countries, and other nations.

A tenet all red and bloody with those most barbarous and tiger-like massacres of so many thousand and ten thousands formerly in France and other parts, and so lately and so horribly in Ireland: of which, whatever causes be assigned, this chiefly will be found the true, and while this continues (to wit, violence against conscience) this bloody issue, sooner or later, must break forth again (except God wonderfully stop it) in Ireland and other places too.

A tenet that stunts the growth and flourishing of the most likely and hopefulest commonweals and countries, while consciences, the best, and the best deserving subjects are forced to fly (by enforced or voluntary banishment) from their native countries; the lamentable proof whereof England hath felt in the flight of so many worthy English, into the Low Countries and New England, and from New England into Old again and other foreign parts.

A tenet whose gross partiality denies the principles of common justice, while men weigh out to the consciences of all others that which they judge not fit nor right to be weighed out to their own: since the persecutor's rule is, to take and persecute all consciences, only himself must not be touched.

A tenet that is but Machiavellianism, and makes a religion but a cloak or stalking horse to policy and private ends of Jeroboam's crown and the priests' benefice, etc.

A tenet that corrupts and spoils the very civil honesty and natural conscience of a nation. Since conscience to God violated proves (without repentance) ever after, a very jade, a drug, loose and unconscionable in all converse with men.

Lastly, a tenet in England most unseasonable, as pouring oil upon those flames which the high wisdom of the Parliament (by easing the yokes on men's consciences) had begun to quench.

In the sad consideration of all which (dear Peace) let Heaven and earth judge of the washing and colour of this tenet. For thee, sweet heavenly guest, go lodge thee in the breasts of the peaceable and humble witnesses of Jesus, that love the truth in peace! Hide thee from the world's tumults and combustions in the breasts of thy truly noble children, who profess and endeavour to break the irony and insupportable yokes upon the souls and consciences of any of the sons of men.

Peace. Methinks, dear Truth, if any of the least of these deep charges be found against this tenet, you do not wrong it when you style it bloody; but since, in the woeful proof of all ages past, since Nimrod (the hunter or persecutor before the Lord) these and more are lamentably evident and undeniable. It gives me wonder that so many and so excellent eyes of God's servants should not espy so foul a monster, especially considering the universal opposition this tenet makes against God's glory and the good of all mankind.

Truth. There hath been many foul opinions with which the old serpent hath infected and bewitched the sons of men (touching God, Christ, the Spirit, the Church, against holiness, against peace, against civil obedience, against chastity) insomuch that even sodomy itself hath been a tenet maintained in print by some of the very pillars of the Church of Rome. But this tenet is so universally opposite to God and man, so pernicious and destructive to both (as hath been declared) that like the powder-plot, it threatens to blow up all religion, all civility, all humanity, yea the very being of the world, and the nations thereof at once.

Peace. He that is the father of lies, and a murderer from the beginning, he knows this well and this ugly blackamoor needs a mask or vizard.

Truth. Yea, the bloodiness and inhumanity of it is such that not only Mr. Cotton's more tender and holy breast, but even the most bloody Bonners and Gardiners have been forced to arm themselves with the fair shows and glorious pretences of the glory of God and zeal for that glory, the love of his truth, the gospel of Christ Jesus, love and pity to men's souls, the peace of the Church, uniformity, order, the peace of the commonweal, the wisdom of the state, the kings, queens and Parliaments proceedings, the odiousness of sects, heresies, blasphemies, novelties, seducers, and their infections: the obstinacy of heretics after all means, disputations, examinations, synods, yea and after conviction in the poor heretics' own conscience. Add to these the flattering sound of those glossing titles, the Godly Magistrate, the Christian Magistrate, the Nursing Fathers and Mothers of the Church, Christian Kings and Queens. But all other kings and magistrates (even all the nations of the world over, as Mr. Cotton pleads) must suspend and hold their hands, and not meddle in matters of religion until they be informed, etc.

Peace. The dreadful righteous hand of God, the eternal and avenging God, is pulling off these masks and vizards, that thousands, and the world may see this bloody tenet's beauty.

Truth. But see (my heavenly sister and true stranger in this sea-like restless, raging world) see here what fires and swords are come to part us! Well: Our meetings in the heavens shall not thus be interrupted, our kisses thus distracted, and our eyes and cheeks thus wet, unwiped. For me, though censured, threatened, persecuted, I must profess, while Heaven and earth lasts, that no one tenet that either London, England, or the world doth harbour, is so heretical, blasphemous, seditious, and dangerous to the corporeal, to the spiritual, to the present, to the eternal good of all men, as the bloody tenet (however washed and whited) I say, as is the bloody tenet of persecution for cause of conscience.

84. Massachusetts laws on heresy (1646, 1656)

Legislation for the purpose of controlling religious dissent was perhaps more stringent in Massachusetts than in any other colony. The first of the two Acts which follow is against heresy in general, and the second is aimed at the Quakers. Printed: William A. Whitmore, ed., *The Colonial Laws of Massachusetts Reprinted from the Edition of 1672, with the Supplements through 1686* (Boston, 1890), pp. 58–59, 61–62.

[Law of 1646]

Although no human power be Lord over the faith and consciences of men, yet because such as bring in damnable heresies, tending to the subversion of the Christian faith, and destruction of the souls of men, ought duly to be restrained from such notorious impieties:

It is therefore ordered and declared by the court that if any Christian within this jurisdiction shall go about to subvert and destroy the Christian faith and religion by broaching and maintaining any damnable heresies: as denying the immortality of the soul, or resurrection of the body, or any sin to be repented of in the regenerate, or any evil done by the outward man to be accounted sin, or denying that Christ gave himself a ransom for our sins, or shall affirm that we are not justified by his death and righteousness but by the perfections of our own works, or shall deny the morality of the fourth commandment, or shall openly condemn or oppose the baptizing of infants, or shall purposely depart the congregation at the administration of that ordinance, or shall deny the ordinance of magistracy, or their lawful authority, to make war, or to punish the outward breaches of the first Table, or shall endeavour to seduce others to any of the errors or heresies abovementioned; every such person continuing obstinate therein, after the due means of conviction, shall be sentenced to banishment.

[Law of 1656]

Whereas there is a pernicious sect, commonly called Quakers, lately arisen, who by word and writing have published and maintained many dangerous and horrid tenets, and do take upon them to change and alter the received laudable customs of our nation, in giving civil respect to equals, or reverence to superiors, whose actions tend to undermine the authority of civil government, as also to destroy the order of the churches, by denying all established forms of worship, and by withdrawing from the orderly church assemblies, allowed and approved by all orthodox professors of the truth; and instead thereof, and opposition thereunto, frequenting private meetings of their own, insinuating themselves into the minds of the simpler, or such as are less affected to the order and government of the church and commonwealth, whereby divers of our inhabitants have been infected and seduced, notwithstanding all former laws made (upon experience of their arrogant bold obtrusions, to disseminate their principles amongst us) prohibiting their coming into this jurisdiction, they have not been deterred from their impetuous attempts to undermine our peace and hasten our ruin:

For prevention thereof, this court doth order and enact, that every person or persons of the cursed sect of the Quakers who is not an inhabitant of, but found within this jurisdiction, shall be apprehended (without warrant, where no magistrate is at hand) by any constable, commissioner, or selectman, and conveyed from constable to constable until they come before the next magistrate, who shall commit the said person or persons to close prison, there to remain without bail until the next Court of Assistants, where they shall have a legal trial by a special jury, and being convicted to be of the sect of the Quakers, shall be sentenced to banishment upon pain of death.

And that every inhabitant of this jurisdiction, being convicted to be of the aforesaid sect, either by taking up, publishing and defending the horrid opinions of the Quakers, or by stirring up mutiny, sedition, or rebellion against the government, or by taking up their absurd and destructive practices, viz., denying civil respect and reverence to equals and superiors, withdrawing from our church assemblies, and instead thereof frequenting private meetings of their own in opposition to church order, or by adhering to, or approving of any known Quakers that are opposite to the orthodox received opinions and practices of the godly, and endeavouring to disaffect others to civil government and church order, and condemning the practice and proceedings of this court against the Quakers, manifesting thereby compliance with those whose design is to overthrow the order established in church and commonwealth: every such person upon examination and legal conviction before the Court of Assistants in manner as aforesaid, shall be committed to close prison for one month, and then unless they choose voluntarily to depart the jurisdiction, shall give bond for their good abearance and appearance at the next Court of Assistants, where continuing obstinate, and refusing to retract and reform the aforesaid opinions and practices, shall be sentenced to banishment upon pain of death. And in case of the aforesaid voluntary departure, not to remain or again to return into this jurisdiction without the allowance of the major part of the Council first had and published, on penalty of being banished upon pain of death, and any one magistrate, upon information given him of any such person, shall cause them to be apprehended, and if upon examination of the case he shall according to his best discretion find just ground for such complaint, he shall commit such person to prison, until he comes to his trial as is above expressed.

85A–B. Persecution of Quakers in Massachusetts

The early Quakers aroused opposition everywhere, and legislation banishing them was adopted in Virginia and New England. Only in Rhode Island did they find a haven. That colony stuck to its principles even though men like Roger Williams disliked Quakers. Banishment was not the only punishment provided. Ears were cropped, tongues were drilled with hot irons and bare backs were whipped with tarred ropes. Neither punishment, fines, nor imprisonment could stop Quaker missionaries. Some of those banished returned to carry on their work. In Massachusetts four such people were hanged, including one woman, Mary Dyer. Two of the men sentenced to death wrote a spirited attack on the Puritans and a defence of their own position while in jail awaiting execution (No. 85A). The General Court in its turn published a justification for their executions (No. 85B).

When the news reached England, Charles II himself ordered Massachusetts to stop the persecution and ordered all Quakers held in jail in Massachusetts to be sent to England for trial. The
point was made even plainer because Samuel Shattuck, a Quaker of Salem who had been banished
on pain of death if he returned, was selected as the king's special messenger to carry the order to
Massachusetts. After 1677 Quakers were no longer persecuted in New England, and they made a
place for themselves in other colonies.

85A. William Robinson and Marmaduke Stevenson: protest against the persecution of Quakers (1659)

Printed: Massachusetts Historical Society *Proceedings*, XLII, pp. 359-363.

To all you magistrates and priests in the town of Boston and elsewhere in the nation
of New England who have had a hand and is guilty of persecuting the innocent
and servants of the living God who in obedience to his command did come among
you to declare his mind and will concerning you; for you be a stiff-necked people
gotten up high in your own wisdom, as the Scribes and Pharisees were who put
Christ to death under the name of a blasphemer and a deceiver of the people, because
he declared his Father's will and counsel to them; but they would not hear him nor
hearken to his words but rejected his pure counsel and set at naught his reproof,
because he came in a low manner and in the way which they despised, who had a
seal of God, but not according to knowledge, though they professed him in words,
yet in the life and in the power, they were strangers to him, for their hearts were
adulterated from him as yours is at this day to that of God in all your consciences
I speak, which is my witness which will say you naked and bare with whom we
have to do, for he is a God that will not wink at wickedness nor let the transgressor
go unpunished, to whom you must all give an account, and receive according to
your deeds. Therefore consider of it and lay it to heart, for the Lord hath a controversy
with you because you have done that which is evil in his sight in whipping and
imprisoning his servants and children, whom you have despised and set at naught:
you who make mention of his name, but not in truth and righteousness. Oh, you
hypocrites and dissemblers who profess God in words but the life and power of truth
you deny and will not own his appearance but trampled upon his pure witness in
your consciences, which will testify to your faces that you do not that which pleaseth
the Lord, but you have grieved his good spirit, and have vexed his righteous soul
and provoked him to anger against you. Yet he is even with bearing your sins and
iniquities, for they are great, and is likely to exceed your forefathers which is gone
before you, which Christ cried woe against, for in their steps you are walking and
bear forth their image. To all those that see you who are in the light, they may read
you with the measure of God which makes all things manifest, and with it you are
seen and made manifest, whose children you are and whose kingdom you uphold.
Oh, consider of it, ye children of anti-Christ who are fighting against Christ and is
seeking as much as in you lies to put him to death, in his appearance. Oh, ye ungodly and unwise, do you think to prosper who fight against God? I tell you, nay.
For the Lord God is arisen in his mighty power for the redemption of his seed
which you seek to keep in bondage; but this all know from the least to the greatest
of you who have given consent, and is joined together as one in making a law

contrary to that of God in your consciences, to banish upon pain of death all those whom the Lord hath sent, and doth send among you to declare his will to you; and what he will bring upon you if you go on in your iniquities and execute your law which you have made in your own wills for to put the innocent to death. For thus saith the Lord, to whom you must all bend and bow: it shall surely come to pass if you execute your law upon my servants in putting them to death, I the Lord will execute my judgments speedily upon you, and will add to your torment seven-fold; for a fire I will kindle in the midst of you, even in your bosoms, which shall consume you and eat you up as doth a canker, and in my wrath and in my fury will I destroy you with a sore destruction, saith the Lord God Almighty, if you do not speedily repent. For none among you shall escape my righteous judgments who are found fighting against me in this day of my power, when I am arisen in my might to overturn my enemies, that rise up in opposition against me and will not have me to reign over you as Lord and King, but sets me at naught, and rejects my pure witness in you because it testifies against you that your deeds are evil. Therefore cease from your oppression and repent at your bloodshed. It cries to the God of Heaven for a vengeance against you for you be a deceitful people, and your iniquities doth abound, and the sound of it is going over the nations that are about you. Oh, consider and lay it to heart, ye priests and magistrates in the town of Boston, and elsewhere in the nation who is exalted in your own wisdom, and seeks honour one of another and is called to your places by one another, and so receives your commissions from man and not from the Lord. How do you think the Lord can own you when you are not chosen by him, but by one another, and so holds upon one another in your abominations, and joins hand in hand to persecute the innocent? Oh, blush for shame, all ye who had some tenderness in you time past, which made some of you leave your own native country for consciences' sake. But you fled the cross when you should have stood in it, and so lost the sense of the law of God that his fear departed from you. Then did your hearts grow hard when your minds were adulterated from him, and so have remained in the dark. Yet have you professed him in words, as the Scribes and Pharisees did, and have drawn near him with your lips and with your mouths, as they did; that the true prophet Isaiah spoke to, but your hearts is removed far from him as theirs was, for thus saith the Lord of hosts, the God of his people Israel: when you make long prayers in your own wills, I will not hear you, for you seek to shed the blood of my servants which I have sent unto you, and to trap them in your snares. Therefore will I not have regard unto your fasts which you make, nor your meetings together, for it is abomination unto me, saith the Lord. My sense loathes it and abhors it, for it is an ill savour in my nostrils, and I will spread it as dung upon your faces if you will not let the oppressed go free and let me reign in my own. I will consume you in my anger, and you shall become an abhorring to all that know you, for my eternal decree is gone over you all, and that which I have spoken shall be accomplished if you do not speedily repent. In the wine-press of my wrath shall you be trodden if you hate to be reformed and refuse to return and hearken to my call; who would not have you to perish and die in your sins, and whether you will hear or forbear, this is my word, saith the

Lord, to you here declared, which shall be as arrows in your sides, to wound you to the heart, if you go on in your stiffneckedness, and will fully resist me in my way: which I have made known to my people to walk in who are of an upright heart and stands in my pure counsel, and abides in my fear–all such you hate and hails out of your assemblies they who come among you to declare against your abominations, which you have long lived in, for the wise in heart sees you, though you be gotten high in your own wisdoms and airy imaginations, out of the cross and from the life and out of the covenant which is to the seed whom the Lord hath blessed; for all that joins with the seed, they join with Christ and all that joins with him are taught of him, and such comes into his image, to be meek and lowly as he was; to bear all things with patience that can be inflicted upon them; and all who takes up his cross must follow him through sufferings, and be reviled with the world wherever they go, and be called fools and deceivers, wanderers and vagabonds by the adulterous generation whose hearts are removed far from the Lord. Oh, consider this, ye priests and rulers of New England, and let the faithful and true witness of God in you all arise and answer, and if it will let you see that you are the wanderers and deceivers whose hearts are adulterated from the Lord. For time was that some of you was tender and tasted something of the love of God, but now you have lost it again, and the sense of your condition which you were then in is now vanished away, and so you are become strangers to what you once did know. In letting your minds go out after other lovers, you have lost your first love, and so is adulterated from the Lord and separated from the God of your life, and have not a habitation in him and so is seen to be in Cain's nature labouring to put the innocent to death, as the Scribes and Pharisees did, who were enemies to the truth as you are at this day, for you are persecuting the same spirit that they persecuted. So remember whose children they were who called Christ a deceiver and the apostle a mad man. You are their brethren, for their image you bear and into their nature you are grown, and is labouring to bring forth the same fruit which they brought forth in persecuting the innocent as they did. But remember what was their portion for what they had done; and so it will be yours if you continue in your iniquity and fulfil your law which you have made in putting the innocent to death. You shall surely perish and die in your sins, and this from the Lord God do I declare unto you: that sorrow and torment shall come speedily upon you as upon a woman in travail, and you shall in no wise escape it nor fly from it. So remember what the Lord hath spoken aforehand to you before the thing to be executed, that so if you perish it is through your own wilfulness. So slight not the counsel of the Lord nor make a mock of his reproof in hardening your hearts and stopping your ears from hearing of his word lest he come suddenly upon you at unawares and sweep you away with the besom of his wrath into the pit of perdition. And verily it will be so with you if you harden your hearts still against the Lord and wilfully resist him in his way which he is making known to his sons and daughters for to walk in; to bear forth their testimony of him in this day of his mighty power, wherein he will break down all his enemies that are gotten into high swelling words, and into great and large professions, out of the possession of what they do profess; and such are the hypocrites and dissemblers and enemies to God who persecutes the life and substance of that in others which they themselves are gone from, and truly this your state. Therefore put it not from you, for many is come in this day of the Lord's love, to taste much of the good things of God and doth enjoy the substance and life of God which you who are high in profession have not. Therefore do you storm and rage against them because they are in that which you are gone from, for you have slain the witness in yourselves, and you seek to slay it in others, for you labour to shut up the kingdom of Heaven against men, and will not enter in yourselves, nor suffer others, and all you who are found in this condition, your state is sad and miserable, which causeth my heart to be broken and my eyes to run down with tears, to see how your hearts is hardened and your eyes is blinded; yet you do nor will not see what you are striving and fighting against. Oh, consider you are striving against him which is too hard for you, who will try you in your law which you have, in your own wills. For some among you are ready to balk because you have made some to fly out of your jurisdiction where they had outward subsistence to live upon; because they could not bow down to you nor submit to your wills. Therefore have you banished them away, upon pain of death. Oh, consider and see if that spirit do not rule in you at present which ruled in them of old England which caused some of you for to leave them. Oh, what a filthy and abominable thing this is to hear: that you should be persecuted for conscience sake and live to come to persecute others even unto death, because they are come to possess the life and substance of that which you profess in words, and therefore is your hatred against them. Therefore hath the Lord required it and laid it upon some of his servants for to try you unto death, that if you satisfy your wills upon them, the Lord will do with you as he hath determined. So remember you are warned of the thing in your lifetime, before the evil day come upon you. By the spirit of the living God. From us who was counted fools among you but is content to be so. Whose names in the flesh is

WILLIAM ROBINSON AND
MARMADUKE STEVENSON

85B. The General Court's justification of the persecution of Quakers (1659)

Printed: Massachusetts Historical Society *Proceedings*, XLII, p. 203.

Although the justice of our proceedings against William Robinson, Marmaduke Stevenson, and Mary Dyer, supported by the authority of this court, the laws of the country, and the law of God, may rather persuade us to expect encouragement and commendation from all prudent and pious men, than convince us of any necessity to apologize for the same, yet for as much as men of weaker parts, out of pity and commiseration (a commendable and Christian virtue, yet easily abused, and susceptible of sinister and dangerous impressions) for want of full information, may be less satisfied, and men of perverser principles may take occasion hereby to calumniate us, and render us as bloody persecutors; to satisfy the one, and stop the mouths of the other, we thought it requisite to declare: That about three years since divers persons, professing themselves Quakers (of whose pernicious opinions and practices we had received intelligence from good hands, from Barbados to England, arrived at Boston), whose persons were only secured to be sent away by the first opportunity, without censure or punishment, although their professed tenets, turbulent, and contemptuous behaviour to authority would have justified a severer animadversion; yet the prudence of this court was exercised only in making provision to secure the peace and order here established, against their attempts, whose design (we were well assured of by our own experience, as well as by the example of their predecessors in Münster) was to undermine and ruin the same; and accordingly a law was made and published prohibiting all masters of ships to bring any Quakers into this jurisdiction, and themselves from coming in, on penalty of the house of correction, till they could be sent away. Notwithstanding which, by a back door they found entrance, and the penalty inflicted on themselves, proving insufficient to restrain their impudent and insolent obtrusions, was increased by the loss of the ears of those that offended the second time, which also being too weak a defence against their impetuous frantic fury, necessitated us to endeavour our security, and upon serious consideration, after the former experiments, by their incessant assaults, a law was made, that such persons should be banished, on pain of death, according to the example of England in their provision against Jesuits, which sentence being regularly pronounced at the last Court of Assistants against the parties above named, and they either returning, or continuing presumptuously in this jurisdiction, after the time limited, were apprehended, and owning themselves to be the persons banished, were sentenced (by the court) to death, according the law aforesaid, which hath been executed upon two of them. Mary Dyer upon the petition of her son, and the mercy and clemency of this court, had liberty to depart within two days, which she hath accepted of. The consideration of our gradual proceeding will vindicate us from the clamorous accusations of severity; our own just and necessary defence, calling upon us (other means failing) to offer the point which these persons have violently and wilfully rushed upon, and thereby become *felons de se*, which might it have been prevented, and the sovereign law *salus populi* been preserved, our former proceedings, as well as the sparing of Mary Dyer, upon an inconsiderable intercession, will manifestly evince, we desire their lives absent, rather than their death present.

86A–C. The Great Awakening

The Great Awakening was a revival movement which swept through the American colonies. It began among the Dutch Reformed churches in the Middle Colonies and reached its peak in the early 1740's during the first American tour of George Whitefield. Theologically the movement was a protest against liberal religious ideas which were making headway in the colonies, and particularly the Arminian doctrine that man was free to choose or reject salvation. Most of the preachers of the Great Awakening supported the Calvinist idea of election and predestination and inveighed against the wickedness of preachers of the new doctrines. But the Great Awakening went far beyond theological controversy. Whatever church they belonged to, its preachers gave up the intellectual formalism of seventeenth-century sermons and indulged in emotional appeals that brought about extraordinary and hysterical outbursts on the part of their audiences. Many of these men became itinerant evangelists, following the example of Whitefield.

The Great Awakening had many results. The movement had political overtones as well as religious, for the 'New Lights' gained their greatest following among back-country farmers and the common people of the colonial towns and won the enmity of the planter and merchant aristocracies and their ministerial allies. These latter, the 'Old Lights', on the whole defended liberal ideas in religion and deplored the mass emotionalism of the New Lights. Church membership increased remarkably, but established churches were weakened because many congregations split into rival churches. Educationally the movement resulted in the founding of many colleges, for the New Lights deplored the unorthodoxy of such institutions as Harvard and Yale.

86A. Jonathan Edwards: from "A Faithful Narrative of the Surprising Work of God" (1737)

The intellectual leader of the Great Awakening was Jonathan Edwards (1703–1758), pastor at Northampton, Massachusetts from 1729 to 1750. In 1734 he began preaching a series of sermons against Arminian ideas which led to an extraordinary outburst of religious enthusiasm. In 1737 he published a remarkably detached account of the religious experiences he had witnessed in his congregation under the title, *A Faithful Narrative of the Surprising Work of God, in the Conversion of Many Hundred Souls, in Northampton, And the Neighbouring Towns and Villages of New Hampshire, in New England: in a Letter to the Reverend Dr. Colman, of Boston*. The following document is the "general introductory statement" from this work. By 1750 the fervour of the movement had declined so far that he was forced from his pastorate and became a missionary to the Stockbridge Indians in western Massachusetts. While among them he wrote *Freedom of the Will* in answer to Arminian and deistic ideas against which he had so long preached. In 1757 he became president of the College of New Jersey (Princeton), which had been founded as a result of the Great Awakening, but he died within a few weeks after taking office. Printed: *The Works of President Edwards* (8 vols., London, 1817), III, pp. 9–23.

The people of the country in general, I suppose, are as sober, orderly, and good sort of people as in any part of New England, and I believe they have been preserved the freest by far of any part of the country from error and variety of sects and opinions. Our being so far within the land, at a distance from seaports, and in a corner of the country, has doubtless been one reason why we have not been so much corrupted with vice as most other parts. But without question, the religion and good order of the county, and purity in doctrine, has, under God, been very much owing to the great abilities and eminent piety of my venerable and honoured grandfather, [Solomon] Stoddard. I suppose we have been the freest of any part of the land from unhappy divisions and quarrels in our ecclesiastical and religious affairs till the late lamentable Springfield contention.

Being much separated from other parts of the province and having comparatively but little intercourse with them, we have always managed our ecclesiastical affairs within ourselves. It is the way in which the country from its infancy has gone on, by the practical agreement of all, and the way in which our peace and good order has hitherto been maintained.

The town of Northampton is of about 82 years standing, and has now about 200 families which mostly dwell more compactly together than any town of such a size in these parts of the country. This probably has been an occasion, that both our corruptions and reformations have been, from time to time, the more swiftly propagated from one to another through the town. Take the town in general, and so far as I can judge, they are as rational and intelligent a people as most I have been acquainted with. Many of them have been noted for religion and particularly remarkable for their distinct knowledge in things that relate to heart religion and Christian experience, and their great regards thereto.

I am the third minister who has been settled in the town. The Rev. Mr. Eleazer Mather, who was the first, was ordained in July, 1669. He was one whose heart was much in his work, and abundant in labours for the good of precious souls. He had the high esteem and great love of his people, and was blessed with no small success. The Rev. Mr. Stoddard, who succeeded him, came first to the town the November after his death, but was not ordained till September 11, 1672, and died February 11, 1728–9. So that he continued in the work of the ministry here from his first coming to town, near 60 years. And as he was eminent and renowned for his gifts and grace, so he was blessed from the beginning with extraordinary success in his ministry, in the conversion of many souls. He had five harvests, as he called them. The first was about 57 years ago; the second about 53; the third about 40; the fourth about 24; the fifth and last about 18 years ago. Some of these times were much more remarkable than others and the ingathering of souls more plentiful. Those about 53 and 40, and 24 years ago, were much greater than either the first or the last, but in each of them, I have heard my grandfather say, the greater part of the young people in the town seemed to be mainly concerned for their eternal salvation.

After the last of these, came a far more degenerate time (at least among the young people), I suppose, than ever before. Mr. Stoddard, indeed, had the comfort, before he died, of seeing a time where there were no small appearances of a divine work among some, and a considerable ingathering of souls, even after I was settled with him in the ministry, which was about two years before his death, and I have reason to bless God for the great advantage I had by it. In these two years there were nearly twenty that Mr. Stoddard hoped to be savingly converted, but there was nothing of any general awakening. The greater part seemed to be at that time very insensible of the things of religion, and engaged in other cares and pursuits. Just after my grandfather's death, it seemed to be a time of extraordinary dullness in religion. Licentiousness for some years greatly prevailed among the youth of the town; they were many of them very much addicted to night-walking, and frequenting the tavern, and lewd practices, wherein some, by their example, exceedingly corrupted others. It was their manner very frequently to get together, in conventions of both sexes, for mirth and jollity, which they called frolics; and they would often spend the greater part of the night in them, without regard to any order in the families they belonged to, and indeed family government did too much fail in the town. It was become very customary with many of our young people to be indecent in their carriage at meeting, which doubtless would not have prevailed in such a degree, had it not been that my grandfather through his great age (though he retained his powers surprisingly to the last), was not so able to observe them. There had also long prevailed in the town a spirit of contention between two parties, into which they had for many years been divided; by which they maintained a jealousy one of the other, and were prepared to oppose one another in all public affairs.

But in two or three years after Mr. Stoddard's death, there began to be a sensible amendment of these evils. The young people showed more of a disposition to hearken to counsel and by degrees left off their frolics; they grew observably more decent in their attendance on the public worship, and there were more who manifested a religious concern than there used to be.

At the latter end of the year 1733 there appeared a very unusual flexibleness and yielding to advice in our young people. It had been too long their manner to make the evening after the Sabbath, and after our public lecture, to be especially the times of their mirth and company-keeping. But a sermon was now preached on the Sabbath before the lecture, to show the evil tendency of the practice and to persuade them to reform it; and it was urged on heads of families that it should be a thing agreed upon among them, to govern their families, and keep their children at home, at these times. It was also more privately moved that they should meet together the next day, in their several neighbourhoods, to know each other's minds, which was accordingly done, and the motion complied with throughout the town. But parents found little or no occasion for the exercise of government in the case. The young people declared themselves convinced by what they had heard from the pulpit, and were willing of themselves to comply with the counsel that had been given; and it was immediately, and I suppose, almost universally complied with, and there was a thorough reformation of these disorders thenceforward, which has continued ever since.

Presently after this, there began to appear a remarkable religious concern at a little village belonging to the congregation called Pascommuck, where a few families were settled, at about three miles distance from the main body of the town. At this place, a number of persons seemed to be savingly wrought upon. In the April following, *Anno* 1734, there happened a very sudden and awful death of a young man in the bloom of his youth, who being violently seized with a pleurisy, and taken immediately very delirious, died in about two days, which (together with what was preached publicly on that occasion) much affected many young people. This was followed with another death of a young married woman who had been considerably exercised in mind about the salvation of her soul, before she was ill, and was in great distress in the beginning of her illness; but seemed to have satisfying evidences of God's saving mercy to her before her death so that she died very full of comfort, in a most earnest and moving manner warning and counselling others. This seemed to contribute to render solemn the spirits of many young persons and there began evidently to appear more of a religious concern on people's minds.

In the fall of the year I proposed it to the young people, that they should agree among themselves to spend the evenings after lectures in social religion and to that end divide themselves into several companies to meet in various parts of the town; which was accordingly done and those meetings have been since continued and the example imitated by elder people. This was followed with the death of an elderly person, which was attended with many unusual circumstances, by which many were much moved and affected.

About this time began the great noise, in this part of the country, about Arminianism, which seemed to appear with a very threatening aspect upon the interest of religion here. The friends of vital piety trembled for fear of the issue, but it seemed, contrary to their fear, strongly to be over-ruled for the promoting of religion. Many who looked on themselves as in a Christless condition, seemed to be awakened by it with fear that God was about to withdraw from the land, and that we should be given up to heterodoxy and corrupt principles and that then their opportunity for obtaining salvation would be past. Many who were brought a little to doubt about the truth of the doctrines they had hitherto been taught seemed to have a kind of trembling fear with their doubts, lest they should be led into bypaths, to their eternal undoing; and they seemed, with much concern and engagedness of mind, to inquire what was indeed the way in which they must come to be accepted with God. There were some things said publicly on that occasion concerning justification by faith alone.

Although great fault was found with meddling with the controversy in the pulpit, by such a person, and at that time–and though it was ridiculed by many elsewhere–yet it proved a word spoken in season here and was most evidently attended with a very remarkable blessing of heaven to the souls of the people in this town. They received thence a general satisfaction, with respect to the main thing in question, which they had been in trembling doubts and concern about; and their minds were engaged the more earnestly to seek that they might come to be accepted of God, and saved in the way of the gospel, which had been made evident to them to be the true and only way. And then it was, in the latter part of December, that the Spirit of God began extraordinarily to set in and wonderfully to work amongst us; and there were, very suddenly, one after another, five or six persons who were to all appearance savingly converted, and some of them wrought upon in a very remarkable manner.

Particularly I was surprised with the relation of a young woman who had been one of the greatest company-keepers in the whole town. When she came to me I had never heard that she was become in any wise serious, but by the conversation I then had with her, it appeared to me that what she gave an account of was a glorious work of God's infinite power and sovereign grace and that God had given her a new heart, truly broken and sanctified. I could not then doubt of it, and have seen much in my acquaintance with her since to confirm it.

Though the work was glorious, yet I was filled with concern about the effect it might have upon others. I was ready to conclude (though too rashly) that some would be hardened by it, in carelessness and looseness of life, and would take occasion from it to open their mouths in reproaches of religion. But the event was the reverse, to a wonderful degree. God made it, I suppose, the greatest occasion of awakening to others of anything that ever came to pass in the town. I have had abundant opportunity to know the effect it had, by my private conversation with many. The news of it seemed to be almost like a flash of lightning upon the hearts of young people all over the town, and upon many others. Those persons amongst us who used to be farthest from seriousness and that I most feared would make an ill improvement of it, seemed greatly to be awakened with it. Many went to talk with her concerning what she had met with and what appeared in her seemed to be to the satisfaction of all that did so.

Presently upon this, a great and earnest concern about the great things of religion and the eternal world became universal in all parts of the town and among persons of all degrees and all ages. The noise amongst the dry bones waxed louder and louder; all other talk but about spiritual and eternal things was soon thrown by; all the conversation, in all companies and upon all occasions, was upon these things only, unless so much as was necessary for people carrying on their ordinary secular business. Other discourse than of the things of religion would scarcely be tolerated in any company. The minds of people were wonderfully taken off from the world, it was treated amongst us as a thing of very little consequence. They seemed to follow their worldly business more as a part of their duty than from any disposition they had to it; the temptation now seemed to lie on that hand, to neglect worldly affairs too much and to spend too much time in the immediate exercise of religion. This was exceedingly misrepresented by reports that were spread in distant parts of the land, as though the people here had wholly thrown by all worldly business and betook themselves entirely to reading and praying, and such like religious exercises.

But although people did not ordinarily neglect their worldly business, yet religion was with all sorts the great concern, and the world was a thing only by the by. The only thing in their view was to get the kingdom of heaven, and everyone appeared pressing into it. The engagedness of their hearts in this great concern could not be hid, it appeared in their very countenances. It then was a dreadful thing amongst us to lie out of Christ, in danger every day of dropping into hell, and what persons' minds were intent upon was to escape for their lives and to fly from the wrath to come. All would eagerly lay hold of opportunities for their souls and were wont very often to meet together in private houses for religious purposes, and such meetings, when appointed, were greatly thronged.

There was scarcely a single person in the town, old or young, left unconcerned about the great things of the eternal world. Those who were wont to be the vainest and loosest; and those who had been most disposed to think and speak slightly of vital and experimental religion, were now generally subject to great awakenings. And the work of conversion was carried on in a most astonishing manner, and increased more and more; souls did, as it were, come by flocks to Jesus Christ. From day to day, for many months together, might be seen evident instances of sinners brought out of darkness into marvellous light, and delivered out of an horrible pit and from the miry clay, and set upon a rock with a new song of praise to God in their mouths.

This work of God, as it was carried on, and the number of true saints multiplied, soon made a glorious alteration in the town, so that in the spring and summer following, *Anno* 1735, the town seemed to be full of the presence of God. It never was so full of love, nor of joy, and yet so full of distress, as it was then. There were remarkable tokens of God's presence in almost every house. It was a time of joy in families on account of salvation being brought unto them; parents rejoicing over their children as new born, and husbands over their wives, and wives over their husbands. The doings of God were then seen in his sanctuary, God's day was a delight, and his tabernacles were amiable. Our public assemblies were then beautiful; the congregation was alive in God's service, everyone earnestly intent on the public worship, every hearer eager to drink in the words of the minister as they came from his mouth; the assembly in general were, from time to time, in tears while the word was preached; some weeping with sorrow and distress, others with joy and love, others with pity and concern for the souls of their neighbours.

Our public praises were then greatly enlivened; God was then served in our psalmody, in some measure, in the beauty of holiness. It has been observable, that there has been scarce any part of divine worship wherein good men amongst us have had grace so drawn forth and their hearts so lifted up in the ways of God, as in singing his praises. Our congregation excelled all that ever I knew in the external part of the duty before, the men generally carrying regularly and well three parts of music, and the women a part by themselves; but now they were evidently wont to sing with unusual elevation of heart and voice, which made the duty pleasant indeed.

In all companies, on other days, on whatever occasions persons met together, Christ was to be heard of and seen in the midst of them. Our young people, when they met, were wont to spend the time in talking of the excellency and dying love of Jesus Christ, the glory of the way of salvation, the wonderful, free, and sovereign grace of God, his glorious work in the conversion of a soul, the truth and certainty of the great things of God's word, the sweetness of the views of his perfections, etc. And even at weddings, which formerly were mere occasions of mirth and jollity, there was now no discourse of anything but religion, and no appearance of any but spiritual mirth. Those amongst us who had been formerly converted, were greatly enlivened, and renewed with fresh and extraordinary incomes of the spirit of God; though some much more than others, according to the measure of the gift of Christ. Many who before had laboured under difficulties about their own state, had now their doubts removed by more satisfying experience, and more clear discoveries of God's love.

When this work first appeared and was so extraordinarily carried on amongst us in the winter, others round about us seemed not to know what to make of it. Many scoffed at and ridiculed it and some compared what we called conversion to certain distempers. But it was very observable of many who occasionally came amongst us from abroad with disregardful hearts, that what they saw here cured them of such a temper of mind. Strangers were generally surprised to find things so much beyond what they had heard and were wont to tell others that the state of the town could not be conceived of by those who had not seen it. The notice that was taken of it by the people who came to town on occasion of the court that sat here in the beginning of March, was very observable. And those who came from the neighbourhood to our public lectures were for the most part remarkably affected. Many who came to town, on one occasion or other, had their consciences smitten and awakened, and went home with wounded hearts and with those impressions that never wore off till they had hopefully a saving issue; and those who before had serious thoughts had their awakenings and convictions greatly increased. There were many instances of persons who came from abroad on visits, or on business, who had not been long here before; to all appearance they were savingly wrought upon and partook of that shower of divine blessing which God rained down here, and went home rejoicing, till at length the same work began evidently to appear and prevail in several other towns in the county.

In the month of March the people in South Hadley began to be seized with deep concern about the things of religion, which very soon became universal. The work of God has been very wonderful there; not much, if anything, short of what it has been here, in proportion to the size of the place. About the same time it began to break forth in the west part of Suffield (where it also has been very great) and it soon spread into all parts of the town. It next appeared at Sunderland, and soon overspread the town, and I believe was, for a season, not less remarkable than it was here. About the same time it began to appear in a part of Deerfield, called Green River, and afterwards filled the town, and there has been a glorious work there. It began also to be manifest in the south part of Hatfield, in a place called the Hill, and the whole town, in the second week in April, seemed to be seized, as it were at once, with concern about the things of religion, and the work of God has been great there. There has been also a very general awakening at West Springfield and Long Meadow; and in Enfield there was for a time a pretty general concern amongst some who before had been very loose persons. About the same time that this appeared at Enfield, the Rev. Mr. Bull, of Westfield, informed me that there had been a great alteration there and that more had been done in one week than in seven years before. Something of this work likewise appeared in the first precinct in Springfield, principally in the north and south extremes of the parish. And in Hadley Old Town there gradually appeared so much of a work of God on souls as at another time would have been thought worthy of much notice. For a short time there was also a very great and general concern of the like nature at Northfield. And wherever this concern appeared, it seemed not to be in vain, but in every place God brought saving blessings with him and his word attended with his spirit (as we have all reason to think) returned not void. It might well be said at that time, in all parts of the county, *who are these that fly as a cloud, and as doves to their windows?*

As what other towns heard of and found in this, was a great means of awakening them; so our hearing of such a swift and extraordinary propagation and extent of this work, did doubtless for a time serve to uphold the work amongst us. The continual news kept alive the talk of religion and did greatly quicken and rejoice the hearts of God's people, and much awakened those who looked on themselves as still left behind, and made them the more earnest that they also might share in the great blessings that others had obtained.

This remarkable pouring out of the Spirit of God, which thus extended from one end to the other of this county, was not confined to it but many places in Connecticut have partaken in the same mercy. For instance, the first parish in Windsor, under the pastoral care of the Rev. Mr. Marsh, was thus blest about the same time as we in Northampton, while we had no knowledge of each other's circumstances. There has been a very great ingathering of souls to Christ in that place, and something considerable of the same work begun afterwards in East Windsor, my honoured father's parish, which has in times past been a place favoured with mercies of this nature, above any on this western side of New England, excepting Northampton, there having been four or five seasons of the pouring out of the spirit to the general awakening of the people there since my father's settlement amongst them.

There was also the last spring and summer a wonderful work of God carried on at Coventry, under the ministry of the Rev. Mr. Meacham. I had opportunity to converse with some Coventry people, who gave me a very remarkable account of the surprising change that appeared in the most rude and vicious persons there. The like was also very great at the same time in a part of Lebanon, called the Crank, where the Rev. Mr. Wheelock, a young gentleman, is lately settled; and there has been much of the same at Durham, under the ministry of the Rev. Mr. Chauncey, and to appearance, no small ingathering of souls there. Likewise amongst many of the young people in the first precinct in Stratford, under the ministry of the Rev. Mr. Gould, where the work was much promoted by the remarkable conversion of a young woman who had been a great company-keeper, as it was here.

Something of this work appeared in several other towns in those parts, as I was informed when I was there, the last fall. And we have since been acquainted with something very remarkable of this nature at another parish in Stratford, called Ripton, under the pastoral care of the Rev. Mr. Mills. There was a considerable revival of religion last summer at Newhaven Old Town, as I was once and again informed by the Rev. Mr. Noyes, the minister there, and by others, and by a letter which I very lately received from Mr. Noyes, and also by information we have had other ways. This flourishing of religion still continues, and has lately much increased. Mr. Noyes writes that many this summer have been added to the church, and particularly mentions several young persons that belong to the principal families of that town.

There has been a degree of the same work at a part of Guildford, and very considerable at Mansfield, under the ministry of the Rev. Mr. Eleazar Williams; and an unusual religious concern at Tolland, and something of it at Hebron and Bolton. There was also no small effusion of the spirit of God in the north parish in Preston, in the eastern part of Connecticut, of which I was informed and saw something when I was the last autumn at the house, and in the congregation of the Rev. Mr. Lord, the minister there, who, with the Rev. Mr. Owen of Groton, came up hither in May, the last year, on purpose to see the work of God. Having heard various and contradictory accounts of it, they were careful when here to satisfy themselves; and to that end particularly conversed with many of our people, which they declared to be entirely to their satisfaction, and that the one half had not been told them, nor could be told them. Mr. Lord told me that when he got home he informed his congregation of what he had seen and that they were greatly affected with it and that it proved the beginning of the same work amongst them, which prevailed till there was a general awakening, and many instances of persons who seemed to be remarkably converted. I also have lately heard that there has been something of the same work at Woodbury.

But this shower of divine blessing has been yet more extensive: there was no small degree of it in some parts of the Jerseys, as I was informed when I was at New York (in a long journey I took at that time of the year for my health) by some people of the Jerseys, whom I saw. Especially the Rev. William Tennent, a minister who seemed to have such things much at heart, told me of a very great awakening of many in a place called the Mountains, under the ministry of one Mr. Cross; and of a very considerable revival of religion in another place under the ministry of his brother, the Rev. Gilbert Tennent; and also at another place, under the ministry of a very pious young gentleman, a Dutch minister, whose name, as I remember, was Freelinghousa [Theodorus Frelinghuysen].

This seems to have been a very extraordinary dispensation of providence; God has in many respects gone out of, and much beyond his usual, and ordinary way. The work in this town, and some others about us, has been extraordinary on account of the universality of it, affecting all sorts, sober and vicious, high and low, rich and poor, wise and unwise. It reached the most considerable families and persons, to all appearance, as much as others. In former stirrings of this nature, the bulk of the young people have been greatly affected; but old men and little children have been so now. Many of the last have, of their own accord, formed themselves into religious societies, in different parts of the town. A loose careless person could scarcely be found in the whole neighbourhood; and if there was any one that seemed to remain senseless or unconcerned, it would be spoken of as a strange thing.

This dispensation has also appeared very extraordinary in the numbers of those on whom we have reason to hope it has had a saving effect. We have about six hundred and twenty communicants, which include almost all our adult persons. The church was very large before, but persons never thronged into it as they did in the late extraordinary time. Our sacraments are eight weeks asunder, and I received into our communion about a hundred before one sacrament, fourscore of them at one time, whose appearance, when they presented themselves together to make an open explicit profession of Christianity, was very affecting to the congregation. I took in near sixty before the next sacrament day, and I had very sufficient evidence of the conversion of their souls, through divine grace, though it is not the custom here, as it is in many other churches in this country, to make a credible relation of their inward experiences the ground of admission to the Lord's Supper.

I am far from pretending to be able to determine how many have lately been the subjects of such mercy; but if I may be allowed to declare anything that appears to me probable in a thing of this nature, I hope that more than 300 souls were savingly brought home to Christ, in this town, in the space of half a year, and about the same number of males as females. By what I have heard Mr. Stoddard say, this was far from what has been usual in years past, for he observed that in his time many more women were converted than men. Those of our young people who are on other accounts most considerable, are mostly, as I hope, truly pious, and leading persons in the ways of religion. Those who were formerly looser young persons are generally, to all appearance, become true lovers of God and Christ, and spiritual in their dispositions. I hope that by far the greater part of persons in this town, above sixteen years of age, are such as have the saving knowledge of Jesus Christ. By what I have heard I suppose it is so in some other places, particularly at Sunderland and South Hadley.

This has also appeared to be a very extraordinary dispensation in that the spirit of God has so much extended not only his awakening, but regenerating influences, both to elderly persons and also those who are very young. It has been heretofore rarely heard of, that any were converted past middle age, but now we have the same ground to think that many such have at this time been savingly changed as that others have been so in more early years. I suppose there were upwards of fifty persons converted in this town above forty years of age; more than twenty of them above fifty; about ten of them above sixty; and two of them above seventy years of age.

It has heretofore been looked on as a strange thing when any have seemed to be savingly wrought upon and remarkably changed in their childhood. But now, I suppose, near thirty were, to appearance, savingly wrought upon between ten and fourteen years of age; two between nine and ten, and one of about four years of age; and because I suppose this last will be with most difficulty believed, I will hereafter give a particular account of it. The influences of God's Holy Spirit have also been very remarkable on children in some other places: particularly at Sunderland, South Hadley, and the west part of Suffield. There are several families in this town who are all hopefully pious. Yea, there are several numerous families in which, I think, we have reason to hope that all the children are truly godly, and most of them lately become so. There are very few houses in the whole town into which salvation has not lately come in one or more instances. There are several Negroes who from what was seen in them then, and what is discernible in them since, appear to have been truly born again in the late remarkable season.

God has also seemed to have gone out of his usual way in the quickness of his work and the swift progress his Spirit has made in his operations on the hearts of many. It is wonderful that persons should be so suddenly, and yet so greatly changed. Many have been taken from a loose and careless way of living and seized with strong convictions of their guilt and misery, and in a very little time old things have passed away, and all things have become new with them.

God's work has also appeared very extraordinary in the degrees of his influences; in the degrees both of awakening and conviction, and also of saving light, love, and joy that many have experienced. It has also been very extraordinary in the extent of it and its being so swiftly propagated from town to town. In former times of the pouring out of the Spirit of God on this town, though in some of them it was very remarkable, it reached no further . . .; the neighbouring towns all around continued unmoved.

This work seemed to be at its greatest height in this town in the former part of the spring, in March and April. At that time God's work in the conversion of souls was carried on amongst us in so wonderful a manner that, so far as I can judge, it appears to have been at the rate, at least, of four persons in a day, or near thirty in a week, take one with another, for five or six weeks together. When God in so remarkable a manner took the work into his own hands, there was as much done in a day or two as at ordinary times, with all endeavours that men can use, and with such a blessing as we commonly have, is done in a year.

I am very sensible how apt many would be, if they should see the account I have here given, presently to think with themselves that I am very fond of making a great many converts, and of magnifying the matter; and to think that for want of judgment I take every religious pang and enthusiastic conceit for saving conversion. I do not much wonder if they should be apt to think so, and for this reason I have forborne to publish an account of this great work of God, though I have often been solicited. But having now a special call to give an account of it, upon mature consideration

I thought it might not be beside my duty to declare this amazing work, as it appeared to me to be indeed divine, and to conceal no part of the glory of it; leaving it with God to take care of the credit of his own work, and running the venture of any censorious thoughts which might be entertained of me to my disadvantage. That distant persons may be under as great advantage as may be to judge for themselves of this matter, I would be a little more large and particular.

86B. George Whitefield in Middletown, Connecticut (23 October 1740)

The most eloquent and effective preacher during the Great Awakening was George Whitefield. The following account of his impact is virtually unique. It is taken from the "Spiritual Travels" of Nathan Cole, a farmer and carpenter in Connecticut. It is printed here with the permission of the Connecticut Historical Society and of Professor Leonard W. Labaree, who wrote an introduction and prepared it for publication. Printed: "George Whitefield Comes to Middletown", in *The William and Mary Quarterly*, 3rd Series, VII (1950), pp. 590–591.

Now it pleased God to send Mr. Whitefield into this land; and my hearing of his preaching at Philadelphia, like one of the old apostles, and many thousands flocking to hear him preach the Gospel, and great numbers were converted to Christ, I felt the Spirit of God drawing me by conviction; I longed to see and hear him and wished he would come this way. I heard he was come to New York and the Jerseys and great multitudes flocking after him under great concern for their souls which brought on my concern more and more, hoping soon to see him; but next I heard he was at Long Island, then at Boston, and next at Northampton. Then on a sudden, in the morning about 8 or 9 of the clock there came a messenger and said Mr. Whitefield preached at Hartford and Wethersfield yesterday and is to preach at Middletown this morning at ten of the clock. I was in my field at work. I dropped my tool that I had in my hand and ran home to my wife, telling her to make ready quickly to go and hear Mr. Whitefield preach at Middletown, then run to my pasture for my horse with all my might, fearing that I should be too late. Having my horse, I with my wife soon mounted the horse and went forward as fast as I thought the horse could bear; and when my horse got much out of breath, I would get down and put my wife on the saddle and bid her ride as fast as she could and not stop or slack for me except I bade her, and so I would run until I was much out of breath and then mount my horse again, and so I did several times to favour my horse. We improved every moment to get along as if we were fleeing for our lives, all the while fearing we should be too late to hear the sermon; for we had twelve miles to ride double in little more than an hour and we went round by the upper housen parish. And when we came within about half a mile or a mile of the road that comes down from Hartford, Wethersfield, and Stepney to Middletown, on high land I saw before me a cloud or fog rising. I first thought it came from the great river, but as I came nearer the road I heard a noise something like a low rumbling thunder and presently found it was the noise of horses' feet coming down the road, and this cloud was a cloud of dust made by the horses' feet. It arose some rods into the air over the tops of hills and trees; and when I came within about 20 rods of the road, I could see men and horses slipping along in the cloud like shadows, and as I drew nearer it seemed like a steady stream of horses and their riders, scarcely a horse more than his length behind another, all of a lather and foam with sweat, their breath rolling out of their nostrils every jump. Every horse seemed to go with all his might to carry his rider to hear news from heaven for the saving of souls. It made me tremble to see the sight, how the world was in a struggle. I found a vacancy between two horses to slip in mine and my wife said "Law, our clothes will be all spoiled, see how they look," for they were so covered with dust that they looked almost all of a colour, coats, hats, shirts, and horses. We went down in the stream but heard no man speak a word all the way for 3 miles but every one pressing forward in great haste; and when we got to Middletown old meeting house, there was a great multitude, it was said to be 3 or 4000 of people, assembled together. We dismounted and shook off our dust, and the ministers were then coming to the meeting house. I turned and looked towards the Great River and saw the ferry boats running swift backward and forward bringing over loads of people, and the oars rowed nimble and quick. Everything, men, horses, and boats seemed to be struggling for life. The land and banks over the river looked black with people and horses; all along the 12 miles I saw no man at work in his field, but all seemed to be gone. When I saw Mr. Whitefield come upon the scaffold, he looked almost angelical; a young, slim, slender youth before some thousands of people with a bold undaunted countenance. And my hearing how God was with him everywhere as he came along, it solemnized my mind and put me into a trembling fear before he began to preach; for he looked as if he was clothed with authority from the Great God, and a sweet solemn solemnity sat upon his brow, and my hearing him preach gave me a heart wound. By God's blessing, my old foundation was broken up, and I saw that my righteousness would not save me.

86c. Protestation of a Presbyterian synod at Philadelphia (1 June 1741)

As the preachers of the Great Awakening went up and down the colonies they were met with more and more opposition from established ministers, both as individuals and as groups. The opposition took the form of sermons and of public statements of embodying their objections. The following 'protestation' was signed by twelve ministers and eight elders at a synod in Philadelphia. It gives reasons which the signers believe justify depriving certain members of the synod of their membership in it. In some form or other similar statements were adopted in most of the colonies by ministers who objected to the ideas and practices of the 'New Light' preachers. Printed: Joseph Tracy, *The Great Awakening. A History of the Revival of Religion in the time of Edwards and Whitefield* (Boston, 1845), pp. 71-72.

1. Their heterodox and anarchical principles, expressed in an "Apology", which had been published by the New Brunswick Presbytery. These principles are enumerated. Blair in his "Vindication", already quoted, denies that they held them.

2. Their protesting against the synod's act in relation to the examination of candidates, together with their proceeding to license and ordain men to the ministry of the gospel, in opposition to, and in contempt of said act of synod.

3. Their making irregular irruptions upon the congregations to which they have no immediate relation, without order, concurrence, or allowance of the Presbyteries or ministers to which congregations belong; thereby sowing the seeds of division among the people, and doing what they can to alienate and fill their minds with unjust prejudices against their lawfully called pastors.

4. Their principles and practice of rash judging and condemning all who do not

fall in with their measures, both ministers and people, as carnal, graceless, and enemies to God's work, and what not; as appears in Mr. Gilbert Tennent's sermon against unconverted ministers, and in his and Mr. Blair's papers of May last, which were read in open synod: which rash judging hath been the constant practice of our protesting brethren and their irregular probationers, for above these twelve months past, in their disorderly itinerations and preaching through our congregations; by which (alas for it!) most of our congregations, through weakness and credulity, are so shattered and divided and shaken in their principles that few or none of us can say we enjoy that comfort, or have that success among our people which otherwise we might, and which we enjoyed heretofore.

5. Their industriously persuading people to believe that the call of God whereby he calls men to the ministry, does not consist in their being regularly ordained and set apart to that work, according to the institution and rules of the word; but in some invisible motions and workings of the Spirit, which none can be conscious or sensible of but the person himself, and with respect to which he is liable to be deceived or play the hypocrite. That the gospel preached in truth by unconverted ministers can be of no saving benefit to souls; and their pointing out such ministers whom they condemn as graceless by their rash judging spirit, thus effectually carry the point with the poor credulous people, who, in imitation of their example, under their patrociny, judge their ministers to be graceless, and forsake their ministers as hurtful rather than profitable.

6. Their preaching the terrors of the law in such manner and dialect as has no precedent in the word of God, but rather appears to be borrowed from a worse dialect; and so industriously working on the passions and affections of weak minds as to cause them to cry out in a hideous manner, and fall down in convulsion-like fits, to the marring of the profiting both of themselves and others, who are so taken up in seeing and hearing these odd symptoms that they cannot attend to or hear what the preacher says; and then, after all, boasting of these things as the work of God, which we are persuaded do proceed from an inferior or worse cause.

7. Their, or some of them, preaching and maintaining, that all true converts are as certain of their gracious state as a person can be of what he knows by his outward senses; and are able to give a narrative of the time and manner of their conversion, or else they conclude them to be in a natural or graceless state; and that a gracious person can judge of another's gracious state otherwise than by his profession and life. That people are under no sacred tie or relation to their own pastors lawfully called, but may leave them when they please, and ought to go where they think they get most good.

87A–B. Religious diversity in the eighteenth century

The great migration to the colonies in the eighteenth century brought with it an extraordinary variety of new religious sects and it also witnessed the spread of older sects to the newly settled portions of the colonies. Religious diversity was greatest in the back country from Pennsylvania to Georgia. Gottlieb Mittelberger, a German pastor, describes conditions in Pennsylvania (No. 87A). James Reed, a missionary of the Society for the Propagation of the Gospel in Foreign Parts, writes of conditions in North Carolina in a letter to the Secretary of the Society. His letter is like those of other Anglican missionaries, whose lot was seldom happy (No. 87B).

87A. Gottlieb Mittelberger: account of religious conditions in Pennsylvania (c. 1750)

Printed: *Journey to Pennsylvania*, pp. 54–55, 61–63.

Coming to speak of Pennsylvania again, that colony possesses great liberties above all other English colonies, inasmuch as all religious sects are tolerated there. We find there Lutherans, Reformed, Catholics, Quakers, Mennonists or Anabaptists, Herrnhuters or Moravian Brethren, Pietists, Seventh Day Baptists, Dunkers, Presbyterians, Newborn, Freemasons, Separatists, Freethinkers, Jews, Mohammedans, Pagans, Negroes, and Indians. The Evangelicals and Reformed, however, are in the majority. But there are many hundred unbaptized souls there that do not even wish to be baptized. Many pray neither in the morning nor in the evening, neither before nor after meals. No devotional book, not to speak of a Bible, will be found with such people. In one house and one family, four, five, and even six sects may be found. . . .

The preachers in Pennsylvania receive no salaries or tithes, except what they annually get from their church members, which varies very much; for many a father of a family gives according to his means and of his own free will, 2, 3, 4, 5, or 6 florins a year, but many others give very little. For baptizing children, for funeral sermons and marriage ceremonies they generally receive a dollar. The preachers have no free dwellings or other *beneficia*. But they receive many presents from their parishioners. The same is true of the schoolmasters. But since 1754 England and Holland give annually a large sum of money for the general benefit of the many poor in Pennsylvania, and for the support of six Reformed English churches and as many Reformed English free schools. Nevertheless, many hundred children cannot attend these schools, on account of their great distance and the many forests. Many planters lead, therefore, a very wild and heathenish life; for as it is with the schools, so it is also with the churches in the rural districts, because churches and school-houses are usually built around at such places only where most neighbours and church members live.

The preachers throughout Pennsylvania have no power to punish anyone, or to compel anyone to go to church; nor has anyone a right to dictate to the other, because they are not supported by any *Consistorio*. Most preachers are hired by the year like the cowherds in Germany; and if one does not preach to their liking, he must expect to be served with a notice that his services will no longer be required. It is, therefore, very difficult to be a conscientious preacher, especially as they have to hear and suffer much from so many hostile and often wicked sects. The most exemplary preachers are often reviled, insulted, and scoffed at like the Jews, by the young and old, especially in the country. I would, therefore, rather perform the meanest herdsman's duties in Germany than be a preacher in Pennsylvania. Such unheard of rudeness and wickedness spring from the excessive liberties of the land, and from the blind zeal of the many sects. To many a one's soul and body, liberty in Pennsylvania is more hurtful than useful. There is a saying in that country: Pennsylvania is the heaven of the farmers, the paradise of the mechanics, and the hell of the officials and preachers.

87B. James Reed: account of religious conditions in North Carolina (26 June 1760)

Printed: *Colonial Records of North Carolina*, VI, pp. 264–266.

Reverend Sir:

I wrote you the 5th of last March by three different conveyances and have now sent you, according to promise, my No. 1 Paroch, which though imperfect, is the most exact and regular I could possibly form in four or five months, and since the receipt of the Society's orders and instructions. In the number of white inhabitants I believe I have come very nigh the truth, exclusive of children under six years of age. In the number of children and infants baptized I have been very exact; three white adults are now under instruction for baptism. In the number of those who have received the sacrament of the Lord's Supper I have been very exact, but cannot as yet ascertain the number of actual communicants of the Church of England in the whole county, for the county is so very large that 'tis not in my power to administer the sacrament of the Lord's Supper at the several chapels above once a year. Therefore I have allotted the spring of the year for the discharge of that part of my duty, and as the last spring was the most sickly season that has ever happened in this part of the province for these seven years past, and great numbers are prevented by sickness from attending the chapels, I shall not be able to inform the Society of the number of actual communicants of the Church of England in the whole county before this time twelve months. As to the number of dissenters and of those who profess themselves members of the Church of England I cannot pretend at present to be very exact. There are too many that can hardly be said to be members of any particular Christian society, and great number of dissenters of all denominations come and settled amongst us from New England, particularly Anabaptists, Methodists, Quakers, and Presbyterians. The Anabaptists are obstinate, illiterate, and grossly ignorant; the Methodists ignorant, censorious, and uncharitable; the Quakers rigid, but the Presbyterians are pretty moderate except here and there a bigot or rigid Calvinist. As for Papists, I cannot learn there are above nine or ten in the whole county. I have estimated the number of infidels and heathens to be about 1,000. We have no Indians amongst us, but the greatest part of the Negroes in the whole county may too justly be accounted heathens. 'Tis impossible for ministers in such extensive counties to instruct them in the principles of the Christian religion and their masters will not take the least pains to do it themselves. I baptize all those whose masters become sureties for them, but never baptize any Negro infants or children upon any other terms. I have not ventured to put down any particular number of converts for I cannot boast of the success of my labours. I trust in God there are several reformed, if not by my ministry, by the perusal of excellent pious tracts which the Society was pleased to send me and which I have with the utmost care and diligence distributed among my parishioners. Besides attending my own county and parish, I have for four or five years past frequently visited St. John's parish in Carteret County. This county and parish, tho' contiguous to Craven, is very difficult to attend on account of its being very much broken and divided by creeks and rivers, and the inhabitants are so poor and few in number that 'twill probably be a great many years before they will be able to maintain a minister. They have built a neat wooden chapel upon Newport River, where a small regular congregation constantly attends divine service, performed by a layman every Sunday. I have visited this parish twice very lately, once at a private house where I baptized eight children, and once at the chapel where I baptized ten children, and administered the sacrament of the Lord's Supper to nineteen communicants.

88. Memorial of the Presbytery of Hanover County, Virginia (24 October 1776)

The long struggle for the disestablishment of State churches and for religious freedom for all sects culminated during the American Revolution. The following memorial is characteristic of the arguments used by dissenters in demanding a freedom which they believed to be consistent with the principles of the American Revolution. Printed: Charles F. James, *Documentary History of the Struggle for Religious Liberty in Virginia* (Lynchburg, Va., 1900), pp. 222–225.

The Memorial of the Presbytery of Hanover humbly represents: that your memorialists are governed by the same sentiments which have inspired the United States of America; and are determined that nothing in our power and influence shall be wanting to give success to their common cause. We would also represent that dissenters from the Church of England in this country have ever been desirous to conduct themselves as peaceable members of the civil government, for which reason they have hitherto submitted to several ecclesiastical burdens and restrictions that are inconsistent with equal liberty. But now when the many and grievous oppressions of our mother country have laid this continent under the necessity of casting off the yoke of tyranny, and of forming independent governments upon equitable and liberal foundations, we flatter ourselves that we shall be freed from all the incumbrances which a spirit of domination, prejudice, or bigotry have interwoven with most other political systems. This we are the more strongly encouraged to expect by the Declaration of Rights, so universally applauded for that dignity, firmness, and precision with which it delineates and asserts the privileges of society, and the prerogatives of human nature; and which we embrace as the *magna charta* of our commonwealth, that can never be violated without endangering the grand superstructure it was destined to sustain. Therefore we rely upon this Declaration, as well as the justice of our honourable legislature, to secure us the *free exercise of religion according to the dictates of our consciences*; and we should fall short in our duty to ourselves, and the many and numerous congregations under our care, were we, upon this occasion, to neglect laying before you a state of the religious grievances under which we have hitherto laboured; that they no longer may be continued in our present form of government.

It is well known that in the frontier counties, which are justly supposed to contain a fifth part of the inhabitants of Virginia, the dissenters have borne the heavy burdens of purchasing glebes, building churches, and supporting the established clergy, where there are very few Episcopalians, either to assist in bearing the expenses, or to reap the advantage; and that throughout the other parts of the country there are also many thousands of zealous friends and defenders of our state, who, beside the invidious, and disadvantageous restrictions to which they have been subjected, annually pay large taxes to support an establishment from which their consciences and principles oblige them to dissent; all which are confessedly so many violations of their natural rights, and in their consequences a restraint upon freedom of inquiry and private judgment.

In this enlightened age, and in a land where all of every denomination are united in the most strenuous efforts to be free, we hope and expect that our representatives will cheerfully concur in removing every species of religious, as well as civil, bondage. Certain it is that every argument for civil liberty gains additional strength when applied to liberty in the concerns of religion; and there is no argument in favour of establishing the Christian religion but what may be pleaded, with equal propriety, for establishing the tenets of Mohammed by those who believe the Alcoran; or if this be not true, it is at least impossible for the magistrate to adjudge the right of preference among the various sects that profess the Christian faith without erecting a chair of infallibility, which would lead us back to the Church of Rome.

We beg leave farther to represent that religious establishments are highly injurious to the temporal interests of any community. Without insisting upon the ambition and the arbitrary practices of those who are favoured by government; or the intriguing, seditious spirit which is commonly excited by this, as well as every other kind of oppression; such establishments greatly retard population, and consequently the progress of arts, sciences, and manufactories: witness the rapid growth and improvements of the northern provinces, compared with this. No one can deny that the more early settlement and the many superior advantages of our country would have invited multitudes of artificers, mechanics, and other useful members of society to fix their habitation among us, who have either remained in their place of nativity, or preferred worse civil governments, and a barren soil, where they might enjoy the rights of conscience more fully than they had a prospect of doing it in this.

From which we infer that Virginia might have now been the capital of America, and a match for the British arms, without depending on others for the necessaries of war, had it not been prevented by her religious establishment.

Neither can it be made to appear that the gospel needs any such civil aid. We rather conceive that when our blessed Saviour declares his kingdom is not of this world, he renounces all dependence upon state power, and as his weapons are spiritual, and were only designed to have influence on the judgment and heart of man, we are persuaded that if mankind were left in the quiet possession of their unalienable rights and privileges, Christianity, as in the days of the Apostles, would continue to prevail and flourish in the greatest purity by its own native excellence and under the all disposing providence of God.

We would humbly represent that the only proper objects of civil government are the happiness and protection of men in the present state of existence, the security of the life, liberty, and property of the citizens, and to restrain the vicious and encourage the virtuous by wholesome laws, equally extending to every individual. But that the duty which we owe our Creator and the manner of discharging it, can only be directed by reason and conviction, and as nowhere cognizable but at the tribunal of the universal Judge.

Therefore we ask no ecclesiastical establishments for ourselves; neither can we approve of them when granted to others. This, indeed, would be giving exclusive or separate emoluments or privileges to one set of men, without any special public services, to the common reproach and injury of every other denomination; and for the reasons recited we are induced earnestly to entreat that all laws now in force in this commonwealth which countenance religious denomination, may be speedily repealed–that all, of every religious sect, may be protected in the full exercise of their several modes of worship, and exempted from all taxes for the support of any church whatsoever further than what may be agreeable to their own private choice, or voluntary obligation. This being done, all partial and invidious distinctions will be abolished, to the great honour and interest of the state, and every one be left to stand or fall, according to merit, which can never be the case so long as any one denomination is established in preference to others.

That the great Sovereign of the Universe may inspire you with unanimity, wisdom, and resolution, and bring you to a just determination on all the important concerns before you, is the fervent prayer of your memorialists.

Signed by order of the Presbytery.

John Todd, Moderator

Caleb Wallace. P. Clerk

B. EDUCATION IN THE COLONIES

MOST of the English colonists soon showed an interest in providing for the education of the young, but both schools and colleges faced many difficulties and grew slowly. The colonists first of all had to carve homes from the wilderness, defend themselves against Indian enemies, and establish the economic bases on which their very existence depended. The surprising thing, therefore, is not how slowly education developed but how much attention was given to it despite the magnitude of the essential needs of the early colonies.

The Virginia Company and the House of Burgesses in 1618 and 1619 proposed the creation of a university in Virginia. Funds were raised and a teacher hired, but whatever 'university' was started was wiped out in the Indian massacre of 1622. For a long time thereafter there was little or no official interest in education in the colony. In 1671 Governor William Berkeley reported that he thanked God there were "no free schools nor printing in Virginia". Not until William and Mary College was founded at the end of the century did the colonial government once more take part in the fostering of education in the colony.[1]

The New England colonies rather than the 'Old Dominion' were the centre of educational developments during the first century of colonial history. Many of the Puritan leaders were graduates of Oxford and Cambridge and were familiar with the free grammar schools of England. From the start they assumed responsibility for the encouragement of education on both the elementary and college level, and they soon established the principle that the education of the young in society was a responsibility of the government. However inadequate the working out of this principle in practice, it was never lost sight of as a principle and ultimately it became a practice as well as a principle in the nation that arose from the English colonies in America.

A Latin school was established in Boston in 1635. The next year the General Court of the colony voted money for the establishment of a college. It began instruction in the autumn of 1638. Shortly thereafter it was named Harvard College in honour of John Harvard, who left it his library and a share of his property.[2] While a fundamental concern of the college was the training of a learned ministry, it was never limited to this task. It provided broad training of both a classical and a humanistic character and provided an increasing number of schoolmasters and lay readers for all the New England colonies.

The Puritan leaders showed an equal concern for elementary education. In 1642 and in 1647 the Massachusetts legislature laid down the legal foundations for free public education. Responsibility was placed upon the individual towns for educating their children. The legislature of Connecticut likewise established the principle of free public education.[3] It is easy to scoff at such legislation and even easier to point out the failure to carry out its purposes, but it remains a basic legacy of the Puritan leaders of the seventeenth century.

The legislatures to the south of New England did not usually establish elementary schools, yet such schools were to be found in every colony during the eighteenth century, sometimes at the direction of legislatures, and occasionally with their support.

[1] No. 91.   [2] No. 89.   [3] No. 90.

Pennsylvania required parents to teach their children to read and write. The South Carolina legislature gave funds to support a schoolmaster in each parish.

However, education was a vital concern of virtually every religious group, and the various churches did much to establish schools. The Anglican Church, working through the Society for the Propagation of the Gospel, supported schools in the southern colonies as a part of its missionary work. The Presbyterians likewise showed a persistent interest in education. Clergymen of every denomination eked out small incomes by running schools in their homes. Many a colonial leader like Thomas Jefferson got a portion of his elementary education in the home of a clergyman. Numerous wandering teachers came to the colonies, for the eighteenth-century newspapers are replete with advertisements of such men seeking pupils. As wealth developed, men left endowments in their wills for the establishment of free schools. In the southern colonies, planters often hired private tutors for their children or bought the contracts of educated indentured servants who were then used as teachers. An increasing number of planters and merchants sent their sons to England or the Continent to be educated. Thus in one way or another, there were a great many opportunities for the acquisition of the elements of reading, writing, and arithmetic in each of the colonies by the middle of the eighteenth century, and the opportunities were not limited to the children of the well-to-do.

The most remarkable development of the eighteenth century was the rapid expansion of the number of colonial colleges. For a half-century Harvard stood alone. Then in 1693 a royal charter was granted for the establishment of William and Mary College in Virginia under the auspices of the Anglican Church. It experienced many political and financial difficulties before achieving a position as one of the distinguished colonial colleges by the middle of the eighteenth century.[1] In New England some of the more orthodox were alarmed at the new tendencies at Harvard. After many difficulties, what was expected to be a more religiously sound institution was established at New Haven, Connecticut, in 1716. In 1718 it was named Yale College in honour of Elihu Yale, who gave it books and some bales of goods for sale. Yale had been born in Boston, but had been taken to England at the age of three. Eventually he went to India, where he acquired a large fortune in the service of the East India Company. He was forced to retire under a cloud of charges of corruption and he returned to England, where he gained a reputation as a philanthropist. It was this reputation which led New England leaders to approach him in search of gifts and offering the hope that a college in the New World would be named in his honour, in return.

The religious interest in the establishment of colonial colleges was intensified with the Great Awakening. The leaders of the movement inveighed against the radicalism of the 'old' colleges and various religious sects determined to establish colleges controlled by themselves. The Baptists established the College of Rhode Island (Brown); the Presbyterians, the College of New Jersey (Princeton); the Dutch Reformed, Queens (Rutgers) in New Jersey; the Anglicans, King's (Columbia), in New York. Dartmouth, which received a royal charter in 1769, grew out of a school for Indians.

Each of these colleges faced many difficulties and particularly that of adequate finance. Some of them got grants from legislatures. Lotteries were used. Emissaries were sent to England to secure donations and often competed with one another for

[1] No. 91.

the favour of donors. Many of them were involved in local political disputes. Despite all such difficulties, by 1775 the colonial colleges were graduating hundreds of men every year.

The religious impulse was not the only one leading to the foundation of colleges and to the broadening of the base of education. By the middle of the century there was a widening demand for more practical education and for secular as opposed to religious control of schools. One evidence of the demand for 'practical' education was the increasing number of Americans who went to Europe to study, particularly in medicine and law. At least seventy Americans studied law at the Middle Temple in London before 1760. Between 1728 and 1759 sixty-three Americans studied medicine at the University of Edinburgh, and still others at the universities of Paris and Leyden. The demand for medical education, in particular, was reflected in the founding of a medical college at Philadelphia in 1765 and of a medical department at King's College in 1767.

The demand for 'practical' education and for the limitation of religious control affected even those colleges that were established under the auspices of a church. Thus the 'Advertisement' for King's College in 1754 promised that the college would not impose the tenets of any particular sect upon the students but only those principles of Christianity and morality upon which all denominations were agreed. Further-more, the college promised to teach not only the traditional subjects, but such things as surveying, navigation, husbandry, and science.[1] The outstanding advocate of college education along practical lines and freed from religious control was Benjamin Franklin. In 1749 he set forth a series of 'proposals' for the establishment of such an institution.[2] Funds were soon raised and the 'Academy' was opened in 1751. After the Revolution, it became the University of Pennsylvania.

Whatever the merits of the colonial colleges and elementary schools, it is plain that a great number of American leaders at the end of the colonial period were men of wide education. Many of them built up large libraries and read a variety of languages. A part of the process was self-education, it is true, and the growing number of newspapers, book publishers, public libraries, and societies for furthering knowledge all contributed to this end. It was a matter for comment by travellers that they often found, even among back-country farmers, men who read not only English, but Latin as well. By 1776 the foundations were laid for the extraordinary expansion of education, both private and public, which was to characterize the United States after 1783 and which was for long to be a unique feature of American society.

89A–B. The founding of Harvard College

In 1636 the General Court of Massachusetts voted money for the establishment of a college. It began instruction in the autumn of 1638. Shortly thereafter John Harvard, who had come from England in 1637, died and left his library and a share of his property to the college. The bequest was so much greater than any other gifts to the college that the legislature named it in his honour in the spring of 1638–1639. In 1642 the first class of nine men was graduated from the college. The following year an anonymous promotion tract was published in London. Among other things, it contained the following account of Harvard College (No. 89A). It is given as it appears in the source from which it was transcribed. In 1650 the General Court of Massachusetts granted the college a formal charter of incorporation (No. 89B).

---

[1] No. 93.   [2] No. 92.

89A. Description of Harvard College, from "New England's First Fruits" (1643)

Printed: Perry Miller and Thomas H. Johnson, eds., *The Puritans* (New York, 1938), pp. 701-704.

In Respect of the Colledge, and the Proceedings of Learning Therein

1. After God had carried us safe to *New-England*, and wee had builded our houses, provided necessaries for our liveli-hood, rear'd convenient places for Gods worship, and setled the Civill Government: One of the next things we longed for, and looked after was to advance Learning and perpetuate it to Posterity; dreading to leave an illiterate Ministery to the Churches, when our present Ministers shall lie in the Dust. And as wee were thinking and consulting how to effect this great Work; it pleased God to stir up the heart of one Mr. *Harvard* (a godly Gentleman, and a lover of Learning, there living amongst us) to give the one halfe of his Estate (it being in all about 1700.l.) towards the erecting of a Colledge, and all his Library: after him another gave 300.l. others after them cast in more, and the publique hand of the State added the rest: the Colledge was, by common consent, appointed to be at *Cambridge*, (a place very pleasant and accommodate) and is called (according to the name of the first founder) *Harvard Colledge*.

The Edifice is very faire and comely within and without, having in it a spacious Hall; (where they daily meet at Common Lectures) Exercises, and a large Library with some Bookes to it, the gifts of diverse of our friends, their Chambers and studies also fitted for, and possessed by the Students, and all other roomes of Office necessary and convenient, with all needfull Offices thereto belonging: And by the side of the Colledge a faire *Grammar* Schoole, for the training up of young Schollars, and fitting of them for *Academicall Learning*, that still as they are judged ripe, they may be received into the Colledge of this Schoole: Master *Corlet* is the Mr., who hath very well approved himselfe for his abilities, dexterity and painfulnesse, in teaching and education of the youth under him.

Over the Colledge is master *Dunster* placed, as President, a learned conscionable and industrious man, who hath so trained up, his Pupills in the tongues and Arts, and so seasoned them with the principles of Divinity and Christianity, that we have to our great comfort, (and in truth) beyond our hopes, beheld their progresse in Learning and godlinesse also; the former of these hath appeared in their publique declamations in *Latine* and *Greeke*, and Disputations Logicall and Philosophicall, which they have beene wonted (besides their ordinary Exercises in the Colledge-Hall) in the audience of the Magistrates, Ministers, and other Schollars, for the probation of their growth in Learning, upon set dayes, constantly once every moneth to make and uphold: The latter hath been manifested in sundry of them by the savoury breathings of their Spirits in their godly conversation. Insomuch that we are confident, if these early blossomes may be cherished and warmed with the influence of the friends of Learning and lovers of this pious worke, they will by the help of God, come to happy maturity in a short time.

Over the Colledge are twelve Overseers chosen by the generall Court, six of them are of the Magistrates, the other six of the Ministers, who are to promote the best good of it, and (having a power of influence into all persons in it) are to see that every one be diligent and proficient in his proper place.

2. *Rules, and Precepts that are observed in the Colledge*

1. When any Schollar is able to understand *Tully*, or such like classical Latine Author *extempore*, and make and speake true Latine in Verse and Prose, *suo ut aiunt Marte*; And decline perfectly the Paradigm's of *Nounes* and *Verbes* in the *Greek* tongue: Let him then and not before be capable of admission into the Colledge.

2. Let every Student be plainly instructed, and earnestly pressed to consider well, the maine end of his life and studies is, *to know God and Jesus Christ which is eternall life*, Joh. 17. 3. and therefore to lay *Christ* in the bottome, as the only foundation of all sound knowledge and Learning.

And seeing the Lord only giveth wisedome, Let every one seriously set himselfe by prayer in secret to seeke it of him *Prov.* 2, 3.

3. Every one shall so exercise himselfe in reading the Scriptures twice a day, that he shall be ready to give such an account of his proficiency therein, both in *Theoretticall* observations of the Language, and *Logick*, and in *Practicall* and spirituall truths, as his Tutor shall require, according to his ability; seeing *the entrance of the word giveth light, it giveth understanding to the simple*, Psalm. 119. 130.

4. That they eshewing all profanation of Gods Name, Attributes, Word, Ordin-ances and times of Worship, doe studie with good conscience, carefully to retaine God, and the love of his truth in their mindes, else let them know, that (notwith-standing their Learning) God may give them up *to strong delusions*, and in the end *to a reprobate minde*, 2 Thes. 2. 11, 12. Rom. 1. 28.

5. That they studiously redeeme the time; observe the generall houres appointed for all the Students, and the speciall houres for their owne *Classes:* and then diligently attend the Lectures, without any disturbance by word or gesture. And if in anything they doubt, they shall enquire, as of their fellowes, so, (in case of *Non satisfaction*) modestly of their Tutors.

6. None shall under any pretence whatsoever, frequent the company and society of such men as lead an unfit, and dissolute life.

Nor shall any without his Tutors leave, or (in his absence) the call of Parents or Guardians, goe abroad to other Townes.

7. Every Schollar shall be present in his Tutors chamber at the 7th. houre in the morning, immediately after the sound of the Bell, at his opening the Scripture and prayer, so also at the 5th. houre at night, and then give account of his owne private reading, as aforesaid in Particular the third, and constantly attend Lectures in the Hall at the houres appointed? But if any (without necessary impediment) shall absent himself from prayer or Lectures, he shall bee lyable to Admonition, if he offend above once a weeke.

8. If any Schollar shall be found to transgresse any of the Lawes of God, or the Schoole, after twice Admonition, he shall be lyable, if not *adultus*, to correction, if *adultus*, his name shall be given up to the Overseers of the Colledge, that he may bee admonished at the publick monethly Act.

3. *The times and order of their Studies, unlesse experience shall shew cause to alter.*

The second and third day of the weeke, read Lectures, as followeth.

To the first yeare at 8th. of the clock in the morning *Logick*, the first three quarters, *Physicks* the last quarter.

To the second yeare, at the 9th. houre, *Ethicks* and *Politicks*, at convenient distances of time.

To the third yeare at the 10th. *Arithmetick* and *Geometry*, the three first quarters, *Astronomy* the last.

Afternoone.

The first yeare disputes at the second houre.

The 2d. yeare at the 3d. houre.

The 3d. yeare at the 4th. every one in his Art.

The 4th. day reads Greeke.

To the first yeare the *Etymologie* and *Syntax* at the eighth houre.

To the 2d. at the 9th. houre, *Prosodia* and *Dialects*.

Afternoone.

The first yeare at 2d. houre practice the precepts of *Grammar* in such Authors as have variety of words.

The 2d. yeare at 3d. houre practice in *Poësy*, [with] *Nonnus, Duport*, or the like.

The 3d. yeare perfect their *Theory* before noone, and exercise *Style, Composition, Imitation, Epitome*, both in Prose and Verse, afternoone.

The fift[h] day reads Hebrew, and the Easterne Tongues.

Grammar to the first yeare houre the 8th.

To the 2d. *Chaldee* [i.e. Aramaic] at the 9th. houre.

To the 3d. *Syriack* at the 10th houre.

Afternoone.

The first yeare practice in the Bible at the 2d. houre.

The 2d. in *Ezra* and *Dan[i]el* at the 3d. houre.

The 3d. at the 4th. houre in *Trostius* New Testament.

The 6th. day reads Rhetorick to all at the 8th houre.

Declamations at the 9th. So ordered that every Scholler may declaime once a moneth. The rest of the day *vacat Rhetoricis studiis. The 7th. day reads Divinity Catecheticall at the 8th. houre, Common places at the 9th houre.*

Afternoone.

The first houre reads history in the Winter,

The nature of plants in the Summer

The summe of every Lecture shall be examined, before the new Lecture be read.

Every Schollar, that on proofe is found able to read the Originalls of the *Old* and *New Testament* into the Latine tongue, and to resolve them *Logically*; withall being of godly life and conversation; And at any publick Act hath the Approbation of the Overseers and Master of the Colledge, is fit to be dignified with his first Degree.

Every Schollar that giveth up in writing a *System*, or *Synopsis*, or summe of *Logick*, Naturall and Morall *Phylosophy*, *Arithmetick*, *Geometry* and *Astronomy*: and is ready to defend his *Theses* or positions: withall skilled in the Originalls as abovesaid: and of godly life & conversation: and so approved by the Overseers and Master of the Colledge, at any publique *Act*, is fit to be dignified with his 2d. Degree.

89B. Charter of Harvard College (31 May 1650)

Printed: Colonial Society of Massachussetts *Publications*, vol. xxxi, pp. 3–6.

Whereas through the good hand of God many well devoted persons have been and daily are moved and stirred up to give and bestow sundry gifts, legacies, lands, and revenues for the advancement of all good literature, arts, and sciences in Harvard College in Cambridge in the County of Middlesex, and to the maintenance of the President and Fellows, and for all accommodations of buildings and all other necessary provisions that may conduce to the education of the English and Indian youth of this country in knowledge and godliness: It is therefore ordered and enacted by this Court and the authority thereof that for the furthering of so good a wcrk and for the purposes aforesaid from henceforth that the said college in Cambridge in Middlesex in New England shall be a corporation consisting of seven persons (to wit): a President, five Fellows, and a Treasurer or Bursar, and that Henry Dunster shall be the first president; Samuel Mather, Samuel Danford, Masters of Art; Jonathan Mitchell, Comfort Starr, and Samuel Eaton, Bachelors of Art, shall be the five fellows, and Thomas Danford to be present treasurer; all of them being inhabitants in the Bay, and shall be the first seven persons of which the said corporation shall consist. And that the said seven persons, or the greater number of them, procuring the presence of the Overseers of the college, and by their counsel and consent shall have power and are hereby authorized at any time or times to elect a new president, fellows, or treasurer, so oft[en] and from time to time as any of the said person or persons shall die or be removed; which said president and fellows for the time being shall forever hereafter in name and fact be one body politic and corporate in law, to all intents and purposes, and shall have perpetual succession; and shall be called by the name of President and Fellows of Harvard College and shall from time to time be eligible as aforesaid. And by that name they and their successors shall and may purchase and acquire to themselves, or take and receive upon free gift and donation, any lands, tenements, or hereditaments within this jurisdiction of the Massachusetts, not exceeding the value of five hundred pounds per annum and any goods and sums of money whatsoever to the use and behoof of the said president, fellows, and scholars of the said college, and also may sue and plead, or be sued and impleaded, by the name aforesaid, in all courts and places of judicature within the jurisdiction aforesaid; and that the said president, with any three of the fellows, shall have power and are hereby authorized, when they shall think fit, to make and appoint a common seal for the use of the said corporation. And the president and fellows, or the major part of them, from time to time, may meet and choose such officers and servants for the college and make such allowance to them and them also to remove, and after death or removal, to choose such others and to make from time to time such orders and by-laws for the better ordering and carrying on the work of the college as they shall think fit, provided the said orders be allowed by the overseers. And also that the president and fellows, or major part of them, with the treasurer, shall have power to make conclusive bargains for lands and tenements to be purchased by the said corporation for valuable consideration. And for the better ordering of the government of the said college and corporation, be it enacted by the authority aforesaid: that the president and three more of the fellows shall, and may from time to time, upon due warning or notice given by the president to the rest, hold a meeting for the debating and concluding of affairs concerning the profits and revenues of any lands and disposing of their goods. Provided that all the said disposings be according to the will of the donors. And for direction in all emergent occasions, execution of all orders and by-laws, and for the procuring of a general meeting of all the overseers and society in great and difficult cases, and in cases of nonagreement; in all which cases aforesaid the conclusion shall be made by the major part, the said president having a casting voice, the overseers consenting thereunto. And that all the aforesaid transactions shall tend to and for the use and behoof of the president, fellows, scholars, and officers of the said college, and for all accommodations of buildings, books, and all other necessary provisions and furnitures as may be for the advancement and education of youth in all manner of good literature, arts, and sciences. And further be it ordered by this court and the authority thereof that all the lands, tenements or hereditaments, houses, or revenues within this jurisdiction to the aforesaid president or college appertaining, not exceeding the value of five hundred pounds per annum, shall from henceforth be freed from all civil impositions, taxes, and rates. All goods to the said corporation or to any scholars thereof appertaining shall be exempt from all manner of toll, customs, and excise whatsoever. And that the said president, fellows, and scholars, together with the servants and other necessary officers to the said president or college appertaining, not exceeding ten, viz., three to the president and seven to the college belonging, shall be exempted from all personal civil offices, military exercises or services, watchings and wardings, and such of their estates not exceeding one hundred pounds a man, shall be free from all country taxes or rates whatsoever, and none others. In Witness whereof the Court hath caused the Seal of the Colony to be hereunto affixed. Dated the One and thirtieth day of the third month called May. Anno 1650.

THO : DUDLEY
Governor

90A–C. New England school laws

The following laws, so far as it could be done in such form, express the educational ideals and policies of the Puritan leaders of New England. The first New England law on education was the Massachusetts law of 1642 (No. 90A). It placed upon parents and the masters of indentured servants the responsibility for educating and training in useful work the children of the colony. The

Massachusetts law of 1647 made mandatory the establishment of elementary schools by the towns, and of secondary or 'grammar' schools by larger towns for the purpose of preparing students for college (No. 90B). The Connecticut law of 1690 sought to enforce earlier legislation and in addition provided for free education at the secondary level (No. 90C).

90A. Massachusetts School Law (14 June 1642)

Printed: Shurtleff, *Records of Massachusetts Bay*, II, pp. 8–9.

This Court, taking into consideration the great neglect in many parents and masters in training up their children in learning and labour, and other employments which may be profitable to the commonwealth, do hereupon order and decree that in every town the chosen men appointed for managing the prudential affairs of the same shall henceforth stand charged with the care of the redress of this evil, so as they shall be liable to be punished or fined for the neglect thereof, upon any presentment of the grand jurors, or other information or complaint in any plantations in this jurisdiction; and for this end they, or the greater part of them, shall have power to take account from time to time of their parents and masters, and of their children, concerning their calling and employment of their children, especially of their ability to read and understand the principles of religion and the capital laws of the country, and to impose fines upon all those who refuse to render such account to them when required; and they shall have power (with consent of any court or magistrates) to put forth apprentice the children of such as shall not be able and fit to employ and bring them up, nor shall take course to dispose of them themselves; and they are to take care that such as are set to keep cattle be set to some other employment withal as spinning up on the rock, knitting, weaving tape, etc.; and that boys and girls be not suffered to converse together so as may occasion any wanton, dishonest, or immodest behaviour; and for their better performance of this trust committed to them, they may divide the town amongst them, appointing to every of the said townsmen a certain number of families to have special oversight of; they are also to provide that a sufficient quantity of materials as hemp, flax, etc., may be raised in their several towns, and tools and implements provided for working out the same; and for their assistance in this so needful and beneficial employment, if they meet with any difficulty or opposition which they cannot well master by their own power, they may have recourse to some of the magistrates, who shall take such course for their help and encouragement as the occasion shall require, according to justice; and the said townsmen, at the next court in those limits, after the end of their year, shall give a brief account in writing of their proceedings herein; provided that they have been so required by some court or magistrate a month at least before; and this order to continue for two years, and till the Court shall take further order.

90B. Massachusetts School Law (11 November 1647)

Printed: Shurtleff, *Records of Massachusetts Bay*, II, p. 203.

It being one chief project of that old deluder, Satan, to keep men from the knowledge of the Scriptures, as in former times by keeping them in an unknown tongue, so in these latter times by persuading from the use of tongues, that so at least the true sense and meaning of the original might be clouded by false glosses of saint-seeming deceivers, that learning may not be buried in the grave of our fathers in the church and commonwealth, the Lord assisting our endeavours.

It is therefore ordered, that every township in this jurisdiction, after the Lord hath increased them to the number of fifty householders, shall then forthwith appoint one within their town to teach all such children as shall resort to him to write and read, whose wages shall be paid either by the parents or masters of such children, or by the inhabitants in general, by way of supply, as the major part of those that order the prudentials of the town shall appoint; provided those that send their children be not oppressed by paying much more than they can have them taught for in other towns; and it is further ordered that where any town shall increase to the number of 100 families or householders, they shall set up a grammar school, the master thereof being able to instruct youth so far as they may be fitted for the university, provided that if any town neglect the performance hereof above one year, that every such town shall pay £5 to the next school till they shall perform this order.

90C. Connecticut School Law (13 May 1690)

Printed: *Public Records of the Colony of Connecticut*, IV, pp. 30-31.

This Court, observing that notwithstanding the former orders made for the education of children and servants, there are many persons unable to read the English tongue, and thereby incapable to read the holy word of God, or the good laws of the colony, which evil, that it grow no farther upon their Majesties' subjects here, it is hereby ordered that all parents and masters shall cause their respective children and servants, as they are capable, to be taught to read distinctly the English tongue, and that the grand jury men in each town do once in the year at least visit each family they suspect to neglect this order, and satisfy themselves whether all children under age and servants in such suspect families can read well the English tongue, or be in a good procedure to learn the same or not; and if they find any such children and servants not taught as their years are capable of, they shall return the names of the parents or masters of the said children so untaught to the next county court, where the said parents or masters shall be fined twenty shillings for each child or servant whose teaching is or shall be neglected, contrary to this order, unless it shall appear to the satisfaction of the court that the said neglect is not voluntary but necessitated by the incapacity of the parents or masters, or their neighbours, to cause them to be taught as aforesaid, or the incapacity of the said children or servants to learn.

This Court considering the necessity and great advantage of good literature, do order and appoint that there shall be two free schools kept and maintained in this colony, for the teaching of all such children as shall come there, after they can first read the psalter, to teach such reading, writing, arithmetic, the Latin and Greek tongues; the one at Hartford, the other at New Haven, the masters whereof shall be chosen by the magistrates and ministers of the said county, and shall be inspected and again displaced by them if they see cause, and that each of the said masters shall have annually for the same the sum of sixty pounds in country pay, thirty pounds of it to be paid out [of the] country treasury, the other thirty to be paid in the school revenue given by particular persons, or to be given to that use, so far as it will extend, and the rest to be paid by the respective towns of Hartford and New Haven.

This Court considering the necessity many parents or masters may be under to improve their children and servants in labour for a great part of the year, do order that if the town schools in the several towns, as distinct from the free school, be, according to law already established, kept up six months in each year to teach to read and write the English tongue, the said towns so keeping their respective schools six months in every year shall not be presentable or fineable by law for not having a school according to law, notwithstanding any former law or order to the contrary.

91A–B. The founding of William and Mary College

William and Mary was the second college founded in the English colonies. Most of the colonial colleges were involved in political disputes at one time or another and William and Mary was no exception, particularly during its first years. Its early history is set forth by Robert Beverley who held various official posts in Virginia and was a member of the House of Burgesses. In 1703 he went to England to protect his interests before the Privy Council. While there a publisher showed him a manuscript relating to Virginia which was to be published as a part of John Oldmixon's *The British Empire in America*. Beverley was so irritated with the errors in it that he wrote and published the book from which the following account of William and Mary College is taken (No. 91A). Another view of the college is set forth by Mungo Ingles, headmaster of the grammar school, in a document which tells of the difficulties of the college (No. 91B). The president to whom he refers was Commissary James Blair, one of the leaders of the party in Virginia seeking the removal of Francis Nicholson as governor (see No. 33).

91A. Robert Beverley: account of the founding of the college, from "The History and Present State of Virginia" (1705)

Printed: *The History and Present State of Virginia* (Louis B. Wright, ed., Chapel Hill, N.C., 1947), pp. 97–100, 101–102.

During that gentleman's presidency, which began *Anno* 1689, the project of a college was first agreed upon. The contrivers drew up their scheme and presented it to the president and council. This was by them approved, and referred to the next assembly. But Col. [Nathaniel] Bacon's administration being very short and no assembly called all the while, this pious design could proceed no further.

Anno 1690. Francis Nicholson, Esq., being appointed lieutenant-governor under the Lord Effingham, arrived there. This gentleman's business was to fix himself in my lord's place, and recommend himself to the supreme government. For that end, he studied popularity, discoursing freely of country improvements. He made his court to the people by instituting Olympic games, and giving prizes to all those that should excel in the exercises of riding, running, shooting, wrestling, and backsword. When the design of a college was communicated to him, he foresaw what interest it might create him with the bishops in England, and therefore promised it all imaginable encouragement. The first thing desired of him in its behalf was the calling of an assembly; but this he would by no means agree to, being under obligations to the Lord Effingham, to stave off assemblies as long as he could, for fear there might be further representations sent over against his lordship, who was conscious to himself how uneasy the country had been under his despotic administration.

When that could not be obtained, then they proposed that a subscription might pass through the colony to try the humour of the people in general, and see what voluntary contributions they could get towards it. This he granted, and he himself, together with the Council, set a generous example to the other gentlemen of the country, so that the subscriptions at last amounted to about two thousand five hundred pounds, in which sum is included the generous benevolences of several merchants of London.

Anno 1691, an assembly being called, this design was moved to them, and they espoused it heartily; and soon after made an address to King William and Queen Mary in its behalf, and sent the Reverend Mr. James Blair their agent to England, to solicit their Majesties' charter for it.

It was proposed that three things should be taught in this college, viz., languages, divinity, and natural philosophy.

They appointed a certain number of professors, and their salaries.

And they formed rules for the continuation and good government thereof to perpetuity. But of this I shall speak more particularly in the last part of my book, wherein the present state will be considered.

The Assembly was so fond of Governor Nicholson at that time that they presented him with the sum of three hundred pounds as a testimony of their good disposition towards him. But he having an instruction to receive no present from the country, they drew up an address to their Majesties, praying that he might have leave to accept it.

This he took an effectual way to secure by making a promise that if their Majesties would please to permit him to accept it, he would give one half thereof to the college; and so he secured at once both the money and the character of being a generous person.

Their Majesties were well pleased with that pious design of the plantation, and granted a charter, according to their desire; in obtaining which the address and assiduity of Mr. Blair, their agent, was highly to be admired.

Their Majesties were graciously pleased to give near two thousand pounds sterling, the balance due upon the account of quit-rents, towards the founding the college; and towards the endowing of it, they allowed twenty thousand acres of choice land, together with the revenue arising by the penny per pound, on tobacco exported from Virginia and Maryland to the other plantations.

It was a great satisfaction to the archbishops and bishops to see such a nursery of religion founded in that new world; especially for that it was begun in an Episcopal way, and carried on wholly by zealous conformists to the Church of England. . . .

. . . With Sir Edmund Andros [in 1692] was sent over the college charter and the subsequent Assembly declared that the subscriptions which had been made to the college were due and immediately demandable. They likewise gave a duty on the exportation of skins and furs, for its more plentiful endowment.

The subscription money did not come in with the same readiness with which it had been underwritten. However, there was enough given by their Majesties and gathered from the people to keep all hands at work and carry on the building, the foundation whereof they then laid.

91B. Mungo Ingles: The several sources of the odium and discouragement which the College of William and Mary in Virginia lies under (1704)

Printed: *The Virginia Magazine of History and Biography*, VII (1900), pp. 391–393.

The College of William and Mary in Virginia (through an odium it has lain under ever since the charter was brought in) has not as yet arrived to any greater perfection than a grammar school. There be several sources whence this odium had its original, as (1) The prejudices of the former collectors of the penny per pound before it was given to the college, for these gentlemen, finding that the current of that money was directed from their coffers into another channel by being given to the college, began personally to entertain an odium against it, and being all of the Council and colls [colonels] of the county [country], the little people that depended on them, began to write after their copy; others (but without any reason) are angry at the place where the college is situated, which yet is absolutely the best of the whole country; but it fares with the college in this point as with towns–everyone would have one in his own county and neighbourhood, and yet the college can be but in one place; and if it had been in another place, others would have had as much to say against that. Others are enemies to it on the account of their subscriptions toward it, for his excellency (when lieutenant-governor) having issued forth a brief for subscription toward a college, to oblige and curry favour with his excellency, the principal promoter of it; others hoping and supposing it would come to nothing; and others for company's sake that they might not be thought singular or enemies to so good a work, put their hand to the brief and could never be reconciled to the college since. But a fourth source, and which has done the college most mischief than all the rest, is Mr. Blair's demanding and taking his full salary as president all this while when the college had been no more but a grammar school, by which means the master and usher and writing master had much ado (when Mr. Blair went last for England) to get any more than half salary for that year, and this is the only reason why we have had not any more of the six masters, for while the president carried away yearly 150 pounds and there remained no more money than will barely pay the master and usher and writing master, which in the above named year came very short even of that, we can never expect to have any more masters, for as no money, no swizer, so no salary, no master.

But notwithstanding that the college is the only contrivance by which Mr. Blair has got both all his gains and his grandeur, he has not stuck of late to strike at all to serve a turn–the schools, the master, the college itself must all fall a sacrifice rather than a design of turning out the governor (though the great patron and promoter of it and best friend yet that ever it had went to King William and Queen Mary and her present Majesty), should miscarry, not that he designed the ruin of the college for good, for it is by it he gets all his gains. But he has endeavoured to ruin the schools (which is all the college at present) by taking away his own brother's son from it and so breaking the ice for six more of his party who all and only they took their sons away from schools after his laudable example, that he and they might have it to say that the Governor had not interest enough to keep it up and that it could not be a school nor a college without Mr. Blair, he being then in England (affidaviting against his excellency) when he writ to his lady to take his brother's sons from the college. This proceeding of Mr. Blair and his party of making a stalking horse of the college was understood by me to such a degree that I had much ado to prevail with myself to continue my charge after such discouragement, but that I was resolved to counterplot those men of design and so stand by his excellency, the great Maecenas of the college, of whom it may be said as of the emperor in Juvenal "Et Spedet Ratio Studiorum, etc." Mr. Blair was never quiet nor easy until we had our present good governor and kindly nursing father, as he was wont formerly to call him, and yet is now doing all that he can to get him removed, from which reason the master, following the wise man's advice is not meddling with them that are given to change, is resolved that he will have no more to do with the college whenever his excellency leaves the country. Mr. Blair has shot at his excellency through my body, and I am resolved to see what he will make of the college without his excellency or any of her governments whom she pleased. But I may without either flattery or ostentation say that if her Majesty should send us a new government every fleet, we can never have any that will do so much either for the country or the college, the church or the clergy, which together have cost his excellency some thousands of pounds sterling, and of which Mr. Blair has had a considerable share. And since ingratitude is so heinous a sin (being as unpardonable in morality as the sin against the Holy Ghost is in Divinity), I am resolved to have no more to do with such a man and will no longer be a member of the body or corporation of which he is the head. Besides I am none of Mr. Blair's party and can never expect to live easy in his society. Moreover the matter is gone too far to be revoked. I have both given it out here and have writ for England to some of the best quality that I am resolved to quit the college if his excellency, the great patron of it, was removed by Mr. Blair's means, and I am not one that will give myself the lie. I am not apt to resolve but on mature deliberation and am satisfied that I have good reasons for what I do. I do not understand the turning of a good design into bad use, a design of breeding up youth in learning and virtue and all commendable qualities into a stalking horse to serve a turn upon occasion, or to enrich a particular man and to carry on the designs of a party. My soul come not than into their secrets and unto their Assembly. Mine honour be not than united.

92. Benjamin Franklin: proposals relating to the education of youth in Pennsylvania (1749)

Among American leaders in the eighteenth century, no man was more concerned with the practical aspects of life than Benjamin Franklin. He was interested in science, in the founding of libraries, and in education of a secular character. His 'Proposals' outline his conception of the kind of education that was fit for youth in the eighteenth century. History, politics, economics were to be taught. The English language was to have an equal place with Latin in the curriculum. Above all, the school was to be free from religious control. Franklin's plan was successful. The Academy of Philadelphia opened in 1751 and was incorporated in 1754. It was the first secular institution of higher learning in the colonies. Printed: Albert H. Smyth, ed., *The Writings of Benjamin Franklin* (10 vols., New York, 1905-1907), II, pp. 386-396.

ADVERTISEMENT TO THE READER

I t has long been regretted as a misfortune to the youth of this province that we have no academy in which they might receive the accomplishments of a regular education. The following paper of hints towards forming a plan for that purpose is so far approved by some public spirited gentlemen to whom it has been privately communicated, that they have directed a number of copies to be made by the press and properly distributed, in order to obtain the sentiments and advice of men of learning, understanding, and experience in these matters; and have determined to use their interest and best endeavours to have the scheme when completed carried gradually into execution; in which they have reason to believe they shall have the hearty concurrence and assistance of many who are well-wishers to their country. Those who incline to favour the design with their advice either as to the parts of learning to be taught, the order of study, the method of teaching, the economy of the school, or any other matter of importance to the success of the undertaking, are desired to communicate their sentiments as soon as may be, by letter directed to B. Franklin, Printer, in Philadelphia.

PROPOSALS

The good education of youth has been esteemed by wise men in all ages as the surest foundation of the happiness both of private families and of commonwealths. Almost all governments have therefore made it a principal object of their attention to establish and endow with proper revenues such seminaries of learning as might supply the succeeding age with men qualified to serve the public with honour to themselves and to their country.

Many of the first settlers of these provinces were men who had received a good education in Europe, and to their wisdom and good management we owe much of our present prosperity. But their hands were full and they could not do all things. The present race are not thought to be generally of equal ability. for though the American youth are allowed not to want capacity, yet the best capacities require cultivation, it being truly with them as with the best ground, which unless well tilled and sowed with profitable seed produces only ranker weeds.

That we may obtain the advantages arising from an increase of knowledge, and prevent as much as may be the mischievous consequences that would attend a general ignorance among us, the following hints are offered towards forming a plan for the education of the youth of Pennsylvania, viz:

It is proposed that some persons of leisure and public spirit apply for a charter by which they may be incorporated, with power to erect an academy for the education of youth, to govern the same, provide masters, make rules, receive donations, purchase lands, etc., and to add to their number from time to time such other persons as they shall judge suitable.

That the members of the corporation make it their pleasure, and in some degree their business, to visit the academy often, encourage and countenance the youth, countenance and assist the masters, and by all means in their power advance the usefulness and reputation of the design; that they look on the students as in some sort their children, treat them with familiarity and affection, and, when they have behaved well and gone through their studies and are to enter the world, zealously unite, and make all the interest that can be made to establish them, whether in business, offices, marriages, or any other thing for their advantage, preferably to all other persons whatsoever even of equal merit.

And if men may, and frequently do, catch such a taste for cultivating flowers, for planting, grafting, inoculating, and the like, as to despise all other amusements for their sake, why may not we expect they should acquire a relish for that more useful culture of young minds. Thompson says:

> "'Tis Joy to see the human Blossoms blow,
> When infant Reason grows apace, and calls
> For the kind Hand of an assiduous Care.
> Delightful Task! to rear the tender Thought,
> To teach the young Idea how to shoot;
> To pour the fresh Instruction o'er the Mind,
> To breathe th' enliv'ning Spirit, and to fix
> The generous Purpose in the glowing Breast."

That a house be provided for the academy, if not in the town, not many miles from it; the situation high and dry, and if it may be, not far from a river, having a garden, orchard, meadow, and a field or two.

That the house be furnished with a library (if in the country; if in the town, the town libraries may serve) with maps of all countries, globes, some mathematical instruments, an apparatus for experiments in natural philosophy, and for mechanics; prints of all kinds, prospects, buildings, machines, etc.

That the rector be a man of good understanding, good morals, diligent and patient, learned in the languages and sciences, and a correct pure speaker and writer of the English tongue; to have such tutors under him as shall be necessary.

That the boarding scholars diet together, plainly, temperately, and frugally.

That to keep them in health, and to strengthen and render active their bodies, they be frequently exercised in running, leaping, wrestling, and swimming, etc.

That they have peculiar habits to distinguish them from other youth, if the academy be in or near the town; for this, among other reasons, that their behaviour may be the better observed.

As to their studies, it would be well if they could be taught everything that is useful, and everything that is ornamental; but Art is long, and their time is short. It is therefore proposed that they learn those things that are likely to be most useful and most ornamental, regard being had to the several professions for which they are intended.

All should be taught to write a fair hand, and swift, as that is useful to all. And with it may be learnt something of drawing, by imitation of prints, and some of the first principles of perspective.

Arithmetic, accounts, and some of the first principles of geometry and astronomy.

The English language might be taught by grammar in which some of our best writers, as Tillotson, Addison, Pope, Algernon Sidney, Cato's Letters, etc., should be classics; the styles principally to be cultivated being the clear and the concise. Reading should also be taught, and pronouncing, properly, distinctly, emphatically; not with an even tone, which underdoes, nor a theatrical, which overdoes Nature.

To form their style they should be put on writing letters to each other, making abstracts of what they read; or writing the same things in their own words; telling or writing stories lately read in their own expressions. All to be revised and corrected by the tutor, who should give his reasons and explain the force and import of words, etc.

To form their pronunciation, they may be put on making declamations, repeating speeches, delivering orations, etc.; the tutor assisting at the rehearsals, teaching, advising, correcting their accent, etc.

But if history be made a constant part of their reading, such as the translations of the Greek and Roman historians, and the modern histories of ancient Greece and Rome, etc., may not almost all kinds of useful knowledge be that way introduced to advantage, and with pleasure to the student? As

Geography, by reading with maps, and being required to point out the places where the greatest actions were done, to give their old and new names, with the bounds, situation, extent of the countries concerned, etc.

Chronology, by the help of Helvicus or some other writer of the kind, who will enable them to tell when those events happened; what princes were contemporaries, what states or famous men flourished about that time, etc. The several principal epochs to be first well fixed in their memories.

Ancient Customs, religious and civil, being frequently mentioned in history, will give occasion for explaining them; in which the prints of medals, basso-relievos, and ancient monuments will greatly assist.

Morality, by descanting and making continual observations on the causes of the rise or fall of any man's character, fortune, power, etc., mentioned in history; the advantages of temperance, order, frugality, industry, perseverance, etc., etc. Indeed the general natural tendency of reading good history must be to fix in the minds of youth deep impressions of the beauty and usefulness of virtue of all kinds, public spirit, fortitude, etc.

History will show the wonderful effects of oratory in governing, turning and leading great bodies of mankind, armies, cities, nations. When the minds of youth are struck with admiration at this, then is the time to give them the principles of that art, which they will study with taste and application. Then they may be made acquainted with the best models among the ancients, their beauties being particularly pointed out to them. Modern political oratory being chiefly performed by the pen and press, its advantages over the ancient in some respects are to be shown, as that its effects are more extensive, more lasting, etc.

History will also afford frequent opportunities of showing the necessity of a public religion from its usefulness to the public; the advantage of a religious character among private persons; the mischiefs of superstition, etc., and the excellency of the Christian religion above all others ancient or modern.

History will also give occasion to expatiate on the advantage of civil orders and constitutions; how men and their properties are protected by joining in societies and establishing government; their industry encouraged and rewarded, arts invented, and life made more comfortable; the advantages of liberty, mischiefs of licentiousness, benefits arising from good laws and a due execution of justice, etc. Thus may the first principles of sound politics be fixed in the minds of youth.

On historical occasions, questions of right and wrong, justice and injustice, will naturally arise and may be put to youth, which they may debate in conversation and in writing. When they ardently desire victory for the sake of the praise attending it, they will begin to feel the want, and be sensible of the use of logic, or the art of reasoning to discover truth, and of arguing to defend it, and convince adversaries. This would be the time to acquaint them with the principles of that art. Grotius, Pufendorf, and some other writers of the same kind may be used on these occasions to decide their disputes. Public disputes warm the imagination, whet the industry, and strengthen the natural abilities.

When youth are told that the great men whose lives and actions they read in history spoke two of the best languages that ever were, the most expressive, copious, beautiful; and that the finest writings, the most correct compositions, the most perfect productions of human wit and wisdom are in those languages, which have endured ages and will endure while there are men; that no translation can do them justice or give the pleasure found in reading the originals; that those languages contain all science; that one of them is become almost universal, being the language of learned men in all countries; that to understand them is a distinguishing ornament, etc., they may be thereby made desirous of learning those languages, and their industry sharpened in the acquisition of them. All intended for divinity should be taught the Latin and Greek; for physic, the Latin, Greek, and French; for law, the Latin and French; merchants, the French, German, and Spanish. And though all should not be compelled to learn Latin, Greek, or the modern foreign languages, yet none that have an ardent desire to learn them should be refused; their English, arithmetic, and other studies absolutely necessary being at the same time not neglected.

If the new Universal History were also read, it would give a connected idea of human affairs, so far as it goes, which should be followed by the best modern histories, particularly of our mother country; then of these colonies, which should be accompanied with observations on their rise, increase, use to Great Britain, encouragements, discouragements, etc., the means to make them flourish, secure their liberties, etc.

With the history of men, times, and nations, should be read at proper hours or days some of the best histories of nature, which would not only be delightful to youth, and furnish them with matter for their letters, etc., as well as other history, but afterwards of great use to them, whether they are merchants, handicrafts, or divines; enabling the first the better to understand many commodities, drugs, etc.; the second to improve his trade or handicraft by new mixtures, materials, etc., and the last to adorn his discourses by beautiful comparisons, and strengthen them by new proofs of divine providence. The conversation of all will be improved by it as occasions frequently occur of making natural observations which are instructive, agreeable, and entertaining in almost all companies. Natural history will also afford opportunities of introducing many observations relating to the preservation of health, which may be afterwards of great use. Arbuthnot on air and aliment, Sanctorius on perspiration, Lemery on foods, and some others may now be read, and a very little explanation will make them sufficiently intelligible to youth.

While they are reading natural history, might not a little gardening, planting, grafting, inoculating, etc., be taught and practised, and now and then excursions made to the neighbouring plantations of the best farmers, their methods observed and reasoned upon for the information of youth? The improvement of agriculture being useful to all, and skill in it no disparagement to any.

The history of commerce, of the invention of arts, rise of manufactures, progress of trade, change of its seats, with the reasons, causes, etc., may also be made entertaining to youth, and will be useful to all. And this, with the accounts in other history of the prodigious force and effect of engines and machines used in war, will naturally introduce a desire to be instructed in mechanics, and to be informed of the principles of that art by which weak men perform such wonders, labour is saved, manufactures expedited, etc. This will be the time to show them prints of ancient and modern machines, to explain them, to let them be copied, and to give lectures in mechanical philosophy.

With the whole should be constantly inculcated and cultivated that benignity of mind which shows itself in searching for and seizing every opportunity to serve and to oblige, and is the foundation of what is called good breeding, highly useful to the possessor, and most agreeable to all.

The idea of what is true merit should also be often presented to youth, explained and impressed on their minds, as consisting in an inclination joined with an ability to serve mankind, one's country, friends and family, which ability is (with the blessing of God) to be acquired or greatly increased by true learning, and should indeed be the great aim and end of all learning.

93. Samuel Johnson: The "Advertisement" for King's College (31 May 1754)

King's College in New York, the forerunner of Columbia University, was one of the several colonial colleges founded in the middle of the eighteenth century, but its founding was attended by a storm of political controversy such as no other college was subjected to. In 1746 a group of Anglicans proposed a college to be supported by the colonial government, but which would at the same time be affiliated with the Anglican Church. A number of Presbyterians at once attacked the proposal and insisted that the college be nonsectarian. In the ensuing fight the project became involved in the struggle between the Livingston and De Lancey factions in New York politics. There was a vast amount of newspaper and pamphlet writing on education, and amidst all the polemic, there was much of new educational theories of the time. Money was raised but the college did not offer classes until July 1754. Samuel Johnson, a noted Anglican divine, was appointed president. His advertisement for the college sets forth his aims. While there is much emphasis on religion, all sects were to be welcome, and 'practical' subjects as well as the traditional ones were to be offered. Printed: *The New York Mercury*, 3 June 1754.

ADVERTISEMENT

To such parents as have now (or expect to have) children prepared to be educated in the College of New York.

I. As the gentlemen who are appointed by the Assembly to be trustees of the intended seminary or college of New York have thought fit to appoint me to take the charge of it, and have concluded to set up a course of tuition in the learned languages and in the liberal arts and sciences, they have judged it advisable that I should publish this advertisement to inform such as have children ready for a college education that it is proposed to begin tuition upon the first day of July next at the vestry room in the new schoolhouse adjoining to Trinity Church in New York, which the gentlemen of the vestry are so good as to favour them with the use of in the interim 'till a convenient place may be built.

II. The lowest qualifications they have judged requisite in order to admission into the said college are as follows, viz.: that they be able to read well and write a good legible hand, and that they be well versed in the five first rules in arithmetic, i.e., as far as division and reduction; and as to Latin and Greek, that they have a good knowledge in the grammars and be able to make grammatical Latin; and both in construing and parsing to give a good account of two or three of the first select orations of Tully and of the first books of Virgil's *Aeneid* and some of the first chapters of the Gospel of St. John in Greek. In these books, therefore, they may expect to be examined; but higher qualifications must hereafter be expected. And if there be any of the higher classes in any college or under private instruction that incline to come hither, they may expect admission to proportionably higher classes here.

III. And that people may be the better satisfied in sending their children for education to this college, it is to be understood that as to religion, there is no intention to impose on the scholars the peculiar tenets of any particular sect of Christians, but to inculcate upon their tender minds the great principles of Christianity and morality in which true Christians of each denomination are generally agreed. And as to the daily worship in the college, morning and evening, it is proposed that it should ordinarily consist of such a collection of lessons, prayers, and praises of the liturgy of the Church as are for the most part taken out of the Holy Scriptures, and such as are agreed on by the trustees to be in the best manner expressive of our common Christianity. And as to any peculiar tenets, everyone is left to judge freely for himself and to be required only to attend constantly at such places of worship on the Lord's Day as their parent or guardians shall think fit to order or permit.

IV. The chief thing that is aimed at in this college is to teach and engage the children to know God in Jesus Christ and to love and serve Him in all sobriety, godliness, and righteousness of life, with a perfect heart and a willing mind, and to train them up in all virtuous habits and all such useful knowledge as may render them creditable to their families and friends, ornaments to their country, and useful to the public weal in their generations. To which good purposes it is earnestly desired that their parents, guardians, and masters would train them up from their cradles under strict government and in all seriousness, virtue, and industry, that they may be qualified to make orderly and tractable members of this society. And above all, that in order hereunto they be very careful themselves to set them good examples of true piety and virtue in their own conduct. For as examples have a very powerful influence over young minds, and especially those of their parents, in vain are they solicitous for a good education for their children if they themselves set before them examples of impiety and profaneness or of any sort of vice whatsoever.

Vth and lastly. A serious, virtuous, and industrious course of life being first provided for, it is further the design of this college to instruct and perfect the youth in the learned languages and in the arts of reasoning exactly, of writing correctly, and speaking eloquently; and in the arts of numbering and measuring, of surveying and navigation, of geography and history, of husbandry, commerce, and government; and in the knowledge of all nature in the heavens above us, and in the air, water, and earth around us, and the various kinds of meteors, stones, mines and minerals, plants and animals, and of every thing useful for the comfort, the convenience, and elegance of life in the chief manufactures relating to any of these things. And finally, to lead them from the study of nature to the knowledge of themselves and of the God of nature and their duty to Him, themselves, and one another, and everything that can contribute to their true happiness both here and hereafter.

Thus much, gentlemen, it was thought proper to advertise you of concerning the nature and design of this college. And I pray God it may be attended with all the success you can wish for the best good of the rising generations to which, while I continue here, I shall willingly contribute my endeavours to the utmost of my power.

Gentlemen,

Your real friend and most humble servant,

Samuel Johnson

N.B. The charge of the tuition is established by the trustees to be only twenty-five shillings for each quarter.

Part VI
EXPANSION AND SOCIAL DISCONTENT

EXPANSION AND SOCIAL DISCONTENT

Introduction

SOCIAL discontent of various sorts was a constant factor in the history of the American colonies. Religious dissenters protested against established churches from the founding of Massachusetts to the American Revolution. The efforts of the imperial government to exercise more and more control after 1660 was met with opposition everywhere in the colonies, and the Revolution of 1688 in England was followed by revolts in Massachusetts, New York, and Maryland. The attempts of the proprietors to exercise the great powers given them in their charters produced opposition, and upon occasion outright rebellion, as in Maryland and the Carolinas.

However, the most important causes of political and social tensions, which at times led to outright rebellions, are to be found in two basic facts of colonial life: in the constant expansion into new frontier areas and all the problems arising therefrom, and in the development of indigenous colonial aristocracies that exercised an extraordinary amount of control over the political and economic life of most of the colonies.[1] Although men of wealth and family were to be found in the colonies from the outset, the majority of the members of the colonial aristocracies gained their wealth and political power within the framework of colonial society.

By the eighteenth century, the aristocracy tended to become an hereditary one, particularly in the southern colonies. Nevertheless, there are any number of men who started out as poor men, or as apprentices or indentured servants, who in their own lifetimes became members of the ruling class. Basically, it was aristocracy founded on wealth: wealth in the form of land, slaves, ships, stores, and goods, rather than on ancestry. The acquisition of wealth made one a member; the loss of wealth meant the loss of social and political importance.

As the colonies developed, wealth and political power concentrated in the seaport towns of the north and in the plantations of the tidewater south. The rising merchant class in the northern towns – as importers and exporters, as creditors, and, increasingly, as speculators in unsettled lands – held a tight economic grip on the vast majority of the people who were made up of artisans, shopkeepers, and small farmers. The planters of the southern tidewater played a similar role as creditors, and, above all, as speculators in land.[2]

Geographically, the aristocracy was centred along the coast. The great expansion in area and population within the colonies, especially during the eighteenth century, was westward and south-westward, and had reached the western edge of the Appalachian ranges by 1763. It was the fact of concentrated settlement along the coast during the seventeenth century and the rapid expansion away from it during the eighteenth century that helps to explain the political control exercised by the colonial aristocracies. The early governments provided for representation of townships, counties, and cities in colonial legislatures.[3] But the creation of new townships and counties

---

[1] See Nos. 94 to 96. [2] No. 50. [3] Nos. 37, 38, 47.

did not keep pace with the rapid expansion of population. The aristocracies, in control of the older areas and hence of the colonial legislatures, refused to create new areas of representation, or if they did so, they were so large as to be politically meaningless. Hence by 1763 the great majority of back-country farmers had little direct political influence in colonial legislatures.[1] The policy was a deliberate one on the part of the colonial ruling classes, and even when they relented from time to time, the British government refused its consent.

Coupled with the refusal to grant adequate representation to new areas was the imposition of a property qualification for the suffrage–an effective means of keeping the poorer inhabitants of the towns from voting. Many of the colonies had no property qualification for the suffrage to begin with, but all of them had adopted one by the eighteenth century. Thus, while the colonies as a whole had won effective self-government from Great Britain by 1763, it was not extended to the ever-growing population within the colonies.

Although the people of the colonial towns had reasons for discontent, they did not express that discontent so violently as did the farmers, at least until the events leading to the outbreak of the war for independence. In the century before the Declaration of Independence, American farmers revolted a remarkable number of times. The first outright revolt was Bacon's Rebellion in Virginia in 1676.[2] The last rebellion was that of the Regulators in North Carolina, which ended with the battle of Alamance Creek in May 1771.[3] The farmers had many reasons for their discontent. The back country, particularly from Pennsylvania to Georgia, was settled by a great variety of religious dissenters who objected to paying taxes to support the Anglican Church.[4] As debtors, they demanded a more adequate money supply. As settlers, they resented the control of land granting by the colonial aristocracies, a process which led to vast accumulations of land by those who granted it. They demanded the creation of smaller counties with court-houses at more convenient locations. They wanted more protection from the Indians than they received.[5] They needed roads and bridges in order to get their crops to the seaport markets. They objected to taxation of land by the acre rather than according to its value. Where they had no local governments, they demanded them;[6] where they had corrupt local governments, they were embittered.[7]

Both the nature and intensity of grievances varied from colony to colony, but in some form existed in all of them. The result was armed revolt over and over again, and most seriously in the years after 1763. In South Carolina, the Regulator Movement aimed to create local government where none existed. In North Carolina, the Regulator Movement fought corrupt local government. The uprising of the Paxton Boys in Pennsylvania sought to eliminate Indians supported by the colonial government.[8] In New York, tenant farmers rose in rebellion against their landlords.

Agrarian discontent in the colonies, which rose to a peak after 1763, paralleled the rise of the opposition to Great Britain which led to the war for independence. The colonial aristocracies thus fought a battle on two fronts: against increasing British control, and against agrarian demands for what amounted to more self-government within the colonies. The agrarian revolts in New York, North Carolina, and South Carolina were suppressed ruthlessly, in some cases by the same men who were leading the movement in opposition to Great Britain. It is not surprising therefore that many

---

[1] Nos. 94, 95, 96.   [2] No. 94.   [3] No. 95.   [4] No. 88.
[5] No. 96.   [6] No. 95A.   [7] No. 95B.   [8] No. 96.

back-country men viewed the war for independence with scepticism, and in New York and North Carolina in particular, many back-country farmers were loyalists. However, in some colonies, such as Pennsylvania, the back-country leaders worked with popular leaders along the coast. Furthermore, back-country discontent and demand for political and economic change were to become a vital force in the history of the states in the years after 1776. The overturn of old governments and the creation of new ones provided opportunities, not always fully realized, for wide-sweeping changes in the structure of American society.

SELECT BIBLIOGRAPHY

(a) COLONIAL EXPANSION

The serious scholarly study of American expansion, of the 'westward movement', was the result of the work of FREDERICK JACKSON TURNER. His essay of 1893, "The Significance of the Frontier in American History", opened up a field of study that has produced a vast amount of published source materials and many detailed monographs. TURNER's essay marks a major turning point in American historiography although of late it has been subjected to a variety of criticisms. All too often the critics have spent their time in a microscopic analysis of TURNER's preliminary essay and have ignored the importance of American expansion. For the controversy, see EVERETT E. EDWARDS, *References to the Significance of the Frontier in American History* (U.S. Dept. of Agric. Library, Bibliographical Contributions, No. 25, 2nd ed., Washington, 1939). TURNER's essay is reprinted in his *The Frontier in American History* (New York, 1921), along with two important studies of the colonial frontier: "The First Official Frontier of the Massachusetts Bay" and "The Old West".

Of the works relating specifically to the colonial frontier, aside from those cited subsequently, the following are important. FRANCIS W. HALSEY, *The Old New York Frontier . . .* (New York, 1901); the early portion of LOIS K. MATTHEWS, *The Expansion of New England* (New York, 1909); VERNER W. CRANE, *The Southern Frontier, 1670–1732*; ROBERT L. MERIWETHER, *The Expansion of South Carolina, 1729–1765* (Kingsport, Tenn., 1940). The most recent study of the southern frontier is the third chapter of CARL BRIDENBAUGH, *Myths and Realities*, "The Back Settlements". In addition to such specific works, the works on immigration already cited have much to say of colonial expansion since most immigrants were frontier settlers.

(b) THE COLONIAL ARISTOCRACIES

The only book discussing the colonial aristocracies as a whole, and particularly their political importance, is LEONARD W. LABAREE, *Conservatism in Early American History* (New York, 1948). The aristocracy of Virginia has been the subject of more study than any similar group in the other colonies. Of the older works, PHILIP A. BRUCE, *Social Life of Virginia in the Seventeenth Century . . .* (Richmond, Va., 1907) and *Institutional History of Virginia in the Seventeenth Century . . .* give the general background. JOHN S. BASSETT's introduction to The Writings of "Colonel William Byrd . . ." (New York, 1901) is a concise study of one family. LOUIS B. WRIGHT and MARION TINLING, eds., *The Secret Diary of William Byrd of Westover, 1709–1712* (Richmond, Va., 1941), and MAUDE H. WOODFIN and MARION TINLING, eds., *Another Secret Diary of William Byrd of Westover, 1739–1741* (Richmond, Va., 1942), present a unique picture of the daily life of one of the leading planters of eighteenth-century Virginia. THOMAS J. WERTENBAKER's *Patrician and Plebian in Virginia . . .* (Charlottesville, Va., 1910) and his *The Planters of Colonial Virginia* emphasize the middle-class origins of the aristocracy and their techniques of economic and political control. WILLIAM E. DODD, "The Emergence of the First Social Order in the United States", *Amer. Hist. Rev.*, vol. XL (1934–1935) and *The Old South: Struggles for Democracy* (New York, 1937), are criticized for errors, but are important for showing the interest of the Restoration politicians in England in building up an aristocracy in the colonies, and particularly in Virginia. LOUIS B. WRIGHT, *The First Gentlemen of Virginia*, and CARL BRIDENBAUGH, *Myths and Realities*, chapter i, "The Chesapeake Society", present two different but useful approaches. Chapter ii of the latter book, "The Carolina Society", is an invaluable discussion of the rapidly rising merchant-planter aristocracy centring in Charleston.

The merchants of the various colonies have never received, as a group, the kind of attention that has been paid to the Virginia planters. However, material for such a study can be found in various works on commerce and on individual merchants. W. B. WEEDEN's *Economic and Social History of New England* has material on the rise of various merchants. Of the modern works, FREDERICK B. TOLLES, *Meeting House and Counting House*, treats of the Quaker merchants of Philadelphia. VIRGINIA D. HARRINGTON, *The New York Merchant on the Eve of the Revolution*, has valuable information for that city. DAVID D. WALLACE, *The Life of Henry Laurens . . .* (New York, 1915), W. T. BAXTER, *The House of Hancock*, and JAMES B. HEDGES, *The Browns of Providence Plantations*, are invaluable for the individuals and the areas concerned.

The political role of the colonial aristocracies is discussed either directly or indirectly in several of the works listed in the bibliography on "Government within the Colonies", as well as in those listed above.

(c) REBELLIONS IN THE COLONIES

The most convenient collection of sources for seventeenth-century rebellions is CHARLES M. ANDREWS, *Narratives of the Insurrections, 1675–1690 (Original Narratives of American History*, New York, 1915). A great deal of material on Bacon's Rebellion in Virginia has been published. The best guide to it is in E. G. SWEM, *Virginia Historical Index*. Many of the sources for the Regulator Movement in North Carolina have also been published. See ARCHIBALD HENDERSON, "The Origin of the Regulation in North Carolina", *Amer. Hist. Rev.*, vol. XXI (1915–1916); W. K. BOYD, ed., *Some Eighteenth Century Tracts Concerning North Carolina* (Raleigh, 1927); and ARTHUR P. HUDSON, "Songs of the North Carolina Regulators", *William and Mary Quarterly*, 3rd Series, vol. IV (1947). A unique collection of sources for the Regulator Movement in South Carolina is brought together in RICHARD J. HOOKER, ed., *The Carolina Back-country on the Eve of the Revolution: The Journal and other Writings of Charles Woodmason, Anglican Itinerant* (Chapel Hill, N.C., 1953).

The following are important specialized studies of rebellions in the colonies and contain many references to printed and manuscript materials: JEROME R. REICH, *Leisler's Rebellion: A Study of Democracy in New York, 1664–1720* (Chicago, 1953); IRVING MARK, *Agrarian Conflicts in Colonial New York, 1711–1775*; BROOKE HINDLE, "The March of the Paxton Boys", *William and Mary Quarterly*, 3rd Series, vol. III (1946); JOHN S. BASSETT, "The Regulators of North Carolina (1765–1771)", Amer. Hist. Assoc. *Annual Report* (1894); and RICHARD J. HOOKER's introduction to *The South Carolina Back-country on the Eve of the Revolution*. DONALD KEMMERER, *Path to Freedom*, discusses the tenant farmer riots in New Jersey. JOHN C. MILLER, "Religion, Finance, and Democracy in Massachusetts", *New England Quarterly*, vol. VI (1933), has some suggestive interpretations of the various causes of discontent in Massachusetts in the 1730's. ROY H. AKAGI, *The Town Proprietors of the New England Colonies*, discusses the rise of land speculation as a source of discontent. For religion and financial issues as sources of discontent, see the bibliography on "Religion in the Colonies", and the bibliography on "Colonial Money Problems".

94A–C. Bacon's Rebellion (1676)

Bacon's Rebellion in Virginia was the first popular revolt in the English colonies. Governor William Berkeley built up a corrupt and efficient political machine in the colony after 1660. He got a legislature which he could control in 1661 and did not call a new election for fourteen years. In 1670 non-landowners were disfranchised. Heavy taxes were laid. Tobacco prices were low and the small farmers were in difficulties. The governor and his clique did not provide for adequate protection against Indian raids. The result was a rebellion led by Nathaniel Bacon (1647–1676), who had come to Virginia only a short time before and had settled on a frontier plantation. Bacon and his followers drove out the Indians and were denounced by the Governor. Within a short time the rebels demanded changes in the government of the colony. Governor Berkeley was driven out and the legislature, under Bacon's control, passed a series of reform acts including one restoring the suffrage to all adult males.

Bacon's sudden death brought about a collapse of the rebellion. Berkeley and his followers regained control and hunted down the rebels, hanged their leaders, and confiscated their property. When news of the rebellion reached England, a commission was appointed to go to Virginia to investigate and more than a thousand troops were sent along to suppress the rebellion. However, the rebellion was over before the fleet got to Virginia in January 1677.

The following documents are samples of a large body of materials relating to the rebellion. Bacon's "Manifesto" states the case of the rebels (No. 94A). Governor Berkeley's view is given in his "Declaration" against Bacon (No. 94B). The commissioners sent over from England asked the county sheriffs to collect statements of the grievances of the counties. The nature of the discontent giving rise to the rebellion is set forth at large in such county statements. That of Isle of Wight County is given here (No. 94C).

94A. Nathaniel Bacon: manifesto concerning the troubles in Virginia (1676)

Printed: *The Virginia Magazine of History and Biography*, 1 (1894), pp. 55–61.

If virtue be a sin, if piety be guilt, all the principles of morality, goodness and justice be perverted, we must confess that those who are now called rebels may be in danger of those high imputations. Those loud and several bulls would affright innocents and render the defence of our brethren and the inquiry into our sad and heavy oppressions, treason. But if there be, as sure there is, a just God to appeal to; if religion and justice be a sanctuary here; if to plead the cause of the oppressed; if sincerely to aim at his Majesty's honour and the public good without any reservation or by interest; if to stand in the gap after so much blood of our dear brethren bought and sold; if after the loss of a great part of his Majesty's colony deserted and dispeopled, freely with our lives and estates to endeavour to save the remainders be treason; God Almighty judge and let guilty die. But since we cannot in our hearts find one single spot of rebellion or treason, or that we have in any manner aimed at the subverting the settled government or attempting of the person of any either magistrate or private man, notwithstanding the several reproaches and threats of some who for sinister ends were disaffected to us and censured our innocent and honest designs, and since all people in all places where we have yet been can attest our civil, quiet, peaceable behaviour far different from that of rebellion and tumultuous persons, let truth be bold and all the world know the real foundations of pretended guilt. We appeal to the country itself what and of what nature their oppressions have been, or by what cabal and mystery the designs of many of those whom we call great men have been transacted and carried on; but let us trace these men in authority and favour to whose hands the dispensation of the country's wealth has been committed. Let us observe the sudden rise of their estates composed with the quality in which they first entered this country, or the reputation they have held here amongst wise and discerning men. And let us see whether their extractions and education have not been vile, and by what pretence of learning and virtue they could so soon [come] into employments of so great trust and consequence. Let us consider their sudden advancement and let us also consider whether any public work for our safety and defence or for the advancement and propagation of trade, liberal arts, or sciences is here extant in any way adequate to our vast charge. Now let us compare these things together and see what sponges have sucked up the public treasure, and whether it has not been privately contrived away by unworthy favourites and juggling parasites whose tottering fortunes have been repaired and supported at the public charge. Now if it be so, judge what greater guilt can be than to offer to pry into these and to unriddle the mysterious wiles of a powerful cabal; let all people judge what can be of more dangerous import than to suspect the so long safe proceedings of some of our grandees, and whether people may with safety open their eyes in so nice a concern.

Another main article of our guilt is our open and manifest aversion of all, not only the foreign but the protected and darling Indians. This, we are informed, is rebellion of a deep dye for that both the governor and council are by Colonel Cole's assertion bound to defend the queen and the Appamatocks with their blood. Now, whereas we do declare and can prove that they have been for these many years enemies to the king and country, robbers and thieves and invaders of his Majesty's right and our interest and estates, but yet have by persons in authority been defended and protected even against his Majesty's loyal subjects, and that in so high a nature that even the complaints and oaths of his Majesty's most loyal subjects in a lawful manner proffered by them against those barbarous outlaws, have been by the right honourable governor rejected and the delinquents from his presence dismissed, not only with pardon and indemnity, but with all encouragement and favour; their firearms so destructful to us and by our laws prohibited, commanded to be restored them, and open declaration before witness made that they must have ammunition, although directly contrary to our law. Now what greater guilt can be than to oppose and endeavour the destruction of these honest, quiet neighbours of ours?

Another main article of our guilt is our design not only to ruin and extirpate all Indians in general, but all manner of trade and commerce with them. Judge who can be innocent that strike at this tender eye of interest: since the right honourable the governor hath been pleased by his commission to warrant this trade, who dare oppose it, or opposing it can be innocent? Although plantations be deserted, the blood of our dear brethren spilled; on all sides our complaints; continually murder upon murder renewed upon us; who may or dare think of the general subversion of all manner of trade and commerce with our enemies who can or dare impeach any of . . . traders at the heads of the rivers, if contrary to the wholesome provision made by laws for the country's safety; they dare continue their illegal practises and dare asperse the right honourable governor's wisdom and justice so highly to pretend to have his warrant to break that law which himself made; who dare say that these men at the heads of the rivers buy and sell our blood, and do still, notwithstanding the late act made to the contrary, admit Indians painted and continue to commerce; although these things can be proved, yet who dare be so guilty as to do it?

Another article of our guilt is to assert all those neighbour Indians as well as others, to be outlawed, wholly unqualified for the benefit and protection of the law, for that the law does reciprocally protect and punish, and that all people offending must either in person or estate make equivalent satisfaction or restitution, according to the manner and merit of the offences, debts, or trespasses. Now since the Indians cannot, according to the tenure and form of any law to us known, be prosecuted, seized, or complained against, their persons being difficultly distinguished or known; their many nations' languages, and their subterfuges such as makes them incapable to make us restitution or satisfaction, would it not be very guilty to say they have been unjustly defended and protected these many years?

If it should be said that the very foundation of all these disasters, the grant of the beaver trade to the right honourable governor was illegal, and not grantable by any power here present as being a monopoly, were not this to deserve the name of rebel and traitor?

Judge, therefore, all wise and unprejudiced men who may or can faithfully or truly with an honest heart, attempt the country's good, their vindication, and liberty without the aspersion of traitor and rebel, since as so doing they must of necessity gall such tender and dear concerns. But to manifest sincerity and loyalty to the world, and how much we abhor those bitter names; may all the world know that we do unanimously desire to represent our sad and heavy grievances to his most sacred Majesty as our refuge and sanctuary, where we do well know that all our causes will be impartially heard and equal justice administered to all men.

THE DECLARATION OF THE PEOPLE

For having upon specious pretences of public works, raised unjust taxes upon the commonalty for the advancement of private favourites and other sinister ends, but no visible effects in any measure adequate.

For not having during the long time of his government in any measure advanced this hopeful colony, either by fortification, towns or trade.

For having abused and rendered contemptible the majesty of justice, of advancing to places of judicature scandalous and ignorant favourites.

For having wronged his Majesty's prerogative and interest by assuming the monopoly of the beaver trade.

By having in that unjust gain bartered and sold his Majesty's country and the lives of his loyal subjects to the barbarous heathen.

For having protected, favoured and emboldened the Indians against his Majesty's most loyal subjects, never contriving, requiring, or appointing any due or proper means of satisfaction for their many invasions, murders, and robberies committed upon us.

For having, when the army of the English was just upon the track of the Indians, which now in all places burn, spoil, and murder, and when we might with ease have destroyed them who then were in open hostility, for having expressly countermanded and sent back our army by passing his word for the peaceable demeanour of the said Indians, who immediately prosecuted their evil intentions, committing horrid murders and robberies in all places, being protected by the said engagement and word passed of him, the said Sir William Berkeley, having ruined and made desolate a great part of his Majesty's country, have now drawn themselves into such obscure and remote places and are by their successes so emboldened and confirmed, and by their confederacy so strengthened that the cries of blood are in all places, and the terror and consternation of the people so great, that they are now become not only a difficult, but a very formidable enemy who might with ease have been destroyed, etc. When upon the loud outcries of blood, the Assembly had with all care raised and framed an army for the prevention of future mischiefs and safeguard of his Majesty's colony.

For having with only the privacy of some few favourites, without acquainting the people, only by the alteration of a figure, forged a commission by we know not what hand, not only without but against the consent of the people, for raising and effecting of civil wars and distractions, which being happily and without bloodshed prevented.

For having the second time attempted the same thereby calling down our forces from the defence of the frontiers, and most weak exposed places, for the prevention of civil mischief and ruin amongst ourselves, whilst the barbarous enemy in all places did invade, murder, and spoil us, his Majesty's most faithful subjects.

Of these, the aforesaid articles, we accuse Sir William Berkeley, as guilty of each and every one of the same, and as one who has traitorously attempted, violated and injured his Majesty's interest here, by the loss of a great part of his colony, and many of his faithful and loyal subjects by him betrayed, and in a barbarous and shameful manner exposed to the incursions and murders of the heathen.

And we further declare these, the ensuing persons in this list, to have been his wicked, and pernicious counsellors, aiders and assisters against the commonalty in these our cruel commotions:

Sir Henry Chicherly, Knt.	Jos. Bridger
Col. Charles Wormley	Wm. Clabourne
Phil. Dalowell	Thos. Hawkins, Jr.
Robert Beverly	William Sherwood
Robert Lee	Jos. Page, Clerk
Thos. Ballard	Jo. Cliffe, ,,
William Cole	Hubberd Farrell
Richard Whitacre	John West
Nicholas Spencer	Thos. Reade

Mathew Kemp

And we do further demand, that the said Sir William Berkeley, with all the persons in this list, be forthwith delivered up, or surrender themselves, within four days after the notice hereof, or otherwise we declare as followeth: that in whatsoever house, place, or ship any of the said persons shall reside, be hid, or protected, we do declare that the owners, masters, or inhabitants of the said places, to be confederates and traitors to the people, and the estates of them, as also of all the aforesaid persons, to be confiscated. This we, the commons of Virginia, do declare desiring a prime union amongst ourselves, that we may jointly, and with one accord defend ourselves against the common enemy. And let not the faults of the guilty be the reproach of the innocent, or the faults or crimes of the oppressors divide and separate us, who have suffered by their oppressions.

These are therefore in his Majesty's name, to command you forthwith to seize the persons above mentioned as traitors to the king and country, and them to bring to Middle Plantation, and there to secure them, till further order, and in case of opposition, if you want any other assistance, you are forthwith to demand it in the name of the people of all the counties of Virginia.

[signed]　　　　NATH BACON, Gen'l.

By the Consent of the People.

94B. Governor William Berkeley: declaration and remonstrance (29 May 1676)

Printed: Massachusetts Historical Society *Collections*, 4th Series, IX, pp. 178–181.

The declaration and remonstrance of Sir William Berkeley, his most sacred Majesty's governor and captain-general of Virginia, shows: That about the year 1660 Colonel Mathews, the then governor died, and then in consideration of the service I had done the country in defending them from and destroying great numbers of the Indians without the loss of three men in all the time that war lasted, and in contemplation of the equal and uncorrupt justice I had distributed to all men, not only the Assembly, but the unanimous votes of all the country concurred to make me governor in a time when, if the rebels in England had prevailed, I had certainly died for accepting it. 'Twas, gentlemen, an unfortunate love showed to me, for to show myself grateful for this I was willing to accept of this government again, when by my gracious king's favour I might have had other places much more profitable and less toilsome than this hath been. Since that time that I returned into the country, I call the great God, judge of all things in heaven and earth, to witness that I do not know of anything relative to this country wherein I have acted unjustly, corruptly, or negligently, in distributing equal justice to all men, and taking all possible care to preserve their proprieties and defend them from their barbarous enemies.

But for all this, perhaps I have erred in things I know not of. If I have, I am so conscious of human frailty and my own defects that I will not only acknowledge them, but repent of and amend them, and not, like the rebel Bacon, persist in an error only because I have committed it; and tells me in divers of his letters that it is not for his honour to confess a fault, but I am of opinion that it is only for devils to be incorrigible, and men of principles like the worst of devils; and these he hath, if truth be reported to me of divers of his expressions of atheism, tending to take away all religion and laws.

And now I will state the question betwixt me as a governor and Mr. Bacon, and say that if any enemies should invade England, any counsellor, justice of peace, or other inferior officer might raise what forces they could to protect his Majesty's subjects. But I say again, if, after the king's knowledge of this invasion, any the greatest peer of England should raise forces against the king's prohibition, this would be now – and ever was in all ages and nations – accounted treason. Nay, I will go further, that though this peer was truly zealous for the preservation of his king and subjects, and had better and greater abilities than all the rest of his fellow-subjects to do his king and country service, yet if the king (though by false information) should suspect the contrary, it were treason in this noble peer to proceed after the king's prohibition: and for the truth of this I appeal to all the laws of England, and the laws and constitutions of all other nations in the world. And yet further, it is declared by this Parliament that the taking up arms for the king and Parliament is treason; for the event showed that whatever the pretence was to seduce ignorant and well-affected people, yet the end was ruinous both to king and people, as this will be if not prevented. I do therefore again declare that Bacon, proceeding against all laws of all nations modern and ancient, is rebel to his sacred Majesty and this country; nor will I insist upon the swearing of men to live and die together, which is treason by the very words of the law.

Now, my friends, I have lived thirty-four years amongst you, as uncorrupt and diligent as ever governor was; Bacon is a man of two years among you; his person and qualities unknown to most of you, and to all men else, by any virtuous action that ever I heard of. And that very action which he boasts of was sickly and foolishly, and, as I am informed, treacherously carried to the dishonour of the English nation. Yet in it he lost more men than I did in three years' war; and by the grace of God will put myself to the same dangers and troubles again when I have brought Bacon to acknowledge the laws are above him, and I doubt not but by God's assistance to have better success than Bacon hath had. The reason of my hopes are, that I will take counsel of wiser men than myself; but Mr. Bacon hath none about him but the lowest of the people.

Yet I must further enlarge, that I cannot without your help do anything in this but die in defence of my king, his laws, and subjects, which I will cheerfully do, though alone I do it; and considering my poor fortunes, I cannot leave my poor wife and friends a better legacy than by dying for my king and you: for his sacred Majesty will easily distinguish between Mr. Bacon's actions and mine, and kings have long arms either to reward or punish.

Now, after all this, if Mr. Bacon can show one precedent or example where such actings in any nation whatever was approved of, I will mediate with the king and you for a pardon and excuse for him; but I can show him a hundred examples where brave and great men have been put to death for gaining victories against the command of their superiors.

Lastly, my most assured friends, I would have preserved those Indians that I knew were hourly at our mercy, to have been our spies and intelligence, to find out our bloody enemies; but as soon as I had the least intelligence that they also were treacherous enemies, I gave out commissions to destroy them all, as the commissions themselves will speak it.

To conclude, I have done what was possible both to friend and enemy; have granted Mr. Bacon three pardons, which he hath scornfully rejected, supposing himself stronger to subvert than I and you to maintain the laws, by which only, and God's assisting grace and mercy, all men must hope for peace and safety. I will add no more, though much more is still remaining to justify me and condemn Mr. Bacon, but to desire that this declaration may be read in every county court in the country, and that a court be presently called to do it before the Assembly meet, that your approbation or dissatisfaction of this declaration may be known to all the country and the king's Council, to whose most revered judgments it is submitted.

Given the 29th day of May, a happy day in the 28th year of his most sacred Majesty's reign, Charles the second, who God grant long and prosperously to reign, and let all his good subjects say amen.

94C. Grievances of Isle of Wight County (5 March 1677)

Printed: *The Virginia Magazine of History and Biography*, II (1895), pp. 380–392.

We have seen the declaration from his Majesty's honourable commissioners to the poor, yet his Majesty's most loyal, subjects of the Isle of Wight County. We have presumed to return this to your honours that we have cause to believe there are many persons who have endeavoured to infuse into you very sinister opinions of our proceedings in relation to the disturbance which was in this country, the which to the outmost of our knowledges and intents we will declare. We having a long time lain under great oppressions, and every year being more and more oppressed with great taxes, and still do load us with greater and unnecessary burdens. It was enacted by the governor and Assembly for the building of forts back in the woods upon several great men's lands, under pretence of security for us against the Indians, which we perceiving and very well knowing that their pretence was no security for us, but rather a ruin to the country, which was the cause of our rising with intents to have our taxes lowered; not that we rose in any ways of rebellion against our most dread sovereign lord the king as by our actions may appear, for we no sooner rose but we sent in a petition and our grievances to Sir William Berkeley, knight, who was not at home. But the Lady Berkeley promised that she would acquaint his honour with our business, and by her request or command, we every man returned home, and as for our being in arms, we was commanded thereto by one act of Governor, Council, and Assembly.

2. After this it was the governor's pleasure to send an order for a new election of burgesses which was in May last, to the best of our remembrance, the which was done according to his order, which privilege we had not in twelve years before. So we all expected redress from this assembly, but nothing answered but only to the Indian war. There was fifty-seven men levied for to go out of the Isle of Wight County under the command of Nathaniel Bacon, a person whom we knew not nor till that time never heard of, though notwithstanding in reference to the command of the governor and Assembly, our men was raised and sent with two months' provision, at which time, whenas our men was gone and under the command of

Squire Bacon, Sir William Berkeley was raising of men against them in Gloucester to the quantity of four or five hundred men, as we are credibly informed; whom, when they understood upon what account they were raised, told his honour to fight against the county men, neighbours and friends, they would not; upon which the governor went away and all the great men whither we know not, and left us as sheep without a shepherd to the mercy of the heathen, yet under the command of Nathaniel Bacon, and this as much as we can say of this disturbance.

3. As to our oppressions: whereas Col. Joseph Bridger for entertaining of Col. William Cole, Col. Charles Morrison, Col. Lemuel Mason, two or three days in dividing of the counties, had between fourteen or fifteen thousand pounds of tobacco from our country, which we humbly conceive is on [one] great oppression.

4. That Col. Bridger had fined several men for not coming to trooping or elsewhere which were fined some 100, 200, 300 pounds of tobacco, all the which we desire to know to what use it is put and that it may be produced for a public good, it amounting to several thousands of tobacco, the which, as we do suppose, Col. Bridger makes use to his own private interest.

5. Whereas formerly it was accounted a great levy that was 40 or 50 pounds of tobacco per each when we were not half so many tithables and a continual war to be maintained, and now we know no occasion extraordinary, yet we paying near 200 a head yearly, but for what we know not.

6. That great quantities of tobacco that was levied upon the poor people to the building of houses at Jamestown, which was not made habitable but fell down again before they were finished.

7. That notwithstanding the great quantities of ammunition paid by ships for fort duties for the country's service, and considerable sums of tobacco raised to maintain a magazine, yet upon all occasions we are forced to provide powder and shot at our proper charges or else fined.

8. That we have been compelled to buy ourselves guns, pistols and other arms to maintain several of our commanders honours and keep ourselves from fining, having been several times threatened before we could procure them, which some of us bought it at a dear rate of them, have now taken them away from us, the which we desire to be restored to us again.

9. The more to encourage the Indians against us they have sent several of them out armed to look after our Christian neighbours who are gone somewhere to secure themselves.

10. That several persons' estates are seized and part taken away before the owners is convicted of any crime, notwithstanding they laid hold of the honourable governor's act of indemnity and have taken the oath of allegiance to his gracious Majesty and fidelity to his Majesty's governor.

11. We desire you, our burgesses, to give none of our estates away as formerly you have done, but if you must give such great sums, dispose of your own.

12. Whereas it was formerly a custom for sheriffs to remain in their place but one year, now it is altered, for they do find such a great benefit by it, that they will buy the

office, and hold it two years so that they predominate over the poor comentrie [*sic*]; whereas the sheriffs are allowed ten pound for every hundred that a hogshead contains besides his salary; he allows us but thirty, the which we desire he may be taken off from it or allow us as much.

13. Also we desire that there may be a continual war with the Indians that we may have once have done with them.

14. We desire we may have liberty to choose our vestries once in three year, and that there may no member of the court be therein.

15. That no Councillor may sit in any inferior court.

16. Also we desire that every man may be taxed according to the tracts of land they hold.

17. That Major Powell had a hundred pounds of tobacco a day for going along with the gentlemen who divided the counties, being as we conceive nothing concerned.

18. And more to exact, he had twelve pounds of tobacco per poll to buy us ammunition, the which we never had.

19. We desire you, our burgesses, to call to account and examine the collectors for the collecting of the two shillings and two pence a hogshead, which have been this many years received but to what use it is put, we, the poor, ignorant inhabitants knows [not], nor how disposed of, being sensible that the merchant exhaust the same in selling his goods and that we pay it, and how and by what power and law the collector demands two pence a hogshead, for what we do request to know, and if not legal, to disannul it for the future. We do humbly conceive that the two shilling a hogshead was raised for to discharge our country taxes; therefore we desire our burgesses to admit our honourable Governor to have his just due out of it, which is 12 hundred pounds a year, and the remainder to assist us, the poor inhabitants towards these great burdens and taxes which we groan under this many years, being not further able to bear it.

20. That by a late act of the Grand Assembly to load us with further taxes, hath enacted forts to be built in several places of this colony, which is as we humbly conceive, for nothing else but for the private use of some particular persons and not at all for the common good; neither to our certain knowledge anyway a defence for us against our most barbarous enemies, who are, as we humbly conceive, too much favoured, emboldened, and encouraged to war with us, but not we with them, being bound absolutely to the peace, as our apprehension tells us, by that act. We therefore desire that we may not be burdened by the building of the foresaid forts, nor that we have any built, and that they may be quite taken off and quitted from all and every one of the pretended charges that may or shall be presented by any, let them be of what nature and quality soever they may be, pretended as an order to the erecting of the foresaid forts, we not being able to undergo so chargeable a compulsion wherein there is neither security nor defence.

21. We do also desire to know for what purpose or use the late public levies of 50 pounds of tobacco and cask per poll and the 12 pound per poll is for, and what benefit we are to have for it, which if it be for our, or our children's good, and that it doth plainly appear so, we are willing to the payment thereof, but otherwise those

that have received our tobacco, to return it us again to the relief of ourselves, and poor families being very unable to pay it.

22. We desire to know for what we do pay our levies every year and that it may no more be laid in private, but that we may have free liberty to hear and see every particular for what it is raised, and that there may no more gifts be given to no particular person or persons whatsoever; neither in public or by private, which hath been only means to make us poor and miserable.

23. Whereas formerly it was the custom of masters of ships to pay the castle duties in powder and shot, which was a safety for this colony at all times, and at war against our Indian enemy or others which should assault us; now it is as we understand, converted, and that duly altered by paying it in shoes, stockings, linen and other merchantable goods as the collectors pleaseth, and disposed of to their own advantages, being no profit or care to country or people, nor no ease to our intolerable taxes. Therefore we desire your honours to have an account of this great bank of money and where it lies, that it may be produced for the country's good, and for the future that it may be paid in powder and shot as formerly, and remain as a magazine for the service of country.

24. Whereas there is one act that burdens the country with amercements in the general and county courts, to know what it is for and to what use it is put and who hath pocketed it, which is against all reason, for many an honest and good paymaster may be sued by too rigid a creditor for what he is willing to pay it if he had it, and it is enough to have judgement for his debt and this amercement exhaust from him; beside which, [it] is too much to the ruin of the debtor.

25. Whereas there are some great persons both in honour rich [and] in estate, and have several ways of gains and profits, are exempted from paying levies, and the poorest inhabitant being compelled to pay the great taxes which we are burdened with, having a hogshead or two of tobacco to pay for rent, and near 200 yearly for levies; having a wife and two or three children to maintain; whether our taxes [are] not the greater by such favour and privileges granted them, which we desire to be eased of by their paying of levies as well as we, they having no necessity from being so exempted.

26. And as for the oath that was sent down to us by Nathaniel Bacon [it] was first concluded by several of the militia officers, Lieutenant-Colonel Arthur Smith being the chief in our county, who was with Squire Bacon at the Middle Plantation and there received the oath, yet so as saving our allegiance to the king.

Whereas there are several clerks in county courts hath enacted their fees on several persons, and especially upon widows and orphans to both their ruins, we desire that a certain rate may be put upon the administration and all other fees thereunto belonging.

We also desire you who are his Majesty's commissioners for to take a view, or cause to be taken, of the forts that we have here made which have cost the country many hundred thousands pounds of tobacco and that we conceive that one fort at Point Comfort had been better and more securer for the King and country, for had there been a fort there by all men's relation, the Dutch had never attempted to a come up the river and burned so many sloops as they did.

       [Signed] Richard Penny, A very busy man in these times.
         John Marshall
         Richard Sharpe
         Richard Jorden, Senior, One of Bacon's representatives.
         Edward Miller,
         A harmless poor man
         John ‡ Davis
           His Mark
One that hath been in arms against the government.

        ANTHONY FULGHAM,
       A busy person that brought this paper
       to the rest to subscribe which was
       written by Marshall's Servant at the
       desire of the subscribers hereof.

          [Indorsed]

       Isle of Wight Grievances
         Brought March 5
         For the Burgesses
     To be perused and returned
         to his Majesty's Commissioners.
         [Signed] Sd. Wiseman

95A–C. The Regulator Movement

The Regulator Movement in the Carolinas during the 1760's was the most violent and prolonged upheaval of back-country settlers in colonial times. In South Carolina the aristocracy had refused to establish adequate local government, particularly courts, and lawlessness was rampant in a rapidly settling area. In North Carolina local governments were established, but they were in the hands of corrupt officials. The legislatures of the two colonies did nothing to alleviate grievances.

By 1764 South Carolina back-country men had begun to take things into their own hands. They organized 'Regulator' associations which enforced law and order in a rough and arbitrary fashion, much like the vigilante associations on later American frontiers. Meanwhile they petitioned the legislature for the establishment of local governmental agencies and for other necessities (No. 95A). The government of the colony planned to suppress the Regulators by force, but at the same time it made concessions by establishing a more adequate court system in the western part of the colony. The organized Regulator Movement subsided, but the back country remained thoroughly distrustful of the low-country leaders and were reluctant to participate in the revolutionary movement because of that distrust.

In North Carolina, unlike South Carolina, county governments were established, but the justices of county courts and other officials were appointees of the governor and council. These officials co-operated with land speculators, merchants, and lawyers in exploiting the back-country settlers for their own benefit. After repeated petitions for relief had been denied, the settlers began organizing Regulator associations to defend themselves. When their leaders were seized, they stormed the jails and removed them. Governor William Tryon led a force into the back country in 1768 but avoided open fighting by promising reforms. In 1769 the Regulators captured control of the Assembly, but Tryon dissolved it because of its attitude towards British measures, and no reforms were forthcoming. The Regulators now became more violent. They intimidated county courts, whipped enemies, and burned houses and barns. In response, Governor Tryon raised a small army and, in May 1771, defeated the Regulator in battle at Alamance Creek, and summarily executed some of their leaders. The movement collapsed but the animosity towards the aristocracy remained, and many back-country men in North Carolina, as in South Carolina, refused to support a revolutionary movement led by their low-country enemies.

The following documents illustrate phases of the discontent which led to the Regulator Movement in the Carolinas. The petition and remonstrance of the South Carolina back country in 1767 is the most eloquent of all the many petitions from the colonial west (No. 95A). The Anson County petition of 1769 is characteristic of many other county petitions to the North Carolina legislature (No. 95B). Governor Josiah Martin's letter of August 1772, to the earl of Hillsborough, gives a far more balanced view of the situation in the North Carolina back country than do the letters of Tryon, whom he replaced (No. 95C).

95A. Remonstrance and petition of the South Carolina back country (7 November 1767)

Although signed by four planters in the name of 4,000 of the inhabitants, the following petition was written by the Reverend Charles Woodmason, one of the most colourful figures in the history of the colony. Woodmason was born in England on an unknown date and came to South Carolina about 1752. In 1766 he went to England where he was ordained. On his return to South Carolina he became a wandering Anglican missionary in the back country. In 1774 he was a Loyalist and returned to England.

The petition is an eloquent and forceful statement of the grievances of the back country. Backed by a threat of a march on Charleston, it jarred the legislature into action. Although the legislature in this and during the next years by no means met all the demands of the petition, it did prevent the open warfare that prevailed during the Regulator Movement in North Carolina. The petition is printed in Richard J. Hooker, ed., *The Carolina Back-country on the Eve of the Revolution: The Journal and other Writings of Charles Woodmason, Anglican Itinerant* (Chapel Hill, N.C., 1953), pp. 213–233.

The Remonstrance and Petition of the Inhabitants of the Upper and Interior Parts of this Province on behalf of themselves, and all other the Settlers of the Back Country,

Humbly Showeth

That for many years past, the back parts of this province hath been infested with an infernal gang of villains, who have committed such horrid depredations on our properties and estates, such insults on the persons of many settlers, and perpetrated such shocking outrages throughout the back settlements, as is past description.

Our large stocks of cattle are either stolen and destroyed, our cow pens are broke up, and all our valuable horses are carried off. Houses have been burned by these rogues, and families stripped and turned naked into the woods. Stores have been broken open and rifled by them (wherefrom several traders are absolutely ruined). Private houses have been plundered; and the inhabitants wantonly tortured in the Indian manner for to be made confess where they secreted their effects from plunder. Married women have been ravished, virgins deflowered, and other unheard of cruelties committed by these barbarous ruffians, who, by being let loose among us (and connived at) by the acting magistrates, have hereby reduced numbers of individuals to poverty, and for these three years last past have laid (in a manner) this part of the province under contribution.

No trading persons (or others) or with money or goods; no responsible persons and traders dare keep cash or any valuable articles by them. Nor can women stir abroad but with a guard, or in terror. The chastity of many beauteous maidens have been threatened by these rogues. Merchants' stores are obliged for to be kept constantly guarded (which enhances the price of goods). And thus we live not as under a British government (every man sitting in peace and security under his own vine, his own fig tree), but as if [we] were in Hungary or Germany, and in a state of war, continually exposed to the incursions of hussars and pandours; obliged to be constantly on the watch and on our guard against these intruders, and having it not in our power to call what we possess our own, not even for an hour; as being liable daily and hourly to be stripped of our property.

Representations of these grievances and vexations have often been made by us to those in power, but without redress. Our cries must have pierced their ears, though not entered into their hearts. For, instead of public justice being executed on many of these notorious robbers (who have been taken by us at much labour and expense and committed) and on others (who with great difficulty and charge have been arraigned and convicted), we have to lament that such have from time to time been pardoned; and afresh set loose among us to repeat their villainies, and strip us of the few remaining cattle, horses, and moveables, which after their former visits they had left us.

Thus distressed, thus situated and unrelieved by government, many among us have been obliged to punish some of these banditti and their accomplices in a proper manner; necessity (that first principle) compelling them to do what was expected that the executive branch of the legislature would long ago have done.

We are free men, British subjects, not born slaves. We contribute our proportion in all public taxations, and discharge our duty to the public equally with our fellow provincials, yet we do not participate with them in the rights and benefits which they enjoy, though equally entitled to them.

Property is of no value, except it be secure. How ours is secured appears from the forementioned circumstances, and from our now being obliged to defend our families by our own strength, as legal methods are beyond our reach, or not as yet extended to us.

We may be deemed too bold in saying "That the present constitution of this province is very defective, and become a burden, rather than being beneficial to the back inhabitants". For instance: to have but one place of judicature in this large and growing colony, and that seated not central but in a nook by the seaside; the back inhabitants to travel two, three hundred miles to carry down criminals, prosecute offenders, appear as witnesses (though secluded to serve as jurors), attend the courts and suits of law, the governor and Court of Ordinary, all land matters, and on every public occasion, are great grievances and call loudly for redress. For 'tis not only loss of time which the poor settlers sustain therefrom, but the toil of travelling, and heavy expenses therefrom arising. Poor suitors are often driven to great distresses, even to the spending their last shilling, or to sell their only horse, for to defray their travelling and town costs. After which, they are obliged to trudge home on foot, and beg for subsistence by the way. And after being subpoenaed and then attending court as witnesses or as constables, they oft are never called for on trials but are put off to next court, and then the same services must be repeated. These are circumstances experienced by no individuals under British government save those in South Carolina.

It is partly owing to these burdens on our shoulders that the gangs of robbers who infest us have so long reigned without repression: for if a party hath twenty cattle, or the best of his stallions stolen from him, the time and charge consequent on a prosecution of the offenders is equal to, or greater than his loss, as to prosecute would make him doubly a sufferer. And poor persons have not money to answer the cravings of rapacious lawyers. As proceedings at law are now managed, it may cost a private person fifty pounds to bring a villain to justice; and in civil cases the recovery of twenty pounds will frequently be attended with seventy pounds costs, if not treble that sum.

When cattle and horses are stolen and the thief is publicly known (at [sic] they will commit their robberies openly at noonday). Persons who see and know of these evils are backward in making information as they thereby are certain to subject themselves to much trouble and expense, beside the risk they run of being plundered themselves by the rogues in revenge for informing against them. And in consequence of being subpoenaed to attend the courts of Charleston (under great disadvantages), they are often obliged to sell their substance at half value to defray road charges, the public having made no provision on this head. These long journeys are often required too at some critical juncture, very detrimental to the poor planter; who therefrom, will endeavour to avoid appearing against rogues when they are brought to trial. From which circumstances, many rogues have been acquitted at court for want of evidence, the trials of others delayed, the province (as well as individuals) put to grievous expense; and the gangs of robbers (herefrom recruited and spirited) have still reigned without control, ranging and plundering the country with impunity. We can truly say they reign, as by their menaces they intimidate many whom they have injured from laying hold on and bringing of them to justice.

If we are thus insecure, if our lives and properties are thus at stake, if we cannot be protected, if these villains are suffered to range the country uncontrolled and no redress to be obtained for our losses; all of us and our families must quit the province and retire where there are laws, religion and government. For as the laws now stand, it is of no import to bind lawless profligate persons to their good behaviour. Recognizances are laughed at because never put in suit, nor can be but at the private expense of the suffering party. Wherefrom the clergy, magistracy, and all in public authority (who ought to be protected in execution of the laws and honoured in their public stations) are insulted and abused by licentious and insolent persons without redress.

The trial of small and mean causes by a single magistrate (a wise institution in the infancy of the colony) is now become an intolerable grievance, partly through the ignorance of some justices, and the bigotry and partiality of others. Individuals are rather oppressed than relieved by their decisions, for persons are ofttimes saddled with ten or twelve pounds costs on a debt of as many shillings. Through the indolence, connivance, or corruption of several justices, it is owing that the thieves have gained such strength and risen to such a pitch of audacity. They well know that if warrants are issued out against them that they will be slowly pursued, or that they shall have timely notice given them for to avoid the officers. We could enumerate many flagrant instances of this sort, but as every complaint of this nature from the country have hitherto been disregarded, we can only close this article with saying that through the venality of mean persons now in the Commission, contempt instead of respect is thrown on this so honourable and necessary an office.

By poor persons being obliged to travel to Charleston to obtain patents for small tracts of land or to renew their warrants, his Majesty's kindness to his subjects is defeated as it causes land to come as dear, or prove as expensive in running out, as if for to be purchased, the same fees being paid on a grant of ten as on one of ten thousand acres. The like grievance exists in respect to the proving of wills or taking out letters of administration, the fees on which are treble to what is charged at home, even though clogged with stamps. When effects of a deceased party doth not exceed £40 or £50, half this sum must be expended in court fees, no distinction being made, it being alike the same if the effects are fifty or fifty thousand pounds. These are great hardships on the poor, especially as the fees now claimed at the public offices are double to what were formerly demanded, which merits the serious attention of the legislature.

As the laws are now modelled, any malicious, malevolent party, may arrest any stranger, any innocent person, for any sum whatever, without showing cause of action or making oath of his debt or giving security for joining issue, which often prevents persons from getting bail, for though the debt or balance may not be six-pence, yet the sum alleged may be six thousand pounds. This intimidates persons from becoming securities and subjects many to wrongful and injurious imprisonment whereby their credit and families are entirely ruined, health impaired, lives sacrificed by lying in a close and stinking gaol; crowded with thieves and vagabonds! No separation, no distinction made of parties, not hardly even of the sexes. Who can boast of British liberty that is not safe one hour from so dreadful an oppression! A stranger, or vagrant in this province, who can pay a lawyer ten pounds, may at his pleasure or for his frolic, send to prison (at 200 miles distance) the best person here among us without his knowing on what account or for what reason, and this in as arbitrary a manner as in France, by a *lettre de cachet*, or in Spain, by warrant from the Inquisition. Most sore are these evils! Especially too when a poor wretch who has inadvertently broke the peace (for which in Britain he would be ordered a few lashes or a small fine, and be dismissed) must lie five or six months in this loathsome gaol amidst thieves and robbers, in the heat of summer, and then afterwards be discharged by proclamation. Punishments ought to bear some proportion to trespasses. Nor should small and great offences be treated with equal severity. To be confined six months in Charleston gaol at 200 or 300 miles distance from friends or family, and to live in this hot clime on bread and water is a far heavier punishment than for to be in the French King's galleys, or a slave in Barbary. And for persons to lie there session after session for small sums or petty offences, is contrary to all humanity. And more so (as we observed) when persons of every class and each sex are promiscuously confined together in a space where they have not room to lie, and no distinction made between offenders; but thieves and murderers, debtors to the king, offenders in penal laws, vagrants and idle persons are closely huddled in one mixed crowd.

When persons are unwarrantably arrested by vexatious pettifoggers or litigious miscreants (as such will infest every society), and bail is given; in this case, should the plaintiff discontinue and refuse joining issue and drop the suit, we apprehend (from the sufferings of many) that no remedy at present lies for relief of any innocent person who is so treated, consistent with the liberty of the subject. But the defendant must submit to £40 or £50 charge and loss. Or if he sue for damages or costs expended, or for false imprisonment after being ruined and undone, what satisfaction is to be obtained against insolvent prosecutors?

By our birthright as Britons we ought for to be tried by a jury of our peers. This is the glorious liberty of free-born subjects, the darling privilege that distinguishes Britain from all other nations. But we poor distressed settlers enjoy only the shadow, not the substance of this happiness. For can we truly be said to be tried by our peers when few or no persons on this north side of Santee River (containing half the province) are on the jury list? The juries of every court are generally composed of the inhabitants of Charleston or its environs—persons who never perhaps travelled beyond Charleston Neck; who know not even the geography, much less the persons and concerns of the back country. These determine boundaries of our lands, without a view, and decide on matters of which they [have] no proper conception. We think these proceedings as absurd as if affairs of shipping and trade were to be settled by twelve residents in our woods who never saw a town, the sea, or a ship in their lives.

Herefrom, the lives and properties of us back settlers, may accidentally be affected through the judge or jurors having no personal knowledge of parties who depose in court, or of their quality, estate, or character they bear where they dwell. All persons, without exception, are now admitted to give evidence, according to the mode of their profession, and stand *recta in curia*. Now, as we are a mixed people, and many concealed papists among us (especially in the disguise of Quakers), and as such are often admitted as witnesses and jurors, a wrong verdict may often pass through this general admission of persons of all countries' complexions and characters being suffered to be on juries, and so give evidence without distinction or restriction.

Nor can we be said to possess our legal rights as freeholders when we are so unequally represented in Assembly. The south side of Santee River, electing 44 members, and the north side, with these upper parts of the province (containing 2/3 of the white inhabitants), returning but six. It is to this great disproportion of representatives on our part that our interests have been so long neglected, and the back country disregarded. But it is the number of free men, not black slaves, that constitute the strength and riches of a state.

The not laying out the back country into parishes is another most sensible grievance. This evil we apprehend to arise from the selfish views of those whose fortune and estates are in or near Charleston, which makes them endeavour that all matters and things shall centre there, however detrimental to the body politic. Hence it arises that Assemblies are kept sitting for six months when the business brought before them might be dispatched in six weeks, to oblige us (against inclination) to choose such persons for representatives who live in or contiguous to Charleston, and to render a seat in the Assembly too heavy a burden for any country planter of a small estate for to bear. From this, our non-representation in the House, we conceive it is that sixty thousand pounds public money (of which we must pay the greater part, as being levied on the consumer) hath lately been voted for to build an Exchange for the merchants, and a ball-room for the ladies of Charleston; while near sixty thousand of us back settlers have not a minister or a place of worship to repair to! As if we were not worth even the thought of, or deemed as savages, and not Christians!

To leave our native countries, friends, and relations, the service of God, the enjoyment of our civil and religious rights for to breathe here (as we hoped) a purer air of freedom, and possess the utmost enjoyment of liberty and independency; and instead hereof, to be set adrift in the wild woods among Indians and outcasts; to live in a state of heathenism, without law or government or even the appearance of religion; exposed to the insults of lawless and impudent persons, to the depredations of thieves and robbers, and to be treated by our fellow provincials who hold the reins of things as persons hardly worthy the public attention, not so much as their Negroes. These sufferings have broken the hearts of hundreds of our new settlers, made others quit the province; some return to Europe (and therefrom prevent others coming this way), and deterred numbers of persons of fortune and character (both at home and in America) from taking up of lands here and settling this, our back country, as otherwise they would have done.

But whatever regulations, whatever emoluments are offered for the embellishment or benefit of the metropolis, such are readily admitted while we are considered by its inhabitants (and if they could, they would make us) hewers of wood and drawers of water, for service of the town; who treat us not as brethren of the same kindred, united in the same interests, and subjects of the same prince, but as if we were of a different species from themselves; reproaching us for our ignorance and unpoliteness, while they themselves contribute to it, and would chain us to these oars, as unwillingly that either us or our posterity should emerge from darkness to light, and from the power of Satan unto God. Their very follies and extravagancies would afford us means of knowledge and refinement. What they waste and throw away would lay for us the foundations of good things. The sums trifled away in a play house there would have raised us fifty new churches. And the heavy annual charges which the public is saddled with, attending the conveying of prisoners to town, summoning juries, and other incident expenses, together with Mr. Provost Marshal's and Mr. Attorney General's bills, would, if thrown together for these last seven years, have defrayed the expense of building gaols and court houses in every parish of the province, and all other public edifices. But this is not comparable to the damage done the mother country and the West India trade by the thieves stealing of all our best horses, and then selling of them to Dutch agents, for to be transported to the French islands to work their sugar mills. Add to this the depression of our lands in value, prevention of their sale and culture of any improvements in planting or public works through the insecurity of all property by incursions of the thieves; the bad character which the back settlements hath gained hereby (both in Britain and America); the rise of provisions through loss of our stocks of meat cattle; the length of time and great expense it will cost us to raise again a fine breed of horses; the dread which persons of condition and character entertain even of their persons should they travel among us (which deters them from sending of any slaves for to improve their lands in the back country through fear of their being stolen), prevents their paying us any attention or regard or attempting any new branches of commerce though excited thereto by the Society of Arts at home. In short, the dread impressed on all travellers, and which prevents itinerants from visiting us (and thereby making cash to circulate); the damp put on our spirits through the disregards shown us by the Legislature which has prevented, as beforesaid, many thousands from settling among us and lessening thereby the weight of taxes, and adding to the increase of provisions and commodities for the market; the drawing of merchants and mechanics among us, thereby lowering the present exorbitant prices of goods and labour, and opening new channels of trade; all these, and other striking circumstances, have been little thought of or considered in Charleston, midst scenes of luxury and dissipation.

Oppression will make wise men mad. And many sober persons among us are become almost desperate in seeing the non-attention given to these and other matters of serious concern, and which so nearly affects the foundation of things. They seem weary of living (as they have done for years past) without exercise of their civil and religious rights which they ought to share in common with the lower settlements, and being deemed and treated as if not members of the same body politic. For, can we vote for members of Assembly, or choose vestry men, or elect parish officers when we have no churches to repair to, or they are situated one, two hundred miles from us? Can our poor be taken charge of when there hath been neither minister, church wardens, or vestry in St. Marks or St. Matthews parish for these three years past? Nor either a church built, or parish laid out in any of the upper parts of the province? Does not hereby a great and heavy incumbrance fall on the generous and humane? On all who have feelings for the sufferings of others? For the poor, the sick, the aged and infirm must be relieved and supported in some manner, and not left to perish. What care is or can be taken of poor orphans and their effects (no proper laws or provisions being yet made on this head)? Are they not liable to become the prey of every invader? Nor is here any security to the merchant or trader who may credit out their goods, as knaves and villains may remove with their substance unmolested into the neighbouring provinces and there bid defiance to their creditors. Herefrom, no credit can be given among us for no writ can be obtained without going to Charleston. No attachment can be sued out but in Charleston, and while these are preparing, your debtor has taken flight and is quite out of reach. And no marriage licence can be obtained but in Charleston, and there every person must repair to get married that would marry judicially and according to law, for we have not churches wherein to publish banns, or ministers to marry persons. Wherefrom, the generality marry each other, which causes the vilest abominations, and that whoredom and adultery overspreads our land. Thus we live and have lived for years past as if without God in the world, destitute of the means of knowledge, without law or gospel, esteem, or credit. For we know not even the laws of this country we inhabit, for where are they to be found but in the Secretary's office in Charleston? The printing a code of the laws hath been long petitioned for, often recommended by the Crown, and delineated in the presentments of grand juries as a matter long wanting and of the utmost consequence. But like all other their presentments, it lies totally unregarded.

Of what service have been, of what use are the parish churches of Prince George, Prince Frederic and St. Mark, to the inhabitants of Williamsburgh, Great and Little Pedee, Lynch's Creek, Waccamaw, the Congarees, Waxhaws, Waterees, Saluday, Long Canes, Ninety-Six, or Broad River; places and settlements containing fifty thousand souls? These fabrics were placed where they are to serve some local occasion or particular persons or purposes but are not (at least at present) of the least benefit to the back country. What church can we repair to for divine service nearer than Dorchester or Charleston, several parishes being now destitute of ministers and no effectual plan settled for their being properly supplied?

It is notorious that through the want of churches and ministers, new sects have arisen and now greatly prevail, especially those called New Lights. Profaneness and infidelity abound; ignorance, vice, and idleness prevail; and to the great indifference shown by all ranks to promote the interests of religion and virtue, it is in great measure owing that such few checks have been given to the villains and outlaws who have devoured us. For the common people hardly know the first principles of religion; and so corrupt are their morals that a reformation of manners among them in our time is more to be wished for than expected.

Through want of churches and ministers many persons go into the north province, there to be married by magistrates; which hath encouraged many of our magistrates (so venal are they) for to take on them also to solemnize marriages, and this without any previous publication of banns or any set form, but each after his own fancy, which occasions much confusion as they ask no questions but couple persons of all ages and every complexion, to the ruin and grief of many families. Their examples have been followed by the low lay teachers of every petty sect and also copied by itinerant and straggling preachers of various denominations, who traverse the back country (sent this way from Pennsylvania and New England to poison the minds of the people). From these irregular practices the sacred bond of marriage is so greatly slighted as to be productive of many great and innumerable evils. For many loose wretches are fond of such marriages on supposition that they are only temporary, or *durante placito*; dissoluble whenever their interests or passions incite them to separate. Thus they live *ad libitum*, quitting each other at pleasure, intermarrying year after year with others; changing from hand to hand as they remove from place to place, and swapping away their wives and children as they would horses or cattle. Great scandal arises herefrom to the back country, and loss to the community; for the issue of such are too often exposed, deserted, and disowned; beggars are hereby multiplied, concubinage established (as it were) by law. The most sacred obligations are hereby trampled on, and bastardy, adultery, and other heinous vices become so common, so openly practised and avowed, as to lose the stigma annexed to their commission. These are some of the main roots from whence the reigning gangs of horse thieves have sprung up from.

Through the nonestablishment of public schools, a great multitude of children are now grown up in the greatest ignorance of everything save vice, in which they are adepts. Consequently they lead idle and immoral lives for they having no sort of education, naturally follow hunting, shooting, racing, drinking, gaming, and every species of wickedness. Their lives are only one continual scene of depravity of manners and reproach to the country, being more abandoned to sensuality and more rude in manners than the poor savages around us. They will learn no trade or mechanic arts whereby to obtain an honest livelihood, or practise any means of industry; or if they know, they will not practise them, but range the country with their horse and gun, without home or habitation, all persons, all places, all women being alike to them. These are other deep roots from which the hordes of mulattoes and villains we are pestered with have shot up, whereas, had we churches and ministers, schools and catechists, children would be early taught the principles of religion and goodness, and their heads and hands be employed in exercises of the manual and useful arts; tradesmen would increase; manufactures be followed up; agriculture be improved; the country wear a new face, and peace and plenty smile around us.

But in our present unsettled situation, when the bands of society and government hang loose and ungirt about us; when no regular police is established but everyone left to do as seemeth him meet, there is not the least encouragement for any individual to be industrious, emulous in well-doing, or enterprising in any attempt that is laudable or public-spirited. Cunning, rapine, fraud, and violence are now the studies and pursuits of the vulgar. If we save a little money for to bring down to town wherewith to purchase slaves, should it be known, our houses are beset and robbers plunder us even of our clothes. If we buy liquor for to retail, or for hospitality, they will break into our dwellings and consume it. If we purchase bedding, linen, or decent furniture, they have early notice, and we are certain for to be stripped of it. Should we raise fat cattle, or prime horses for the market, they are constantly carried off, though well guarded (as a small force is insufficient for their security). Or if we collect gangs of hogs for to kill and to barrel up for sale, or plant orchards or gardens, the rogues, and other idle, worthless, vagrant people with whom we are overrun, are continually destroying of them, and subsisting on the stocks and labours of the industrious planter. If we are in any wise injured in our persons, fame, or fortune, what remedy have we? What redress can be obtained without travelling two hundred miles to Charleston? Where (through the chicanery of lawyers, slowness of law proceedings, and expenses thence arising), we are greater sufferers than before, and only thereby add evil to evil. Nay, we have had, and daily do see those very horses and creatures which have been stolen from us (and for which we have endeavoured to bring villains to justice); we have seen these our creatures sold before our faces for to raise money to fee lawyers to plead against us and to save rogues from the halter. And what defence are the laws (as they are now dispensed) to us against such as are below the law? For in many cases (as in branding and killing of cattle) fines only being imposed and no provision made for the sufferer, should the injurer be a vagrant, or insolvent, incapable of paying the fine, what redress lies in this case? The confining of the transgressor for six months (at the private expense of the sufferer, beside his charges of prosecution) in the common gaol of Charleston, where it is as agreeable to him to live an idle life in as out of it, work being the article he would avoid at any rate, and we have not a bridewell, whipping post, or pair of stocks in the province, and the workhouse of Charleston is only so in name.

As the back country is now daily increasing by imports of people from Ireland and elsewhere (most of whom are very poor), the number of the idle and worthless must also increase if our settlements long remain in their present neglected state. Many of these new settlers greatly repent their coming out here, to languish away life in a country that falls so very short of their expectations; and the sober part of them would more willingly return than remain here. They have indeed land given them, and may with industry, raise a bare subsistence; but they are discouraged from any bold pursuits or exerting their laudable endeavours to make improvements through the uncertainty that attends us all; i.e., whether in the end they may reap the fruits of their labour; for such number of idle and vagrant persons from the northern colonies traverse and infest this province that if a spot of ground be planted (especially with fruit trees for cider, etc.), the proprietor cannot be certain of gathering the produce but may see it carried off before his face without control. So great is the weakness of government in these parts that our magistrates are weary of committing persons to Charleston for petty offences and they have no authority to inflict punishments. It is therefore in vain for us to attempt the laying out of vineyards, sheepwalks, or bleaching grounds, as it would only be working for these indolent, unsettled, roving wretches.

Property being thus insecure, no improvements are attempted, no new plans can take place, nothing out of the common road can be executed, till legislation is extended to us. A damp is now put on all spirited endeavours to make matters run in their proper channel. And (shameful to say), our lands (some of the finest in America) lie useless and uncleared, being rendered of small value from the many licentious persons intermixed among us whom we cannot drive off without force or violence.

But these our lands would be of infinite value, and in time, the most desirable in the province, were proper regulations to take place, and good manners and order be introduced among us. Our soil is not only fruitful but capable of producing any grain whatever. Our vales and woods are delightful, our hills healthful and pleasant. This single consideration merits the public attention. For, was the country to be once cleared of lawless and idle people (or were they only for to be put under proper restraint), were courts of justice once established, the roads repaired and improved, bridges built in proper places, and travelling rendered safe and commodious, we should no longer be pestered with insolvent and licentious persons from the neighbouring governments. Nor would this province be the sink (as now it is) of the refuse of other colonies. Such abandoned wretches would no longer seek shelter or find protection here, nor set bad examples to our rising progeny. We should chase them away as beasts of prey. And was the country once cleared of such vermin, it would induce genteel persons to make the tour of their native country and not embark annually for Rhode Island or New York for the benefit of cool air. They may breathe equal as salubrious on our hills. And the specie which is now carried out of the province by our travelling gentry (never to return!) would circulate among the poor back inhabitants and quickly find its way down to Charleston.

We may be despised or slighted for our poverty but poor the country ever will be if it long remains in its present disordered state as the few persons of property among us must be obliged to quit their farms instead of their engaging of new adventurers to sit down among us. Were our interests (which is the interest of the community) but properly attended to and the laws duly administered among us, our industry and application to raise staple articles for the foreign market would render this province in few years a most valuable country and one of the brightest jewels in the crown of Great Britain.

By our urging of these particulars and thus bringing them home to the attention of the legislature, we do not presume to reflect on or to censure the conduct, much less to prescribe or dictate to those in authority; but we humbly submit ourselves and our cause to the wisdom of our superiors, professing ourselves dutiful and loyal subjects to His Majesty King George, true lovers of our country, zealous for its true interests, the rights and liberties of the subject, and the stability of our present happy constitution in church and state. We only enumerate plain and glaring facts and all we crave is the enjoyment of those native rights which as freeborn subjects we are entitled unto but at present are debarred of; and also the proper establishment of religion and dispensation of the laws in the upper part of the country. All which our petitions we humbly beg leave (with the greatest deference and submission) to sum up in the following articles, humbly praying that the legislature would be pleased to grant us such relief as may be conducive to the public welfare, the honour of the Crown, the good of the church, and the peace and prosperity of all His Majesty's liege people in this his province.

With all due respect, we humbly request:

First) That circuit or county courts for the due and speedy administration of justice be established in this, as is in the neighbouring provinces.

2d) That some subordinate courts to consist of justices and freeholders be erected in each parish for the trial of slaves, small and mean causes, and other local matters. And that (under the Governor) they may grant probate of wills and letters of administration for all effects under £100. Also to pass small grants of lands, renew warrants, etc., paying the common fees, to prevent poor persons from travelling down to Charleston on account of these and other such petty matters.

3d) That these circuits or county courts may decide all suits not exceeding £100 currency without appeal, and that no *nolle prosequis* or *traverses* be filed against informations made against transgressors of the local or penal laws.

4th) That the clerk of the circuit or county court may issue writs or attachments for any sum, all above £100 currency to be made returnable to the Supreme Court in Charleston and all under that sum, returnable by the sheriff of each county to his particular court, and that justices of the peace, or clerk of the court may issue attachments (as now they do executions) for sums under £20 currency.

5th) That the poor laws be amended and some better provision made for the care of poor orphans and their estates; also of the effects of strangers, travellers, and transient persons dying within the province.

6th) That court houses, gaols, and bridewells be built in proper places and coercive laws framed for the punishment of idleness and vice and for the lessening the number of vagrant and indolent persons, who now prey on the industrious. And that none such be allowed to traverse the province without proper licences or passes.

7th) That the laws respecting public houses and taverns be amended, and the prices of articles vended by them, for to be ascertained as to quality and quantity. And that none be permitted for to retail liquors on the public roads but such as can lodge travellers and provide entertainment for man and horse.

8th) That the laws concerning the stealing and branding of cattle, tolling of horses, taking up of strays, etc., be amended; that hunters be put under some restrictions and obliged not to leave carcasses unburied in the woods; and that some few regulations be made in respect to swine.

9th) That the provincial laws be digested into a regular code, and be printed as soon as possible.

10th) That gentlemen who may be elected as members of Assembly, commissioners of the roads, and into other public offices, be obliged to serve, or fine.

11th) That the interior and upper parts of the province, and all beyond Black River, be laid out into parishes, or chapels, churches and parsonages be founded among them.

12th) That ministers be provided for these new as well as vacant old parishes, and that some method be devised for an immediate supply of parishes with ministers, on the death or cession of incumbents, also for the better care (than at present) of vacant churches and parsonages.

13th) That the salaries of the country clergy be augmented and some provision made for their widows, thereby that learned and goodly men may be excited to come over to us, and not profligates.

14th) That all magistrates, lay persons, and itinerant preachers and teachers be inhibited from marrying, and the mode and authenticity of marriages be settled; and that dissenting teachers be obliged to register their meeting houses and to take the state oaths agreeable to the statute (1 William and Mary); and that none but such settled pastors be allowed to teach or preach among the people.

15th) That some expedient be devised for His Majesty's Attorney General to put recognizances in suit; and that he may be empowered for to prosecute on all recognizances given for the observance of the provincial laws.

16th) That a proper table of fees be framed for all ministers, ecclesiastical and civil, to govern themselves by; and that the length and enormous expense of law suits be moderated, this province being harder rode at present by lawyers than Spain or Italy by priests.

17th) That juries be impanelled from, and all offences tried in that county wherein crimes, trespasses, and damages have been committed or sustained—agreeable to Magna Charta.

18th) That no attorney be put into commission of the peace, and that their number be limited in the Commons House of Assembly.

19th) That some public schools be founded in the back settlements for training up of the rising generation in the true principles of things, that so they may become useful and not pernicious members of society.

20th) That proper premiums be annually distributed for promoting agriculture, the raising of articles for exportation, and establishing useful arts, on the plan of the Dublin Society and that of Arts and Commerce in London.

21) That the statute for limitation of actions and that for preventing frivolous and vexatious suits be enforced and elucidated; and that the liberty of the subject as to arrests and wrongful imprisonments be better secured.

22) That the lines of the several counties be run out from the sea to the Cherokee boundary; also that the lines of each old and new parish be ascertained and known, that we may no longer wander in the mazes of supposition.

23) Lastly we earnestly pray that the legislature would import a quantity of Bibles, Common Prayers, and devotional tracts, to be distributed by the ministers among the poor, which will be of far greater utility to the province than erecting the statue of Mr. Pitt.

The above particulars are with the greatest deference and respect submitted to the wisdom of the Legislature.

In the name, by desire, and on behalf of the back inhabitants, and signed in their presence, by us, their deputies

BENJAMIN HART

JOHN SCOTT

MOSES KIRKLAND

THOMAS WOODWARD

95B. Petition of Anson County, North Carolina (9 October 1769)

Printed: *Colonial Records of North Carolina*, VIII, pp. 75–78.

Mr. Speaker and Gentlemen of the Assembly:
     The Petition of the inhabitants of Anson County, being part of the Remonstrance of the Province of North Carolina, humbly showeth:

That the province in general labour under general grievances, and the western part thereof under particular ones which we not only see, but very sensibly feel, being crouched beneath our sufferings; and notwithstanding our sacred privileges, have too long yielded ourselves slaves to remorseless oppression. Permit us to conceive it to be our inviolable right to make known our grievances and to petition for redress, as appears in the Bill of Rights passed in the reign of King Charles the first, as well as the Act of Settlement of the Crown of the revolution. We therefore beg leave to lay before you a specimen thereof that your compassionate endeavours may tend to the relief of your injured constituents, whose distressed condition calls aloud for aid. The alarming cries of the oppressed possibly may reach your ears, but without your zeal how shall they ascend the throne–how relentless is the breast without sympathy, the heart that cannot bleed on a view of our calamity; to see tenderness removed, cruelty stepping in, and all our liberties and privileges invaded and abridged by, as it were, domestics who are conscious of their guilt and void of remorse. O how daring!

how relentless! whilst impending judgments loudly threaten and gaze upon them, with every emblem of merited destruction.

A few of the many grievances are as follows:

1. That the poor inhabitants in general are much oppressed by reason of disproportionate taxes, and those of the western counties in particular, as they are generally in mean circumstances.

2. That no method is prescribed by law for the payment of the taxes of the western counties in produce (in lieu of a currency) as is in other counties within this province, to the peoples' great oppression.

3. That lawyers, clerks, and other pensioners in place of being obsequious servants for the country's use, are become a nuisance, as the business of the people is often transacted without the least degree of fairness, the intention of the law evaded, exorbitant fees extorted, and the sufferers left to mourn under their oppressions.

4. That an attorney should have it in his power, either for the sake of ease or interest, or to gratify their malevolence and spite, to commence suits to what courts he pleases, however inconvenient it may be to the defendant, is a very great oppression.

5. That all unlawful fees taken on indictment, where the defendant is acquitted by his country (however customary it may be) is an oppression.

6. That lawyers, clerks, and others, extorting more fees than is intended by law, is also an oppression.

7. That the violation of the king's instructions to his delegates, their artfulness in concealing the same from him, and the great injury the people thereby sustains, is a manifest oppression.

And for remedy whereof we take the freedom to recommend the following mode of redress, not doubting audience and acceptance, which will not only tend to our relief, but command prayers as a duty from your humble petitioners.

1. That at all elections each suffrage be given by ticket and ballot.

2. That the mode of taxation be altered, and each person to pay in proportion to the profits arising from his estate.

3. That no future tax be laid in money until a currency is made.

4. That there may be established a Western as well as a Northern and Southern District, and a treasurer for the same.

5. That when a currency is made it may be let out by a loan office on land security, and not to be called in by a tax.

6. That all debts above 40s. and under £10 be tried and determined without lawyers, by a jury of six freeholders, impanelled by a justice, and that their verdict be entered by the said justice and be a final judgment.

7. That the chief justice have no perquisites, but a salary only.

8. That clerks be restricted in respect to fees, costs, and other things within the course of their office.

9. That lawyers be effectually barred from exacting and extorting fees.

10. That all doubts may be removed in respect to the payment of fees and costs

on indictments where the defendant is not found guilty by the jury, and therefore acquitted.

11. That the Assembly make known by remonstrance to the king the conduct of the cruel and oppressive receiver of the quit-rents, for omitting the customary easy and effectual method of collecting by distress, and pursuing the expensive mode of commencing suits in the most distant courts.

12. That the Assembly in like manner make known that the governor and Council do frequently grant lands to as many as they think proper without regard to head rights, notwithstanding the contrariety of his Majesty's instructions, by which means immense sums has been collected, and numerous patents granted, for much of the most fertile lands in this province, that is yet uninhabited and uncultivated, environed by great numbers of poor people who are necessitated to toil in the cultivation of bad lands whereon they hardly can subsist, who are thereby deprived of his Majesty's liberality and bounty; nor is there the least regard paid to the cultivation clause in said patent mentioned, as many of the said council as well as their friends and favourites enjoy large quantities of lands under the above mentioned circumstances.

13. That the Assembly communicates in like manner the violation of his Majesty's instructions respecting the land office by the governor and Council, and of their own rules, customs, and orders, if it be sufficiently proved that after they had granted warrants for many tracts of land, and that the same was in due time surveyed and returned, and the patent fees timely paid into the said office; and that if a private council was called on purpose to avoid spectators, and peremptory orders made that patents should not be granted; and warrants by their orders arbitrarily to have issued in the names of other persons for the same lands, and if when entreated by a solicitor they refused to render so much as a reason for their so doing, or to refund any part of the money by them extorted.

14. That some method may be pointed out that every improvement on lands in any of the proprietors' part be proved when begun, by whom, and every sale made, that the eldest may have the preference of at least 300 acres.

15. That all taxes in the following counties be paid as in other counties in the province (i.e.) in the produce of the country and that warehouses be erected as follows:

In Anson County at Isom Haley's Ferry Landing on Pedee River,

Rowan and Orange at Cambleton in Cumberland County,

Mecklenburg at ———— on the Catawba River, and in Tryon County at ———— on ———— River.

16. That every denomination of people may marry according to their respective mode, ceremony, and custom, after due publication or licence.

17. That Dr. Benjamin Franklin, or some other known patriot, be appointed agent to represent the unhappy state of this province to his Majesty, and to solicit the several boards in England.

95C. Governor Josiah Martin: letter to the Earl of Hillsborough on the North Carolina Regulators (30 August 1772)

Printed: *Colonial Records of North Carolina*, IX, pp. 329–333.

Since I had the honour of writing to your lordship of my intention to visit that part of this province lying to the westward of this place, I have made a tour through the most broken, difficult, and rough country I have ever seen as far as Salisbury in my circuit, taking in the Moravian settlements where I was irresistibly detained beyond my intention in admiration of the virtuous industry and perfect economy of that people who are notable examples to the supine and licentious inhabitants of this colony who live in their neighbourhood and must, I think, sooner or later feel their influence beneficially.

On my route, my lord, I passed through the county of Guilford, the residence of the principal insurgents who had lately made their submissions to me. I received from them here the most pressing solicitations to be permitted to present themselves before me, and after some debate with myself about the decency of compliance and considering that a refusal might to their ignorant minds imply apprehensions of personal violence or predetermined rigour, I consented that they should meet me at an appointed place; they came accordingly before me bearing in their countenances every mark of truest contrition and penitence, and after the most solemn protestation of their innocence and abhorrence of the design to subvert the government of which they had been misled to crimes and violences they had never intended, and for which they felt the severest remorse, they declared their resolution to submit to the royal pleasure and implored my pity and good offices. I set before them in the strongest light I was able their criminality aggravated by their long forbearance to submit themselves to justice. I reprehended Hunter, who was among them, more particularly for his indecent defiance of a court of justice by appearing in the face of it while he stood in so criminal a state, with any other design than to render himself, to which he submissively replied that if he had offended by so doing, it was innocently and ignorantly and that he heartily asked pardon for it. After exhorting them to deserve his Majesty's mercy to which they had now submitted themselves by future right good conduct and informing them that I should soon apprise them of the measures to be taken in consequence of their surrender, I dismissed them and I must own to your lordship, with sentiments of pity and compassion I never should have felt if I had not seen them and made myself acquainted with their barbarous ignorance that really surpasses all description.

My progress through this country, my lord, hath opened my eyes exceedingly with respect to the commotions and discontents that have lately prevailed in it. I now see most clearly that they have been provoked by insolence and cruel advantages taken of the people's ignorance by mercenary tricking attorneys, clerks, and other little officers who have practised upon them every sort of rapine and extortion, by which having brought upon themselves their just resentment, they engaged government in their defence by artful misrepresentations that the vengeance the wretched people in folly and madness aimed at their heads was directed against the constitution, and by this stratagem they threw an odium upon the injured people that by degrees begat a prejudice which precluded a full discovery of their grievances. Thus, my lord, as far as I am able to discern, the resentment of government was craftily worked up against the oppressed, and the protection which the oppressors treacherously acquired where the injured and ignorant people expected to find it, drove them to acts of desperation, and confederated them in violences which, as your lordship knows, induced bloodshed, and I verily believe, necessarily. Inquiries of this sort, my lord, I am sensible are invidious, nor would anything but a sense of duty have drawn from me these opinions of the principles of the past troubles of this country.

Since I became acquainted with the barbarism and profound ignorance of the wretched people of this country, I perceive all the resentment subsided which the representations of the people in general (styling themselves the friends of Government) in spite of all my endeavours to hold myself impartial, had wrought into my mind, and my indignation is not only disarmed but converted to pity; nevertheless, my lord, as I had been led by misrepresentations in the whole course of my correspondence with your lordship to hold up the delinquents here to his Majesty as people against whom the proceedings at law had been complete and final, and in a state depending solely on the royal pleasure, I thought it my indispensable duty as soon as I discovered my error, and after receiving his Majesty's commands, to propose to the legislature an act of pardon and oblivion, which I might presume were given in that opinion to advise whether they could not be brought into that predicament wherein I had represented them. I therefore summoned the judges to attend here pursuant to my intention communicated to your lordship by a former letter, and on their arrival I proposed to their consideration the questions which together with their answers, and the attorney general's opinion, I now have the honour to transmit to your lordship. Another principle, my lord, that engaged me in this inquiry was an opinion that if exceptions should be made in the act of grace to be proposed, they would be impotent unless the criminals were in a state wherein the royal pleasure might operate effectually and conclusively against them. And further, that it behooved me to guard against future omissions and irregularities in the proceedings at law which might tend to restrain its influence, as well as more fully and clearly to understand the past erroneous transactions which had placed the offenders in a light so different to that in which they have been heretofore universally considered and represented by me.

From the several opinions I have now the honour to lay before your lordship, you will see that the judges who have consented hitherto to the common error, and deemed the prosecuted offenders here outlaws, think them no longer so, and are doubtful as well about the possibility as the expediency of ascertaining or punishing their past crimes. Wherefore, my lord, it hath been determined with the advice of his Majesty's Council and the judges, that I shall signify to the people who have desired to surrender themselves, that they will on their appearance, be bound in recognizances to appear at the Superior Court from term to term to answer such matters as shall be brought against them at the suit of the Crown until his Majesty's pleasure concerning them shall be finally declared, the only measure, it seems, by which they can be kept in hold, and which may at the same time, I think, have the effect of protecting their neighbourhood from the injuries which have been committed in it since their return to their habitations, and are by some supposed (although perhaps unjustly) to have been done by them. I do not apprehend that the Assembly will make other exceptions in the act of grace than were made in the late Assembly's address to me, and I confess, my lord, I am of opinion none other will be necessary. The measure which his Majesty hath been pleased to authorize me to propose, will, I am persuaded, have the best tendency to harmonize the discord that has prevailed in this country, but cordial union can never take place until the victors forget to exult on the last year's triumph at Alamance.

96A–B. Frontier discontent in Pennsylvania

The rapid growth of Pennsylvania created a sectional cleavage as sharp as existed in any other colony. The Quakers dominated the three eastern counties and the city of Philadelphia. The back country was settled mainly by Scotch-Irish and Germans. By the middle of the eighteenth century these two groups made up more than half of the population of the colony; yet the Quaker aristocracy in the east managed to retain political control by refusing to grant representation in the legislature to the newer and more populous areas of the colony. The Scotch-Irish in particular were aggressive leaders, whereas the Germans on the whole maintained a more neutral position in the struggles between east and west. There were disputes over land, over transportation facilities, over "taxation without representation", but above all, over the question of frontier defence.

As a rule, the Scotch-Irish settled on the frontiers and were therefore subject to constant attack by the Indians. Although the Scotch-Irish were more than willing to match violence with violence, they expected and demanded aid from the government of the colony. This, as men of peace, the Quakers refused to give.

During the French and Indian war the struggle was particularly bitter, and it was complicated by the refusal of the Assembly to vote money for defence unless it was in turn allowed to tax the vast tracts of ungranted proprietary lands.

During the war the frontier was raided repeatedly, and many settlements were abandoned. In 1763 the great Indian uprising led by Chief Pontiac threatened to wipe out all frontier settlements, but again the Pennsylvania legislature was slow to grant aid, for the dispute over taxation continued. Frontiersmen were furious and massacred some 'tame' Indians who were under the protection of the colonial government, which then took steps to protect the Indians.

The outraged frontiersmen then organized a large body of men who called themselves Paxton Boys, taking the name of one of the townships which was a centre of discontent. They proceeded to march on Philadelphia, where they arrived early in February 1764. Some of the leading officials of the colony met them at Germantown, outside Philadelphia. After several hours of parleying, the frontiersmen agreed to return home, but they left two of their leaders behind to prepare a declaration of their grievances for presentation to the Assembly. The declaration was virtually ignored by the legislature, and few concessions were made to the west before 1776. The frontiersmen joined with the popular leaders in Philadelphia in the revolutionary movement, which in Pennsylvania was more clearly an internal revolution than in any other colony. Most of the demands of the frontiersmen, particularly for equality of representation, were to find expression in the Pennsylvania Constitution of 1776.

Henry Melchior Muhlenberg's account of the march of the Paxton Boys (No. 96A) is one of the few temperate accounts that exist. Muhlenberg (1711–1787) was born in Hanover, Germany, and educated at the University of Göttingen. In 1742 he came to Pennsylvania as the pastor of three Lutheran churches known as the United Congregations. A man of extraordinary ability, his influence soon spread throughout the Lutheran congregations in the middle colonies. He was in a very real sense the founder of the Lutheran Church in America.

The statement of grievances (No. 96B) was prepared by Matthew Smith and James Gibson who had remained behind for that purpose after the main body of the Paxton Boys had returned home.

96A. Henry Melchior Muhlenberg: account of the Paxton Boys (1–7 February 1764)

Printed: *The Journals of Henry Melchior Muhlenberg* (translated by Theodore G. Tappert and John W. Doberstein, 2 vols., Philadelphia, 1942, 1945), II, pp. 18–22, 22–23.

February 1, Wednesday. . . . This afternoon all citizens were summoned to the state house by the governor and Council through the constable where the governor made a public proclamation to the effect:

1. That it had been learned that a large mob of frontier settlers, who had killed several Indians in Lancaster, were coming to Philadelphia to kill the Indian families who had been brought down from Bethlehem and taken under the protection of the government.

2. That since such procedure could be considered as being none other than a breach of the peace, revolution, or rebellion against our gracious king and the law of the land, the Act of Riot was invoked and one hundred and some regular soldiers were set apart to guard and protect the Bethlehem Indian families in the barracks.

3. That the governor and council called upon citizens who were willing to lend armed assistance and resist the rebellion, to band themselves together and hand in their names.

4. That because there was a pouring rain at the time and the Germans did not enlist and sign their names with the rest, the governor and others were much offended, conjecturing that perhaps the Germans might be making common cause with the malcontents or so-called rebels, etc.

As far as I can learn the opinion and sentiment of various ones of our German citizens are as follows:

1. They are of the opinion that it could be proved that the Indians who had lived among the so-called Moravian Brethren had secretly killed several [D: a number of German][1] settlers.

2. That the Quakers and [D: Herrnhuters] Bethlehemites had [D: only used] some of the aforesaid Indians [D: as spies and] that they had in view only their own selfish interests, without considering at all that they had murdered their fellow Christians.

3. Indeed, that they had loaded down the said Indians with presents and taken them, their secret enemies, to their bosom only for the sake of this selfish interest, which explained why the [D: Quakers] Friends, etc. in Philadelphia did not exhibit the least evidence of human sympathy, etc. when Germans and other settlers on the frontiers were massacred and destroyed in the most inhuman manner by the Indians. On the contrary, these Bethlehem Indians, despite this [D: despite their congenital craftiness, etc.], were brought to Philadelphia and maintained and supported at the expense of the inhabitants. Besides, the young male Indians had already escaped and were probably doing harm, while the old men and women and children were living off the fat of the land at the expense of the province.

4. And now because there was a rumour that the remote settlers, some of whom had lost their wives and others their children and relatives through those atrocious Indian massacres, were intending to come to Philadelphia in a corps and revenge themselves upon these Indians, therefore our German citizens should enlist to fight, resist, or even kill their own flesh and blood, their fellow citizens and fellow Christians, and seek to protect the lives of the Bethlehem Indians! Why, they say, that would be quite contrary to nature and contrary to the law of Christ, for He did

[1] The editors of the *Journal* state that "[D:]" indicates a deletion in the original journals which has been restored.

not say, "Thou shalt hate thy friend and love thine enemy." That is the general tone among some. They would unhesitatingly and gladly pour out their possessions and their blood for our most gracious king and [D: his] officers, but they would not wage war against their own suffering fellow citizens for the sake of the Quakers and Herrnhuters and their creatures or instruments, the double-dealing Indians.

It is difficult in such a crisis to say anything or give any judgment in such a strange republic which has caught a fever, or, rather, is suffering from *colica pituitosa*.

February 5, Sunday. . . . Toward evening the rumour sprang up that a corps of backwoods settlers–Englishmen, Irishmen, and Germans–were on the march toward Philadelphia to kill the Bethlehem Indians at the barracks outside the city. Some reported that they numbered 700, others said 1500, etc. The Friends, or so-called Quakers, and the Herrnhuters ran furiously back and forth to the barracks, and there was a great to-do over constructing several small fortresses or ramparts near the barracks. Cannons were also set up. Some remarked concerning all this that it seemed strange that such preparations should be made against one's own fellow citizens and Christians, whereas no one ever took so much trouble to protect from the Indians his Majesty's subjects and citizens on the frontier.

. . . After two o'clock at night the watchmen began to cry, "Fire!" I asked our watchman, who is a member of our congregation, where the fire was. He said there was no fire but that the watchmen had orders to cry out, "Fire," because the above-mentioned backwoodsmen were approaching. Thereupon all the alarm bells began to ring at once and a drum was sounded to summon the inhabitants of the city to the town hall plaza. The ringing sounded dreadful in the night. I asked a German neighbour to go to the town hall and bring me news of what was happening there. He reported that the market place was crowded with all sorts of people and that arms were being distributed to those who would take them. He had not, however, seen many Germans. The sounding of the tocsin continued on through the night until near dawn and the inhabitants were ordered to place lights inside the doors and windows, which was done. Meanwhile, all sorts of rumours were flying in every direction: the rebels had divided into three groups and were going to attack the open city in three places simultaneously; then they were near; then they were still far away; now they were coming from the east, then from the west, and so on.

February 6, Monday. The alarm bells finally ceased at daylight. About nine o'clock his reverence Dr. Wrangel came and told us that he had been invited to attend upon the governor and Council and that the *vener[abile] concilium* was annoyed because few or none of our German church people had reported on Saturday or last night to take up arms against the rebels, which might give rise to evil reflections, etc. Dr. Wrangel therefore felt himself compelled by motives of the common good, and especially the good of our German nation, to urge our Germans who had stood idly in the market place to take up arms. Because I was still weak from my illness and was unable to go out, Dr. Wrangel ordered Pastor Brycelius, who was still with me, to drive to Germantown with all haste and in our names (a) warn the elders of our congregation there not to join the approaching rebels, but rather to stand on the side of the government, and (b) since it had been bruited about that there were many Germans among the so-called rebels, Mr. Brycelius was to try and see whether he could not give them an earnest and kindly admonition, etc.

His reverence Dr. Wrangel left us and roused up a number of our Germans. Mr. Brycelius rode to Germantown because the word was going around that the mob was coming toward Germantown from Whitemarsh. Several hours later Mr. Metzger and other craftsmen gathered together, formed themselves into a small mounted company furnished with proper arms, sounded the trumpets, and made a several hours' tour in and around the city. They were almost shot by inadvertence, for cannons loaded with small balls had been placed here and there and the ignorant constable was just on the point of blazing away at them because he thought they were rebels. It seems almost inconceivable, but a number of older and younger Quakers also formed themselves into companies and took up arms, etc. At any rate, it was a strange sight to the children on the streets. A whole troop of small boys followed a prominent Quaker down the street shouting in amazement, "Look, look! a Quaker carrying a musket on his shoulder!" Indeed, the older folks also looked upon it as a miraculous portent to see so many old and young Quakers arming themselves with flintlocks and daggers, or so-called murderous weapons! What heightened their amazement was this: that these pious sheep, who had such a tender conscience during the long Spanish, French, and Indian War, and would rather have died than lift a hand for defence against the most dangerous enemies, were now all of a sudden willing to put on horns of iron like Zedekiah, the son of Chenaanah (1 Kings 22), and shoot and smite a small group of their poor, oppressed, driven, and suffering fellow inhabitants and citizens from the frontier!

February 7, Tuesday. [D: Early in the day I heard that the Governor had gone out to Germantown with several other members of the government in order to make peace with the band that was camping there.]

[MS: At five o'clock in the morning several members of the governor's Council, who intended to go to Germantown as deputies, assembled. They were: Mr. [Benjamin] Franklin, royal agent, [attorney-general Benjamin] Chew, [Joseph] Galloway, City Mayor [Thomas] Willing, William Logan, Dr. Wrangell, and Mr. [Daniel] Roberdo [Roberdeau]. They rode together until they were half way to Germantown. Then Dr. Wrangel deemed it advisable to ride on ahead of the others with Mr. Roberdeau in order to prepare the so-called rioters by a speech. It was about seven o'clock in the morning when Dr. Wrangel and Mr. Roberdeau arrived at Coleman's tavern where the largest band was assembled. Dr. Wrangel asked them if they would give him their ears. Answer: Yes. Thereupon Dr. Wrangel delivered an address suitable to the occasion. He depicted the characteristics of true Christians and of faithful subjects of his royal Majesty. He expressed the hearty desire and hope that these characteristics might be found among them *in minori propositione* and that they might become known by their fruits. In the second part of his speech Dr. Wrangel discussed the great danger which would confront Christian and sensible subjects if, seduced by improper sentiments, they transgressed the bounds of Christian and civil laws.

Since this address, seasoned as it was with salt or with love and earnestness, lasted somewhat more than half an hour, it was hardly concluded when the gentlemen of the Council reached the house and dismounted. The first to enter was Mr. William Logan. When the warriors saw him they shouted, "There is that scoundrel Logan, that Quaker!" And he immediately mounted his horse again and prepared [to ride away]. . . .

The rest of the gentlemen entered and were conducted to a room upstairs, where the conference was to be held. Those present in the conference were Messrs. Chew, Willing, Franklin, Galloway, Dr. Wrangel, Roberdeau, and Col. [John] Armstrong. The last named was perhaps the chief agent of the frontier inhabitants. But the conference could not be opened until the spokesman of the militant frontiersmen had arrived. Strange to say, he had been in the barracks and had observed the preparations which had been made, incognito, and he had also spoken with the governor and the Council early in the morning before the deputies had started out from the city. As soon as this spokesman, Matthew Smith by name, had arrived in Germantown, the conference was begun in the upper room. The said spokesman, M. Smith, also had with him two assistants to represent his side–Messrs. Brown and Gibson.

The spokesman stated why they had come down with their weapons. (1) They, the backwoodsmen, had for years been left to cope with the distressing warfare on the frontiers without any help. They had been plundered by the Indians and had fought much and suffered much. Although they had repeatedly sent their *gravamina* to the government in Philadelphia, both in writing and by word of mouth, they had received neither help nor hearing. (2) After the Indians had been taken to Philadelphia, they, the backwoodsmen, were insulted by Quakers and other disorderly people who jeered at them, "See there! There are the murderers of Paxton who have slain the Indians!" (3) More than that, the leading Quakers took those Bethlehem Indians (among whom were murderers) into the city and treated them like lords at public expense. Meanwhile nothing at all was done for the suffering frontiersmen. On the contrary, it was said that they were nothing but a mixed crowd of Scotch-Irishmen and Germans; it did not matter whether they lived or died. (4) They were in a position to give assurances that they were loyal subjects of our king and friends of the province. In fact, they had proved this by risking life and limb against the enemy. They said that they had no intention of using their weapons against the government or of doing harm to loyal fellow citizens, but that they intended only to defend themselves against attack, to take the Indians out of the barracks, and to conduct them out of the province. They proposed to do this without killing them, and they were ready to offer an adequate guarantee to this effect. (5) Now, however, that they were informed that the Bethlehem Indians had been taken into custody, not by private Quakers but by the government, and that they were being guarded by his Majesty's soldiers, they had no desire to use their weapons and even less to apply pressure to the government by force of arms. Instead, they would select three deputies from their midst and through these lay their grievances and remonstrances before the government. In particular they requested that Mr. Franklin and City Mayor Willing help them to get their *gravamina* on paper, which request was granted. Thereupon the conference was concluded—on condition that the frontiersmen disperse at once and return to their homes.

96B. Matthew Smith and James Gibson: remonstrance of the Pennsylvania frontiersmen (13 February 1764)

Printed: *Minutes of the Provincial Council of Pennsylvania*, IX, pp. 138–142.

We, Matthew Smith and James Gibson, in behalf of ourselves and his Majesty's faithful and loyal subjects, the inhabitants of the frontier counties of Lancaster, York, Cumberland, Berks, and Northampton, humbly beg leave to remonstrate and lay before you the following grievances, which we submit to your wisdom for redress.

First. We apprehend that as freemen and English subjects, we have an indisputable title to the same privileges and immunities with his Majesty's other subjects who reside in the interior counties of Philadelphia, Chester, and Bucks, and therefore ought not to be excluded from an equal share with them in the very important privilege of legislation; nevertheless, contrary to the proprietor's charter and the acknowledged principles of common justice and equity, our five counties are restrained from electing more than ten representatives, viz.: four for Lancaster, two for York, two for Cumberland, one for Berks, and one for Northampton, while the three counties and city of Philadelphia, Chester, and Bucks elect twenty-six. This we humbly conceive is oppressive, unequal, and unjust, the cause of many of our grievances, and an infringement of our natural privileges of freedom and equality; wherefore, we humbly pray that we may be no longer deprived of an equal number with the three aforesaid counties to represent us in Assembly.

Secondly. We understand that a bill is now before the House of Assembly, wherein it is provided that such persons as shall be charged with killing any Indians in Lancaster County shall not be tried in the county where the fact was committed, but in the counties of Philadelphia, Chester, or Bucks. This is manifestly to deprive British subjects of their known privileges, to cast an eternal reproach upon whole counties, as if they were unfit to serve their country in the quality of jurymen, and to contradict the well known laws of the British nation in a point whereon life, liberty, and security essentially depend, namely, that of being tried by their equals in the neighbourhood where their own, their accusers, and the witnesses' character and credit, with the circumstances of the fact, are best known, and instead thereof putting their lives in the hands of strangers, who may as justly be suspected of partiality to as the frontier counties can be of prejudices against Indians; and this, too, in favour of Indians only, against his Majesty's faithful and loyal subjects. Besides, it is well known that the design of it is to comprehend a fact committed before such a law was thought of. And if such practices were tolerated, no man could be secure in his most valuable interest. We are also informed, to our great surprise, that this bill has actually received the assent of a majority of the House, which we are persuaded could not have been the case, had our frontier counties been equally represented in Assembly. However, we hope that the legislature of this province will never enact a law of so dangerous a tendency, or take away from his Majesty's good subjects a privilege so long esteemed sacred by Englishmen.

Thirdly. During the late and present Indian War, the frontiers of this province had been repeatedly attacked and ravaged by skulking parties of the Indians, who have with the most savage cruelty murdered men, women, and children, without distinction, and have reduced near a thousand families to the most extreme distress. It grieves us to the very heart to see such of our frontier inhabitants as have escaped savage fury with the loss of their parents, their children, their wives or relatives, left destitute by the public, and exposed to the most cruel poverty and wretchedness, while upwards of an hundred and twenty of these savages, who are with great reason suspected of being guilty of these horrid barbarities, under the mask of friendship, have procured themselves to be taken under the protection of the government, with a view to elude the fury of the brave relatives of the murdered, and are now maintained at the public expense. Some of these Indians now in the barracks of Philadelphia, are confessedly a part of the Wyalusing Indians, which tribe is now at war with us, and the others are the Moravian Indians, who, living with us under the cloak of friendship, carried on a correspondence with our known enemies on the Great Island. We cannot but observe, with sorrow and indignation, that some persons in this province are at pains to extenuate the barbarous cruelties practised by these savages on our murdered brethren and relatives, which are shocking to human nature, and must pierce every heart but that of the hardened perpetrators or their abettors; nor is it less distressing to hear others pleading that, although the Wyalusing Tribe is at war with us, yet that part of it which is under the protection of the government may be friendly to the English, and innocent. In what nation under the sun was it ever the custom that when a neighbouring nation took up arms, not an individual should be touched but only the persons that offered hostilities? Who ever proclaimed war with a part of a nation, and not with the whole? Had these Indians disapproved of the perfidy of their tribe, and been willing to cultivate and preserve friendship with us, why did they not give notice of the war before it happened, as it is known to be the result of long deliberations, and a preconcerted combination among them? Why did they not leave their tribe immediately and come among us before there was ground to suspect them, or war was actually waged with their tribe? No, they stayed amongst them, were privy to their murders and ravages, until we had destroyed their provisions, and when they could no longer subsist at home, they come, not as deserters, but as friends, to be maintained through the winter, that they may be able to scalp and butcher us in the spring.

And as to the Moravian Indians, there are strong grounds at least to suspect their friendship, as it is known they carried on a correspondence with our enemies on the Great Island. We killed three Indians going from Bethlehem to the Great Island with blankets, ammunition, and provisions, which is an undeniable proof that the Moravian Indians were in confederacy with our open enemies; and we cannot but be filled with indignation to hear this action of ours painted in the most odious and detestable colours, as if we had inhumanly murdered our guides, who preserved us from perishing in the woods, when we only killed three of our known enemies, who attempted to shoot us when we surprised them. And besides all this, we understand that one of these very Indians is proved by the oath of Stinton's widow to be the very person that murdered her husband. How then comes it to pass that he alone, of all the Moravian Indians, should join with the enemy to murder that family? Or can it be supposed that any enemy Indians, contrary to their known custom of making war, should penetrate into the heart of a settled country, to burn, plunder, and murder the inhabitants, and not molest any houses in their return, or ever be seen or heard of? Or how can we account for it, that no ravages have been committed in Northampton County since the removal of the Moravian Indians, when the Great Cove has been struck since? These things put it beyond doubt with us that the Indians now at Philadelphia are his Majesty's perfidious enemies, and therefore to protect and maintain them at the public expense, while our suffering brethren on the frontiers are almost destitute of the necessaries of life, and are neglected by the public, is sufficient to make us mad with rage, and tempt us to do what nothing but the most violent necessity can vindicate. We humbly and earnestly pray, therefore, that those enemies of his majesty may be removed as soon as possible out of the province.

Fourthly. We humbly conceive that it is contrary to the maxims of good policy, and extremely dangerous to our frontiers, to suffer any Indians, of what tribe soever, to live within the inhabited parts of this province while we are engaged in an Indian war, as experience has taught us that they are all perfidious, and their claim to freedom and independency puts it in their power to act as spies, to entertain and give intelligence to our enemies, and to furnish them with provisions and warlike stores. To this fatal intercourse between our pretended friends and open enemies, we must ascribe the greatest of the ravages and murders that have been committed in the course of this and the last Indian war. We, therefore, pray that this grievance be taken under consideration and remedied.

Fifthly. We cannot help lamenting that no provision has been hitherto made that such of our frontier inhabitants as have been wounded in defence of the province, their lives and liberties, may be taken care of, and cured of their wounds at the public expense. We, therefore, pray that this grievance may be redressed.

Sixthly. In the late Indian war this province, with others of his Majesty's colonies, gave rewards for Indian scalps, to encourage the seeking them in their own country as the most likely means of destroying or reducing them to reason, but no such encouragement has been given in this war, which has damped the spirits of many brave men who are willing to venture their lives in parties against the enemy. We, therefore, pray that public rewards may be proposed for Indian scalps, which may be adequate to the dangers attending enterprises of this nature.

Seventhly. We daily lament that numbers of our nearest and dearest relatives are still in captivity among the savage heathen, to be trained up in all their ignorance and barbarity, or to be tortured to death with all the contrivances of Indian cruelty, for attempting to make their escape from bondage. We see they pay no regard to the many solemn promises which they have made to restore our friends who are in bondage amongst them. We, therefore, earnestly pray that no trade may hereafter be permitted to be carried on with them until our brethren and relatives are brought home to us.

Eighthly. We complain that a certain society of people in this province, in the late

Indian war, and at several treaties held by the king's representatives, openly loaded the Indians with presents, and that J[ames] P[emberton], a leader of the said Society, in defiance of all government, not only abetted our Indian enemies, but kept up a private intelligence with them, and publicly received from them a belt of wampum, as if he had been our governor, or authorized by the king to treat with his enemies. By this means the Indians have been taught to despise us as a weak and disunited people, and from this fatal source have arose many of our calamities under which we groan. We humbly pray, therefore, that this grievance may be redressed, and that no private subject be hereafter permitted to treat with, or carry on a correspondence with our enemies.

Ninthly. We cannot but observe with sorrow that Fort Augusta, which has been very expensive to this province, has afforded us but little assistance during this or the last war. The men that were stationed at that place neither helped our distressed inhabitants to save their crops, nor did they attack our enemies in their towns, or patrol on our frontiers. We humbly request that proper measures may be taken to make that garrison more serviceable to us in our distress, if it can be done.

N.B. We are far from intending any reflection against the commanding officer stationed at Augusta, as we presume his conduct was always directed by those from whom he received his orders.

Signed on behalf of ourselves, and by appointment of a great number of the frontier inhabitants.

MATTHEW SMITH
JAMES GIBSON

Part VII

BRITISH COLONIAL POLICIES AND THE GROWTH OF COLONIAL OPPOSITION
1763–1773

BRITISH COLONIAL POLICIES AND THE
GROWTH OF COLONIAL OPPOSITION
1763–1773

Introduction

THE SEVEN YEARS WAR (1756–1763) marked a fundamental turning-point in the relationship between Great Britain and the American mainland colonies. The war began in 1754 as a struggle between the Virginians and the French for the control of the forks of the Ohio River, and the French won the first encounter. In 1755 an expedition under General Braddock was sent to recapture the forks, but it ended in disaster for the British and colonial troops. The war thus begun in America became world-wide in 1756, but not until 1757, when William Pitt became prime minister, did the British start on the road to victory. By 1760 the conquest of Canada was completed. The Treaty of Paris of 1763 left Britain the dominant colonial power of the world. She acquired Canada, the region between the Mississippi River and the Appalachian Mountains, the Floridas, some of the French islands in the West Indies, and on the other side of the world she got control of most of India.[1] Yet within a decade this vast empire was disrupted by the revolt of thirteen of the American mainland colonies.

What were the causes of the revolt? What policies and what men were to blame? Were they British, or American, or both? The debate has gone on from the eighteenth century to the present, and no answers have ever been agreed upon. Participants, of course, had definite convictions. Those Americans who remained loyal to Great Britain looked on the war for independence as a movement made up of smuggling merchants, debt-ridden planters, and the property-less rabble, each of whom sought their own selfish ends. The patriots justified the war on the grounds that they had been bitterly oppressed by Great Britain. The Declaration of Independence listed a series of specific charges ranging from economic to political and social limitations on self-governing colonies which could do nothing but revolt, considering their English heritage, their rights as men, and the tyranny and unconstitutional behaviour of the king.

Such ideas are threads running through the interpretations of the Revolution down to the present day. Historians have argued as to whether or not the Revolution was primarily an economic, a constitutional, or a political movement, and within any one of these categories have offered conflicting arguments to explain it.

The war for independence had far more tangled roots than either most participants or later historians have ever made clear. This is true whether one looks at the evolution of British policy towards the colonies or at political developments within the colonies. One thing stands out clearly in the complex history of British politics after 1763: clear-cut and consistent colonial policy was often sacrificed in order to secure immediate political advantage in the struggle between warring factions in Parliament and

---

[1] For documents on the Seven Years War, see *English Historical Documents*, vol. x.

in the series of ministries that followed one after another until 1770. The spoils of office rather than a realistic administration of colonial affairs was the aim and end of plot and counterplot, even though colonial affairs were often a central issue in the debates of the times.

It is true that two groups emerged, one of which can be called pro-colonial and the other anti-colonial in their attitudes. However, the lines between them are blurred. Neither group, except a few who believed in outright coercion of the colonies, supported a consistent policy. Leaders of both groups insisted that Parliament had the 'right' to legislate for the colonies; yet they differed widely on the point of expediency, and even their definition of what was expedient varied from time to time.

When one turns to the colonies, the situation is even more complex. There was a separate revolutionary movement in each of the thirteen colonies. Furthermore, there were sharp divisions of opinion within each colony on virtually every measure taken by the British government after 1763. Some colonial leaders consistently supported the 'right' of Parliament to legislate for the colonies, although they doubted the wisdom of most of the Acts passed. Other leaders denied the 'right' of Parliament to legislate for the colonies, but admitted the necessity of parliamentary regulation of trade. When one moves from the realm of constitutional argument to that of practical means of opposition to British measures, the division in every colony is even sharper. The more conservative leaders insisted that the only proper means of opposition was a dutiful petition to the king and Parliament for a redress of grievances. The most radical soon showed that they were willing to oppose British measures by non-consumption and non-importation agreements, and if these failed, to use open violence.

Each of the colonies, too, was characterized by political and social cleavages which had more than once resulted in popular rebellions against the established political order in the colonies.[1] In the years after 1763 there was a growing demand by farmers and the citizenry of the towns for what amounted to more political and economic democracy. Yet at the same time, many of the outstanding popular leaders, who were willing in the end to lead a war for independence, wanted no change in the internal political and economic structure of the colonies, although most of their support came from the people who wanted such change.

This multiplicity of facts must be considered in any discussion of the American Revolution. The documents presented in this part and in the part which follows do not presume to explain the 'causes' of the Revolution nor to fix responsibility on individuals or groups of them. Instead, they are offered to illustrate the nature of British policies after 1763, the various types of colonial opposition to those policies, the progress, step by step, which led to the actual warfare between the British and the colonists, and, finally, to the Declaration of Independence by thirteen colonies in 1776.

[1] Nos. 94, 95, 96.

SELECT BIBLIOGRAPHY
on the background of the American Revolution

I. ORIGINAL SOURCES

In addition to the printed sources previously cited, such as legislative journals, and other colonial records which cover the years 1763–1776, a great body of letters, journals, and diaries has been published. Only a few of the more important can be included here. Despite the quantity of published material, the bulk remains in manuscript. The guides to manuscript collections which have been cited should be consulted.

(a) THE SEVEN YEARS WAR AND THE WEST, 1750–1776

The most convenient guide to printed and manuscript sources and to secondary materials for the Seven Years War is to be found in the notes in L. H. GIPSON, *The British Empire before the American Revolution* (vols. IV–VIII, New York, 1939–1954). THEODORE C. PEASE, ed., *Anglo-French Boundary Disputes in the West, 1749–1763* (Springfield, Ill., 1936) is a useful collection. STANLEY M. PARGELLIS, ed., *Military Affairs in North America, 1748–1765* (New York, 1936) contains a wide range of documents drawn from the Cumberland Papers at Windsor Castle. ALFRED P. JAMES, ed., *The Writings of General John Forbes* . . . (Menasha, Wis., 1938) and J. C. WEBSTER, ed., *The Journal of Jeffrey Amherst* . . . (Toronto, 1931) are important for the work of two of the British commanders in America. S. K. STEVENS and D. H. KENT, eds., *The Papers of Colonel Henry Bouquet* (19 vols., mimeographed, Harrisburg, Pa., 1940–1943). Vol. II, printed, Harrisburg, 1951) are invaluable for the war in the West and for the career of the Swiss soldier who was one of the ablest British officers in the colonies. C. H. LINCOLN, ed., *Correspondence of William Shirley, Governor of Massachusetts and Military Commander in America, 1731–1760* (2 vols., New York, 1912) contains much material on the war and on the career of the most active of the colonial governors in fighting it. JAMES SULLIVAN, A. C. FLICK, *et al.*, eds., *The Papers of Sir William Johnson* (10 vols., Albany, N.Y., 1921–1951) are replete with materials on the war, on Indian relations, and on land speculation after the war. GERTRUDE S. KIMBALL, ed., *Correspondence of William Pitt, when Secretary of State, with Colonial Governors and Military and Naval Commissioners in America* (2 vols., New York, 1906) is important, both for overall policy and for the events of the war in the colonies.

There are several valuable collections for the history of the West after 1763. CLARENCE W. ALVORD and CLARENCE E. CARTER, eds., *The Critical Period, 1763–1765, The New Regime, 1765–1767,* and *Trade and Politics, 1767–1769* (Illinois State Historical Library Collections, British Series, vols. X, XI, XVI, Springfield, Ill., 1915–1921) contain letters, journals and other documents of first importance for British policy as well as for events in the West. R. G. THWAITES and LOUISE P. KELLOG, eds., *Documentary History of Dunmore's War, 1774* and *The Revolution on the Upper Ohio, 1775–1777* (State Historical Society of Wisconsin Collections, Draper Series, vols. I–II. Madison, Wis., 1905, 1908) are gleanings from the Draper Manuscript Collection in the State Historical Society of Wisconsin.

Documents illustrating the Seven Years War have not been included in this volume. For such materials, see *English Historical Documents*, vol. x.

(b) BRITISH COLONIAL POLICY, 1763–1776

Previously cited sources such as the *Journals* of the House of Commons and the House of Lords, the parliamentary debates, the *Acts of the Privy Council, Colonial Series,* the *Journal* of the Board of Trade, and the *Statutes at Large,* are all essential. J. A. REDINGTON and R. A. ROBERTS, eds., *Calendar of Home Office Papers of the Reign of George the Third, 1760–1776* (4 vols., London, 1878–1899) also contains material on colonial affairs.

W. B. DONNE, *The Correspondence of King George the Third with Lord North from 1768 to 1783* (2 vols., London, 1867); SIR JOHN FORTESCUE, ed., *The Correspondence of King George III from 1760 to December 1783* . . . (6 vols., London, 1927-1928), and ROMNEY SEDGWICK, ed., *Letters from George III to Lord Bute, 1756-1766* (London, 1939) are all important. Fortescue's careless editing is illustrated in SIR LEWIS NAMIER, *Additions and Corrections to Sir John Fortescue's Edition of the Correspondence of George III* (vol. 1) (Manchester, 1937).

Smaller collections of value are W. J. SMITH, ed., *The Grenville Papers* . . . (4 vols., London 1852-1853); N. S. JUCKER, ed., *The Jenkinson Papers, 1760-1766* (London, 1949); and VERNER S. CRANE, ed., *Benjamin Franklin's Letters to the Press, 1758-1775* (Chapel Hill, N.C., 1950). Franklin's activities as a pro-colonial propagandist are fully revealed in the latter volume. For additional printed sources for the period see STANLEY PARGELLIS and D. J. MEDLEY, *Bibliography of British History: The Eighteenth Century, 1714-1789* and vol. x of *English Historical Documents*.

(c) CORRESPONDENCE, DIARIES, JOURNALS, AND MISCELLANEOUS COLLECTIONS

A part of the correspondence of British officials in the colonies, and particularly of the governors, has been printed. This is notably the case in the New York *Colonial Documents*, the *Archives* of New Jersey, the Pennsylvania *Archives*, the Maryland *Archives*, the North Carolina *Colonial Records*, and Georgia *Colonial Records*. In most cases, such collections also include selections from the letters of officials in England to the governors. EDWARD CHANNING and A. C. COOLIDGE, eds., *The Barrington-Bernard Correspondence* . . . *1760-1770* (Cambridge, Mass., 1912) is a selection from the voluminous correspondence between Francis Bernard, governor of Massachusetts, and Lord Barrington, Secretary at War. The letters and papers of Cadwallader Colden, lieutenant-governor of New York, and often acting governor between 1760 and 1776, have been published at large by the New York Historical Society in its *Collections* (11 vols., 1877-1936).

The writings of several British army officers in the colonies have been published. The most important collection is CLARENCE E. CARTER, ed., *The Correspondence of General Thomas Gage with Secretaries of State and with the War Office and the Treasury, 1763-1775* (2 vols., New Haven, Conn., 1931-1933). These are taken from the Gage papers in the Clements Library, Ann Arbor, Mich. Other accounts are G. D. SCULL, ed., *The Montresor Journals* (N.Y. Hist. Soc. *Collections*, 1881); H. M. LYDENBERG, ed., *Archibald Robertson, Lieutenant-General, Royal Engineers. His Diaries and Sketches in America, 1762-1780* (New York Public Library *Bulletin*, vol. XXXVII, 1933); *Diary of Frederick Mackenzie* . . . *1775-1781* (2 vols., Cambridge, Mass., 1930); ELIZABETH E. DANA, ed., *The British in Boston, being the diary of Lieutenant John Barker of the King's Own Regiment from November 15, 1774 to May 31, 1776* (Cambridge, Mass., 1924); EDWARD H. TATUM, ed., *The American Journal of Ambrose Serle* . . . (The Huntington Library, San Marino, Cal., 1940). *The Journal of Nicholas Cresswell, 1774-1777* (New York, 1924) is an account by a young English civilian.

The published colonial records, the colonial newspapers, and the writings of American leaders are basic sources. Some of the writings of American leaders – letters, diaries, journals, and the like – have been published.

The following are among the most important of the collected writings of American leaders: C. F. ADAMS, ed., *The Works of John Adams* (10 vols., Boston, 1856); H. A. CUSHING, ed., *The Writings of Samuel Adams* (4 vols., New York, 1904-1908); W. C. FORD, ed., *The Warren-Adams Letters* (2 vols., Boston, 1917, 1925. Mass. Hist. Soc. *Collections*, vols. LXXII-LXXIII); A. H. SMYTH, ed., *The Writings of Benjamin Franklin* (10 vols., New York, 1905-1907); CARL VAN DOREN, ed., *Letters and Papers of Benjamin Franklin and Richard Jackson 1753-1785* (Philadelphia, 1947); W. W. HENRY, *Patrick Henry: Life, Correspondence, and Speeches* (3 vols., New York, 1891); H. P. JOHNSTON, ed., *The Correspondence and Public Papers of John Jay* (4 vols., New York, 1890-1893; JULIAN P. BOYD, et al., eds., *The Papers of Thomas Jefferson* (8 vols. to date, Princeton, 1950-1953); JAMES C. BALLAGH, ed., *Letters of Richard Henry Lee* (2 vols., New York, 1911-1914); PHILIP S. FONER, ed., *The Complete Writings of Thomas Paine* (2 vols., New York, 1945); W. B.

REED, *Life and Correspondence of Joseph Reed* (2 vols., Philadelphia, 1847); GEORGE H. RYDEN, ed., *Letters to and from Caesar Rodney, 1756-1784* (Philadelphia, 1933); L. H. BUTTERFIELD, ed., *Letters of Benjamin Rush* (2 vols., Princeton, 1951); JOHN C. FITZPATRICK, ed., *The Writings of George Washington . . . 1745-1799* (39 vols., Washington, 1931-1944); JARED SPARKS, ed., *Correspondence of the American Revolution: Being Letters of Eminent Men to George Washington . . .* (4 vols., Washington, 1853); and S. M. HAMILTON, ed., *Letters to Washington and Accompanying Papers, 1752-1775* (5 vols., Boston, 1898-1902).

For the most part, the collected writings of the above men include only a small part of their own papers, and with one exception, do not include the letters written to them. The Fitzpatrick edition of Washington's writings includes virtually all of Washington's letters. The new edition of Jefferson's writings includes both Jefferson's letters and either the text or a summary of the letters written to him. A new edition of Franklin's writings is now under way at Yale University.

There are several important smaller collections. P. L. FORD, ed., *The Writings of John Dickinson* (Penn. Hist. Soc. *Memoirs*, vol. XIV, Philadelphia, 1895) and C. F. MULLETT, ed., *Some Political Writings of James Otis* (Univ. of Missouri *Studies*, Columbia, Mo., 1929) are devoted to political tracts rather than private correspondence. A. R. CUNNINGHAM, ed., *Letters and Diary of John Rowe, Boston Merchant* (Boston, 1903); *Letter Book of John Watts . . .* (N.Y. Hist. Soc. *Collections*, 1928) and *The Bowdoin and Temple Papers* (Mass. Hist. Soc. *Collections*, 6th Series, vol. IX) are representative samples of important source materials.

Among the diaries, journals, and reminiscences, good examples are JONATHAN BOUCHER, ed., *Reminiscences of an American Loyalist, 1738-1789, being the Autobiography of the Reverend Jonathan Boucher . . .* (Boston, 1925); LANDON CARTER, "Diaries", 1770-1776, *William and Mary College Quarterly*, 1st Series, vols. XIII-XXI (1904-1913); P. O. HUTCHINSON, ed., *The Diary and Letters of . . . Thomas Hutchinson . . .* (2 vols., Boston, 1884-1886); WILLIAM DUANE, ed., *Extracts from the Diary of Christopher Marshall . . . 1774-1781* (Albany, N.Y., 1877); T. G. TAPPERT and J. W. DOBERSTEIN, eds., *The Journals of Henry Melchior Muhlenberg* (vol. II [1764-1776] Philadelphia, 1945); JOSIAH QUINCY, Jr., "A Journal, 1773" (Mass. Hist. Soc. *Proceedings*, vol. XLIX, 1916). An excellent guide to published diaries is WILLIAM MATTHEWS, *American Diaries: an Annotated Bibliography of American Diaries Written Prior to the Year 1861* (Berkeley, Cal., 1945).

The events of the two years preceding the Declaration of Independence are particularly well represented in printed sources. PETER FORCE, ed., *American Archives . . .* 4th Series (6 vols., Washington, 1837-1846) and 5th Series (3 vols., Washington, 1848-1853) is a monumental collection of every kind of source material, some of which is no longer available. It covers the period from 7 March 1774 to 31 December 1776. A much smaller but still useful collection is HEZEKIAH NILES, ed., *Principles and Acts of the Revolution in America . . .* (Baltimore, 1822. Republished, Philadelphia, 1786). FRANK MOORE, ed., *The Diary of the Revolution . . . 1775 to 1784* (Hartford, Conn., 1875) is a day by day account taken principally from contemporary newspapers.

W. C. FORD, et al., eds., *The Journals of the Continental Congress, 1774-1789* (34 vols., Washington, 1904-1937) is the official record of the central body which directed the American Revolution. EDMUND C. BURNETT, ed., *Letters of Members of the Continental Congress* (8 vols., Washington, 1921-1936) provides the necessary background without which the *Journals* would be relatively barren.

Among the several useful collections for the literary aspects of the Revolution are FRANK MOORE, ed., *Songs and Ballads of the American Revolution* (New York, 1856) and *Illustrated Ballad History of the American Revolution 1765-1783* (1876); SAMUEL W. PATTERSON, *The Spirit of the American Revolution as revealed in the Poetry of the Period . . .* (Boston, 1915); WINTHROP SARGENT ed., *Loyalist Poetry of the Revolution* (Philadelphia, 1857); and JOHN W. THORNTON, ed., *The Pulpit of the American Revolution . . .* (Boston, 1860); ARTHUR M. SCHLESINGER, "A Note on Songs as Patriot Propaganda, 1765-1776", *William and Mary Quarterly*, 3rd Series, vol., XI (1954) is a tentative list of such material, and indicates where it may be found. The best account of the literature of the Revolution, as well as a guide to it, is MOSES COIT TYLER, *The Literary History of the American Revolution, 1763-1783* (2 vols., New York, 1897. Republished: New York, 1941).

(d) SOURCES FOR SPECIAL ASPECTS OF COLONIAL OPPOSITION

The "State of the Trade, 1763", Col. Soc. Mass. *Publications*, vol. XIX (1918) was drawn up by Boston merchants in 1763 to combat the renewal of the Molasses Act of 1733, and presents a picture of trade conditions as seen by the merchants. Documents illustrating opposition to customs officials are given in G. G. WOLKINS, "The Seizure of John Hancock's Sloop *Liberty*," Mass. Hist. Soc. *Proceedings*, vol. LV (1923), "A History of the Destruction of . . . *Gaspee*", Rhode Island *Colonial Records*, vol. VII, and "Gaspee Papers, 1772–1773", Rhode Island Hist. Soc. *Publications*, new Series, vol. VII (1899); O. M. DICKERSON, *Boston under Military Rule*, *1768–1769* (Boston, 1936), reprints "A Journal of the Times", a widely circulated series of articles on the iniquities of British customs officials and soldiers from September 1768 to August 1769.

A valuable collection of documents on the Boston Massacre is printed by RANDOLPH G. ADAMS in "New Light on the Boston Massacre", Amer. Antiq. Soc. *Proceedings*, new Series, vol. XLVII (1937). FRANCIS S. DRAKE, *Tea Leaves* . . . (Boston, 1884) is a collection of letters and other documents on the crisis in 1773.

II. MODERN WORKS ON THE PERIOD 1763–1776

(a) GENERAL HISTORIES

The following histories are but a few of the many that have been written. They are listed because they represent a variety of interpretations of the Revolution. Most of them are in one way or another inadequate, yet material of value may be found in each of them.

Among the works written by participants in the Revolution, three are outstanding. The third volume of THOMAS HUTCHINSON's *History of . . . Massachusetts Bay* is a detailed account of events in Massachusetts before the Revolution. Dr. David Ramsay's *A History of the Revolution in South Carolina* . . . (2 vols., Trenton, N.J., 1785) is the narrative of an active participant in many phases of the Revolution. The REVEREND WILLIAM GORDON's *The History of the Rise, Progress, and Establishment of the Independence of the United States of America* . . . (4 vols., London, 1788) is the work of an English clergyman who came to the colonies in 1770 and who returned to England in 1786. GORDON lived in Massachusetts but travelled everywhere. He determined to write the history of the war from the outset. He knew or corresponded with many of the American leaders. He searched through their papers. Despite the doubt that has been cast upon his work it contains much valuable material that cannot be found elsewhere.

GEORGE BANCROFT was for long the most influential American interpreter of the Revolution. His *History of the United States* (6 vols., New York, 1834–1874, and many subsequent editions) was based on much research. Although he treated the Revolution as a democratic movement, his view was that colonial opposition to the Navigation Acts was the basic cause of the Revolution. His interpretation has been followed by many English and American historians. One example is W. E. H. LECKY, *A History of England in the Eighteenth Century* (8 vols., London, 1879–1890). LECKY's chapters on the Revolution are reprinted in JAMES A. WOODBURN, ed., *The American Revolution, 1763–1783* (New York, 1912). American writers who have seen the English commercial system as the root cause of the Revolution are G. E. HOWARD, *Preliminaries of the Revolution, 1763–1775* (New York, 1905) and EDWARD CHANNING, *The American Revolution, 1761–1789* (*History of the United States*, vol. III. New York, 1912).

A second interpretation was established mainly by the Whig historians of nineteenth-century England. They denounced the behaviour of George III and a 'Tory' party and argued if such 'Whigs' as Pitt and Burke had been in power, there would not have been an American Revolution. The culmination of this school of writing was SIR GEORGE OTTO TREVELYAN's *The American Revolution* (4 vols., London, 1899–1907) and *George the Third and Charles Fox. The Concluding Part of the American Revolution* (2 vols., London, 1912–1914). In America, JOHN FISKE in *The War for Independence* (New York, 1889) and in *The American Revolution* (2 vols., Boston, 1891) put the same idea into somewhat different form. C. H. VAN TYNE, whose earlier work had done much to demonstrate the over-simplification in such interpretations, returned to an essentially Whig interpretation of the Revolution after World War I in his *The Causes of the War of Independence* (Boston, 1922). Such essentially political interpretations of the Revolution have been followed in the recent study of JOHN MILLER, *Origins of the American Revolution* (Boston, 1943) and in the most recent study by an English historian, H. E. EGERTON, *The Causes and Character of the American Revolution* (Oxford, 1923).

A third thread of interpretation has appeared as a result of detailed studies which have been made of the revolutionary movement in individual colonies. Some of these studies assert or imply that the Revolution arose from conditions within the colonies themselves, and tend to relegate British policies to a secondary place: to view the Revolution as an internal revolution. This is particularly true of the studies of CHARLES H. LINCOLN, CARL BECKER, and JAMES T. ADAMS, which are cited hereafter in the section on "Works on Particular Colonies".

There are several interpretative essays on the nature of the Revolution which offer a convenient means of becoming aquainted with various concepts held by historians. MAX FARRAND, "The West and the Principles of the Revolution", *Yale Review*, vol. XVII (1908–1909) emphasizes the importance of the back country. A differing interpretation is presented by PHILIP DAVIDSON, "The Southern Back Country on the Eve of the Revolution", in AVERY CRAVEN, ed., *Essays in Honor of William E. Dodd . . .* (Chicago, 1935).

CLARENCE W. ALVORD, "Virginia and the West; an Interpretation", *Miss. Valley Hist. Rev.*, vol. III (1916–1917) upholds the idea that Virginians were driven into the Revolution by British western policy, and in "Politics in the Revolution", *American Mercury*, vol. V (1925) he sees the Revolution as a whole as the outgrowth of a "rising consciousness of American nationality" on one hand, and of political muddling in England on the other. ARTHUR M. SCHLESINGER, "The American Revolution Reconsidered", *Pol. Sci. Quarterly*, vol. XXXIV (1919) considers the sectional differences among the colonies, their reactions to British policies, and their interaction upon one another as leading to the Revolution. CHARLES M. ANDREWS in *The Colonial Background of the American Revolution* (New Haven, 1924) and in "The American Revolution: an Interpretation", *Amer. Hist. Rev.*, vol. XXXI (1925–1926) holds to an essentially political and constitutional interpretation as opposed to an economic one. LOUISE M. HACKER, "The First American Revolution", *Columbia University Quarterly*, vol. XXVII (1935) argues that the Revolution came about because of the exploitation of colonial capitalists for the benefit of British capitalists, particularly in the field of manufacturing. "The American Revolution: A Symposium", *Canadian Historical Review*, vol. XXIII (1942) consists of important discussions by LAURENCE A. HARPER, W. T. ROOT, O. M. DICKERSON, and LAWRENCE H. GIPSON on various interpretations of the Revolution.

(b) SPECIAL WORKS ON BRITISH POLITICS AND COLONIAL POLICY

Major works by American and English scholars during the twentieth century have provided the basis for more adequate interpretation of the American Revolution. CLARENCE W. ALVORD, *The Mississippi Valley in British Politics* (2 vols., Cleveland, 1917) was one of the first to point out the fallacies of the 'Whig' interpretation of the Revolution, and in addition he focused attention on expansion into the Mississippi Valley as playing a vital role in both the colonies and in British politics. SIR LEWIS NAMIER in *The Structure of Politics at the Accession of George III* (2 vols., London, 1929) and in *England in the Age of the American Revolution* (London, 1930) completed the demolition of the Whig myth by a detailed study of politics in the years 1760–1763. Recent works in more or less the same vein are SIR KEITH FEILING, *The Second Tory Party, 1714–1832* (London, 1938); G. H. GUTTRIDGE, *English Whiggism and the American Revolution* (Berkeley, Cal., 1942); RICHARD PARES, *King George III and the Politicians* (Oxford, 1953). VINCENT T. HARLOW has a valuable chapter, "The Argument about North America", in volume one of his *The Founding of the Second British Empire, 1763–1793* (London, 1952).

Special studies of the details of colonial policy are GEORGE L. BEER, *British Colonial Policy, 1754–1765* (New York, 1907) and O. M. DICKERSON, *The Navigation Acts and the American*

Revolution (Philadelphia, 1951). BEER, as in his earlier works, is more concerned with the British side than the American, and views British policies sympathetically. DICKERSON attacks and demolishes the idea of the Navigation Acts as a cause of the Revolution, but insists that it was their perversion after 1763: the shift from a policy of protection and encouragement of trade before 1763 to a policy of trade taxation and customs 'racketeering' afterwards, that brought on the Revolution. DICKERSON's bibliography contains a valuable list of the contemporary pamphlet literature as well as a guide to manuscript sources.

C. F. MULLETT, "English Imperial Thinking, 1764–1783", *Pol. Sci. Quarterly*, vol. XLV (1930) is a convenient summary. KLAUS KNORR, *British Colonial Theories, 1570–1850*, chaps. iii and iv presents more material on the same subject. FRED J. HINKHOUSE, *The Preliminaries of the American Revolution as Seen in the English Press, 1763–1775* (New York, 1926) and DORA M. CLARK, *British Opinion and the American Revolution* (New Haven, Conn., 1930) cover public opinion. In addition to the various works listed in the following topical bibliographies, the following should be consulted: ARTHUR H. BASYE, "The Secretary of State for the Colonies, 1768–1782", *Amer. Hist. Rev.*, vol. XXVIII (1922–1923); MARGARET MARION SPECTOR, *The American Department of the British Government, 1768–1780*; LUCY S. SUTHERLAND, "Edmund Burke and the First Rockingham Ministry", *Eng. Hist. Rev.*, vol. XLVII (1932); R. A. HUMPHREYS, "Lord Shelburne and British Colonial Policy, 1766–1768", *Eng. Hist. Rev.*, vol. L (1935); and "Lord Shelburne and a Projected Recall of Colonial Governors in 1767", *Amer. Hist. Rev.*, vol. XXXVII (1931–1932).

(c) CONSTITUTIONAL AND POLITICAL THEORY

Among many such studies, the following are the most useful. RANDOLPH G. ADAMS, *Political Ideas of the American Revolution* (Durham, N.C., 1932) is essentially a study of various conceptions of the nature of the Empire. CHARLES H. McILWAIN, *The American Revolution: a Constitutional Interpretation* (New York, 1923) denies that Parliament had any authority outside the realm of England while ROBERT L. SCHUYLER, *Parliament and the British Empire* (New York, 1929) says that it did. EDMUND S. MORGAN, "Colonial Ideas of Parliamentary Power 1764–1766", *William and Mary Quarterly*, 3rd Series, vol. V (1948), argues that the colonists made no distinction between internal and external taxation.

Other aspects are treated in CARL BECKER, *The Declaration of Independence. A Study in the History of Political Ideas* (New York, 1922), chap. ii, "Historical Antecedents of the Declaration: The Natural Rights Philosophy", and in C. F. MULLETT, *Fundamental Law and the American Revolution, 1760–1776* (New York, 1933).

The most recent and detailed study of American political thought 1763–1776 are the last three chapters of CLINTON ROSSITER, *Seedtime of the Republic*. The footnotes are a detailed guide to the sources and the scholarly writing on the subject.

(d) WORKS ON PARTICULAR COLONIES

Although there are some good studies of the revolutionary movements in individual colonies, there is need for more detailed work on most of them. The following are the principal works which are useful.

Connecticut. The most recent work is OSCAR ZEICHNER, *Connecticut's Years of Controversy, 1750–1776* (Chapel Hill, N.C., 1949). EDITH A. BAILEY, *Influences Towards Radicalism in Connecticut, 1754–1775* (Smith College *Studies in History*, vol. V, Northampton, Mass., 1920) and JULIAN P. BOYD, "Connecticut's Experiment in Expansion; The Susquehanna Company, 1753–1803", *Journal of Economic and Business History*, vol. IV (1931–1932) should also be consulted.

Georgia. The only worthwhile study is KENNETH COLEMAN, "The American Revolution in Georgia, 1763–1789", an unpublished doctoral thesis (1952) in the Library of the University of Wisconsin.

Maryland. CHARLES A. BARKER, *The Background of the Revolution in Maryland* (New Haven, Conn., 1940) is thorough but does not go beyond the year 1774.

Massachusetts. JAMES T. ADAMS, *Revolutionary New England, 1691–1776* (Boston, 1923) covers the New England colonies but concentrates on Massachusetts. ELLEN E. BRENNAN, *Plural Office Holding in Massachusetts, 1760–1780* (Chapel Hill, N.C., 1945) contains important material. LEE N. NEWCOMER, *The Embattled Farmers. A Massachusetts Countryside in the American Revolution* (New York, 1953) is useful but too brief. The best biography of Samuel Adams is RALPH V. HARLOW, *Samuel Adams, Promoter of the American Revolution* (New York, 1923). The psychological interpretation can be ignored. Thorough use was made of the newspapers in this biography and it comes nearer to setting forth the intricacies of politics than any other single work. The third volume of THOMAS HUTCHINSON, *History of . . . Massachusetts Bay* is still of great value. Other items relevant to the history of Massachusetts are cited elsewhere.

New Hampshire. RICHARD F. UPTON, *Revolutionary New Hampshire* (Hanover, N.H., 1936) is good. It should be supplemented by LAWRENCE MAYO, *John Wentworth* (Cambridge, Mass., 1921) and his *John Langdon of New Hampshire* (Concord, N.H., 1937).

New Jersey. DONALD L. KEMMERER, *Path to Freedom: The Struggle for Self-Government in New Jersey, 1703–1776* (Princeton, 1940) is excellent.

New York. CARL BECKER, *The History of Political Parties in the Province of New York, 1760–1776* (Madison, Wis., 1909) was one of the first thorough studies of the revolutionary movement in a single colony, and is still the one upon which all writers on New York depend. DOROTHY R. DILLON, *The New York Triumvirate: A study of the Legal and Political Careers of William Livingston, John Morin Scott, and William Smith, Jr.* (New York, 1949) is a recent account. Consult also, VIRGINIA HARRINGTON, *The New York Merchant on the Eve of the Revolution.*

Pennsylvania. CHARLES H. LINCOLN, *The Revolutionary Movement in Pennsylvania, 1760–1776* (Philadelphia, 1901) ranks along with BECKER's work on New York, which it preceded. It nevertheless needs revision and amplification. J. PAUL SELSAM, *The Pennsylvania Constitution of 1776 . . .* (Philadelphia, 1936) fills in some of the gaps left by LINCOLN.

South Carolina. There is no study of the revolutionary movement as such. DAVID D. WALLACE, *The History of South Carolina*, contains the best and most recent account. RICHARD HOOKER, *The South Carolina Back Country on the Eve of the Revolution* has valuable material. So too does the contemporary history of DAVID RAMSAY, *History of the Revolution in South Carolina.*

Vermont. Although Vermont did not become a state until after the Revolution, it played an important role in American politics. CHILTON WILLIAMSON, *Vermont in Quandary: 1763–1825* (Montpelier, Vt., 1949) is the best account.

Virginia. H. J. ECKENRODE, *The Revolution in Virginia* (New York, 1916); FREEMAN H. HART, *The Valley of Virginia in the American Revolution 1763–1789* (Chapel Hill, N.C., 1942); ISAAC S. HARRELL, *Loyalism in Virginia: Chapters in the Economic History of the Revolution* (Philadelphia, 1926); and T. P. ABERNETHY, *Western Lands and the American Revolution* (New York, 1937), all contain valuable materials as well as differing viewpoints, as do biographies of Washington, Jefferson, and other Virginia leaders. The most important recent study, which is far more than a biography, is DAVID J. MAYS, *Edmund Pendleton, 1721–1803: A Biography* (2 vols., Cambridge, Mass., 1952). A satisfactory study of the revolutionary movement in Virginia remains to be done.

(e) THE SEVEN YEARS WAR

The Seven Years War was a vital turning point in the history of Britain and the mainland colonies and has been the subject of many works. The most comprehensive is L. H. GIPSON, *The British Empire Before the American Revolution* (8 vols., Caldwell, Idaho, and New York, 1936–1954). The first three volumes survey the entire British Empire, and the next five volumes recount the history of the war throughout the world. FRANCIS PARKMAN's classic volumes, *A Half Century of Conflict* (2 vols., Boston, 1892), and *Montcalm and Wolfe* (2 vols., Boston, 1884) concentrate on the conflict in North America. GEORGE M. WRONG, *The Rise and Fall of New France* (2 vols., New York, 1928) is a thorough study. CHARLES M. ANDREWS, "Anglo-French Rivalry, 1700–1750: The Western Phase", *Amer. Hist. Rev.*, vol. XX (1914–1915) is a brief but useful study.

The struggle for the Ohio–Mississippi valleys is set in perspective by CLARENCE W. ALVORD,

The Illinois Country, 1673-1818 (Springfield, Ill., 1920). More detailed are LOUISE P. KELLOGG, *The French Regime in Wisconsin and the Northwest* (Madison, Wis., 1925); MAX SAVELLE, *The Diplomatic History of the Canadian Boundary, 1749-1763* (New Haven, Conn., 1940); and WILBUR R. JACOBS, *Diplomacy and Indian Gifts: Anglo-French Rivalry Along the Ohio and Northwest Frontiers, 1748-1763* (Stanford, Cal., 1950). GERALD S. GRAHAM, *Empire of the North Altantic: The Maritime Struggle for North America* (Toronto, 1950) emphasizes the Canadian aspects.

The conflict of interests in the West Indies and Spanish America among England, France, and Spain can best be followed in RICHARD PARES, *War and Trade in the West Indies, 1739-1763* and in his *Colonial Blockade and Neutral Rights, 1739-1763* (Oxford, 1938).

For the war itself, GIPSON's work is the most thorough, although he maintains some debatable interpretations. Special studies of note are STANLEY PARGELLIS, *Lord Loudoun in North America* (New Haven, Conn., 1933); EUGENE I. McCORMAC, *Colonial Opposition to Imperial Authority during the French and Indian War* (Berkeley, Cal., 1911); L. K. KOONTZ, *The Virginia Frontier, 1754-1763* (Baltimore, 1925); HAYES BAKER-CROTHERS, *Virginia and the French and Indian War* (Chicago, 1928); KATE HOTBLACK, *Chatham's Colonial Policy . . .* (London, 1917); W. L. GRANT, "Canada versus Guadeloupe, An Episode of the Seven Years War", *Amer. Hist. Rev.*, vol. XVII (1911-1912); W. R. SHEPHERD, "The Cession of Louisiana to Spain", *Pol. Sci. Quarterly*, vol. XIX (1904).

For further materials, consult the bibliographies in *English Historical Documents*, vol. X.

(*f*) THE WEST, 1763-1776

CLARENCE W. ALVORD's *The Mississippi Valley in British Politics* is the major study. R. A. HUMPHREYS, "Lord Shelburne and the Proclamation of 1763", *Eng. Hist. Rev.*, vol. XLIX (1934) corrects Alvord and views Shelburne far more dimly. CLARENCE E. CARTER, *Great Britain and the Illinois Country, 1763-1774* (Washington, 1910) has much useful detail, as does LOUISE P. KELLOGG, *The British Regime in Wisconsin and the Old Northwest* (Madison, Wis., 1935). A. L. BURT, *The Old Province of Quebec* (Toronto, 1935) offers a different and important perspective.

Among the many specialized studies the following are among the best: FRANCIS PARKMAN, *The Conspiracy of Pontiac* (2 vols., Boston, 1851); and HOWARD H. PECKHAM, *Pontiac and the Indian Uprising* (Princeton, N.J., 1947) are thorough accounts of the Indian uprising in 1763 which did much to determine British western policy after the war. JOHN R. ALDEN, *John Stuart and the Southern Colonial Frontier . . .* (Ann Arbor, Mich., 1944); THOMAS P. ABERNETHY, *Western Lands and the American Revolution*; A. T. VOLWILER, *George Croghan and the Westward Movement, 1741-1782* (Cleveland, 1926); KENNETH P. BAILEY, *The Ohio Company of Virginia and the Westward Movement, 1748-1792* (Glendale, Cal., 1939); GEORGE E. LEWIS, *The Indiana Company, 1763-1798; A Study in Eighteenth Century Frontier Land Speculation and Business Venture* (Glendale, Cal., 1941); W. S. LESTER, *The Transylvania Colony* (Spencer, Ind., 1935); MARJORIE C. REID, "The Quebec Fur-Traders and Western Policy, 1763-1774", *Canadian Historical Review*, vol. VI (1925).

On the West immediately before the Revolution, see RANDOLPH C. DOWNES, "Dunmore's War: an Interpretation", *Miss. Valley Hist. Rev.*, vol. XXI (1934-1935); VICTOR COFFIN, *The Province of Quebec and the Early American Revolution . . .* (Madison, Wis., 1896); CHARLES H. METZGER, S. J., *The Quebec Act: A Primary Cause of the American Revolution* (New York, 1936). The latter work emphasizes the anti-Catholic feeling aroused by the Quebec Act as a cause, rather than the restriction on western expansion.

(*g*) THE STAMP ACT CRISIS, 1765-1766

Much attention has been devoted to the Stamp Act in a great variety of monographic articles. The first full-length book is EDMUND S. and HELEN M. MORGAN, *The Stamp Act Crisis: Prologue to Revolution* (Chapel Hill, N.C., 1953). It is the most thorough study but with some overemphasis on the political and constitutional aspects and too little attention to internal political conditions. A somewhat different view as to the origins of the Act may be found in

CHARLES R. RITCHESON, "The Preparation of the Stamp Act", *William and Mary Quarterly*, 3rd Series, vol. x (1953). Specialized articles of note are EDWARD HUGHES, "The English Stamp Duties, 1664–1764", *Eng. Hist. Rev.*, vol. LVI (1941); WILLIAM T. LAPRADE, "The Stamp Act in British Politics", *Amer. Hist. Rev.*, vol. xxxv (1929–1930); A. M. SCHLESINGER, "The Colonial Newspapers and the Stamp Act", *New England Quarterly*, vol. VIII (1935). The Stamp Act riots are treated in many periodical articles and in all the books covering the period.

(h) THE BRITISH ARMY IN THE COLONIES, 1763–1776

A thorough study of the British army in America after 1763 is much needed. Lacking this, JOHN R. ALDEN, *General Gage in America* (Baton Rouge, La., 1948) is the best account. Special studies are CLARENCE E. CARTER, "The Significance of the Military Office in America, 1763–1775", *Amer. Hist. Rev.*, vol. XXVIII (1922–1923); ROBERT L. SCHUYLER, "The Recall of the Legions: a Phase of the Decentralization of the British Empire", *Amer. Hist. Rev.*, vol. XXVI (1920–1921); CHARLES L. MOWAT, "The Southern Brigade: A Sidelight on the British Military Establishment in America, 1763–1775", *Journal of Southern History*, vol. x (1944); and DORA M. CLARK, "The British Treasury and the Administration of Military Affairs in America, 1754–1774", *Pennsylvania History*, vol. II (1935).

(i) CUSTOMS REFORMS AND COLONIAL OPPOSITION, 1763–1774

The most recent and detailed analysis of the new reforms and of colonial opposition to them is in O. M. DICKERSON, *The Navigation Acts and the American Revolution*. G. L. BEER, *British Colonial Policy, 1754–1765* emphasizes the British background. Special studies of the customs service in the colonies which should be consulted are EDWARD CHANNING, "The American Board of Commissioners of the Customs", *Mass. Hist. Soc. Proceedings*, vol. XLIII (1910); DORA M. CLARK, "The American Board of Customs, 1767–1783", *Amer. Hist. Rev.*, vol. XLV (1939–1940); WINSLOW WARREN, "The Colonial Customs Service in Massachusetts in its Relation to the American Revolution", *Mass. Hist. Soc. Proceedings*, vol. XLVI (1913); ALFRED E. MARTIN, "The King's Customs: Philadelphia, 1763–1774", *William and Mary Quarterly*, 3rd Series, vol. v (1948). There is no study in print concerning the important role of the admiralty courts during this period. CARL W. UBBELOHDE, "The Vice-Admiralty Courts of British North America, 1763–1776", an unpublished doctoral thesis (1954) in the library of the University of Wisconsin is a thorough study.

The colonial merchants who led the initial opposition to the new measures are discussed at length in ARTHUR M. SCHLESINGER, *The Colonial Merchants and the American Revolution, 1763–1776* (New York, 1918); VIRGINIA HARRINGTON, *The New York Merchant on the Eve of the Revolution*; C. C. CRITTENDEN, *The Commerce of North Carolina, 1763–1789*; and LEILA SELLERS, *Charleston Business on the Eve of the American Revolution*.

Special studies are F. B. WIENER, "The Rhode Island Merchants and the Sugar Act", *New-England Quarterly*, vol. III (1930); CHARLES M. ANDREWS, "The Boston Merchants and the Non-Importation Movement", *Col. Soc. Mass. Publications*, vol. XIX (1918); G. C. SMITH, "An Era of Non-Importation Associations, 1768–1773", *William and Mary Quarterly*, 2nd Series, vol. xx (1940); R. L. BRUNHOUSE, "The Effect of the Townshend Acts in Pennsylvania", *Penn. Mag. of Hist. and Biog.*, vol. LIV (1930). G. G. WOLKINS, "Daniel Malcolm and Writs of Assistance", *Mass. Hist. Soc. Proceedings*, vol. LVIII (1925) is a case study of opposition to customs enforcement. FRANK W. C. HERSEY, "Tar and Feathers: the Adventures of Captain John Malcolm", *Col. Soc. Mass. Publications*, vol. XXXIV (1943) documents the plight of a customs official who was brother to the smuggler cited above. O. M. DICKERSON, "John Hancock: Notorious Smuggler or Near Victim of British Revenue Racketeers?" *Miss. Valley Hist. Rev.*, vol. XXXII (1945–1946) states here the thesis elaborated in his *Navigation Acts and the American Revolution*: namely that 'racketeering' by British customs officials in the colonies drove large numbers of American merchants into the revolutionary movement.

(j) PUBLIC OPINION AND PROPAGANDA

The most thorough study of propaganda and of the role of newspapers and other publications in the Revolutionary movement is PHILIP G. DAVIDSON, *Propaganda and the American Revolution* (Chapel Hill, N.C., 1941). Useful too is MOSES C. TYLER, *Literary History of the American Revolution*. Important special studies are CHESTER N. GREENOUGH, "New England Almanacs, 1766-1775, and the American Revolution", *Amer. Antiq. Soc. Proceedings*, vol. XLV (1935); HOMER L. CALKIN, "Pamphlets and Public Opinion during the American Revolution", *Penn. Mag. of Hist. and Biog.*, vol. LXIV (1940); STELLA DUFF, "The Case Against the King: *The Virginia Gazettes* Indict George III", *William and Mary Quarterly*, 3rd Series, vol. VI (1949); A. M. SCHLESINGER, "Politics, Propaganda, and the Philadelphia Press, 1767-1770", *Penn. Mag. of Hist. and Biog.*, vol. LX (1936); JOHN J. STOUDT, "The German Press in Pennsylvania and the American Revolution", *Penn. Mag. of Hist. and Biog.*, vol. LIX (1935); A. SCHLESINGER, "Propaganda and the Boston Newspaper Press, 1767-1770", *Col. Soc. Mass. Publications*, vol. XXXII (1937); FRANK L. MOTT, "The Newspaper Coverage of Lexington and Concord", *New England Quarterly*, vol. XVII (1944).

The considerable influence of the clergy in the formation of public opinion is discussed in C. H. VAN TYNE, "Influence of the Clergy, and of Religious and Sectarian Forces, on the American Revolution", *Amer. Hist. Rev.*, vol. XIX (1913-1914). ALICE M. BALDWIN, *The New England Clergy and the American Revolution* (Durham, N.C., 1928) emphasizes, perhaps overmuch, the role of the clergy of New England. G. A. KOCH, *Republican Religion: The American Revolution and the Cult of Reason* (New York, 1933) and E. F. HUMPHREY, *Nationalism and Religion in America, 1774-1789* (Boston, 1924) are important for a fuller understanding of the impact of new religious ideas.

(k) THE DEVELOPMENT OF INTERCOLONIAL CO-OPERATION

The efforts of various groups in the several colonies to co-operate in opposition have not been adequately studied. ARTHUR M. SCHLESINGER, *The Colonial Merchants and the American Revolution* has considerable material on the attempts of the merchants to work together. The efforts of the popular leaders to combine the Sons of Liberty in the various colonies are more difficult to discover since much of it was done secretly. HENRY B. DAWSON, *The Sons of Liberty in New York* (Poughkeepsie, 1859); HERBERT M. MORAIS, "The Sons of Liberty in New York" in RICHARD B. MORRIS, ed., *The Era of the American Revolution*, and PHILIP DAVIDSON, "Sons of Liberty and Stamp Men", *N.C. Hist. Rev.*, vol. IX (1932) have some material without in any way being complete accounts of the organization.

The development of co-operation among colonial legislatures is inadequately treated in EDWARD D. COLLINS, "Committees of Correspondence of the American Revolution", *Amer. Hist. Assoc. Annual Report* (1901), vol. I; AGNES HUNT, *The Provincial Committees of Safety* (Cleveland, 1904); and JAMES M. LEAKE, *The Virginia Committee System and the American Revolution* (Baltimore, 1917).

The idea of a constitutional union among the colonies dated from the beginning of the century. An excellent survey of these attempts may be found in CHARLES M. ANDREWS, *The Colonial Period* (New York, 1912), chap. ix. The various plans are printed in HAMPTON L. CARSON, ed., *History of the Celebration of the One Hundredth Anniversary of the Promulgation of the Constitution of the United States* (2 vols., Philadelphia, 1889). LOIS K. MATTHEWS, "Benjamin Franklin's Plans for a Colonial Union, 1750-1775", *American Political Science Review*, vol. VIII (1914) is a thorough study. See also chap. iv, MERRILL JENSEN, *The Articles of Confederation: An Interpretation of the Social-Constitutional History of the American Revolution 1774-1781* (Madison, Wis., 1940). JULIAN P. BOYD, *Anglo-American Union: Joseph Galloway's Plans to Preserve the British Empire, 1774-1788* (Philadelphia, 1941) discusses the efforts of a leading loyalist and includes his various plans of union.

The various attempts at reconciliation between Britain and the colonies after 1774 are discussed in WELDON A. BROWN, *Empire or Independence; a Study in the Failure of Reconciliation*,

1774–1783 (Baton Rouge, La., 1941); G. H. GUTTRIDGE, *David Hartley, M.P., An Advocate of Conciliation, 1774–1783* (Berkeley, Cal., 1926); SAMUEL F. BEMIS, *The Hussey-Cumberland Mission and American Independence* (Princeton, 1931). BEMIS, *The Diplomacy of the American Revolution* (New York, 1935) outlines the general diplomatic history of the period.

(l) COLONIAL LOYALISTS AND THE LOYAL COLONIES

Studies of those Americans who remained loyal to Great Britain reveal much of the American Revolution. LORENZO SABINE, *Biographical Sketches of Loyalists of the American Revolution* (2 vols., Boston, 1864) was a pioneer work. Twentieth-century historians have devoted more and more attention to the Loyalists. C. H. VAN TYNE, *The Loyalists in the American Revolution* (New York, 1902) is still the only overall study, and it has been outmoded by many specialized monographs. LEONARD W. LABAREE, "The Nature of American Loyalism", Amer. Antiq. Soc. *Proceedings*, new Series, vol. LIV (1944) and chap. vi in his *Conservatism in Early American History* are studies of loyalist thought. HUGH EGERTON, ed., *The Royal Commission on the Losses and Services of the American Loyalists, 1783–1785* (Oxford, 1915) contains valuable source materials. Studies of loyalism in particular colonies are E. A. JONES, *The Loyalists of Massachusetts* (London, 1930); G. A. GILBERT, "The Connecticut Loyalists", Amer. Hist. Rev., vol. IV (1898–1899); A. C. FLICK, *Loyalism in New York During the American Revolution* (New York, 1901); E. ALFRED JONES, *The Loyalists of New Jersey* . . . (N.J. Hist. Soc. Collections, vol. X, 1927); WILBUR H. SIEBERT, *The Loyalists of Pennsylvania* (Ohio State University Bulletin, No. 23, Columbus, 1920); ISAAC S. HARRELL, *Loyalism in Virginia* . . .; ROBERT O. DeMOND, *The Loyalists in North Carolina During the Revolution* (Durham, N.C., 1940), ISAAC S. HARRELL, "North Carolina Loyalists", N.C. Hist. Rev., vol. III (1926); ROBERT W. BARNWELL, "The Migration of Loyalists from South Carolina", S.C. Hist. Assoc. Proceedings (1937); ELLA P. LEVETT, "Loyalism in Charleston, 1761–1784", ibid. (1936). ARTHUR G. BRADLEY, *United Empire Loyalists* . . . (London, 1932) is an account of those Americans who migrated to Canada, published in New York in 1932 as *Colonial Americans in Exile: Founders of British Canada*.

There are a few worthwhile studies of the colonies which did not revolt. AGNES M. WHITSON, "The Outlook of the Continental American Colonies on the British West Indies, 1760–1775", Pol. Sci. Quarterly, vol. XLV (1930) stresses the differing economic interests as being more important than the constitutional agreement between the two groups of colonies. WILFRED B. KERR, *Bermuda and the American Revolution* (Princeton, 1936) and *The Maritime Provinces of British North America and the American Revolution* (Sackville, New Brunswick, 1941?); JOHN B. BREBNER, *The Neutral Yankees of Nova Scotia* (New York, 1937); A. L. BURT, *The Old Province of Quebec*; and GEORGE M. WRONG, *Canada and the American Revolution*, are all thorough works on the colonies concerned.

(m) THE BEGINNING OF THE WAR FOR INDEPENDENCE

The East India Act and the colonial 'tea parties' which followed are discussed in MAX FARRAND, "The Taxation of Tea, 1767–1773", Amer. Hist. Rev., vol. III (1897–1898); FREDERICK D. STONE, "How the Landing of Tea was Opposed in Philadelphia by Colonel William Bradford and Others in 1773", Penn. Mag. Hist. and Biog., vol. XV (1891); ARTHUR M. SCHLESINGER, "The Uprising against the East India Company", Pol. Sci. Quarterly, vol. XXXII (1917); FRANCIS S. DRAKE, *Tea Leaves*, which includes many letters and documents, and the various histories cited previously.

The Continental Congress which met in 1774 as a result of the passage of the 'Intolerable Acts', and directed American destinies until 1789, is the subject of EDMUND C. BURNETT, *The Continental Congress* (New York, 1941), a full-scale work. Chap. vi of CARL BECKER's *History of Political Parties in the Province of New York* is a remarkable analysis of the first Congress in 1774. A somewhat different view is taken by MERRILL JENSEN, *The Articles of Confederation*, chap. iii, where the emphasis is on the struggle over independence in the first and second congresses from 1774 to 1776.

The military history of the Revolution has been and continues to be the subject of a vast variety of books and articles. This is particularly true of the first battle of the war at Lexington and Concord, Massachusetts, in April, 1775. A few examples are HARROLD MURDOCK, *The Nineteenth of April, 1775* ... (Boston, 1923); ALLEN FRENCH, *The Day of Concord and Lexington, the Nineteenth of April, 1775* (Boston, 1923), and the same author's *General Gage's Informers* (Ann Arbor, Mich., 1932), and *The First Year of the American Revolution* (Boston, 1934). FRENCH's work is of first importance, utilizing for the first time as it does the papers of General Thomas Gage in the Clements Library. For Gage's role, JOHN R. ALDEN's *General Gage in North America* is an excellent work. The most recent and the best survey of the military history of the Revolution is WILLARD M. WALLACE, *Appeal to Arms* (New York, 1951). JOHN R. ALDEN, *The American Revolution, 1775-1783* (New American Nation Series, New York, 1954) is largely military history and should be used in conjunction with WALLACE.

The Declaration of Independence is the subject of several excellent books. CARL BECKER, *The Declaration of Independence* emphasizes the intellectual backgrounds. JULIAN P. BOYD, *The Declaration of Independence* ... (Washington, 1943) is a study of the evolution of the final text of the document, with photographic reproductions of the various drafts. An older work which is still useful is HERBERT FRIEDENWALD, *The Declaration of Independence, An Interpretation and an Analysis* (New York, 1907). There are many other books and articles of varying merit. Some relate to the validity of the various charges against the king. Examples are S. G. FISHER, "The Twenty-eight Charges against the King in the Declaration of Independence", *Penn. Mag. of Hist and Biog.*, vol. XXXI (1907) argues the essential validity of the charges, as does EDWARD DUMBAULD at much greater length in *The Declaration of Independence and What it means Today* (Norman, Okla., 1950). On the other hand, CARL BECKER in his *Declaration of Independence* takes a somewhat more sceptical view of the charges.

A. THE INSTRUMENTS OF BRITISH POLICY
1763–1765

THE broad outlines of British colonial policy after 1763 are clear, however much befogged by the vagaries of administrative decisions and legislative actions. In brief, those policies were to maintain a standing army in the colonies in peace-time,[1] to enforce the Acts of trade and navigation effectively,[2] to regulate western expansion and the Indian trade,[3] to raise at least enough revenue from the customs service to enable it to pay for itself,[4] and finally, to collect new revenues in the colonies through taxation by Parliament in order to help maintain the army and to free British civil officials from dependence on colonial legislatures.[5]

The charge was made at the time that such policies were new and unprecedented, that they injured the economic life of the colonies, and that they threatened to destroy the political institutions which the colonists looked upon as theirs by right. Such charges have been made repeatedly since then and the 'new' policies have been attributed to the 'Tories', and particularly to George Grenville and Charles Townshend. The Whig historians of the nineteenth century, and notably Sir George Otto Trevelyan, did much to establish this view in Anglo-American historiography, and only within the last generation have scholars been able to undo this hopelessly inadequate view of British politics and British colonial policy.

Two facts were implicit in British policy, however, that justified the colonial argument: that policy did involve the limitation of the colonial self-government which had been built up during the early part of the eighteenth century, and it also involved a sharp restriction of the expanding economy of the colonies. These facts were clear to every colonial leader of whatever shade of political opinion. They, too, like the later Whig historians, charged that such policies were new and they argued that the solution of the problem was a return to happy days before 1763. Some policies were new, particularly the establishment of a standing army in the colonies and the effort to raise money by parliamentary taxation; but many of the policies were old ones. The purpose of British colonial policy since the middle of the seventeenth century had been to regulate and channelize the political and economic life of the colonies for the benefit of the mother country. The passage of laws, the appointment of new officials, and the development of administrative policies were all means to implement this purpose. Yet in practice, despite all such means and measures, the colonies managed to retain their self-government, and even to strengthen it. When they chose to do so, they ignored the Navigation Acts and the customs officials, although the bulk of their economy flowed within channels established by British policy and British economic power.

By 1750 it was a fact recognized on both sides of the Atlantic that the colonies were virtually self-governing. Almost from the first they had insisted on the right of self-government and they used every political device to achieve it in practice. They were aided by the fact that British officials were dependent on colonial legislatures for money. When it came to providing money for the representatives of the king,

---

[1] Nos. 102, 117, 129, 130.
[2] Nos. 97, 99, 114, 115, 116, 119.
[3] Nos. 98, 118.   [4] No. 97.   [5] Nos. 99, 101, 114, 115.

every colonial legislature could and did quote the traditions and practices of Parliament. The colonists were aided also by the relative indifference of the ministry towards the colonies during most of the early part of the eighteenth century. Sir Robert Walpole, for example, believed in letting the colonies develop pretty much as they pleased, with the result that colonial governors and the Board of Trade got little backing for the policies they tried to enforce.

This attitude changed at the middle of the century and a series of steps were taken to remedy what were, from the British point of view, defects in the administration of the colonies. In 1752 royal governors were ordered to promote a revision of all colonial laws so as to bring them into conformity with royal instructions to the governors. In the same year the governors were ordered to abide by their instructions in all cases whatsoever, something which few of them had ever done consistently. Investigations of the 'subversion' of colonial constitutions, as set forth in royal commissions and instructions, were undertaken. These efforts at tighter control were abandoned during the Seven Years War, but they were not forgotten. In fact, British experience with the colonies during the war fortified the determination to exercise closer control over them afterwards.

During the war some of the colonies supplied troops and went heavily into debt to assist in the struggle for Canada. Others were reluctant to help, or refused outright to do so. Meanwhile the British spent large sums on the army and navy in America, and, in addition, gave large cash grants to reimburse the colonies which gave military aid. It seemed obvious during the war that the colonies would never come to any agreement on a common frontier defence policy, once the war was over. Furthermore, the acquisition of vast new regions to the north and west of the coastal settlements raised, as never before, the questions of Indian relations and frontier expansion. Hence, before the end of the war, the decision was reached to keep a standing army in America in peace-time. Although in theory the troops were to be maintained in America for the purposes of frontier defence, the bulk of them were not sent to the frontiers after 1763. Most of them were maintained along the coast and in time were moved into political storm centres like Boston.[1]

Coupled with the decision to maintain a standing army in the colonies was the adoption of a policy of British control of the Indian trade and of western expansion –two related matters that had always been the province of the individual colonial governments. This, too, was decided upon before the end of the war. At best, it was a vacillating policy, but its overall tendency was in the direction of greater royal control, and the colonies looked upon it as an infringement of their charter rights.[2]

A third aspect of post-war policy that arose immediately from the war, but which had roots running back to the seventeenth century, was that dealing with the colonial customs service and the question of illegal trade. There were enough examples to lend colour, if not entire validity, to official charges.[3] But during the Seven Years War trading with the enemy became notorious. William Pitt began a vigorous attempt to stamp out such trade, and the navy was used to assist the customs officers. This led to investigations of the colonial customs service, and by the end of the war it was clear that the service was inefficient at best, and entirely corrupt at worst, and that it cost far more to maintain than it collected in the colonies.[4]

Such were the policies and the conditions inherited by the Grenville ministry when it took over in 1763. The war had left Britain with a debt which for the times was

[1] Nos. 118, 122, 129, 130.   [2] Nos. 98, 118.   [3] Nos. 53, 97.   [4] No. 97.

astronomical. British taxpayers demanded economy and reform. George Grenville, as prime minister from 1763 to 1765, was charged with the responsibility for making administrative changes and securing parliamentary legislation to achieve those ends.

And inevitably the question of colonial policy was an important part of the whole programme. Between 1763 and 1765 there came a series of administrative decisions and parliamentary Acts which sought to improve the enforcement of the Acts of Navigation and the collection of customs. While this was an end in itself, it had the additional purpose of increasing revenue to the point where the colonial customs service would pay for itself and, in addition, provide some portion of the cost of the army in America. It was obvious, however, that even a completely reformed and efficient customs organization would not produce enough to materially assist in the payment of military expenditures. Barring the improbable solution of voluntary support by the colonies, the only alternative was parliamentary taxes levied upon them, and this too was tried.

In 1763 the first step was an Act of Parliament authorizing the use of naval vessels to help enforce the Acts of trade and navigation.[1] Meanwhile the Treasury investigated the colonial customs service and issued a report stating what it had done in the way of reform and urging new legislation. The Privy Council enacted this report as an Order in Council.[2] The Proclamation of 1763 established policies for regulating affairs with the western Indians and for the organization and control of new areas acquired as a result of the war.[3] In 1764 the so-called 'Sugar Act' was enacted. It made some changes in duties and drawbacks and declared the Molasses Act of 1733 to be perpetual. But above all, it was a sweeping reform of colonial customs procedures and of the methods of trying cases of violation.[4] The Currency Act of 1764 forbade the colonies to issue any more legal tender paper currency.[5] In 1765 came the Stamp Act, which was the first attempt to raise money within the colonies through direct taxes levied by Parliament.[6] During the same year a Quartering Act set forth regulations requiring colonial legislatures to pay for certain specified articles used by the British troops in the colonies.[7]

Shortly after the completion of this administrative and legislative programme the Grenville ministry was forced from power, for reasons that had nothing to do with colonial affairs, and was replaced by one headed by the Marquis of Rockingham. The new ministry was thus left to face the storm of opposition which had been brewing ever since 1763 in the colonies, and which became violent with the news of the passage of the Stamp Act.

97. Order in Council on the reform of the customs service (4 October 1763)

The following document was originally drawn up as a memorial of the Treasury and was subsequently enacted as an Order in Council. It was based upon an investigation of the colonial customs service and gives an account of the administrative reforms that had already been made. Its suggestions for new legislation were to be followed out by Parliament during the next few years. By and large, the memorial laid down the broad outlines of policy that were to be followed until the outbreak of the American Revolution. The adoption of the memorial as an Order in Council was followed by new instructions to the colonial governors, and Secretary of State Halifax directed the commander-in-chief in America to use the army to support customs officials. Printed: W. L. Grant and J. Munro, eds., *Acts of the Privy Council of England, Colonial Series* (6 vols., London, 1908–1912), IV, pp. 569–572.

W e, the Commissioners of your Majesty's Treasury beg leave humbly to represent to your Majesty that having taken into consideration the present state of the duties of customs imposed on your Majesty's subjects in America and the West

[1] 3 Geo. III, c. 22.   [2] No. 97.   [3] No. 98.   [4] No. 99.   [5] No. 100.   [6] No. 101.   [7] No. 102.

Indies, we find that the revenue arising therefrom is very small and inconsiderable, having in no degree increased with the commerce of those countries, and is not yet sufficient to defray a fourth part of the expense necessary for collecting it. We observe with concern that through neglect, connivance, and fraud, not only the revenue is impaired, but the commerce of the colonies is diverted from its natural course and the salutary provisions of many wise laws to secure it to the mother country are in great measure defeated. Attention to objects of so great importance we are sensible is at all times our duty, but at this it is more indispensable when the military establishment necessary for maintaining these colonies requires a large revenue to support it, and when their vast increase in territory and population makes the proper regulation of their trade of immediate necessity lest the continuance and extent of the dangerous evils above-mentioned may render all attempts to remedy them hereafter infinitely more difficult, if not utterly impracticable. We have endeavoured therefore to discover, and as far as the power of our department will allow, remove the causes, to which the deficiency of this revenue and the contraband trade with other European nations are owing. For this purpose we have ordered all the officers belonging to the customs in America and the West Indies to be fully instructed in their duty to repair forthwith to their respective stations and constantly to reside there for the future; and where we find that a sufficient number of proper officers are not yet established, it is intended to supply the deficiency by the appointment of others. We have directed that all the officers of the revenue in your Majesty's plantations should be furnished with new and ample instructions, enforcing in the strongest manner the strictest attention to their duty, and requiring that by regular and constant correspondence they give an account, as well of their own proceedings as of the conduct of the officers under them, and inform us likewise of any obstructions they may meet with in discharging the business of their respective offices. We have ordered them to transmit exact accounts of the imports and exports in their several districts, of the state of the revenue, and of the illicit commerce with other European states from time to time in consequence of these directions, with such observations as may occur to them in regard either to the efficacy and inefficacy of any subsisting regulations, or to such alterations as they may judge conducive to the farther improvement of the revenue, to the prevention of those frauds by which it is impaired, and to the suppression of the contraband trade which has been hitherto carried on with too much impunity; and we have directed the Commissioners of your Majesty's Customs immediately to dismiss every officer that shall fail to pay obedience to these instructions or be any way deficient in his duty. But as the restraint and suppression of practices which have unhappily prevailed too long will certainly be encountered with great difficulties in such distant parts of your Majesty's dominions, we apprehend that these our regulations will not fully answer the end for which they are designed, unless in consequence of your Majesty's commands, the other departments of your government afford their utmost assistance in support of them. With this view we thought it became us thus to lay our proceedings before your Majesty, and further humbly to represent that it appears to us of the highest importance that strict orders should be given to the governors of all the colonies to make the suppression of the clandestine and prohibited trade with foreign nations, and the improvement of the revenue the constant and immediate objects of their care, and by a vigorous discharge of the duty required of them by several acts of Parliament and a due exertion of their legal authority, to give the officers of the revenue the necessary protection and support, and that they from time to time transmit such observations as occur to them on the state of the illicit and contraband trade, and on the conduct of all persons whose duty it is to prevent the same, in order that the necessary directions may be given for punishing such persons as shall appear to be guilty of any misbehaviour, and correcting all abuses for the future. We are further humbly of opinion that it will greatly contribute to the same salutary ends, and to the carrying of the several laws and regulations into execution with success, if all officers, both civil and military, are strictly commanded to give their assistance upon all proper occasions, and if the commanders-in-chief of your Majesty's ships and troops in America and the West Indies are directed to attend to this object with the utmost care, and to make such a disposition of the force under their respective commands as will be most serviceable in suppressing these dangerous practices, and in protecting the officers of the revenue from the violence of any desperate and lawless persons who shall attempt to resist the due execution of the laws in the same manner as is practised in England. The advantages of a sea guard, more especially in those parts, are sufficiently obvious. We depend upon it as the likeliest means for accomplishing these great purposes, and the good effects that have already been experienced from the measures lately taken for that purpose at home, make us earnestly wish that the same may not only be continued but even extended and strengthened as far as the naval establishment will allow. And lastly, it appears to us highly necessary that there should be established by law a new and better method of condemning seizures made in the colonies. The Commissioners of the Customs have reported to us that they have received various complaints of great difficulties and partialities in the trials on these occasions, and the several statutes in force from the 12th of Charles the second to the third of your Majesty, vary so much both as to the mode and place of trial that the officers of the revenue, when they have made a seizure, cannot but be under great doubt and uncertainty in what manner they should proceed to the condemnation of it. It is therefore humbly submitted to your Majesty, whether from the importance of this object, it would not be of the greatest public utility that an uniform plan be prepared for establishing the judicature of the courts of admiralty in that country under persons qualified for so important a trust, in order that justice may hereafter in all cases be diligently and impartially administered and that such regulations as Parliament may think proper to make may be duly carried into execution.

98. The Proclamation of 1763 (7 October 1763)

The Proclamation of 1763 had a dual purpose. The first was to provide for the establishment of governments in the new territories acquired as a result of the Seven Years War. The second was to provide for imperial control of Indian affairs in the new lands acquired by the Crown. This question had been under consideration during the war and was given point by the news of a great Indian uprising in the west, Pontiac's Rebellion, which began in May 1763, and resulted in the capture of all the British posts in the west except Fort Pitt and Detroit. The rebellion was suppressed in 1764, but the news of it had influence on the Proclamation of 1763. It drew a boundary line along the headwaters of rivers running into the Atlantic. The colonists were forbidden to settle beyond it, although some had already established themselves there. The right to purchase land west of the line was reserved to the Crown. The Indian trade, which had caused so much discontent among the Indians, was to be regulated by imperial officers. The British attitude towards the Indians and westward expansion was to be less consistent than almost any other phase of policy in the years after 1763 (No. 118). Printed: Brigham, *British Royal Proclamations Relating to America*, pp. 212–218.

Whereas we have taken into our royal consideration the extensive and valuable acquisitions in America, secured to our crown by the late definitive treaty of peace concluded at Paris the 10th day of February last; and being desirous that all our loving subjects, as well of our kingdoms as of our colonies in America, may avail themselves, with all convenient speed, of the great benefits and advantages which must accrue therefrom to their commerce, manufactures, and navigation; we have thought fit, with the advice of our Privy Council, to issue this our royal proclamation, hereby to publish and declare to all our loving subjects, that we have, with the advice of our said Privy Council, granted our letters patent under our great seal of Great Britain, to erect within the countries and islands, ceded and confirmed to us by the said treaty, four distinct and separate governments, styled and called by the names of Quebec, East Florida, West Florida, and Grenada.... [Description of boundaries omitted.]

And to the end that the open and free fishery of our subjects may be extended to, and carried on upon the coast of Labrador and the adjacent islands, we have thought fit, with the advice of our said Privy Council, to put all that coast, from the river St. John's to Hudson's Straits, together with the islands of Anticosti and Magdalen, and all other smaller islands lying upon the said coast, under the care and inspection of our governor of Newfoundland.

We have also, with the advice of our Privy Council, thought fit to annex the islands of St. John and Cape Breton, or Isle Royale, with the lesser islands adjacent thereto, to our government of Nova Scotia.

We have also, with the advice of our Privy Council aforesaid, annexed to our province of Georgia, all the lands lying between the rivers Altamaha and St. Mary's.

And whereas it will greatly contribute to the speedy settling our said new governments, that our loving subjects should be informed of our paternal care for the security of the liberties and properties of those who are, and shall become inhabitants thereof; we have thought fit to publish and declare, by this our proclamation, that we have, in the letters patent under our great seal of Great Britain, by which the said governments are constituted, given express power and direction to our governors of our said colonies, respectively, that so soon as the state and circumstances of the said colonies will admit thereof, they shall, with the advice and consent of the members of our council, summon and call general assemblies within the said governments respectively, in such manner and form as is used and directed in those colonies and provinces in America, which are under our immediate government; and we have also given power to the said governors, with the consent of our said councils, and the representatives of the people, so to be summoned as aforesaid, to make, constitute, and ordain laws, statutes, and ordinances for the public peace, welfare, and good government of our said colonies, and of the people and inhabitants thereof, as near as may be, agreeable to the laws of England, and under such regulations and restrictions as are used in other colonies; and in the meantime, and until such assemblies can be called as aforesaid, all persons inhabiting in, or resorting to, our said colonies, may confide in our royal protection for the enjoyment of the benefit of the laws of our realm of England; for which purpose we have given power under our great seal to the governors of our said colonies respectively, to erect and constitute, with the advice of our said councils respectively, courts of judicature and public justice within our said colonies, for the hearing and determining all causes as well criminal as civil, according to law and equity, and as near as may be agreeable to the laws of England, with liberty to all persons who may think themselves aggrieved by the sentences of such courts, in all civil cases, to appeal, under the usual limitations and restrictions, to us, in our Privy Council.

We have also thought fit, with the advice of our Privy Council as aforesaid, to give unto the governors and councils of our said three new colonies upon the continent, full power and authority to settle and agree with the inhabitants of our said new colonies, or with any other persons who shall resort thereto, for such lands, tenements, and hereditaments, as are now, or hereafter shall be, in our power to dispose of, and them to grant to any such person or persons, upon such terms, and under such moderate quit-rents, services, and acknowledgments, as have been appointed and settled in our other colonies, and under such other conditions as shall appear to us to be necessary and expedient for the advantage of the grantees, and the improvement and settlement of our said colonies.

And whereas we are desirous, upon all occasions, to testify our royal sense and approbation of the conduct and bravery of the officers and soldiers of our armies, and to reward the same, we do hereby command and impower our governors of our said three new colonies, and all other our governors of our several provinces on the continent of North America, to grant, without fee or reward, to such reduced officers as have served in North America during the late war, and to such private soldiers as have been or shall be disbanded in America, and are actually residing there, and shall personally apply for the same, the following quantities of lands, subject, at the expiration of ten years, to the same quit-rents as other lands are subject to in the province within which they are granted, as also subject to the same conditions of cultivation and improvement, viz.

To every person having the rank of a field officer, five thousand acres. To every captain, three thousand acres. To every subaltern or staff officer, two thousand acres. To every non-commission officer, two hundred acres. To every private man, fifty acres.

We do likewise authorize and require the governors and commanders-in-chief of all our said colonies upon the continent of North America to grant the like quantities of land, and upon the same conditions, to such reduced officers of our navy of like rank, as served on board our ships of war in North America at the times of the reduction of Louisburg and Quebec in the late war, and who shall personally apply to our respective governors for such grants.

And whereas it is just and reasonable, and essential to our interest, and the security of our colonies, that the several nations or tribes of Indians with whom we are connected, and who live under our protection, should not be molested or disturbed in the possession of such parts of our dominions and territories as, not having been ceded to, or purchased by us, are reserved to them, or any of them, as their hunting grounds; we do therefore, with the advice of our Privy Council, declare it to be our royal will and pleasure, that no governor, or commander-in-chief, in any of our colonies of Quebec, East Florida, or West Florida, do presume, upon any pretence whatever, to grant warrants of survey, or pass any patents for lands beyond the bounds of their respective governments, as described in their commissions; as also that no governor or commander-in-chief in any of our other colonies or plantations in America, do presume for the present, and until our further pleasure be known, to grant warrants of survey, or pass patents for any lands beyond the heads or sources of any of the rivers which fall into the Atlantic Ocean from the west and northwest; or upon any lands whatever, which not having been ceded to, or purchased by us, as aforesaid, are reserved to the said Indians, or any of them.

And we do further declare it to be our royal will and pleasure, for the present, as aforesaid, to reserve under our sovereignty, protection, and dominion, for the use of the said Indians, all the lands and territories not included within the limits of our said three new governments, or within the limits of the territory granted to the Hudson's Bay Company, as also all the lands and territories lying to the westward of the sources of the rivers which fall into the sea from the west and northwest as aforesaid; and we do hereby strictly forbid, on pain of our displeasure, all our loving subjects from making any purchases or settlements whatever, or taking possession of any of the lands above reserved, without our especial leave and licence for that purpose first obtained.

And we do further strictly enjoin and require all persons whatever, who have either wilfully or inadvertently seated themselves upon any lands within the countries above described, or upon any other lands, which not having been ceded to, or purchased by us, are still reserved to the said Indians as aforesaid, forthwith to remove themselves from such settlements.

And whereas great frauds and abuses have been committed in the purchasing lands of the Indians, to the great prejudice of our interests, and to the great dissatisfaction of the said Indians; in order, therefore, to prevent such irregularities for the future, and to the end that the Indians may be convinced of our justice and determined resolution to remove all reasonable cause of discontent, we do, with the advice of our Privy Council, strictly enjoin and require, that no private person do presume to make any purchase from the said Indians of any lands reserved to the said Indians within those parts of our colonies where we have thought proper to allow settlement; but that if at any time any of the said Indians should be inclined to dispose of the said lands, the same shall be purchased only for us, in our name, at some public meeting or assembly of the said Indians, to be held for that purpose by the governor or commander-in-chief of our colonies respectively within which they shall lie: and in case they shall lie within the limits of any proprietary government, they shall be purchased only for the use and in the name of such proprietaries, conformable to such directions and instructions as we or they shall think proper to give for that purpose:

and we do, by the advice of our Privy Council, declare and enjoin, that the trade with the said Indians shall be free and open to all our subjects whatever, provided that every person who may incline to trade with the said Indians, do take out a licence for carrying on such trade, from the governor or commander-in-chief of any of our colonies respectively, where such person shall reside, and also give security to observe such regulations as we shall at any time think fit, by ourselves or by our commissaries, to be appointed for this purpose, to direct and appoint for the benefit of the said trade; and we do hereby authorize, enjoin, and require the governors and commanders-in-chief of all our colonies respectively, as well those under our immediate government, as those under the government and direction of proprietaries, to grant such licences without fee or reward, taking especial care to insert therein a condition that such licence shall be void, and the security forfeited, in case the person to whom the same is granted, shall refuse or neglect to observe such regulations as we shall think proper to prescribe as aforesaid.

And we do further expressly enjoin and require all officers whatever, as well military as those employed in the management and direction of Indian affairs within the territories reserved, as aforesaid, for the use of the said Indians, to seize and apprehend all persons whatever, who standing charged with treasons, misprisions of treason, murders, or other felonies or misdemeanours, shall fly from justice and take refuge in the said territory, and to send them under a proper guard to the colony where the crime was committed of which they stand accused, in order to take their trial for the same.

Given at our court at St. James's, the seventh day of October, one thousand seven hundred and sixty three, in the third year of our reign.

99. The Revenue Act of 1764 (5 April 1764)

The Revenue Act of 1764 (4 Geo. III, c. 15) the so-called 'Sugar Act', had two purposes. One was to raise more money through the colonial customs service and to apply it to the maintenance of the military establishment in the colonies. Only two Acts of Parliament provided for the collection of money in the colonies: the Navigation Act of 1673 (No. 51C) which imposed duties on enumerated articles shipped from colony to colony; and the Molasses Act of 1733 (No. 51E) which imposed various duties on molasses, rum, and sugar brought from foreign colonies into the British colonies. The latter Act had not been enforced or had been evaded by the American colonists, customs officials, and British West India planters alike. The Revenue Act of 1764 made the Molasses Act perpetual but reduced the duty on molasses from six pence to three pence a gallon. Additions were made to the list of enumerated articles. Rebates on certain European manufactures shipped from Britain to the colonies were abolished.

The second and more far-reaching purpose of the Act was the strengthening of the customs service and the trials of seizures. Under the Navigation Acts, seizures had been tried either in colonial Vice-Admiralty courts or in common law courts within the jurisdiction where the seizure took place. Under the Act of 1764, the seizer or informer could elect to take the case to a court within the jurisdiction or to a new Vice-Admiralty court to be established at Halifax, Nova Scotia. The Act also provided for new trial procedures which virtually freed customs officers from all responsibility and freed them from effective civil suits for damages in colonial courts. The Act also set up elaborate new provisions for the shipping of goods in and out of the colonies: new bonds, cockets, and permits were required for every item loaded or unloaded.

The enforcement provisions, with some changes, remained a basic part of the British policy. They were effective in increasing customs revenue and lay at the bottom of much colonial opposition. The revenue features of the Act were changed in the Revenue Act of 1766 (No. 114). The requirement of section XXVIII that all iron and lumber sent to Europe must be landed in Great Britain aroused so much opposition that in 1765 an Act was passed (5 Geo. III, c. 45) which allowed the exportation of iron to Ireland and lumber to Ireland and to Europe south of Cape Finisterre. Printed: Pickering, *Statutes at Large*, XXVI, pp. 33-52.

Whereas it is expedient that new provisions and regulations should be established for improving the revenue of this kingdom, and for extending and securing the navigation and commerce between Great Britain and your Majesty's dominions in America, which, by the peace, have been so happily enlarged; and whereas it is just and necessary that a revenue be raised in your Majesty's said dominions in America for defraying the expenses of defending, protecting, and securing the same . . . be it enacted, . . . that from and after the twenty-ninth day of September, one thousand seven hundred and sixty-four, there shall be raised, levied, collected, and paid unto his Majesty, his heirs and successors, for and upon all white or clayed sugars of the produce or manufacture of any colony or plantation in America, not under the dominion of his Majesty, his heirs and successors; for and upon indigo, and coffee of foreign produce or manufacture; for and upon all wines (except French wine); for and upon all wrought silks, bengals, and stuffs, mixed with silk or herba, of the manu-- facture of Persia, China, or East India, and all calico painted, dyed, printed, or stained there; and for and upon all foreign linen cloth called cambric and French lawns which shall be imported or brought into any colony or plantation in America, . . . the several rates and duties following:

For every hundredweight avoirdupois of such foreign white or clayed sugars, one pound, two shillings, over and above all other duties imposed by any former Act of Parliament.

For every pound weight avoirdupois of such foreign indigo, six pence.

For every hundredweight avoirdupois of such foreign coffee which shall be imported from any place except Great Britain, two pounds, nineteen shillings, and nine pence.

For every tun of wine of the growth of the Madeiras, or of any other island or place from whence such wine may be lawfully imported, and which shall be so imported from such islands or places, the sum of seven pounds.

For every tun of Portugal, Spanish, or any other wine (except French wine) imported from Great Britain, the sum of ten shillings.

For every pound weight avoirdupois of wrought silks, bengals, and stuffs, mixed with silk or herba, of the manufacture of Persia, China, or East India, imported from Great Britain, two shillings.

For every piece of calico painted, dyed, printed, or stained, in Persia, China, or East India, imported from Great Britain, two shillings and six pence.

For every piece of foreign linen cloth called cambric, imported from Great Britain, three shillings.

For every piece of French lawn imported from Great Britain, three shillings.

And after those rates for any greater or lesser quantity of such goods respectively.

II-III. [Coffee and pimento grown in any British colony if loaded on any British vessel to be shipped to any place except Great Britain must pay the following duties: coffee, seven shillings per hundredweight; pimento, one half penny per pound.]

IV-V. [Molasses Act of 1733 (6 Geo. III, c. 13) continued and made perpetual, subject to changes made by the present Act.]

VI. [Instead of duties imposed in Molasses Act of 1733, each gallon of molasses and syrups grown in foreign colonies and plantations and imported into the British colonies shall pay a duty of three pence per gallon.]

XI. . . . All the monies which . . . shall arise by the several rates and duties herein-before granted; and also by the duties which, from and after the said twenty-ninth day of September, one thousand seven hundred and sixty-four, shall be raised upon sugars and paneles, by virtue of the said Act made in the sixth year of the reign of his said late Majesty King George the second (except the necessary charges of raising, collecting, levying, recovering, answering, paying, and accounting for the same) shall be paid into the receipt of his Majesty's exchequer, and shall be entered separate and apart from all other monies paid or payable to his Majesty, his heirs or successors; and shall be there reserved to be from time to time disposed of by Parliament towards defraying the necessary expenses of defending, protecting, and securing the British colonies and plantations in America.

XVIII. . . . No rum or spirits of the produce or manufacture of any of the colonies or plantations in America not in the possession or under the dominion of his Majesty, his heirs or successors, shall be imported or brought into any of the colonies or plantations in America which now are, or hereafter may be, in the possession or under the dominion of his Majesty, his heirs or successors, upon forfeiture of all such rum or spirits, together with the ship or vessel in which the same shall be imported, with the tackle, apparel, and furniture thereof; to be seized by any officer or officers of his Majesty's customs, and prosecuted in such manner and form as hereinafter is expressed; any law, custom, or usage to the contrary notwithstanding.

XX. And for the better preventing frauds in the importation of foreign sugars and paneles, rum and spirits, molasses and syrups, into any of his Majesty's dominions, under pretence that the same are the growth, produce, or manufacture of the British colonies or plantations; . . . every person or persons loading on board any ship or vessel, in any of the British colonies or plantations in America, any rum or spirits, sugars or paneles, molasses or syrups, as of the growth, product, or manufacture of any British colony or plantation, shall before the clearing out of the said ship or vessel, produce and deliver to the collector or other principal officer of the customs at the loading port, an affidavit signed and sworn to before some justice of the peace in the said British colonies or plantations, either by the grower, maker, or shipper of such goods, or his or their known agent or factor, expressing in words at length and not in figures, the quality of the goods so shipped, with the number and denomination of the packages, and describing the name or names of the plantation or plantations, and the name of the colony where the same grew or were produced and manufactured; which affidavit shall be attested, under the hand of the said justice of the peace, to have been sworn to in his presence; who is hereby required to do the same without fee or reward; and the collector or other principal officer of the customs to whom such affidavit shall be delivered, shall thereupon grant to the master, or other person having the charge of the ship or vessel, a certificate under his hand and seal of office (without fee or reward) of his having received such affidavit pursuant to the directions of this Act; which certificate shall express the quality of the goods shipped on board such ship or vessel, with the number and denomination of the packages; and such collector or other principal officer of the customs shall also (without fee or reward) within thirty days after the sailing of the ship or vessel, transmit an exact copy of the said affidavit to the secretary's office for the respective colony or plantation where the goods were shipped, on forfeiture of five pounds.

XXI. And it is further enacted, that upon the arrival of such ship or vessel into the port of her discharge, either in Great Britain or any other port of his Majesty's dominions, where such goods may be lawfully imported, the master or other person taking the charge of the ship or vessel shall, at the time he makes his report of his cargo, deliver the said certificate to the collector or other principal officer of the customs, and make oath before him that the goods so reported are the same that are mentioned in the said certificate, on forfeiture of one hundred pounds; and if any rum or spirits, sugars or paneles, molasses or syrups, shall be imported or found on board any such ship or vessel, for which no such certificate shall be produced, or which shall not agree therewith, the same shall be deemed and taken to be foreign rum and spirits, sugar and paneles, molasses and syrups, and shall be liable to the same duties, restrictions, regulations, penalties, and forfeitures, in all respects as rum, spirits, sugar, paneles, molasses, and syrups, of the growth, produce, or manufacture, of any foreign colony or plantation would respectively be liable to by law.

XXIII. [Despite Acts in force requiring bonds to be given for the landing of all enumerated commodities in Great Britain or the colonies, it is feared that many such commodities are taken to foreign ports. Furthermore, great quantities of foreign molasses and syrups are "clandestinely run on shore" in the British colonies. Therefore, bonds must be given for all non-enumerated commodities produced in the British colonies before being loaded on vessels. If foreign molasses and syrups are loaded as well, bond must be given to unload them either in colonial or British ports. All foreign molasses and syrups must be reported by the master of a vessel immediately on arrival in a British or colonial port. If non-enumerated commodities are loaded before bonds are given, the goods and vessel shall be forfeit.]

XXIV. [Every shipmaster, before leaving a colonial port, must obtain a certificate from the principal customs officer showing that he has given bond and must deliver this certificate to the principal customs officer on arrival in a British or colonial port.]

XXV. [If British vessels laden with American goods or foreign molasses or syrups are found within two leagues of any British colony by any customs officer, and the master is unable to show a certificate indicating that a bond has been given, or is unable to show such bond at the port of arrival, the goods and ship shall be forfeit.]

XXVII. [Adds coffee, pimento, cocoa nuts, whale fins, raw silk, hides, skins, pot and pearl ashes produced in the British colonies to the list of enumerated articles which may be shipped only to Great Britain or to British colonies.]

XXVIII. [Bonds to be given for all colonial iron and lumber exported. All iron and lumber sent to Europe may be landed only in Great Britain.]

XXIX. [No goods of any kind may be loaded in any British colony to be shipped to any other British colony without a "sufferance or warrant" obtained from the proper customs official before the goods are loaded. Before the goods leave port the master of a vessel must take out a cocket or cockets listing quality and quantity of goods, marks on the packages, with names of merchants by whom shipped and of merchants to whom consigned. If goods are liable to duties, either on importation into or exportation from the colonies, cockets shall specify at what time the goods were entered and by whom the duties were paid. Master must show such cockets to the principal customs officer at any port or place in the colonies where the ship shall arrive before any part of the goods is unloaded. If any goods are loaded without sufferance, or the ship shall sail without cocket or cockets, or if goods are unloaded without showing such cockets, or if the goods do not agree with the cockets, the goods shall be forfeit. Customs officers are empowered to stop any ship within two leagues of the shore of any British colony and take from the ship any goods for which cockets cannot be produced.]

XXX. [Since British vessels arrive in Great Britain from foreign parts loaded with goods "pretended to be destined to some foreign plantation" and take on board parcels entered outward for some British colony, and cockets and clearance are provided for such goods, "under cover of which the whole cargoes of such vessels are clandestinely landed in the British American dominions," therefore, no ship may be cleared outward from Great Britain for the British colonies unless the whole cargo shall be laden and shipped in Great Britain. Any customs officer is empowered to seize any British ship arriving from any part of Europe within two leagues of any British colony and take from thence any goods for which the master of the ship cannot produce a cocket showing that the goods were loaded in some British port.]

XXXI. [Excepted from the above are salt loaded in Europe for colonial fisheries; wines of the Madeiras and Azores; and horses, victuals, and linens from Ireland.]

XXXII. [Penalties for those producing or using false papers.]

XXXIII. [Foreign vessels found anchored or hovering within two leagues of any of the American colonies, and not leaving within forty-eight hours after being ordered to do so by any customs officer, shall be forfeit with the goods on board.]

XXXIV. [Exempts French vessels fishing off Newfoundland coast from the above.]

XXXV. [Restricts trade with French islands of Saint Pierre and Miquelon.]

XXXVI. [Goods concealed on vessels and not reported by master of vessel when reporting to customs officers shall be forfeit. If it can be proved that master of vessel was privy to fraud, he shall forfeit treble the value of the goods.]

XXXVII. [If goods subject to customs duties are loaded on a vessel or landed from it before duties are paid, or if prohibited goods are imported into or exported from the colonies, every person involved shall forfeit treble the value of the goods, and also all boats, carriages, horses, etc., used in handling such goods.]

XXXVIII. [Provides penalties and fines for customs officers who take bribes or connive in breaking the laws.]

XXXIX. [Provides oath to support Acts of trade and navigation which must be taken by all governors and commanders-in-chief in the colonies.]

XLI. [Provides that all forfeitures and penalties inflicted by this Act or any other Acts of Parliament relating to] the trade and revenues of the said British colonies or plantations in America which shall be incurred there, shall and may be prosecuted, sued for, and recovered in any court of record, or in any court of admiralty, in the said colonies or plantations where such offence shall be committed, or in any court of vice-admiralty which may or shall be appointed over all America (which court of admiralty or vice-admiralty are hereby respectively authorized and required to proceed, hear, and determine the same) at the election of the informer or prosecutor.

XLII-XLIII. [Provides for distribution of proceeds from sales of ships and cargoes seized under provision of this and previous Acts of Parliament.]

XLIV. [Provides that no one may enter a claim to seized ships or goods until sufficient security is given to answer the costs of prosecution in the court where seizure is prosecuted. If security is not given, ships or goods shall be judged forfeit.]

XLV. [If goods or ships are seized for any cause, and any dispute shall arise as to payment of duties, origin of goods, etc., the burden of proof is to be provided by owner or claimant rather than by seizing officer.]

XLVI. [In cases brought to trial under this or any other Act of Parliament, and the verdict is favourable to the claimant, and the judge or court indicates there was probable cause for seizure, the claimant shall not be entitled to costs of the suit, nor shall the seizing officers be liable to any suit or action because of the seizure. If seized goods or ships are not brought to trial, but the seizing officers are sued, and the judge or court certify that there was probable cause for seizure, the plaintiff, in addition to his ship or goods, shall not be entitled to more than two pence damages, nor to any costs, nor shall the defendant be fined more than one shilling.]

XLVII. And be it further enacted by the authority aforesaid, that if any action or suit shall be commenced, either in Great Britain or America, against any person or persons for anything done in pursuance of this or any other Act of Parliament relating to his Majesty's customs, the defendant or defendants in such action or suit may plead the general issue, and give the said Acts, and the special matter, in evidence at any trial to be had thereupon, and that the same was done in pursuance and by the authority of such Act; and if it shall appear so to have been done, the jury shall find for the defendant or defendants; and if the plaintiff shall be nonsuited, or discontinue his action after the defendant or defendants shall have appeared, or if judgment shall be given upon verdict or demurrer against the plaintiff, the defendant or defendants shall recover treble costs, and have the like remedy for the same as defendants have in other cases by law.

100. The Currency Act of 1764 (19 April 1764)

Questions of currency and government finance were the subject of internal debate in the colonies and of controversy between Britain and the colonies from early in the eighteenth century (see Nos. 58-62). During the Seven Years War British restrictions were suspended and most of the colonies issued large sums of paper money. As soon as the war was over, British merchants, particularly those trading to Virginia, demanded parliamentary legislation. The result was the Act of 1764.

It provoked widespread opposition, especially in those colonies where the currency had been well managed. There were repeated demands for relaxation and official circles in Britain realized that the problem of colonial money supply had not been solved by the Act of 1764. In 1769 Parliament passed an Act permitting New York to issue a limited amount of currency to be legal tender in payments due to the public treasury (10 Geo. III, c. 35). Finally in 1773 Parliament passed a similar Act applying to all except the New England colonies (13 Geo. III, c. 57). However, it came too late to have any effect on colonials who had been irked or injured by British restrictions. Printed: Pickering, *Statutes at Large*, XXVI, pp. 103-105.

Whereas great quantities of paper bills of credit have been created and issued in his Majesty's colonies or plantations in America by virtue of acts, orders, resolutions, or votes of assembly, making and declaring such bills of credit to be legal tender in payment of money; and whereas such bills of credit have greatly depreciated in their value, by means whereof debts have been discharged with a much less value than was contracted for, to the great discouragement and prejudice of the trade and commerce of his Majesty's subjects, by occasioning confusion in dealings, and lessening credit in the said colonies or plantations; for remedy whereof, may it please your most excellent Majesty, that it may be enacted . . . that from and after the first day of September, one thousand seven hundred and sixty-four, no act, order, resolution, or vote of assembly, in any of his Majesty's colonies or plantations in America, shall be made for creating or issuing any paper bills, or bills of credit of any kind or denomination whatsoever, declaring such paper bills, or bills of credit to be legal tender in payment of any bargains, contracts, debts, dues, or demands whatsoever; and every clause or provision which shall hereafter be inserted in any act, order, resolution, or vote of assembly, contrary to this act, shall be null and void.

II. And whereas the great quantities of paper bills, or bills of credit, which are now actually in circulation and currency in several colonies or plantations in America, emitted in pursuance of acts of assembly declaring such bills a legal tender, make it highly expedient that the conditions and terms, upon which such bills have been emitted, should not be varied or prolonged, so as to continue the legal tender thereof beyond the terms respectively fixed by such acts for calling in and discharging such bills; be it therefore enacted by the authority aforesaid, that every act, order, resolution, or vote of assembly in any of the said colonies or plantations, which shall be made to prolong the legal tender of any paper bills, or bills of credit, which are now subsisting and current in any of the said colonies or plantations in America, beyond the times fixed for the calling in, sinking, and discharging of such paper bills, or bills of credit, shall be null and void.

III. And be it further enacted by the authority aforesaid, that if any governor or commander-in-chief for the time being, in all or any of the said colonies or plantations, shall, from and after the said first day of September, one thousand seven hundred and sixty-four, give his assent to any act or order of assembly contrary to the true intent and meaning of this act, every such governor or commander-in-chief shall, for every such offence, forfeit and pay the sum of one thousand pounds, and shall be immediately dismissed from his government, and forever after rendered incapable of any public office or place of trust.

IV. Provided always, that nothing in this Act shall extend to alter or repeal an Act passed in the twenty-fourth year of the reign of his late Majesty King George the second, entitled, An Act to regulate and restrain paper bills of credit in his Majesty's Colonies or Plantations of Rhode Island and Providence Plantations, Connecticut, the Massachusetts Bay, and New Hampshire, in America, and to prevent the same being legal tenders in payments of money.

V. Provided also, that nothing herein contained shall extend, or be construed to extend, to make any of the bills now subsisting in any of the said colonies a legal tender.

101A–B. The Stamp Act

Among the resolutions offered to the House of Commons in 1764 as a basis for the Revenue Act of 1764 (No. 99) was one which declared that it was proper to levy stamp duties in the colonies. However, action on this resolution was delayed to give the colonists time to suggest other means of raising revenues in the colonies. The Americans offered nothing but objections, and in 1765 the Stamp Act was passed (5 Geo. III, c. 12). The law became effective on 1 November 1765 and was repealed 22 March 1766 (see No. 112).

The following account of the debate in Parliament over the passage of the Act was written to Governor Thomas Fitch of Connecticut by Jared Ingersoll, who at the time was the colonial agent of Connecticut in London (No. 101A). The Stamp Act itself runs to twenty-five closely printed pages. Only two brief excerpts are given here: the preamble and the section specifying the use to which the revenues collected were to be put (No. 101B).

101A. Jared Ingersoll's account of the debate on the Stamp Act (11 February 1765)

Printed: Connecticut Historical Society *Collections*, XVIII, pp. 317–326.

Since my last to you I have been honoured with yours of the 7th of December in which you inform me that the General Assembly have been pleased to desire my assistance while here in any matters that may concern the colony. Be so good, sir, in return as to assure the Assembly that I have not only a due sense of the honour they have done me by placing this confidence in me, but that I have ever since my arrival here, from motives of inclination as well as duty, done everything in my power to promote the colony's interests.

The principal attention has been to the stamp bill that has been preparing to lay before Parliament for taxing America. The point of the authority of Parliament to impose such tax I found on my arrival here was so fully and universally yielded that there was not the least hopes of making any impressions that way. Indeed it has appeared since that the House would not suffer to be brought in, nor would any one member undertake to offer to the House any petition from the colonies that held forth the contrary of that doctrine. I own I advised the agents if possible to get that point canvassed that so the Americans might at least have the satisfaction of having the point decided upon a full debate, but I found it could not be done, and here, before I proceed to acquaint you with the steps that have been taken in this matter, I beg leave to give you a summary of the arguments which are made use of in favour of such authority.

The House of Commons, say they, is a branch of the supreme legislature of the nation, and which in its nature is supposed to represent, or rather to stand in the place of, the Commons; that is, of the great body of the people who are below the dignity of peers; that this House of Commons consists of a certain number of men chosen by certain people of certain places, which electors, by the way, they insist are not a tenth part of the people, and that the laws, rules, and methods by which their number is ascertained have arose by degrees and from various causes and occasions, and that this House of Commons therefore is now fixed and ascertained and is a part of the supreme unlimited power of the nation, as in every state there must be some unlimited power and authority; and that when it is said they represent the commons of England it cannot mean that they do so because those commons choose them, for in fact by far the greater part do not, but because by their constitution they must themselves be commoners and not peers, and so the equals, or of the same class of subjects, with the commons of the kingdom. They further urge that the only reason why America has not been heretofore taxed in the fullest manner has been merely on account of their infancy and inability; that there have been, however, not wanting instances of the exercise of this power in the various regulations of the American trade, the establishment of the post office, etc., and they deny any distinction between what is called an internal and external tax as to the point of the authority imposing such taxes. And as to the charters in the few provinces where there are any, they say in the first place the king cannot grant any that shall exempt them from the authority of one of the branches of the great body of legislation, and in the second place say the king has not done or attempted to do it. In that of Pennsylvania the authority of Parliament to impose taxes is expressly mentioned and reserved; in ours 'tis said, our powers are generally such as are *according to the course of other corporations in England* (both which instances by way of sample were mentioned and referred to by Mr. Grenville in the House); in short, they say a power to tax is a necessary part of every supreme legislative authority, and that if they have not that power over America, they have none, and then America is at once a kingdom of itself.

On the other hand, those who oppose the bill say it is true the Parliament have a supreme unlimited authority over every part and branch of the king's dominions, and as well over Ireland as any other place, yet we believe a British Parliament will never think it prudent to tax Ireland. 'Tis true they say that the commons of England and of the British Empire are all represented in and by the House of Commons, but this representation is confessedly on all hands by construction and virtually only as to those who have no hand in choosing the representatives, and that the effects of this implied representation here and in America must be infinitely different in the article of taxation. Here in England the member of Parliament is equally known to the neighbour who elects and to him who does not; the friendships, the connections, the influences are spread through the whole. If by any mistake an Act of Parliament is made that prove injurious and hard, the member of Parliament here sees with his own eyes and is moreover very accessible to the people; not only so, but the taxes are laid equally by one rule and fall as well on the member himself as on the people. But as to America, from the great distance in point of situation, from the almost total unacquaintedness, especially in the more northern colonies, with the members of Parliament, and they with them, or with the particular ability and circumstances of one another, from the nature of this very tax laid upon others not equally and in common with ourselves, but with express purpose to ease ourselves, we think, say they, that it will be only to lay a foundation of great jealousy and continual uneasiness, and that to no purpose, as we already by the regulations upon their trade draw from the Americans all that they can spare. At least they say this step should not take place until or unless the Americans are allowed to send members to Parliament; for *who of you*, said Col. [Isaac] Barré nobly in his speech in the House upon this occasion; *who of you reasoning upon this subject feels warmly from the heart* (putting his hand to his own breast) *for the Americans as they would for themselves or as you would for the people of your own native country?* And to this point Mr. Jackson produced copies of two Acts of Parliament granting the privilege of having members to the county palatine of Chester and the bishopric of Durham upon petitions preferred for that purpose in the reign of King Henry the eighth and Charles the first, the preamble of which statutes counts upon the petitions from those places as setting forth that being in their general civil jurisdiction exempted from the common law courts, etc., yet being subject to the general authority of Parliament, were taxed in common with the rest of the kingdom, which taxes by reason of their having no members in Parliament to represent their affairs, often proved hard and injurious, etc., and upon that ground they had the privilege of sending members granted them—and if this, say they, could be a reason in the case of Chester and Durham, how much more so in the case of America.

Thus I have given you, I think, the substance of the arguments on both sides of that great and important question of the right and also of the expediency of taxing America by authority of Parliament. I cannot, however, content myself without giving you a sketch of what the aforementioned Mr. Barré said in answer to some remarks made by Mr. Charles Townshend in a speech of his upon this subject. I ought here to tell you that the debate upon the American stamp bill came on before the House for the first time last Wednesday, when the same was opened by Mr. Grenville, the Chancellor of the Exchequer, in a pretty lengthy speech, and in a very able, and I think, in a very candid manner he opened the nature of the tax, urged the necessity of it, endeavoured to obviate all objections to it—and took occasion to desire the House to give the bill a most serious and cool consideration and not suffer themselves to be influenced by any resentments which might have been kindled from anything they might have heard out of doors—alluding, I suppose, to the New York and Boston Assemblies' speeches and votes—that this was a matter of revenue which was of all things the most interesting to the subject, etc. The argument was taken up by several who opposed the bill (viz.) by Alderman Beckford, who, and who only, seemed to deny the authority of Parliament, by Col. Barré, Mr. Jackson, Sir William Meredith, and some others. Mr. Barré, who by the way, I think, and I find I am not alone in my opinion, is one of the finest speakers that the House can boast of, having been some time in America as an officer in the army, and having while there, as I had known before, contracted many friendships with American gentlemen, and I believe entertained much more favourable opinions of them than some of his profession have done, delivered a very handsome and moving speech upon the bill and against the same, concluding by saying that he was very sure that most who should hold up their hands to the bill must be under a necessity of acting very much in the dark, but added, perhaps as well in the dark as any way.

After him Mr. Charles Townshend spoke in favour of the bill—took notice of several things Mr. Barré had said, and concluded with the following or like words: and now will these Americans, children planted by our care, nourished up by our indulgence until they are grown to a degree of strength and opulence, and protected by our arms, will they grudge to contribute their mite to relieve us from the heavy weight of that burden which we lie under? When he had done, Mr. Barré rose, and having explained something which he had before said and which Mr. Townshend had been remarking upon, he then took up the before mentioned concluding words of Mr. Townshend, and in a most spirited and I thought an almost inimitable manner, said:

"They planted by your care? No! Your oppressions planted 'em in America. They fled from your tyranny to a then uncultivated and unhospitable country where they exposed themselves to almost all the hardships to which human nature is liable, and among others to the cruelties of a savage foe, the most subtle, and I take upon me to say, the most formidable of any people upon the face of God's earth. And yet, actuated by principles of true English liberty, they met all these hardships with pleasure, compared with those they suffered in their own country, from the hands of those who should have been their friends.

"They nourished by *your* indulgence? They grew by your neglect of 'em. As soon as you began to care about 'em, that care was exercised in sending persons to rule over 'em, in one department and another, who were perhaps the deputies of deputies to some member of this house, sent to spy out their liberty, to misrepresent their actions and to prey upon 'em; men whose behaviour on many occasions has caused the blood of those sons of liberty to recoil within them; men promoted to the highest seats of justice; some who to my knowledge were glad by going to a foreign country to escape being brought to the bar of a court of justice in their own.

"They protected by *your* arms? They have nobly taken up arms in your defence, have exerted a valour amidst their constant and laborious industry for the defence of a country, whose frontier while drenched in blood, its interior parts have yielded all its little savings to your emolument. And believe me, remember I this day told you so, that same spirit of freedom which actuated that people at first, will accompany them still. But prudence forbids me to explain myself further. God knows I do not at this time speak from motives of party heat; what I deliver are the genuine sentiments of my heart; however superior to me in general knowledge and experience the reputable body of this House may be, yet I claim to know more of America than most of you, having seen and been conversant in that country. The people I believe are as truly loyal as any subjects the king has, but a people jealous of their liberties and who will vindicate them if ever they should be violated; but the subject is too delicate and I will say no more."

These sentiments were thrown out so entirely without premeditation, so forceably and so firmly, and the breaking off so beautifully abrupt, that the whole House sat a while as amazed, intently looking and without answering a word.

I own I felt emotions that I never felt before and went the next morning and thanked Col. Barré in behalf of my country for his noble and spirited speech.

However, sir, after all that was said, upon a division of the House upon the question there was about 250 to about 50 in favour of the bill.

The truth is, I believe some who inclined rather against the bill voted for it, partly because they are loath to break the measures of the ministry, and partly because they don't undertake to inform themselves in the fullest manner upon the subject. The bill comes on to a second reading tomorrow when ours and the Massachusetts petitions will be presented and perhaps [there] may be some further debate upon the subject, but to no purpose, I am very sure, as to the stopping or preventing the Act taking place.

The agents of the colonies have had several meetings, at one of which they were pleased to desire Mr. Franklin and myself as having lately come from America and knowing more intimately the sentiments of the people, to wait on Mr. Grenville, together with Mr. Jackson and Mr. Garth, who, being agents are also members of Parliament, to remonstrate against the stamp bill, and to propose in case any tax must be laid upon America, that the several colonies might be permitted to lay the tax themselves. This we did Saturday before last. Mr. Grenville gave us a full hearing—told us he took no pleasure in giving the Americans so much uneasiness as he found he did—that it was the duty of his office to manage the revenue—that he really was made to believe that considering the whole of the circumstances of the mother country and the colonies, the lat[t]er could and ought to pay something, and that he knew of no better way than that now pursuing to lay such tax, but that if we could tell of a better, he would adopt it. We then urged the method first mentioned as being a method the people had been used to—that it would at least seem to be their own act and prevent that uneasiness and jealousy which otherwise we found would take place—that they could raise the money best by their own officers, etc.

Mr. Jackson told him plainly that he foresaw [by] the measure now pursuing, by enabling the Crown to keep up an armed force of its own in America and to pay the governors in the king's governments, and all with the Americans' own money, the assemblies in the colonies would be subverted—that the governors would have no occasion as for any ends of their own or of the Crown, to call 'em, and that they never would be called together in the king's governments. Mr. Grenville warmly rejected the thought, said no such thing was intended nor would, he believed, take place. Indeed, I understand since, there is a clause added to the bill applying the monies that shall be raised to the protecting and defending America *only*. Mr. Grenville asked us if we could agree upon the several proportions each colony should raise. We told him no. He said he did not think anybody here was furnished with materials for that purpose; not only so, but there would be no certainty that every colony would raise the sum enjoined and to be obliged to be at the expense of making stamps to compel some one or two provinces to do their duty, and that perhaps for one year only, would be very inconvenient; not only so, but the colonies by their constant increase will be constantly varying in their proportions of numbers and ability and which a stamp bill will always keep pace with, etc.

Upon the whole he said he had pledged his word for offering the stamp bill to the House, that the House would hear all our objections and would do as they thought best; he said he wished we would preserve a coolness and moderation in America; that he had no need to tell us that resentments indecently and unbecomingly expressed on one side the water would naturally produce resentments on tother side, and that we could not hope to get any good by a controversy with the mother country; that their ears will always be open to any remonstrances from the Americans with respect to this bill, both before it takes effect and after, if it shall take effect, which shall be expressed in a becoming manner, that is, as becomes subjects of the same common prince.

I acquainted you in my last that Mr. Whately, one of the secretaries of the Treasury, and who had under his care and direction the business of preparing the stamp bill, had often conferred with me on the subject. He wanted, I know, information of the several methods of transfer, law process, etc., made use of in the colony, and I believe has been also very willing to hear all objections that could be made to the bill or any part of it. This task I was glad to undertake, as I very well knew the information I must give would operate strongly in our favour; as the number of our law-suits, deeds, tavern licences, and in short, almost all the objects of the intended taxation and duties are so very numerous in the colony that the knowledge of them would tend to the imposing a duty so much the lower as the objects were more in number. This effect, I flatter myself, it has had in some measure. Mr. Whately, to be sure, tells me I may fairly claim the honour of having occasioned the duty's being much lower than was intended, and three particular things that were intended to be taxed I gave him no peace till he dropped; these were licences for marriage–a duty that would be odious in a new country where every encouragement ought to be given to matrimony, and where there was little portion; commissions of the justices of peace, which office was, generally speaking, not profitable and yet necessary for the good order and government of the people; and notes of hand which with us were given and taken so very often for very small sums.

After all, I believe the people in America will think the sums that will be raised will be quite enough, and I wish they may'nt find it more distressing than the people in power here are aware of.

The merchants in London are alarmed at these things; they have had a meeting with the agents and are about to petition Parliament upon the Acts that respect the trade of North America.

What the event of these things will be I don't know, but am pretty certain that wisdom will be proper and even very necessary, as well as prudence and good discretion to direct the councils of America.

101B. The Stamp Act (22 March 1765)

Printed: Pickering, *Statutes at Large*, XXVI, pp. 179, 201.

Whereas by an Act made in the last session of Parliament, several duties were granted, continued, and appropriated towards defraying the expenses of defending, protecting, and securing the British colonies and plantations in America;

and whereas it is just and necessary that provision be made for raising a further revenue within your Majesty's dominions in America towards defraying the said expenses; ... be it enacted ... that from and after the first day of November, one thousand seven hundred and sixty-five, there shall be raised, levied, collected, and paid unto his Majesty, his heirs, and successors, throughout the colonies and plantations in America which now are, or hereafter may be, under the dominion of his Majesty, his heirs and successors. ... [Stamp duties on newspapers, pamphlets, cards, dice, and on each sheet of an extensive, varied, and complicated list of legal papers such as court proceedings and associated papers, wills, certificates of academic degrees, licences, bills of lading, clearances, appointments to public office, licences for selling spirits, letters of administration, surveys, warrants, grants or conveyances of land, indentures, leases, conveyances, bills of sale, contracts, notarial acts, deeds, and letters of attorney. It then describes the administration and enforcement of the Act and specifies penalties for violations.]

LIV. And be it further enacted by the authority aforesaid, that all the moneys which shall arise by the several rates and duties hereby granted (except the necessary charges of raising, collecting, recovering, answering, paying, and accounting for the same, and the necessary charges from time to time incurred in relation to this Act, and the execution thereof) shall be paid into the receipt of his Majesty's Exchequer, and shall be entered separate and apart from all other moneys, and shall be there reserved to be from time to time disposed of by Parliament, towards further defraying the necessary expenses of defending, protecting, and securing the said colonies and plantations.

102. The Quartering Act (15 May 1765)

The purpose of the Quartering Act (5 Geo. III, c. 33) was to provide for the maintenance of British troops in the colonies. Section VII was the cause of much trouble. It provided that when British troops were quartered in barracks belonging to the colonial government, those governments must provide certain supplies. However, they refused to do so. Even Georgia, which wanted troops for frontier defence, refused to provide supplies. The controversy over the Act in New York led to the suspension of the New York Assembly in 1767 by an Act of Parliament (No. 117). Printed: Pickering, *Statutes at Large*, XXVI, pp. 305-309.

Whereas in and by an Act made in the present session of Parliament entitled, An Act for punishing mutiny and desertion, and for the better payment of the army and their quarters; several regulations are made and enacted for the better government of the army, and their observing strict discipline, and for providing quarters for the army, and carriages on marches and other necessary occasions, and inflicting penalties on offenders against the same Act, and for many other good purposes therein mentioned; but the same may not be sufficient for the forces that may be employed in his Majesty's dominions in America; and whereas, during the continuance of the said Act there may be occasion for marching and quartering of regiments and companies of his Majesty's forces in several parts of his Majesty's dominions in America; and whereas the public houses and barracks, in his Majesty's dominions in America may not be sufficient to supply quarters for such forces; and whereas it is expedient and necessary that carriages and other conveniences, upon the march of troops in his Majesty's dominions in America should be supplied for that purpose: be it enacted . . . that for and during the continuance of this Act, and no longer, it shall and may be lawful to and for the constables, tithingmen, magistrates, and other civil officers of villages, towns, townships, cities, districts, and other places, within his Majesty's dominions in America, and in their default or absence, for any one justice of the peace inhabiting in or near any such village, township, city, district, or place, and for no others; and such constables, tithingmen, magistrates, and other civil officers as aforesaid, are hereby required to quarter and billet the officers and soldiers in his Majesty's service, in the barracks provided by the colonies; and if there shall not be sufficient room in the said barracks for the officers and soldiers, then and in such case only, to quarter and billet the residue of such officers and soldiers for whom there shall not be room in such barracks, in inns, livery stables, ale-houses, victualling houses, and the houses of sellers of wine by retail to be drunk in their own houses or places thereunto belonging, and all houses of persons selling of rum, brandy, strong water, cider, or metheglin, by retail, to be drunk in houses; and in case there shall not be sufficient room for the officers and soldiers in such barracks, inns, victualling and other public ale-houses, that in such and no other case, and upon no other account, it shall and may be lawful for the governor and council of each respective province in his Majesty's dominions in America, to authorize and appoint, and they are hereby directed and empowered to authorize and appoint such proper person or persons as they shall think fit, to take, hire and make fit, and, in default of the said governor and council appointing and authorizing such person or persons, or in default of such person or persons so appointed neglecting or refusing to do their duty, in that case it shall and may be lawful for any two or more of his Majesty's justices of the peace in or near the said villages, towns, townships, cities, districts, and other places, and they are hereby required to take, hire, and make fit for the reception of his Majesty's forces, such and so many uninhabited houses, outhouses, barns, or other buildings, as shall be necessary, to quarter therein the residue of such officers and soldiers for whom there should not be room in such barracks and public houses as aforesaid, and to put and quarter the residue of such officers and soldiers therein.

V-VI. [Soldiers quartered in other than public barracks are to be provided with supplies by innkeepers, etc., at certain rates and to be reimbursed out of soldiers' subsistence money.]

VII. And whereas there are several barracks in several places in his Majesty's said dominions in America, or some of them, provided by the colonies, for the lodging and covering of soldiers in lieu of quarters, for the ease and conveniency as well of the inhabitants of and in such colonies, as of the soldiers; it is hereby further enacted, that all such officers and soldiers so put and placed in such barracks, or in hired uninhabited houses, outhouses, barns, or other buildings, shall, from time to time be furnished and supplied there by the persons to be authorized or appointed for that purpose by the governor and council of each respective province, or upon neglect or refusal of such governor and council in any province, then by two or more justices of the peace residing in or near such place, with fire, candles, vinegar, and salt, bedding, utensils for dressing their victuals, and small beer or cider, not exceeding five pints, or half a pint of rum mixed with a quart of water, to each man, without paying anything for the same.

VIII. And that the several persons who shall so take, hire, and fit up as aforesaid, such uninhabited houses, outhouses, barns, or other buildings, for the reception of the officers and soldiers, and who shall so furnish the same, and also the said barracks with fire, candles, vinegar, and salt, bedding, utensils for dressing victuals, and small beer and cider, or rum, as aforesaid, may be reimbursed and paid all such charges and expenses they shall be put to therein, be it enacted by the authority aforesaid, that the respective provinces shall pay unto such person or persons all such sum or sums of money so by them paid, laid out, or expended, for the taking, hiring, and fitting up such uninhabited houses, outhouses, barns, or other buildings, and for furnishing the officers and soldiers therein, and in the barracks with fire, candles, vinegar, and salt, bedding, utensils for dressing victuals, and small beer, cider, or rum, as aforesaid; and such sum or sums are hereby required to be raised in such manner as the public charges for the provinces respectively are raised.

B. COLONIAL OPPOSITION AND BRITISH RETREAT, 1764–1766

THE British determination to tighten political and economic control over the colonies and to raise more money from them would have met with opposition at any time, but after 1763 a variety of internal conditions produced a reaction that was far more serious than would have been the case earlier. To begin with, there was a post-war depression that lasted, in the northern colonies at least, until the end of the decade. There was a relatively heavy burden of taxation in some of the colonies to pay the debts incurred during the war. The depression meant unemployment in the towns along the coast, and hence a problem of discontent that could be and was channelled into political activity. The back-country farmers showed increasing irritation at the continued dominance of merchant and planter aristocracies along the coast, and during the decade of the 1760's several of the colonies were the scene of civil war.[1]

Such factors, although not unknown in Britain, were either ignored or misunderstood by British policy makers, with the result that many of the policies adopted were certain to irritate most colonials for one reason or another. The commercial towns of the northern colonies were the first to react. Before the end of 1763 colonial newspapers were printing lists of naval vessels stationed in American waters, and merchants were warning one another privately to be careful. The appointment of new customs officers and the news of new enforcement policies brought expressions of alarm. Merchants concerned with the West India trade were well aware that the Molasses Act of 1733 was up for renewal in 1764 and recognized that if it were to be enforced (as it never had been), it would seriously affect them. The Boston merchants therefore prepared a "State of Trade" in 1763 which was a defence of trade with the foreign West India islands and an analysis of the economic problems facing New England merchants. The Rhode Island legislature was called into special session, and it prepared a remonstrance objecting to the proposed renewal of the Molasses Act. It insisted that trade with the foreign islands was indispensable to the economy of the colonies and that it made possible their imports from Great Britain.

The Boston Town Meeting expressed its alarm at the declining state of trade and instructed its representatives in the legislature to protest against the passage of the Act, or, if passed, to endeavour to secure its repeal. In addition, the instructions raised the constitutional issue "for if our trade may be taxed why not our lands? Why not the produce of our lands and everything we possess or make use of? This we apprehend annihilates our charter right to govern and tax ourselves."[2]

The passage of the sweeping Revenue Act of 1764[3] and the news of the proposed Stamp Act widened and intensified colonial opposition. The Rhode Island legislature appointed a committee to correspond with other colonial legislative committees to secure the repeal of the Revenue Act and to prevent the passage of a Stamp Act. The legislatures of Massachusetts,[4] New York, Pennsylvania, and Virginia[5] adopted memorials against the new measures and the proposed Stamp Act. In some form or other these legislatures asserted that the colonists should be taxed only by representatives of their own choosing. They all elaborated upon the economic hardships of

[1] Nos. 95, 96.   [2] No. 103.   [3] No. 99.   [4] No. 104.   [5] No. 105.

the colonies, and the Virginia legislature declared that it was "inconsistent with the fundamental principles of the constitution" for Parliament to impose taxes on the colonies, and even if such taxes were proper, they would be economically ruinous for Virginia.[1] The New York legislature in a petition to the House of Commons adopted on 18 October 1764 specifically denied the right of Parliament to tax the colonies.

These preliminary protests were ignored in Britain. The colonists offered no alternative suggestions as to how the colonies might provide a portion of the cost of the army in America. Therefore, with relatively little opposition, the Stamp Act was passed, to take effect 1 November 1765.[2] It was direct taxation by Parliament, and as such was diametrically opposed to a basic colonial conviction that Americans should be taxed only by representatives of their own choosing. Economically it threatened to be a heavy burden, for the stamps were to be paid for in specie, and specie had always been so scarce in the colonies that it was almost never used as a medium of exchange. Furthermore, the taxes on virtually all business and legal transactions, as well as on newspapers and pamphlets, united, as nothing else could have done, the three most vocal and influential classes in the colonies: the merchants, the lawyers, and the printers. It also brought about an alliance of the planting colonies of the south with the commercial colonies of the north. The former, despite difficult economic conditions, had not shown overmuch concern over stricter customs regulations, but the Stamp Act aroused all their fervour.

Thus in 1765 colonial opposition was perhaps more united than it was to be again until 1774. The legislature of Virginia in its Stamp Act Resolves in the spring of 1765 set the pattern for statements of constitutional rights by other colonial legislatures.[3] The Stamp Act Congress, a voluntary meeting in New York of delegates from nine of the mainland colonies, wrote a measured statement of the rights of the colonies,[4] but, even more importantly, pointed the way to the intercolonial organization which resulted in the First and Second Continental Congresses which carried the colonies into the war for independence. In local governments, which were far more responsive to the citizenry, particularly in New England, resolutions were adopted which proclaimed the principles later to be embodied in the Declaration of Independence. Thus New London, Connecticut, in December 1765, declared that it was the duty of every citizen to oppose the execution of the Stamp Act, and, failing this, it was their duty to "reassume their natural rights, and the authority the laws of Nature and of God have vested them with".[5]

During 1764 and 1765 the colonies thus set forth their conception of the relationship that should exist between the colonies and the British government and of their rights as colonists and Englishmen. In the years that followed there was little fundamental alteration in such statements: they were merely sharpened and stated more strongly. On the whole, the colonial legislatures were more cautious than the local governments such as the New England town meetings, but they moved eventually to the same position. Such statements had little effect in Britain except to irritate the ministry and Parliament. The vacillations in British policy towards the colonies between 1765 and 1774 were not due to constitutional arguments, however much the colonies believed in them, but to more concrete realities.

First of all, the Stamp Act was prevented from going into operation by sheer violence and open defiance of the law. A secret organization, the "Sons of Liberty",

[1] No. 105.   [2] No. 101.   [3] No. 106.   [4] No. 109.   [5] No. 107.

sprang into being. It took its name from a speech of Colonel Isaac Barré in which he opposed the passage of the Stamp Act and spoke of Americans as "those sons of liberty",[1] a speech widely reported in American newspapers. The story was the same in every colony: the men appointed to sell stamps were forced by popular violence to resign and the mobs were supported for the most part, though secretly, by many of the most substantial citizens.[2]

On 1 November 1765, when the law went into effect, few if any stamps were to be had in the mainland colonies, or if they were, few citizens dared use them. The result was that courts stopped proceedings, ships were tied up at wharves, and many newspapers suspended publication. The next step was to bring about the resumption of all business in open defiance of the law. Conservative minded men were hesitant and some openly opposed such an extreme measure; but popular pressure was so great that within a few months most of the courts were open, ships were entering and clearing harbours, and the law was a nullity.

Meanwhile a movement to apply economic pressure gained ground, particularly in the northern colonies. As a result of the depression after 1763, various proposals had been made to reduce the consumption of British goods and to encourage domestic manufactures in order to better economic conditions in the colonies. The Stamp Act gave real focus to such ideas, and merchants in the northern provinces took the lead in non-importation agreements, a role quite in contrast with their reluctance to adopt similar agreements two years later in opposition to the Townshend Revenue Act. The merchants of New York, Philadelphia, and Boston all signed agreements to stop importation of most goods from England until the Stamp Act was repealed.[3]

However, the most significant pressure for the repeal of the Stamp Act came from those British merchants and manufacturers who were concerned primarily with the trade to the colonies. They had been seriously alarmed at the decline of exports which accompanied the depression after 1763. They had welcomed Grenville's programme of economy and reform at first, but they soon came to blame it for worsening business conditions in Britain and the colonies. Thus as complaints from the colonies against the new customs reforms and regulations appeared, British merchants and manufacturers echoed them and demanded 'reforms'. An opportunity was presented to them as a result of the difficulties in which the Rockingham ministry found itself as soon as it took office. Aside from Rockingham himself, it was made up mostly of younger men of no particular influence, while the powerful Grenville and Bedford Whigs and William Pitt stood ready to topple it from power whenever the opportunity offered. Thus the Rockingham Whigs looked for support wherever it could be found, either inside or outside of Parliament. Merchants and manufacturers soon found this situation suited to their purposes and offered to trade their political support for the 'reforms' they demanded. As early as the autumn of 1764 merchants of Bristol and London were demanding changes in the Revenue Act of 1764. They pointed to the decline of American trade and to the complaints of Americans against the Act as justification for their demands.

The scattered efforts of British merchants and manufacturers were brought to a head in December 1765, as mounting protests against the Stamp Act poured into Britain from the colonies. The merchants of London, encouraged by the Rockingham ministry, proceeded to organize. With Barlow Trecothick as chairman, they appointed a committee of twenty-eight to manage a national movement for commercial reform

[1] No. 101A.　　　　　[2] No. 110.　　　　　[3] No. 108.

and the repeal of the Stamp Act. The result was that petitions were sent to Parliament from most of the leading commercial and manufacturing towns of Great Britain. They demanded relief for the colonies quite as vigorously as the Americans did.

Parliament proceeded to hold an inquiry into economic conditions in Britain and the colonies. All sorts of people were interrogated: colonials like Benjamin Franklin, and British merchants and manufacturers.[1] By this means support was built up for the repeal of the Stamp Act, and when William Pitt threw his weight behind repeal, success was assured. Grenville and his followers fought bitterly against repeal, but the Bill was passed.[2] As a concession, and doubtless a necessary one to the opponents of repeal, it was accompanied by the Declaratory Act, which asserted the sovereignty of Parliament over the colonies.[3]

But the demand for reform was not satisfied by the repeal of the Stamp Act. The merchants and manufacturers demanded more. They asked that restraints be placed on the colonial admiralty courts. They insisted that the duty on foreign molasses imported into the colonies should be lowered, pointing out that the trade with the foreign West Indies brought the specie into the colonies which was used to pay colonial debts to British merchants.

The desire to increase the flow of bullion from foreign colonies in America led to a further demand: that certain ports in the British West Indies be opened up as free ports to ships from the foreign colonies. Here the British merchants and manufacturers and the West India planter interest met in collision. They had united in seeking repeal of the Stamp Act, to which the West Indies objected as strenuously as the mainland colonies, but the West Indians were opposed to the idea of free ports. They feared that the mainland colonies would use them to enlarge their trade with the foreign islands, to the detriment of the British.

The merchants swept away such objections, and for the first time the West India planters suffered a serious defeat in Parliament. The result was the passage of the Revenue Act of 1766, which, among other things, reduced the duty on foreign molasses imported into the colonies from 3d. to 1d. a gallon, and in addition required molasses from the British colonies to pay the same duty.[4] This was accompanied by an Act making several ports on the islands of Jamaica and Dominica free ports to encourage the bullion trade from foreign colonies.[5]

The reform legislation of 1766 was thus primarily the work of British merchants and manufacturers, whose concern was their own economic interest, and of the Rockingham ministry, which used every means possible to stay in power. Neither group had any basic concern with the welfare of the colonies and both were horrified by the reports of violence in America. In fact, British merchants complained to their American correspondents that the Stamp Act would have been repealed sooner if the Americans had kept quiet. The opposition in Parliament, led by George Grenville, consistently opposed all concession to the colonies and insisted that they should be compelled to obey the laws of Parliament and the directives of the ministry.

The Americans were delighted with the repeal of the Stamp Act, and celebrations were held in honour of George III and William Pitt. The Declaratory Act was ignored. There was some protest at the penny duty on molasses in the Revenue Act of 1766, but no colonial seemed to realize its real significance. The penny duty made smuggling unprofitable, with the result that ever-increasing revenues were produced by it. When compared with customs collections before 1763, the increase after 1766

[1] No. 111.   [2] No. 112.   [3] No. 113.   [4] No. 114.   [5] 6 Geo III, c. 49.

was astonishing, and at least eighty per cent of all revenues collected in the American colonies in the years just before the Revolution came from this penny duty. Eventually, after Parliament gave up the effort to raise money in the colonies through direct taxation, the money could be and was used to support civil officials, at least in the case of Massachusetts. Thus the Act promised to fulfil the basic purpose of the Townshend Revenue Act of 1767,[1] although no one on either side of the Atlantic seems to have been aware of this possibility when it was passed.

103. Boston instructions to its delegates in the Massachusetts Legislature (24 May 1764)

It was the common practice of voters in the townships and counties in the American colonies to prepare instructions for the delegates they elected to the colonial legislatures. In the years after 1763 such instructions were much used by popular leaders of the opposition to Great Britain. Those leaders, particularly in New England, got control of local governments long before they were able to dominate the legislatures. They were thus able to force the legislatures to consider controversial issues which the legislatures might otherwise have avoided. In fact the rejection of popular demands by colonial legislatures was often as useful for purposes of propaganda as acceptance would have been.

No political agency in the colonies was more important in the growth of the revolutionary movement than the Boston Town Meeting which could be called into session at any time on the petition of a few inhabitants. Its leaders, who were usually its delegates to the legislature as well, were thus in position to push legislative programmes through the adoption of instructions to themselves. News of the Revenue Act of 1764 reached Boston before the regular spring meeting of the town. When it met it approved of instructions which outlined the programme of the popular party. These instructions show clearly how local political issues and the opposition to British policies are linked together. The first part of the instructions (omitted here) attack plural officeholding. They urge that judges who hold other posts be denied their salaries. They urge the passage of a colonial equivalent of the British Place Act to provide for vacating the seats of members of the legislature who receive appointments from the Crown or the governor. These proposals were aimed at the Hutchinson oligarchy which dominated the politics of the colony. Thomas Hutchinson, the leader of the oligarchy, was chief justice, lieutenant-governor, and as councillor, a member of the legislature. He was the particular target of the Boston Town Meeting.

That part of the instructions printed here outlines the ideas of the popular leaders on the subject of British policy. The instructions object to that policy on both economic and constitutional grounds. They propose in effect that the legislature deny that Parliament has any right to tax the colonies. Printed: *A Report of the Record Commissioners of the City of Boston, Containing the Boston Town Records, 1758 to 1769* (Boston, 1886), pp. 121–122.

You will join in any proposals that may be made for the better cultivating the lands and improving the husbandry of this province; and as you represent a town which lives by its trade, we expect in a very particular manner that you make it the object of your attention to support our commerce in all its just rights, to vindicate it from all unreasonable impositions and promote its prosperity. Our trade has for a long time laboured under great discouragements, and it is with the deepest concern that we see such further difficulties coming upon it as will reduce it to the lowest ebb, if not totally obstruct and ruin it. We cannot help expressing our surprise that when so early notice was given by the agent of the intention of the ministry to burden us with new taxes so little regard was had to this most interesting matter that the Court was not even called together to consult about it till the latter end of the year, the consequence of which was that instructions could not be sent to the agent, though solicited by him, till the evil had got beyond an easy remedy. There is now no room for further delay. We therefore expect that you will use your earliest endeavours in the General Assembly that such methods may be taken as will effectually prevent their proceedings against

[1] No. 115.

us. By a proper representation we apprehend it may easily be made to appear that such severities will prove detrimental to Great Britain itself, upon which account we have reason to hope that an application, even for a repeal of the Act, should it be already passed, will be successful. It is the trade of the colonies that render them beneficial to their mother country. Our trade as it is now, and always has been conducted, centres in Great Britain, and in return for her manufactures, affords her more ready cash, beyond any comparison that [than] can possibly be expected by the most sanguine promoters of these extraordinary methods. We are, in short, ultimately yielding large supplies to the revenues of the mother country while we are labouring for a very moderate subsistence for ourselves. But if our trade is to be curtailed in its most valuable branches, and burdens beyond possible bearings laid upon that which is suffered to remain, we shall so far be able to take off the manufactures of Great Britain that it will be scarce possible for us to earn our bread. But what still heightens our apprehensions is that those unexpected proceedings may be preparatory to new taxations upon us; for if our trade may be taxed, why not our lands? Why not the produce of our lands and everything we possess or make use of? This we apprehend annihilates our charter right to govern and tax ourselves. It strikes at our British privileges which, as we have never forfeited them, we hold in common with our fellow subjects who are natives of Britain. If taxes are laid upon us in any shape without ever having a legal representation where they are laid, are we not reduced from the character of free subjects to the miserable state of tributary slaves?

We therefore earnestly recommend it to you to use your utmost endeavours to obtain in the General Assembly all necessary instructions and advice to our agent at this most critical juncture, that while he is setting forth the unshaken loyalty of this province and this town–its unrivalled exertions in supporting his Majesty's government and rights in this part of his dominion–its acknowledged dependence upon and subordination to Great Britain, and the ready submission of its merchants to all just and necessary regulations of trade, he may be able in the most humble and pressing manner to remonstrate for us all those rights and privileges which justly belong to us either by charter or birth.

As his Majesty's other northern American colonies are embarked with us in this most important bottom, we further desire you to use your endeavours that their weight may be added to that of this province; that by the united applications of all who are aggrieved, all may happily obtain redress.

104. Petition from the Massachusetts Legislature to the House of Commons (3 November 1764)

In the spring of 1764 the Boston Town Meeting instructed its delegates in the provincial legislature to oppose the Revenue Act of 1764 on constitutional as well as on economic grounds, and they proposed that the legislature ask other colonial legislatures to co-operate with that of Massachusetts (No. 103). When the legislature met in the spring it refused to follow the lead of the Boston members. But near the end of the session, after many members had started home, the Boston members secured the appointment of a committee which sent a letter to the colonial agent in London, in which was asserted the right of the colonies to tax themselves.

Opposition grew during the summer as news of the proposed Stamp Act spread through the colony. Governor Bernard was persuaded to call a special session of the legislature in October 1764. The events of this session illuminate the internal conflict as to methods of opposition. The popular party, led by the Boston members, insisted that colonial opposition to the Revenue Act of 1764 and the proposed Stamp Act should be based on the idea of colonial 'rights' as proposed in the instructions of the Boston Town Meeting in May (No. 103). The conservatives, led by Thomas Hutchinson, objected to any protest based on 'rights' and insisted that a petition should be based only on the 'privileges' of the colonies. Furthermore, they insisted that any protest should be based on economic rather than on constitutional grounds. In this controversy the conservatives won out. The petition to the House of Commons is an elaborate statement of the economic difficulties created by the Revenue Act, the new Admiralty court, and the economic threat involved in the proposed Stamp Act. Printed: Alden Bradford, ed., *Speeches of the Governors of Massachusetts from 1765 to 1775; And the Answers of the House of Representatives* . . . (Boston, 1818), pp. 21–23.

The petition of the Council and House of Representatives of his Majesty's Province of Massachusetts Bay, Most humbly showeth:

That the Act passed in the last session of Parliament, entitled "An act for granting certain duties in the British colonies and plantations in America," etc., must necessarily bring many burdens upon the inhabitants of these colonies and plantations, which your petitioners conceive would not have been imposed if a full representation of the state of the colonies had been made to your honourable House.

That the duties laid upon foreign sugars and molasses by a former Act of Parliament entitled "an Act for the better securing and encouraging the trade of his Majesty's sugar colonies in America," if the Act had been executed with rigour, must have had the effect of an absolute prohibition.

That the duties laid on those articles by the present Act still remain so great that, however otherwise intended, they must undoubtedly have the same effect.

That the importation of foreign molasses into this province in particular is of the greatest importance, and a prohibition will be prejudicial to many branches of its trade and will lessen the consumption of the manufactures of Great Britain.

That this importance does not arise merely, nor principally, from the necessity of foreign molasses in order to its being consumed or distilled within the province.

That if the trade for many years carried on for foreign molasses can be no longer continued, a vent cannot be found for more than one half the fish of inferior quality which are caught and cured by the inhabitants of the province, the French not permitting fish to be carried by foreigners to any of their islands, unless it be bartered or exchanged for molasses.

That if there be no sale of fish of inferior quality it will be impossible to continue the fishery, the fish usually sent to Europe will then cost so dear that the French will be able to undersell the English at all the European markets; and by this means one of the most valuable returns to Great Britain will be utterly lost, and that great nursery of seamen destroyed.

That the restraints laid upon the exportation of timber, boards, staves, and other lumber from the colonies to Ireland and other parts of Europe, except Great Britain, must greatly affect the trade of this province and discourage the clearing and improving of the lands which are yet uncultivated.

That the powers given by the late Act to the court of vice-admiralty, instituted over all America, are so expressed as to leave it doubtful, whether goods seized for illicit importation in any one of the colonies may not be removed, in order to trial, to any other colony where the judge may reside, although at many hundred miles distance from the place of seizure.

That if this construction should be admitted, many persons, however legally their goods may have been imported, must lose their property, merely from an inability of following after it, and making that defence which they might do if the trial had been in the colony where the goods were seized.

That this construction would be so much the more grievous, seeing that in America the officers by this Act are indemnified in case of seizure whenever the judge of admiralty shall certify that there was probable cause; and the claimant can neither have costs nor maintain an action against the person seizing, how much soever he may have expended in defence of his property.

That the extension of the powers of courts of vice-admiralty has, so far as the jurisdiction of the said courts hath been extended, deprived the colonies of one of the most valuable of English liberties, trials by juries.

That every Act of Parliament, which in this respect distinguishes his Majesty's subjects in the colonies from their fellow subjects in Great Britain, must create a very sensible concern and grief.

That there have been communicated to your petitioners sundry resolutions of the House of Commons in their last session for imposing stamp duties or taxes upon the inhabitants of the colonies, the consideration whereof was referred to the next session.

That your petitioners acknowledge with all gratitude the tendencies [tenderness] of the legislature of Great Britain of the liberties of the subjects in the colonies, who have always judged by their representatives both of the way and manner in which internal taxes should be raised within their respective governments, and of the ability of the inhabitants to pay them.

That they humbly hope the colonies in general have so demeaned themselves, more especially during the late war, as still to deserve the continuance of all those liberties which they have hitherto enjoyed.

That although during the war the taxes upon the colonies were greater than they have been since the conclusion of it, yet the sources by which the inhabitants were enabled to pay their taxes having ceased, and their trade being decayed, they are not so able to pay the taxes they are subjected to in time of peace as they were the greater taxes in time of war.

That one principal difficulty which has ever attended the trade of the colonies, proceeds from the scarcity of money, which scarcity is caused by the balance of trade with Great Britain, which has been continually against the colonies.

That the drawing sums of money from the colonies from time to time must distress the trade to that degree that eventually Great Britain may lose more by the diminution of the consumption of her manufactures than all the sums which it is possible for the colonies thus to pay can countervail.

That they humbly conceive if the taxes which the inhabitants of this province are obliged annually to pay towards the support of the internal government, the restraint they are under in their trade for the benefit of Great Britain, and the consumption thereby occasioned of British manufactures, be all considered and have their due weight, it must appear that the subjects of this province are as fully burdened as their fellow subjects in Britain, and that they are, whilst in America, more beneficial to the nation than they would be if they should be removed to Britain and there held to a full proportion of the national taxes and duties of every kind.

Your petitioners, therefore, most humbly pray that they may be relieved from the burdens which, they have humbly represented to have been brought upon them by the late Act of Parliament, as to the wisdom of the honourable House shall seem meet, that the privileges of the colonies relative to their internal taxes which they have so long enjoyed, may still be continued to them, or that the consideration of such taxes on the colonies may be referred, until your petitioners, in conjunction with the other governments, can have opportunity to make a more full representation of the state and condition of the colonies and the interest of Great Britain with regard to them.

105. Petition of the Virginia House of Burgesses to the House of Commons (18 December 1764)

In the northern colonies the aggressive leaders against British policy worked through the local governments and particularly the Boston Town Meeting. In the southern colonies such leadership came from within the colonial legislatures, and particularly the Virginia House of Burgesses. By 1763 the Virginians had behind them a long tradition of self-government and a well-established pattern for the formulation of their ideas concerning their constitutional position within the Empire. After 1763 both conservative and popular leaders were ready and willing to state their position with forthright vigour. While various colonial legislatures protested against the Revenue Act of 1764 and the proposed Stamp Act, it was the Virginia legislature which took the leadership that it was to maintain until the Declaration of Independence. In December 1764 the House of Burgesses prepared three petitions. They asked the king to protect them in their right to taxation only by their own consent. They declared to the House of Lords that a fundamental principle of the British constitution was that a people could be taxed only by their own consent. They pointed to the distress caused by the heavy debt left by the war, the low price of tobacco, and the entire lack of specie in the colony, and declared that the late restrictions on trade were causing even further distress. The petition to the House of Commons objected to the proposed Stamp Act and elaborated upon the Virginians' conception of their rights as colonists and as Englishmen. Printed: *Journals of the House of Burgesses, 1761–1765*, pp. 303–304.

To the Honourable the Knights, Citizens, and Burgesses of Great Britain in Parliament assembled:

The Remonstrance of the Council and Burgesses of Virginia.

It appearing by the printed votes of the House of Commons of Great Britain in Parliament assembled that in a committee of the whole House, the 17th day of March last, it was resolved that towards defending, protecting, and securing the British colonies and plantations in America, it may be proper to charge certain stamp duties in the said colonies and plantations; and it being apprehended that the same subject, which was then declined, may be resumed and further pursued in a succeeding session, the Council and Burgesses of Virginia, met in General Assembly, judge it their indispensable duty, in a respectful manner but with decent firmness, to remonstrate against such a measure, that at least a cession of those rights, which in their opinion must be infringed by that procedure, may not be inferred from their silence, at so important a crisis.

They conceive it is essential to British liberty that laws imposing taxes on the people ought not to be made without the consent of representatives chosen by themselves; who, at the same time that they are acquainted with the circumstances of their constituents, sustain a proportion of the burden laid on them. This privilege, inherent in the persons who discovered and settled these regions, could not be renounced or forfeited by their removal hither, not as vagabonds or fugitives, but licensed and encouraged by their prince and animated with a laudable desire of enlarging the British dominion, and extending its commerce. On the contrary, it was secured to them and their descendants, with all other rights and immunities of British subjects, by a royal charter, which hath been invariably recognized and confirmed by his Majesty and his predecessors in their commissions to the several governors, granting a power, and prescribing a form of legislation; according to which, laws for the administration of justice, and for the welfare and good government of the colony, have been hitherto enacted by the Governor, Council, and General Assembly, and to them requisitions and applications for supplies have been directed by the Crown. As an instance of the opinion which former sovereigns entertained of these rights and privileges, we beg leave to refer to three acts of the General Assembly passed in the 32^d year of the reign of King Charles II (one of which is entitled An Act for raising a Public Revenue for the better Support of the Government of his Majesty's Colony of Virginia, imposing several duties for that purpose) which they thought absolutely necessary, were prepared in England, and sent over by their then governor, the Lord Culpepper, to be passed by the General Assembly, with a full power to give the royal assent thereto; and which were accordingly passed, after several amendments were made to them here. Thus tender was his Majesty of the rights of his American subjects; and the remonstrants do not discern by what distinction they can be deprived of that sacred birthright and most valuable inheritance by their fellow subjects, nor with what propriety they can be taxed or affected in their estates by the Parliament, wherein they are not, and indeed cannot, constitutionally be represented.

And if it were proper for the Parliament to impose taxes on the colonies at all, which the remonstrants take leave to think would be inconsistent with the fundamental principles of the constitution, the exercise of that power at this time would be ruinous to Virginia, who exerted herself in the late war, it is feared, beyond her strength, insomuch that to redeem the money granted for that exigence her people are taxed for several years to come; this with the large expenses incurred for defending the frontiers against the restless Indians, who have infested her as much since the peace as before, is so grievous that an increase of the burden will be intolerable; especially as the people are very greatly distressed already from the scarcity of circulating cash amongst them, and from the little value of their staple at the British markets.

And it is presumed that adding to that load which the colony now labours under will not be more oppressive to her people than destructive of the interests of Great Britain; for the plantation trade, confined as it is to the mother country, hath been a principal means of multiplying and enriching her inhabitants; and if not too much discouraged, may prove an inexhaustible source of treasure to the nation. For satisfaction in this point, let the present state of the British fleets and trade be compared with what they were before the settlement of the colonies; and let it be considered that whilst property in land may be acquired on very easy terms, in the vast un-cultivated territory of North America, the colonists will be mostly, if not wholly, employed in agriculture; whereby the exportation of their commodities of Great Britain, and the consumption of their manufactures supplied from thence, will be daily increasing. But this most desirable connection between Great Britain and her colonies, supported by such a happy intercourse of reciprocal benefits as is continually advancing the prosperity of both, must be interrupted, if the people of the latter, reduced to extreme poverty, should be compelled to manufacture those articles they have been hitherto furnished with from the former.

From these considerations it is hoped that the honourable House of Commons will not prosecute a measure which those who may suffer under it cannot but look upon as fitter for exiles driven from their native country, after ignominiously forfeit-ing her favours and protection, than for the prosperity of Britons who have at all times been forward to demonstrate all due reverence to the mother kingdom, and are so instrumental in promoting her glory and felicity; and that British patriots will never consent to the exercise of anticonstitutional power, which even in this remote corner may be dangerous in its example to the interior parts of the British Empire, and will certainly be detrimental to its commerce.

106. The Virginia Stamp Act resolutions (30 May 1765)

The Virginia resolves, proposed by Patrick Henry, were the most extreme statement from a colonial legislature in opposition to the Stamp Act after its passage. The first four resolutions were adopted by the House but the remaining three were rejected as being too radical. Nevertheless, all the resolves soon appeared in many of the colonial newspapers and furnished a platform for popular opposition everywhere. Printed: *Journals of the House of Burgesses, 1761-1765*, pp. lxvi-lxvii, 360.

Whereas, the honourable House of Commons in England, have of late draw[n] into question how far the General Assembly of this colony hath power to enact laws for laying of taxes and imposing duties payable by the people of this, his Majesty's most ancient colony; for settling and ascertaining the same to all future times, the House of Burgesses of this present General Assembly have come to the following resolves.

Resolved, that the first adventurers, settlers of this his Majesty's colony and dominion of Virginia, brought with them and transmitted to their posterity, and all other his Majesty's subjects since inhabiting in this his Majesty's colony, all the privileges and immunities that have at any time been held, enjoyed, and possessed by the people of Great Britain.

Resolved, that by two royal charters granted by King James the first, the colonists aforesaid are declared and entitled to all privileges and immunities of natural born subjects, to all intents and purposes as if they had been abiding and born within the realm of England.

Resolved, that the taxation of the people by themselves, or by persons chosen by themselves to represent them, who can only know what taxes the people are able to bear, or the easiest method of raising them, and must themselves be affected by every tax laid on the people, is the only security against a burdensome taxation, and the distinguishing characteristic of British freedom, without which the ancient constitution cannot exist.

Resolved, that his Majesty's liege people of this ancient colony have enjoyed the right of being thus governed by their own Assembly in the article of taxes and internal police, and that the same have never been forfeited, or any other way yielded up, but have been constantly recognized by the king and people of Great Britain.

Resolved, therefore, that the General Assembly of this colony, together with his Majesty or his substitutes, have in their representatives capacity, the only exclusive right and power to lay taxes and imposts upon the inhabitants of this colony; and that every attempt to vest such power in any other person or persons whatever than the General Assembly aforesaid, is illegal, unconstitutional, and unjust, and has a manifest tendency to destroy British as well as American liberty.

Resolved, that his Majesty's liege people, the inhabitants of this colony, are not bound to yield obedience to any law or ordinance whatever, designed to impose any taxation whatsoever upon them, other than the laws or ordinances of the General Assembly aforesaid.

Resolved, that any person who shall, by speaking or writing, assert or maintain that any person or persons other than the General Assembly of this colony, have any right or power to impose or lay any taxation on the people here, shall be deemed an enemy to his Majesty's colony.

107. New London, Connecticut resolutions on the Stamp Act (10 December 1765)

Among the many resolutions adopted by town meetings in New England in 1765, none were more striking than those of New London, Connecticut. Not only do they contain a clear threat of independence, but they base government entirely on the consent of the people and thus foreshadow the Declaration of Independence. Such resolutions indicate that local governments were far in advance of most colonial legislatures in their willingness to take a strong stand in opposition to British policies. Printed: *The Massachusetts Gazette*, 19 December 1765.

At a meeting of a large assembly of the respectable populace in New London the 10th of December 1765, the following resolves were unanimously come into. Resolved, 1st. That every form of government rightfully founded, originates from the consent of the people.

2d. That the boundaries set by the people in all constitutions are the only limits within which any officer can lawfully exercise authority.

3d. That whenever those bounds are exceeded, the people have a right to reassume the exercise of that authority which by nature they had before they delegated it to individuals.

4th. That every tax imposed upon English subjects without consent is against the natural rights and the bounds prescribed by the English constitution.

5th. That the Stamp Act in special, is a tax imposed on the colonies without their consent.

6th. That it is the duty of every person in the colonies to oppose by every lawful means the execution of those acts imposed on them, and if they can in no other way be relieved, to reassume their natural rights and the authority the laws of nature and of God have vested them with.

And in order effectually to prevent the execution thereof, it is recommended:

1st. That every officer in this colony duly execute the trust reposed in him, agreeable to the true spirit of the English constitution and the laws of this colony.

2d. That every officer neglecting the exercise of his office may justly expect the resentment of the people, and those who proceed may depend on their protection.

3d. It is presumed no person will publicly, in the pulpit or otherwise, inculcate the doctrine of passive obedience, or any other doctrine tending to quiet the minds of the people, in a tame submission to any unjust impositions.

4th. We fully concur with the respectable body of the populace in all their Resolves made at Windham the 26th November 1765 and published in the *New-London Gazette*.

108. Non-importation agreement of New York merchants (31 October 1765)

During 1765 merchants in many of the northern towns adopted agreements to stop importation of most British goods until the Stamp Act was repealed. The first such agreement was that of New York which is printed here. It was also adopted by the merchants of Albany. The Philadelphia merchants adopted an agreement in November and the Boston merchants in December. The latter agreement was copied by the merchants of other Massachusetts towns, including Salem and Marblehead. Such agreements, and letters from American merchants to their English correspondents, did much to reinforce the determination of English merchants to bring about general commercial reform as well as the repeal of the Stamp Act. Printed: *New York Mercury*, 7 November 1765.

At a general meeting of the merchants of the city of New York, trading to Great Britain, at the house of Mr. George Burns, of the said city, innholder, to consider what was necessary to be done in the present situation of affairs with respect to the Stamp Act, and the melancholy state of the North American commerce, so greatly restricted by the impositions and duties established by the late acts of trade, they came to the following resolutions, viz.

First. That in all orders they send out to Great Britain for goods or merchandise of any nature, kind, or quality whatsoever, usually imported from Great Britain, they will direct their correspondents not to ship them unless the Stamp Act be repealed. It is nevertheless agreed that all such merchants as are owners of and have vessels already gone, and now cleared out for Great Britain, shall be at liberty to bring back in them, on their own accounts, crates and casks of earthen ware, grind-stones, pipes, and such other bulky articles as owners usually fill up their vessels with.

Secondly. It is further unanimously agreed that all orders already sent home, shall be countermanded by the very first conveyance; and the goods and merchandise thereby ordered, not to be sent unless upon the condition mentioned in the foregoing resolution.

Thirdly. It is further unanimously agreed that no merchant will vend any goods or merchandise sent upon commission from Great Britain that shall be shipped from thence after the first day of January next, unless upon the condition mentioned in the first resolution.

Fourthly. It is further unanimously agreed that the foregoing resolutions shall be binding until the same are abrogated at a general meeting hereafter to be held for that purpose.

In witness whereof we have hereunto respectively subscribed our names.

[This was subscribed by upwards of two hundred principal merchants.]

In consequence of the foregoing resolutions the retailers of goods of the city of New York subscribed a paper in the words following, viz.

We, the underwritten, retailers of goods, do hereby promise and oblige ourselves not to buy any goods, wares, or merchandises of any person or persons whatsoever that shall be shipped from Great Britain after the first day of January next unless the Stamp Act shall be repealed–as witness our hands.

109. The Declarations of the Stamp Act Congress (19 October 1765)

The meeting of the Stamp Act Congress in New York in October 1765 was the culmination of the development of formal opposition to the Stamp Act in the colonies. In June 1765, the Massachusetts legislature invited the other colonial legislatures to send delegates to a congress to meet in New York. On 7 October twenty-seven men from nine of the colonies met in New York. New Hampshire, Virginia, North Carolina, and Georgia did not send delegates. After considerable debate, of which they kept no record, they adopted "The Declarations" which follow. In addition they prepared petitions to the king, the House of Lords, and the House of Commons. The congress adjourned on 24 October.

The members of the Stamp Act Congress were far more conservative in their statements than members of colonial legislatures had been. Even so some of its members refused to sign the documents it produced. Despite the relative mildness of the petitions, Parliament refused to receive them. Printed: Hezekiah Niles, *Principles and Acts of the Revolution in America* (New York, 1876), p. 163. The documents of the Stamp Act Congress have also been reprinted in *Old South Leaflets*, No. 223 (Boston, 1948).

The members of this congress, sincerely devoted, with the warmest sentiments of affection and duty to his Majesty's person and government; inviolably attached to the present happy establishment of the Protestant succession, and with minds deeply impressed by a sense of the present and impending misfortunes of the British colonies on this continent; having considered as maturely as time would permit, the circumstances of the said colonies, esteem it our indispensable duty to make the following declarations, of our humble opinion, respecting the most essential rights and liberties of the colonists, and of the grievances under which they labour, by reason of several late acts of Parliament.

I. That his Majesty's subjects in these colonies, owe the same allegiance to the Crown of Great Britain, that is owing from his subjects born within the realm, and all due subordination to that august body, the Parliament of Great Britain.

II. That his Majesty's liege subjects in these colonies are entitled to all the inherent rights and liberties of his natural born subjects within the kingdom of Great Britain.

III. That it is inseparably essential to the freedom of a people, and the undoubted right of Englishmen, that no taxes should be imposed on them, but with their own consent, given personally, or by their representatives.

IV. That the people of these colonies are not, and from their local circumstances, cannot be represented in the House of Commons in Great Britain.

V. That the only representatives of the people of these colonies, are persons chosen therein, by themselves; and that no taxes ever have been, or can be constitutionally imposed on them, but by their respective legislature.

VI. That all supplies to the Crown, being free gifts of the people, it is unreasonable and inconsistent with the principles and spirit of the British constitution, for the people of Great Britain to grant to his Majesty the property of the colonists.

VII. That trial by jury is the inherent and invaluable right of every British subject in these colonies.

VIII. That the late Act of Parliament, entitled, An Act for granting and applying certain Stamp Duties, and other Duties in the British Colonies and Plantations in America, etc., by imposing taxes on the inhabitants of these colonies, and the said Act, and several other Acts, by extending the jurisdiction of the courts of admiralty beyond its ancient limits, have a manifest tendency to subvert the rights and liberties of the colonists.

IX. That the duties imposed by several late Acts of Parliament, from the peculiar circumstances of these colonies, will be extremely burdensome and grievous, and from the scarcity of specie, the payment of them absolutely impracticable.

X. That as the profits of the trade of these colonies ultimately centre in Great Britain, to pay for the manufactures which they are obliged to take from thence, they eventually contribute very largely to all supplies granted there to the Crown.

XI. That the restrictions imposed by several late Acts of Parliament, on the trade of these colonies, will render them unable to purchase the manufactures of Great Britain.

XII. That the increase, prosperity and happiness of these colonies, depend on the full and free enjoyment of their rights and liberties, and an intercourse with Great Britain, mutually affectionate and advantageous.

XIII. That it is the right of the British subjects in these colonies, to petition the king or either house of Parliament.

Lastly, that it is the indispensable duty of these colonies to the best of sovereigns, to the mother country, and to themselves, to endeavour by a loyal and dutiful address to his Majesty, and humble applications to both houses of Parliament, to procure the repeal of the Act for granting and applying certain stamp duties, of all clauses of any other Acts of Parliament, whereby the jurisdiction of the admiralty is extended as aforesaid, and of the other late Acts for the restriction of American commerce.

110A–D. Accounts of popular opposition to the Stamp Act (1765)

While town meetings and legislatures were passing resolutions and merchants were adopting non-importation agreements, a popular upheaval took place in every colony. Before 1 November 1765 every stamp agent appointed for the thirteen mainland colonies had been forced to resign by threats of mob violence. It is clear that many of the gentry encouraged this violence in order to prevent the law from going into effect. It is also evident that the mob got out of hand in many places. Thus in Boston it destroyed the house of Thomas Hutchinson, the chief political enemy of the popular leaders of the town. Most of the accounts of violence came from men who supported the Stamp Act, or who at least believed it should be acquiesced in until repealed. Naturally, the leaders who encouraged popular opposition did not admit their part in it. Where action was taken, the violence was deplored only in official terms. Thus a special town meeting was called in Boston the day after Hutchinson's house was destroyed. The meeting voted "utter detestation of the extraordinary and violent proceedings of a number of persons unknown" on the previous night. Hutchinson's comment on this was that some of the loudest mourners in the town meeting were the very people who had attacked his house.

The accounts which follow are by William Almy of Newport, Rhode Island, Governor Francis Bernard of Massachusetts, Lieutenant-Governor William Bull of South Carolina, and Lieutenant-Governor Cadwallader Colden of New York.

110A. William Almy to Elisha Story (29 August 1765)

Printed: Massachusetts Historical Society *Proceedings*, LV, pp. 235-237.

In my last I promised to give you the particulars of our transactions here concerning the stamp affair, which I now shall endeavour to do. In the first place I'll just inform you concerning Mr. Martin Howard Jr. and Doctor Moffatt, who was hung in effigy with the Stamp Master. Mr. Howard and the doctor, you must know, have made themselves very busy with their pen (by all accounts) in writing against the colonies and in favour of the Stamp Act, etc.

In the morning of the 27 instant between five and six a mob assembled and erected a gallows near the Town House and then dispersed, and about ten o'clock reassembled and took the effigies of the above men and the Stamp Master and carted them up Thames Street, then up King Street to the said gallows where they was hung up by the neck and suspended near 15 feet in the air; and on the breast of the Stamp Master was this inscription, THE STAMP MAN, and holding in his right hand the Stamp Act. And upon the breast of the Doctor was wrote: THAT INFAMOUS, MISCREATED, LEERING JACOBITE DOCTOR MURFY. In his right hand was a folded letter with this direction: To that Mawgazeene of Knowledge Doct'r Muffy in Rhode Island; and on the same arm was wrote: If I had but rec'd this Letter from the Earl of Bute But One Week sooner. And upon a strip of paper hanging out of his mouth was wrote: It is too late Martinius to Retract, for we are all Aground.

And upon Mr. Howard's breast was wrote: THAT FAWNING, INSIDIOUS, INFAMOUS MISCREANT AND PARACIDE MARTINIUS SCRIBLERIUS; and upon his right arm was wrote: THE ONLY FILIAL PEN. Upon his left arm was wrote: CURS'D AMBITION AND YOUR CURSED CLAN HAS RUIN'D ME and upon the same arm a little below was this: WHAT THO' I BOAST OF INDEPENDENCE POSTERITY WILL CURSE MY MEMORY. And upon one of the posts of the gallows was wrote: We have an Heriditary Indefeasible Right to a Halter, Besides we Encourag'd the Growth of Hemp you know. And underneath that was a new song (made upon the occasion) which I have here enclosed. And upon the other post was wrote: That Person who shall Efface this Publick Mark of Resentment will be Deem'd an Enemy to liberty and Accordingly meet with Proper Chastisement. And about five o'clock in the afternoon they made a fire under the gallows which consumed the effigies, gallows and all, to ashes. I forgot to tell you that a boot hung over the doctor's shoulder with the devil peeping out of it, etc. I've enclosed you a piece that was stuck up in the Town House at the same time. And after the effigies were burnt the mob dispersed and we thought it was all over. But last night about dusk they all mustered again, and first they went to Martin Howard's and broke every window in his house, frames and all; likewise chairs, tables, pictures, and everything they could come across. They also sawed down two trees which stood before his door and brought them and stuck them up in two great guns which have been fixed at the bottom of the Parade some years as posts. When they found they had entirely demolished all his furniture and done what damage they could, they left his house and proceeded to Dr. Moffatts where they behaved much in the same manner. I can't say which came off the worst for all the furniture of both houses

were entirely destroyed; petitions [partitions] of the houses broke down, fences
levelled with the ground, and all the liquors which were in both houses were entirely
lost. Dear Doctor, this moment I've received a piece of news which effects me so
much that I can't write any more, which is the demolition of your worthy daddy's
house and furniture, etc. But I must just let you know that the Stamp Master has
resigned; the copy of his resignation and oath I now send you. I hope, my friend,
you'll send me the particulars of your daddy's misfortune.
[address] To Doctor Elisha Story, Boston

A NEW SONG

He who for a Post or Base sordid Pelf
His Country Betrays, Makes a Rope for himself.
Of this an Example, Before you we Bring
In these Infamous Rogues, Who in Effigy Swing.

Huzza my Brave Boys, Ev'ry man Stand his Ground
With Liberty's Praise, Let the Welkin Resound
Eternal Disgrace On those Miscreants Fall
Who Through Pride or for Wealth, Wou'd Ruin us All.

Let us Make wise Resolves and to them stand strong
Your Puffs and your Vapours will Ne'er last Long
To Ma[i]ntain Our Just Rights, Every Measure Pursue
To Our King we'll be Loyal, To Ourselves we'll be True.

Those Blessings Our Fathers, Obtain'd by their Blood
We are Justly Oblig'd to Our Sons to make Good
All internal Taxes let us then Nobly spurn
These Effigy's First, The Next The Stamp Papers Burn.

Chorus

Sing Tantarara, Burn All, Burn All
Sing Tantarara, Burn All.

110B. Governor Francis Bernard to the earl of Halifax (31 August 1765)

From: British Public Record Office, C.O. 5/755.

It is with the utmost concern that I am obliged to continue the subject of my last
letters of the 15th and 16th and of the 22nd instant; the disorders of the town
having been carried to much greater lengths than what I have before informed
your lordship of.

After the demolition of Mr. Oliver's house was found so practicable and easy
that the government was obliged to look on without being able to take any one step

to prevent it, and the principal people of the town publicly avowed and justified the act; the mob, both great and small, became highly elated, and all kinds of ill humours were set on float. Everything that for years past had been the cause of any popular discontent was revived and private resentments against persons in office worked themselves in and endeavoured to execute themselves under the mask of the public cause. Among others the affairs of the attack upon the Admiralty and Custom House above four years ago (which after a contestation of a year, by the steadiness and resolution of myself, I may truly say, and the other officers of the Crown, ended entirely in conclusions on the side of the Crown) was brought up again and became as fresh as if it had been a business of yesterday. One B—— H—— of this town, who was in London about two years ago, had got a sight of the depositions which were sent home on the behalf of the Crown. Upon his return to Boston he took upon him to report the substance of these with additions of his own, and concluded with an assertion that the whole body of merchants had been represented as smugglers. This occasioned some murmuring at that time but it soon passed over. All this story has been now revived with fresh circumstances of acrimony and inflammation, and a diligent pointing out the persons who in the former contest had acted on the side of the Crown, and H——, instead of telling his story verbally, reduced it into writing, which was handed about the town. This occasioned much clamour among some of the merchants, who were told, without the least foundation in truth, that they were represented at home by name; and the clamour, as usual, soon descended from the top to the bottom of the town, and several persons' houses began to be threatened. This was truly the principal if not the sole cause of the second insurrection, which has had such shocking effects.

On Monday, August 26 there was some small rumour that mischief would be done that night, but it was in general disregarded. Towards evening some boys began to light a bonfire before the Town House, which is an usual signal for a mob. Before it was quite dark a great company of people gathered together crying liberty and property, which is the usual notice of their intention to plunder and pull down an house. They first went to Mr. Paxton's house (who is marshal of the Court of Admiralty and surveyor of the port); and finding before it the owner of the house (Mr. Paxton being only a tenant), he assured them that Mr. Paxton had quitted the house with his best effects; that the house was his; that he had never injured them; and finally invited them to go to the tavern and drink a barrel of punch. The offer was accepted and so that house was saved. As soon as they had drinked the punch, they went to the house of Mr. Story, registrar deputed of the Admiralty, broke into it and tore it all to pieces; and took out all the books and papers, among which were all the records of the Court of Admiralty, and carried them to the bonfire and there burnt them. They also looked about for him with an intention to kill him. From thence they went to Mr. Hallowell's, comptroller of the customs, broke into his house and destroyed and carried off everything of value, with about 30 pounds sterling in cash. This house was lately built by himself and fitted and furnished with great elegance. But the grand mischief of all was to come.

The lieutenant-governor had been apprised that there was an evil spirit gone forth against him, but being conscious that he had not in the least deserved to be made a party in regard to the Stamp Act or the Custom House, he rested in full security that the mob would not attack him, and he was at supper with his family when he received advice that the mob were coming to him. He immediately sent away his children and determined to stay in the house himself, but happily his eldest daughter returned and declared she would not stir from the house unless he went with her; by which means she got him away, which was undoubtedly the occasion of saving his life. For as soon as the mob had got into the house, with a most irresistible fury they immediately looked about for him to murder him, and even made diligent enquiry whither he was gone. They went to work with a rage scarce to be exemplified by the most savage people. Everything moveable was destroyed in the most minute manner except such things of value as were worth carrying off, among which was near 1000 pounds sterling in specie, besides a great quantity of family plate, etc. But the loss to be most lamented is that there was in one room kept for that purpose a large and valuable collection of manuscripts and original papers which he had been gathering all his lifetime, and to which all persons who had been in possession of valuable papers of a public kind had been contributing as to a public museum. As these related to the history and policy of the country from the time of its settlement to the present and was the only collection of its kind, the loss to the public is great and irretrievable as it is to himself, the loss of the papers of a family which had made a figure in this province for 130 years. As for the house, which from its structure and inside finishing seemed to be from a design of Inigo Jones or his successor, it appears that they were a long while resolved to level it to the ground. They worked for 3 hours at the cupola before they could get it down, and they uncovered part of the roof; but I suppose that the thickness of the walls which were of very fine brickwork, adorned with Ionic pilasters worked into the wall, prevented their completing their purpose though they worked at it till daylight. The next day the streets were found scattered with money, plate, gold rings, etc., which had been dropped in carrying off. The whole loss in this house only is reckoned at 3,000 pounds sterling.

As soon as I received advice of this at the Castle, I immediately sent an order to the secretary to summon a Council at Cambridge early in the afternoon, not thinking Boston a safe place to sit at. As I was going thither, on the road I received a letter from the secretary desiring that I would hold the Council in Boston; for that this affair had given such a turn to the town that all the gentlemen in the place were ready to support the government in detecting and punishing the actors in the last horrid scene, and there was a town meeting appointed to testify their abhorrence of it. I accordingly went to the Council and there issued orders to the colonel of the regiment of militia, the captain of the company of cadet guards; the captains of the batteries and of the companies of militia in Charles Town, Cambridge, and Roxbury, to raise their several corps and make detachments therefrom to keep a constant guard; and I recommended to the gentlemen of the town who were excused from military duty to enroll themselves as volunteers in some of the corps, many of which did, especially in the cadets, which were doubled upon this occasion; to whom I assigned the guard of the Custom House where there were several thousand pounds of the king's money. And these measures were but just taken in time for otherwise a much greater mischief would have happened the second night than the former. For, it seems, the mob had set down no less than 15 houses in or near the town to be attacked the next night, among which was the Custom House and the houses of some of the most respectable persons in the government. It was now becoming a war of plunder, of general levelling and taking away the distinction of rich and poor so that those gentlemen who had promoted and approved the cruel treatment of Mr. Oliver became now as fearful for themselves as the most loyal person in the town could be. They found, as I told some of them, that they had raised the devil and could not lay him again. However, by means of the military guards the town was kept quiet that night without anything happening except that the cadets were obliged once to present their pieces, but did not fire.

After I had established these guards, which took up all that day, I considered whether it would not be proper to call in assistance from without. By an instruction, I am directed to have the advice of Council whenever I call for military aid. I knew that the Council would never advise me to call in the king's troops in cases more desperate than this. Their own situation and dependence would make them afraid of being answerable to the people for so disagreeable a step. I therefore put the question whether it was expedient to advertise General Gage and Lord Colville of what had happened at Boston. But they advised in the negative, saying that such advertisement would amount to a tacit request for forces; and though they expected such forces would be ordered hither some time or other, they would not help to bring them here nor hasten them before their time. I therefore transmitted to General Gage a copy of this resolution of Council, copies of my proclamations, with advice of the intention of lodging the stamps in the Castle, and augmenting the garrison for that purpose; from all which he will see the restraints I am under. I then acquainted the Council with the various reports I had heard of the Castle being threatened if the stamps were put in there, represented the present state of the garrison, and proposed that an independent company should be raised for augmenting the garrison, which they readily came into, and I immediately dispatched orders for that purpose. I am also by all means in my power strengthening the Castle so that if I can get the reinforcement here in time, I shan't be afraid for the Castle against any number, though I cannot think that any people will be desperate enough to attack it, notwithstanding what has been given out.

When first the town took this new turn, I was in hopes that they would have disavowed all the riotous proceedings, that of the first night as well as the last. But it is no such thing: great pains are taken to separate the two riots; what was done against Mr. Oliver is still approved of as a necessary declaration of their resolution not to submit to the Stamp Act; and even the cruel treatment of him and his family is justified by its consequences – the frightening him into a resignation; and it has been publicly hinted that if a line is not drawn between the first riot and the last, the civil power will not be supported by the principal people of the town, as it is assured it shall be now. And indeed, if the last riot had been the only one, the civil government would appear to be in full power. Many people concerned in the last riot are daily taken up and committed to gaol, where a constant guard is kept by the militia, and the town cries aloud for some of them to be made examples of. And yet if one was to offer to take one of the persons concerned in the first riot only, things would again be flung into confusion and the civil power would become as weak as ever. So that the present authority of the government is only exercised upon condition and with prescribed limitations.

It seems therefore that the horror of this last affair has not at all abated the spirit of the people against the Stamp Act. I am again and again assured that this town and country about it (how far deep I can't say) are as resolute as ever to oppose the execution of the Stamp Act and to suffer the utmost extremities rather than submit to it. There are but two things which are like to produce a change in these resolutions: the one is a nearer and fuller prospect of the anarchy and confusion which must take place when the courts of justice and public offices are shut up, as they must be on the first of November, unless stamps are allowed to be used. These must necessarily alarm all serious people and especially those who have much property. The other is the meeting of the Assembly, which I believe I shall be obliged to call at the time it is prorogued to, the 25th of September, though I could have wished that it might have been postponed till I could have received orders from England. I should have much dependence upon the prudence of the Assembly in common cases, but I know not how to expect that they will act against the voice of the people, if it is such as I am told it is. On the other hand, they must be greatly staggered when they are called upon to assist the execution of an Act of Parliament which is opposed by violence. Hitherto the opposition is chargeable upon private persons only; it will then be adopted by the legislature, and if that should fail in so important a duty, they must expect that a forfeiture of their rights will be the consequence. If these two causes, the apprehension of confusion when all business shall cease, and the prudence, or what is the same, the fear of the Assembly, should cooperate together, it is possible that the Act may be yet carried into execution at its day. I shall watch every opportunity and improve every incident to produce so happy an event.

I labour under many difficulties, and none more than that the Council, which I have to advise with, is composed almost wholly of gentlemen whose connections and properties are in Boston. They that live out of Boston will not come in; I have had but 2 or 3 such since the last riot and I have known some that have been afraid to come to Boston. By these means nothing can pass the Council that is like to be displeasing to Boston; expedients are thereby rendered very few and spirited measures are quite impracticable. I submitted to the Council whether it would not be best to call the Assembly at a distance from Boston, that it might sit free from intimidation or undue influence: it passed in the negative. I then asked if I should call a general Council by summoning every member to meet at Cambridge, and I urged that several members, naming them, objected to coming to Boston: it passed in the negative. I then proposed calling such general Council at Boston, which was approved of, and it is appointed for Thursday next, September 5. It is true that I can without advice of Council call the Assembly and the Council to what place I please, but it is the business of the Council, among other things, to guard the Governor against popular odium from his taking unpopular measures necessary to government by concurring with him and advising such measures; and when they refuse so to do, it would be dangerous as well as impolitic for the Governor to expose himself solely to the resentment of the people by acting without or contrary to the advice of Council. I must however add that it is become now much safer to meet at Boston than it was a week ago. The town is now become as quiet as ever it was, and the principal gentlemen have desired me, who have of late slept in the Castle, although I have been in town almost every day, and sometimes all day long, to live more at the Province House, assuring me that I shall have a guard of what number of gentlemen I please; and I shall go to the Province House on Monday and stay there some days, to show that I don't keep out of the town for fear of it. There will therefore remain only the objection to the Assembly's meeting at Boston upon account of undue influence, which I own has considerable weight with me; though perhaps it may not have so much weight with the Council, by whom I must be determined concerning the sitting of the Assembly.

P.S.—I have taken the liberty to use only initial letters in one name as the person is of no significance and has a brother who is a very faithful officer of the king. . . .

110C. Lieutenant-Governor William Bull to the Board of Trade (3 November 1765)

From: British Public Record Office, C.O. 5/378.

I think it my duty to acquaint your lordships with some very extraordinary and universal commotions which have happened in this town[1] upon the arrival of the stamp papers.

Accounts had been received from Boston of the outrages committed there on the 14th and 26th of August last, and also of those at Rhode Island, to show their determined resolutions to prevent or elude the execution of the Stamp Act in those provinces, and also of the intentions which other provinces at the northward had expressed to the like purpose, though not with so much violence, all which have undoubtedly been transmitted to your lordships and I now presume to mention them only as the unhappy cause of what has happened here.

New England vaunts its numbers and arrogates glory to itself in taking the lead of North America. For before those accounts came, the people of this province, though they conceived it too great a burden, seemed generally disposed to pay a due obedience to the Act, and at the same time in a dutiful and respectful manner to represent to his Majesty the hardships which it would lay them under, and to pray relief therein. I must do them the justice to add that in all other respects the king has no subjects that express and show more loyalty to his majesty than the people of this province.

But by the artifices of some busy spirits the minds of men here were so universally poisoned with the principles which were imbibed and propagated from Boston and Rhode Island (from which towns, at this time of the year vessels very frequently arrive) that after their example, the people of this town resolved to seize and destroy

[1] Charleston, South Carolina.

the stamp papers, and to take every means of deterring the stamp officers from executing their duty.

Upon the arrival of the stamp papers on the 20th ultimo a great concourse of men assembled. Application was thereupon made to me for protection of the papers. As the intention of the populace were too well known to be doubted, I thought it my duty to secure them from destruction or even insult and therefore requested Capt. Fanshawe of his Majesty's sloop *Speedwell* to receive them on board until it should be necessary to remove them on shore for the execution of the Act. His ship was then heaving down at Hobcaw to career and he thought it not safe to have them on board as he lay at a wharf; I then desired he would send his boats armed to take the packages of stamp papers out of the ship which brought them before night, at which time the populace vowed to execute their design. This he readily complied with, and I sent the papers down to Fort Johnson, and lest their madness should attempt to carry their scheme into execution, I reinforced the garrison with a detachment of a sergeant and 12 Royal Americans who happened to be in town, that the appearance of military troops joining the few provincials there might deter them from the rash undertaking; and I gave directions to Col. Howorth, who commands in that fort, to take every precaution against a surprise, and put it in the best posture of defence against an escalade. These measures happily prevented their making any attempt on the papers. Their fury was then directed towards striking a terror into the stamp officers if they persisted to perform their duty; which was done by night in great numbers, battering the house of Mr. Saxby, who was suspected to be arrived, though he then was not, and hunting after Mr. Caleb Lloyd, searching his lodgings, who prudently had withdrawn himself.

On the same day the information was given to me that the stamp papers were arrived, I summoned the Council, acquainting them therewith and what I had done thereon, and took my oath to use my utmost endeavours to carry the Act into execution, and as this commotion began on Saturday while the Court of General Sessions for the whole province was sitting in town, I thought proper to recommend to the chief justice to require all peace officers to exert themselves in suppressing such unlawful assemblies. But the infection was too generally spread to receive any check from his authority. On the Monday, being informed what had happened on Saturday and Sunday nights, I published a proclamation offering a reward from my own pocket of £50 sterling to any person who would discover the author of the outrage, and a pardon to any informer who was an accomplice, and commanded all judges, etc., to do their duty in preserving the public peace, but all this produced not the desired effect. And some insults having been committed on several persons' houses under pretext of searching for stamp papers, I ordered an advertisement to be published that they were by my order lodged in Fort Johnson. The commotions upon this in some measure subsided till the arrival of Mr. Saxby from London on the 27th when everything was again set in motion by a very great concourse of people threatening everything against the persons and effects of Mr. Saxby and Mr. Lloyd to deter them or any other person from doing their duty under that Act. Mr. Saxby having been apprised of these dispositions by his friends on the first arrival of the ship, prudently declined coming up to town but went on shore at Fort Johnson, whither Mr. Lloyd had also retired for his safety, which was all the protection my power could afford them. The commotions still continued and all this during the sitting of the Court of Sessions which by law is vested with the powers of the King's Bench in criminal matters, till on Monday these two officers, prevailed upon by the importunate request of their friends, consented to decline acting until the sense of the Parliament of Great Britain should be known upon the joint petition of the colonies which is now on the anvil at New York. These two gentlemen wrote me a letter on the occasion of their declining to act, a copy whereof I have the honour to transmit to your lordships.

Although these very numerous assemblies of the people bore the appearance of common populace, yet there is great reason to apprehend they were animated and encouraged by some considerable men who stood behind the curtain. This contagion has spread through this whole country and many are alarmed by various false representations, not only of what this act enjoins, but with fears of what is to follow from future laws of the like nature.

As there are no stamp papers can be issued during this situation, a stop is now put to all business in every office where they are required, and notwithstanding the great inconveniences and detriments which it will occasion, the people at present seem determined to submit to them patiently till they see the fate of New England, which I presume they will follow, in returning to their duty in this matter, as soon as they know that province is brought to theirs.

I have thus endeavoured, my lords, to represent to your lordships a faithful and circumstantial account of the unhappy situation of this province on account of this spirit of opposition to the Stamp Act, in which relation I thought it my duty to be very particular that your lordships might be the better enabled to judge what was necessary to be done for his Majesty's service thereupon, and at the same time, my lords, may I humbly hope to appear to your lordships to have performed everything in my power for the service of his Majesty and the preserving the public peace of the province; and I flatter myself I shall, when your lordships will please to consider that I had none but the civil magistracy to enforce my orders, and that they are to be supported by the *posse comitatus*, of which these concourses of people were composed; and I am morally certain, my lords, any attempt to quell them by force would have occasioned the shedding of blood without effecting the end proposed thereby.

The new elected General Assembly met on the 29th ultimo and in their answer to my recommending to them to form their deliberations upon the principle of duty to his Majesty and the considering the service of the king and their country as inseparable and as the surest foundation whereon to establish the tranquillity, prosperity, and happiness of their country, they declared their resolution to proceed upon those dutiful and loyal principles, which they trusted would produce freedom and happiness to their constituents. Being too early to enter upon the ordinary business of the year, they had my leave to adjourn to the 25th instant. Whether a little longer time and the examples of the assemblies of several other provinces in coming to bold resolutions which assert the independency of America in taxing themselves, exclusive of any other power, will contaminate our Assembly and lead them to come to such resolutions also, is what I do not think impossible, though it may be at present somewhat doubtful, wherefore I will not flatter your lordships or myself with too sanguine expectations therein.

I humbly beg your lordships to be assured that I shall do everything in my power to prevent the prerogative of the Crown from receiving any indignity, though as I had the honour to observe before to your lordships, my power can extend its influence but a little way under the present almost universal disposition of the people against the admitting the execution of the Stamp Act.

As the *Grenville* packet is daily expected here, I may probably receive the Stamp Act by that opportunity; in the meantime I shall continue to acquaint your lordships with the proceedings in this province on this subject and with great punctuality perform any commands with which his Majesty or your lordships shall be pleased to honour me.

110D. Lieutenant-Governor Colden's account of the state of the province of New York (6 December 1765)

In the first part of the letter, which is omitted here, Lieutenant-Governor Colden analyses the structure of New York society, and particularly the political alliance between the great landholders and a powerful legal profession. Colden tells how he sought to limit the control of the lawyers by refusing to issue commissions to judges "during good behaviour" and insisting on issuing them "during the King's pleasure", as his instructions required. He says this united the legal profession against him and that the opposition grew more violent as he insisted on the right of appeal of cases from the Supreme Court of the colony to the Governor and Council. This is the background for the following account of events in the fall of 1765. Printed: *New York Colonial Documents*, VII, pp. 795–800.

When the king's order in his Privy Council of the 26 of July arrived in September last, it renewed all the rage of the profession of the law, and they, taking the advantage of this spirit of sedition which was raised in all the colonies against the Act of Parliament for laying a stamp duty in the colonies, they turned the rage of the mob against the person of the lieutenant-governor, after all the other methods which their malice had invented for that purpose had failed. The malice of the faction against the lieutenant-governor is so evident that their inclination to expose every failing in his administration cannot be doubted, and when they have nothing to charge him with besides his supporting the right of the subject to appeal to the king, it gives the strongest presumption in his favour that they cannot otherwise blame any part of his administration.

In the night of the first of November a great mob came up to the fort gate with two images carried on a scaffold, one representing their old grey-haired governor, the other the devil whispering him in the ear. After continuing thus at the fort gate with all the insulting ribaldry that malice could invent, they broke open the lieutenant-governor's coach house which was without the walls of the fort, carried his chariot round the streets of the town in triumph with the images, returned a second time to the fort gate and finished their insult in an open place near the fort with all the indignities the malice of their leaders could invent. Their view certainly was to pro-voke the garrison then placed in the ramparts to some act which might be called a commencement of hostilities, in which case it cannot be said what was further intended. Being disappointed in this, the mob expended their rage by destroying everything they found in the house of Major James of the Royal Artillery for which no reason can be assigned other than his putting the fort in a proper posture of defence, as his duty in his department required of him.

While the lieutenant-governor was in the country as usual during the heat of summer, he received a letter from General Gage informing him that "the public papers were cramm'd with treason – the minds of the people disturbed, excited and encouraged to revolt against the government to subvert the constitution, and trample on the laws – that every falsehood that malice can invent is propagated as truth to sow dissension and create animosities between Great Britain and the colonies," concluding with an offer of such military assistance as the lieutenant-governor should think requisite in support of the civil authority. The lieutenant-governor immediately answered this letter with his opinion that one battalion would be requisite, with the garrison of the fort, but that he would immediately return to town and take the advice of the Council on the subject. The advice of the Council appears on the minutes of Council transmitted to Mr. Secretary Conway by the first packet after the advice was given. Though this advice was contrary to the lieutenant-governor's private sentiments, he thought it most prudent to submit the matter to the General. The argument made use of by the Council that it would be more safe to show confidence in the people than to discover a distrust of them by calling in any assistance to the civil power, in the lieutenant-governor's opinion, goes too far as it discouraged every precaution. The event has shown that it was not well judged, for it is most probable that had a battalion of regulars been brought to New York, all the riot and insults upon government had been prevented. The acting with vigour seemed the more necessary as the eyes of all the other colonies were on New York where the king had a fort allwise garrisoned with regular troops. The General kept his headquarters there and two frigates and a sloop of war were in the port.

When the lieutenant-governor came to town he found the General had ordered Major James to carry in such artillery and military stores as he thought necessary for the defence of the fort, and two companies of artillery having opportunely arrived at that time from England, they had likewise been ordered into the fort to strengthen the garrison. Major James is certainly a benevolent, humane man, and has distinguished himself on several occasions in the late war. No objection could be made to him, but his daring to put the king's fort in a state of defence against the sovereign lords the people, as they styled themselves, and for which offence they resolved to make him an example of their displeasure.

Before these additional defences were made, and while the garrison consisted of 44 privates and two subaltern officers, the fort could not have been defended against 100 resolute men, in which case the governor must have submitted to every shameful condition which the insolence of the leaders of the mob should think fit to impose upon him. They certainly had this in view while the fort remained in its defenceless state, but after it was in that state of offence as well as defence in which the engineers of the army put it after the first of November, the style of the leaders of the mob was changed from threatening to deprecating, and they only wanted some colour for desisting from their designs, and save their credit with the deluded people. It became evident that the fort could not be carried by assault, and that in the attempt the town would be exposed to desolation. In the state the fort then was, it was the opinion of the gentlemen of the army that one regiment in the city would have been sufficient to have subdued the seditious spirit that then prevailed.

The authors of the sedition place their security in the number of offenders and that no jury in the colonies will convict any of them. Were it possible that these men could succeed in their hope of independency on a British Parliament, many judicious persons think (though they dare not declare what they think) we shall become a most unhappy people. The obligation of oaths daringly profaned and every bond of society dissolved; the liberty and property of individuals will become subject to the avarice and ambition of wicked men who have art enough to keep the colony in perpetual factions by deluding an ignorant mob, and the colonies must become thereby useless to Great Britain.

It may in the last place be proper to observe that the authors of this seditious spirit in the colonies have extended their views even to Great Britain in hopes of raising a spirit of discontent among the manufacturers there. They publish in the newspapers that the importation of British manufactures are greatly decreased since the duties on the American trade, and that the colonies are under a necessity of setting up the manufactures which they otherwise would import from Great Britain. The importation from Great Britain had surprisingly increased during the war; the lessening of them from what it was in that time is unavoidable–from the recalling or disbanding the greatest part of the army, but chiefly to the entire stop to the trade with the French colonies, who were supplied from the British colonies, while their commerce with France was shut up.

What has been published of the manufactures lately set up are absolute falsehoods, and yet they are not ashamed to publish them where they are known to be such. All the wool in America is not sufficient to make stockings for the inhabitants, and the severe winters in North America render the production of wool in great quantities impracticable.

The merchants in New York and some other places, have entered into an agreement not to import any goods from England the next year unless the Stamp Act is repealed; this scheme is calculated solely to influence the people in England, and should it be executed, the people in America will pay an extravagant price for old moth-eaten goods, and such as the merchants could not otherwise sell. The merchants may likewise have views of getting goods in that case from Holland and other foreign ports, while the mob can deter the Custom House officers from attempting to do their duty.

In forming a judgment of the subject of the above narrative, it may be impossible in many cases to procure what is called legal evidence, and at the same time numerous circumstances may give the strongest conviction of the truth to the mind.

III. Testimony of British merchants on colonial trade and the effects of the Stamp Act (1766)

As a result of the agitation of British merchants and of American opposition to the Stamp Act, Parliament undertook an investigation of the economic effects of the various laws and measures adopted since 1763. The documents which follow consist of the testimony of three merchants involved in the trade with America. Barlow Trecothick was chairman of the committee of London merchants organized in 1765 to bring about a relaxation of those colonial policies which were held responsible for worsening economic conditions in the colonies and in Britain. William Reeve was a merchant of Bristol and John Glasford was a merchant of Glasgow. The questions and answers are not only an indication of the merchants' demands, but are also an illuminating commentary on the nature of the trade between Britain and the colonies. From: United States Library of Congress Transcripts from the British Museum, Additional Manuscripts, No. 33030, ff. 214-215, 146-162.

Extract from the petition to the House of Commons of the merchants of London trading to North America of such allegations as relate immediately to the commerce of the Northern Colonies and Great Britain, with Mr. Trecothick's proofs and observations thereupon.

1. That your petitioners have long been concerning in carrying on the trade between this country and the British colonies on the continent of North America.

Answer. This [is] true of my own knowledge for many years past.

2. That they have annually exported large quantities of British manufactures, consisting of woollen goods of all kinds, cottons, linens, hardware, shoes, household furniture, and almost without exception, of every species of goods manufactured in these kingdoms; besides other articles imported from abroad, chiefly purchased with our manufactures, and with the produce of our colonies, by all [of] which many thousands [of] manufacturers, seamen, and labourers have been employed to the very great and increasing benefit of this nation.

Answer. This I also know to be true, and is, with the former allegations, evident from the custom house books.

If the amount of the goods exported to North America should be called in question, I have endeavoured to obtain an account of the exact value. But many of the merchants declining to give precise details of their affairs, I have been able to procure it only from eight houses whose joint exports appear to be as follows:

For the year 1763 —	£431,901.	4. 4
1764	537,614.13.	7
1765	404,644.14.10	

3. That in return for these exports your petitioners have received from the colonies rice, indigo, tobacco, naval stores, oil, whale fins, and lately potash, with other commodities, besides remittances by bills of exchange, and bullion, obtained by the colonists in payment for articles of their produce not required for the British market, and therefore exported to other places.

Answer. That the articles of produce mentioned in this allegation are imported by the petitioners I likewise know to be true, and may likewise be proved by the custom house books. Bills of exchange are obtained and remitted by the colonists for fish, corn, flour, rum, lumber sold in Portugal, Spain, and Italy, at Gibraltar and Port Mahon; for slaves purchased with rum on the coast of Africa and sold in the

Sugar Islands; for rum, molasses, and provisions supplied the fishery at Newfoundland; for flaxseed and lumber sold in Ireland; for provisions, ships, lumber, horses, and cattle sold in the West India islands.

Bullion in times of peace has been remitted by almost every merchant ship for a long course of years back. I remember this to have been the case for thirty years past, particularly from the more northern colonies. The specie are usually pistoles and pieces of eight. This may be proved by the Bank account; by Messrs. Howe and Masterman, and John Bland, bankers, and by the merchants themselves, for a great part of the bullion imported went to the merchants directly and not through the hands of either the Bank or private bankers. This bullion is obtained in the course of their trade with the foreign and British southern settlements for flour sold at Jamaica for the Spanish trade, for British manufactures, occasionally introduced into the Spanish settlements at such times as a scarcity of provisions obliges them to admit of a free trade, and from the coast of Africa for rum sold there for gold dust.

4. That from the nature of the trade, consisting of British manufactures exported, and of the import of raw materials from America, many of them used in our manufactures, and all of them tending to lessen our dependence on neighbouring states, it must be deemed of the highest importance in the commercial system of this nation.

Answer. In this trade the benefit of labour, in the imports as well as the exports, remains to Great Britain, for iron, copper ore, logwood, furs, skins, indigo, tobacco, and potash, all for manufacture, and with masts, pitch, tar, turpentine, oil, whale fins, and lumber, tend greatly to lessen the dependence of Great Britain on its neighbours.

5. That this commerce so beneficial to the state and so necessary for the support of multitudes, now lies under such difficulties and discouragements that nothing less than its utter ruin is apprehended without the immediate interposition of Parliament.

Answer. Among the discouragements this trade now labours under, the following may be enumerated, viz: drawbacks retained here; custom house bonds multiplied; heavy duties on American trade; these universal disorders in the American provinces; courts of justice shut; no recovery of debts by law; no legal security to be obtained for debts; navigation and commerce obstructed; failure of remittances; decay and loss of credit; restrictions of orders for goods, etc., all which have disabled the petitioners from continuing their exports.

6. That in consequence of the trade between the colonies and the mother country, as established and as permitted for many years, and of the experience which your petitioners have had of the readiness of the Americans to make their just remittances to the utmost of their real abilities, they have been induced to make and venture such large exportation of British manufactures as to leave the colonies indebted to the merchants of Great Britain in the sum of several millions sterling.

Answer. The whole trade is here meant, as well the circuitous trade of the colonies in search of remittances to Great Britain, as the direct export hence and import here.

That the petitioners have experienced a disposition in the Americans to make due remittances when in their power, is evinced by their continuance of the trade and the credit they have given them.

Many tedious methods of remittance have been adopted and submitted to from necessity, occasioned by the deficiency of commodities to remit to Great Britain directly; but these delays cannot be deemed intentional, or impeach the willingness of the Americans to pay their debts.

Four or five voyages are sometimes necessary to bring about a remittance: viz., first to fish, to carry that fish to the foreign West India islands, bring back molasses, manufacture that molasses into rum, carry that rum to Africa, from thence slaves to the West Indies, there to procure bills of exchange, bullion, or produce to remit to Great Britain.

In consequence of what is alleged of several millions being owing, etc., endeavours have been used to obtain an exact account of the sums due to the merchants, but only eight principal houses in London have been given in billets of the balances at present due to them from the continent of North America, which amount to the sum of £956,579 sterling.

The Committee of Merchants of London trading to North America have deliberated upon the matter and do unanimously authorize me to give it as their opinion that at the lowest computation there is due to the merchants of London only:

	£2,900,000
The agents for the merchants in Bristol authorize me in the same manner to say that there is due to that town	800,000
Ditto from Glasgow (Virginia and Maryland only)	500,000
Ditto from Liverpool	150,000
Ditto from Manchester	100,000
	£4,450,000

Besides sums due to Lancaster, Whitehaven, Birmingham, Sheffield, Leeds, Norwich, Wakefield, Halifax, and other manufacturing towns, which must considerably augment the balance due from North America.

William Reeve, merchant at Bristol, has been concerned thirty years in American trade: something less than £100,000 per annum.

On an average the merchants have traded to £500,000 per annum.

The trade have suffered diminution lately.

To what extent?

At present it is totally stagnated.

Owing to what?

To the confusion they are in on account of the Stamp Act.

Have you any particular evidence of that?

I have many letters that mention the cause of it.

Reads a letter from Boston of the 4th November last. Has 500 letters to the same purpose: that the Americans will not send orders unless Act is repealed.

Do you think the want of British manufactures will not oblige them to abandon
their.... [?]

They can do without some of our coarse manufactures but the fine manufactures they cannot do without. The merchants of Bristol have debts in America
to £500,000 at the least, which stood at present on a very precarious footing. I
am owed a very large sum and upwards of £150,000 in my own and partner's name.
I have several ships in North America loaded with rice, wheat, and flour, some
bound hither and some to Portugal; they remaining there for want of ships, many
mine. If the Act is not repealed I will send no more and totally withdraw myself.

What part of the Stamp Act is ruinous?

I can't define the particular parts.

Is not the opposition to the Act the cause of the stagnation?

I submit to the judgment of this house I know the Stamp Act is the grievance.

If the Stamp Act had been submitted to would your ships have remained there?

I know they do remain there.

Have you heard that any ships were sent over?

Nothing but from the newspapers.

Do you know there was a riot?

I have no immediate account of it.

When did you leave off exportation to North America?

None this four months.

How many nailmakers dismissed since that?

Since my orders countermanded for nails from £16,000 to £20,000, 300 men
turned off in one day.

Have any been discharged since?

I have been attending here for five weeks and can't speak, but my correspondents at Manchester say they shall be obliged to turn off several, but said they
would employ the men out of compassion for two or three days in a week.

In your letters have they said there are no stamps?

They say nothing about it but thought some are burnt.

Why were they burnt?

I can't say the reason.

If the Act should be repealed would you ship goods immediately or wait further orders?

I would ship immediately without waiting.

Were not the exportations in [17]64 large?

I cannot remember, not having taken it out of my books.

Is not the opinion of merchants at Bristol that the North American merchants had
ever traded themselves?

Before this Stamp Act the North Americans remitted as well as ever.

Question repeated.

I can judge only by the remittances, which if they are sufficient, he inquires
no further.

Are the exports of [17]64 paid for?

Great sums have been paid and much remains behind.

Is a great proportion of it paid? Is as much remained in [17]65 of the goods in [17]64 as usual?

Has not.

What credit do you give?

Different to different traders. Some goods bought for ready money, some at six months, nine, and twelve months. Would reckon nine months good payment. If they don't pay punctually, they pay interest.

Will not you reckon twelve months good pay?

With interest.

What part of the debt bears interest?

Cannot tell how long the debt has been contracting.

Can you recover your debt as easily if the Stamp Act [is] continued as repealed?

I can now recover nothing. I never gave twelve months' credit in my life. Nine months is the usual, and then it bears interest.

If now in the present situation you was to receive orders, would you comply with it?

Not a single one.

Would you if your correspondent [said] he would comply with the Act?

No. One swallow does not make summer.

Would you if the Americans generally submitted to the Act?

No.

Why?

Because my affairs are in my own hands and if the Stamp Act is not repealed I will never ship or lance [sic] off goods for America. That is explicit.

Withdrew

Mr. Glasford

John Glasford from Glasgow resides there, deals with Virginia and Maryland. To what extent?

To a considerable extent.

On order or your own account?

Principally on my own account.

What debts due?

To a considerable extent.

What is the quantity of tobacco annually imported into Glasgow?

About 25,000 hogsheads. Lately more, very considerable. Debts owing to merchants of Glasgow I believe £500,000 to [be] the whole.

Are these debts con[tained] in large or small sums?

Some in large but many in small, from £30 upwards.

There are the supreme court in the colony and county courts. [Are] these small debts recoverable in the county courts?

The goods I send are to the agents and factors who compose of [the] county courts. I am told in Virginia the judges are made by the governor from the freeholders.

Have they any salaries?

I am told they are not compellable by law to act.

Will they then sit while there is anything disagreeable from the stamp law according to an information?

No courts are held since 1st November. The sums above £5 currency are by juries.

If the Stamp Act was repealed do you hear the judges would act?

I hope and believe so.

Would they if the Stamp Act was not repealed only?

From our past information they would not.

Is not the method of trading on your account?

19/20 the[re] are on the part of merchants of Glasgow. They trust to the ability and considerable part to the labourer.

Are not the debts small?

Yes. The greater part [are] under £30 sterling.

How long is it before the return?

The payments fall not so much short of four years.

So this £500,000 is a debt of near four years?

Yes, near it.

If America should be again quieted would they not again trade with the colonies?

I believe they would send the goods because they could not otherwise recover the debts, but they would endeavour to retrench that trade.

Were there more tobacco imported last year than usual?

Yes, more than for several years.

Will they for the future allow the Americans to be four years in your debt?

They would endeavour to retrench.

Can it be less than two or three years in the common course for the returns?

Ever since I have been concerned I have known it in two years, some in five years. I mean by retrenching, retrench the sums owing. And this whether the Stamp Act was repealed or not.

What is the value of tobacco imported into Great Britain?

Into Glasgow, £150,000 at the rate they have imported. This is the price at Virginia, exclusive of freight.

What is the value of exports?

Yearly to the same amount.

Whence then comes the debt of £500,000?

I said it might be four years collecting in the return. They will endeavour to lessen the sum when the Act is repealed.

112A–B. Repeal of the Stamp Act

The first document which follows (No. 112A) consists of two letters of Henry Cruger, one to his father in New York and one to Aaron Lopez, a merchant of Newport, Rhode Island. Cruger's grandfather had gone from Bristol to New York where he became a merchant. In 1757 he sent his grandson to enter a Bristol counting-house. Henry Cruger became a well-to-do merchant in Bristol and was elected to Parliament in 1774. He lost his seat in 1780 but was elected mayor of

Bristol in 1781 and elected to Parliament again in 1784. In 1790 he returned to New York and in 1792 he was elected to the New York Senate. He died in 1827. During the period of the Stamp Act, Cruger was active in support of the merchant agitation for its repeal and for commercial reform. His letters present an interesting picture of the politics of the time and of the merchants' aims.

The Act repealing the Stamp Act (6 Geo. III, c. 11) was passed by the House of Commons, 11 March 1766 by a vote of 275 to 167 and passed the Lords a week later by a vote of 105 to 71. It received the royal assent on 18 March (No. 112B).

112A. Letters of Henry Cruger, Jr. on the repeal of the Stamp Act

Printed: Massachusetts Historical Society *Collections*, 7th Series, IX, pp. 139-143, 145-146.

[To Henry Cruger, Sr., Bristol, 14 February 1766]

The debates in Parliament lasting so long on the Stamp Act determined me to return to my business ere it was terminated. I was three weeks in London, and every day with some one member of Parliament, talking as it were for my own life. It is surprising how ignorant some of them are of trade and America. The House at last came to a resolution to examine only one person from each place that brought petitions. Mr. William Reeve, being the senior of us who went from Bristol, was put in the votes. Upon hearing of this resolve, I set out and arrived here late last night; it is now afternoon, and not until this moment would Mr. Penington let me know his vessel was bound to New York. He assures me no man in Bristol knows it but Mr. Hayes and myself. I will employ what little time I have in scribbling as much news to you as I can, supposing everybody on your side are impatient for the Stamp Act. Tuesday the 11th instant Mr. Trecothick was ordered to the bar of the House of Commons, where he was examined, and X examined 3½ hours; the last question Lord Strange (your enemy) asked was this: if he did not think the Americans would rather submit to the S[tamp] Act than remain in the confusion they are in? It was not a proper question. Mr. Trecothick was ordered to withdraw; some debates ensued; he was recalled to the bar and told the House had altered the question to this: if it was not his opinion the Americans would acquiesce with the Stamp Act provided it was mitigated? Mr. Trecothick answered it was his opinion that no modification of the Act would reconcile it and that the Americans would be contented with nothing less than a *Total Repeal*.

This inflamed Grenville's party. They called you insolent rebels. I dread his party coming into power before the Act is repealed. If they do, they'll certainly scourge you although some English merchants are ruined by it.

We have proved the debt from the continent of America to England is five millions sterling. This Grenville attempted to disprove, and is what makes the examinations at the bar so tedious.

All the principal manufacturing towns have sent petitions for a repeal of the Stamp Act. A manufacturer from Leeds was ordered to the bar, who said since the stagnation of the American trade he has been constrained to turn off 300 families out of 600 he constantly employed. This fact will have great weight when added to many more evidences of the like kind. The country members are somewhat alarmed at so many people losing employ; if anything repeals the Act, it must be this. The present ministry see and have declared the expediency of repealing on this ground. If the late ministers come in again and enforce the Act, they will have 20,000 unemployed poor in a suppliant manner petitioning a repeal of the S[tamp] Act; otherwise they must starve, or so I think. There is no doubt but it must be repealed on some grounds, or some cause or other, especially if you stick to your engagements of having no English goods until it is effectuated. This resolution I hope you'll abide by. Nay! it is my opinion this tiresome procrastination would never have happened if you had sent no ships away till it was decided, for Mr. Grenville has declared he will try to keep it off this 6 weeks in hopes you will at last submit, saying it is a proof you are tired by venturing to send your ships away, and that he has no doubt you will also soon be tired of the lawless state you are in. Retrospect to the question Lord Strange put to Mr. Trecothick, I attended the House of Commons all day Tuesday the 11th instant. In the evening a member (who is in the administration) told me things were doubtful, and went vastly hard with them; that the k[ing] was not staunch to his ministers; that although he assured them he would support them, yet he had deceived them; that they daily and hourly experience Lord Bute's dreadful influence, that the k[ing] had empowered Lord Bute and Lord Strange to say his private wish was not for a repeal of the Stamp Act as it would be derogatory to the honour of his Crown and dignity of his Parliament to be compelled to repeal an Act that had been so disrespectfully treated without first exercising their authority by enforcing it. He further told me that the k[ing] acted with great duplicity–it is amazing what power Lord Bute continues to have over him! My friend further said he thought notwithstanding all this they would yet have a repeal of the Stamp Act. At one time the present ministry were bent upon resigning, on finding the duke of York and duke of Gloucester were against them, also all the k[ing]'s *immediate* servants such as the lords of the bed chamber and nine bishops; they were for carrying fire and sword to America with this argument: that since you snarl and begin to show your teeth, they ought to be knocked out before you are able to bite.

Enclosed is a minute or two I made the days they happened. By them you'll see the sentiments of the great.

You also have an exact copy of Mr. Grenville's motion in the House which I had address enough to get, he little thinking what use was to be made of it, though if he knew I don't suppose it would give him any concern. He was backed upon a division (after debating till 11 o'clock at night) by 134 though lost it by a majority of 140. I saw the list of the minority. In it were Sir Charles Hardy and General Abercrombie. These are the thanks for the old Madeira you have given them. O! Curse them! About 10 o'clock when the House were almost wearied out, old General Howard stood up. At his martial appearance a profound silence ensued. He spoke (I don't pretend to give you his words, only the substance) to this effect: that he shuddered at the unnatural motion; he hoped in God it would not succeed, for in all likelihood he might be ordered to execute it, and before he would imbrue his hands in the blood of his countrymen who were contending for English liberty he would, if ordered, draw his sword, but would soon after sheath it in his own body. Secretary Conway said (though not at the same time) that he would sooner cut off his right arm than sign an order for soldiers to enforce the Act. The majority against it in the House of Commons were 274; yet, when you reflect that 134 were for it, it is enough to make you tremble. When I left London the 12th instant it was about three to one the Act would be repealed, but for three weeks past there has been no dependence on anything we hear—neither king nor Parliament knew. Today the ministry would have the best of it, and things would look well; tomorrow Grenville and his party would gain the power, and then of course no repeal. The vox populi now begins to gain ground, and I think since the legality of taxation is allowed, the Act will be repealed upon the grounds of expediency.

These particulars, few and inconclusive as they are, I thought would still be agreeable, for the authenticity of them I will answer.

As so much politics may confound business, I will do myself the honour to write you a few lines on the latter subject in another epistle. I remain with all due respect in haste my Dear Sir Your Most Dutiful Son etc.

H. C. Jr.

P.S.—The Parliament have not yet done anything about the Sugar Act and other destructive restraints on your trade. It will come as soon as ever the Stamp Act is settled. I imagine they will rescind all the restrictive clauses, and grant you everything you ask. Their eyes are at last opened and they seem convinced what vast benefit will accrue to this kingdom by giving you almost an unlimited trade, so far as doth not interfere with British manufactures. The West Indians are collecting all their force to oppose us; I have reason to say they will at length be defeated.

'Tis said French sugars, coffee, cotton, etc., the produce of foreign islands, will have the indulgence of being imported in our colonies duty free, but must be put in king's warehouses, and the proprietors constrained to ship them off again (to any part of the world they please) in a stipulated time.

The duty on molasses will be reduced to 1d per gallon.

[To Aaron Lopez, Bristol, 1 March 1766]

The confusion of American affairs hath affected us equally. I have been very deeply involved in them, and think myself amply rewarded with the bare aspect which now abounds with looks and promises of success to America. The Stamp Act is not yet repealed, but it is as good as done. A motion was made in the House of Commons for a bill to be brought in for a repeal and was carried by 275 against 167; the latter were only for a modification of the Act. The debates pro and con have been very warm and serious. As I have not time now to be particular, will trouble you with a copy of my last letter to my father just for your amusement. There is little doubt but the affairs will be finished in a few days and the Act repealed. You'll be informed that the Parliament have settled their *right* of taxing you. When that was done they proceeded to the expediency of repealing the Act, which never would have come to pass had it not been for the merchants and manufacturers of England. Trade here was totally stagnated; not one American merchant gave out a single order for goods on purpose to compel all manufacturers to engage with us in petitioning Parliament for a repeal of the Stamp Act, by which thousands were out of employ and in a starving condition. You, dear sir, shared in the common calamity. I hope and persuade myself you will not murmur at this momentary disappointment when so much good will come out of it. I hug myself the Parliament will never trouble America again. I could not think of giving out any of your orders until I saw which way this momentous affair would turn and terminate. I congratulate you on our success and with redoubled joy—as the contrary was at one time much dreaded. The letter I shall enclose you will give you a great insight into the actions and sentiments of our British senators.

Immediately upon hearing by express that a bill was to be brought in the House of Commons for a total repeal, I set about providing your orders, all which I hope to have shipped on board the *Charlotte*, Captain Brown, by the latter end of this month. No doubt you'll wonder at not hearing from me oftener of late. I have the best excuse that ever I had for not writing, even a serving my country, which I have been doing day and night. I am no politician, but in this matter of America and its trade I embarked body and soul. I have been in London with all the great men in the kingdom. The Stamp and Sugar Acts were my two objects. I think you American gentlemen will have all your wishes gratified, but more of this in my next. I only claim a share of the merit if all comes to pass that I expect. See the P.S. of the letter to my father. I will be very punctual in future to make amends for my past silence; have patience and you'll reap the advantages.

112B. Act repealing the Stamp Act (18 March 1766)

Printed: Pickering, *Statutes at Large*, XXVII, p. 19.

Whereas an Act was passed in the last session of Parliament entitled, An Act for granting and applying certain stamp duties, and other duties in the British colonies and plantations in America towards further defraying the expenses of defending, protecting, and securing the same; and for amending such parts of the several Acts of Parliament relating to the trade and revenues of the said colonies and plantations as direct the manner of determining and recovering the penalties and forfeitures therein mentioned; and whereas the continuance of the said Act would be attended with many inconveniencies, and may be productive of consequences greatly detrimental to the commercial interests of these kingdoms; may it therefore please your most excellent Majesty that it may be enacted; and be it enacted by the king's most excellent Majesty, by and with the advice and consent of the Lords Spiritual and Temporal, and Commons, in this present Parliament assembled, and by the authority of the same, that from and after the first day of May, one thousand seven hundred and sixty-six, the above-mentioned Act, and the several matters and things therein contained, shall be, and is and are hereby repealed and made void to all intents and purposes whatsoever.

113. The Declaratory Act (18 March 1766)

The Declaratory Act (6 Geo. III, c. 12) asserting the absolute sovereignty of Parliament received royal assent the same day as the Act repealing the Stamp Act. Printed: Pickering, *Statutes at Large*, XXVII, pp. 19-20.

Whereas several of the houses of representatives in his Majesty's colonies and plantations in America, have of late, against law, claimed to themselves, or to the general assemblies of the same, the sole and exclusive right of imposing duties and taxes upon his Majesty's subjects in the said colonies and plantations; and have, in pursuance of such claim, passed certain votes, resolutions, and orders, derogatory to the legislative authority of Parliament, and inconsistent with the dependency of the said colonies and plantations upon the Crown of Great Britain: may it therefore please your most excellent Majesty that it may be declared; and be it declared by the King's most excellent Majesty, by and with the advice and consent of the Lords Spiritual and Temporal, and Commons, in this present Parliament assembled, and by the authority of the same, that the said colonies and plantations in America have been, are, and of right ought to be, subordinate unto, and dependent upon the imperial Crown and Parliament of Great Britain; and that the King's Majesty, by and with the advice and consent of the Lords Spiritual and Temporal, and Commons of Great Britain, in Parliament assembled, had, hath, and of right ought to have, full power and authority to make laws and statutes of sufficient force and validity to bind the colonies and people of America, subjects of the Crown of Great Britain, in all cases whatsoever.

II. And be it further declared and enacted by the authority aforesaid, that all resolutions, votes, orders, and proceedings, in any of the said colonies or plantations, whereby the power and authority of the Parliament of Great Britain, to make laws and statutes as aforesaid, is denied, or drawn into question, are, and are hereby declared to be, utterly null and void to all intents and purposes whatsoever.

114. The Revenue Act of 1766 (6 June 1766)

This Act (6 Geo. III, c. 52), coupled with the Act creating free ports for foreign produce in Jamaica and Dominica (6 Geo. III, c. 49), represents a continuation of the programme of the British merchants whose first victory was the repeal of the Stamp Act. While the Revenue Act was in part a concession to the colonists, it actually added to the burdens of which they complained. The reduction of the duty on molasses to one penny a gallon and the requirement that both British and foreign molasses pay it, converted this portion of the Act from a regulatory to a revenue producing measure. Furthermore, since the low duty made smuggling unprofitable, the Act produced more revenue in the colonies than any other Act ever passed by Parliament. In addition, the revenue was set aside in a special fund to be used for the same purpose as the Stamp Act. The duties on certain kinds of foreign cloth collected at colonial customs houses under the Act of 1764 were repealed, but they were replaced by duties on the same cloth when imported into England, and thus the colonial consumer gained no advantage.

Finally, the Act provided for closer control of colonial trade. The Revenue Act of 1764 provided that bonds must be given for non-enumerated goods loaded in the colonies, if a vessel also loaded foreign sugars and molasses. The Act of 1766 extended this idea to provide that bonds must be given for all non-enumerated goods loaded in the colonies. Not only did this add to the duties of customs officers, it added to the complications of carrying on trade and to the irritation of colonial merchants. Printed: Pickering, *Statutes at Large*, XXVII, pp. 275-286, *passim*.

Whereas the several duties hereinafter mentioned, imposed by certain Acts of Parliament to be raised in the British colonies and plantations in America, have been attended with great inconveniencies to the trade of his Majesty's dominions, and it is therefore necessary that the same should be discontinued, and that other duties should be granted in lieu thereof, ... be it enacted ... that all the duties imposed by any Act or Acts of Parliament upon molasses or syrups of the growth, product, or manufacture, of any foreign American colony or plantation, imported into any British colony or plantation in America; and also the duties imposed by an Act made in the twenty-fifth year of the reign of King Charles the second (for the encouragement of the Greenland and Eastland trades, and for the better securing the plantation trade) upon sugar, of the growth, production, and manufacture, of the British plantations in America, which should be laden there; and also the duties imposed by an Act made in the fourth year of the reign of his present Majesty for granting certain duties in the British colonies and plantations in America, and for other purposes in the said Act mentioned, upon coffee and pimento, of the growth and produce of any British colony or plantation in America, which should be shipped to be carried out from thence, except to Great Britain, shall, from and after the first day of November, one thousand seven hundred and sixty-six, cease, determine, and be no longer paid.

II. And be it further enacted by the authority aforesaid, that the several duties imposed by the last-mentioned Act upon wrought silks, bengals, and stuffs mixed with silk or herba, of the manufacture of Persia, China, or East India, and upon calicoes painted, dyed, printed, or stained there, and upon foreign linen cloth called cambric, and upon French lawns, imported into any British colony or plantation in America, from Great Britain, shall, from and after the first day of October, one thousand seven hundred and sixty-six, cease, determine, and be no longer paid.

IV. And be it further enacted by the authority aforesaid, that from and after the said first day of November, one thousand seven hundred and sixty-six, there shall be raised, levied, collected, and paid unto his Majesty, his heirs, and successors, the several and respective rates and duties hereinafter mentioned; that is to say:

For every gallon (wine-measure) of molasses and syrups which shall be imported or brought (except as is hereinafter mentioned) into any colony or plantation in America, which now is, or hereafter may be, under the dominion of his Majesty, his heirs and successors, one penny.

For every hundredweight avoirdupois of coffee of the growth and produce of any British colony or plantation in America which shall be imported or brought from thence into any other British colony or plantation in America, seven shillings.

And for every pound weight avoirdupois of such British pimento, which shall in like manner be imported or brought into any such British colony or plantation, one halfpenny; except only such British coffee and pimento as shall be warehoused under the regulations and restrictions hereinafter mentioned; and after those rates for any greater or less quantity of such goods respectively.

XII. . . . That all the monies that shall arise by the said duties (except the necessary charges of raising, collecting, levying, recovering, answering, paying, and accounting for the same) shall be paid into the receipt of his Majesty's exchequer, and shall be entered separate and apart from all other monies paid or payable to his Majesty, his heirs or successors, and shall be there reserved to be from time to time disposed of by Parliament, towards defraying the necessary expenses of defending, protecting, and securing the British colonies and plantations in America.

XVI. [No duty shall be paid on foreign sugars, coffee, or indigo brought into any British colony on the continent of America if they are warehoused and re-exported within twelve months, upon condition that sugar shall be exported directly to Great Britain or to Europe south of Cape Finisterre, that foreign indigo shall be exported to

Great Britain only, and that foreign coffee shall not be brought back or relanded in any part of the British Dominions in America.]

XXIII. And it is hereby further enacted by the authority aforesaid, that from and after the first day of January, one thousand seven hundred and sixty-seven, all sugars which shall be imported into Great Britain, from any part of the British colonies or plantations on the continent of America, shall be deemed and taken to be French sugars, and the importer or proprietor shall, upon the importation thereof, pay down in ready money to the collector of his Majesty's customs, only three pence per hundred-weight avoirdupois for such sugars, which shall not be afterwards drawn back or repaid upon the exportation of the same goods. . . .

XXX. And whereas by an Act made in the twelfth year of the reign of King Charles the second, entitled, An act for encouraging and increasing of shipping and navigation, and several subsequent Acts of Parliament which are now in force, it is, amongst other things, enacted, that for every ship or vessel which shall load any commodities, in those Acts particularly enumerated, at any British plantation, being the growth, product, or manufacture thereof, bonds shall be given, with one surety, to the value of one thousand pounds if the ship be of less burden than one hundred tons, and of the sum of two thousand pounds if the ship be of greater burden; that the same commodities shall be brought by such ship or vessel to some other British plantation, or to some port in Great Britain. Now, in order more effectually to prevent such goods being privately carried from any British colony or plantation in America into foreign parts of Europe in vessels that clear out with non-enumerated goods, as well as to prevent the clandestine importation of foreign European goods into the said British colonies; be it further enacted by the authority aforesaid, that from and after the first day of January, one thousand seven hundred and sixty-seven, bond and security, in the like penalty, shall also be given to the collector, or other principal officer of the customs, at any port or place in any of the British American colonies or plantations, with one surety besides the master of every ship or vessel that shall lade or take on board there any goods not particularly enumerated in the said Acts, with condition that such goods shall not be landed at any part of Europe to the northward of Cape Finisterre, except in Great Britain. . . .[1]

[1] This provision of the Act was interpreted to exclude all exports to Ireland. In 1767 an Act was passed (7 Geo. III, c. 2) which specifically stated that the term "Great Britain" in this section was meant to include Ireland.

C. THE PITT-GRAFTON MINISTRY AND THE COLONIES, 1767–1768

IN the eyes of George III the Rockingham ministry was a stopgap affair and throughout its existence he was engaged in tortuous negotiations to bring William Pitt back into power. An agreement was at last arrived at and Pitt took office in August 1766, with the duke of Grafton as the nominal head of the ministry. Pitt himself went into the House of Lords as the earl of Chatham and shortly thereafter became ill and went into seclusion and refused to see his supporters or to make political decisions. The formation of the ministry had little or no relation to the question of colonial policy, although nominally it could be regarded as friendly to the colonies since Pitt himself had supported the repeal of the Stamp Act. Shelburne, as Secretary of State for the southern department, was in charge of colonial affairs, and he too was looked upon as, and proved himself to be, a friend of the colonies. Nevertheless within a few months after taking office, the ministry embarked on a programme that was to irritate the colonies anew, and by 1768 it was to be controlled by men who insisted on coercion of the colonies.

The duke of Grafton was little interested in administration, and Shelburne was dilatory, with the result that when colonial affairs became an issue in Parliament, Charles Townshend, Chancellor of the Exchequer, took the lead in a legislative programme which in many respects represented a continuation of the Grenville policies.[1] After Townshend died in September 1767 a series of Cabinet changes took place which swung the ministry over to the side of a forceful policy towards the Americans. The Bedford Whigs, who had supported Grenville, made an alliance with Grafton and placed some of their men in power. Lord North was brought into the Cabinet as Chancellor of the Exchequer. Shortly thereafter a third secretaryship of state was created for the purpose of handling American affairs. In January 1768 Lord Hillsborough was appointed to the post and thus Shelburne was removed from control of the colonies. As head of the "American Department" Hillsborough supported a vigorous policy towards the colonies, a policy that included the use of the army to support civil officials and customs officers. Later in the same year Shelburne resigned and Chatham aroused himself enough to resign as well, and the ministry was thus left entirely in the hands of those unfriendly to colonial claims.

While these changes were taking place, the Americans demonstrated that they did not intend to yield to the demands of British policy despite the repeal of the Stamp Act and the passage of the Revenue Act of 1766. They persistently opposed the strengthening of customs enforcement.[2] They objected to and refused to obey the provisions of the Quartering Act. The legislatures of New York, Massachusetts, New Jersey, South Carolina, and Georgia, all refused to provide funds, and in the case of Georgia, did so at the same time it was asking for British troops for frontier defence.

The legislatures of Massachusetts and New York were reluctant to comply with the demand of the ministry that the victims of the Stamp Act riots be compensated for their losses. New York finally gave compensation although it refused to reimburse Lieutenant-Governor Cadwallader Colden. Massachusetts delayed for a long time,

[1] Nos. 115, 116, 117, 119, 122.   [2] Nos. 127A, 128, 131.

and then its Act of compensation was accompanied by an Act of indemnity for the rioters. Such behaviour irritated men like Pitt, Shelburne, and Townshend, while George Grenville and his followers looked upon it as a clear demonstration of the futility of making concessions to the colonists. The ministry considered a variety of measures: voiding the Massachusetts charter, bringing James Otis to England for trial, recalling governors like Francis Bernard of Massachusetts, and so on, but it did nothing.

In January 1767 the issue of colonial policy was placed squarely before Parliament by George Grenville. In the course of a debate over army estimates, Grenville demanded that the Americans be made to pay for at least part of the expense of the army in America, an item of some £400,000 a year in the British budget. Charles Townshend, Chancellor of the Exchequer, without consulting his Cabinet colleagues, declared that he knew how to raise revenue in America without offending the colonists. Shortly thereafter the opposition led by Grenville called his bluff by voting a one-shilling reduction in the proposed land tax of four shillings. When Townshend proposed his budget in April, he declared that the American distinction between internal and external taxes was "perfect nonsense". He therefore proposed and secured the passage of legislation to collect import duties on glass, paper, painters' colours, and tea brought into colonial ports. A revenue of £40,000 was predicted. The duties paid on the importation of tea, coffee, and cocoa brought into England were given back when re-exported to the colonies, a measure which in the case of tea meant that its cost to the colonial consumer was less than to the English consumer.

But the Townshend Revenue Act[1] meant far more than the collection of duties at colonial ports of entry. Its political purpose was far more significant than its economic. It dealt directly with a basic problem of administration within the colonies. The proceeds of the Act were to be set aside to pay the salaries of governors, judges, and other royal officials, and thus to render them independent of colonial legislatures. The purpose was clear, and every colonial leader recognized it. A second piece of legislation passed during this session of Parliament was an even more direct blow at the power of colonial legislatures. The New York legislature was only one among many which had refused to comply with the provisions of the Quartering Act. New York was the headquarters of the British Army in America, and therefore an example was to be made of her. Hence Parliament passed an Act suspending the New York Assembly until it complied with the Quartering Act.[2]

On the same day this Act was proposed Townshend offered another measure to further strengthen the customs service. An American Board of Customs, independent of the Customs Commissioners in England, had long been talked of. Parliament now made it a reality by passing an Act establishing a board of five commissioners to be located in Boston and to have charge of the North American customs service.[3]

During 1768 a further step was taken to improve customs enforcement. The Revenue Act of 1764 had provided for a court of Vice-Admiralty for all of North America which would have both original and appellate jurisdiction. One had actually been established at Halifax, Nova Scotia, although it seems not to have functioned. The distance of this court from colonial commercial centres and from the Vice-Admiralty courts of the individual colonies guaranteed that it would be much objected to and little used. Hence in 1768 Parliament authorized the creation of additional

[1] No. 115.   [2] No. 117.   [3] No. 116.

courts of vice-admiralty. Following this legislation, the Privy Council authorized the establishment of courts at Halifax, Boston, Philadelphia, and Charleston.[1]

Only one phase of colonial policy was handled by the ministry rather than by Parliament in 1767–1768: that relating to the American west. During the Seven Years War two Indian superintendents – Sir William Johnson, north of the Ohio River, and John Stuart to the south – had been appointed to supervise Indian affairs in the west. The proclamation of 1763 had drawn a boundary between white and Indian territory,[2] but the line was looked upon as temporary. Stuart had proceeded with treaty negotiations for the purpose of drawing a permanent boundary south of the Ohio, but Sir William Johnson did nothing north of the river. However, both men did what they could to supervise and regulate the fur trade between the whites and the Indians.

The colonies disliked the idea of a boundary line and both settlements and speculative land claims were to be found in the region beyond the proclamation line of 1763. Fur traders objected to any control which interfered with their exploitation of the Indians. Land speculators on both sides of the Atlantic opposed any limitation of their activities and promoted the idea of the establishment of new colonies in the west. Meanwhile, there was steady opposition in Britain to the expense of maintaining the army in frontier posts. Out of these multiple pressures a new western policy was decided upon.[3]

The British surrender of any serious effort to regulate western expansion and the fur trade had disastrous results. A 'permanent' boundary line was drawn but land speculators and settlers ignored it. The regulation of the fur trade was handed back to the colonies, and the result was anarchy, for the colonial legislatures did nothing to control it. By 1773 the results were plain, and the ministry once more undertook to regulate western expansion. An investigation of colonial land grants was made, and governors were forbidden to issue warrants for survey or to issue patents except by permission of the Crown or the Privy Council. In 1774 a drastic step was taken when the region north-west of the Ohio River was attached to the province of Quebec in the Quebec Act of that year. But by this time the American Revolution was under way, and British efforts to control the west did nothing except to further incite the Americans to rebellion.

115. The Revenue Act of 1767 (26 June 1767)

This Act (7 Geo. III, c. 46) marks the renewal of the effort to raise additional funds in the colonies by Parliamentary taxation. This time the method was to collect colonial import duties on certain British manufactures and on tea. Unlike the Stamp Act, the funds to be raised were for the support of civil government in the colonies. In addition, it legalized the use of writs of assistance in the colonies, and, like the Revenue Act of 1764, virtually exempted British officials in the colonies from suits in colonial courts. Printed: Pickering, *Statutes at Large*, XXVII, pp. 505–512, *passim*.

Whereas it is expedient that a revenue should be raised, in your Majesty's dominions in America, for making a more certain and adequate provision for defraying the charge of the administration of justice, and the support of civil government in such provinces where it shall be found necessary, and towards further defraying the expenses of defending, protecting, and securing the said dominions; we, your Majesty's most dutiful and loyal subjects, the commons of Great Britain, in Parliament assembled, have therefore resolved to give and grant unto your Majesty the several

[1] No. 119.   [2] No. 98.   [3] No. 118.

rates and duties hereinafter mentioned; and do most humbly beseech your Majesty that it may be enacted, and be it enacted . . . that from and after the twentieth day of November, one thousand seven hundred and sixty-seven, there shall be raised, levied, collected, and paid, unto his Majesty, his heirs and successors, for and upon the respective goods hereinafter mentioned, which shall be imported from Great Britain into any colony or plantation in America which now is, or hereafter may be, under the dominion of his Majesty, his heirs or successors, the several rates and duties following [on glass, red and white lead, painters' colours, three pence a pound on tea, and on many varieties of paper].

IV. And it is hereby further enacted by the authority aforesaid, that the said rates and duties, charged by this Act upon goods imported into any British American colony or plantation, shall be deemed, and are hereby declared to be, sterling money of Great Britain; and shall be collected, recovered, and paid, to the amount of the value which such nominal sums bear in Great Britain; and that such monies may be received and taken, according to the proportion and value of five shillings and sixpence the ounce in silver. . . .

V. And be it further enacted by the authority aforesaid, that his Majesty and his successors shall be, and are hereby, empowered, from time to time, by any warrant or warrants under his or their royal sign manual or sign manuals, countersigned by the high treasurer, or any three or more of the commissioners of the treasury for the time being, to cause such monies to be applied out of the produce of the duties granted by this Act, as his Majesty or his successors shall think proper or necessary, for defraying the charges of the administration of justice, and the support of the civil government within all or any of the said colonies or plantations. . . .

X. [Because earlier Acts to prevent frauds in trade authorized writs of assistance but did not expressly provide for any particular court to grant them to the officers of the customs in the colonies] it is doubted whether such officers can legally enter houses and other places on land, to search for and seize goods, in the manner directed by the said recited Acts: To obviate which doubts for the future, and in order to carry the intention of the said recited Acts into effectual execution, be it enacted, . . . that from and after the said twentieth day of November, one thousand seven hundred and sixty-seven, such writs of assistance, to authorize and empower the officers of his Majesty's customs to enter and go into any house, warehouse, shop, cellar, or other place, in the British colonies or plantations in America, to search for and seize prohibited or uncustomed goods, in the manner directed by the said recited Acts, shall and may be granted by the said superior or supreme court of justice having jurisdiction within such colony or plantation respectively.

116. Act creating the American Board of Customs Commissioners (29 June 1767)

The creation of an American Board of Customs (7 Geo. III, c. 41) was essentially a continuation of the policy of reform begun by George Grenville in 1763. The establishment of the Board in the colonies undoubtedly did much to make the customs service more efficient, but at the same time the activities of the Board did much to increase the opposition of the Americans to all British policies. Printed: Pickering, *Statutes at Large*, XXVII, pp. 447-449, *passim*.

Whereas in pursuance of an Act of Parliament made in the twenty-fifth year of the reign of King Charles the second, entitled, An Act for the encouragement of the Greenland and Eastland trades, and for the better securing the plantation trade, the rates and duties imposed by that, and several subsequent Acts of Parliament, upon various goods imported into, or exported from, the British colonies and plantations in America, have been put under the management of the commissioners of the customs in England for the time being, by and under the authority and directions of the high treasurer, or commissioners of the treasury for the time being; and whereas the officers appointed for the collection of the said rates and duties in America are obliged to apply to the said commissioners of the customs in England for their special instructions and directions upon every particular doubt and difficulty which arises in relation to the payment of the said rates and duties; whereby all persons concerned in the commerce and trade of the said colonies and plantations are greatly obstructed and delayed in the carrying on and transacting of their business; and whereas the appointing of commissioners to be resident in some convenient part of his Majesty's dominions in America, and to be invested with such powers as are now exercised by the commissioners of the customs in England by virtue of the laws in being, would relieve the said merchants and traders from the said inconveniences, tend to the encouragement of commerce, and to the better securing of the said rates and duties by the more speedy and effectual collection thereof. be it therefore enacted . . . that the customs and other duties imposed, by any Act or Acts of Parliament, upon any goods or merchandises brought or imported into, or exported or carried from, any British colony or plantation in America, may, from time to time, be put under the management and direction of such commissioners, to reside in the said plantations, as his Majesty . . . by his . . . commission . . . under the great seal of Great Britain, shall judge to be most for the advantage of trade, and security of the revenue of the said British colonies; any law, custom, or usage to the contrary notwithstanding.

II. And it is hereby further enacted . . . that the said commissioners so to be appointed, or any three or more of them, shall have the same powers and authorities for carrying into execution the several laws relating to the revenues and trade of the said British colonies in America as were, before the passing of this Act, exercised by the commissioners of the customs in England, by virtue of any Act or Acts of Parliament now in force: and it shall and may be lawful to and for his Majesty . . . in such commission . . . to make provision for putting in execution the several laws relating to the customs and trade of the said British colonies.

117. Act suspending the New York assembly (2 July 1767)

The Act suspending the New York assembly (7 Geo. III, c. 59) was the most drastic step taken by Parliament before 1774. Although Parliament was forced to compromise with New York within two years, the damage done from the point of view of Americans was irreparable. Printed: Pickering, *Statutes at Large*, XXVII, pp. 609–610.

[Because the House of Representatives of New York have refused to provide supplies according to the Quartering Act of 1765 (5 Geo. III, c. 33), and subsequent Acts, it is enacted] that from and after the first day of October, one thousand seven hundred and sixty-seven, until provision shall have been made by the said assembly of New York for furnishing his Majesty's troops within the said province, with all such necessaries as are required by the said Acts of Parliament, or any of them, to be furnished for such troops, it shall not be lawful for the governor, lieutenant-governor, or person presiding or acting as governor or commander-in-chief, or for the council for the time being, within the colony, plantation, or province of New York in America, to pass, or give his or their assent to, or concurrence in, the making or passing of any act of assembly; or his or their assent to any order, resolution, or vote, in concurrence with the House of Representatives for the time being within the said colony, plantation, or province; or for the said house of representatives to pass or make any bill, order, resolution, or vote (orders, resolutions, or votes, for adjourning such house only, excepted) of any kind, for any other purpose whatsoever; and that all acts of assembly, orders, resolutions, and votes whatsoever, which shall or may be passed, assented to, or made, contrary to the tenor and meaning of this Act, after the said first day of October, one thousand seven hundred and sixty-seven, within the said colony, plantation, or province, before and until provision shall have been made for supplying his Majesty's troops with necessaries as aforesaid, shall be, and are hereby declared to be null and void, and of no force or effect whatsoever.

II. Provided nevertheless, and it is hereby declared to be the true intent and meaning of this Act, that nothing herein before contained shall extend, or be construed to extend, to hinder, prevent, or invalidate, the choice, election, or approbation, of a speaker of the House of Representatives for the time being within the said colony, plantation, or province.

118. The earl of Hillsborough: letter to General Thomas Gage on the new western policy (15 April 1768)

As a result of the demand for economy and of the combined pressure of land speculators and fur traders, both British and American, a new western policy was decided upon in 1768. The part of the letter which follows outlines the policy and some of the reasons for it. Printed: Clarence E. Carter, ed., *The Correspondence of General Thomas Gage with the Secretaries of State, and with the War Office and the Treasury, 1763-1775* (2 vols., New Haven, 1931-1933), II, pp. 61-64. The report of the Board of Trade dated 7 March 1768 upon which the policy was based is printed in *New York Colonial Documents*, VIII, pp. 19-31.

In my letter to you dated the 12th instant (No. 2) I acquainted you that had I taken the earliest opportunity of submitting to the committee of his Majesty's servants some propositions respecting the system to be finally adopted for the management of our interests with the savages in America, and for the future disposition of his Majesty's troops in consequence thereof, and that it was intended to enter into a full discussion of this business in the ensuing week.

The opinions formed upon the fullest consideration of this very important matter have been laid before his Majesty, who has examined them with the deepest attention and with the greatest solicitude for the interests and welfare of his subjects both in this kingdom and in his colonies.

Upon this occasion his Majesty has had recourse, not only to such of your letters as relate to those points which were the subject of this deliberation, but also to a report thereupon, made by the Lords of Trade, in consequence of a reference from the earl of Shelburne, and as his Majesty does in general approve not only the propositions contained in that report but also the principles on which they are founded, I have thought fit, in order to avoid unnecessary repetition, to send you herewith a copy of it for your information.

It appears to his Majesty that, in the present state of this kingdom, its future safety and welfare do in great measure depend upon the relieving it from every expense that is not of absolute necessity, and therefore, though his Majesty applauds the motives which induced the first institution of the present plan of superintendency for Indian affairs, which was evidently calculated to regain the confidence and combine the force of the savages against a then powerful enemy, yet, as in the present state of America, the main objects of that plan, if not entirely removed, are at least greatly diminished, his Majesty trusts that the continuance of it is rendered the less necessary, at least in its full extent, and that whatever regulations may be proper, they are more desirable for the sake of commerce than necessary for public security.

Upon this view of the state of this service, his Majesty has given the fullest attention to every circumstance that accompanies the present plan, as well in respect to the expense as to the difficulties that have been represented by the superintendents to attend the execution of it, and when his Majesty considers that the one is as far beyond the value of the object to be attained as the other is out of reach of any effectual remedy, his Majesty concurs in opinion with his Board of Trade, that the laying aside that part of it which relates to the Indian trade and entrusting the entire management of that trade to the colonies themselves, will be of public utility and advantage as a means of avoiding much difficulty, and saving much expense to this country, both in present and in future.

As his Majesty observes however that both yourself and Sir William Johnson have, in several of your letters, expressed some apprehensions of ill consequences that might follow from a neglect in the colonies to establish those regulations which might prevent or correct the frauds and abuses of private traders, and that such neglect might operate to endanger the public peace, his Majesty has not been wanting in a due attention to so important a consideration.

His Majesty is convinced from the experience of former times that antecedent to the establishment of the present regulations by superintendents, the traders were guilty of the grossest frauds and abuses; that little care was taken to correct those abuses; and that this neglect occasioned the Indians to break out into frequent hostilities. The same experience however serves to show that these were evils merely of a local operation and would have produced their own remedy, perhaps at no other expense than the temporary abandonment of a few straggling settlements upon the frontiers, had not the consideration of the safety of the posts in the interior country, which from their situation necessarily became the first objects of the resentment of the savages, involved this kingdom (upon every rupture between them and the colonies) in the necessity of carrying on a war in the Indian country at an enormous and ruinous expense.

The propriety therefore of entrusting the management of the trade with the Indians to the colonies does, in this view of the case, appear to his Majesty to depend in great measure upon a reduction of such posts in the interior country as are, by their situation, exposed to the resentment of the savages, it being evident that in proportion as the number of such posts is diminished, the necessity of carrying on an Indian war at the expense of this kingdom will be the less, and the colonies themselves will be more attentive to their own security by adopting such of the regulations established under the present plan of superintendency as have evidently operated to the benefit of the trade and to the giving that satisfaction and content to the Indians, from which alone the colonies can hope to derive either immediate profit or lasting peace. It is not however from this consideration alone that his Majesty is induced to wish for a reduction of the posts in the interior country. The great expense of these establishments and the effect they have to destroy all useful discipline by keeping the troops divided into small parties, are inconveniences which have been severely felt, and strongly represented. But at the same time it is not his Majesty's intention that any of these reasons, however just and cogent, should operate to induce such a reduction in the military establishments, or a reform in the plan for the management of Indian affairs as shall be inconsistent with public safety, by withdrawing that protection which may be thought necessary to give facility to commerce, or may weaken those alliances between his Majesty and the Indians, which both his Majesty's honour and the public interests require to be preserved.

His Majesty therefore concurs in opinion with his Board of Trade, that the offices of superintendents of Indian affairs should be continued for all those purposes enumerated in their report to his Majesty.

That provision should be made by a stated estimate for a salary of £1,000 per annum to each superintendent, and for an allowance of £3,000 per annum to each for annual or occasional presents to the Indians, and to answer all other contingent expenses, which allowance is on no account to be exceeded.

That all the establishments made with a view to the execution of the regulations for the trade (which is now to be left to the management of the colonies) be discontinued.

That the line between the settlements of his Majesty's subjects and the Indian country, as described in the report of the Board of Trade, be everywhere finally ratified and confirmed, and that the several colonies be required and enjoined in the strongest manner to provide by provincial laws for the punishment of any persons who shall make settlements beyond such line, or be guilty of any frauds or abuses in carrying on the trade with the Indians.

That the forts of Niagara, Detroit, and Michilimakinac be kept up and garrisoned in such manner as you shall think fit; and that such a naval force be maintained upon the lakes as you shall judge necessary for keeping up a proper communication, and giving all reasonable facility and protection to the trade of his Majesty's subjects, taking care that the establishment be so formed as that the expense be reduced to some certain annual estimate, and in this you will have regard to the report of the Board of Trade, and to any contracts already made.

His Majesty has not failed in this great and extensive consideration to give due attention to propositions which have been made with regard to establishments on the rivers Mississippi, Ohio, and Illinois; but as his Majesty has doubts concerning the utility of establishments in such remote situations, which consequently cannot be kept up but at an immense expense, it is the king's pleasure that you should report your opinion with regard to the continuance of any of the forts in those situations, and in the meantime that you should keep up for the present Fort Chartres, or some proper post in the Illinois, and Pittsburgh, as also either the works at Ticonderoga, or the fort at Crown Point, as a communication between New York and Quebec, and that you should in like manner report your opinion upon the necessity of this last.

These, sir, are the only establishments in the interior country of the utility of which his Majesty has sufficient information to give any directions. As to all other posts and establishments, as well in the interior country as in the settled parts of the colonies, and the islands dependent thereon, which you shall think not absolutely necessary for public safety in general, his Majesty trusts that the present state of his colonies, under the security they derive from the important cessions made to his Majesty by the Treaty of Paris, may with propriety admit of their entire reduction, and that the fifteen battalions employed for the service of North America may be so stationed in large bodies in the provinces of Quebec, Nova Scotia, East Florida, and the middle colonies, as to be in a proper state with regard to discipline and situation to serve effectually upon any emergency whatever. . . .

119. Order in Council establishing four courts of Vice-Admiralty in the colonies (6 July 1768)

By the authority of the Revenue Act of 1764 (No. 99), a Vice-Admiralty court for all the colonies was established at Halifax, Nova Scotia, in 1765. It was soon recognized, however, that this court was too far from the commercial centres of the colonies, and in 1768 Parliament passed an Act (8 Geo. III, c. 22) authorizing the establishment of additional courts. Acting on the basis of this legislation, the Privy Council ordered the Admiralty to establish four courts: at Halifax, Boston, Philadelphia, and Charleston. These courts were given original jurisdiction in all cases arising within their districts as well as the right to hear appeals from provincial Vice-Admiralty courts. Printed: *Acts of the Privy Council, Colonial Series*, v, pp. 151–153.

[Order in accordance with the following Treasury representation of 2 July.] Whereas by an Act passed in the last session of the last Parliament entitled an Act for the more easy and effectual recovery of the penalties and forfeitures inflicted by the Acts of Parliament relating to the trade or revenues of the British colonies and plantations in America, it is enacted that from and after the first day of September 1768 all forfeitures and penalties inflicted by any Act or Acts of Parliament relating to the trade or revenues of the British colonies or plantations in America may be prosecuted, sued for, and recovered in any court of vice-admiralty appointed or to be appointed, and which shall have jurisdiction within the colony, plantation, or place where the cause of such prosecution shall have arisen, and that in all cases where any prosecution or suit shall be commenced and determined for any penalty or forfeiture inflicted by any such Act or Acts of Parliament in any court of admiralty in the respective colony or plantation where the offence shall be committed, either party who shall think himself aggrieved by such determination may appeal from such determination to any court of vice-admiralty appointed or to be appointed, and which shall have jurisdiction within such colony, plantation, or place; and whereas it will greatly contribute to the due collection of your Majesty's revenue; and to the prevention and punishment of frauds committed against the same, and will likewise tend to the more speedy and effectual administration of justice within the said colonies and plantations, and be agreeable to the intention of the legislature in passing the said Act that a sufficient number of such courts of vice-admiralty be constituted and established at proper and convenient places within the said colonies and plantations: we humbly submit to your Majesty whether it may not be expedient and necessary for the purposes above-mentioned to revoke the commission appointing one only court of vice-admiralty over all America, and in lieu thereof, to establish four other courts of vice-admiralty, the first at Halifax in the province of Nova Scotia; the second at Boston in the province of New England; the third at Philadelphia in the colony of Pennsylvania, and the fourth at Charles Town in the colony of South Carolina: the said courts to have jurisdiction within certain districts to be allotted to them respectively by your Majesty [a plan of which districts is submitted], each of the judges of the said courts respectively to be allowed such salary as your Majesty shall think proper, to be paid in the first place out of your Majesty's moiety of the money arising from any penalties and forfeitures to be levied within the said colonies and plantations, and if this fund shall not be sufficient, out of the money arising from the sale of old naval stores; and the said judges to be expressly enjoined in their commissions, upon pain of losing their offices, not to take any fee or gratuity whatsoever for any judgment given, or business done, in their respective courts.

[Plan of the districts. (1) Halifax: original jurisdiction in all cases (a) arising within the limits of Quebec, Newfoundland, and Nova Scotia, and within three leagues of the shores thereof; (b) arising from the capture of ships to the northward of 43° 15′ N. or of ships whose port of destination is within the above colonies.

(2) Boston: (a) New Hampshire, Massachusetts Bay, Rhode Island, and Connecticut; (b) between 40° 30′ N. and 44° 30′ N.

(3) Philadelphia: (a) New York, New Jersey, Pennsylvania, Delaware, Maryland, and Virginia; (b) between 41° N. and 36° 15′ N.

(4) Charleston: (a) N. and S. Carolina, Georgia, E. and W. Florida; (b) to the southward of 36° 45′ N.]

Each court to have appellate jurisdiction from vice-admiralty courts in these colonies.

[On an Admiralty memorial of 25 August the judges' salary is fixed at £600 each.]

D. THE COLONIES v. THE MINISTRY, 1767–1770

COLONIAL opposition to the various Acts sponsored by Charles Townshend was immediate. Regardless of the variety of political opinions in the colonies, most Americans objected for one reason or another. The most conservative colonial leader could agree with the most radical that he wanted none of the interference with colonial self-government implicit in the proposal to use the funds from the Revenue Act of 1767 to pay British civil officials in the colonies. The withholding of salaries, or the threat to do so, was perhaps more important as a symbol than as an actual political weapon, yet it had been one device by which colonial legislatures had acquired virtual independence. Aside from its political implications, the colonists looked upon the Act as an economic threat as well. The duties levied, as in the case of the Stamp Act, were to be payable only in specie. The colonies had always lacked an adequate supply of specie, and this legislation, coupled with the deflationary Currency Act of 1764[1] and the post-war depression, all added fuel to discontent with British policy. The suspension of the New York Assembly[2] was an unprecedented intervention by Parliament in the internal affairs of the colonies and its political and constitutional implications were even clearer than those of the Revenue Act of 1767.[3]

Colonial opposition took various forms. The legislation of 1767 was denounced in colonial legislatures, in town meetings, in extra-legal meetings of merchants and of popular political organizations, and in newspaper and pamphlet publications. The most striking pamphlet was that of John Dickinson of Pennsylvania. His *Letters from a Farmer in Pennsylvania to the Inhabitants of the British Colonies* began appearing in colonial newspapers in December 1767, and by March 1768 were in pamphlet form. Several editions appeared in the colonies, two in London, one in Dublin, and a French translation was circulated widely in Europe. The argument presented was legalistic, but few colonials found difficulty in accepting it, for it was essentially the argument they had used against the Revenue Act of 1764 and the Stamp Act of 1765. Parliament had no right to tax the colonies. It could regulate trade by the imposition of duties but if it levied duties on trade to raise revenue, it was a tax. The Townshend duties were a tax, for the framers of that Act had admitted that it was for the purpose of raising revenue.

But, as in the case of the Stamp Act, the colonists turned to more direct methods of opposition. On 11 February 1768 the Massachusetts legislature adopted a circular letter to be sent to the other colonial legislatures. It urged a union of forces in opposing the Townshend duty Act and other measures of Parliament and flatly denied the constitutionality of much parliamentary legislation for the colonies.[4] Hillsborough's response was immediate. He wrote to Governor Bernard of Massachusetts ordering him to have the legislature rescind the circular letter. If the legislature refused, it was to be dissolved. A circular letter to the governors of other colonies ordered them to use their influence to prevent consideration of the Massachusetts letter in their colonies. If their legislatures did so, they were to be dissolved.[5] These orders merely spurred the colonists to further opposition. Colonial legislatures defied the ministry and supported

---

[1] No. 100.   [2] No. 117.   [3] No. 115.   [4] No. 120.   [5] No. 121.

Massachusetts. New elections after the dissolutions resulted in strengthening the opponents of Great Britain in virtually every colonial legislature.

Meanwhile the opposition to the strengthening of the customs service had been continuous. The story was the same in almost every colony: seizures of ships and goods for supposed violations were often followed by mob action resulting in the recovery of whatever had been seized. Customs officers were treated violently or so intimidated that they did not dare to function.[1] The famous affair of John Hancock's sloop, the *Liberty*, in June 1768 was only one of many similar cases. It was not entirely a one-sided matter, however, for some of the customs officials were plainly 'racketeers', as were those in South Carolina.

The American Board of Customs arrived in Boston in November 1767. Popular opposition was immediate and increasingly violent, and more and more merchants in Boston moved or were driven in the direction of open defiance of enforcement. The customs commissioners were frightened by mob action and demanded protection. Governor Bernard wanted troops sent in, but he was unwilling to ask for them; in fact, he could not make the request of General Gage in New York without the consent of the Massachusetts Council, and this would not have been given if asked for. Gage was eager to send troops, but he could not do so without a request from the governor and council. The only person who acted with decision was Commodore Samuel Hood, who was in charge of the British Navy in American waters. When the customs commissioners appealed to him, he promptly sent the warship *Romney* to Boston harbour.

When the news of increasing violence in Massachusetts reached London, Hillsborough promptly ordered General Gage to send one or more regiments to be quartered in the town of Boston for the purpose of supporting the civil government in maintaining peace and aiding the customs officials in doing their duty.[2] Commodore Hood's action in sending a warship was ratified and further ships were ordered to Boston harbour. Eventually the headquarters of the British Navy in North America were removed from Halifax to Boston.

There was an immediate reaction in Massachusetts to the news of troops being ordered to Boston. The Boston town meeting asked Governor Bernard to call a special session of the legislature. The governor refused, explaining that he could not call a new session until he received permission from Britain, a situation that existed because of the refusal of the legislature to rescind the circular letter of February 1768.[3] The town meeting thereupon adopted a forthright statement of the rights of the colonists, and then proceeded to the extraordinary step of calling a provincial convention to meet in Boston on 22 September.[4] This was outright defiance of royal authority in the colony and was looked upon with horror by royal officials. The convention was widely attended, but it was cautious in its deliberations. The popular leaders in Boston plainly wanted to take extreme measures in opposition to the coming of the troops, but members from the country towns were extremely dubious. The result was a series of letters and petitions by no means as extreme in statement as many of the documents being produced by colonial legislatures.

During November and December 1768 and January 1769 the ministry laid before Parliament various reports of the difficulties with the colonies, and particularly with Massachusetts. The result was that both houses adopted a series of resolutions and an

<hr />

[1] Nos. 127A, 128, 131. [2] No. 122. [3] No. 120. [4] No. 123.

address to the king, in which they declared among other things that the Massachusetts convention had been called for the purpose of setting up a "new and unconstitutional authority independent of the Crown of Great Britain". Parliament urged the king to secure evidence of treason on the part of Massachusetts leaders and to bring them to England for trial under a statute of 35 Henry VIII.[1]

No action was ever taken as a result of this proposal, but it further alarmed and angered the colonists. The Virginia legislature adopted a series of spirited resolves reiterating the 'sole right' of taxing themselves, their right to join with other colonists in petitioning the Crown, and denouncing the proposal for taking a citizen from his own colony to England for trial.[2] The Virginia legislature sent its resolutions to other colonial legislatures and they supported Virginia.[3]

While orders, petitions, and resolutions were being sent back and forth across the Atlantic, the Americans, as during the Stamp Act crisis, were taking more forceful means to oppose British policies. Again the town of Boston took the lead. When the news of the suspension of the New York Assembly reached Boston in August 1767, a public meeting was held. Governor Bernard reported that a "Son of Liberty" proposed that "we shall do as we have done before, agree to send for no more English goods". This proposal for an economic boycott came from the popular leaders of the town and not from the merchants, who were reluctant to suspend trade and worried over the activities of their political opponents in the popular party. The Boston leaders then demanded a special session of the legislature, and when Governor Bernard refused, they called a special town meeting on 28 October.

The town meeting blamed the depression on heavy taxes, the loss of trade, the lack of money, and the unfavourable trade balance with Britain. The meeting then resolved to encourage local manufactures and authorized the preparation of a non-consumption agreement to be signed by those who would bind themselves not to purchase certain imported goods, and particularly high-priced cloth. The proposal was mild and the agreement was to be voluntary, but it met with opposition. Governor Bernard was convinced that "the principal people" were disposed to "prevent popular commotions in the future". While this was doubtless the case, the movement spread. At least thirty Massachusetts towns adopted the Boston agreement, and similar agreements were adopted in Providence and Newport, Rhode Island, and in several Connecticut towns before the end of the year.

The next step in the development of opposition was taken by the Massachusetts legislature, which, as we have seen, had adopted the circular letter of February 1768.[4] But the legislature balked at adopting a colony-wide non-consumption agreement which was proposed by the Boston members. While the legislature was debating this proposal, the popular leaders in Boston and some of the more radical merchants met on 4 March and adopted an agreement to stop the importation of European commodities except for salt, coal, fishing-supplies, lead and shot, for the period of a year. However, the agreement was not to go into effect unless New York and Philadelphia would adopt similar measures. In April the New York merchants adopted a non-importation agreement but made its operation depend on acceptance by Boston and Philadelphia. The Boston merchants agreed, but those of Philadelphia refused.

British measures, however, provided the necessary ammunition for those who wanted to use economic pressure to oppose British policy. Hillsborough's order to rescind the Massachusetts circular letter and his order to send troops to Boston made

[1] No. 124.   [2] No. 125A.   [3] No. 125B.   [4] No. 120.

it possible to apply even greater pressure on the reluctant Boston merchants. On 1 August 1768 a Boston meeting agreed to the non-importation of all British goods, except articles necessary for the fisheries, for the year 1769.[1] This was an unconditional agreement and not dependent upon the co-operation of other commercial towns in the colonies. Many of the Boston merchants refused to sign the agreement but Governor Bernard predicted, correctly for once, that they would "be brought to reason by mob law. . . ." It seems clear that if the Boston merchants had been left to themselves, few of them would have agreed to a non-importation agreement of any kind. While they did not like the duty Act, they were increasingly alarmed at the popular leaders in Boston who had won their first real victories at the time of the Stamp Act and who were to gain power steadily in the town and the province until 1770.

Similar developments took place in other colonies. There was increasing popular pressure in both New York and Philadelphia, and this, coupled with the opposition of even the most conservative Americans to the political and economic aims of British policy, brought one colony after another into the non-importation movement. In August 1768 the New York merchants adopted an agreement to stop the importation of British goods, except for a specific list of items, after 1 November. A few days later the retailers and tradesmen of New York adopted an agreement that they would not purchase goods brought in contrary to the merchants' agreement, a measure calculated to keep the merchants firm in the cause.

In Philadelphia, John Dickinson had supported the Boston proposal for non-importation in the spring of 1768. The Philadelphia merchants, however, could not be persuaded, and they were charged with preferring profits to patriotism. After Boston and New York adopted their agreements in August 1768, the Philadelphia merchants again refused to co-operate and seemed quite content to await the result of a memorial from the legislature to Parliament. However, they did agree to non-importation in the spring of 1769 if the memorial did not achieve results. Since it did not, the Philadelphia merchants on 10 March 1769 adopted a non-importation agreement with the usual list of articles excepted.

In the southern colonies where, except for South Carolina, the planters were the dominant element, there was less haste in the adoption of non-importation agreements. Virginia adopted an agreement in May 1769, and Maryland in June. South Carolina merchants were reluctant to enter any agreement. Nevertheless the legislature took a vigorous stand on the issues of the times. It instructed the colonial agent in London to work for the repeal of the Townshend Acts, and it approved of the Massachusetts circular letter in defiance of Hillsborough's order to ignore it. It was prorogued for its pains in the autumn of 1768, but when it met again in June 1769 it took an even firmer stand. It refused supplies for British troops, and when the Virginia resolves in opposition to the resolutions of Parliament of February 1769 were laid before it, the South Carolina legislature approved and adopted a vigorous set of resolutions of their own.[2]

Meanwhile there was increasing agitation for outright non-consumption of British goods by planters and mechanics in order to force the merchants to stop importation. An agreement was adopted on 29 June 1769, and the very next day the merchants met to plan an agreement of their own. Eventually the three groups— merchants, planters, and mechanics—agreed upon a non-importation agreement.[3] It

[1] No. 126A.   [2] No. 125B.   [3] No. 126B.

was the most comprehensive and probably the most vigorously enforced of any of those adopted in the colonies.

The whole non-consumption and non-importation movement in the colonies is of extraordinary importance, both in terms of internal politics and in terms of relations with Britain. It is plain, in the light of recent research, that in virtually every colony the economic opposition to the Townshend Acts was begun by the leaders of popular parties in the colonies, and not by the merchants. With some exceptions, the popular leaders proposed non-consumption of British goods, a measure which merchants looked upon as aimed at themselves as much as at British policy. Although reluctant merchants countered with the proposal that only the goods taxed in the Townshend Revenue Act be the object of non-importation agreements, they were forced by popular pressure to adopt agreements of far wider scope.

The question of the effectiveness of the non-importation agreements on British policy is debatable. The agreements were not uniform in character throughout the colonies nor was enforcement at all complete. Nevertheless, colonial imports from England did drop sharply in some colonies, particularly in New England, New York, Pennsylvania, and South Carolina. This drop, however, did not excite British merchants and manufacturers as had the decline of exports in 1764 and 1765. For one thing, economic conditions were better in England in 1768 and 1769 than they had been. For another, British merchants had been alienated by the violence of colonial opposition to the Stamp Act. Then, too, the colonial insistence on the 'unconstitutionality' of the Townshend Revenue Act was deeply disturbing. Many English merchants were willing to oppose the duties on economic grounds but were unwilling to agree with the constitutional arguments of the Americans.

As a revenue measure the Act was a failure. In 1768, £13,202 were collected. The next year collections dropped to £5,561, and in 1770, although repeal did not take effect until 1 December, the collections were but £2,727. Even before this was clear, the ministry began to display doubts of the wisdom of the Act.

In February 1769, Hillsborough proposed to the Cabinet that Virginia and the West India colonies, which had permanent civil lists, be exempted from the Act and that it remain in force in the other colonies only until they provided permanent funds for the civil establishment. The king declared that the conduct of the Virginians had been so offensive during the last spring that he objected to any change in the law during the present session of Parliament. However, he said it would be proper to 'hint' that those colonies which submitted to the law and made proper establishments for governors and other services might be exempted from the law in another year, except for the duty on tea.

Shortly after the session of Parliament ended in May 1769, Hillsborough sent a circular letter to all the governors in America. He told them no measure ought to be taken that would in any way "derogate from the legislative authority of Great Britain over the colonies" and went on to say that despite insinuations to the contrary, the ministry had no intention of proposing that Parliament lay any further taxes upon America to raise a revenue. Furthermore, he announced it as the intention of the ministry to propose that the next session of Parliament remove the duties on glass, papers, and colours, "upon consideration of such duties having been laid contrary to the true principles of commerce".

The North ministry took office in January 1770, and North carried through the repeal. He justified it on the ground that the duties were levied on British manufactures and were therefore injurious to British commercial interests. However, the tax on tea was to be retained to maintain the principle of the right of Parliament to tax the colonies. The effort of the opposition to repeal the tax on tea was beaten down and the final Bill repealing the Townshend Revenue Act passed the House of Commons 12 April 1770, to take effect 1 December 1770.[1]

The effort to raise revenue in the colonies by direct taxation was thus abandoned. The retention of the tax on tea was to maintain a principle, and it produced little revenue: the effect was the reinforcement of the American principle that the American colonies could not be taxed by Parliament, for the Americans smuggled tea as never before. Nevertheless, the course of events in the colonies since 1765 caused many an American leader to accept the situation in 1770. Many Americans who had been vigorous opponents of British policy in 1765 were frightened by the rise of popular leaders and popular parties and the violence that accompanied that rise; therefore they welcomed an excuse to come to terms with Great Britain in order to suppress internal commotions. The repeal of the Townshend Revenue Act gave them the opportunity they wanted to regain control of the political life of the colonies, and they seized upon it gladly.

120. Massachusetts Circular Letter to the Colonial Legislatures (11 February 1768)

As early as August 1767 popular leaders in Boston proposed a non-consumption policy to oppose the Townshend Revenue Act of 1767, but the majority of Boston merchants were opposed. The Boston leaders then demanded a special session of the legislature, but Governor Bernard refused to call one. Before the legislature met in regular session in December the Boston town meeting instructed its delegation to urge measures to encourage domestic manufactures, to discourage imports, and to object to the Revenue Act of 1767 on both economic and constitutional grounds. When the legislature met, it appointed a committee on the state of the province which wrote letters to various members of the ministry and prepared a petition to the king. The committee then proposed a circular letter to be sent to the other colonies urging them to join with Massachusetts in defeating the Revenue Act. At first this motion was rejected two to one, but within two weeks it was passed and all mention of the previous defeat erased from the journals. The circular letter marks a step forward in the control of the popular party, for it based Massachusetts objections on constitutional as well as on economic grounds, a stand which the Boston town meeting took as early as 1764 but which the legislature had refused to accept (see Nos. 103 and 104). Printed: Bradford, ed., *Speeches of the Governors of Massachusetts . . .*, pp. 134–136.

The House of Representatives of this province have taken into their serious consideration the great difficulties that must accrue to themselves and their constituents by the operation of several Acts of Parliament, imposing duties and taxes on the American colonies.

As it is a subject in which every colony is deeply interested, they have no reason to doubt but your house is deeply impressed with its importance, and that such constitutional measures will be come into as are proper. It seems to be necessary that all possible care should be taken that the representatives of the several assemblies, upon so delicate a point, should harmonize with each other. The House, therefore, hope that this letter will be candidly considered in no other light than as expressing a disposition freely to communicate their mind to a sister colony, upon a common concern, in the same manner as they would be glad to receive the sentiments of your or any other house of assembly on the continent.

[1] 10 Geo. III, c. 17.

The House have humbly represented to the ministry their own sentiments, that his Majesty's high court of Parliament is the supreme legislative power over the whole empire; that in all free states the constitution is fixed, and as the supreme legislative derives its power and authority from the constitution, it cannot overleap the bounds of it without destroying its own foundation; that the constitution ascertains and limits both sovereignty and allegiance, and, therefore, his Majesty's American subjects, who acknowledge themselves bound by the ties of allegiance, have an equitable claim to the full enjoyment of the fundamental rules of the British constitution; that it is an essential, unalterable right in nature, engrafted into the British constitution, as a fundamental law, and ever held sacred and irrevocable by the subjects within the realm, that what a man has honestly acquired is absolutely his own, which he may freely give, but cannot be taken from him without his consent; that the American subjects may, therefore, exclusive of any consideration of charter rights, with a decent firmness, adapted to the character of free men and subjects, assert this natural and constitutional right.

It is, moreover, their humble opinion, which they express with the greatest deference to the wisdom of the Parliament, that the Acts made there, imposing duties on the people of this province, with the sole and express purpose of raising a revenue, are infringements of their natural and constitutional rights; because, as they are not represented in the British Parliament, his Majesty's commons in Britain, by those Acts, grant their property without their consent.

This House further are of opinion that their constituents, considering their local circumstances, cannot, by any possibility, be represented in the Parliament; and that it will forever be impracticable, that they should be equally represented there, and consequently, not at all; being separated by an ocean of a thousand leagues. That his Majesty's royal predecessors, for this reason, were graciously pleased to form a subordinate legislature here, that their subjects might enjoy the unalienable right of a representation; also, that considering the utter impracticability of their ever being fully and equally represented in Parliament, and the great expense that must unavoidably attend even a partial representation there, this House think that a taxation of their constituents, even without their consent, grievous as it is, would be preferable to any representation that could be admitted for them there.

Upon these principles, and also considering that were the right in Parliament ever so clear, yet, for obvious reasons, it would be beyond the rules of equity that their constituents should be taxed on the manufactures of Great Britain here, in addition to the duties they pay for them in England, and other advantages arising to Great Britain, from the Acts of trade, this House have preferred a humble, dutiful, and loyal petition, to our most gracious sovereign, and made such representations to his Majesty's ministers, as they apprehended would tend to obtain redress.

They have also submitted to consideration, whether any people can be said to enjoy any degree of freedom if the Crown, in addition to its undoubted authority of constituting a governor, should appoint him such a stipend as it may judge proper, without the consent of the people, and at their expense; and whether, while the judges of the land, and other civil officers, hold not their commissions during good behaviour, their having salaries appointed for them by the Crown, independent of the people, hath not a tendency to subvert the principles of equity, and endanger the happiness and security of the subject.

In addition to these measures, the House have written a letter to their agent which he is directed to lay before the ministry; wherein they take notice of the hardships of the Act for preventing mutiny and desertion, which requires the governor and council to provide enumerated articles for the king's marching troops, and the people to pay the expenses; and also, the commission of the gentlemen appointed commissioners of the customs, to reside in America, which authorizes them to make as many appointments as they think fit, and to pay the appointees what sum they please, for whose malconduct they are not accountable; from whence it may happen that officers of the Crown may be multiplied to such a degree as to become dangerous to the liberty of the people, by virtue of a commission, which does not appear to this House to derive any such advantages to trade as many have supposed.

These are the sentiments and proceedings of this House; and as they have too much reason to believe that the enemies of the colonies have represented them to his Majesty's ministers, and to the Parliament, as factious, disloyal, and having a disposition to make themselves independent of the mother country, they have taken occasion, in the most humble terms, to assure his Majesty, and his ministers, that, with regard to the people of this province, and, as they doubt not, of all the colonies, the charge is unjust. The House is fully satisfied that your assembly is too generous and liberal in sentiment to believe that this letter proceeds from an ambition of taking the lead, or dictating to the other assemblies. They freely submit their opinions to the judgment of others; and shall take it kind in your house to point out to them anything further that may be thought necessary.

This House cannot conclude, without expressing their firm confidence in the king, our common head and father, that the united and dutiful supplications of his distressed American subjects will meet with his royal and favourable acceptance.

121. Circular letter to the governors in America (21 April 1768)

When the Massachusetts circular letter reached London in April, it was laid before the Cabinet. A few days later Hillsborough wrote Governor Bernard ordering him to have the Massachusetts legislature rescind the circular letter at its next session. He told Bernard that if the legislature refused, he wanted a complete account of its proceedings to be laid before Parliament so that steps could be taken to prevent such extraordinary and unconstitutional conduct in the future. (C.O. 5/757.) In addition, the following circular letter was sent to the other governors on the mainland.

The Massachusetts legislature refused to rescind the letter on 30 June 1768 by a vote of 92 to 17, and Governor Bernard dissolved it the next day. The other colonial legislatures refused to obey their governors' orders. Thus Hillsborough's letter achieved the result which the Massachusetts circular letter had not been able to: common defiance by the colonial legislatures. In addition, it greatly strengthened the position of the popular leaders in Massachusetts. Printed: *New York Colonial Documents*, VIII, pp. 58-59.

I have his Majesty's commands to transmit to you the enclosed copy of a letter from the speaker of the House of Representatives of the colony of Massachusetts Bay, addressed by order of that House to the speaker of the assembly of each colony upon the continent of North America.

As his Majesty considers this measure to be of a most dangerous and factious tendency, calculated to inflame the minds of his good subjects in the colonies, to promote an unwarrantable combination, and to excite and encourage an open opposition to and denial of the authority of Parliament, and to subvert the true principles of the constitution; it is his Majesty's pleasure that you should immediately upon the receipt hereof exert your utmost influence to defeat this flagitious attempt to disturb the public peace by prevailing upon the Assembly of your province to take no notice of it, which will be treating it with the contempt it deserves.

The repeated proofs which have been given by the Assembly of [   ] of their reverence and respect for the laws, and of their faithful attachment to the constitution, leave little room in his Majesty's breast to doubt of their showing a proper resentment of this unjustifiable attempt to revive those distractions which have operated so fatally to the prejudice of this kingdom and the colonies; and accordingly his Majesty has the fullest confidence in their affections. But if, notwithstanding these expectations and your most earnest endeavours, there should appear in the Assembly of your province a disposition to receive or give any countenance to this seditious paper, it will be your duty to prevent any proceeding upon it by an immediate prorogation or dissolution.

122. The earl of Hillsborough: letter to General Thomas Gage ordering British troops to be stationed in Boston (8 June 1768)

Opposition to British customs officers was greater in Massachusetts than in any other colony except Rhode Island. Report after report of violent opposition in Boston and of general political and civil strife was sent to London. The news of the riots in Boston in March and April 1768 was the immediate occasion for the following letter to General Thomas Gage. For the results of this momentous decision see Nos. 129 and 130. Printed: Carter, ed., *Gage Correspondence*, II, pp. 68–69.

I transmit to you, for your private information, copies of a letter from his Majesty's commissioners of the revenue to the lords of the Treasury; of my circular letter to the several governors upon the continent in consequence of it, and of Governor Bernard's three last letters to my office.

The contents of these papers will evince to you how necessary it is become that such measures should be taken as will strengthen the hands of government in the province of Massachusetts Bay, enforce a due obedience to the laws, and protect and support the civil magistrates and the officers of the Crown in the execution of their duty.

For these purposes I am to signify to you his Majesty's pleasure that you do forthwith order one regiment, or such force as you shall think necessary, to Boston, to be quartered in that town and to give every legal assistance to the civil magistrate in the preservation of the public peace; and to the officers of the revenue in the execution of the laws of trade and revenue. And as this appears to be a service of a delicate nature, and possibly leading to consequences not easily foreseen, I am directed by the king to recommend to you to make choice of an officer for the command of these troops upon whose prudence, resolution, and integrity you can entirely rely.

The necessary measures for quartering and providing for these troops must be entirely left to your direction, but I would submit to you whether, as troops will probably continue in that town, and a place of some strength may in case of emergency be of great service, it would not be advisable to take possession of, and repair if repairs be wanting, the little castle, or fort of William and Mary, which belongs to the Crown.

123. Resolutions of the Boston town meeting (13 September 1768)

The following resolutions were adopted after Governor Bernard refused a request of the town meeting to call a special session of the legislature to consider the expected arrival of British troops in Boston. The resolutions are notable, not only for their statement of colonial rights, but because the town meeting took the revolutionary step of calling a provincial convention. The proceedings were ordered printed in the newspapers, and copies sent by express to the other towns in the province. Printed: *Boston Town Records, 1758–1769*, pp. 261–264.

The committee appointed to take the state of our public affairs into consideration reported the following declaration and resolves:

Whereas it is the first principle in civil society, founded in nature and reason, that no law of the society can be binding on any individual without his consent, given by himself in person, or by his representative of his own free election; and whereas in and by an Act of the British Parliament passed in the first year of the reign of King William and Queen Mary, of glorious and blessed memory, entitled an Act declaring the Rights and Liberties of the Subject, and Settling the Succession of the Crown; the Preamble of which Act is in these words, viz: "Whereas the late King James the Second, by the assistance of diverse evil councillors, judges, and ministers employed by him, did endeavour to subvert and extirpate the Protestant religion, and the laws and liberties of this kingdom," it is expressly among other things declared, that the levying money for the use of the Crown, by pretence of prerogative, without grant of Parliament for a longer time or in other manner than the same is granted, is illegal. And whereas in the third year of the reign of the same King William and Queen Mary, their Majesties were graciously pleased by their royal charter to give and grant to the inhabitants of his Majesty's province all the territory therein described, to be held in free and common socage; and also to ordain and grant to the said inhabitants certain rights, liberties, and privileges therein expressly mentioned; among which it is granted, established, and ordained, that all and every the subjects of them, their heirs and successors, which shall go to inhabit within said province and territory, and every of their children which shall happen to be born there, or on the seas in going thither, or returning from thence, shall have and enjoy all liberties and immunities of free and natural subjects, within any of the dominions of them, their heirs and successors, to all intents, purposes, and constructions whatever, as if they and every of them were born within the realm of England.

And whereas by the aforesaid Act of Parliament made in the first year of the said King William and Queen Mary, all and singular the premises contained therein, are claimed, demanded, and insisted on as the undoubted rights and liberties of the subjects born within the realm.

And whereas the freeholders and other inhabitants of this town, the metropolis of the province in said charter mentioned, do hold all the rights and liberties therein contained to be sacred and inviolable; at the same time publicly and solemnly acknowledging their firm and unshaken allegiance to their alone and rightful sovereign King George the third, the lawful successor of the said King William and Queen Mary to the British throne.

Resolved, that the said freeholders and other inhabitants of the Town of Boston will at the utmost peril of their lives and fortunes take all legal and constitutional measures to defend and maintain the person, family, crown, and dignity of our said sovereign Lord George the third; and all and singular the rights, liberties, privileges, and immunities granted in the said royal charter, as well as those which are declared to be belonging to us as British subjects by birthright, as all others therein specially mentioned.

And whereas by the said royal charter it is specially granted to the Great and General Court or assembly therein constituted, to impose and levy proportionable and reasonable assessments, rates, and taxes upon the estates and persons of all and every the proprietors and inhabitants of said province or territory, for the service of the king in the necessary defence and support of his government of this province, and the protection and preservation of his subjects therein, therefore:

Voted, as the opinion of this town, that the levying money within this province for the use and service of the Crown in other manner than the same is granted by the Great and General Court or assembly of this province is in violation of the said royal charter; and the same is also in violation of the undoubted natural rights of subjects, declared in the aforesaid Act of Parliament, freely to give and grant their own money for the service of the Crown, with their own consent, in person, or by representatives of their own free election.

And whereas in the aforesaid Act of Parliament it is declared that the raising or keeping a standing army within the kingdom in time of peace, unless it be with the consent of Parliament, is against law; it is the opinion of this town that the said declaration is founded in the indefeasible right of the subjects to be *consulted*, and to give their *free consent in person*, or by representatives of their own free election, to the raising and keeping a standing army among them; and the inhabitants of this town being free subjects, have the same right derived from nature and confirmed by the British constitution, as well as the said royal charter; and therefore the raising or keeping a standing army, without their consent in person or by representatives of their own free election, would be an infringement of their natural, constitutional, and charter rights; and the employing such army for the enforcing of laws made without the consent of the people, in person, or by their representatives, would be a grievance.

The aforegoing report being divers times distinctly read, and considered by the town, the question was put: whether the same shall be accepted and recorded, and passed unanimously in the affirmative.

Upon a motion made and seconded, the following votes was unanimously passed, viz:

Whereas by an Act of Parliament of the first of King William and Queen Mary, it is declared that for the redress of all grievances, and for amending, strengthening, and preserving the laws, parliaments ought to be held frequently, and inasmuch as it is the opinion of this town that the people labour under many intolerable grievances which unless speedily redressed threaten the total destruction of our invaluable natural, constitutional, and charter rights:

And furthermore as his excellency the governor has declared himself unable, at the request of this town, to call a general court, which is the assembly of the states of this province for the redress of such grievances:

Voted, that this town will now make choice of a suitable number of persons to act for them as a committee in convention, with such as may be sent to join them from the several towns in this province, in order that such measures may be consulted and advised as his Majesty's service, and the peace and safety of his subjects in this province may require; whereupon the Hon. James Otis, Esq., The Hon. Thomas Cushing, Esq., Mr. Samuel Adams, and John Hancock, Esq., were appointed a committee for the said purpose, the town hereafter to take into consideration what recompense shall be made them for the service they may perform.

Voted, that the selectmen be directed to write to the selectmen of the several towns within this province informing them of the aforegoing vote, and to propose that a convention be held, if they shall think proper, at Faneuil Hall, in this town, on Tuesday the 22d day of September, instant, at 10 o'clock before noon.

124. Resolves of Parliament and address to the king (9 February 1769)

When Parliament met in November 1768, Lord North laid before it from time to time various papers relating to troubles in Massachusetts. Parliamentary consideration resulted in the following resolutions and in the address to the king recommending that if evidence of treason or misprision of treason could be secured, those guilty should be brought to England for trial. A motion to recommit the address to the king was defeated by a vote of 169 to 65. Printed: *Journals of the House of Commons*, XXXII, pp. 185-186, 194.

[Resolves of Parliament]

Resolved, By the Lords Spiritual and Temporal, and Commons, in Parliament assembled, that the votes, resolutions, and proceedings of the House of Representatives of Massachusetts Bay, in the months of January and February, one thousand seven hundred and sixty-eight, respecting several late Acts of Parliament, so far as the said votes, resolutions, and proceedings do import a denial of, or do draw into question the power and authority of his Majesty, by and with the advice and consent of the Lords Spiritual and Temporal, and Commons, in Parliament assembled, to make laws and statutes of sufficient force and validity to bind the colonies and people of America, subjects to the Crown of Great Britain, in all cases whatsoever, are illegal, unconstitutional, and derogatory of the rights of the Crown and Parliament of Great Britain.

Resolved ... that the resolution of the said House of Representatives of the province of Massachusetts Bay, to write letters to the several houses of representatives of the British colonies on the continent desiring them to join with the said House of Representatives of the province of Massachusetts Bay in petitions which do deny, or draw into question, the right of Parliament to impose duties and taxes upon his Majesty's subjects in America; and in pursuance of the said resolution, the writing such letters in which certain late Acts of Parliament, imposing duties and taxes, are stated to be infringements of the rights of his Majesty's subjects of the said province, are proceedings of a most unwarrantable and dangerous nature, calculated to inflame the minds of his Majesty's subjects in the other colonies, tending to create unlawful combination, repugnant to the laws of Great Britain, and subversive of the constitution.

Resolved ... that it appears that the town of Boston, in the province of Massachusetts Bay has for some time past been in a state of great disorder and confusion, and that the peace of the said town has at several times been disturbed by riots and tumults of a dangerous nature, in which the officers of his Majesty's revenue there have been obstructed by acts of violence in the execution of the laws, and their lives endangered.

Resolved ... that it appears that neither the Council of the said province of Massachusetts Bay nor the ordinary civil magistrates did exert their authority, for suppressing the said riots and tumults.

Resolved ... that in these circumstances of the province of the Massachusetts Bay and of the town of Boston, the preservation of the public peace and the due execution of the laws became impracticable without the aid of a military force to support and protect the civil magistrate and the officers of his Majesty's revenue.

Resolved ... that the declarations, resolutions, and proceedings in the town meetings at Boston, on the 14th of June, and 12th September, were illegal and unconstitutional, and calculated to excite sedition and insurrections in his Majesty's province of Massachusetts Bay.

Resolved ... that the appointment at the town meeting on the 12th September of a convention to be held in the town of Boston on the 22d of that month to consist of deputies from the several towns and districts in the province of the Massachusetts Bay, and the writing a letter by the selectmen of the town of Boston to each of the said towns and districts, for the election of such deputies were proceedings subversive of his Majesty's government and evidently manifesting a design in the inhabitants of the said town of Boston, to set up a new and unconstitutional authority independent of the Crown of Great Britain.

Resolved ... that the elections by several towns and districts in the province of Massachusetts Bay of deputies to sit in the said convention and the meeting of such convention, in consequence thereof were daring insults offered to his Majesty's authority, and audacious usurpations of the powers of government.

[Address to the King]

Resolved, That it is the opinion of this committee [of the Committee of the Whole to Commons] to agree to the address sent from the Lords, and referred to this comittee; viz:

Most Gracious Sovereign,

We, your Majesty's most dutiful and loyal subjects, the Lords Spiritual and Temporal [and Commons], in Parliament assembled, return your Majesty our humble thanks for the communication your Majesty has been graciously pleased to make to your Parliament, of several papers relative to public transactions in your Majesty's province of Massachusetts Bay.

We beg leave to express to your Majesty our sincere satisfaction in the measures which your Majesty has pursued for supporting the constitution, and for inducing a due obedience to the authority of the legislature; and to give your Majesty the strongest assurances that we will effectually stand by and support your Majesty in such further measures as may be found necessary to maintain the civil magistrates in a due execution of the laws within your Majesty's province of Massachusetts Bay; and as we conceive that nothing can be more immediately necessary, either for the maintenance of your Majesty's authority in the said province, or for guarding your Majesty's subjects therein from being further deluded by the arts of wicked and designing men than to proceed, in the most speedy and effectual manner, for bringing to condign punishment the chief authors and instigators of the late disorders, we most humbly beseech your Majesty that you will be graciously pleased to direct your Majesty's governor of Massachusetts Bay to take the most effectual methods for procuring the fullest information that can be obtained, touching all treasons, or misprisions of treason committed within his government, since the thirtieth day of December [1767] and to transmit the same, together with the names of the persons who were most active in the commission of such offences, to one of your Majesty's principal secretaries of state, in order that your Majesty may issue a special commission for inquiring of, hearing, and determining the said offences within this realm, pursuant to the provisions of the statute of the thirty-fifth year of the reign of King Henry the eighth, in case your Majesty shall, upon receiving the said information, see sufficient ground for such a proceeding. . . .

125A–B. Colonial answers to the resolutions of Parliament

Colonial response to the parliamentary resolutions of 9 February 1769 (No. 124) was prompt and spirited. On 16 May 1769 the Virginia House of Burgesses passed a series of resolves, copies of which were sent to other colonial legislatures. On 19 August 1769 the South Carolina Commons House of Assembly adopted a series of resolutions patterned on those of Virginia.

125A. Virginia resolutions (16 May 1769)

Printed: *Journals of the House of Burgesses, 1766–1769*, pp. 214–215.

Resolved, *nem. con.*, that the sole right of imposing taxes on the inhabitants of this his Majesty's colony and dominion of Virginia is now, and ever has been, legally and constitutionally vested in the House of Burgesses, lawfully convened according to the ancient and established practice, with the consent of the Council, and of his Majesty the king of Great Britain, or his governor for the time being.

Resolved, that it is the undoubted privilege of the inhabitants of this colony to petition their sovereign for redress of grievances; and that it is lawful and expedient to procure the concurrence of his Majesty's other colonies in dutiful addresses, praying the royal interposition in favour of the violated rights of America.

Resolved, that all trials for treason, misprision of treason, or for any felony or crime whatsoever committed and done in this his Majesty's said colony and dominion by any person or persons residing therein, ought of right to be had and conducted in and before his Majesty's courts held within the said colony, according to the fixed and known course of proceeding; and that the seizing any person or persons residing in this colony, suspected of any crime whatsoever committed therein, and sending such person or persons to places beyond the sea to be tried, is highly derogatory of the rights of British subjects, as thereby the inestimable privilege of being tried by a jury from the vicinage, as well as the liberty of summoning and producing witnesses on such trial, will be taken away from the party accused.

Resolved, that an humble, dutiful, and loyal address be presented to his Majesty to assure him of our inviolable attachment to his sacred person and government, and to beseech his royal interposition, as the father of all his people, however remote from the seat of his empire, to quiet the minds of his loyal subjects of this colony, and to avert from them those dangers and miseries which will ensue from the seizing and carrying beyond the sea any persons residing in America suspected of any crime whatsoever, to be tried in any other manner than by the ancient and long established course of proceeding.

125B. South Carolina resolutions (19 August 1769)

From: British Public Record Office, C.O. 5/379.

The house (according to order) proceeded to take into consideration the letter from the Honourable Peyton Randolph, Esquire, late speaker of the House of Burgesses of Virginia, to the speaker of this house, and also the resolutions which were entered into by the said House of Burgesses of Virginia; and the said letter and resolutions being severally read, the house came to the following resolutions thereupon.

Resolved, Nemine Contradicente, that the sole right of imposing taxes on the inhabitants of the province of South Carolina, is now and ever has been legally and constitutionally vested in the Commons House of Assembly lawfully convened according to the ancient and established practice, with the consent of the Council, and of his Majesty the king of Great Britain, or his governor for the time being.

Resolved, Nemine Contradicente, that it is the undoubted privilege of the inhabitants of this colony to petition their sovereign for redress of grievances; and that it is lawful and expedient to procure the concurrence of his Majesty's other colonies in dutiful addresses, praying the royal interposition in favour of the violated rights of America.

Resolved, Nemine Contradicente, that all trials for treason, misprision of treason, or for any felony or crime whatsoever, committed and done in this his Majesty's said province, by any person or persons residing therein, ought of right to be had and conducted in and before his Majesty's courts, held within the said province, according to the fixed and known course of proceeding; and that the seizing any person or persons residing in this province suspected of any crime whatsoever, committed therein, and sending such person or persons to places beyond the sea to be tried is oppressive and illegal, and highly derogatory of the rights of British subjects; as thereby the inestimable privilege of being tried by a jury from the vicinage, as well as the benefit of summoning and producing witnesses on such trial, will be taken away from the party accused.

Resolved, Nemine Contradicente, that the statute made in the thirty-fifth year of the reign of King Henry the VIII, Chapter II, entitled "An Act for the trial of Treasons committed out of the King's Dominions," does not extend, and cannot but by an arbitrary and cruel construction of the said Act, be construed to extend to treasons, misprisions of treasons, or concealments of treasons, committed in any of his Majesty's American colonies where there is sufficient provision by the laws of the land for the impartial trial of all such persons as are charged with, and for the due punishment of such as are convicted, of those offences.

Resolved, Nemine Contradicente, that an humble, dutiful, and loyal address be presented to his Majesty, to assure him of our inviolable attachment to his sacred person and government; and to beseech his royal interposition, as the father of all his people, however remote from the seat of his empire, to quiet the minds of his loyal subjects of this colony, and to avert from them those dangers and miseries which will ensue from the seizing and carrying beyond sea any person residing in America, suspected of any crime whatsoever, to be tried in any other manner than by the ancient and long established course of proceeding.

126A–B. Colonial non-importation agreements (1768–1769)

Proposals to stop the importation of various goods were made shortly after the arrival of the news of the passage of the Revenue Act of 1767 (see No. 120). Several agreements to stop the consumption of 'superfluities' were adopted in New England before the end of 1767. During the spring of 1768 non-importation agreements among the large northern commercial towns fell through because the Philadelphia merchants refused to co-operate. But on 1 August 1768 an independent agreement was adopted in Boston. The movement spread slowly, but by the end of 1769 every colony had adopted some form of non-importation. The documents which follow are examples of such agreements.

126A. Boston non-importation agreement (1 August 1768)

Printed: Colonial Society of Massachusetts *Publications*, XIX, p. 205.

The merchants and traders in the town of Boston, having taken into consideration the deplorable situation of the trade and the many difficulties it at present labours under on account of the scarcity of money, which is daily decreasing for want of the other remittances to discharge our debts in Great Britain, and the large sums collected by the officers of the customs for duties on goods imported; the heavy taxes levied to discharge the debts contracted by the government in the late war; the embarrassments and restrictions laid on the trade by the several late Acts of Parliament; together with the bad success of our cod fishery this season, and the discouraging prospect of the whale fishery, by which our principal sources of remittances are like to be greatly diminished, and we thereby rendered unable to pay the debts we owe the merchants in Great Britain, and to continue the importation of goods from thence:

We, the subscribers, in order to relieve the trade under those discouragements, to promote industry, frugality, and economy, and to discourage luxury and every kind of extravagance, do promise and engage to and with each other as follows:

That we will not send for or import from Great Britain this fall, either on our own account, or on commission, any other goods than what are already ordered for the fall supply.

That we will not send for or import any kind of goods or merchandise from Great Britain, either on our own account, or on commissions, or any otherwise, from January 1, 1769, to January 1, 1770, except salt, coals, fish-hooks and lines, hemp, duck, bar lead and shot, wool-cards, and card-wire.

That we will not purchase of any factors, or others, any kind of goods imported from Great Britain from January 1, 1769, to January 1, 1770.

That we will not import on our own account, or on commission, or purchase from any who shall import from any other colony in America, from January 1, 1769, to January 1, 1770, any tea, glass, paper, or other goods commonly imported from Great Britain.

That we will not, from and after January 1, 1769, import into the province any tea, paper, glass, or painters' colours, until the Acts imposing duties on these articles have been repealed.

126B. Charleston non-importation agreement (22nd July 1769)

Printed: Colonial Society of Massachusetts *Publications*, XIX, pp. 217–219.

We, his Majesty's dutiful and loving subjects, the inhabitants of South Carolina, being sensibly affected with the great prejudice done to Great Britain, and the abject and wretched condition to which the British colonies are reduced by several Acts of Parliament lately passed; by *some of which* the moneys that the colonists usually and cheerfully spent in the purchase of all sorts of goods imported from Great Britain, are now, to their great grievance, wrung from them, without their consent, or even their being represented, and applied by the ministry, in prejudice of, and without regard to, the real interest of Great Britain, or the manufactures thereof, almost totally, to the support of new-created commissioners of customs, place-men, parasitical and novel ministerial officers; and *by others of which acts* we are not only deprived of those invaluable rights, trial by our peers and the common law, but are also made subject to the arbitrary and oppressive proceedings of the civil law, justly abhorred and rejected by our ancestors, the freemen of England; and finding that the most dutiful and loyal petitions from the colonies alone, for redress of those grievances, have been rejected with contempt so that no relief can be expected from that method of proceedings; and being fully convinced of the absolute necessity of stimulating our fellow subjects and sufferers in Great Britain to aid us in this our distress, and of joining the rest of the colonies in some other loyal and vigorous methods that may most probably procure such relief, which we believe may be most effectually promoted by strict economy, and by encouraging the manufactures of America in general, and of this province in particular: we therefore, whose names are underwritten, do solemnly promise, and agree to and with each other, that, until the colonies be restored to their former freedom by the repeal of the said Acts, we will most strictly abide by the following

RESOLUTIONS

I. That we will encourage and promote the use of North American manufactures in general, and those of this province in particular. And any of us who are vendors thereof, do engage to sell and dispose of them at the same rates as heretofore.

II. That we will upon no pretence whatsoever, either upon our own account or on commission, import into this province any of the manufactures of Great Britain, or any other European or East India goods, either from Great Britain, Holland, or any other place, other than such as may have been shipped in consequence of former orders; excepting only Negro cloth, commonly called white and coloured plains, not exceeding one shilling and six pence sterling per yard, canvas, bolting cloths, drugs and family medicines, plantation and workmen's tools, nails, firearms, bar steel, gunpowder, shot, lead, flints, wire cards and card-wire, mill and grindstones, fish-hooks, printed books and pamphlets, salt, coals, and saltpeter. And exclusive of these articles, we do solemnly promise and declare that we will immediately countermand all orders to our correspondents in Great Britain for shipping any such goods, wares, and merchandise; and we will sell and dispose of the goods we have on hand, or that may arrive in consequence of former orders at the same rates as heretofore.

III. That we will use the utmost economy in our persons, houses, and furniture; particularly, that we will give no mourning, or gloves, or scarves at funerals.

IV. That from and after the 1st day of January, 1770, we will not import, buy, or sell any Negroes that shall be brought into this province from Africa; nor after the 1st day of October next, any Negroes that shall be imported from the West Indies, or any other place excepting from Africa as aforesaid; and that if any goods or Negroes shall be sent to us contrary to our agreement in this subscription, such goods shall be re-shipped or stored, and such Negroes re-shipped from this province, and not by any means offered for sale therein.

V. That we will not purchase from, or sell for, any masters of vessels, transient persons, or non-subscribers, any kind of European or East India goods whatever, excepting coals and salt, after the 1st day of November next.

VI. That as wines are subject to a heavy duty, we agree not to import any on our account or commission, or purchase from any master of vessel, transient person, or non-subscriber, after the 1st day of January next.

VII. Lastly, that we will not purchase any Negroes imported, or any goods or merchandise whatever, from any resident in this province, that refuses or neglects to sign this agreement within one month from the date hereof; excepting it shall appear he has been unavoidably prevented from doing the same. And every subscriber who shall not strictly and literally adhere to this agreement, according to the true intent and meaning hereof, ought to be treated with the utmost contempt.

E. THE RISE OF REVOLUTIONARY ORGANIZATIONS, 1765-1773

IN the years after 1763, as Britain sought to govern the colonies more strictly and to enforce tighter economic controls, 'popular' parties grew up in each of the colonies, or gained strength where they were already in existence. With each new restrictive law or policy that Britain tried to put into effect, such parties gained wider and wider support. They were the most ardent defenders of colonial liberties. They were likewise proponents of more extreme measures of opposition than were most of the members of the conservative ruling groups in the colonies.

The leaders of the popular parties were an able group of men and they came from all ranks of colonial society. Some of them, such as Richard Henry Lee and Thomas Jefferson of Virginia, were from the ranks of the planter aristocracy. Others like Samuel Adams of Massachusetts and Patrick Henry of Virginia came from solid middle-class families. There were merchants like Christopher Gadsden of Charleston and Alexander McDougall of New York. A good many were lawyers, particularly younger men such as John Morin Scott in New York and John Adams in Boston. Others had particular personal grievances against the royal government as did James Otis in Boston.[1] Most of these men were not ordinarily associated with the group in colonial society which supported the royal governors, and who enjoyed the political and financial rewards of such support.

An outstanding example of this was to be found in Massachusetts, where Thomas Hutchinson, his family and political connexions, monopolized most of the positions at the disposal of the Crown. Hutchinson himself held simultaneously the posts of chief justice of the Superior Court and lieutenant-governor of the colony as well as several minor offices, while his relatives filled a variety of other positions at the disposal of the governor. It is significant that the leaders of the popular party (and it was called that in Massachusetts) fought against both the Hutchinson oligarchy and British 'tyranny', which, with some justice, the oligarchy was said to support. So intertwined was the fight against Hutchinson and his followers with the fight against British policies, that it is difficult and sometimes impossible to distinguish between the two aspects of the programme of the popular party.

Whatever the motives of popular leaders, they were all aggressive in the defence of colonial right against British encroachments, and they showed extraordinary ability in organizing the discontented people of the colonies in support of their programme.[2] However, few if any of them, at least before 1776, seemed to have any programme of internal social or political reform to alleviate the discontent which existed within the colonies. Most of them had little sympathy for the back-country farmers who revolted during the 1760's. John Morin Scott sat on the court which convicted the leader of the tenant farmer rebellion in New York. The Charleston leaders of the popular party helped suppress the Regulator Movement in back-country South Carolina. Samuel Adams was thoroughly distrustful of the farmers in Massachusetts, and he was slow to seek their support. Pennsylvania was the only colony in which there was co-operation between popular leaders in an urban centre and in the back

[1] No. 127a.   [2] No. 127.

country. The result was that in 1776 a large number of back-country farmers, particularly in New York and in the Carolinas, remained loyal to the Crown. It was natural enough for such men to charge the popular leaders along the coast with hypocrisy when they talked of liberty and freedom as opposed to Great Britain, while refusing to yield to the demands for political changes within the colonies.

Despite this, American farmers as a whole were supporters of the Revolution, once it had started. Popular leaders had also the support of a great many members of the planter and merchant aristocracies who were vastly irritated by British efforts to tax the colonies, by the more effective enforcement of the laws of trade, and by the efforts to control western expansion. Such men therefore backed the popular leaders in their violent opposition to Britain at the time of the Stamp Act. Although some were alarmed at the fury of the outburst and began to withdraw, enough men of property supported popular agitation to give it strength and respectability. It is plain, for instance, that a great merchant like Henry Laurens of Charleston was driven to support the revolutionary movement because he believed he was victimized by corrupt customs officials, and not because he believed in independence as the solution of colonial ills.

A second source of strength for the popular party was the existence of depression and unemployment in most of the commercial towns of the colonies. This was a fact that could be and was exploited. Artisans, mechanics, shopkeepers, and others rallied behind the popular leaders who pointed to members of the colonial aristocracy in league with the royal governments, as well as to British policies, as the source of all the ills of the people. Thus the populace of the leading towns was organized and ready and more than willing to attack customs officials, royal officials, and merchants who were the political enemies of the popular leaders or the supporters of British policies.[1] Hence it was that the urban areas, rather than the discontented back country, were the centres of the revolutionary movement until the outbreak of warfare in 1775. This is particularly true of the four largest cities: Philadelphia, New York, Boston, and Charleston. These and other cities near or on the coast were the seats of colonial governments. Here too were the printing presses from which flowed an increasing quantity of news and propaganda. It was in these towns that the first and most effective popular parties grew up and that again and again led the opposition to British measures, usually in advance of the colonial legislatures. The most important exception was the legislature of Virginia where the planter aristocracy dominated the affairs of the colony. The Virginia planters had behind them a long tradition of proud self-government with which few royal governors dared interfere. If they did so, it was to their sorrow and inevitable defeat.

The colonial aristocracies in every colony found themselves in an extraordinarily difficult position after 1763. At home they were faced with growing popular parties that demanded a greater share in the government of the colonies. Such things as representation of the rapidly growing west were opposed by the aristocracy, and in this they were supported by the British government. But at the same time the British showed every intention of sharply limiting the control that the aristocracies had long exercised. Colonial writers and legislatures protested that British measures were unconstitutional, but argument alone was inadequate. Hence at the time of the Stamp Act many aristocratic leaders secretly encouraged the mobs to riot against the operation of the law.[2]

[1] Nos. 110, 127, 128.   [2] No. 110.

But the mob was a weapon that could be and was turned against the aristocracy to achieve the aims of popular leaders.[1] It was the threat of force that brought reluctant merchants into the non-importation agreements of 1768 and 1769. When the news came that the Townshend Revenue Act was to be repealed, merchants everywhere welcomed it and at once proposed to give up non-importation. Not only did they want to resume trade, they had become increasingly frightened at the violence that had accompanied the rise of the popular parties since 1765. The popular leaders, on the other hand, proposed even more extreme measures. A Boston town meeting in October 1769 demanded that non-importation be continued until Parliament had repealed all the Revenue Acts, abolished the American Board of Customs, and recalled the troops. They adopted a new agreement for this purpose, but New York and Philadelphia merchants refused to subscribe to it. Meanwhile the existing agreement was rigidly enforced by mob action and the Boston merchants were helpless.

When the news of actual repeal of the Act reached the colonies in June and July 1770, the New York merchants took the lead in breaking the non-importation agreements. The popular party in New York demanded that non-importation be kept up rigidly, but the merchants countered by making a house-to-house canvass of the town, and found that a majority of the people were on the side of the merchants. The merchants then abolished the agreement and ordered goods from Great Britain. New Yorkers were denounced as the enemies of freedom, but their example was followed as agreement after agreement was broken in other colonies. The pattern was much the same everywhere: the popular leaders wanted to keep up the agreements; the merchants wanted to break them, and in the end were successful. Even in Boston, where the popular leaders had more merchant support than in perhaps any other colony, the merchants were alienated by violence; and in September 1770 the merchants began ordering goods.

In repealing the Townshend Act, except for the tax on tea, the British yielded the substance of what the Americans demanded while retaining the principle of parliamentary supremacy. Nevertheless it is clear that the ministry had every intention of avoiding issues of principle which might arouse the Americans. At the end of 1769, for instance, Hillsborough wrote General Gage that South Carolina's protests against complying with the Quartering Act had "a trace of plausibility", and declared that there was little hope of executing the Act as it existed. The next year, after Parliament allowed New York to issue paper currency, he expressed the "hope" that New York would reimburse officers who provided firewood for the troops. There was no yielding, however, on the continued enforcement of customs regulations; and there was continued concern with Massachusetts, the focal-point of revolutionary activity.

In America members of the colonial aristocracy, and particularly the merchants, were likewise content to let disputes die, although they continued the non-importation agreements against tea. Many of them were convinced that the popular leaders' ardent defence of colonial liberties was merely a cloak to hide their real aim, which was to gain political power in the colonies. Hence, conservative leaders were willing to come to terms with Britain as they had not been in the first few years after 1763. As a result there was a conservative reaction in virtually every colony. The depression that had existed in the commercial towns was over by 1770, and during the next three years trade grew rapidly. Economic discontent was no longer a factor that could be utilized for political agitation.

[1] No. 169.

Nevertheless the opposition continued and by 1773 the groundwork of inter-colonial co-operation had been laid on a solid foundation. Although the British government tried to avoid conflict, certain policies remained a source of trouble. The enforcement of trade laws was a continuous irritant, and Americans in colony after colony made it difficult for customs officers to carry on their duties. William Shepherd's account of his troubles in Philadelphia in 1769 is one example of an individual official in a minor post who was attacked for his activities.[1] The *Gaspee* affair in Rhode Island in 1772 is an example of virtually a whole colony, including the governor, the leading merchants, and the ordinary citizens, uniting to oppose the British customs service.[2]

A second source of opposition was the presence of British troops, particularly in Boston. The populace of Boston kept the troops under continuous attack in news-papers and poured abuse upon them in the streets of the town. The culmination was the Boston Massacre on 5 March 1770.[3] Although the officers and soldiers involved were acquitted, the 'massacre' provided the popular leaders with a rich source of anti-British propaganda and helped them to keep alive party spirit.[4]

Despite the conservative reaction after 1770, the popular leaders thus managed to keep up agitation and to build a political organization. The rise of the popular parties can be best illustrated in Massachusetts. The leaders of the party were James Otis, Samuel Adams, Thomas Cushing, Joseph Warren, and a large number of less well-known but no less able men. Governor Francis Bernard's accounts of their aims is prejudiced, yet he had a realistic appreciation of their methods.[5] So too did John Adams, who associated with the popular leaders.[6] Although they suffered set-backs in the legislature, they kept control of the Boston town meeting. Lacking larger issues such as parliamentary taxation, they seized upon local ones. Thus in 1772, when the popular leaders discovered that the salaries of Thomas Hutchinson, who was appointed governor of the colony in 1770, and the judges of the Superior Court of the colony were being paid from customs receipts, the uproar was immediate. Samuel Adams wrote revealingly: "I wish we could arouse the Continent." The next day the Boston town meeting met and petitioned Governor Hutchinson to tell them whether or not judges were to be paid by the Crown. The governor refused, and the town meeting then demanded that he allow the legislature to meet at the time to which it stood prorogued in order that "that constitutional body" may examine into "a matter so important and alarming". The governor replied that such matters were not the business of town meetings. Thereupon Samuel Adams moved the appointment of a committee of correspondence to state the rights of the colonists and to communicate with other towns and with the world.[7] The Boston committee of correspondence thus established soon became the centre of an effective political organization within the colony, and its influence spread to other colonies as well.

Meanwhile the popular leaders carried on the fight against crown salaries for royal officials in the colony. By 1774 the party was again strong enough to influence the legislature. The superior court judges were brought before it and the four associate judges promised to renounce their salaries from the Crown.

Chief Justice Peter Oliver refused. The House at once impeached him for high crimes and misdemeanours, but Governor Hutchinson stopped the proceedings by a prorogation. This is but one example of the kind of activity by which the popular leaders in one colony built up their organization. There were other issues in other colonies which kept popular parties active if not so influential as in Massachusetts.

[1] No. 128.   [2] No. 131.   [3] No. 129.   [4] No. 130.   [5] No. 127A.   [6] No. 127B.   [7] No. 132.

Anti-British activities were not purely intracolonial. Since 1764 there had been repeated examples of intercolonial co-operation to meet special situations. The Rhode Island legislature set up a committee of correspondence to write to other colonial legislatures to secure support for opposition to the Revenue Act of 1764. In 1765 the Stamp Act Congress, representing nine of the colonial legislatures, met to protest against the Stamp Act.[1] At the same time the Sons of Liberty organized. While it was a secret society, it was clear that the Sons of Liberty in various colonies were in touch with one another and agreed upon common courses of action. The Massachusetts circular letter invited common action.[2] Meanwhile, merchants in every colony were in touch with one another as crisis after crisis arose.

The popular leaders in most of the colonies were convinced that some permanent organization should be formed. In 1768 Richard Henry Lee proposed the appointment of permanent committees of correspondence by the legislatures of each of the colonies. In 1771 Samuel Adams wrote to Arthur Lee in London, declaring that societies should be formed in every colony and that their deputies should meet once a year. Furthermore, he proposed that they should correspond with a similar society that should be formed in London. The occasion for the actual establishment of intercolonial committees of correspondence grew out of the *Gaspee* affair.[3] When news of it reached Britain, a commission consisting of the chief justices of New York, New Jersey, and Massachusetts, the governor of Rhode Island, and the judge of the Vice-Admiralty court at Boston, was appointed to investigate the matter. The commission was utterly baffled by conflicting evidence despite its desire, as one of them said, to discover the perpetrators of "that most abandoned piece of villainy". The appointment of the commission had an entirely different result than was intended, for it was seized upon by Patrick Henry, Richard Henry Lee, and Thomas Jefferson, who persuaded the Virginia legislature to appoint "a standing committee of correspondence and enquiry". This committee was given the responsibility of acquiring information as to the Acts of Parliament or proceedings of the ministry that might affect the colonies, and to "keep up and maintain" correspondence with the other colonies. They were particularly instructed to inquire into the commission appointed to investigate the *Gaspee* affair in Rhode Island.[4] These resolutions were sent to the speakers of the legislatures of other colonies inviting them to ask their legislatures to appoint committees like that of Virginia. The Virginia resolutions met with widespread response. In April the Boston committee of correspondence printed a circular containing the news and sent it to all the town clerks in the colony. The circular, in addition, quoted a letter purporting to come from a gentleman in Virginia to a friend in Boston to the effect that ". . . we [in Virginia] are endeavouring to bring our sister colonies into the strictest union with us that we may RESENT IN ONE BODY any steps that may be taken by administration to deprive ANY ONE OF US of the least particle of our rights and liberties". In May the Massachusetts legislature heartily agreed to the Virginia resolutions and sent copies of its proceedings to the other colonial legislatures.[5]

The news was likewise sent to England where a good number of men, both English and American, had been in correspondence with American leaders such as Samuel Adams and Richard Henry Lee. John Wilkes, among others, was a correspondent of Adams. Men like William and Arthur Lee, brothers of Richard Henry Lee, carried on correspondence with many of the popular leaders. Benjamin Franklin was

[1] No. 109.   [2] No. 120.   [3] No. 131.   [4] No. 133A.   [5] No. 133B.

in intimate touch with popular leaders everywhere and had provided considerable ammunition for the Boston politicians. When he heard news of the establishment of the intercolonial committees of correspondence, he wrote to Thomas Cushing, speaker of the Massachusetts House: "it is natural to suppose, as you do, that if the oppressions continue a congress may grow out of that correspondence".

The popular leaders had thus by the middle of 1773 created an organization to oppose any British measures that might be taken. Since the *Gaspee* commission failed completely to fix guilt upon anyone, it did not provide an issue. The payment of judges' salaries in Massachusetts had little interest for the people in other colonies. What was needed was an issue that could unite all the colonies as the Stamp Act and the Townshend Act had done. This was provided by the Tea Act of 1773, which the ministry and Parliament passed in an effort to extricate the East India Company from its perennial financial difficulties.[1]

127A-B. Rise of the popular party in Massachusetts

New England, and particularly Massachusetts, was the focal point of the revolutionary movement from 1765 onwards. Although the Massachusetts legislature was behind others in taking an advanced constitutional position in opposition to Britain, this was not true of the local governments within Massachusetts and in the other New England colonies. The New England town meetings had been self-conscious self-governing bodies from the foundation of the colonies. It was these local communities, and particularly the Boston town meeting, which expressed popular opposition to Britain and to the royal governor and his supporters among colonial leaders most forcefully.

During the spring of 1766 the popular leaders in Massachusetts charged, quite falsely, that Governor Bernard, Thomas Hutchinson, and others were the real authors of the Stamp Act. The popular party won the election and got control of the House of Representatives. Since the upper house, the Council, was elected annually by the representatives, the popular leaders got control of that as well. From 1766 to 1770, the leaders of the Boston town meeting, as delegates to the legislature, were virtually managers of both houses. The accounts of some of these things by Governor Francis Bernard and John Adams are revealing.

127A. Letters of Governor Francis Bernard to the Secretary of State (1766, 1768)

The most elaborate accounts of political events in the colonies during the 1760's were written by Governor Francis Bernard of Massachusetts to the secretaries of state and the Board of Trade. Bernard was Governor of New Jersey from 1758 to 1760, when he was appointed Governor of Massachusetts. In August 1769, he was recalled to England and made a baronet. From his hundreds of letters, the two following are given as examples. It is clear that his view of the events that took place is supported by a great deal of collateral evidence. He perhaps places too much emphasis on the leadership of James Otis; yet Otis was the outstanding spokesman of the popular party until mental illness disabled him. This was at least in part the result of a blow on the head from the sword of a British officer during a political controversy in a tavern. Otis, on the other hand, attributed the worst of motives to Bernard. In letters to officials in Britain, Bernard was continually accused by the popular leaders of distorting accounts of what happened. Whatever Bernard's prejudices, his letters are still one of the most valuable sources for the history of Massachusetts while he was governor.

[Bernard to the Earl of Shelburne (22 December 1766)]

From: British Public Record Office, C.O. 5/892.

I am extremely sorry that I am obliged to enter minutely into the civil divisions of this province and the causes and effects of the same. I should have been glad to have saved your lordship the trouble of reading so unpleasing a report and myself the disagreeable task of making it. I should also have been glad to have concealed the present unhappy state of the province if there was any prospect of its amendment;

[1] 13 Geo. III, c. 44.

although in truth the disgrace arising therefrom is chargeable but to few persons, for though the driven and the led are many, the drivers and the leaders are but few. But since the faction which has raised itself upon the public calamity knows no bounds and seems determined to persist in bringing all authority down to the level of the people (preserving nevertheless the form of the government which may be made consistent with such a scheme) and to make an example of a governor who has dared to stand in the gap, and to endeavour to support the royalty of the government, I can not any longer excuse myself laying open this system to the bottom. Not only my own defence, for that I might have safely left to a review of my general conduct since I have been governor, but my duty in discovering designs and proceedings full of danger to the king's government require it of me.

I would avoid personalities, but in the present case it is impossible. The troubles of this country take their rise from and owe their continuance to one man, so much that his history alone would contain a full account of them. This man, James Otis, Esq., was a lawyer at Boston when I came to the government. He is by nature a passionate, violent, and desperate man, which qualities sometimes work him up to an absolute frenzy. I say nothing of him which is not known to be his certain character, confirmed by frequent experience. Soon after my entrance upon the government the place of chief justice of the province became vacant. The lieutenant-governor was proposed for that office by the best men in the government. Mr. Otis (the father of *the* Otis) proposed himself for a seat on the bench in case one of the judges was made chief. Both these proposals could not be complied with and there was no balancing between the two candidates. But Mr. Otis, Senior, urged his pretensions by telling me and the lieutenant-governor that if he (the lieutenant-governor) was appointed, we should both of us repent it. Otis, Junior, did not confine himself to hints but declared publicly, with oaths, that "if his father was not appointed judge, he would set the whole province in a flame though he perished in the attempt". This was proved by the oaths of two gentlemen of credit, whose depositions are now in the public offices at home. However I appointed the lieutenant-governor with the general approbation of the whole province and Messrs. Otis immediately proceeded to make good their promises.

In less than half a year they stirred up a persecution against the Court of Admiralty and the custom house, promising nothing less than the abolishment of the activity of both. In this it was unavoidable, as it was intended, that I should be involved, as well as the chief justice. This persecution (it may be truly called so) lasted two years. In the course of it five actions were brought against different custom house officers, one (made bailable) against the surveyor general (not the present) for £7500 sterling, all by the advice and direction of Otis, Junior. In the course of these proceedings Otis everywhere appeared the principal. He was chief director, chamber council, counsellor at the bar, popular haranguer, and assembly orator; for the merit of this opposition to the king's officers procured him a seat in the house. However, after about two years harassment this matter subsided with the maintenance of the king's rights, which were preserved, I may truly say, by my firmness and perseverance and by the steadiness of the chief justice and the other judges of the Superior Court. A full account of these proceedings, chiefly supported by oath, was returned to the Treasury and to the Board of Trade, and will appear further from my letters to the Secretary of State and the Lords of Trade, in 1761 and 1762.

When this was over he still continued in a constant opposition to government, except during an interval when his father was soliciting for two offices, which put him at the head of his county. These I gave to him, together with a good place to one of his sons, and was assured that this would wipe away all the ill humour which his former disappointment had occasioned. But no sooner were these patents sealed than Otis renewed his hostilities against government with fresh vigour; but to no purpose, as the Council and House was then filled with men of worth and ability, who greatly outweighed and outnumbered the opposers of government; and as I had at that time a credit with the province equal at least to any of my predecessors at any time. The business of the government was carried on with the utmost harmony and good humour, and I never met the Assembly without giving and receiving mutual testimonies of our satisfaction with one another. All this fair form of civil power, which had its chief foundation upon the prudence and good temper of the constituent members of the government and the confidence of the people, and had scarce any coercive power to resort to upon occasion, was at once overturned by the fatal and unfortunate Stamp Act. This let loose all the ill humours of the common people and put them into the hands of designing men, to be employed not so much for the defence of their real and constitutional rights, as to humble the government and bring it to the level of the very people.

I desire not to revive the disputes concerning the Stamp Act; I wish they were buried beyond the reach of memory, and they would have been buried before now if the opposition had not had further views than the defeat of the taxation. But, my lord, the opposing the Stamp Act has been made a mask for a battery, a stalking horse to take a better aim at the royalty of the government. This was apparent whilst the repeal was in suspense, but since it has passed, it is put out of all doubt. For this purpose, when the people's passions were thoroughly worked up; when their fears, jealousy, and credulity were got to such a pitch that it was dangerous as well as impracticable to reason with them, they were told that the scheme of the Stamp Act was formed in this province; the principal officers of the government and others of the first men of the province were pointed out as the contrivers of it. Otis himself said, in the House as well as out of it, that he knew the room (meaning in my house), the time, and the company when the plan was settled. All persons who had any weight or influence in the province, and had been used to exercise it in the support of the government, were branded by the name of friends to the Stamp Act; when the propagators of these calumnies knew in their conscience that there did not exist within the province a friend to the Stamp Act, not even in the stamp officer himself, who to my knowledge at no time wished for the continuance of the Act.

These being the purposes of the faction, means were taken to distress the government quite foreign to the repeal of the Stamp Act, and such as if they had been known in Parliament, would have tended to prevent it. I shall mention a few particulars which will divide these matters into heads. Mr. Otis in a speech in the House directed against the government of Great Britain said that "he wished that the island was sunk in the sea so that the king and his family were saved": this proviso I suppose was to qualify the treasonableness of the wish. Of the king's governors he has said that "those who were appointed to the American governments were such as were obliged either by their crimes or their debts to fly their country". Of the Council (who had given no other offence than by assisting me to secure the stamp papers at the castle) he said in the House "it was an infernal divan and deserved to be sent to the place from whence they derived their councils". In the House it was common for him to tell a member who spoke on the side of government that he should not sit in that House the next year. And accordingly as soon as the General Court was dissolved in order for a new election, there was published in a weekly paper conducted by Otis and his junto, a list of 32 members, the most respectable in the House and noted for their attachment to government, who were proscribed as enemies to their country because they had given their testimony against the violences lately committed; and of these 32, 19 lost their election.

Most of the foregoing passed whilst the event of the Stamp Act was in suspense and therefore might have well been forgot, if the party himself had desired that they should. But when the same violent measures are pursued after the repeal of the Stamp Act is made known, as before; when the king's government and all that bear office in it are persecuted with the same unrelenting acrimony as if nothing had been done for the people and they were under no obligations to the king and his Parliament; when the servant, to whom his king had forgiven ten thousand talents, takes his fellow-servant by the throat for one hundred pence, it is difficult not to connect the proceedings before and after the repeal. However I shall draw a line between them in order to show that the repeal occasioned no relaxation in the disposition and designs of the faction which had raised itself by the Act.

It was the general opinion that Otis himself wished that the Act might not be repealed as that would answer his inflammatory purposes better. This was collected partly from a declaration he made about the time of the advice of the event being expected, that he hoped it would not be repealed; for, said he, "We will repeal it ourselves." As soon as the advice of the repeal came Otis published an advertisement which all the printers were obliged to insert under pain of mob execution. I enclose this advertisement which Otis owned to be his till he found it to be generally reprobated, after which he would neither own it nor deny it. By the terms of this, it is plain that the repeal was to produce no remission either of the pretensions against Parliament, or the persecution of the friends of the government. The week after this came out a republication of the list of the 32 members who had been proscribed as friends of the Stamp Act and therefore enemies to their country, accompanied with observations, among which it was said "that a general purgation in both Houses was of absolute necessity". That is, that every member of either House who professed to have a regard for the support of the government and the royal rights thereof should lose his seat. About this time Mr. Otis began to declare that they had fixed upon 15 councillors, who were to be turned out at the next election. This threat was continued almost to the day of election. I must add one transaction more which passed in this interval, which will properly conclude this paragraph. Mr. Otis at a meeting at the town hall (which I think was to fix a time for public rejoicings for the repeal) in a set speech told the people that "the distinction between inland taxes and port duties was without foundation for whoever had a right to impose one had a right to impose the other: and therefore as the Parliament had given up the one (for he said the Act for securing the dependency had no relation to taxes), they had given up the other; and the merchants were great fools if they submitted any longer to the laws restraining their trade, which ought to be free." This speech made a great deal of noise, and it was observed by serious men that Otis had thereby made himself answerable for all the disturbances which should thereafter happen in the execution of the laws of trade. But the natural consequence, and what immediately followed, was that a common talk prevailed among the people that there should be no more seizures in this town. There have been but two seizures made in the province since, and they have been both rescued with an high hand. In that at Boston it is remarkable that the man who opposed the officers sent for Otis and he went thither as his counsellor. This is the manner in which this man and his faction, after they had heard of the repeal of the Stamp Act, prepared to make a return for it on the part of this province.

As I have now got to the opening of the new Assembly, I will finish this letter; that if your lordship shall think, as I fear will be the case, that I encumber you too much with writings, you may lay this preliminary account aside without giving it a formal consideration. However, as I have thought it necessary to explain what follows, I could not excuse myself prefixing it.

[Bernard to the Earl of Hillsborough (19 March 1768)]
From: British Public Record Office, C.O. 5/757.

I expected that the appointment of commissioners of customs in America would have made it unnecessary for me to have troubled your lordship with any representations upon the subject of the customs; but I see such an opposition to the commissioners and their officers, and such a defiance of the authority by which they are appointed continually growing, that I can no longer excuse my informing your lordship of the detail of facts from whence the most dangerous consequences are to be expected.

It is some time since there have been frequent reports of insurrections intended, in which it has been said the houses of one or more of the commissioners and their officers would be pulled down; two were more particularly fixed upon. Upon one of these nights a number of lads, about 100, paraded the town with a drum and horns, passed by the council chamber whilst I was sitting there in Council, assembled before Mr. Paxton's (a commissioner's) house, and huzzaed; and to the number of at least 60 lusty fellows (as I am assured) invested Mr. Burch's (another commissioner's) house for some time, so that his lady and children were obliged to go out of the back door to avoid the danger which threatened. This kind of disturbance was kept up all the evening and after all, was treated as the diversion of a few boys, a matter of no consequence. This was, I think, on March 4th.

After this it was reported that the insurrection was postponed till March 18th, which was the anniversary of the repeal of the Stamp Act, upon which day effigies were to be exhibited; and two persons, Mr. Paxton, a commissioner, and Mr. Williams, one of the inspectors general, were mentioned as devoted to the resentment of the mob. I took all the pains I could to discover the truth of this report but could get no other answer but assurances that no such thing would be done or suffered. On the very day before I spoke with the most knowing men I could procure who were very positive that no effigies would be hung up. And yet late that evening I had certain advice that effigies were prepared, but it was too late to do anything, and my information was of that nature I could not make use of it in public.

Early the next morning the sheriff came to me to inform me that the effigies of Mr. Paxton and Mr. Williams were hanging upon Liberty Tree. I had the day before appointed a Council to meet, and I now sent round to get them together as soon as possible it might be. Before I went to Council I learned that the effigies had been taken down by some of the neighbours without any opposition. At Council I set forth in strong terms the atrociousness of this insult, the danger of its being followed by actual violence, and the necessity there was of providing for the preservation of the peace of the town. But all I could say made no impression upon the Council; they persevered in treating the affair as of no consequence, and assuring me that there was no danger of any commotion. After they had given their opinion, as in the inclosed copy of the minutes, I received a letter from the commissioners setting forth the insult they had received, the danger they apprehended, and desiring the protection of the government. I communicated this to the Council and proposed that they should reconsider this business; but finding them not inclined to depart from their opinion as before given, I adjourned the reconsideration till the afternoon. In the afternoon, upon the question being again put to them, they adhered to their former opinion.

I should have mentioned before that under all the assurances I had that there would be no disturbances, it was never understood that the day, the anniversary of the repeal of the Stamp Act, should not be celebrated. Accordingly at break of day there were beating of drums and firing of guns heard, and the whole town was adorned with ship's colours; and to add to the celebration, the feast of St. Patrick being the day before, was postponed to this day. However, great pains were taken by the selectmen of the town and some other gentlemen, that the festivity should not produce a riot in the evening, and so far it succeeded that it produced terror only and not actual mischief. There was a number of gentlemen dined at two taverns near the town house upon the occasion of the day. These broke up in good time, after which many of the same, and other gentlemen, kept together at the Coffee House (one of the taverns) all the evening. These prevented the lighting a bonfire in that street, which was several times attempted, and would probably have been a prelude to action. But the assembling a great number of people of all kinds, sex, and ages, many of which showed a great disposition to the utmost disorder, could not be prevented. There were many hundreds of them paraded the streets with yells and outcries which were quite terrible. I had in my house Mr. Burch, one of the commissioners, and his lady and children, who had the day before moved to our house for safety. I had also with me the lieutenant-governor and the sheriff of the county. But I had taken no steps to fortify my house, not being willing to show an apprehension of danger to myself; but at one time there was so terrible a yell from the mob going by that it was apprehended that they were breaking in, but it was not so. However it caused the same terror as if it had been so, and the lady, a stranger to this country who chose our house for an asylum, has not recovered it as yet. They went on and invested Mr. Williams' house, but he showed himself at a window and told them that he was ready for their reception, and they went off, and either did not intend or dared not to attack his house. They also at two different times about midnight made outcries about Mr. Paxton's house out of mere wantonness to terrify his family. The whole made it a very terrible night to those who thought themselves objects of the popular fury; and yet if I should complain of it, I should be told that it was nothing but the common effects of festivity and rejoicing and there was no harm intended.

Your lordship will perhaps ask what I have been doing all this while, that this spirit of disorder is got to such a pitch; I answer, everything in my power to prevent it. Since first these tumults were apprehended, the commissioners with whom (I mean 4 of the 5) I am upon the most intimate terms, have often asked me what support to their office or protection for themselves I can afford; I answer, none in the world. For though I am allowed to proceed in the ordinary business of the government without interruption, in the business of a popular opposition to the laws of Great Britain founded upon pretensions of rights and privileges, I have not the shadow of authority or power. I am just now in the situation I was in about two years ago, sure to be made obnoxious to the madness of the people by the testimony I am obliged to bear against it, and yet left exposed to their resentment without any possible resort for protection. I am then asked why I don't apply for troops, as well to support the king's government as to protect the persons of his officers. I answer, because I don't think it proper or prudent to make such application upon my own opinion only. All the king's governors are directed to take the advice of the Council in military movements, and in this government where the governor is in a more peculiar manner obliged to have the advice of the Council for almost everything he does, it would be dangerous to act in such an important business without such advice. And it is in vain to put such a question to the Council; for, considering the influence they are under from their being creatures of the people, and the personal danger they would be subject to in assisting in the restraining them, it is not probable that the utmost extremity of mischief and danger would induce them to advise such a measure. I have once before tried the experiment when the danger was more urgent and immediate than it is now, and the success then fully convinced me that it is to no purpose ever again to repeat the question. His Majesty's ministers have within these three years been fully acquainted with the defenceless state of this government, and therefore I trust that I shall be excused leaving it entirely to the administration to determine upon a measure which they are much more able to judge of and be answerable for than I can be. I shall have trouble and danger enough when such orders arrive, though I keep ever so clear of advising or promoting them. These, my lord, are the answers I have given to the commissioners in the course of conversation, which I have thought proper to recapitulate in this place for my own vindication if it should be needful.

I should have mentioned before, but for not interrupting the narrative, that in the debate at the Council one gentleman said that there were associations formed for preserving the peace of the town. I said that I had not been made acquainted with them; that if there were any such they ought to have been formed with my privity and confirmed by my authority. That if a general association for supporting the authority of the government and preserving the peace of the town could be brought about it would be of great service, and I should be glad to see it set about immediately. Upon this a councillor got up with vehemence and said that such a subscription was illegal and unconstitutional and he should protest against it as tending to bring an opprobrium on the town. I said that at a time when a subscription was handed about the town in direct opposition to the Parliament and people of Great Britain, and was every day enforced by menaces and other unfair methods, it was very extraordinary at that board to hear a subscription for the support of government and preservation of peace called illegal. That I should not endeavour to press a measure which would derive its chief efficacy from being voluntary, but I feared they would see the expediency of such a measure when it was too late. From this, and the generality of the assurances that no mischief would be done, I am to understand that the preservation of the peace of this town is to depend upon those who have the command of the mob, and can restrain them (and of course let them loose) when they please, and civil authority is not to interpose in this business. And indeed I have with attention observed that all the assurances that no mischief was intended at present are founded upon the impropriety of using violence at a time when they were applying to the government and Parliament of Great Britain for redress. But it is inferred, and sometimes expressly declared, that when they have advice that the redress which they expect is denied, they will immediately proceed to do themselves justice. And it is now become common talk that they will not submit to duties imposed by Parliament, not only those imposed by the late Acts, but all others which raise a revenue. This is public talk; as for the sanguine expectations which the faction from whose cabinet all these troubles have arisen has formed for controlling and triumphing over Great Britain, I dare not repeat what I have heard till their purposes become more apparent.

In this narrative I have taken no notice of the town meetings, meetings of merchants and subscriptions for not importing English goods, proposals for manufactures, etc., which have been carrying on before and during the whole forementioned time. I intend to make a separate letter upon these subjects which possibly may accompany this, as I am not at present apprised of a conveyance safe enough to trust this by.

127B. Excerpts from the diary of John Adams (1763, 1766, 1769)

John Adams of Braintree, Massachusetts was a distant cousin of Samuel Adams of Boston. As a rising young lawyer he was associated with the popular leaders in the colony, yet he always stood somewhat aside from them. He approved of their opposition to British policy and to the Hutchinson oligarchy, yet he disliked most of their methods. His diary is a remarkable commentary on the events preceding the Revolution. The first excerpt from his diary tells of the Caucus Club which was the steering committee of the Boston leaders. The excerpt for 1766 relates to the events following the spring election of 1766. As a result of that election the popular leaders got control of the legislature and refused to elect most of the Hutchinson oligarchy to the Council. The two excerpts for 1769 are self-explanatory. Printed: John Adams, *Works*, II, pp. 144, 195–196, 218–219.

Diary, February 1763

Boston. This day learned that the Caucus Club meets at certain times in the garret of Tom Dawes, the adjutant of the Boston Regiment. He has a large house, and he has a movable partition in his garret which he takes down, and the whole club meets in one room. There they smoke tobacco till you cannot see from one end of the garret to the other. There they drink flip, I suppose, and there they choose a moderator who puts questions to the vote regularly; and selectmen, assessors, collectors, wardens, fire-wards, and representatives are regularly chosen before they are chosen in the town. Uncle Fairfield, Story, Ruddock, Adams, Cooper, and a *rudis indigestaque moles* of others are members. They send committees to wait on the merchant's club, and to propose and join in the choice of men and measures. Captain Cunningham says they have often solicited him to go to those caucuses; they have assured him benefit in his business, etc.

Diary, 28 May 1766

General election. At Boston. After lecture, dined at Mr. Austin's, the wine-cooper, with the Rev. Messrs. Prentice of Charlestown and Adams of Roxbury. Adams and Austin were the disputants in politics. Prentice a moderator.

This morning [Samuel] Adams was chosen clerk, and Otis speaker. Governor Bernard negatived him. Cushing was chosen. In the afternoon they proceeded to choose councillors when Hutchinson and the two Olivers were dropped, and Trowbridge was dropped, and Mr. Pitts, Colonel Gerrish, Colonel White, Bowers, Powell, and Mr. Saunders, and Dexter were chosen. What a change! This day seems to be the literal accomplishment of a prophecy of Mr. Otis, published two or three winters ago in the newspaper: "The day is hastening on with large strides when a dirty, very dirty, witless rabble, I mean the great vulgar, shall go down with deserved infamy to all posterity." Thus the triumph of Otis and his party are complete. But what changes are yet to come? Will not the other party soon be uppermost?

Diary, 29 May 1766

The governor negatived Otis, Sparhawk, Dexter, Saunders, Gerrish, and Bowers, and made the two Houses a most nitrous, sulphureous speech.

What will be the consequence?

Diary, 14 August 1769

Dined with three hundred and fifty Sons of Liberty at Robinson's, the sign of Liberty Tree, in Dorchester. We had two tables laid in the open field, by the barn, with between three and four hundred plates and an awning of sailcloth over head, and should have spent a most agreeable day had not the rain made some abatement in our pleasures. Mr. Dickinson, the Farmer's[1] brother, and Mr. Reed, the secretary of New Jersey, were there; both cool, reserved, and guarded all day. After dinner was over and the toasts drunk, we were diverted with Mr. Balch's mimicry. He gave us

[1] John Dickinson of Pennsylvania.

the lawyer's head, and the hunting of a bitch fox. We had also the Liberty Song–that by the farmer and that by Dr. Church, and the whole company joined in the chorus. This is cultivating the sensations of freedom. There was a large collection of good company. Otis and Adams are politic in promoting these festivals; for they tinge the minds of the people; they impregnate them with the sentiments of liberty; they render the people fond of their leaders in the cause and averse and bitter against all opposers. To the honour of the Sons, I did not see one person intoxicated or near it.

Between four and five o'clock the carriages were all got ready, and the company rode off in procession, Mr. Hancock first, in his chariot, and another chariot bringing up the rear. I took my leave of the gentlemen and turned off for Taunton, oated at Doty's, and arrived long after dark at Noice's; there I put up. I should have been at Taunton if I had not turned back in the morning from Roxbury, but I felt as if I ought not to lose this feast; as if it was my duty to be there. I am not able to conjecture of what consequence it was whether I was there or not. Jealousies arise from little causes, and many might suspect that I was not hearty in the cause if I had been absent, whereas none of them are more sincere and steadfast than I am.

Diary, 3 September 1769

Heard Dr. Cooper in the forenoon, Mr. Champion of Connecticut in the afternoon, and Mr. Pemberton in the evening at the charity lecture. Spent the remainder of the evening and supped with Mr. Otis in company with Mr. Adams, Mr. William Davis, and Mr. John Gill. The evening spent in preparing for the next day's newspaper, a curious employment, cooking up paragraphs, articles, occurrences, &c., working the political engine! Otis talks all; he grows the most talkative man alive; no other gentleman in company can find a space to put in a word; as Dr. Swift expressed it, he leaves no elbow room. There is much sense, knowledge, spirit, and humour in his conversation; but he grows narrative like an old man; abounds with stories.

128. William Shepherd's account of opposition to the customs service in Philadelphia (1 April 1769)

There are many accounts of the opposition to the customs service and of the violence often used to defeat its operation. Shepherd's letter to the commissioners of customs in Boston is a fairly characteristic account of the treatment received by minor officials in the customs service. It is notable in the fact that Philadelphia was relatively more quiet than towns like Boston. Printed: Massachusetts Historical Society *Collections*, 4th Series, x, pp. 611–617.

Having obtained the inspector general's leave of absence for the recovery of my health, I returned here on the 13th instant. I now in obedience to your commands signified to me when I had the honour to attend the board, do lay before your honours the following account of the disturbances which happened at Philadelphia, viz.

On Saturday 1st instant, about ten o'clock in the morning, a seizure was made by the collector in consequence of an order from the inspector general, of near fifty pipes of Madeira wine, which was lodged in a store belonging to Mr. Andrew Hodge.

The supposed owner of the wine was one Captain Caldwell. In about half an hour after the seizure was made, I received a letter from the inspector general directing me to attend my duty. I show[ed] the same to the collector, who required me to go to the store where the wines was, and take an account of the number of casks therein. He gave me the key of the padlock which he had put on the door; when I got there I took the same off but found the store fastened with the lock that was on it before the collector made the seizure, upon which I went to Mr. Hodge's house to get the key of the same but was told that he was not at home and that they did not know where he was. I asked the family for the key, but they said it was not in the house and that they did not know who had got it. Between 11 and 12 o'clock I waited upon the inspector general and acquainted him that I had great reason to suspect that it was the intention of some of the inhabitants to rescue the wines from the officers. He told me that he would take care to prevent it. I informed the collector of my not being able to get the key of the store, and with my apprehensions of the design of the inhabitants, and recommended the wines being removed as soon as possible. He told me that he had no stores to put them in and that if he had, it was not in his power to get it removed on account of the rain. The rain was over about four o'clock in the afternoon, when the collector went down to the store but was denied admittance therein by a man unknown who had armed himself with pistols, and swore that if he pretended to enter it he would blow his brains out, or words to that effect; upon which the collector retired and went to the chief justice and procured a writ of assistance, and a number of constables to assist him in the execution of his duty, and they returned to the store about five o'clock in the afternoon, but they were not able to afford him any help, the mob being so numerous. They ordered the constables off of the wharf, though I think they tarried there long enough to read the Riot Act or writ of assistance, but which I do not know. They likewise prevented the collector's executing his duty, obliging him to go away, swearing they would shoot him if he attempted it. They pelted him with stones, glass bottles, etc., one of which struck him in the lip and hurt it considerably. It was by this time near dusk. The collector not being able to proceed in the execution of his duty, communicated the same to the inspector general, who thereupon waited upon the governor and made him acquainted therewith and renewed his desire for support and assistance, having about 5 o'clock wrote to him on that subject. This procured an order for [a] captain and 50 men to assist the king's officers, but they did not get to the custom house till ten o'clock that night, near an hour before which the lock which the collector put on the store was broke off by the mob, and the door forced open and all the wines therein taken out and put on board three lighters or shallops and carried up the river. All the time they were transacting this matter they swore revenge and destruction against me, taking it for granted that I was the cause of making the seizure. Some time in the night a number of people went to the custom house which is held at the collector's house, where Mr. Williams lodged, and broke many of the windows. There being one or two constables in the house, they run out and took three that was concerned in the act, and secured them in gaol, since which they have been tried and found guilty. One of them was fined 25 pounds, the other two, five or ten pounds each. On Sunday 2d instant, I found in the necessary house belonging to my lodgings the following abusive letter directed "To the infamous Scoundrel Sheppard–altho I sign no name yet I sware by God Almighty that I will be revenged on you for this day's affair and put it out of your Power ever to hurt any body else for the future, believe what I say." I gave the inspector general, Mr. Williams, the above letter, who told me he would show it to the governor. The affair of the seizure was matter of conversation all Sunday. Everybody inveterate against me, saying they were sure it would not have happened if I had not informed the collector thereof. Some particular persons told me they thought it would be dangerous for me to venture out. The gentleman that I boarded with was advised not to let me tarry in his house; that if he did it would be in danger of being pulled down, but he kindly said that he would run the risque of it. I could not be persuaded that my person was in danger, and thought that if I appeared to be intimidated, the inhabitants would think it arose from a consciousness of guilt. I therefore went out as usual. I spent the evening out, taking care for fear I should be insulted, to put a pair of pistols in my pockets. Upon my return home about a quarter past ten o'clock, two men of a sudden came up to me, one of them without saying a word to me, struck me as hard as he could in the pit of my stomach, which immediately deprived me of breath and I fell down. He took the advantage with some weapon, I apprehend a knife, and slit my nose. I suppose his intention was to slit it up to my eyes. He did not altogether succeed in this, though he did in part, having cut the inside thereof considerably and more than a quarter of an inch clear through. I received several blows upon my face which bruised it greatly, caused a large swelling. While this piece of cruelty was transacted I recovered strength enough to endeavour to defend myself. I got my right hand into my pocket and cocked the pistol that was in it, intending to discharge the same at him through my pocket, but as soon as he heard the guard of the pistol spring back he run from me. I, upon his retreat, fired it at him but am uncertain whether I hit him or not, am apt to think I did. I can not hear or find out who the person was. I lay some time upon the ground, being faint with the blows, and bleeding considerably, at last got home. The family was much frightened seeing me very bloody. When I had recruited a little, I waited upon Mr. Williams accompanied by Mr. Hill and his servant, armed, to know what I should do. Mr. Hill acquainted him he had received a message from Mr. Hodge, delivered by his son, that if he harboured me in his house he would be in danger, and that if the mob came, he would recommend to him to consent to let some of them go over his house to see if I was in it or not. This message was delivered about three quarters of an hour before I received the abuse above mentioned. Mr. Williams and Mr. Swift procured a number of watchmen belonging to the city to guard the house that night. The severity of the blow that I received in my stomach was so great as to cause me to bring up a considerable quantity of blood the next morning but one. I have had a constant pain in my breast ever since, besides a kind of inward favour [fever?] which hangs about me, no appetite to my victuals, and spirits very much depressed. On the morning of the 6th instant I was advised to let blood, which I consented to, and was in hopes it would have made feel better, but was disappointed. I could not think of tarrying among a set of people, under my present circumstances, whose greatest pleasure would be to have an opportunity of burying me. The few acquaintance that I had at Philadelphia were afraid of being seen to keep company with me. that so I was in a manner alone in the city without a friend to assist me in any trouble. I was obliged to confine myself at home a nights, as I did not know what murderous intentions the people had determined to execute against me. As I passed through the streets I was the object that everybody stared and gazed at. I at present think myself unable to persevere any longer at Philadelphia, for the trouble and abuse I meet with there appears to be impossible for me to encounter with, and yet my desires are so great to be continued and fixed in it, that notwithstanding their opposition, I can't think of quitting the field. Therefore if the honourable board should think it most for his Majesty's service to order me to return, I am determined to obey them, if the consequence should be the loss of my life, which I really apprehend may be the case. Mr. Williams acquainted me that he had recommended to the board that a number of officers be made at Philadelphia. If the honourable board should think proper to appoint them, the inhabitants would think that I was the procuring cause of them, which if possible, would make them more inveterate against me. If the honourable board should think it best not to order me to return, I hope they will be pleased kindly to take into consideration the abusive treatment I have received for exerting myself in order to prevent his Majesty's being defrauded of that part of his revenue which is due to him at that port, and make such provision for me elsewhere as they in their great goodness may think I am deserving of. Whether the governor has or intends to do anything in consequence of the abuse that I have received, I know not. Mr. Williams acquainted me that the merchants had so far interfered in the affair of the wines as to engage that they should be all returned back to the store from whence they were taken, and that he and the collector had promised them if that was done, no further notice should be taken of the behaviour of the mob on Saturday evening. Mr. Williams engaged that I had not nor would not represent the behaviour or treatment I had met with if the wines were returned. This request I think the merchants ought to have applied to me to grant, but as Mr. Williams had given his honour that I should not write anything of the matter, I did not. I don't mean to cast any reflection upon Mr. Williams for I dare say what he did he meant well in; yet I can't but say that I think the behaviour of the people in general on Saturday night and on the Sunday night following when I was so injuriously treated, to be of too high a nature to be hushed up. Notwithstanding the merchants agreed to return the same wines that were taken from the store as far as possible, they did not do it till five or six days after and then returned not near the quantity that was taken, and instead [of] delivering Madeira wine, it was no better than mean Fayal, as Mr. Swift, the collector, declared, who tasted of them, and said that it was his opinion they would not fetch more than the cost of condemnation and sale. Mr. Williams, when he was informed of this, declared that he would not receive them and that he would make a full representation of their conduct. I left Philadelphia the day after the wines were [returned] and so am unable to give any account of what took place after I came away. I have thus endeavoured as faithfully and truly to represent to the board the conduct of the people at Philadelphia in consequence of the seizure on the fifth instant as nearly as I can recollect. If I should be wrong in some particulars, though I believe I am not, Mr. Williams will more correctly and fully acquaint the honourable board, which he said he should do very soon after I left Philadelphia.

129A–B. The Boston Massacre (5 March 1770)

The first British troops arrived in Boston in October 1768. From then on, there was continuous antagonism between the populace and the soldiers. Every kind of delaying tactic was used to prevent the troops from being quartered. The newspapers, week after week, printed accounts of the 'atrocities' committed by the soldiers. The town meeting denounced them. Mobs hooted at them and attacked them from time to time. British officers made every effort to prevent trouble, but minor difficulties were unavoidable. Meanwhile the presence of the troops made it safe for the customs commissioners and other British officials to remain in the town, something that had not been true previous to their arrival. Governor Bernard commented that while the troops might protect the person of the governor, they could not restore the authority of the government although they might in time enable the governor to pursue the means to do so.

Antagonism between the populace and the troops came to a head in the spring of 1770. During several days, fighting between groups of soldiers and the people of the town had been almost continuous. Then on 5 March came the 'massacre'. The evidence as to what happened is completely contradictory. About the only thing that the accounts agree upon is that the event took place on 5 March and that several men were killed.

There was danger of open warfare, but Thomas Hutchinson, who had succeeded Bernard as governor, acted with firmness. Captain Preston and some of the soldiers were arrested and held for trial. The two regiments were removed to Castle William, an old fort on an island in Boston harbour. One regiment was soon removed from the colony, while one regiment was maintained at Castle William until the outbreak of the war for independence. Meanwhile, the popular leaders demanded that the soldiers be tried at once. But Hutchinson delayed the trials until October to allow passions to cool. When the trials were held, John Adams acted as one of the defence counsel. Captain Preston and six of the soldiers were acquitted and two were convicted of manslaughter.

The removal of the troops and the trial had a healthy effect. Substantial people in the town were thoroughly disgusted with the violence that had been almost continuous since 1765. The merchants defied the popular leaders and broke the non-importation agreement. For the next two years Boston was relatively quiet although the popular leaders continued their agitation. In doing so, the Boston Massacre was an invaluable source of propaganda (see No. 130).

The two documents that follow are striking examples of contradictory accounts of the events on 5 March 1770. The first is from the newspaper of the popular party. The second is by Captain Thomas Preston, who was in charge of the troops which fired on the mob.

129A. Newspaper account of the Boston Massacre

Printed: *The Boston Gazette and Country Journal*, 12 March 1770.

The town of Boston affords a recent and melancholy demonstration of the destructive consequences of quartering troops among citizens in a time of peace, under a pretence of supporting the laws and aiding civil authority; every considerate and unprejudiced person among us was deeply impressed with the apprehension of these consequences when it was known that a number of regiments were ordered to this town under such a pretext, but in reality to enforce oppressive measures; to awe and control the legislative as well as executive power of the province, and to quell a spirit of liberty, which however it may have been basely opposed and even ridiculed by some, would do honour to any age or country. A few persons amongst us had determined to use all their influence to procure so destructive a measure with a view to their securely enjoying the profits of an American revenue, and unhappily both for Britain and this country they found means to effect it.

It is to Governor Bernard, the commissioners, their confidants and coadjutors, that we are indebted as the procuring cause of a military power in this capital. The Boston Journal of Occurrences, as printed in Mr. Holt's *New York Gazette*, from time to time, afforded many striking instances of the distresses brought upon the inhabitants by this measure; and since those Journals have been discontinued, our troubles from that quarter have been growing upon us. We have known a party of soldiers in the face of day fire off a loaden musket upon the inhabitants, others have been pricked with bayonets, and even our magistrates assaulted and put in danger of their lives, when offenders brought before them have been rescued; and why those and other bold and base criminals have as yet escaped the punishment due to their crimes may be soon matter of enquiry by the representative body of this people. It is natural to suppose that when the inhabitants of this town saw those laws which had been enacted for their security, and which they were ambitious of holding up to the soldiery, eluded, they should more commonly resent for themselves; and accordingly it has so happened. Many have been the squabbles between them and the soldiery; but it seems their being often worsted by our youth in those rencounters, has only served to irritate the former. What passed at Mr. Gray's rope-walk has already been given the public and may be said to have led the way to the late catastrophe. That the rope-walk lads, when attacked by superior numbers, should defend themselves with so much spirit and success in the club-way, was too mortifying, and perhaps it may hereafter appear that even some of their officers were unhappily affected with this circumstance. Divers stories were propagated among the soldiery that served to agitate their spirits; particularly on the Sabbath that one Chambers, a sergeant, represented as a sober man, had been missing the preceding day and must therefore have been murdered by the townsmen. An officer of distinction so far credited this report that he entered Mr. Gray's rope-walk that Sabbath; and when required of by that gentleman as soon as he could meet him, the occasion of his so doing, the officer replied that it was to look if the sergeant said to be murdered had not been hid there. This sober sergeant was found on the Monday unhurt in a house of pleasure. The evidences already collected show that many threatenings had been thrown out by the soldiery, but we do not pretend to say that there was any preconcerted plan. When the evidences are published, the world will judge. We may, however, venture to declare that it appears too probable from their conduct that some of the soldiery aimed to draw and provoke the townsmen into squabbles, and that they then intended to make use of other weapons than canes, clubs, or bludgeons.

Our readers will doubtless expect a circumstantial account of the tragical affair on Monday night last; but we hope they will excuse our being so particular as we should have been, had we not seen that the town was intending an enquiry and full representation thereof.

On the evening of Monday, being the fifth current, several soldiers of the 29th Regiment were seen parading the streets with their drawn cutlasses and bayonets, abusing and wounding numbers of the inhabitants.

A few minutes after nine o'clock four youths, named Edward Archbald, William Merchant, Francis Archbald, and John Leech, jun., came down Cornhill together, and separating at Doctor Loring's corner, the two former were passing the narrow alley leading to Murray's barrack in which was a soldier brandishing a broad sword of an uncommon size against the walls, out of which he struck fire plentifully. A person of mean countenance armed with a large cudgel bore him company. Edward Archbald admonished Mr. Merchant to take care of the sword, on which the soldier turned round and struck Archbald on the arm, then pushed at Merchant and pierced through his clothes inside the arm close to the armpit and grazed the skin. Merchant then struck the soldier with a short stick he had; and the other person ran to the barrack and brought with him two soldiers, one armed with a pair of tongs, the other with a shovel. He with the tongs pursued Archbald back through the alley, collared and laid him over the head with the tongs. The noise brought people together; and John Hicks, a young lad, coming up, knocked the soldier down but let him get up again; and more lads gathering, drove them back to the barrack where the boys stood some time as it were to keep them in. In less than a minute ten or twelve of them came out with drawn cutlasses, clubs, and bayonets and set upon the unarmed boys and young folk who stood them a little while but, finding the inequality of their equipment, dispersed. On hearing the noise, one Samuel Atwood came up to see what was the matter; and entering the alley from dock square, heard the latter part of the combat; and when the boys had dispersed he met the ten or twelve soldiers aforesaid rushing down the alley towards the square and asked them if they intended to murder people? They answered Yes, by G-d, root and branch! With that one of them struck Mr. Atwood with a club which was repeated by another; and being unarmed, he turned to go off and received a wound on the left shoulder which reached the bone and gave him much pain. Retreating a few steps, Mr. Atwood met two officers and said, gentlemen, what is the matter? They answered, you'll see by and by. Immediately after, those heroes appeared in the square, asking where were the boogers? where were the cowards? But notwithstanding their fierceness to naked men, one of them advanced towards a youth who had a split of a raw stave in his hand and said, damn them, here is one of them. But the young man seeing a person near him with a drawn sword and good cane ready to support him, held up his stave in defiance; and they quietly passed by him up the little alley by Mr. Silsby's to King Street where they attacked single and unarmed persons till they raised much clamour, and then turned down Cornhill Street, insulting all they met in like manner and pursuing some to their very doors. Thirty or forty persons, mostly lads, being by this means gathered in King Street, Capt. Preston with a party of men with charged bayonets, came from the main guard to the commissioner's house, the soldiers pushing their bayonets, crying, make way! They took place by the custom house and, continuing to push to drive the people off, pricked some in several places, on which they were clamorous and, it is said, threw snow balls. On this, the Captain commanded them to fire; and more snow balls coming, he again said, damn you, fire, be the consequence what it will! One soldier then fired, and a townsman with a cudgel struck him over the hands with such force that he dropped his firelock; and, rushing forward, aimed a blow at the Captain's head which grazed his hat and fell pretty heavy upon his arm. However, the soldiers continued the fire successively till seven or eight or, as some say, eleven guns were discharged.

By this fatal manœuvre three men were laid dead on the spot and two more struggling for life; but what showed a degree of cruelty unknown to British troops, at least since the house of Hanover has directed their operations, was an attempt to fire upon or push with their bayonets the persons who undertook to remove the slain and wounded!

Mr. Benjamin Leigh, now undertaker in the Delph manufactory, came up; and after some conversation with Capt. Preston relative to his conduct in this affair, advised him to draw off his men, with which he complied.

The dead are Mr. Samuel Gray, killed on the spot, the ball entering his head and beating off a large portion of his skull.

A mulatto man named Crispus Attucks, who was born in Framingham, but lately belonged to New-Providence and was here in order to go for North Carolina, also killed instantly, two balls entering his breast, one of them in special goring the right lobe of the lungs and a great part of the liver most horribly.

Mr. James Caldwell, mate of Capt. Morton's vessel, in like manner killed by two balls entering his back.

Mr. Samuel Maverick, a promising youth of seventeen years of age, son of the widow Maverick, and an apprentice to Mr. Greenwood, ivory-turner, mortally wounded; a ball went through his belly and was cut out at his back. He died the next morning.

A lad named Christopher Monk, about seventeen years of age, an apprentice to Mr. Walker, shipwright, wounded; a ball entered his back about four inches above the left kidney near the spine and was cut out of the breast on the same side. Apprehended he will die.

A lad named John Clark, about seventeen years of age, whose parents live at Medford, and an apprentice to Capt. Samuel Howard of this town, wounded; a ball entered just above his groin and came out at his hip on the opposite side. Apprehended he will die.

Mr. Edward Payne of this town, merchant, standing at his entry door received a ball in his arm which shattered some of the bones.

Mr. John Green, tailor, coming up Leverett's Lane, received a ball just under his hip and lodged in the under part of his thigh, which was extracted.

Mr. Robert Patterson, a seafaring man, who was the person that had his trousers shot through in Richardson's affair, wounded; a ball went through his right arm, and he suffered a great loss of blood.

Mr. Patrick Carr, about thirty years of age, who worked with Mr. Field, leather breeches-maker in Queen Street, wounded; a ball entered near his hip and went out at his side.

A lad named David Parker, an apprentice to Mr. Eddy, the wheelwright, wounded; a ball entered in his thigh.

The people were immediately alarmed with the report of this horrid massacre, the bells were set a-ringing, and great numbers soon assembled at the place where this tragical scene had been acted. Their feelings may be better conceived than expressed; and while some were taking care of the dead and wounded, the rest were in consultation what to do in those dreadful circumstances. But so little intimidated were they, notwithstanding their being within a few yards of the main guard and seeing the 29th Regiment under arms and drawn up in King Street, that they kept their station and appeared, as an officer of rank expressed it, ready to run upon the very muzzles of their muskets. The lieutenant-governor soon came into the town house and there met some of his Majesty's Council and a number of civil magistrates. A considerable body of the people immediately entered the council chamber and expressed themselves to his honour with a freedom and warmth becoming the occasion. He used his utmost endeavours to pacify them, requesting that they would let the matter subside for the night and promising to do all in his power that justice should be done and the law have its course. Men of influence and weight with the people were not wanting on their part to procure their compliance with his Honour's request by representing the horrible consequences of a promiscuous and rash engagement in the night, and assuring them that such measures should be entered upon in the morning as would be agreeable to their dignity and a more likely way of obtaining the best satisfaction for the blood of their fellow townsmen. The inhabitants attended to these suggestions; and the regiment under arms being ordered to their barracks, which was insisted upon by the people, they then separated and returned to their dwellings by one o'clock. At three o'clock Capt. Preston was committed, as were the soldiers who fired, a few hours after him.

Tuesday morning presented a most shocking scene, the blood of our fellow citizens running like water through King Street and the Merchants' Exchange, the principal spot of the military parade for about eighteen months past. Our blood might also be tracked up to the head of Long Lane, and through divers other streets and passages.

At eleven o'clock the inhabitants met at Faneuil Hall; and after some animated speeches becoming the occasion, they chose a committee of fifteen respectable gentlemen to wait upon the lieutenant-governor in Council to request of him to issue his orders for the immediate removal of the troops.

[The Funeral]

Last Thursday, agreeable to a general request of the inhabitants and by the consent of parents and friends, were carried to their grave in succession the bodies of Samuel Gray, Samuel Maverick, James Caldwell, and Crispus Attucks, the unhappy victims who fell in the bloody massacre of the Monday evening preceding!

On this occasion most of the shops in town were shut, all the bells were ordered to toll a solemn peal, as were also those in the neighbouring towns of Charlestown, Roxbury, etc. The procession began to move between the hours of four and five in the afternoon, two of the unfortunate sufferers, viz. Messrs. James Caldwell and Crispus Attucks who were strangers, borne from Faneuil Hall attended by a numerous train of persons of all ranks; and the other two, viz. Mr. Samuel Gray, from the house of Mr. Benjamin Gray (his brother) on the north side the Exchange, and Mr. Maverick, from the house of his distressed mother, Mrs. Mary Maverick, in Union Street, each followed by their respective relations and friends, the several hearses forming a junction in King Street, the theatre of the inhuman tragedy, proceeded from thence through the Main Street, lengthened by an immense concourse of people so numerous as to be obliged to follow in ranks of six, and brought up by a long train of carriages belonging to the principal gentry of the town. The bodies were deposited in one vault in the middle burying ground. The aggravated circumstances of their death, the distress and sorrow visible in every countenance, together with the peculiar solemnity with which the whole funeral was conducted, surpass description.

129B. Captain Thomas Preston's account of the Boston Massacre (13 March 1770)

From: British Public Record Office, C.O. 5/759.

It is [a] matter of too great notoriety to need any proofs that the arrival of his Majesty's troops in Boston was extremely obnoxious to its inhabitants. They have ever used all means in their power to weaken the regiments, and to bring them into contempt by promoting and aiding desertions, and with impunity, even where there has been the clearest evidence of the fact, and by grossly and falsely propagating untruths concerning them. On the arrival of the 64th and 65th their ardour seemingly began to abate; it being too expensive to buy off so many, and attempts of that kind rendered too dangerous from the numbers. But the same spirit revived immediately on its being known that those regiments were ordered for Halifax, and has ever since their departure been breaking out with greater violence after their embarkation. One of their justices, most thoroughly acquainted with the people and their intentions, on the trial of a man of the 14th Regiment, openly and publicly in the hearing of great numbers of people and from the seat of justice, declared "that the soldiers must now take care of themselves, *nor trust too much to their arms*, for they were but a handful; that the inhabitants carried weapons concealed under their clothes, and would destroy them in a moment, *if they pleased*". This, considering the malicious temper of the people, was an alarming circumstance to the soldiery. Since which several disputes have happened between the townspeople and the soldiers of both regiments, the former being encouraged thereto by the countenance of even some of the magistrates, and by the protection of all the party against government. In general such disputes have been kept too secret from the officers. On the 2d instant two of the 29th going through one Gray's rope-walk, the rope-makers insultingly asked them if they would empty a vault. This unfortunately had the desired effect by provoking the soldiers, and from words they went to blows. Both parties suffered in this affray, and finally the soldiers retired to their quarters. The officers, on the first knowledge of this transaction, took every precaution in their power to prevent any ill consequence. Notwithstanding which, single quarrels could not be prevented, the inhabitants constantly provoking and abusing the soldiery. The insolence as well as utter hatred of the inhabitants to the troops increased daily, insomuch that Monday and Tuesday, the 5th and 6th instant, were privately agreed on for a general engagement, in consequence of which several of the militia came from the country armed to join their friends, menacing to destroy any who should oppose them. This plan has since been discovered.

On Monday night about 8 o'clock two soldiers were attacked and beat. But the party of the townspeople in order to carry matters to the utmost length, broke into two meeting houses and rang the alarm bells, which I supposed was for fire as usual, but was soon undeceived. About 9 some of the guard came to and informed me the town inhabitants were assembling to attack the troops, and that the bells were ringing as the signal for that purpose and not for fire, and the beacon intended to be fired to bring in the distant people of the country. This, as I was captain of the day, occasioned my repairing immediately to the main guard. In my way there I saw the people in great commotion, and heard them use the most cruel and horrid threats against the troops. In a few minutes after I reached the guard, about 100 people passed it and went towards the custom house where the king's money is lodged. They immediately surrounded the sentry posted there, and with clubs and other weapons threatened to execute their vengeance on him. I was soon informed by a townsman their intention was to carry off the soldier from his post and probably murder him. On which I desired him to return for further intelligence, and he soon came back and assured me he heard the mob declare they would murder him. This I feared might be a prelude to their plundering the king's chest. I immediately sent a non-commissioned officer and 12 men to protect both the sentry and the king's money, and very soon followed myself to prevent, if possible, all disorder, fearing lest the officer and soldiers, by the insults and provocations of the rioters, should be thrown off their guard and commit some rash act. They soon rushed through the people, and by charging their bayonets in half-circles, kept them at a little distance. Nay, so far was I from intending the death of any person that I suffered the troops to go to the spot where the unhappy affair took place without any loading in their pieces; nor did I ever give orders for loading them. This remiss conduct in me perhaps merits censure; yet it is evidence, resulting from the nature of things, which is the best and surest that can be offered, that my intention was not to act offensively, but the contrary part, and that not without compulsion. The mob still increased and were more outrageous, striking their clubs or bludgeons one against another, and calling out, come on you rascals, you bloody backs, you lobster scoundrels, fire if you dare, G-d damn you, fire and be damned, we know you dare not, and much more such language was used. At this time I was between the soldiers and the mob, parleying with, and endeavouring all in my power to persuade them to retire peaceably, but to no purpose. They advanced to the points of the bayonets, struck some of them and even the muzzles of the pieces, and seemed to be endeavouring to close with the soldiers. On which some well behaved persons asked me if the guns were charged. I replied yes. They then asked me if I intended to order the men to fire. I answered no, by no means, observing to them that I was advanced before the muzzles of the men's pieces, and must fall a sacrifice if they fired; that the soldiers were upon the half cock and charged bayonets, and my giving the word fire under those circumstances would prove me to be no officer. While I was thus speaking, one of the soldiers having received a severe blow with a stick, stepped a little on one side and instantly fired, on which turning to and asking him why he fired without orders, I was struck with a club on my arm, which for some time deprived me of the use of it, which blow had it been placed on my head, most probably would have destroyed me. On this a general attack was made on the men by a great number of heavy clubs and snowballs being thrown at them, by which all our lives were in imminent danger, some persons at the same time from behind calling out, damn your bloods–why don't you fire. Instantly three or four of the soldiers fired, one after another, and directly after three more in the same confusion and hurry. The mob then ran away, except three unhappy men who instantly expired, in which number was Mr. Gray at whose rope-walk the prior quarrels took place; one more is since dead, three others are dangerously, and four slightly wounded. The whole of this melancholy affair was transacted in almost 20 minutes. On my asking the soldiers why they fired without orders, they said they heard the word fire and supposed it came from me. This might be the case as many of the mob called out fire, fire, but I assured the men that I gave no such order; that my words were, don't fire, stop your firing. In short, it was scarcely possible for the soldiers to know who said fire, or don't fire, or stop your firing. On the people's assembling again to take away the dead bodies, the soldiers supposing them coming to attack them, were making ready to fire again, which I prevented by striking up their firelocks with my hand. Immediately after a townsman came and told me that 4 or 5000 people were assembled in the next street, and had sworn to take my life with every man's with me. On which I judged it unsafe to remain there any longer, and therefore sent the party and sentry to the main guard, where the street is narrow and short, there telling them off into street firings, divided and planted them at each end of the street to secure their rear, momently expecting an attack, as there was a constant cry of the inhabitants to arms, to arms, turn out with your guns; and the town drums beating to arms, I ordered my drums to beat to arms, and being soon after joined by the different companies of the 29th regiment, I formed them as the guard into street firings. The 14th regiment also got under arms but remained at their barracks. I immediately sent a sergeant with a party to Colonel Dalrymple, the commanding officer, to acquaint him with every particular. Several officers going to join their regiment were knocked down by the mob, one very much wounded and his sword taken from him. The lieutenant-governor and Colonel Carr soon after met at the head of the 29th regiment and agreed that the regiment should retire to their barracks, and the people to their houses, but I kept the picket to strengthen the guard. It was with great difficulty that the lieutenant-governor prevailed on the people to be quiet and retire. At last they all went off, excepting about a hundred.

A Council was immediately called, on the breaking up of which three justices met and issued a warrant to apprehend me and eight soldiers. On hearing of this procedure I instantly went to the sheriff and surrendered myself, though for the space of 4 hours I had it in my power to have made my escape, which I most undoubtedly should have attempted and could easily executed, had I been the least conscious of any guilt. On the examination before the justices, two witnesses swore that I gave the men orders to fire. The one testified he was within two feet of me; the other that I swore at the men for not firing at the first word. Others swore they heard me use the word "fire," but whether do or do not fire, they could not say; others that they heard the word fire, but could not say if it came from me. The next day they got

5 or 6 more to swear I gave the word to fire. So bitter and inveterate are many of the malcontents here that they are industriously using every method to fish out evidence to prove it was a concerted scheme to murder the inhabitants. Others are infusing the utmost malice and revenge into the minds of the people who are to be my jurors by false publications, votes of towns, and all other artifices. That so from a settled rancour against the officers and troops in general, the suddenness of my trial after the affair while the people's minds are all greatly inflamed, I am, though perfectly innocent, under most unhappy circumstances, having nothing in reason to expect but the loss of life in a very ignominous manner, without the interposition of his Majesty's royal goodness.

130. Joseph Warren's Boston Massacre oration (5 March 1772)

Beginning in 1771, and annually until some time after the Revolution, the anniversary of the Boston Massacre was the occasion for a commemorative oration. The popular leaders used it from 1771 onwards to stir up antagonism towards the British troops and towards Britain itself. The oration by Joseph Warren in 1772 is one of the most eloquent and effective of these speeches. Printed: Niles, ed., *Principles and Acts of the Revolution in America*, pp. 20–24.

When we turn over the historic page and trace the rise and fall of states and empires, the mighty revolutions which have so often varied the face of the world strike our minds with solemn surprise, and we are naturally led to endeavour to search out the causes of such astonishing changes.

That man is formed for social life is an observation, which, upon our first enquiry, presents itself immediately to our view, and our reason approves that wise and generous principle which actuated the first founders of civil government; an institution which hath its origin in the weakness of individuals, and hath for its end the strength and security of all; and so long as the means of effecting this important end are thoroughly known, and religiously attended to, government is one of the richest blessings to mankind, and ought to be held in the highest veneration.

In young and new formed communities, the grand design of this institution is most generally understood, and the most strictly regarded; the motives which urged to the social compact, cannot be at once forgotten, and that equality which is remembered to have subsisted so lately among them, prevents those who are clothed with authority from attempting to invade the freedom of their brethren; or if such an attempt is made, it prevents the community from suffering the offender to go unpunished: every member feels it to be his interest and knows it to be his duty, to preserve inviolate the constitution on which the public safety depends, and he is equally ready to assist the magistrate in the execution of the laws, and the subject in defence of his right; and so long as this noble attachment to a constitution, founded on free and benevolent principles, exists in full vigour, in any state, that state must be flourishing and happy.

It was this noble attachment to a free constitution which raised ancient Rome, from the smallest beginnings, to that bright summit of happiness and glory to which she arrived; and it was the loss of this which plunged her from that summit into the black gulf of infamy and slavery. It was this attachment which inspired her senators with wisdom; it was this which glowed in the breast of her heroes; it was this which guarded her liberties and extended her dominions, gave peace at home and commanded respect abroad: and when this decayed, her magistrates lost their reverence for justice and the laws, and degenerated into tyrants and oppressors—her senators, forgetful of their dignity, and seduced by base corruption, betrayed their country—her soldiers, regardless of their relation to the community, and urged only by the hopes of plunder and rapine, unfeelingly committed the most flagrant enormities; and hired to the trade of death, with relentless fury, they perpetrated the most cruel murders, whereby the streets of imperial Rome were drenched with her noblest blood. Thus this empress of the world lost her dominions abroad, and her inhabitants, dissolute in their manners, at length became contented slaves; and she stands to this day, the scorn and derision of nations, and a monument of this eternal truth, that *public happiness depends on a virtuous and unshaken attachment to a free constitution.*

It was this attachment to a constitution, founded on free and benevolent principles, which inspired the first settlers of this country—they saw with grief the daring outrages committed on the free constitution of their native land—they knew nothing but a civil war could at that time restore its pristine purity. So hard was it to resolve to embrue their hands in the blood of their brethren, that they chose rather to quit their fair possessions and seek another habitation in a distant clime. When they came to this new world, which they fairly purchased of the Indian natives, the only rightful proprietors, they cultivated the then barren soil by their incessant labour, and defended their dear-bought possessions with the fortitude of the Christian, and the bravery of the hero.

After various struggles, which, during the tyrannic reigns of the house of Stuart, were constantly kept up between right and wrong, between liberty and slavery, the connection between Great Britain and this colony was settled in the reign of King William and Queen Mary, by a compact, the conditions of which were expressed in a charter, by which all the liberties and immunities of British subjects, were confided to this province, as fully and as absolutely as they possibly could be by any human instrument which can be devised. And it is undeniably true, that the greatest and most important right of a British subject is, that *he shall be governed by no laws but those to which he, either in person or by his representatives hath given his consent*: and this I will venture to assert, is the great basis of British freedom: it is interwoven with the constitution; and whenever this is lost, the constitution must be destroyed.

The British constitution (of which ours is a copy) is a happy compound of the three forms (under some of which all governments may be ranged) viz., monarchy, aristocracy, and democracy; of these three the British legislature is composed, and without the consent of each branch, nothing can carry with it the force of a law; but when a law is to be passed for raising a tax, that law can originate only in the democratic branch, which is the House of Commons in Britain, and the House of Representatives here. The reason is obvious: they and their constituents are to pay much the largest part of it; but as the aristocratic branch, which, in Britain, is the House of Lords, and in this province, the Council, are also to pay some part, their consent is necessary; and as the monarchic branch, which in Britain is the king, and with us, either the king in person, or the governor whom he shall be pleased to appoint to act in his stead, is supposed to have a just sense of his own interest, which is that of all the subjects in general, his consent is also necessary, and when the consent of these three branches is obtained, the taxation is most certainly legal.

Let us now allow ourselves a few moments to examine the late Acts of the British Parliament for taxing America. Let us with candour judge whether they are constitutionally binding upon us; if they are, in the name of justice let us submit to them, without one murmuring word.

First, I would ask whether the members of the British House of Commons are the democracy of this province? If they are, they are either the people of this province, or are elected by the people of this province to represent them, and have therefore a constitutional right to originate a bill for taxing them; it is most certain they are neither; and therefore nothing done by them can be said to be done by the democratic branch of our constitution. I would next ask, whether the lords, who compose the aristocratic branch of the legislature, are peers of America? I never heard it was (even in those extraordinary times) so much as pretended, and if they are not, certainly no act of theirs can be said to be the act of the aristocratic branch of our constitution. The power of the monarchic branch, we, with pleasure, acknowledge resides in the king, who may act either in person or by his representative; and I freely confess that I can see no reason why a proclamation for raising in America issued by the king's sole authority would not be equally consistent with our own constitution, and therefore equally binding upon us with the late Acts of the British Parliament for taxing us; for it is plain, that if there is any validity in those Acts, it must arise altogether from the monarchical branch of the legislature; and I further think that it would be at least as equitable; for I do not conceive it to be of the least importance to us by whom our property is taken away, so long as it is taken without our consent; and I am very much at a loss to know by what figure of rhetoric, the inhabitants of this province can be called free subjects, when they are obliged to obey implicitly, such laws as are made for them by men three thousand miles off, whom they know not, and whom they never empowered to act for them, or how they can be said to have property, when a body of men, over whom they have not the least control, and who are not in any way accountable to them, shall oblige them to deliver up any part, or the whole of their substance without even asking their consent; and yet whoever pretends that the late Acts of the British Parliament for taxing America ought to be deemed binding upon us, must admit at once that we are absolute slaves, and have no property of our own; or else that we may be freemen, and at the same time under a necessity of obeying the arbitrary commands of those over whom we have no control or influence, and that we may have property of our own which is entirely at the disposal of another. Such gross absurdities, I believe, will not be relished in this enlightened age: and it can be no matter of wonder that the people quickly perceived, and seriously complained of the inroads which these Acts must unavoidably make upon their liberty, and of the hazard to which their whole property is by them exposed; for, if they may be taxed without their consent, even in the smallest trifle, they may also, without their consent, be deprived of everything they possess, although never so valuable, never so dear. Certainly it never entered the hearts of our ancestors, that after so many dangers in this then desolate wilderness, their hard-earned property should be at the disposal of the British Parliament; and as it was soon found that this taxation could not be supported by reason and argument, it seemed necessary that one act of oppression should be enforced by another, and therefore, contrary to our just rights as possessing, or at least having a just title to possess, all the liberties and immunities of British subjects, a standing army was established among us in time of peace; and evidently for the purpose of effecting *that*, which it was one principal design of the founders of the constitution to prevent (when they declared a standing army in a time of peace to be *against law*), namely, for the enforcement of obedience to acts which, upon fair examination, appeared to be unjust and unconstitutional.

The ruinous consequences of standing armies to free communities may be seen in the histories of Syracuse, Rome, and many other once flourishing states; some of which have now scarce a name! Their baneful influence is most suddenly felt when they are placed in populous cities; for, by a corruption of morals, the public happiness is immediately affected! And that this is one of the effects of quartering troops in a populous city, is a truth, to which many a mourning parent, many a lost despairing child in this metropolis must bear a very melancholy testimony. Soldiers are also taught to consider arms as the only arbiters by which every dispute is to be decided between contending states; they are instructed implicitly to obey their commanders, without enquiring into the justice of the cause they are engaged to support; hence it is, that they are ever to be dreaded as the ready engines of tyranny and oppression. And it is too observable that they are prone to introduce the same mode of decision in the disputes of individuals, and from thence have often arisen great animosities between them and the inhabitants, who, whilst in a naked, defenceless state, are frequently insulted and abused by an armed soldiery. And this will be more especially the case when the troops are informed that the intention of their being stationed in any city is to overawe the inhabitants. That this was the avowed design of stationing an armed force in this town is sufficiently known; and we, my fellow citizens, have seen, we have felt the tragical effects! *The fatal fifth of March, 1770, can never be forgotten.* The horrors of *that dreadful night* are but too deeply impressed on our hearts. Language is too feeble to paint the emotion of our souls, when our streets were stained with the blood of our brethren – when our ears were wounded by the groans of the dying, and our eyes were tormented with the sight of the mangled bodies of the dead.

When our alarmed imagination presented to our view our houses wrapped in flames, our children subjected to the barbarous caprice of the raging soldiery, our beauteous virgins exposed to all the insolence of unbridled passion, our virtuous wives, endeared to us by every tender tie, falling a sacrifice to worse than brutal violence, and perhaps like the famed Lucretia, distracted with anguish and despair, ending their wretched lives by their own fair hands. When we beheld the authors of our distress parading in our streets, or drawn up in a regular *battalia*, as though in a hostile city, our hearts beat to arms; we snatched our weapons, almost resolved by one decisive stroke to avenge the death of our slaughtered brethren, and to secure from future danger all that we held most dear: but propitious heaven forbade the bloody carnage and saved the threatened victims of our too keen resentment, not by their discipline, not by their regular array, no, it was royal George's livery that proved their shield – it was that which turned the pointed engines of destruction from their breasts. The thoughts of vengeance were soon buried in our inbred affection to Great Britain, and calm reason dictated a method of removing the troops more mild than an immediate resource to the sword. With united efforts you urged the immediate departure of the troops from the town – you urged it, with a resolution which ensured success – you obtained your wishes, and the removal of the troops was effected without one drop of their blood being shed by the inhabitants.

The immediate actors in the tragedy of that night were surrendered to justice. It is not mine to say how far they were guilty. They have been tried by the country and *acquitted* of murder! And they are not to be again arraigned at an earthly bar; but, surely the men who have promiscuously scattered death amidst the innocent inhabitants of a populous city ought to see well to it that they be prepared to stand at the bar of an omniscient judge! And all who contrived or encouraged the stationing troops in this place have reasons of eternal importance to reflect with deep contrition on their base designs, and humbly to repent of their impious machinations.

The infatuation which hath seemed, for a number of years, to prevail in the British councils, with regard to us, is truly astonishing! What can be proposed by the repeated attacks made upon our freedom, I really cannot surmise; even leaving justice and humanity out of question. I do not know one single advantage which can arise to the British nation from our being enslaved. I know not of any gains which can be wrung from us by oppression which they may not obtain from us by our own consent in the smooth channel of commerce. We wish the wealth and prosperity of Britain; we contribute largely to both. Doth what we contribute lose all its value because it is done voluntarily? The amazing increase of riches to Britain, the great rise of the value of her lands, the flourishing state of her navy, are striking proofs of the advantages derived to her from her commerce with the colonies; and it is our earnest desire that she may still continue to enjoy the same emoluments, until her streets are paved with *American gold*; only, let us have the pleasure of calling it our own whilst it is in our own hands; but this it seems is too great a favour. We are to be governed by the *absolute command of others; our property is to be taken away without our consent.* If we complain, our complaints are treated with contempt; if we assert our rights, that assertion is deemed insolence; if we humbly offer to submit the matter to the impartial decision of reason, the *sword* is judged the most proper argument to silence our murmurs! But this cannot long be the case. Surely the British nation will not suffer the reputation of their justice and their honour to be thus sported away by a capricious ministry; no, they will in a short time open their eyes to their true interest. They nourish in their own breasts a noble love of liberty; they hold her dear, and they know that all who have once possessed her charms had rather die than suffer her to be torn from their embraces. They are also sensible that Britain is so deeply interested in the prosperity of the colonies that she must eventually feel every wound given to their freedom; they cannot be ignorant that more dependence may be placed on the affections of a brother than on the forced service of a slave; they must approve your efforts for the preservation of your rights; from a sympathy of soul they must pray for your success. And I doubt not but they will, ere long, exert themselves effectually, to redress your grievances. Even in the dissolute reign of King Charles II, when the House of Commons impeached the earl of Clarendon of high treason, the first article on which they founded their accusation was, that *"he had designed a standing army to be raised, and to govern the kingdom thereby"*. And the eighth article was that *"he had introduced an arbitrary government into his Majesty's plantation"*. A terrifying example to those who are now forging chains for this country.

You have, my friends and countrymen, frustrated the designs of your enemies by your unanimity and fortitude. It was your union and determined spirit which expelled those troops who polluted your streets with innocent blood. You have appointed this anniversary as a standard memorial of the *bloody consequences of placing an armed force in a populous city*, and of your deliverance from the dangers which then seemed to hang over your heads; and I am confident that you never will betray the least want of spirit when called upon to guard your freedom. None but they who set a just value upon the blessings of liberty are worthy to enjoy her. Your illustrious fathers were her zealous votaries. When the blasting frowns of tyranny drove her from public view they clasped her in their arms, they cherished her in their generous bosoms, they brought her safe over the rough ocean and fixed her seat in this then dreary wilderness; they nursed her infant age with the most tender care; for her sake they patiently bore the severest hardships; for her support they underwent the most rugged toils, in her defence they boldly encountered the most alarming dangers; neither the ravenous beasts that ranged the woods for prey, nor the more furious savages of the wilderness could damp ardour! Whilst with one hand they broke the stubborn glebe, with the other they grasped their weapons, ever ready to protect her from danger. No sacrifice, not even their own blood, was esteemed too rich a libation for her altar! God prospered their valour, they preserved her brilliancy unsullied; they enjoyed her whilst they lived, and dying, bequeathed the dear inheritance to your care. And as they left you this glorious legacy, they have undoubtedly transmitted to you some portion of their noble spirit, to inspire you with virtue to merit her, and courage to preserve her. You surely cannot, with such examples before your eyes, as every page of the history of this country affords, suffer your liberties to be ravished from you by lawless force, or cajoled away by flattery and fraud.

The voice of your fathers' blood cries to you from the ground, *my sons scorn to be slaves!* In vain we met the frowns of tyrants. In vain we crossed the boisterous ocean, found a new world and prepared it for the happy residence of liberty. In vain we toiled. In vain we fought. We bled in vain, if you, our offspring, want valour to repel the assaults of her invaders! Stain not the glory of your worthy ancestors, but like them resolve never to part with your birthright; be wise in your deliberations, and determined in your exertions for the preservation of your liberties. Follow not the dictates of passion, but enlist yourselves under the sacred banner of reason; use every method in your power to secure your rights; at least prevent the curses of posterity from being heaped upon your memories.

If you, with united zeal and fortitude, oppose the torrent of oppression; if you feel the true fire of patriotism burning in your breasts; if you, from your souls, despise the most gaudy dress that slavery can wear; if you really prefer the lonely cottage (whilst blest with liberty) to gilded palaces surrounded with the ensigns of slavery, you may have the fullest assurance that tyranny, with her whole accursed train, will hide their hideous heads in confusion, shame, and despair. If you perform your part, you must have the strongest confidence that the same Almighty Being who protected your pious and venerable forefathers – who enabled them to turn a barren wilderness into a fruitful field, who so often made bare his arm for their salvation, will still be mindful of you, their offspring.

May this Almighty Being graciously preside in all our councils. May he direct us to such measures as he himself shall approve, and be pleased to bless. May we ever be a people favoured of God. May our land be a land of liberty, the seat of virtue, the asylum of the oppressed, a name and a praise in the whole earth, until the last shock of time shall bury the empires of the world in one common undistinguished ruin!

131. The *Gaspee* affair (10 June 1772)

The burning of the British naval vessel *Gaspee* by citizens of Rhode Island was an outstanding example of colonial opposition to the enforcement of the Acts of Trade and Navigation. Rhode Island citizens had previously destroyed two naval vessels, and the *Gaspee*, commanded by Lieutenant William Dudingston, was one of the two sent to replace them. Dudingston arrived in Rhode Island waters 22 March 1772. He was in difficulty at once and was threatened with arrest by local sheriffs for the seizure of merchant vessels. He wrote of his troubles to Admiral Montagu in Boston. The admiral protested to Governor Joseph Wanton, who returned a sharp reply.

On the night of 9 June, the *Gaspee* ran aground a few miles from Providence. Early the next morning the ship was boarded. Dudingston was wounded, and he and his crew were put ashore, and the vessel was burned. A Rhode Island sheriff promptly arrested Dudingston for 'illegal' seizure of casks of rum and sugar. He stood three trials, all of which he lost, and eventually the British Navy subjected him to court-martial proceedings for the loss of his ship.

Meanwhile, depositions and statements concerning the destruction of the ship were sent to England. The result was the appointment of a royal commission consisting of Governor Wanton, the judge of the Vice-Admiralty court at Boston, and the chief justices of Massachusetts, New York, and New Jersey. This commission met in the spring of 1773. In its final report, 22 June 1773, the commission concluded that it was impossible to identify the guilty parties because of conflicting evidence and perjured testimony. Most of the relevant documents are printed: *Rhode Island Colonial Records*, VII, pp. 58–192. The following letters are from pp. 62–64, 86–87.

[Admiral Montagu to the Governor of Rhode Island]

Boston, 8th April, 1772

Sir:

Lieutenant Dudingston, commander of his Majesty's armed schooner, and a part of the squadron under my command, has sent me two letters he received from you, of such a nature I am at a loss what answer to give them, and ashamed to find they come from one of his Majesty's governors. He informs me that he waited upon you and showed you the Admiralty and my orders for his proceedings; which, agreeably to his instructions, he is to do, that you may be acquainted that he is on that station to protect your province from pirates, and to give the trade all the assistance he can, and to endeavour, as much as lays in his power, to protect the revenue officer, and to prevent (if possible) the illicit trade that is carrying on at Rhode Island.

He, sir, has done his duty and behaved like an officer, and it is your duty, as a governor, to give him your assistance, and not endeavour to distress the king's officers for strictly complying with my orders. I shall give them directions that in case they receive any molestation in the execution of their duty, they shall send every man so taken in molesting them to me. I am also informed the people of Newport talk of fitting out an armed vessel to rescue any vessel the king's schooner may take carrying on an illicit trade. Let them be cautious what they do, for as sure as they attempt it, and any of them are taken, I will hang them as pirates. I shall report your two insolent letters to my officer, to his Majesty's secretaries of state, and leave them to determine what right you have to demand a sight of all orders I shall give to all officers of my squadron; and I would advise you not to send your sheriff on board the king's ship again on such ridiculous errands. The captain and lieutenants have all my orders to give you assistance whenever you demand it, but further, you have no business with them; and be assured, it is not their duty to show you any part of my orders or instructions to them.

[The Governor of Rhode Island to Admiral Montagu]

Rhode Island, May 8, 1772

Sir:

Your letter dated April the 8th at Boston, I have received. Lieutenant Dudingston has done well in transmitting my letters to you, which I sent him; but I am sorry to be informed there is anything contained in them that should be construed as a design of giving offence, when no such thing was intended. But Mr. Dudingston has not behaved so well in asserting to you "he waited on me, and showed me the Admiralty and your orders for his proceedings, which, agreeably to his instructions, he is so to do"; but in that he has altogether misinformed you, for he at no time ever showed me any orders from the Admiralty or from you; and positively denied that he derived any authority either from you or the commissioners; therefore, it was altogether out of my power to know whether he came hither to protect us from pirates, or was a pirate himself. You say, "he has done his duty and behaved like an officer". In this, I apprehend you must be mistaken, for I can never believe it is the duty of any officer to give false information to his superiors. As to your attempt to point out what was my duty as governor, please to be informed that I do not receive instructions for the administration of my government from the king's admiral stationed in America.

You seem to assert that I have endeavoured to distress the king's officers for strictly complying with your orders. In this you are altogether mistaken, for I have at all times heretofore, and shall constantly for time to come, afford them all the aid and assistance in my power in the execution of their office.

The information you have received, "that the people of Newport talked of fitting out an armed vessel to rescue any vessel the king's schooner might take carrying on an illicit trade", you may be assured is without any foundation, and a scandalous imposition; for, upon inquiring into this matter, I cannot find that any such design was ever conceived, or so much as talked of; and therefore I hope you will not hang any of his Majesty's subjects belonging to his colony upon such false information.

I am greatly obliged for the promise of transmitting my letters to the secretary of state. I am, however, a little shocked at your impolite expression, made use of upon that occasion. In return for this good office, I shall also transmit your letter to the secretary of state, and leave to the king and his ministers to determine on which side the charge of insolence lies.

As to your advice, not to send the sheriff on board any of your squadron, please to know that I will send the sheriff of this colony at any time, and to any place, within the body of it, as I shall think fit.

In the last paragraph of your letter you are pleased flatly to contradict what you wrote in the beginning, for there you assert that Dudingston, by his instructions, was directed to show me the Admiralty and your orders to him; and here you assert that I have no business with them and assure me that it is not his duty to show me them, or any part thereof.

[Lieutenant Dudingston to Admiral Montagu]

Pawtuxet, 12th June, 1772

Sir:

On Wednesday morning about one o'clock, as his Majesty's schooner was lying upon a spit of sand called Namcutt, the sentinels discovered a number of boats coming down the river towards us.

As soon as I was acquainted with it I came upon deck and hailed the boats, forbidding them to come near the schooner or I should order them to be fired upon.

They made answer they had the sheriff with them and must come on board.

I told them the sheriff could not be admitted on board at that time of night, on which they set up a halloa and rowed as fast as they could towards the vessel's bows. I was then using every means in my power to get the guns to bear upon them, which I could not effect, as they came right ahead of the vessel, she being aground. I then ordered the men to come forward with their small arms and prevent them from boarding.

As I was standing myself to oppose them, and making a stroke with my sword at the man who was attempting to come up, at that instant I found myself disabled in my left arm, and shot through the groin. I then stepped from the gunwale, with an intention to order them retire to close quarters, but soon saw that most of them were knocked down, and myself twice (after telling them I was mortally wounded).

They damned me and said I was not wounded; if I was, my own people had done it. As loss of blood made me drop down upon deck, they ordered me to beg my life, and commanded the people to surrender. As I saw there was no possibility of defending the vessel against such numbers, who were in every respect armed, and commanded with regularity by one who personated the sheriff, I thought it best for the people's preservation to propose to them that I would order them to surrender if they assured me they should not be hurt, which they did.

I then called out, which was immediately echoed by the people round me, that I had given them orders to surrender. They hurried all the people below and ordered them up, one by one, and tied their hands behind their backs, then ordered them into different boats.

I then begged they would either dispatch me or suffer my wounds to be dressed; upon that they allowed my servant to be unbound to get me things for dressing, and carried me below. But what was my surprise when I came down in the cabin, two surgeons were ordered down from the deck to dress me, who were furnished with drops, and began to scrape lint for that purpose.

During this time I had an opportunity of observing the persons of about a dozen who were in the cabin. They appeared to me to be merchants and masters of vessels, who were at my bureau, reading and examining my papers. They promised to let me have the schooner's books and my clothes; instead of which, as they were handing me up to go into the boat, they threw them overboard, or into some of the boats. I was soon afterwards thrust into a boat, almost naked.

During the time they were rowing me on shore I had an opportunity of observing the boat, which appeared to me to be a very large longboat. I saw by the man who steered her a cutlass lying by him, and directing the men to have their arms ready. As soon as they put off, the sheriff gave them orders to land me on some neck, and the boat to come off immediately, and told me if I did not consent to pay the value of the rum I must not expect to have anything belonging to me saved.

I made answer, whatever reparation the law would give, I was ready and willing; as to my things, they might do with them as they pleased. They were accordingly going to land me on this neck when I told them they had better throw me overboard. One man who had a little more humanity than any of the rest said they had better land me at the Point of Pawtuxet. As I was unable to stand, they unbound five of the men and gave them a blanket to carry me up. When I was half way on shore I heard some of the schooner's guns go off and heard the people say she was on fire.

I had not been carried far when the people exclaimed I was on an island and they saw no house; on which they laid me down and went in quest of one. Soon after they came to acquaint me they saw one, which I was carried to; a man was immediately dispatched to Providence for a surgeon. A little after, the people joined me, with the midshipman, all of whom that I could persuade are sent on board his Majesty's sloop *Beaver*.

The schooner is utterly destroyed, and everything appertaining to her, me, and the schooner's company. If I live, I am not without hope of being able to convict some of the principal people that were with them. The pain, with the loss of blood, rendered me incapable of informing you before of the particulars. There are none of the people anyways wounded, but bruised with handspikes.

132. Establishment of the Boston Committee of Correspondence (2 November 1772)

The occasion for establishment of the Boston Committee of Correspondence was the news that certain royal officials, including the judges of the Superior Court, were to be paid from British funds rather than by grant from the legislature. The Boston town meeting demanded a special session of the legislature, and when this was refused by Governor Hutchinson, Samuel Adams proposed the establishment of the Committee of Correspondence. The men on this committee were soon in touch with like-minded men in all the other Massachusetts towns. The committee functioned as a clearing-house for news and propaganda and built up an effective organization within the colony and kept in touch with popular leaders in all the other colonies. Printed: *Boston Town Records, 1770–1777*, pp. 92–93.

Resolved as the opinion of the inhabitants of this town that they have ever had, and ought to have a right to petition the king or his representatives for the redress of such grievances as they feel, or for preventing of such as they have reason to apprehend, and to communicate their sentiment to other towns.

It was then moved by Mr. Samuel Adams that a committee of correspondence be appointed to consist of twenty-one persons: to state the rights of the colonists, and of this province in particular, as men, as Christians, and as subjects; to communicate and publish the same to the several towns in this province and to the world as the sense of this town, with the infringements and violations thereof that have been, or from time to time may be made; also requesting of each town a free communication of their sentiments on this subject; and the question being accordingly put, passed in the affirmative. *Nem. Con.*

133A–B. Establishment of inter-colonial committees of correspondence (1773)

The establishment of a permanent inter-colonial organization was achieved in 1773 as a result of the appointment of a court of inquiry in the *Gaspee* affair in Rhode Island in 1772 (see No. 131). It was a common practice of colonial legislatures to have standing committees to correspond with the colonial agents in London at times when the legislatures were not in session. Now the device was extended to the establishment of colonial legislative committees to correspond with one another. On 12 March 1773 the Virginia legislature established such a committee and invited other colonial legislatures to do likewise. On 28 May the Massachusetts legislature adopted the proposal and notified the other colonial legislatures. Within a short time all the colonial legislatures had appointed similar committees.

A working organization was now in effect, ready to meet any issue that might arise. One soon did with the colonial opposition to the East India Company Act and the passage of what the Americans at once called the "Intolerable Acts" by Parliament in the spring of 1774 (see No. 138).

133A. Virginia resolutions establishing a committee of correspondence (12 March 1773)

Printed: *Journals of the House of Burgesses, 1773–1776*, p. 28.

Whereas, the minds of his Majesty's faithful subjects in this colony have been much disturbed by various rumours and reports of proceedings tending to deprive them of their ancient, legal, and constitutional rights.

And whereas, the affairs of this colony are frequently connected with those of Great Britain, as well as of the neighbouring colonies, which renders a communication of sentiments necessary; in order, therefore, to remove the uneasinesses and to quiet the minds of the people, as well as for the other good purposes above mentioned:

Be it resolved, that a standing committee of correspondence and inquiry be appointed to consist of eleven persons, to wit: the Honourable Peyton Randolph, Esquire; Robert Carter Nicholas, Richard Bland, Richard Henry Lee, Benjamin Harrison, Edmund Pendleton, Patrick Henry, Dudley Digges, Dabney Carr,

Archibald Cary, and Thomas Jefferson, Esquires, any six of whom to be a committee, whose business it shall be to obtain the most early and authentic intelligence of all such Acts and resolutions of the British Parliament, or proceedings of administration, as may relate to or affect the British colonies in America, and to keep up and maintain a correspondence and communication with our sister colonies, respecting these important considerations; and the result of such their proceedings, from time to time, to lay before this House.

Resolved, that it be an instruction to the said committee that they do, without delay, inform themselves particularly of the principles and authority on which was constituted a court of inquiry, said to have been lately held in Rhode Island, with powers to transmit persons accused of offences committed in America to places beyond the seas to be tried.

The said resolutions being severally read a second time, were, upon the question severally put thereupon, agreed to by the House, *nemine contradicente*.

Resolved, that the speaker of this House do transmit to the speakers of the different assemblies of the British colonies on the continent, copies of the said resolutions, and desire that they will lay them before their respective assemblies, and request them to appoint some person or persons of their respective bodies, to communicate from time to time with the said committee.

133B. Resolutions of the Massachusetts House of Representatives agreeing to the Virginia Proposal (28 May 1773)

Printed: Niles, *Principles and Acts of the Revolution*, pp. 94-95.

Whereas, the speaker hath communicated to this House a letter from the truly respectable House of Burgesses, in his Majesty's ancient colony of Virginia, enclosing a copy of the resolves entered into by them on the 12th of March last, and requesting that a committee of this House may be appointed to communicate, from time to time, with a corresponding committee, then appointed by the said House of Burgesses in Virginia:

And, whereas this House is fully sensible of the necessity and importance of a union of the several colonies in America, at a time when it clearly appears that the rights and liberties of all are systematically invaded; in order that the joint wisdom of the whole may be employed in consulting their common safety:

Resolved, that this House have a very grateful sense of the obligations they are under to the House of Burgesses, in Virginia, for the vigilance, firmness and wisdom, which they have discovered, at all times, in support of the rights and liberties of the American colonies; and do heartily concur with their said judicious and spirited resolves.

Resolved, that a standing committee of correspondence and enquiry be appointed, to consist of fifteen members, any eight of whom to be a quorum; whose business it shall be to obtain the most early and authentic intelligence of all such Acts and resolutions of the British Parliament, or proceedings of administration as may relate to, or affect the British colonies in America, and to keep up and maintain a correspondence and communication with our sister colonies, respecting these important considerations: and the result of such their proceedings, from time to time, to lay before the House.

Resolved, that it be an instruction to the said committee, that they do, without delay, inform themselves particularly of the principles and authority, on which was constituted a court of enquiry, held in Rhode Island, said to be vested with powers to transport persons, accused of offences committed in America, to places beyond the seas, to be tried.

Resolved, that the said committee be further instructed to prepare and report to this House, a draft of a very respectful answer to the letter, received from the speaker of the honourable House of Burgesses in Virginia, and another, to a letter received from the speaker of the honourable House of Representatives, of the colony of Rhode Island; also, a circular letter to the several other houses of assembly on this continent, enclosing the aforesaid resolves, and requesting them to lay the same before their respective assemblies, in confidence, that they will readily and cheerfully comply with the wise and salutary resolves of the House of Burgesses, in Virginia.

[The committee of correspondence, chosen in pursuance of the resolves aforesaid, were Mr. Cushing (the speaker), Mr. Adams, Hon. John Hancock, Mr. William Phillips, Captain William Heath, Hon. Joseph Hawley, James Warren, Esq., R. Derby, Jun., Esq., Mr. Elbridge Gerry, J. Bowers, Esq., Jedediah Foster, Esq., Daniel Leonard, Esq., Captain T. Gardner, Capt. Jonathan Greenleaf, and J. Prescott, Esq.]

Part VIII

THE COMING OF THE WAR FOR AMERICAN INDEPENDENCE
1773–1776

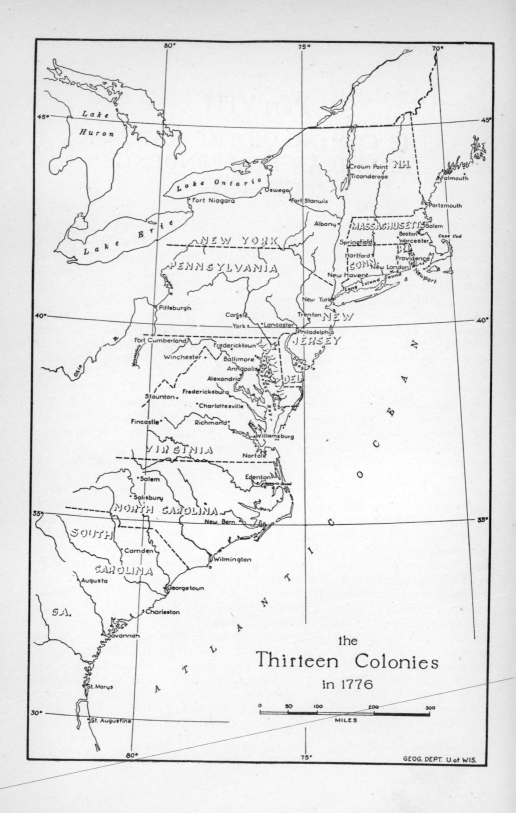

the
Thirteen Colonies
in 1776

GEOG. DEPT. U. of WIS.

THE COMING OF THE WAR FOR AMERICAN INDEPENDENCE
1773—1776

A. THE BACKGROUND OF THE FIRST CONTINENTAL CONGRESS

ALTHOUGH the popular leaders of colonial opposition to Great Britain had created an intercolonial organization by the middle of 1773 as a result of the *Gaspee* inquiry, there was no real issue to unite the colonies.[1] It seems plain that they looked forward to a continental congress; yet there was no occasion to call one, and if they tried to do so, there would be strong opposition. The members of the colonial aristocracy, and particularly the merchants, were anxious for peaceful relations with Britain. They had had their fill of popular leaders and mob violence between 1765 and 1770. On the other side of the Atlantic the ministry also wanted to avoid raising any issues that would stir up the colonies. Benjamin Franklin pointed this out during 1773 in several letters to Thomas Cushing, speaker of the Massachusetts House of Representatives. In January he wrote that circumstances were working in favour of the colonies. Britain had a favourable balance of trade in 1772, and he predicted that even the tax on tea might be removed. He urged, however, that the colonists remain quiet and stop sending memorials about colonial rights. In April and May he reported that Lord Dartmouth, now secretary of state for the colonies, was much irritated by the dispute in Massachusetts between Governor Hutchinson and the legislature. Hutchinson had opened the January 1773 session with a speech to the legislature in which he asserted the sovereignty of Parliament over the colonies. The legislature had returned a spirited answer denying his assertion. These papers had been sent to the ministry. After a conference with Dartmouth on the subject, Franklin reported that "the administration are chagrined with his [Hutchinson's] officiousness, their intention having been to let all contention subside, and by degrees suffer matters to return to their old channels". Dartmouth told Franklin that the ministry was embarrassed because Parliament, if the dispatches were laid before it, would not let the declaration of the Massachusetts legislature "asserting its independence, to pass unnoticed".

Despite the desire of the ministry to maintain peaceful relations with the colonies, action was taken by Parliament in the spring of 1773 that was to inaugurate the chain of events leading directly to the war for American independence. Ironically enough, this action was not the result of concern with colonial policy but of the British government's preoccupation with the tangled affairs of the East India Company. Previous legislation had not served to keep the company out of debt nor to dispose of its surplus of tea. In 1773, therefore, Parliament passed a regulating Act giving to the government a share in the control of India.[2] This was accompanied by another Act designed to increase the market for tea in America and Ireland.[3] This was the "Tea Act" to which the colonists objected so violently and so fatefully.

[1] Nos. 132, 133.　　　　[2] 13 Geo. III, c. 63.　　　　[3] 13 Geo. III, c. 44.

When the revenue features of the Revenue Act of 1767 were repealed in 1770, the threepenny duty on each pound of tea imported into the colonies had been retained. A certain amount of revenue had been derived from the duty, but there were repeated charges that the colonists continued to smuggle large amounts of tea from the Dutch. The Tea Act of 1773 retained the threepenny duty on tea imported into the colonies, but it added an entirely new feature. It provided that the East India Company might export tea directly to the colonies and appoint its own agents to sell it. Prior to this the company had been required to sell its tea at auction in London to wholesalers and retailers. Now it entered the retail business for itself.

In picking agents, the company for the most part picked colonial merchants who were opponents of the popular leaders. In Massachusetts, for instance, the list included two sons and a nephew of Governor Hutchinson, a fact guaranteed to arouse popular opposition even if nothing else had been at stake. In New York it was reported that the tea smugglers were the leading opponents of the Act which made tea so cheap they could no longer afford to smuggle, and that they therefore gave enthusiastic support to the popular leaders in their opposition. Everywhere there were loud cries that the East India Company was a vast monopoly with which no colonial merchant could afford to compete, and much of this concern was sincere.

Despite these various motives for opposition, it seems plain that the basic fact in the uprising against the Tea Act was that the popular leaders in the colonies seized upon it as an issue that might further their cause politically. The first public action was taken in Philadelphia where a mass meeting on 16 October 1773 passed a series of resolutions denying the right of parliamentary taxation and asserting that the Tea Act was a violent attack on the liberties of America.[1] The meeting demanded that the tea agent resign, and that when the tea came it should be sent back to England. There were threats of violence[2] that did not need to be carried out, and the tea was sent back. In Charleston the tea was landed and placed in a warehouse and three years later was sold for the benefit of the Revolutionary cause. In New York denunciations of the Tea Act began appearing in the newspapers in October. In November the tea agents were requested to resign. On 29 November appeared a document called The Association of the Sons of Liberty. It declared a boycott against those who disagreed with the resolutions it contained.[3] By December the popular leaders were threatening the use of force to prevent the tea from being landed. Governor Tryon came to the conclusion that the tea could be landed only "under the protection of the point of the bayonet and muzzle of the cannon". However, because of the weather, no tea arrived in New York until the spring of 1774. When it did arrive, the cargo of tea on board one of the ships was dumped in the harbour, and another ship returned to England without attempting to unload.

The dispute between popular leaders and the merchants is evident in both New York and Philadelphia, but it is clearest of all in Boston, where the most drastic events took place. In October the popular leaders met in a caucus and decided to oppose the sale of any tea shipped by the company. Soon there was a demand that the tea consignees resign. A mass meeting was held on 3 November to receive their resignations, but the tea agents refused to appear. The next step was to call a town meeting on 5 November. This meeting adopted the Philadelphia resolutions of 16 October and demanded the resignation of the tea agents. Again the agents refused, as they did again after another town meeting on 18 November. Thereafter matters were left in

[1] No. 134A.   [2] No. 134B.   [3] No. 135.

the hands of the Boston Committee of Correspondence. Samuel Adams called a meeting of the committees from nearby towns. This meeting announced that it would use all its influence to prevent the tea from being landed and sold.

The first tea ship arrived in Boston harbour on 27 November and two more came a few days later. A mass meeting in Boston, to which many came from surrounding towns, demanded that the tea ships be sent back, but Governor Hutchinson refused to allow it. The mob took over, and on 16 December men disguised as Indians dumped the tea into Boston harbour.[1] The next day Samuel Adams in a letter to kindred spirits in New York and Philadelphia reported that "in a very little time every ounce of tea . . . was immersed in the bay, without the least injury to private property". The tea was valued at more than £10,000, a fact that he omitted to mention.

When the news of colonial opposition, and particularly that of Boston, reached England, any hope of compromise was at an end. The emotions of the ministry and Parliament rose to a high pitch. Benjamin Franklin wrote from London to Thomas Cushing in March of 1774 that "I suppose we have never had since we are a people, so few friends in Britain. The violent destruction of the tea seems to have united all parties here against our province. . . ." Dartmouth wrote to Hutchinson that as a result of the destruction of the tea, it was necessary "to vindicate the insulted authority of this kingdom and to protect its commerce. . . ." He said that Boston would be deprived of all its privileges as a seat of government and a place of trade, and that the guilty would be punished. He declared that the Crown alone could not do this, and that the king had seen fit to lay the whole matter before Parliament. In addition, the ministry took a major step by appointing General Thomas Gage governor of Massachusetts while retaining him as commander-in-chief of the British army in America. Dartmouth's first letter to Gage as governor sets forth clearly the determination of the ministry to force the submission of Massachusetts. [2]

In the meantime Parliament rapidly passed one Act after another. The Boston Port Act closed the port of Boston until the tea was paid for.[3] The Massachusetts Government Act was a sweeping revision of the charter of Massachusetts for the purpose of lessening the power of the people and increasing that of the governor.[4] The Quartering Act applied to all British America and authorized governors to requisition vacant buildings to quarter troops.[5] The Administration of Justice Act provided that British officials in Massachusetts accused of capital crimes while performing their duties might be removed to other colonies or to Britain for trial if a fair trial could not be had in Massachusetts.[6]

The colonists promptly labelled these four Acts the "Intolerable Acts", and by that name they are known to this day. Coupled with them was another Act, the Quebec Act, that related primarily to the problems of government in Canada.[7] However, two parts of it excited colonial alarm and bitterness. The restoration of French law and the Catholic religion to the French inhabitants of Quebec aroused the alarm and anger of the New Englanders. The attachment of the region north-west of the Ohio River (the "Old Northwest"), to the province of Quebec, alienated the Virginians whose charter claims extended over the whole region.

When the news of the Boston Port Act reached Boston, a town meeting was called on 13 May. The Act was read to the meeting. The Committee of Correspondence was directed to speed special messengers to the other colonies, informing them

[1] Nos. 136, 137. [2] No. 139. [3] No. 138A. [4] No. 138B.
[5] No. 138D. [6] No. 138C. [7] 14 Geo. III, c. 83.

of the Port Act and of the actions of the town meeting. Merchants were urged to write their friends everywhere to seek co-operation. The meeting declared that if the other colonies would join with Massachusetts in a complete stoppage of trade with Britain and the West Indies until the Port Act was repealed, "the same will be the salvation of North America and her liberties . . .", but that if they continued to trade, there was reason to fear that "fraud, power, and the most odious oppression, will rise triumphant over right, justice, social happiness, and freedom . . .". This resolution and others were ordered sent to all the other colonies by special messenger, and special missions were sent to nearby Massachusetts towns. The Committee of Correspondence drafted a circular letter to the colonies appealing for help and for the complete stoppage of trade.[1] The Boston merchants were alarmed, but they agreed to the proposal if the merchants of Philadelphia and New York would also agree.

The Boston appeal for the stoppage of trade met with a mixed response. New York and Philadelphia merchants had looked with horror on the destruction of the tea. Although they disliked the Boston Port Act, they were even more alarmed at the activities of the popular leaders in New York and Philadelphia. The latter were as eager as the popular leaders of Boston to take drastic action against Britain. The merchants of New York therefore joined in popular demonstrations in an effort to control events. The Philadelphia merchants likewise participated in a mass meeting. The merchants were successful, with the result that the letters drafted by New York and Philadelphia in answer to the letter from the Boston Committee of Correspondence evaded the request that all trade be stopped. Instead, the letters proposed that a continental congress be called to consider the whole question of opposition.[2]

Elsewhere the Boston letter met with enthusiastic support. Other New England towns denounced the British in language far more violent than that of the Boston town meeting.[3] When the news of the Port Act reached Virginia, the House of Burgesses at once adopted a resolution setting a day of fasting. The governor, Lord Dunmore, promptly dissolved the House for its temerity and declared that he would not issue writs for a new election. A large number of the burgesses thereupon adjourned to the Raleigh Tavern. This meeting proposed that a continental congress meet in Philadelphia in September and issued a call for a special election for a convention to meet in Williamsburg in August. Not only did it thus defy royal authority, it proposed that the courts be stopped and that the payment of debts be suspended until the issue with Great Britain had been settled.

When the Virginia convention met in August it elected seven delegates to the Continental Congress and adopted an association. The agreement provided that Virginians would stop all importations from Great Britain in November, and that they would stop all exportations on 10 August 1775 unless American grievances had been redressed by that time.[4] Meanwhile events in Boston were illuminating the rapidly growing split between the popular leaders and the conservatives that was taking place, particularly in the northern colonies. No one in Boston liked the Port Act or the other Acts of Parliament that followed it, but they could not agree on the method of opposition. The Boston merchants objected strenuously to the town-meeting proposal that all trade be stopped. Many of them had agreed to non-importation unwillingly in 1768 and had wanted to give it up long before the popular leaders were defeated in their efforts to maintain it. When the New York and Philadelphia merchants refused to agree to non-intercourse, the Boston merchants

[1] No. 140.   [2] Nos. 141, 144, 169.   [3] Nos. 142, 143.   [4] No. 145.

were desperate. They disclaimed all responsibility for the destruction of the tea, but they told Governor Hutchinson that they would pay for it in order to have the port reopened. When General Gage arrived as governor, they repeated the offer. The basis for the offer was explained by one of them, John Andrews. He wrote that unless the port was reopened, there would be civil war in the colony. The merchants were ready to pay for the tea, but he said "those who have governed the town for years past and were in a great measure the author of all our evils, by their injudicious conduct, are grown more obstinate than ever, and seem determined to bring total destruction upon us . . . ".

The popular leaders now decided to force the reluctant merchants to adopt non-intercourse. On 30 May 1774 the town meeting instructed a committee to prepare a 'paper' to be taken to each family in the town. The document was to be an agreement to refuse to buy British manufactures and to refuse to purchase anything from "those who shall counter work the salutary measure of the town". The result was the "Solemn League and Covenant". The merchants now made a desperate effort to capture the town meeting, a body they had long ignored. Their purpose was to abolish the Solemn League and Covenant and the Boston Committee of Correspondence. The effort was a dismal failure. According to Gage they were "outvoted by a great majority of the lower class".

But by this time the question of method of opposition had been transferred to the First Continental Congress which had been called to meet in Philadelphia in September. The struggle between the popular leaders and the merchants of the northern colonies was transferred to a body representing the colonies as a whole. Upon its decisions, rather than upon those of the individual colonies acting separately, the future was to depend.

134A–B. Philadelphia opposition to the Tea Act

The first public statement in opposition to the Tea Act was a series of resolutions adopted by the inhabitants of Philadelphia on 16 October 1773 (No. 134A). Widely publicized, these resolutions were used as models by other colonies and were adopted by the Boston Town Meeting on 5 November. As the time for the arrival of the tea ships neared, handbills threatening violence appeared in Philadelphia (No. 134B). Handbills such as these were a common device in the period. Appearing anonymously, and usually posted at night, they were a safe means of expressing the more violent sentiments of the times, and perhaps are a better expression of popular feeling than the more formal resolutions usually adopted in public meetings.

134A. The Philadelphia resolutions (16 October 1773)

Printed: *The Pennsylvania Gazette*, 20 October 1773.

1. That the disposal of their own property is the inherent right of freemen; that there can be no property in that which another can, of right, take from us without our consent; that the claim of Parliament to tax America is, in other words, a claim of right to levy contributions on us at pleasure.

2. That the duty imposed by Parliament upon tea landed in America is a tax on the Americans, or levying contributions on them without their consent.

3. That the express purpose for which the tax is levied on the Americans, namely, for the support of government, administration of justice, and defence of his Majesty's dominions in America, has a direct tendency to render assemblies useless and to introduce arbitrary government and slavery.

4. That a virtuous and steady opposition to this ministerial plan of governing America is absolutely necessary to preserve even the shadow of liberty and is a duty which every freeman in America owes to his country, to himself, and to his posterity.

5. That the resolutions lately entered into by the East India Company to send out their tea to America, subject to the payment of duties on its being landed here, is an open attempt to enforce this ministerial plan and a violent attack upon the liberties of America.

6. That it is the duty of every American to oppose this attempt.

7. That whoever shall, directly or indirectly, countenance this attempt or in any wise aid or abet in unloading, receiving, or vending the tea sent or to be sent out by the East India Company while it remains subject to the payment of a duty here, is an enemy to his country.

8. That a committee be immediately chosen to wait on those gentlemen who, it is reported, are appointed by the East India Company to receive and sell said tea and request them, from a regard to their own characters and the peace and good order of the city and province, immediately to resign their appointment.

134B. Philadelphia handbills

Printed: *The Pennsylvania Magazine of History and Biography*, xv (1891), pp. 390-391.

TO THE
DELAWARE PILOTS

We took the pleasure, some days since, of kindly admonishing you to do your duty if perchance you should meet with the (tea) ship *Polly*, Captain Ayres, a three decker which is hourly expected.

We have now to add that matters ripen fast here; and that much is expected from those lads who meet with the tea ship. There is some talk of a handsome reward for the pilot who gives the first good account of her. How that may be, we cannot for certain determine. But all agree that tar and feathers will be his portion who pilots her into this harbour. And we will answer for ourselves that whoever is committed to us as an offender against the rights of America will experience the utmost exertion of our abilities, as

THE COMMITTEE FOR TARRING AND FEATHERING

P.S.—We expect you will furnish yourselves with copies of the foregoing and following letter which are printed for this purpose, that the pilot who meets with Captain Ayres may favour him with a sight.

COMMITTEE OF TARRING AND FEATHERING

TO
CAPT. AYRES

Of the Ship *Polly*, on a Voyage from London to Philadelphia

Sir,

We are informed that you have, imprudently, taken charge of a quantity of tea which has been sent out by the India Company, under the auspices of the ministry as a trial of American virtue and resolution.

Now, as your cargo, on your arrival here, will most assuredly bring you into hot water; and as you are perhaps a stranger to these parts, we have concluded to advise you of the present situation of affairs in Philadelphia–that, taking time by the forelock, you may stop short in your dangerous errand–secure your ship against the rafts of combustible matter which may be set on fire and turned loose against her; and more than all this, that you may preserve your own person from the pitch and feathers that are prepared for you.

In the first place, we must tell you that the Pennsylvanians are, to a man, passionately fond of freedom, the birthright of Americans, and at all events are determined to enjoy it.

That they sincerely believe no power on the face of the earth has a right to tax them without their consent.

That in their opinion the tea in your custody is designed by the ministry to enforce such a tax which they will undoubtedly oppose, and in so doing, give you every possible obstruction.

We are nominated to a very disagreeable, but necessary service–to our care are committed all offenders against the rights of America; and hapless is he, whose evil destiny has doomed him to suffer at our hands.

You are sent out on a diabolical service; and if you are so foolish and obstinate as to complete your voyage by bringing your ship to anchor in this port, you may run such a gauntlet as will induce you in your last moments most heartily to curse those who have made you the dupe of their avarice and ambition.

What think you Captain, of a halter around your neck–ten gallons of liquid tar decanted on your pate–with the feathers of a dozen wild geese laid over that to enliven your appearance?

Only think seriously of this–and fly to the place from whence you came–fly without hesitation–without the formality of a protest–and above all, Captain Ayres, let us advise you to fly without the wild geese feathers.

Your friends to serve

THE COMMITTEE, as before subscribed

Philadelphia, Nov. 27, 1773.

TO THE
DELAWARE
PILOTS

The regard we have for your characters and our desire to promote your future peace and safety are the occasion of this third address to you.

In our second letter we acquainted you that the tea ship was a three decker. We are now informed by good authority she is not a three decker, but an old black ship without a head or any ornaments.

The Captain is a short fat fellow, and a little obstinate withal. So much the worse for him. For, so sure as he rides rusty, we shall heave him keel out and see that his bottom be well fired, scrubbed, and paid. His upper-works, too, will have an over-hauling; and as it is said he has a good deal of quick work about him, we will take particular care that such part of him undergoes a thorough rummaging.

We have a still worse account of his owner; for it is said the ship *Polly* was bought by him on purpose to make a penny of us and that he and Captain Ayres were well advised of the risk they would run in thus daring to insult and abuse us.

Captain Ayres was here in the time of the Stamp Act and ought to have known our people better than to have expected we would be so mean as to suffer his rotten tea to be funnelled down our throats with the Parliament's duty mixed with it.

We know him well and have calculated to a gill and a feather how much it will require to fit him for an American exhibition. And we hope not one of your body will behave so ill as to oblige us to clap him in the cart along side of the Captain.

We must repeat that the ship *Polly* is an old black ship of about two hundred and fifty tons burthen, without a head, and without ornaments, and that Captain Ayres is a thick, chunky fellow. As such, take care to avoid them.

Your old friends,

THE COMMITTEE FOR TARRING AND FEATHERING

Philadelphia, December 7, 1773.

135. Association of the Sons of Liberty in New York (15 December 1773)

There were threats of violence against the tea consignees in New York and they resigned on 1 December. On 15 December the following 'Association' was drafted. It purported to be a common platform for all classes in society, but it plainly implied that violence would be forthcoming if any attempt was made to land the tea. This fact was made clear at a mass meeting the next day, which ratified the document. Printed: Niles, *Principles and Acts of the Revolution*, pp. 169-170.

The following association is signed by a great number of the principal gentlemen of the city, merchants, lawyers, and other inhabitants of all ranks, and it is still carried about the city to give an opportunity to those who have not yet signed, to unite with their fellow citizens, to testify their abhorrence to the diabolical project of enslaving America.

The Association of the Sons of Liberty of New York

It is essential to the freedom and security of a free people, that no taxes be imposed upon them but by their own consent, or their representatives. For "What property have they in that which another may, by right, take when he pleases to himself?" The former is the undoubted right of Englishmen, to secure which they expended millions and sacrificed the lives of thousands. And yet, to the astonishment of all the world, and the grief of America, the Commons of Great Britain, after the repeal of the memorable and detestable Stamp Act, reassumed the power of imposing taxes on the American colonies; and insisting on it as a necessary badge of parliamentary supremacy, passed a bill, in the seventh year of his present Majesty's reign, imposing duties on all glass, painters' colours, paper, and teas, that should, after the 20th of November, 1767, be "imported from Great Britain into any colony or plantation in

America". This bill, after the concurrence of the Lords, obtained the royal assent. And thus they who, from time immemorial, have exercised the right of giving to, or withholding from the crown, their aids and subsidies, according to their *own free will and pleasure*, signified by their representatives in Parliament, do, by the Act in question, deny us, their brethren in America, the enjoyment of the same right. As this denial, and the execution of that Act, involves our slavery, and would sap the foundation of our freedom, whereby we should become slaves to our brethren and fellow subjects, born to no greater stock of freedom than the Americans–the merchants and inhabitants of this city, in conjunction with the merchants and inhabitants of the ancient American colonies, entered into an agreement to decline a part of their commerce with Great Britain, until the above mentioned Act should be totally repealed. This agreement operated so powerfully to the disadvantage of the manufacturers of England that many of them were unemployed. To appease their clamours, and to provide the subsistence for them, which the non-importation had deprived them of, the Parliament, in 1770, repealed so much of the Revenue Act as imposed a duty on glass, painters' colours, and paper, and left the duty on tea, as *a test of the parliamentary right to tax us*. The merchants of the cities of New York and Philadelphia, having strictly adhered to the agreement, so far as it is related to the importation of articles subject to an American duty, have convinced the ministry, that some other measures must be adopted to execute parliamentary supremacy over this country, and to remove the distress brought on the East India Company, by the ill policy of that Act. Accordingly, to increase the temptation to the shippers of tea from England, an Act of Parliament passed the last session, which gives the whole duty on tea, the company were subject to pay, upon the importation of it into England, to the purchasers and exporters; and when the company have ten millions of pounds of tea in their warehouses exclusive of the quantity they may want to ship, they are allowed to export tea, discharged from the payment of that duty with which they were before chargeable. In hopes of aid in the execution of this project, by the influence of the owners of the American ships, application was made by the company to the captains of those ships to take the tea on freight; but they virtuously rejected it. Still determined on the scheme, they have chartered ships to bring the tea to this country, which may be hourly expected, to make an important trial of our virtue. If they succeed in the sale of that tea, we shall have no property that we can call our own, and then we may bid adieu to American liberty. Therefore, to prevent a calamity which, of all others, is the most to be dreaded–slavery and its terrible concomitants–we, the subscribers, being influenced from a regard to liberty, and disposed to use all lawful endeavours in our power, to defeat the pernicious project, and to transmit to our posterity those blessings of freedom which our ancestors have handed down to us; and to contribute to the support of the common liberties of America, which are in danger to be subverted, *do*, for those important purposes, agree to associate together, under the name and style of the *sons of New York*, and engage our honour to, and with each other faithfully to observe and perform the following resolutions, viz.

1st. Resolved, that whoever shall aid or abet, or in any manner assist, in the introduction of tea from any place whatsoever, into this colony, while it is subject, by a British Act of Parliament, to the payment of a duty, for the purpose of raising a revenue in America, he shall be deemed an enemy to the liberties of America.

2d. Resolved, that whoever shall be aiding, or assisting, in the landing, or carting of such tea, from any ship, or vessel, or shall hire any house, storehouse, or cellar or any place whatsoever, to deposit the tea, subject to a duty as aforesaid, he shall be deemed an enemy to the liberties of America.

3d. Resolved, that whoever shall sell, or buy, or in any manner contribute to the sale, or purchase of tea, subject to a duty as aforesaid, or shall aid, or abet, in transporting such tea, by land or water, from this city, until the 7th George III, chap. 46, commonly called the Revenue Act, shall be totally and clearly repealed, he shall be deemed an enemy to the liberties of America.

4th. Resolved, that whether the duties on tea, imposed by this Act, be paid in Great Britain or in America, our liberties are equally affected.

5th. Resolved, that whoever shall transgress any of these resolutions, we will not deal with, or employ, or have any connection with him.

136. Boston handbill signed "The People" (2 December 1773)

The following handbill is characteristic of the many used during the period. It was sent to Britain by Governor Hutchinson. From: British Public Record Office, C.O. 5/763.

WHEREAS it has been reported that a permit will be given by the Custom house for landing the tea now on board a vessel laying in this harbour, commanded by Capt. Hall: this is to remind the public that it was solemnly voted by the body of the people of this and the neighbouring towns assembled at the Old South meeting-house on Tuesday the 30th day of November, that the said tea never should be landed in this province, or pay one farthing of duty. And as the aiding or assisting in procuring or granting any such permit for landing the said tea, or any other tea so circumstanced, or in offering any permit, when obtained, to the master or commander of the said ship, or any other ship in the same situation, must betray an inhuman thirst for blood, and will also in a great measure accelerate confusion and civil war; this is to assure such public enemies of this country that they will be considered and treated as wretches unworthy to live, and will be made the first victims of our just resentment.

THE PEOPLE

N.B.—Captain Bruce is arrived laden with the same detestable commodity; and 'tis peremptorily demanded of him, and all concerned, that they comply with the same requisitions. [Endorsement: Taken down from the place where it had been posted in Boston.]

137. Newspaper report of the Boston Tea Party (16 December 1773)

After the arrival of the first tea ship, the *Dartmouth*, on 27 November, a series of mass meetings were held in Boston which were attended by people from surrounding towns. These meetings insisted that the duty should not be paid and that the tea should be shipped back. Governor Hutchinson ordered such meetings to disperse but they refused. Meanwhile the *Dartmouth* entered at the customs house and was liable to seizure if the duties were not paid within twenty days. The twentieth day was Thursday, 16 December. On that morning people began pouring into Boston by the hundreds to attend a mass meeting. The consignee of the tea on the *Dartmouth* was willing to return the cargo but Governor Hutchinson refused a permit and ordered warships in the harbour to prevent the ship from sailing. His effort was courageous but futile. When the mass meeting heard the report, Samuel Adams rose and declared: "This meeting can do no more to save the country." What followed is described in the newspaper report. Printed: *Massachusetts Gazette and Boston Weekly News-Letter*, 23 December 1773.

Just before the dissolution of the meeting, a number of brave and resolute men, dressed in the Indian manner, approached near the door of the Assembly, gave the war whoop, which rang through the house and was answered by some in the galleries, but silence being commanded, and a peaceable deportment was again enjoined till the dissolution. The Indians, as they were then called, repaired to the wharf where the ships lay that had the tea on board, and were followed by hundreds of people to see the event of the transactions of those who made so grotesque an appearance. They, the Indians, immediately repaired on board Capt. Hall's ship, where they hoisted out the chests of tea, and when upon deck stove the chests and emptied the tea overboard; having cleared this ship, they proceeded to Capt. Bruce's and then to Capt. Coffin's brig. They applied themselves so dextrously to the destruction of this commodity that in the space of three hours they broke up 342 chests, which was the whole number in those vessels, and discharged their contents into the dock. When the tide rose it floated the broken chests and the tea insomuch that the surface of the water was filled therewith a considerable way from the south part of the town to Dorchester Neck, and lodged on the shores. There was the greatest care taken to prevent the tea from being purloined by the populace. One or two, being detected in endeavouring to pocket a small quantity, were stripped of their acquisitions and very roughly handled. It is worthy of remark that although a considerable quantity of goods were still remaining on board the vessels, no injury was sustained. Such attention to private property was observed that a small padlock belonging to the captain of one of the ships being broke, another was procured and sent to him. The town was very quiet during the whole evening and night following. Those persons who were from the country returned with a merry heart; and the next day joy appeared in almost every countenance, some on occasion of the destruction of the tea, others on account of the quietness with which it was effected. One of the Monday's papers says that the masters and owners are well pleased that their ships are thus cleared.

138A–D. The Intolerable Acts

Of the four Acts so named, selections from which follow, three were directed at Massachusetts. The Boston Port Act (14 Geo. III, c. 19) closed the port of Boston to all commerce except fuel and food necessary for the use of the inhabitants of the town, and to military stores for the use of the royal forces. The port could be opened only after the tea had been paid for and officials reimbursed for losses suffered in riots during 1773 and 1774 (No. 138A). The Massachusetts Government Act (14 Geo. III, c. 45) made significant alterations in the charter of 1691. The governor was given wide power of appointment and removal and freed from the requirement that he have consent of members of the Council in such matters. The Council was to be appointed by the Crown instead of elected by the House of Representatives. Special town meetings were forbidden except by consent of the governor. The freeholders were forbidden to elect jurors; instead they were to be selected by the sheriffs (No. 138B). The Administration of Justice Act (14 Geo. III, c. 39) provided that British officials in Massachusetts could be removed from the colony for trial for capital crimes if a fair trial could not be had within the colony (No. 138C). While the Quartering Act (14 Geo. III, c. 54) applied to all British America, it was lumped together with the three previous Acts as being 'intolerable' (No. 138D).

138A. The Boston Port Act (31 March 1774)

Printed: Pickering, *Statutes at Large*, XXX, pp. 336-341.

Whereas dangerous commotions and insurrections have been fomented and raised in the town of Boston, in the province of Massachusetts Bay in New England, by divers ill-affected persons, to the subversion of his Majesty's government and to the utter destruction of the public peace and good order of the said town; in which commotions and insurrections certain valuable cargoes of teas, being the property of the East India Company and on board certain vessels lying within the bay or harbour of Boston, were seized and destroyed; and whereas, in the present condition of the said town and harbour the commerce of his Majesty's subjects cannot be safely carried on there, nor the customs payable to his Majesty duly collected; and it is therefore expedient that the officers of his Majesty's customs should be forthwith removed from the said town: ... be it enacted ... [that it is unlawful to load on any vessel goods for shipment to any other part of the province or to any other colony or country, and that it is unlawful to unload goods from any other part of the province or any other colony or country in the town of Boston and in the bay called the harbour of Boston. Penalty for violation is forfeiture of ship and goods.]

IV. Provided always, that nothing in this Act contained shall extend, or be construed to extend to any military or other stores for his Majesty's use, or to the ships or vessels whereon the same shall be laden, which shall be commissioned by, and in the immediate pay of his Majesty, his heirs or successors; nor to any fuel or victual brought coastwise from any part of the continent of America, for the necessary use and sustenance of the inhabitants of the said town of Boston, provided the vessels wherein the same are to be carried shall be duly furnished with a cocket and let-pass, after having been duly searched by the proper officers of his Majesty's customs at Marblehead, in the port of Salem in the said province of Massachusetts Bay; and that some officer of his Majesty's customs be also there put on board the said vessel, who is hereby authorized to go on board and proceed with the said vessel, together with a sufficient number of persons, properly armed, for his defence, to the said town or harbour of Boston; nor to any ships or vessels which may happen to be within the said harbour of Boston on or before the first day of June, one thousand seven hundred and seventy-four, and may have either laden or taken on board, or be there with intent to load or take on board, or to land or discharge any goods, wares, and merchandise, provided the said ships and vessels do depart the said harbour within fourteen days after the said first day of June, one thousand seven hundred and seventy-four.

X. Provided also, and it is hereby declared and enacted, that nothing herein contained shall extend, or be construed, to enable his Majesty to appoint such port, harbour, creeks, quays, wharfs, places, or officers, in the said town of Boston, or in the said bay or islands, until it shall sufficiently appear to his Majesty that full satisfaction has been made by or on behalf of the inhabitants of the said town of Boston to the United Company of Merchants of England Trading to the East Indies, for the damage sustained by the said company by the destruction of their goods sent to the said town of Boston, on board certain ships or vessels as aforesaid; and until it shall be certified to his Majesty in Council by the governor or lieutenant-governor of the said province, that reasonable satisfaction hath been made to the officers of his Majesty's revenue, and others, who suffered by the riots and insurrections above mentioned, in the months of November and December, in the year one thousand seven hundred and seventy-three, and in the month of January, in the year one thousand seven hundred and seventy-four.

138B. The Massachusetts Government Act (20 May 1774)

Printed: Pickering, *Statutes at Large*, **xxx**, pp. 381–390.

Whereas by letters patent under the great seal of England, made in the third year of the reign of their late Majesties King William and Queen Mary, for uniting, erecting, and incorporating the several colonies, territories, and tracts of land therein mentioned, into one real province by the name of their Majesties' province of the Massachusetts Bay in New England; whereby it was, amongst other things, ordained and established, that the governor of the said province should from thenceforth be appointed and commissioned by their Majesties, their heirs and successors; it was, however, granted and ordained that from the expiration of the term for and during which the eight and twenty persons named in the said letters patent were appointed to be the first councillors or assistants to the governor of the said province for the time being, the aforesaid number of eight and twenty councillors or assistants should yearly, once in every year, forever thereafter, be, by the general court or assembly, newly chosen; and whereas the said method of electing such councillors or assistants, to be vested with the several powers, authorities, and privileges therein mentioned, although conformable to the practice theretofore used in such of the colonies thereby united, in which the appointment of the respective governors had been vested in the general courts or assemblies of the said colonies hath, by repeated experience, been found to be extremely ill-adapted to the plan of government established in the province of the Massachusetts Bay, by the said letters patent hereinbefore mentioned, and has been so far from contributing to the attainment of the good ends and purposes thereby intended, and to the promoting of the internal welfare, peace, and good government of the said province, or to the maintenance of the just subordination to, and conformity with, the laws of Great Britain that the manner of exercising the powers, authorities, and privileges aforesaid, by the persons so annually elected, hath for some time past been such as had the most manifest tendency to obstruct, and, in great measure, defeat, the execution of the laws; to weaken the attachment of his Majesty's well-disposed subjects in the said province to his Majesty's government, and to encourage the ill-disposed among them to proceed even to acts of direct resistance to, and defiance of, his Majesty's authority; and it hath accordingly happened that an open resistance to the execution of the laws hath actually taken place in the town of Boston and the neighbourhood thereof, within the said province; and whereas it is, under these circumstances, become absolutely necessary, in order to the preservation of the peace and good order of the said province, the protection of his Majesty's well-disposed subjects therein resident, the continuance of the mutual benefits arising from the commerce and correspondence between this kingdom and the said province, and the maintaining of the just dependance of the said province upon the Crown and Parliament of Great Britain that the said method of annually electing the councillors or assistants of the said province should no longer be suffered to continue but that the appointment of the said councillors or assistants should henceforth be put upon the like footing as is established in such other of his Majesty's colonies or plantations in America, the governors whereof are appointed by his Majesty's commission, under the great seal of Great Britain. Be it therefore enacted . . . that from and after the first day of August, one thousand seven hundred and seventy-four . . . the council or court of assistants of the said province for the time being, shall be composed of such of the inhabitants or proprietors of lands within the same as shall be thereunto nominated and appointed by his Majesty, his heirs and successors, from time to time, by warrant under his or their signet or sign manual, and with the advice of the Privy Council, agreeable to the practice now used in respect to the appointment of councillors in such of his Majesty's other colonies in America, the governors whereof are appointed by commission under the great seal of Great Britain; provided that the number of the said assistants or councillors shall not at any one time exceed thirty-six, nor be less than twelve.

II. And it is hereby further enacted, that the said assistants or councillors, so to be appointed as aforesaid, shall hold their offices respectively, for and during the pleasure of his Majesty. . . .

III. And be it further enacted, . . . that from and after the first day of July, one thousand seven hundred and seventy-four, it shall and may be lawful for his Majesty's governor for the time being of the said province, or in his absence, for the lieutenant-governor, to nominate and appoint, under the seal of the province, from time to time, and also to remove, without the consent of the council, all judges of the inferior courts of common pleas, commissioners of oyer and terminer, the attorney general, provosts, marshals, justices of the peace, and other officers to the council or courts of justice belonging. . . .

V. And be it further enacted by the authority aforesaid, that from and after the said first day of July, one thousand seven hundred and seventy-four, it shall and may be lawful for his Majesty's governor, or in his absence, for the lieutenant-governor for the time being of the said province, from time to time, to nominate and appoint the sheriffs without the consent of the council, and to remove such sheriffs with such consent, and not otherwise.

VI. And be it further enacted by the authority aforesaid, that upon every vacancy of the offices of chief justice and judges of the Superior Court of the said province, from and after the said first day of July, one thousand seven hundred and seventy-four, the governor for the time being, or in his absence, the lieutenant-governor, without the consent of the Council, shall have full power and authority to nominate and appoint the persons to succeed to the said offices, who shall hold their commissions during the pleasure of his Majesty, his heirs and successors. . . .

VII. And whereas, by several acts of the General Court, which have been from time to time enacted and passed within the said province, the freeholders and inhabitants of the several townships, districts, and precincts, qualified, as is therein expressed, are authorized to assemble together, annually, or occasionally, upon notice given, in such manner as the said acts direct, for the choice of selectmen, constables, and other officers, and for the making and agreeing upon such necessary rules, orders, and by-laws, for the directing, managing, and ordering, the prudential affairs of such townships, districts, and precincts, and for other purposes; and whereas a great abuse has been made of the power of calling such meetings, and the inhabitants have, contrary to the design of their institution, been misled to treat upon matters of the most general concern, and to pass many dangerous and unwarrantable resolves; for remedy whereof, be it enacted, that from and after the said first day of August, one thousand seven hundred and seventy-four, no meeting shall be called by the selectmen, or at the request of any number of freeholders of any township, district, or precinct, without the leave of the governor, or in his absence, of the lieutenant-governor, in writing, expressing the special business of the said meeting, first had and obtained, except the annual meeting in the months of March or May, for the choice of selectmen, constables, and other officers, or except for the choice of persons to fill up the offices aforesaid, on the death or removal of any of the persons first elected to such offices, and also, except any meeting for the election of a representative or representatives in the general court; and that no other matter shall be treated of at such meetings, except the election of their aforesaid officers or representatives, nor at any other meeting, except the business expressed in the leave given by the governor, or in his absence, by the lieutenant-governor.

VIII. And whereas the method at present used in the province of Massachusetts Bay in America, of electing persons to serve on grand juries, and other juries, by the freeholders and inhabitants of the several towns, affords occasion for many evil practices, and tends to pervert the free and impartial administration of justice; for remedy whereof, be it further enacted . . . that, from and after the respective times appointed for the holding of the general sessions of the peace in the several counties within the said province, next after the month of September, one thousand seven hundred and seventy-four, the jurors to serve at the superior courts of judicature, courts of assize, general gaol delivery, general sessions of the peace, and inferior court of common pleas, in the several counties within the said province, shall not be elected, nominated, or appointed, by the freeholders and inhabitants of the several towns within the said respective counties, nor summoned or returned by the constables of the said towns; but that, from thenceforth, the jurors to serve at the superior courts of judicature, courts of assize, general gaol delivery, general sessions of the peace, and inferior court of common pleas within the said province, shall be summoned and returned by the sheriffs of the respective counties within the said province; and all writs of *Venire Facias*, or other process or warrants to be issued for the return of jurors to serve at the said courts, shall be directed to the sheriffs of the said counties respectively, any law, custom, or usage to the contrary notwithstanding.

138C. The Administration of Justice Act (20 May 1774)

Printed: Pickering, *Statutes at Large*, XXX, pp. 367-371.

Whereas in his Majesty's province of Massachusetts Bay, in New England, an attempt has lately been made to throw off the authority of the Parliament of Great Britain over the said province, and an actual and avowed resistance by open force, to the execution of certain Acts of Parliament, has been suffered to take place, uncontrolled and unpunished, in defiance of his Majesty's authority, and to the utter subversion of all lawful government; and whereas, in the present disordered state of the said province it is of the utmost importance to the general welfare thereof, and to the re-establishment of lawful authority throughout the same, that neither the magistrates acting in support of the laws, nor any of his Majesty's subjects aiding and assisting them therein, or in the suppression of riots and tumults raised in opposition to the execution of the laws and statutes of this realm, should be discouraged from the proper discharge of their duty by an apprehension that in case of their being questioned for any acts done therein, they may be liable to be brought to trial for the same before persons who do not acknowledge the validity of the laws, in the execution thereof, or the authority of the magistrate in the support of whom such acts had been done: in order therefore to remove every such discouragement from the minds of his Majesty's subjects, and to induce them, upon all proper occasions, to exert themselves in support of the public peace of the province, and of the authority of the king and Parliament of Great Britain over the same, be it enacted . . . that if any inquisition or indictment shall be found, or if any appeal shall be sued or preferred against any person for murder, or other capital offence, in the province of Massachusetts Bay, and it shall appear by information given upon oath to the governor, or, in his absence, to the lieutenant-governor of the said province, that the fact was committed by the person against whom such inquisition or indictment shall be found, or against whom such appeal shall be sued or preferred as aforesaid, either in the execution of his duty as a magistrate for the suppression of riots, or in the support of the laws of revenue, or in acting in his duty as an officer of revenue, or in acting under the direction and order of any magistrate for the suppression of riots, or for the carrying into effect the laws of revenue, or in aiding and assisting in any of the cases aforesaid; and if it shall also appear to the satisfaction of the said governor, or lieutenant-governor respectively, that an indifferent trial cannot be had within the said province; in that case it shall and may be lawful for the governor or lieutenant-governor to direct, with the advice and consent of the council, that the inquisition, indictment, or appeal shall be tried in some other of his Majesty's colonies, or in Great Britain; and for that purpose, to order the person against whom such inquisition or indictment shall be found, or against whom such appeal shall be sued or preferred as aforesaid, to be sent, under sufficient custody, to the place appointed for his trial, or to admit such person to bail, taking a recognizance (which the said governor, or, in his absence, the lieutenant-governor, is hereby authorized to take), from such person, with sufficient sureties, to be approved of by the said governor, or, in his absence, the lieutenant-governor, in such sums of money as the said governor, or in his absence, the lieutenant-governor, shall deem reasonable for the personal appearance of such person, if the trial shall be appointed to be had in any other colony, before the governor, or lieutenant-governor, or commander-in-chief of such colony; and if the trial shall be appointed to be had in Great Britain, then before his Majesty's Court of King's Bench, at a time to be mentioned in such recognizances; and the governor or lieutenant-governor, or commander-in-chief of the colony where such trial shall be appointed to be had, or Court of King's Bench, where the trial is appointed to be had in Great Britain, upon the appearance of such person, according to such recognizance, or in custody, shall either commit such person, or admit him to bail, until such trial; and which the said governor, or lieutenant-governor, or commander-in-chief, and Court of King's Bench, are hereby authorized and empowered to do.

138D. The Quartering Act (2 June 1774)

Printed: Pickering, *Statutes at Large*, xxx, p. 410.

Whereas doubts have been entertained, whether troops can be quartered otherwise than in barracks, in case barracks have been provided sufficient for the quartering of all the officers and soldiers within any town, township, city, district, or place, within his Majesty's dominions in North America; and whereas it may frequently happen, from the situation of such barracks that, if troops should be quartered therein they would not be stationed where their presence may be necessary and required: be it therefore enacted . . . that, in such cases it shall and may be lawful for the persons who now are, or may be hereafter, authorized by law, in any of the provinces within his Majesty's dominions in North America, and they are hereby respectively authorized, empowered, and directed, on the requisition of the officer who, for the time being, has the command of his Majesty's forces in North America, to cause any officers or soldiers in his Majesty's service to be quartered and billeted in such manner as is now directed by law, where no barracks are provided by the colonies.

II. And be it further enacted by the authority aforesaid, that if it shall happen at any time that any officers or soldiers in his Majesty's service shall remain within any of the said colonies without quarters for the space of twenty-four hours after such quarters shall have been demanded, it shall and may be lawful for the governor of the province to order and direct such and so many uninhabited houses, outhouses, barns, or other buildings, as he shall think necessary to be taken (making a reasonable allowance for the same) and make fit for the reception of such officers and soldiers, and to put and quarter such officers and soldiers therein for such time as he shall think proper.

III. And be it further enacted by the authority aforesaid, that this Act, and everything herein contained, shall continue and be in force in all his Majesty's dominions in North America, until the twenty-fourth day of March, one thousand seven hundred and seventy-six.

139. Lord Dartmouth: Instructions to General Thomas Gage on securing the submission of Massachusetts (9 April 1774)

The following letter was the first written by Dartmouth, secretary of state for the colonies, to General Gage after he had been appointed governor of Massachusetts, and it was delivered before Gage left England to return to the colonies. The letter indicates even more clearly than the "Intolerable Acts" the determination of the government to force the submission of Massachusetts. Printed: Carter, ed., *Gage Correspondence*, II, pp. 158–162.

The king having thought fit that you should return immediately to your command in North America, and that you should proceed directly to Boston on board his Majesty's ship *Lively*, now lying at Plymouth ready to sail with the first fair wind, I send you herewith by his Majesty's command a commission under the great seal, appointing you captain-general and governor-in-chief of his Majesty's province of Massachusetts Bay; together with such instructions as have been usually given to governors of that province for their guidance in the exercise of the ordinary and more permanent powers and authorities incident to that command.

What is further necessary for your direction in the present state of disorder and commotion within that province, and for enabling you to carry into execution the measures that have been, and probably will be adopted for reducing it to a state of obedience to lawful authority, is of a more delicate and important nature, and requires more precise and particular instructions. With this letter you will receive an Act of Parliament passed in the present session for discontinuing the loading and unloading of goods and merchandise at the town and within the harbour of Boston; and also a minute of the Treasury Board, containing the substance of such instructions as their lordships have thought fit to give to their officers in consequence thereof, and it is the king's command that you do give them all proper and necessary assistance and support in the execution thereof.

To this end it will be expedient that you do, immediately upon your arrival and so soon as your commission has been read and published in the usual form, appoint a meeting either at the town, or within the castle (as circumstances shall point out) with the commander-in-chief of his Majesty's ships, the lieutenant-governor, the commissioners of the customs, the chief justice, and the secretary of the province, in order to consider what steps it may be proper to take for carrying the Act into execution, and for enforcing, if necessary, a due obedience thereto; and if Mr. Hutchinson should not be come away in consequence of the leave he has obtained for that purpose, his advice and assistance in this case, as well as in the execution of every other part of your instructions, will be of very great use and advantage to you.

His Majesty trusts that no opposition will, or can, with any effect, be made to the carrying the law into execution, nor any violence or insult offered to those to whom the execution of it is intrusted. Should it happen otherwise, your authority as the first magistrate, combined with your command over the king's troops, will, it is hoped, enable you to meet every opposition, and fully to preserve the public peace by employing those troops with effect, should the madness of the people on the one hand, or the timidity or want of strength of the peace officers on the other hand, make it necessary to have recourse to their assistance. The king trusts, however, that such necessity will not occur, and commands me to say that it will be your duty to use every endeavour to avoid it, to quiet the minds of the people, to remove their prejudices, and by mild and gentle persuasion, to induce such a submission on their part to this law, and such a proper compliance with the just requisitions it contains, as may give full scope to his Majesty's clemency, and enable his Majesty to exercise the discretionary power given him by the Act, of again restoring to the town of Boston those commercial privileges and advantages which it hath so long enjoyed, and which have raised it to its present state of opulence and importance.

At the same time, the sovereignty of the king in his Parliament over the colonies requires a full and absolute submission, and his Majesty's dignity demands that until that submission be made the town of Boston, where so much anarchy and confusion have prevailed, should cease to be the place of the residence of his governor, or of any other officer of government who is not obliged by law to perform his functions there. It is therefore his Majesty's further pleasure that so soon as the law for discontinuing the port shall have taken place, and every step has been pursued that is necessary to insure the execution of it, you do make the town of Salem the place of your residence; that you do require all officers (not included in the above exception) to attend you there, and that the General Court and all other courts and offices which are not by law fixed at Boston, be appointed and held at Salem until his Majesty, satisfied upon your representation that the laws of this kingdom will be duly observed, and government be again administered at the town of Boston without opposition, shall have signified his royal will and pleasure for the return of his governor to, and for holding of the General Court at that town.

The proceedings of the body of the people at the town of Boston in the months of November and December last were of such a nature and criminality as to have fixed a deep degree of guilt upon those who were the principal ringleaders and abettors of those proceedings, and the measures proper to be taken for inducing the punishment of such guilt become a very necessary part of the present consideration relative to the state of the province of Massachusetts Bay.

The enclosed copy of a report made to me by his Majesty's attorney and solicitor-general will point out to you their opinion of the extent of the criminality attending those transactions; and the copy of the narrative on which that opinion was given, accompanied with copies of certain depositions taken before the lords of the Council (all of which are herewith enclosed) will fully inform you as well of the facts as of the persons to which the opinion applies.

The object of the enquiry made here was to have established such a charge against the ringleaders in those violences as might have enabled his Majesty to have proceeded against them in this kingdom. It was found, however, upon the result that it would be difficult (clear and positive as the evidence was with respect to some parts of the proceedings) to establish such a connection between the acts of the body of the people and the destruction of the tea as to have no doubt of the propriety and effect of bringing over the persons charged to be tried here.

In this dilemma there seemed to be no other method of proceeding against them but in the ordinary courts of justice within the colony. It will therefore be your duty, with the advice and assistance of such of his Majesty's law servants as it may be proper for you to consult upon such occasion, to make all possible inquiry into every particular of the transactions pointed out in the attorney and solicitor-generals' report, and to employ your utmost endeavours to obtain sufficient evidence against the principal actors therein; and in case the acts stated in the report of the attorney and solicitor-general, to have been acts of treason, can by full and clear evidence be brought home to any individuals, or that such transactions have been attended with any other degree of guilt that is an object of criminal prosecution against any persons, and you shall be of opinion that upon indictment of them there is a probability of their being brought to punishment, it is his Majesty's pleasure that you do, in such case, direct the proper steps to be taken for their prosecution.

The king considers the punishment of these offenders as a very necessary and essential example to others of the ill consequences that must follow from such open and arbitrary usurpations as tend to the subversion of all government, and the rendering civil liberty unsafe and precarious. And his Majesty's subjects in the province of Massachusetts Bay in general cannot give a better test of their love of justice, and respect for the constitution, than in their zealous endeavours to render effectual a due prosecution of such offenders.

If, however, the prejudices of the people should appear to you to be such as would, in all probability, prevent a conviction, however clear and full the evidence might be, in that case it would be better to desist from prosecution, seeing that an ineffectual attempt would only be triumph to the faction, and disgraceful to government.

You will observe, sir, that I have throughout the whole of this letter avoided making any mention of the Council for the province of Massachusetts Bay, and I have been thus silent with regard to them from an apprehension that from what has already appeared respecting their conduct, any hope of proper advice or assistance from them would be vain; at the same time I do not mean that any constitutional power or authority, vested in them, should be set aside by any part of these instructions, or that you should not be at liberty to give them full confidence and communication, in case you shall perceive such an alteration in their conduct as will justify such a behaviour towards them.

There are, however, some amongst those who constitute the present Council there, upon whose attachment to the constitution no reliance can be had in any case where the sovereignty of the king in his Parliament is in question, and his Majesty thinks it essential to the due support of that sovereignty, that the principal of those who insisted upon the report of the committee of the Council on the 27th day of September [November] last, in which report that sovereignty is questioned, at a time when the execution of the laws was openly opposed by force and violence, should not have seats at the council board. It is therefore his Majesty's pleasure that if those persons, or any of them, shall be chosen at the next general election, you do put your negative upon such election.

The foregoing is all that I have at present in command from the king to say to you. I need not suggest to you the very great advantage that will result from your obtaining a just and perfect knowledge of the characters, inclinations, and tempers of the principal people in the colony; such information must, of necessity, be of great benefit, and your own discretion will point out to you the use that is to be made of it.

The last advices from Boston are of a nature to leave but little room to hope that order and obedience are soon likely to take the place of anarchy and usurpation. His Majesty, however, confides in your fortitude and discretion, and doubts not that all other officers, civil and military, animated by your example, will exert themselves in such manner, in support of the constitution, and for enforcing obedience to the laws, as will recommend them to his Majesty's royal grace and favour.

140. Circular letter of the Boston Committee of Correspondence (13 May 1774)

This letter, urging the complete stoppage of trade, was sent throughout the colonies. It precipitated public meetings everywhere to prepare an answer. Although there was some immediate support for it within Massachusetts, the general reaction was that the whole question should be left to a continental congress. The outstanding exception was Virginia (see No. 145). Printed: Harry A. Cushing, ed., *The Writings of Samuel Adams* (4 vols., New York, 1904-1908), III, pp. 109-111.

We have just received the copy of an Act of the British Parliament passed in the present session whereby the town of Boston is treated in a manner the most ignominious, cruel, and unjust. The Parliament have taken upon them, from the representations of our governor and other persons inimical to and deeply prejudiced against the inhabitants, to try, condemn, and by an Act to punish them, *unheard*; which would have been in violation of *natural justice* even if they had an acknowledged jurisdiction. They have ordered our port to be entirely shut up, leaving us barely so much of the means of subsistence as to keep us from perishing with cold and hunger; and it is said that [a] fleet of British ships of war is to block up our harbour until we shall make restitution to the East India Company for the loss of their tea, which was destroyed therein the winter past, obedience is paid to the laws and authority of Great Britain, and the revenue is duly collected. This Act fills the inhabitants with indignation. The more thinking part of those who have hitherto been in favour of the measures of the British government look upon it as not to have been expected even from a barbarous state. This attack, though made immediately upon us, is doubtless designed for every other colony who will not surrender their sacred rights and liberties into the hands of an infamous ministry. Now therefore is the time when *all* should be united in opposition to this violation of the liberties of *all*. Their grand object is to divide the colonies. We are well informed that another bill is to be brought into Parliament to distinguish this from the other colonies by repealing some of the Acts which have been complained of and ease the American trade; but be assured, *you* will be called upon to surrender your rights if ever they should succeed in their attempts to suppress the spirit of liberty *here*. The single question then is, whether you consider Boston as now suffering in the common cause, and sensibly feel and resent the injury and affront offered to her? If you do (and we cannot believe otherwise), may we not from your approbation of our former conduct in defense of American liberty, rely on your suspending your trade with Great Britain at least, which it is acknowledged, will be a great but necessary sacrifice to the cause of liberty and will effectually defeat the design of this act of revenge. If this should be done, you will please to consider it will be, though a voluntary suffering, greatly short of what we are called to endure under the immediate hand of tyranny.

We desire your answer by the bearer; and after assuring you that, not in the least intimidated by this inhumane treatment, we are still determined to maintain to the utmost of our abilities the rights of America, we are, gentlemen,

Your friends and fellow countrymen.

141A–B. New York reply to the Boston circular letter

When the letter from the Boston Committee of Correspondence, asking for a complete stoppage of trade, arrived in New York, the popular leaders called a mass meeting. The merchants turned out in force and manœuvred the appointment of a committee of fifty-one, dominated by themselves, to draft an answer to the Boston letter. The merchants had no desire for a stoppage of trade, but they were anxious to maintain their tenuous control of the popular movement. Therefore the letter sympathized with Boston's predicament but suggested that only a continental congress could handle the matter properly (No. 141A). Lieutenant-Governor Cadwallader Colden's letter to Lord Dartmouth explains the motives of the merchants in seeking control of the popular movement (No. 141B). A more elaborate account of the mass meeting and of the history behind it is contained in the letter from Gouverneur Morris to John Penn (see No. 169).

141A. Letter from the New York Committee of Fifty-One to the Boston Committee of Correspondence (23 May 1774)

Printed: Peter Force, ed., *American Archives*, 4th Series, 1 (Washington, 1837), pp. 297-298.

The alarming measures of the British Parliament relative to your ancient and respectable town, which has so long been the seat of freedom, fill the inhabitants of this city with inexpressible concern. As a sister colony, suffering in defence of the rights of America, we consider your injuries as a common cause, to the redress of which it is equally our duty and our interest to contribute. But what ought to be done in a situation so truly critical, while it employs the anxious thoughts of every generous mind, is very hard to be determined.

Our citizens have thought it necessary to appoint a large committee, consisting of fifty-one persons to correspond with our sister colonies on this and every other matter of public moment, and at ten o'clock this forenoon we were first assembled. Your letter, enclosing the vote of the town of Boston, and the letter of your Committee of Correspondence, were immediately taken into consideration.

While we think you justly entitled to the thanks of your sister colonies for asking their advice on a case of such extensive consequences, we lament our inability to relieve your anxiety by a decisive opinion. The cause is general, and concerns a whole continent, who are equally interested with you and us; and we foresee that no remedy can be of avail unless it proceeds from the joint act and approbation of all; from a virtuous and spirited union which may be expected while the feeble efforts of a few will only be attended with mischief and disappointment to themselves and triumph to the adversaries of our liberty.

Upon these reasons we conclude that a congress of deputies from the colonies in general is of the utmost moment; that it ought to be assembled without delay, and some unanimous resolution formed in this fatal emergency, not only respecting your deplorable circumstances, but for the security of our common rights. Such being our sentiments, it must be premature to pronounce any judgment on the expedient which you have suggested. We beg, however, that you will do us the justice to believe that we shall continue to act with a firm and becoming regard to American freedom, and to co-operate with our sister colonies in every measure which shall be thought salutary and conducive to the public good.

We have nothing to add, but that we sincerely condole with you in your un-exampled distress, and to request your speedy opinion of the proposed congress, that if it should meet with your approbation, we may exert our utmost endeavours, to carry it into execution.

141B. Letter from Lieutenant-Governor Colden to the earl of Dartmouth (1 June 1774)

Printed: *New York Colonial Documents*, VIII, pp. 433-434.

The Act of Parliament shutting up the port of Boston was brought to this place by a merchant vessel a few days before I received it from your lordship's office.

The Act was immediately published in all our newspapers and was the subject of all conversation. I knew that people universally in this colony had received such ideas of being taxed at the pleasure of Parliament, that I was particularly anxious upon this occasion to discover the sentiments of those who might have most influence over others, and was assured by the gentlemen of the Council and others of weight in the city, that no means would be omitted to prevent the hot-headed people taking any measures that might endanger the peace and quiet of the colony.

The men who at that time called themselves the committee, who dictated and acted in the name of the people, were many of them of the lower rank, and all the warmest zealots of those called the Sons of Liberty. The more considerable merchants and citizens seldom or never appeared among them, but I believe were not displeased with the clamour and opposition that was shown against internal taxation by Parliament.

The principal inhabitants, being now afraid that these hot-headed men might run the city into dangerous measures, appeared in a considerable body at the first meeting of the people after the Boston Port Act was published here. They dissolved the former committee and appointed a new one of fifty-one persons, in which care was taken to have a number of the most prudent and considerate people of the place. Some of them have not before joined in the public proceedings of the opposition, and were induced to appear in what they are sensible is an illegal character, from a consideration that if they did not, the business would be left in the same rash hands as before.

Letters had been received from Boston with an invitation from that town to the sister colonies immediately to come into a resolution to refrain from any commerce with Great Britain and the West India Islands till the Act for shutting up the port of Boston was repealed. A printed handbill of this proposal is enclosed.

I am informed that the new committee in their answer to Boston have given them no reason to expect that the merchants of this place will adopt so extravagant a measure, and people with whom I converse assure me that they think it cannot be brought about by the most zealous advocates of opposition. As yet no resolutions have been taken by the people of this colony, and the cool, prudent men will endeavour to keep measures in suspense till they have an opportunity of adopting the best. I am told that they have proposed that the colonies be invited to send deputies to meet to-gether, in order to petition the king for redress of grievances, and to deliberate upon some plan whereby the jealousies between Great Britain and her colonies may be removed. It is allowed by the intelligent among them that these assemblies of the people, without authority of government, are illegal, and may be dangerous, but they deny that they are unconstitutional when a national grievance cannot otherwise be removed. What resolutions will be taken I cannot as yet say. The government of this province has no coercive power over these assemblies of the people, but the authority of the magistrates in all other cases is submitted to as usual.

142. Proceedings of Farmington, Connecticut, on the Boston Port Act (19 May 1774)

The following account of events is typical of what took place in many of the smaller New England towns during 1774. Printed: Force, ed., *American Archives*, 4th Series, I, p. 336.

Early in the morning was found the following handbill, posted up in various parts of the town, viz:

> To pass through the fire at six o'clock
> this evening, in honour to the immortal
> goddess of Liberty, the late infamous
> Act of the British Parliament for farther
> distressing the American Colonies; the
> place of execution will be the public
> parade, where all Sons of Liberty are
> desired to attend.

Accordingly, a very numerous and respectable body were assembled of near one thousand people, when a huge pole, just forty-five feet high was erected, and consecrated to the shrine of liberty; after which the Act of Parliament for blocking up the Boston harbour was read aloud; sentenced to the flames, and executed by the hands of the common hangman; then the following resolves were passed, *nem. con.*:

1st. That it is the greatest dignity, interest, and happiness of every American to be united with our parent state, while our liberties are duly secured, maintained, and supported by our rightful sovereign, whose person we greatly revere; whose government while duly administered, we are ready with our lives and properties to support.

2d. That the present ministry, being instigated by the devil, and led on by their wicked and corrupt hearts, have a design to take away our liberties and properties, and to enslave us forever.

3d. That the late Act which their malice hath caused to be passed in Parliament, for blocking up the port of Boston, is unjust, illegal, and oppressive; and that we, and every American, are sharers in the insults offered to the town of Boston.

4th. That those pimps and parasites who dared to advise their master to such detestable measures be held in utter abhorrence by us and every American, and their names loaded with the curses of all succeeding generations.

5th. That we scorn the chains of slavery; we despise every attempt to rivet them upon us; we are the sons of freedom, and resolved, that, till time shall be no more, that god-like virtue shall blazon our hemisphere.

143. Newport, Rhode Island handbill, "Join or Die" (30 May 1774)

The following handbill from Newport indicates that Boston had hearty support, even in a town dominated by conservative merchants. Printed: *Rhode Island Colonial Records*, VII, p. 293.

The Act of Parliament for blocking up the harbour of Boston in order to reduce its spirited inhabitants to the most servile and mean compliances ever attempted to be imposed on a free people, is allowed to be infinitely more alarming and dangerous to our common liberties than even that hydra, the Stamp Act (which was defeated by our firmness and union) and must be read with a glowing indignation by every real friend of freedom in Europe and America.

Though the town of Boston is now intended to be made a victim to ministerial wrath; yet the insult and indignity offered to our virtuous brethren in that capital, who have so nobly stood as a barrier against slavery, ought to be viewed in the same odious light as a direct, hostile invasion of every province on the continent, whose inhabitants are now loudly called upon by interest, honour, and humanity to stand forth with firmness and unanimity for the relief, support, and animation of our brethren in the insulted, besieged capital of Massachusetts Bay.

The generals of despotism are now drawing the lines of circumvallation around our bulwarks of liberty; and nothing but unity, resolution, and perseverance can save ourselves and posterity from what is worse than death–slavery!

Newport, Rhode Island, May 30th, 1774.

144. Proceedings of the inhabitants of Philadelphia (18 June 1774)

Paul Revere arrived in Philadelphia on 19 May with a copy of the circular letter of the Boston Committee of Correspondence. There followed weeks of complicated political manœuvring in which the popular leaders, supported by the artisans, fought the conservative Quaker merchant group for control of the various meetings and committees that were organized to consider the questions presented by British policy towards Massachusetts. The popular leaders, Charles Thomson, Joseph Reed, and Thomas Mifflin, called a mass meeting for 20 May to consider the Boston letter. The conservatives turned out and joined in appointing a committee of nineteen to write the answer. The letter of 21 May, which was written in reply to that of Boston, indicates that the more moderate elements in Philadelphia were in control. The letter deplored the destruction of property, urged that the tea should be paid for, and suggested that a continental congress be called for the purpose of petitioning the king. Stoppage of trade, said the letter, was a last resort.

Popular pressure continued and grew so, as in New York, one committee after another was chosen. The merchants participated in each of them in order to control, and on the whole they were successful. Yet step by step, in spite of themselves, the merchants were pushed in the direction of revolutionary activity. The resolutions of the meeting of 18 June which follow, called for a continental congress, but in addition, provided for the establishment of a committee of correspondence.

This committee reluctantly became the centre of a revolutionary organization which in time was to carry Pennsylvania into the war for independence. Printed: Niles, *Principles and Acts of the Revolution*, pp. 203–204.

I. Resolved, that the Act of Parliament, for shutting up the port of Boston, is unconstitutional; oppressive to the inhabitants of that town; dangerous to the liberties of the British colonies; and that, therefore, we consider our brethren at Boston as suffering in the common cause of America.

II. That a congress of deputies from the several colonies in North America is the most probable and proper mode of procuring relief for our suffering brethren, obtaining redress of American grievances, securing our rights and liberties, and re-establishing peace and harmony between Great Britain and these colonies on a constitutional foundation.

III. That a large and respectable committee be immediately appointed for the city and county of Philadelphia, to correspond with their sister colonies and with the several counties in this province, in order that all may unite in promoting and endeavouring to attain the great and valuable ends mentioned in the foregoing resolution.

IV. That the committee nominated by this meeting shall consult together, and on mature deliberation determine what is the most proper mode of collecting the sense of this province, and appointing deputies for the same, to attend a general congress: and having determined thereupon, shall take such measures, as by them shall be judged most expedient, for procuring this province to be represented at the said congress, in the best manner that can be devised for promoting the public welfare.

V. That the committee be instructed immediately to set on foot a subscription for the relief of such poor inhabitants of the town of Boston, as may be deprived of the means of subsistence by the operation of the Act of Parliament, commonly styled the Boston Port Bill. The money arising from such subscription to be laid out as the committee shall think will best answer the ends proposed.

VI. That the committee consist of forty-three persons, viz., John Dickinson, Edward Pennington, John Nixon, Thomas Willing, George Clymer, Samuel Howell, Joseph Reed, John Roberts (miller), Thomas Wharton, Jun., Charles Thomson, Jacob Barge, Thomas Barclay, William Rush, Robert Smith (carpenter), Thomas Fitzimons, George Roberts, Samuel Ervin, Thomas Mifflin, John Cox, George Gray, Robert Morris, Samuel Miles, John M. Nesbit, Peter Chevalier, William Moulder, Joseph Moulder, Anthony Morris, Jr., John Allen, Jeremiah Warder, Jr., Rev. Dr. William Smith, Paul Engle, Thomas Penrose, James Mease, Benjamin Marshall, Reuben Haines, John Bayard, Jonathan B. Smith, Thomas Wharton, Isaac Howell, Michael Hillegas, Adam Hubley, George Schlosser, and Christopher Ludwick.

Thomas Willing, John Dickinson, Esquires, chairmen.

145. The Association of the Virginia convention (1–6 August 1774)

Aside from the smaller towns of New England, the most forceful support of Boston came from Virginia and Maryland. After the House of Burgesses was dissolved in May, a rump session of the House called a convention to meet in August. During the summer before the convention met, at least a majority of the sixty-one counties in Virginia held meetings and passed resolutions. Virtually all the resolutions that remain urge some form of commercial coercion. Several of the counties recommended that suits for recovery of debt owing British merchants be suspended until the repeal of the Boston Port Bill. The counties expressed sympathy for Boston and provided for the collection of supplies to be sent there. Most of them approved of the proposed convention and of a continental congress. Some of them took high constitutional grounds, as did Albemarle County, whose resolutions, written by Thomas Jefferson, categorically denied the legislative authority of Parliament. The Fairfax County resolves, written by George Mason, and approved of at a meeting presided over by George Washington, were the model for the Association adopted by the Virginia convention in August. When the convention met, it elected delegates to the continental congress and adopted the following association, which in large measure spelled out the proposal of the Boston circular letter of 13 May. Printed: Niles, *Principles and Acts of the Revolution*, pp. 272–274.

We, his Majesty's dutiful and loyal subjects, the delegates of the freeholders of Virginia, deputed to represent them at a general meeting in the city of Williamsburg, avowing our inviolable and unshaken fidelity and attachment to our most gracious sovereign, our regard and affection for all our friends and fellow subjects in Great Britain and elsewhere, protesting against every act or thing which may have the most distant tendency to interrupt, or in any wise disturb his Majesty's peace, and the good order of government, within this his ancient colony, which we are resolved to maintain and defend at the risk of our lives and fortunes, but at the same time affected with the deepest anxiety, and most alarming apprehensions of those grievances and distresses by which his Majesty's American subjects are oppressed, and having taken under our most serious deliberation the state of the whole continent, find that the present unhappy situation of our affairs is chiefly occasioned by certain ill-advised regulations, as well of our trade as internal policy, introduced by several unconstitutional Acts of the British Parliament, and at length attempted to be enforced by the hand of power; solely influenced by these important and weighty considerations, we think it an indispensable duty which we owe to our country, ourselves, and latest posterity, to guard against such dangerous and extensive mischiefs, by every just and proper means.

If, by the measures adopted, some unhappy consequences and inconveniences should be derived to our fellow subjects, whom we wish not to injure in the smallest degree, we hope and flatter ourselves, that they will impute them to their real cause— the hard necessity to which we are driven.

That the good people of this colony may, on so trying an occasion, continue steadfastly directed to their most essential interests, in hopes that they will be influenced and stimulated by our example to the greatest industry, the strictest economy, and frugality, and the execution of every public virtue, persuaded that the merchants, manufacturers, and other inhabitants of Great Britain, and above all, that the British Parliament will be convinced how much the true interest of that kingdom must depend on the restoration and continuance of that mutual friendship and cordiality which so happily subsisted between us, we have unanimously, and with one voice, entered into the following resolutions and association, which we do oblige ourselves, by those sacred ties of honour and love to our country, strictly to observe; and further declare before God and the world, that we will religiously adhere to and keep the same inviolate in every particular, until redress of all such American grievances as may be defined and settled at the general congress of delegates from the different colonies shall be fully obtained, or until this association shall be abrogated or altered by a general meeting of the deputies of this colony, to be convened, as is hereinafter directed. And we do with the greatest earnestness recommend this our association to all gentlemen, merchants, traders, and other inhabitants of this colony, hoping that they will cheerfully and cordially accede thereto.

1st. We do hereby resolve and declare that we will not, either directly or indirectly, after the first day of November next, import from Great Britain, any goods, wares, or merchandises whatever (medicines excepted), nor will we after that day, import any British manufactures, either from the West Indies or any other place, nor any article whatever, which we shall know or have reason to believe, was brought into such countries from Great Britain, nor will we purchase any such articles so imported of any person or persons whatsoever, except such as are now in the country, or such as may arrive on or before the said first day of November, in consequence of orders already given, and which cannot now be countermanded in time.

2dly. We will neither ourselves import nor purchase any slave or slaves, imported by any person, after the first day of November next, either from Africa, the West Indies, or any other place.

3dly. Considering the article of tea as the detestable instrument which laid the foundation of the present sufferings of our distressed friends in the town of Boston, we view it with horror, and therefore resolve that we will not from this day, either import tea of any kind whatever, nor will we use or suffer, even such of it as is now at hand, to be used in any of our families.

4thly. If the inhabitants of the town of Boston, or any other colony, should by violence or dire necessity, be compelled to pay the East India Company for destroying any tea which they have lately by their agents unjustly attempted to force into the colonies, we will not, directly or indirectly, import or purchase any British East India commodity whatever till the company, or some other person on their behalf, shall refund and fully restore to the owners all such sum or sums of money as may be so extorted.

5thly. We do resolve that unless American grievances be redressed before the 10th day of August, 1775, we will not after that day, directly or indirectly, export tobacco or any other article whatever to Great Britain; nor will we sell any such articles as we think can be exported to Great Britain with a prospect of gain, to any person or persons whatever, with a design of putting it into his or their power to export the same to Great Britain, either on our own, his or their account. And that this resolution may be the more effectually carried into execution, we do hereby recommend it to the inhabitants of this colony to refrain from the cultivation of tobacco as much as conveniently may be, and in lieu thereof that they will, as we resolve to do, apply their attention and industry to the cultivation of all such articles as may form a proper basis for manufactures of all sorts, which we will endeavour to encourage throughout this colony to the utmost of our abilities.

6thly. We will endeavour to improve our breed of sheep and increase their number to the utmost extent, and to this end we will be as sparing as we conveniently can in killing of sheep, especially those of the most profitable kind, and if we should at any time be overstocked and can conveniently spare any, we will dispose of them to our neighbours, especially the poorer sort of people, upon moderate terms.

7thly. Resolved, that the merchants and others, venders of goods and merchandises within this colony, ought not to take advantage of the scarcity of goods that may be occasioned by this association, but that they ought to sell the same at the rates they have been accustomed to for twelve months past, and if they shall sell any such goods on higher terms, or shall in any manner, or by any device whatever, violate or depart from this resolution, we will not, and are of opinion that no inhabitant of this colony ought, at any time thereafter, to deal with any such persons, their factors, or agents, for any commodity whatever; and it is recommended to the deputies of the several counties that committees be chosen in each county, by such persons as accede to this association, to take effectual care that these resolves be properly observed, and for corresponding occasionally with the general committee of correspondence in the city of Williamsburg. Provided that, if exchange should rise, such advance may be made in the prices of goods as shall be approved by the committee of each county.

8thly. In order the better to distinguish such worthy merchants and traders who are well wishers to this colony from those who may attempt, through motives of self-interest, to obstruct our views, we do hereby resolve that we will not, after the first day of November next, deal with any merchant or trader who will not sign this association, nor until he hath obtained a certificate of his having done so from the county committee, or any three members thereof. And if any merchant, trader, or other persons shall import any goods or merchandise after the first day of November, contrary to this association, we give it as our opinion that such goods and merchandise should be either forthwith reshipped, or delivered up to the county committee, to be stored at the risk of the importer, unless such importer shall give a proper assurance to the said committee that such goods or merchandises shall not be sold within this colony during the continuance of this association; and if such importer shall refuse to comply with one or the other of these terms, upon application and due caution given to him or her, by the said committee, or any three members thereof, such committee is required to publish the truth of the case in the gazettes, and in the county where he or she resides, and we will thereafter consider such person or persons as inimical to this country, and break off every connection and all dealings with them.

9thly. Resolved, that if any person or persons shall export tobacco, or any other commodity, to Great Britain, after the 10th day of August, 1775, contrary to this association, we shall hold ourselves obliged to consider such person or persons as inimical to the community, *and as an approver of* American *grievances*; and give it as our opinion that the public should be advertised of his conduct, as in the 8th article is desired.

10thly. Being fully persuaded that the united wisdom of the general congress may improve these our endeavours to preserve the rights and liberties in British America, we decline enlarging at present, but do hereby resolve that we will conform to, and strictly observe, all such alterations, or additions, assented to by the delegates for this colony, as they may judge it necessary to adopt, after the same shall be published and made known to us.

11thly. Resolved, that we think ourselves called upon by every principle of humanity and brotherly affection, to extend the utmost and speediest relief to our distressed fellow subjects in the town of Boston, and therefore most earnestly recommend it to all the inhabitants of this colony, to make such liberal contributions as they can afford; to be collected and remitted to Boston in such manner as may best answer so desirable a purpose.

12thly, and lastly. Resolved, that the moderator of this meeting, and, in case of his death, Robert Carter Nicholas, Esquire, be empowered on any future occasion that may in his opinion require it, to convene the several delegates of this colony at such time and place as he may judge proper; and in case of the death or absence of any delegate, it is recommended that another be chosen in his place.

B. THE FIRST CONTINENTAL CONGRESS

THE calling of the First Continental Congress transferred the problem of deciding on measures to be adopted in opposition to Britain from the separate colonies to a central body, illegal and unconstitutional though it might be. Popular and conservative leaders alike tacitly agreed to this, though for quite different reasons. The Congress represented a goal towards which the popular leaders had been working for years; to the conservatives in some of the colonies, at least, it represented an escape from the threat of popular control, and particularly from the policy of complete stoppage of trade as proposed by the Boston town meeting.[1] The Congress was therefore the scene of a crucial struggle for control between the popular and conservative leaders who made up the delegations from the twelve colonies represented. (Georgia alone did not send delegates.)

By 1774 most of the popular leaders were openly denying the right of Parliament to legislate for the colonies in any case whatever. The conservative leaders, although opposed to most British colonial policies, insisted that there must be a supreme legislature in the empire and that only Parliament could be that legislature.[2] However, very few of them would go so far as to accept Thomas Hutchinson's view that Parliament had absolute sovereignty. Therefore the conservatives were in a weak position between the two extremes represented by the popular leaders on one hand and the attitude of the British ministry on the other. That attitude was no better expressed than by Lord Dartmouth in a private letter to Joseph Reed of Pennsylvania in the summer of 1774. He declared that "the supreme legislature of the whole British Empire has laid a duty (no matter for the present whether it has or has not the right so to do, it is sufficient that we conceive it has). . . . The question then is whether these laws are to be submitted to? If the people of America say no, they say in effect they will no longer be a part of the British Empire."[3] There was no compromise possible between these two positions, nor did their proponents offer any. The British soon showed that they intended to use the army to compel colonial obedience; the popular leaders, and many conservatives as well, soon took the position that force must be met with force if the colonies were to retain any of their rights and privileges.

The First Continental Congress met on 5 September, and its first decisions were straws in a wind which indicated the final outcome. Charles Thomson, the "Sam Adams of Philadelphia", was elected secretary, a post he was to hold until 1789. Carpenter's Hall, rather than the Pennsylvania State House, was selected as the meeting-place. These two decisions, wrote one delegate, were "highly agreeable to the mechanics and citizens in general but mortifying to the last degree to Mr. Joseph Galloway and his party". It was next decided that each colony should have one vote. Although delegates from the large colonies demanded that voting should be according to population, no one had accurate figures as to population, and furthermore, the smaller colonies were a majority. On 7 September two committees were appointed: one to state the rights of the colonies, and the other to examine and report on the various laws affecting the trade and manufactures of the colonies.

[1] Nos. 140, 141, 144.   [2] Cf. Nos. 142, 152, 149.   [3] Cf. No. 139.

The two committees debated day after day but were deadlocked. The conservatives wanted to petition for a redress of grievances while the popular leaders demanded a more forceful form of opposition. The popular leaders proposed to base colonial rights on the "laws of nature" and to deny the authority of Parliament; the conservatives insisted that colonial rights be based on the colonial charters and the English constitution and that the "laws of nature" be excluded. Furthermore, they insisted that Parliament must have the right to regulate trade.[1]

The deadlock was broken by the strategy of Samuel Adams. On 6 September, Suffolk County, Massachusetts, had adopted a series of resolutions written by Joseph Warren, one of the ablest popular leaders in Boston. On 16 September, Paul Revere arrived in Philadelphia with the resolutions. The Suffolk resolves were an able statement of the popular position. They cited the law of nature, acknowledged George III as sovereign "agreeable to compact", indirectly denied the authority of Parliament by declaring that the colonists did not have to obey the Intolerable Acts, and recommended the stoppage of trade. The Massachusetts delegation promptly presented these resolves to Congress for approval. The conservatives were faced with a hopeless dilemma · if they approved, they would give up what they had been struggling for in Congress; if they disapproved, they would, in effect, give tacit support to British measures with which few indeed were in sympathy. Therefore they gave reluctant approval to the resolves, and from that time on the course was clear.[2]

On 22 September, Congress asked the merchants to suspend importations until it could make public the means to be taken to preserve the liberties of America. On 27 September the non-importation of goods from Britain and Ireland after 1 December 1774 was agreed to. On 30 September, Congress resolved that after 10 September 1775 all exportations to Britain, Ireland, and the West Indies should stop and appointed a committee to prepare a plan for carrying the resolutions into effect. These resolutions were the basis for the Association that Congress agreed to on 18 October and which the members signed on 20 October.[3]

In the midst of the debate on these measures the conservatives countered with a proposal of their own: the Galloway Plan of Union.[4] Joseph Galloway, the speaker of the Pennsylvania Assembly, laid the plan before Congress on 28 September. Later to become a loyalist, Galloway made a fervent plea for an attempt to arrive at some constitutional definition of the relationship between Britain and the colonies. His speech introducing the plan and the debates that followed set forth clearly the diametrically opposed views of the two groups in Congress.[5] The Galloway plan was finally rejected and all record of it erased from the journals of Congress by the triumphant popular leaders.

The final draft of the Declaration of Rights was somewhat of a compromise between popular and conservative views. Colonial rights were based on the "immutable laws of nature, the English constitution and the several charters or compacts...". On the disputed question of the authority of Parliament, John Adams worked out a compromise statement to the effect that "from the necessity of the case" we "cheerfully consent" to the regulation of purely external trade by Parliament, but excluding external and internal taxation of Americans without their consent. But on the whole, the declaration was another triumph for the popular leaders.[6] Further addresses and

[1] No. 147.   [2] No. 146.   [3] No. 151.   [4] No. 150.   [5] No. 149.   [6] No. 148.

memorials—to the king, to the inhabitants of the colonies, to the people of Great Britain, and to the inhabitants of the province of Quebec—elaborated upon the ideas contained in the Declaration of Rights and in the Association.

Congress took even further steps as letters from Massachusetts came in. The Boston Committee of Correspondence reported that British forts were being built and that Boston would become a garrison town. What would Congress advise? Should Boston be evacuated or should the inhabitants remain as hostages? Again the conservatives faced a dilemma which forced them to agree to a resolution stating that unless the actions of the British soldiers were stopped, all America would be involved in the horrors of civil war. The next day Congress adopted a resolution approving the opposition of Massachusetts to the Acts of Parliament and stating that if Britain tried to carry those Acts into effect by force, all Americans ought to support Massachusetts. This was virtually a declaration that Americans were ready to fight.

It was little wonder that a Maryland merchant wrote that "Adams with his crew and the haughty Sultans of the South juggled the whole conclave of delegates". The Congress adjourned 27 October, agreeing to meet again on 10 May 1775 unless their grievances had been redressed. Yet there was little chance that this would happen, and the day after adjournment John Dickenson wrote that the Congress had taken such grounds that either Britain must give in or civil war would follow. General Gage reported that the proceedings of the Congress had astonished and terrified all moderate men, but that its proceedings would be accepted because the moderate people lacked the resolution and the strength to defeat them. Conservatives predicted utter disaster but they were unable to prevent the Association from being put into effect. Only one legislature, the New York Assembly, repudiated the proceedings of the Congress, but this had no effect except to increase the strength of the popular organization in New York City.

Newspaper articles and pamphlets poured forth denouncing and defending the Congress. Early in 1775 an embittered Joseph Galloway published a pamphlet in which he included his plan of union and charged the popular leaders with aiming at independence. The popular leaders, of course, denied that their aim was independence: they could not safely affirm that it was otherwise. But this did not inhibit anonymous newspaper writers from debating the matter openly. The "Political Observations without Order" that appeared in a Philadelphia newspaper on 12 November 1774 admitted frankly that independence was the ultimate goal.[1] Much of its language was an anticipation of the ideas of Thomas Paine's *Common Sense*, which did not appear until January 1776. The answer to the "Political Observations", which appeared in a New York newspaper, presents with equal clarity the view of those Americans who, though disapproving of British policy, had no desire to follow the popular leaders down the road to independence.[2]

The lines were now drawn. The popular leaders in New England began to prepare for war. Britain continued to increase her forces in Massachusetts. The First Continental Congress had stated its position. The ministry and Parliament could yield, they could offer a compromise, or they could reject the results of the Congress. Given the attitude expressed by Lord Dartmouth in the summer of 1774, the last choice was inevitable, and equally inevitable was the war for American independence.

[1] No. 152.   [2] No. 153.

146. Joseph Galloway on the First Continental Congress (1780)

Joseph Galloway, speaker of the Pennsylvania Assembly, had, since 1765, consistently upheld the right of Parliament to legislate for the colonies. In the First Congress in 1774 he led the conservative forces in a futile effort to take a stand which would provide grounds for compromise of the dispute between Britain and the colonies. His comments on the Congress, published in 1780, though biased, represent his feelings in 1774. The excerpts which follow are notable for the analysis of party divisions. the sketch of Samuel Adams, and the reasons lying behind the presentation of his plan of union. Printed: Joseph Galloway, *Historical and Political Reflections on the Rise and Progress of the American Rebellion* (London, 1780), pp. 66–70.

Upon the meeting of Congress, two parties were immediately formed, with different views, and determined to act upon different principles. One intended candidly and clearly to define American rights, and explicitly and dutifully to petition for the remedy which would redress the grievances justly complained of – to form a more solid and constitutional union between the two countries, and to avoid every measure which tended to sedition, or acts of violent opposition. The other consisted of persons whose design, from the beginning of their opposition to the Stamp Act, was to throw off all subordination and connection with Great Britain; who meant by every fiction, falsehood, and fraud to delude the people from their due allegiance, to throw the subsisting governments into anarchy, to incite the ignorant and vulgar to arms, and with those arms to establish American independence. The one were men of loyal principles and possessed the greatest fortunes in America; the other were Congregational and Presbyterian republicans, or men of bankrupt fortunes, over-whelmed in debt to the British merchants. The first suspected the designs of the last, and were therefore cautious; but as they meant to do nothing but what was reasonable and just, they were open and ingenuous. The second, fearing the opposition of the first, were secret and hypocritical, and left no art, no falsehood, no fraud unessayed to conceal their intentions. The loyalists rested, for the most part, on the defensive, and opposed, with success, every measure which tended to violent opposition. Motions were made, debated and rejected, and nothing was carried by either.

While the two parties in Congress remained thus during three weeks on an equal balance, the republicans were calling to their assistance the aid of their factions without. Continual expresses were employed between Philadelphia and Boston. These were under the management of Samuel Adams–a man, who though by no means remark-able for brilliant abilities, yet is equal to most men in popular intrigue, and the management of a faction. He eats little, drinks little, sleeps little, thinks much, and is most decisive and indefatigable in the pursuit of his objects. It was this man, who by his superior application managed at once the faction in Congress at Philadelphia, and the factions in New England. Whatever these patriots in Congress wished to have done by their colleagues without, to induce General Gage, then at the head of his Majesty's army at Boston, to give them a pretext for violent opposition, or to promote their measures in Congress, Mr. Adams advised and directed to be done; and when done, it was dispatched by express to Congress. By one of these expresses came the inflammatory resolves of the county of Suffolk, which contained a complete declaration of war against Great Britain. By these resolves it is declared, "that no obedience is due to Acts of Parliament affecting Boston";

That "the justices of the superior courts of judicature, court of assize, etc., are unconstitutional officers, and that *no regard ought to be paid to them by the people*";

That "the county will support and bear harmless all sheriffs and their deputies, constables, jurors, and other officers who shall *refuse to carry into execution the orders of the said courts*";

That "the collectors of taxes, constables, and other officers, retain in their hands *all public moneys*, and not make any payment thereof to the provincial county treasurer";

And that "the persons who had accepted seats at the council-board, by *virtue of a mandamus from the king*, should be considered as *obstinate and incorrigible enemies to their country*".

They advise the people "to elect the officers of militia, and to use their *utmost diligence to acquaint themselves with the art of war* as soon as possible, and for that purpose to appear under arms once in every week".

And to carry these and other measures into execution, among many other things equally treasonable, they recommend it to the several towns to "choose a provincial congress".

Upon these resolves being read, a motion was made that the Congress should give them their sanction. Long and warm debates ensued between the parties. At this time the republican faction in Congress had provided a mob, ready to execute their secret orders. The cruel practice of tarring and feathering had been long since introduced. This lessened the firmness of some of the loyalists; the vote was put and carried. Two of the dissenting members presumed to offer their protest against it in writing, which was negatived. They next insisted that the tender of their protest and its negative should be entered on the minutes; this was also rejected.

By this treasonable vote the foundation of military resistance throughout America was effectually laid. The example was now set by the people of Suffolk, and the measure was approved of by those who called themselves *the representatives of all America*. The loyal party, although they knew a great majority of the colonists were averse to the measure, perceived the improbability of stemming the torrent. They had no authority, no means in their own power to resist it; they saw those who held the powers of government inactive spectators, and either shrinking from their duty, or uniting in the measures of sedition; they saw the flame of rebellion spreading with more rapidity in a province under the eye of his Majesty's army than in any other; and that no effectual measures were taking by government in Britain to suppress it; and yet, as a petition to his Majesty had been ordered to be brought in, they resolved to continue their exertions. They hoped to prevail in stating the rights of America on just and constitutional principles; in proposing a plan for uniting the two countries on those principles, and in a clear, definitive, and decent prayer to ask for what a majority of the colonies wished to obtain; and as they had no reason to doubt the success of this measure in a British Parliament, they further hoped that it would stop the effusion of blood and the ruin of their country.

With this view, as well as to probe the ultimate design of the republicans, and to know with certainty whether any proposal, short of the absolute independence of the colonies, would satisfy them, a plan of union was drawn by a member of the loyal party, and approved by the rest. It was so formed as to leave no room for any reasonable objection on the part of the republicans, if they meant to be united to Great Britain on any grounds whatever. It included a restoration of all their rights, and a redress of all their grievances, on constitutional principles; and it accorded with all the instructions given to them as members of Congress.

147. Debate in the Committee to state the rights of the colonies (8 September 1774)

The following notes were taken by John Adams. Fragmentary though they are, they demonstrate the sharp difference of opinion that existed as to the theoretical foundation of colonial rights. Printed: John Adams, *Works*, II, pp. 370–373.

September 8. In the Committee for stating rights, grievances, and means of redress. Colonel [Richard Henry] Lee, [Virginia]: The rights are built on a fourfold foundation: on nature, on the British constitution, on charters, and on immemorial usage. The Navigation Act, a capital violation.

Mr. [John] Jay, [New York]: It is necessary to recur to the law of nature and the British constitution to ascertain our rights. The constitution of Great Britain will not apply to some of the charter rights.

A mother country surcharged with inhabitants, they have a right to emigrate. It may be said, if we leave our country we cannot leave our allegiance. But there is no allegiance without protection, and emigrants have a right to erect what government they please.

Mr. J[ohn] Rutledge, [South Carolina]: Emigrants would not have a right to set up what constitution they please. A subject could not alienate his allegiance.

Lee: Can't see why we should not lay our rights upon the broadest bottom, the ground of nature. Our ancestors found here no government.

Mr. [Edmund] Pendleton, [Virginia]: Consider how far we have a right to interfere with regard to the Canada constitution. If the majority of the people there should be pleased with the new constitution, would not the people of America and of England have a right to oppose it, and prevent such a constitution being established in our neighbourhood?

Lee: It is contended that the Crown had no right to grant such charters as it has to the colonies, and therefore we shall rest our rights on a feeble foundation if we rest them only on charters; nor will it weaken our objections to the Canada bill.

Mr. Rutledge: Our claims, I think, are well founded on the British constitution, and not on the law of nature.

Colonel [Eliphalet] Dyer, [Connecticut]: Part of the country within the Canada bill is a conquered country, and part not. It is said to be a rule that the king can give a conquered country what law he pleases.

Mr. Jay: I can't think the British constitution inseparably attached to the person of every subject. Whence did the constitution derive its authority? From compact; might not that authority be given up by compact?

Mr. William Livingston, [New Jersey]: A corporation cannot make a corporation;

charter governments have done it. King can't appoint a person to make a justice of peace; all governors do it. Therefore it will not do for America to rest wholly on the laws of England.

Mr. [Roger] Sherman, [Connecticut]: The ministry contend that the colonies are only like corporations in England and therefore subordinate to the legislature of the kingdom. The colonies not bound to the king or Crown by the act of settlement, but by their consent to it. There is no other legislative over the colonies but their respective assemblies.

The colonies adopt the common law, not as the common law, but as the highest reason.

Mr. [James] Duane, [New York]: Upon the whole, for grounding our rights on the laws and constitution of the country from whence we sprung, and charters, without recurring to the law of nature; because this will be a feeble support. Charters are compacts between the Crown and the people, and I think on this foundation the charter governments stand firm.

England is governed by a limited monarchy and free constitution. Privileges of Englishmen were inherent, their birthright and inheritance, and cannot be deprived of them without their consent.

Objection: that all the rights of Englishmen will make us independent. I hope a line may be drawn to obviate this objection.

James was against Parliament interfering with the colonies. In the reign of Charles II the sentiments of the Crown seem to have been changed. The Navigation Act was made; Massachusetts denied the authority but made a law to enforce it in the colony.

Lee: Life and liberty, which is necessary for the security of life, cannot be given up when we enter into society.

Mr. Rutledge: The first emigrants could not be considered as in a state of nature; they had no right to elect a new king.

Mr. Jay: I have always withheld my assent from the position that every subject discovering land (does it) for the state to which he belongs.

Mr. [Joseph] Galloway, [Pennsylvania]: I never could find the rights of Americans in the distinction between taxation and legislation, nor in the distinction between laws for revenue and for the regulation of trade. I have looked for our rights in the law of nature but could not find them in a state of nature, but always in a state of political society.

I have looked for them in the constitution of the English government, and there found them. We may draw them from this source securely.

Power results from the real property of the society. The states of Greece, Macedon, Rome were founded on this plan. None but landholders could vote in the comitia or stand for offices.

English constitution founded on the same principle. Among the Saxons the land-holders were obliged to attend, and shared among them the power. In the Norman period, the same. When the landholders could not all attend, the representatives of the freeholders came in. Before the reign of Henry IV an attempt was made to give the tenants *in capite* a right to vote. Magna Charta–archbishops, bishops, abbots, earls, and barons, and tenants *in capite* held all the lands in England.

It is of the essence of the English constitution that no laws shall be binding but such as are made by the consent of the proprietors in England.

How then did it stand with our ancestors when they came over here? They could not be bound by any laws made by the British Parliament, excepting those made before. I never could see any reason to allow that we are bound to any law made since, nor could I ever make any distinction between the sorts of law.

I have ever thought we might reduce our rights to one–an exemption from all laws made by British Parliament since the emigration of our ancestors. It follows, therefore, that all the Acts of Parliament made since are violations of our rights.

These claims are all defensible upon the principles even of our enemies–Lord North himself, when he shall inform himself of the true principles of the constitution, etc.

I am well aware that my arguments tend to an independency of the colonies and militate against the maxims that there must be some absolute power to draw together all the wills and strength of the empire.

148. The Declaration of Colonial Rights and Grievances (14 October 1774)

The following statement was the result of the work of the committee appointed on 7 September "to state the rights of the colonies in general, the several instances in which these rights are violated or infringed, and the means most proper to be pursued for obtaining a restoration of them". The two most heated issues were the theoretical foundation of colonial rights and the question of the regulation of trade by Parliament (see No. 147). Although the final declaration represented a compromise of views it was in essence a victory for the popular leaders since it contained most of their ideas, including the "law of nature" as one basis for colonial rights, and made 'consent' and 'necessity' rather than 'right' the basis for the regulation of trade by Parliament. Printed: Worthington C. Ford, *et al.*, eds., *Journals of the Continental Congress, 1774–1789* (34 vols., Washington, 1904–1937), I, pp. 63–73.

Whereas, since the close of the last war the British Parliament, claiming a power of right to bind the people of America by statute in all cases whatsoever, hath in some Acts expressly imposed taxes on them, and in others, under various pretences, but in fact for the purpose of raising a revenue, hath imposed rates and duties payable in these colonies, established a board of commissioners with unconstitutional powers, and extended the jurisdiction of courts of admiralty, not only for collecting the said duties, but for the trial of causes merely arising within the body of a county.

And whereas, in consequence of other statutes, judges, who before held only estates at will in their offices, have been made dependent on the Crown alone for their salaries, and standing armies kept in times of peace:

And it has lately been resolved in Parliament, that by force of a statute, made in the thirty-fifth year of the reign of King Henry the eighth, colonists may be transported to England, and tried there upon accusations for treasons, and misprisions, or concealments of treasons committed in the colonies; and by a late statute, such trials have been directed in cases therein mentioned.

And whereas, in the last session of Parliament, three statutes were made; one, entitled "An Act to discontinue, in such manner and for such time as are therein mentioned, the landing and discharging, lading, or shipping of goods, wares and merchandise, at the town, and within the harbour of Boston, in the province of Massachusetts Bay in North America"; another entitled "An Act for the better regulating the government of the province of the Massachusetts Bay in New England"; and another entitled "An Act for the impartial administration of justice, in the cases of persons questioned for any act done by them in the execution of the law, or for the suppression of riots and tumults, in the province of the Massachusetts Bay in New England". And another statute was then made "for making more effectual provision for the government of the province of Quebec, etc." All which statutes are impolitic, unjust, and cruel, as well as unconstitutional, and most dangerous and destructive of American rights.

And whereas, assemblies have been frequently dissolved, contrary to the rights of the people, when they attempted to deliberate on grievances; and their dutiful, humble, loyal and reasonable petitions to the Crown for redress have been repeatedly treated with contempt by his Majesty's ministers of state:

The good people of the several colonies of New Hampshire, Massachusetts Bay, Rhode Island and Providence Plantations, Connecticut, New York, New Jersey, Pennsylvania, New Castle, Kent and Sussex on Delaware, Maryland, Virginia, North Carolina and South Carolina, justly alarmed at these arbitrary proceedings of Parliament and administration, have severally elected, constituted, and appointed deputies to meet and sit in general congress, in the city of Philadelphia, in order to obtain such establishment, as that their religion, laws, and liberties may not be subverted.

Whereupon the deputies so appointed being now assembled, in a full and free representation of these colonies, taking into their most serious consideration the best means of attaining the ends aforesaid, do, in the first place, as Englishmen, their ancestors in like cases have usually done, for asserting and vindicating their rights and liberties, declare,

That the inhabitants of the English colonies in North America, by the immutable laws of nature, the principles of the English constitution, and the several charters or compacts, have the following rights:

Resolved, N. C. D. 1. That they are entitled to life, liberty and property, and they have never ceded to any sovereign power whatever, a right to dispose of either without their consent.

Resolved, N. C. D. 2. That our ancestors who first settled these colonies, were at the time of their emigration from the mother country, entitled to all the rights, liberties, and immunities of free and natural-born subjects, within the realm of England.

Resolved, N. C. D. 3. That by such emigration they by no means forfeited, surrendered, or lost any of those rights, but that they were, and their descendants now are, entitled to the exercise and enjoyment of all such of them, as their local and other circumstances enable them to exercise and enjoy.

Resolved, 4. That the foundation of English liberty, and of all free government, is a right in the people to participate in their legislative council: and as the English colonists are not represented, and from their local and other circumstances, cannot properly be represented in the British Parliament, they are entitled to a free and exclusive power of legislation in their several provincial legislatures, where their right of representation can alone be preserved, in all cases of taxation and internal polity, subject only to the negative of their sovereign, in such manner as has been heretofore used and accustomed. But, from the necessity of the case, and a regard to the mutual interest of both countries, we cheerfully consent to the operation of such Acts of the British Parliament, as are *bona fide*, restrained to the regulation of our external commerce, for the purpose of securing the commercial advantages of the whole empire to the mother country, and the commercial benefits of its respective members; excluding every idea of taxation, internal or external, for raising a revenue on the subjects in America, without their consent.

Resolved, N. C. D. 5. That the respective colonies are entitled to the common law of England, and more especially to the great and inestimable privilege of being tried by their peers of the vicinage, according to the course of that law.

Resolved, 6. That they are entitled to the benefit of such of the English statutes as existed at the time of their colonization; and which they have, by experience, respectively found to be applicable to their several local and other circumstances.

Resolved, N. C. D. 7. That these, his Majesty's colonies, are likewise entitled to all the immunities and privileges granted & confirmed to them by royal charters, or secured by their several codes of provincial laws.

Resolved, N. C. D. 8. That they have a right peaceably to assemble, consider of their grievances, and petition the king; and that all prosecutions, prohibitory proclamations and commitments for the same, are illegal.

Resolved, N. C. D. 9. That the keeping a standing army in these colonies, in times of peace, without the consent of the legislature of that colony, in which such army is kept, is against law.

Resolved, N. C. D. 10. It is indispensably necessary to good government, and rendered essential by the English constitution, that the constituent branches of the legislature be independent of each other; that, therefore, the exercise of legislative power in several colonies, by a council appointed, during pleasure, by the Crown, is unconstitutional, dangerous, and destructive to the freedom of American legislation.

All and each of which the aforesaid deputies, in behalf of themselves and their constituents, do claim, demand, and insist on, as their indubitable rights and liberties; which cannot be legally taken from them, altered or abridged by any power whatever, without their own consent, by their representatives in their several provincial legislatures.

In the course of our inquiry, we find many infringements and violations of the foregoing rights, which, from an ardent desire, that harmony and mutual intercourse of affection and interest may be restored, we pass over for the present, and proceed to state such acts and measures as have been adopted since the last war, which demonstrate a system formed to enslave America.

Resolved, N. C. D. That the following Acts of Parliament are infringements and violations of the rights of the colonists; and that the repeal of them is essentially necessary in order to restore harmony between Great Britain and the American colonies, viz:

The several Acts of 4 Geo. III, c. 15 and c. 34; 5 Geo. III, c. 25 · 6 Geo. III, c. 52; 7 Geo. III, c. 41 and c. 46; 8 Geo. III, c. 22, which impose duties for the purpose of raising a revenue in America, extend the powers of the admiralty courts beyond their ancient limits, deprive the American subject of trial by jury, authorize the judges' certificate to indemnify the prosecutor from damages that he might otherwise be liable to, requiring oppressive security from a claimant of ships and goods seized, before he shall be allowed to defend his property, and are subversive of American rights.

Also the 12 Geo. III, c. 24, entitled "An Act for the better securing his Majesty's dockyards, magazines, ships, ammunition, and stores", which declares a new offence in America, and deprives the American subject of a constitutional trial by a jury of the vicinage, by authorizing the trial of any person charged with the committing any offence described in the said Act, out of the realm, to be indicted and tried for the same in any shire or county within the realm.

Also the three Acts passed in the last session of Parliament, for stopping the port and blocking up the harbour of Boston, for altering the charter and government of the Massachusetts Bay, and that which is entitled "An Act for the better administration of justice", etc.

Also the Act passed in the same session for establishing the Roman Catholic religion in the province of Quebec, abolishing the equitable system of English laws, and erecting a tyranny there, to the great danger, from so total a dissimilarity of religion, law, and government of the neighbouring British colonies, by the assistance of whose blood and treasure the said country was conquered from France.

Also the Act passed in the same session for the better providing suitable quarters for officers and soldiers in his Majesty's service in North America.

Also that the keeping a standing army in several of these colonies, in time of peace, without the consent of the legislature of that colony in which such army is kept, is against law.

To these grievous acts and measures, Americans cannot submit, but in hopes that their fellow subjects in Great Britain will, on a revision of them, restore us to that state in which both countries found happiness and prosperity, we have for the present only resolved to pursue the following peaceable measures:

1. To enter into a non-importation, non-consumption, and non-exportation agreement or association.

2. To prepare an address to the people of Great Britain, and a memorial to the inhabitants of British America, and

3. To prepare a loyal address to his Majesty, agreeable to resolutions already entered into.

149. Debate on the Galloway plan of union ([28 September] 1774)

John Adams's notes of the debates on the Galloway plan reveal even more clearly than the notes of the debates in the committee to state the rights of the colonies (No. 147), the division of opinion between the popular and conservative leaders. Galloway explained his motives for introducing his

plan later (see No. 146) but his speech at the time elaborated the conservative view of the necessity
of a sovereign central government. It was a view which continued to be held by those conservatives
who became revolutionists after 1776, and notably by John Jay and James Duane, who supported
Galloway's plan. Printed: John Adams, *Works*, II, pp. 387–391.

Mr. [Joseph] Galloway [Pennsylvania]. The proposal I intended to make having
been opposed, I have waited to hear a more effectual one. A general non-
importation from Great Britain and Ireland has been adopted, but I think this will
be too gradual in its operation for the relief of Boston. A general non-exportation
I have ever looked on as an undigested proposition. It is impossible America can
exist under a total non-exportation. We, in this province, should have tens of thousands
of people thrown upon the cold hand of charity. Our ships would lie by the walls,
our seamen would be thrown out of bread, our shipwrights out of employ, and it
would affect the landed interest. It would weaken us in another struggle, which I fear
is too near.

To explain my plan I must state a number of facts relative to Great Britain and
relative to America. I hope no facts which I shall state will be disagreeable.

In the last war America was in the greatest danger of destruction. This was held
up by the Massachusetts, and by the Congress in 1754. They said we are disunited
among ourselves. There is no indifferent arbiter between us.

Requisitions came over. A number of the colonies gave most extensively and
liberally; others gave nothing or late. Pennsylvania gave late, not for want of zeal
or loyalty, but owing to their disputes with proprietors, their disunited state. These
delinquencies were handed up to the parent state, and these gave occasion to the Stamp
Act. America, with the greatest reason and justice, complained of the Stamp Act.

Had they proposed some plan of policy, some negotiation been set afoot, it would
have terminated in the most happy harmony between the two countries. They repealed
the Stamp Act, but they passed the Declaratory Act.

Without some supreme legislature, some common arbiter, you are not, say they,
part of the state.

I am as much a friend of liberty as exists; and no man shall go further in point of
fortune, or in point of blood, than the man who now addresses you.

Burlamaqui, Grotius, Pufendorf, Hooker. There must be a union of wills and
strength; distinction between a state and a multitude; a state is animated by one soul.

As we are not within the circle of the supreme jurisdiction of the Parliament,
we are independent states. The law of Great Britain does not bind us in any case
whatever.

We want the aid and assistance and protection of the arm of our mother country.
Protection and allegiance are reciprocal duties. Can we lay claim to the money and
protection of Great Britain upon any principles of honour or conscience? Can we
wish to become aliens to the mother state?

We must come upon terms with Great Britain.

Some gentlemen are not for negotiation. I wish I could hear some reason against it.

The minister must be at twenty or thirty millions [expense] to enforce his measures.

I propose this proposition. The plan: two classes of laws. 1. Laws of internal
policy. 2. Laws in which more than one colony are concerned,–raising money for

war. No one act can be done without the assent of Great Britain. No one without the assent of America. A British American legislature.

Mr. [James] Duane [New York]. As I mean to second this motion, I think myself bound to lay before the Congress my reasons. New York thought it necessary to have a congress for the relief of Boston and Massachusetts, and to do more, to lay a plan for a lasting accommodation with Great Britain.

Whatever may have been the motive for departing from the first plan of the Congress, I am unhappy that we have departed from it. The Post-office Act was before the year 1763. Can we expect lasting tranquillity? I have given my full assent to a non-importation and non-exportation agreement.

The right of regulating trade, from the local circumstances of the colonies, and their disconnection with each other, cannot be exercised by the colonies. Massachusetts disputed the Navigation Act, because not represented, but made a law of their own, to enforce that Act. Virginia did the same nearly.

I think justice requires that we should expressly cede to Parliament the right of regulating trade. In the Congress of 1754, which consisted of the greatest and best men in the colonies, this was considered as indispensable.

A civil war with America would involve a national bankruptcy.

Colonel [Richard Henry] Lee [Virginia]. How did we go on for one hundred and sixty years before the year 1763? We flourished and grew. This plan would make such changes in the legislature of the colonies that I could not agree to it without consulting my constituents.

Mr. [John] Jay [New York]. I am led to adopt this plan. It is objected that this plan will alter our constitutions and therefore cannot be adopted without consulting constituents. Does this plan give up any one liberty or interfere with any one right?

Mr. [Patrick] Henry [Virginia]. The original constitution of the colonies was founded on the broadest and most generous base. The regulation of our trade was compensation enough for all the protection we ever experienced from her.

We shall liberate our constituents from a corrupt House of Commons, but throw them into the arms of an American legislature, that may be bribed by that nation which avows, in the face of the world, that bribery is a part of her system of government.

Before we are obliged to pay taxes as they do, let us be as free as they; let us have our trade open with all the world.

We are not to consent by the representatives of representatives. I am inclined to think the present measures lead to war.

Mr. Edward Rutledge [South Carolina]. I came with an idea of getting a bill of rights and a plan of permanent relief. I think the plan may be freed from almost every objection. I think it almost a perfect plan.

Mr. Galloway. In every government, patriarchal, monarchial, aristocratical, or democratical, there must be a supreme legislature.

I know of no American constitution; a Virginia constitution, a Pennsylvania constitution we have; we are totally independent of each other.

Every gentleman here thinks the Parliament ought to have the power over trade because Britain protects it and us. Why then will we not declare it?

Because Parliament and ministry is wicked and corrupt, and will take advantage of such declaration to tax us, and will also reason from this acknowledgment to further power over us.

Answer. We shall not be bound further than we acknowledge it.

Is it not necessary that the trade of the empire should be regulated by some power or other? Can the empire hold together without it? No. Who shall regulate it? Shall the legislature of Nova Scotia or Georgia regulate it? Massachusetts or Virginia? Pennsylvania or New York? It can't be pretended. Our legislative powers extend no further than the limits of our governments. Where then shall it be placed? There is a necessity that an American legislature should be set up, or else that we should give the power to Parliament or king.

150. The Galloway plan of union (28 September 1774)

The idea of a common colonial constitution was not new in 1774. Throughout the early part of the century plans for such a constitution had been proposed both in Britain and in the colonies, but nothing had ever been achieved. Most of the plans had been concerned with the creation of an effective intercolonial organization for the purpose of fighting the French and Indians. After 1763, as the constitutional arguments between Britain and the colonies were elaborated and multiplied, a good many men, including such governors as Francis Bernard of Massachusetts, became convinced that some constitutional definition of the relationship between mother country and colonies must be established. Galloway's plan, which was supported by the conservatives in the First Congress, was a simple constitution clearly defining the powers of the proposed American legislature and its relationship to Parliament. The plan was rejected by the popular leaders and all record erased from the published journals of the Congress. Printed: *Journals of the Continental Congress*, I, pp. 49–51.

Resolved. That the Congress will apply to his Majesty for a redress of grievances under which his faithful subjects in America labour; and assure him that the colonies hold in abhorrence the idea of being considered independent communities on the British government, and most ardently desire the establishment of a political union, not only among themselves, but with the mother state, upon those principles of safety and freedom which are essential in the constitution of all free governments, and particularly that of the British legislature; and as the colonies from their local circumstances cannot be represented in the Parliament of Great Britain, they will humbly propose to his Majesty and his two houses of Parliament, the following plan, under which the strength of the whole empire may be drawn together on any emergency, the interest of both countries advanced, and the rights and liberties of America secured.

A Plan of a proposed Union between Great Britain and the Colonies

That a British and American legislature, for regulating the administration of the general affairs of America, be proposed and established in America, including all the said colonies; within, and under which government, each colony shall retain its present constitution, and powers of regulating and governing its own internal police, in all cases whatsoever.

That the said government be administered by a president-general, to be appointed by the king, and a grand council, to be chosen by the representatives of the people of the several colonies, in their respective assemblies, once in every three years.

That the several assemblies shall choose members for the grand council in the following proportions, viz.

New Hampshire	Delaware Counties
Massachusetts Bay	Maryland
Rhode Island	Virginia
Connecticut	North Carolina
New York	South Carolina
New Jersey	Georgia
Pennsylvania	

Who shall meet at the city of   for the first time, being called by the president-general, as soon as conveniently may be after his appointment.

That there shall be a new election of members for the grand council every three years; and on the death, removal or resignation of any member, his place shall be supplied by a new choice, at the next sitting of assembly of the colony he represented.

That the grand council shall meet once in every year, if they shall think it necessary, and oftener, if occasions shall require, at such time and place as they shall adjourn to, at the last preceding meeting, or as they shall be called to meet at, by the president-general, on any emergency.

That the grand council shall have power to choose their speaker, and shall hold and exercise all the like rights, liberties and privileges as are held and exercised by and in the House of Commons of Great Britain.

That the president-general shall hold his office during the pleasure of the king, and his assent shall be requisite to all acts of the grand council, and it shall be his office and duty to cause them to be carried into execution.

That the president-general, by and with the advice and consent of the grand council, hold and exercise all the legislative rights, powers, and authorities necessary for regulating and administering all the general police and affairs of the colonies in which Great Britain and the colonies, or any of them, the colonies in general, or more than one colony, are in any manner concerned, as well civil and criminal as commercial.

That the said president-general and the grand council be an inferior and distinct branch of the British legislature, united and incorporated with it, for the aforesaid general purposes; and that any of the said general regulations may originate and be formed and digested, either in the Parliament of Great Britain, or in the said grand council, and being prepared, transmitted to the other for their approbation or dissent; and that the assent of both shall be requisite to the validity of all such general acts or statutes.

That in time of war, all bills for granting aid to the Crown, prepared by the grand council, and approved by the president-general, shall be valid and passed into a law, without the assent of the British Parliament.

151. The Association of the First Continental Congress (20 October 1774)

The Association was a victory for the popular method of opposition to Britain: the complete suspension of trade. In effect it was an implementation of the idea of the non-consumption of British goods which had been proposed as early as 1767. Economically the Association was effective, for it has been estimated that colonial imports dropped over ninety per cent between 1774 and 1775. It had little if any influence on British policy for the British were now determined to exact obedience no matter what the economic consequences might be.

Its political consequences were far more important than its economic. In effect, it forced all Americans to choose between support of the proposals of Congress and obedience to the laws of Parliament. Furthermore, it was a major step in the development of revolutionary political organizations. The committees created in every community to enforce the Association were largely controlled by the popular leaders. Within a short time many of these committees were ignoring local governments, and in time they were to supplant most of them. Printed: *Journals of the Continental Congress,* 1, pp. 75–80.

We, his Majesty's most loyal subjects, the delegates of the several colonies of New Hampshire, Massachusetts Bay, Rhode Island, Connecticut, New York, New Jersey, Pennsylvania, the three lower counties of Newcastle, Kent, and Sussex on Delaware, Maryland, Virginia, North Carolina, and South Carolina, deputed to represent them in a continental congress, held in the city of Philadelphia, on the 5th day of September, 1774, avowing our allegiance to his Majesty, our affection and regard for our fellow-subjects in Great Britain and elsewhere, affected with the deepest anxiety and most alarming apprehensions, at those grievances and distresses, with which his Majesty's American subjects are oppressed; and having taken under our most serious deliberation the state of the whole continent, find that the present unhappy situation of our affairs is occasioned by a ruinous system of colony administration, adopted by the British ministry about the year 1763, evidently calculated for enslaving these colonies, and with them, the British Empire. In prosecution of which system, various Acts of Parliament have been passed for raising a revenue in America, for depriving the American subjects, in many instances, of the constitutional trial by jury, exposing their lives to danger, by directing a new and illegal trial beyond the seas, for crimes alleged to have been committed in America; and in prosecution of the same system, several late, cruel and oppressive Acts have been passed, respecting the town of Boston and the Massachusetts Bay, and also an Act for extending the province of Quebec, so as to border on the western frontiers of these colonies, establishing an arbitrary government therein, and discouraging the settlement of British subjects in that wide extended country; thus, by the influence of civil principles and ancient prejudices, to dispose the inhabitants to act with hostility against the free Protestant colonies, whenever a wicked ministry shall choose so to direct them.

To obtain redress of these grievances which threaten destruction to the lives, liberty, and property of his Majesty's subjects, in North America, we are of opinion that a non-importation, non-consumption, and non-exportation agreement, faithfully adhered to, will prove the most speedy, effectual, and peaceable measure: and therefore, we do, for ourselves, and the inhabitants of the several colonies whom we represent, firmly agree and associate, under the sacred ties of virtue, honour and love of our country, as follows:

1. That from and after the first day of December next, we will not import into British America, from Great Britain or Ireland, any goods, wares or merchandise

whatsoever, or from any other place, any such goods, wares, or merchandise, as shall have been exported from Great Britain or Ireland; nor will we, after that day, import any East India tea from any part of the world; nor any molasses, syrups, paneles, coffee, or pimento, from the British plantations or from Dominica; nor wines from Madeira, or the Western Islands; nor foreign indigo.

2. We will neither import nor purchase any slave imported after the first day of December next; after which time we will wholly discontinue the slave trade and will neither be concerned in it ourselves, nor will we hire our vessels, nor sell our commodities or manufactures to those who are concerned in it.

3. As a non-consumption agreement, strictly adhered to, will be an effectual security for the observation of the non-importation, we, as above, solemnly agree and associate, that from this day we will not purchase or use any tea imported on account of the East India Company, or any on which a duty hath been or shall be paid; and from and after the first day of March next, we will not purchase or use any East India tea whatever; nor will we, nor shall any person for or under us, purchase or use any of those goods, wares or merchandise we have agreed not to import, which we shall know, or have cause to suspect, were imported after the first day of December, except such as come under the rules and directions of the tenth article hereafter mentioned.

4. The earnest desire we have not to injure our fellow-subjects in Great Britain, Ireland, or the West Indies, induces us to suspend a non-exportation until the tenth day of September, 1775; at which time, if the said Acts and parts of Acts of the British Parliament hereinafter mentioned are not repealed, we will not, directly or indirectly, export any merchandise or commodity whatsoever to Great Britain, Ireland or the West Indies, except rice to Europe.

5. Such as are merchants, and use the British and Irish trade, will give orders, as soon as possible, to their factors, agents and correspondents, in Great Britain and Ireland, not to ship any goods to them, on any pretence whatsoever, as they cannot be received in America; and if any merchant residing in Great Britain or Ireland shall directly or indirectly ship any goods, wares, or merchandise for America, in order to break the said non-importation agreement, or in any manner contravene the same, on such unworthy conduct being well attested, it ought to be made public; and on the same being so done, we will not, from thenceforth, have any commercial connection with such merchant.

6. That such as are owners of vessels will give positive orders to their captains, or masters, not to receive on board their vessels any goods prohibited by the said non-importation agreement, on pain of immediate dismission from their service.

7. We will use our utmost endeavours to improve the breed of sheep and increase their number to the greatest extent; and to that end we will kill them as seldom as may be, especially those of the most profitable kind; nor will we export any to the West Indies or elsewhere; and those of us who are or may become overstocked with, or can conveniently spare any sheep, will dispose of them to our neighbours, especially to the poorer sort, on moderate terms.

8. We will, in our several stations, encourage frugality, economy, and industry,

and promote agriculture, arts, and the manufactures of this country, especially that of wool; and will discountenance and discourage every species of extravagance and dissipation, especially all horse-racing, and all kinds of gaming, cock-fighting, exhibitions of shows, plays, and other expensive diversions and entertainments; and on the death of any relation or friend, none of us, or any of our families, will go into any further mourning-dress than a black crepe or ribbon on the arm or hat, for gentlemen, and a black ribbon and necklace for ladies, and we will discontinue the giving of gloves and scarves at funerals.

9. Such as are vendors of goods or merchandise will not take advantage of the scarcity of goods, that may be occasioned by this association but will sell the same at the rates we have been respectively accustomed to do for twelve months last past. And if any vendor of goods or merchandise shall sell any such goods on higher terms, or shall, in any manner, or by any device whatsoever violate or depart from this agreement, no person ought, nor will any of us deal with any such person, or his or her factor or agent, at any time thereafter, for any commodity whatever.

10. In case any merchant, trader, or other person, shall import any goods or merchandise after the first day of December, and before the first day of February next, the same ought forthwith, at the election of the owner, to be either reshipped or delivered up to the committee of the county or town wherein they shall be imported, to be stored at the risk of the importer until the non-importation agreement shall cease, or be sold under the direction of the committee aforesaid; and in the last mentioned case, the owner or owners of such goods shall be reimbursed out of the sales, the first cost and charges, the profit, if any, to be applied towards relieving and employing such poor inhabitants of the town of Boston as are immediate sufferers by the Boston Port Bill; and a particular account of all goods so returned, stored or sold to be inserted in the public papers; and if any goods or merchandises shall be imported after the said first day of February, the same ought forthwith to be sent back again, without breaking any of the packages thereof.

11. That a committee be chosen in every county, city, and town by those who are qualified to vote for representatives in the legislature, whose business it shall be attentively to observe the conduct of all persons touching this Association; and when it shall be made to appear to the satisfaction of a majority of any such committee that any person within the limits of their appointment has violated this Association, that such majority do forthwith cause the truth of the case to be published in the gazette; to the end that all such foes to the rights of British America may be publicly known, and universally condemned as the enemies of American liberty; and thenceforth we respectively will break off all dealings with him or her.

12. That the committee of correspondence, in the respective colonies, do frequently inspect the entries of their custom houses, and inform each other, from time to time, of the true state thereof, and of every other material circumstance that may occur relative to this Association.

13. That all manufactures of this country be sold at reasonable prices, so that no undue advantage be taken of a future scarcity of goods.

14. And we do further agree and resolve that we will have no trade, commerce,

dealings, or intercourse whatsoever, with any colony or province in North America which shall not accede to, or which shall hereafter violate this Association, but will hold them as unworthy of the rights of freemen, and as inimical to the liberties of their country.

And we do solemnly bind ourselves and our constituents, under the ties aforesaid, to adhere to this Association, until such parts of the several Acts of Parliament passed since the close of the last war, as impose or continue duties on tea, wine, molasses, syrups, paneles, coffee, sugar, pimento, indigo, foreign paper, glass, and painters' colours imported into America, and extend the powers of the admiralty courts beyond their ancient limits, deprive the American subject of trial by jury, authorize the judge's certificate to indemnify the prosecutor from damages, that he might otherwise be liable to from a trial by his peers, require oppressive security from a claimant of ships or goods seized, before he shall be allowed to defend his property, are repealed. And until that part of the Act of the 12 Geo. III, c. 24, entitled "An Act for the better securing his Majesty's dock-yards, magazines, ships, ammunition, and stores", by which any persons charged with committing any of the offences therein described, in America, may be tried in any shire or county within the realm, is repealed–and until the four Acts, passed the last session of Parliament, viz. that for stopping the port and blocking up the harbour of Boston–that for altering the charter and government of the Massachusetts Bay–and that which is entitled "An act for the better administration of justice, etc."–and that "for extending the limits of Quebec, etc." are repealed. And we recommend it to the provincial conventions, and to the committees in the respective colonies, to establish such farther regulations as they may think proper, for carrying into execution this Association.

The foregoing Association being determined upon by the Congress, was ordered to be subscribed by the several members thereof; and thereupon, we have hereunto set our respective names accordingly.

152. Political Observations, without Order: addressed to the People of America (14 November 1774)

The following essay with its emphasis on the depravity of kings, the sovereignty of the people, and the desirability of independence, shows that popular opinion was far in advance of that expressed in official documents such as the various papers of the First Continental Congress. Whatever the private opinions of the popular leaders may have been in 1774, they could not afford to admit publicly that independence was their goal. If that was their aim, and doubtless it was, they would have lost much of their support and the organized opposition to Britain might well have collapsed. This did not affect newspaper writers, who could remain anonymous while stirring up popular support. Printed: Force, *American Archives*, 4th Series, I, pp. 976–977.

1. All power of government is derived from God through the instrumentality of kings or the people. Has the impartial governor of the universe communicated his attributes of power, wisdom, justice, and mercy to kings only, and denied the least portion of them to every other class of mankind? Let history decide this question. The history of kings is nothing but the history of the folly and depravity of human nature.

2. To live (says Bishop Hoadly) by one man's will became the cause of all men's misery. If the Bible was silent, analogy would teach us that the depravity and misery

of one man could contaminate and render miserable a whole race of men. Look up then, mortals, to kings with humility. They are living histories of your first calamity. One man still continues to be the source of misery and depravity in all the kingdoms of the world. God deals with all mankind as he did with the Jews. He gives them kings only in his anger. We read now and then, it is true, of a good king; so we read likewise of a prophet escaping unhurt from a lion's den, and of three men walking in a fiery furnace without having even their garments singed. The order of nature is as much inverted in the first as it was in the last two cases. A good king is a miracle.

3. The American Congress derives all its power, wisdom, and justice, not from scrolls of parchment signed by kings, but from the people. A more august, and a more equitable legislative body never existed in any quarter of the globe. It is founded upon the principles of the most perfect liberty. A freeman in honouring and obeying the Congress, honours and obeys himself. The man who refuses to do both is a slave. He knows nothing of the dignity of his nature. He cannot govern himself. Expose him for sale at a public vendue. Send him to plant sugar with his fellow slaves in Jamaica. Let not the air of America be contaminated with his breath.

4. The Congress like other legislative bodies, have annexed penalties to their laws. They do not consist of the gallows, the rack, and the stake. These punishments belong to vindictive states, and are proper only for a corrupted people. They have held out no punishments but infamy, a species of infamy which sound more dreadful to a freeman than the gallows, the rack, or the stake. It is this, he shall be declared in the public papers to be an enemy to his country.

5. The wisdom and revenge of man have been exhausted to find out a suitable punishment for treason, or for those crimes which affect the liberty and happiness of a people. The least deviation from the resolves of the Congress will be treason—such treason as few villains have ever had an opportunity of committing. It will be treason against the present inhabitants of the colonies—against the millions of unborn generations who are to exist hereafter in America; against the only liberty and happiness which remain to mankind; against the last hopes of the wretched in every corner of the world. In a word, it will be treason against God. It will be to take from him (with reverence be it spoken) the power of making his creatures happy. I do not attempt to hint a punishment for such extensive and complicated guilt. Infamy is a punishment of the soul. It can only affect a free man. The body of the wretch who is capable of violating the resolves of the Congress is the only part of him which can be punished. But here all ingenuity fails us. The tortures of Damien and Ravillac would be rendered abortive for this purpose by the longest possible duration of human life.

6. There is a strange veneration for antiquity and disinclination for innovations in all civil as well as religious bodies. We are now laying the foundation of an American constitution. Let us therefore hold up everything we do to the eye of posterity. They will probably measure their liberties and happiness by the most careless of our footsteps. Let no unhallowed hand touch the precious seed of liberty. Let us form the glorious tree in such a manner, and impregnate it with such principles of life that it shall last forever. Greece, Rome, and Britain would still have been free had not the

principles of corruption been concealed in the elements of their constitutions. Let us not avail ourselves of the just spirit of the times, but bind up posterity to be freemen. Our Congress were actuated with this prophetic benevolence when they dissolved themselves, and recommended a new choice of delegates in the spring.

7. There is some reason to fear that the steps we are obliged to take to defend our liberties will render us careless in establishing them. Wise and good men in Britain have lifted up the curtain of futurity in America. Let us not be afraid to look through it. Ye intuitive spirits who see through the connection of cause and effect: ye holy spirits who have been accustomed to trace the operations of Divine Providence: ye decisive spirits who resolve and execute at once–ye know what I mean. "*In eternitatem pingo*" said a poet. Let us neither think, write, speak, nor act without keeping our eyes fixed upon the period which shall dissolve our connection with Great Britain. The delirium of the present ministry may precipitate it, but the ordinary course of human things must accomplish it. Britain may relax from her present arbitrary measures, but political necessity, not justice, must hereafter be the measure of her actions. Free men cannot bear a middle state between liberty and slavery. It is essential to the happiness of liberty that it should be secure and perpetual.

8. A rotation of offices is one of the life-guards of liberty. The right as well as the obligations to legislation are alike binding upon all men. To prevent pride and excessive popularity, and to diffuse knowledge and virtue, are the surest methods of securing and perpetuating public liberty. These are to be obtained only by a constant rotation of offices.

9. I almost wish to live to hear the triumphs of the Jubilee in the year 1874; to see the medals, pictures, fragments of writings, etc., that shall be displayed to revive the memory of the proceedings of the Congress in the year 1774. If any adventitious circumstance shall give precedency on that day, it shall be to inherit the blood or even to possess the name of a member of that glorious assembly. I cannot after this be understood to mean the least reflection upon any one of that body when I urge that only one half, or at most two thirds of the old members should be returned from each colony to attend the next Congress. The good dispositions in human nature sometimes lead us astray in public affairs. Do not, illustrious senators, avail yourselves of the gratitude and veneration of your countrymen. You have, we trust, made them free. But a nobler task awaits you. Instruct them, instruct posterity in the great science of securing and perpetuating freedom.

153. 'M' to the Printer of the *New York Gazetteer*

The appearance of "Political Observations, Without Order" (No. 152) was greeted as proof of the charge that the popular leaders, the 'Republicans', really wanted independence despite their denials. The following newspaper essay is typical of the many articles and pamphlets attacking the proceedings of the First Continental Congress. Printed: Force, *American Archives*, 4th Series, I, pp. 978–979.

Happening to be in several companies lately where the conversation fell upon a most extraordinary piece published in the *Pennsylvania Packet* and afterwards transcribed into the *New-York Journal*, entitled "Political Observations, without Order, addressed to the People of America", it was by all present except myself, condemned as a vile, inflammatory, and treasonable publication. As I could wish my reasons for dissenting from the opinions of so many respectable persons were more generally known, I beg leave, through the channel of your paper, to lay them before the public.

Every essay that makes its appearance in a paper which is confessedly under the influence of the republican party and is copied into other papers of the same stamp I consider as containing the sentiments of that party; it is their general way of broaching a new doctrine, to try how it will be relished by the palates of the people. As to myself, I am without a doubt that the republicans of North America, particularly those of New England, have long been aiming at independency, and that they have eagerly seized this golden opportunity when discontent prevails throughout the colonies, to establish a grand American commonwealth; but there are many honest, well-meaning people who join heartily in contending for what they esteem their privileges, without knowing that they are in danger of being precipitated into the other extreme–of being awakened from their pleasing dreams of liberty by the shackles of a republican commonwealth. It is to open the eyes of these secure politicians that so many pens have lately been drawn; but no argument strikes so forcibly, or carries more conviction to the mind, than those voluntary effusions of a hair-brained republican. Such persons cannot be tied down to secrecy by their adherents till a proper time arrives for a disclosure of the grand arcana; their zeal hurries them on beyond the bounds of reason and their own shallow judgment, and then it is no wonder they should let the cat out of the bag before they are aware.

I never take up a newspaper which I know to be under republican influence but I expect to be put to the trouble of deciphering some enigmatical sentence, or of developing some deep laid scheme; on the contrary, the author of the Political Considerations saves me all this trouble; he stands acquitted, at least, of bearing the hypocritical badge of his party. Commend me to the man who speaks his sentiments undisguised, whatever they may be; and let me not be deceived by one who wears a vizor to hide his deformity and endeavours to win me over by stratagem; this writer makes no scruple of throwing off the mask, and appears in all the terrible pomp of his own horrid visage.

Notwithstanding the secrecy enjoined, and so strongly insisted on by the republican part of the Congress, it is now pretty generally known and believed that the first grand question proposed was the throwing off all subordination to Great Britain; and when the republicans found this point could not be carried, many of the members threatening to return home if it was not given up, they were compelled to adopt the present plan with a view of distressing the parent country; that by causing intestine broils at home, it would force her to recall her troops from America, and then they might usurp the reins of government unmolested; and yet this plan, moderate as it may appear compared with the idea of an immediate usurpation, was not obtained without the meanest arts and the vilest intrigues, both in and out of Congress. It is even now a matter of doubt whether some of the members did not sign the Association more out of fear of popular resentment than from the calm dictates of their own unbiased judgment.

In a little time I expect to lay before the public some secrets that will equally astonish and confound the generality of your readers. There are matters yet to be disclosed, the bare relation of which will

> "Make mad the guilty, and appal the free,
> Confound the ign'rant, and amaze indeed
> The very faculties of eyes and ears."

C. WARFARE BEGINS, 1774–1775

DURING the autumn and winter of 1774–1775 the various colonies began to prepare for war by collecting arms and ammunition and by urging the encouragement of local manufactures. On 12 September General Gage wrote Dartmouth that "the country people are exercising in arms in this province, Connecticut, and Rhode Island, and getting magazines of arms and ammunition in the country, and such artillery as they can procure, good and bad. They threaten to attack the troops in Boston, and are very angry at a work throwing up at the entrance of the town. . . ." In letter after letter during the following months Gage continued to report on the growing preparations for war.

In September 1774 Gage issued writs for an election for the Massachusetts House of Representatives. The election was held, but Gage decided not to meet the House since virtually all the members of the new royally appointed council had been so intimidated that they refused to serve. Nevertheless, a group of the men elected proceeded to meet and declared themselves a provincial congress. In October the congress appointed a committee to survey the armed resources of the colony, appointed generals, and began organizing the militia.[1] Minute Men companies were formed, ready for action at a moment's notice.[2] A second provincial congress met in February and took further steps to prepare for war. It appointed more generals and directed them to oppose the British by force, if necessary. It ordered the gathering of military stores. On 5 April it adopted articles of war.[3]

On 8 April the congress formally resolved by a vote of 96 out of 103 members present that it was necessary for defence and security to establish an army. Messages were sent to the other New England colonies asking them to furnish quotas "for the general defence".

Similar events were taking place in other colonies. In December 1774 Lord Dunmore, governor of Virginia, reported that royal authority was at an end. A second provincial convention met in Virginia in March 1775. As the counties elected delegates, many of them instructed their delegates specifically to prepare the colony for defence.[4] A few days after the convention met, Patrick Henry offered a series of resolutions concluding with one which proposed that the colony "be immediately put in a posture of defence" and that a committee be appointed to "prepare a plan for the embodying, arming, and disciplining such a number of men as may be sufficient for that purpose".[5] It was on this occasion that Patrick Henry gave the most famous speech of the Revolutionary era, at least in the eyes of posterity, for no contemporary account of it exists. Many years later his biographer, depending on the memories of old men who heard the speech, wrote that Henry concluded by saying: "Is life so dear, or peace so sweet, as to be purchased at the price of chains and slavery? Forbid it, Almighty God! I know not what course others may take; but as for me, give me liberty or give me death!"

Not all the delegates were swept off their feet by Henry's oratory. They still believed that reconciliation was possible, but in the end the convention agreed to the

[1] No. 154.   [2] No. 155.   [3] No. 158.   [4] No. 156.   [5] No. 157.

appointment of a committee to arm the colony and a second committee to prepare a plan for encouraging the "arts and manufactures in this colony".

It was, however, in Massachusetts that the event occurred which set the colonies ablaze. General Gage had fortified Boston, and from time to time had sent out expeditions to capture stores of ammunition gathered together by the Americans. No open clash came until General Gage dispatched a body of troops to confiscate a supply of arms and ammunition stored at Concord. Paul Revere carried word in advance that the troops were coming. When they got to Lexington on the morning of 19 April 1775, they were met by Minute Men, and the fighting began. The British moved on to Concord, but by this time the entire countryside had been aroused. The British were driven back to Boston.

As a purely military operation the event was insignificant, but it had an explosive effect on American opinion everywhere. The Massachusetts provincial congress secured depositions describing British atrocities and prepared messages which were sent everywhere describing the brutalities committed by the soldiers. According to the British, the Americans likewise committed atrocities. General Gage's own account of the event was strictly factual.[1]

As the news reached other colonies, popular resentment flared to great heights. Lieutenant-Governor Colden in New York wrote that when the report reached New York "the moment of consternation and anxiety was seized. The people were assembled, and that scene of disorder and violence begun which has entirely prostrated the powers of government, and produced an association by which this province has solemnly united with the others in resisting the Acts of Parliament." New York City was virtually in the hands of a mob for a time. The arsenal was broken into and arms distributed to the people; the customs house was closed. In Philadelphia, Richard Henry Lee, who had just arrived to attend the Second Continental Congress, declared the event had "roused such an universal resentment against this savage ministry and their detestable agents, that now no doubt remains of their destruction with the establishment of American rights". Even a mild Quaker could write in his diary: "it's admirable to see the alteration of the Tory class in this place, since the account of the engagement in New England; their language is quite softened, and many of them have so far renounced their former sentiments as that they have taken up arms, and are joined in the Association; nay, even many of the stiff Quakers. . . ." When the news reached South Carolina on 8 May, regiments were raised at once and the South Carolina provincial congress declared its support of the cause in a resounding association. Back-countrymen in North Carolina met and declared that civil and military commissions under the Crown were null and void.

In Massachusetts the provincial congress resolved that an army of 30,000 men should be raised immediately and declared that Massachusetts' quota would be 13,600. Within a few days General Gage and his army were blockaded in the town of Boston, then virtually an island. Men poured in from all over New England to join the Massachusetts troops. The first real battle of the war took place on 17 June, the battle of Bunker Hill. The Americans occupied the heights above Charlestown to the north of Boston, and the British ferried across the river and drove them off. The British victory was a costly one. It has been estimated that of all the British officers killed during the entire war, one-eighth lost their lives at Bunker Hill. Though the Americans were defeated, General Gage declared that "the trials we have had show

[1] No. 159A, B, and C.

that the rebels are not the despicable rabble too many have supposed them to be, and I find it owing to a military spirit encouraged amongst them for a few years past, joined with an uncommon degree of zeal and enthusiasm. . ."

American 'enthusiasm' for war was probably never higher than in the summer and autumn of 1775, but the final determination between peace and war lay in the hands of the king and Parliament on one hand, and the Second Continental Congress on the other. Step by step the former made it clear that war it would be if the Americans refused to surrender. But the Second Continental Congress debated month after month before coming to an equally clear decision. It agreed to oppose British force with American force, but it continued to delay a complete break with Britain because large numbers of its members hoped for a reconciliation that would make it possible to stay within the British Empire. It was not until after the first great upsurge of popular enthusiasm had cooled that the Second Continental Congress adopted the Declaration of Independence.

154. Resolutions of the Massachusetts provincial congress recommending the development of manufactures (8 December 1774)

Recommendations that home manufactures be developed and used in the colonies had been a part of the pattern of opposition to Britain ever since 1763. From 1774 onward the threat of war lent a real urgency to such recommendations, for the colonies lacked many domestic resources and particularly arms and ammunition. The following recommendations adopted by the Massachusetts provincial congress are some of the earliest of the kind adopted by virtually every colony before the end of 1775. Printed: William Lincoln, ed., *The Journals of each Provincial Congress of Massachusetts in 1774 and 1775* (Boston, 1838), pp. 62–65.

As the happiness of particular families arises in a great degree from their being more or less dependent upon others; and as the less occasion they have for any article belonging to others, the more independent; and consequently the happier they are; so the happiness of every political body of men upon earth is to be estimated in a great measure upon their greater or less dependence upon any other political bodies; and from hence arises a forcible argument, why every state ought to regulate their internal policy in such a manner as to furnish themselves, within their own body, with every necessary article for subsistence and defence. Otherwise their political existence will depend upon others who may take advantage of such weakness and reduce them to the lowest state of vassalage and slavery. For preventing so great an evil, more to be dreaded than death itself, it must be the wisdom of this colony at all times, more especially at this time, when the hand of power is lashing us with the scorpions of despotism, to encourage agriculture, manufactures and economy, so as to render this state as independent of every other state as the nature of our country will admit. From the consideration thereof, and trusting that the virtue of the people of this colony is such that the following resolutions of this congress, which must be productive of the greatest good, will by them be effectually carried into execution. And it is therefore resolved:

1st. That we do recommend to the people the improvement of their breed of sheep, and the greatest possible increase of the same; and also the preferable use of our own woollen manufactures; and to manufacturers, that they ask only reasonable prices for their goods; and especially a very careful sorting of the wool, so that it may be manufactured to the greatest advantage, and as much as may be, into the best goods.

2nd. We do also recommend to the people the raising of hemp and flax; and as large quantities of flax-seed, more than may be wanted for sowing, may be produced, we would also farther recommend the manufacturing the same into oil.

3rd. We do likewise recommend the making of nails; which we do apprehend must meet with the strongest encouragement from the public, and be of lasting benefit both to the manufacturer and the public.

4th. The making of steel, and the preferable use of the same, we do also recommend to the inhabitants of this colony.

5th. We do in like manner recommend the making tin-plate, as an article well worth the attention of this people.

6th. As fire-arms have been manufactured in several parts of this colony, we do recommend the use of such, in preference to any imported. And we do recommend the making gun-locks, and furniture and other locks, with other articles in the iron way.

7th. We do also earnestly recommend the making of salt-petre, as an article of vast importance to be encouraged, as may be directed hereafter.

8th. That gunpowder is also an article of such importance, that every man among us who loves his country, must wish the establishment of manufactories for that purpose, and, as there are the ruins of several powder mills, and sundry persons among us who are acquainted with that business, we do heartily recommend its encouragement, by repairing one or more of said mills, or erecting others, and renewing said business as soon as possible.

9th. That as several paper mills are now usefully employed, we do likewise recommend a preferable use of our own manufactures in this way; and a careful saving and collecting of rags, etc., and also that the manufacturers give a generous price for such rags, etc.

10th. That it will be the interest, as well as the duty of this body, or of such as may succeed us, to make such effectual provision for the further manufacturing of the several sorts of glass, as that the same may be carried on to the mutual benefit of the undertaker and the public, and firmly established in this colony.

11th. Whereas buttons of excellent qualities and of various sorts are manufactured among us, we do earnestly recommend the general use of the same; so that the manufactories may be extended to the advantage of the people and the manufacturers.

12th. And whereas salt is an article of vast consumption within this colony, and in its fisheries, we do heartily recommend the making the same, in the several ways wherein it is made in several parts of Europe; especially in the method used in that part of France where they make bay-salt.

13th. We do likewise recommend an encouragement of horn-smiths in all their various branches, as what will be of public utility.

14th. We do also recommend the establishment of one or more manufactories for making wool-comber's combs, as an article necessary in our woollen manufactures.

15th. We do in like manner heartily recommend the preferable use of the stockings and other hosiery wove among ourselves, so as to enlarge the manufactories thereof, in such a manner as to encourage the manufacturers and serve the country.

16th. As madder is an article of great importance in the dyer's business, and which may be easily raised and cured among ourselves, we do therefore earnestly recommend the raising and curing the same.

17th. In order the more effectually to carry these resolutions into effect, we do earnestly recommend, that a society or societies be established for the purposes of introducing and establishing such arts and manufactures as may be useful to this people, and are not yet introduced, and the more effectually establishing such as we already have among us.

18th. We do recommend to the inhabitants of this province to make use of our own manufactures, and those of our sister colonies, in preference to all other manufactures.

155. Agreement of the Ipswich, Massachusetts Minute Men (24 January 1775)

On 29 October 1774 the Massachusetts provincial congress ordered the publication of various resolutions which had been adopted. One of these urged militia companies that had not done so, to meet and choose officers, the officers to form regiments and companies. These companies, of at least fifty privates each, "shall equip and hold themselves in readiness to march at the shortest notice . . .". Such companies were formed throughout Massachusetts and took the name of Minute Men. The agreement which follows is typical of those drawn up by these voluntary companies. Printed: *Essex Institute Historical Collections*, XIV, pp. 237-238.

We whose names are hereunto subscribed do voluntarily enlist ourselves as minute men, to be ready for military operation upon the shortest notice. And we hereby promise and engage that we will immediately, each of us, provide for and equip himself with an effective fire-arm, bayonet, pouch, knapsack, and round of cartridges ready made. And that we may obtain the skill of complete soldiers, we promise to convene for exercise in the art military, at least twice every week; and oftener, if our officers shall think necessary. And as soon as such a number shall be enlisted as the present captain, lieutenant, and ensign of the company of militia shall think necessary, we will proceed to choose such officers as shall appear to them and to the company to be necessary; the officers to be chosen by a majority of the votes of the enlisted company. And when the officers are duly chosen, we hereby promise and engage that we will punctually render all that obedience to them respectively as is required by the laws of this province, or practised by any well regulated troops. And if any officer or soldier shall neglect to attend the time and place of exercise, he shall forfeit and pay the sum of two shillings lawful money for the use of the company unless he can offer such an excuse to the officers of the company as to them shall appear sufficient.

N.B.—It is to be understood that when nine companies of fifty men each are enlisted, that then the said officers of the minute companies proceed to choose their field officers, agreeable to the proposal of the provincial congress.

156. Instructions of the freeholders of Cumberland County, Virginia to their delegates to the Second Provincial Convention (March 1775)

As provincial congresses and conventions met more and more frequently during 1774 and 1775, the voters in the townships and counties continued to instruct the delegates as they had done when electing members of the colonial legislatures. The following instructions demonstrate the local support behind the activities of the provincial meetings. Printed: Niles, *Principles and Acts of the Revolution*, p. 276.

We, the freeholders of Cumberland County, having elected you to represent us in a provincial convention to be held in the town of Richmond on Monday the 20th of this instant, and being convinced that the safety and happiness of British America depend on the unanimity, firmness, and joint efforts of all the colonies, we expect you will, on your parts, let your measures be as much for the common safety as the peculiar interests of this colony will permit; and that you, in particular, comply with the recommendation of the Continental Congress in appointing delegates to meet in the city of Philadelphia in May next.

The means of constitutional legislation in this colony, being now interrupted, and entirely precarious, and being convinced that some rule is necessary for speedily putting the colony in a state of defence, we, in an especial manner, recommend this matter to your consideration in convention; and you may depend that any general tax, by that body imposed, for such purposes, will be cheerfully submitted to and paid by the inhabitants of this county.

We desire that you will consider the Bostonians as suffering in the common cause, and cheerfully join in their support to the utmost of your power.

That you will direct the deputies to congress, on the parts of this colony, to use their best endeavours to establish a trade between the colonies; and to procure a quantity of gunpowder and a number of cotton and wool cards from the northward, or elsewhere.

We desire further that you will not depart from the Association formed by the Continental Congress in September last, but will strictly adhere to it in every particular.

157. Resolutions of the Provincial Convention of Virginia (23 March 1775)

The following resolutions, proposed by Patrick Henry and supported by him in his "give me liberty or give me death" speech, placed the Virginia Convention firmly in line with the preparations for war being made in Massachusetts, and did so before the outbreak of hostilities in that colony. Printed: Force, *American Archives*, 4th Series, ii, pp. 167-168.

Resolved, that a well regulated militia composed of gentlemen and yeomen is the natural strength and only security of a free government; that such a militia in this colony would forever render it unnecessary for the mother country to keep among us, for the purpose of our defence, any standing army of mercenary forces, always subversive of the quiet, and dangerous to the liberties of the people, and would obviate the pretext of taxing us for their support.

That the establishment of such a militia is at this time peculiarly necessary, by the state of our laws for the protection and defence of the country, some of which have already expired, and others will shortly do so; and that the known remissness of government in calling us together in a legislative capacity renders it too insecure, in this time of danger and distress, to rely that opportunity will be given of renewing them in General Assembly or making any provision to secure our inestimable rights and liberties from those farther violations with which they are threatened.

Resolved therefore, that this colony be immediately put into a posture of defence; and that Patrick Henry, Richard Henry Lee, Robert Carter Nicholas, Benjamin Harrison, Lemuel Riddick, George Washington, Adam Stephen, Andrew Lewis, William Christian, Edmund Pendleton, Thomas Jefferson, and Isaac Zane, Esquires, be a committee to prepare a plan for the embodying, arming, and disciplining such a number of men as may be sufficient for that purpose.

158. Preamble to the Articles of War adopted by the Massachusetts provincial congress (5 April 1775)

Throughout the winter of 1774-1775 the Massachusetts provincial congress steadily prepared for war. Early in April it adopted fifty-three articles of war, to which the following preamble was attached. Printed: *Journals of each Provincial Congress of Massachusetts*, pp. 120-121.

Whereas the lust of power, which of old oppressed, persecuted, and exiled our pious and virtuous ancestors from their fair possessions in Britain, now pursues with tenfold severity us, their guiltless children, who are unjustly and wickedly charged with licentiousness, sedition, treason, and rebellion, and being deeply impressed with a sense of the almost incredible fatigues and hardships our venerable progenitors encountered, who fled from oppression for the sake of civil and religious liberty, for themselves and their offspring, and began a settlement here *on bare creation*, at their own expense; and having seriously considered the duty we owe to God, to the memory of such invincible worthies, to the king, to Great Britain, our country, ourselves, and posterity, do think it our indispensable duty, by all lawful ways and means in our power, to recover, maintain, defend, and preserve the free exercise of all those civil and religious rights and liberties for which many of our forefathers fought, bled, and died, and to hand them down entire, for the free enjoyment of the latest posterity; and whereas the keeping a standing army in any of these colonies in times of peace, without the consent of the legislature of that colony in which such army is kept is against law; and whereas such an army with a large naval force is now placed in the town and harbour of Boston for the purpose of subjecting us to the power of the British Parliament; and whereas we are frequently told by the tools of administration, dupes to ministerial usurpation, that Great Britain will not, in any degree, relax in her measures until we acknowledge her "right of making laws binding upon us in all cases whatever"; and that if we refuse by our denial of her claim, the dispute must be decided by arms; in which, it is said by our enemies, "we shall have no chance, being undisciplined, cowards, disobedient, impatient of command, and possessed of that spirit of levelling which admits of no order, subordination, rule, or government"; and whereas, from the ministerial army and fleet now at Boston, the large re-enforcement of troops expected, the late circular letters to the governors upon the continent, the general tenor of intelligence from Great Britain, and the hostile preparations making here; as also, from the threats and repeated insults of our enemies in the capital town, we have reason to apprehend that the sudden destruction of this province is in contemplation, if not determined upon;

And whereas the great law of self-preservation may suddenly require our raising and keeping an army of observation and defence, in order to prevent or repel any further attempts to enforce the late cruel and oppressive Acts of the British Parliament, which are evidently designed to subject us and the whole continent to the most ignominious slavery; and whereas in case of raising and keeping such an army it will be necessary that the officers and soldiers in the same be fully acquainted with their duty, and that the articles, rules, and regulations thereof be made as plain as possible; and having great confidence in the honour and public virtue of the inhabitants of this colony that they will readily obey the officers chosen by themselves, and will cheerfully do their duty when known, without any such severe articles and rules (except in capital cases), and cruel punishments as are usually practised in standing armies; and will submit to all such rules and regulations as are founded in reason, honour, and virtue; it is therefore *Resolved*, that the following articles, rules, and regulations for the army that may be raised for the defence and security of our lives, liberties, and estates, be, and hereby are, earnestly recommended to be strictly adhered to by all officers, soldiers, and others concerned, as they regard their own honour and the public good.

159A–C. The Battle of Lexington and Concord (19 April 1775)

Few events of the American Revolution were so widely and diversely reported as the first clash between Americans and the British troops. The Massachusetts provincial congress gathered depositions from participants and supposed onlookers and sent copies everywhere. In addition, it prepared various accounts such as the following to the people of Great Britain, which painted a black picture of the behaviour of the British troops (No. 159A). On the other side, some of the British at least, took an equally dim view of the behaviour of the Americans. Ann Hulton had come to Boston with her brother Henry Hulton, one of the customs commissioners, in 1767. Her letters to her friend Mrs. Adam Lightbody of Bristol, from 1767 to 1775, present the Americans in a very unpleasant light. Her account of the battle is in direct contrast to that of the provincial congress (No. 159B). General Gage's account of the event in his letter to Lord Dartmouth is factual (No. 159C).

159A. Massachusetts provincial congress to the Inhabitants of Great Britain (26 April 1775)

Printed: *Journals of each Provincial Congress of Massachusetts*, pp. 154-156.

To the Inhabitants of Great Britain.
Friends and Fellow-Subjects:

Hostilities are at length commenced in this colony by the troops under the command of General Gage, and it being of the greatest importance that an early, true, and authentic account of this inhuman proceeding should be known to you, the congress of this colony have transmitted the same and from want of a session of the honourable Continental Congress, think it proper to address you on this alarming occasion.

By the clearest depositions relative to this transaction, it will appear that on the night preceding the 19 of April instant, a body of the king's troops, under the command of Colonel Smith, were secretly landed at Cambridge with an apparent design to take or destroy the military and other stores provided for the defence of this colony, and deposited at Concord; that some inhabitants of the colony on the night aforesaid, whilst travelling peaceably on the road between Boston and Concord, were seized and greatly abused by armed men who appeared to be officers of General Gage's army; that the town of Lexington by these means was alarmed, and a company of the inhabitants mustered on the occasion; that the regular troops on their way to Concord marched into the said town of Lexington, and the said company, on their approach, began to disperse; that, notwithstanding this, the regulars rushed on with great violence and first began hostilities by firing on said Lexington Company, whereby they killed eight and wounded several others; that the regulars continued their fire until those of said company who were neither killed nor wounded had made their escape; that Colonel Smith with the detachment then marched to Concord, where a number of provincials were again fired on by the troops, and two of them killed, and several wounded, before the provincials fired on them; and that these hostile measures of the troops produced an engagement that lasted through the day in which many of the provincials, and more of the regular troops, were killed and wounded.

To give a particular account of the ravages of the troops as they retreated from Concord to Charlestown, would be very difficult, if not impracticable. Let it suffice to say that a great number of the houses on the road were plundered and rendered unfit for use; several were burnt; women in childbed were driven by the soldiery naked into the streets; old men, peaceably in their houses were shot dead; and such scenes exhibited as would disgrace the annals of the most uncivilized nation.

These, brethren, are marks of ministerial vengeance against this colony for refusing, with her sister colonies, submission to slavery, but they have not yet detached us from our royal sovereign. We profess to be his loyal and dutiful subjects, and so hardly dealt with as we have been, are still ready with our lives and fortunes to defend his person, family, crown, and dignity. Nevertheless, to the persecution and tyranny of his cruel ministry, we will not tamely submit. Appealing to Heaven for the justice of our cause, we determine to die or be free.

We cannot think that the honour, wisdom, and valour of Britons will suffer them to be longer inactive spectators of measures in which they themselves are so deeply interested: measures pursued in opposition to the solemn protests of many noble lords and [the] expressed sense of conspicuous commoners whose knowledge and virtue have long characterized them as some of the greatest men in the nation; measures executing contrary to the interest, petitions, and resolves of many large, respectable, and opulent counties, cities, and boroughs in Great Britain; measures highly incompatible with justice, but still pursued with a specious pretence of easing the nation of its burdens; measures which, if successful, must end in the ruin and slavery of Britain, as well as the persecuted American colonies.

We sincerely hope that the great Sovereign of the universe who hath so often appeared for the English nation, will support you in every rational and manly exertion with these colonies for saving it from ruin, and that in a constitutional connection with the mother country we shall be altogether a free and happy people.

159B. Ann Hulton to Mrs. Adam Lightbody [April, 1775]

Printed: *Letters of a Loyalist Lady* (Cambridge, Mass., 1927), pp. 77-80.

On the 18th instant at 11 at night, about 800 grenadiers and light infantry were ferried across the bay to Cambridge, from whence they marched to Concord, about 20 miles. The congress had been lately assembled at that place, and it was imagined that the general had intelligence of a magazine being formed there and that they were going to destroy it.

The people in the country (who are all furnished with arms and have what they call minute companies in every town ready to march on any alarm) had a signal, it's supposed, by a light from one of the steeples in town, upon the troops embarking. The alarm spread through the country so that before daybreak the people in general were in arms and on their march to Concord. About daybreak a number of the people appeared before the troops near Lexington. They were called to, to disperse, when they fired on the troops and ran off. Upon which the light infantry pursued them and brought down about fifteen of them. The troops went on to Concord and executed the business they were sent on, and on their return found two or three of their people lying in the agonies of death, scalped and their noses and ears cut off and eyes bored out, which exasperated the soldiers exceedingly, a prodigious number of people now occupying the hills, woods, and stone walls along the road. The light troops drove some parties from the hills but all the road being enclosed with stone walls served as a cover to the rebels, from whence they fired on the troops still running off whenever they had fired, but still supplied by fresh numbers who came from many parts of the country. In this manner were the troops harassed in their return for seven [or] eight miles. They were almost exhausted and had expended near the whole of their ammunition when to their great joy they were relieved by a brigade of troops under the command of Lord Percy with two pieces of artillery. The troops now combated with fresh ardour and marched in their return with undaunted countenances, receiving sheets of fire all the way for many miles, yet having no visible enemy to combat with, for they never would face 'em in an open field, but always skulked and fired from behind walls and trees, and out of windows of houses, but this cost them dear for the soldiers entered those dwellings and put all the men to death. Lord Percy has gained great honour by his conduct through this day of severe service; he was exposed to the hottest of the fire and animated the troops with great coolness and spirit. Several officers are wounded and about 100 soldiers. The killed amount to near 50; as to the enemy we can have no exact account but it is said there was about ten times the number of them engaged and that near 1,000 of 'em have fallen.

The troops returned to Charlestown about sunset after having some of 'em marched near fifty miles, and being engaged from daybreak in action, without respite or refreshment, and about ten in the evening they were brought back to Boston. The next day the country poured down its thousands, and at this time from the entrance of Boston Neck at Roxbury round by Cambridge to Charlestown is surrounded by at least 20,000 men, who are raising batteries on three or four different hills. We are now cut off from all communication with the country and many people must soon perish with famine in this place. Some families have laid in store of provisions against a siege. We are threatened, that whilst the outlines are attacked, with a rising of the inhabitants within, and fire and sword, a dreadful prospect before us, and you know how many and how dear are the objects of our care. The Lord preserve us all and grant us an happy issue out of these troubles.

For several nights past I have expected to be roused by the firing of cannon. Tomorrow is Sunday and we may hope for one day of rest. At present a solemn dead silence reigns in the streets, numbers have packed up their effects and quitted the town, but the general has put a stop to any more removing and here remains in town about 9,000 souls (besides the servants of the Crown). These are the greatest security; the general declared that if a gun is fired within the town, the inhabitants shall fall a sacrifice. Amidst our distress and apprehension I am rejoiced our British hero was preserved. My Lord Percy had a great many and miraculous escapes in the late action. This amiable young nobleman with the graces which attracts admiration, possesses the virtues of the heart and all those qualities that form the great soldier–vigilant, active, temperate, humane, great command of temper, fortitude in enduring hardships and fatigue, and intrepidity in dangers. His lordship's behaviour in the day of trial has done honour to the Percys. Indeed, all the officers and soldiers behaved with the greatest bravery, it is said.

159C. General Thomas Gage to the earl of Dartmouth ([22] April 1775)

Printed: Carter, ed., *Gage Correspondence*, I, pp. 396–397.

I am to acquaint your lordship that having received intelligence of a large quantity of military stores being collected at Concord, for the avowed purpose of supplying a body of troops to act in opposition to his Majesty's government, I got the grenadiers and light infantry out of town under the command of Lieutenant-Colonel Smith of the 10th Regiment, and Major Pitcairne of the marines, with as much secrecy as possible, on the 18th at night, and with orders to destroy the said military stores; and supported them the next morning by eight companies of the 4th, the same number of the 23d, 47th, and marines, under the command of Lord Percy. It appears from the firing of alarm guns and ringing of bells that the march of Lieutenant-Colonel Smith was discovered, and he was opposed by a body of men within six miles of Concord, some few of whom first began to fire upon his advanced companies which brought on a fire from the troops that dispersed the body opposed to them; and they proceeded to Concord, where they destroyed all the military stores they could find. On the return of the troops they were attacked from all quarters where any cover was to be found, from whence it was practicable to annoy them, and they were so fatigued with their march that it was with difficulty they could keep out their flanking parties to remove the enemy to a distance, so that they were at length a good deal pressed. Lord Percy then arrived opportunely to their assistance with his brigade and two pieces of cannon, and notwithstanding a continual skirmish for the space of fifteen miles, receiving fire from every hill, fence, house, barn, etc., his lordship kept the enemy off, and brought the troops to Charlestown, from whence they were ferried over to Boston.

Too much praise cannot be given Lord Percy for his remarkable activity and conduct during the whole day. Lieutenant-Colonel Smith and Major Pitcairne did everything men could do, as did all the officers in general, and the men behaved with their usual intrepidity. I send your lordship Lord Percy's and Lieutenant-Colonel Smith's letters to me on this affair, to which I beg leave to refer your lordship for a more circumstantial account of it. I have likewise the honour to transmit your lordship a return of the killed, wounded, and missing. The loss sustained by those who attacked is said to be great.

The whole country was assembled in arms with surprising expedition, and several thousand are now assembled about this town, threatening an attack and getting up artillery. And we are very busy in making preparations to oppose them.

D. KING AND PARLIAMENT v. THE CONTINENTAL CONGRESS, 1775–1776

BEFORE the proceedings of the First Continental Congress were received in Britain, the king, the ministry, and Parliament made it plain that British policy in the colonies would be maintained by force. Lord Dartmouth wrote General Gage in June 1774 that no matter what violence was committed, it must be resisted and "the constitutional authority of the kingdom over its colonies must be vindicated, and its laws obeyed throughout the whole empire. It is not only its dignity and reputation, but its power–nay its very existence depends upon the present moment; for should those ideas of independence which some dangerous and ill-designing persons here are artfully endeavouring to instill into the minds of the king's American subjects once take root, that relation between this kingdom and its colonies which is the bond of peace and power, will soon cease to exist, and destruction must follow disunion." The king was more succinct in his letters to Lord North. In September 1774 he wrote: "the die is now cast, the colonies must either submit or triumph. . . ." A month later he declared that "the New England governments are in a state of rebellion, blows must decide whether they are to be subject to this country or independent. . . ." On the same day in another note, rejecting a proposal by General Gage that certain Acts be suspended, the king said: "we must either master them or totally leave them to themselves and treat them as aliens. . . ."

When Parliament met in November, after the election of 1774, the king's speech reported on events in Massachusetts and declared that he would take every measure to maintain the supremacy of the Crown and of Parliament over the colonies. Both houses returned addresses expressing their abhorrence of events in the colonies and promising the fullest support for necessary measures. The minority in both houses favouring lenity towards the colonies was overridden by decisive majorities. Lord Dartmouth sent a circular letter to the American governors reporting Parliament's approval of the measures of the Crown and expressing the hope that this would remove false impressions and put an end to the hope of support in Britain for the "unwarrantable pretensions which have been held forth by artful and designing men".

The British still had no realization of how widespread colonial opposition had become and how determined many Americans were in that opposition. Furthermore, it took the British some time to realize that Massachusetts was not the only centre of opposition. That colony had been a focal-point of discontent for so long that it was perhaps natural to think that colonial resistance could be ended by solving the problem there, but it was futile to think that it could be done by the issuance of laws, proclamations, speeches, and addresses. General Gage recognized this, but at first his advice was ignored. During 1774 he came to the conclusion that only a large army could suppress colonial resistance, not only in Massachusetts, but in other colonies as well, but the ministry was at first reluctant to increase either the army or navy because of the costs involved.

An even more fundamental defect in British thinking about the colonies was the fact that the king, the ministry, and a majority of Parliament had little or no under-standing of basic American attitudes; attitudes which were held in common by virtually every American political leader, whatever he might think of British policy or of independence. During a century and a half the colonists, steeped in the political and constitutional traditions of England, had built up the tradition and practice of colonial self-government within each of the colonies. They had developed a complex economic life which they felt should be administered in the interests of the colonies. They had evolved a social structure headed by a small but wealthy, self-conscious, and intellectually sophisticated aristocracy of merchants and planters. It was an aristo-cracy which had great vitality for it was constantly being recruited from the ablest men in the colonies as they acquired wealth. Neither birth nor nationality nor religion was a barrier to membership in it. The broad base of colonial society was made up of a small but politically articulate artisan group and a vast majority of independent-minded small farmers who were as politically conscious as the artisans, and many of whom owned the land on which they lived and thus had the right to vote.

Most British officials seemed unaware of these things, or ignored their significance. Nor did they recognize the fact that by 1774 colonial opposition was supported in every colony by well-organized political groups led by extremely able men from all ranks in colonial society and that they possessed power because they had won wide-spread popular support. Yet in 1774 Lord Dartmouth was still insisting that events in the colonies were the work of "the rabble". It is true that the popular leaders often used mob violence to achieve particular ends, but mob violence alone does not explain American opposition. In the end the power of the popular leaders was based on the fact that they expressed forcefully and clearly their conviction that the colonial legis-latures had a position within the colonies equal to that of Parliament in Great Britain. Furthermore, it was a conviction supported by a multiplicity of economic, social, and political conditions. Although these varied from colony to colony, taken together they combined to convince a growing number of Americans that the colonies must be self-governing units within the empire, or entirely independent of it.

Not only did British officials lack understanding of such matters, but their prevail-ing attitude was one of contempt for Americans as individuals as well as for American constitutional theories. Such contempt was never better expressed than by Henry Hulton, who had come to Boston in 1767 as one of the members of the American Board of Customs. In June 1775, in describing the siege of Boston by the Americans, he wrote: "in this army [the British] are many men of noble family, virtuous and amiable characters, and it grieves one that gentlemen, brave British soldiers, should fall by the hands of such despicable wretches as compose the banditti of the country, amongst whom there is not one that has the least pretension to be called a gentleman. They are a most rude, depraved, degenerate race, and it is a mortification to us that they speak English and can trace themselves from that stock." Such being the attitude of a typical minor official in the colonies, it is little wonder that those in London had little awareness of the realities of the problems facing the British in America.

Hence the proclamations issued, the laws passed, and the orders sent to governors, combined above all with the use of force, did little except to convince an increasing number of Americans, including many who wanted to stay within the empire, that independence was the only solution. In October 1774 the Privy Council forbade the export of arms and ammunition from Britain. In January 1775 the colonial governors were ordered to prevent the election of delegates to the Second Continental Congress.

When Parliament met on 19 January, Lord North laid before it a great number of papers relating to American affairs, including those prepared by the First Continental Congress. Shortly thereafter merchants and manufacturers all over Britain began sending in petitions appealing for reconciliation and the avoidance of civil war and citing the economic hardships resulting from the troubles with the colonies.[1] Parliament treated the proceedings of the Continental Congress with scorn. The petitions of British merchants and manufacturers were heard but ignored. A minority in both houses of Parliament made a vigorous but futile attempt to secure a temperate discussion of colonial affairs in terms that had some relation to the realities of the situation.

The upshot of parliamentary consideration was an address by Parliament to the king on 9 February which declared that a rebellion existed in Massachusetts and that it was aided by other colonies. As in November 1774, Parliament urged the king to take the most effectual measures "to enforce due obedience to the laws and authority of the supreme legislature. . . ." A minority in the House of Lords dissented vigorously. It declared that the merchants' petitions should be considered, for merchants knew far more about the colonies than either colonial governors or British officials in the colonies. They urged that there should be time for deliberation before being "driven headlong into a declaration of civil war".

But the majority of Parliament was in no mood for deliberation, conciliation, or delay. The address was presented to the king and received his hearty approval. He wrote Lord North that if its language did not "open the eyes of the deluded Americans . . . it must set every delicate man at liberty to avow the propriety of the most coercive measures". The next day he sent a message to the House of Commons, asking for an increase in the naval and military forces.

The use of the club was not palliated by the extension of a somewhat puny olive branch. Lord North proposed a resolution for reconciliation with the colonies which was adopted by the House of Commons on 28 February. The resolution promised that if any colony agreed to provide money for defence and civil government, and the provision was approved by the king and Parliament, Parliament would not tax the colony concerned.[2] This resolution ignored completely the stand taken by the First Continental Congress. It seems clear from the correspondence between the king and Lord North that the purpose of the resolution was more to appease the opposition in Parliament than to appease the colonies, and, in particular, that it was put forth to win support for further coercive measures. At the same time as the resolution was under consideration, a Bill was being prepared to restrain the commerce of the New England colonies, and a further one was in contemplation which would limit the commerce of certain of the colonies to the south of New England. The New England Restraining Act was approved 30 March 1775. It limited the commerce of New England to Great Britain and the British West Indies, and forbade them to fish on the Newfoundland Banks.[3] Two weeks later another Act restricted the commerce of New Jersey, Pennsylvania, Maryland, Virginia, and South Carolina.[4]

When the Second Continental Congress met in Philadelphia on 10 May 1775 it had to face the fact that fighting had begun in Massachusetts in April and that an army of New Englanders was besieging General Gage in Boston. Popular enthusiasm was at a high point, and in every colony men were preparing for war. Although many members were reluctant, Congress sanctioned the use of force to meet force.

[1] No. 160.   [2] No. 161.   [3] 15 Geo. III, c. 10.   [4] 15 Geo. III, c. 18.

In June, Congress appointed George Washington commander in chief of the troops in New England. To justify its actions, Congress on 6 July adopted the Declaration of the Causes and Necessity for Taking up Arms,[1] a spirited anticipation of the Declaration of Independence.

Despite its approval of the use of force, Congress was not united. The popular leaders were openly willing to engage in warfare, whatever the outcome. But there were almost an equal number of conservative leaders who, although they agreed to the use of force, still hoped for reconciliation with Great Britain. Thus, while they agreed to the Declaration of the Causes for Taking up Arms, they insisted that Congress should again petition the king for redress of grievances. The popular leaders thought it was foolish to petition. John Adams declared that "powder and artillery are the most efficacious sure and infallible conciliatory measures we can adopt". Nevertheless the conservatives had their way, and on 8 July a second petition to the king was agreed to.[2]

Meanwhile Lord North's motion on reconciliation had been laid before Congress late in May. Even if the motion had offered to meet the colonies half-way, the use of the British army and the passage of the restraining Acts made it meaningless. Even those members of Congress who most ardently wanted reconciliation could not accept the terms laid down by Lord North. The second restraining Act had obviously been designed to divide the colonies, since it exempted New York, North Carolina, and the Delaware counties, and Congress recognized its purpose. The New York merchants did argue that if they traded, it would benefit all the colonies, but Congress rejected this proposal out of hand. On 31 July, Congress rejected Lord North's motion in a declaration that further elaborated the colonial claim to the right of self-government and denounced the hypocrisy involved in offering reconciliation while at the same time passing the restraining Acts.[3]

During the autumn of 1775 Congress forged ahead steadily, preparing for further hostilities. From time to time the popular leaders offered proposals which, if adopted, would have been indirect declarations of independence. They urged that customs houses be abolished, that independent governments be set up in the colonies, that a confederation be formed, and that the ports of the colonies be opened to all the world. The conservative members of Congress were frightened by such proposals and managed to defeat them during 1775. They realized that the adoption of any one of them would be a long step in the direction of independence and make reconciliation impossible. To defeat any overt move for a declaration of independence which the popular leaders might make, the conservatives adopted a new strategy in November 1775. By now the conservative leader was John Dickinson of Pennsylvania. Throughout the years preceding 1775 he had denied the legislative supremacy of Parliament, but he did not want independence. As a member of the Pennsylvania Assembly he secured the adoption of instructions to the Pennsylvania delegates in Congress. These instructions forbade the delegates to vote for independence if the issue was raised in Congress.[4] New York, Maryland, Delaware, and South Carolina, where the conservative element was still in control, soon adopted similar instructions.

Meanwhile the king, ministry, and Parliament continued to cut the ground from beneath the feet of those Americans who wanted to stay within the empire. Never once between 1774 and 1776 did the British give such men an opportunity either to stay in control, or to regain control in those colonies in which they had lost it. Time

[1] No. 163.   [2] No. 164.   [3] No. 162.   [4] No. 170.

after time the conservative leaders in Congress were able to block extreme measures by arguing that they would defeat the hope of reconciliation; yet each new ship from England brought news of measures that rendered their arguments futile and proved to more and more Americans that the popular leaders were right in saying that the hope of reconciliation was a delusion. In August 1775 the king issued a proclamation of rebellion aimed at the British supporters of the Americans.[1] In September 1775, when Richard Penn and Arthur Lee brought to Lord Dartmouth the second petition to the king, he told them that it would not be presented to the king. When Parliament met in October, the king's speech declared that the Americans were fighting to establish "an independent empire". In addition, it promised to send commissioners to America to receive the submission of any colony desiring to return to its former allegiance.[2]

The news of the king's speech reached Philadelphia early in January 1776. The conservatives grasped at once at the hope of commissioners and proposed that an address be prepared and sent to the colonies denying that independence was the aim of Congress. The popular leaders were furious at the proposal and got consideration delayed. The address was prepared, however, but on 13 February it was defeated. At the time of the vote the news had just arrived of the American prohibitory Bill which had been introduced in Parliament in November and which was to receive royal approval on 22 December. This Bill, in effect, declared all Americans to be outlaws. It declared the commerce of all the American colonies at an end and the ships and goods of Americans subject to capture and confiscation by British naval vessels.[3]

The news of this Bill was a crushing blow to those who hoped for reconciliation. Their address was defeated and before the end of February, members of Congress were talking openly of a declaration of independence. Only the instructions against independence adopted previously by Pennsylvania and some of the other colonies prevented action at this time. The popular leaders declared that the Prohibitory Act was itself a declaration of independence by Act of Parliament, and wondered that Americans hesitated to accept the gift.[4] But there were other measures they could adopt, and Congress was rapidly swinging over to their side as hope of reconciliation faded. Early in April Congress declared the ports of America open to all the world, a measure the popular leaders had proposed as early as July 1775. In May Congress adopted a resolution that was a virtual declaration of independence. Its purpose was to invite the revolutionary leaders to take control of colonies, such as Pennsylvania, where the old colonial legislatures were still in control. The resolution recommended that governments deriving their power from royal charters should be replaced by governments deriving their power from the consent of the people.[5] John Adams declared at the time that it was the most important resolution ever taken in America. Within a matter of weeks an overt declaration of independence was being prepared.

160. Petition of the London merchants for reconciliation with the colonies (23 January 1775)

The following petition was the first of many which poured in from the merchants and manufacturers of England asking that Parliament put an end to the troubles with the colonies. These petitions were heard but had no influence, for the majority of Parliament was now committed, as never before, to the maintenance of British supremacy in America. Printed: Hansard, *Parliamentary History*, XVIII, pp. 168–171.

---

[1] No. 165.   [2] No. 166.   [3] No. 167.   [4] No. 172.   [5] No. 168A and B.

That the petitioners are all essentially interested in the trade to North America, either as exporters and importers, or as venders of British and foreign goods for exportation to that country; and that the petitioners have exported, or sold for exportation, to the British colonies in North America, very large quantities of the manufacture of Great Britain and Ireland, and in particular the staple articles of woollen, iron, and linen; also those of cotton, silk, leather, pewter, tin, copper, and brass, with almost every British manufacture; also large quantities of foreign linens and other articles imported into these kingdoms from Flanders, Holland, Germany, the East Countries, Portugal, Spain, and Italy, which are generally received from those countries in return for British manufactures; and that the petitioners have likewise exported, or sold for exportation, great quantities of the various species of goods imported into this kingdom from the East Indies, part of which receive additional manufacture in Great Britain; and that the petitioners receive returns from North America to this kingdom directly, viz., pig and bar iron, timber, staves, naval stores, tobacco, rice, indigo, deer and other skins, beaver and furs, train oil, whale-bone, beeswax, pot and pearl ashes, drugs, and dyeing woods, with some bullion, and also wheat flour, Indian corn and salted provisions, when on account of scarcity in Great Britain those articles are permitted to be imported; and that the petitioners receive returns circuitously from Ireland (for flax seed, etc., exported from North America) by bills of exchange on the merchants of this city trading to Ireland, for the proceeds of linens, etc., imported into these kingdoms from the West Indies; in return for provisions, lumber, and cattle, exported from North America, for the use and support of the West India islands, by bills of exchange on the West India merchants, for the proceeds of sugar, molasses, rum, cotton, coffee, or other produce, imported from those islands into these kingdoms; from Italy, Spain, Portugal, France, Flanders, Germany, Holland, and the East Countries, by bills of exchange or bullion in return for wheat flour, rice, Indian corn, fish, and lumber exported from the British colonies in North America, for the use of those countries; and that the petitioners have great reason to believe, from the best informations they can obtain, that on the balance of this extensive commerce there is now due from the colonies in North America to the said city only, £2,000,000 sterling and upwards; and that by the direct commerce with the colonies and the circuitous trade thereon depending, some thousands of ships and vessels are employed, and many thousands of seamen are bred and maintained, thereby increasing the naval strength and power of Great Britain; and that in the year 1765 there was a great stagnation of the commerce between Great Britain and her colonies in consequence of an Act for granting and applying certain stamp duties, and other duties, in the British colonies and plantations in America, by which the merchants trading to North America, and the artificers employed in the various manufactures consumed in those countries were subjected to many hardships; and that in the following year the said Act was repealed, under an express declaration of the legislature that the continuance of the said Act would be attended with many inconveniences, and might be productive of consequences greatly detrimental to the commercial interests of these kingdoms; upon which repeal the trade to the British colonies immediately resumed its former flourishing state; and that in the year 1767 an Act passed for granting certain duties in the British colonies and plantations in America, which imposed certain duties, to be paid in America, on tea, glass, red and white lead, painters' colours, paper, pasteboard, millboard, and scaleboard, when the commerce with the colonies was again interrupted; and that in the year 1770 such parts of the said Act as imposed duties on glass, red and white lead, painters' colours, paper, pasteboard, millboard, and scaleboard, were repealed, when the trade to America soon revived except in the article of tea, on which a duty was continued, to be demanded on its importation into America, whereby that branch of our commerce was nearly lost; and that in the year 1773 an Act passed to allow a drawback of the duties of customs on the exportation of tea to his Majesty's colonies or plantations in America, and to empower the Commissioners of the Treasury to grant licences to the East India Company, to export tea, duty free; and by the operations of those and other laws, the minds of his Majesty's subjects in the British colonies have been greatly disquieted, a total stop is now put to the export trade with the greatest and most important part of North America, the public revenue is threatened with a large and fatal diminution, the petitioners with grievous distress, and thousands of industrious artificers and manufacturers with utter ruin; under these alarming circumstances the petitioners receive no small comfort from a persuasion that the representatives of the people, newly delegated to the most important of all trusts, will take the whole of these weighty matters into their most serious consideration; and therefore praying the House that they will enter into a full and immediate examination of that system of commercial policy which was formerly adopted and uniformly maintained, to the happiness and advantage of both countries, and will apply such healing remedies as can alone restore and establish the commerce between Great Britain and her colonies on a permanent foundation; and that the petitioners may be heard by themselves, or agents, in support of the said petition.

161. Lord North's motion on reconciliation with the colonies (27 February 1775)

This motion was the only gesture of conciliation towards the colonies made by Parliament between 1774 and 1776. But it was a gesture which could not be accepted by the Americans and it is doubtful that the ministry had much hope that it would. The evidence indicates that its purpose was to divide parliamentary opposition to ministerial policy and to win support for further coercive measures, and particularly the Acts restraining the commerce of the colonies. Printed: *Journals of the House of Commons*, xxxv, p. 161.

That it is the opinion of this committee that when the governor, council, and assembly, or general court, of any of his Majesty's provinces or colonies in America shall propose to make provision, according to the condition, circumstances, and situation of such province or colony, for contributing their proportion to the common defence (such proportion to be raised under the authority of the general court or general assembly of such province or colony, and disposable by Parliament) and shall engage to make provision also for the support of the civil government and the administration of justice in such province or colony, it will be proper, if such proposal shall be approved by his Majesty and the two houses of Parliament, and for so long as such provision shall be made accordingly, to forbear, in respect of such province or colony, to levy any duty, tax, or assessment, or to impose any further duty, tax, or assessment, except only such duties as it may be expedient to continue to levy or to impose for the regulation of commerce; the net produce of the duties last mentioned to be carried to the account of such province or colony respectively.

162. Rejection of Lord North's motion on reconciliation by the Second Continental Congress (31 July 1775)

Lord North's motion was laid before Congress late in May after it had been rejected by several colonial legislatures. Not until late in July was a committee appointed to report on it. The committee consisted of Benjamin Franklin, Thomas Jefferson, Richard Henry Lee, and John Adams, each of whom believed in taking a vigorous stand in opposition to Britain. The answer was largely the work of Jefferson, who followed closely the argument of the Virginia legislature, which had previously rejected the motion. Printed: *Journals of the Continental Congress*, II, pp. 225-234.

The Congress took the said resolution into consideration, and are thereupon of opinion,

That the colonies of America are entitled to the sole and exclusive privilege of giving and granting their own money; that this involves a right of deliberating whether they will make any gift, for what purposes it shall be made, and what shall be its amount; and that it is a high breach of this privilege for any body of men, extraneous to their constitutions, to prescribe the purposes for which money shall be levied on them, to take to themselves the authority of judging of their conditions, circumstances, and situations, and of determining the amount of the contribution to be levied.

That as the colonies possess a right of appropriating their gifts, so are they entitled at all times to inquire into their application, to see that they be not wasted among the venal and corrupt for the purpose of undermining the civil rights of the givers, nor yet be diverted to the support of standing armies, inconsistent with their freedom and subversive of their quiet. To propose, therefore, as this resolution does, that the moneys given by the colonies shall be subject to the disposal of Parliament alone, is to propose that they shall relinquish this right of inquiry and put it in the power of others to render their gifts ruinous, in proportion as they are liberal.

That this privilege of giving or of withholding our moneys is an important barrier against the undue exertion of prerogative, which, if left altogether without control may be exercised to our great oppression; and all history shows how efficacious is its intercession for redress of grievances and re-establishment of rights, and how improvident it would be to part with so powerful a mediator.

We are of opinion that the proposition contained in this resolution is unreasonable and insidious: unreasonable, because if we declare we accede to it, we declare without reservation we will purchase the favour of Parliament, not knowing at the same time at what price they will please to estimate their favour. It is insidious because individual colonies, having bid and bidden again till they find the avidity of the seller too great for all their powers to satisfy; are then to return into opposition, divided from their sister colonies whom the minister will have previously detached by a grant of easier terms, or by an artful procrastination of a definitive answer.

That the suspension of the exercise of their pretended power of taxation being

expressly made commensurate with the continuance of our gifts, these must be perpetual to make that so. Whereas no experience has shown that a gift of perpetual
revenue secures a perpetual return of duty or of kind disposition. On the contrary, the
Parliament itself, wisely attentive to this observation, are in the established practice
of granting their supplies from year to year only.

Desirous and determined as we are to consider, in the most dispassionate view,
every seeming advance towards a reconciliation made by the British Parliament, let
our brethren of Britain reflect what would have been the sacrifice to men of free
spirits had even fair terms been proffered, as these insidious proposals were, with
circumstances of insult and defiance. A proposition to give our money, accompanied
with large fleets and armies, seems addressed to our fears rather than to our freedom.
With what patience would Britons have received articles of treaty from any power
on earth when borne on the point of the bayonet by military plenipotentiaries?

We think the attempt unnecessary to raise upon us by force or by threats, our
proportional contributions to the common defence, when all know, and themselves
acknowledge, we have fully contributed whenever called upon to do so in the
character of freemen.

We are of opinion it is not just that the colonies should be required to oblige
themselves to other contributions while Great Britain possesses a monopoly of their
trade. This of itself lays them under heavy contribution. To demand, therefore,
additional aids in the form of a tax is to demand the double of their equal proportion.
If we are to contribute equally with the other parts of the empire, let us equally with
them enjoy free commerce with the whole world. But while the restrictions on our
trade shut to us the resources of wealth, is it just we should bear all other burdens
equally with those to whom every resource is open?

We conceive that the British Parliament has no right to intermeddle with our
provisions for the support of civil government, or administration of justice. The
provisions we have made are such as please ourselves, and are agreeable to our own
circumstances. They answer the substantial purposes of government and of justice,
and other purposes than these should not be answered. We do not mean that our
people shall be burdened with oppressive taxes to provide sinecures for the idle or the
wicked, under colour of providing for a civil list. While Parliament pursue their
plan of civil government within their own jurisdiction, we also hope to pursue ours
without molestation.

We are of opinion the proposition is altogether unsatisfactory because it imports
only a suspension of the mode, not a renunciation of the pretended right to tax us:
because, too, it does not propose to repeal the several Acts of Parliament passed for the
purposes of restraining the trade and altering the form of government of one of our
colonies; extending the boundaries and changing the government of Quebec;
enlarging the jurisdiction of the courts of admiralty and vice-admiralty; taking from
us the rights of trial by a jury of the vicinage in cases affecting both life and property;
transporting us into other countries to be tried for criminal offences; exempting, by
mock trial the murderers of colonists from punishment; and quartering soldiers on us
in times of profound peace. Nor do they renounce the power of suspending our own

legislatures, and of legislating for us themselves in all cases whatsoever. On the contrary, to show they mean no discontinuance of injury, they pass Acts, at the very time of holding out this proposition, for restraining the commerce and fisheries of the provinces of New England, and for interdicting the trade of other colonies with all foreign nations, and with each other. This proves unequivocally they mean not to relinquish the exercise of indiscriminate legislation over us.

Upon the whole, this proposition seems to have been held up to the world to deceive it into a belief that there was nothing in dispute between us but the *mode* of levying taxes, and that the Parliament having now been so good as to give up this, the colonies are unreasonable if not perfectly satisfied. Whereas, in truth our adversaries still claim a right of demanding *ad libitum*, and of taxing us themselves to the full amount of their demand if we do not comply with it. This leaves us without anything we can call property. But what is of more importance, and what in this proposal they keep out of sight, as if no such point was now in contest between us, they claim a right to alter our charters and established laws and leave us without any security for our lives or liberties. The proposition seems also to have been calculated more particularly to lull into fatal security our well-affected fellow subjects on the other side the water till time should be given for the operation of those arms which a British minister pronounced would instantaneously reduce the 'cowardly' sons of America to unreserved submission. But when the world reflects how inadequate to justice are these vaunted terms; when it attends to the rapid and bold succession of injuries which during the course of eleven years have been aimed at these colonies; when it reviews the pacific and respectful expostulations which during that whole time were the sole arms we opposed to them; when it observes that our complaints were either not heard at all or were answered with new and accumulated injury; when it recollects that the minister himself on an early occasion declared "that he would never treat with America, till he had brought her to his feet", and that an avowed partisan of ministry has more lately denounced against us the dreadful sentence, "*delenda est Carthago*"; that this was done in the presence of a British senate, and being unreproved by them must be taken to be their own sentiment (especially as the purpose has already in part been carried into execution by their treatment of Boston and burning of Charlestown); when it considers the great armaments with which they have invaded us and the circumstances of cruelty with which these have commenced and prosecuted hostilities; when these things, we say, are laid together and attentively considered, can the world be deceived into an opinion that we are unreasonable, or can it hesitate to believe with us that nothing but our own exertions may defeat the ministerial sentence of death or abject submission?

163. Declaration of the causes and necessity for taking up arms (6 July 1775)

During the summer of 1775 Congress prepared several addresses to justify armed resistance to Great Britain. The most notable was the following declaration which was published by General George Washington on his arrival in Massachusetts to take charge of the army there. The declaration was the joint production of Thomas Jefferson and John Dickinson. It is the opinion of the editors of *The Papers of Thomas Jefferson* (I, pp. 187-219) that the issues as between Jefferson's and Dickinson's versions were essentially questions of style and method of presentation rather than of radicalism and conservatism. For a different view of this see Merrill Jensen, *The Articles of Confederation*, pp. 83-84. Printed: *Journals of the Continental Congress*, II, pp. 140-157.

A declaration by the representatives of the United Colonies of North America, now met in General Congress at Philadelphia, setting forth the causes and necessity of their taking up arms.

If it was possible for men who exercise their reason to believe that the Divine Author of our existence intended a part of the human race to hold an absolute property in, and an unbounded power over others, marked out by his infinite goodness and wisdom, as the objects of a legal domination never rightfully resistible, however severe and oppressive, the inhabitants of these colonies might at least require from the Parliament of Great Britain some evidence that this dreadful authority over them has been granted to that body. But a reverence for our great Creator, principles of humanity, and the dictates of common sense, must convince all those who reflect upon the subject, that government was instituted to promote the welfare of mankind, and ought to be administered for the attainment of that end. The legislature of Great Britain, however, stimulated by an inordinate passion for a power, not only unjustifiable, but which they know to be peculiarly reprobated by the very constitution of that kingdom, and desperate of success in any mode of contest where regard should be had to truth, law, or right, have at length, deserting those, attempted to effect their cruel and impolitic purpose of enslaving these colonies by violence, and have thereby rendered it necessary for us to close with their last appeal from reason to arms. Yet, however blinded that assembly may be, by their intemperate rage for unlimited domination, so to slight justice and the opinion of mankind, we esteem ourselves bound, by obligations of respect to the rest of the world, to make known the justice of our cause.

Our forefathers, inhabitants of the island of Great Britain, left their native land, to seek on these shores a residence for civil and religious freedom. At the expense of their blood, at the hazard of their fortunes, without the least charge to the country from which they removed, by unceasing labour, and an unconquerable spirit, they effected settlements in the distant and inhospitable wilds of America, then filled with numerous and warlike nations of barbarians. Societies or governments, vested with perfect legislatures, were formed under charters from the Crown, and an harmonious intercourse was established between the colonies and the kingdom from which they derived their origin. The mutual benefits of this union became in a short time so extraordinary as to excite astonishment. It is universally confessed that the amazing increase of the wealth, strength, and navigation of the realm arose from this source; and the minister who so wisely and successfully directed the measures of Great Britain in the late war, publicly declared that these colonies enabled her to triumph over her enemies.

Towards the conclusion of that war it pleased our sovereign to make a change in his counsels. From that fatal moment, the affairs of the British empire began to fall into confusion, and gradually sliding from the summit of glorious prosperity, to which they had been advanced by the virtues and abilities of one man, are at length distracted by the convulsions that now shake it to its deepest foundations. The new ministry finding the brave foes of Britain, though frequently defeated, yet still contending, took up the unfortunate idea of granting them a hasty peace, and of then subduing her faithful friends.

These devoted colonies were judged to be in such a state as to present victories without bloodshed, and all the easy emoluments of statutable plunder. The uninterrupted tenor of their peaceable and respectful behaviour from the beginning of colonization, their dutiful, zealous, and useful services during the war, though so recently and amply acknowledged in the most honourable manner by his Majesty, by the late king, and by Parliament, could not save them from the meditated innovations. Parliament was influenced to adopt the pernicious project, and assuming a new power over them, have, in the course of eleven years, given such decisive specimens of the spirit and consequences attending this power as to leave no doubt concerning the effects of acquiescence under it. They have undertaken to give and grant our money without our consent, though we have ever exercised an exclusive right to dispose of our own property; statutes have been passed for extending the jurisdiction of courts of admiralty and vice-admiralty beyond their ancient limits; for depriving us of the accustomed and inestimable privilege of trial by jury, in cases affecting both life and property; for suspending the legislature of one of the colonies; for interdicting all commerce to the capital of another; and for altering fundamentally the form of government established by charter, and secured by acts of its own legislature solemnly confirmed by the Crown; for exempting the 'murderers' of colonists from legal trial, and in effect, from punishment; for erecting in a neighbouring province, acquired by the joint arms of Great Britain and America, a despotism dangerous to our very existence; and for quartering soldiers upon the colonists in time of profound peace. It has also been resolved in Parliament, that colonists charged with committing certain offences, shall be transported to England to be tried.

But why should we enumerate our injuries in detail? By one statute it is declared that Parliament can "of right make laws to bind us IN ALL CASES WHATSOEVER". What is to defend us against so enormous, so unlimited a power? Not a single man of those who assume it is chosen by us; or is subject to our control or influence; but, on the contrary, they are all of them exempt from the operation of such laws, and an American revenue, if not diverted from the ostensible purposes for which it is raised, would actually lighten their own burdens in proportion as they increase ours. We saw the misery to which such despotism would reduce us. We for ten years incessantly and ineffectually besieged the throne as supplicants; we reasoned, we remonstrated with Parliament, in the most mild and decent language. But administration, sensible that we should regard these oppressive measures as freemen ought to do, sent over fleets and armies to enforce them. The indignation of the Americans was roused, it is true; but it was the indignation of a virtuous, loyal, and affectionate people. A congress of delegates from the united colonies was assembled at Philadelphia on the fifth day of last September. We resolved again to offer an humble and dutiful petition to the king, and also addressed our fellow-subjects of Great Britain. We have pursued every temperate, every respectful measure: we have even proceeded to break off our commercial intercourse with our fellow-subjects, as the last peaceable admonition, that our attachment to no nation upon earth should supplant our attachment to liberty. This, we flattered ourselves, was the ultimate step of the controversy: But subsequent events have shown how vain was this hope of finding moderation in our enemies.

Several threatening expressions against the colonies were inserted in his Majesty's speech; our petition, though we were told it was a decent one, and that his Majesty had been pleased to receive it graciously, and to promise laying it before his Parliament, was huddled into both houses amongst a bundle of American papers, and there neglected. The Lords and Commons in their address, in the month of February, said that "a rebellion at that time actually existed within the province of Massachusetts Bay; and that those concerned in it had been countenanced and encouraged by unlawful combinations and engagements, entered into by his Majesty's subjects in several of the other colonies; and therefore they besought his Majesty, that he would take the most effectual measures to enforce due obedience to the laws and authority of the supreme legislature". Soon after, the commercial intercourse of whole colonies, with foreign countries, and with each other, was cut off by an Act of Parliament; by another, several of them were entirely prohibited from the fisheries in the seas near their coasts, on which they always depended for their sustenance; and large reinforcements of ships and troops were immediately sent over to General Gage.

Fruitless were all the entreaties, arguments and eloquence of an illustrious band of the most distinguished peers and commoners who nobly and strenuously asserted the justice of our cause, to stay, or even to mitigate the heedless fury with which these accumulated and unexampled outrages were hurried on. Equally fruitless was the interference of the city of London, of Bristol, and many other respectable towns in our favour. Parliament adopted an insidious manœuvre calculated to divide us, to establish a perpetual auction of taxations where colony should bid against colony, all of them uninformed what ransom would redeem their lives; and thus to extort from us, at the point of the bayonet, the unknown sums that should be sufficient to gratify, if possible to gratify, ministerial rapacity, with the miserable indulgence left to us of raising, in our own mode, the prescribed tribute. What terms more rigid and humiliating could have been dictated by remorseless victors to conquered enemies? In our circumstances to accept them would be to deserve them.

Soon after the intelligence of these proceedings arrived on this continent, General Gage, who in the course of the last year had taken possession of the town of Boston in the province of Massachusetts Bay, and still occupied it as a garrison, on the 19th day of April, sent out from that place a large detachment of his army, who made an unprovoked assault on the inhabitants of the said province, at the town of Lexington, as appears by the affidavits of a great number of persons, some of whom were officers and soldiers of that detachment, murdered eight of the inhabitants, and wounded many others. From thence the troops proceeded in warlike array to the town of Concord, where they set upon another party of the inhabitants of the same province, killing several and wounding more, until compelled to retreat by the country people suddenly assembled to repel this cruel aggression. Hostilities, thus commenced by the British troops have been since prosecuted by them without regard to faith or reputation. The inhabitants of Boston being confined within that town by the general, their governor, and having, in order to procure their dismission, entered into a treaty with him, it was stipulated that the said inhabitants having deposited their arms with their own magistrates, should have liberty to depart, taking with them their other effects. They accordingly delivered up their arms, but in open violation of honour, in defiance of the obligation of treaties, which even savage nations esteemed sacred, the governor ordered the arms deposited as aforesaid, that they might be preserved for their owners, to be seized by a body of soldiers; detained the greatest part of the inhabitants in the town, and compelled the few who were permitted to retire, to leave their most valuable effects behind.

By this perfidy wives are separated from their husbands, children from their parents, the aged and the sick from their relations and friends, who wish to attend and comfort them; and those who have been used to live in plenty and even elegance, are reduced to deplorable distress.

The general, further emulating his ministerial masters, by a proclamation bearing date on the 12th day of June, after venting the grossest falsehoods and calumnies against the good people of these colonies, proceeds to "declare them all, either by name or description, to be rebels and traitors, to supersede the course of the common law, and instead thereof to publish and order the use and exercise of the law martial". His troops have butchered our countrymen, have wantonly burnt Charlestown, besides a considerable number of houses in other places; our ships and vessels are seized; the necessary supplies of provisions are intercepted, and he is exerting his utmost power to spread destruction and devastation around him.

We have received certain intelligence that General Carleton, the governor of Canada, is instigating the people of that province and the Indians to fall upon us; and we have but too much reason to apprehend that schemes have been formed to excite domestic enemies against us. In brief, a part of these colonies now feels, and all of them are sure of feeling, as far as the vengeance of administration can inflict them, the complicated calamities of fire, sword and famine. We are reduced to the alternative of choosing an unconditional submission to the tryranny of irritated ministers, or resistance by force. The latter is our choice. We have counted the cost of this contest and find nothing so dreadful as voluntary slavery. Honour, justice, and humanity forbid us tamely to surrender that freedom which we received from our gallant ancestors, and which our innocent posterity have a right to receive from us. We cannot endure the infamy and guilt of resigning succeeding generations to that wretchedness which inevitably awaits them, if we basely entail hereditary bondage upon them.

Our cause is just. Our union is perfect. Our internal resources are great, and, if necessary, foreign assistance is undoubtedly attainable. We gratefully acknowledge, as signal instances of the Divine favour towards us, that his Providence would not permit us to be called into this severe controversy, until we were grown up to our present strength, had been previously exercised in warlike operation, and possessed of the means of defending ourselves. With hearts fortified with these animating reflections, we most solemnly, before God and the world, declare, that, exerting the utmost energy of those powers which our beneficent Creator hath graciously bestowed upon us, the arms we have been compelled by our enemies to assume, we will in defiance of every hazard, with unabating firmness and perseverance, employ for the preservation of our liberties; being with our [one] mind resolved to die free men rather than live slaves.

Lest this declaration should disquiet the minds of our friends and fellow-subjects in any part of the empire, we assure them that we mean not to dissolve that union which has so long and so happily subsisted between us, and which we sincerely wish to see restored. Necessity has not yet driven us into that desperate measure, or induced us to excite any other nation to war against them. We have not raised armies with ambitious designs of separating from Great Britain, and establishing independent states. We fight not for glory or for conquest. We exhibit to mankind the remarkable spectacle of a people attacked by unprovoked enemies, without any imputation or even suspicion of offence. They boast of their privileges and civilization, and yet proffer no milder conditions than servitude or death.

In our own native land, in defence of the freedom that is our birthright, and which we ever enjoyed till the late violation of it, for the protection of our property, acquired solely by the honest industry of our forefathers and ourselves, against violence actually offered, we have taken up arms. We shall lay them down when hostilities shall cease on the part of the aggressors, and all danger of their being renewed shall be removed, and not before.

With an humble confidence in the mercies of the supreme and impartial Judge and Ruler of the universe, we most devoutly implore his divine goodness to protect us happily through this great conflict, to dispose our adversaries to reconciliation on reasonable terms, and thereby to relieve the empire from the calamities of civil war.

164. The second petition to the king (8 July 1775)

As the Second Continental Congress moved step by step in the direction of open war, the conservative element in it continued to demand that the door be left open for reconciliation. John Dickinson of Pennsylvania was the leader of this group. It was largely because of his prestige and influence that Congress agreed to a second petition to the king. The petition was almost solely his work. He was proud of the fact that in it "we make no *Claim*, and mention no *Right*". But the popular leaders were furious. John Adams wrote that "a certain great fortune and piddling genius, whose fame has been trumpeted so loudly, has given a silly cast to our whole doings. We are between hawk and buzzard." Printed: *Journals of the Continental Congress*, II, pp. 158–161.

We, your Majesty's faithful subjects of the colonies of New Hampshire, Massachusetts Bay, Rhode Island and Providence Plantations, Connecticut, New York, New Jersey, Pennsylvania, the counties of New Castle, Kent, and Sussex on Delaware, Maryland, Virginia, North Carolina and South Carolina, in behalf of ourselves and the inhabitants of these colonies, who have deputed us to represent them in general congress, entreat your Majesty's gracious attention to this our humble petition.

The union between our mother country and these colonies, and the energy of mild and just government, produced benefits so remarkably important, and afforded such an assurance of their permanency and increase that the wonder and envy of other nations were excited, while they beheld Great Britain rising to power the most extraordinary the world had ever known.

Her rivals, observing that there was no probability of this happy connection being broken by civil dissensions, and apprehending its future effects if left any longer undisturbed, resolved to prevent her receiving such continual and formidable accessions of wealth and strength by checking the growth of these settlements from which they were to be derived.

In the prosecution of this attempt, events so unfavourable to the design took place that every friend to the interests of Great Britain and these colonies entertained pleasing and reasonable expectations of seeing an additional force and extension immediately given to the operations of the union hitherto experienced, by an enlargement of the dominions of the Crown and the removal of ancient and warlike enemies to a greater distance.

At the conclusion, therefore, of the late war, the most glorious and advantageous that ever had been carried on by British arms, your loyal colonists having contributed to its success by such repeated and strenuous exertions as frequently procured them the distinguished approbation of your Majesty, of the late king, and of Parliament, doubted not but that they should be permitted, with the rest of the empire, to share in the blessings of peace, and the emoluments of victory and conquest. While these recent and honourable acknowledgments of their merits remained on record in the journals and acts of that august legislature, the Parliament, undefaced by the imputation or even the suspicion of any offence, they were alarmed by a new system of statutes and regulations adopted for the administration of the colonies, that filled their minds with the most painful fears and jealousies; and, to their inexpressible astonishment, perceived the dangers of a foreign quarrel quickly succeeded by domestic dangers, in their judgment, of a more dreadful kind.

Nor were their anxieties alleviated by any tendency in this system to promote the welfare of the mother country. For though its effects were more immediately felt by them, yet its influence appeared to be injurious to the commerce and prosperity of Great Britain.

We shall decline the ungrateful task of describing the irksome variety of artifices, practised by many of your Majesty's ministers, the delusive pretences, fruitless terrors, and unavailing severities that have, from time to time, been dealt out by them in their attempts to execute this impolitic plan, or of tracing through a series of years past, the progress of the unhappy differences between Great Britain and these colonies, which have flowed from this fatal source.

Your Majesty's ministers, persevering in their measures, and proceeding to open hostilities for enforcing them, have compelled us to arm in our own defence, and have engaged us in a controversy so peculiarly abhorrent to the affections of your still faithful colonists that when we consider whom we must oppose in this contest, and if it continues, what may be the consequences, our own particular misfortunes are accounted by us only as parts of our distress.

Knowing to what violent resentments and incurable animosities, civil discords are apt to exasperate and inflame the contending parties, we think ourselves required by indispensable obligations to Almighty God, to your Majesty, to our fellow-subjects, and to ourselves, immediately to use all the means in our power not incompatible with our safety, for stopping the further effusion of blood, and for averting the impending calamities that threaten the British Empire.

Thus called upon to address your Majesty on affairs of such moment to America, and probably to all your dominions, we are earnestly desirous of performing this office with the utmost deference for your Majesty; and we therefore pray that your royal magnanimity and benevolence may make the most favourable construction of our expressions on so uncommon an occasion. Could we represent in their full force the sentiments that agitate the minds of us, your dutiful subjects, we are persuaded your Majesty would ascribe any seeming deviation from reverence in our language, and even in our conduct, not to any reprehensible intention, but to the impossibility of reconciling the usual appearances of respect with a just attention to our own preservation against those artful and cruel enemies who abuse your royal confidence and authority for the purpose of effecting our destruction.

Attached to your Majesty's person, family, and government, with all devotion that principle and affection can inspire, connected with Great Britain by the strongest ties that can unite societies, and deploring every event that tends in any degree to weaken them, we solemnly assure your Majesty that we not only most ardently desire the former harmony between her and these colonies may be restored, but that a concord may be established between them upon so firm a basis as to perpetuate its blessings, uninterrupted by any future dissensions, to succeeding generations in both countries, and to transmit your Majesty's name to posterity, adorned with that signal and lasting glory that has attended the memory of those illustrious personages whose virtues and abilities have extricated states from dangerous convulsions, and, by securing happiness to others, have erected the most noble and durable monuments to their own fame.

We beg leave further to assure your Majesty that notwithstanding the sufferings of your loyal colonists during the course of the present controversy, our breasts retain too tender a regard for the kingdom from which we derive our origin to request such a reconciliation as might in any manner be inconsistent with her dignity or her welfare. These, related as we are to her, honour and duty as well as inclination, induce us to support and advance; and the apprehensions that now oppress our hearts with unspeakable grief being once removed, your Majesty will find your faithful subjects on this continent ready and willing at all times, as they ever have been, with their lives and fortunes to assert and maintain the rights and interests of your Majesty, and of our mother country.

We, therefore, beseech your Majesty that your royal authority and influence may be graciously interposed to procure us relief from our afflicting fears and jealousies, occasioned by the system before mentioned, and to settle peace through every part of your dominions, with all humility submitting to your Majesty's wise consideration whether it may not be expedient for facilitating those important purposes, that your Majesty be pleased to direct some mode by which the united applications of your faithful colonists to the throne, in pursuance of their common councils, may be improved into a happy and permanent reconciliation; and that, in the mean time, measures may be taken for preventing the further destruction of the lives of your Majesty's subjects; and that such statutes as more immediately distress any of your Majesty's colonies may be repealed.

For by such arrangements as your Majesty's wisdom can form for collecting the united sense of your American people, we are convinced your Majesty would receive such satisfactory proofs of the disposition of the colonists towards their sovereign and parent state that the wished for opportunity would soon be restored to them of evincing the sincerity of their professions by every testimony of devotion becoming the most dutiful subjects, and the most affectionate colonists.

That your Majesty may enjoy a long and prosperous reign, and that your descendants may govern your dominions with honour to themselves and happiness to their subjects, is our sincere and fervent prayer.

165. The king's proclamation for suppressing rebellion and sedition (23 August 1775)

This proclamation was the first official recognition of rebellion in the colonies and was aimed primarily at those people in England who sympathized with the colonial position, and who were suspected by the king and ministry of aiding and abetting them. Printed: Brigham, *British Royal Proclamations Relating to America, 1603-1783*, pp. 228-229.

Whereas many of our subjects in divers parts of our colonies and plantations in North America, misled by dangerous and ill-designing men, and forgetting the allegiance which they owe to the power that has protected and sustained them, after various disorderly acts committed in disturbance of the public peace, to the obstruction of lawful commerce and to the oppression of our loyal subjects carrying on the same, have at length proceeded to an open and avowed rebellion by arraying themselves in hostile manner to withstand the execution of the law, and traitorously preparing, ordering, and levying war against us; and whereas there is reason to apprehend that such rebellion hath been much promoted and encouraged by the traitorous correspondence, counsels, and comfort of divers wicked and desperate persons within this realm; to the end therefore that none of our subjects may neglect or violate their duty through ignorance thereof, or through any doubt of the protection which the law will afford to their loyalty and zeal; we have thought fit, by and with the advice of our Privy Council, to issue this our royal proclamation, hereby declaring that not only all our officers, civil and military, are obliged to exert their utmost endeavours to suppress such rebellion and to bring the traitors to justice; but that all our subjects of this realm and the dominions thereunto belonging are bound by law to be aiding and assisting in the suppression of such rebellion, and to disclose and make known all traitorous conspiracies and attempts against us, our Crown, and dignity; and we do accordingly strictly charge and command all our officers, as well civil as military, and all other our obedient and loyal subjects, to use their utmost endeavours to withstand and suppress such rebellion, and to disclose and make known all treasons and traitorous conspiracies which they shall know to be against us, our Crown and dignity; and for that purpose, that they transmit to one of our principal secretaries of state, or other proper officer, due and full information of all persons who shall be found carrying on correspondence with, or in any manner or degree aiding or abetting the persons now in open arms and rebellion against our government within any of our colonies and plantations in North America, in order to bring to condign punishment the authors, perpetrators and abettors of such traitorous designs.

Given at our court at St. James the twenty-third day of August, one thousand seven hundred and seventy-five, in the fifteenth year of our reign.

166. The king's speech to Parliament (26 October 1775)

The following speech declared that Americans were fighting for independence before the Americans officially admitted it themselves. It also made plain that Britain would take every measure to defeat them. The promise that commissioners would be sent to grant pardons and receive submissions gave hope to Americans who were opposed to independence but had little effect except to delay an open declaration of independence for a time. Printed: *Journals of the House of Commons*, xxxv, pp. 397–398.

The present situation of America, and my constant desire to have your advice, concurrence, and assistance on every important occasion, have determined me to call you thus early together.

Those who have long too successfully laboured to inflame my people in America by gross misrepresentations and to infuse into their minds a system of opinions repugnant to the true constitution of the colonies, and to their subordinate relation to Great Britain, now openly avow their revolt, hostility, and rebellion. They have raised troops, and are collecting a naval force; they have seized the public revenue, and assumed to themselves legislative, executive, and judicial powers, which they already exercise in the most arbitrary manner over the persons and properties of their fellow subjects; and although many of these unhappy people may still retain their loyalty and may be too wise not to see the fatal consequence of this usurpation, and wish to resist it; yet the torrent of violence has been strong enough to compel their acquiescence till a sufficient force shall appear to support them.

The authors and promoters of this desperate conspiracy have in the conduct of it derived great advantage from the difference of our intentions and theirs. They meant only to amuse by vague expressions of attachment to the parent state and the strongest protestations of loyalty to me, whilst they were preparing for a general revolt. On our part, though it was declared in your last session that a rebellion existed within the province of the Massachusetts Bay, yet even that province we wished rather to reclaim than to subdue. The resolutions of Parliament breathed a spirit of moderation and forbearance; conciliatory propositions accompanied the measures taken to enforce authority, and the coercive acts were adapted to cases of criminal combinations amongst subjects not then in arms. I have acted with the same temper; anxious to prevent, if it had been possible, the effusion of the blood of my subjects and the calamities which are inseparable from a state of war; still hoping that my people in America would have discerned the traitorous views of their leaders and have been convinced that to be a subject of Great Britain, with all its consequences, is to be the freest member of any civil society in the known world.

The rebellious war now levied is become more general and is manifestly carried on for the purpose of establishing an independent empire. I need not dwell upon the fatal effects of the success of such a plan. The object is too important, the spirit of the British nation too high, the resources with which God hath blessed her too numerous, to give up so many colonies which she has planted with great industry, nursed with great tenderness, encouraged with many commercial advantages, and protected and defended at much expense of blood and treasure.

It is now become the part of wisdom, and (in its effects) of clemency, to put a speedy end to these disorders by the most decisive exertions. For this purpose I have increased my naval establishment, and greatly augmented my land forces, but in such a manner as may be the least burdensome to my kingdoms.

I have also the satisfaction to inform you that I have received the most friendly offers of foreign assistance; and if I shall make any treaties in consequence thereof, they shall be laid before you. And I have, in testimony of my affection for my people who can have no cause in which I am not equally interested, sent to the garrisons of Gibraltar and Port Mahon a part of my Electoral troops in order that a larger number of the established forces of this kingdom may be applied to the maintenance of its authority; and the national militia, planned and regulated with equal regard to the rights, safety, and protection of my Crown and people, may give a farther extent and activity to our military operations.

When the unhappy and deluded multitude against whom this force will be directed shall become sensible of their error, I shall be ready to receive the misled with tenderness and mercy; and in order to prevent the inconveniences which may arise from the great distance of their situation, and to remove as soon as possible the calamities which they suffer, I shall give authority to certain persons upon the spot to grant general or particular pardons and indemnities, in such manner and to such persons as they shall think fit, and to receive the submission of any province or colony which shall be disposed to return to its allegiance. It may be also proper to authorize the persons so commissioned to restore such province or colony so returning to its allegiance to the free exercise of its trade and commerce and to the same protection and security as if such province or colony had never revolted.

Gentlemen of the House of Commons:

I have ordered the proper estimates for the ensuing year to be laid before you; and I rely on your affection to me and your resolution to maintain the just rights of this country, for such supplies as the present circumstances of our affairs require. Among the many unavoidable ill consequences of this rebellion none affects me more sensibly than the extraordinary burden which it must create to my faithful subjects.

My Lords and Gentlemen:

I have fully opened to you my views and intentions. The constant employment of my thoughts, and the most earnest wishes of my heart tend wholly to the safety and happiness of all my people, and to the re-establishment of order and tranquillity through the several parts of my dominions, in a close connection and constitutional dependence. You see the tendency of the present disorders and I have stated to you the measures which I mean to pursue for suppressing them. Whatever remains to be done that may farther contribute to this end, I commit to your wisdom. And I am happy to add that as well from the assurances I have received as from the general appearance of affairs in Europe, I see no probability that the measures which you may adopt will be interrupted by disputes with any foreign power.

167. The American Prohibitory Act (22 December 1775)

This Act (16 Geo. III, c. 5) ending the trade of the American colonies and making their goods and ships subject to capture and confiscation, in effect declared them to be outlaws. A member of the opposition in Parliament said that the Bill answered all the purposes of the most violent Americans and that its title should be altered to fit its purpose and be called "a Bill for carrying more effectively into execution the resolves of Congress". Its effect was precisely that. The popular leaders labelled it independence by Act of Parliament and cited it as further proof of their contention that there was no hope of reconciliation with Britain. Printed: Pickering, *Statutes at Large*, XXXI, pp. 135-154.

Whereas many persons in the colonies of New Hampshire, Massachusetts Bay, Rhode Island, Connecticut, New York, New Jersey, Pennsylvania, the three lower counties on Delaware, Maryland, Virginia, North Carolina, South Carolina, and Georgia, have set themselves in open rebellion and defiance to the just and legal authority of the king and Parliament of Great Britain, to which they ever have been, and of right ought to be, subject; and have assembled together an armed force, engaged his Majesty's troops, and attacked his forts; have usurped the powers of government, and prohibited all trade and commerce with this kingdom and the other parts of his Majesty's dominions; for the more speedily and effectually suppressing such wicked and daring designs, and for preventing any aid, supply, or assistance being sent thither during the continuance of the said rebellious and treasonable commotions, be it therefore declared and enacted . . . that all manner of trade and commerce is and shall be prohibited with the colonies of New Hampshire, Massachusetts Bay, Rhode Island, Connecticut, New York, New Jersey, Pennsylvania, the three lower counties on Delaware, Maryland, Virginia, North Carolina, South Carolina, and Georgia; and that all ships and vessels of or belonging to the inhabitants of the said colonies, together with their cargoes, apparel, and furniture, and all other ships and vessels whatsoever, together with their cargoes, apparel, and furniture, which shall be found trading in any port or place of the said colonies, or going to trade, or coming from trading, in any such port or place, shall become forfeited to his Majesty, as if the same were the ships and effects of open enemies, and shall be so adjudged, deemed, and taken in all courts of admiralty, and in all other courts whatsoever.

III. And, for the encouragement of the officers and seamen of his Majesty's ships of war, be it further enacted, that the flag officers, captains, commanders, and other commissioned officers in his Majesty's pay, and also the seamen, marines, and soldiers on board shall have the sole interest and property of and in all and every such ship, vessel, goods, and merchandise, which they shall seize and take (being first adjudged lawful prize in any of his Majesty's courts of admiralty) to be divided in such proportions, and after such manner, as his Majesty shall think fit to order and direct by proclamation or proclamations hereafter to be issued for those purposes.

168A–B. Congress recommends the overthrow of governments deriving authority from the Crown (10, 15 May 1776)

By the spring of 1776 the main obstacle to independence was the fact that the middle colonies were still controlled by men opposed to it. Revolutionary organizations existed in each of these colonies, but the old legislatures were still in control, elected delegates to the Continental Congress, and instructed those delegates to oppose independence. The problem of the revolutionary leaders in Congress was to bring about the establishment of revolutionary governments, particularly in

Pennsylvania. Therefore, they introduced the resolution of 10 May and the preamble of 15 May to provide the Pennsylvania revolutionary leaders with a justification for taking over control of the colony. The passage of the resolution and preamble was followed three days later by a mass meeting in Philadelphia which declared that the Pennsylvania Assembly had no power to form a new government. This was followed by a call for a convention to meet in June. On 8 June the Assembly, in a desperate effort to retain control, rescinded its instructions against independence but thereafter was unable to obtain a quorum and so passed from existence.

John Adams's notes of the debates on 15 May show that the conservative leaders of the middle colonies still hoped for reconciliation and that they wanted to avoid a political revolution within colonies where one had not yet occurred.

168A. Resolution of 10 May and preamble of 15 May 1776

Printed: *Journals of the Continental Congress*, IV, pp. 342, 357-358.

Whereas his Britannic Majesty, in conjunction with the Lords and Commons of Great Britain has, by a late Act of Parliament, excluded the inhabitants of these united colonies from the protection of his Crown; and whereas no answer whatever to the humble petitions of the colonies for redress of grievances and reconciliation with Great Britain has been or is likely to be given, but the whole force of that kingdom, aided by foreign mercenaries, is to be exerted for the destruction of the good people of these colonies; and whereas it appears absolutely irreconcilable to reason and good conscience for the people of these colonies now to take the oaths and affirmations necessary for the support of any government under the Crown of Great Britain and it is necessary that the exercise of every kind of authority under the said Crown should be totally suppressed and all the powers of government exerted under the authority of the people of the colonies for the preservation of internal peace, virtue, and good order as well as for the defence of their lives, liberties, and properties against the hostile invasions and cruel depredations of their enemies; therefore,

Resolved, that it be recommended to the respective assemblies and conventions of the united colonies where no government sufficient to the exigencies of their affairs have been hitherto established, to adopt such government as shall, in the opinion of the representatives of the people, best conduce to the happiness and safety of their constituents in particular and America in general.

168B. John Adams: notes on debates (15 May 1776)

Printed: *Works*, II, pp. 489-491.

Mr. [James] Duane [New York] moves that the delegation from New York might be read.

When we were invited by Massachusetts Bay to the first Congress, an objection was made to binding ourselves by votes of Congress. Congress ought not to determine a point of this sort about instituting government. What is it to Congress how justice is administered? You have no right to pass the resolution, any more than Parliament has. How does it appear that no favourable answer is likely to be given to our petitions? Every account of foreign aid is accompanied with an account of commissioners. Why all this haste? Why this urging? Why this driving? Disputes about independence are in all the colonies. What is this owing to but our indiscretion? I shall take the liberty of informing my constituents that I have not been guilty of a breach of trust.

I do protest against this piece of mechanism, this preamble. If the facts in this pre-amble should prove to be true, there will not be one voice against independence. I suppose the votes have been numbered, and there is to be a majority.

[Thomas] McKean [Pennsylvania] construes the instructions from New York as Mr. Sherman does, and thinks this measure the best to procure harmony with Great Britain. There are now two governments in direct opposition to each other. Don't doubt that foreign mercenaries are coming to destroy us. I do think we shall lose our liberties, properties, and lives too, if we do not take this step.

S[amuel] Adams [Massachusetts]. We have been favoured with a reading of the instructions from New York; I am glad of it. The first object of that colony is no doubt the establishment of their rights. Our petitions have not been heard, yet answered with fleets and armies, and are to be answered with myrmidons from abroad. The gentleman from New York, Mr. Duane, has not objected to the preamble, but this, that he has not a right to vote for it. We cannot go upon stronger reasons than that the king has thrown us out of his protection. Why should we support governments under his authority? I wonder that people have conducted so well as they have.

Mr. [James] Wilson [Pennsylvania]. Was not present in Congress when the resolution passed, to which this preamble is proposed. I was present, and one of the committee who reported the advice to Massachusetts Bay. New Hampshire, Carolina, and Virginia had the same advice, and with my hearty concurrence.

The claim of Parliament will meet with resistance to the last extremity. Those colonies were royal governments; they could not subsist without some government. A maxim, that all government originates from the people. We are the servants of the people, sent here to act under a delegated authority. If we exceed it, voluntarily, we deserve neither excuse nor justification. Some have been put under restraints by their constituents; they cannot vote without transgressing this line. Suppose they should hereafter be called to an account for it. This province has not by any public act authorized us to vote upon this question; this province has done much and asked little from this Congress; the Assembly, largely increased, will (not) meet till next Monday. Will the cause suffer much if this preamble is not published at this time? If the resolve is published without the preamble? The preamble contains a reflection upon the conduct of some people in America. It was equally irreconcilable to good conscience nine months ago to take the oaths of allegiance, as it is now. Two respectable members, last February, took the oath of allegiance in our Assembly. Why should we expose any gentlemen to such an invidious reflection? In Magna Charta there is a clause which authorizes the people to seize the king's castles and oppose his arms when he exceeds his duty.

In this province if that preamble passes, there will be an immediate dissolution of every kind of authority; the people will be instantly in a state of nature. Why then precipitate this measure? Before we are prepared to build the new house, why should we pull down the old one and expose ourselves to all the inclemencies of the season?

R[ichard] H[enry] Lee [Virginia]. Most of the arguments apply to the resolve, not to the preamble.

E. THE DEBATE OVER INDEPENDENCE, 1774–1776

FROM 1763 onward, the idea of American independence was a subject of comment and conjecture by various writers both in England and America. One objection to the taking of Canada in 1763 had been that it might make the colonies less dependent on Great Britain. In 1766 Josiah Tucker, an English clergyman, wrote a pamphlet in which he charged that the Americans obviously wanted independence and that their opposition to the Stamp Act was a demonstration of the proposition. In 1768 General Gage declared "that they will struggle for independency, if the good folks at home are not already convinced of it, they soon will be convinced. From the denying the right of internal taxations, they next deny the right of duties on imports, and thus they mean to go on step by step 'till they throw off all subjections to your laws. They will acknowledge the king of Great Britain to be their king, but soon deny the prerogatives of the Crown, and acknowledge their king no longer than it shall be convenient for them to do so. It is very easy to gather all I have said, as well from the writings as the frequent conversations of the popular leaders." After the end of the First Continental Congress, the debate was in the open. The men who had lost the battle for control of the Congress charged in newspaper essay, pamphlet, and private letter that the popular leaders were aiming at independence.

But the popular leaders did not admit that this was their goal. Instead they stated and restated their views of the constitutional relationship that should exist between Britain and the colonies; they urged union among the colonies to maintain colonial rights; they made it plain that they would not compromise in their demand for colonial self-government; and they showed themselves willing to use forceful means to oppose British policies and British efforts to enforce them. In vain did their opponents charge the popular leaders with hypocrisy and insist that the measures they proposed in the first and second congresses were declarations of independence in fact, if not in name.

It is difficult and perhaps impossible to say just when the popular leaders came to believe that independence was the only possible solution of the dispute with Great Britain. If they believed it in 1774, they did not admit it, and if they had done so, they would have lost the support of many men such as George Washington, who were to support the movement for independence a year later. Furthermore, as they must have known, the minute they admitted that they wanted independence, they were chargeable with treason. Therefore, as wise men and cautious politicians, they remained silent as to their convictions, even in their most private letters. They were entirely content to allow anonymous newspaper essayists and the pamphleteers to debate the issue in public.

Why did they believe or come to believe in independence? Their American opponents charged them with various low motives; of being for independence because they were "republicans", or because they wanted to escape the payment of their debts to British merchants, or because they were smugglers, or because they were men without property, whose only hope of making a living was during a time of confusion. Although some of the revolutionary leaders were in these categories, a majority were plainly not smugglers, debtors, or rabble rousers. There is little alternative except to accept their public statements that they believed in freedom and liberty and self-government, and that since Britain was determined to impose her will on the colonies with the brute force of an army, independence was the only solution. Whatever the mixture of motives, this had become the basic issue by the middle of 1775 and even the strongest opponents of American independence had to face it, and one by one were converted to the position of the popular leaders.

By 1775 such men are more properly called revolutionary leaders. They would never have achieved their goal of independence had it not been for British measures. As each new one appeared, it was further proof of the argument that Britain was bent on tyranny and that the hope of reconciliation was a delusion. The men who were reluctant to face independence, but who objected just as strongly to British measures, were forced by the facts, in 1776, to concede the rightness of the argument. One by one they were won over to independence as in 1775 they had been won over to the necessity of meeting a British army with an American one.

Yet the opposition to independence remained deeply rooted and widely spread among many Americans. The strongest element in that opposition was the elusive but very real loyalty they felt for Great Britain, a loyalty that was the result of history–of the fact that England was literally the "Mother Country"–and it was a loyalty reinforced by family ties, education, and social and economic relationships. On another level there was a loyalty born of self-interest. Many of those closely associated with the royal officials of the colonies, the "court party" as they were often called, tended to loyalism. So too did many merchants who could not conceive of carrying on trade outside the bounds of the British Empire. Loyalist too were farmers such as those in the Carolina back country, who looked with dubious eye upon a movement carried on in the name of liberty and freedom, but led by their political enemies along the coast.

Perhaps the greatest factor behind the opposition to independence was the fear of many members of the colonial aristocracy that a war for independence would lead to social and political revolution at home, to the triumph of what they were shortly to call democracy. That fear is no better demonstrated than in the language used to describe the popular leaders and their followers. They were called among other things, "the rabble", "the mob", "Presbyterian republicans", and "New England republicans". Although most southern planters were far more active revolutionary leaders than the merchants of the north, even they spoke contemptuously of the "darling Democracy" of the New Englanders, and feared that they would try to spread it to the other colonies.

The revolutionary movement in the middle colonies, particularly in New York and Pennsylvania, was far different from that in the planting colonies. In New York it was centred in the city itself, and it was largely a popular movement of which the great merchants and landlords were afraid. In Pennsylvania the popular leaders in the city of Philadelphia had the co-operation of the aggressive Scotch-Irish of the back country who hated the aristocracy of Philadelphia. Although in these two colonies the aristocracy managed to retain a measure of control until 1776, their fear of an internal revolution grew more rather than less intense, and does much to explain their opposition to independence.

One of the first and clearest statements of their conviction was that contained in a letter of Gouverneur Morris written in May 1774, in which he declared that if the dispute with Britain continued, the aristocracy would be overthrown and New York would be ruled by a "riotous mob".[1] Morris became a patriot in the fight for independence, but he never changed his conviction that America should continue to be ruled by an aristocracy. Such sentiments abounded among members of the colonial aristocracy, some of whom remained loyal to Great Britain, but many of whom were leaders in the fight for independence as was Morris after 1776. These sentiments were expressed in diaries and private letters and sometimes in public as well. In January 1775 Thomas Wharton, a merchant of Philadelphia, wrote to his brother in England that the thoughtful people cannot help asking what will happen if England is beaten in a war. England is wrong, he wrote, but we expect her to redress our grievances. But no redress can be expected nor any civil or religious liberty if 'others' gain the ascendency. By 'others' he meant the "Presbyterian republicans" of back-country Pennsylvania, men who had little love for Quaker merchants such as Wharton.

The diary of James Allen, member of a wealthy Philadelphia family, is particularly revealing. In July of 1775 he wrote that many thinking people believed that America had seen its best days and that even if there was a victorious peace it would be difficult to restore order. Yet, he wrote, "if we fall, liberty no longer continues an inhabitant of this globe for England is running fast to slavery". In October 1775 he joined a battalion for the defence of the city. "My inducement principally to join them is that a man is suspected who does not, and I choose to have a musket on my shoulder to be on a par with them; and I believe discreet people mixing with them may keep them in order." By March of 1776 he was in despair. "The plot thickens; peace is scarcely thought of. Independency predominant. Thinking people uneasy, irresolute and inactive. The Mobility triumphant." He then went on to say: "I love the cause of liberty, but cannot heartily join in the prosecution of measures totally foreign to the original plan of resistance. The madness of the multitude is but one degree better than submission to the Tea Act."

Over and over again such men as Allen bewailed the fact that the cause of resistance had fallen into "low hands" and that "new men" one had never heard of before had come to take the lead. The revolutionary leaders recognized this feeling as a cause of opposition. Thus in October 1776 the Connecticut Committee of Safety, in listing the various causes for the growth of "toryism", cited as the most important the fact that many "disapprove of the men in power and the measures in their respective states". John Adams believed profoundly in independence and worked to achieve it, but at the same time he was convinced that independence might bring a democratic upheaval with it. On 3 July, the day after Congress adopted the Virginia resolution for independence, he wrote that "the people will have unbounded power and the people are extremely addicted to corruption and venality, as well as the great".

The fear of "the people" and what they might do was thus a significant element in the thinking of American leaders during 1775 and 1776. Another thing that many of them feared was civil war among the colonies if independence was declared. In the first Congress in 1774 Joseph Galloway had argued that a supreme legislature was a necessity, and declared that British power alone prevented civil war among the colonies. There was real reason for such fear for many of the colonies had boundary disputes that threatened warfare. Pennsylvania and Virginia were engaged in a dispute over the region around Fort Pitt. Connecticut claimed the Wyoming Valley along

[1] No. 169.

the Susquehanna River in Pennsylvania and had moved settlers into it. Virginia's neighbours were alarmed at what they believed to be her imperialistic ambitions.

It is in the light of such attitudes that American opposition to independence must be considered. It was because of them that the conservative leaders in Congress in 1774 and 1775 fought every measure which tended towards independence by indirection. Hence, where they were in control of colonies in 1775, they adopted instructions to their delegates in Congress to vote against independence if the question should arise.[1] But in February 1776 they failed in an attempt to secure the adoption of an address to the colonies denying that the purpose of Congress was independence. Thereafter all they could do was to delay action in the hope of an offer of reconciliation from Britain. Some of them came bitterly and reluctantly to the conclusion that all that was left to do was to fight.[2] Even so, the word 'independence' was an alarming thing as late as March 1776. "Independence", wrote John Adams, "is a hobgoblin of so frightful mien, that it would throw a delicate person into fits to look it in the face."[3]

From February 1776 onward, the revolutionary leaders in Congress were increasingly aggressive. They urged their colonies to send them instructions favourable to independence in order to counter the instructions opposed to it. In April Congress declared the ports of the colonies open to the world in answer to the American Prohibitory Bill.[4] In May Congress recommended that all old colonial governments deriving their powers from the Crown be replaced by new ones deriving their power from the people.[5]

Meanwhile, pamphlets and newspaper articles in increasing numbers demanded independence, beginning with the publication of Thomas Paine's *Common Sense* early in January 1776. In April 1776 "A Planter" addressed the inhabitants of Virginia, declaring that "we have not armed from one end of the continent to the other, and expended so many millions, merely to drown a chest of tea, but to oppose the dangerous authority the English House of Representatives has usurped, pretending to bind us in all cases whatever. . . ." "Where is the wisdom of this squeamishness about independence pretended by the Assembly of Pennsylvania or any other assembly or convention on the continent? There appears to be moderation in it, indeed; but it is the moderation of a spaniel dog that grows more tame in proportion to the ill usage he receives."

As the result of such opinion, and of the manœuvring between the revolutionary leaders in Congress and the leaders within the colonies, the pressure for open declaration of independence grew stronger. On 12 April the North Carolina convention authorized its delegates in Congress to join with others in declaring independence and forming foreign alliances. On 4 May Rhode Island declared its independence of Great Britain. On 15 May the Virginia convention took decisive action and instructed its delegates in Congress to move for independence, foreign alliances, and the formation of a confederation.[6] On 27 May the Virginia and North Carolina delegates laid their instructions before Congress and on 7 June Richard Henry Lee of Virginia moved in Congress: "Resolved, that these United Colonies, are, and of right ought to be, free and independent states, that they are absolved from all allegiance to the British Crown and that all political connection between them and the state of Great Britain, is and ought to be, totally dissolved."[7] It was entirely fitting that John Adams seconded the motion.

[1] No. 170.　[2] Nos. 171, 173.　[3] No. 172.　[4] No. 167.　[5] No. 168.　[6] No. 174.　[7] No. 175.

Lee's resolution was debated for two days, in the course of which many of the old arguments against independence were reiterated.[1] A final vote was put off for three weeks because of the instructions against independence from such colonies as Pennsylvania. Meanwhile, a committee consisting of Thomas Jefferson of Virginia, Benjamin Franklin of Pennsylvania, Roger Sherman of Connecticut, John Adams of Massachusetts, and Robert R. Livingston of New York was appointed to draft a declaration of independence.[2] At the same time a committee of one from each colony, headed by John Dickinson of Pennsylvania, was appointed to draft articles of confederation.

On 1 July Lee's motion was again debated. John Dickinson made a formal speech in opposition.[3] Nine colonies voted for the resolution. Pennsylvania and South Carolina voted against it. The New York delegates did not vote because of their instructions. The two delegates from Delaware were divided. At the request of a South Carolina delegate the final decision was postponed until the next day. On 2 July South Carolina voted for the resolution and the arrival of a third member from Delaware broke the tie in that delegation. On 1 July the majority of the Pennsylvania delegation was opposed to independence. The next day John Dickinson and Robert Morris stayed away and James Wilson switched his vote, thus allowing the Pennsylvania delegation to vote for the resolution. Only the New York delegation, still bound by its instructions, refused to vote.

There was now no turning back, as perhaps there had not been since the First Continental Congress. Men now had to choose between loyalty to Great Britain and loyalty to America. Men like Thomas Hutchinson and Joseph Galloway had chosen loyalty to Britain long before; others like Samuel Adams, John Adams, Patrick Henry, Richard Henry Lee, and Thomas Jefferson had likewise taken their stand in favour of America. But others who had delayed could no longer do so. Reluctantly, some now chose loyalty to Britain, and equally reluctantly, others chose to become American patriots. The motives and emotions lying behind the choices were complex and not to be sorted into neat categories. Writing in 1807, John Adams said that "the principles of the American Revolution may be said to have been as various as the thirteen states that went through it and in some sense almost as diversified as the individuals who acted in it. In some few principles, or perhaps in one single principle, they all united."

169. Gouverneur Morris to [John] Penn (20 May 1774)

The following letter was written on the day of the mass meeting held in New York to consider an answer to the letter from Boston asking for the stoppage of trade with Great Britain as a result of the Boston Port Act (see Nos. 140 and 141). Morris, a younger member of the New York aristocracy, was one of the most realistic and even cynical participants in the Revolution. His letter describes lucidly the events in New York after 1763. The aristocracy at first encouraged mob action to oppose British measures but in doing so inadvertently created a popular movement which eventually was turned against the aristocracy itself. Morris illuminates the thinking of many members of the colonial aristocracy who opposed independence because they feared that it would mean an internal revolution. Like many other members of the aristocracy, Morris became a patriot leader, and like them too, he fought all his life to limit and check the democratic potential unleashed by the Revolution. Printed: Force, *American Archives*, 4th Series, I, pp. 342-343.

---

[1] Nos. 176, 177.   [2] No. 179.   [3] No. 178.

You have heard, and you will hear a great deal about p   ap of chaff *you* may find some grains of good sense. Bel   n and religion are only watchwords. We have appointed a cor   e have nominated one. Let me give you the history of it. It is   that the lower orders of mankind are more easily led by speciou   ose of a more exalted station. This, and many similar proposi   tter than your humble servant.

The troubles in America during Grenville's admi   ntry upon this finesse. They stimulated some daring coxcombs   o an attack upon the bounds of order and decency. These fello   Cades of the day, the leaders in all the riots, the bell-wethers   eason of the manœuvre in those who wished to keep fair with   d at the same time to receive the incense of popular applause,   rceive. On the whole, the shepherds were not much to blame i   view. The bell-wethers jingled merrily and roared out liberty   religion, and a multitude of cant terms which everyone thought he underst   was egregiously mistaken. For you must know the shepherds kept the dictionary of the day, and like the mysteries of the ancient mythology, it was not for profane eyes or ears. This answered many purposes; the simple flock put themselves entirely under the protection of these most excellent shepherds. By and by, behold a great metamorphosis without the help of Ovid or his divinities, but entirely effectuated by two modern Genii, the god of Ambition and the goddess of Faction. The first of these prompted the shepherds to shear some of their flock, and then in conjunction with the other, converted the bell-wethers into shepherds. That we have been in hot water with the British Parliament ever since everybody knows. Consequently these new shepherds had their hands full of employment. The old ones kept themselves least in sight, and a want of confidence in each other was not the least evil which followed. The port of Boston has been shut up. These sheep, simple as they are, cannot be gulled as heretofore. In short, there is no ruling them, and now, to leave the metaphor, the heads of the mobility grow dangerous to the gentry, and how to keep them down is the question. While they correspond with the other colonies, call and dismiss popular assemblies, make resolves to bind the consciences of the rest of mankind, bully poor printers, and exert with full force all their other tribunitial powers, it is impossible to curb them.

But art sometimes goes farther than force, and therefore, to trick them handsomely a committee of patricians was to be nominated, and into their hands was to be committed the majesty of the people, and the highest trust was to be reposed in them by a mandate that they should take care, *quod respublica non capiat injuriam*. The tribunes, through the want of good legerdemain in the senatorial order, perceived the finesse; and yesterday I was present at a grand division of the city, and there I beheld my fellow-citizens very accurately counting all their chickens, not only before any of them were hatched, but before above one half of the eggs were laid. In short, they fairly contended about the future forms of our government, whether it should be founded upon aristocratic or democratic principles.

I stood in the balcony, and on my right hand were ranged all the people of property, with some few poor dependents, and on the other all the tradesmen, etc., who thought it worth their while to leave daily labour for the good of the country. The spirit of the English constitution has yet a little influence left, and but a little. The remains of it, however, will give the wealthy people a superiority this time, but would they secure it they must banish all schoolmasters and confine all knowledge to themselves. This cannot be. The mob begin to think and to reason. Poor reptiles! It is with them a vernal morning; they are struggling to cast off their winter's slough, they bask in the sunshine, and ere noon they will bite, depend upon it. The gentry begin to fear this. Their committee will be appointed, they will deceive the people and again forfeit a share of their confidence. And if these instances of what with one side is policy, with the other perfidy, shall continue to increase and become more frequent, farewell aristocracy. I see, and I see it with fear and trembling, that if the disputes with Great Britain continue, we shall be under the worst of all possible dominions; we shall be under the domination of a riotous mob.

It is the interest of all men, therefore, to seek for reunion with the parent state. A safe compact seems, in my poor opinion, to be now tendered. Internal taxation is to be left with ourselves. The right of regulating trade to be vested in Great Britain, where alone is found the power of protecting it. I trust you will agree with me that this is the only possible mode of union. Men by nature are free as air. When they enter into society, there is, there must be, an implied compact, for there never yet was an express one, that a part of this freedom shall be given up for the security of the remainder. But what part? The answer is plain. The least possible, considering the circumstances of the society, which constitute what may be called its political necessity.

And what does this political necessity require in the present instance? Not that Britain should lay imposts upon us for the support of government, nor for its defence; not that she should regulate our internal police. These things affect us only. She can have no right to interfere. To these things we ourselves are competent. But can it be said that we are competent to the regulating of trade? The position is absurd, for this affects every part of the British Empire, every part of the habitable earth. If Great Britain, if Ireland, if America, if all of them are to make laws of trade, there must be a collision of these different authorities, and then who is to decide the *vis major*? To recur to this, if possible to be avoided, is the greatest of all great absurdities.

Political necessity, therefore, requires that this power should be placed in the hands of one part of the empire. Is it a question which part? Let me answer by taking another. Pray, which part of the empire protects trade? Which part of the empire receives almost immense sums to guard the rest? And what danger is in the trust? Some men object that England will draw all the profits of our trade into her coffers. All that she can, undoubtedly. But unless a reasonable compensation for his trouble be left to the merchant here, she destroys the trade, and then she will receive no profit from it.

If I remember, in one of those kind letters with which you have honoured me, you desire my thoughts on matters as they rise. How much pleasure I take in complying with your requests let my present letter convince you. If I am faulty in telling things which you know better than I do, you must excuse this fault, and a thousand others, for which I can make no apology.

170. Pennsylvania Assembly instructions against independence (9 November 1775)

Although Pennsylvania had a series of revolutionary conventions from 1774 onward, the legal Assembly of the province remained in control of the functions of government. The Assembly was dominated by a conservative group of merchants and lawyers who opposed independence because they feared, and correctly, that they would lose control of the province in a political upheaval. The instructions below order the delegates in the Second Continental Congress to oppose both independence and any change in government. These instructions were also adopted by New York, Maryland, Delaware, and South Carolina, and for months provided an effective barrier against independence. Printed: *Pennsylvania Archives*, 8th Series, VIII, pp. 7352-7353.

The trust reposed in you is of such a nature and the modes of executing it may be so diversified in the course of your deliberations, that it is scarcely possible to give you particular instructions respecting it.

We, therefore, in general, direct that you, or any four of you, meet in Congress the delegates of the several colonies now assembled in this city and any such delegates as may meet in Congress next year; that you consult together on the present critical and alarming state of public affairs; that you exert your utmost endeavours to agree upon, and recommend such measures as you shall judge to afford the best prospect of obtaining redress of American grievances, and restoring that union and harmony between Great Britain and the colonies so essential to the welfare and happiness of both countries.

Though the oppressive measures of the British Parliament and administration have compelled us to resist their violence by force of arms, yet we strictly enjoin you that you, in behalf of this colony, dissent from and utterly reject any propositions, should such be made, that may cause or lead to a separation from our mother country or a change of the form of this government.

You are directed to make report of your proceedings to this House.

171. Joseph Hewes to Samuel Johnston (20 March 1776)

Joseph Hewes, a North Carolina merchant, is a typical example of a colonial leader who felt driven into independence by British policy. In July of 1775 he wrote: "we do not want to be independent; we want no revolution, unless a change of ministry and measures would be deemed such." By 1 December 1775 he wrote: "no plan of separation has been offered, the colonies will never agree to any till drove to it by dire necessity. I wish the time may not come too soon. I fear it will be the case if the British ministry pursue their present diabolical schemes." By 20 March 1776, when he wrote the following letter, he was convinced that "nothing is left now but to fight it out", but he was reluctant to do it and pessimistic about the outcome. Printed: Edmund C. Burnett, ed., *Letters of Members of the Continental Congress* (8 vols., Washington, 1921-1936), I, p. 401.

. . . The Act of Parliament prohibiting all trade and commerce between Great Britain and the colonies has been lately brought here by a Mr. Temple from London. It makes all American property found on the sea liable to seizure and confiscation, and I fear it will make the breach between the two countries so wide as never more to be reconciled. We have heard much talk of commissioners to be sent to treat with us.

I do not expect any. The Act of Parliament empowers the king to appoint commissioners to receive submissions and grant pardons but no further. Doctor Franklin told me last evening he had a letter from London dated the 25th December. No commissioners were then appointed; Parliament was prorogued to 25th of January. I see no prospect of a reconciliation. Nothing is left now but to fight it out, and for this we are not well provided, having but little ammunition, no arms, no money, nor are we unanimous in our councils. We do not treat each other with that decency and respect that was observed heretofore. Jealousies, ill-natured observations and recriminations take place of reason and argument. Our tempers are sound. Some among us urge strongly for independency and eternal separation, others wish to wait a little longer and to have the opinion of their constituents on that subject. You must give us the sentiment of your province when your convention meets. Several merchants and others have petitioned the Congress for leave to fit out privateers to cruise against British vessels. It was granted yesterday. The restrictions are not yet completed or I would have sent you a copy of them. I send you the last newspaper enclosed to which refer for news.

172. John Adams to General Horatio Gates (23 March 1776)

John Adams's letter is a revealing statement by one of the most ardent yet one of the most realistic of the supporters of American independence. He was convinced that the American Prohibitory Act (No. 167) was an act of independence, yet he was keenly aware of the reasons why many Americans opposed independence. Printed: Burnett, *Letters of Members of the Continental Congress*, I, pp. 405-406.

. . . I agree with you that in politics the middle way is none at all. If we finally fail in this great and glorious contest, it will be by bewildering ourselves in groping after this middle way. We have hitherto conducted half a war, acted upon the line of defence, etc., etc. But you will see by tomorrow's paper, that for the future we are likely to wage three quarters of a war. The continental ships-of-war and provincial ships-of-war and letters of marque and privateers are permitted to cruise upon British property wherever found on the ocean. This is not independency you know, nothing like it.

If a post or two more should bring you unlimited latitude of trade to all nations, and a polite invitation to all nations to trade with you, take care that you don't call it or think it independency. No such matter. Independency is a hobgoblin of so frightful mien that it would throw a delicate person into fits to look it in the face.

I know not whether you have seen the Act of Parliament called the restraining act, or prohibitory act, or piratical act, or plundering act, or act of independency, for by all these titles is it called. I think the most apposite is the act of independency, for king, Lords, and Commons have united in sundering this country from that, I think forever. It is a complete dismemberment of the British Empire. It throws thirteen colonies out of the royal protection, levels all distinctions, and makes us independent in spite of our supplications and entreaties.

It may be fortunate that the act of independency should come from the British Parliament rather than the American Congress; but it is very odd that Americans should hesitate at accepting such a gift from them. However, my dear friend Gates, all our misfortunes arise from a single source – the reluctance of the southern colonies to republican government. The success of this war depends on a skilful steerage of the political vessel. The difficulty lies in forming constitutions for particular colonies and a continental constitution for the whole. Each colony should establish its own government, and then a league should be formed between them all. This can be done only on popular principles and maxims which are so abhorrent to the inclinations of the barons of the south and the proprietary interests in the middle colonies as well as to that avarice of land which has made upon this continent so many votaries to Mammon that I sometimes dread the consequences. However, patience, fortitude, and perseverance with the help of time will get us over these obstructions.

Thirteen colonies under such a form of government as that of Connecticut, or one not quite so popular, leagued together in a faithful confederacy, might bid defiance to all the potentates of Europe if united against them. . . .

173. Carter Braxton to Landon Carter (14 April 1776)

Braxton, a Virginia planter and merchant, opposed independence but became a patriot when forced to choose. The following letter, written while he was attending the Second Continental Congress, sets forth his reasons for opposition. He was alarmed at New England 'democracy' and feared the outbreak of war over rival land claims. Like many another conservative, he wanted the formation of a central government prior to a declaration of independence, if that proved inevitable. Printed: Burnett, *Letters of the Members of the Continental Congress*, I, pp. 420–421.

. . . Independency and total separation from Great Britain are the interesting subjects of all ranks of men and often agitate our body. It is in truth a delusive bait which men inconsiderately catch at without knowing the hook to which it is affixed. It is an object to be wished for by every American when it can be obtained with safety and honour. That this is not the moment I will prove by arguments that to me are decisive and which exist with certainty. Your refined notion of our public honour being engaged to await the terms offered by commissioners operates strongly with me and many others and makes the first reason I would offer. My next is that America is in too defenceless a state for the declaration, having no alliance with a naval power nor as yet any fleet of consequence of her own to protect that trade which is so essential to the prosecution of the war, without which I know we cannot go on much longer. It is said by the advocates for separation that France will undoubtedly assist us after we have asserted the state, and therefore they urge us to make the experiment. Would such a blind precipitate measure as this be justified by prudence, first to throw off our connection with G. Britain and then give ourselves up to the arms of France? Would not the court so famous for intrigues and deception avail herself of our situation and from it exact much severer terms than if we were to treat with her (G.B.) beforehand and settle the terms of any future alliance. Surely she would, but the truth of the matter is, there are some who are afraid to await the arrival of commissioners, lest the dispute should be accommodated much against their will even upon the admission of our own terms. For however strange it may appear I am satisfied that the eastern colonies do not mean to have a reconciliation and in this I am justified by public and private reasons. To illustrate my opinion I will beg leave to mention them.

Two of the New England colonies enjoy a government purely democratical, the nature and principle of which, both civil and religious, are so totally incompatible with monarchy that they have ever lived in a restless state under it. The other two, though not so popular in their frame, bordered so near upon it that monarchical influence hung very heavy on them. The best opportunity in the world being now offered them to throw off all subjection and embrace their darling democracy, they are determined to accept it. These are aided by those of a private nature, but not less cogent. The colonies of Massachusetts and Connecticut, who rule the other two, have claims on the province of Pennsylvania in the whole for near one third of the land within their provincial bounds, and indeed the claim extended to its full extent comes within four miles of this city. This dispute was carried to the king and council, and with them it now lies. The eastern colonies, unwilling they should now be the arbiter, have asserted their claims by force, and have at this time eight hundred men in arms upon the upper part of this land called Wyoming, where they are peaceable at present only through the influence of the Congress. Then naturally, there arises a heartburning and jealousy between these people and they must have two very different objects in view. The province of New York is not without her fears and apprehensions from the temper of her neighbours, their great swarms, and small territory. Even Virginia is not free from claim on Pennsylvania nor Maryland from those on Virginia. Some of the delegates from our colony carry their ideas of right to lands so far to the eastward that the middle colonies dread their being swallowed up between the claims of them and those from the east. And yet, without any adjustment of those disputes and a variety of other matters, some are for lugging us into independence. But so long as these remain unsettled and men act upon the principles they ever have done, you may rely, no such thing will be generally agreed on. Upon reviewing the secret movements of men and things I am convinced the assertion of independence is far off. If it was to be now asserted the continent would be torn in pieces by intestine wars and convulsions. Previous to independence all disputes must be healed and harmony prevail. A grand continental league must be formed and a superintending power also. When these necessary steps are taken and I see a coalition formed sufficient to withstand the power of Britain, or any other, then am I for an independent state and all its consequences, as then I think they will produce happiness to America. It is a true saying of a wit – we must hang together or separately. I will not beg your pardon for intruding this long letter upon your old age, which I judged necessary in my situation, and to conclude by assuring you I am with great regard . . .

[P.S.] If any of our newspapers will be agreeable, say so in your next.

174. The resolutions of the Virginia convention (15 May 1776)

The Virginia convention met anew on 6 May 1776 and on the next day resolved itself into a committee of the whole to consider the state of the colony. The result of its deliberations was the following set of resolutions, unanimously agreed to by the 112 men present, declaring that there was no alternative to independence and instructing the Virginia delegates in Congress to propose a declaration of independence and to assent to the formation of foreign alliances and a confederation of the colonies. The final resolve provided for the formation of a constitution for Virginia, a task completed before Congress voted for independence in July. Printed: Force, *American Archives*, 4th Series, VI, p. 1524.

Forasmuch as all the endeavours of the united colonies by the most decent repre-sentations and petitions to the king and Parliament of Great Britain to restore peace and security to America under the British government and a reunion with that people upon just and liberal terms, instead of a redress of grievances, have produced from an imperious and vindictive administration increased insult, oppression, and a vigorous attempt to effect our total destruction. By a late Act, all these colonies are declared to be in rebellion and out of the protection of the British Crown, our properties subjected to confiscation, our people, when captivated, compelled to join in the murder and plunder of their relations and countrymen, and all former rapine and oppression of Americans declared legal and just. Fleets and armies are raised, and the aid of foreign troops engaged to assist these destructive purposes. The king's representative in this colony has not only withheld all the powers of government from operating for our safety, but, having retired on board an armed ship, is carrying on a piratical and savage war against us, tempting our slaves by every artifice to resort to him, and training and employing them against their masters. In this state of extreme danger we have no alternative left but an abject submission to the will of those overbearing tyrants, or a total separation from the Crown and government of Great Britain, uniting and exerting the strength of all America for defence, and forming alliances with foreign powers for commerce and aid in war. Wherefore, appealing to the Searcher of hearts for the sincerity of former declarations, expressing our desire to preserve the connection with that nation, and that we are driven from that inclina-tion by their wicked councils and the eternal law of self-preservation:

Resolved, unanimously. That the delegates appointed to represent this colony in general congress be instructed to propose to that respectable body to declare the united colonies free and independent states, absolved from all allegiance to, or dependence upon, the Crown or Parliament of Great Britain; and that they give the assent of this colony to such declaration, and to whatever measures may be thought proper and necessary by the congress for forming foreign alliances, and a confederation of the colonies, at such time, and in the manner, as to them shall seem best. Provided, that the power of forming government for, and the regulations of the internal concerns of each colony be left to the respective colonial legislatures.

Resolved, unanimously. That a committee be appointed to prepare a declaration of rights, and such a plan of government as will be most likely to maintain peace and order in this colony, and secure substantial and equal liberty to the people.

175. The Virginia resolutions for independence (7 June 1776)

The Virginia resolutions of 15 May (No. 174) were laid before Congress on 27 May along with instructions from North Carolina permitting the delegation of that colony to vote for independence. On 7 June Richard Henry Lee of Virginia offered the following resolutions to Congress. They were debated on Saturday, 8 June and on Monday, 10 June. Consideration was postponed for three weeks in order to permit the delegations not having authority to vote for independence to secure a change of instructions. Printed: *Journals of the Continental Congress*, v, p. 425.

Resolved, that these united colonies are, and of right ought to be, free and inde-pendent states, that they are absolved from all allegiance to the British Crown, and that all political connection between them and the state of Great Britain is, and ought to be, totally dissolved.

That it is expedient forthwith to take the most effectual measures for forming foreign alliances.

That a plan of confederation be prepared and transmitted to the respective colonies for their consideration and approbation.

176. Edward Rutledge to John Jay [8 June 1776]

Rutledge of South Carolina opposed Richard Henry Lee's resolution of 7 June. The following letter amplifies somewhat the arguments given in Jefferson's notes on the debates (No. 177). Printed: Burnett, *Letters of Members of the Continental Congress*, I, pp. 476–477.

The Congress sat till 7 o'clock this evening in consequence of a motion of R. H. Lee's rendering ourselves free and independent state. The sensible part of the house opposed the motion–they had no objection to forming a scheme of a treaty which they would send to France by proper persons and uniting this continent by a confederacy. They saw no wisdom in a declaration of independence, nor any other purpose to be enforced by it, but placing ourselves in the power of those with whom we mean to treat, giving our enemy notice of our intentions before we had taken any steps to execute them and thereby enabling them to counteract us in our intentions and rendering ourselves ridiculous in the eyes of foreign powers by attempting to bring them into an union with us before we had united with each other. For daily experience evinces that the inhabitants of every colony consider themselves at liberty to do as they please upon almost every occasion. And a man must have the impudence of a New Englander to propose in our present disjointed state any treaty (honourable to us) to a nation now at peace. No reason could be assigned for pressing into this measure but the reason of every madman, a show of our spirit. The event, however, was that the question was postponed; it is to be renewed on Monday when I mean to move that it should be postponed for 3 weeks or months. In the meantime the plan of confederation and the scheme of treaty may go on. I don't know whether I shall succeed in this motion; I think not, it is at least doubtful. However, I must do what is right in my own eyes, and consequences must take care of themselves. I wish you had been here. The whole argument was sustained on one side by R[obert] Livingston, [James] Wilson, [John] Dickinson and myself and by the power of all N[ew] England, Virginia, and Georgia at the other.

177. Thomas Jefferson's notes on the debates and proceedings on the Virginia resolution of independence (8, 10 June, July 1776)

Thomas Jefferson made notes on the debates of 8 and 10 June and on the proceedings of 1 July, and following. At a later date he rewrote the rough notes, which subsequently disappeared. Jefferson sent a copy of his transcription to James Madison on 1 June 1783, and later inserted it in his "Auto-biography", which was written during the early part of 1821. The editors of *The Papers of Thomas Jefferson* (I, pp. 299–301), after a careful analysis of the problems involved, conclude that the transcript was probably prepared during the summer of 1776. Despite certain errors it remains the only significant account of the crucial debate on 8 and 10 June 1776. The following document is a copy of the one sent to James Madison on 1 June 1783. Printed: *Journals of the Continental Congress*, VI, pp. 1087–1093.

In Congress, Friday, June 7, 1776

The delegates from Virginia moved in obedience to instructions from their constituents that the Congress should declare that these United Colonies are and of right ought to be free and independent states; that they are absolved from all obedience to the British Crown, and that all political connection between them and the state of Great Britain is and ought to be totally dissolved; that measures should be immediately taken for procuring the assistance of foreign powers, and a confederation be formed to bind the colonies more closely together.

The house being obliged to attend at that time to some other business, the proposition was referred to the next day when the members were ordered to attend punctually at ten o'clock.

Saturday June 8th they proceeded to take it into consideration, and referred it to a committee of the whole, into which they immediately resolved themselves, and passed that day and Monday the 10th in debating on the subject.

It was argued by [James] Wilson, Robert R. Livingston, E[dward] Rutledge, [John] Dickinson, and others:

That though they were friends to the measures themselves and saw the impossibility that we should ever again be united with Great Britain, yet they were against adopting them at this time;

That the conduct we had formerly observed was wise and proper now, of deferring to take any capital step till the voice of the people drove us into it;

That they were our power and without them our declarations could not be carried into effect;

That the people of the middle colonies (Maryland, Delaware, Pennsylvania, the Jersies, and N[ew] York) were not yet ripe for bidding adieu to British connection; but that they were fast ripening and in a short time would join in the general voice of America;

That the resolution entered into by this house on the 15th of May for suppressing the exercise of all powers derived from the Crown had shown, by the ferment into which it had thrown these middle colonies, that they had not yet accommodated their minds to a separation from the mother country;

That some of them had expressly forbidden their delegates to consent to such a declaration, and others had given no instructions, and consequently no powers to give such consent;

That if the delegates of any particular colony had no power to declare such colony independent, certain they were the others could not declare it for them, the colonies being as yet perfectly independent of each other;

That the Assembly of Pennsylvania was now sitting above stairs, their convention would sit within a few days; the convention of New York was now sitting, and those of the Jersies and Delaware counties would meet on the Monday following, and it was probable these bodies would take up the question of independence, and would declare to their delegates the voice of their state;

That if such a declaration should now be agreed to, these delegates must retire and possibly their colonies might secede from the union;

That such a secession would weaken us more than could be compensated by any foreign alliance;

That in the event of such a division foreign powers would either refuse to join themselves to our fortunes, or having us so much in their power as that desperate declaration would place us, they would insist on terms proportionably more hard and prejudicial;

That we had little reason to expect an alliance with those to whom alone as yet we had cast our eyes;

That France and Spain had reason to be jealous of that rising power which would one day certainly strip them of all their American possessions;

That it was more likely they should form a connection with the British court who, if they should find themselves unable otherwise to extricate themselves from their difficulties, would agree to a partition of our territories, restoring Canada to France and the Floridas to Spain to accomplish for themselves a recovery of these colonies;

That it would not be long before we should receive certain information of the disposition of the French court from the agent whom we had sent to Paris for that purpose;

That if this disposition should be favourable, by waiting the event of the present campaign, which we all hoped would be successful, we should have reason to expect an alliance on better terms;

That this would in fact work no delay of any effectual aid from such ally, as, from the advance of the season and distance of our situation, it was impossible we could receive any assistance during this campaign;

That it was prudent to fix among ourselves the terms on which we would form alliance before we declared we would form one at all events;

And that if these were agreed on and our declaration of independence ready by the time our ambassador should be ready to sail, it would be as well as to go into that declaration at this day.

On the other side it was urged by J[ohn] Adams, [Richard Henry] Lee, [George] Wythe, and others:

That no gentleman had argued against the policy or the right of separation from Britain, nor had supposed it possible we should ever renew our connection; that they had only opposed its being now declared;

That the question was not whether, by a declaration of independence we should make ourselves what we are not, but whether we should declare a fact which already exists;

That as to the people or Parliament of England, we had always been independent of them, their restraints on our trade deriving efficacy from our acquiescence only and not from any rights they possessed of imposing them, and that so far our connection had been federal only and was now dissolved by the commencement of hostilities;

That as to the king, we had been bound to him by allegiance, but that this bond was now dissolved by his assent to the late Act of Parliament by which he declares us out of his protection and by his levying war on us, a fact which had long ago proved us out of his protection, it being a certain position in law that allegiance and protection are reciprocal, the one ceasing when the other is withdrawn;

That James II never declared the people of England out of his protection; yet his actions proved it, and the Parliament declared it;

No delegates then can be denied, or ever want a power of declaring an existent truth;

That the delegates from the Delaware counties having declared their constituents ready to join, there are only two colonies, Pennsylvania and Maryland, whose delegates are absolutely tied up, and that these had by their instructions only reserved a right of confirming or rejecting the measure;

That the instructions from Pennsylvania might be accounted for from the times in which they were drawn, near a twelvemonth ago, since which the face of affairs has totally changed;

That within that time it had become apparent that Britain was determined to accept nothing less than a carte blanche, and that the king's answer to the lord mayor, aldermen, and common council of London, which had come to hand four days ago, must have satisfied everyone of this point;

That the people wait for us to lead the way;

That *they* are in favour of the measure, though the instructions given by some of their *representatives* are not;

That the voice of the representatives is not always consonant with the voice of the people, and that this is remarkably the case in these middle colonies;

That the effect of the resolution of the 15th of May has proved this, which, raising the murmurs of some in the colonies of Pennsylvania and Maryland, called forth the opposing voice of the freer part of the people and proved them to be the majority, even in these colonies;

That the backwardness of these two colonies might be ascribed partly to the influence of proprietary power and connections, and partly to their having not yet been attacked by the enemy;

That these causes were not likely to be soon removed, as there seemed no probability that the enemy would make either of these the seat of this summer's war;

That it would be vain to wait either weeks or months for perfect unanimity, since it was impossible that all men should ever become of one sentiment on any question;

That the conduct of some colonies from the beginning of this contest had given reason to suspect it was their settled policy to keep in the rear of the confederacy, that their particular prospect might be better, even in the worst event;

That therefore it was necessary for those colonies who had thrown themselves forward and hazarded all from the beginning to come forward now also and put all again to their own hazard;

That the history of the Dutch revolution, of whom three states only confederated at first, proved that a secession of some colonies would not be so dangerous as some apprehended;

That a declaration of independence alone could render it consistent with European delicacy for European powers to treat with us, or even to receive an ambassador from us;

That till this they would not receive our vessels into their ports nor acknowledge the adjudications of our courts of admiralty to be legitimate in cases of capture of British vessels;

That though France and Spain may be jealous of our rising power, they must think it will be much more formidable with the addition of Great Britain and will therefore see it their interest to prevent a coalition; but should they refuse, we shall be but where we are; whereas without trying we shall never know whether they will aid us or not;

That the present campaign may be unsuccessful, and therefore we had better propose an alliance while our affairs wear a hopeful aspect;

That to wait the event of this campaign will certainly work delay because during this summer France may assist us effectually by cutting off those supplies of provisions from England and Ireland on which the enemy's armies here are to depend, or by setting in motion the great power they have collected in the West Indies and calling our enemy to the defence of the possessions they have there;

That it would be idle to lose time in settling the terms of alliance, till we had first determined we would enter into alliance;

That it is necessary to lose no time in opening a trade for our people, who will want clothes and will want money too for the payment of taxes;

And that the only misfortune is that we did not enter into alliance with France six months sooner, as, besides opening their ports for the vent of our last year's produce, they might have marched an army into Germany and prevented the petty princes there from selling their unhappy subjects to subdue us.

It appearing in the course of these debates that the colonies of N[ew] York, N[ew] Jersey, Pennsylvania, Delaware, and Maryland were not yet matured for falling from the parent stem, but that they were fast advancing to that state, it was thought most prudent to wait a while for them, and to postpone the final decision to July 1. But that this might occasion as little delay as possible, a committee was appointed to prepare a declaration of independence. The committee were J[ohn] Adams, Dr. Franklin, Roger Sherman, Robert R. Livingston, and myself. Committees were also appointed at the same time to prepare a plan of confederation for the colonies, and to state the terms proper to be proposed for foreign alliance. The committee for drawing the declaration of independence desired me to do it. It was accordingly done, and being approved by them, I reported it to the house on Friday the 28th of June, when it was read and ordered to lie on the table. On Monday the 1st of July the house resolved itself into a committee of the whole and resumed the consideration of the original motion made by the delegates of Virginia, which being again debated through the day, was carried in the affirmative by the votes of N[ew] Hampshire, Connecticut, Massachusetts, Rhode Island, N[ew] Jersey, Maryland, Virginia, N[orth] Carolina, and Georgia. S[outh] Carolina and Pennsylvania voted against it. Delaware having but two members present, they were divided. The delegates for N[ew] York declared they were for it themselves and were assured their constituents were for it but that their instructions, having been drawn near a twelvemonth before, when reconciliation was still the general object, they were enjoined by them to do nothing which should impede that object. They therefore thought themselves not justifiable in voting on either side and asked leave to withdraw from the question which was given them. The committee rose and reported their resolution to the house. Mr. Rutledge of S[outh] Carolina then requested the determination might be put off to the next day as he believed his colleagues, though they disapproved of the resolution, would then join in it for the sake of unanimity. The ultimate question whether the house would agree to the resolution of the committee, was accordingly postponed to the next day, when it was again moved and S[outh] Carolina concurred in voting for it. In the meantime a third member had come post from the Delaware counties and turned the vote of that colony in favour of the resolution. Members of a different sentiment attending that morning from Pennsylvania also, their vote was changed so that the whole twelve colonies who were authorized to vote at all gave their voices for it; and within a few days the convention of N[ew] York approved of it, and thus supplied the void occasioned by the withdrawing of their delegates from the vote.

178. John Dickinson's speech against independence (1 July 1776)

John Dickinson won wide fame as a defender of colonial rights in 1767-1768 for his letters of a "Pennsylvania Farmer" in opposition to the Townshend Acts. Because he denied the authority of Parliament he was looked upon as a radical by the Pennsylvania Assembly which at first refused to elect him a delegate to the First Continental Congress. Yet he consistently opposed independence and by the end of 1775 was the recognized leader of those who fought measures which might prevent reconciliation with Britain (see Nos. 164 and 170). By the end of May 1776 he was at least partially reconciled to the inevitability of independence although he continued to argue for delay. During the nine-hour debate on 1 July 1776 he made his last formal protest against a declaration. Because no contemporary record of the speech could be found, and because participants like John Adams remembered it in their old age, the speech was for generations thought apocryphal. Recently, however, among some manuscripts given to the Historical Society of Pennsylvania there was found a document in Dickinson's handwriting which is indisputably the basis for the speech he gave on 1 July. A part of the document is written out in full but much of it consists of brief notes. The speech has been reconstructed by Dr. John H. Powell who has supplied missing letters, words, and clauses and careful editorial notes. The document as given below omits all the remarkable editorial apparatus in order to present Dickinson's ideas clearly and simply. Although Dickinson doubted the wisdom of independence and did not sign the Declaration, he became an important leader in winning that independence which he so sincerely opposed in 1776. Printed: *The Pennsylvania Magazine of History and Biography*, LXV (1941), pp. 468-481.

The consequences involved in the motion now lying before you are of such magnitude that I tremble under the oppressive honour of sharing in its determination. I feel myself unequal to the burden assigned me. I believe; I had almost said, I rejoice, that the time is approaching when I shall be relieved from its weight. While the trust remains with me I must discharge the duties of it as well as I can – and I hope I shall be the more favourably heard, as I am convinced that I shall hold such language as will sacrifice my private emolument to general interests. My conduct this day I expect will give the finishing blow to my once too great, and my integrity considered now, too diminished popularity. It will be my lot to know that I had rather vote away the enjoyment of that dazzling display, that pleasing possession, than the blood and happiness of my countrymen – too fortunate amidst their calamities, if I prove (a truth known in Heaven) that I had rather they should hate me than that I should hurt them. I might indeed practise an artful, an advantageous reserve upon this occasion. But thinking as I do on the subject of debate, silence would be guilt. I despise its arts, I detest its advantages. I must speak, though I should lose my life, though I should lose the affections of my country. Happy at present, however, I shall esteem myself if I can so far rise to the height of this great argument as to offer to this honourable assembly, in a full and clear manner, those reasons that have so invariably fixed my own opinion.

It was a custom in a wise and virtuous state to preface propositions in council with a prayer, that they might redound to the public benefit. I beg leave to imitate the laudable example. And I do most humbly implore Almighty God, with whom dwells wisdom itself, so to enlighten the members of this house that their decision may be such as will best promote the liberty, safety, and prosperity of these colonies, and for myself, that his divine goodness may be graciously pleased to enable me to speak the precepts of sound policy on the important question that now engages our attention.

Sir, gentlemen of very distinguished abilities and knowledge differ widely in their sentiments upon the point now agitated. They all agree that the utmost prudence is required in forming our decision, but immediately disagree in their notion of that prudence. Some cautiously insist that we ought to obtain that previous information which we are likely quickly to obtain, and to make those previous establishments that are acknowledged to be necessary. Others strenuously assert that though regularly such information and establishment ought to precede the measure proposed, yet, confiding in our fortune more boldly than Caesar himself, we ought to brave the storm in a skiff made of paper.

In all such cases where every argument is adorned with an eloquence that may please and yet mislead, it seems to me the proper method of discovering the right path, to inquire which of the parties is probably the most warmed by passion. Other circumstances being equal or nearly equal, that consideration would have influence with me. I fear the virtue of Americans. Resentment of the injuries offered to their country may irritate them to counsels and to actions that may be detrimental to the cause they would die to advance.

What advantages could it be claimed would follow from the adoption of this resolution? (1) It might animate the people. (2) It would convince foreign powers of our strength and unanimity and we would receive their aid in consequence thereof. As to the first point, it is unnecessary. The preservation of life, liberty, and property is a sufficient motive to animate the people. The general spirit of America is animated. As to the second, foreign powers will not rely on words.

The event of the campaign will be the best evidence of our strength and unanimity. This properly the first campaign. Who has received intelligence that such a proof of our strength and daring spirit will be agreeable to France? What must she expect from a people that begin their empire in so high a style when on the point of being invaded by the whole power of Great Britain aided by formidable afor [foreign?] aid, unconnected with foreign powers? She and Spain must perceive the immediate danger of their colonies lying at our doors, their seat of empire is in another world. Masserano – Intelligence from Cadiz.

It would be more respectful to act in conformity to the views of France. Let us take advantage of their pride; let us give them reason to believe that we confide in them; that we desire to act in conjunction with their policies and interests. Let us know how they would regard this stranger in the states of the world. People are fond of what they have attained in producing; they regard it as a child. A cement of affection exists between them. Let us allow them the glory of appearing the vindicators of liberty. It will please them.

It is treating them with contempt to act otherwise, especially after the application made to France which by this time has reached them. Bermuda, 5 May. Consider the abilities of the persons sent. What will they think if now so quickly afterwards, without waiting for their determination, totally slighting their sentiments on such a prodigious issue, we haughtily pursue our own measures?

May they not say to us: Gentlemen, you falsely pretended to consult us and disrespectfully proceeded without waiting our resolution. You must abide the consequences. We are not ready for a rupture. You should have negotiated till we were. We will not be hurried by your impetuosity. We know it is our interest to support you but we shall be in no haste about it. Try your own strength and resources in which you have such confidence. We know now you dare not look back. Reconciliation is impossible without declaring independence, now that you have reached the stage you have. Yours is the most rash and at the same time, the most contemptible senate that ever existed on earth! Suppose on this event Great Britain should offer Canada to France and Florida to Spain with an extension of the old limits. Would not France and Spain accept them? Gentlemen say the trade of all America is more valuable to France than Canada. I grant it; but suppose she may get both? If she is politic, and none doubt that, I aver she has the easiest game to play for attaining both that ever presented itself to a nation.

When we have bound ourselves to a stern quarrel with Great Britain by a declaration of independence, France has nothing to do but to hold back and intimidate Great Britain till Canada is put into her hands; then to intimidate us into a most disadvantageous grant of our trade. It is my firm opinion these events will take place, and arise naturally from our declaring independence.

As to aid from foreign powers: our declaration can procure us none during this present campaign though made today. It is impossible.

Now let us consider if all the advantages expected from foreign powers cannot be attained in a more unexceptional manner. Is there no way of giving notice of a nation's resolution than by proclaiming it to all the world? Let us in the most solemn manner inform the House of Bourbon, at least France, that we wait only for her determination to declare our independence. We must not talk generally of foreign powers but only of those we expect to favour us. Let us assure Spain that we never will give any assistance to her colonies. Let France become guarantee for us in arrangements of this kind.

Besides. first we ought to establish our governments and take the regular form of a state. These preventive measures will show deliberation, wisdom, caution, and unanimity.

It is our interest to keep Great Britain in the opinion that we mean reconciliation as long as possible. The wealth of London, etc., is poured into the treasury. The whole nation is ardent against us. We oblige her by our attitude to persevere in her spirit. See the last petition of London.

Suppose we shall ruin her. France must rise on her ruins. Her ambition. Her religion. Our dangers from thence. We shall weep at our [?]. We shall be overwhelmed with debt. Compute that debt at 6 millions of Pennsylvania money a year.

The war will be carried on with more severity. The burning of towns, the setting loose of Indians on our frontiers has not yet been done. Boston might have been burned, though it was not.

What advantage is to be expected from a declaration? (1) The animating of our troops? I answer, it is unnecessary. (2) Union of the colonies? I answer, this is also unnecessary. It may weaken that union when the people find themselves engaged in a cause rendered more cruel by such a declaration without prospect of an end to their calamities, by a continuation of the war.

People are changeable. In bitterness of soul they may complain against our rashness and ask why we did not apply first to foreign powers; why we did not settle differences among ourselves; why we did not take care to secure unsettled lands for easing their burdens instead of leaving them to colonies; why we did not wait till we were better prepared, or till we had made an experiment of our strength.

(3) A third advantage to be expected from a declaration is said to be the proof it would furnish of our strength of spirit. But this is possibly only the first campaign of the war. France and Spain may be alarmed and provoked with each other; Masserano was an insult to France. There is not the least evidence of her granting us favourable terms. Her probable condition. The glory of recovering Canada will be enough for her. She will get that and then dictate terms to us.

A partition of these colonies will take place if Great Britain can't conquer us. To escape from the protection we have in British rule by declaring independence would be like destroying a house before we have got another in winter with a small family; then asking a neighbour to take us in and finding he is unprepared.

(4) It is claimed that the spirit of the colonies calls for such a declaration. I answer that the spirit of the colonies is not to be relied on. Not only treaties with foreign powers but among ourselves should precede this declaration. We should know on what grounds we are to stand with regard to one another. We ought to settle the issues raised by the declaration of Virginia about colonists in their limits. And too, the committee on confederation dispute almost every article. Some of us totally despair of any reasonable terms of confederation.

We cannot look back. Men generally sell their goods to most advantage when they have several chapmen. We have but two to rely on. We exclude one by this declaration without knowing what the other will give.

Great Britain after one or more unsuccessful campaigns may be induced to offer us such a share of commerce as would satisfy us, to appoint councillors during good behaviour, to withdraw her armies, to protect our commerce, establish our militias–in short to redress all the grievances complained of in our first petition. Let us know if we can get terms from France that will be more beneficial than these. If we can, let us declare independence. If we cannot, let us at least withold that declaration till we obtain terms that are tolerable.

We have many points of the utmost moment to settle with France–Canada, Acadia, and Cape Breton. What will content her? Trade or territory? What conditions of trade? Barbary pirates, Spain, Portugal? Will she demand an exclusive trade as a compensation, or grant us protection against piratical states only for a share of our commerce?

When our enemies are pressing us so vigorously; when we are in so wretched a state of preparation; when the sentiments and designs of our expected friends are so unknown to us, I am alarmed at this declaration being so vehemently presented. A worthy gentleman told us that people in this house have had different views for more than a twelvemonth. This is amazing after what they have so repeatedly declared in this house and private conversations, that they meant only reconciliation. But since they can conceal their views so dextrously, I should be glad to read a little more in the Doomsday Book of America–not all–that, like the Book of Fate, might be too dreadful–title page–binding. I should be glad to know whether in 20 or 30 years this commonwealth of colonies may not be thought too unwieldy, and Hudson's River be a proper boundary for a separate commonwealth to the northward. I have a strong impression on my mind that this will take place.

179. The Declaration of Independence

The Declaration of Independence has been reprinted innumerable times. The following text is taken from the first volume of the new edition of Thomas Jefferson's writings being prepared under the editorship of Julian P. Boyd, of Princeton University. The volume also contains various preliminary drafts, with editorial comments and notes. Printed: Julian P. Boyd, *et al.*, eds., *The Papers of Thomas Jefferson* (Princeton, 1950), I, pp. 429-432.

THE UNANIMOUS DECLARATION

OF THE THIRTEEN UNITED STATES

OF AMERICA,

When in the Course of human events, it becomes necessary for one people to dissolve the political bands which have connected them with another, and to assume among the powers of the earth, the separate and equal station to which the Laws of Nature and of Nature's God entitle them, a decent respect to the opinions of mankind requires that they should declare the causes which impel them to the separation. We hold these truths to be self-evident, that all men are created equal, that they are endowed by their Creator with certain unalienable Rights, that among these are Life, Liberty and the pursuit of Happiness. That to secure these rights, Governments are instituted among Men, deriving their just powers from the consent of the governed, That whenever any Form of Government becomes destructive of these ends, it is the Right of the People to alter or to abolish it, and to institute new Government, laying its foundation on such principles and organizing its powers in such form, as to them shall seem most likely to effect their Safety and Happiness. Prudence, indeed, will dictate that Governments long established should not be changed for light and transient causes; and accordingly all experience hath shewn, that mankind are more disposed to suffer, while evils are sufferable, than to right themselves by abolishing the forms to which they are accustomed. But when a long train of abuses and usurpations, pursuing invariably the same Object evinces a design to reduce them under absolute Despotism, it is their right, it is their duty, to throw off such Government, and to provide new Guards for their future security. Such has been the patient sufferance of these Colonies; and such is now the necessity which constrains them to alter their former Systems of Government. The history of the present King of Great Britain is a history of repeated injuries and usurpations, all having in direct object the establishment of an absolute Tyranny over these States. To prove this, let Facts be submitted to a candid world. He has refused his Assent to Laws, the most wholesome and necessary for the public good. He has forbidden his Governors to pass Laws of immediate and pressing importance, unless suspended in their operation till his Assent should be obtained; and when so suspended, he has utterly neglected to attend to them. He has refused to pass other Laws for the accommodation of large districts of people, unless those people would relinquish the right of Representation in the Legislature, a right inestimable to them and formidable to tyrants only. He has called together legislative bodies at places unusual, uncomfortable, and distant from the depository of their public Records, for the sole purpose of fatiguing them into compliance with his measures. He has dissolved Representative Houses repeatedly, for opposing with manly firmness his invasions on the rights of the people. He has refused for a long time, after such dissolutions, to cause others to be elected; whereby the Legislative powers, incapable of Annihilation, have returned to the People at large for their exercise; the State remaining in the mean time exposed to all the dangers of invasion from without, and convulsions within. He has endeavoured to prevent the population of these States; for that purpose obstructing the Laws for Naturalization of Foreigners; refusing to pass others to encourage their migrations hither, and raising the conditions of new Appropriations of Lands. He has obstructed the Administration of Justice, by refusing his Assent to Laws for establishing Judiciary powers. He has made Judges dependent on his Will alone, for the tenure of their offices, and the amount and payment of their salaries. He has erected a multitude of New Offices, and sent hither swarms of Officers to harass our people, and eat out their substance. He has kept among us, in times of peace, standing Armies without the Consent of our legislatures. He has affected to render the Military independent of and superior to the Civil power. He has combined with others to subject us to a jurisdiction foreign to our constitution, and unacknowledged by our laws; giving his Assent to their Acts of pretended Legislation: For Quartering large bodies of armed troops among us: For protecting them, by a mock Trial, from punishment for any Murders which they should commit on the Inhabitants of these States: For cutting off our Trade with all parts of the world: For imposing Taxes on us without our Consent: For depriving us in many cases of the benefits of Trial by Jury: For transporting us beyond Seas to be tried for pretended offences: For abolishing the free System of English Laws in a neighbouring Province, establishing therein an Arbitrary government, and enlarging its Boundaries so as to render it at once an example and fit instrument for introducing the same absolute rule into these Colonies: For taking away our Charters, abolishing our most valuable

Laws, and altering fundamentally the Forms of our Governments: For suspending our own Legislatures, and declaring themselves invested with power to legislate for us in all cases whatsoever. He has abdicated Government here, by declaring us out of his Protection and waging War against us. He has plundered our seas, ravaged our Coasts, burnt our towns, and destroyed the Lives of our people. He is at this time transporting large Armies of foreign Mercenaries to compleat the works of death, desolation and tyranny, already begun with circumstances of Cruelty & perfidy scarcely paralleled in the most barbarous ages, and totally unworthy the Head of a civilized nation. He has constrained our fellow Citizens taken Captive on the high Seas to bear Arms against their Country, to become the executioners of their friends and Brethren, or to fall themselves by their Hands. He has excited domestic insurrections amongst us, and has endeavoured to bring on the inhabitants of our frontiers, the merciless Indian Savages, whose known rule of warfare, is an undistinguished destruction of all ages, sexes and conditions. In every stage of these Oppressions We have Petitioned for Redress in the most humble terms: Our repeated Petitions have been answered only by repeated injury. A Prince, whose character is thus marked by every act which may define a Tyrant, is unfit to be the ruler of a free people. Nor have We been wanting in attentions to our Brittish brethren. We have warned them from time to time of attempts by their legislature to extend an unwarrantable jurisdiction over us. We have reminded them of the circumstances of our emigration and settlement here. We have appealed to their native justice and magnanimity, and we have conjured them by the ties of our common kindred to disavow these usurpations, which would inevitably interrupt our connections and correspondence. They too have been deaf to the voice of justice and of consanguinity. We must, therefore, acquiesce in the necessity, which denounces our Separation, and hold them, as we hold the rest of mankind, Enemies in War, in Peace Friends.

We, therefore, the Representatives of the united States of America, in General Congress, Assembled, appealing to the Supreme Judge of the world for the rectitude of our intentions, do, in the Name, and by Authority of the good People of these Colonies, solemnly publish and declare, That these United Colonies are, and of Right ought to be Free and Independent States; that they are Absolved from all Allegiance to the British Crown, and that all political connection between them and the State of Great Britain, is and ought to be totally dissolved; and that as Free and Independent States, they have full Power to levy War, conclude Peace, contract Alliances, establish Commerce, and to do all other Acts and Things which Independent States may of right do. And for the support of this Declaration, with a firm reliance on the protection of divine Providence, we mutually pledge to each other our Lives, our Fortunes and our sacred Honour.

John Hancock

Button Gwinnett	Thos. Nelson jr.	Richd. Stockton
Lyman Hall	Francis Lightfoot Lee	Jno Witherspoon
Geo Walton	Carter Braxton	Fras. Hopkinson
Wm. Hooper	Robt. Morris	John Hart

Joseph Hewes
John Penn
Edward Rutledge
Thos. Heyward Junr.
Thomas Lynch Junr.
Arthur Middleton
Samuel Chase
Wm. Paca
Thos. Stone
Charles Carroll of
   Carrollton
George Wythe
Richard Henry Lee
Th: Jefferson
Benja. Harrison

Benjamin Rush
Benja. Franklin
John Morton
Geo Clymer
Jas. Smith
Geo. Taylor
James Wilson
Geo. Ross
Caesar Rodney
Geo Read
Tho M: Kean
Wm. Floyd
Phil. Livingston
Frans. Lewis
Lewis Morris

Abra Clark
Josiah Bartlett
Wm: Whipple
Saml. Adams
John Adams
Robt. Treat Paine
Elbridge Gerry
Step. Hopkins
William Ellery
Roger Sherman
Saml. Huntington
Wm. Williams
Oliver Wolcott
Matthew Thornton

INDEX

INDEX TO TEXTS

The figures refer to the numbered documents, not to the pages. Documents with known authors are indexed under the names of the authors. In addition, such of these as have reference to particular colonies, as well as other documents so referring, are indexed under the name of the colony concerned. All other documents are indexed under such headings as Petitions and Resolutions, Proclamations, Statutes of Parliament and the like.